Advances in Intelligent Systems and Computing

Volume 738

About this series

The series "Advances in Intelligent Systems and Computing" contains publications on theory, applications, and design methods of Intelligent Systems and Intelligent Computing. Virtually all disciplines such as engineering, natural sciences, computer and information science, ICT, economics, business, e-commerce, environment, healthcare, life science are covered. The list of topics spans all the areas of modern intelligent systems and computing such as: computational intelligence, soft computing including neural networks, fuzzy systems, evolutionary computing and the fusion of these paradigms, social intelligence, ambient intelligence, computational neuroscience, artificial life, virtual worlds and society, cognitive science and systems, Perception and Vision, DNA and immune based systems, self-organizing and adaptive systems, e-Learning and teaching, human-centered and human-centric computing, recommender systems, intelligent control, robotics and mechatronics including human-machine teaming, knowledge-based paradigms, learning paradigms, machine ethics, intelligent data analysis, knowledge management, intelligent agents, intelligent decision making and support, intelligent network security, trust management, interactive entertainment, Web intelligence and multimedia. The publications within "Advances in Intelligent Systems and Computing" are primarily proceedings of important conferences, symposia and congresses. They cover significant recent developments in the field, both of a foundational and applicable character. An important characteristic feature of the series is the short publication time and world-wide distribution. This permits a rapid and broad dissemination of research results.

More information about this series at http://www.springer.com/series/11156

Shahram Latifi

Editor

Information Technology – New Generations

15th International Conference on Information Technology

 Springer

Editor
Shahram Latifi
Department of Electrical & Computer Engineering
University of Nevada, Las Vegas
Las Vegas, Nevada, USA

ISSN 2194-5357   ISSN 2194-5365   (electronic)
Advances in Intelligent Systems and Computing
ISBN 978-3-030-08352-6   ISBN 978-3-319-77028-4   (eBook)
https://doi.org/10.1007/978-3-319-77028-4

This Springer imprint is published by the registered company Springer International Publishing AG part of Springer Nature.
The registered company address is: Gewerbestrasse 11, 6330 Cham, Switzerland

Contents

Part V Data Mining/Machine Learning

ITNG 2018 Organization

General Chair and Editor

Shahram Latifi, UNLV, USA

Vice General Chair

Doina Bein, California State University, Fullerton, USA

Track Chairs and Associate Editors

Glauco Carneiro, University of Salvador (UNIFACS), Brazil
L. A. Vieira Dias, ITA, Brazil
Ray Hasehmi, Armstrong State University, USA
Yenumula Reddy, Grambling state University
Fangyan Shen, New York City College of Technology (CUNY), USA
Ping Wang, Robert Morris University, USA
Christoph Thuemmler, Edinburgh Napier University, UK

Track Co-Chairs and Session Chairs

Thomas Jell, Siemens, Germany
Michel Soares, Federal University of Sergipe (UFS), Brazil
Mei Yang, UNLV, USA

Program Committee Members

Kohei Arai, Japan
Nader Bagherzadeh, USA
Wolfgang Bein, USA
Glauco Carneiro, Brazil
Narayan Debnath, USA
Vieira Dias, Brazil
Laxmi Gewali, USA
James McCaffrey, USA
Teruya Minamoto, Japan
Yenumula Reddy, USA
Kashif Saleem, SA

Anna Scaglione, USA
Hal Sudborough, USA
Christoph Thuemmler, UK
Ping Wang, USA

Conference Secretary

Mary Roberts, Premier Hall for Advancing Science and Engineering, USA

Industry Partnership

Microsoft, Siemens

Chair Message

 Welcome to the 15th International Conference on Information Technology—New Generations—ITNG 2018. It is a pleasure to report that we have another successful year for the ITNG 2018. Gaining popularity and recognition in the IT community around the globe, the conference was able to attract many papers from authors worldwide. The papers were reviewed for their technical soundness, originality, clarity, and relevance to the conference. The conference enjoyed expert opinion of over 100 author and nonauthor scientists who participated in the review process. Each paper was reviewed by at least two independent reviewers. A total of 89 articles were accepted as regular papers and 12 were accepted as short papers (posters).

The chapters in this book address the most recent advances in such areas as Wireless Communications and Networking, Software Engineering, Information Security, Data Mining and Machine Learning, Informatics, High-Performance Computing Architectures, Internet, and Computer Vision.

As customary, the conference features two keynote speakers on Monday and Tuesday. There will be a short tutorial session Wednesday morning on Deep Learning. The presentations for Monday, Tuesday, and Wednesday are organized in two meeting rooms simultaneously, covering a total of 20 technical sessions. Poster presentations are scheduled for the morning and afternoon of these days. The award ceremony, conference reception and dinner are scheduled for Tuesday evening.

Many people contributed to the success of this year's conference by organizing symposia or technical tracks for the ITNG. Dr. Doina Bein served in the capacity of conference vice chair. We benefited from the professional and timely services of Dr. Ping Wang who not only organized the Security Track but also helped in shaping the students' book of abstracts to be published online at the ITNG website. Dr. Yenumula Reddy deserves much credit for spearheading the review process and running a symposium on Wireless Communications and Networking. My sincere thanks go to other symposium and major track organizers and associate editors namely—Glauco Carneiro, Luiz Alberto Vieira Dias, Ray Hashemi, Thomas Jell, Kashif Saleem, Fangyan Shen, Michel Soares, and Christoph Thuemmler.

Others who were responsible for solicitation, review and handling the papers submitted to their respective tracks/sessions include Drs Azita Bahrami, Wolfgang Bein, Alessio Bucaioni, Federico Ciccozzi, Saad Mubeen, Armin Schneider, and Mei Yang.

The help and support of Springer in preparing the ITNG book is specially appreciated. Many thanks are due to Michael Luby, the Senior Editor, and Nicole Lowary, the Assistant Editor of Springer, supervisor of Publications, for the timely handling of our publication order. We also appreciate the hard work by Murugesan Tamilselvan, the Springer Project Coordinator, and Mario Gabriele, the Springer Project Manager, who looked very closely at every single article to make sure they are formatted correctly according to the publisher guidelines. Finally, the great efforts of the conference secretary, Ms. Mary Roberts, who dealt with the day-to-day conference affairs, including the timely handling of volumes of emails, are acknowledged.

The conference venue is Tuscany Suites Hotel. The hotel, conveniently located within half a mile of the Las Vegas Strip, provides an easy access to other major resorts and recreational centers. I hope and trust that you have an academically and socially fulfilling stay in Las Vegas.

Shahram Latifi
The ITNG General Chair

List of Reviewers

Abbas, Haider	Durelli, Rafael	Li, Shujun	Romano, Breno
Abreu, Fernando	Eldefrawy, Mohamed	Machado, Ivan	Rossi, Gustavo
Ahmad, Aftab	Eler, Marcelo	Maglaras, Leandros	Saleem, Kashif
Ahmed, Adel	El-Ziq, Yacoub	Maia, Paulo	Sant'anna, Cláudio
Andro-Vasko, James	Faria, João	Marques, Johnny	Santos, Katyusco
Anikeev, Maxim	Figueiredo, Eduardo	Mascarenhas, Ana	Sarijari, Mohd
Araújo, Marco	Ford, George	Mateos, Cristian	Sbeit, Raed
Baguda, Yaqoub	França, Joyce	Mialaret, Lineu	Schneider, Armin
Bein, Doina	Garcia, Vinicius	Monteiro, Miguel	Shen, Fangyang
Bein, Wolfgang	Gawanmeh, Amjad	Montini, Denis	Shoraka, Babak
Caetano, Paulo	Girma, Anteneh	Mukkamala, Ravi	Silva, Bruno
Cagnin, Maria	Gofman, Mikhail	Munson, Ethan	Soares, Michel
Camargo, Valter	Gueron, Shay	Nguyen, Nikyle	Suzana, Rita
Canedo, Edna	Huang, Yingsong	Nunes, Eldman	Thuemmler, Christoph
Carneiro, Glauco	Ibrahim, Ahmed	Nwaigwe, Adaeze	Tsetse, Anthony
Chapman, Matthew	Imran, Muhammad	Orgun, Mehmet	Wang, Jau-Hwang
Cheng, Wen	Jell, Thomas	Owen, Richard	Wang, Ping
Christos, Kalloniatis	Ji, Yanqing	Paiva, Ana	Wang, Yi
Colaço, Jr Methanias	Kannan, Sudesh	Pang, Les	Williams, Hank
Cunha, Adilson	Khan, Zahoor	Pathan, Al-Sakib	Xu, Weifeng
Daniels, Jeff	Khanduja, Vidhi	Paulin, Alois	Yang, Mei
Darwish, Marwan	Kim, Hak	Peiper, Chad	Zhang, Jun
David, José	Kinyua, Johnson	Popa, Vlad	
Dawson, Maurice	Koch, Fernando	Rehmani, Mubashir	
Dias, Luiz Alberto	Laskar, John	Resende, Antonio	

Part I

Cybersecurity

Safeguarding Personal Health Information: Case Study

Holly Gandarilla

Abstract

Password cracking tools have given hackers the ability to solve hashes in minutes. These same tools can also be used for penetration testing to determine weak passwords within our own infrastructure. In using products, such as, Cain and Abel or Ophcrack, organizations can gain insight and awareness that could be the stronghold in keeping accounts and personal health information (PHI) safe. Cain and Abel, and Ophcrack, which are the two password cracking tools tested, can be both useful and very dangerous at the same time. While many can learn from these products, so can their adversaries. In using these products to test our own password strengths we can foresee vulnerabilities that we may have been overlooked. As new software is created, passwords will become easier to crack. Technology knows no boundaries in many aspects, which is why securing our networks, strengthening our physical and logical security, and mitigating every risk possible, becomes of utmost importance in this technology-ridden world.

Keywords

PHI · Personal health information · Password · Cracking · Penetration · Safeguard · Hackers · Study

1.1 Introduction

Technology is ever-advancing and constantly creating new avenues for vulnerabilities in our information systems to be exploited. Midyear 2016, 60% of data breaches were attributed to hacking [1]. An organization's duty to protect their patients' PHI should remain top priority. With a more comprehensive security posture, organizations can barricade these vicious avenues from negatively impacting their patients.

The CIA triad refers to the confidentiality, integrity, and availability of information—in our case, PHI. The confidentiality of information is protected by a system's access controls. Those who require access to the system are granted it, and those who do not are denied. The confidentiality of information is pertinent because it ensures that patient and employee information have not been compromised. The integrity of information is backed by encryption procedures. Per HIPAA Security Rule, medical facilities should be encrypting PHI when deemed appropriate [2]. For many, this means when it is static, or stored in file systems, and while in transmission. While these HIPAA guidelines are addressable, organizations should stress this to employees who handle PHI frequently and implement organizational policies identifying proper procedures. The availability of PHI is maintained by Disaster Recovery and Business Continuity Plans [3]. By making this information constantly available the CIA triad is being enforced.

1.2 Proposed Work

In order to effectively control unauthorized access, the identities of individuals should be validated. It is not enough to impose partial security standards. Multiple methods should be in place to protect the failure of any one of them. For example, if password requirements are that the key must be 14 characters in length, include upper and lowercase letters, and numbers—that's a great first step. Given enough time, passwords could still be compromised via password cracking tools. However, if an account lockout policy were in place after three incorrect attempts, the chances of a brute force attack could be mitigated.

H. Gandarilla (✉)
Department of Cybersecurity, University of Maryland University College, Adelphi, MD, USA

© Springer International Publishing AG, part of Springer Nature 2018
S. Latifi (ed.), *Information Technology – New Generations*, Advances in Intelligent Systems and Computing 738,
https://doi.org/10.1007/978-3-319-77028-4_1

Fig. 1.1 Cisco's recommended
network topology for
medium-sized clinics

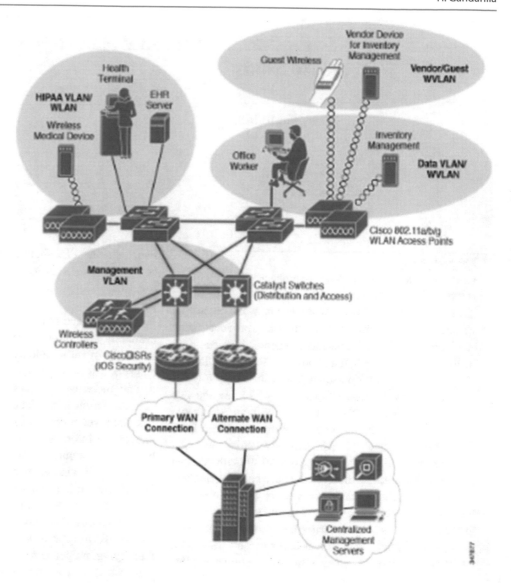

The issuance of identification badges that dual as common access cards (CACs) are perfect examples of authentication. Two-factor authentication is a method of authentication that requires two of the following: something you have, something you know, or something you are (i.e. biometrics). The combination of CAC and password mitigates the risk of losing a badge and systems automatically being compromised. A CAC alone would not be enough to breach the system.

Authorization is the method of permittance to a system. Often times, authentication and authorization are seen as one entity. Authorization is the process in which users are granted or denied access based on their permissions. Controlling access to systems assists in solidifying one's security posture as a whole. Organizations that are partially enforcing these measures should implement multiple methods. Thus, the failure of just one method does not permit access.

Access control lists (ACLs) determine who is authorized access to a network. As opportunity arises through open ports, even settings, such as, access lists can protect against unauthorized traffic. With the settings deny and allow, administrators can dictate who is granted access. Additionally, unused ports should always be turned off to prevent intruders from gaining access to the network (Fig. 1.1).

Role-based access controls (RBAC) are set based upon the role or position an employee holds. If they are a nurse or a doctor, they have access based on what their position requires access to. For example, nurses should be permitted access to levels of PHI that are relevant to the care that they give. In turn, doctors are authorized greater access to view entire records, so that they may better diagnose health issues.

With the influx of mobile platforms, hospitals have become more productive as they can work on the go. However, with easier access for users comes easier access for intruders. Mobile devices are more difficult to secure as they have weaker protocols without being hard wired, not to mention, that wireless access is never as secure as a wired connection.

Nonetheless, mobile devices and their connectivity has become essential to the welfare of patients. This means strong passwords, CAC readers connected via USB or built-in, and implementing protection displays and locks. In 2016, 78% of data breaches in U.S. hospitals were due to the loss or theft of information [1]. These devices, although they are made to be portable, should have emergency procedures in place in the event of loss or theft. Remote wipe should certainly be considered an option. Encrypting PHI is the most secure method in providing confidentiality to this information [4].

The importance of having strong password requirements is paramount. Passwords that are alpha-numeric and short, or contain words from the dictionary are easily guessed and cracked using password cracking tools. Tools, such as, Ophcrack, and Cain and Abel are specifically designed to figure out passwords in as little time as possible. Even more concerning, the word lists that are used to perform dictionary attacks are a dime a dozen.

1.3   Findings and Results

Cain and Abel, and Ophcrack, two password cracking tools tested in this case study, can be both useful and very dangerous at the same time. While organizations can learn from these products, so can our adversaries. In using these products to test internal account password strengths, organizations can foresee vulnerabilities that perhaps may have been overlooked.

Dictionary attacks can be debilitating for users who use full words in their passwords. Word lists can be uploaded to password cracking programs, making it almost effortless to solve hashes. Ensuring that password policies do not allow for words that can be found in the dictionary, this threat can be mitigated. While it may be difficult to remember complex passwords, users can also spell out words using various characters. For example, the password floridagators could be turned into a more secure one by substituting characters that look similar; Fl0R!d@G@t0R5. It does take some extra steps to make a password secure, but if this is what an organization requires to keep PHI safe, users will become more skilled in creating stronger passwords.

"A brute-force attack is a method of defeating a cryptographic scheme by trying a large number of possibilities" [4]. In simpler terms, brute force attacks occur when multiple password entries are sent to overload a system. Sometimes a correct password is guessed, or sometimes a system becomes overloaded. In both scenarios, neither one is particularly good. Limiting the amount of times an incorrect password can be entered before the account locks is one way to keep these types of attacks from debilitating our systems. The most common is the number three—after three incorrect attempts, an account should lock, and administrators can now control access to the user's account. In many cases users are required to verify their identity either in person, via video teleconferencing, or by giving identifying information about themselves. Organizational policies should provide more than one way of validating an individual's identity and should be approved by the Chief Security Officer.

The speed in which these programs cracked passwords was impressive. For simpler passwords, such as xmen and M00n, both programs almost immediately solved the hashes. Ophcrack was easier and faster to use, but only performs by using Rainbow tables. Whereas, Cain and Abel can use a variety of attacks. Cain and Abel was precise in solving hashes when the correct attack was chosen. Being that not all passwords include dictionary words in them, a dictionary attack can certainly be unsuccessful. The good news—Cain and Abel attacks in more than one way. Rainbow tables are easily found for use in Ophcrack and make it easier to solve multiple account passwords in one function. However, for passwords that the hash is unknown, Ophcrack will not be able to find it on its own.

Password strength was the most determining factor for cracking account passwords. The longer the password, the more time consuming it becomes. Likewise, the more difficult a password is by including not just letters and numbers, but also symbols, can be the saving grace or end all in these situations. Requiring passwords to be at least 14 characters in length, with two uppercase letters, two lowercase letters, two numbers and two symbols makes solving them more difficult and time consuming for hackers.

Both programs were successful in solving for simple hashes, dictionary words and short passwords. Essentially, if the password was weak, these programs could crack them in under a minute. While both programs differ in ability, they both can be useful to our organization.

1.4   Conclusions

Both programs were successful in solving for simple hashes, dictionary words, and short passwords. Essentially, if the password was weak, these programs could crack them in under a minute. While both programs differ in ability, they both can be useful to an organization. It is my recommendation that both programs be used for penetration testing. Because they are open source products, this comes at no cost to organizations, but with a plethora of benefits. In using these programs, they will be flagged as malware. The simple solution would be to advise the IT department to download the programs and leave their testing lab equipment offline when not in use. During penetration testing, these machines can be connected to the network to perform their duties, scanning for weak security and then once again disconnected so that they are not constantly flagged on the network. Deploying both tools on networks for penetration testing will significantly decrease the ability of intruders to hack networks effortlessly. In keeping machines that house these tools offline until weekly testing is done, the chances of false positives in anti-virus software can be mitigated. The ability to know what hackers can do and where the faults lie, will strengthen security posture to the best of our ability. Most importantly, this will show patients that we care about their personal information and we will continue to keep it secure.

References

1. Major 2016 healthcare data breaches: mid year summary. HIPAA J. (2017), [Online]. http://www.hipaajournal.com/major-2016-healthcare-data-breaches-mid-year-summary-3499/
2. R.A. Leo, *The HIPAA Program Reference Handbook* (CRC Press, Boca Raton, FL, 2005)
3. M. Korolov, Healthcare organizations face unique security challenges. CSO Online, (2015), [Online]. https://www.csoonline.com/article/2932978/data-protection/health-care-organization-face-unique-security-challenges.html
4. N. Daras (ed.), *Applications of Mathematics and Informatics in Military Science* (Springer, Berlin, 2014), p. 208

Cybersecurity as People Powered Perpetual Innovation

Mansur Hasib

Abstract

While tools and technology are important, people are the most important element of a cybersecurity strategy. A properly implemented cybersecurity strategy engages every member of an organization in achieving mission success and in perpetually improving its cybersecurity posture.

Keywords

Cybersecurity governance · Cybersecurity leadership

2.1 Introduction

Cybersecurity is not a one-brain sport. The offensive and defensive cybersecurity capability and ultimate posture of any organization depends on the actions of every individual associated with the organization. While tools and technology are important, the most powerful offensive and defensive weapon for any organization is the collective brainpower of its people [1].

Each human brain is unique. Given the right conditions, each brain has an unlimited capacity to innovate. Brains can also atrophy. Leadership and teamwork can inspire, unleash, nurture, and sustain this force toward a mission. Human brains produce higher levels of innovation when people are happy because happiness produces benign chemicals, which inspire innovation. Conversely, stress and unhappy conditions create an amygdala hijack condition, which significantly reduces a human brain's capacity to think rationally and to innovate. Team and social environments accelerate innovation because social interactions produce inspiration chemicals [2].

Therefore the key to perennial success and superiority for any organization is to implement a culture of perpetual innovation. This requires leadership [1].

People in any organization succeed in fulfilling the mission of the organization most effectively when they can tie their respective roles to the mission. Such connection helps people understand the importance of each role and how the role ties back to the mission. Such a connection inspires better action.

This is the role of risk management and governance, which provide structure, yet allow methodical innovation and the channeling of limited resources towards optimal solutions, which focus on the mission.

2.2 Leadership

Leadership is highly misunderstood. Many academic programs and books incorrectly discuss it and classify it into mystical characteristics and a variety of styles. These sources profess that leaders must possess charisma and several key characteristics, which allow them to influence others. Leadership is often equated to authority and even celebrity status. Some use it synonymously with management. Such confusion results in people believing they are not leaders; nor can they be leaders!

Yet, leaders are not anointed people on a pedestal. Leadership is a frame of mind and not a position. Leadership is also the feeling of empowerment, discretion, and freedom to make a decision and to act. Every person is capable of being a leader. Every person has knowledge, which others do not have. Everyone can use their knowledge to guide others and to gain knowledge from others to make more informed and higher quality decisions and to reduce the risk of their actions.

M. Hasib (✉)
Cybersecurity Technology, The Graduate School, University of Maryland University College (UMUC), Marlboro, MD, USA
e-mail: mansur.hasib@umuc.edu

© Springer International Publishing AG, part of Springer Nature 2018
S. Latifi (ed.), *Information Technology – New Generations*, Advances in Intelligent Systems and Computing 738,
https://doi.org/10.1007/978-3-319-77028-4_2

Leadership through knowledge sharing allows a higher degree of accuracy with a better probability of success; informed decisions are stronger than uninformed decisions. Empowerment allows more decisions and actions to happen at any given time. This results in higher levels of productivity and better outcomes [2].

Every one of us can use our knowledge to guide others and to help others succeed. This is what true leadership is. It can be practiced by anyone and can be the culture of any organization. An organization full of such leaders is a powerful organization!

2.3   People as Expenses

Despite lip service vocalizing people as assets, accounting systems and business schools regard people as simple labor and expenses. Elite MBA schools profess that in order to be successful, executives must discard their emotions; and in their psychopathic pursuit of money and profits—usually designed to benefit themselves at the cost of the organizations, they also toss out their ethical barometers.

In all organizations, including government, people are viewed as the single largest expense and are therefore the bane of Chief Financial Officers. The fact that people produce innovation and are repositories of intellectual capital is largely lost in the vagaries of the accounting system. Therefore, a layoff results in an immediate reduction in expenses; it is frequently used as the first resort. The social and economic costs of the layoff are borne by society and not by the organization conducting the layoff. The intellectual capital loss is not accounted for either.

The professional financial executives groomed by MBA schools are frequently viewed as saviors of organizations and are touted as turnaround executives. The rise to power of these types of executives since the 1970s, has taken an excessive toll on the workforce and the society at large. Gone are retirement benefits, job security, living wages, healthcare, and other key foundational elements required for people to innovate. A culture of annual layoffs, perpetual job insecurity, and unpredictable economic cycles have caused people to worry about their basic needs; people do not have the mental equilibrium needed to inspire innovation and to seek higher levels of purpose.

Chief Financial Officers and Chief Executive Officers with Marketing and Finance backgrounds lead many organizations. Often the mission of the organization or the development of innovative products, which fulfill societal needs and create lasting value for the organization are cast aside in the relentless pursuit of money or profits through cost reduction—usually by laying off people or reducing benefits. Yet, laying off people does not require business genius.

Dramatic levels of corporate consolidation through mergers and acquisitions and other financial games have also driven out competitive forces, reduced investments in people, and dramatically reduced innovation—and even the safety and sanctity of human lives. There has been a general decline in the proportion of US national funds spent in research and development. Even federal research money has declined dramatically.

However, the financial turnaround expert is a myth of dramatic proportions! Examples of these executives causing the demise and malaise of erstwhile healthy or promising organizations such as Enron, AIG, Lehman Brothers, JC Penney, Sears and others are plentiful. Even government organizations, which earlier touted job stability in return for service and a substantially reduced level of compensation are no longer inure from a culture of layoffs.

To facilitate layoffs, government executives have also dramatically increased the use of contractors. Some have argued fallaciously that information technology and cybersecurity are not mission critical and therefore, should be outsourced. While this phenomenon has further reduced job stability for workers, along with a concomitant decline in innovation, it has not reduced government expenses. Rather, it has given rise to large procurement and contracting bureaucracies and actually increased total government expenses; in many cases the expenses are three to ten times more than what it would have been if the government had hired employees.

The situation has been exacerbated further because in an environment of job instability, people are stingy about sharing or documenting their knowledge for the benefit of others; many people view such hoarding of knowledge as job security. The divide in knowledge sharing between the contracting organizations and the government workers is even more dramatic. This is a deadly phenomenon in any organization.

Knowledge in our heads is useless; its power is unleashed only when it is shared. This can mean the difference between someone being able to fulfill a mission or being destroyed in the process. Teamwork and knowledge sharing is at the core of cybersecurity and innovation.

2.4   Ethical Leadership and Innovation

Another serious problem plaguing the federal government sector is the rise of federal contracting companies with unilateral contracts with their workers. These companies require workers to sign away any intellectual property workers may produce. In addition, many of these companies require non-compete clauses for prolonged periods of time, which can take away the ability of workers to earn a living. These companies will purposefully develop a W-2 based employee relationship simply to avoid paying someone overtime even though they may be billing the government or other clients for the overtime worked by the employee. Therefore, when they can get away with it, these employees refuse to work overtime if they can—often resulting in delays in citizens receiving critical service.

One of the foundations of a free market capitalist society is the promise that if you work hard and you produce great results and innovation, you get to enjoy a fair share of the benefits of that innovation. Certainly the company, which invested in you and provided you the environment and tools, deserves to benefit as well. However, if you are hired with a significant level of experience and pre-existing intellectual capital, there is a serious danger that you will lose rights to your own intellectual capital.

Therefore, with unilateral contracts and a decline in ethical leadership, which promises innovators a fair share of the benefits of innovation, there is no incentive to innovate. People therefore remain unengaged; they clock and bill hours perfunctorily and simply look out for themselves and their next opportunity. Loyalty to the organization has no value and therefore people's association with organizations is temporal. People therefore become a major source of internal threats—both for intellectual property loss as well as accidental and malicious cybersecurity threat vectors. It does not have to be this way! We can and should do something about it. The first step is accepting the criticality of people to cybersecurity and innovation.

2.5 Cybersecurity

Cybersecurity is another highly misunderstood topic. People associate it with computers and networks; they look for a technical solution to every cybersecurity problem. However, cybersecurity at its core is perpetual innovation by people at all levels of an organization.

The mission of any modern organization today is driven by information technology, systems, and data. Therefore their uninterrupted functioning, reliability, access management and protection are critical. In addition, the safety and privacy of legislatively protected data processed and maintained in these systems has to be assured.

Cybersecurity is not a state but a process. Modern cybersecurity has moved from a static 1991 model of information security to a modern dynamic model. In such a model, data exist in three possible states: Transmission, Storage and Processing. Cybersecurity seeks to maintain confidentiality (right people have access to information and the wrong people do not), integrity (information is trustworthy and can be relied upon to make accurate decisions), and availability (information is available when you need it) of systems and information.

We use three tools: people, policy, and technology to achieve cybersecurity goals [3]. However, organizations have limited resources. Every organization has a mission and must prioritize spending so it enhances the mission and maximizes positive risks, which are financially rewarding, while minimizing negative risks, which might harm the mission of the organization. Therefore, mission, risk, and governance are the foundation of an organizational cybersecurity strategy.

Innovation or improvement over time is critical. Through proactive monitoring, refinement, and perennial innovation, an organization can maintain a healthy cybersecurity posture perpetually. Since everyone handles data and information systems, everyone must innovate in their job roles. Everyone must learn to lead as well as follow and a culture of leadership and innovation must exist throughout the organization.

Cybersecurity is the mission focused and risk optimized governance of information, which maximizes confidentiality, integrity, and availability using a balanced mix of people, policy, and technology, while perennially improving over time [1].

A properly implemented cybersecurity strategy engages every member of an organization in achieving mission success and in perpetually improving its cybersecurity posture. The strategy enhances productivity and innovation of all workers of the organization. In addition, such a strategy provides key analytical data and metrics to the executive leadership team so they can maintain executive oversight, actively manage risks, and make optimal business decisions.

As organizations move from the old and static compliance model to the dynamic perpetual innovation model, every organization must be able to perform several key cybersecurity governance activities.

People are the most critical element of all these activities. As a matter of national security, the critical role of people and innovation in cybersecurity has to be recognized and accepted. Devastating cycles of intellectual capital loss, a perpetual state of low innovation and reduced teamwork as a result of contracting and churn has to be obviated.

2.6 Cybersecurity Is Interdisciplinary

Another major fallacy persistent in the minds of many people is that cybersecurity is a Science, Technology, Engineering, and Math (STEM) discipline. Cybersecurity is a business discipline. Disciplinary diversity of people is essential for a successful organizational cybersecurity strategy. People from almost any discipline such as sociology, linguistics, psychology, political science, language, arts, business, law, finance, criminal justice, or forensics can succeed is some aspect of cybersecurity and must be welcomed into the field. Indeed they are critical and cybersecurity education must embrace and teach all aspects of the cybersecurity model.

2.7 The Role of Governance

Governance is another misunderstood topic. Governance is frequently confused with compliance and control. However, governance is simply an organizational framework for ensuring the following [1, 4, 5]:

- Establish Culture and Tone for Conduct [6]
- Provide a Process for Decision-Making
- Establish Accountability, Roles, and Responsibilities [7]
- Establish Strategic Direction
- Encourage and Influence All to Achieve Goals
- Align Risks with Mission
- Implement Effective Controls, Metrics, and Enforcement
- Provides Clarity on Policies
- Provide Avenues for Idea Generation and Prioritization
- Foster Continuous Improvement

Governance requires the engagement of all possible stakeholders for an organization.

Governance must provide a structure, which encourages innovation and safe behavior similar to lanes and other controls on highways.

2.8 People Are Our Greatest Strength in Cybersecurity

People have frequently been maligned as the "weakest link" in cybersecurity. Those who adhere to this jaundiced view, resort to more control, cybersecurity awareness programs, and surveillance of people, which create a police state and stifle innovation.

Cybersecurity, by itself is meaningless and irrelevant to most people. Training must be relevant to the jobs people do. Training should stress job relevant technology usage and associated data safety practices. Forcing people to take cybersecurity awareness training, based on an outdated 1991 information security model, is dubious.

Phishing tests have dubious results as well because people fall for such schemes due to an amygdala hijack condition and the only way to fix this is to train people to move away from the stimulus even for 10 s before doing anything so that the chemical reaction caused by the amygdala hijack can subside [1]. People should be rewarded for ideas, successful innovations and improvements. People do not respond to purely negative policies.

2.9 Recommendation

Based on the principles identified in this paper, use cybersecurity leadership to implement a people powered perpetual innovation strategy as a lasting offensive and defensive cybersecurity strategy.

References

1. M. Hasib, *Cybersecurity Leadership: Powering the Modern Organization*, 3rd edn. (Tomorrow's Strategy Today, LLC., 2015)
2. K. Zachery, *The Leadership Catalyst: A New Paradigm for Helping Leadership Flourish in Organizations* (Bravo Zulu Consulting, LLC., 2012)
3. W.V. Maconachy, C.D. Schou, D. Ragsdale, D. Welch, A model for information assurance: an integrated approach, in *Proceedings of the 2001 IEEE Workshop on Information Assurance and Security*, United States Military Academy, West Point, New York, 5–6 June 2001, pp. 306–310
4. L. Corriss, Information security governance: integrating security into the organizational culture, in *Proceedings of the Governance of Technology, Information and Policy, 26th Annual Computer Security Applications Conference*, United States Military Academy, West Point, New York, 7 December 2010, pp. 35–41
5. T. Schlienger, S. Teufel, Information security culture: from analysis to change. S. Afr. Comput. J. **31**, 46–52 (2003)
6. T.E. Deal, A.A. Kennedy, *Corporate Cultures: The Rites and Rituals of Corporate Life* (Addison-Wesley, Reading, 1982)
7. A. Dutta, K. McCrohan, Management's role in information security in a cyber economy. Calif. Manag. Rev. **45**(1), 67–87 (2002)

Performance Study of the Impact of Security on 802.11ac Networks

3

Anthony Tsetse, Emilien Bonniord, Patrick Appiah-Kubi, and Samuel Tweneboah-Kodua

Abstract

Wireless Local Area Networks (WLAN) are gaining popularity due to the ease of use and ubiquity. Notwithstanding, their inherent characteristics make them more vulnerable to security breaches compared to wired networks. IEEE 802.11ac specification is currently the widely used WLAN standard deployed by most organizations.

We study the impact of security on 802.11AC WLANs using different security modes (No Security, Personal and Enterprise Security) using a test WLAN. The performance analysis is based on throughput, delay, jitter, loss ratio and connection time. Our experiments indicate a performance improvement when no security is implemented relative to other security modes. For throughput performance, improvements ranged between 1.6 and 8.2% depending on the transport (TCP/UDP) and network (IPv4/IPv6) layer protocol. Improvements between 2.8 and 7.9% was observed when no security is implemented for delay. Jitter, Loss Ratio and connection time experienced between 1.3 and 18.6% improvement in performance. Though the performance degradation because of implementing security measures on 802.11ac WLANs appear relatively insignificant per the study, we believe the situation could be different when a heterogeneously complex setup is used. However, other factors (e.g. channel congestion, interference etc.) may equally be responsible for the performance degradation in WLANs that may not be necessarily security related.

Keywords

Security · Wireless Network Performance · 802.11ac · IPv4 · IPv6

3.1 Introduction

In recent times, there has been tremendous advancement in Wireless Local Area Network (WLAN) Technology. The ubiquitous nature of Wireless network architecture has made the system one of the preferred data communication medium in the industry. 802.11ac [1] is one of current wireless communication standards deployed by most organizations and is part of the Wi-Fi (802.11) family of standards developed by IEEE. The specification indicates a default frequency of 5GHz and backward compatibility with earlier [1] standards (e.g. 802.11n) which operate in the 2.4GHz frequency range. The 802.11ac standard extends the capability of its predecessors at the MAC layer. Some of the enhancements in the 802.11ac standard include [2–4];

- extended channel binding
- Multi-user Multiple-input multiple-output (MU-MIMO)
- Spatial streams beam forming.
- Larger channel bandwidths of 80 and 160 MHz
- 256-quadrature amplitude modulation (QAM)
- A theoretical maximum aggregate bit rate of 6.7Gbps at the physical layer is achievable by 802.11ac access points using eight spatial streams.

A. Tsetse (✉)
Department of Computer Science, Northern Kentucky University, Highland Heights, KY, USA
e-mail: tsetse@nku.edu

E. Bonniord
IUT Laninion, University De Rennes, Rennes, France
e-mail: emilien.bonniord@etudiant.univ-rennesl.fr

P. Appiah-Kubi
Information and Technology University of Maryland University College, Largo, MD, USA
e-mail: Patrick.appiahkubi@umuc.edu

S. Tweneboah-Kodua
School of Technology, Ghana Institute of Management and Public Administration, Accra, Ghana
e-mail: stkoduah@gimpa.edu.gh

© Springer International Publishing AG, part of Springer Nature 2018
S. Latifi (ed.), *Information Technology – New Generations*, Advances in Intelligent Systems and Computing 738,
https://doi.org/10.1007/978-3-319-77028-4_3

Wireless Networks by virtue of their characteristics are vulnerable to various security threats compared to wired networks. Most WLANs operate in three security modes; no security, personal and enterprise security. 802.11i [5] standard is the defacto protection standard used in protecting WLANs. Wi-Fi Protected Access version 2 (WPA2) is widely used in the implementation of 802.11i. With Enterprise Security mode, a server is required to provide Authentication, Authorization and Auditing services to the connected nodes. In this study, a Remote Authentication Dial-In User Service (RADIUS) [6] Server running on Linux is used to implement the enterprise security protocols.

We have attempted to study the extent to which the security modes mentioned above impact 802.11ac WLAN performance by running several experiments using a test WLAN. The remainder of this paper is organized as follows. In Sect. 3.2, we briefly discuss related work. In Sect. 3.3, we describe our testbed network, and in Sect. 3.4, a discussion of our finding is presented. The conclusion and future work is given in Sect. 3.5.

3.2 Related Research

IEEE 802.11ac is a new wireless technology standard aimed at improving the speed of transmission, improve throughput, lower latency and improve power usage in wireless devices [7]. As a relatively new standard, research on 802.11ac is very elementary and attracting research interest. A study in [8] investigated the signal strength performance of IEEE 802.11ac in Wi-Fi communication and concluded that the technology can provide good signal quality over distance of up to 1 km as compared to IEEE 802.11n. An empirical study of performance and fairness of 802.11ac feature for an indoor WLAN was conducted in [9]. The study evaluated performance characteristics of the achievable data values of throughput, jitter and fairness in WLAN. Findings of the study showed 802.11ac achieved higher throughput and was fairer with wider channels compared to 802.11a/n. Enhancement for very high throughput in WLAN through IEEE 802.11ac was discussed in [10]. The paper introduced key features as well as MAC enhancements in 802.11ac that affect the performance. The paper further demonstrated that the aggregate MAC service data unit (A-MSDU), aggregate MAC protocol data unit (A-MPDU) and a hybrid of both units outperformed similar configurations in 802.11n. In [11], performance analysis of IEEE 802.11ac Distributed coordination function (DCF) with hidden nodes was conducted and the authors demonstrated that the traditional RTS/CTS handshake had shortcomings that had to be modified to support 802.11ac [21]. The power-throughput tradeoffs of 802.11n/ac in smartphone was discussed in [10]. Theory and practical Wi-Fi capacity analysis for 802.11ac/n was conducted in [12].

To the best of our knowledge, few known security studies have been performed on 802.11ac. Most security studies conducted on wireless standards were conducted on 802.11b/g/n [13–18]. These papers studied the effect of security on performance in WLANs and the robustness of the security standards implemented in these wireless standards.

3.3 Experimental Setup

A test WLAN was configured to run the experiments. Figure 3.1 depicts the topology of the testbed. In Fig. 3.1, Nodes 1 and 2 communicate with each other through the Wireless router and the Server. The experiments involved transmitting data between Nodes 1 and 2 and between Nodes and the webserver. Depending on the experiment run, the Server (Fig. 3.1) functions as a RADIUS Server or Webserver (Apache).

For experiments with no security, the wireless access point was configured such that no security credentials were required from connecting devices. Thus, the no security configuration was an open access network. The personal security mode involved setting up the wireless access point to require connecting devices to enter a paraphrase for authentication and traffic encrypted using AES. In Enterprise mode, clients have to enter a user name and password in other to gain access. The access point verifies these credentials through the RADIUS server prior to granting clients access. The RADIUS server uses Challenge Handshake Authentication Protocol (CHAP) for authentication.

Throughput, Delay, Jitter, Loss Ratio and connection time were used as the performance metrics. On the webserver, a webpage was hosted, allowing Nodes to request resources. The connection time for a Node to successfully establish a TCP connection with the webserver was measured using Wireshark [19]. IPerf3 [20] an open-source traffic analyzer was used as the packet generator to transmit data

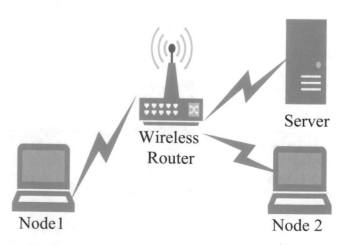

Fig. 3.1 Experimental testbed

Table 3.1 Technical specifications

Equipment/software	Function	Technical specification
Dell Latitude Laptop	Wireless nodes	4GBRAM Intel Core i5- 2410M CPU @ 2.3 GH × 4,64 bit Ubuntu 16.04,802.1ac NIC
Dell OptiPlex 790	Radius server/Apache server	8 GB RAM Intel Core i5- 2400M CPU @ 3.1 GH × 4 64 bit Ubuntu
Talon AD7200 Multi-Band Wi-Fi Router	Wireless router	10/100/1000 Mbps LAN Ports, 60 GHz, 2.4 GHz and 5 GHz bands, IEEE 802.11a/b/g/n/ac/ad
Iperf3	Traffic generator	
Wireshark	Packet capture/analyzer	

between Nodes and measured the metrics of interest. For each measured performance metric, we run 30 experiments for a duration of 30 s and the average value noted. Prior to running connection time related experiments, we cleared the browser cache of traces of any prior TCP connections with the webserver to avoid inaccurate results. The wireless router was configured to use 5GHz frequency range. Table 3.1 provides the technical specifications of equipment used.

3.4 Discussion of Results

Per the objectives of the study, three security modes were used: No security—representing the baseline scenario, Personal Security—using WPA2/AES and Enterprise Security using a WPA2/AES and RADIUS server. For each of these scenarios, IPv4 and IPv6 traffic was used with TCP and UDP as transport layer protocols. Loss Ratio and Jitter were measured only for UDP traffic.

3.4.1 Throuhgput

Figures 3.2, 3.3, 3.4, 3.5 and 3.6 indicate test results obtained for throughput using different payload sizes and varying the type of security mode and the network layer protocol (IPv4 or IPv6) used. In Figs. 3.2 and 3.3, it can be observed that throughput increases with increasing payload size for TCP and UDP traffic irrespective of the security mechanism deployed.

Figures 3.4 and 3.5 depict IPv6 TCP and UDP throughput respectively. From the diagrams, IPv6 traffic exhibits similar characteristic as IPv4. In Fig. 3.6, we compare throughput for various security modes and different network layer protocols. This figure serves as a summary of our findings for throughput. It is observed that regardless of the type of protocols deployed, throughput is generally higher when no security is

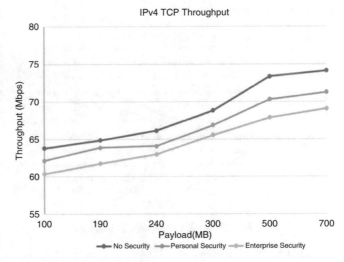

Fig. 3.2 IPv4 TCP throughput

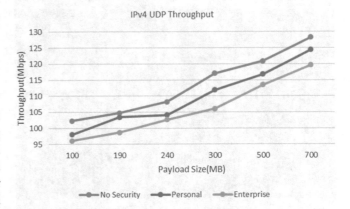

Fig. 3.3 IPv4 UDP throughput

deployed in the network. Thus, when no security is implemented, the WLAN experiences throughput improvements ranging from 1.1 to 6.7% over personal security. The performance improvement experience when Enterprise security is used ranges from 2.2 to 8.2%.The percentage improvement

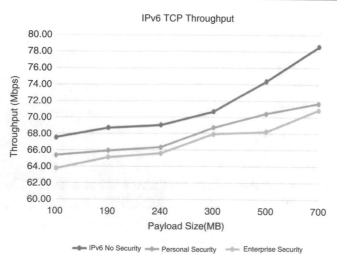

Fig. 3.4 IPv6 TCP throughput

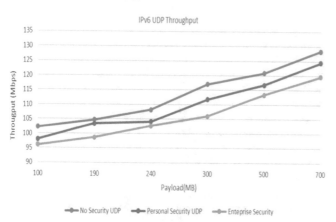

Fig. 3.5 IPv6 UDP throughput

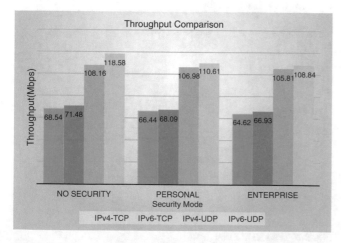

Fig. 3.6 Throughput comparison using different security modes

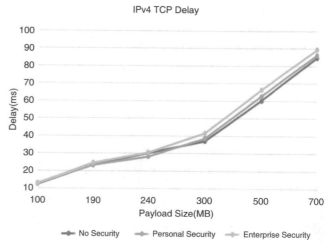

Fig. 3.7 IPv4 TCP delay

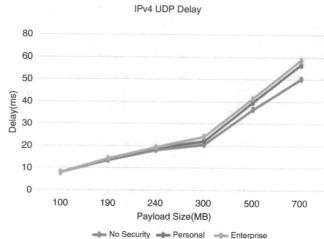

Fig. 3.8 IPv4 UDP delay

3.4.2 Delay

Delay as used here is defined as the time it takes to transfer data between two Nodes. This includes the time taken to establish a connection between nodes in the case of TCP traffic streams. Figures 3.7, 3.8, 3.9, 3.10 and 3.11 provide delay related data for our test network. For both UDP and TCP traffic as indicated in Figs. 3.7, 3.8, 3.9, 3.10 and 3.11, delay increases with increasing payload size. The same trend is true for IPv4 and IPv6 data. It can also be deduced that, consistently, when no security is implemented, the network tends to perform better in terms of delay.

In Fig. 3.11, we compare the delay under various security settings to determine the extent to which the various metrics and protocols impact delay. Based on the results in Fig. 3.11, a 5% performance improvement in delay is experienced for IPv6 relative to IPv4 when TCP is used as the transport layer protocol. Similarly, for UDP traffic, the performance improvement of IPv6 over IPv4 is 3%. In terms of security,

of IPv6 traffic over IPv4 traffic with regards to throughput ranges between 3 and 5% depending on the transport layer protocol used. The relatively better performance of IPv6 over IPv4 traffic can be attributed to the simple nature of the IPv6 header which reduces the amount of overhead processing.

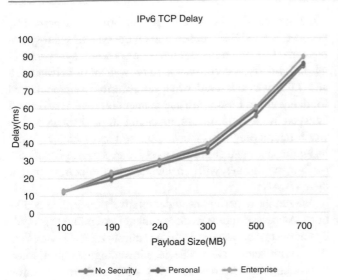

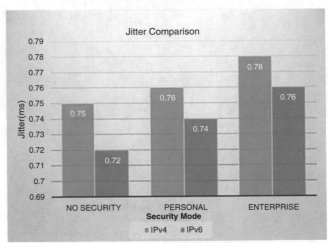

Fig. 3.9   IPv6 TCP delay

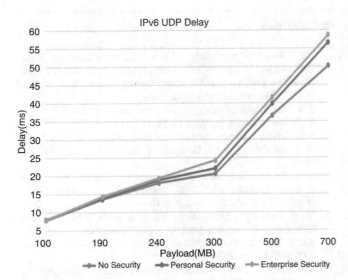

Fig. 3.10   IPv6 UDP delay

Fig. 3.12   Jitter comparison with different security modes

for TCP traffic when no security is implemented, there is a performance improvement of 3.3–4.5% over personal security and 5.7–8.8% over enterprise security. For UDP traffic, with no security, a 2.8–7.9% improvement is realized over personal security whiles an 8.0–11% enhancement of enterprise security is observed.

3.4.3   Jitter

The relatively simple nature of the testbed with no background traffic or congestion accounts for the low values obtained for jitter. It is likely these results may vary significantly when the network is scaled up. Furthermore (as shown in Fig. 3.12), for jitter, it is realized, a performance degradation of 3% using IPv4 traffic relative to IPv6. A 1.3–2.8% performance improvement is recorded when no security is used relative to personal security and 4–5.6% relative to enterprise security.

3.4.4   Connection Time

We define the connection time as the time it takes for a TCP connection to be established by measuring delay between the SYN and the ACK from the client. In Fig. 3.13, we observe no significant difference in connection time for cases where no security is implemented and personal security. However, there is an increase of about 14.2–18.6% when enterprise security is used. The extra time required by the RADIUS server to authenticate the client explains the increase in connection time.

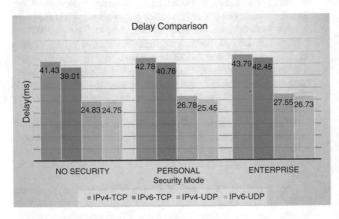

Fig. 3.11   Delay comparison with different security modes

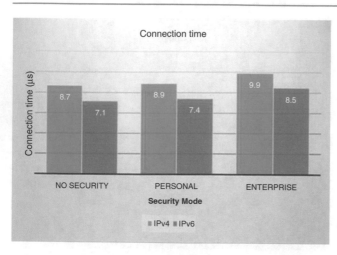

Fig. 3.13 Connection time

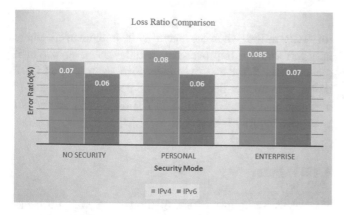

Fig. 3.14 Loss ratio comparison with different security modes

3.4.5 Loss Ratio

The Loss Ratio shows a similar trend as the other metrics used as shown in Fig. 3.14. Unlike the other metrics though, the performance improvements reported are quite significant in some cases. In particular, a 16.7–21.4% improvement is realized for no security over enterprise security. It is worth noting from Fig. 3.13 that, for IPv6 traffic there was no change in loss ratio when personal security is deployed relative to no security. Further experiments would be necessary, perhaps, to ascertain the validity or otherwise of this specific result.

3.5   Conclusion and Future Work

In this paper, we studied the extent to which various security modes impact the performance of 802.11ac WLANs by measuring throughput, delay, jitter, Loss Ratio and connection time. The results indicate a slight performance degradation when various security mechanisms are implemented on

802.11ac WLANs. For throughput performance degraded by between 1.6 and 8.2% depending on the type of security implemented and the transport and network work layer protocol used. Similarly, a performance improvement of between 2.8 and 7.9% was observed when no security is implemented for delay. Jitter, Loss Ratio and connection time experienced between 1.3 and 18.6% improvement in performance. It is worth mentioning that, much as these results may be quite insignificant, organization are likely to experience significant performance issues with an increase in the complexity of their WLANs.

We run the experiments under relatively controlled conditions. As part of future work, we intend extending the topology of the test network to include multiple Basic Service Sets (BSS) with heterogeneous devices including, but not limited to mobile handheld devices with some background traffic introduced in the network.

References

1. IEEE Standards Association, Wireless LAN medium access control wireless LAN (MAC) and physical layer (PHY) specifications. (2016), http://standards.ieee.org/getieee802/download/802.11-2016.pdf. Accessed 2 Aug 2017
2. R.V. Nee, Breaking the gigabit-per-second barrier with 802.11ac. IEEE Wirel. Commun. Mag. **18**(2), 4 (2011)
3. S.N. Kelkar, A survey and performance analysis of IEEE 802.11ac Wi-Fi networking. Int. J. Comput. Sci. Inf. Technol. **3**(2), 808–814 (2015)
4. M.-D. Dianu, J. Riihijarvi, M. Petrova, Measurement- based study of the performance of IEEE 802.11ac in an indoor environment, in *IEEE International Conference on Communications*, Sydney, 2014
5. IEEE Standards Association, Wireless LAN medium access control (MAC) and physical layer (PHY) specifications. (2007), [Online]. http://standards.ieee.org/getieee802/download/802.11-2007.pdf. Accessed 2 Aug 2017
6. FreeRADIUS, FreeRADIUS, [Online]. http://freeradius.org/. Accessed 1 Aug 2017
7. Nescout, Netscout White Paper, The impact of 802.11ac wireless networks on network technicians, Nescout, [Online]. http://enterprise.netscout.com/edocs/white-paper-impact-80211ac-wireless-networks-network-technicians. Accessed 1 Aug 2017
8. P. Li, S.S. Kolahi, M. Safdari, M. Argawe, Effect of WPA2 security on IEEE 802.11n bandwidth and round trip time in peer-peer wireless local area networks. Workshops of International Conference on Advanced Information Networking and Applications, in *International Conference on Advanced Information Networking and Applications*, 2011
9. L. Kriaia, E.C. Molero, T. R. Gross, Evaluating 802.11ac features in indoor WLAN: an empirical study of performance and fairness. in *ACM International Workshop on Wireless Network Testbeds, Experimental evaluation & CHaracterization*, New York City, 2016
10. H. Ong, J. Kneckt, O. Alanen, Z. Chang, T.T. Huovinen, T. Nihtila, EEE 802.11ac: Enhancements for very high throughput WLANs, in *IEEE Personal Indoor Mobile Radio Communitcations*, 2011
11. Z. Chang, O. Alanen, T. Huovinen, T. Nihtila, H. Ong, J. Kneckt, T. Ristaniemi, Performance analysis of IEEE 802.11ac DCF with hidden nodes, in *EEE 75th Vehicular Technology Conference (VTC Spring)*, 2012

12. T. Vanhatupa, *Wi-Fi Capacity Analysis for 802.11ac and 802.11n: Theory and Practice* (Ekahau Inc, 2015)
13. R. Mardeni, K. Anuar, A. Salamat, M.G.I. Yusop, Investigation of IEEE 802.11ac signal strength performance in Wi-Fi communication systems, in *Research World International Conference*, Osaka, 2016
14. P.D and B.D, The impact of security overheads on 802.11 WLAN throughput
15. H. Ce, *Effects of Security Features on the Performance of Voice over WLAN* (Stanford University Press, Stanford, 2004)
16. P. Likhar, R.S. Yadav, K.M. Rao, Securing IEEE 802.11g WLAN using OpenVPN and its impact analysis. IJNSA **3**(6), 97–113 (2011)
17. W. Agosto-Padilla, A. Loukili, A. Tsetse, A. Wijesinha, R. Karne, 802.11n wireless LAN performance for mobile devices, in *IEEE/ACS International Conference of Computer Systems and Applications (AICCSA)*, 2016
18. P. Jindal, B. Singh, Quantitative analysis of the security performance in WLANs. J. King Saud. Univ. **29**(3), 246–268 (2014)
19. Wireshark, Wireshark protocol analyzer, [Online]. https://www.wireshark.org/. Accessed 1 Aug 2017
20. IPerf, [Online]. https://iperf.fr/iperf-download.php. Accessed 2 Aug 2017
21. S. Saha, P. Deshpande, P. Inamdar, R. Sheshadri, D. Koutsonikolas, Power-throughput tradeoffs of 802.11ac in smartphones, in *IEEE Conference on Computer Communications (INFOCOM)*, 2015

Training Neural Tensor Networks with the Never Ending Language Learner

4

Flávio A. O. Santos, Filipe B. do Nascimento, Matheus S. Santos, and Hendrik T. Macedo

Abstract

Neural Networks have become the state-of-the-art technique in the field of Natural Language Processing (NLP). Many models attempt to learn and extend facts on graph-based knowledge bases (KBs). These datasets and models are valuable resources for many NLP tasks but are occasionally limited by data incompleteness. Previous work limited the number of relationships the model would learn from. In this paper we attempt to train a Neural Tensor Network (NTN) using 97 relationships from the Never Ending Language Learner (NELL) knowledge base. We compare its performance with previous NTNs trained with 11 relationships from Wordnet and 13 relationships from Freebase. Our model has achieved significant accuracy given the limited number of tuples per relationship in NELL's KB.

Keywords

Neural Tensor Network · Never Ending Language Learning · Knowledge base

4.1 Introduction

Natural Language Processing (NLP) is the field of Artificial Intelligence dedicated to giving machines the capacity to process and understand human language. Many NLP tasks rely on Machine Learning (ML) techniques [3]. State-of-the-art results come from Deep Learning (DL) techniques [13], which process and learn information in many layers of non-linear representations in order to understand and model relationships among complex data [11].

Most NLP solutions that exploit DL techniques use *word embeddings*, a vectorial space representation for words that estimates and attempts to quantify the likelihood of a relation between entities [5]. In order to learn word embeddings, these methods use data from Knowledge Bases (KB), which are graph-based datasets that represent facts in a relational manner.

Recent works have used a limited subset of relationships for each knowledge base with each relationship describing a large number of entities. We have trained a Neural Tensor Network (NTN) [20] using a bigger quantity of relationships from NELL's knowledge base (with fewer triples per relationship) in an attempt to verify the model's behavior in a more practical scenario.

The remainder of this paper is structured in four sections. In Sect. 4.2, we present related models that learn from knowledge bases and their respective cost functions. Section 4.3 details the NELL system and the Neural Tensor Network. The experiments are described and discussed in Sect. 4.4. Finally, our conclusions are presented in Sect. 4.5.

4.2 Related Works

There are knowledge bases that use semantic information about words, e.g. Freebase [4], WordNet [16], Dbpedia [2], NELL [8]. This information can be represented in the form of $t = (w_i, R, w_j)$, where R is a relation (semantic relationship) between words w_i and w_j.

There are also some models that learn the word representation through this semantic information. These models take tuple t as input and output a *score* value, expressing how close to the truth is the relationship R between the words w_i and w_j.

F. A. O. Santos (✉) · H. T. Macedo
Computer Science Postgraduate Program, Federal University of Sergipe, São Cristóvão, Brazil
e-mail: flavio.santos@dcomp.ufs.br; hendrik@dcomp.ufs.br

F. B. do Nascimento · M. S. Santos
Computer Science Department, Federal University of Sergipe, São Cristóvão, Brazil
e-mail: filipe.nascimento@dcomp.ufs.br; matheusss@dcomp.ufs.br

© Springer International Publishing AG, part of Springer Nature 2018
S. Latifi (ed.), *Information Technology – New Generations*, Advances in Intelligent Systems and Computing 738,
https://doi.org/10.1007/978-3-319-77028-4_4

The TransE model [6] represents a relationship R as a translation. If a relationship R between the words w_i and w_j exists, then w_i and w_j should be close to each other after translating w_i by R. Thus, the goal of the model TransE is:

$$S_{TransE}(v_i, R, v_j) = -||v_i + R - v_j||^2 \qquad (4.1)$$

where v_i and v_j are the w_i and w_j word embeddings, respectively.

The work of [23] introduces the RCM model. Its objective function is similar to the one used in word2vec [15]. The only difference is that, instead of considering the words in a sentence context as a neighbor, the RCM model uses all the words that have a semantic relationship with the current word. Thereby, its objective function is:

$$\frac{1}{T} \sum_{t=1}^{T} \sum_{w \in R_{w_i}} \log p(w|w_i) \qquad (4.2)$$

where R_{w_i} is the set of all the words that have a semantic relationship with w. $p(w|w_i)$ is estimated according to the Skip-gram formula:

$$p(w_{t+j}|w_t) = \frac{\exp(v'_{w_{t+1}}{}^T v_{w_t})}{\sum_{n=1}^{N} \exp(v'_{w_n}{}^T v_{w_t})} \qquad (4.3)$$

A modified version of the RCM model is proposed in [21]. Whereas this model's architecture is the same, they add functions that adjust the learning rate according to how often the words occur in the training *corpus*. They argue that this modification is necessary because the *word embeddings* of low frequency words cannot provide context diversity and as a consequence there is not enough information to capture the meaning of these words. details and clarity in Sect. 4.3 (Method) is insufficient.

The work of [22] introduces the RC-NET *framework*. It's main purpose is to incorporate knowledge into word representations. It is composed by three models: C-NET, R-NET and RC-NET. Given a set S of triples in the form of $t = (w_i, r, w_j)$, where w_i and w_j belong to the vocabulary W and r is the semantic relationship between these words. The R-NET foundation is that if the relation $t = (w_i, r, w_j)$ persists, then the distance between the representation of w_j and w_i plus r should be close. The cost function which R-NET attempts to minimize is:

$$C = [\gamma + d(w_i + r, w_j) - d(w'_i + r, w'_j)]_+ \qquad (4.4)$$

$$E_r = \sum_{(w_i,r,w_j) \in S} \sum_{(w'_i,r,w'_j) \in S'_{(w_i,r,w_j)}} C \qquad (4.5)$$

where $[x]_+$ represents the positive part of x, γ is a parameter and $d(x, y)$ is the euclidean distance between the vectors x and y. $S'_{(w_i,r,w_j)}$ is defined as follows:

$$A = \{(w'_i, r, w_j)| w'_i \in W\} \qquad (4.6)$$

$$B = \{(w_i, r, w'_j)| w'_j \in W\} \qquad (4.7)$$

$$S'_{(w_i,r,w_j)} = A \cup B \qquad (4.8)$$

where $S'_{(w_i,r,w_j)}$ is the set of noise tuples used to train via *noise contrastive estimation* (4.10). It is obtained from the set S such that $S'_{(w_i,r,w_j)} \cap S = \emptyset$. The RC-NET authors also propose training the C-NET along with the Skip-gram, so this combination's goal is to minimize the following cost function:

$$E_{r-join} = E_r - E_{sk} \qquad (4.9)$$

$$error = max(0, 1 - Score(x) + Score(x_c)) \qquad (4.10)$$

The R-NET is responsible for encoding word features in a way that words with the same features are close to each other. The authors define a function s that returns how similar two words are according to their attributes, so that given a word w_i:

$$\sum_{j=1}^{V} s(w_i, w_j) = 1 \qquad (4.11)$$

where V is the set of words from the vocabulary. To encode the features, the C-NET minimizes the following error function:

$$E_c = \sum_{i=1}^{V} \sum_{j=1}^{V} s(w_i, w_j)d(w_i, w_j) \qquad (4.12)$$

where d(x, y) is the euclidean distance between the vectors x and y. Finally, the RC-NET is a combination of the models C-NET, R-NET and Skip-gram. Its main goal is to minimize the following equation:

$$J_{rc} = E_c + E_r - E_{sk} \qquad (4.13)$$

4.3 Method

4.3.1 NELL

The Never-Ending Language Learner (NELL) is a semi-supervised learning agent based on an extension [18] of the prototype implementation proposed by Carlson et al. [8]. Its main task is to read the web and learn new information from it. It has been running since January 2010, extracting beliefs

Fig. 4.1 NELL's software architecture [18]

Fig. 4.1 NELL's software
architecture [18]

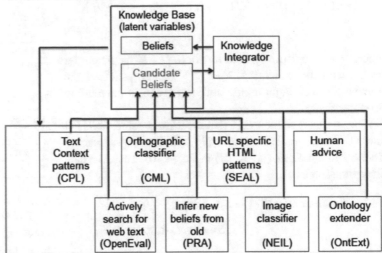

NELL Architecture

and using the facts to retrain itself every day, improve its reading capabilities and extend its knowledge base[18].

NELL's architecture is designed around a group of learning components that share a common knowledge base. The modules depicted in Fig. 4.1 are based on different learning methods, working collectively and interacting in order to perform learning, reading and inference tasks.

According to Mitchell et al. [18], these subsystems handle the following types of tasks:

1. CMC (*Coupled Morphological Classifier*): represents the noun phrase based on string features [9];
2. CPL (*Coupled Pattern Learning*): learns from context and uses patterns and co-occurrence statistics to extract information [8];
3. CSEAL (*Coupled SEAL*): Extracts information from semi-structured sources, namely HTML documents [9];
4. OpenEval: given a few seed predicates, this module evaluates the truth of new predicate instances by querying the web and processing the resulting web pages [19];
5. PRA (*Path Ranking Algorithm*): infers new relation instances from the graph representation of the knowledge base using random walks [12];
6. NEIL (*Never-Ending Image Learner*): module which extracts knowledge from images, restricted to a subset of NELL's categories [10].

The Knowledge Integrator is responsible for integrating beliefs proposed for the KB updates if the belief has high confidence from a single source or if it has been proposed with less confidence by multiple sources. The facts are stored in a Theo-based [17] knowledge base implementation that is able to handle millions of values on a single machine.

Initially, NELL was given an input ontology of categories (locations, people, animals, etc.), relations (e.g. *playsInstru-*

ment(George_Harrison, guitar)) and seed instances (10–15 examples for each relation and category). It has also been given access to 500 million English web pages from the ClueWeb09 data set and access to 100,000 Google API queries per day [18]. Since then, the research team started providing small human feedback in order to improve the learning process. Additionally, users are able to mark beliefs as correct or incorrect while browsing the knowledge base's web page.

NELL's ontology was manually provided at first, but it is now capable of extending itself by coming up with new relations using the OntExt system. Its learning capacity has proved to be very promising and has become a reliable source for neural network models, such as the Neural Tensor Network, described in the following section.

4.3.2 Neural Tensor Network

The Neural Tensor Network (NTN), proposed by Socher et al. [20], is a neural network model for knowledge bases that attempts to learn new true beliefs from an existing database. Instead of extracting information from text corpora, the NTN represents entities as vectors capable of storing facts related to a certain entity and also their probability of pertaining to a certain relation. Also, each entity is represented as the average of its word vectors so as to share statistical strength between words with similar substrings (e.g. *Bank of China* and *China*).

The NTN is a two-layer neural network with h units and a bilinear tensor that relates two words w_i and w_j. Given the word embeddings v_i and v_j, the score describing how likely it is that the two entities are in a relationship is modeled by the NTN-based function:

$$S_{NTN}(v_i, R, v_j) = \mathbf{U}^T f(v_i^T \mathbf{W_T} v_j + V_R \begin{bmatrix} v_i \\ v_j \end{bmatrix} + b_R),$$

$$(4.14)$$

where f is a logistic sigmoid function, $U \in R^h$ is the output layer vector, $W_R \in R^{d \times d \times h}$, $V_R \in R^{h \times 2d}$ and $b_R \in R^h$ are the bilinear tensor, weight matrix and bias vector of the relation R, respectively.

This model is trained via noise-contrastive estimation [14] and stochastic gradient descent [7] techniques by replacing $Score(x)$ with $S_{NTN}(v_i, R, v_j)$ in Eq. (4.10). Thus, the new error function is:

$$error = max(0, 1 - S_{NTN}(v_i, R, v_j) +$$
$$S_{NTN}(v_i, R, v_c))$$

$$(4.15)$$

where v_c is a random word that does not have a relationship with v_i.

4.4 Experiments

In Sect. 4.4.1, we describe the dataset as well as the training details for the experiment. Next, the results are presented and discussed.

4.4.1 Dataset and Training Details

From more than 430 relationships extracted from NELL's KB, 97 were selected for the following experiment. The NTN experiments [20] used a smaller amount of relationships (11 and 13 relationships for the Freebase and Wordnet datasets, respectively) and for each one there were a substantial amount of triples. On the other hand, our experiment with NELL attempts to work with the opposite: more relationships with less triples per relationship. The 97 relationships with the highest triple per relationship ratio were selected.

Table 4.1 shows statistical information about our proposed model using NELL in comparison to Socher's [20] experiments with Wordnet and Freebase. Although there are 430 relationships in NELL, most of them have a low triple frequency and therefore might not provide a good generalization capacity for the model. For the 97 relationships selected, 51,792 entities can be observed in a total of 158,490 triples. The training, testing and development sets were split using the distribution rates used by the NTN authors when applied to the Wordnet and Freebase datasets, which are 90%, 7% and 3%, respectively. In the end, the resulting amount of triples for training is 142,725, 11,053 for testing and 4712 for development.[1]

Table 4.1 Dataset statistics

Dataset	#R.	#Ent.	#Train	#Dev	#Test
Wordnet	11	38,696	112,581	2609	10,544
Freebase	13	75,043	316,232	5908	23,733
NELL	97	51,792	142,725	4712	11,053

Table 4.2 Dataset-accuracy comparison

Dataset	Accuracy.
Wordnet	86.2
Freebase	90.0
NELL	69.3

The NTN was trained with a learning rate of 0.01 and L2 regularization $\alpha = 0.0001$. The dimension of the hidden layer and the vectors for each entity was $d = 100$ and we used a Gaussian distribution in order to initialize every weight in the model. Also, the model was trained for 20 epochs and implemented on TensorFlow [1].

4.4.2 Results

Once the model was trained, the best achieved accuracy was 69.3%. Although it is worse than that achieved from experiments with Wordnet and Freebase datasets (Table 4.2), it is an acceptable value considering that the amount of triplets per relationship is indeed smaller in NELL than on the other KBs, which could have potentially hampered the model's generalization capacity, even though the most relevant relationships have been selected. For instance, the *concept-competeswith*, *concept-companyeconomicsector* and *concept-thinghascolor* relationships have 1401, 1378 and 367 triples, respectively.

The curve behavior seen in Fig. 4.2 shows that after achieving the highest accuracy around epoch 15, accuracy starts to decline without any further improvements.

4.5 Conclusion

Whereas the amount of triples per relationship is smaller in the dataset we used to train the NTN model, our experiment has shown that it is possible to use NELL's KB as a training dataset, which, due to the amount of relationships, is more likely to provide results that are closer to a real-life scenario.

Our work thus presents two main contributions: (1) enable the usage of a new dataset to train and test models such as the NTN and (2) experimental validation confirming that the NTN is able to learn from relations with low triple frequency.

As future work, we intend to improve experimentation with NELL's KB, perhaps increasing the number of re-

---

[1]The dataset used in this experiment is available at https://goo.gl/BZD12W.

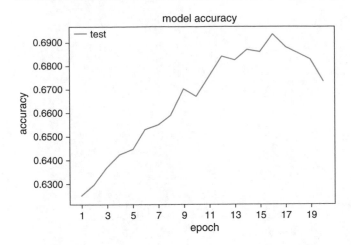

Fig. 4.2 Model accuracy

lationships extracted and certainly observing the behavior of accuracy curve with the variation of learning rate and regularization parameter value.

Acknowledgements The authors thank FAPITEC-SE for granting a graduate scholarship to Flávio Santos, CNPq for granting a graduate scholarship to Filipe Nascimento and a productivity scholarship to Hendrik Macedo [DT-II, Processo 310446/2014-7] and LCAD-UFS for providing a cluster for the execution of the experiments.

References

1. M. Abadi, A. Agarwal, P. Barham, E. Brevdo, Z. Chen, C. Citro, G.S. Corrado, A. Davis, J. Dean, M. Devin, S. Ghemawat, I.J. Goodfellow, A. Harp, G. Irving, M. Isard, Y. Jia, R. Józefowicz, L. Kaiser, M. Kudlur, J. Levenberg, D. Mané, R. Monga, S. Moore, D.G. Murray, C. Olah, M. Schuster, J. Shlens, B. Steiner, I. Sutskever, K. Talwar, P.A. Tucker, V. Vanhoucke, V. Vasudevan, F.B. Viégas, O. Vinyals, P. Warden, M. Wattenberg, M. Wicke, Y. Yu, X. Zheng, Tensorflow: large-scale machine learning on heterogeneous distributed systems, CoRR, abs/1603.04467 (2016)
2. S. Auer, C. Bizer, G. Kobilarov, J. Lehmann, R. Cyganiak, Z. Ives, Dbpedia: a nucleus for a web of open data, in *The Semantic Web* (Springer, Berlin, 2007), pp. 722–735
3. C.M. Bishop, *Pattern Recognition and Machine Learning* (Springer, New York, 2006)
4. K. Bollacker, C. Evans, P. Paritosh, T. Sturge, J. Taylor, Freebase: a collaboratively created graph database for structuring human knowledge, in *Proceedings of the 2008 ACM SIGMOD International Conference on Management of Data* (ACM, New York, 2008), pp. 1247–1250
5. A. Bordes, J. Weston, R. Collobert, Y. Bengio, et al., Learning structured embeddings of knowledge bases, in *AAAI*, vol. 6 (2011), p. 6
6. A. Bordes, N. Usunier, A. Garcia-Duran, J. Weston, O. Yakhnenko, Translating embeddings for modeling multi-relational data, in *Advances in Neural Information Processing Systems* (2013), pp. 2787–2795
7. L. Bottou, Stochastic gradient descent tricks, in *Neural Networks: Tricks of the Trade* (Springer, Berlin, 2012), pp. 421–436
8. A. Carlson, J. Betteridge, B. Kisiel, B. Settles, E.R. Hruschka Jr., T.M. Mitchell, Toward an architecture for never-ending language learning, in *AAAI*, vol. 5 (2010), p. 3
9. A. Carlson, J. Betteridge, R.C. Wang, E.R. Hruschka Jr., T.M. Mitchell, Coupled semi-supervised learning for information extraction, in *Proceedings of the Third ACM International Conference on Web Search and Data Mining* (ACM, New York, 2010), pp. 101–110
10. X. Chen, A. Shrivastava, A. Gupta, Neil: extracting visual knowledge from web data, in *Proceedings of the IEEE International Conference on Computer Vision* (2013), pp. 1409–1416
11. L. Deng, D. Yu, et al., Deep learning: methods and applications. Found. Trends Signal Process. **7**(3–4), 197–387 (2014)
12. M. Gardner, P.P. Talukdar, J. Krishnamurthy, T. Mitchell, Incorporating vector space similarity in random walk inference over knowledge bases (2014)
13. Y. Goldberg, A primer on neural network models for natural language processing. J. Artif. Intell. Res. (JAIR) **57**, 345–420 (2016)
14. M. Gutmann, A. Hyvärinen, Noise-contrastive estimation: a new estimation principle for unnormalized statistical models, in *Proceedings of the Thirteenth International Conference on Artificial Intelligence and Statistics* (2010), pp. 297–304
15. T. Mikolov, I. Sutskever, K. Chen, G.S. Corrado, J. Dean, Distributed representations of words and phrases and their compositionality, in *Advances in Neural Information Processing Systems* (2013), pp. 3111–3119
16. G.A. Miller, Wordnet: a lexical database for english. Commun. ACM **38**(11), 39–41 (1995)
17. T.M. Mitchell, J. Allen, P. Chalasani, J. Cheng, O. Etzioni, M. Ringuette, J.C. Schlimmer, Theo: a framework for self-improving systems. *Architectures for Intelligence* (1991), pp. 323–355
18. T.M. Mitchell, W.W. Cohen, E.R. Hruschka Jr., P.P. Talukdar, J. Betteridge, A. Carlson, B.D. Mishra, M. Gardner, B. Kisiel, J. Krishnamurthy, et al., Never ending learning, in *AAAI* (2015), pp. 2302–2310
19. M. Samadi, M.M. Veloso, M. Blum, Openeval: web information query evaluation, in *AAAI* (2013)
20. R. Socher, D. Chen, C.D. Manning, A.Y. Ng, Reasoning with Neural Tensor Networks for knowledge base completion, in *Advances in Neural Information Processing Systems* (2013), pp. 926–934
21. H.-Y. Wang, W.-Y. Ma, Integrating semantic knowledge into lexical embeddings based on information content measurement, in *EACL 2017* (2017), p. 509
22. C. Xu, Y. Bai, J. Bian, B. Gao, G. Wang, X. Liu, T.-Y. Liu, Rc-net: a general framework for incorporating knowledge into word representations, in *Proceedings of the 23rd ACM International Conference on Conference on Information and Knowledge Management* (ACM, New York, 2014), pp. 1219–1228
23. M. Yu, M. Dredze, Improving lexical embeddings with semantic knowledge, in *ACL (2)* (2014), pp. 545–550

PERIA-Framework: A Prediction Extension Revision Image Annotation Framework

Umer Rashid and Bakhtawar Arif

Abstract

Image annotation is a procedure to interpret the semantic concepts associated with image objects and represent them as their textual descriptions. Automatic and manual techniques have been extensively discussed in recent years to annotate the image objects, but are not without limitations. Automatic image annotation techniques mainly consider a single classifier and a descriptor type to annotate the image objects. Furthermore, thesaurus based extensions and human-centered revisions of the annotations are usually not possible. The fine-tuning of classifiers is generally not supported. In contrast to this, manual image annotation improves the accuracy, but tedious to annotate huge collections of image objects. Alternatively, semi-automatic image annotation techniques are human-centered, enhances the efficiency, and also speed-up the annotation process by machine intervention. In this research, a semi-automatic image annotation framework is proposed to address limitations in automatic and manual image annotation techniques. Our image annotation framework considers multiple descriptors and artificial neural networks to annotate the image objects. Along with that, a voting mechanism is provided to recommend the suitable annotations extendible by thesaurus and human revisions. Revised and extended annotations employed further to fine-tune the classifiers. Image annotation framework is instantiated and tested on a real dataset by implementing an image annotation tool.

Keywords

Annotation · Descriptors · Extension · Framework · Image · Prediction · Revision · Semi-automatic · Tool

U. Rashid (✉)
Quaid-i-Azam University, Islamabad, Pakistan
e-mail: umerrashid@qau.edu.pk

B. Arif
iENGINEERING Pakistan (Private) Limited, Islamabad, Pakistan

5.1 Introduction

Image annotation is described well in 'Paivio' dual coding theory; which portrays the image as mental imagery defined by logical or semantic concepts [1]. The 'Paivio' dual coding theory suggests basic mental imaginary as 'Logogens,' 'Imagens,' and an association in them. The imagens deal with the visual perception of image objects. Alternatively, the logogens are the textual interpretations and representations of individual perceptions about the image objects. Image annotation techniques have been exploited to associate imagens and logogens. In fact, in an image annotation technique, imagens and logogens are identified, interpreted, and mapped. An image annotation technique make it possible to identify, describe, and retrieve imagens by exploiting logogens [2]. An annotation procedure annotates an image object with the individual's textual description of the mental perceptions about the fundamental concepts or contents may exist in the image objects. The image resources can be better retrieved by the utilization of text retrieval techniques [3].

Image annotation techniques can be classified into automatic and manual [4]. Automatic image annotation techniques are widely accepted and utilized to tag a large number of image objects [4–6]. Automatic image annotation techniques usually consider a single descriptor type extracted from the image objects and a classifier in the annotation procedure. They also shorten the utility of the automatic classifiers. In fact, they confine the diverse conceptual and perceptual information in the few predefined annotations of image objects in the training examples.

In contrast to this, manual image annotation techniques confer more accurate results, by considering the human cognitive capabilities. Manual image annotation mechanisms are usually provided in social media applications. For example,

© Springer International Publishing AG, part of Springer Nature 2018
S. Latifi (ed.), *Information Technology – New Generations*, Advances in Intelligent Systems and Computing 738,
https://doi.org/10.1007/978-3-319-77028-4_5

Flickr,[1] Facebook,[2] and YouTube[3] are examples of social media application providing human-centered manual annotation procedures. They require human interventions to annotate the visual contents including image objects. The involvement of the community in the annotation procedure make annotation attractive. Despite that the process makes the entire annotation procedure awkward due to scalability issues associated with the manual annotations of visual contents.

In this research, we defined, instantiated, and evaluated an image annotation framework to annotate the image objects in a semi-automatic image annotation environment. In fact, we exploited automatic and manual image annotation techniques to annotate the image objects. Our image annotation framework utilizes multiple low-level image descriptors and classifiers to predict the image annotations. In our image annotation framework, the annotations are recommended via a voting mechanism. The annotation recommendation is an automatic process, while the extension and revision of image annotations are human-centered and are performed manually by the human intervention. The recommended annotations are also extendable by using thesaurus based extensions. Revised and extended image annotations by humans and thesaurus respectively are exploited further to fine-tune the existing trained classifiers. The predictions of image annotation are fully automatic and performed via automatic machine learning classifiers.

Our image annotation framework overcomes the deficiencies in the automatic as well as manual image annotation techniques. The image annotation process by the utilization of the multiple descriptors and classifiers can improve the precision and accuracy of the predicted annotations. The manual revision of the automatic annotations by humans and their thesaurus based extension make the annotation procedure human-centered. Furthermore, our image annotation framework speed-up the annotation procedure by employing automated classifiers. Furthermore, adaptation and fine-tuning of the trained classifiers improves image annotation accuracy.

The predictions of image annotation in an automated way decreases human cognitive load. Similarly, the extensions of the image annotations via thesaurus exploits the human recognition capabilities. Image annotation framework is instantiated, by implementing a full-fledged image annotation tool. Our image annotation tool employs multiple Artificial Neural Networks (ANNs) with feed-forward algorithms. The ANNs are trained on various types of color and texture based descriptors. The accuracy of image annotations via our framework evaluated via sample and average error rates

over a real dataset of image objects of natural scenes. The evaluation gives satisfactory results.

This article is organized as follows. We discussed background and motivation of the research work in Sect. 5.2. The image annotation framework is defined in Sect. 5.3. Framework instantiation is elaborated in Sect. 5.4. Evaluation and significance of image annotation framework is discussed in Sect. 5.5. We finally concluded our discussion in Sect. 5.6.

5.2 Background and Motivation

An image object is a symphony of the concepts and their context. An annotation technique tags an image with the textual description of the ideas confined in a given image object. Image annotation techniques can be broadly classified into automatic and manual. In the following sections, we will discuss image annotation techniques and motivational factors behind this research.

5.2.1 Automatic Image Annotation

Automatic image annotation techniques mostly exploit machine learning techniques to annotate the given image objects [7]. They exploit low-level image descriptors categorized into color, texture, edge, shape, etc., in training and automatic annotation of the image objects [8–11]. Classifiers are usually trained on pre-annotated sample datasets of image objects. In automatic image annotation techniques, a dataset containing the image objects is pre-annotated and used in the training. Descriptors are extracted from the image objects. They are used as example attributes and are mapped on annotations using automatic classifiers like neural networks, decision trees, and Naïve Bayes classifier [12–14]. Trained classifiers are exploited further to annotate the image objects in an automated way. An interactive image annotation system (I^2A) [15], new image auto-annotation method based on building simple Multivariate Gaussian Models for images (MAGMA) [16], A Hierarchical automatic Image Annotation System Using Holistic Approach (HANOLISTIC) [17], and Semantic Image Annotation and Retrieval (SIA) [18] are examples of automatic image annotation tools. In these image annotation tools annotation are usually performed via supervised machine learning techniques and the low-level descriptors extracted from the image objects in the training dataset.

5.2.2 Manual Image Annotation

In manual image annotation techniques, the domain experts perceive and interpret concepts to tag the image objects

---

in an image annotation process. The domain experts are considered as annotators; they perceive concepts in the given image and interpret their perceptions usually in precise and single word textual descriptions. The textual interpretations of the concepts of an image are identifiable concepts. Manual image annotation techniques are more accurate as compared to the automatic annotation techniques. Flickr, Facebook, YouTube, etc., are online tools providing manual annotation of visual contents. The users mostly annotate the visual contents via textual descriptions. Combinformation [19], PhotoStuff [20], LabelMe [21], DoctorEye [22], and a volume-object image annotation system (VANO) [23] are examples of tools providing manual annotation of image objects. In these search tools mostly an integrated and conducive environment is provided to present and annotate the image objects effectively by the human involvement.

5.2.3 Issues and Motivations

Automatic image annotation approaches usually associates few predefined concepts with image descriptors. In this way, the procedure is biased due to the strict association of predefined descriptors and concepts. Furthermore, classifiers also limit the annotations by the confinement of concepts and descriptors. In fact, in an automatic image annotation, differently perceived logogens can't be appropriately interpreted in few predefined annotations. Mostly the automated image annotation techniques exploit a single descriptor type and a classifier to annotate the image objects. The manual image annotations are usually influenced by the individual's visual perceptions and the thinking process. Manual image annotation techniques are highly biased by annotators' mental perceptions and imagery models, which negatively affects the image annotation process. Alternatively, manual image annotation techniques are not capable of annotating a considerable number of image objects in digital image archives.

Automatic as well as manual image annotations are common but not without the drawbacks. The semi-automatic image annotation techniques are candidates to annotation the image objects because they employ the best features of both techniques and give human-centered and accurate results. In this research to address the limitation of the existing image annotation techniques, our objective is to define, instantiate, and evaluate a semi-automatic framework to annotate the image objects. We are interested to propose a human-centered semi-automatic image annotation procedure. The objective is to extend and revise automatic image annotation by the humans. We are also interested in exploiting the extended and revised image annotations in fine-tuning of supervised machine learning techniques.

5.3 PERIA-Framework

In this research we proposed a **P**rediction **E**xtension **R**evision **I**mage **A**nnotation Framework (PERIA-Framework) mainly to provide the semi-automatic annotation of image objects. Particularly, PERIA-Framework is describe via an **I**mage **A**nnotation **P**rocess **M**odel (IAPM) constituted by prediction, extension, and revision phases. Image annotation is the outcome of progressive iterations in prediction, extension, and revision phases of IAPM. Figure 5.1 depicts prediction, extension, and revision mechanism provided in IAPM.

It is shown in Fig. 5.1 that annotations are evolved iteratively from prediction, extension, and revision phases. In fact, image annotation is performed in three stages. Firstly, the proposed process predicts the annotations via multiple predictors. The descriptors are in fact classifiers to suggest annotations by considering low-level features associated with image objects. Secondly, the recommendations are extended by the thesaurus and also by the user's intervention. The system provides a dictionary for extending the image annotations suggested in prediction phase. Thirdly, image annotators, which are, in fact, humans revise the image annotations. The revisions of image annotations provided by the predictors make the annotation procedure human-centered. The prediction is fully automatic while the extensions and revisions are manually performed via human interventions. The extended and revised image annotations are exploited further in adaptation and fine-tuning of the automatic image annotation classifiers.

In IAPM multiple classifiers are trained on the various descriptors representing color and texture information connected with image objects. In fact, descriptors are extracted from the image objects and further employed in the training of classifiers. Voting performed among the annotations

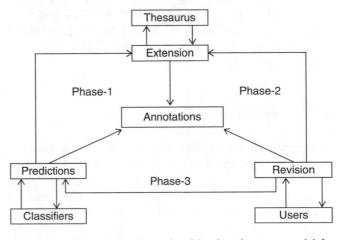

Fig. 5.1 Prediction, extension and revision based process model for semi-automatic image annotation

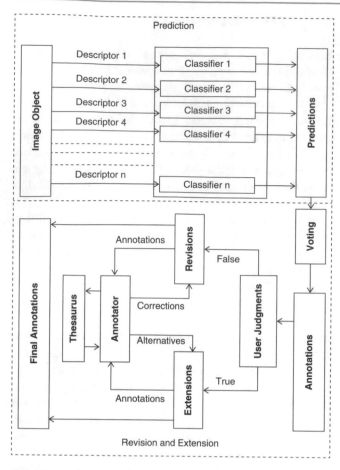

Fig. 5.2 Prediction, extension, and revision mechanism in PERIA-framework

mechanism recommends the final set of annotations. The annotations suggested by the highest number of classifiers are recommended as final set of annotations. Figure 5.2 depicts annotation prediction mechanism. Let $F_{ann} = C_1(D_{set1}) + C_2(D_{set2}) + C_3(D_{set3}) + \ldots + C_n(D_{setn})$ represents the annotation prediction mechanism adopted by different classifiers by employing particular descriptors. F_{ann} is a set of annotations of an image recommended by classifiers $C_1, C_2, C_3 \ldots C_n$. $C_1, C_2, C_3 \ldots C_n$ are trained on descriptors $D_{set1}, D_{set2}, D_{set3}, \ldots, D_{setn}$ respectively. The F_{ann} is calculated by voting of the annotations predicted by n different classifiers. In fact, the selected annotations are recommended by the maximum number of classifiers.

5.3.2 Extension Mechanism

The annotations recommended by the prediction mechanism are extendible by the utilization of the thesaurus. At this stage, annotator's intervention will become started in the annotation process. Extension mechanism provides an alternative way to predict collectively the annotations. Extension mechanism strengthens the annotations by selecting the appropriate perceptions of the annotations by the humans. Extensions of the correct annotations update the training dataset to fine-tune trained classifiers. Figure 5.2 represents the extension mechanism in PERIA-Framework. Let $F_{ext-ann} = F_{ext}(F_{ann}, H)$ represents extension mechanism. $F_{ext-ann}$ are extended annotations and F_{ext} is a function to provide extensions of annotations. The function gives thesaurus based extensions of the predicted annotations recommended in the previous phase. The extensions are performed by human annotators 'H' interventions.

5.3.3 Revision Mechanism

In the revision mechanism, annotators revise the wrong annotations manually. The revised annotations will become the part of a vocabulary. The revised annotations will update the training dataset by an addition of new and adaption of existing examples in the training dataset. The inclusion of a new example or updating of the existing example in the training dataset improves the accuracy of the classifiers. This process provides adaptation to the existing classifiers. Figure 5.2 represents revision mechanism. Let $F_{update-ann} = F_{update}(F_{ann}, H)$ denotes the revision mechanism. $F_{update-ann}$ be the updated annotations, and F_{update} be the functions that perform updates in the final annotations F_{ann} recommended in the prediction mechanism. The function is performed by human's 'H' intervention.

provided by predictors to select best recommendations. Since the annotations recommended by multiple classifiers and we are interested in choosing the annotations provided by a maximum number of classifiers. Predictions, extensions, and revisions iteratively performed in a conducive environment to annotate the image objects in a semi-automatic way by exploiting multiple classifiers, descriptors, thesaurus, and possible human interventions. Figure 5.2 represents the prediction, extension, and revision mechanisms adopted in PERIA-Framework.

5.3.1 Prediction Mechanism

The prediction mechanism utilizes multiple classifiers and descriptors to predict the annotations. In fact, in this mechanism multiple classifiers are trained on distinct descriptors associated with the image objects. The inputs and outputs of classifier are descriptors and concepts respectively. The concepts are associated with the image objects. A voting

5.4   PERIA-Framework Instantiation

We instantiated PERIA-Framework by implementing an Interactive Semi-Automatic Image aNnotations Tool (IT-SAIN). Our image annotation tool suggests automatically the image annotations by mapping low-level image object descriptors on the explicitly specified concepts in the training dataset. ANNs with feed-forward algorithms are employed as classifiers to map descriptors on the concepts in the image objects to provide automatic annotations. Recommended image annotations by ANNs are updated manually and extended by the thesaurus. The manually updated image annotations are further encountered in the training dataset. In this way, PERIA-Framework improves the accuracy of image annotation via retraining of the classifiers. The combination of automatic and manual techniques provides a semi-automatic technique to annotate the image objects.

IT-SAIN exploits five distinct, ANNs and descriptors (one ANN for one descriptor set). The descriptors include foreground color, background color, 3-D color histogram, edge, and, corner Information. The inputs of the ANNs are the numeric values of the extracted descriptors and outputs are the image annotations. In fact, we trained five ANNs separately on the extracted descriptors. The ANNs predicts the concepts for given input descriptors. The detailed structure of the ANNs and the descriptors extraction mechanisms is not discussed in this article due to space limitations.

In the implementation of IT-SAIN, we utilized C# and MatLab. We constructed and trained ANNs in MatLab and import them in a Matlab MAT-file. In this way, trained ANNs are permanently stored as a workspace and used to predict the annotations in IT-SAIN. We encapsulated MAT-file in a component and integrate into a C# application to predict the annotations. The descriptor extractors are also implemented in Matlab and finally integrated into the C# application to extract the descriptors associated with image objects. The application interface, extension, and revision mechanisms are also implemented in C#. Figure 5.3 represents the snapshot of implemented IT-SAIN Tool.

5.5   Evaluation and Discussion

IT-SAIN provides the instantiation of prediction, extension, and revision mechanisms. We evaluated the performance of predictor mechanism in terms of accuracy and error. The evaluation of extension and revision mechanisms is out of the scope of this research. We assessed the performance of multiple classifiers and descriptors employed in the prediction of annotations via a dataset of 150 images of natural

Fig. 5.3 IT-SAIN interface design

Table 5.1 The experimental results of image annotation prediction mechanism

Experiments	Test instances	Average (suggestions)	Misclassified	Correct classified	Sample error (error(h))	Average error (error(h))
Exp1	25	10	04	21	0.16	0.20
Exp2	25	09	06	19	0.24	
Exp3	25	09	03	22	0.12	
Exp4	25	10	07	18	0.28	
Exp5	25	11	06	19	0.24	
Exp6	25	07	04	21	0.16	

scenes. The 15 undergraduate students manually annotate the image objects with five distinct perceived concepts. We resolved the issue associated with the small number of training examples. We make use Jackknife mechanism with six folds in training and validation of the multiple ANNs employed in training. It is revealed from the experimentation that performance of the IT-SAIN reaches to 80%, without utilizing the extension, revision, and ANNs fine-tuning. It is also revealed that adaptation of the predictor's module can improve the accuracy of the IT-SAIN. Table 5.1 represents the experimental results.

PERIA-Framework utilizes the best features of automatic as well as manual image annotation techniques. Automatic by employing multiple classifiers and the descriptors to annotate the image objects and manual by extensions and revisions in the automatic image annotations. PERIA-Framework provides a mechanism for the automatic predictions of image annotations along with the explicit control to the users in the annotation process. The automatic annotation prediction mechanism is adaptable by employing user's image annotation experience that can be incorporated in future predictions. Now we will discuss some key features representing the significance of the proposed image annotation framework.

Classifiers are trained on the multiple descriptors associated with the image objects in the dataset. This type of training is advised because in some particular examples one descriptor type may give more accurate results as compared to the other kind of descriptors. Training may improve the accuracy of the classifiers, which may cause biasing in the interrelation of some particular descriptors with some specific concepts. This biasing is useful because it can target identification of the best descriptors in concept mapping. We also remove the biasing associated with particular classifiers and descriptors by considering the image annotations recommended by multiple classifiers.

Best annotations are selected using a particular voting mechanism. Multiple ANNs commonly choose annotations may be considered the best candidates for the future reference of image objects via annotations. The voting process tries to recommend the best predictions for image annotations. It may improve the accuracy of the automatic annotation process by extending and revising the image annotations.

The concept that is commonly recognized by the multiple ANNs using varying types of different descriptors may improve the overall accuracy of the predicted annotations.

Presenting annotations to users for revisions and extensions may speed-up the annotation process unlike in manual annotation techniques; since users are not forced to think about the annotations. They are just requested to revise the annotations. It may also decrease their cognitive burden and exploits their recognition capabilities by showing them the alternative image annotations. In PERIA-Framework automatic annotations are predicted and provide cues in the selection of appropriate annotations. The recommended annotations by the predictor may limit the different perceptual process, and best utilize the human recognition abilities.

Revision of the wrong annotations by the user can improve the quality of annotations since we enable the users to revise and correct the annotations. ANNs in the prediction mechanism is adopted according to the new, extended training datasets after retraining. Thesaurus-based extensions of the correct annotations by users also improve quality of annotations since updated annotations are reflected in the database. These concepts and image objects also update training dataset which may provide adaptations of the existing ANNs after re-training. The user interaction will evolve new dataset, so it includes diversities which are finally reflected in the predictions of the adapted ANNs.

5.6 Conclusion and Future Works

We defined, instantiated, and evaluated PERIA-Framework based on the three-factor process model to annotate image objects in a semi-automated way. Three factors are predictions, extensions, and revisions. PERIA-Framework utilizes the best properties of automatic as well as manual annotation techniques. Our framework uses individual classifiers using different descriptors extracted from the image objects. A voting mechanism will recommend the best annotations among predicted annotations. Automatic annotations are updated using thesaurus based extension and corrections. Updated image annotations take part in the adaptations of the existing classifiers. IT-SAIN is designed and developed to annotate image objects. IT-SAIN suggests image annotations by exploiting multiple ANNs and descriptors. IT-SAIN also facilitates prediction and extension mechanism defined in PERIA-Framework. The prediction accuracy of IT-SAIN is 80%, which can be further improved by the utilization of extension and revision mechanisms available in IT-SAIN. In future, we will elaborate the design, implementation, and work of IT-SAIN. We will deploy IT-SAIN in web settings and perform exhaustive experimentation to evaluate the proposed prediction, extension, and revision mechanisms.

Acknowledgements The authors would like to acknowledge the provision of the research facilities provided by Department of Computer Sciences, Quaid-i-Azam University, Islamabad, Pakistan to carry out this research work. Authors would also acknowledge the finical support offered by Higher Education Commission, Pakistan to present this research work in the conference.

References

1. M.G. Van Doorn, A.P. de Vries, The psychology of multimedia databases, in *Proceedings of the Fifth ACM Conference on Digital Libraries* (ACM, New York, 2000), pp. 1–9
2. M. Kolodnytsky, N.O. Bernsen, L. Dybkjær, A visual interface for a multimodal interactivity annotation tool: design issues and implementation solutions, in *Proceedings of the Working Conference on Advanced Visual Interfaces* (ACM, New York, 2004), pp. 407–410
3. R. Baeza-Yates, B. Ribeiro-Neto, et al., *Modern Information Retrieval*, vol. 463 (ACM, New York, 1999)
4. A. Hanbury, A survey of methods for image annotation. J. Vis. Lang. Comput. **19**(5), 617–627 (2008)
5. Y. Jin, L. Khan, L. Wang, M. Awad, Image annotations by combining multiple evidence & wordnet, in *Proceedings of the 13th Annual ACM International Conference on Multimedia* (ACM, New York, 2005), pp. 706–715
6. P.G. Enser, C.J. Sandom, P.H. Lewis, Automatic annotation of images from the practitioner perspective, in *Proceedings of International Conference on Image and Video Retrieval* (Springer, Cham, 2005), pp. 497–506
7. J. Li, J.Z. Wang, Real-time computerized annotation of pictures. IEEE Trans. Pattern Anal. Mach. Intell. **30**(6), 985–1002 (2008)
8. P. Rogelj, S. Kovacic, Local similarity measures for multimodal image matching, in *Proceedings of the First International Workshop on Image and Signal Processing and Analysis* (IEEE, Piscataway, 2000), pp. 81–86
9. K. Zagoris, S.A. Chatzichristofis, N. Papamarkos, Y.S. Boutalis, Automatic image annotation and retrieval using the joint composite descriptor, in *Proceedings of 14th Panhellenic Conference on Informatics (PCI)* (IEEE, Piscataway, 2010), pp. 143–147
10. O.A. Penatti, E. Valle, R.d.S. Torres, Comparative study of global color and texture descriptors for web image retrieval. J. Vis. Commun. Image Represent. **23**(2), 359–380 (2012)
11. A. Yavlinsky, E. Schofield, S.M. Rüger, Automated image annotation using global features and robust nonparametric density estimation, in *Proceedings of International Conference on Image and Video Retrieval*, vol. 3568 (Springer, Cham, 2005), pp. 507–517
12. Y. Zhao, Y. Zhao, Z. Zhu, J.-S. Pan, A novel image annotation scheme based on neural network, in *Proceedings of Eighth International Conference on Intelligent Systems Design and Applications*, vol. 3 (IEEE, Piscataway, 2008), pp. 644–647
13. L. Jiang, J. Hou, Z. Chen, D. Zhang, Automatic image annotation based on decision tree machine learning, in *Proceedings of International Conference on Cyber-Enabled Distributed Computing and Knowledge Discovery* (IEEE, Piscataway, 2009), pp. 170–175
14. S. Rui, W. Jin, T.-S. Chua, A novel approach to auto image annotation based on pairwise constrained clustering and semi-naive bayesian model, in *Proceedings of 11th International Conference on Multimedia Modeling* (IEEE, Piscataway, 2005), pp. 322–327
15. M. Dong, C. Yang, F. Fotouhi, I^2a: an interactive image annotation system, in *Proceedings of IEEE International Conference on Multimedia and Expo* (IEEE, Piscataway, 2005), pp. 1–4
16. B. Broda, H. Kwasnicka, M. Paradowski, M. Stanek, Magma—efficient method for image annotation in low dimensional feature space based on multivariate Gaussian models, in *Proceeding of International Multiconference on Computer Science and Information Technology* (IEEE, Piscataway, 2009), pp. 131–138
17. O.O. Karadag, F.T.Y. Vural, Hanolistic: a hierarchical automatic image annotation system using holistic approach, in *Proceedings of IEEE Computer Society Conference on Computer Vision and Pattern Recognition Workshops* (IEEE, Piscataway, 2009), pp. 16–21
18. P. Koletsis, E.G. Petrakis, Sia: semantic image annotation using ontologies and image content analysis, in *Proceedings of International Conference Image Analysis and Recognition* (Springer, Cham, 2010), pp. 374–383
19. A. Kerne, E. Koh, B. Dworaczyk, J.M. Mistrot, H. Choi, S.M. Smith, R. Graeber, A. Caruso, A. Webb, R. Hill, et al., Combinformation: a mixed-initiative system for representing collections as compositions of image and text surrogates, in *Proceedings of the 6th ACM and IEEE-CS Joint Conference on Digital Libraries* (ACM, New York, 2006), pp. 11–20
20. C. Halaschek-Wiener, J. Golbeck, A. Schain, M. Grove, B. Parsia, J. Hendler, Photostuff-an image annotation tool for the semantic web, in *Proceedings of the 4th International Semantic Web Conference* (2005)
21. A. Torralba, B.C. Russell, J. Yuen, Labelme: online image annotation and applications. Proc. IEEE **98**(8), 1467–1484 (2010)
22. E. Skounakis, V. Sakkalis, K. Marias, K. Banitsas, N. Graf, Doctoreye: a multifunctional open platform for fast annotation and visualization of tumors in medical images, in *Proceedings of Annual International Conference of the IEEE Engineering in Medicine and Biology Society International Conference of the IEEE* (IEEE, Piscataway, 2009), pp. 3759–3762
23. H. Peng, F. Long, E.W. Myers, Vano: a volume-object image annotation system. Bioinformatics **25**(5), 695–697 (2009)

The Modern State and the Further Development Prospects of Information Security in the Republic of Kazakhstan

Askar Boranbayev, Seilkhan Boranbayev, Assel Nurusheva, and Kuanysh Yersakhanov

Abstract

As information technologies are embedding in increasing number of spheres of life of states and societies, dependence on the use of them transforms in new vulnerabilities and security concerns for entire states. The article is devoted to the analysis of the modern state of information security in the Republic of Kazakhstan. This article reviews the law, standards, technologies and incidents in the field of information security. Some statistics of information security events, threats and incidents are considered. The measures to provide information security in Kazakhstan including the basic norms of information security of information systems, resources and networks are described. The importance of timely elimination of vulnerabilities, exclusion and prevention of information security threats and incidents is highlighted. In conclusion the authors emphasizes that effective ways to solve the existing problems of low security clearance is full implementation of the specific recommendations are made to improve the information security of the country.

Keywords

Information security · Information technology · Vulnerability · Incident · Threat · Standard

A. Boranbayev
Department of Computer Science, Nazarbayev University, Astana, Kazakhstan
e-mail: aboranbayev@nu.edu.kz

S. Boranbayev (✉) · A. Nurusheva · K. Yersakhanov
Department of Information Systems, L.N. Gumilyov Eurasian National University, Astana, Kazakhstan
e-mail: sboranba@yandex.kz

6.1 Introduction

The global trends, which are actual for today, signal about the formation of the new types of threats to the security of Kazakhstan, among which the issues of information security are the most prioritized. The immediacy of this issue in the country, as well as all over the world, is growing every day: articles about ".KZ" Kazakhstan domain Internet-resources hacking, a bank robbery by electronic intruders, phishing links, DDoS attacks, etc. are publishing more and more often.

Let us consider some statistics of the most popular companies in this field. So, according to APWG, in the period from October to December 2016 there were about 277.7 thousand unique sites-traps and 211 thousand phishing mails. Over the year, the cumulative number of phishers' attacks was increased by 65% and exceeded 1.22 million. Intruders continued to favor the retail sector (41.85% of attacks) and financial organizations (19.60%). 12.58% of phishing attacks was for Internet services, 11.33%—for payment services [1].

APWG statistics on infections were presented by PandaLabs: in the 4th quarter of 2016 experts on average recorded 190 thousand new malware samples, three-quarters of them were Trojans. The top three infected countries in the world are: China (47.09%), Turkey (42.88%) and Taiwan (38.98%). The most "clean" countries were the Scandinavian countries.

Among the most recent media publications we can emphasize following: Kazakh policemen curbed the activities of the hacker group, which stole about 60 million tenge from accounts of domestic enterprises and clients of banks. The actions of hackers who steal money from accounts of financial institutions are qualified according to art. 188, par. 2 of the Criminal Code of Kazakhstan as illegal access into the information system [2].

Information security is a strategic category that can be considered in the aspect of social and economic development as a policy aimed at ensuring the protection of information, its influence on the consciousness of society and individual, monitoring of existing and possible threats and prevention of wars in the field of informatization. Thus, we can note that the main areas of the national security system are such tasks as the searching of the abovementioned factors and the appropriate countermeasures development [3].

The active development of information technologies has expanded the specialists' technical capabilities in the field of information security. Information security depends largely on the security of technical structures, the failure of which can lead to disruption of the integrated security system. So, at present, information and communication technologies are the main factors determining the level of socio-economic development and the state of international information security [4].

In this regard, in recent years a number of measures have been implemented to improve the system of state information security in Kazakhstan. The regulatory documentation and technologies, which used both in the private organizations and in the development of "e-Government", have been constant improvement. The main trend in the field of information security is aimed at the timely detection and further prevention of the information security threats and incidents.

The Law of the Republic of Kazakhstan on National Security is the most priority document aimed at regulating relations in the sphere of security ensuring in Kazakhstan, which separately highlights information security as a security state of the information space of Kazakhstan, human, society and state rights and interests in the information sphere from threats, while ensuring of sustainable development and information independence of the country [5]. The law defines the following threats to national security: the informational impact on the consciousness of the public and the individual, related to the information propagation to the detriment of national security; reducing the security of the information space of the country, national information resources against unauthorized access, etc. Thus, security determines the quality of national security, which allows assessing the effectiveness of measures to prevent the threats and their timely elimination.

6.2 Measures to Provide Information Security in Kazakhstan

According to the Law of the Republic of Kazakhstan on Informatization, information security in the field of informatization is defined as security of the information resources and systems and information and communication infrastructure against the threats [6].

Let us consider some basic requirements to the state information systems. One of the basic requirements is the implementation of the creation, operation and development of information systems in accordance with the lifecycle,

the standards in force in Kazakhstan and the law, including the unified requirements in the field of information and communication technologies (ICT) and information security (hereinafter—unified requirements).

Thus, the state information system is created and developed taking into account several basic measures of information security:

- the operation testing in accordance with unified requirements, including testing for compliance with information security requirements, optimization and elimination of defects with correction of the defects;
- the attestation of the state information system and Internet-resource, information and communication platform of "e-Government" for compliance with information security requirements in the commissioning period;
- the implementation of the state information system in accordance with the standards in force in Kazakhstan, etc.

During industrial use of the state information system the following requirements are provided:

- the unified requirements implementation;
- their protection and recovery in case of failure and damage;
- the information security events monitoring with the transfer of its results to the monitoring system of State technical service, etc.

On January 9, 2017, the Decree of the Government "On the Approval of Unified Requirements in the Field of ICT and Information Security" came into force.

To determine the critical objects of information and communication infrastructure, the Rules and criteria for assigning objects of information and communication infrastructure to critical objects of information and communication infrastructure work in Kazakhstan [7].

Unified requirements represent a kind of codification consisting of the previously disparate norms and harmonized in Kazakhstan technical standards in the field of information technologies and information security. The document describes the procedures and rules for the use of information technologies with regard to processing of types of information that protected by law and do not contain state secrets [8].

It is necessary to note the importance of the appropriate measures organizing at the pointed lifecycle phases.

At present in Kazakhstan at the phase of operation testing of the state information system it is mandatory to pass testing for compliance with the information security requirements, at the commissioning phase—to pass attestation for compliance with information security requirements and at the production phase—to conduct monitoring of the protection, information security and safe functioning of the state information system and monitoring of the unchanged conditions of functioning and functionality of the state information system in accordance with the information security requirements.

During the attestation and monitoring of the securing of the information system, it is carried out an instrumental scanning—a scanning for a remote or local diagnosis of communication channels, nodes, servers, workstations, application and system software, databases and network elements by software tools to detect vulnerabilities in it (weakness of an object that can disrupt the operation of the object, or lead to unauthorized access bypassing used information security tools) [9]. The information objects owners themselves should promptly eliminate all identified vulnerabilities to secure of information objects. For example, in April 2016, the information about the existence of vulnerability on "egov.kz" was published [10]. The vulnerability allowed downloading a document without authorization through a direct link, as well as attacking by direct enumeration to obtain documents or citizens' documents through their UIN. As a result of the taken measures, the vulnerability was deleted.

IP-networks are also vulnerable to many methods of unauthorized intrusion into the data exchange process. As the technologies develop, the list of possible types of network attacks to IP-networks is constantly expanding [11]. The most growing threats are the following: sniffing, data changing, network traffic analyzing, IP-spoofing, mediation, mediation in the exchange of unencrypted keys, session hijacking, denial of service (DoS), password attacks, key guessing, application level attacks, Web intelligence, abuse of trust attack, computer viruses, network worms, "Trojan horse" program [12].

The state networks connection to Internet is provided through unified access gateway to the Internet, which significantly reduces the number of information security incidents. It is a hardware-software complex, which protect networks of the state bodies of Kazakhstan.

In 2010, Kazakhstan was the leader in the spam spreading in Central Asia (89.2% of the total volume of unwanted mail in the region, but only 0.66% of the global volume: 32nd place in the world) [13]. According to the information of Kaspersky Lab, in 2013 Kazakhstan ranked 7th place in the world in spam spreading (3.4%) [14], and in 2016 Kazakhstan already left the leading positions [15].

The unified e-mail gateway of "e-Government is a hardware-software complex, which secure the e-mail of the "e-Government" in Kazakhstan.

The specialists note that Kazakhstan's state systems are not a priority for the attack: the country is not in conflict relations and Kazakhstan's data are of less value than the information of the departments of more developed states. If you evaluate how a country is prepared in terms of technical information security, you can pay attention to the passport of cybernetic well-being, which is maintained by the International Telecommunication Union at the United Nations. Union specialists note that today in Kazakhstan they remain unrealized next measures: lack of an officially recognized basis for the implementation of international information security standards; lack of a basis for accreditation and certification of national agencies or specialists; lack of a state road map for cybersecurity; lack of standards for assessing of the cybersecurity development; lack of officially recognized national or sectorial programs for research and development of best practices on cybersecurity; lack of training programs for professional development of specialists; lack of the necessary number of the specialists certified according to international security standards; lack of officially recognized national or sectorial programs for the exchange of experience within the public and private sectors in Kazakhstan.

Among the executed items we can see the work of legislation, and that Computer Emergency Response Teams (CERT/CSIRT) were also established in Kazakhstan as in other countries of the world.

It should be noted that the Committee of Information security of the Ministry of Defense and Aerospace Industry of the Republic of Kazakhstan has been established. It exercises regulatory, implementation and control functions, participates in the implementation of the strategic functions of the Ministry in the field of information security. One of the functions of this body is "the development of legal, administrative and other measures to ensure information security, control of its implementation and compliance, as well as interdepartmental coordination of the activities to ensure information security". Also, the Committee has the task to organize work on the development of regulations and national standards within own competence.

It is important to note that the security and efficiency of information systems should be based on compliance with the basic requirements for information security according to the following standards:

ST RK ISO/IEC 27001-2008 "Information technology. Security Techniques. Information security management systems. Requirements";

ST RK ISO/IEC 27002-2009 "Information technologies. Security Techniques. Code of practice for information security management".

Technical means of the information system must meet the regulatory requirements for security in accordance with the following State Standards ("GOST"):

1. GOST 25861-83—on computer equipment;
2. GOST 12.2.007.0-75—on electro technical products;

3. GOST 12.1.003-83—on the level of noise and sound power;
4. GOST 12.1.019-79—for electrical safety. General requirements and nomenclature of security types;
5. GOST 12.1.030-81—for electrical safety. Protection earth. Neutralling.

The information system must comply with the regulatory framework of the Republic of Kazakhstan ST RK 34.023-2006 "Information technology. Method for assessing the compliance of information systems with security requirements".

However, the introduction of this type of certification does not a guarantee of complete safety. President of the Center for Analysis and Investigation of Cyber Attacks O. Satiev notes that all banks are certified by PCI-DSS (the security standard for payment cards developed by the Council for the Payment Card Industry Data Security Standards), however, there are occasional news about hacking of this or another bank in Kazakhstan.

Also, according to President's address of the Republic of Kazakhstan N. Nazarbayev, one of the strategic priorities for the development of Kazakhstan is the development of the national system "Cybershield". Currently, work is actively being carried out to develop proposals aimed at implementing this system.

6.3   Overview of Information Security Incidents in Kazakhstan

National Computer Emergency Response Team KZ-CERT is the single centre for national information systems users and Internet segment providing collection and analysis of security incidents reports as well as assistance to users in prevention of cyberthreats. Primary goal of KZ-CERT is the counteracting of cyberthreats to Internet users. KZ-CERT collection, analysis and storing statistical information concerning malware, hacker attacks or other existing threats to cybersecurity of the Republic of Kazakhstan. KZ-CERT processes computer security incidents listed below to prevent and neutralize them in the future: attacks on network infrastructure in order to render them unavailable to legitimate users (DoS и DDoS) and to endanger the confidentiality of information; unauthorized access to information resources; spreading the malware and unsolicited mail (spam); hostile scanning of national information networks and hosts; brute-forcing of passwords or other authentication data; hacking security systems, including planting of malicious software (sniffers, rootkits, keyloggers etc) [16].

Thus, according to KZ-CERT.KZ statistics, for the period from 2011 to 2015, 45,179 incidents were monitored by Computer Emergency Response Teams, where 432 of them were found on the resources of the state bodies. Figure 6.1 shows detailed information on number of the processed incidents for the period from 2011 to 2015. Figure 6.2 shows detailed information on the types of the processed incidents for the period from 2011 to 2015 [17].

As can be seen from the figures, the greatest number of incidents is associated with botnet—one of the most significant and ever growing threats to the Internet, which can lead to devastating consequences. The infected computer armies can control the computers to harm others even if their owners do not know and do not use them. They are controlled as a whole one through the Internet, using various management strategies. Botnet can be used for spamming, phishing or as spyware, but often they are used to implement distributed denial of service (DDoS) attacks. This type of cyberattack makes Internet service unavailable for the users, creating a huge amount of traffic consuming all of the victim's resources [18].

Also, the Center for Analysis and Investigation of Cyber-attacks created the first private Kazakhstan Computer Emergency Response Center (CERT.KZ) in Kazakhstan. The main activity of the Center is to assist the competent authorities of Kazakhstan and private structures in the detection and analysis of cyber-crime, the development of Information Security Institute, as well as conducting an information security audit, etc. [19].

Publications in the media confirm that the risks in the field of data protection in Kazakhstan are very high. In 2014, according to Kaspersky Lab, 25% of Kazakhstan companies were subjected to DDoS attacks [20]. This share among the organizations reaches 38%. 40% of these companies lost contracts because of these attacks, 10%—lost current customers, and 20%—suffered reputational losses [21]. Often, the protection of companies is limited to the installation of anti-virus programs on corporate computers, whereas in fact, it is necessary to systematically change the business process itself, change the habits of employees, etc.

6.4   Conclusion

Analysis of the modern state of information security in the Republic of Kazakhstan shows the growth of information security threats. Today to prevent these threats it is implemented the abovementioned measures.

Thus, we can note the positive dynamics of the information security state in Kazakhstan. However, it is important to develop the abovementioned measures, as well as the implement the following areas:

- the control of timely elimination of vulnerabilities, exclusion and prevention of information security threats and incidents;

Fig. 6.1 Number of the incidents for the period from 2011 to 2015

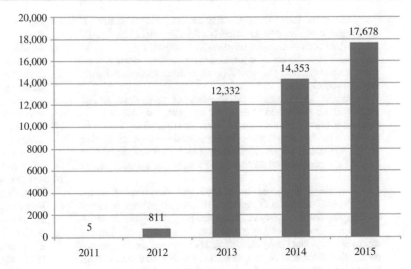

Fig. 6.2 Types of the incidents for the period from 2011 to 2015

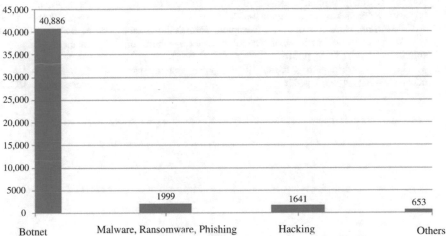

- the opening of additional specialties in the universities (bachelors, masters, PhD doctors) and the training of specialists certified in accordance with international security standards and training programs;
- the development of the domestic information security industry: the stimulation of domestic software and hardware manufacturers;
- the organization of research and development work in the field of cybersecurity, development of the domestic certification laboratories;
- the development of the national standards and techniques in the field of information security, including harmonization with international standards and technical regulations;
- the development of the cybersecurity standards and an officially recognized framework for the implementation of recognized international information security standards;
- the development of the basis for accreditation and certification of national agencies or specialists;
- the development of the state road map on cybersecurity;

- the development of international cooperation and officially recognized national and sectorial programs for the exchange of experience within the public and private sectors in Kazakhstan, as well as research and development of best practices on cybersecurity, etc.

It must be remembered that the information security requires an integrated approach. Non-fulfillment of any component in information security can lead to increased risks of implementation of negative consequences [22, 23].

References

1. https://docs.apwg.org/reports/apwg_trends_report_q4_2016.pdf
2. http://profit.kz/news/38114/V-Kazahstane-pojmali-hakerov-ukravshih-u-bankov- okolo-60-mln-tenge/
3. A.A. Streltsov, Actual problems of information security. Secur. Technol. **11**, 54 (2004)
4. A.I. Ahmetyanova, A.R. Kuznetsova, Problems of information security in Russia and its regions. Fundam. Res. **8**(1), 82–86 (2016)

5. The Law of the Republic of Kazakhstan on National Security of the Republic of Kazakhstan dated 6th January, 2012 No. 527-IV. [Online]. http://adilet.zan.kz/rus/docs/Z1200000527

6. The Law of the Republic of Kazakhstan on Informatization dated 24th November, 2015 No. 418-V. [Online]. http://adilet.zan.kz/rus/docs/Z1500000418

7. Government Regulations of the Republic of Kazakhstan on Approval of the Rules and Criteria for assigning of objects of information and communication infrastructure to critically important objects in the sphere of informatization dated 8th September, 2016 No. 529. [Online]. http://adilet.zan.kz/rus/docs/P1600000529

8. http://www.zakon.kz/4838230-kak-v-kazakhstane-budut-borotsja-s.html

9. Order of the Minister of investments and development of the Republic of Kazakhstan On approval of the methodology and rules for carrying out the testing of the service programm product, information and communication platform of "eGovernment", Internet resource of the state body and information system for compliance with information security requirements dated 28th January, 2016 No. 108. [Online]. http://adilet.zan.kz/rus/docs/V1600013207

10. http://www.computerworld.kz/news/10054/

11. A.V. Galitskiy, S.D. Ryabko, V.F. Shanguin, Information security in the network—analysis of technologies and synthesis of solutions—2004, (2004), p. 616

12. V. Shangin, Information security of computer systems and networks—2011, (2011), p. 416

13. http://profit.kz/news/6616/Kazahstan-spam-lider-v-Centralnoj-Azii/

14. https://usa.kaspersky.com/internet-security-center/threats/spam-statistics-report-q2-2013#.WOicKNLyjIV

15. https://securelist.com/analysis/quarterly-spam-reports/75764/spam-and-phishing-in-q2-2016/

16. http://kz-cert.kz/about

17. http://www.kz-cert.kz/page/524

18. S. Ramanauskaite, N. Goranin, A. Čenys, J. Juknius, Modelling influence of Botnet features on effectiveness of DDoS attacks. Secur. Commun. Netw. **8**, 2090–2101 (2015)

19. http://cert.kz/ru/o-nas

20. http://tengrinews.kz/internet/DDoS-atakam-podvergalas-chetvert-kazahstanskih-onlayn-272508/

21. http://tengrinews.kz/internet/40-protsentov-kompaniy-kazahstane-poteryali-kontraktyi-iz-za-275955/

22. S. Boranbayev, S. Altayev, A. Boranbayev, Applying the method of diverse redundancy in cloud based systems for increasing reliability, in *Proceedings of the 12th International Conference on Information Technology: New Generations (ITNG 2015)*, Las Vegas, Nevada, USA, 2015, pp. 796–799

23. S. Boranbayev, A. Boranbayev, S. Altayev, A. Nurbekov, Mathematical model for optimal designing of reliable information systems. in *Proceedings of the 2014 IEEE 8th International Conference on Application of Information and Communication Technologies-AICT2014*, Astana, Kazakhstan, 2014, pp. 123–127

Evaluating Cyber Threats to the United Kingdom's National Health Service (NHS) Spine Network

7

Michael Gibbs

Abstract

This report serves as a brief review of United Kingdom's (UK) National Health Service's (NHS) information system infrastructure and the various security threats that could lead to potential breaches of personal health information hosted on the network. Specifically, the document will address details of the NHS Spine infrastructure and how its components, users, and security mechanisms have a great impact on the NHS' overall ability to provide quality service to the UK's healthcare customers. The report will also provide an overview of the NHS system, its sub-components, and how they are all connected via the Spine infrastructure to serve UK citizens seeking healthcare assistance. Lastly, the report will touch on recommendations for role-based access control and identity management.

Keywords

Cybersecurity · National healthcare system · NHS · Spine network · United Kingdom

7.1 UK NHS Information System Infrastructure

The UK originally established the NHS in 1948 as a way to provide health care for all citizens [1]. Today, the organization provides leadership for the strategy and implementation of all health care services to the UK. NHS has one of the world's largest workforces that number over one and a half million who strive toward providing services to approximately 54 million UKresidents [2]. NHS

M. Gibbs (✉)
University Maryland University College, Evans, GA, USA

uses the NHS Digital organization to operate all networks, collect all user data, and ensure all security standards are enforced [3, 4].

The NHS falls under the Department of Health and is mostly comprised of approximately 211 clinical commissioning groups (CCG). The CCGs are the organizations providing most of the direct care to UK citizens. There are also other elements to include dentists, opticians, pharmacists, and trusts that fall outside any specific CCG [2].

NHS Digital operates a large backbone network known as Spine or N3 that interconnects 23,000 healthcare information technology (IT) systems used by 20,500 organizations [3, 4].

The Spine network infrastructure allows for all healthcare patients and providers to access databases that store personal health records, as well as a way to communicate health care planning across the entire country. To do this, Spine can be broken up into five major components.

The Legitimate Relationship Service (LRS) manages how health practitioners access patient records [5]. The National Care Record (NCR). This is where local health organizations store pertinent information allowing for staff to support customers [5]. The Personal demographics system (PDS) is where both customers and practitioners can access personal health information (PHI) [5]. The Spine directory service (SDS) database system houses all information associated with the healthcare organizations supporting the NHS [5]. The Transaction and Messaging Spine (TMS) component serves as the backbone routing element for all other systems through the use of the HL7 version three messaging standard [5].

The Spine network hardware consists of routers and switches that manage traffic paths across its thousands of systems. Additionally, Spine includes databases and application servers that provide access to patient and provider information. Because patients can also access personal information stored within the network, end users' devices such as desktop computers, laptops, and mobile devices might also be considered part of the network.

The Spine network requires that systems use many flavors of software and operating systems, but all of them must be able to interface with HL7's Fast Healthcare Interoperability Resources (FHIR) message standard. The TMS uses FHIR to transmit messages across all databases, application servers, practitioners, and patients. FHIR does this using the Extensible Markup Language (XML) over the Hypertext Transport Protocol (HTTP) [5]. HTTP is an application protocol found at the seventh layer of the Open System Interconnections (OSI) model that uses the TCP/IP suite to transmit and control connections between clients and servers [6].

The NHS Spine relies on end user devices to be running fully patched operating systems as well as updated antivirus applications. Should end users become compromised due to failed security practices, hackers might then access NHS databases and application servers in an unauthorized manner. NHS Spine administrators should implement intrusion prevention systems (IPS) at core nodes to identify and mitigate malicious activities based on known signatures.

7.2 Threats

Due to the enormous number of systems that comprise the NHS network, the threat to its resources and data are equally large. Hackers would likely consider the NHS network a relatively easy target based on the volume of end users accessing the system on a regular basis. Should hackers compromise any of the end users' devices, they would be able to use the access to protected services in an unauthorized manner. Hackers might leverage the access to deny services or data to NHS end users by incorporating ransomware or dynamic denial of service (DDoS) tools into their attacks.

The NHS TMS network is based on transferring network messages via HTTP. Doing so creates a huge premium on web-based security protocols. Administrators must ensure that all web servers are properly patched and limit servers running processes not required for legitimate end user applications.

The insider threat poses the greatest risk to the network as it is usually the most difficult to identify and mitigate. Insiders normally have intimate knowledge of their employer's network systems and are privy to security protocols designed to limit unauthorized access. One of the best ways to stop this would be to log and audit all administrator actions on the network.

Healthcare practitioners can pose a security risk as they may become complacent with respect to cybersecurity since they are primarily focused their patients. These providers may ignore standard protocols designed to protect network components or even purposely subvert them if practitioners find them unduly restrictive or intrusive.

Motives driving intruders can span a range of reasons. One of the primary motives would be financial gain. Cyber criminals are always looking for ways to make money and one of the easiest ways is ransomware. NHS experienced a ransomware intrusion in 2017 and it served as an expensive lesson for NHS as some of its end users were not adhering to security protocols [7]. Another motive for insiders may be retribution. Disgruntled employees may seek to create financial hardships or cause public scrutiny against an employer at any point. Because of this, logging and auditing for critical positions should be mandatory.

To understand how breaches in the cybersecurity realm have become so prevalent, professionals charged with securing networks should maintain an awareness of hacking tradecraft. One of the most effective means of gaining unauthorized access to victims is through social engineering. These attacks prey on the psychological aspects of those they mean to exploit. Social engineering campaigns usually seek to take advantage of a potential victim's sense of fear, obedience, greed, or helpfulness [8]. Senior security staff should consider mandating training for all employees that provide education on how to spot social engineering attacks.

7.3 Vulnerabilities to Identity Management

One of the biggest threats to identity management would be end users losing their common access cards (CAC). These cards are instrumental in protecting the public key infrastructure (PKI) currently used to authenticate all users before they are granted access to network resources and databases [9].

Network administrators and senior security executives must ensure identify management is properly addressed. Currently, NHS employs the use of a PKI system that implements OAuth2 protocol authentication using tokens issued to end user devices. This construct helps to limit the possibilities of hackers gaining unauthorized access to network resources.

Authentication is handled through the PKI system and the OAuth2 database via the authorization server. End users must have a CAC and the correct credentials to successfully authorize themselves for access to resources.

After authentication, the authorization process affords the end users with access to those resources they are entitled based on their role. Patients should be restricted to only those services related to their personal information while practitioners should have access to all databases required for treatment. Managers and network administrators would also have different access to resources based on their jobs and responsibilities.

Table 7.1 Role-based access control recommendations

Role	Role-based controls	File-based controls	Access list controls	Database controls	Mobile-device controls
NHS Administrators	Allow access to all relevant files and network resources	Allow access to all files	Allow connections to all network resources	Allow connections to all databases	Deny mobile device access to critical files and network resources
Practitioners	Allow access to relevant files/resources, deny all else	Allow access to relevant files/resources, deny all else	Allow only connection to pertinent network resources	Allow only connection to pertinent database resources	Deny mobile device access to critical files and network resources
Patients	Allow access to relevant files/resources, deny all else	Allow access to relevant files/resources, deny all else	Allow only connection to pertinent network resources	Allow only connection to pertinent database resources	Deny mobile device access to critical files and network resources

Managing users' access to resources with the NHS network is critical to increasing the security of the entire organization. The following controls should be put in place.

NHS Spine core routers should be updated with access control lists that only allow connections coming from verified and trusted points of network infrastructure. As an example, the SDS should be restricted to only those IP addresses used owned by one of the CCGs.

User accounts should be assigned privileges based on their need for resources associated with their roles. Administrators should only be given administrator-level access to those systems they manage. Conversely, patients should be restricted to normal user permissions to those systems hosting personal information. These roles should be managed via the authorization server after authentication.

Much like server and database resources, sensitive files should be protected against unauthorized access. Administrators should restrict access to files and folders only to those roles needing to use them for official business. Examples might include router configuration backup files need to be restricted to those local administrators. Web-based services specific for a CCG would be locked down to only those computers within that same CCG network.

Database information is the lifeblood of the NHS and its ability to afford patients with quality care. Because they contain such sensitive data, administrators must restrict access to databases with regard to an end user's role. Patients should be able to access the PDS via approved web forms and approved application programming interfaces, but not others such as the NCR or SDS.

Mobile devices can pose threats to the network as they are not managed by the NHS and have a higher likelihood of risk. Patients and NHS employees with mobile devices should be limited to a small set of resources that are not critical to the overall functionality of the Spine. Enforcing these restrictions will drastically reduce the potential for unauthorized access to occur from a device that isn't managed by NHS administrators.

Administrators should also consider implementing a role-based access control construct to effectively manage risks to key infrastructure. The following chart provides recommendations for role-based access control measures (Table 7.1).

7.4 Identity Management Protection

Protecting NHS resources by way of authentication and authorization applications is useless if administrators are unable to ensure identity management is appropriately implemented across the network; for this password fidelity is instrumental to success. Administrators should enforce a password policy consistent with the latest suggestions from the cybersecurity field.

Properly constructed passwords significantly reduce the chances of successful password attacks. NHS should consider adhering to NIST's latest recommendations on enforcing password policies that prevent unauthorized access while also remaining palatable to end users. NIST now recommends that organizations simply enforce a requirement of eight characters or longer, but not mandate the use of the four types of characters [10].

Applications used for testing password strength can be helpful, but can also pose serious security risks to authentication systems. NHS should seriously consider this matter moving forward if it hopes to ensure it is limiting risk to patient data.

Password cracking tools can help security professionals if improper password choices are being chosen by end users. Finding weaknesses in password choice can result in policy changes that effectively increase authentication processes.

If used improperly, these tools could result in hackers or disgruntled employees acquiring access to end user account information and network resources.

7.5 Conclusions

The NHS Spine is a vast network that interconnects thousands of networks and millions of end users. Its availability and security is critical to UK citizens receiving vital healthcare. NHS Digital must enforce policies that ensure the network is reliable and secure. Most of the network traffic is handled by the TMS through the HTTP protocol and HL7 version three standard. NHS' authentication and authorization functions are managed through PKI and the OAuth2 database. To keep these elements secure, NHS should enforce a password policy requiring users to create passwords at least eight characters in length, as well as forbidding any NHS-managed computer to run password cracking tools. Taking these steps will help to severely reduce the threats that hackers or disgruntled employees pose to NHS' authentication and authorization systems.

References

1. T. Powell, The structure of the NHS in England. From NHShistory.net, (2016). http://www.nhshistory.net/Parliament%20NHS%20Structure.pdf
2. www.nhs.uk, The NHS in England. From www.nhs.uk, (2017). http://www.nhs.uk/NHSEngland/thenhs/about/Pages/overview.aspx
3. NHS Digital, Spine. From NHS digital, (2017). https://digital.nhs.uk/spine
4. NHS Digital, What is NHS digital. From digital.nhs.uk, (2017). https://digital.nhs.uk/article/219/What-is-NHS-Digital
5. R. Spronk, The Spine, an English National Programme. From Ringholm Whitepaper, (2007). http://www.ringholm.de/docs/00970_en.htm
6. B. Mitchell, Understanding the open systems interconnection model? From Lifewire, (2017). https://www.lifewire.com/open-systems-interconnection-model-816290
7. BBC News. NHS cyber-attack: GPs and hospitals hit by ransomware. From BBC Health News, (2017). http://www.bbc.com/news/health-39899646
8. A. Whipple, Hacker psychology: understanding the 4 emotions of social engineering. From Network World, (2016). https://www.networkworld.com/article/3070455/cloud-security/hacker-psychology-understanding-the-4-emotions-of-social-engineering.html
9. K. Mayfield, HL7 FHIR Plus OAuth2 in a NHS Trust. From Slide Share, (2015). https://www.slideshare.net/KevinMayfield/hl7-fhir-plus-oauth2-in-a-nhs-trust
10. Passwordping, Surprising new password guidelines from NIST. From Passwordping, (2017). https://www.passwordping.com/surprising-new-password-guidelines-nist/

A Virtual Animated Commentator Architecture for Cybersecurity Competitions

Ruth Agada, Jie Yan, and Weifeng Xu

Abstract

Cybersecurity competitions are exciting for the game participants; however, the excitement and educational value do not necessarily transfer to audiences because audiences may not be experts in the field. To improve the audiences' comprehension and engagement levels at these events, we have proposed a virtual commentator architecture for cybersecurity competitions. Based on the architecture, we have developed a virtual animated agent that serves as a commentator in cybersecurity competition. This virtual commentator can interact with audiences with facial expressions and the corresponding hand gestures. The commentator can provide several types of feedback including causal, congratulatory, deleterious, assistive, background, and motivational responses. In addition, when producing speech, the lips, tongue, and jaw provide visual cues that complement auditory cues. The virtual commentator is flexible enough to be employed in the Collegiate Cyber Defense Competitions environment. Our preliminary results demonstrate the architecture can generate phonemes with timestamps and behavioral tags. These timestamps and tags provide solid building blocks for implementing desired responsive behaviors.

Keywords

Virtual agent · Software architecture · Cybersecurity · Education · Animation

R. Agada (✉) · J. Yan · W. Xu
Department of Computer Science, Bowie State University, Bowie, MD, USA
e-mail: ragada@bowiestate.edu; jyan@bowiestate.edu; wxu@bowiestate.edu

8.1 Introduction

Cybersecurity is a field that is continually garnering much interest as it is now pervasive in the everyday lives of people. To educate the public and train prospective security specialists, the academic community and industry has been responding by developing new programs in information assurance and devising creative ways to attract and train the next generation of cybersecurity professionals [1–3]. One such means has been to create a cybersecurity competitions [4]. These competitions serve to educate its participants and spectators alike. However, the number of student participants engaged in these competitions has still been relatively small. One of the reasons for this lack of interest may be attributed to the fact that, to date, the competitions have been beneficial mainly to anticipants, such as student teams, cybersecurity experts, and administrators and judges of the games. However, for an audience of the sport, the excitement and educational value do not necessarily transfer. This may be because there are audiences who are not experts in the field, and the information and visualization tools are too high level for them to understand.

To help the audiences to comprehend cybersecurity competitions and encourage their engagements at these events, many educators use video game format [5] to educate their participants. Researchers have observed that audiences become engaged in the activity and gain educational content vicariously [2, 6, 7].

Considering the effectiveness of applying video game in education, this paper presents a system to build a game-like virtual commentator that aims to help non-expert audiences comprehend the concepts and engage audiences in cybersecurity-related events, and therefore, promote cybersecurity education among non-expert audiences. Specifically, the commentator is able to: (1) perform various human-like behaviors which range from various valenced facial

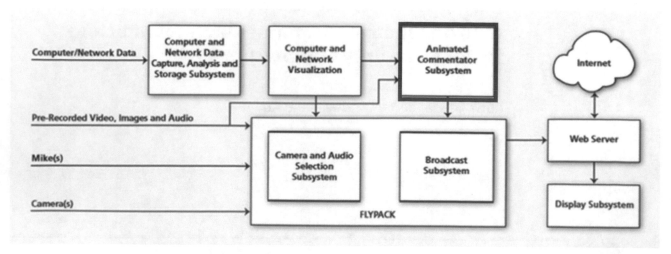

Fig. 8.1 Logical view of the LUCID visualization system

expressions to gestures, gaze and emotions conveyed in speech, (2) interacting with audiences, and providing several types of feedback including causal, congratulatory, deleterious, assistive, background, and motivational responses, and (3) when producing speech, the lips, tongue, and jaw provide visual cues that complement auditory cues. In addition, the virtual commentator is flexible enough to be employed in the Collegiate Cyber Defense Competitions environment.

NSF mainly supports this research "LUCID: A Spectator Targeted Visualization System to Broaden Participation at Cyber Defense Competitions". The proposed virtual commentator is built as part of the LUCID framework shown in Fig. 8.1. The goal of this project was to stimulate interest in cybersecurity competitions through the development of a visualization and broadcast system targeted to enhancing learning and understanding among spectators. The LUCID framework is comprised of five basic subsystems: a computer and Networking data capture, analysis, and storage subsystem, a computer and networking visualization system, a camera and audio selection subsystem, a broadcast subsystem, and display subsystem. Each system collects their respective data and in concert with one another relaying the necessary information in some fashion to the spectator [2].

The animated commentator subsystem, highlighted by the red box in Fig. 8.2, takes video, images, and audio information, as well as computer and network visualization information, to generate semantic tags, that control various behaviors from facial expressions to gestural motion of animated agent to make it believable, personable and emotional. These behaviors are broadcasted and displayed on the camera and audio subsystem.

The rest of this paper is organized as follows: Sect. 8.2 describe the architecture of the commentator subsystem. Section 8.3 demonstrates some preliminary development results.

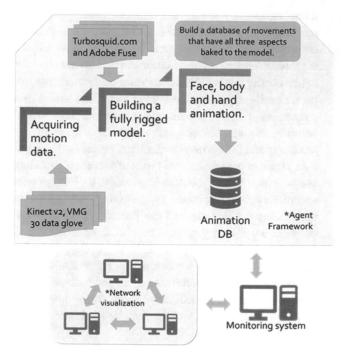

Fig. 8.2 Animated commentator subsystem architecture

Section 8.4 reviews the related work. Section 8.5 concludes the paper.

8.2 The Commentator Subsystem

As stated earlier, the commentator subsystem in the LUCID framework aims to engage the spectators in a similar fashion [8] as with video games. The commentator subsystem focuses on the visual and auditory component in terms of a virtual environment.

8.2.1 Virtual Commentary Architecture

The architecture of the animated commentator subsystem is shown in Fig. 8.2.

The core of the architecture consists of three components:

- An integrated hardware and software interface for acquiring motion data from a variety of hardware device, including Kinect v1 camera and VMG 30 data glove.
- A software system to build a fully rigged behavioral model for the commentary based on motion data.
- An animation software to combine face, body and hand tags for the agent's behavioral models.

For modeling different affective states exhibited by most engaging sports casters, we develop a system to generate images in the 3-D scene in two steps. Firstly, in the modeling step, the system produces a precise description of the agent, in terms of graphics primitives. Then it acquires the vertex data required for the primitives from 3-D modeling software that can generate vertex data. The data provided for the development of the animated agent contain over one thousand points in 3-D space. Secondly, in the rendering step, the vertex data also serve to draw the model to the screen.

For the system to simulate a smooth transition in the model's facial expression, as well as different full body gestures, our method generates a sequence of vertices given that only known vertices are the start and end vertices. By studying and annotating the video clips we collected, we can model realistic animation patterns. With the help of third-party applications, the animation is natural-looking and includes head and face movements, combined with the movements of facial components (eyes, eyebrows, nose, cheeks, etc.) and full body movements (arms, hands, fingers, torso, legs, etc.).

8.2.2 Motion Generation

For the agent to simulate human commentator behavior, initially, we used video footage of various contact sports commentators. Sample footage of commentator came from NFL roundtable discussions, super bowl commentators, and Apollo Robbins' TED talks. Each video file is roughly 9 min in length. These contain commentator motion data that can be applied to the animated agent. The videos used in this project were sourced from YouTube.com. To further analyze behaviors of commentators from non-contact sports, especially from cybersecurity events, we collected data from the Maryland Cyber Challenge. In 2014, we attended one such event in which we interviewed (and recorded) one of the sponsors of the competition. The interview lasted 30 min, and from that, we created frame-by-frame shots to aid in the analysis of facial and body gestures. Again in 2015, we performed a similar data collection, which provided us with data 1 h and 30 min in duration.

We observed several motions/gestures across all the collected data. To annotate the footage, we used a tool called ELAN [9]. With ELAN [9], we created three tiers to represent the different commentator behaviors we analyzed. Further to that we added another tier to represent the dialog phase of the interaction between the interviewer, spectators, and event sponsors. Figure 8.3 shows the interface of ELAN and the different tiers which allow the user to analyze different media corpora by adding descriptive tags that are either be time-aligned to the media or it can refer to other existing annotations.

From the analyzed video clips, we observed typical animation pattern for a commentator with individual personalities. We represent this animation pattern by using tagged meta-animation sequence. Based on behaviors of interest in the expression and gestural behaviors, we developed tagged animations sequences that correspond to the tier of behavior. To capture the requisite gestures and facial expressions used by sports commentators several hardware devices and software applications. Microsoft's Kinect v2 captured face and body motion data, while the virtual motion glove—VMG30—captured relevant hand motion. To process the data stream from both the Kinect v2 and VMG30, we used the Brekel and VMG SDK to map the input motion data to the animated model.

8.2.3 Speech Generation

The animated agent is required to give commentary on the cybersecurity competition, and to give this commentary while maintaining human-like expressions, hand gestures, and movements. The facial expression demonstrated by the agent is dependent on sentences being narrated by the agent. Having this work seamlessly for the different scenarios that may arise based on the activities in the competition involves two parts. Firstly, a database that provides the appropriate triggers for the agent to speak based on different conditions in the form of text, and secondly, a system that takes this text and converts it into speech while using the appropriate facial expressions.

The database used in this system is the MySQL database. For our system, the events happening during the competition, mainly the services that are up or down (up indicating this it is currently still running, and down indicating that the service has been compromised and shut down), cause data to be stored in the MySQL database. This data contains keywords that the agent needs to narrate. We created scripts that query

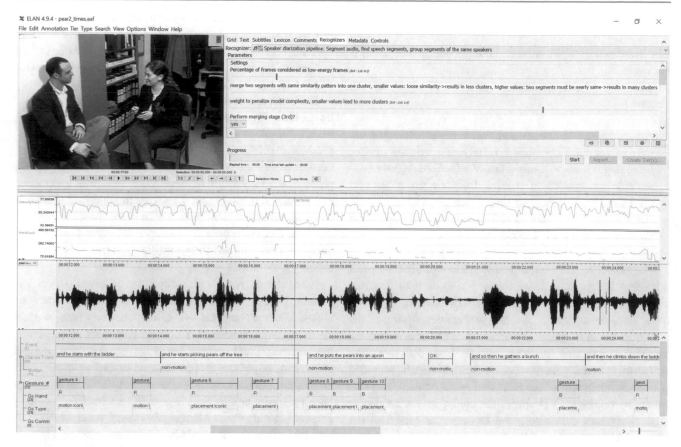

Fig. 8.3 Annotated video clip using ELAN and the associated annotation tiers

this database whenever the virtual agent needs to announce information to the spectators.

The second part of the system is the TTS. For this part of our system, we used several third-party systems to provide speech functionality and to ensure that the text spoken by the agent also creates appropriate lip movement and facial expressions to generate a full and realistic virtual commentator. We use two separate software for the text-to-speech because of the different advantages they provide. MaryTTS [10, 11] is an open-source, multilingual Text-to-Speech Synthesis platform written in Java. Being open-source means that it is available for free online. We chose this because of its availability, user-friendliness, and ease of use. The result of the query, i.e., the text, is inputted into this software to generate the necessary phonemes contained in each word. A phoneme is the basic unit of sound in any word in a specified language. The phoneme is used to determine the way the agent's lips move. Phonemes affect how words are pronounced, things like accent, the shape of the mouth, language all affect the way the mouth and lips move. This phoneme list is generated and then used to facilitate the mouth shapes of the agent when pronouncing each word. The second software is CereVoice [12, 13], which is another TTS software. This is also open source and available through

different license tiers. We use CereVoice because it produces a much more natural sounding synthesized speech than MaryTTS [10, 11]. It also takes in the same text as input and is responsible for producing the final audio that will be heard by the spectators. To tie the model's speech capabilities to its motion, we use the Lip Sync pro system [14] to provide a window for synchronizing phonemes generated, emotions and gestures to dialogue in an audio file, and a component for playing back these dialogue clips on a character using totally customizable poses.

8.3 Preliminary Results

Our preliminary results include: (1) developed expressions/gestures of an animated virtual commentator and (2) generated a marked-up animation sequence.

8.3.1 Generating Expressions and Gestures

Figure 8.4 shows some of the expressions and gestures of an animated virtual commentator we have developed to engage spectators in the Collegiate Cyber Defense Compe-

Fig. 8.4 Diverse expression of an emotional embodied conversational agent. Top row: smile with teeth, smile closed mouth, and sadness. Middle row: surprise, anger, and disgust. Bottom row: fear, pursed lips and pursed lips with closed eyes

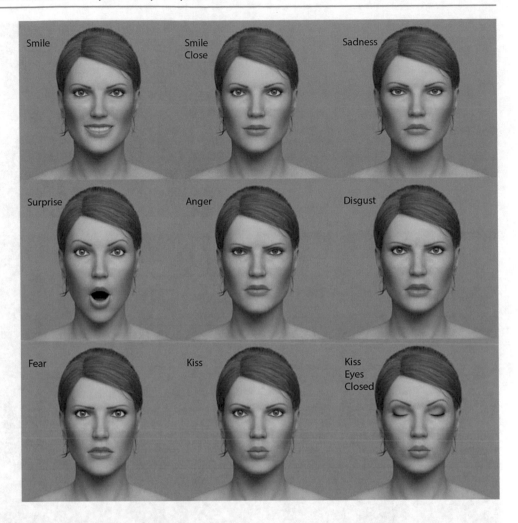

titions (CCDCs) environment. By recording and observing the interactional behaviors of different professional human commentator working with various groups of spectators in a set of CCDCs, we have identified specific coordinated verbal and nonverbal signals exchanged during the class session. The nonverbal cues include head nods, the direction of eye gaze (including eye contact), facial expressions, posture shifts and hand and arm gestures. Once these have been codified and analyzed to determine their temporal organization and contexts of occurrence, we conducted several experiments and noted the common behaviors exhibited by the observed commentators and mapped those behaviors unto the animated agent.

The current interface, while independent of other external systems, as seen in Fig. 8.5, contains the current virtual environment for one of the virtual commentators created for the system. The current scene is a 3D mock-up of the bridge of the starship Enterprise from the popular science fiction show Star Trek™: The Next Generation. On initialization of the system, the agent checks if it has established a connection to the MySQL database that houses the data collected from the network monitoring system. If there is any connection

issue, the agent reports that to the spectator in randomly selected over emphasized gestures with matching speech generation as seen in Fig. 8.6.

8.3.2   Generate a Marked-up Animation Sequence

To generate a marked-up animation sequence or to add additional markup to a sequence, we need to insert a series of animation tags to the phoneme.

Here is an example to describe how it works as seen in Table 8.1. Suppose the input text string is the prompt "didn't know you know so much," with associated phoneme string and animation sequence and, that a meta animation sequence will be imposed on this animation sequence automatically.

Using for example, the meta animation sequence example: 0.2 s—<FET = SMILE>—0.2 s—<EYEB = (3000, B)>—0.2 s—<HGT = (−2,0,0)>—0.3 s—<HGT = (2,0,0)> <FET = RAISEEYEBROW>—0.3 s—<HGT = (4,0,2)>— 0.3 s—<FET = SMILE>. The smile target is inserted on a phoneme boundary close to the 0.2 s into the animation as

Fig. 8.5 System interface with a
virtual agent in an idle animation

Fig. 8.6 Top: Model behavior for successful MySQL connection by showing an exaggerated thumbs up gesture and returning to the idle animation.
Bottom: Model behavior for failed MySQL connection by showing disappointment by shrugging its shoulders

Table 8.1 Phoneme generation with time stamps and no behavioral tags

Phoneme	Duration	Word boundary	Tag<s>
D	0.054	1	
I	0.09	0	
d	0.08	0	
&	0.06	0	
n	0.06	0	
n	0.1	1	
oU	0.2	0	
j	0.12	1	
u	0.069	0	
n	0.04	1	
u	0.27	0	
s	0.14	1	
oU	0.14	0	
m	0.109	1	
^	0.23	0	
tS	0.348	0	
. pau	0.4	1	

Table 8.2 Phoneme generation with desired effective behavioral tags

Phoneme	Duration	Word boundary	Tag<s>
D	0.054	1	
I	0.09	0	<FET = SMILE>
d	0.08	0	
&	0.06	0	
n	0.06	0	<EYEB = (3000, B)>
n	0.1	1	<HGT = (−2,0,0)>
oU	0.2	0	
j	0.12	1	
u	0.069	0	
n	0.04	1	<HGT = (2,0,0)>
			<FET = RAISEEYEBROW>
u	0.27	0	
s	0.14	1	
oU	0.14	0	<HGT = (4,0,2)>
m	0.109	1	
^	0.23	0	<FET = SMILE>
tS	0.348	0	
.pau	0.4	1	

specified by the meta-animation sequence but not at exactly 0.2 s as such, allowing semi-random behavior and ensuring temporal variability while ensuring speech synchronized behavior. The animation sequence may alternatively have specified that the tag be inserted only at a word boundary, probabilistically or in other ways.

Tags in the meta-animation sequence are inserted in order, and the movements from all channels are finally combined to generate a final animation sequence. For the previous example the result may look like Table 8.2.

8.4 Related Work

Cybersecurity competitions are becoming increasingly prominent parts of the landscape of cybersecurity education. Most notably is the National Collegiate Cyber Defense Competition (NCCDC) with its precursor regional events [6] and the UCSB International Capture the Flag Competition (iCTF) [7]. These are both large national and international competitions with scores of institutions and hundreds of students [4]. There are several other competitions held at regional levels [4] and those organized by other faculty and security specialists [7, 15–21].

As O'Leary noted [4], these competitions require the students a certain level of competence in defensive and administrative skills. The teams of participating students work to defend identical networks from a group of designated attackers. The team that successfully keeps most of their services on their network, as well as their network operational are declared winners of the event.

Most of these games favor the war game mode of hands-on exercises for participants. These war games are either organized as capture-the-flag (CTF) [22, 23], king of the hill (KOTH), defend the flag—a variation of KOTH, computer simulations and online programming-level war-games [24, 25]. The issue with these modes is there is no opportunity for the spectator to actively participate in the competition, granted they are prevented from engaging with actual participants of the competition. The lack of a system that involves spectators in the event continues to unintentionally exclude that potential population of security specialists in a field that suffers from reduced engagement from different groups. Hence, we propose the use of an effective pedagogical virtual agent with commentator status that engages the spectators.

8.5 Conclusion

This paper presents a virtual animated commentator architecture for cybersecurity competitions. We have developed a commentator based on the architecture. The commentator is able to generate expressions/gestures and a marked-up animation sequence. Specifically, we have identified a set of verbal and nonverbal signals and cues exchanged during the interactions between spectators and the commentator. To that end, we take advantage of the capabilities the Kinect v2 and VMG 30 glove to model those behaviors and map them to our 3D animated models to better simulate the realistic performance of human commentators. We anticipate that the system will ultimately improve the educational value and excitement for the spectator and broaden interest in the field of cybersecurity. Our future work is based on two hypotheses in terms of the audience's interaction with the system and the method to educate and engage them. For the spectator, we hypothesize that the excitement and learning outcomes are associated with the ability to extract, visualize and comprehend the details of the game as they unfold will improve [2], thus opening cybersecurity events to a broader group. Secondly, the use of a pedagogically effective animated commentator will aid in the comprehension and engagement at these events.

Acknowledgment This work is mainly supported by grant NSF-DUE 1303424 and partially supported by grant NSF-HBCU-UP 1714261.

References

1. R.S. Cheung, J.P. Cohen, H.Z. Lo, F. Elia, V. Carrillo-Marquez, Effectiveness of cybersecurity competitions, in *Proceedings of the International Conference on Security and Management (SAM)*, (2012), p. 1
2. C. Turner, J. Yan, D. Richards, P.O. Brien, J. Odubiyi, Q. Brown, LUCID: A visualization and broadcast system for cyber defense competitions. ACM Inroads **6**(2), 70–76 (2015)
3. R. Agada, J. Yan, Leveraging automated animated agent commentary to improve sense-making for novice users at cybersecurity competitions. Natl. Cybersecurity Inst. J. **3**(1), 47–55 (2016)
4. M. O'Leary, Small-scale cyber security competitions, in *Proceeding of the 16th Colloquium for Information Systems Education*, (2012)
5. A. Groen, How video games are becoming the next great North American spectator sport, *arstechnica*, (2012), [Online]. https://arstechnica.com/gaming/2012/09/how-video-games-are-becoming-next-great-north-america-spectator-sport/. Accessed 1 Jan 2017
6. History of CCDC, *National collegiate cyber defense competition*. [Online]. http://www.nationalccdc.org/index.php/competition/about-ccdc/history. Accessed 1 Jan 2017
7. A. Conklin, The use of a collegiate cyber defense competition in information security education. in *Proceedings of the 2nd Annual Conference on Information Security Curriculum Development—InfoSecCD'05*, (2005), p. 16
8. G. Cheung, J. Huang, Starcraft from the stands: understanding the game spectator, in *Proc. SIGCHI Conf. Hum. Factors Comput. Syst.*, (2011), pp. 763–772
9. P. Wittenburg, H. Brugman, A. Russel, A. Klassmann, H. Sloetjes, ELAN: a professional framework for multimodality research, in *Proceedings of LREC 2006, Fifth International Conference on Language Resources and Evaluation*, (2006)
10. M. Schröder, J. Trouvain, The German text-to-speech synthesis system MARY: a tool for research, development and teaching. Int. J. Speech Technol. **6**, 365–377 (2003)
11. M. Schröder, M. Schröder, Interpolating expressions in unit selection, in *Proceedings of the 2nd International Conference on Affective Computing and Intelligent Interaction*, **2**(2), 718–720 (2007)
12. CereVoice Engine Text-to-Speech SDK, CereProc. [Online]. https://www.cereproc.com/en. Accessed 1 Jan 2017
13. M. Aylett, C. Pidcock, The CereVoice characterful speech synthesiser SDK. AISB **2007**, 174–178 (2007)
14. LipSync Documentation, Rogo Digital, (2016), [Online]. https://lipsync.rogodigital.com/documentation/. Accessed 5 May 2017
15. G.B. White, D. Williams, The Collegiate Cyber Defense Competition, in *9th Colloq. Inf. Syst. Secur. Educ.*, (2005), pp. 26–31
16. G.B. White, D. Ph, I. Assurance, The National Collegiate Cyber Defense, in *10th Colloquium for Information Systems Security Education*, (2006)
17. T. Rosenberg, W.W. Security, C.O. Brien, The growth of the Mid-Atlantic CCDC: public—private partnerships at work, in *Proceedings of the 12th Colloquium for Information Systems Security Education*, (2008), pp. 72–76
18. A. Carlin, D.P. Manson, J. Zhu, Developing the cyber defenders of tomorrow with regional collegiate cyber defense competitions (CCDC). Inf. Syst. Educ. J. **8**(14), 3–10 (2010)
19. A. Cook, R.G. Smith, L. Maglaras, H. Janicke, SCIPS: using experiential learning to raise cyber situational awareness in industrial control system. Int. J. Cyber Warf. Terror. **7**, (2017)
20. B. Hallaq, A. Nicholson, R. Smith, L. Maglaras, H. Janicke, K. Jones, CYRAN: a hybrid cyber range for testing security on ICS/SCADA systems, in *Security Solutions and Applied Cryptography in Smart Grid Communications*, (2017)
21. A. Furfaro, A. Piccolo, D. Sacca, A. Parise, A virtual environment for the enactment of realistic cyber security scenarios, in *Proc. 2016 Int. Conf. Cloud Comput. Technol. Appl. CloudTech 2016*, (2017), pp. 351–358
22. J. Werther, M. Zhivich, T. Leek, N. Zeldovich, Experiences in cyber security education: the MIT Lincoln Laboratory capture-the-flag exercise, in *Proceedings of the 4th Workshop on Cyber Security Experimentation and Test*, (2011)
23. N. Capalbo, T. Reed, M. Arpaia, RTFn: enabling cybersecurity education through a mobile capture the flag client, in *Proceedings of SAM'11*, (2011), pp. 500–506
24. M.E. Whitman, H.J. Mattord, A. Green, Incident response: planning, in *Principles of Incident Response and Disaster Recovery*, 2nd edn. (Cengage Learning, 2013), p. 131
25. S. Jajodia, S. Noel, P. Kalapa, M. Albanese, J. Williams, Cauldron mission-centric cyber situational awareness with defense in depth, in *2011—MILCOM 2011 Military Communications Conference*, (2011), pp. 1339–1344

Malicious Software Classification Using VGG16 Deep Neural Network's Bottleneck Features

9

Edmar Rezende, Guilherme Ruppert, Tiago Carvalho, Antonio Theophilo, Fabio Ramos, and Paulo de Geus

Abstract

Malicious software (malware) has been extensively employed for illegal purposes and thousands of new samples are discovered every day. The ability to classify samples with similar characteristics into families makes possible to create mitigation strategies that work for a whole class of programs. In this paper, we present a malware family classification approach using VGG16 deep neural network's bottleneck features. Malware samples are represented as byteplot grayscale images and the convolutional layers of a VGG16 deep neural network pre-trained on the ImageNet dataset is used for bottleneck features extraction. These features are used to train a SVM classifier for the malware family classification task. The experimental results on a dataset comprising 10,136 samples from 20 different families showed that our approach can effectively be used to classify malware families with an accuracy of 92.97%, outperforming similar approaches proposed in the literature which require feature engineering and considerable domain expertise.

Keywords

Malicious software · Classification · Machine learning · Deep learning · Transfer learning

E. Rezende (✉)
University of Campinas, Campinas, SP, Brazil

Center for Information Technology Renato Archer, Campinas, SP, Brazil

G. Ruppert · A. Theophilo
Center for Information Technology Renato Archer, Campinas, SP, Brazil

T. Carvalho
Federal Institute of São Paulo, Campinas, SP, Brazil

F. Ramos
University of Sydney, Sydney, NSW, Australia

P. de Geus
University of Campinas, Campinas, SP, Brazil

9.1 Introduction

Over the past years, the number of programs developed for malicious and illegal purposes has grown at an extremely high rate. Thousands of new malicious software (malware) samples are discovered every day. Malware authors often reuse code to generate different variants with similar characteristics that can be grouped into one malware family. The ability to identify samples that belong to the same malware family makes significantly easier to derive generalized signatures, implement removal procedures and create new mitigation strategies that work for a whole class of programs.

Several feature extraction approaches based on static and dynamic malware analysis have been used to train machine learning classifiers in order to automate malware classification task. However, designing a feature extractor able to transform raw data into a suitable feature vector from which the learning algorithm can detect patterns requires careful engineering and considerable domain expertise.

In this work we investigate the use deep learning algorithms [1] to learn good malware representations. Deep learning are representation learning methods with multiple levels of representation able to transform the raw input into a representation at a higher and more abstract level. Deep learning's key aspect is that these feature layers are not designed by human engineers, rather they are learned from data using a general purpose learning procedure.

Deep Neural Networks (DNN) have become the standard approach for many classification tasks within the last few years, due to the overwhelming performance of DNNs on image recognition challenges. Tremendous progress has been made in image recognition, primarily due to the availability of large-scale annotated datasets and the use of DNNs. Large-scale well-annotated datasets are crucial to learning more accurate or generalizable models. The ImageNet [2] is a dataset containing 1.28 million images of 1000 classes. By the use of transfer learning [3], DNN models trained upon this dataset have been used to significantly improve many

© Springer International Publishing AG, part of Springer Nature 2018
S. Latifi (ed.), *Information Technology – New Generations*, Advances in Intelligent Systems and Computing 738,
https://doi.org/10.1007/978-3-319-77028-4_9

image classification tasks using other datasets in different domains.

In this paper we present an approach for malware family classification using the DNN proposed by Visual Geometry Group with 16 layers (VGG16) [4]. First, we represent malware samples as byteplot images, where each byte corresponds to one pixel in a grayscale image. Through transfer learning, we extract the filter activation maps (usually called bottleneck features) using the convolutional layers of VGG16 pre-trained on the ImageNet dataset. The bottleneck features are then used to train a Support Vector Machine (SVM) classifier for the malware family classification task.

Our hypothesis is that despite the disparity between natural images and malware byteplot images, VGG16 parameters may still be transferred to make malware image recognition tasks more effective. The experimental results on a dataset comprising 10,136 samples from 20 different malware families showed that our approach can effectively be used to classify malware families with an accuracy of 92.97%, outperforming similar approaches proposed in the literature which require careful feature engineering and considerable domain expertise.

The remaining of the paper is organized as follows: Sect. 9.2 presents malware classification related work. Section 9.3 describes the method proposed in this work in details. Section 9.4 presents our experimental results. The conclusions follow in Sect. 9.5.

9.2 Related Work

The use of machine learning for automatically classifying malware families has been extensively studied in the literature. Kolter and Maloof [5] extracted byte n-grams from Windows executables and trained several classifiers. They used a one-versus-all classification approach and combined the predictions of the individual classifiers. Shabtai et al. [6] evaluated various settings of opcode n-gram sizes and classifiers. The authors concluded that the 2-gram opcodes outperformed the others and the use of byte n-grams appears to produce less accurate classifiers than using opcode n-grams.

Some approaches based on the use of visualization techniques have been proposed to support malware analysis with respect to feature extraction and pattern recognition of malware samples. Nataraj et al. [7] proposed a method for classifying malware represented as byteplot grayscale images using image processing techniques. Using Gabor filters to extract GIST descriptors from the byteplot grayscale images and then using a k-nearest neighbors (kNN) classifier, they obtained an accuracy of 97.18% in a dataset consisting of 25 malware families, totaling 9458 malware samples.

In the last few years, researchers have applied deep learning techniques to learn patterns in a set of features extracted from static and dynamic malware analysis in order to classify new samples. Kolosnjaji et al. [8] used a hierarchical feature extraction architecture that combines convolutional and recurrent neural network layers for malware classification using system call n-grams obtained from dynamic analysis. Their evaluation results achieved an average accuracy of 89.4% in a dataset containing 4753 malware samples from ten different families.

Unlike previous work, our approach does not require any feature engineering, using raw pixel values of byteplot images as our underlying malware representation. Additionally, we employ knowledge transfer from a deep neural network trained for object detection task on a different dataset to discover good malware representations, improving the classification results.

9.3 Methodology

An overview of the entire method's pipeline is given in Fig. 9.1.

In the first step, we convert the malware executable to a byteplot grayscale image. The byteplot representation of binary executables can be used for automatic identification of visual patterns in static malware analysis.

The byteplot grayscale image consists of a variable-resolution image with only one channel, while our DNN model requires constant input dimensionality with three channels (RGB). Therefore, in the second step we convert the grayscale image to RGB and rescale it to a fixed resolution of 224×224. Additionally, we subtract the mean RGB value computed on the ImageNet dataset from each pixel of the resulting $224 \times 224 \times 3$ image, as suggested by Krizhevsky et al. [9]. These mean-centered raw RGB values of the pixels are used as input features to our DNN model.

In the third step, we build a Deep Neural Network (DNN) model by transferring convolutional layers of VGG16 model pre-trained on the ImageNet dataset to our DNN model. The transferred convolutional layer's parameters are used to extract the bottleneck features.

In the last step, the bottleneck features are used to train a SVM classifier for malware family classification. This approach is equivalent to replace the fully-connected layers of VGG16 by the SVM classifier freezing the parameters of the convolutional layers during the training process, with the advantage of a much smaller training time.

Finished the training process, the SVM classifier is stacked on the top of the convolutional layers and the whole model is used to classify the test samples.

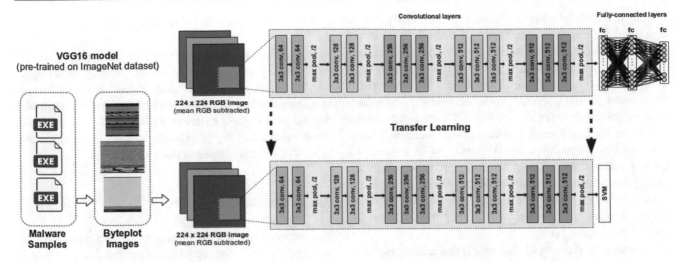

Fig. 9.1 Overview of proposed method

Fig. 9.2 Byteplot visualization of malware samples from six different families

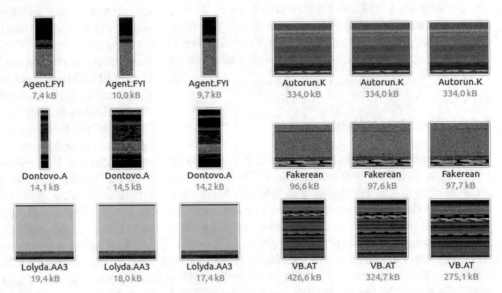

9.3.1 Byteplot Visualization

The byteplot visualization method was initially proposed by Conti et al. [10] to represent binary data objects as grayscale images, where each byte corresponds to one image pixel color rendered as a grayscale (zero is black, 255 is white and other values are intermediate shades of gray). They presented a visual reverse engineering system arguing that visual analysis of binary data presented as grayscale graphical depictions helps distinguish structurally different regions of data and thus facilitates a wide range of analytic tasks such as fragment classification, file type identification, location of regions of interest and other tasks that require an understanding of the primitive data types.

Later, Nataraj et al. [7] observed significant visual similarities in image texture for malware belonging to the same family, as shown in Fig. 9.2, possibly explained by the common practice of reusing code to create new malware variants.

To transform malware samples into byteplot images, a given malware binary is read as a vector of 8-bit unsigned integers and then organized into a 2D array, where the width is defined by the file size, based on empirical observations made by Nataraj et al. [7]. The height is allowed to vary depending on the width and the file size.

9.3.2 VGG16 Architecture

The VGG network architecture was initially proposed by Simonyan and Zisserman [4]. The VGG models with 16 layers (VGG16) and with 19 layers (VGG19) were the basis of their ImageNet Challenge 2014 submission, where the Visual Geometry Group (VGG) team secured the first and the second places in the localization and classification tracks respectively.

The VGG16 architecture, shown at the top of Fig. 9.1, is structured starting with five blocks of convolutional layers followed by three fully-connected layers. Convolutional layers use 3×3 kernels with a stride of 1 and padding of 1 to ensure that each activation map retains the same spatial dimensions as the previous layer. A rectified linear unit (ReLU) activation is performed right after each convolution and a max pooling operation is used at the end of each block to reduce the spatial dimension. Max pooling layers use 2×2 kernels with a stride of 2 and no padding to ensure that each spatial dimension of the activation map from the previous layer is halved. Two fully-connected layers with 4096 ReLU activated units are then used before the final 1000 fully-connected softmax layer.

A downside of the VGG16 model is that it is expensive to evaluate and use a lot of memory and parameters. VGG16 has approximately 138 million parameters. Most of these parameters (approximately 123 million) are in the fully-connected layers, that are replaced by a SVM classifier in our model, significantly reducing the number of necessary parameters.

9.3.3 Transfer Learning

Transfer learning consists in transferring the parameters of a neural network trained with one dataset and task to another problem with a different dataset and task [3]. Many deep neural networks trained on natural images exhibit a curious phenomenon in common: on the first layers they learn features that appear not to be specific to a particular dataset or task, but general in that they are applicable to many datasets and tasks. When the target dataset is significantly smaller than the base dataset, transfer learning can be a powerful tool to enable training a large target network without overfitting.

In the proposed transfer learning approach, we have used VGG16 as the base model, pre-trained for object detection task on the ImageNet dataset. We use the convolutional layers of the VGG16 to extract the bottleneck features of malware byteplot images, that are used as input to train a SVM classifier. Then, we replace the fully-connected layers by the trained SVM classifier in the proposed model.

Our hypothesis is that despite the disparity between natural images and malware byteplot images, VGG16 parameters trained on the large-scale well-annotated ImageNet may still be transferred to make malware image recognition tasks more effective. Collecting and annotating large numbers of malware samples still poses significant challenges. Accordingly, the VGG16 architecture contains millions of parameters to train and thus requires sufficiently large numbers of labeled malware samples.

9.4 Experimental Results

In this section, we evaluate the performance of the proposed model and present the experimental results. We applied transfer learning techniques using VGG16 as the base model to extract the bottleneck features of our malware samples, that are used as input to train a SVM classifier. To perform a comparative analysis, we reproduced some approaches used by similar work proposed in the literature.

9.4.1 Dataset

The proposed method has been tested over a dataset created with samples collected from VirusSign[1] from August 1, 2014 to January 18, 2015. We obtained 10,136 malware samples and submitted them to Virustotal[2] service to identify their antivirus (AV) labels. Using AVCLASS [11] we have obtained a unique malware family label for each sample. AVCLASS is an automatic labeling tool that given the AV labels for a number of malware samples, outputs the most likely family names for each sample, implementing techniques to address AV label normalization, removal of generic tokens, and alias detection, ranking each candidate family name by the number of AV engines assigned to each sample. The samples are distributed in 20 malware families.

To evaluate the performance of proposed models we used a stratified tenfold cross-validation, randomly partitioning the samples into ten disjoint sets of equal size containing roughly the same proportions of the class labels in each fold, selecting one as a testing set and combining the remaining nine to form a training set. We conducted ten such runs using each partition as the testing set and reported the accuracy by fold, the average classification accuracy and the standard deviation.

9.4.2 Feature Extraction Analysis

To perform a comparative analysis of our model with similar work proposed in the literature, we implemented feature extraction approaches using Gabor filters to extract GIST descriptors from the byteplot grayscale images [7], byte n-grams ($n = 1$) [5] and opcode n-grams ($n = 1$) [6].

We are interested in evaluate how good the VGG16 bottleneck features are compared with other feature extraction methods. To perform a qualitative analysis, we generated data visualization using the t-Distributed Stochastic Neighbor Embedding (t-SNE) algorithm [12]. The goal of t-SNE is to reduce the dimensionality so that the closer two nodes

---

[1] Available at http://www.virussign.com.

[2] Available at http://www.virustotal.com.

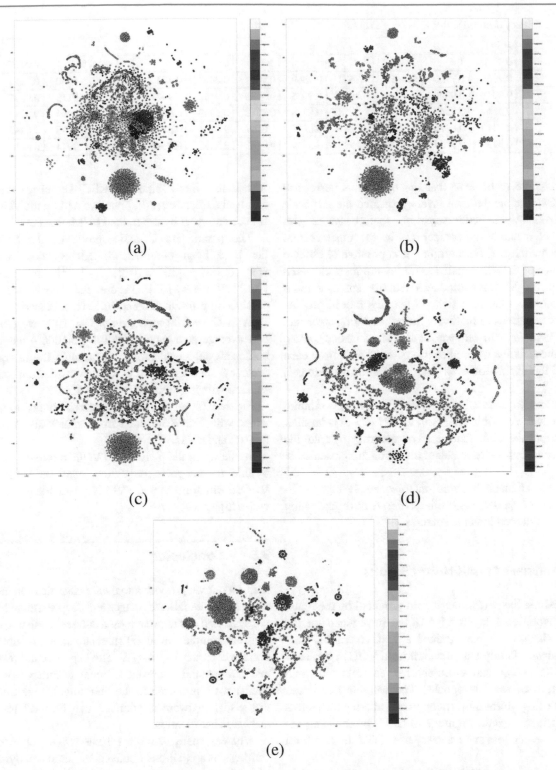

Fig. 9.3 t-SNE visualization of extracted features: (**a**) grayscale image pixels, (**b**) VGG16 bottleneck features, (**c**) GIST descriptors, (**d**) Byte 1-gram and (**e**) Opcode 1-gram

are to each other in the original high-dimensional space, the closer they would be in the 2-dimensional space.

Figure 9.3 provides a t-SNE visualization of the dataset using different feature extraction approaches. Each node cor-

responds to one malware sample and each color represents one malware family. Note that the t-SNE dimensionality reduction process is completely unsupervised and the labels are used for coloring the nodes at plotting time only.

Table 9.1 Accuracy obtained with a kNN (k = 1) classifier

Features	Fold										Avg acc	Std dev
	0	1	2	3	4	5	6	7	8	9		
Grayscale	0.7705	0.7769	0.7765	0.7520	0.7569	0.7587	0.7453	0.7540	0.7664	0.7550	0.7612	0.0108
VGG16	0.9043	0.9090	0.9108	0.8967	0.9075	0.8981	0.9138	0.9077	0.9135	0.9153	0.9077	0.0064
GIST	0.9014	0.8943	0.8961	0.8858	0.8878	0.8912	0.8949	0.8899	0.9016	0.9004	0.8943	0.0057
Byte 1-gram	0.8340	0.8415	0.8363	0.8297	0.8248	0.8437	0.8404	0.8393	0.8380	0.8406	0.8368	0.0058
Opcode 1-gram	0.8799	0.9031	0.8971	0.8996	0.8839	0.8783	0.8890	0.8919	0.8897	0.9014	0.8914	0.0089

It is possible to observe that the operations performed by the VGG16 convolutional layers projected the grayscale image pixels into a better separable feature space, with a degree of separability comparable to the other feature extraction techniques. Furthermore, it is possible to observe that samples of the same malware family are most clustered together in the VGG16 bottleneck features space, demonstrating that the VGG16 activation features indeed provide good representations of malware. Some clustering errors are expected here (as can be seen in the visualization), since many of these malware families use parts of code from each other, and the distinction even among antivirus detections is blurred.

To perform a quantitative analysis of features, we implemented malware classification with a kNN ($k = 1$) classifier using as input the same features. The accuracy by fold, the average accuracy and the standard deviation are presented in Table 9.1.

VGG16 bottleneck features obtained an average accuracy of 0.9077 (± 0.0064), while other feature extraction approaches obtained lower accuracies.

9.4.3 Malware Classification Results

To demonstrate the performance gain provided by the transfer of convolutional layers of VGG16 pre-trained on the ImageNet dataset, we have trained a VGG16 from scratch for the malware family classification task. VGG16 has been trained with categorical cross-entropy cost function and Adam optimizer for 100 epochs. The weights have been initialized using glorot uniform approach and the bias terms were initialized to zero. Figure 9.4a and b present, respectively, the average loss and accuracy of VGG16 trained from scratch.

The network converges quickly to an extremely low average accuracy of 0.1128 (± 0.0434). While in principle VGG16 network is a powerful model, in practice, it is hard to train properly. The reasons why this model is so unwieldy are the vanishing and exploding gradient problems.

In the proposed approach, we use the convolutional layers of VGG16 pre-trained on the ImageNet dataset to extract bottleneck features which are used to train a SVM classifier

with Radial Basis Function (RBF) kernel for the malware family classification task. Then, we replace the VGG16 fully-connected layers by the trained SVM classifier.

The parameters C and gamma of the SVM classifier have been obtained through a gridsearch process with $C \in \left[10^{-2}, 10^{-1}, \ldots, 10^{10}\right]$ and $gamma \in \left[10^{-9}, 10^{-8}, \ldots, 10^{3}\right]$. Figure 9.5 shows the accuracy obtained in gridsearch using VGG16 bottleneck features.

With $C = 100$ and $gamma = 10^{-6}$ we obtained the best average accuracy of 0.9297 (± 0.0063) using VGG16 bottleneck features. Table 9.2 presents the comparison of accuracy obtained with VGG16 trained from scratch and VGG16 with transfer and SVM.

Figure 9.6 presents the normalized confusion matrix obtained with VGG16 trained from scratch and VGG16 with transfer and SVM.

As shown in the picture, the VGG16 trained from scratch is able to recognize only four malware families, while VGG16 with transfer and SVM is able to identify all families with a high accuracy.

9.5 Conclusion

In this work we propose a malware classification mechanism using byteplot malware images and deep learning techniques. We evaluated our approach on a dataset consisting of 10,136 malware samples from 20 malware families, obtaining an average accuracy of 92.97%. The experimental results show that our method achieved a better accuracy compared to similar work proposed in the literature. Our results confirm that visual malware similarities can be used for accurate malware classification.

Whereas many solutions have relied solely on hand-crafting representations obtained by static and dynamic feature extraction procedures, the use of deep learning algorithms seems to be a promising alternative to discover good malware representations without laborious feature engineering process. Moreover, we demonstrated that the knowledge obtained in the ImageNet classification task can be successfully transferred to malware classification. In our experiments, the accuracy obtained with VGG16 using transfer learning and SVM outperformed VGG16 trained from scratch.

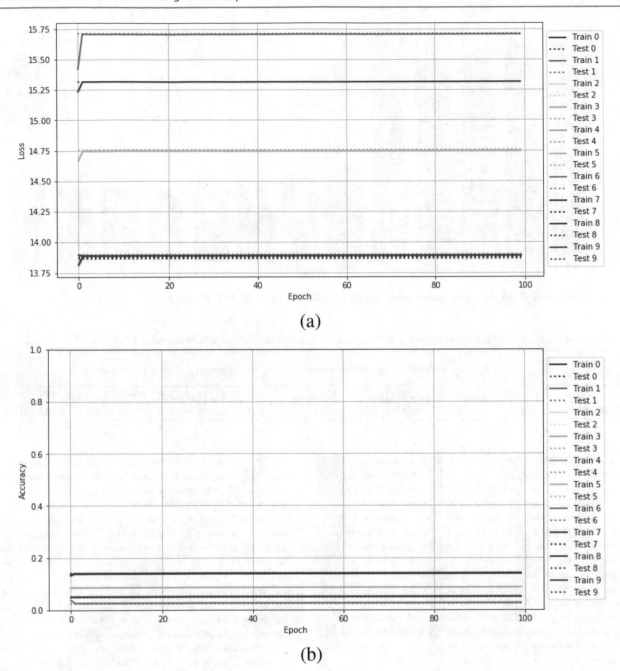

Fig. 9.4 VGG16 train/test average (**a**) loss and (**b**) accuracy

The VGG16 learned feature extractor can still be fine-tuned to malware classification, backpropagating the errors from the last layers into the VGG16 transferred convolutional layers to fine-tune them, possibly improving the performance of the classifier.

Acknowledgements This work has been partially supported by Brazilian National Council for Scientific and Technological Development (grants 302923/2014-4 and 313152/2015-2). We gratefully acknowledge the support of NVIDIA Corporation with the donation of the Titan Xp GPUs used for this research.

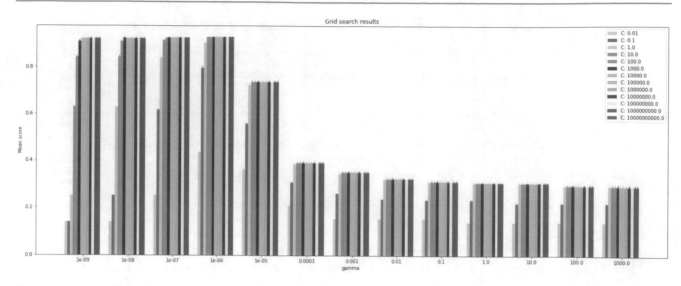

Fig. 9.5 Gridsearch of C and gamma parameters using VGG16 bottleneck features with SVM classifier

Table 9.2 Comparison of accuracy obtained with VGG16 trained from scratch and VGG16 with transfer and SVM

Model	Transfer	Top	Fold										Avg acc	Std dev
			0	1	2	3	4	5	6	7	8	9		
VGG16	No	Fully-connected	0.1377	0.0254	0.1373	0.0846	0.1378	0.1385	0.1388	0.1389	0.0497	0.1394	0.1128	0.0434
VGG16	Yes	SVM	0.9297	0.9364	0.9333	0.9154	0.9301	0.9268	0.9376	0.9276	0.9264	0.9333	0.9297	0.0063

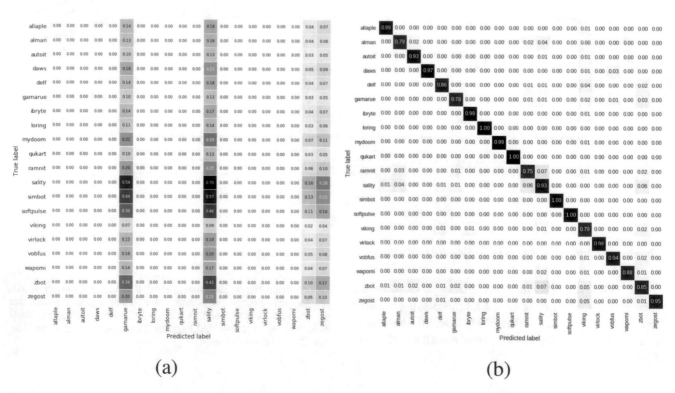

(a)   (b)

Fig. 9.6 Normalized confusion matrix of (**a**) VGG16 trained from scratch and (**b**) VGG16 with transfer and SVM

References

1. Y. Bengio et al., Learning deep architectures for AI. Found. Trends Mach. Learn. **2**(1), 1–127 (2009)
2. O. Russakovsky, J. Deng, H. Su, J. Krause, S. Satheesh, S. Ma, Z. Huang, A. Karpathy, A. Khosla, M. Bernstein, et al., Imagenet large scale visual recognition challenge. Int. J. Comput. Vis. **115**(3), 211–252 (2015)
3. J. Yosinski, J. Clune, Y. Bengio, H. Lipson, How transferable are features in deep neural networks? in *Advances in Neural Information Processing Systems* (2014), pp. 3320–3328
4. K. Simonyan, A. Zisserman, Very deep convolutional networks for large-scale image recognition (2014). arXiv preprint arXiv:1409.1556
5. J.Z. Kolter, M.A. Maloof, Learning to detect and classify malicious executables in the wild. J. Mach. Learn. Res. **7**, 2721–2744 (2006)
6. A. Shabtai, R. Moskovitch, C. Feher, S. Dolev, Y. Elovici, Detecting unknown malicious code by applying classification techniques on opcode patterns. Secur. Inform. **1**(1), 1–22 (2012)
7. L. Nataraj, S. Karthikeyan, G. Jacob, B. Manjunath, Malware images: visualization and automatic classification, in *Proceedings of the 8th International Symposium on Visualization for Cyber Security* (ACM, New York, 2011), p. 4
8. B. Kolosnjaji, A. Zarras, G.D. Webster, C. Eckert, Deep learning for classification of malware system call sequences, in *Australasian Conference on Artificial Intelligence* (2016), pp. 137–149
9. A. Krizhevsky, I. Sutskever, G.E. Hinton, Imagenet classification with deep convolutional neural networks, in *Advances in Neural Information Processing Systems* (2012), pp. 1097–1105
10. G. Conti, E. Dean, M. Sinda, B. Sangster, Visual reverse engineering of binary and data files, in *Visualization for Computer Security* (Springer, Berlin, 2008), pp. 1–17
11. M. Sebastián, R. Rivera, P. Kotzias, J. Caballero, Avclass: a tool for massive malware labeling, in *International Symposium on Research in Attacks, Intrusions, and Defenses* (Springer, Cham, 2016), pp. 230–253
12. L. van der Maaten, G. Hinton, Visualizing data using t-SNE. J. Mach. Learn. Res. **9**, 2579–2605 (2008)

Cybersecurity Vulnerabilities Assessment (A Systematic Review Approach)

Hossein Zare, Mohammad Jalal Zare, and Mojgan Azadi

Abstract

For analysis information technology and computer system vulnerabilities, this paper benefits from *"systematic review analysis: 2000–2015"* with two-time searches: One established using suitable keywords, the second performed inside references used by selected papers.

A detailed approach for analysis vulnerabilities of an organization includes physical and infrastructure of an organization, software, networks, policies, and information system vulnerabilities.

Our findings highlight the following to be the most important vulnerabilities of networks: buffer overruns, operating environment, resource exhaustion, race conditions, standardization of canonical form, and violation of trust, injection attacks, cross-site scripting, non-secure cryptography storage and failure to restrict URL access.

Keywords

Cyber-attack · IT system · vulnerability · Software · Network · Systematic review · Vulnerability assessment

10.1 Introduction

Vulnerability is defined as a *"security weakness,"* the *"capability of being physically damaged"* and "open to attack, harm, or damage." In computers and in the information technology (IT) industry, vulnerability is defined as an existing weakness in operating systems (OS), computer and networks, physical and infrastructure of an organization as well as policies and procedures connecting to internal and external networks. The importance of each weakness depends on the organization's function; however, there are some well-known vulnerabilities for IT in literally all organizations.

Our approach for listing and discussing the most common vulnerabilities in institutes and organizations in this paper is based on a "systematic review" for professional papers published between 2000 and 2015.

10.2 Methodology

We conducted a search in the SCOPUS [1] database for literature published from 2000 to 2015 up to 10/01/2015. We used the following search strategy:

"Known vulnerabilities" AND/OR "cyber-attacks" AND "LIMIT-TO ((LANGUAGE, "English"))
"Computer vulnerabilities" AND/OR "cyber-attacks" AND "LIMIT-TO ((LANGUAGE, "English")).

From 120 published documents, almost 61% were conference papers, 24% articles, 8% book chapters and 3.4% peer-articles. The remaining 3.6% were business articles, reviews and conference reviews.

Most of the documents (80%) were published after 2010, 40 from the U.S.; 67% covered computer science areas, with 59 documents on engineering and mathematics, with 37 and 12% located in second and third level of publications. Abstracts of all documents were reviewed for additional relevant studies.

Bibliographies of selected articles and relevant review articles were evaluated. Sixty-one documents were used for full-text review. In addition, documents published by institutes responsible for cyber-security in the U.S. such as the *National Institute of Standards and Technology* (NIST), U.S. *Computer Emergency Team, Microsoft TechCenter*, and the *Security TechCenter* were reviewed for explanatory and standard measures.

H. Zare (✉) · M. J. Zare · M. Azadi
University of Maryland University College, Upper Marlboro, MD, USA

The Johns Hopkins Center for Disparities Solution, Department of Health Policy and Management, Johns Hopkins Bloomberg School of Public Health, Baltimore, MD, USA
e-mail: Hossein.Zare@Faculty.UMUC.edu

© Springer International Publishing AG, part of Springer Nature 2018
S. Latifi (ed.), *Information Technology – New Generations*, Advances in Intelligent Systems and Computing 738,
https://doi.org/10.1007/978-3-319-77028-4_10

Considering the scope of this assignment, I did not report any systematic review tables, but I saw classified vulnerabilities in five main areas.

10.3 Vulnerabilities

Vulnerabilities can exist in almost all parts of computing systems. Some facilitate physical or cyber access, others can be categorized as providing or facilitating access, or simplifying misuse. Hackers exploit these vulnerabilities and use a variety of tools, skills, and techniques to attack systems and try to hack into software, crack passwords, sniff data, spoof information, identify social networks, and steal data and information [2]. Here are the most important vulnerabilities for improving organizational efforts against physical and cyber-attacks:

10.3.1 Postponing the Update of Software

Systems need to be updated manually or by auto-update. Having an old version of software may not provide needed protection. Installing the most updated version is necessary for security purposes. *The Canadian Cyber Incident Response Centre* (CCIRC, 2014) suggests four essential strategies to improve security of systems against cyber-attacks: *"Application whitelisting," "Patch common use applications," "Patch operating systems,"* and *"Restrict administrative privileges."*

10.3.2 Lack of Backup for Critical Assets and Services

To maintain secure systems, procedures need to be available in case of attack or damage to critical assets and services. Given the history of attacks against critical assets and services, this is especially important for data and important documents [3].

10.3.3 Lack of Protection for Portable Assets and Services

Hardware including (i.e. storage, machines, transmission) is one of the most important components of computers. The main reasons for a physical security strategy is to keep them available and secure by guarding and preventing them from misuse [4]. Sensitive assets and data need more protection. More security is needed for portable systems (laptops and external hard drives) to avoid them being stolen or compro-

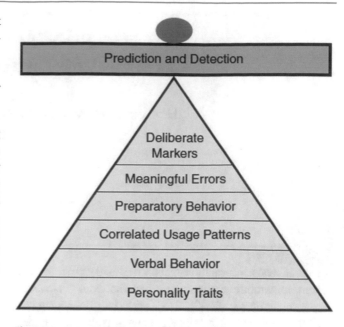

Fig. 10.1 Potential indicators of insider attacks

mised and to ensure that they can be recovered. Policies and step-by-step procedures are needed to keep critical data as safe as possible [5].

10.3.4 Unauthorized Staff and Attacks from Inside

Information security professionals believe that "most attacks come from inside", these users have much more knowledge about type of system, firewall, information systems and storing data. They are able to use a security professional level of authority to violate the security policies of organizations. The potential indicators for insider hackers are presented in Fig. 10.1 [6].

To protect against this vulnerability, critical resources need to be restricted by the level of accessibility for each employee. This simple policy could provide more protection against; stealing data or sensitive equipment, damaging critical data and sensitive data, making unauthorized changes in the system such as connections, spoofing and sniffing of data and information.

10.3.5 Insufficient Physical-Cyber Security for Remotely Monitoring Systems

New capabilities in remotely monitoring systems such as electricity, gas, water, and even security monitoring systems have lots of advantages associated with efficiency, faster response in case of problems and quality controls. However, these data are available on a network and these systems are vulnerable to different types of malicious attacks. Companies not only need to protect systems with security controls and check up to prevent access by unauthorized users, but also need to identify new risk and vulnerabilities of systems, both physically and over their networks [7]. Here are common vulnerabilities reported for this system [8]:

- Inadequate testing, weak design, updating and complexity make this software so vulnerable against cyber-attacks.
- Working as non-stop assets and cannot be updated quickly.
- Using non-standard, old versions of Windows in the central office. They need to be fixed first before updating assets in sites, but this process takes a long time and a lot of money.
- This system is more likely to be known as real-time control systems. For improving economic performance, companies store data in a cloud, which potentially creates another vulnerability and increased risk of spoofing through the cloud.
- This system generates a lot of data during a very short period of time. Most of these infrastructure systems are connected by external network connections, and any possible attack from the Internet could be considered as a vulnerability of this system. ICS-CERT reported more than 239 registered attacks of these facilities in the US between 2010 and 2011 [9].

10.3.6 Lack of a Cover Power System for Emergency Situations

Lack of backup power for all or part of an organization in case of disaster could potentially put an organization at risk of physical or unsafe environments. It could also impact the real-time understanding. (We will talk about Real-time understanding in a separate section). These internal weaknesses for a "power system" in the national level or country (on the macro-level) potentially increases the risk of threats for other organizations, although this situation on the micro-level could be considered a vulnerability [7].

10.4 Software Vulnerabilities

Any weakness in software that could be exploitable by a hacker is defined as vulnerability. This part reported the most common software vulnerabilities, that allow hackers to exploit such weaknesses during operational software.

10.4.1 Buffer Overrun

Viega and McGraw claim that buffer overruns—"the most common vulnerabilities in software" [10]—happen when a program tries to use "outside of a storage buffer" for reading or writing.

Injection and DOS attacks are common types of attacks because of this vulnerability. The basic strategies for avoiding these buffer overruns are:

- Avoid the specific weakness of each language, constructs, and runtime libraries while coding
- Avoid using non-executable memory locations
- Process runtime environment and check performance of bounds for all data
- Check the complier before performing integrity function

10.4.2 Operating Environment

The source of many vulnerabilities collected in the operating environment include the following: system files, operating systems (OS), services provided by the OS, user accounts, and other environment elements. The most recommended treats for this vulnerability are as follow: (a) the first step for treating this vulnerability is to limit the access of entrusted users, and then (b) generate a unique temporary file with strong name far from guessing names and control access control from unauthorized users [11].

10.4.3 Resource Exhaustion

Having limited bounds and resources—with unlimited access to the same resource—increase the chance of resource amplification. This vulnerability occurs during an asymmetric attack [11]. Using stronger access controls is the most effective way to control this weakness.

10.4.4 Race Conditions

In this situation, a malicious program benefits from "time of check" and "time of use" and tries to change the content of a file for malicious behavior. Usually the race condition used to exploit the file system and the technique for controlling this attack need the cooperation of the OS, and using the "atomic" operating mechanism recommended for race condition treatment [12].

Fig. 10.2 Level of awareness in an organization

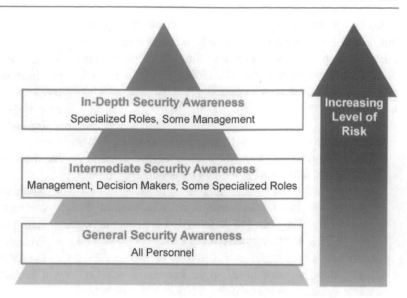

10.4.5 Standardization of Canonical Form

Converting a "set of symbols to their standard forms" is called standardization. Most resources in the computer are named by the person who uses the system. Howard and LeBlanc recommend, "Do not make any security decision based on the name of a resource" [13]. Associated vulnerabilities with the non-standard form occur in all Operating System Information (OSI) network models that are included, making decisions by IP address or directory names. Dot-dot attack is a common type of attack that benefits from this vulnerability [14].

10.4.6 Violation of Trust

A simple example is the viewpoint of the computer system in authenticating a user with the real user name and password (even if a hacker stole it). "Cross-site scrapping" and SQL code injection are examples of vulnerabilities using violation of trust [15, 16].

10.4.7 Use of Software and an Operating System (OS) with Well-Discussed Issues Are Not-Strong Enough

Lack of a penetration test for software and OS could leave the door open for hackers and malicious malware. During this authorized process, not only are software vulnerabilities identified but the concept of proof attacks are collected to treat the system. There are well-known programs for monitoring the vulnerabilities of OSs (such as Microsoft Baseline Security Analyzer) to run a white-hat attack (ethical computer hackers, who utilize hacking in a helpful way) and recognize the OS weaknesses [17].

Windows OSs are more likely to be vulnerable than Linux or most of the *Transmission Control Protocols (TCP)*. The TCP windows allows transmitting many packets before the recognizing reply. This vulnerability opens an opportunity to inject a malicious program such as the bogus reset control packet [18].

10.4.8 Lack of Awareness

Role-based security responsibility based on personnel job function is an important indicator not only to determine the level of access, but training and level of awareness are essential, as presented in Fig. 10.2. Researchers define three level requirements to determine financial organization security requirements: "identifying level of accountability," "determining minimum standard awareness," and "identifying the level of training program" [19]. These three level requirements could be recommended for similar organizations.

10.5 Vulnerabilities with Policies and Procedure

With the increasing number of cyber-attacks in recent decades, organizations need strong, clear, and updated policies to protect against potential cyber-attacks. They also need to revise and keep updated procedures especially for the most valuable assets and resources. The six most common vulnerabilities for policies and procedures in organizations include the following [20]:

- Inadequate security policies
- Lack of formal training program for employees
- Absent, inadequate, or not-well-defined guidelines
- Lack of administrative enforcement for responsibility and accountability
- Lack of continuous quality control, audit and monitoring
- Lack of strong disaster management policies [21].

The above-mentioned vulnerabilities could potentially put facilities at risk of attacks targeting the OS, supervisory control and data acquisition (SCADA) application, network, restoring the cloud in field [22].

10.5.1 Password Protection Policies

Hacker-targeted password by hacking system end, communication networks or end user—the last one is the most popular category because this attack needs a minimum level of skills and technical knowledge to implement and more probability of success. Ignoring password protocols and policies by careless users makes them the "weakest link" for cyberattacks [23]. Passwords are the most vulnerable issues for all companies to be explained more, as follows:

10.5.1.1 Lack of Password Policies
Hackers using the *"weakest link"* principle are constantly searching to find the weakest link possible to give them access to a network or computer; that *"weakest link"* is often a weak password.

10.5.1.2 Lack of "Password Expiration Policy," Password History," and "Minimum Password Age"
Having a successful "password expiration" policy—the process of forcing users to change their passwords and select a new password after a certain period of time—will not be helpful if companies do not complete it with *"Password history,"* *"minimum password age"* protocols and other essential requirements. Based on the first protocol (password history), systems need to keep previous passwords or password hashes (at least two recent passwords) to compare against new passwords or password hashes. The amount of time that must pass between password changes called "minimum password age" [24].

10.5.1.3 Passwords Size and Type of Characters
The type of cryptographic algorithm used for the password hashes has significant impact on the cracking speed. The other important indicators are the size and type of characters. The *National Institute of Standards and Technology* (NIST) reported that the estimated time for cracking a password will significantly increase with increasing size and type of characters [24].

10.5.2 Outdated Malware Protection

Malicious software attacks organizations and takes advantage of weaknesses in the system and results in loss of availability, stealing, or deleting data. Companies need to keep their software updated to protect systems from being infected. Outdated antivirus programs leave the door open for potential malware.

10.5.3 Lack of Cyclic Redundancy Check

Policies, procedures and performance of critical components need to be checked several times to find possible failures.

10.6   Network Vulnerability

10.6.1 Web Application Vulnerabilities

10.6.1.1 SQL Injection Attacks
SQL injection is another type of vulnerability that belongs to injection flows. In this attack, both the attacker and user have access to the Internet. Vulnerable web applications permit hackers to inject malicious codes to SQL servers and use a SQL command to find user information. An unauthorized hacker can attack the SQL server, discover the passwords then have free rein over the system [25].

10.6.1.2 Cross-Site Scripting (XSS)
Cross-Site Scripting vulnerability happens when there is a possibility of injection to a web application by malicious code; *"reflected," "stored"* and *"document object model"* (DOM) are three main known XSS vulnerabilities. *Nonpersist* is another XSS vulnerability. It occurs when a web applicant accepts a malicious code from a hacker and injects the code into the web server. *Stored persists* happens by storing a malicious code into the server and that code will send information later. Finally, with the DOM model, hackers modify a client site script with a fake application and steal data [26].

10.6.1.3 Weak Authentication
Using a *"weak authentication"* process with insufficient protection gives attackers an edge to find user credential easy and hack information. A combination of *social engineering*, *brute force* and *dictionary attacks* helps hackers find the secret questions from a user and discover the passwords [27].

10.6.1.4 Direct Object Reference Insecure
Some OSs such as *Unix* OS save passwords in the main directory. Attackers with *"directory travel methods"* are able to crack a password and take advantage of the OS.

10.6.1.5 Cross-Site Scripting; HTTP

In this type of attack, hackers take advantage of a weak website and from a pre-authenticated HTTP. For example, a hacker could send a virus that forces a bank account holder to open a link or fill out the form which results in the hacker stealing account user cookies and finding their personal information.

10.6.1.6 Insecure Cryptography Storage

A Web applicant who saves critical information without encryption increases the chance of successful *dictionary* or *brute force* attacks.

10.6.1.7 Failure to Restrict URL Access

An experienced hacker equipped with "crawling tools" could browse the URL enter an authorized URL for a specific person, and then take advantage of the user's account.

10.6.1.8 Insufficient Transport Layer Protection (ITLP)

ITLP is a common vulnerability with Web applicants failing to encrypt sensitive data, using weak ciphering or providing inefficient protection for network traffic. The common example of this vulnerability is transmitting sensitive data by HTTPS instead of using secure encryption channels.

10.6.1.9 Redirect to Non-valid URL

Web applicants with inadequate security can permit malicious URLs to redirect other applicants onto fake browsers.

In addition to the mentioned network browsing vulnerabilities, there are other vulnerabilities not touched upon previously that targeted equipment and infrastructure of networks. Here are the most common vulnerabilities:

10.6.2 Lack of Security for Network Infrastructure Such as Architecture, Equipment and Inadequate Network Devices

In spite of advances in technologies and equipment for computers and IT industries, in most institute networks, environments and infrastructure were not modified and developed according to essential security standards. Most of this equipment has security gaps that could be used for keeping the backdoor open for hackers. In almost all institutes there are unnecessary open-access ports or inappropriate routers that make networks unsecure.

10.6.3 Lack of Backup and Storing Systems for Network Devices

Equipment and infrastructure network devices need to be stored and prepared for restoring in case of disaster and for keeping system maintenance for essential changes and updates.

10.6.4 Lack of Encrypting Passwords for Critical Networks Transit and Identifying the Existence of Network Devices

In some institutes—especially some ICS organizations with older models—passwords are sent through the network with clear text and without encryption. Hackers with access codes could be able to monitor network and OSs and disrupt the network.

10.6.5 Lack of Distribution Network Protocols

In most organizations, protocol information is available for anyone. Having standard protocols is a necessary part of networks.

10.6.6 Lack of Physical and Environment Protection for Network Devices

Critical assets such as network devices not only need soft protection (password and secure programming to access through the Intranet and Internet) but need physical protection, especially for ports and modems, and for continued monitoring for possible physical damage or attacks.

10.6.7 Inappropriate or Non-existent Firewalls

Lack of appropriate firewalls increase the chance of passing unnecessary data between networks and, in spite of raising network traffic, increase the chance of spreading malware between networks, and open the window for monitoring critical data by other networks and synergize the likelihood of unauthorized access to networks [28].

10.6.8 Lack of Security Monitoring and Keeping Eyes Open on Network Trafficking

Any unusual increase in network traffic should be considered as a possible cyber-attack. In addition to setting automatic sensors and alarm systems, IT managers need to monitor the systems. Documenting the history of network traffic and control network traffic with standards could provide better protection for critical assets and data.

10.7 Communication Vulnerabilities and Information Systems

In spite of an information system being single or multiple source, a common vulnerability is "ambiguous text-based description" for the communication between and within sources [29]. As discussed earlier, using a text-approach communication protocol not only decreases the security of your system but protocols cannot be analyzed by an automatic control system.

With the interaction of this common vulnerability, studies have reported other weaknesses that we explain in more depth, as follows:

10.7.1 Lack of Standard Documentation Protocols for Communication

Every institute needs to have protocols to decode data before transmitting to receivers. These documents need to be encrypted and kept out of the hands of unauthorized users, otherwise hackers could use and analyze the documents using these protocols.

10.7.2 Lack of Users, Data, or Authentications

Identifying users, data and devices with level of access for each user and considering his/her job description could potentially protect against unauthorized access to data and company resources.

10.7.3 Lack of Communication Control Protocols Between Clients/Customers and Access Points

Transferring critical data between clients and points of access not only needs encryption protocols; it is also essential to limit each client to a specific level of access. On the other hand, IT managers need to define multi-layer access, considering client levels for keeping the company secure enough [30].

10.7.4 Lack of Strong Information Systems to Show Line Load

Having critical data in the dashboard control helps IT managers understand the circulation of data inside the systems. Availability of key information is the other indicator to verify system vulnerabilities with simulating patterns of data. Most companies do not use enough strong sensors in terms of defining the upper and lower limit circulations. These information helps organizations to find the source of attack in a shorter time and decrease system vulnerabilities [29].

10.7.4.1 Real-Time Understanding
"*Real-time security* is the time between attack and understanding the attack" [31]. A *real-time security operation* is a system to generate output of the risk assessment process and information for recognizing and managing the attack in the shortest time and to recognize the vulnerability of the information system [31] to decrease the marginal impact of any threat or attacks, as presented in Fig. 10.3. The most vulnerable time with the highest impact on systems under attack is the time between the analysis data and stopping the attack [31].

When hackers are uncertain about the types of attack and period of time they need to accomplish their attack, maximizing the impact and minimizing the duration are the key indicators. From the IT managers' viewpoint, there is different situation maximizing during an attack and minimizing the impact of attacks on systems [32].

10.8 Conclusion

Vulnerabilities reported in this paper are the most frequently incurred in spite of an organization's functions. Systems that are storing higher amounts of classified information, not only need to cover the multiple vulnerabilities reported in this study, they also need to follow the following advised steps:

- Perform risk and vulnerability assessment systematically and randomly for system with high levels of security and chances for attacks.
- Document the main vulnerabilities used to attack a system and calibrate those specific vulnerabilities after treatment and learn from incurred mistakes.
- Control internal misuse. It is crucial to have a strong policy for limiting access for top-level authorized individuals immediately after leaving classified information storage organizations, and monitor and mapping their information systems and networks.

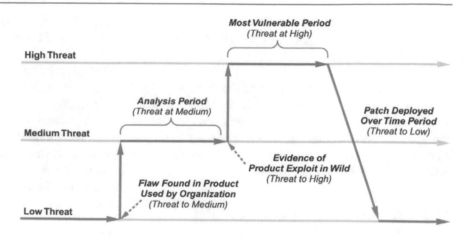

Fig. 10.3 Security position trends based on activity and response

---

References

1. Elsevier: SCOPUS Database, www.scopus.com
2. P. Baybutt, Cyber security vulnerability analysis: an asset-based approach. Process. Saf. Prog. **22**, 220–228 (2003)
3. I. Linkov, D.A. Eisenberg, K. Plourde, T.P. Seager, J. Allen, A. Kott, Resilience metrics for cyber systems. Environ. Syst. Decis. **33**, 471–476 (2013)
4. H. Bidgoli, *The Internet Encyclopedia* (Wiley, Hoboken, NJ, 2004)
5. C.A. Sennewald, J.H. Christman, *Retail Crime, Security, and Loss Prevention: An Encyclopedic Reference* (Butterworth-Heinemann, Burlington, MA, 2011)
6. E.E. Schultz, A framework for understanding and predicting insider attacks. Comput. Secur. **21**, 526–531 (2002)
7. H. Umberger, A. Gheorghe, Cyber security: threat identification, risk and vulnerability assessment, in *NATO Science for Peace and Security Series C: Environmental Security*, vol. 109, (2011), pp. 247–269
8. K. Stouffer, J. Falco, K. Scarfone, *Guide to Industrial Control Systems (ICS) Security* (NIST special publication, 2011), pp. 800–882
9. C. Wilson, Cyber threats to critical information infrastructure, in *Cyberterrorism: Understanding, Assessment, and Response* (2014), pp. 123–136
10. J. Viega, G. McGraw, *Building Secure Software: How to Avoid Security Problems the Right Way* (Pearson Education, Upper Saddle River, NJ, 2001)
11. P. Meunier, Resource exhaustion. in *Secure Programming Educational Material* (2004)
12. J. Viega, G. McGraw, *Building Secure Software: How to Avoid Security Problems the Right Way (paperback)* (Addison-Wesley Professional Computing Series, Addison-Wesley Professional, 2011)
13. M. Howard, D. LeBlanc, *Writing Secure Code* (Pearson Education, Upper Saddle River, NJ, 2003)
14. S.T. Redwine Jr., *Software Assurance: A Guide to the Common Body of Knowledge to Produce, Acquire and Sustain Secure Software, version 1.1* (US Department of Homeland Security, Washington, DC, 2006)
15. M. Bishop, S. Engle, The software assurance CBK and university curricula, in *Proceedings of the 10th Colloquium for Information Systems Security Education* (2006)
16. H. Zare, M. Azadi, P. Olsen, Techniques for detecting and preventing denial of service attacks (a systematic review approach), in *Information Technology-New Generations* (Springer, 2018), pp. 151–157
17. P. Engebretson, *The Basics of Hacking and Penetration Testing: Ethical Hacking and Penetration Testing Made Easy* (Elsevier, 2013)
18. P. Watson, Slipping in the Window: TCP reset attacks. Presentation at (2004)
19. PCI-DSS, PCI Data Security Standard. Information Supplement: Best Practices for Implementing a Security Awareness Program (October 2014), https://www.pcisecuritystandards.org/documents/PCI_DSS_V1.0_Best_Practices_for_Implementing_Security_Awareness_Program.pdf
20. T.D. Graham, J.C. Hudson, *Dynamic File Access Control and Management* (Google Patents, 2010)
21. NAS, National Academy of Sciences, Disaster resilience: a national imperative. Washington, DC (2012), http://www.nap.edu/catalog.php?record_id=13457
22. A. Amantini, M. Choraś, S. D'Antonio, E. Egozcue, D. Germanus, R. Hutter, The human role in tools for improving robustness and resilience of critical infrastructures. Cogn. Tech. Work **14**, 143–155 (2012)
23. G. Notoatmodjo, *Exploring the 'Weakest Link': A Study of Personal Password Security* (Citeseer, 2007)
24. K. Scarfone, M. Souppaya, *Guide to Enterprise Password Management (Draft): Recommendations of the National Institute of Standards and Technology* (US Dept of Commerce, Technology Administration, National Institute of Standards and Technology, Gaithersburg, MD, 2009)
25. WASC, Threat Classification, WASC-23: XML Injection (2015), http://projects.webappsec.org/w/page/13247004/XML%20Injection
26. WASC Threat Classification: WASC-31: OS Commanding (2015), http://projects.webappsec.org/w/page/13246950/OS%20Commanding
27. WASC Threat Classification. Category:OWASP Top Ten Project (2015), https://www.owasp.org/index.php/Category:OWASP_Top_Ten_Project
28. J.R. Vacca, S. Ellis, *Firewalls: Jumpstart for Network and Systems Administrators* (Elsevier, Burlington, MA, 2004)
29. E. Bompard, R. Napoli, F. Xue, Vulnerability of interconnected power systems to malicious attacks under limited information. Eur. T. Electr. Power **18**, 820–834 (2008)
30. J. Hall, *Multi-Layer Network Monitoring and Analysis* (University of Cambridge, Cambridge, 2003)
31. E.G. Amoroso, Cyber attacks: awareness. Netw. Secur. **2011**, 10–16 (2011)
32. M. Krotofil, A. Cárdenas, J. Larsen, D. Gollmann, Vulnerabilities of cyber-physical systems to stale data-Determining the optimal time to launch attacks. Int. J.Crit. Infrastruct. Prot. **7**, 213–232 (2014)

A Self Proxy Signature Scheme Over NTRU Lattices

11

Sonika Singh and Sahadeo Padhye

Abstract

The concept of self proxy signature (SPS) scheme was proposed by Kim and Chang in 2007. In a self proxy signatures, the signer wants to protect his original keys by generating temporary key pairs for a time period and then revoke them. The temporary keys can be generated by delegating the signing right to himself. Thus, in SPS the user can prevent the exposure of his private key from repeated use. If we are considering the existence of quantum computers, then scheme proposed by Kim and Chang's is no more secure since its security is based on the hardness of discrete logarithm assumption. In this paper we propose the first lattice based self proxy signature scheme. Since hard problems of lattices are secure against quantum attacks, therefore, our proposed scheme is secure against quantum computer also. We designed our scheme on NTRU lattices since NTRU lattices are most efficient lattices than general lattices.

Keywords

NTRU lattices · Proxy signature scheme · Random oracle · SIS problem · Identity based signatures

11.1 Introduction

Digital signature schemes are very important and significant primitives for constructing secure systems and are used in most of real world applications and security protocols. The proxy signature scheme is a kind of digital signature scheme firstly proposed by Mambo et al. [12] in 1996. It can be widely used in different situations, such as e-election, cloud computing, e-commerce etc. In proxy signature scheme, an original signer can delegate his signing rights to a proxy signer to sign on any document for a period of time. The proxy signer constructs a proxy private key by using the information given to him. Then he can use his signing rights to sign any document with his proxy private key by using a normal digital signature scheme. After getting the message and signatures from proxy signer, the verifier gets the public proxy key and verifies the correctness of signatures by using a normal digital signature scheme. After the concept of a proxy signature scheme proposed by Mambo et al., many effective proxy signature schemes [9, 10, 17, 22, 25, 27] etc. have been proposed by researchers based on discrete logarithmic problem (DLP). In 2007, Y.S. Kim and J.H. Chang [8] proposed a new type of digital signature scheme using DLP and they called it self proxy signature scheme. The idea behind self proxy signature is to keep the private key secret and generate temporary proxy keys to sign on any document on behalf of original key. So, in a self proxy signature scheme, a user Alice can delegates her signing rights to herself recursively. By using a self proxy signature scheme, the user Alice can generate many proxy public and private key pairs and can use them simultaneously. He can revoke the temporary private and public keys pair easily. Due to this fact, Kim et al. [8] considered their self proxy signature scheme for practical purposes and secure since their scheme satisfies all the security requirements of a proxy signature scheme. But, due to Shor's algorithm [18, 19], schemes based on DLP are not safe against quantum computers. Additionally, this scheme was analysed later in 2012 by S. Mashhadi [14, 24]. They showed that an adversary can forge a valid self proxy signature for any message by using different ways and proposed an improvement to remove the pointed out security leaks in Kim et al.'s scheme. After Kim et al. [8] scheme, several self proxy schemes have been proposed . As like, in 2010, Salevi et al. proposed ID Based self proxy signatures [16]. They gave a formal security model for identity based self proxy signatures and showed

S. Singh (✉) · S. Padhye
Department of Mathematics, Motilal Nehru National Institute of Technology, Allahabad, India

© Springer International Publishing AG, part of Springer Nature 2018
S. Latifi (ed.), *Information Technology – New Generations*, Advances in Intelligent Systems and Computing 738,
https://doi.org/10.1007/978-3-319-77028-4_11

that the scheme by Kim et al. [8] is existentially forgeable. They proposed a generic identity based self proxy signature scheme and proved the security in random oracle assumption. Later, in 2012, V. Verma also gave identity based version of a self proxy signature scheme with warrant [23]. Later, in 2013, Tahat et al. [21] proposed an efficient self proxy signature scheme based on ECDLP(elliptic curve discrete logarithm problem). They claimed that their scheme require less number of operations than Mashhadi scheme [14] and so is more efficient than Mashhadi scheme. The discrete logarithm problem is no more intractable after the quantum computers become reality. Therefore it is quite better to construct a scheme based on lattices, since lattices are considered as the best and strongest candidate for post quantum cryptography. The cryptographic schemes based on lattices are supported by worst case hardness assumption and Bernstein's conjuncture [1] that lattice can withstand quantum attacks. The running time of lattice based scheme are quadratic polynomial in respect of cubic polynomial of DLP and Factoring based scheme. The NTRU lattices [4–7] are better than general lattices. With general lattices, a scheme can suffer with large key sizes and large signature sizes. By motivating and considering all these facts, here, we are proposing a self proxy signature scheme relies on NTRU lattices in this paper and prove that it holds all the security requirements like distinguishability, unforgeability, verifiability and undeniabilty.

Rest of the sections in this paper is organized as follows. In Sect. 11.2, we give some required preliminaries used in our proposed scheme and then some related work (Kim and Chang self proxy scheme) is described in Sect. 11.3. The proposed self proxy signature scheme over NTRU lattices is given in Sect. 11.4. In Sect. 11.5, we provide a formal security proof for our scheme. Finally, in section 5 we conclude the paper.

11.2 Preliminaries

11.2.1 Notations

We will use the following notations throughout the paper- N is being security parameter and some power of 2. R is a polynomial ring $\frac{Z[X]}{X^N+1}$. The polynomials in ring R have degree $N-1$. R_q is a polynomial ring R with coefficients in Z_q i.e. $\frac{Z_q[X]}{X^N+1}$. q is a large modulus to which each coefficient is reduced. The polynomial f is the NTRU's private key polynomial and g is a polynomial used for generating the public key of NTRU cryptosystem [5, 6] from its private key f. The operation $\star$ is convolution multiplication operation. The polynomial h is NTRU's public key, given by

$h = f_q^{-1} \star g \mod q$. $||x||$ denotes the Euclidean norm of x and $||x||_1$ is l_1- norm which is given by $||x||_1 = \sum_{i=1}^{N} |x|_i$.

11.2.2 Definitions

We are giving some definitions that are very useful in this article.

Definition 1 (Self Proxy Signature Scheme) A self proxy signature scheme consists of the following algorithms—(assume Alice is the signer and Bob is the verifier.)

1. **Setup:** In this algorithm, Alice generates her private and public key pair as in a normal digital signature scheme.
2. **ProxyKeyGen:** Here, Alice constructs her temporary self proxy private and public key pair for a given time period. She publishes the proxy public key publicly available and can be revoked publicly.
3. **SelfProxySignGen:** The signer Alice here generates the signature on a message by using her private self proxy key and sends the signature and message pair to a verifier.
4. **SelfProxysignVfy:** The verifier Bob (say) using public proxy key checks the signature and message for verification.

Definition 2 (Secure Self Proxy Signature Scheme) A self proxy signature scheme is called secure if it satisfies following properties.

1. **Undeniability:** According to this property, a signer can not repudiate that he signed the document.
2. **Verifiability:** According to this property, a self proxy signature should be verified by anyone.
3. **Unforgeability:** No one can generate the valid self proxy signature except the original signer.
4. **Distinguish-ability:** The self proxy signatures should be distinguishable from normal signatures.

Definition 3 (NTRU Lattice) The NTRU lattice related to h and q is a full rank lattice in $\mathbb{Z}^{2N}$, given by

$$L_{h,q} = \{(u, v) : u + v \star h = 0 \, mod \, q\}.$$

The NTRU lattices are generated by the rows of the matrix

$$A_{h,q} = \begin{bmatrix} \mathcal{A}_{N,q}(h) & I_N \\ qI_N & O_N \end{bmatrix}$$

where $\mathcal{A}_N(h)$ is an anti-circulant matrix whose ith row contains of the coefficients of the polynomial $hx^i \mod (X^N+1)$.

11.2.3 Gaussian on Lattices

Discrete Gaussian Distribution: Gaussian sampling is a method given by Gentry et al. [3] to use a short basis as a trapdoor without revealing any information about the short basis. The $N-$ dimensional Gaussian distribution

$$\rho_{s,c}(x) = e^{-\pi \frac{||(x-c)||^2}{s^2}}$$

where $s \in R^m$ is standard deviation and vector $c \in Z^m$ is center.

For any lattice L, $\rho_{s,c}(L) = \sum_{x \in L} \rho_{s,c}(x)$. The probability mass function of the discrete Gaussian distribution is $D_{L,s,c}(x) = \rho_{s,c}(x)/s,c(L)$.

Some Important Results about discrete Gaussian distribution [11, 15]:

1. For a real positive α and any $v \in Z^m$, if $\sigma = \omega(||v||\sqrt{logm})$, then

$$Pr[x \leftarrow D_\sigma^m : \frac{D_\sigma^m(x)}{D_{\sigma,v}^m(x)} < e^{\frac{12}{\alpha}+\frac{1}{2\alpha^2}}] = 1 - 2^{100}$$

where $\omega(.)$ is the non-asymptotic tight lower bound. If $\sigma = \alpha||v||$, then

$$Pr[x \leftarrow D_\sigma^m : \frac{D_\sigma^m(x)}{D_{\sigma,v}^m(x)} = O(1)] = 1 - 2^{\omega(logm)}$$

2. For any $\sigma > 0$ and positive integer m,

$$Pr[x \leftarrow D_\sigma^1 : ||x|| > 12\sigma] < 2^{-100}$$

$$Pr[x \leftarrow D_\sigma^m : ||x|| > 2\sigma\sqrt{m}] < 2^{-m}$$

3. For given any $N-$dimensional lattice L, center $c \in R^N$, $\varepsilon > 0$ and $s > 2\eta_\varepsilon(L)$, for any $x \in L$,

$$D_{L,s,c}(x) \leq \frac{1+\varepsilon}{1-\varepsilon}2^{-N}$$

where $2\eta_\varepsilon(L)$ is the smoothing parameter of lattice L.

11.2.4 Master Key Generation

Master key generation algorithm is the most important part of a lattice based signature scheme because it generates secret keys. It works as follows:

Algorithm-1 $MasterKeyGen(N, q)$

Input : $N, q \in Z, \sigma > 0$
Output : $(msk, mpk) \in R^{2N \times 2N} \times R_q^\star$
1 Sample f and g from $D_{Z^N,\sigma}$
2 **if** $||f|| > \sigma\sqrt{N}$ or $||g|| > \sigma\sqrt{N}$ or f (mod q) $\notin R_q^\star$ or g (mod q) $\notin R_q^\star$ **then**
3 Restart
4 **end if**
5 **if** max($||(g, -f)||$, $||(\frac{g\bar{f}}{f\bar{f}+g\bar{g}})||) > 1.17\sqrt{g}$ **then**
6 Restart
7 **end if**
8 Define $\rho_f = \prod_{i=2}^{n-1} f(x^i)$ mod $(x^N + 1)$ and ρ_g similarly.
9 Compute k_f and k_g satisfy $\rho_f f + k_f(x^N + 1) = R_f$, $\rho_g f + k_g(x^N + 1) = R_g$ where $R_f = resultant(f, x^N + 1)$, $R_g = resultant(g, x^N + 1)$
10 **if** $(R_f, R_g) \neq 1$ **then**
11 Restart
12 **end if**
13 Find α and β satisfy $\alpha R_f + \beta R_g = 1$ by extended Euclidean algorithm i.e. $(\alpha\rho_f)f + (\beta\rho_g)g = 1 + k(x^N + 1)$
14 Let $F = q\beta\rho_g$, $G = q\alpha\rho_f$, then $f \star G - g \star F = q$.
15 **return** KGC's public key $mpk = h = f^{-1}g$, KGC's secret keys msk as

$$msk = B = \begin{bmatrix} \mathcal{A}(g) & -\mathcal{A}(f) \\ \mathcal{A}(G) & -\mathcal{A}(F) \end{bmatrix}$$

where $\mathcal{A}(g), -\mathcal{A}(f), \mathcal{A}(G), -\mathcal{A}(F)$ are anti-circulant matrices whose ith row contains the coefficients of the polynomial gx^i mod $(X^N + 1)$, fx^i mod $(X^N + 1)$, Gx^i mod $(X^N + 1)$ and Fx^i mod $(X^N + 1)$, respectively.

Note. In our proposed scheme, we are assuming KGC as signer Alice itself.

11.2.5 Hardness Assumption

Our signature scheme relies on small integer solution (SIS) problem and approximate shortest vector problem over NTRU lattices.

Definition 4 (SIS (Small Integer Solution) Problem Over Ring) $R(SIS_{q,m,\beta}^\phi)$. With the parameters q, m, ϕ and β, SIS problem can be defined as—If we are given m uniformly and independently chosen polynomials $a_1, a_2, \ldots, a_m$ in R_q, then to find non-zero $t \in \bar{a}$ satisfying the conditions $||t|| \leq \beta$ where $\bar{a} = \{(t_1, t_2, \ldots, t_m) \in R^m$ such that $\sum_i t_i a_i = 0$ mod $q\}$.

Definition 5 (SIS Problem Over NTRU Lattices)
$(SIS^\kappa_{q,1,2,\beta})$. Stehle and Steinfeld [20] showed that statistical distance between R^* and the distribution of $h = \frac{g}{f}$ is $2^{10N}q^{-\lfloor \epsilon N \rfloor}$, which is negligible.

For SIS problem on NTRU lattice, set $R = \frac{Z[x]}{x^{N+1}}$ and let κ be distribution that chooses small f and g according to sampling algorithm $Sampler(B, \sigma, c)$, $A_{h,q} = (h, 1) \in R^{1\times 2}_q$ and $h = \frac{g}{f}$. The problem is to find (z_1, z_2) that satisfies the conditions $A_{h,q}(z_1, z_2)^T = 0 \mod q$ and $||(z_1, z_2)|| \leq \beta$.

Definition 6 (γ Approximate Shortest Vector Problem)
$(\gamma- \text{SVP})$. For the NTRU lattice $L_{h,q}$ generated by the basis $A_{h,q}$, the shortest vector problem is to find the vector $(u, v) \in L_{h,q}$ such that $||(u, v)|| \leq ||(s, t)||$, $(s, t) \in L_{h,q}$. So, $\gamma- \text{SVP}$ is to find the vector $(u, v) \in L_{h,q}$ such that $||(u, v)|| \leq \gamma \lambda_1 L_{h,q}$, where $\lambda_1 L_{h,q}$ is the successive minimum of $L_{h,q}$.

Remark 1 According to the definitions of $\gamma- \text{SVP}$ and $(SIS^\kappa_{q,1,2,\beta})$, smallest integer solution problem is equal to the approximate shortest vector problem when $\frac{\beta}{\lambda_1 L_{h,q}} = \gamma$. Hence, our proposed scheme relies on the hardness of approximate shortest vector problem on the NTRU lattices against polynomial time algorithms and approximate shortest vector problem $\gamma-\text{SVP}$ is a NP-hard problem with $\gamma < 1 + 1/n^\epsilon$ [2].

11.3 The Proposed Self Proxy Signature Over NTRU Lattice

We are presenting here a new self proxy signature scheme over NTRU lattices. Only two candidates are participating in the proposed self proxy signature scheme, an original signer Alice and a verifier Bob. The proposed scheme have three probabilistic polynomial time algorithms, *Setup*, *SelfProxySignKeyGen*, *SelfProxySignGen* and a deterministic algorithm *SelfProxySignVfy* algorithm. The underlying hardness of the proposed scheme is the hardness of $\gamma-\text{SVP}$ and SIS problem over NTRU lattices. These algorithms are as follows :

1. **Setup** (N): Here we consider the same parameter setup as given in [26]. On input of the security parameter N, this algorithm outputs the public parameters as follows:
   Let $q = \text{Poly}(N)(q \geq 3)$, $\varepsilon \in (0, \frac{lnN}{lnq})$, $s = \Omega(N^{3/2}\sigma)$, where $\Omega(.)$ is the asymptotic lower bound and $\text{Poly}(N)$ is the polynomial function of security parameter N. Then,
   1. Choose two hash functions $H_1 : \{0, 1\}^\star \to Z^{N\times k}_q$ and $H_2 : \{0, 1\}^\star \to \{v : v \in \{-1, 0, 1\}^k, ||v||_1 \leq k\}(k$ being a positive integer).

2. Run the algorithm $MasterKeyGen$ to generate system's master key (msk, mpk).
3. Public parameters of our proxy signature system are (N, q, H_1, H_2).
   The signer Alice computes $t = H_1(ID_A)$, where ID_A is Alice's identity and sets her private signing key $SK = (S_1, S_2)$ such that $S_1 + S_2 \star h = t$ by using master secret key msk and applying $Sampler(B, \sigma, (t, 0))$.

2. **SelfProxySignKeyGen:** In this phase, signer Alice constructs a message warrant W and the temporary self proxy signing private and public key pair with her original signing key $SK = (S_1, S_2)$ as follows:
   Alice construct a warrant W consists of public key of signer Alice and a valid time period T i.e. $W = (PK, T)$.
   For constructing self proxy keys, Alice first chooses $r_1, r_2 \in_R Z^{N\times k}_q$ randomly and computes $r_1 + r_2 \star h = u$ and makes u is a public quantity. Then, she sets her self proxy private signing key $SK_{sp} = (S_3, S_4)$ with $S_3 = S_1 t H_1(W) - r_1$ and $S_4 = S_2 t H_1(W) - r_2$. The self proxy signing public key is $PK_{sp} = t^2 H_1(W) - u$.

3. **SelfProxySignGen:** Let m be the message to be signed. The self proxy signature on message m is generated as follows.
   1. Randomly select $y_1, y_2 \in D_{Z^N, \sigma}$.
   2. Compute $U = H_2(y_1 + y_2 h, m)$
   3. Now, the signer computes $Z_1 = S_3 U + y_1$ and $Z_2 = S_4 U + y_2$.
   4. The signer generates the triplets (Z_1, Z_2, U) with probability $min\left(\frac{D_{Z^N, \sigma}}{MD_{Z^N, \sigma, SK_{sp}U}}, 1\right)$, where $M = O(1)$.
   5. Now, As a result, (W, Z_1, Z_2, U) is defined as the self proxy signature on message m of signer Alice by using temporary self proxy signing key.

4. **SelfProxySignVefy:** Now, after obtaining self proxy signature from the signer, the verifier verifies the signature in the following manner.
   1. Obtain the public key of signer from the public ID board.
   2. Verify whether $||Z_1, Z_2|| \leq 2s\sqrt{2N}$ and $H_2(hZ_2 + Z_1 - [t^2 - u]H_1(W)U, m) = U$ holds or not. If holds, then accept the signature as a valid signature, otherwise reject it.

Correctness: The correctness of the scheme is given as follows
$$hZ_2 + Z_1 - [t^2 H_1(W) - u]U$$
$$= h(S_4U + y_2) + (S_3U + y_1) - [t^2 H_1(W) - u]U$$
$$= hS_4U + hy_2 + S_3U + y_1 - [t^2 H_1(W) - u]U$$
$$= (hS_4 + S_3)U + (hy_2 + y_1) - [t^2 H_1(W) - u]U$$
$$= [(hS_2t + S_1t)H_1(W) - (r_2 \star h + r_1)]U + (hy_2 + y_1) - [t^2 H_1(W) - u]U$$
$$= [(hS_2 + S_1)tH_1(W) - u]U + (hy_2 + y_1) - [t^2 H_1(W) - u]U$$

$$= [t^2 H_1(W) - u]U + (hy_2 + y_1) - [t^2 H_1(W) - u]U$$
$$= (hy_2 + y_1)$$

Hence, $H_2(hZ_2 + Z_1 - [t^2 H_1(W) - u]U, m) = U$.

By combining the results of [11], the distribution of Z_i is very close to $D_{Z^N,s}$. Therefore, we have $||Z_i|| < 2s\sqrt{N}$ by the result of [15] with a probability of at least $1 - 2^N$. Hence, the inequality $||Z_1, Z_2|| \leq 2s\sqrt{2N}$ is with an overwhelming probability.

11.4 Security Analysis

In this section we describe that the proposed scheme satisfies all security properties of a self proxy signature scheme.

Theorem 1 *The proposed self proxy signature scheme entertains the unforgeability property.*

Proof The proposed self proxy signature scheme relies on SIS problem (or in particular $\gamma - SVP$). The security against forgeability is explained as follows :

We are assuming that an attacker wants to forge the self proxy signature. He can mount attack on the scheme in two manners—the first manner is to compute the private self proxy key SK_{sp}, and the second manner is to forge the valid self proxy signature without the self proxy private key. In the first way, the attacker has to compute SK_{sp} from PK_{sp} or to generate SK_{sp} with the help of the information (W, Z_1, Z_2, U) that is transferred from signer to verifier. Howbeit, it is computationally difficult to compute SK_{sp} from PK_{sp} or from (W, Z_1, Z_2, U) because it is SIS problem over NTRU lattices. Therefore, it is computationally hard to compute SK_{sp} for the attacker. In the second manner, the attacker has to get the valid signature (Z_1, Z_2, U) on the message document m without the private key SK_{sp}. Since the second condition for verification is also a SIS problem over NTRU lattices, so attacker has to solve SIS problem to forge the signature [26].

Since both the two attacks are not viable, therefore, it is computationally difficult to the attacker to forge the self proxy signature. Therefore, the proposed scheme holds the unforgeability property. □

Theorem 2 *The self proxy signature scheme satisfies the undeniability property.*

Proof As the requirement of undeniability property, the signer can not repudiate the valid message and its signature. In our proposed self proxy signature scheme, at the time of verification of the self proxy signature (W, Z_1, Z_2, U), the warrant W is also checked, and the publicly available information t^2 and u of the proxy signer and the master's

public key h are used in the verification step. Therefore, the signer can not deny after signing on any message. □

Theorem 3 *The self proxy signature scheme holds the distinguish-ability property.*

Proof In the proposed self proxy signature scheme, the signer's identity, temporary public key and message warrant are used at the verification step of the self proxy signature (W, Z_1, Z_2, U). Thus, we can assume it as a self proxy signature instead of a normal signature. Hence, anyone can distinguish the self proxy signatures from normal signatures. If the signer sign the document with his original keys, the verification process will not hold. Therefore, the proposed signature scheme holds the distinguish-ability property. □

Theorem 4 *The proposed self proxy signature scheme entertains the verifiability property.*

Proof A scheme is said to be verifiable if the verifier can be assured of the signer's agreement on the signed message. In the proposed scheme, the verification phase is done with the help of the signer's identity and temporary public key. Therefore, any verifier can verify the signer's agreement on the signed message. Moreover, the verifier can recover the self proxy public key by public information. Hence, the proposed scheme satisfies the verifiability property. □

11.5 Conclusion

We proposed a new self proxy signature over NTRU lattices which is secure against quantum computer. Using this scheme, a user can delegate his signing right to himself for a period of time. The signer can have several ephemeral public and private key pairs and use them simultaneously. Our signature scheme is secure because it entertains all the security properties—verifiability, undeniability, distinguish-ability and unforgeability of a proxy signature scheme.

References

1. D.J. Bernstein, Introduction to post-quantum cryptography, in *Post-Quantum Cryptography*, ed. by D.J. Bernstein, J. Buchmann, E. Dahmen (Springer, Berlin, 2009), pp. 1–14
2. J.Y. Cai, A. Nerurkar, Approximating the SVP to within a factor (1+1/dim) is NP-hard under randomized reductions. J. Comput. Syst. Sci. **59**(2), 221–239 (1998)
3. C. Gentry, C. Peikert, V. Vaikuntanathan, Trapdoors for hard lattices and new cryptographic constructions, in *40th Annual ACM Symposium on Theory of Computing* (2008), pp. 197–206
4. J. Hermans, F. Vercauteren, B. Preneel, Speed records for NTRU, in *Topics in Cryptology-CT-RSA* (Springer, Basel, 2010), pp. 73–88

5. J. Hoffstein, J. Pipher, J.H. Silverman, NTRU: a new high speed public key cryptosystem (1996, preprint). Presented at the rump session of Crypto96

6. J. Hoffstein, J. Pipher, J.H. Silverman, NTRU : a ring based public key cryptosystem, in *Proceedings of ANTS*, LNCS, vol. 1423 (Springer, Cham, 1998), pp. 267–288

7. J. Hoffstein, J.H. Silverman, Optimizations for NTRU, in *Public-key Cryptography and Computational Number Theory* (DeGruyter, Berlin, 2000)

8. Y.S. Kim, J.H. Chang, Self proxy signature scheme. Int. J. Comput. Sci. Netw. Secur. **7**(2), 335–338 (2007)

9. S. Lal, A.K. Awasthi, Proxy blind signature scheme. J. Inf. Sci. Eng. Cryptol. ePrint Archive. Report 2003/072. Available at http://eprint.iacr.org/

10. Z.H. Liu, Y.P. Hu, H. Ma, Secure proxy multi-signature scheme in the standard model, in *Proceeding of the 2nd International Conference on Provable Security (ProvSec'08), Oct 30 Nov 1, Shanghai*. LNCS, vol. 5324 (Springer, Berlin, 2008), pp. 127–140

11. V. Lyubashevsky, Lattice signatures without trapdoors, in *31st Annual International Conference on the Theory and Applications of Cryptographic Techniques* (2012), pp. 738–755

12. M. Mambo, K. Usuda, E. Okamoto, Proxy signatures: delegation of the power to sign messages. IEICE Trans. Fundam. Electron. Commun. Comput. Sci. **79**(9), 1338–1354 (1996)

13. M. Mambo, K. Usuda, E. Okamoto, Proxy signatures for delegating signing operation, in *3rd ACM Conference on Computer and Communication Security(CCS'96)* (1996), pp. 48–57

14. S. Mashhadi, A novel secure self proxy signature scheme. Int. J. Netw. Secur. **14**(1), 2226 (2012)

15. P.Q. Nguyen, O. Regev, Learning a parallelepiped : cryptanalysis of GGH and NTRU signatures, in *24th Annual International Conference on the Theory and Applications of Cryptographic Techniques* (2006), pp. 271–288

16. S.S.D. Selvi, S.S. Vivek, S. Gopinath, C.P. Rangan, Identity based self delegated signature-self proxy signatures, in *Network and System Security (NSS)* (2010), pp. 568–573

17. S.H. Seo, K.A. Shim, S.H. Lee, A mediated proxy signature scheme with fast revocation for electronic transaction, in *Proceeding of the 2nd International Conference on Trust, Privacy and Security in Digital Business, Aug 22–26, Copenhagen*. LNCS, vol. 3592 (Springer, Cham, 2005), pp. 216–225

18. P. Shor, Algorithms for quantum computation: discrete logarithms and factoring, in *Proceedings of 35th Annual IEEE Symposium on Foundations of Computer Science* (IEEE, Piscataway, 1994), pp. 124–134

19. P. Shor, Polynomial-time algorithms for prime factorization and discrete logarithms on a quantum computer. SIAM J. Comput. **26**, 1484–1509 (2006)

20. D. Stehle, R. Steinfeld, Making NTRUEncrypt and NTRUSign as secure as standard worst-case problems over ideal lattices (2013), Cryptology ePrint Archive 2013/004. Available from http://eprint.iacr.org/2013/004

21. N. Tahat, K.A. Alzubi, I. Abu-Falahah, An efficient self proxy signature scheme based on elliptic curve discrete logarithm problems. Appl. Math. Sci. **7**(78), 3853–3860 (2013)

22. Z. Tan, Z. Liu, C. Tang, Digital proxy blind signature schemes based on DLP and ECDLP. MM Research Preprints, No. 21, MMRC AMMS (Academia Sinica, Beijing, 2002), pp. 212–217

23. V. Verma, An efficient identity based selff proxy signature scheme with warrant. Int. J. Comput. Sci. Commun. **3**(1), 111–113 (2012)

24. G. Wang, Designated-verifier proxy signature schemes, in *Security and Privacy in the Age of Ubiquitous Computing (IFIP/SEC 2005)* (Springer, New York, 2005), pp. 409–423

25. G. Wang, F. Bao, J. Zhou, R.H. Deng, Security analysis of some proxy signatures, in *Information Security and Cryptology - ICISC 2003*. LNCS, vol. 2971 (Springer, Cham, 2004), pp. 305–319

26. J. Xie, Y.P. Hu, J.T. Gao, W. Gao, Efficient identity based signature over NTRU lattice. Front. Inf. Technol. Electron. Eng. **17**(2), 135–142 (2016)

27. Y. Yu, Y. Sun, B. Yang, Multi-proxy signature without random oracles. Chin. J. Electron. **17**(3), 475–480 (2008)

Towards an Ontology of Security Assessment: A Core Model Proposal

12

Ferrucio de Franco Rosa, Mario Jino, and Rodrigo Bonacin

Abstract

SecAOnto (Security Assessment Ontology) aims at formalizing the knowledge on "Security Assessment". A conceptual formalization of this area is needed, given that there is an overlap of the "Information Security" and "Systems Assessment" areas, concepts are ambiguous, terminology is confounding, and important concepts are not defined. Nineteen papers on ontology, out of 80 papers of interest, have been selected to be discussed. Most of them are proposals of ontologies on information security; here we propose an ontology to deal specifically with security assessment aspects and particularities. SecAOnto is OWL-based, is publicly available and is devised to be used as a common and extensible model for security assessment. Its foundation comes from glossaries, vocabularies, taxonomies, ontologies, and market's guidelines. The initial version of the ontology, its core model, as well as an application are presented. Our proposal is meant to be useful for security researchers who wish to formalize knowledge in their systems, methods and techniques.

Keywords

Security assessment · Information security · Knowledge formalization · OWL · Ontology

F. de Franco Rosa
Information Technology Center Renato Archer, Campinas, SP, Brazil
e-mail: ferrucio.rosa@cti.gov.br

M. Jino
FEEC–University of Campinas, Campinas, SP, Brazil
e-mail: jino@dca.fee.unicamp.br

R. Bonacin (✉)
Information Technology Center Renato Archer, Campinas, SP, Brazil

Faculty of Campo Limpo Paulista, Campo Limpo Paulista, SP, Brazil
e-mail: rodrigo.bonacin@cti.gov.br

12.1 Introduction

Software assessment comprises key processes to ensure software quality in general. At the heart of the intersection between "Information Security" and "Software Assessment" there is "Security Assessment". It encompasses concepts, processes, methods and techniques crucial to the development and maintenance of secure systems.

Software systems, networks, and threats as well are becoming more complex and evolving fast. Organizations are increasing investments in security assessment of their systems to identify critical security vulnerabilities. However, despite its growing importance, knowledge available on security assessment is not structured enough; there are various types of terminological misconceptions, for instance, the use of same terms to denote different concepts [1].

Ontologies can be developed to represent, organize and make knowledge on security assessment to be explicit and available to both humans and machines. There are efforts using ontologies and other formal models to make explicit knowledge on information security; nevertheless, we identified a lack of ontologies that address the relationship between "Information Security" and "Software Assessment" [2, 3].

A core model of SecAOnto (Security Assessment Ontology) is presented. The main objective of the ontology is to formalize the main concepts of the security assessment area. Security assessment methods are usually based on attack and vulnerability analysis paradigms; the proposed model aims to support methods based on rigorous assessment criteria.

First, papers on ontologies and taxonomies of information security and system assessment were studied. Next, the following engineering procedure, based on Guarino's ontology classification [4], were performed: (1) reuse of concepts and structures modeled by information security ontologies as a domain ontology; (2) reuse of system assessment models as a task ontology; and (3) development of SecAOnto as a novel application ontology describing concepts that consider both domain and task. The conceptualization of core concepts of

© Springer International Publishing AG, part of Springer Nature 2018
S. Latifi (ed.), *Information Technology – New Generations*, Advances in Intelligent Systems and Computing 738,
https://doi.org/10.1007/978-3-319-77028-4_12

security assessment in an ontology connects well defined concepts of both "Information Security" and "Software Assessment" domains.

The remainder of this paper is organized as follows: Sect. 12.2 presents a summary of a literature review on ontologies and taxonomies on information security and system assessment, and related work; Sect. 12.3 describes how SecAOnto was developed; Sect. 12.4 presents the core concepts of the ontology, including a scenario of use; finally, Sect. 12.5 presents the conclusion and future work.

12.2 Literature Review and Related Work

We followed the guidelines for performing systematic reviews by Biolchini [5] and Kitchenham [6] to perform a quasi-systematic review. We summarized the results of the papers, focusing on aspects we considered in the development of SecAOnto. The complete literature review can be found in [7]. Out of 88 papers of interest from the literature review, 19 papers were considered closely related work discussed in this article. Most of them aim to describe domains or sub-domains of software security and software test, including their various sub-domains.

In Fig. 12.1 we present a summary of the complete mapping [7] with an excerpt of the 19 closely related works. Knowledge formalization is the most frequent focus of the selected works, 31.6% of the works, followed by works focusing on detecting attacks and risk assessment, with 10.5% each. Other studies include: trust calculation, measuring information security, e-Voting systems, security policies, coverage of standards, security requirements, and SIEM (Security Information and Event Management). Information security is the domain of 52.6% of the selected papers; security requirements are addressed by 15.8%. Other studies discuss the following domains: e-privacy laws and acts, trust, software testing, risk management, SIEM, and security standards. The most common contributions are ontologies. They are proposed by 57.9% of the studies, while 21.1% proposed concepts on information security. Other contributions include: glossaries, concepts for trust calculation, mapping standards to academic works, and security requirements.

As presented in [8], various questions were raised concerning how to represent knowledge in the security field. A formalization of information security knowledge interpretable by machines is presented in [9]. Ontologies by Herzog [10] and Fenz [11] represent a general view of the security area, providing more concepts than other ontologies. An ontology to support the process of measuring information security is proposed in [12].

A UML software testing model with high-level abstractions used for validation by humans is presented in [13]. An ontology of security requirements for web applications is proposed in [14]. An ontology to detect attacks on Web systems is proposed in [15]; it uses semantic web concepts

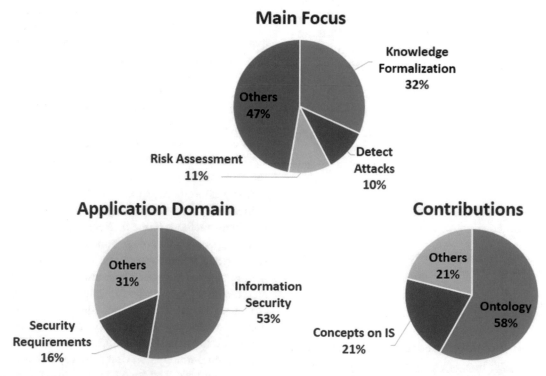

Fig. 12.1 Summary of the related works mapping

and ontologies to analyze security logs and identify potential security problems.

Some of the selected studies focus on application domains, such as e-Voting [16] and e-Gov [17]. Other studies focus on the formalization of specific aspects of information security. Trust and interoperability aspects are addressed in [1]. A domain ontology to formalize knowledge on risk management is proposed in [18]. An ontology of security metrics is presented in [19]. The Ontology presented in [20] for identifying security requirements in the development process. In [21] The Security Toolbox: Attacks & Countermeasures ontology is aimed at aiding developers in the design of secure applications.

The security assessment process is usually standard-aided. In [22] the regulatory requirements contained in standards are used as reference. A standard-based ontology is proposed in [23].

Privacy is another important environment issue [24]. In [25] a top-level ontology to model concepts related to privacy is presented.

The selected works deal with a wide spectrum of issues, applications and use of ontologies in information security. This fact highlights the need for an in-depth exploration of the subject. The available ontologies are the starting point of our work; nonetheless, none of the analyzed works focuses on relating concepts of information security and software assessment.

12.3 Developing SecAOnto

The creation process of an ontology can be done through the following activities: planning, requirements specification, knowledge capture, delivery, integration, implementation, development, documentation, and maintenance. With this in mind and taking into consideration the methodology proposed in [26], we have adopted the following:

1. *Harvesting, requirements specification and knowledge capture.* Here, we focus on the capture and formalization of knowledge, and explain how the references are used or are integrated into the proposed ontology;
2. *Creating, integration, implementation and development.* The main knowledge sources of the proposed ontology are concepts from glossaries and vocabularies, taxonomies and ontologies on security information (e.g., [1, 8, 10, 11, 23]), systems assessment (e.g., [13, 27]), and market's practice guides aimed at assessing the security of systems (e.g., [28]). We used concepts taken from references, but most of them are defined from a novel perspective, due to the particularities of the security assessment context. Specifically, we have adapted concepts related to countermeasures, assets and attacks;

3. *Applying and Sharing. Apply to validate concepts and document to share.* We have applied the main concepts in the development of a coverage calculus algorithm and we have shared the conceptualization in the GitHub Repository [29].

SecAOnto was developed using the Web Ontology Language (OWL). The ontology was developed with the participation of a senior security assessment specialist and a senior specialist (full professor) in software assessment, and was reviewed by other two senior specialists in software development. In total, close to ten versions of the ontology were produced in 2 years through an iterative reviewing process. Our ontology was used in an algorithm for coverage calculus of assessment dimensions and security properties.

12.4 The SecAOnto Core Model

A core ontology can be understood as a mid-level ontology between the top-level and domain ontologies. In the context of this work, we refer to core model as the model containing the key concepts of our ontology, which are used to structure and understand all other concepts.

12.4.1 SecAOnto.owl: Core Model Description

Security assessment inherits concepts from systems assessment and information security. Hence, it is important to point out the specific definitions, based on the views of lead authors, and propose a common vocabulary for the security assessment process. Figure 12.2 presents the core concepts of SecAOnto, including concepts related to: (1) Systems Assessment; (2) Information Security; (3) Security Assessment.

12.4.1.1 Conceptualization: Systems Assessment

Assessment, Test, Verification and Evaluation—Test is the dynamic activity aimed at running a program or a model in a controlled manner using specific entries and verifying whether the behavior is in accordance to specifications to identify defects or to ensure its reliability. There are various kinds of tests, e.g., *Functional, Penetration, Fuzzing, Fault or Defect Injection,* and *Exploratory. Verification* is the activity aimed at verifying whether a requirement is present, without a test of the functionality. There are various kinds of verification, e.g., *Compliance, Formal Methods, Vulnerability Analysis, Reverse engineering, Social engineering,* and *Business Rules.* The term *Assessment* is more generic and includes testing and verifying activities. *Evaluation* is considered synonymous of *Assessment* in this context.

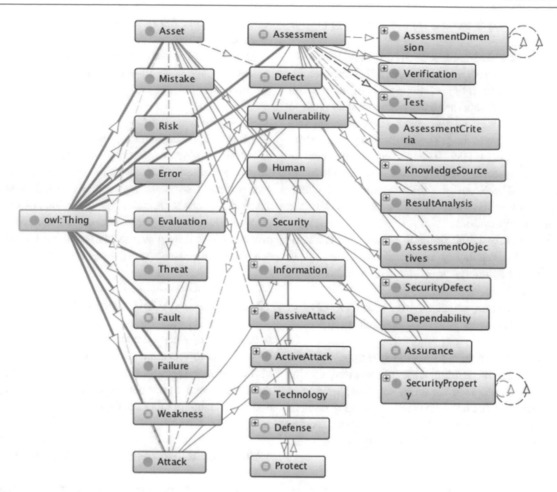

Fig. 12.2 Core classes of SecAOnto

ResultAnalysis of the assessment can be classified as *Homologation* or *Certification*. *Homologation* is related to ratify, affirm, confirm, and approve. *Certification* is related to certify, formal concession, and submission to regulation.

Mistake is a human action, which can produce a *Defect*. *Programmers*, *Engineers* or *Operators* make mistakes for various reasons (e.g., forgetfulness, lack of knowledge).

Defect, Fault—It is a deficiency or lack in a step, process or in definition of data. If present in a program, a defect may cause an error when executed.

Error is an inconsistent or unexpected condition of the program. It is an incorrect value or sequence in a given state of the program. It is caused by the execution of a defect. *Failure* is result from error propagation. A failure is noticed when the produced result is different from the expected result.

AssessmentCriteria are rules that define how we will execute the assessment. Assessment criteria define requirements to be satisfied.

AssessmentDimension are the scope of assessment, i.e., defines under which view or perspective the system must be evaluated. Assessment Dimensions are: *Business Logic,*

System Architecture, Process, System in Runtime; *Source Code*; and *Operating Environment*. Assessment Dimensions are related to each other, and the distances between them are proposed by means of an adjacency matrix. We expressed the distances between assessment dimensions by creating instances of classes and annotations in those instances.

KnowledgeSource are documents, standards, Web sites, etc., which can be used in an assessment process to provide a set of assessment items. *AssessmentItems* are assessment requirements, such as test cases, verification items, standard controls, aimed at finding defects or faults in systems.

12.4.1.2 Conceptualization: Information Security

Security is an objective, i.e., to protect the asset against misuse. *Security* is detailed in security properties. *Dependability* and *Assurance* are considered synonymous to *Security* in this context.

Asset is information or any system component valuable for the institution, e.g., data, device, or other component of the operational environment. *Defenses* (or *Protections*) are methods, processes or mechanisms aimed at protecting an asset from misuse. *Vulnerability* is a defect, i.e., a weakness or incapacity of a system that can be exploited by attackers. An *Attack* is an attempt to access improperly an asset with malicious purpose. *Attacks* exploit defects.

Risk as a probability of an adverse event to happen and impact an asset, and *Threat* is an asset can be under a risk of being attacked. *SecurityProperties* are principles or specific security characteristics of information or systems. We propose eleven security properties, namely: *Availability, Integrity, Confidentiality, Authenticity, Traceability, Privacy, Auditability, Legality, Resilience,* and *Nonretroactivity*. Other properties may be included, especially when specific knowledge fields are addressed.

12.4.1.3 Conceptualization: Security Assessment

The security assessment process includes rules that define how to perform the assessment, with emphasis on finding security defects. Security assessment has two important particularities, namely: (a) Continuous test, due to the uncertainty on the completeness of requirements; and, (b) User profiles and other interoperable systems are always considered malicious. Security assessment also has objectives, namely: (a) measuring the level of security or insecurity; (b) defining maturity; (c) verifying compliance; and, (d) finding defects or vulnerabilities.

SecurityDefects impact, directly or indirectly, the security level of a system. We can define three kinds of security defects, namely: (1) *DesignDefect*—It is an incorrect specification of business logic, such as rules, requirements, architecture, resources, etc.; (2) *DevelopmentDefect*—It is an incorrect coding of functionality; and (3) *OperationDefect*— It is an inappropriate operating environment or incorrect use of system features; lack of proper maintenance and constant evolution of system.

12.4.2 An Application Scenario

We applied SecAOnto as the core element in the development of a coverage calculus algorithm. *SecAOnto.OWL* is used for identifying concepts in descriptions of assessment items, i.e., using the Apache JENA Framework we search for concepts represented in the knowledge source; we then assign assessment dimensions and security properties with their distances to each assessment item. Distances represented in the ontology are used to calculate the coverage of security characteristics.

We have developed two software prototypes. The first application receives lists containing the assessment items and their assessment dimensions and security properties, calculates the coverage and returns the coverage data. The second application provides the graphical interface and yields visual information for generation of assessment designs.

The coverage calculus algorithm aims to provide the following main coverage measures: (1) Coverage of Assessment Dimensions; (2) Coverage of Security Properties; and (3) Local Coverage of the Assessment Item. Global Coverage of the Knowledge Source and Total Coverage of the Assessment Design are calculated later based on the main coverage.

The second application enables the selection of assessment items, in accordance with the chosen criteria. It aims to support the building process of assessment designs, by allowing the generation of security assessment designs in a structured manner; it is also capable of using the ontology concepts to describe labels contained in its web forms.

12.4.3 Discussion

SecAOnto is a proposal for conceptualization of an important field, whose concepts were always considered separately and ambiguously. We have created a relatively clean ontology focused on security assessment instead of information security in general. OntoMetric [30] methodology allows a more precise judgment on security ontologies rather than general comparison, because it enables an evaluation of the content of compared ontologies. Evaluation marks are very dependable on the evaluator's opinion and requirements for the ontology. SecAOnto is an ALCHIQ(D) ontology with 758 Axioms, 290 Logical Axioms, 156 Classes, 37 Object Properties, 14 Object Property Domains, 56 Individual Axioms, and 202 Annotation Axioms.

Due to the complexity of formalizing the security assessment field of applied research, SecAOnto must still be improved. A better analysis on the expressivity of SecAOnto is in order. We are working on increasing its expressivity by including technical details in some branches of concepts and by creating instances close to real-world conditions.

SecAOnto is also limited to security assessment and is not intended to describe the entire assessment field or the entire information security domain. For example, we do not deal with risk management process, vulnerability analysis, and other topics. SecAOnto can also be applied in other algorithms or tools whenever a conceptual formalization of security assessment is required.

12.5 Conclusions

We propose the SecAOnto aimed at formalizing concepts from information security and systems assessment. SecAOnto is extensible, human and machine readable, and the OWL source file is available for researchers use, edit or merge it.

We have presented the development of the core concepts of the ontology, as well as an application scenario. We defined the concepts in natural language to make it easier for humans to understand them. Our proposal is meant to be useful for security researchers who wish to formalize knowledge in their systems, methods and techniques.

As future work, we intend to use SecAOnto as a conceptual reference of a novel approach for security assessment. We expect to continue expanding the ontology and improving its expressivity, by incorporating other concepts, relations, properties and individuals. We also expect to validate some novel concepts with the collaboration of security assessment experts.

References

1. L. Viljanen, Towards an ontology of trust. Computer (Long. Beach. Calif) **3592**, 175–184 (2005)
2. F.F. Rosa, M. Jino, A survey of security assessment ontologies, in *Advances in Intelligent Systems and Computing (AISC)*, 569th edn, ed. by J. Kacprzyk (Springer, 2017), pp. 166–173
3. C.P. de Barros, F. de Franco Rosa, A.F. Balcão Filho, Software testing with emphasis on finding security defects, in *IADIS—The 12th International Conference on WWW/Internet* (2013), pp. 226–228
4. N. Guarino, Formal ontology and information systems, in *ACM International Conference in Formal Ontology and Information Systems* (1998)
5. J. Biolchini, P.G. Mian, A. Candida, C. Natali, Systematic review in software engineering. Engineering **679**, 165–176 (2005)
6. B. Kitchenham, Procedures for performing systematic reviews (Keele Univ., Keele, UK) **33**, no. TR/SE-0401, 28 (2004)
7. F. de Franco Rosa, M. Jino, R. Bonacin, *The Security Assessment Domain: A Survey of Taxonomies and Ontologies* (Renato Archer Information Technology Center (CTI), Campinas, Brazil, 2017)
8. A. Souag, C. Salinesi, R. Mazo, I. Comyn-Wattiau, *A Security Ontology for Security Requirements Elicitation* (2015)
9. D. Feledi, S. Fenz, Challenges of web-based information security knowledge sharing, in *2012 Seventh Int. Conf. Availability, Reliab. Secur.* (2012), pp. 514–521
10. A. Herzog, N. Shahmehri, C. Duma, An ontology of information security. Int. J. Inf. Secur. Priv. **1**(4), 1–23 (2007)
11. S. Fenz, A. Ekelhart, Formalizing information security knowledge, in *… 4th Int. Symp. Inf. …* (2009), p. 183
12. A. Evesti, R. Savola, E. Ovaska, J. Kuusijarvi, The design, instantiation, and usage of information security measuring ontology, in *Proc. 4th IEEE Int. Conf. Self-Adaptive Self-Organizing Syst., no. c* (2011), pp. 204–212
13. H. Zhu, Q. Huo, Developing a software testing ontology in UML for a software growth environment of web-based applications, in *Softw. Evol. with UML* (2005), pp. 1–34
14. P. Salini, S. Kanmani, Ontology-based representation of reusable security requirements for developing secure web applications (2013)
15. A.D. Khairkar, D.D. Kshirsagar, S. Kumar, Ontology for detection of web attacks, in *Proc.—2013 Int. Conf. Commun. Syst. Netw. Technol. CSNT 2013* (2013), pp. 612–615
16. P. Salini, S. Kanmani, A knowledge-oriented approach to security requirements engineering for e-voting system. Int. J. Comput. Appl. **49**(11), 21–25 (2012)
17. M. Grobler, J.J. van Vuuren, L. Leenen, Implementation of a cyber security policy in South Africa: reflection on progress and the way forward. ICT Crit. Infrastruct. Soc. **386**(2012), 215–225 (2012)
18. F.-H. Liu, W.-T. Lee, Constructing enterprise information network security risk management mechanism by ontology. J. Appl. Sci. Eng. **13**(1), 79–87 (2010)
19. I. Kotenko, O. Polubelova, I. Saenko, E. Doynikova, The ontology of metrics for security evaluation and decision support in SIEM systems, in *Proc.—2013 Int. Conf. Availability, Reliab. Secur. ARES 2013* (2013), pp. 638–645
20. W. Kang, Y. Liang, A security ontology with MDA for software development, in *Proc.—2013 Int. Conf. Cyber-Enabled Distrib. Comput. Knowl. Discov. CyberC 2013* (2013), pp. 67–74
21. A. Gyrard, C. Bonnet, K. Boudaoud, A. Gyrard, C. Bonnet, K. Boudaoud, T. Stac, S. Toolbox, A. Gyrard, C. Bonnet, The STAC (Security Toolbox: Attacks & Countermeasures) ontology (2014)
22. U. Koinig, S. Tjoa, J. Ryoo, Contrology—an ontology-based cloud assurance approach, in *2015 IEEE 24th Int. Conf. Enabling Technol. Infrastruct. Collab. Enterp.* (2015), pp. 105–107
23. S. Ramanauskaite, D. Olifer, N. Goranin, A. Čenys, Security ontology for adaptive mapping of security standards. Int. J. Comput. Commun. Control **8**(6), 878–890 (2013)
24. D. Jutla, L. Xu, Privacy agents and ontology for the semantic web. Am. Conf. Inf. Syst., 1760–1767 (2004)
25. V. Raskjn, C. F. Hempelmann, S. Nirenburg, W. Lafayette, Ontology in information security: a useful theoretical foundation and methodological tool, in *Work. New Secur. Paradig.* (2002), pp. 53–59
26. L. Obrst, P. Chase, R. Markeloff, Developing an ontology of the cyber security domain, in *Seventh Int. Conf. Semant. Technol. for. Intell. Defense, Secur.—STIDS 2012* (2012), pp. 49–56
27. P.M.S. Bueno, M. Jino, W.E. Wong, Diversity oriented test data generation using metaheuristic search techniques. Inf. Sci. (NY). **259**, 490–509 (2011)
28. ISO/IEC, *ISO/IEC 27001:2013 Information Technology—Security Techniques—Information Security Management Systems—Requirements* (2013)
29. F. de Franco Rosa, M. Jino, L.A.L. Teixeira Junior, Security Assessment Ontology—SecAOnto (2017), https://github.com/ferruciof/Files/blob/master/SecAOnto/SecAOnto_V4.owl. Accessed 12 Jan 2017
30. A. Lozano-Tello, A. Gomez-Perez, ONTOMETRIC: a method to choose the appropriate ontology. J. Database Manag. **15**(2), 1–18 (2004)

13

Ping Wang, Matt Rosenberg, and Hubert D'Cruze

Abstract

Mobile forensics has been gaining in demand and significance with fast-growing number of users for mobile devices such as smartphones. Mobile forensics tools provide important capabilities for digital forensic investigators to extract, examine, and analyze evidence data uncovered from mobile devices. Due to the limitations of various tools, this paper argues for an integrated approach to mobile forensic tool capabilities through combined use of different tools. This study provides empirical data that demonstrates the benefit of integrating the strengths of two different mobile forensic tools, Cellebrite UFED and Oxygen Forensics, in evidence extraction from two sample Samsung Galaxy smartphones.

Keywords

Mobile forensic tools · Evidence extraction · Smartphone · Cellebrite UFED · Oxygen Forensics

13.1 Introduction

Mobile devices such as smartphones have increasingly become an integral part of people's life and work today. In the United States alone, about 80% of the population are now owners of smartphones [1]. Smartphones, including both Android and iOS devices, have also become attractive targets for online attacks and criminal activities, such as thefts

P. Wang (✉)
Robert Morris University, Moon, PA, USA
e-mail: wangp@rmu.edu

M. Rosenberg
Allegheny County Police Department, Pittsburgh, PA, USA

H. D'Cruze
University of Maryland, College Park, MD, USA

of sensitive personal information and money extortion [2]. Therefore, mobile forensic investigations into smartphones has been gaining in demand and significance.

As more and more users store data and communicate with others via smartphones, the smartphone devices may provide potentially valuable evidence for digital investigations. The potential evidence items from various smartphone devices may include: (1) incoming, outgoing, and missed calls and voicemail records; (2) Multimedia Message Service (MMS) text messages and Short Message Service (SMS) messages; (3) Instant Messaging (IM) logs, Email accounts, and accessed Web pages; (4) Pictures, videos, music files, and voice recordings; (5) Calendars and address books; and (6) Social media account information and GPS data [3].

Mobile forensic tools with capable features are needed in order to uncover and extract or acquire valuable data from mobile devices for further examination, analysis, and reporting. The discussion of this paper focuses on software tools. There are a number of mobile forensic tools available. Examples of commercial software tools include EnCase Smartphone Examiner, AccessData FTK Imager, Cellebrite UFED (Universal Forensic Extraction Device). Examples of free or open source tools include the Sleuth Kit/Autopsy, DEFT (Digital Evidence & Forensics Toolkit), Helix, etc. However, "the growing number and variety of mobile devices makes it difficult to develop a single process or tool to address all eventualities" [4]. While all tools try to include features to address investigative needs for a wide range of mobile devices, their capabilities and performance may vary considerably, such as in recovering deleted data, in product support and documentation, and in searching, bookmarking, and reporting capabilities [5].

Comparative studies on the performance of mobile forensic tools indicated that it is not feasible to use a single forensic tool or kit for all mobile device platforms [6]. Conducting a successful digital investigation on a mobile device using a single forensic software tool is a very challenging task. Discrepancies, such as inconsistencies, errors, and data trun-

© Springer International Publishing AG, part of Springer Nature 2018
S. Latifi (ed.), *Information Technology – New Generations*, Advances in Intelligent Systems and Computing 738,
https://doi.org/10.1007/978-3-319-77028-4_13

cations in recovering and reporting data residing on mobile devices have been reported in previous testing of tools [5]. There are multiple factors contributing to the challenges and limitations facing mobile forensic software tools, including the continuous functioning of the mobile device clock in bitstream copying of memory contents, wide variety of mobile device hardware and customized operating systems (OS), various connection protocols, lack of standard data format, and the inability of mobile forensic software vendors to keep up to date with the mobile device OS releases [6].

To address the limitations of individual mobile forensic tools, this paper argues for an integrated approach of using multiple tools to combine and optimize the effect of different tools which complement each other in capabilities. Using two or more forensic tools to obtain identical results also helps to validate the tools and the data extraction results in addition to the data authentication via hashing [1].

To demonstrate the integrated approach of using more than one software tool in digital forensic investigations of mobile devices, this paper will present sample data captures from two Samsung Galaxy smartphones using two different mobile forensic tools—Cellebrite UFED and Oxygen Forensic. The rest of the paper will review relevant research literature on mobile forensic tools, describe the experiment methodology, and present and discuss the findings.

13.2 Literature Review

This section reviews important performance criteria and capability requirements and options for evaluating mobile forensic software tools. The features and capabilities of some major mobile forensic tools are also discussed.

A standard evaluation process is necessary for mobile forensic tools to behave reasonably and meet the required performance standard. According to the latest mobile device tool specification published by the US National Institute of Standards and Technology (NIST), all mobile device forensic tools capable of acquiring internal memory are required to have these core features and be able to: (a) recognize supported devices via suggested interfaces; (b) notify the user of connectivity errors between the device and application during data extraction; and (c) perform a logical data extraction of supported data objects without modification [7]. However, NIST also specifies optional features that may not apply to all mobile forensic tools. The optional features include physical data extraction, UICC (Universal Integrated Circuit Card) or identity module data extraction, and authentication mechanism (e.g. password) bypass [7]. In addition, mobile forensic tools should be able to acquire data that must be well documented and repeatable at any point in time [1]. The main principle for a sound forensic examination of digital evidence is that the original evidence must not be modified.

A sound forensic tool must produce evidence that is useful and admissible to the court of law. The five evidence rules guiding the performance and integrity of a mobile forensic tool are that the digital evidence must be authentic, complete, reliable, believable and admissible [8]. Mobile forensic tools and their updates and new versions should be thoroughly evaluated and validated to ensure their acceptability [5, 9].

AccessData's Mobile Phone Examiner (MPE) is a commercial mobile forensic tool and a good example of capability integration. MPE's key features include broad support of mobile devices, automated smart application recovery, built in iOS and Android parsers, Hex Interpreter, SIM and USIM Support and SQLite DB Browser [1]. MPE can be used as a standalone application or as a fully integrated part of Forensic Toolkit (FTK) interface. Digital forensic investigators in the mobile field have the option of a quick and easy acquisition via interfaces such as a cable or Bluetooth/infrared connection to maintain the integrity of the data on the device. When integrated with FTK, MPE can take advantage of leading digital forensic technology validated by courts and organizations such as Federal Bureau of Investigations (FBI) or Internal Revenue Service (IRS). This integration would allow MPE to perform forensic analysis on multiple smartphones simultaneously within the same FTK interface as well as to manage the evidence data for simplified interpretation. Reports produced by the integrated suite are instantly ready to be used as evidence in court and include both phone and computer analysis allowing for easy correlation of evidence data from a smartphone to the data from a computer or another mobile device [10].

Cellebrite, an Israel-based company with global operations, offers an extensive range of software tools for mobile forensics under their Universal Forensic Extraction Device (UFED) umbrella. UFED Physical Analyzer, UFED Logical Analyzer, UFED Phone Detective, UFED Cloud Analyzer, and more are available from Cellebrite [11]. The essential physical extraction of UFED tools allows the examiner to access target data by creating a bit-for-bit copy of the mobile device's flash memory. Seeing where the data is located within the device's memory greatly facilitates forensic interpretation of the acquired data [1]. The main feature of UFED open to integration is that the logical extraction of data is performed mainly through a designated API (Application Programming Interface) allowing third party apps to communicate with the device operating system to enable forensically sound data extraction. In addition, Cellebrite UFED Physical Analyzer includes other advanced capabilities for logical acquisition, such as the abilities to extract device keys needed to decrypt raw disk images as well as keychain items, crack and reveal device passwords, and generate reports in several popular formats such as Microsoft Excel, PDF, or HTML [8]. These additional versatile features may complement other mobile forensic tool products which may not have all the capabilities of Cellebrite UFED.

Oxygen Forensic offers some strong mobile forensic capabilities with advanced all-in-one acquisition and analysis toolkits supporting more than 12,000 unique device models via physical, logical, and cloud data acquisitions. Oxygen Forensic toolkit comes with the ability to exploit unique properties of certain chipsets and OEMs, which is a powerful feature allowing investigators to dump the entire contents of the device while bypassing the bootloader lock and screen lock altogether [11]. Oxygen forensic software can perform logical analysis of mobile devices such as smartphones to extract crucial information such as text messages, call logs, calendar data or event logs. The software suite also has features of timeline analysis and is able to detect and decrypt user passwords, track device owner's movements and analyze application data and generate forensic reports of the findings. It is also able to recover deleted data automatically and provide access to raw files for manual examination and analysis. In addition, the software tools provides an intuitive and user-friendly user interface to browse the extracted data as well as keyword lists and a regular expression library for searching [8].

Given the fact that there are multiple forms of data on mobile devices such as smartphones, which may use different and customized operating systems with a variety of known and unknown manufacturers and models, there has been increased challenge and difficulty for digital investigators to select a forensic tool to acquire evidence data from mobile devices across the board [1]. One single forensic tool is not capable and powerful enough to extract the various forms of data from diverse mobile devices. Thus, it is recommended not to rely on just one forensic tool to acquire, examine, analyze, and report pertinent and true evidence admissible to the court of law. It is necessary to adopt an integrated approach and compare and make combined use of strong features and capabilities from more than one software tool. For example, a forensic examiner may have a better chance of obtaining thorough evidence data from smartphones by using capabilities from both the Cellebrite UFED Logical Analyzer Tool and the Oxygen Forensics Suite Tool. While Cellebrite UFED has strong essential features for data acquisition, the Oxygen Forensics tool is able to extract more data such as the Device Status "Rooted", Device Internal Name, Device Serial Number, Owner Phone Number, Owner Accounts and Network Information; and it is a more favorable method to use the Oxygen Forensics Suite to support Cellebrite UFED logical acquisition such as in detecting device manufacturer and model, phone revision, date/time, or IMEI [12].

13.3 Methodology

To demonstrate the benefit of the integration approach to using mobile forensic tool capabilities, this study tests data acquisition on two smartphones using two different mobile forensic tools. The four material items (two smartphone devices and the two mobile forensic tools) used in the study are as follows:

1. Samsung Galaxy On5 (SM-G550T1), running Android v6.0.1
2. Samsung Galaxy S III (SCH-I535), running Android v4.1.2
3. Cellebrite UFED 4PC v6.3.1
4. Oxygen Forensic Detective v9.6.2

In this study, both phones, the Samsung Galaxy On5 (SM-G550T1) (Fig. 13.1) and Samsung Galaxy S III (SCH_I535) (Fig. 13.2), were donated and due to be destroyed so all personal information and identifying factors have been removed for the privacy of the previous owners.

Mobile device information is important for digital forensic examiners in preparation for data acquisition. Each smartphone that an examiner receives may be different and can

Fig. 13.1 Samsung Galaxy On5 (SM-G550T1)

Fig. 13.2 Samsung Galaxy S III (SCH_I535)

Table 13.1 Mobile device information

	Samsung Galaxy (Sm-G550T1)	Samsung Galaxy S III (SCH-I535)
Technology	LTE (Cat 3)	LTE (Cat 3)
Launched	October 2015	June 2012
SIM	Nano (4FF)	Micro (3FF)
OS	Launched with Android 5.1	Launched with Android 4.0.4
Internal memory	8 GB raw hardware 3.7 GB available to user	16 GB raw hardware 12 GB available to user
WLAN	Wi-Fi 802.11 b/g/n, Wi-Fi Direct, hotspot	Wi-Fi 802.11 a/b/g/n, dual-band, Wi-Fi Direct, DLNA, hotspot
Bluetooth	Yes	Yes
USB	Yes Micro-USB	Yes Micro-USB
Processor	1.3 GHz Samsung Exynos 3475	1.5 GHz Qualcomm Snapdragon S4

cause issues when it comes to extraction of data. An examiner also needs to know the system and connection details of the phone so as to decide on the capabilities of his/her tools

especially when it comes to what can or cannot be retrieved. Table 13.1 above shows the system and connection details for the two smartphones used in this study.

The primary forensic tool used in the study is Cellebrite UFED 4PC. Figure 13.3 below is an example of all the extractions that are possible using Cellebrite UFED 4PC for the Samsung Galaxy On5 (SM-G550T1). Similar features are also available to the Samsung Galaxy S III device. There are three options to bypass the lock on this phone, as well as a logical extraction if the phone is unlocked. The limitation is that Cellebrite can perform a physical extraction with lock bypass on most but not all devices, thus resorting to retrieving deleted data directly from the memory chip without having the passcode.

13.4 Findings and Discussions

This section presents the data extraction findings using the Cellebrite UFED and Oxygen Forensic tools on the two Samsung smartphones for this study. The strengths and limitations for the two tools are also discussed.

Table 13.2 below shows the performance results of both Cellebrite UFED 4PC and Oxygen Forensic Detective on the Samsung Galaxy On5 (SM-G550T1) smartphone. Both Cellebrite UFED and Oxygen Forensic tools have multiple options to extract data from the device. However, Oxygen was not able to obtain data results in recovering contacts, SMS and MMS messages, Web history, device locations, and deleted information as Cellebrite UFED did. Also, the Oxygen Forensic tool did not provide lock bypassing on the phone, and the USB debugging had to be activated for it to work.

Figures 13.4 and 13.5, and Table 13.3 jointly present comparative results of the Cellebrite UFED and Oxygen Forensic tools on the second smartphone, Samsung Galaxy S III (SCH-I535). Cellebrite UFED performance is consistent on this device and better than Oxygen Forensic. For example, the Cellebrite UFED tool retrieved considerably more SMS and MMS text messages and contacts than Oxygen did. With a different version of OS, an older version of Android than the first device, Oxygen Forensic performed better on Galaxy S III than previously on Galaxy On5, especially in recovering

Fig. 13.3 Cellebrite features for Galaxy On5

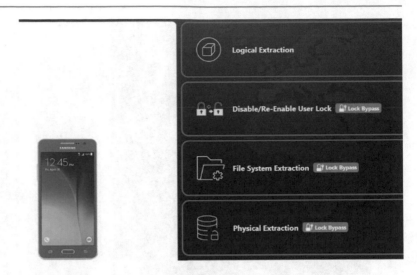

Table 13.2 Performance results on Galaxy On5

Mobile device evidence	Cellebrite UFED 4PC	Oxygen forensic detective
Pictures	Yes	Yes
Contacts	Yes	No
SMS	Yes	No
Videos	Yes	Yes
MMS	Yes	No
Web history	Yes	No
Device locations	Yes	No
TimeLine	Yes	Yes
Deleted information	Yes	No

contacts, text messages, Web history, device locations and deleted information. It should be noted that Oxygen Forensic also performs slightly better than Cellebrite in detecting the device information, such as manufacturer information and model, of older mobile devices. Therefore, it would be beneficial to use both tools. An additional benefit of using both tools is that they help to check and validate the results of each other.

13.5 Conclusions

The demand for digital forensic investigations of mobile devices has been growing with increasing significance and abundant mobile forensic software tools available. However, the features, capabilities, and performance of the tools may vary with diverse hardware and software of mobile devices and smartphones. It is difficult to depend on a single software tool to perform all forensic acquisition, examination, analysis, and reporting of evidence data from all mobile devices as there are strengths and limitations with all software tools. The best way is to integrate the forensic capabilities of different tools through combined use of the strengths of more than one tool. The integration approach also helps to validate the forensic results in addition to the hashing solution. The preliminary comparative results of the tests on the two Samsung smartphones using Cellebrite UFED and Oxygen Forensic tools support the integration approach. Future studies may include more mobile forensic tools and mobile devices for more conclusive results.

Fig. 13.5 Oxygen's results on Galaxy S III

Fig. 13.4 Cellebrite's results on Galaxy S III

Table 13.3 Performance results on Galaxy S III

Mobile device evidence	Cellebrite UFED 4PC	Oxygen forensic detective
Pictures	Yes	Yes
Contacts	Yes	Yes (not as many)
SMS	Yes	Yes (not as many)
Videos	Yes	Yes
MMS	Yes	Yes (not as many)
Web history	Yes	Yes
Device locations	Yes	Yes
TimeLine	Yes	Yes
Deleted information	Yes	Yes (not as many)

References

1. R. Wilson, H. Chi, A case study for mobile device forensics tools, in *Proceedings of the South East Conference on—ACM SE '17* (2017), https://doi.org/10.1145/3077286.3077564
2. Symantec, Internet security threat report (2016), http://www.symantec.com/threatreport/
3. B. Nelson, A. Phillips, C. Steuart, *Guide to Computer Forensics and Investigations*, 5th edn. (Cengage Learning, Boston, 2016)
4. E. Casey, B. Turnbull, Digital evidence on mobile devices, in *Digital Evidence and Computer Crime*, 3rd edn, ed. by E. Casey, (Elsevier, Inc., London, 2011), pp. 1–44
5. NIST (National Institute of Standards and Technology). Guidelines on mobile device forensics (Special Publication 800-101 Revision 1) (2014), http://nvlpubs.nist.gov/nistpubs/SpecialPublications/NIST.SP.800-101r1.pdf
6. O. Osho, S.O. Ohida, Comparative evaluation of mobile forensic tools. I.J. Inform. Technol. Comput. Sci. **1**, 74–83 (2016)
7. NIST (National Institute of Standards and Technology). Mobile device tool specification (2016), https://www.cftt.nist.gov/documents/Mobile%20Device%20Tool%20Secification_v2.0.pdf
8. S. Bommisetty, R. Tamma, H. Mahalik, Practical mobile forensics (2014), http://proquestcombo.safaribooksonline.com.ezproxy.umuc.edu/book/hardware-and-gadgets/9781783288311
9. NIST, Cell phone forensic tools: an overview and analysis update (2007), https://www.hsdl.org/?view&did=7414
10. M. Yates, Practical investigations of digital forensics tools for mobile devices, in *2010 Information Security Curriculum Development Conference on—InfoSecCD '10* (2010), https://doi.org/10.1145/1940941.1940972
11. O. Afonin, Mobile forensic tools and case studies, in *Mobile Forensics—Advanced Investigative Strategies* (2016), http://proquestcombo.safaribooksonline.com.ezproxy.umuc.edu/book/networking/forensic-analysis/9781786464484
12. K.A. Zaabi, Android forensics: investigating social networking cybercrimes against man-in-the-middle attacks, in *2016 Cybersecurity and Cyberforensics Conference (CCC)* (2016), https://doi.org/10.1109/ccc.2016.15

Deep Packet Inspection: A Key Issue for Network Security

Hannah Bartus

Abstract

As the number of cyber-attacks continue to increase, the need for data protection increases as well. Deep Packet Inspection is a highly effective way to reveal suspicious content in the headers or the payloads in any packet processing layer, except when the payload is encrypted. DPI is an essential inspector of packet payloads as it is applied to many different layers of the OSI model. The DPI tasks include intrusion detection, exfiltration detection and parental filtering. This can be a great advantage as layer-independent attacks are becoming more prevalent. It allows for inspection of all layers for attacks. However, there are challenges that come with Deep Packet Inspection. Some include the decrease of throughput of the system, attacks through the Secured Socket Layer and intrusion fingerprint matching. These challenges do not constitute as grounds to eliminate DPI as a method, but instead obstacles to be aware of in case difficulties with implementation prevails.

Keywords

Deep Packet Inspection · Network intrusion detection system · Secure socket layer · Network security · Network traffic · Pattern matching

14.1 Introduction

In approaching the investigation of network attacks, the use of Deep Packet Inspection (DPI) must be analyzed. This technique is used to closely examine packets and its fields that flow within the network. This will allow for anomaly detection within the network flow. The anomalies can be used to determine important information for dealing with and responding to security incidents. This could be in the form of IP addresses involved, the type of attack, the time of the incident as well as the incident duration. With all of the data from this inspection as well as what is gathered during the incident, security professionals are then able to mitigate risks and consequently, incidents [1].

At this point in time, the use of DPI is limited to end-host. This is because the edge and core routers do not have the processing power needed to inspect the entire content of a packet at wire speed. The edge router typically only examines the head of that packet, whereas the core routers examine the packet's destination address for forwarding. The problem arises when these routers perform at such high line speeds that this leaves very few nanoseconds to analyze the entire packet content. As the line rates increase between an edge router and a core router, the task becomes more difficult as the time to process each byte of the packet decreases [2]. Usually, an intrusion detection system for Deep Packet Inspection consists of two different parts. The first is a header rule that includes a 5-tuple packet classification being performed on the packet's header. The second focuses on content at given points within the packet's payload. However, only 60–80% of instructions are executed in the fraction of time of 40–70% with network intrusion detection [3]. Any type of design for improving network security must have efficiency in mind. A high throughput is very prevalent and cannot be the solution of throwing more processing power at string matching due to other restrictions in the network. This would cause an increase in cost as the need for cooling would increase with maintenance expenses.

Deep Packet Inspection must be implemented in such a way in order to avoid the main problems that come with it. DPI is quite complex and is extremely difficult to customize. Without a team directly working on implementation of a custom network intrusion detection system, users ought to depend on commercial products to perform the actions

H. Bartus (✉)
Robert Morris University, Moon, PA, USA
e-mail: hcbst109@mail.rmu.edu

© Springer International Publishing AG, part of Springer Nature 2018
S. Latifi (ed.), *Information Technology – New Generations*, Advances in Intelligent Systems and Computing 738,
https://doi.org/10.1007/978-3-319-77028-4_14

needed within DPI. However, one of the biggest concerns is DPI of the Secure Socket Lay (SSL). Due to the encryption of the HTTPS packet, SSL creates a blind spot for the firewall. This occurs because the firewall inspects the data broken into packets and a traditional firewall cannot inspect encrypted traffic on its own—and anything behind that encryption will enter the network untouched [4]. As the need for encrypted services like HTTPS increases, unfortunately the security risks also increase due to the level of insecurity behind the secure socket layer.

14.2 Literature Review

The goal of this research is to explore solutions to the obstacles with Deep Packet Inspection. DPI has been implemented in many workplace settings to aid in the security of the network. However, there is not one solution that results in 100% accuracy regarding network monitoring through DPI.

14.2.1 Pattern Matching Algorithms

The standard function of a Network Intrusion Detection System (nIDS) is based on a set of signatures, each describing one known intrusion threat. The nIDS examines the network's traffic for any matches to known intrusion attempts. NIDS's rule set is a two-dimensional data-structure chain that tests chain headers against packet header rules. When the packet header rule is matched, a pattern matching algorithm begins. However, this is the most financially detrimental operation of the nIDS [3]. No single algorithm performs best in all conditions, however a possible hybrid of multiple algorithms may be the best solution for such an obstacle.

14.2.1.1 The Boyer-Moore Algorithm
The Boyer-Moore Algorithm is the most well-known pattern matching algorithm for examining an input against a single pattern. This algorithm starts at the rightmost character of the search pattern and analyzes leftward. When a mismatch occurs, both heuristics are triggered. The bad character heuristic is the first one triggered. This heuristic operates by shifting the search pattern to the rightmost position of where it appears if the mismatching character appears in the search pattern. However, if the mismatching character does not appear in the search pattern, then it is shifted to one position past that character. The good suffixes heuristic, when triggered due to a mismatch in the middle of the search pattern, shifts the search pattern to the next occurrence of the suffix in the pattern [3]. The Boyer-Moore algorithm has been adjusted many times, whether it was reduced to its bad character heuristic solely, or a modified version of

the algorithm then integrated and tested with an enterprise internet connection.

14.2.1.2 The Wu-Manber Algorithm
The Wu-Manber algorithm is used in some variant in the nIDS known as Snort. This algorithm is based on the bad character heuristic of Boyer-Moore but uses up to two-byte bad shift tables. These were created to process the entirety of the patterns instead of just one at a time. This creates a table similar to that of a rainbow list that can then be used to detect intrusion threats. The Wu-Manber algorithm "performs a hash on the two-character prefix of the current input to index into a group of patterns, which are then checked starting from the last character, as in Boyer-Moore" [3]. Although this algorithm performs well on large sets, it struggles with short patterns in rules.

14.2.2 Hardware

The A10 network middlebox is not only praised for the throughput that it can handle, but also the additional tools and operations that can be utilized. A10 allows for visibility and security in the form of hardware, software or in the cloud. This network analyzer has both the ability to scan for intrusions and DoS attacks, as well as scan through the SSL. This hardware can decrypt packets to further analyze their contents and therefore better secure the network they are passing through [5]. Many federal contractors use this hardware because of its protection against their highest threat of intrusion through the SSL.

The FortiGate is a similar solution to the A10 network middlebox. However, FortiGate's hardware is known as a Next Generation Firewall (NGFW). This hardware also has the ability to decrypt the SSL for further security. The NGFW can be combined with pattern-matching algorithms to perform at its best and create a secure and intrusion-free environment [6]. Both of these hardware solutions are ones that can be implemented in any size organization or network due to their flexibility.

14.2.3 Software

Although hardware is a great permanent DPI solution, software can also help an organization test out what they may need in a DPI tool. For example, SolarWinds is a network managing tool that can analyze network performance as well as track network traffic. SolarWinds offers performance monitors that would assist in finding anomalies within the network [7].

A second software option is Snort, an open source nIDS. This free software can help sort out where possible vulnerabilities are. This software can also perform real-time traffic analysis and packet logging on IP networks as well as protocol analysis to detect anomalies within the network and catch intrusions [8]. Although each of these software systems are not permanent solutions, they can assist in quick scans of the network to then perform a more intense evaluation of vulnerabilities.

14.3   Proposed Solution

To begin, the highest vulnerabilities must be assessed. Across the board, one of the greatest vulnerabilities is the SSL. Although this allows for information to be encrypted and protected, it also causes a blind spot in network detection. HTTPS and other encryption protocols have grown rapidly over the past years and therefore protected the private data in those encrypted packets from eavesdroppers. However, this category also includes middleboxes, like the A10 network, which are also, by definition, eavesdropping on the network traffic. Therefore, malicious encrypted packets are not inspected and are able to accomplish their malicious tasks. However, many middleboxes "mount a man-in-the middle attack on SSL and decrypt the traffic at the middlebox" which is an incredibly insecure way of attempting to support HTTPS [9]. However, HTTPS must be supported through some available method. Below is a diagram of how middleboxes interact with the SSL and their rules detailed in the rule generator.

Different DPI tools perform different tasks. This being established, one must know and understand the company's needs prior to being able to choose the tool that best suits them. A company must have an organization-wide security assessment to accurately install what is needed. For example, if throughput is not a major concern due to the fact that it is a different network than what customer-facing employees use, then throughput does not need to be analyzed as heavily. The organization must make sure they are not using too many resources with DPI and SSL inspection. Therefore, it is important to know the traffic primarily.

14.3.1 Know the Traffic

In understanding the traffic, it is worth noting how much traffic is expected and how much of that traffic is encrypted. From here, the allowance of encrypted traffic can be edited and customized [4]. The first step in DPI implementation is testing out open source software to see if the data produced on the user interface is what is imperative for the organization. The Fortigate user interface details the IP address of the source as well as the destinations in which they are headed.

Besides the source, this interface also shows the amount of data sent and received. This is the most significant step in remaining aware of the traffic in the network.

14.3.2 Be Selective

Secure Socket Layer inspection should only be placed where it is needed. This will not only assist the throughput in the system, but also the policy limitations that are caused by such an inspection [4]. This selectivity could also be related to the amount of customization added to any type of hardware used.

14.3.3 Use Hardware Acceleration

For most SSL security with DPI, a hardware accelerator is the best step in inspection. However, with this accelerator, it is important for customization that matches the business needs of the company. This is where custom or known algorithms can be added for the greatest amount of security [4]. Depending on the company, the algorithm needs as well as the hardware needs may vary. Once these needs are determined, implementation can occur.

14.3.4 Test Real-World SSL Inspection Performance

Using the hardware accelerator, the best way to enforce this policy would be to gradually deploy SSL inspection to test SSL inspection performance. The SSL Inspection performance test would need to be managed like any other security protocol. This inspection may cause a decrease of the allowed throughput during the actual process, but it would become alike to any other scan made on a default schedule.

Security Information exchange programs can help explore algorithms just as many do with patches when attacks happen on the firewall. However, creating continued algorithms customized to the organization can be the greatest factor for SSL inspection [10].

14.4   Conclusion

When all of the above steps are performed, DPI can be properly initiated and SSL will no longer be as serious of a security issue now that the proper controls are in place. Although many DPI tools were tested throughout our research, we were not able to test every DPI tool. We also met with a representative from SolarWinds, but decided it was not the right solution due to the lack of possible uses with DPI and

SSL inspection. With the increase of ecommerce throughout the workplace, SSL inspections are more necessary than they have ever been. Luckily with the progressive technology of DPI, encrypted data is able to be decrypted, pattern matched and then re-encrypted and sent wherever needed.

References

1. G.A.P. Rodrigues, R. de Oliveira Albuquerque, F.E.G. de Deus, R.T. de Sousa Jr., G.A. de Oliveira Júnior, L.J.G. Villalba, T.-H. Kim, Cybersecurity and network forensics: Analysis of malicious traffic towards a Honeynet with Deep Packet Inspection. Appl. Sci. **7**(10), 1082 (2017)
2. A. Kennedy, X. Wang Z. Liu, B. Liu, Ultra-high throughput string matching for Deep Packet Inspection, in *2010 Design, Automation & Test in Europe Conference & Exhibition (2010)*, Dresden, 2010, pp. 399–404
3. S. Antonatos, K.G. Anagnostakis, E.P. Markatos, Generating realistic workloads for network intrusion detection systems. SIGSOFT Softw. Eng. Notes **29**(1), 207–215 (2004)
4. V. Martin, Why you should use SSL inspection—Fortinet Cookbook. [Online] Fortinet Cookbook (2017). http://cookbook.fortinet.com/why-you-should-use-ssl-inspection
5. A10 Networks, Thunder SSLi|A10 Networks (2017) [Online]. https://www. a10networks.com/products/thunder-series/ssl-decryption-encryption-and-inspection-ssl-insight
6. Fortinet, Next-Generation Firewalls (2017). [Online]. https://www.fortinet.com/products/next-generation-firewall.html
7. Solarwinds, IT Management Software & Monitoring Tools|SolarWinds (2017). [Online]. https://www.solarwinds.com/?&CMP=KNC-TAD-GGL-SW_NA_US_PP_CPC_LD_EN_PBR DE_DWA-X-X_X_X_X_X-775928844_40237439985_g_c_Solar winds-e~185579782075~&kwid=iDVonkDn&gclid=CjwKCAiA xarQBRAmEiwA6YcGKOxRegq5tt6yVv_1LfkFMzd51MDaZX-JCVc0l2077adKbim-1GosPhoCL58QAvD_BwE
8. Snort.org, What is Snort? (2017) [Online]. https://www.snort.org/faq/what-is-snort
9. J. Sherry, C. Lan, R.A. Popa, S. Ratnasamy, Blindbox: Deep packet inspection over encrypted traffic. Comput. Commun. Rev. **45**(5), 213 (2015). https://doi.org/10.1145/2829988.2787502
10. M. Pyatkovskiy, Fast SSL testing using precalculated cryptographyc data (2017). Patents, [Online] p. 9. https://www.google.com/patents/US8649275

What Petya/NotPetya Ransomware Is and What Its Remidiations Are

15

Sharifah Yaqoub A. Fayi

Abstract

Ransomware attacks have been growing worldwide since they appeared around 2012. The idea of ransomware attacks is, encrypting and locking the files on a computer until the ransom is paid. These attacks usually enter the system by using Trojans, which has malicious programs that run a payload that encrypts and locks the files. The basic goal of this type of attack is getting money, so hackers usually unlock the files when they receive the money, but really there is no guarantee of that. Ransomware attacks have various versions such as Reveton, CryptoWall, WannaCry, and Petya. The Petya attack is the attack that this paper discusses, especially the most recent version of it, which is referred as NotPetya. This paper defines the NotPetya attack, explains how it works, and where and how it spreads. Also, this paper discusses four solutions available to recover after a system infected by the NotPetya attack and propose the best solution depending on intense research about the recovering solutions of this attack.

Keywords

NotPetya recovering · NotPetya ransomware · NotPetya ransomware removing · NotPetya ransomware solutions · NotPetya ransomware prevention

15.1 Introduction

This paper especially discusses the most recent ransomware attack, which appeared on June 27, 2017, called NotPetya ransomware and recently has been the second global infor-mation security issue in the world [1, 2]. This ransomware is a modified version of Petya that is referred as NotPetya to distinguish this attack from the old version of Petya attacks. NotPetya differs from old versions by taking a high level of encryption that doesn't encrypt just the files but it also encrypts the whole system. It encrypts the Master File Table (MFT) after rebooting the infected system, therefore the Master Boot Record (MBR) becomes impracticable [3, 4]. As a result, by locking the MBR, the infected system eventually becomes useless, so you can't reach your files or even the operating system on the drive because the MBR, which is a sector of a hard drive, is essential to identify the location of the operating system and files. NotPetya spreads by taking advantages of the EternalBlue, which is a vulnerability in the Windows operating system, and this vulnerability also exploits by the WannaCry attack. In addi-tion, the EternalBlue is not the only vulnerability NotPetya uses, it tries to exploit other Windows vulnerabilities, such as PsExec, Windows Management Instrumentation (WMI), and EternalRomance to propagate through the infected network [1]. NotPetya attack can for example, use the WMI tool to propagate by getting the administrator access information in one unpatched computer in the network and propagate itself to other computers in the same network. Robert Lipovsky who is an ESET researcher said, "It only takes one unpatched computer to get inside the network, and the malware can get administrator rights and spread to other computers." [6]. Also, this ransomware can extend and affect other computers through the network by getting the users' logins information [5]. Another way the attack uses to spread is by phishing emails that contain malware-laden attachments [2, 7]. After that, if the computer is affected by NotPetya, a message telling your computer files are encrypted will appear, and it demands you $300 Bitcoins to decrypt the files as Fig. 15.1 shown [6].

Ukraine is the country where the attack started and af-fected many government offices, banks and the airport [2]. According to the Ukrainian Cyber Police, the attack is

S. Y. A. Fayi (✉)
Department of Computer and Information Systems, Robert Morris University, Moon Township, PA, USA

© Springer International Publishing AG, part of Springer Nature 2018
S. Latifi (ed.), *Information Technology – New Generations*, Advances in Intelligent Systems and Computing 738,
https://doi.org/10.1007/978-3-319-77028-4_15

Fig. 15.1 Note displays on computers infected with NotPetya

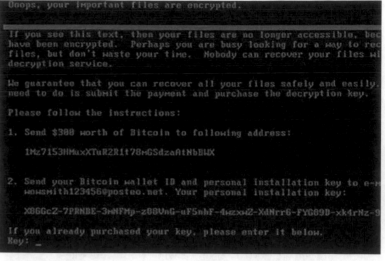

Fig. 15.2 Top 20 countries depend on number of infected organizations

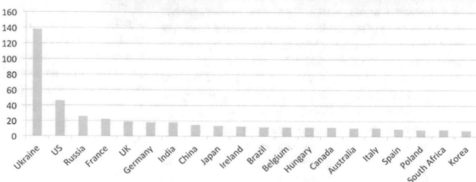

distributed through the accounting software, which is called MeDo, which Ukrainian companies need to work with the government [2].

This attack doesn't affect just Ukraine, it is also detected in other 64 countries in the world including Europe and the USA [6]. Based on the following Fig. 15.2, the USA is the second highest country affected by the NotPetya after Ukraine [8].

It is obvious from the number of countries and organizations which NotPetya infected that this ransomware attack spreads rapidly and affects great spots of the world. In addition, this spreading of the NotPetya leads to significant disruptions because it targets the important organizations in a country like advertising firm WPP, shipping giant Maersk, and Heritage Valley Health System [2, 5]. Such organizations require their systems to be operational all the time to do their job completely and perfectly. As a result, and as we know that prevention is better than remediation, you must prevent your network from being infected this by, for example, requesting help from IT specialists if you have a big organization or learning about security threats if you have a small business and don't want to spend much money for an IT expert. To prevent your network, US CERT recommends you, for instance, to update your computer system to last Microsoft's

patch for MS17-010 SMB vulnerability, to make regular backups for your data and test them, to set anti-virus & anti-malware regularly scanning, to manage the use of privileged account, to secure the use of WMI by setting permissions [1]. However, if your prevention system is not that strong and the NotPetya ransomware is running in your computer or your network, there are some solutions to recover from it and this paper reviews four solutions.

15.2 Literature Review

The aim of this paper is to discuss four existed solutions to remediate infected devices after NotPetya Ransomware in a clear and easy way that doesn't require a depth experience in computer fields or a technician who cost much money.

The first solution is a solution that CrowdStrike Blog explains. This blog explains tools for decrypting the MFT, which has the system files and their information and helps recovering files after the attack. These tools exploit the shortcomings of the implementation of the Salsa20 cipher in NotPetya to restore the files from MFT by at first extracting the MFT from a corrupted hard disk, then using the De-cyptpetya.py tool that you can find in the CrowdStrike code warehouse [9]. This solution in my opinion is a good solution because CrowdStrike Blog has proved that their tools can extract and decrypt the most decryption MFT records. However, this solution requires depth technical information in the computer and technology fields, so I think it is difficult for the people who don't have enough technical information or small businesses that don't have enough budget to follow this solution that requires a technician who costs a lot. I suggest those businesses or any person who uses a computer for personal purposes to use an easier way that doesn't cost much money to recover their files because those people and the small business in my opinion don't have that much of sensitive data or files that deserve spending much money to a technician to restore their files. They can try the one of other following solutions that the paper discusses, which doesn't require intensive information in dealing with NotPetya ransomware threats.

The idea of the second solution which, the @HackerFantastic mentioned on Twitter, is interrupting the encryption process by utilizing the waiting time that NotPetya ransomware takes to reboot the system. The account advises you to turn off your computer instantaneously if you see the following message (Fig. 15.3) [2].

The second solution seems to be a great solution to prevent files from encryption, but I assume that the disadvantages of it are, you must be concentrated and turn off your computer as quickly as you can without any delay, which is sometimes easier said than done, and there is no practical proof that I can find. As a result, I believe that if you don't have that much information about security attacks, you can't do this quick response.

The third solution which 2-SpyWare.com provides, is recommending you use some anti-spyware like, Reimage and Malwarebytes Anti Malware for removing the attack [10]. They explain two manual removal methods which eliminate NotPetya by using Safe Mode with Networking or by using System Restore. In the first method, you must enter the Safe Mode after you restart the system to escape NotPetya and access a security tool, so you can download any anti-spyware software that helps you to eliminate the NotPetya, but if the ransomware denies the Safe Mode with Networking, try the second method [10]. The second method is removing NotPetya by using System Restore which also required to reboot the computer to the Safe Mode, but with Command Prompt. When the Command Prompt appears, you can use some commands that 2-SpyWare.com demonstrates visibly to restore your system to prior date. After that, you should

Fig. 15.3 Message shows encryption process

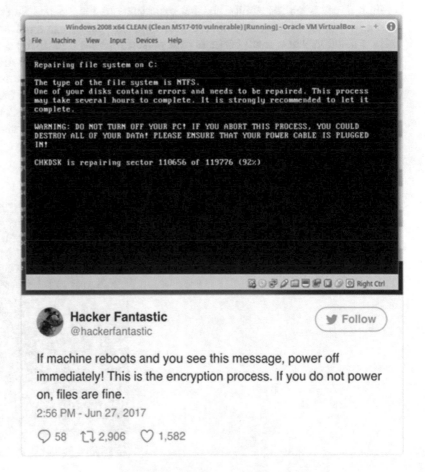

scan your computer and make sure that NotPetya is successfully removed [10]. After that, you can try to restore data by using Data Recovery Pro Method software, which can help to restore damaged files or ShadowExplorer, which can help to decrypt infected files [10]. Even if you cannot decrypt the files by an official NotPetya decryption program because 2-SpyWare.com indicates that "NotPetya decryption is not available yet.", I think the third solution if you have plenty technical information is the perfect way to recover your computer by just following the clearly guide in the website.

The final solution is acceptable for those who want the easiest and clearest way to eliminate NotPetya and their files worthless to try hardly and costly to redeem them. The solution is formatting the infected hard drive and reinstalling the operating system and after that, with a fluke you can restore the files from backups if you back up your files routinely [2, 6]. Consequently, keep your anti-virus up to date and set automatically backup for your files even if on another device or on the cloud [2, 6].

15.3   Proposed Solution

I reviewed four solutions in this paper that deal with NotPetya ransomware, and I believe that the best and easiest solution depends on the ability and the experience of the person in dealing with security attacks. However, I propose to try a solution that a small business or a person who has enough information in technology can follow. This solution obviously is not paying the ransom to obtain the key that decrypts the files because there is no guarantee of that but the solution is the third one in this paper that I think is the perfect solution you can follow to recover after the ransomware attack. The idea of this solution is restarting your computer

and entering the Safe Mode, then removing NotPetya by downloading an anti-spyware and after that restore your infected files by using some software that help you in this recovering.

At first, to access your files, you have to eliminate NotPetya from your system by following the manual removing guidelines that 2-SpyWare.com clearly explains. The first step in this guide is requiring you to enter the Safe Mode to discard the NotPetya ransomware and then you can access a security tool. There are two methods to enter the Safe Mode which are, entering by using Safe Mode with Networking or using Safe Mode with Command Prompt, but in this paper, I will review just how to enter the Safe Mode with Networking in Windows 7, and assume that the ransomware doesn't block entering Safe Mode with Networking.

The first step to enter the Safe Mode with Networking in Windows 7 is restarting your computer and when your computer turns on, press F8 button many times until the Advanced Boot Options window appears and then choose the Safe Mode with Networking from the menu [10] (Fig. 15.4).

The second step is opening the browser in your infected account and downloading one of the anti-spyware software that 2-SpyWare.com recommends like Reimage, or Malwarebytes Anti-malware. Before you start scanning and removing the ransomware, ensure that the anti-spyware that you downloaded is up to date. In this paper, I choose Malwarebytes to delete NotPetya because it is a free removal program, and it can remove malicious files and programs easily by its tools [11]. You can download the Malwarebytes on your Windows from My Anti Spyware website and follow provided instructions to complete set it up. After downloading it, double-click the setup file called "mb3-setup" and click 'Yes' if the User Account Control Window appears [11].

After that, follow the Setup Wizard to install Malwarebytes on your computer and don't change the default settings

Fig. 15.4 Advanced boot options window

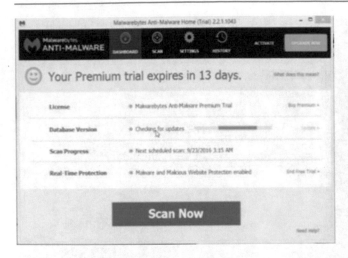

Fig. 15.5 Malwarebytes main screen

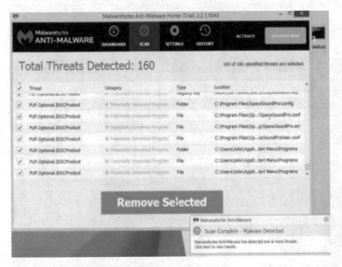

Fig. 15.6 Threats detected report window

[11]. When the installation is completed successfully, the main screen of the software will appear automatically as shown in Fig. 15.5 [11].

After checking the update version, press the Scan Now button and therefore the scanning process will begin to detect the NotPetya ransomware and any other malicious programs [11]. After that, assess the report, which usually you wait much time until it appears, and click the Remove Selected button [11] (Fig. 15.6).

As a result, the Malwarebytes software begins to remove NotPetya and any security threats found [11]. After the cleansing process finishes, a prompt window that requires you to restart your computer will appear and after restarting your computer, it should be free of malicious software or files [11].

The second step is recovering the corrupted files by trying one of the procedures that 2-SpyWare.com suggests.

The first method is downloading Data Recovery Pro software, which helps you to recover corrupted and encrypted files, and then follow the instructions that Viruses Removal Pro website provides in its guide to remove NotPetya ransomware [11, 12]. After downloading the software and opening it, choose Quick Scan or Full Scan as shown in Fig. 15.7 and then click Start Scan to find the files that NotPetya corrupts [12].

After that, check the type of all files you need to restore and then press the Recover button as Fig. 15.8 shown [12].

The second recovering method is decrypting files with ShadowExplorer software that has a high chance to restore infected files successfully because as 2-SpyWare.com states that "At the moment, the malware does not manifest the ability to delete volume shadow copies, so you are likely to succeed in restoring affected files with the assistance of this tool" [10]. After downloading the software, you can follow the guideline that the Security Affairs website explains [13]. After you choose the drive and identify the files that you need to recover from the list in the main window of ShadowExplorer, then you can export the files by pressing right-click on the folder as Fig. 15.9 shown below [13].

In the case that the Security Affairs website used, they can successfully recover 100% of the files that you can see in Fig. 15.10 [13].

As a result, by following the solution that I suggested, you can recover your system after the NotPetya Ransomware infection. In addition, based on what I represented previously that demonstrates the success of the recovering process, you obviously have a great chance in removing the ransomware and restoring your files [14].

15.4 Conclusion

To sum up, this paper explains what NotPetya is, how it works, and when and where it appears. Also, it mentioned some ways to prevent NotPetya and reviewed four existed solutions that can help to remove NotPetya and restore files. The four solutions are, using tools for decrypting the MFT, which you can use to recover files by taking advantage of the limitation of the Salsa20 cipher in NotPetya and you can find the full explanation of this solution in CrowdStrike Blog, the interception of the encryption process by exploiting the waiting time that NotPetya need to reboot the system, entering the Safe Mode, removing the NotPetya and then restoring the files by using the way that 2-SpyWare.com provides, and reinstalling the operating system and then restoring the files from a backup if you usually back up your files. When I reviewed these four solutions I tried to focus on showing their disadvantages to help you choose the appropriate solution for you.

Fig. 15.7 Data recovery Pro
scanning options

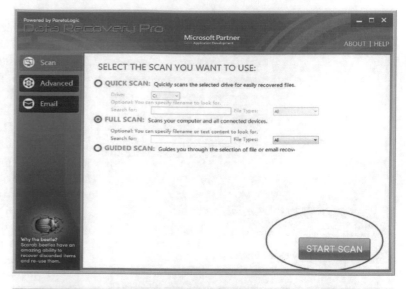

Fig. 15.8 Items available to
recover

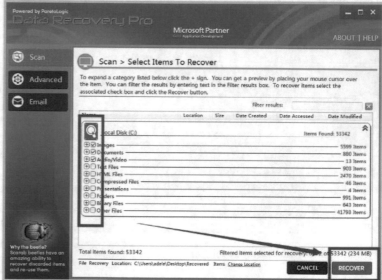

Fig. 15.9 Files available to
export

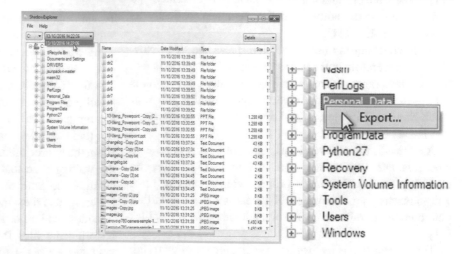

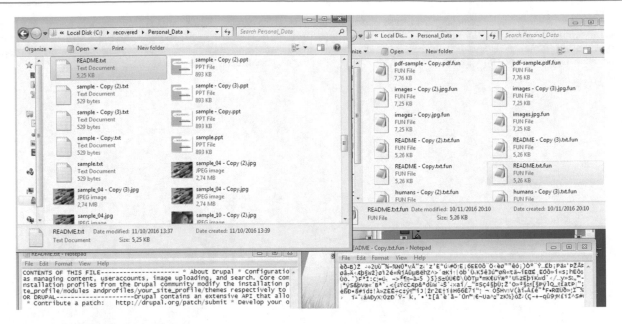

Fig. 15.10 Files after recovering successfully

After reviewing all four solutions, I state that the second solution, which is entering the Safe Mode, removing the NotPetya and then restoring the files by using the way that 2-SpyWare.com provides is a perfect solution because it covers how to remove the NotPetya ransomware and how to restore the files. I support this solution by adding more details to how removing NotPetya by using Malwarebytes software, and how to restore your files by using Data Recovery Pro software or ShadowExplorer software.

At the end, don't forget that deciding which the best or easiest solution depends on you, on your ability and on your experience in dealing with security threats, and on the solution that makes the least possible losses. Moreover, don't forget that prevention is better than remediation, so always back up your files on another device or in the cloud and test these backups, make sure that patches and anti-viruses or anti-spyware on your computer are up to date. Finally, always be aware of everything on security threats to secure your system or your organization's system.

References

1. Alert (TA17-181A) Petya Ransomware, *US-CERT* (2017). [Online]. https://www.us-cert.gov/ncas/alerts/TA17-181A. Accessed 7 Nov 2017

2. O. Solon, A. Hern, Petya' ransomware attack: what is it and how can it be stopped?, *The Guardian* (2017) [Online]. https://www.theguardian.com/technology/2017/jun/27/petya-ransomware-cyber-attack-who-what-why-how. Accessed 7 Nov 2017

3. Q. Yeh, A.J. Chang, Threats and countermeasures for information system security: a cross-industry study. Inf. Manag. **44**, 480–491 (2007)

4. P. Bedwell, A deep dive into the NotPetya ransomware attack, *Lastline* (2017) [Online]. https://www.lastline.com/blog/notpetya-ransomware-attack/. Accessed 7 Nov 2017

5. L. Abrams, Petya Ransomware skips the Files and Encrypts your Hard Drive Instead, *BleepingComputer* (2016). [Online]. https://www.bleepingcomputer.com/news/security/petya-ransomware-skips-the-files-and-encrypts-your-hard-drive-instead/. Accessed 7 Nov 2017

6. A. Kharpal, 'Petya' ransomware: All you need to know about the cyberattack and how to tell if you're at risk, *CNBC* (2017). [Online]. https://www.cnbc.com/2017/06/28/petya-ransomware-cyberattack-explained-how-to-tell-if-youre-at-risk-or-been-attacked.html. Accessed 7 Nov 2017

7. T. Fox-Brewster, 3 Things You Can Do To Stop 'NotPetya' Ransomware Wrecking Your PC, *Forbes* (2017). [Online]. https://www.forbes.com/sites/thomasbrewster/2017/06/28/three-things-you-can-do-to-stop-notpetya-ransomware-wrecking-your-pc/#6f276e377b05. Accessed 7 Nov 2017

8. I. Thomson in San Francisco 2017 at 03:19 tweet_btn(), Everything you need to know about the Petya, er, NotPetya nasty trashing PCs worldwide, The Register®—Biting the hand that feeds IT (2017). [Online]. https://www.theregister.co.uk/2017/06/28/petya_notpetya_ransomware/. Accessed 8 Nov 2017.

9. Symantec Security Response, Petya ransomware outbreak: Here's what you need to know, *Symantec* (2017). [Online]. https://www.symantec.com/connect/blogs/petya-ransomware-outbreak-here-s-what-you-need-know. Accessed 8 Nov 2017

10. S. Eschweiler, Decrypting NotPetya/Petya: Tools for recovering your MFT after an attack, *CrowdStrike* (2017). [Online]. https://www.crowdstrike.com/blog/decrypting-notpetya-tools-for-recovering-your-mft-after-an-attack/. Accessed 7 Nov 2017

11. J. Splinters, NotPetya ransomware virus. How to remove? (Uninstall guide), *2-spyware* (2017). [Online]. https://www.2-spyware.com/remove-notpetya-ransomware-virus.html#data-recovery! Accessed 7 Nov 2017

12. Patrik, Petya.A/NotPetya virus removal——How to protect computer, *My AntiSpyware* (2017). [Online]. http://www.myantispyware.com/2017/06/28/petya-notpetya-virus/. Accessed 7 Nov 2017

13. CASPAR, Guide to remove NotPetya ransomware permanently, *Viruses Removal Pro* (2017). [Online]. http://provirusesremoval.com/guide-remove-notpetya-ransomware-permanently/. Accessed 7 Nov 2017]

14. P. Paganini, Ransomware: How to recover your encrypted files, the last guide, *Security Affairs* (2016). [Online]. http://securityaffairs.co/wordpress/53438/malware/ransomware-recover-guide.html. Accessed 7 Nov 2017

Analysis of Security Vulnerability and Analytics of Internet of Things (IOT) Platform

16

Anteneh Girma

Abstract

The Internet of Things (IOT) has become an attractive and inviting technology that enables gathering information about all interconnected devices on real-time. These interconnected physical devices have a unique identifiers and the ability to communicate each other using its sensor technology and transfer data over a network. The collected information also provide significant opportunity for different businesses to have insight about these data by applying effective data analytics on them. Internet of Things have also revealed a huge security vulnerability that range from its authentication to its trust management, and a threat to its embedded devices. This research paper explores and discusses the challenges of Internet of things (IOT) that includes: its vulnerability, security and Privacy of IOT, current analytics of IOT, Imminent ownership threat, trust management, IOT Models, its road map, and make recommendation on how to resolve its security challenges.

Keywords

IOT · IOT security · IOT models · IOT category · IOT privacy

16.1 Introduction

Since its inception during 1991, the idea of interconnecting objects and sharing information has been advanced a great deal. Electronics devices with embedded smart technologies has become more appealing and being attractive for both business community and both home and business owners. Many different types of IOT platforms could be observed both in private and business sectors. IOT devices in smart home environment includes house appliances like dryer, washer, dish washer, TV, heating, and cooling, refrigerator. The business sectors include health care, transportation, digital city, vehicles, and agriculture.

Internet of things (IOT) is an interconnected environment of physical devices to exchange information among them and collect information from them and apply IOT analytics to take the right action. Internet of things also includes different communication such as Things to Things, Human to Things, and Human to Human interactions [1]. Information technology experts have already starting talking about nearly fifty billion smart devices would be available in 2020 and most of our household objects would be interconnected. An individual could also start managing at least ten devices. Some of these interconnected IoT devices are mobile devices and could lose connectivity due to vulnerability of wireless outages. Some of them could also run out of the battery life time to operate. The use of these heterogeneous interconnected devices in IoT platform could bring both security and interoperability issues [2].

The internet of things deployed on intranet environment for different purposes, and the information collected from these devices are monitored from the remote. The advancement in high speed connectivity has also brought certain progress in the deployment and performance of current IOT devices. The key indicators of the IOT system that is the way its different parts, including the devices and the services where the information are get analyzed, combine to generate new value or better performance.

A. Girma (✉)
Robert Morris University, Moon, PA, USA
e-mail: Girma@rmu.edu

© Springer International Publishing AG, part of Springer Nature 2018
S. Latifi (ed.), *Information Technology – New Generations*, Advances in Intelligent Systems and Computing 738,
https://doi.org/10.1007/978-3-319-77028-4_16

16.2 Background Information

16.2.1 Security and Privacy of IOT

Internet of things could provide an interconnected easily managed computing environment by enabling the individual users to control their digital household items, and also the businesses to enhance the capacity, security, and other related functionalities of these interconnected items by gathering information and applying different IOT analytics operation. The security vulnerabilities of these devices has been the major and critical issue for the researchers around the globe. Because IOT is dealing with number of interconnected devices, any security vulnerability associated with each individual physical device could pose a security threat to the whole interconnected devices. Moreover, as we are also managing and controlling these devices from remote location, the other major security concern is the internet itself, which is always vulnerable and could cause another security threat. Internet is the most widely used data communication route and any access to the information which are carried out via Internet using many types of smart devices, could cause users' identity easily hacked. Other security related issues also include authentication, privacy, trust relationship among the interconnected devices, access control. Researchers reviewed thoroughly the existing authentication techniques used with IOT devices by discussing the existing limitation of those currently available authentication tools. By using their in-depth survey, they further detailed how cryptography could contribute in securing the IOT devices, and provided a well refined summary on the weakness and strength of the existing IOT security tool performances [3].

A cloud based identity framework for resolving some of the security issues associated with IOT has also been proposed [4]. This proposed frame work identified the major components like the physical environment that host the sensors and transmitters that interact with each other and the cloud services. This proposed framework also has two components: *service manager* that handles the authorization module that provides access to the sensors and receivers, and *identity manager* that handle the authentication module. Another researchers [5] also applied the two mostly popularly used keys [6, 7] with the wireless networks, by integrating them in IOT computing environment to mitigate and prevent the malicious attacks.

Other security threats related to privacy due to the involvements of those many number of interconnected devices have been identified [8]. Some middleware layers were recommended to enforce the security of the interconnected devices and the integrity of the data communicated among these devices.

16.2.2 Modelling of Internet of Things

The internet of things has been a huge interest of the business world provided that more billions of devices are expected to be interconnected through the internet in the next few years; and it brings people, data, and process to be more interconnected. The IoT is getting everywhere and its impact on the internetworking business is growing tremendously. Businesses are planning and investing much to have an adaptable and scalable infrastructure that could handle all what it takes to deploy what the IOT computing environment needs. The major capability requirements of modelling the internet of things include model construction, representation across scales, broad accommodation for multiple formalisms, integration and aggregation across models, model evolution, flexibility and modularity, scalability [9].

16.3 IOT Challenges

The number of interconnected devices at every household and every organization are getting too big, the amount of data communicating through the internet is also exploding, the number of smart devices used by every human is getting high in number, and the need for scalable and adaptable computer networking architecture is not only a much more needed but a must considered investment plan. Most importantly, the number of people who will join the computing world could make the internet traffic and the network connectivity more exploded. The interconnected devices with IOT computing environment are very different, the data generated by these different devices are also computed differently, and most importantly the location of this devices could be different. The security of this very complex interconnected network infrastructure is always a concern. The security of the communication and connectivity among these devices is the major threat and a paramount concern. Any attack aimed at one of the interconnected devices could be a security threat for all other devices. Networking systems must be built to reliably route information at rest and in motion. Security should be a major factor while designing the IOT environment. Most of currently available off the shelf IOT devices lacks security requirements and are vulnerable to get easily compromised. Moreover, IOT devices deployed on public network and accessed wirelessly are also subject to malicious attacks. The major security challenges of the IOT include Authentication, Trust, Privacy, Mobile Security, Confidentiality, Secure Middle ware, policy enforcement, and access control. Among the above mentioned security requirements, the three major three key security requirements are Authentication, confidentiality, and access control [9].

The trust level among the interconnected devices should be considered to enhance the IOT security. A dynamically trust management protocol among the interconnected physical devices have been proposed that could adapt and adjust its parameter setting for any real time changing environments. [10]. This protocol deals with physically connected devices that acts differently called malicious nodes and provide the required behavioral resolution by validating the changes in behavior and adapt on real time.

16.4   IOT Analytics

The changing and advancing nature of technology is bringing many changes in our daily life and working environments. Every household is getting smart by getting its major items interconnected. Every devices in the hospital is getting interconnected and provide any patient related information as required. Automobiles are also getting their devices interconnected with different sensors and are making driving easier and somehow safe. All these Interconnected IoT devices are handling the data analysis in a dynamic environment on real time. In most cases these analytics computations are done in cloud computing environment. The elasticity, ease of use, and scalability nature of cloud make it more attractive and convenient except the security issues associated with its service models, deployment models, and its' major characteristics.

Sensors and system logs are critical in order to collect data from each interconnected devices and execute the required data analytics. Among the requirement to analyze the data, the sensor life time and cost are the most critical elements. This is because of its major contribution in detecting and responding to inputs from the other interconnected device in the IOT platform it belongs to. The characteristics of different internet of things data types including streaming, high volume, semi structured, and non-structured data types have been discussed and mentioned that the vast majority of IOT data streams are not useful in broader context [11]. Moreover, it was noted and explained how streaming data analytics play a greater role in unlocking value from the interconnected devices, and present the main difference between IOT analytics and big data analytics.

As the number of interconnected devices is increasing, the amount of data collected and exchanged within the IoT platform is also increasing at the higher rate. Processing and analysis of big data has been a huge issue for researchers as it demand big investment requiring big memory, high level performing infrastructure, and high level of security. To resolve these issues, different analytical algorithms has been proposed to handle applying streaming and batch data feed approach. The existing big data analytics frameworks present the problem associated with big data analytics as a map reduce problem. Incremental algorithm approach using autoregression has been used to improve memory reduction by increasing and allowing each participating devices to handle the request at its node [12]. Even though the autoregression works well to handle the high level memory needs, the security and the performance issue are still continuing and remains to be resolved.

The other very challenging task in IoT is the nonexistence of any form of standards that govern how the interconnected devices exchange information and operate at the cloud computing environment. The security of the cloud operation and the information exchange medium (Internet) are the most known unsecure and vulnerable cases while trying to implement the IoT Analytics. Some form of standards like Message Queue Telemetry Transport (MQTT) and Advanced Message Queuing Protocol (AMQP) was proposed which only could handle lightweight message oriented middleware [13].

Some of those interconnected smart devices have different limitations that include sensor lifetime, bandwidth, battery life, etc. Moreover, the performance and availability of wireless infrastructure to support the required information handling and IoT analytics, is not reliable and remains to be a high level research project to be considered. These issues could result in a catastrophic consequences in Health-IoT infrastructures. For example, a Hadoop-based intelligent care system (HICS) [14] that demonstrates IoT-based collaborative contextual Big Data sharing among all of the devices in a healthcare system was proposed. This proposed system have shown a very positive and promising results in leveraging the capacity and performances of sensors, coordinators, and being flexible based on intelligent building that performs the collecting the IoT data from the interconnected devices and do the analytics. But the security of the proposed system has number of vulnerability mainly with its' confidentiality and user authentication.

16.5   Conclusion

The rapid and dynamic presence of IOT has brought a new direction of computing environment. The number of interconnected devices at every household is increasing at alarming rate, and the needs for having a more secured and powerful infrastructure to handle its data collection and analytics has been very critical. Hospitals, Cities, electrical grids and power systems, automobile systems, are among those already implementing the internet of things technology by deploying as many interconnected devices as needed. In addition to their performance issue during IOT analytics, currently existing IOT frameworks infrastructures and applications are exposed to high degree of security vulnerabilities and lacks the required security assurances. The insecurity of cloud operation where part or all the information are stored, and the insecurity of internet media through which the information exchange is taking place, are the major and critical problems that required an immediate attentions. Security issues associated with the sensors, which are the main source of data about the interconnected devices that requires advance enhancement to leverage both its security vulnerability and performance issues is also another major areas of security problems.

The business communities is embracing the IoT success and are investing a lot. More and more other promising and enhanced IoT platform solutions are well ahead of us. Its' application is limitless. The performance issues are well getting covered. But the IoT-security issue remains to be a big challenge. Different cybersecurity attacks like DDoS, Data Integrity, Information theft, are among the major cyber-attacks that could be launched and result in severe damage in any IoT platform. In our research, we will present our detailed analysis with regard to IoT and its operation in cloud computing environment.

References

1. T. Heer, O. Murchony, R. Hummen, S.L. Keoh, S.S. Kumar, K. Wehlre, Security challenges in the IP-based internet of things. Wirel Pers Commun **61**(3), 527–542 (2011)
2. M. Babar, F. Arf, Smart urban planning using big data analytics based internet of tings, in *UBICOMP/ISWC, Ubicomp' 17 Proceeding of the the* 2017 *ACM International Joint Conference on Pervasive and Ubiqui Plannintous Cimputing, and Ubiquitous Computing and Preceeding of the* 2017 *ACM International on Wearable Computer, "International Conference on Future Internet of Things"*, pp. 191–196
3. Y. Atwald, M. Hammoudeh, A survey on authentication techniques for the internet of things, in *Preceedings of ICFNDS'17*, Cambridge, United Kingdom, July 2017
4. S. Homow, A. Sardana, Identity management framework for cloud based internet of things, in *Secure IT'12*, ACM, Kollam, Kerale, India, August 2012
5. S. Silari, D. Morandi, A. Rizzardi, A. Coen-Porisini, Internet of things: security in the keys, in *Q2SWINET, Preceeding of 12th ACM Symposium on QoS and Security for Wireless and Mobile Networks*, Malta, Malta, November 2016, pp. 129–133
6. R. Di Pietro, L. Mancini, S. Jajodia, Providing secrecy in key management protocols for large wireless sensor networks. Ad Hoc Netw. **1**(4), 455–468 (2003)
7. G. Dini, L. Lopriore, Key propagation in wireless sensor networks. Comput Electr Eng **41**, 426–433 (2015)
8. S. Silari, L.A. Grieco, A. Coen Porisini, Security, privacy, and trust in internet of things: the road ahead. Comput Network **76**(15), 146–164 (2015)
9. S. Breiner, E. Subrahmanian, R.D. Sriram, *Modeling The Internet of Things, Foundational Approach* (ACM, Stuttgart, 2016)
10. F. Bao, R. Chen, Dynamic trust management for internet of things applications, in *Self-IoT'12, Preceeding of the 2012 International Workshop on Self-aware Internet of Things*, San Jose, California, USA., September 2012, pp. 1–6
11. J. Haight, H. Park, "IoT analytics and practice", Blue Hill Research, Analyst Insight, Report number A0173, September 2015, pp. 1–12
12. D. Mukerjee, S. Datta, Incremental time series algorithm for iot analytics: an example from autoregression, in *ICDCN'16, Proceedings of the 17th International Conference on Distributed Computing and Networking Article, Number 13*, Singapore, Singapore, January 2016
13. P. Wlodarczak, M. Ally, J. Soar, Data Mining in IoT Data analysis for a new paradigm on the Internet, in *WI'17 Proceedings of the International Conference on Web Intelligence*, Leipzig, Germany, August 2017, pp. 1100–1103
14. Hadoop-Based Intelligent Care System (HICS). Analytical Approach for Big Data in IoT in M. Mazhar Rathore and Anand Paul, Awais Ahmad, Marco Anisett, Gwanggil Jeon, ACM Transaction on Internet Technology (TOIT)", vol. 8, issue 1, New York, New York, November 2017

New Techniques for Public Key Encryption with Sender Recovery

Murali Godi and Roopa Vishwanathan

Abstract

In this paper, we consider a scenario where a sender transmits ciphertexts to multiple receivers using a public-key encryption scheme, and at a later point of time, wants to retrieve the plaintexts, without having to request the receivers' help in decrypting the ciphertexts, and without having to locally store a separate recovery key for every receiver the sender interacts with. This problem, known as *public key encryption with sender recovery* has intuitive solutions based on hybrid encryption-based key encapsulation mechanism and data encapsulation mechanism (KEM/DEM) schemes. We propose a KEM/DEM-based solution that is CCA2-secure, allows for multiple receivers, only requires the receivers to be equipped with public/secret keypairs (the sender needs only a *single* symmetric recovery key), and uses an analysis technique called *plaintext randomization* that results in greatly simplified, clean, and intuitive proofs compared to prior work in this area. We instantiate our protocol for public key encryption with sender recovery with the Cramer-Shoup hybrid encryption scheme.

Keywords

Cryptography · Authentication · Encryption · Confidentiality · Signatures · Public-key encryption · Hybrid encryption

M. Godi
SUNY Polytechnic, Utica, NY, USA
e-mail: godim@sunyit.edu

R. Vishwanathan (✉)
New Mexico State University, Las Cruces, NM, USA
e-mail: roopav@nmsu.edu

17.1 Introduction

Consider a situation where Alice and Bob exchange e-mails through an untrusted e-mail service provider. Alice sends e-mails to Bob encrypted under his public key, and does not necessarily save a plaintext copy of every e-mail she sends Bob on her local device, or on the untrusted server. In this scenario, Alice cannot retrieve a plaintext message at a later date without the co-operation of Bob, who is presumably the only party who will have the corresponding secret key used to decrypt the message. Ideally, we would like Alice to be able to retrieve the plaintext messages without having to contact Bob (or other recipients), who either may not be available, or may not have any incentive to co-operate with Alice.

A natural solution to this problem involves Alice and Bob setting up a shared session key, and Alice using the session key to send encrypted messages to Bob, and Alice storing copies of the session keys and ciphertexts. The copies could be stored on Alice's device or can be stored in encrypted form on the server. This solution works, but Alice would need to setup a separate session key with every receiver she communicates with, store ciphertexts encrypted under several session keys, and have a separate recovery key associated with each receiver. It would be ideal if we could minimize the storage and computation required on Alice's side.

The problem of a sender being able to decrypt a ciphertext encrypted under the key of a receiver, without the co-operation of the receiver, known as *public key encryption with sender recovery*, was first introduced by Wei et al. [1–3] as a complementary notion to *forward secrecy*, in which past encrypted messages cannot be decrypted using expired keys. In this paper, we construct new solutions for this problem using hybrid encryption-based techniques. Our constructions are CCA2-secure, are based on minimal/relaxed assumptions as compared to prior work in this area, and use a proof technique called *plaintext randomization* [4], which results in simplified protocol constructions, and intuitive and cleaner proofs compared to prior work.

17.1.1 Our Contributions

- We propose a new protocol for public-key encryption with sender recovery, where the sender can independently retrieve a plaintext message that was encrypted under the receiver's public key, without receiving help from the receiver. Potential applications of our protocol include untrusted third party data storage (e.g., Dropbox), and encrypted e-mail recovery services.
- We instantiate our protocol using the classic Cramer-Shoup key/data encapsulation mechanism, KEM/DEM-based hybrid encryption scheme. We prove that our protocols are CCA2 secure if the underlying DEM scheme is CCA2 secure, i.e., we do not require the underlying KEM scheme to be secure in any sense (previous work in this area required the entire KEM/DEM scheme to be CCA2 secure).
- We consider both, the single receiver and multiple receiver models, and make minimal assumptions with respect to key requirements: in particular, we only require the sender to be equipped with a *single* recovery key that can be used across multiple receivers. We use KEM/DEM-based hybrid encryption combined with a technique called *plaintext randomization*, and helps us obtain proofs of CCA2 security that are clean, intuitive, and much simpler compared to prior work in this area.

17.2   Related Work

Wei et al. [3] first introduced the idea of public-key encryption with sender recovery using KEM/DEM-based hybrid encryption protocols. The idea of a sender being able to recover a previously encrypted ciphertext without the receiver's help is somewhat complementary to the better-known notion of forward security [5,6] where the goal is to prevent decryption of ciphertexts using old, expired keys. The scheme of [3] required both, sender and receiver to be equipped with a public/secret keypair, and among other things, [3] provided the sender the ability to authenticate the ciphertext to check if it really originated from her, and worked for multiple receivers. In further work, Wei and Zheng [1,2] presented an efficient public key encryption scheme with sender recovery, but which requires only the receiver to have a public/secret keypair. The efficiency gains though, come at the cost of sacrificing ciphertext authenticity checks, besides their scheme works only in the single receiver model.

The main differences between prior work and our paper are: (1) [1–3] rely on the underlying KEM/DEM scheme to be CCA2 secure in order to prove the security of their protocols. We considerably relax this requirement, and *do not* require the KEM scheme to be CCA2 secure. (2) Furthermore, in our work, we consider the multiple receiver model, where a sender can recover ciphertexts encrypted under the keys of multiple receivers, using just one symmetric recovery key (no requirement for the sender to have a separate recovery key for each receiver). (3) The analysis and security proofs of prior protocols for public-key encryption with sender recovery were tricky, with two CCA2 reductions, and used the game-hopping technique, which involves reductions between a series of several games. We abstract out the analysis of the KEM scheme using a technique called *plaintext randomization*, which results in clean, intuitive proofs, which are much shorter in length than the previous ones. Additionally, prior work also involved the universal one-way functions with collision accessibility assumption (deliberately inducing collisions in a family of one-way functions), which we avoid. A comparison of our work with previous works is given in Table 17.1.

More generally, KEM/DEM schemes have been used in applications such as identity-based password exchange [7], puncturable encryption [8], attribute-based encryption [9], and more. We do not review the vast KEM/DEM literature here, since we are not designing a new KEM/DEM scheme, rather we are using KEM/DEM to build a public-key encryption scheme that allows for sender recovery.

17.3   Plaintext Randomization

The notion of plaintext randomization [4] was introduced to address issues of composability in high-level protocols, where we use one secure protocol as a component of another protocol, while retaining security inside the higher-level protocol. In particular, plaintext randomization deals with situations where a public-key encryption (PKE) scheme is used as a component in a higher-level protocol, and tries to simplify the analysis of the higher-level protocol, by abstracting out the analysis of the PKE scheme. Consider the problem of k-of-n secret sharing, where a secret is divided among n proxies or trusted third parties, such that a combination of any k of them can decrypt the secret. The analysis of this would require using a decryption oracle in the CCA2 game, where the adversary is allowed to query the decryption oracle with any ciphertext of its choice, except for the challenge ciphertext. In a standard CCA2 game, the decryption oracle will not return copies of the decrypted challenge ciphertext. Now, in a secret sharing scheme CCA2 game, the adversary will query the oracle with $m \leq k$ copies of the challenge ciphertext, and will require the oracle to return real, decrypted ciphertexts, for all of the $m \leq k$ share queries. Moreover we must make multiple encryptions,

Table 17.1 Comparison of our work with previous works

Properties	[3]	[1, 2]	Our Work
Number of receivers	n	1	n
Asymmetric keys for sender required?	Yes	Yes	No
Number of symmetric keys to be stored on sender's side	n	1	1
Underlying KEM/DEM security requirements	CCA2-secure KEM/DEM	CCA2-secure KEM/DEM	CCA2-secure DEM only
Authentication provided?	Yes	No	No (can be added if necessary).

and they must be consistent. These issues could possibly be addressed by using Bellare's left-right oracle [10], but the decryption oracle must decrypt some of the shares consistently, and must disallow decryption of a set that will allow reconstruction of the secret. Unfortunately, a standard CCA2 decryption oracle will not allow consistent encryptions *and* correct decryption of some shares of the challenge ciphertext. This composability problem also arises in the context of a hybrid encryption system, where the key encapsulation mechanism (KEM) encrypts either a session key, or a random string, but a KEM is a single-use mechanism, and cannot be used in a consistent way across encryptions. In hybrid encryption, we compose the PKE and shared key encryption (SKE) schemes in the sense that we establish that if the PKE scheme, and the SKE scheme are both secure in some sense (e.g., CCA2 secure), then the resulting hybrid encryption scheme is also secure in the same sense. Although the idea seems intuitive, the security of a hybrid encryption scheme was not established until the work of Cramer and Shoup [11].

The goal of plaintext randomization is to "cut" off the underlying PKE scheme from the rest of the protocol, with the motivation of simplifying proofs for PKE-hybrid systems. In plaintext randomization, each time the encrypt function is called on a plaintext p with some public key, PK, the CCA2 oracle replaces the real plaintext with a random string, r, such that $|r| = |p|$, encrypts r, and stores the tuple $(c = E_{PK}(r), PK, p)$. To provide consistent decryptions on a decryption request, the oracle looks up the stored tuple and returns the plaintext p, rather than the actual decryption of c, which would give r. Intuitively, if we think about using this scheme in a hybrid encryption system, we would first generate a session key k, encrypt a random string r generated by sampling the "plaintext" space (which is the key space), such that $|r| = |k|$. We would then generate $c = E_{PK_{Recv}}(r)$, where "Recv" is the recipient. Then, we would encrypt the message to be sent: $c_{DEM} = E_K(p)$. But, here, c_{KEM} and c_{DEM} are two independent strings – c_{KEM} is an encryption of a random string that bears no relation to c_{DEM}. Hence, in the analysis of the hybrid encryption scheme, we will not have to deal with composability issues.

Real-or-Random Security The notion of plaintext randomization might seem similar to, but has some subtle differences with real-or-random security. In real-or-random security, the

ROR oracle encrypts either the real or random plaintext, and the task of the adversary is to distinguish between the real and random encrypted shares with non-negligible probability. In the context of a k-of-n secret sharing scheme, the ROR oracle is disallowed from decryptions of the "right" challenge ciphertext shares. But it is essential to provide the adversary decrypted shares of the real ciphertexts, to prove that any subset of n less than k will not decrypt the secret correctly. It is this fundamental problem that plaintext randomization was designed to solve. In plaintext randomization, we move the entire PKE scheme inside the oracle, such that the oracle can give consistent decryptions of the challenge ciphertext, for some subset of n, which is less than k: the minimum number of decryptions necessary to correctly decrypt the challenge ciphertext.

17.4 Preliminaries

In this section we review some relevant definitions and concepts that will be used in the construction of our protocols. We start with the basic public-key encryption with sender recovery scheme by Wei and Zhang [2].[1]

Definition 17.4.1 (Basic PKE-SR Scheme [2])

1) $(PK_r, SK_r, K_s) \leftarrow \mathsf{KeyGen}(1^\lambda)$: This is a randomized algorithm that outputs a public/secret keypair for the receiver, (PK_r, SK_r) and a secret recovery key, K_s for the sender. This is run by both parties individually to generate their respective keys.

2) $c \leftarrow \mathsf{Encrypt}(K_s, PK_r, m)$. This is a randomized algorithm run by the sender that takes as input the sender's recovery key, the receiver's public key, a message m, and gives as output a ciphertext c. Internally, it consists of two algorithms, $\mathsf{KEMEncrypt}$ and $\mathsf{DEMEncrypt}$. The sender picks a $\tau \leftarrow \{0, 1\}^\lambda$, and computes $r = F(K_s, \tau, PK_r)$, where F is an injective function. The sender then generates and encrypts an ephemeral, shared, session key, $(c_{KEM}, \kappa) \leftarrow \mathsf{KEMEncrypt}(r, PK_r)$.

---

[1]While it is possible to, and would be trivial to introduce a message authentication code in the scheme for integrity checking, we omit that step here for clarity of presentation.

The sender then encrypts the message using the ephemeral key, $(c_{DEM}) \leftarrow \mathsf{DEMEncrypt}(\kappa, m)$. Set $c = (c_{KEM}, c_{DEM})$. Send c to receiver.

3) $m \leftarrow \mathsf{Decrypt}(c, PK_r, SK_r)$. This is a deterministic algorithm run by the receiver to extract m from the ciphertext $c = (c_{KEM}, c_{DEM})$. The receiver first retrieves the ephemeral key, $\kappa \leftarrow \mathsf{KEMDecrypt}(SK_r, c_{KEM})$. Then the receiver then retrieves the message, $m \leftarrow \mathsf{DEMDecrypt}(\kappa, c_{DEM})$.

4) $m \leftarrow \mathsf{Recover}(K_s, PK_r, c)$: This is a deterministic algorithm run by the sender to recover the message m from the ciphertext $c = (c_{KEM}, c_{DEM})$. The sender first computes $r \leftarrow F(K_s, \tau, PK_r)$, and retrieves κ: $\kappa \leftarrow \mathsf{KEMRecover}(r, PK_r, C_{KEM})$. Finally the sender recovers $m \leftarrow \mathsf{DEMDecrypt}(K_s, c_{DEM})$

□

We next review a few definitions from [4, 12] regarding public-key encryption, plaintext-samplable public-key encryption, public-key encryption with multiple users, secret-key oblivious encryption, and plaintext randomization. We give the security definition of public-key encryption with multiple receivers, and definition of plaintext randomization here. The proofs, and other details are given in the full version posted on the eprint archive [13].

Definition 17.4.2 (Public Key Encryption with Multiple Users Game [12]) The security game for public key encryption in a multi-user setting is defined as follows:

- $\mathsf{PK\text{-}MU}_n^{\mathfrak{S}}.\mathsf{Initialize}(1^\lambda)$: For $i = 1$ to n, the oracle generates keypairs $(pk_i, sk_i) = \mathfrak{S}.KeyGen(1^\lambda)$, picks a random bit $b \in \{0, 1\}$, and sets C as an initially empty set of challenge ciphertexts. $pk_1, \cdots, pk_n$ are returned to the adversary.
- $\mathsf{PK\text{-}MU}_n^{\mathfrak{S}}.\mathsf{Decrypt}(i, x)$: If $(i, x) \in C$, the oracle returns $\perp$; otherwise, it returns $\mathfrak{S}.Decrypt(pk_i, sk_i, x)$.
- $\mathsf{PK\text{-}MU}_n^{\mathfrak{S}}.\mathsf{PEncrypt}(i, x_0, x_1)$: The oracle calculates $c = \mathfrak{S}.Encrypt(pk_i, x_b)$, adds (i, c) to C, and returns c to the adversary.
- $\mathsf{PK\text{-}MU}_n^{\mathfrak{S}}.\mathsf{IsWinner}(a)$: Takes a bit a from the adversary, and returns true if and only if $a = b$.

□

Definition 17.4.3 (Plaintext Randomization of a PKE) Given a plaintext-samplable PKE scheme $\mathfrak{S}$, the **plaintext randomization** of $\mathfrak{S}$ is a set of functions that acts as a PKE scheme, denoted $\mathfrak{S}$-rand, defined as follows:

- $\mathfrak{S}$-rand.$KeyGen(1^\lambda)$ computes $(pk, sk) = \mathfrak{S}.KeyGen(1^\lambda)$ and returns (pk, sk).
- $\mathfrak{S}$-rand.$Encrypt(pk, p)$ first computes $r = \mathfrak{S}.PTSample$ (pk, p), and then $c = \mathfrak{S}.Encrypt(pk, r)$. If a tuple of the form $(pk, c, \cdot)$ is already stored in $\mathfrak{S}$-rand's internal state, then $\perp$ is returned (the operation fails); otherwise, $\mathfrak{S}$-rand stores the tuple (pk, c, p), and returns c as the ciphertext.
- $\mathfrak{S}$-rand.$Decrypt(pk, sk, c)$ looks for a tuple of the form (pk, c, x) for some x. If such a tuple exists, then x is returned as decrypted plaintext; otherwise, $p = \mathfrak{S}.Decrypt(pk, sk, c)$ is called and p is returned.

□

17.5 Our Protocols

We now give a technique for constructing a public-key encryption with sender recovery (PKE-SR) scheme using plaintext randomization. Intuitively, our scheme works by encrypting a session key using the sender's recovery key and storing the encrypted key along with the ciphertext, such that the sender can independently retrieve the ciphertext when required, without having to contact the receiver, and while maintaining $O(n + k)$ storage cost, where n is the size of the ciphertext, and k the session key length.

The main novel contribution of our paper is taking this intuitive idea and applying the plaintext randomization proof technique to the PKE scheme used, which enables us to obtain a simple, natural construction of a PKE-SR scheme, without having to make additional cryptographic assumptions as was done in prior work in this area, such as assuming the existence of hash function families with collision accessibility (inducing hash functions to produce collisions), and without requiring the KEM/DEM scheme to be CCA2 secure. Consequently, our protocols have simple, clean proofs, which are easy to reason about, and which do not require a complicated series of reductions between games. We define our PKE-SR scheme with plaintext randomization for multiple receivers below, the single-receiver model is a simpler variant. Note that the sender needs to be equipped with just one recovery key, even in the presence of multiple receivers.

Definition 17.5.1 PKE-SR using plaintext randomization with multiple receivers

1) $((PK_1, SK_1), \cdots, (PK_n, SK_n), K_s) \leftarrow \mathsf{KeyGen}(1^\lambda)$: This is a randomized algorithm that generates public/secret keys for the receivers and a symmetric recovery key for the sender. Parties run this algorithm individually to generate their respective keys.
2) $c \leftarrow \mathsf{Encrypt}(PK_i, K_s, m)$: This is a randomized algorithm run by the sender that takes as input a receiver's public key, the sender's recovery key, and a message m. The algorithm proceeds as follows:
   a) Compute session key, κ: $\kappa \leftarrow \mathsf{KeyGen}(PK_i, K_s, \{0, 1\}^\lambda)$.
   b) Sample the session keyspace and produce a random string: $\rho \leftarrow \mathsf{PTSample}(\kappa, PK_i)$, such that $|\rho| = |\kappa|$.

c) Compute $c_{KEM} \leftarrow$ KEMEncrypt(PK_i, K_s, ρ). If a tuple of the form $(PK_i, c_{KEM}, \cdot)$ already exists in the PKE's internal state, return $\perp$. Else store the tuple (PK_i, c_{KEM}, κ)

d) Encrypt the message m: $c_{DEM} \leftarrow$ DEMEncrypt(κ, m), and set $c = (c_{KEM}, c_{DEM})$.

e) For enabling recovery at a later stage, compute $c' =$ DEMEncrypt(K_s, κ), and set $c'' = c||c'$.

f) Store c'', and return c.

3) $m \leftarrow$ Decrypt(PK_i, SK_i, c): This is a deterministic algorithm run by the receiver that takes as input a ciphertext c, the receiver's public and secret keys, and outputs the message m. The algorithm follows the steps below:

a) Retrieve the session key κ: $\kappa \leftarrow$ KEMDecrypt (PK_i, SK_i, c). The PKE scheme internally looks for a tuple of the form (PK_i, c_{KEM}, κ). If such a tuple exists, κ is returned as the decrypted session key, else $\kappa \leftarrow$ KEMDecrypt(SK_i, c_{KEM}) is returned.

b) Decrypt the message m: $m \leftarrow$ DEMDecrypt(κ, c_{DEM}).

4) $m \leftarrow$ Recover(c, K_s, PK_i): This is a deterministic algorithm run by the sender that takes in the ciphertext, the sender's secret recovery key, the receiver's public key, and returns the message m. The algorithm proceeds as follows:

a) Retrieve the stored $c'' = c||c'$, and computes $\kappa \leftarrow$ DEMDecrypt(K_s, c').

b) Compute $m \leftarrow$ DEMDecrypt(κ, c).

$\square$

We could, in principle, plaintext-randomize the symmetric encryption part as well, by sampling message m's plaintext-space, and replacing m with a random string of the same length, but that would then be equivalent to the well-known model of real-or-random (ROR) security. The point of plaintext randomization is to replace a public key scheme (PKE) that is internal to some larger operation - essentially the PKE ciphertexts give us something that is incidental to the answer that is wanted, but are not what we are ultimately interested in.

17.6 Analysis and Proofs

In this section, we introduce the plaintext randomization lemma of Tate et al. [4], and propose extensions to it. The original plaintext randomization lemma was for a single sender and receiver PKE game. Since we are working with single sender and multiple receivers PKE games, we require that the plaintext randomization lemma be extended to the multiple receivers model.

Lemma 17.6.1 (Plaintext Randomization Lemma for a Single Receiver [4]) *Let G be a game that makes sk-oblivious use of a plaintext-samplable public key encryption*

scheme $\mathfrak{S}$, and let $\mathfrak{S}$-rand be the plaintext randomization of $\mathfrak{S}$. Then, for any probabilistic adversary A that plays $G^{\mathfrak{S}}$ so that the total game-playing time of A is bounded by t, the number of calls to $\mathfrak{S}.KeyGen$ is bounded by n, and the number of encryption and decryption requests for any individual key is bounded by q_e and q_d, respectively,

$$\left| Adv_{A, G^{\mathfrak{S}}} - Adv_{A, G^{\mathfrak{S}\text{-}rand}} \right| \leq 2 Adv_{PK-MU_n^{\mathfrak{S}}}(t', q_e, q_d),$$

where $t' = t + O(\log(q_e n))$.

Lemma 17.6.2 (Plaintext Randomization Lemma for Multiple Receivers)

Let G be a game that makes sk-oblivious use of n plaintext-samplable public key encryption schemes, $\mathfrak{S}_1, \cdots, \mathfrak{S}_n$, and let $\mathfrak{S}$-rand$_1, \cdots, \mathfrak{S}$-rand$_n$ be the plaintext randomization of $\mathfrak{S}$. Then, for any probabilistic adversary A that plays the $G^{\mathfrak{S}_1}, \cdots, G^{\mathfrak{S}_n}$, so that the total game-playing time of A is bounded by t, the number of calls to $\mathfrak{S}_1.KeyGen, \cdots, \mathfrak{S}_n.KeyGen$ is bounded by m, and the total number of encryption and decryption requests for any individual key is bounded by q_e and q_d respectively, the advantage of A is defined by:

$$\left| Adv_{A, G^{\mathfrak{S}_1, \cdots, \mathfrak{S}_n}} - Adv_{A, G^{\mathfrak{S}\text{-}rand_1, \cdots, \mathfrak{S}\text{-}rand_n}} \right|$$
$$\leq 2 Adv_{PK-MU_m^{\mathfrak{S}_1, \cdots, \mathfrak{S}_n}}(t', q_e, q_d)$$

where $t' = t + O(\log(q_e n))$.

The proof, which involves reducing a adversary for any plaintext-randomized PKE game with multiple receivers into an adversary for a public-key encryption scheme with multiple receivers is omitted for lack of space, but is given in the full version [13]. We now present a theorem that our sender recovery scheme (PKE-SR) with plaintext randomization is CCA2-secure, if the underlying PKE and SKE schemes used are CCA2-secure.

Theorem 17.6.1 *Let A be an adversary that attacks the CCA2 security of our PKE-SR scheme, which uses public-key encryption scheme P as the KEM, and symmetric-key encryption scheme S as the DEM. If A runs in time t in a game that uses at most n keypairs, and performs at most q_e encryptions and q_d decryptions, then*

$$Adv_{A, PK-MU_n^{PKE-SR}}$$
$$\leq 2 Adv_{PK-MU_n^P}(t', q_e, q_d) + Adv_{SK-MU_{q_e n}^S}(t', 1, q_d)$$

where $t' = t + O(\log(q_e n))$.

17.7 Practical Instantiations

In this section, we describe an instantiation of our PKE-SR scheme using the classic Cramer-Shoup KEM/DEM scheme [11], which was the first work to rigorously establish the security of hybrid encryption. The idea of hybrid encryption has been around since the 1980s, primarily due to the inefficiency of public key encryption, and intuition tells us that if the symmetric key scheme and the public key scheme used in hybrid encryption are both secure in some sense (e.g., CCA2 secure), then a hybrid encryption scheme that composes them should be secure as well. In spite of this, the security of hybrid encryption was tricky to formally establish until the work of Cramer and Shoup, who introduced the primitives of key encapsulation mechanism (KEM) for generating and encrypting the session key, and data encapsulation mechanism (DEM) for encrypting data with the session key. Their work was instrumental in establishing a rigorous foundation for the analysis of hybrid encryption schemes. We first review some preliminary definitions from [11].

Computational Group Scheme A computational group scheme $\mathcal{G}$ specifies a sequence S_λ, where $\lambda \in \mathbb{Z}^+$. For every value of λ, S_λ is a probability distribution of group description, where a group description Γ specifies a finite abelian group $\hat{G}$, along with a prime-order subgroup G, a generator g of G, and the order q of G. Let $\Gamma[\hat{G}, G, g, q]$ indicate that Γ specifies $\hat{G}$, G, g and q. The group scheme also provides several algorithms to test membership and group properties, such as closure, existence of identity element, inverse element, associativity.

Target Collision Hash Function Let $k \in \mathbb{Z}^+$, such that k is constant, and let $\mathcal{G}$ be a computational group scheme, specifying a sequence S_λ of group distributions, where $\lambda \in \mathbb{Z}^+$ is a security parameter. Then HF is a k-ary group hashing scheme that specifies two algorithms:

- A family of key spaces indexed by $\lambda \in \mathbb{Z}^+$ and $\Gamma \in |S_\lambda|$. Each such key space is a probability space on bit strings denoted by $HF.KeySPace_{\lambda,\Gamma}$. There must exist a probabilistic, polynomial-time algorithm whose output distribution on input 1^λ and Γ is equal to $HF.KeySpace_{\lambda,\Gamma}$.
- A family of hash functions indexed by $\lambda \in \mathbb{Z}^+$, $\Gamma[\hat{G}, G, g, q] \in [S_\lambda]$, and $hk \in [HF.KeySpace_{\lambda,\Gamma}]$, and $\rho \in G^k$, outputs $HF_{hk}^{\lambda,\Gamma}(\rho)$.

The target collision resistance assumption for HF is then this: for every probabilistic polynomial-time algorithm A, the function $Adv\text{TCR}_{HF,A}(\lambda)$ is negligible in λ.

$$Adv\text{TCR}_{HF,A}(\lambda|\Gamma) = Pr[\rho in G^k \wedge \rho \neq \rho^* \wedge HF_{hk}^{\lambda,\Gamma}(\rho^*)$$

$$= HF_{hk}^{\lambda,\Gamma}(\rho)$$

Key Derivation Functions Let $\mathcal{G}$ be a computational group scheme, specifying a sequence (S_λ) of group distributions. A key derivation function (KDF), associated with $\mathcal{G}$, specifies two items:

- A family of *key spaces* indexed by $\lambda \in \mathbb{Z}^+$, and $\Gamma \in [S_\lambda]$. Each such key space is a probability space, denoted $KDF.KeySpace_{\lambda,\Gamma}$, on bit strings, called derivation keys. There must exist a probabilistic, polynomial time algorithm, whose output distribution on input 1^λ and Γ is equal to $KDF.KeySpace_{\lambda,\Gamma}$.
- A family of *key derivation functions* indexed by $\lambda \in \mathbb{Z}^+$, $\Gamma[\hat{G}, G, g, q] \in [S_\lambda]$, and $dk \in [KDF.KeySpace_{\lambda,\Gamma}]$, where each such function $KDF_{dk}^{\lambda,\Gamma}$ maps a pair $(a, b) \in G^2$ of group elements to a key K. A key k is a bit string of length $KDF.OutLen(\lambda)$. The parameter $KDF.OutLen(\lambda)$ should be computable in deterministic polynomial time, given 1^λ. There must exist a deterministic polynomial-time algorithm that on input 1^λ, $\Gamma[\hat{G}, G, g, q] \in [S_\lambda]$, $dk \in [KDF.KeySpace_{\lambda,\Gamma}]$, and $(a, b) \in G^2$, outputs $KDF_{dk}^{\lambda,\Gamma}(a, b)$.

The key derivation function security assumption is then this: for all probabilistic, polynomial-time algorithms A, and for all $\lambda \in \mathbb{Z}^+$, the function $Adv\text{Dist}_{KDF,A}$ is negligible in λ.

Definition 17.7.1 (PKE-SR Using Plaintext Randomized Cramer-Shoup (CS) Scheme)

- $(PK, SK, K_s) \leftarrow CS.KeyGen(1^\lambda)$: This is a randomized algorithm run by the sender and receiver individually to generate their respective keys. The key generation process proceeds as follows:
  - $\Gamma[\hat{G}, G, g, q] \leftarrow \hat{S}(1^\lambda)$
  - $hk \leftarrow HF.KeySpace_{\lambda,\Gamma}$
  - $dk \leftarrow KDF.KeySpace_{\lambda,\Gamma}$
  - $K_s \leftarrow KDF.KeySpace_{\lambda,\Gamma}$
  - $z_1, z_2 \leftarrow \mathbb{Z}_q; h \leftarrow g^{z_1}\hat{g}^{z_2}$
  - Set $PK = (\Gamma, hk, dk, h)$, $SK = (\Gamma, hk, dk, z_1, z_2)$. Set K_s as the sender's recovery key.
- $(c = (c_{KEM}, c_{DEM})) \leftarrow CS.Encrypt(PK, K_s, m)$: This is a randomized algorithm run by the sender that takes as input the receiver's public key, sender's recovery key, a message m, and outputs a ciphertext. The algorithm proceeds as follows:
  - Compute $u \leftarrow \mathbb{Z}_q$, $a \leftarrow g^u$, $b \leftarrow h^u$, $\kappa \leftarrow KDF_{dk}^{\lambda,\Gamma}(a, b)$.

– Sample the keyspace of κ, and produce a random string: $\hat{\kappa} \leftarrow$ CS.PTSample(PK, κ), such that $|\hat{\kappa}| = |\kappa|$.
– Compute $c_{KEM} =$ CS.KEMEncrypt$(PK, K_s, \hat{\kappa})$. Store (PK, c_{KEM}, κ) in internal state, if it does not already exist.
– Compute $c_{DEM} \leftarrow$ CS.DEMEncrypt(κ, m). Compute $c' =$ CS.DEMEncrypt(κ, K_s), set $c'' = c\|c'$.
– Send c to the receiver, and store c''.

• $\{m, \perp\} \leftarrow$ CS.Decrypt$(SK, c = (c_{KEM}, c_{DEM}))$: This is a deterministic algorithm run by the receiver that takes in the receiver's secret key and the ciphertext, and outputs the message m. The algorithm proceeds as follows:
– Check if the internal state of the KEM scheme contains a tuple (PK, c_{KEM}, κ). If such a tuple is found, then κ is returned as the session key. Else, $\kappa \leftarrow$ CS.DEMDecrypt(SK, c_{KEM}) is returned.
– Compute $b = a^{z_1}\hat{a}^{z_2}$. Compute $\kappa \leftarrow$ KDF$_{dk}^{\lambda,\Gamma}(a, b)$.
– Decrypt the message m: $m \leftarrow$ CS.DEMDecrypt (κ, c_{DEM}).

• $m \leftarrow$ CS.Recover(c''): This is a deterministic algorithm run by the sender when the sender wants to recover message m. The sender retrieves $c'' = c\|c'$, and computes $\kappa =$ CS.DEMDecrypt(K_s, c'). Sender then does $m \leftarrow$ CS.DEMDecrypt(K_s, c_{DEM}).

$\square$

Theorem 17.7.1 *Let A be a probabilistic, polynomial-time adversary that attacks the CCA2 security of the Cramer-Shoup hybrid encryption scheme,* CS(P, S), *where P is the public-key encryption scheme, and S is the shared-key encryption scheme used by the* CS *scheme. If A runs in time t in a game that used at most n keypairs, and performs at most q_e encryptions and q_d decryptions, then,*

$$Adv_{A,\text{PK}-\text{MU}}\text{cs} \leq 2Adv_{\text{PK}-\text{MU}^{P_n}}(t', q_e, q_d)$$
$$+Adv_{\text{SK}-\text{MU}_{q_{en}}^S}(t', 1, q_d)$$

where $t' = t + O(\log(q_e n))$.

The proof, which involves bounding the advantage of a PKE-SR adversary by a DEM adversary is given in the full version [13]. The corollary follows.

Corollary 17.7.1 *If P is a CCA-2 secure PKE scheme, and S is a CCA2-secure SKE scheme, then CS-rand, which is the plaintext randomized version of the Cramer-Shoup hybrid encryption scheme, CS, is a CCA2-secure hybrid encryption scheme.*

Acknowledgment Supported by NSF award no. 1566297.

References

1. P. Wei, Y. Zheng, On the construction of public key encryption with sender recovery. Int. J. Found. Comput. Sci. **26**(1), 1–32 (2015)
2. P. Wei, Y. Zheng, Efficient public key encryption admitting decryption by sender, in *Public Key Infrastructures, Services and Applications - 9th European Workshop on Public Key Cryptography, EuroPKI* (2012), pp. 37–52
3. P. Wei, Y. Zheng, X. Wang, Public key encryption for the forgetful, in *Cryptography and Security*, ed. by D. Naccache (Springer, Berlin, 2012), pp. 185–206
4. S.R. Tate, R. Vishwanathan, S. Weeks, Encrypted secret sharing and analysis by plaintext randomization, in 16th *Information Security Conference ISC* (2013), pp. 49–65
5. M. Bellare, B.S. Yee, Forward-security in private-key cryptography, in *Topics in Cryptology - CT-RSA 2003, The Cryptographers' Track at the RSA Conference 2003, San Francisco, CA, April 13-17, 2003, Proceedings* (2003), pp. 1–18
6. M. Bellare, S.K. Miner, A forward-secure digital signature scheme, in *Advances in Cryptology - CRYPTO '99, 19th Annual International Cryptology Conference, Santa Barbara, California, USA, August 15-19, 1999, Proceedings* (1999), pp. 431–448
7. K.Y. Choi, J. Cho, J.Y. Hwang, T. Kwon, Constructing efficient PAKE protocols from identity-based KEM/DEM, in *IACR Cryptology ePrint Archive*, vol. 2015 (2015), p. 606
8. S. Liu, K.G. Paterson, Simulation-based selective opening CCA security for PKE from key encapsulation mechanisms, in *Public-Key Cryptography - PKC 2015 - 18th IACR International Conference on Practice and Theory in Public-Key Cryptography, Gaithersburg, MD, March 30 - April 1, 2015, Proceedings* (2015), pp. 3–26
9. J. Blömer, G. Liske, Direct chosen-ciphertext secure attribute-based key encapsulations without random oracles, *IACR Cryptology ePrint Archive*, vol. 2013 (2013), p. 646
10. M. Bellare, A. Desai, E. Jokipii, P. Rogaway, A concrete security treatment of symmetric encryption, in *38th Annual Symposium on Foundations of Computer Science, FOCS* (1997), pp. 394–403
11. R. Cramer, V. Shoup, Design and analysis of practical public-key encryption schemes secure against adaptive chosen ciphertext attack. SIAM J. Comput. **33**(1), 167–226 (2003)
12. M. Bellare, A. Boldyreva, S. Micali, Public-key encryption in a multi-user setting: security proofs and improvements, in *Advances in Cryptology - EUROCRYPT* (2000), pp. 259–274
13. M. Godi, R. Vishwanathan, New techniques for public key encryption with sender recovery, Cryptology eprint archive (2018). https://eprint.iacr.org/

Cloud Intrusion Detection and Prevention System for M-Voting Application in South Africa: Suricata vs. Snort

18

Moloiyatsana Dina Moloja

Abstract

Information and Communication Technology is giving rise to new technologies and solutions that were not possible a few years ago. Electronic voting is one of the technologies that has emerged. One of the subsets of e-voting is mobile voting. Mobile voting is the use of mobile phones to cast a vote outside the restricted electoral boundaries. Mobile phones are pervasive; they offer connection anywhere, at any time. However, utilising a fast-growing medium such as the mobile phone to cast a vote, poses various security threats and challenges such as viruses, Trojans and worms. Many approaches for mobile phone security were based on running a lightweight intrusion detection software on the mobile phone. Nevertheless, such security solutions failed to provide effective protection as they are constrained by the limited memory, storage and computational resources of mobile phones. This paper compared and evaluated two intrusion detection and prevention systems named Suricata and Snort to equate, among the two security systems the one suitable to secure mobile voting application called XaP, while casting a vote. Simulations were used to evaluate the two security systems and results indicated that Suricata is more effective, reliable, accurate and secure than Snort when comes to protecting XaP.

Keywords

Mobile phone voting · Cloud computing · Intrusion detection and prevention systems

M. D. Moloja (✉)
Central University of Technology, Westdene, Bloemfontein, South Africa

18.1 Introduction

Mobile phones are pervasive and ambitious; they offer connection anywhere, at any time. The mobile phone penetration is increasing every day, as it becomes more and more affordable to acquire these devices. This is the reason why mobile voting (M-voting) has attracted a lot of attention from researchers and innovators [1–3]. The advantages of mobile phones to provide advanced technology and extra services compared to traditional phones gave people an opportunity to have remote access and be in control of information and communication anywhere and anytime [4, 5]. Also, the rapid development of technology regarding miniaturization and computing, in wireless mobile networks, brings a new dimension to security threats [4–6]. These portable devices have limited memory. They are accompanied with the computing and networking power of personal computers (PCs) [5, 7]. Also, they are involved with various network technologies such as third generation (3G), Bluetooth, infrared and Wireless Local Area Network (WLAN) or IEEE 802.11, which cause them to become extremely vulnerable to different attacks [4, 6]. Denial-of-service (DoS) and flooding attacks are major security threats to internet communications as it disrupts communication over the network and leaves servers inaccessible to legitimate users [6, 7]. It has been reported that wireless networks such as mobile phones, are more susceptible to these types of attacks than wired networks [5].

This paper is concerned with preventing increasing security threats against mobile devices [4–6], even more so during the voting process [2, 3, 7]. The paper argues that there is no cloud security solution for M-voting in South Africa (S.A).

This paper complements a significant contribution to the body of knowledge because no research has been conducted that combines Intrusion detection and prevention system, cloud computing and M-voting.

The paper is organised as follows; Sect. 18.2 discusses what other researchers have done. In Sect. 18.3, the compar-

© Springer International Publishing AG, part of Springer Nature 2018
S. Latifi (ed.), *Information Technology – New Generations*, Advances in Intelligent Systems and Computing 738,
https://doi.org/10.1007/978-3-319-77028-4_18

ison of the two Intrusion Detection and Prevention Systems [IDPSs] is discussed. Sect. 18.4 presents the results obtained after the evaluation. The paper concludes in Sect. 18.5.

18.2 Correlated Work

Multiple approaches to mobile phone security solutions have been introduced before; the literature reviewed indicates that many of these approaches support running light-weight intrusion detection software on the phone [8], some develop a full IDPS running on the mobile phone [9, 10] and lastly, some IDPS solutions employ the cloud environment [11]. Researchers have tried to develop an effective security solution for mobile phones, but their systems fail to cater to both malware detection and prevention while saving the computational resources of mobile phones [12] identified the main challenge when building effective mobile phone security solutions: the computational resources. As a result, these researchers developed a lightweight IDPS that operates on a mobile phone. The mobile phone has to be registered in the emulated environment of the cloud in real time. The IDPS records all information so that the registered mobile phone can be copied. The IDPS records every input taking place to the mobile phone, such as any traffic entering the mobile phone and physical sensors, and replays all the input to the emulator with no need to monitor the events taking place between the mobile phone and the emulator in the cloud. Their results revealed that their security solution is consume a lot of resources, which resulted in high volume of overhead being produced by the mobile phone.

Another study conducted by [8] developed an intrusion detection system for mobiles phones that operated in the cloud. Their system comprised two parts: (1) the mobile host agent, and (2) the proxy server. The mobile host agent is a light system that operated directly on the device and examines every activity taking place. The proxy server acts as an intermediary which mirrors the incoming and ongoing traffic between the mobile phone and the cloud. Also, it is the job of the proxy server to send all traffic to the cloud services where further analysis is performed on the basis of behaviour patterns and code signatures. The researchers' system turned out to be feasible and effective since it provided a 79% rate of true-positive alerts and a 21% rate of false-negative alerts. The system provides more comprehensive security for mobile phone

Currently, there is no single technique for M-voting in S.A that can guarantee threat detection and at the same time prevent those attacks from taking place. A security system is needed to protect the confidentiality and integrity of mobile voting in South Africa while saving mobile phone resources.

Table 18.1 Summary of mobile voting criteria

M-voting applications	Access to code?	Developed in South African context?	References
Mobile voting scheme	No	No	[2]
XaP application	Yes	Yes	[3]
GSM mobile voting	No	No	[1]
m-Voting system	No	No	[8]

18.2.1 Operation of the Security Solution

For this research, a security solution called "A Cloud-based Intrusion Detection and Prevention System" was developed to secure a mobile phone voting application.

The criteria that the researcher used to choose a mobile voting application to secure is as follows:

1. Access to code
2. Developed in South African context.

Table 18.1 summaries the criteria that were used to choose a mobile voting application designations.

The mobile voting application that met the criteria is XaP application. In this paper, XaP application was utilised as a mobile voting application to be secured.

The security solution comprises of two parts: the first part is the client software or "client agent" running on a mobile phone; the second part is the cloud IDPS or "cloud analysis engine" that utilises PaaS as a cloud computing layer. The client agent monitors and records every event taking place on the mobile phone's interface in runtime and direct it to the cloud analysis engine to perform an intensive malware scan. The cloud analysis engine uses a hybrid detection method where the signature and anomaly detection methods work in parallel. The cloud analysis engine makes use of a malware library to scan for intrusions. The client agent listens for notifications from the cloud analysis engine if a threat is detected.

To evaluate how IDPS's acts and its detection accuracy, there were four possible events whose ratio was scrutinized: True Positive (TP), True Negative (TN), False Positive (FP) and False Negative (FN).

When you look at how the four events are defined in the literature that were reviewed, it is safe to conclude that a system is said to be effective when there is a high number of true-positives and true-negatives alerts.

The next section compares two IDPS named: Suricata and Snort.

18.3 Comparison of Suricata and Snort

Before analysis engines, also known as packet sniffers, are technologies that are used to monitor legitimate or bogus traffic on a network. Suricata and Snort are the two analysis engines that were used in this paper:

18.3.1 Suricata

Suricata is an open source IDPS that was developed by the Open Information Security Foundation (OISF) in 2009 and was only released in 2010 [11, 13, 14]. Suricata is a multithreaded system that is more effective and scalable than Snort which is single threaded [11]. It inspects incoming data until the connection with the internet is terminated [13]. The packets are inspected using the sliding window concept (as depicted in Fig. 18.1).

According to [13, 14], Suricata receives the first segment and immediately inspects it. Then it receives the second segment, puts it together with the first, and inspects it. At the end, it catches the third segment, cuts off the first one, puts together the second segment with the third segment, and inspects it. Once the full packet is inspected and no malware was found or intrusion detected, the packet is sent to the receiver [10, 11].

Also, Suricata has two modes that act on intrusion when it is detected, namely a Drop mode and/or a Reject mode [14]:

- Drop (IPS mode):
  - If a signature containing a drop action matches a packet, it is immediately discarded and will not be send any further.
  - The receiver does not receive the message, resulting in a time-out.
  - All following packets from the same sender are dropped.
  - an alert for a packet is generated.

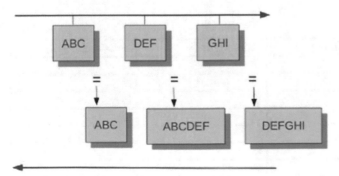

Fig. 18.1 Sliding window used in Suricata [14]

- Reject (both IDS and IPS mode):
  - This is an active rejection of the packet; both the receiver and sender receive a reject packet.
  - If the packet concerns Transmission Control Protocol (TCP), it will be a reset-packet, otherwise it will be an Internet Control Message Protocol (ICMP)-error packet.
  - an alert for a packet is generated.

A study conducted by [11] stated that Suricata is able to use less memory and less CPU utilisation than Snort. Another study that proves the effectiveness of Suricata was conducted by [14]. Their study, which analysed the performance of both analysis engines (Suricata and Snort), revealed that Suricata has better probability to be more effective and capable than Snort [11, 13].

18.3.2 Snort

Snort is a packet-sniffer and logger, utilised as a lightweight IDS [15]. Snort was originally developed in 1998 by Martin Roesch to scan the application layer of system data packets [8]. It is one of the current and commonly used open source signature based IDS, sustained by Source Fire [15].

Snort produces alarms using signature rules and has a semantic way to describe novel rules. Its design creates a way to add novel functionalities when recording events [7, 8]. The filtered traffic passes through the Snort attack detection engine in order to detect various active and passive attacks. With the help of Snort, the researcher was able to analyse and monitor live traffic and packet flow along with anomalies in the network [14].

Snort comprises of the following mechanisms. Below is a description of each component [15]:

- Packet capture: To capture packets, Snort uses a library called libpcap written in Lawrence Berkeley National Laboratories. The packets that are captured are managed by decoding engines, yielding to the network level.
- Pre-processor plugins: packets are conceded over multiple pre-processors. Additionally, before packet are passed to the detection engines, they must be investigated and processed. Each pre-processor inspects the packets for a different trait and makes a verdict whether to pass the packet to the detection engine without altering the packet or not.
- Detection engine: Tests packets for multiple elements that are stated in the Snort-rules definition- file. The plugins of the detection engines offer additional detection functions.
- Output plug-ins: The produced alarms from the detection engine, pre-processors or decoding engines are received by the Snort output plugins.

The following comparison between Snort and Suricata is made on the basis of different parameters, such as signatures, false alarm, flexibility, deployment, interface and operating system capability. (see Table 18.2)

When choosing an intrusion detection and prevention system, the two signature-based detection engines can both function effectively depending on the environment and the deployment of the rule set [14]. The development in Suricata gave the researcher the ability to utilise multithreaded operations for the simulation, which is very important and crucial when it comes to network bandwidth [11]. Both Snort and Suricata were used in the simulations and their results were compared.

The next section discusses the results obtained from evaluating Suricata and Snort.

18.4 Results

As previously mentioned, four ratios were scrutinized to analyse the effectiveness of the two IDPS. The researcher has hoped to obtain a 100% TP rate, a 100% TN rate, a 0% FN rate and a 0% FP rate. Below are the results obtained for Snort and Suricata. The researcher utilised Pytbull as a signature database and geny-motion as a simulation tool.

Table 18.2 Comparison of Suricata and Snort

Parameters	Suricata	Snort
Contextual signatures	Yes	No
Flexible site customisation	High	Medium
False alarm	Small	Medium
Large user community	Yes	Yes
Configuration GUI	Yes	Yes
Installation/deployment	Easy	Easy
Operating system compatibility	Any OS	Any OS

18.4.1 Suricata

Suricata generated 12 FN where it did not detect malicious traffic as depicted in Table 18.3. The most likely reason for these FN is that the rule utilised was not loaded or optimised for a specific threat.

During the client-side attack, Suricata detected both tests, but during the evasion-technique attack, it did not recognise that an evasion attack was underway.

The Pytbull tests revealed that the FP were more difficult to measure because of the composite nature of the Pytbull. If it is clear that an alert is a FP alert, such as Trojan infection during an Nmap scan, that alert is categorised as a FP. Nmap is a protocol that is been used to discover hosts, protocols, open ports, services and vulnerabilities on networks [13].

18.4.2 Snort

Snort generated 16 false-negatives where it did not detect the malicious traffic. As was the case with Suricata, false-negatives were observed and a possible reason for this is that the rule used by both was not loaded or optimised for the particular threat.

During the client side attack, Snort detected only one test and during the evasion-technique attack, it identified that an evasion attempt was underway (compared to Suricata which did not recognise the attack).

Table 18.4 presents the summarised results from the Snort experiment:

To summarise this experiments: In some instances, both analysis engines failed to generate alerts to known malicious traffic when they were both loaded with the same rule set. When they were both unsuccessful in generating alerts, we can say objectively that it can be attributed in the rules and not the detection engines. Additionally, both analysis engines were inconsistent in the alerts. One explanation for this may be the differences between Snort and Suricata regarding the implementation of the rule language.

Table 18.3 Summary of Suricata results

Test types	Suricata true (+)	Suricata true (−)	Suricata false (+)	Suricata false (−)
Client side attack	75	78	8	11
Test rules	85	56	9	12
Bad traffic	77	77	13	15
Fragmented packets	51	77	18	16
Multiple failed logins	65	65	21	9
Evasions techniques	89	91	15	9
Shell-codes	81	58	14	10
Denial-of-service	63	63	14	34
PCAP replay	61	30	47	12

Table 18.4 Summary of Snort results

Test type	Snort true (+)	Snort true (−)	Snort false (+)	Snort false (−)
Client Side attack	71	68	10	13
Test rules	84	56	10	16
Bad traffic	77	77	12	12
Fragmented packets	51	55	16	16
Multiple failed logins	65	71	19	11
Evasions techniques	70	75	17	9
Shell-codes	80	57	15	7
Denial-of-service	63	63	11	9
PCAP replay	61	31	43	10

This study adopted Suricata as a suitable cloud-based analysis engine to protect a mobile voting application called XaP. The researcher established that as much as Snort has been the preferred IDPS in the past, during the evaluation simulation that was run for this paper, Suricata presented more effective and accurate results close to what the researcher anticipated.

18.5 Conclusion

In this paper, two analysis engines were evaluated, namely Snort and Suricata. The researcher tested Suricata and Snort on similar data to provide an informed recommendation for the XaP application. Both analysis engines did well during the tests. Both generated FP and FN, however the weaknesses in the rule set used for the tests are subject to be attributed. In the end, Suricata was adopted as the most suitable cloud analysis engine to protect a mobile voting application such as XaP.

More work needs to be done in order to reduce the false-negatives observed, which were caused by the anomaly-detection method and also on Suricata as the adopted cloud IDPS so that it can be configured to protect any mobile voting application, not only the XaP application.

References

1. F. Breitinger, C. Nickel, User survey on phone security and usage, in *BIOSIG* 2010, pp. 139–144
2. E. Eilu, R. Baguma, J.S. Pettersson, M-voting in developing countries: findings from Uganda. Commonwealth Governance Handbook **15**, 25–28 (2014)
3. N. Mpekoa, A model of mobile phone voting system for South Africa (Masters dissertation, Tshwane University of Technology), 2014
4. E. Chin, A.P. Felt, V. Sekar, D. Wagner, Measuring user confidence in smartphone security and privacy, in *Proceedings of the Eighth Symposium On Usable Privacy and Security*, 2012, p. 1. ACM
5. D. He, S. Chan, M. Guizani, Mobile application security: malware threats and defenses. IEEE Wirel Commun **22**(1), 138–144 (2015)
6. M. La Polla, F. Martinelli, D. Sgandurra, A survey on security for mobile devices. IEEE Commun Surv Tutorials **15**(1), 446–471 (2013)
7. D. Zissis, D. Lekkas, Securing e-Government and e-Voting with an open cloud computing architecture. Gov Inf Q **28**(2), 239–251 (2011)
8. N. Khamphakdee, N. Benjamas, S. Saiyod, Improving intrusion detection system based on snort rules for network probe attacks detection with association rules technique of data mining. J ICT Res Appl **8**(3), 234–250 (2015)
9. M. Ahmed, A.N. Mahmood, J. Hu, A survey of network anomaly detection techniques. J Netw Comput Appl **60**, 19–31 (2016)
10. N. Hubballi, V. Suryanarayanan, False alarm minimization techniques in signature-based intrusion detection systems: a survey. Comput Commun **49**, 1–17 (2014)
11. J.S. White, T. Fitzsimmons, J.N. Matthews, Quantitative analysis of intrusion detection systems: Snort and Suricata. in *SPIE Defense, Security, and Sensing*, 2013, 875704
12. S. Zonouz, A. Houmansadr, R. Berthier, N. Borisov, W. Sanders, Secloud: a cloud-based comprehensive and lightweight security solution for smartphones. Comput Secur **37**(2013), 215–227 (2013)
13. E. Albin, N.C. Rowe, A realistic experimental comparison of the Suricata and Snort intrusion-detection systems, in *26th International Conference on Advanced Information Networking and Applications Workshops (WAINA)*, 2012, pp. 122–127. IEEE
14. D. Day, B. Burns, A performance analysis of snort and suricata network intrusion detection and prevention engines, in *Fifth International Conference on Digital Society, Gosier, Guadeloupe*, 2011, pp. 187–192
15. T. Xing, D. Huang, L. Xu, C.J. Chung, P. Khatkar, Snortflow: a openflow-based intrusion prevention system in cloud environment, in *Research and Educational Experiment Workshop (GREE), 2013 Second GENI*, 2013, pp. 89–92. IEEE

Protecting Personal Data with Blockchain Technology

Alexander Masluk and Mikhail Gofman

Abstract

Service providers depend on the ability to host, analyze, and exchange the personal data of users. Legal and contractual frameworks aim to protect the rights of users regarding this data. However, a confluence of factors render these rights difficult to guarantee. This paper evaluates the potential of blockchain technology as a mechanism for achieving transparency and accountability in the realm of personal data collection.

Keywords

Security · Cybersecurity · Neural networks · Machine learning · Network security · Intrusion detection · Artificial intelligence

19.1 Introduction

Unless a user takes extraordinary protective measures, typical computer use results in the creation of vast quantities of personal and private data and metadata [1–4]. Each day, people upload terabytes of data to storage platforms like Dropbox, Google Drive, and social networking sites like Facebook. In addition, environments such as Google and Windows 10 passively collect even greater quantities of metadata in the form of keystroke dynamics, usage duration logs, and the like. By applying machine learning and data analytics to this data and metadata, service providers are able to refine the interfaces and content of their products, and derive profit through targeted advertising platforms such as Google's AdWords [3, 4, 10].

The benefits both user and provider enjoy in this arrangement are difficult to overstate. Users have access to a wide range of robust, free-to-use internet services, and service providers procure significant profits [5–7]. Yet, with regular data breaches in the news and an increasing public awareness of the depth of information that can be gained through data mining, this arrangement has become a cause of deep concern for users fearing that their privacy may be compromised or their data misused.

Privacy policies and other mechanisms behold service providers to certain practices regarding the data they collect [1–4, 8]. These practices limit the circumstances under which they may retain a user's personal data, share the data with third parties, and so on. However, several challenges impede the efficacy of these agreements and associated enforcement mechanisms. The users may find the privacy policies difficult to understand and draw unwarranted conclusions about the degree to which their data really is private. The service provider may inadvertently or intentionally violate policy without leaving any sort of record of having done so [9].

Our motivation is to better understand the specific data collection and use practices of service providers according to a close reading of the relevant policy agreements, and propose a mechanism by which a greater degree of provider transparency and accountability may be achieved to aid in enforcing said policy. To this end, we will examine the application of blockchain technology as an accounting mechanism for personal data collection, retention, and exchange. We will see that defining a set of data transaction types and recording these in a publicly verifiable ledger helps to achieve this accountability.

The organization of the paper is as follows. Section II establishes the preliminary concepts of data collection and blockchain technology; section III discusses the limitations of allowable use of collected data. In the fourth section we present the concept of our proposed solution for applying

A. Masluk · M. Gofman (✉)
Department of Computer Science, California State University, Fullerton, CA, USA
e-mail: alex.masluk@csu.fullerton.edu; mgofman@fullerton.edu

© Springer International Publishing AG, part of Springer Nature 2018
S. Latifi (ed.), *Information Technology – New Generations*, Advances in Intelligent Systems and Computing 738,
https://doi.org/10.1007/978-3-319-77028-4_19

blockchain to personal data lineage, while in the fifth we touch upon related research. The sixth section concludes the paper.

19.2 Preliminaries

19.2.1 Data Collection Scope

Necessary to any proposed scheme is a realistic view of the breadth and depth of data collected. To that end, we examined the data collection policies of four prominent service providers: Apple, Facebook, Google, and Microsoft.

Each of these entities differ in terms of the business model under which they operate and the nature of services they provide. Nonetheless, we discover a uniformly maximalist approach to the type of data they each afford themselves license to collect, with noteworthy differences.

All four provide cloud-based repositories for data to be stored privately or shared with others. The providers reserve the right to analyze both varieties. So too do each of these providers log and analyze metadata in many or all of the following forms: frequency and duration statistics; details of the hardware, operating system, and file system contents of the device used to access a service; location data; data generated by a device's input peripherals such as keyboards, touch screens, microphones, and webcams; and other sources too numerous to list exhaustively [1–4].

Many web-based services connect and interact with one another. This offers providers additional data collection vectors. For example, Facebook owns the virtual-reality platform Oculus and collects data generated by use of that platform [1]. In general, using one's identity on one of these platforms to access another service allows the provider to collect and link data from each service [1, 2]. Apple and Microsoft distinguish themselves here by enumerating safeguards against linking the data collected from third party or subsidiary services to the user's identity [3, 4].

In the case of social media platforms, information provided about one user by another user may be collected. For example, if Alice uploads a photo of Bob to Facebook, Facebook can link the photo with information it has collected directly from Bob [1].

Additionally, through use of "unique application numbers", Google can link together multiple accounts that have been accessed through a single app installation. This may indicate multiple accounts held by an individual, or a connection between multiple individuals who used the same device [2]. In its own privacy policy, Microsoft specifies that it declines to collect this particular type of data [3].

Though noteworthy differences exist, four privacy policies we examined all took a broad approach to delineating the types of data their policies permit them to collect, and the uses to which the data can be put.

19.2.2 Blockchain

Blockchain is the distributed ledger technology which guarantees the value and controls the inflation rate of Bitcoin. It achieves this through mechanisms such as proof of work and mutual consensus [11].

All Bitcoin transactions are recorded in the blockchain ledger. A transaction records an amount to be transferred from one Bitcoin "wallet" to another. Since a given wallet's balance is calculated as the running summation of ledger-recorded transactions involving that wallet, the ability to guarantee the validity of each transaction guarantees the currency's viability and value [11, 12].

The actual process of recording new ledger transactions takes place in a distributed manner, with multiple nodes competing to conduct the validation process necessary to add the transaction to the ledger. To win the competition, a node must solve a computationally difficult problem ("proof of work"), the answer to which can be evaluated by other competing nodes for correctness. Nodes will attempt to append or "chain" new transactions to previous transactions that they agree are correct ("mutual consensus"). Unless the majority of blockchain nodes are controlled by hostile actors, this system guarantees the validity of ledger transactions [11, 12].

We are particularly interested in blockchain's ability to facilitate trustworthy record keeping in a distributed environment.

19.3 Data Usage Limitations

We hope to propose a mechanism for ensuring transparency and accountability regarding personal data collection. To this end, we must understand what rights and limitations exist regarding the data collection sphere. These are the limitations whose enforcement we intend to support.

Insofar as a user licenses through agreement the provider's right to various uses of their data, we turn again to the privacy policies of four prominent providers. We also examine the EU-U.S. Privacy Shield, a self-certification framework that prescribes additional obligations on the part of the provider.

19.3.1 Limitations Through Organization Policy

Although the four privacy policies we examined tended towards similarity regarding the breadth of data the providers enjoy license to collect, greater distinction can be discovered in the uses to which the data is put. Google and Facebook make significant use of the ability to draw connections between a user's activity across different services, platforms, and accounts in order to build a unified data profile [1, 2]. By contrast, Microsoft and Apple may decline to collect this information; in Apple's case, the privacy policy elaborates the safeguards Apple employs to confound the potential of doing so [3, 4].

Similarities exist as well. Each privacy policy reserves the provider's right to transfer a user's data to a third party entity for data processing purposes. We are assured in each case that their privacy agreement extends to any third party thus employed. None of the policies made it clear how the identity of these potential third parties can be discovered [1–4].

The four providers distinguish between sensitivity levels of the data they collect, subjecting more sensitive data to more stringent protective measures. For example, Facebook promises not to display advertisements based on a user's medical condition. Apple makes a broad distinction between "personal" and "non-personal" data. The policies provide little in the way of a concrete methodology for evaluating and assigning the sensitivity level of data collected [1–4].

Regarding the issue of data retention, each provider's policy stipulates that the provider will remove any individual user datum upon request. However, each also includes a similar caveat, providing for circumstances in which they may fail to fulfill the request. Facebook may decline to remove data if a "good faith belief" implies that the information could be "necessary to … protect ourselves, you and others" [1]. Google may not remove information that resides on their backup systems [2]. Microsoft may elect to "access, transfer, disclose, and preserve personal data" when it believes doing so will "protect our customers" and "protect the rights or property of Microsoft" [3]. Apple can retain data for a "longer retention period" than specified in their privacy policy if doing so is "permitted by law" [4]. We discovered no official company documentation regarding how the decisions to retain or delete data are made.

19.3.2 Limitations through the EU-U.S. Privacy Shield

Many service providers transfer data across state and national boundaries, and in doing so fall subject to a variety of regional privacy laws too numerous to summarize here. In general, European Union member nations possess privacy laws of greater stringency than the U.S [13]. This presents EU nations with the challenge of protecting the privacy rights of its citizens while permitting them to use services that may result in their data residing in more unrestricted nations such as the United States. The EU-U.S. Privacy Shield framework addresses this dilemma [8].

The framework operates under the principle of self-certification. An organization self-certifies that it meets the Privacy Shield's requirements. Among other specifications, these require a member organization to make available a transparent and complete privacy policy, including an exhaustive list of all the uses to which the collected data is put. They must provide a mechanism for responding to user complaints if deviations from the policy should be suspected, and only transfer user data to organizations with equal or greater privacy protection [8]. Microsoft, Facebook, and Google are Privacy Shield member organizations; Apple is not [14].

The specifications of the Privacy Shield strike a balance between permissiveness and restrictiveness. This makes intuitive sense. Given the intent of bounding allowable uses of personal data, such a framework must be restrictive in some degree in order to perform any useful function. Conversely, fewer organizations will find their mode of operation compatible with overly restrictive regulations, and will decline to adopt the certification.

It is easily understood that the Privacy Shield derives its authority from the degree to which a broad number of U.S. organizations attain membership. EU member nations cannot exert any legal authority over U.S. organizations, but an EU data protection authority (DPA) may prohibit data trade with non-certified U.S. organizations. It becomes less advantageous to exert such prohibitions in a circumstance where few U.S. organizations are Privacy Shield members, since it prohibits trade with a vast majority of potential business partners. On the other hand, trade restrictions imposed by DPAs provide a market incentive for U.S. organizations to obtain certification.

A weakness of the Privacy Shield framework stems from our core problem of accountability. How might a user determine, for example, that their data was transferred to a third party that failed to fulfill the "equal or greater" privacy standard, or that the provider neglected to delete data upon request? The framework might be strengthened by insisting the adherence of member organizations to a mechanism guaranteeing transparency in this regard, supposing such a mechanism could be implemented with sufficiently non-restrictive impact.

19.4   Blockchain for Personal Data

How can blockchain be used to promote transparency and accountability in the data collection sphere? Here we will outline the general concept of how we propose to apply the technology.

19.4.1 Premise

For our purpose, we consider the Bitcoin concept of the "wallet". For Bitcoin, the blockchain ledger supports two simple wallet operations: adding or removing funds to and from a wallet. These wallets are pseudonymous and do not reveal the identity of their owner.

We propose to extend the concept of the "wallet" into a hierarchy of data repositories (DRs). At the higher level, a master data repository (MDR) refers to a service provider's primary or backup storage; unlike Bitcoin's wallets, the MDR's owner is publicly known. Sub-DRs correspond to the individual users whose data falls under the provider's possession.

In this context, our blockchain should support the following transaction types: WRITE, COPY, ERASE, and PROCESS. These transactions contain information corresponding to the relevant DR, user datum, and transaction time. Tracing these transactions reveals a sequential chain of custody for

each datum, allowing data lineage to be established. The service provider exposes an interface for users or enforcement entities to examine the ledgers and gain knowledge of these custody chains..

Examples of how the flow of data translates into ledger transactions can be seen in Fig. 19.1. Provider 1 (P1) collects data from users, which result in a series of WRITE transactions in the provider's primary storage, MDR_P. From MDR_P they are also stored in backup, resulting in a COPY entry for MDR_P and a WRITE entry for the backup storage, MDR_B. P1 associates its data with the users that originated them, so we also see a series of COPY operations for MDR_P and corresponding WRITE operations for the SDRs corresponding to each user.

Suppose P1 outsources analysis of its data to a third party, P2. The transfer required for this outsourcing results in COPY transactions for P1's MDR, and WRITE transactions for P2's. Additionally, we will see PROCESS transactions corresponding to P2's MDR, indicating the nature of the operations performed on the data.

Transactions of type PROCESS also indicate instances where processing data results in the creation of derived data distinct from—but based upon—the original data. In this case, the PROCESS ledger entry will indicate both the original data and any data derived from the original data, allowing data lineage to be traced through derivations.

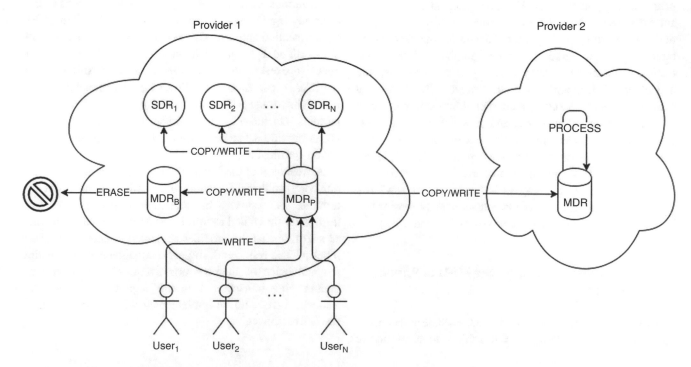

Fig. 19.1 How the flow of data translates into ledger transactions

The complete contents of a ledger transaction include the following:

1. Transaction timestamp
2. Data identifier
3. Transaction type
4. Source MDR
5. Destination MDR
6. Process performed (if applicable)
7. Derived data identifier (if applicable)

This design provides accountability for several typical data collection scenarios.

19.4.1.1 What Data Has Been Collected?

We can examine the ledger of WRITE operations that a given provider has recorded to see exactly what data they have collected about us. The hierarchical nature of the data repositories give us an access control mechanism to allow a user to track the data belonging to their SDRs alone, whereas an enforcement agency may be given broader access to MDR ledger information.

19.4.1.2 Has My Data Been Deleted?

The ERASE ledger entries allows us to verify that data requested for removal has indeed been removed. Since copying data from primary storage to backup storage results in a COPY and WRITE operation in the two respective high-level DRs, we can verify that the data no longer resides in backup by finding the corresponding ERASE entry in the backup DR ledger if necessary.

19.4.1.3 With Whom Has My Data Been Shared?

An examination of the COPY entries allows us to trace each instance in which our data was transferred to a third party DR. The third party may be audited for corresponding ERASE transactions to ensure they have not retained any data.

19.4.1.4 Have Multiple Accounts of Mine Been Correlated?

Because low-level DRs must correspond to individuals, data collected from disparate but correlated accounts must belong to the same low-level DR. We are thus able to confirm the extent to which our activity on various accounts and services have been compiled into a single data profile.

19.4.1.5 What Exactly Are you Doing with My Data?

Because Privacy Shield-compliant organizations must publish an inclusive list of applications for which our data is being used, we speculate that each such organization could publish a list of keywords associated with each. If Google analyzes our search strings for use in AdWords, the corresponding PROCESS ledger entry may include the keyword "ADWORDS" or, more generally, "MARKETING". This allows users to verify their data are being used exclusively for the purposes for which they have been licensed.

19.4.2 Challenges of Implementation

There exist a few generic implementation challenges when it comes to generalizing blockchain from cryptocurrency to other applications. Several scale-related obstacles could affect the viability of implementing our proposal: the Bitcoin network can handle a maximum of seven transactions per second; each copy of the blockchain ledger occupies 50 gb of storage space; the process of validating new transactions and adding them to the chain consumes energy on the order of $15 million USD per day. A blockchain capable of handling the number and frequency of transactions associated with big data collection and processing would be prohibitively resource-intensive if implemented using the same strategy [12, 15, 16].

A few strategies can be leveraged to mitigate the issue of scale. The major factor that causes the Bitcoin network to perform slowly and consume great amounts of energy is the computationally intensive task necessary to validate a block of transactions, the "proof of work" (PoW). Alternatively, we can make use of the faster and less expensive "proof of stake" (PoS). Rather than competing to solve a computationally difficult problem, nodes are awarded the right to add transactions to the chain using a lottery-based system [12]. Kiayias et al. present a provably secure implementation of the PoS model [17, 20].

The Bitcoin network uses a single, permissionless ledger, but this may not be necessary in our case. It may be reasonable to allow each provider to implement a local, closed-participation blockchain that meets a given set of requirements. Using such a stratified approach would help alleviate scaling issue of the storage size required for the ledger itself, since service provider A would not need to store a copy of service provider B's data transactions. This may weaken the efficacy of the design since a provider, controlling all of the nodes participating in the blockchain, could generate counterfeit ledger entries. Nonetheless, an internally distributed blockchain protects against rogue individuals within an organization attempting to falsify records, and against security breaches in which a minority of participating nodes fall under hostile control.

Another issue is the variety of datatypes we see collected, which range from small strings of text to large video files. Hashing can be used to uniformly transform these data into a fixed, manageable size. Existing blockchain implementations make use of this strategy [15]. The strategy could be extended from individual data to datasets. The total set of all data pertaining to a user hashes to a single unique value; any subset of that data transferred or operated upon would hash to a single value as well.

Though beyond the scope of this research, a more detailed design would be needed in order to formally evaluate the efficiency, and therefore viability, of our proposed system.

19.5   Related Works

In the course of our research, we encountered these proposed personal data accountability mechanisms, and applications of blockchain besides cryptocurrency.

Mehmood et al. provide a useful survey of the various strategies proposed and in use for augmenting privacy in the big data context. These consist largely of cryptographic and anonymization techniques. We store user data in an encrypted form to protect against data breaches, and we present data in an anonymized form so that it can be analyzed without revealing the identity of the data's originator. A discussion of integrity verification obliquely touches upon the issue of accountability, but only in terms of providing a mechanism to guarantee the data has not been altered [18].

These concerns, while important, may at odds with the our use cases. Generalizing and suppressing datasets inevitably leads to a loss of integrity in the original dataset; this trade-off may be appropriate when exposing the data to third parties for analysis, but users expect the data we upload to the cloud to be preserved exactly as we created it. Encryption, especially when implemented with a multitude of keys relative to the user's identity or attributes, introduces additional overhead that does not lend itself well to the sort of parallel computing strategies big data consumers use to expediently process data.

Gao and Iwane [19] present a model for social networking with robust privacy features. The model works by introducing trusted intermediaries between social networking providers that guard a user's data and only permit access to the data as specified by the user's preferences. These intermediaries or "virtual-network control centers" (VCCs) facilitate data transfer between participating social media organizations (POs). The VCCs maintain an anonymized copy of the user data to supply to other POs upon request, should the request be permissible given the access controls assigned to the user data. The participating organization must implement connectivity with these VCCs and expose the implementation to the user, who may decline to make use of the system and simply expose their data directly from the PO using the traditional approach. Though Gao and Iwane discuss their model in terms of intentionally created data, the approach likely generalizes to automatically collected metadata as well; a user could, for example, toggle "location history" as a private field in the VCC interface, which will then block social media platforms from sharing this information.

Gao and Iwane's approach addresses the accountability concern with regards to data transfer between parties: if a social media provider wishes to transfer data to a third party entity, it must do so through user-obedient VCCs. It does not, however, promote transparency regarding initial data collection or data retention. The VCC has no awareness of what a PO may be doing with a user's data until a situation arises for which the VCC must act as intermediary.

A potential issue arises from how the VCCs themselves will be implemented, whether through centralized trusted authorities, or an open-participation distributed model similar to certain blockchain implementations. Relying on a trusted third-party to act as intermediary for the huge amounts of data characteristic of social media may create a central bottleneck and point of failure, whereas a distributed model introduces security and privacy concerns.

Setting big data privacy and accountability aside [21, 22], we examine how blockchain technology has been applied to spheres other than cryptocurrency in order to achieve accountability. The organization Everledger attempts to apply distributed ledger technology to luxury goods such as diamonds and fine art. The organization Factom is developing a protocol that they hope will be used to apply distributed ledger methodology in any sphere where record-keeping accountability is needed [15]. Factom and Everledger apply to scenarios in which records are already being kept and trustworthy records must be separated from counterfeit or otherwise illegally-produced records. In the realm of personal data collection, we are concerned not only with the trustworthiness of records, but with ensuring that records are being kept in the first place, and kept in a way that provides data lineage transparency.

As well as use and retention, one of our primary goals is achieving to achieve accountability with regards to data lineage. Backes et al. propose a framework for building data lineage transparency into data exchange at the bit level. This is achieved through "robust watermarking". A data sender alters the data before sending it so that the data contains a detectable watermark uniquely associated with the data receiver. The watermark has the following properties: it preserves the original data's information in such a way that it can be processed according to the original intent, and can coexist with multiple other watermarks such that the order in which they were applied to the data can be discerned [23].

For data lineage, this is in ways a superior approach to our proposed blockchain model, since it functions at the protocol level and avoids the significant overhead of maintaining transaction ledgers; the ledger information is instead stored in the data itself. Our scheme could perhaps be augmented if the concept of robust watermarking could be extended to describe not just data transfers, but various distinguishable data processing operations.

19.6 Conclusion

Computer users enjoy access to a range of robust and inexpensive services and applications. The providers of these rely upon the ability to collect, share, and analyze large amounts of personal data in order to financially support themselves and deliver quality products. Users have the expectation that providers will adhere to a set of rules regarding the collection, use, and retention of their data, but these rules are difficult to enforce given the lack of a mechanism guaranteeing transparency and accountability regarding the life of a given piece of data.

We turn to the distributed ledger technology of blockchain to provide such a mechanism. By suggesting a logical organization of collected data into data repositories, and defining a simple set of data transactions between them, we have shown how a publicly visible ledger of these transactions would facilitate data accountability and empower enforcement agencies.

References

1. Data Policy. Facebook, 2017, www.facebook.com/about/privacy
2. Apple Legal—Legal—Privacy Policy—Apple. Apple, Apple Legal, 2017, www.apple.com/legal/privacy/en-ww/
3. Privacy Policy—Privacy & Terms—Google. Google, 2017, www.google.com/policies/privacy
4. Privacy—Microsoft Privacy. Microsoft, 2017, privacy.microsoft.com/en-US
5. Google's ad revenue from 2001 to 2016 (in billion U.S.dollars). Statista, 2017, www.statista.com/statistics/266249/advertising-revenue-of-google
6. Tam, Donna. Facebook processes more than 500 TB of data daily. CNET, 2012, www.cnet.com/news/facebook-processes-more-than-500-tb-of-data-daily
7. J. Dean, S. Ghemawat, MapReduce: Simplified data processing on large clusters. Commun. ACM **51**(1), 107–113 (2008)
8. Privacy Shield Framework. Privacy Shield, 2017, www.privacyshield.gov/EU-US-Framework
9. Minelli, Michael, et al., *Big Data, Big Analytics: Emerging Business Intelligence and Analytic Trends for Today's Businesses*, Hoboken, Wiley, 2012, pp. 151–167
10. Your guide to AdWords. Google, 2017, support. google.com/adwords/answer/6146252hl=en&ref_topic=311 9071,3181080,3126923
11. Shute, Jeff, et al., F1: the fault-tolerant distributed RDBMS supporting Google's Ad business, in *Proceedings of the 2012 ACM SIGMOD International Conference on Management of Data*, 2012, pp. 777–778
12. Protocol Buffers. Google, 2017, developers. google.com/protocol-buffers/docs/overview
13. C. Garcia, Demystifying MapReduce. Procedia Computer Science **20**, 484–489 (2013)
14. Nakamoto, Satoshi. *Bitcoin: A Peer-to-Peer Electronic Cash System*, Bitcoin, 2008, bitcoin.org/bitcoin.pdf
15. Judmayer, Aljosha, et al, *Blocks and Chains: Introduction to Bitcoin, Cryptocurrencies, and Their Consensus Mechanisms*, 2017
16. Greenleaf, Graham. *Global Data Privacy Laws: 89 Countries, and Accelerating. Privacy Laws & Business International Report, no. 115*, 2012., papers.ssrn.com/sol3/papers.cfm?abstract_id=2000034
17. Participant Search. Export.gov, International Trade Administration, 2017, www.export.gov/participant_search
18. S. Underwood, Blockchain beyond Bitcoin. Commun. ACM **59**(11), 15–17 (2016)
19. J. Yli-Huumo et al., Where is current research on Blockchain technology?-a systematic review. PLoS One **11**(10), e0163477 (2016)
20. A. Kiayias et al., Ouroboros: A provably secure proof-of-stake Blockchain protocol. Advances in Cryptology **10401** (2017)
21. Mehmood, Abid, et al, Protection of big data privacy. Access, IEEE, vol. 4, 2016, pp. 1821–1834
22. Gao, C., & Iwane, N., A social network model for big data privacy preserving and accountability assurance. in *Consumer Communications and Networking Conference (CCNC), 2015 12th Annual IEEE*, pp. 19–22
23. Backes, Michael, et al, Data lineage in malicious environments. in *Dependable and Secure Computing, IEEE Transactions On, vol. 13, no. 2*, 2016, pp. 178–191

The Role of CAE-CDE in Cybersecurity Education for Workforce Development

Maurice Dawson, Ping Wang, and Kenneth Williams

Abstract

With a fast-growing demand for properly trained cybersecurity professionals to defend our cyber space and information systems, effective cybersecurity education programs and courses with consistent and reliable quality control and evaluation are necessary to prepare qualified workforce for the cybersecurity industry. The national Centers of Academic Excellence in Cyber Defense Education (CAE-CDE) designation program jointly sponsored by the US National Security Agency (NSA) and Department of Homeland Security (DHS) is a rigorous certification and national standard for maintaining quality of cybersecurity education. This paper explains the CAE-CDE program criteria and requirements and discusses the important role of the designation in cybersecurity education and workforce development. This paper illustrates the educational value and impact of the CAE-CDE program with case studies of three different institutions: (1) University of Missouri—St. Louis, which has obtained the CAE-CDE and Security Policy Development and Compliance Focus Area designations; (2) American Public University System, which has just completed the application for CAE-CDE; and (3) Robert Morris University, which is in the process of applying for the CAE-CDE designation.

Keywords

Cybersecurity education · Workforce development · Centers of Academic Excellence (CAE) · Cyber Defense Education (CDE) · Designation

M. Dawson
University of Missouri—St. Louis, MO, USA

P. Wang (✉)
Robert Morris University, Moon, PA, USA
e-mail: wangp@rmu.edu

K. Williams
American Public University, Charles Town, WV, USA

20.1 Introduction

Cybersecurity has been a fast-growing career field and an important area with increasing demand and opportunities for higher education. Information security analyst is only one of the cybersecurity career titles. According to U.S. Department of Labor Bureau of Labor Statistics (BLS), employment of information security analysts is projected to grow 18% from 2014 to 2024, much faster than the average growth rates of 7% for all occupations and 12% for all computer related occupations [1].

The latest cybersecurity workforce framework published by the National Initiative for Cybersecurity Education (NICE) recognizes the growing need for an integrated cybersecurity workforce with technical and non-technical roles for organizations to address their cybersecurity challenges and implement their missions and business processes connected to cyberspace. The NICE Cybersecurity Workforce Framework (NCWF) emphasizes that "academic institutions are a critical part of preparing and educating the cybersecurity workforce" [2]. A recent study shows that top U.S. universities were failing at cybersecurity education with a lack of cybersecurity requirements for graduates and a slow change in curriculum and courses [3]. However, it is encouraging to see more and more 2-year and 4-year academic institutions have started to offer cybersecurity degree programs and courses across the country. Quality assurance is needed for cybersecurity-related degree programs to meet high cybersecurity academic standards in order to prepare the graduates for the growing number of cybersecurity positions [4].

The national Centers of Academic Excellence in Cyber Defense Education (CAE-CDE) designation program jointly sponsored by the US National Security Agency (NSA) and Department of Homeland Security (DHS) is a national quality standard for certifying and maintaining high quality of cybersecurity education with rigorous and consistent requirements for program evaluation and close alignment to specific cybersecurity knowledge units. Out of over 5300 colleges and universities in the U.S., only about 200 of them have achieved the CAE-CDE designation status. Attendance at a CAE school will give students confidence in learning, and a degree from a CAE school will give employers confidence in hiring [4].

This paper will describe the background for CAE-CDE program, highlight the important application and designation criteria, and use the case study methodology to present three different cases of academic institutions with different CAE status: University of Missouri—St. Louis (UMSL), American Public University System (APUS), and Robert Morris University (RMU). The goal of the study is to illustrate the important role of the CAE designation and the application process in the cybersecurity education and workforce preparation at these institutions.

20.2 Background

The national CAE-CDE program evolved from the initial national CAE in Information Assurance Education (CAE-IAE) program started by NSA in 1998 with DHS joining as a co-sponsor in 2004, and the CAE in IA Research special designation was added in 2008 to encourage doctoral level research in cybersecurity [5]. In 2010, the CAE2Y component was created to provide the CAE designation opportunity for 2-year institutions, technical schools, and government training centers. Hence, the current CAE-CD program includes these designations: CAE2Y for 2-year institutions, and CAE-CDE for 4-year institutions, and CAE-R for doctoral universities or Department of Defense schools. All regionally accredited 2-year, 4-year and graduate level institutions in the United States are eligible to apply for the appropriate CAE designation. The designation is granted to schools which have demonstrated compliance with rigorous CAE criteria and curricula mapping to a required core set of cyber defense knowledge units (KUs) with optional Focus Areas [5].

20.2.1 Application Requirements

Eligible applicants should submit their CAE applications online, and new applicants should complete a checklist for readiness check to determine if optional application assistance, such as program and curriculum development assistance or application mentoring, is needed. An official Letter of Intent and Endorsement signed by the applicant institution's Provost or higher is a mandatory requirement to be included in online application. This letter should express institutional commitment and support for the CAE program, identify the institution's CAE point of contact, and provide information on regional accreditation and list accomplishments in the cyber defense field [6].

20.2.2 Criteria for Measurement

All applications will be reviewed and assessed by qualified independent cyber professionals and subject matter experts from CAE schools, government, and industry. New applications will be assessed by three reviewers, and applications for re-designations will be reviewed by two reviewers. Initial designation is valid for five academic years, and re-application is required for retaining the designation. The following are the latest criteria for assessing CAE applications for the 2018 cycle [6].

20.2.2.1 Cyber Academic Curriculum Path
This is to demonstrate a relevant and mature cyber curriculum program in place for at least 3 years with mappings to KUs and NCWF and student enrollment and completion data.

20.2.2.2 Student Skill Development and Assessment
This is to show student development activities and assessment in cyber defense, including syllabi, assignments, hands-on labs, competitions, and guest lectures from cybersecurity practitioners.

20.2.2.3 "Center" for Cyber Education
This is to an officially established physical or virtual center to serve as a guidance and resource center with an external advisory board for the institution's cyber curriculum and practice.

20.2.2.4 Cyber Faculty Qualifications and Courses Taught
This is to show the faculty in charge of the cyber defense program, relevant faculty publications, presentations, and faculty support student cyber activities and clubs.

20.2.2.5 Multidisciplinary Practice in Cyber Defense
This is to demonstrate that Cybersecurity is integrated additional degree programs and courses in the same institution.

20.2.2.6 Institutional Security Plan
This is to show the institution's security plans, responsible party, and its implementation of cybersecurity practices.

20.2.2.7 Cyber Outreach and Collaboration

The institution must demonstrate activities to extend cyber defense practices beyond the institution, including faculty and curriculum sharing with community schools, credit transfer agreement, participation in the CAE community, and outreach activities and industry collaboration.

20.3 Case Study: UMSL

20.3.1 School Profile, Demographics, Mission

The University of Missouri—Saint Louis (UMSL) is the largest public research university in eastern Missouri. It provides excellent learning experiences and leadership opportunities to a diverse student body whose influence on the region upon graduation is immense. UMSL is spread across 470 acres in suburban St. Louis County. UMSL's College of Business Administration is accredited by Association to Advance Collegiate Schools of Business (AACSB) International. UMSL is the region's first and only NSA/DHS designated CAE-CDE. UMSL is the only institution within the eight states that border Missouri to hold any of the 17 available focus areas.

20.3.2 Cyber Programs and Data

The cybersecurity program at UMSL is a multidisciplinary effort between the Department of Mathematics and Computer Science in the College of Arts and Sciences and the Department of Information Systems in the College of Business Administration. This collaborative approach allows students to explore the many avenues of information security and adapts to the evolving nature of the field. UMSL has created an undergraduate certificate, graduate certificate, undergraduate minor, and graduate track in cyber security. The programs were created to address the shortfall of 3800+ jobs in the Saint Louis Metropolitan Region [7]. Table 20.1 below displays the courses for the cybersecurity certificate programs in the Information Systems Department which require students take at least one computer science course.

The courses all have a hands-on component which enables students to gain more technical depth in varied programming languages, forensic tools, static code analyzers, and offensive security applications. The courses are developed to address the future of national and international cybersecurity [8]. The UMSL program heavily uses Open Source Software (OSS) as it serves as a means for students to understand low-level coding and to inspect source code for security [9]. Additionally, the labs become reusable learning objects. To enhance student learning, a physical and virtual lab environment was created with both Linux and Windows systems in which the student is given a dedicated Kali Linux virtual machine that allows them to practice offensive security operations in a controlled environment. The lab activities allow students to obtain hands-on experience in offensive and defensive security.

20.3.3 CAE Status and Accomplishments

The cybersecurity program at UMSL received $493,650 from two NSA grants within the last year. This funding will help develop lab infrastructures, enhance equipment and further advance cyber security curricula. Through two Non-Governmental Organizations (NGOs), faculty and students have also received grants of about $35,000 from John Ogonowski and Doug Bereuter Farmer-to-Farmer Program (F2F). The CAE designation also helped a faculty member to secure a 2-year Fulbright Scholar Cybersecurity Specialist Grant valued at about $20,000. Industry partners have provided more than $150,000 to the Information Systems program UMSL in the form of gifts, equipment, internships, and more.

20.4 Case Study: APUS

20.4.1 Profile, Demographics, and Mission

American Public University System (APUS) has completed preparation for submission as a Center of Academic Excellence (CAE) in Cyber Security Defense (CDE). APUS

Table 20.1 UMSL cybersecurity certificate programs

Undergraduate program	Graduate program
INFSYS 3848 Introduction to Information Security	INFSYS 6828 Principles of Information Security
INFSYS 3842 Data Networks and Security	INFSYS 6836 Management of Data Networks and Security
INFSYS 3858 Advanced Security and Information Systems	INFSYS 6858 Advanced Cybersecurity Concepts
INFSYS 3868 Secure Software Development	INFSYS 6868 Software Assurance
INFSYS 3878 Information Security Risk Management and Business Continuity	INFSYS 6878 Management of Information Security
CMP SCI 4700 Computer Forensics	CMP SCI 4700 Computer Forensics

is accredited by the Higher Learning Commission (HLC) and offers online degree and certificate programs through American Military University (AMU) and American Public University (APU). APUS is an online institution of higher learning serving the needs of military, public service and civilian communities through American Military University (AMU) and American Public University (APU). APUS is a subsidiary of American Public Education, Inc. (APEI)—the parent company that also owns Hondros College of Nursing (HCN) which serves students primarily through five Ohio campuses in Cincinnati, Cleveland, Columbus, Dayton and Toledo. Together, these institutions serve more than 85,000 adult learners worldwide and offer more than 200 degree and certificate programs in fields ranging from cybersecurity, homeland security, military studies, intelligence, criminal justice to technology, business administration, public health, nursing and liberal arts [10]. APUS was founded in 1991 as AMU. Since then, approximately 75,000 alumni have graduated from either AMU or APU. As of September 30, 2017, APUS has a student population of over 81,000. APUS student enrollment by degree level consists of 59% Bachelor's, 16% Associate, 16% Master's and 9% Certificate programs. Demographically, APUS student population includes 88% working adults with an average student age of 33 and an average class size of 9 students, and a gender ratio 64% male versus 36% female in over 200 degree and certificate programs [10].

20.4.2 APUS Cybersecurity Programs

At APUS Cybersecurity is taught as a program within the School of Science Technology Engineering and Math. Students may choose to earn cybersecurity education through certificates, Bachelor's or Master's programs. The cybersecurity undergraduate certificate examines the digital forensics tools, techniques, and methods used by cyber analysts to detect cybercrime, cyber terrorism, cyber war, cyberstalking, and cyberbullying. The Bachelor of Science in Cybersecurity provides students with both theory and know-how required to strategically assess, plan, design, and implement effective cybersecurity defenses in the public and private sectors. This Master of Science in Cybersecurity Studies takes a broad, multi-disciplinary approach to preventing and responding to large-scale cyber threats and cyber-attacks. The first half of this program provides students with a foundation in network security, cybersecurity, cybercrime, and digital forensics. The second half of this program focuses on the issues, policies, practices, and perspectives of various sectors, critical infrastructures, agencies, and disciplines, such as national security, intelligence, criminal justice, and emergency management [11].

20.4.3 CAE Status and Accomplishments

APUS started the process to achieve the status as a Center of Academic Excellence in Cyber Defense (CD) Education (CAE-CDE) in mid-2017 with a self-assessment of readiness. The assessment of the APUS readiness for the CAE-CDE designation resulted in the assignment of a mentor to assist in the completion of the application [6]. Following the result of the self-assessment and assignment of a mentor, a core group of subject matter experts (SME) supported by other members of the APUS staff was convened. This core group was managed by the APUS Provost and consisted of SMEs from the Cybersecurity program along with support from the APUS accreditation group and other department including career services, academics, and other schools throughout APUS. Weekly meetings were held with various members of the core group, including both virtual and face-to-face sessions.

The first significant session of the core group consisted of a face-to-face 2-day conference with SMEs and the assigned mentor. During this session, selection of the cybersecurity path was finalized, resulting in the selection of 12 courses from the Bachelor of Science in cybersecurity program. These 12 selected courses formed the core courses used to meet the requirements of the CAE-CDE mandatory core and optional Knowledge Units (KUs). Along with the selection of the core courses for CAE-CDE program, the group selected seven optional Knowledge Units resulting in a total of 22 KUs to measure the readiness for the APUS CAE-CDE designation. Subsequent meetings with the matrix team followed over a 6-month period to complete the CAE-CDE application. Meetings were also held with members of the NSA CAE-CDE office to include two face-to-face sessions to seek feedback and clarification on the application process. Shortly after the availability of the submission portal in September 2017, the submission process began and reached completion as determined by the mentor. The mentor's determination initiated the process of an independent pre-assessment of the APUS application that was returned with a report of no deficiencies for the mapping of the core courses to the 22 KUs and criteria. Following a final review from the APUS leadership, the final submission of the application will occur to meet the deadline of 15 January 2018.

20.4.4 Impact of CAE-CDE Application

The application of the APUS CAE-CDE application is long lasting in its impact on the programs, course, institution, and its students. The cybersecurity program saw changes to the core courses; allowing students to follow a direct path that will result in the achievement of a robust cybersecurity education, ranging from knowledge in software to database security and statistics. All students selecting the cybersecurity program are required to follow this CAE-CDE path. Courses within the CAE-CDE path were also examined to ensure the robustness of the CAE-CDE criteria.

Courses from other schools within APUS were also assessed and selected for submission of the CAE-CDE application. The selected courses resulted in a greater appreciation for the importance of cybersecurity across the APUS; initiating a call for additional cross discipline courses that further increase awareness of cybersecurity threats.

Students within APUS were also impacted by the application for CAE-CDE. As noted above all students selecting the BA in cybersecurity are now expected to complete the path; resulting in a robust cybersecurity education and an enhance career opportunity. Students completing the path can share the news of their completion with potential employers; resulting in an edge over other applicants without equal level of education.

20.5 Case Study: RMU

20.5.1 Profile, Demographics, and Mission

Robert Morris University (RMU), founded in 1921, is a selective private non-profit national university located in the Greater Pittsburgh region in western Pennsylvania. RMU has a total enrollment of 4384 undergraduate and 815 graduate students. RMU is accredited by the Middle States Commission on Higher Education and serves a diverse student population of men and women, working professional, military and veteran students, minorities, and international students. RMU provides a professionally focused education with an emphasis on engaged learning.

20.5.2 RMU Cyber Programs

Housed in RMU's School of Communications and Information Systems (SCIS), the Department of Computer and Information Systems (CIS) offers four B.S. degrees in Cyber Forensics and Information Security (BS-CFIS), Computer Information Systems (BS-CIS), Information Sciences (BS-IS), and Data Analytics (BS-DTAN). The BS-CFIS, BS-CIS, and BS-IS degree programs are all accredited by the Computing Accreditation Commission of ABET [12]. The key cybersecurity courses for the BS-CFIS and other programs include Computer and Network Security, Intro to Computer Forensics, Digital Evidence Analysis, IT Security, Control/Assurance, and Mobile Forensics.

The department also offers five M.S. degrees in Cyber Security and Information Assurance, Information Systems Management, Internet Information Systems, Information Technology Project Management, and Data Analytics, as well as one doctoral degree in Information Systems and Communications. In addition to its degree programs, CIS offers undergraduate and graduate certificate programs in Information Systems, Mobile Forensics and Security, and Enterprise Systems. Most CIS degree and certificate programs are offered in both traditional and online formats.

20.5.3 CAE Status and Accomplishments

RMU is in the process of preparing to submit the application for a CAE-CDE designation. RMU has submitted a New Applicant Inventory to NSA. Based on the review of the New Applicant Inventory submitted, RMU was assessed to be within 1 year of applying for the CAE designation. Hence, RMU was referred to the mentoring program with designated mentor as part of the Application Assistance Program (APP) funded by the National Science Foundation. RMU has confirmed its participation in the APP program with a designated Mentee Point of Contact to apply for the CAE-CDE designation. The application submission is projected to be completed within 1 year. RMU leadership is very supportive of this pursuit, and faculty and students are looking forward to enhanced cybersecurity programs and courses through the CAE-CDE application and designation.

20.6 Conclusions

This paper explains the rigorous quality control criteria and important role of the NSA/DHS CAE-CDE designation in cybersecurity education and workforce development. Three case studies of different institutions with different CAE status are presented to illustrate the importance of the CAE designation in enhancing cybersecurity education at these institutions. Updates to the CAE designation and application status for the two applicant schools with more specific data and accomplishments will be presented and discussed in future research reports.

References

1. U. S. Department of Labor, Occupational outlook handbook. (2015), https://www.bls.gov/ooh/computer-and-information-technology/information-security-analysts.htm#tab-6
2. NICE (National Initiative for Cybersecurity Education), NICE cybersecurity workforce framework (SP800-181). (2017), https://csrc.nist.gov/publications/detail/sp/800-181/final
3. S.K. White, Top U.S. universities failing at cybersecurity education. CIO. (2016), https://www.cio.com/article/3060813/it-skills-training/top-u-s-universities-failing-at-cybersecurity-education.html

4. NICCS (National Initiative for Cybersecurity Careers and Studies), National Centers of Academic Excellence (CAE). (2017), https://niccs.us-cert.gov/formal-education/national-centers-academic-excellence-cae
5. NSA (National Seucrity Agency), National Centers of Academic Excellence in Cyber Defense. (2016), https://www.nsa.gov/resources/educators/centers-academic-excellence/cyber-defense/
6. NIETP (National IA Education & Training Programs), CAE-CDE criteria for measurement 2018. (2018), https://www.iad.gov/NIETP/CAERequirements.cfm
7. CyberSeek, Cybersecurity supply/demand heat map. (n.d.), http://cyberseek.org/heatmap.html. Accessed 15 Dec 2017
8. M. Dawson, M. Omar, J. Abramson, D. Bessette, The future of national and international security on the internet, in *Information Security in Diverse Computing Environments*, ed. By A. Kayem, C. Meinel, (IGI Global, Hershey, 2014), pp. 149–178. https://doi.org/10.4018/978-1-4666-6158-5.ch009
9. M. Dawson, I. Al Saeed, J. Wright, F. Onyegbula, Open source software to enhance the STEM learning environment, in *Handbook of Research on Education and Technology in a Changing Society*, ed. By V. Wang, (IGI Global, Hershey, 2014), pp. 569–580. https://doi.org/10.4018/978-1-4666-6046-5.ch042
10. APEI (American Public Education, Inc.), (n.d.), http://www.americanpubliceducation.com/phoenix.zhtml?c=214618&p=irol-homelanding
11. AMU (American Military University), (n.d.), http://www.amu.apus.edu/
12. ABET, ABET Accredited Program Search, (n.d.), http://main.abet.org/aps/Accreditedprogramsearch.aspx

Shay Gueron and Regev Shemy

Abstract

This paper describes some software optimizations for the classical Data Encryption Standard (DES) cipher DES applicable for modern processor architectures that have SIMD instructions. Performance is gained by processing several messages in parallel, compared to processing single messages serially. An added value that the proposed optimizations offer is that the resulting implementations are also side channel protected, unlike other implementations that are found in open source libraries. For comparison, when measured on the latest Intel server processor (Architecture Codename Skylake), our side channel safe implementation is 3.2× faster than that of OpenSSL.

Keywords

Component · DES · DOCSIS · IPSEC · Software optimizations · 3-DES · Side-channel protection

21.1 Introduction

The proliferation of the block cipher AES [1] together with the dedicated processor instruction that speed up AES encryption by more than an order of magnitude, make AES the most ubiquitous cipher in use. Nevertheless, some legacy systems that use outdated ciphers still need support. We are interested here in the classical Data Encryption Standard (DES) [2], and its 3-DES [3] variant, used in either ECB or CBC modes of operation [4], that are still used in some systems. One example is DOCSIS (Data Over Cable Service Interface Specifications) [5].

S. Gueron (✉)
Department of Mathematics, University of Haifa, Haifa, Israel

R. Shemy
Intel Corporation, Israel Development Center, Haifa, Israel

In general, DES is practically replaced by the more modern cipher AES. Thus, software performance of DES/3-DES is an attractive target for optimization only for better support of legacy systems that still use DES. We note that the performance of AES is accelerated by processor instructions AES-NI [6, 7], which are by now ubiquitous. This makes DES is significantly slower than AES. For example, on the latest architecture Intel Xeon Phi Processor 7230, the DES performance, in CBC mode is 42.77 cycles per byte (C/B hereafter). By comparison, on the same platform, AES (in CBC mode) performs at 2.63 C/B. Similarly, in ECB mode, DES performs at 40.9 C/B, and AES performs at 0.63 C/B. These were measured for a message of 8 KB, using the latest version 1.0.2k of OpenSSL [8].

We point out that the block size of DES is 64 bits (whereas AES operates on blocks of 128 bits). As such, the number of blocks that can be encrypted using the same key is limited to at most 2^{32}. Furthermore, Some cryptanalytic results on DES are reported in [9–14].

In this paper, we present a new method for software implementation of DES in ECB and CBC modes, when multiple messages are processed in parallel. We show that our implementation also has the security advantage of being resistant to side channel attacks. Nonetheless, while our solution described on DES, it is relevant for 3-DES, which is more practical and used today in a real system.

21.2 Preliminaries

DES is defined in the specifications [2–4]. We describe it only briefly here, as needed for the rest of the paper.

DES is a block cipher that operates on a block of 64 bit, using a cipher key of 56 bits (technically, the key is embedded in a 64-bit container, where the 8 extra bits are used as parity bits). The construction is called a Feistel cipher.

Let X be a plaintext block, let Y be the resulting ciphertext, and let K be the key. DES consists of *16* identical rounds (Gj), where, for j = *1, 2, ..., 16*, round j uses round key K_j. Each round key K_j has *48* bits, and is derived from the cipher key K, using some key schedule procedure. The key schedule is independent of the processing of the data, and is not described here. The input X goes through a sequence *19* back-to-back transformations, each one producing a 64-bit output from a 64-bit input. The input for each transformation is the output of the previous one, where X counts as the first input, and Y is the output of the last transformation (IP^{-1} in our case), as follows:

$$Y = IP^{-1} \circ T \circ G_{16} \circ G_{15} \circ \cdots \circ G_1 \circ IP\,(X)$$

The *3* "outer" transformations (IP, IP^{-1}, T) do not depend on the key: IP, called "initial permutation", is a fixed (known), IP^{-1} is its inverse, and T is a transformation that switches the position of the left *32* bits of its state, with that of the right *32* bits. To describe the rounds, let L_{j-1} and R_{j-1} denote the left and right halves of the input to round G_j, and let Lj and Rj denote the output of the round. Then,

$$L_j = R_{j-1}, \quad R_j = L_{j-1} \oplus f\left(R_{j-1}, K_j\right)$$

where f denotes the "Core Function" of DES. It operates on two inputs: one (the right half of the state) of *32* bits and the other (K_j) of *48* bits, and outputs *32* bits. It consists of *3* elements: Expansion (E), Substitution (S) and Permutation (P). The Expansion is a fixed function that takes a 32-bit input and expands it to *48* bits. The function computes the 48-bit result of E (R_{j-1}) $\oplus K_j$. These *48* bits are viewed as *8* 6-bit elements, which pass through *8* (different) S-boxes. Each of these S-boxes represents some nonlinear function, which is a lookup table that maps a *6* bits input to a *4* bits output. The details of all the functions and transformations are found in the above specifications. CBC mode processes a plaintext message of m blocks $P_1, P_2, \ldots P_m$ and produces m ciphertext blocks $C_1, C_2, \ldots, C_m$ by $C_j = DES\,(P_j \oplus C_{j-1})$, j = *1,2, ..., m*, where, by definition, $C_0 = IV$.

We point out the fact that side channel attacks that exploit information from memory access patterns. Therefore, if the DES S-boxes are lookup tables that reside in memory, and software accesses directly, the resulting implementation is considered susceptible to side channel attacks. Indeed, this is the case with the OpenSSL implementation. The same is true, of course, for AES, the presence of AES-NI eliminates the need to use lookup tables for AES (Fig. 21.1).

21.3 Multi Block Approach for DES

Processing multiple independent messages in parallel, using modern SIMD architectures, improves the resulting performance significantly. Examples with some cryptographic algorithms are shown in [15–17] for hashing. Using SIMD is not the only way to introduce software pipelining in order to turn latency bounded computations to throughput bounded computations. For example, consider AES-CBC encryption, which is essentially a serial mode. References [6, 7] show how to process multiple messages in parallel with this mode (in the presence of AES-NI), to get the performance of parallelizable modes of operation. Reference [18, 20] shows a technique that gains a *3×* speedup factor for CRC32 computations when a single message is broken (logically) to three chunks, computations are done on these chunks independently so that the processor's pipeline is filled up, and

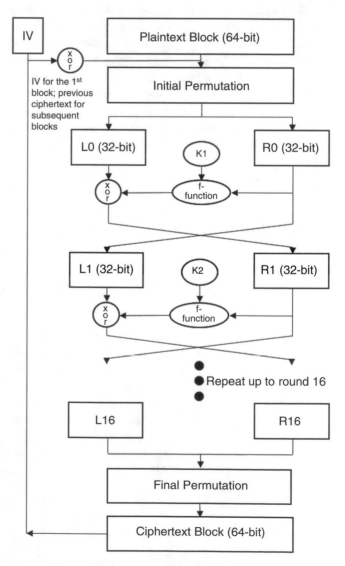

Fig. 21.1 Outline: DES in CBC mode

in the end, the three results are combined to a single CRC32 value by using some mathematical transformation.

We show here how to apply this approach, which we call "Multi Block DES", for DES (and 3-DES) cipher. Our method processes several messages in parallel, at the cost of some added overhead of "transposing" the inputs when they are consumed from memory, in order to make them ready for processing with SIMD instructions. Then, the SIMD capabilities of modern processors can be leveraged. The overall result is significant performance gains.

Transposing: To illustrate the transposing overhead, consider a single message M, pointed to by the pointer p. To encrypt M in CBC mode, it is possible to consume consecutive blocks (of *64* bits) and process them. Now, consider two message M1, M2, with two pointers p1, p2. Suppose that we wish to encrypt both messages in parallel, using a SIMD architecture with 128-bit registers (xmm's). This requires placing two 64-bit blocks B1, B2, of M1, M2, respectively, in a single xmm register, say xmm2. B1 and B2 are read (loaded) from different pointers, into registers, say xmm0, xmm1, populating the low halves of these registers. Subsequently, we need to appropriately shuffle the two 64-bit contents of xmm0, xmm1 into the single xmm2. The following is a code sequence is an example:

vmovdqu (%rsi), %xmm0

vmovdqu (%rdi), %xmm1
vpshufd $0x4e, %xmm1, %xmm1
vpblendd $0x0c, %xmm0, %xmm1, %xmm2

Of course, a more efficient implementation would read two blocks from each pointer, into xmm1, xmm2, and shuffle the contents of these registers into two xmm registers with a similar software flow. The following is a code sequence is an example.

vmovdqu (%rsi), %xmm0
vmovdqu (%rdi), %xmm1
vpunpcklqdq %xmm0, %xmm1, %xmm2
vpunpckhqdq %xmm0,%xmm1, %xmm3

In the context of DES, the algorithm actually processes two halves of the block independently. Denote $B1 = [b1, a1]$ and $B2 = [b2, a2]$, where a1, a2, b1, b2 are the 32-bit halves. An efficient implementation would place these halves in two xmm registers, xmm0, xmm1, as

$$xmm0 = [0, 0, b2, b1], xmm1 = [0, 0, a2, a1]$$

Obviously, it is more efficient to read in *4* blocks and deposit populate the respective halves in *2* xmm registers, in a way that populates them entirely (Fig. 21.2).

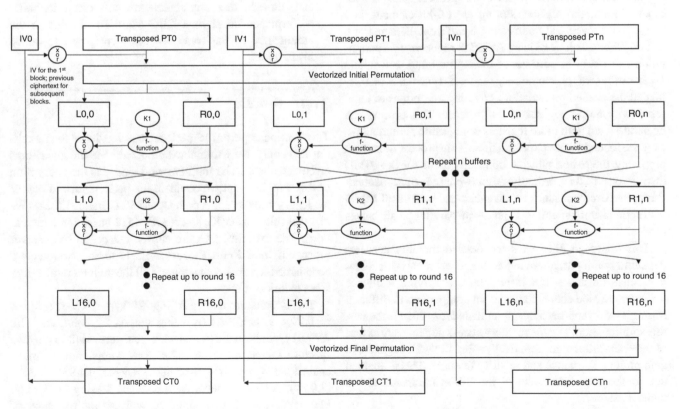

Fig. 21.2 Outline: DES in CBC mode, with a Multi Block implementation

```
vmovdqu (%rsi), %xmm0
vmovdqu (%rdi), %xmm1
vpunpckldq %xmm0, %xmm1, %xmm2
vpunpckhdq %xmm0, %xmm1, %xmm3
```

SIMD processing: Having the input organized in halves blocks on several registers, allows the encryption process to be done in parallel using SIMD instructions. Implementing the Initial Permutation and Final Permutation on the registers is easily done using shift, logical AND and XOR instructions done using SIMD on double word chunks (32- bit, half block data). The "f" core function implementation consists of three main phases. The first phase, E-phase is done using similar SIMD instructions. Both S-phase and P-phase, requires constants to be tailored to their use model. S-phase includes substation of each 6-bit of input to 4-bit according to the 6-bit element of the block. In order to prevent each element of each block from accessing S-box table serially, we load part of the S-box table to a register, permuting several elements of several different blocks in parallel. Result register of this permutation, is eventually blended in using mask registers, deciding whether the permutation was done with the correct part of the S-box table. Iterating through all part of the S-box table, resulting in a final result registers, with all results blended between all result registers, covering all S-box table constants. This technique, available using Intel AVX512 Extension. Using AVX512, we are able to process up to 8 halves blocks in a single register, storing each 6-bit element, in a single bytes, eventually permuting 8 different elements of 8 different halves blocks. Using AVX512 registers, this permutation can load big portions of the S-box table, and within 16 iterations of permutations, whole S-box table is fully loaded the needed permutations covering all options of input result with output register of the S-phase. This process can be parallelized with more registers doing same permutations, over the loaded S-box part each time. This process done with preparing the S-box table of constants to fit for the SIMD instructions used accordingly. After S-phase is done, using of P-box prepared constants in advanced and additional SIMD instructions implementing P-phase in parallel to all halves blocks.

This approach eliminates the needed memory accesses depending on input, removing all branches or cache accesses that relies on any secret information, supplying resilience for software side channel attacks. In comparison to different Multi Blocks approaches implemented on other schemes, this solution eliminate the memory access dependency as part of the encryption algorithm itself, using the wide registers to gain both performance and security features. This is enabled due to the total small size of the S-box compared to the registers size.

Remark 1: The technique detailed here is using Intel latest AVX512 Extension, found on architecture codename Skylake Server. This technique could be downgraded to fit for AVX2 extension, first introduced on Intel architecture codename Haswell. Using AVX2, will result in less parallel streams processed, bigger number of iterations done on processing S-phase of the "f" core function and additional costs. These additional costs withdraw the use of DES CBC mode of operation using Multi Block approach from performance view. Additional security benefit is till gained and describes later on this paper.

Remark 2: The use of AVX512, as similar to remark 1, is first introduced on Intel server processors (Intel Architecture Codename Skylake). Additional future AVX512 instructions, announced to public, including AVX512 VBMI instructions. These future instructions will give extra performance boost to the technique used in S-phase using AVX512 instructions, allowing byte permutations over AVX512 register (512 bit).

Remark 3: The method described in this section us referred to DES CBC mode of operation using Multi Block approach. Similar implementation, excluding the transpose costs, could be implemented on DES ECB mode of operation for single input data stream. DES ECB mode of operation will require additional instructions splitting the blocks in halves and uniting them in the end, though, this implementation will result in better performance boost than CBC Multi Block, due to the redundancy of the transpose costs compared to added instructions.

21.4 Results

This section reports the performance results of our study. For this study, we wrote new optimized code the algorithms discussed above. The measure workload was the encryption of 8 KB inputs, and we compare the performance to that of the legacy code as appears in OpenSSL (version 1.0.2k). We report results for AVX2 and for AVX512 based implementations. The experiments were carried out on an Intel server processer, Intel Xeon Processor E3-1230-v5 (Architecture codename Skylake), that supports all the architectural extensions mentioned above.

The Results are shown in Fig. 21.3. A slowdown factor of $0.79\times$ is achieved by using the AVX2 solution. With AVX512, additional ISA and wider registers result in positive speedup factor, reaching $3.2\times$. The comparison is made against the legacy code, used in the recent OpenSSL version (1.0.2k). All experiments were conducted using Intel Xeon PHI Processor 7230, configured with static frequency of 1.3 GHz. We note that our code executes in constant time: it

Fig. 21.3 Optimized DES implementations through Multi Block processing. Measurements taken on input messages of size *8192* Bytes (total). The results of code that leverages AVX2 and AVX512 are compared to the results of the code implemented on OpenSSL (1.0.2k)

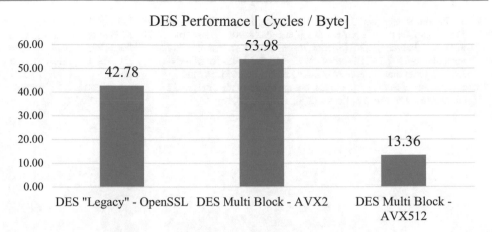

	OpenSSL DES	AVX2 Multi Block DES	AVX512 Multi Block DES
Speedup	1x	0.79x	3.2x

does not use lookup tables for computing the results of the S-boxes. It is therefore side channel protected. Additional DES Multi Block AVX2 solution can be implemented, gaining extra performance speedup but lacks side channel protection and therefore is not discussed on this paper.

21.5   Conclusions

The solution described here, provides a new implementation for the legacy cipher DES. It offers a side channel protected implementation which is *3.2×* faster than the (unprotected) implementation of OpenSSL. Our code was published and is now part of the Intel IPSEC MB public code library [19].

The new approach can be adapted and adjusted to fit for wider area of new solution and defense mechanisms for protecting versus software side channel attacks, eventually providing a new methodology of using the updated hardware and architectures used in the market.

Acknowledgements This research was supported by the Israel Science Foundation (grant No. 1018/16), by the BIU Center for Research in Applied Cryptography and Cyber Security, in conjunction with the Israel National Cyber Bureau in the Prime Minister's Office, and by the Center for Cyber Law & Policy at the University of Haifa.

References

1. National Institue of Standards and Technology, Advance Encryption Standard (AES), FIPS Publication 197, November, (2001), https://csrc.nist.gov/csrc/media/publications/fips/197/final/documents/fips-197.pdf
2. National Burea of Standards, Data Encryption Standard, U.S, Department of Commerece, FIPS pub. 47, January, (1977)
3. National Institue of Standards and Technology, Data Encryption Standard (DES), FIPS Publication 46–3, October, (1999)
4. National Institue of Standards and Technology, DES Modes of Operation, FIPS publications 81, December, (1980), https://csrc.nist.gov/csrc/media/publications/fips/81/archive/1980-12-02/documents/fips81.pdf
5. DOCSIS 3.1 Specfication, September, (2017), https://apps.cablelabs.com/specification/CM-SP-MULPIv3.1
6. S. Gueron, Intel Advanced Encryption Standard (AES) instructions set (Rev. 3), Intel Software Network, (2010), http://software.intel.com/en-us/articles/advanced-encryption-standard-aes-instructions-set/
7. S. Gueron, Intel's New AES Instructions for Enhanced Performance and Security. Fast Software Encryptiom, 16th International Workshop (FSE 2009). Lecture Notes in Computer Science: 5656, (2009), pp. 51–66
8. OpenSSL: The Open Source toolkit for SSL/TLS, project webpage, http://www.openssl.org
9. E. Biham, A. Biryukov, An improvement of Davies' attack on DES. J. Cryptol. **10**(3), 195–206 (1997)
10. E. Biham, A. Shamir, Differential cryptanalysis of DES-like cryptosystems. J. Cryptol. **4**(1), 3–72 (1991)
11. E. Biham, A. Shamir, *Differential Cryptanalysis of the Data Encryption Standard* (Springer, Berlin, 1993). ISBN 0-387-97930-1, ISBN 3-540-97930-1
12. J. Kelsey, B. Schneier, D. Wagner, C. Hall, Side channel cryptanalysis of product ciphers, in *Proc. European Symp. Research in Computer Security (ESORICS '98)*, (1998), pp. 97–110
13. P. Kocher, Timing attacks on implementations of Diffie-Hellman, RSA, DSS and other systems, in *Adavance in Cryptology–CRYPTO '96 Proceedings*, (Springer, 1996), pp. 104–113
14. S. Kumar, C. Paar, J. Pelzl, G. Pfeiffer, A. Rupp, M. Schimmler, *How to Break DES for Euro 8,980, 2nd Workshop on Special-purpose Hardware for attacking Cryptographic Systems—SHARCS 2006*, Cologne, Germany, April, 2006
15. S. Gueron, V. Krasnov, Simultaneous hashing of multiple messages. J. Inf. Secur. **3**, 319–325 (2012)
16. S. Gueron, R. Shemy, [OpenSSL Patch]: Accelerating Multi (MB) CBC SHA256 on architectures that support AVX512 instructions set, January, (2016), http://openssl.6102.n7.nabble.com/openssl-org-4221-PATCH-Accelerating-Multi-Block-MB-CBC-SHA256-on-architectures-that-support-AVX512-it-td62058.html

17. S. Gueron, R. Shemy, [OpenSSL Patch]: Multi Block (MB) SHA 512 for x86_64 Architectures that support AVX2/ AVX512 instructions set, February, (2016), http://openssl.6102.n7. nabble.com/openssl-org-4307-PATCH-Multi-Block-MB-SHA512- for-x86-64-Architectures-that-support-AVX2-AVX512-instrt-td63716.html

18. S. Gueron, Speeding up crc32c computations with intel crc32 instructions. Inf. Process. Lett. **112**(5), 179–185 (2012)

19. Intel IPSEC MB Library, https://github.com/01org/intel-ipsec-mb

20. S. Gueron, V. Krasnov, Fast implementation of AES-CRT mode for AVX capable x86-64 processors, March, (2013), http://rt.openssl.org/Ticket/Display.html?id=3021&user=guest&pass= guest

Part II

Networking and Wireless Communications

Design and Development of VXLAN Based Cloud Overlay Network Monitoring System and Environment

22

Shahzada Khurram and Osman Ghazali

Abstract

Now a day's individuals and organizations are adopting cloud at a faster rate, due to which cloud traffic is increasing at a pace which is difficult to manage (Mamta Madan, Int J Cloud Comput Serv Archit 4:9–20, 2014). The virtualization plays a vital role to implement cloud computing but virtualization technologies add an additional level of complexity for the consumers and cloud providers. Cloud overlay network technology introduces the same visibility challenges as most exist for encapsulation methods. In this paper we present Virtual eXtensible LANs (VXLAN) based packet capturing and filtering mechanism for cloud overlay networks. This mechanism can provide cloud users and providers, detail visibility and information of VXLAN based network traffic traversing in cloud environment. Furthermore, we present design and development of real time VXLAN based virtual cloud overlay network environment. The proposed mechanism was tested in the Linux operating system based virtual environment.

Keywords

Cloud · Monitoring · Overlay networks · Vxlan · Flow monitoring

22.1 Introduction

A multi-tenant nature of cloud [1] can be challenging for smooth management in term of performance constraints and quality of service because the services of the cloud are scalable, flexible and on demand [2]. Which leads to manage physical and as well as virtual resources of cloud infrastructure. Since the growth of cloud computing increased, network traffic also growing rapidly in cloud data centers, which leads to increase the number of virtual machines deployment. Virtual private network (VPN) and virtual local area network (VLAN) are examples of network virtualization. Network virtualization has some limitations and issues. Though, VLAN can only identify a maximum of 4094 virtual LANs, IP addressing and VLAN are often assigned to virtual machines. To overcome this limitation, overlay network technology introduced into a cloud environment. Overlay networks are similar to network virtualization, but with different functionality. Overlay network technology is used in cloud data centers to effectively isolate multiple tenants and automate network-wide virtual machine migration that fully satisfy the requirements of large cloud service providers and enterprises.

A few standards have been proposed to enable overlay networks, which include Virtual extensible LANs (VXLAN) [3], Network Virtualization with GRE (NVGRE) [4] and Stateless Transport Tunneling Protocol (STT) [5]. These overlay protocols use different encapsulation techniques to overcome the current network limitations.

Since cloud overlay network technology is still new and emerging, thus, only mature and widely adopted VXLAN technology in cloud data centers [6] is considered in this research paper for cloud overlay network monitoring.

22.1.1 Cloud Monitoring

Monitoring is the process of observing and tracking applications as well as resources at run time [7]. Cloud monitoring become an essential part to service providers for providing service assurance based on quality of services for managing cloud network resources. Moreover, users require network performance statistics, especially in virtual network envi-

S. Khurram (✉) · O. Ghazali
Department of Computer Science, School of Computing, Universiti Utara Malaysia, Kedah, Malaysia
e-mail: osman@uum.edu.my

© Springer International Publishing AG, part of Springer Nature 2018
S. Latifi (ed.), *Information Technology – New Generations*, Advances in Intelligent Systems and Computing 738,
https://doi.org/10.1007/978-3-319-77028-4_22

ronment, as network performance has a direct impact on perceived quality of the application viewed by the users. To manage large and complex cloud network infrastructure, the monitoring system should be able to precisely capture its state [8]. Few studies deal with monitoring in cloud computing environment [2] and these different monitoring efforts may focus on different aspects of cloud monitoring. However, none of them monitor overlay cloud computing services or performance. Unfortunately, cloud network monitoring features are often limited, which means they can miss out on major performance issues in the cloud overlay network environment. To keep a close watch on cloud networks and catch potential problems, a cloud overlay network monitoring tool for track and report more in-depth on performance is needed [2].

In this paper, we present VXLAN based cloud overlay network monitoring system and real time VXLAN based cloud environment. Proposed monitoring system can capture the VXLAN packets and differentiate from other network traffic. The remainder of this paper proceeds as follows. Section 22.2 describes how to build a VXLAN based cloud network environment and its components. Section 22.3 explains the detail of proposed VXLAN based monitoring system. Section 22.4 present experimental results and analysis. Finally, Sect. 22.5 concludes the paper and briefs future research direction in cloud monitoring.

22.2 Building VXLAN Based Cloud Overlay Network Environment

In this section, we present design and development of real time VXLAN based cloud overlay network environment. Since VXLAN is new technology in cloud overlay network environment therefore, no simulation tool available to create a complete VXLAN based cloud overlay network environment to fulfill our monitoring requirement. Hence, the required components were studied in detail to build a real time cloud overlay network scenario. It has also been emphasized that the mechanism developed as part of this research must be extensible to single cloud environment to multi cloud environment. It is necessary to mention here the complete modeling of cloud overlay network environment is built at single computer machine with virtualized hypervisor and required necessary components.

22.2.1 Required Components to Build the Lab

In order to build a cloud overlay network environment, first we need to build a cloud underlay network. We

came up with a topology that could be easily demonstrate VXLAN based cloud network environment as presented in Fig. 22.1.

We have created three servers on virtualized hypervisor with different network segments on underlay networks, two servers SERVER-1 and SERVER-2 used for multi–tenancy environment for VM to VM communications respectively third server act as router to connect both SERVER-1 and SERVER-2 for underlay network communication to each other. For all the servers we installed Linux Ubuntu 16.04 Server edition [9] with minimum packages. We have created two different IP network segments 172.16.10.0/24 for SERVER-1(Kuala Lumpur) and 172.16.20.0/24 for SERVER-2 (New York) to connect with the SERVER-3 (Network Cloud) for routing purpose to each other underlay network communication. Figure 22.2 demonstrate the detail underlay network connectivity to all server machines.

22.2.2 Modeling Cloud Based Overlay Network

In order to build a VXLAN based cloud overlay network environment on the underlay network. We selected Open vSwtich [10] to build a VXLAN based cloud overlay network. Open vSwitch is the only open source switch which is supported VXLAN technology and IPFIX [11]. It is also operate as a soft switch running within the hypervisor. On other hand to create a multi-tenant cloud environment where each VM isolated with other VM to keep the isolated communication. We need to build virtual network and virtual machines within the environment to communicate with each other. Therefore, we selected mininet [12] emulator to create instant virtual hosts, virtual network links, virtual switches and controller for flexible custom routing using openFlow [13]. It is also supported Open vSwitch within the hypervisor environment. Mininet is an open source emulator software and its VM virtual machines based on standard Linux network software.

We installed mininet with Open vSwitch on both servers SERVER-1 and SERVER-2 in order to create a virtual network environment for cloud overlay network. Furthermore, we also installed python [14] scripting language in order to build a custom based virtual network topology. Figure 22.3 presents the detail version of software installed on both servers.

Following are the components we used in mininet to build the lab environment as presented in Fig. 22.1.

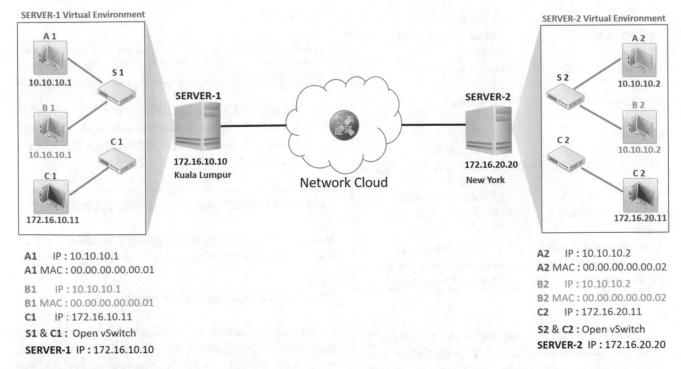

Fig. 22.1 Cloud overlay network environment

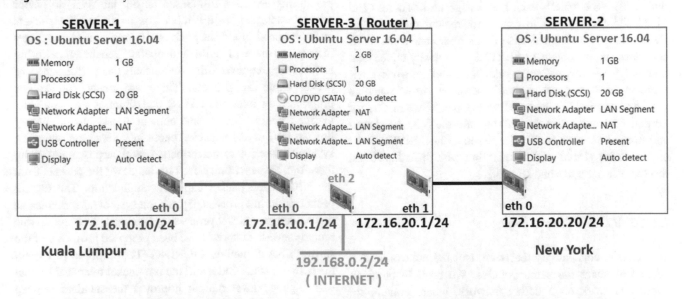

Fig. 22.2 Cloud underlay network environment

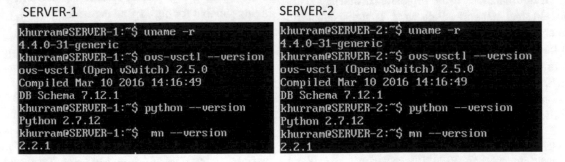

Fig. 22.3 Installed software detail

SERVER-1	SERVER-2
Virtual Machines (VM)	**Virtual Machines (VM)**
A1, B1, C1	A2, B2, C2
Open vSwitch (OVS)	**Open vSwitch (OVS)**
S1, C1	S2, C2
IP Address	**IP Address**
A1—10.0.0.1	A2—10.0.0.2
B1—10.0.0.1	B2—10.0.0.2
C1—172.16.10.11	C2—172.16.20.11
Media Access Control (MAC address)	**Media Access Control (MAC address)**
A1—00:00:00:00:00:01	A2—00:00:00:00:00:02
B1—00:00:00:00:00:01	B2—00:00:00:00:00:02
Links	**Links**
A1 machine connect with S1	A2 machine connect with S2
B1 machine connect with S1	B2 machine connect with S2
C1 machine connect with C1	C2 machine connect with C2

In order to match our lab topology, we created two virtual machines on SERVER-1 with hosts names A1 and B1 for VXLAN communication, both hosts are connected with Open vSwitch S1, each host assign an IP address and MAC address in order to easily understand the topology. Furthermore, we assigned same IP addresses and same MAC addresses on each hosts at SERVER-1 to easily understand how VXLAN technology works at cloud network environment. However, we created one other virtual machine with host name C1 connected with Open vSwitch C1, for normal communication to differentiate the VXLAN based and normal network traffic. On the hand at SERVER-2 we created same virtual environment, but with different virtual machines host names and IP address.

22.2.3 VXLAN Tunneling

To achieve connectivity between isolated networks that needed to share the same policies. We need to build an overlay network on underlay network, where tunnels are created between the hypervisors in different locations allowing virtual machines to be provisioned independently from the physical network. Following is the mechanism to create an overlay virtual Layer 2 network on top of the physical Layer 3, based on VXLAN tunnels between Open vSwitch bridges running on separate machines SERVER-1 and SERVER-2. Following configuration added on Open vSwitchs on mininet at both servers.

SERVER-1:

```
sh ovs-vsctl add-port s1 vtep – set interface vtep type = vxlan
option:remote_ip  =  172.16.20.20  option:key  =  flow
ofport_request = 10
```

SERVER-2:

```
sh ovs-vsctl add-port s2 vtep – set interface vtep type = vxlan
option:remote_ip  =  172.16.10.10  option:key  =  flow
ofport_request = 10
```

We added VXLAN Tunnel Endpoint (VTEP) services on both Open vSwitchs to communicate with each other remotely and also added flow forwarding port functionality using OpenFlow controller.

22.3 VXLAN Based Monitoring System

In this section we describe the proposed monitoring system with detail packet capturing process and filtering techniques.

22.3.1 Packet Capturing Process

Packet capturing performed commonly in two modes in-line mode and mirroring mode. Selection of mode to capture the packets depends on bandwidth, type of analysis and monitoring environment. Based on our lab scenario in our case we selected in-line mode for capturing the packets on high speed cloud network environment. It is necessary to mention here to build and operate reliable monitoring architecture required fully understand the performance of packet capturing process. There are many applications programming interface (APIs) and libraries are available, in open source Linux environment most reliable library libpcap [15] used for packet capturing. Since the operating system network stack performed general purpose networking therefore, libpacp library used for handover the packets from the NIC to the packet capturing application. The overall packet capturing process depends on system performance as they added pre-packet processing overhead. To speedup this process several methods have been proposed [16]. One of the software based method PF_RING [17] proposed to bypass the network stack and avoid the pre-packet overhead to deal with higher packet rate. It improves the standard libpcap mechanism. It allows fast packet capturing mechanism without losing any packet loss and processing load. It is highly suitable for high speed networks.

22.3.2 Packet Filtering Process

Packet filtering is the technique which defines what kind of action perform on every single packet received from the observation point for the selection of particular packets. The role of packet filtering defined in RFC 5475 "separate all the packets having a certain property from those not having it" [18]. This step is adopted for selection of interested packets

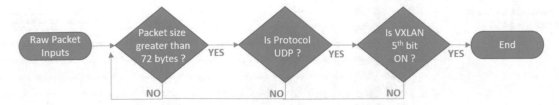

Fig. 22.4 VXLAN based packet filtering mechanism

in our case VXLAN (Virtual eXtensible LANs) packets. Typically, this type of packet filtering required property match filtering technique; a packet is selected if specific fields within packet are equal to a specified value or inside a specified value range [18]. In order to design the filtering technique of cloud overlay packets we need to understand the complete structure of VXLAN packet format which is defined in RFC 7348 [3].

22.3.3 VXLAN Based Packet Filtering Mechanism

Since the cloud overlay is a new technology and packets are encapsulated thus the most critical step is retrieving and sampling the VXLAN packets. Therefore, we proposed new technique to inspect the every captured packet and select only VXLAN packets. All packets are read directly from the observation point with time stamped. Packets are inspected based on header instead of whole payload inspection, to reduce the overhead and minimize the load of packet selection stage. Thus selected packet becomes an element of the output packet stream (Fig. 22.4).

The pseudocode of VXLAN based packet selection is given in Algorithm 22.1. The pseudocode describes the implementation of this filtering mechanism.

22.3.4 Dataset for Simulation

Under Cloud overlay network monitoring mechanism following standard data set used for simulation. Traffic generated through well-known network tool iperf [19] between different virtual machines for monitoring performance measurement in different conditions. Refer to the Fig. 22.1, traffic generated between different network segments based on following dataset.

Transmission duration: 60 min.
Protocol: ICMP
VM-A1 → VM-A2
Sending rate: 200 bytes/s
VM-B1 ← VM-B2
Sending rate: 100 bytes/s
VM-C1 → VM-C2
Sending rate: 200 bytes/s

Algorithm 22.1 VXLAN based packet selection algorithm

OPcount is initialized to zero
Arrival of new packet P_i
Open the new packet Pi and check the packet size
if
    If (the packet size <72 bytes) then
    No action
End if
Else
    If (the packet size >72 bytes) then
    Lookup the protocol
    If (the packet protocol! = UDP) then
    No action
End Else
Else
    If (the packet protocol = UDP) then
    Open the VXLAN header of the packet P_i
    Lookup the 5th bit
    If (5th bit is! = 1) then
    No action
End Else
Else
    If (5th bit is = 1) then
    Select the packet and
    Retrieve the 24-bit value of VNI
    Increment OPcount
End Else

22.4 Experimental Results

To illustrate the difference between standard flow monitoring and proposed VXLAN based flow monitoring for overlay cloud networks. We used dataset refer to Sect. 22.3.4 and simulate the monitoring. We captured the traffic in-line mode using open source tool yaf [20]. Yaf has ability to capture live traffic from an interface using pcap into bidirectional flows, then exports those flows to IPFIX collecting processes. We develop a plugin, based on proposed algorithm, for VXLAN based traffic capturing of cloud overlay networks.

The experiment results shown in Figs. 22.5 and 22.6 with standard monitoring tool which is only capture the total number of packets and bandwidth but could not identify the VXLAN based tunnel traffic. The Figs. 22.7 and 22.8 shows

Fig. 22.5 Standard monitoring with packet capture detail

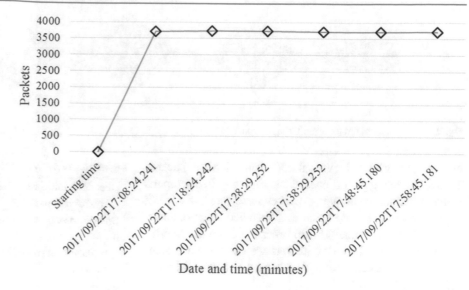

Fig. 22.6 Standard monitoring with bandwidth detail

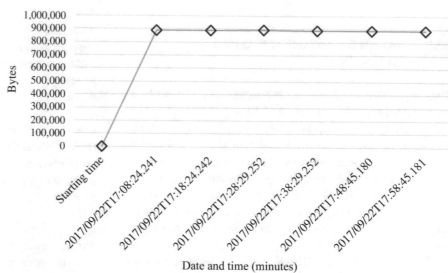

Fig. 22.7 VXLAN monitoring with packet capture detail

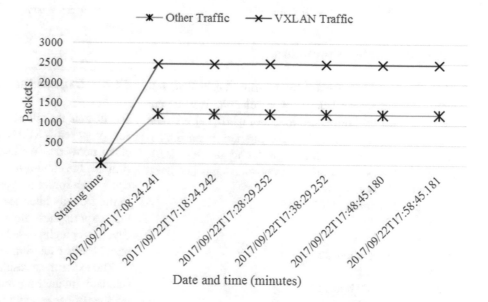

Fig. 22.8 VXLAN monitoring with bandwidth detail

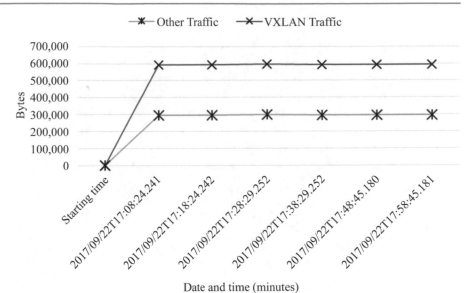

22.5 Conclusion and Future Work

In this paper we presented VXLAN based monitoring system and its environment. Proposed monitoring system can provide network operators with detailed information about the traffic traversing a link. For example, computing traffic volumes by source and destination IP addresses allows operators to identify the end hosts responsible for bulk of load on the network. Achieving network situational awareness depends on an organization's ability to effectively monitor its networks and, ultimately, to analyze that data to detect malicious activity. This is an ongoing PhD studies work and in future studies may we can enhance further monitoring system with flow pattern.

The results with proposed VXLAN based monitoring system which is clearly identify and differentiate the VXLAN based and other traffic.

References

1. M.M. Mamta Madan, Cloud network management model -A novel approach to manage cloud traffic. Int. J. Cloud Comput. Serv. Archit. **4**, 9–20 (2014)
2. S. Khurram, O. Ghazali, F. Shahzad, A.S. Osman, A survey of cloud monitoring: high level, low level, underlay and overlay. in *NETAPPS2015*, (2015), pp. 1–7
3. M. Mahalingam, Virtual eXtensible Local Area Network (VXLAN): A Framework for Overlaying Virtualized Layer 2 Networks over Layer 3 Networks, (2014)
4. K.D.M. Sridharan, A. Greenberg, N. Venkataramiah, Y. Wang, K. Duda, I. Ganga, G. Lin, M. Pearson, NVGRE: Network virtualization using generic routing encapsulation, (2012)
5. B. Davie, J. Gross, A stateless transport tunneling protocol for network virtualization (STT). Draft-Davie-Stt-06, (2012), pp. 1–21
6. N. Bitar, S. Gringeri, J.X. Tiejun, Technologies and protocols for data center and cloud networking. IEEE Commun. Mag. **51**, 24–31 (2013)
7. K. Fatema, V.C. Emeakaroha, P.D. Healy, J.P. Morrison, T. Lynn, A survey of cloud monitoring tools: taxonomy, capabilities and objectives. J. Parallel Distrib. Comput. **74**(10), 2918–2933 (2014)
8. A. Viratanapanu, A. Kamil, A. Hamid, Y. Kawahara, T. Asami, On demand fine grain resource monitoring system for server consolidation. 2010 ITU-T Kaleidoscope: beyond the Internet?—Innovations for Future Networks and Services, (2010), pp. 1–8
9. Ubuntu Server—for scale out workloads | Ubuntu. [Online]. https://www.ubuntu.com/server. Accessed 23 Sept 2017
10. Open vSwitch. [Online]. http://openvswitch.org/. Accessed 23 Sept 2017
11. G. Sadasivan, J. Brownlee, B. Claise, J. Quittek, Architecture for IP flow information export. RFC Editor
12. Mininet: An Instant Virtual Network on your Laptop (or other PC)—Mininet. [Online]. http://mininet.org/. Accessed 23 Sept 2017
13. OpenFlow-Enabling Innovation in Your Network. [Online]. http://openflow.org/. Accessed 23 Sept 2017
14. Welcome to Python.org. [Online]. https://www.python.org/. Accessed 23 Sept 2017
15. S.M.V. Jacobson, C. Leres, The libpcap packet capture library
16. L. Braun, A. Didebulidze, N. Kammenhuber, G. Carle, Comparing and improving current packet capturing solutions based on commodity hardware. in *Proceedings of the 10th Annual Conference on Internet Measurement—IMC '10*, (2010), p. 206
17. L. Deri, PF_Ring, (2012), [Online]. http://www.ntop.org/products/packet-capture/pf_ring/
18. T. Zseby, F. Fokus, M. Molina, F. Raspall, Sampling and Filtering Techniques for IP Packet Selection. RFC 5475
19. iPerf—The TCP, UDP and SCTP network bandwidth measurement tool. [Online]. https://iperf.fr/. Accessed 25 Sept 2017
20. YAF—Yet Another Flowmeter. [Online]. https://tools.netsa.cert.org/yaf/. Accessed 25 Sept 20

Vicente Casares-Giner, Tatiana Ines Navas, Dolly Smith Flórez, and Tito R. Vargas H.

Abstract

We consider a Wireless Sensor Networks (WSN) in a planar structure with uniform distribution of the sensors and with a two-level hierarchical topology. At lower level, the clustering architecture is adopted in which the sensed information is transferred from nodes to a cluster head (CH). At CH level, CHs transfer information, hop-by-hop, towards to the sink located at the center of the sensed area. We propose a Markovian model to evaluate the end-to-end transfer delay. The numerical results reveal that the traffic carried by CHs near the sink is higher than the traffic carried by CHs located near the perimeter of the sensed area, as it could be expected. Furthermore, for a given radial distance between the source and the sink, the transfer delay depends on the angular orientation between both. This asymmetric behavior is revealed by the model.

Keywords

Wireless sensor network · Markov process · Protocol · F-S-ALOHA · TDMA · Delay

23.1 Introduction

A Wireless Sensor Network (WSN) is composed by hundreds or even thousands of small and low cost nodes or motes, that are deployed in a wide area to be sensed. Each node is powered with small and inexpensive batteries, and offers several capabilities such as sensing information (tem-

V. Casares-Giner (✉)
Universitat Politècnica de València, València, Spain
e-mail: vcasares@upv.es

T. I. Navas · D. S. Flórez · T. R. Vargas H.
Universidad de Santo Tomás, Bogotá, Colombia
e-mail: tatiana.navas@ustabuca.edu.co; dolly.florez@ustabuca.edu.co; tivarher@ustabuca.edu.co

perature, humidity, speed of the wind, . . .), data processing (compression, aggregation, ciphering, . . .) and transferring the data packets towards a gateway or central node, named as sink. To those purposes, motes are organized in a hierarchical way, being the clustering technique the most common practical solution. By clustering, a relative few number of nodes are grouped forming a closed set, in which one of them is elected as the cluster head (CH) [11]. The communication within a cluster is typically implemented using some kind of random access protocol (RAP) such as ALOHA, CSMA, CSMA/CD, CSMA/CA, splitting algorithm, ..., [9]. On the other hand, CHs communicate between them with the idea of sending the sensed information to the sink, typically using a deterministic protocol such as TDMA [4]. This topology has been recognized in the open literature as a two tier cluster hierarchical WSN. For communication between CHs two main approaches have been study. The first is hop-by-hop (multi-hop routing) in which each CH forwards the information to another CH located in a position closer to the sink. The second approach is the direct transmission (sensor-to-sink) by which each CH forwards the information directly to the sink, i.e., with no intermediate nodes. In the hop-by-hop option, the CHs near the sink process a large traffic load, a situation that leads to a rapid depletion of the energy of those CHs, which results in the so-called *problem of the energy hole*. In direct routing, we have the opposite effect in which the CHs away from the sink consume more energy per bit, therefore their batteries run out faster than the batteries of the CHs near the sink. These phenomena have been widely discussed quite frequently in the literature [10, 14].

This work deals with the two tier cluster hierarchical topology in which the Framed ALOHA (F-ALOHA) protocol is chosen for intra cluster communication and the TDMA multi-hop routing protocol is chosen for communications between CHs. Our contribution lies in the formulation of the end-to-end transfer delay of an arbitrary data packet from the time it originates at a given mote until it reaches the sink.

© Springer International Publishing AG, part of Springer Nature 2018
S. Latifi (ed.), *Information Technology – New Generations*, Advances in Intelligent Systems and Computing 738,
https://doi.org/10.1007/978-3-319-77028-4_23

Markov chains and processes are the basic tools that support the analysis.

The work is organized as follows: Sect. 23.2 describes the WSN scenario. In Sect. 23.3 we deal with the communication model where the Combi-Frame structure is introduced together with the concept of slot-reuse and routing strategy for load balancing. Sections 23.4 and 23.5 concerns about inter clustering and intra clustering communications, respectively. In Sect. 23.6 we formulate the end-to-end delay analysis. Section 23.7 provides some illustrative results. Finally, conclusions end the work in Sect. 23.8.

23.2 WSN Scenario

We suppose a WSN with a large number (hundreds) of sensor nodes (motes) randomly distributed in a two-dimensional (2D) area. This is illustrated in Fig. 23.1, where sensor nodes or motes are depicted by small white circles.

Motes are homogeneous, with identical hardware and software configuration. Node's antennae are assumed to be omni-directional and model their transmission ranges as circles. There are no slow neither fast fading effects. There is only a single transceiver unit per node. Hence, the WSN operates on a single frequency. We assume that all nodes know their real physical location in the 2D area by applying some known localization technique (for instance, see [3, 7, 8]).

23.2.1 Cells, Motes and Cell Head Selection

We divide the monitored 2D area into *cells* with hexagonal perimeter. Each hexagon has the same size, defined by radius R (in meters) as it is shown in Fig. 23.1. All the motes that are located within a given hexagon will form a cluster. The number of motes within a cluster is a random variable and its distribution is dependent of the statistical distribution of the motes in the monitored 2D area (Poisson, uniform, $\cdots$). Since the details about those distributions are out of the scope of this contribution, here we only assume that M_C, a constant value, is the number of members that belongs to any cluster. For each cluster, a single node among all M_C members, called *cell head node* (CH), will act as the receiver of the information sensed by the other members of the cluster, perhaps also including the information sensed by the CH itself. We indicate that the number of techniques to elect one mote as CH of the group is rather large [5]; but due to space limitations they will not be discussed in this document. Hence, for simplicity in our studies we will assume that the CH is approximately located at the center of the hexagon.

To identify each hexagon or its own CH, we use *hexagonal coordinates*, $\langle x, y \rangle_h = \langle x_h, y_h \rangle$. Also, for convenience, we introduce coordinates in polar-like (or ring) form $\langle r, m \rangle_p = \langle r_p, m_p \rangle$; which we call *polar coordinates*. Both are illustrated in Fig. 23.2 where the sink is located at the center of the sensed area, i.e. $x_h = y_h = r_p = m_p = 0$.

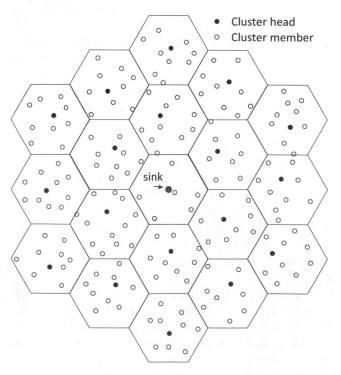

Fig. 23.1 Wireless sensor network scenario

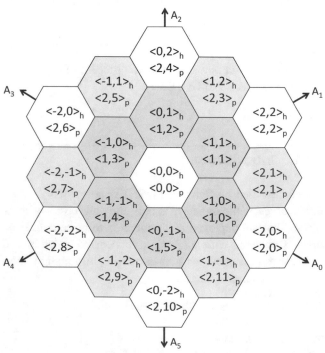

Fig. 23.2 Configuration with flat topped hexagons. Hexagonal coordinates $\langle x, y \rangle_h$, polar coordinates $\langle r, m \rangle_p$, axes A_k and sectors S_k

Table 23.1 Definition of axes A_k and sectors S_k, $0 \leq k \leq 5$

Axes		Sectors	
Axis	Condition	Sector	Condition
A_0	$0 = y_h < x_h$	S_0	$0 < y_h < x_h$
A_1	$0 < y_h = x_h$	S_1	$0 < x_h < y_h$
A_2	$0 = x_h < y_h$	S_2	$x_h < 0 < y_h$
A_3	$x_h < y_h = 0$	S_3	$x_h < y_h < 0$
A_4	$x_h = y_h < 0$	S_4	$y_h < x_h < 0$
A_5	$y_h < x_h = 0$	S_5	$y_h < 0 < x_h$

Finally, we divide the hexagonal grid into twelve disjoint zones: six sectors and six axes. Each sector is located between two axes. Sectors and axes are defined according to Table 23.1.

23.3 Communication

For the communication process we distinguish between intra-cell or intra-cluster communication and inter-cell or inter-cluster communication. The first one refers to the direct, i.e., single-hop communication between motes and its CH and viceversa. It deals with local traffic generated by motes, therefore low traffic load is expected and a RAP seems appropriate, [4]. On the other hand, inter-cluster communications refers to the communication between the CHs that direct the flow of information towards the sink, in our case in a multi-hop way from ring r_p to ring $r_p - 1$ involving only one CH per ring. So, the closer a CH of the sink is, the more traffic it will carry and, therefore, a deterministic protocol like TDMA seems more appropriate in this situation [4].

The communication range, R_C, of intra-cell communication is approximately the radius of the hexagon, R. And the communication range, R_T, of inter-cell communication

R_T becomes $R_C < R_T$ since the distance between two neighbouring CHs is $\sqrt{3}R < R_T$.

23.3.1 Frame Structure

For both communication protocols, we recall the reuse concept that is implemented in cellular networks (see, e.g., [6]). Two motes, or two CHs that are far apart each other can transmit at the same time and using the same frequency if the potential co-channel interference is below a given threshold. As a brief-short refreshment of the reuse concept introduced in [6], we recall that given two positive integer *shift parameters* i and $j \leq i$ the number of cells operating at different frequency, is given by $N = i^2 + ij + j^2$. Therefore, since $R_C < R_T$, two different reuse factors are assumed, (i_x, j_x) $(x = Intra, x = Inter)$, so different number of time slots per frame allocated for the intra clustering communication, N_{Intra}, and for the inter CH's communication N_{Inter}. Obviously, it is expected that $N_{Intra} < N_{Inter}$ and the quantification of both mainly depends on the radio co-channel interference; task that we leave for later studies.

Figure 23.3 shows the proposed *Combi-Frame*. It starts with a short synchronization phase of fixed lengths T_{Syn}. The contention sub-frame for intra-cluster communication follows. It is composed of N_{intra} contention slots, each of duration T_{Intra}, so the duration of the containment subframe is $T_{CONT} = N_{intra} \cdot T_{Intra}$. We specify that each cluster uses exactly one contention slot per contention sub-frame for intra clustering communication. The value of T_{Intra} depends of the RAP that is implemented. In our work we adopt the F-S-ALOHA protocol [12], with N_{Intra} mini-slots per contention slot, each one with duration equal to T_{msC} followed by a time interval T_{ACK-C} for ACKs; then, $T_{Intra} = N_{Intra} \cdot T_{msC} + T_{ACK-C}$.

Fig. 23.3 Combi-frame structure

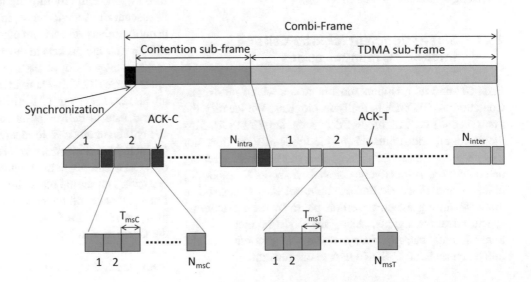

The assumption of low-traffic does not hold for inter-cell traffic, in particular for CHs close to the sink. Hence, the remainder of the Combi-Frame comprises a TDMA sub-frame which is used by the CHs to forward traffic to the sink by using the TDMA protocol. N_{Inter} slots conform the TDMA sub-frame and each slot consists of N_{msT} mini-slots. A single data packet can be transmitted in a single mini-slot. We specify that each CH gets exactly one transmission slot, therefore N_{msT} mini-slots per TDMA sub-frame, hence N_{msT} is the maximum number of data packet per TDMA sub-frame that a CH can transmit. Then, the duration of the TDMA sub-frame is $T_{TDMA} = N_{inter} \cdot T_{Inter}$ where $T_{Inter} = N_{msT} \cdot T_{msT} + T_{ACK-T}$ is the duration of the slot and T_{msT} the duration of the mini-slot. T_{ACK-T} is for ACKs. Therefore, the duration of the Combi-Frame is,

$$
\begin{aligned}
T_{CF} &= T_{Syn} + T_{CONT} + T_{TDMA} = \\
&= T_{Syn} + N_{Intra} \cdot T_{Intra} + N_{Inter} \cdot T_{Inter} = \\
&\approx N_{Intra}(N_{msC} \cdot T_{msC}) + N_{Inter}(N_{msT} \cdot T_{msT}) = \\
&= N_{msCF} \cdot T_{ms}.
\end{aligned}
\tag{23.1}
$$

where the approach in Eq. (23.1) comes from the assumptions $T_{Syn} \approx T_{ACK-C} \approx T_{ACK-T} \approx 0$. For the last equality we set $T_{ms} = T_{msC} = T_{msT}$, i.e. T_{ms} is the transmission time for a data packet (time propagation is considered negligible) and $N_{msCF} = N_{Intra} \cdot N_{msC} + N_{Inter} \cdot N_{msT}$. This assumption involves the choice of the F-S-ALOHA protocol for intra-cluster communication [12]. By choosing the pairs (i_x, j_x) $(x = Intra, Inter)$, we can select cluster sizes N_x and consequently the length of the Combi-Frame (23.1). This allows us to balance the trade-off between interference and network throughput. For example, a high N_{inter} increases the geographical distance between CHs that use the same transmission slot which implies a longer TDMA sub-frame, but each CH experiences a longer interval between two consecutive transmission slots, and consequently longer delay. The same argument applies for N_{intra}.

23.3.2 Slot Assignment for Intra-Cell and Inter-Cell Communications

Each CH and its members must be aware which sub-frame, Contention or TDMA is really in progress. We identify the first (second) case as mode $\mathcal{CONT}$ (mode $\mathcal{TDMA}$). Furthermore, all nodes must been able to identify the time slot it is currently running for reception, transmission, sleeping or contention, respectively denoted as mode $\mathcal{R}$, mode $\mathcal{T}$, mode $\mathcal{S}$ and mode $\mathcal{C}$. For example, all nodes must be in mode $\mathcal{R}$ during synchronization phase to receive external synchronization signals. Also, any node in mode $\mathcal{C}$ will transmit data packet, if any, to its CH according to the implemented RAP, F-S-ALOHA in our illustration.

Table 23.2 Cluster size $N_x = i_x^2 + i_x j_x + j_x^2$, $(x = N_{intra}, N_{inter})$ and slot assignment for transmission from any CH $\langle x, y \rangle_h$

i_x	j_x	N_x	$T(x_h, y_h)$
1	1	3	$(x_h + y_h) \bmod 3$
2	0	4	$2x_h \bmod 4 + y_h \bmod 2$
2	1	7	$[2x_h + y_h] \bmod 7$
2	2	12	$[2x_h + 2y_h + x_h \bmod 2] \bmod 12$
3	0	9	$3x_h \bmod 9 + y_h \bmod 3$
3	1	13	$[3x_h + y_h] \bmod 13$
3	2	19	$[3x_h + 2y_h] \bmod 19$
3	3	27	$[3x_h + 3y_h + x_h \bmod 3] \bmod 27$
4	0	16	$4x_h \bmod 16 + y_h \bmod 4$
4	1	21	$[4x_h + y_h] \bmod 21$
4	2	28	$[4x_h + 2y_h + x_h \bmod 2] \bmod 28$
4	3	37	$[4x_h + 3y_h] \bmod 37$
4	4	48	$[4x_h + 4y_h + x_h \bmod 4] \bmod 48$
5	0	25	$5x_h \bmod 25 + y_h \bmod 5$
5	1	31	$[5x_h + y_h] \bmod 31$
5	2	39	$[5x_h + 2y_h] \bmod 39$
5	3	49	$[5x_h + 3y_h] \bmod 49$
5	4	61	$[5x_h + 4y_h] \bmod 61$
5	5	75	$[5x_h + 5y_h + x_h \bmod 5] \bmod 75$
⋮	⋮	⋮	⋮

Based on its cell coordinates $\langle x, y \rangle_h$ and the cluster size N_z $(z = Intra, Inter)$, each node is able to unambiguously derive the time slot $T(x_h, y_h)$ it may use in the mode $\mathcal{CONT}$ or in the mode $\mathcal{TDMA}$, see Table 23.2.[1] Then, for a tagged slot of the TDMA sub-frame, all nodes are in mode $\mathcal{TDMA}$ and all CHs assigned to that slot, will be in one of the three modes, $\mathcal{T}$, $\mathcal{R}$ or $\mathcal{S}$ while all non-head nodes switch to mode $\mathcal{S}$. In mode $\mathcal{T}$, a CH located at ring r_p can transmit data packets to some other CHs located in the inner neighbor ring $r_p - 1$ while in mode $\mathcal{R}$, the same CH can receive data packets from some other CHs located in the outer neighbor ring $r_p + 1$ (this is part of the routing algorithm that is described in the next section). And viceversa, in the TDMA sub-frame, a CH cannot receive packets from other nodes while it is in mode $\mathcal{T}$ neither transmit packets to other nodes while it is in mode $\mathcal{R}$.

For a tagged slot of the Contention sub-frame, all nodes are in mode $\mathcal{CONT}$. Then, in a cluster assigned to that slot, all nodes except the CH will be in mode $\mathcal{T}$ if they have sensed data to deliver or in mode $\mathcal{S}$ otherwise, while the CH will be in mode $\mathcal{R}$ to receive data from its cell members (or motes). Cell members will send sensed information to its own CH according to the implemented RAP, F-S-ALOHA in our case. During the other time slots of the Contention sub-frame, all nodes of that cluster, including the CH, will remain in mode $\mathcal{S}$. As for CH, when we consider the mode $\mathcal{T}$ in the Contention sub-frame, we will use the mode $\mathcal{C}$ notation

---

[1] Obtained intuitively, with trial and error method.

Fig. 23.4 Routing probabilities for load balancing from ring 5 to ring 2 in sector S_1

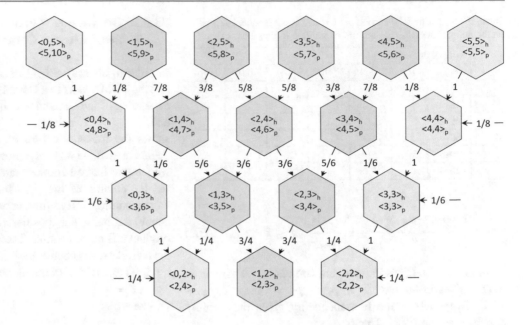

instead; just to avoid possible confusion with the mode $\mathcal{T}$ in the TDMA sub-frame.

Finally, during the ACK period, a given tagged CH is in mode $\mathcal{T}$ and transmits ACKs of the received data packets, ACK-Cs to motes or ACK-Ts to CH neighbors to ours (see the routing algorithm in the next section). In addition, we mention that any mote, including the CHs, could collect data from its own sensor panel at any time, regardless of which sub-frame is actually in progress and regardless of the mode, $\mathcal{R}$, $\mathcal{T}$, $\mathcal{S}$ or $\mathcal{C}$ functioning.

23.3.3 Inter-Cell Routing and Load Balancing

Here we adopt the inter-cell routing protocol between CHs presented in [2]. CHs at ring r_p deliver the information to the nearest CH(s) at ring $r_p - 1$. More specifically, a CH located on one of the axes A_0 to A_5 and ring r_p transfer the information to the CH located in the same axes but at ring $r_p - 1$, for example $\langle 3, 3 \rangle_h \rightarrow \langle 2, 2 \rangle_h$. And non-axis CH can transfer the information to two inner-ring neighbors, for example $\langle 2, 3 \rangle_h \rightarrow \langle 2, 2 \rangle_h$ or $\langle 2, 3 \rangle_h \rightarrow \langle 1, 2 \rangle_h$ where the probability of the first case versus the second one can be chosen following the load balancing principle between CHs of the same ring. Figure 23.4 shows an extract of the set $A_1 \cup S_1 \cup A_2$ for rings $2 \leq r_p \leq 5$ and the generalization to arbitrary rings and sectors can be found in Table II of [2].

23.4 The Intra-Cluster Communication

23.4.1 Traffic Model: The Contention Process

For the contention process in the Contention sub-frame, here we borrow the proposal presented in [1]. Each non

CHs (mote) is equipped with a unit-size buffer and with probability p_{act} generates at most one data packet each T_{ms} (Bernoulli process). M_C motes try to gain the access towards its CH using the F-S-ALOHA protocol. Then, for our Combi-Frame scenario we have derived the corresponding output of the contention process at each CH, i.e. the probability generating function (PGF) in the transform domain,

$$L(z) = \sum_{k=0}^{N_{msC}} l_k z^k$$

where l_k is the probability in steady state that at the end of a contention slot, k data packets win the contention process and successfully reach your CH (obviously $L'(z = 1) = L'(1) < N_{msC}$). Due to the lack of space we omit the details which can be found in [1].

23.5 The Inter-Cluster Communication

23.5.1 The Traffic Load and the Stability Conditions

For analytical tractability we assume that buffer capacity or queue size in each CH is infinite. Let us consider a total number of r_{max} rings. Data packets will flow downstream from external rings towards to the sink. It is quite straightforward to see that for any given CH located at ring k and due to the principle of load balancing, the normalized average number of data packets transmitted per TDMA slot in the TDMA sub-frame, ρ_k, is given by,

Table 23.3 Traffic load carried per CH in a lossless model depending on the number of rings r_{max} present in addition to ring 0 (sink)

r_{max}	Ring (# of nodes)						
	0 (1)	1 (6)	2 (12)	3 (18)	4 (24)	5 (30)	6 (36)
1	6+1	1					
2	18+1	3	1				
3	36+1	6	$^5/_2$	1			
4	60+1	10	$^9/_2$	$^7/_3$	1		
5	90+1	15	$^{14}/_2$	$^{12}/_3$	$^9/_4$	1	
6	126+1	21	$^{20}/_2$	$^{18}/_3$	$^{15}/_4$	$^{11}/_5$	1

$$\rho_k = \left[\frac{C_2^{r_{max}+1} - C_2^{k+1}}{k} + 1 \right] \frac{L'(1)}{N_{msT}} \quad 1 \le k \le r_{max} \quad (23.2)$$

In Eq. (23.2), C_n^m is the standard combinatorial number m over n. Clearly we have $1 > \rho_1 > \rho_2 > \ldots > \rho_{r_{max}} = L'(1)/N_{msT}$ where the first inequality gives the stability condition of the WSN. That is,

$$\rho_1 = C_2^{r_{max}+1} \frac{L'(1)}{N_{msT}} < 1. \quad (23.3)$$

Notice that, in Eq. (23.2) the first term in brackets reflects the exogenous traffic offered to a CH from external rings while the second one, the term "1", takes into account the local traffic. Then, the two terms within brackets is the total traffic offered to a CH located at ring k. Table 23.3 shows those values for several sizes of the WSN.

23.5.2 The Embedded Markov Chain

For a given CH we observe its Combi-Frame at the beginning of a $\mathcal{T}$-slot. Let $F(z) = \sum_{i=0}^{\infty} f_i z^i$ be the PGF of the number of packets that arrive to the tagged CH during a Combi-Frame. $F(z)$ is composed by the local traffic, $L(z)$ and the exogenous traffic that comes from some outer neighbor rings. The instants at which the $\mathcal{T}$-slots begins define an embedded Markov with steady state probabilities given by the following PGF,

$$\pi_T(z) =$$

$$\sum_{k=0}^{\infty} \pi_{T,k} z^k = \frac{\sum_{i=0}^{N_{msT}-1} (z^{N_{msT}} - z^i) \pi_{T,i}}{z^{N_{msT}} - F(z)} F(z), \quad (23.4)$$

The details of how to obtain the set of probabilities $\pi_{T,0}, \pi_{T,1}, \pi_{T,2}, \ldots \pi_{T,N_{msT}-1}$ can be found in [2].

23.5.3 On the Input Process in the Inter-Cluster Communication

In order to quantify $F(z)$, first, notice that Contention slots and the TDMA slots in a Combi-Frame are sorted differently, depending of the CH under study. For $r_{max} = 4$, $N_{Intra} = 3$ and $N_{Inter} = 7$, column $-\mathcal{CONT}\text{-}\mathcal{TDMA}-$ in Table 23.4 shows the frame structure of each CH located in the 60 degree area $A_0 \cup S_0 \cup A_1$. However, for analysis purposes, we assume that all frames start with a transmission slot $\mathcal{T}$; see the column of the right hand side in Table 23.4. The corresponding shift in time between frames is taken into account later on, when considering the transfer delay from the original CH until the sink. Then, assuming independence of the arrival process between disjoint time slots, and denoting by $A_i(z)$ as the PGF of the number of arrivals during the time slot i, $i = 0, 1, \ldots, N_{sCF} - 1$; ($N_{sCF} = N_{Inter} + N_{Intra}$) we can write:

$$F(z) = \prod_{i=0}^{N_{sCF}-1} A_i(z), \text{ with}$$

$$A_i(z) = \begin{cases} L(z) & \text{if } i \in \mathcal{C} \text{ (Contention)} \\ R_{\langle x,y \rangle}(z) & \text{if } i \in \mathcal{R} \text{ slot} \\ 1 & \text{otherwise} \end{cases} \quad (23.5)$$

From Eq. (23.5) time slot 0 is only for transmission, mode $\mathcal{T}$, so $A_0(z) = 1$. While the CH is in mode $\mathcal{S}$ no transmission neither reception happens. During the mode $\mathcal{T}$ data packets are served into consecutive mini-slots of a TDMA slot and

Table 23.4 Frame structure for nodes in $A_0 \cup S_0 \cup A_1$

Ring	CH	Frame structure : $-\mathcal{CONT}\text{-}\mathcal{TDMA}-$	Frame structure : With $\mathcal{T}$ as starting point
4	$\langle 4,4 \rangle$	-SSC-SSSSSTS-	TS-SSC-SSSSS
	$\langle 4,3 \rangle$	-SCS-SSSTSSS-	TSSS-SCS-SSS
	$\langle 4,2 \rangle$	-CSS-STSSSSS-	TSSSSS-CSS-S
	$\langle 4,1 \rangle$	-SSC-SSSSSST-	T-SSC-SSSSSS
	$\langle 4,0 \rangle$	-SCS-SSSSTSS-	TSS-SCS-SSSS
3	$\langle 3,3 \rangle$	-CSS-SSTRRRS-	TRRRS-CSS-SS
	$\langle 3,2 \rangle$	-SSC-TRSRSSS-	TRSRSSS-SSC-
	$\langle 3,1 \rangle$	-SCS-SRSSSTR-	TR-SCS-SRSSS
	$\langle 3,0 \rangle$	-CSS-SRSTRSR-	TRSR-CSS-SSS
2	$\langle 2,2 \rangle$	-SCS-RRRSSST-	T-SCS-RRRSSS
	$\langle 2,1 \rangle$	-CSS-RSSSTRS-	T-SCS-RRRSSS
	$\langle 2,0 \rangle$	-SSC-RSTRSRS-	TRSRS-SSC-RS
1	$\langle 1,1 \rangle$	-SSC-SSSTRRR-	TRRR-SSC-SSS
	$\langle 1,0 \rangle$	-SCS-STRSRSR-	TRSRSR-SCS-S

$(N_{Intra}, N_{Inter}) = (3, 7)$ and Ring ≤ 4

are delivered to one or two CHs inner-ring neighbor. The reception of data packets occurs in two ways. The first one, represented by $L(z)$, refers to the local traffic and it is denoted by mode $\mathcal{C}$. The second way is labeled as $R_{\langle x, y \rangle}$ (mode $\mathcal{R}$), deals with traffic coming from a CH $\langle x, y \rangle$ located in the neighboring outer ring.

Then, denoting by $D_{\langle x, y \rangle}(z)$ (departure) the PDF of the output process at CH $\langle x, y \rangle$ and according to Eq. (23.5) and to Table 23.4 we have, for instance, for CH $\langle 3, 3 \rangle$ with pattern $T\mathcal{RRRS}\text{-}\mathcal{CSS}\text{-}\mathcal{SS}$, and

$$A_1(z) = R_{\langle 4,3 \rangle}(z) = D_{\langle 4,3 \rangle}\left(p_{\langle 4,3 \rangle - \langle 3,3 \rangle} z + 1 - p_{\langle 4,3 \rangle - \langle 3,3 \rangle}\right)$$
$$A_2(z) = R_{\langle 3,4 \rangle}(z) = D_{\langle 3,4 \rangle}\left(p_{\langle 3,4 \rangle - \langle 3,3 \rangle} z + 1 - p_{\langle 3,4 \rangle - \langle 3,3 \rangle}\right)$$
$$A_3(z) = R_{\langle 4,4 \rangle}(z) = D_{\langle 4,4 \rangle}(z)$$
$$A_5(z) = L(z)$$
$$A_i(z) = 1 \quad \text{elsewhere.}$$

The previous expression implies that the routing decision is taken packet by packet. Alternatively, we could decide slot by slot, which means that $D_{\langle x, y \rangle}(pz + 1 - p)$ must be replaced by $p D_{\langle x, y \rangle}(z) + 1 - p$. This second option seems more appropriated from the point of view of energy efficiency, since after detecting an empty mini-slot the CH can enter the mode $\mathcal{S}$, remaining in this state at least until the end of the current time slot.

23.5.4 On the Output Process in the Inter-Cluster Communication

From Eq. (23.4), for each CH the corresponding PGF of number of customers served during one transmission slot (TDMA sub-frame), $D(z)$, can be expressed as,

$$D(z) = \sum_{i=0}^{N_{msT}} d_i z^i = z^{N_{msT}} - \sum_{i=0}^{N_{msT}-1} \pi_{T,i}\left(z^{N_{msT}} - z^i\right)$$

Clearly,

$$D'(1) = N_{msT} - \sum_{i=0}^{N_{msT}-1} \pi_{T,i}\left(N_{msT} - i\right) = F'(1) \quad (23.6)$$

In Eq. (23.6) the last equality comes from the fact that in equilibrium the service rate per Combi-Frame equals to the arrival rate per Combi-Frame. And the average number of packets found at the beginning of a transmission slot $\mathcal{T}$ can be written as, after some simple algebra,

$$\pi'_T(1) = F'(1) + \frac{F''(1) - D''(1)}{2[N_{msT} - F'(1)]} \quad (23.7)$$

23.6   End-to-End Delay Analysis

Here we derive the end-to-end delay of any tagged data packet generated in a given mote until it reach the sink. The derivations are supported by the previous queue model.

23.6.1 Sojourn Times in a CH

For each CH under study, let us denote by $\bar{b}_i$ the mean number of data packets at the beginning of the time slot i ($i = 0, 1, \ldots, N_{sCF} - 1$). $\bar{b}_i$ can be expressed as,

$$\bar{b}_i = \begin{cases} \pi'_T(1), & \text{for } i = 0 \\ \pi'_T(1) - D'(1), & \text{for } i = 1 \\ \bar{b}_1 + \sum_{j=1}^{i-1} A'_j(1), & \text{for } i = 2, \ldots, N_{sCF} \end{cases}$$

We identify $Z_i = N_{msC}$ if $i \in intra$ time slot and $Z_i = N_{msT}$ if $i \in inter$ time slot, and we approximate the mean number of data packets in the system as,

$$\overline{N_p} = \frac{\displaystyle\sum_{i=0}^{N_{sCF}-1} Z_i \bar{b}_i}{N_{msCF}}$$

Therefore, for an arbitrary data packet in a given CH under study, the mean dwell time (waiting + service), expressed in Combi-Frames (in frames, for short) can be estimated as (Little formula),

$$\overline{W}(\text{st, CF}) = \frac{\overline{N_p}}{D'(1)} = \frac{\overline{N_p}}{F'(1)} \quad (23.8)$$

where the last equality in Eq. (23.8) is obtained using Eq. (23.7). Obviously, expressing Eq. (23.8) in minislots we have:

$$\overline{W}(\text{st, ms}) = \overline{W}(\text{st, CF}) N_{msCF} \quad (23.9)$$

23.6.2 Local and Exogenous Traffic

Let r_L (r_E) be the fraction of local (exogenous) traffic carried by a given CH. r_L is given by,

$$r_L = \frac{L'(1)}{L'(1) + \displaystyle\sum_{i \in TDMA} A'_i(1)} = \frac{L'(1)}{F'(1)} = 1 - r_E. \quad (23.10)$$

Then, having in mind Eqs. (23.10), (23.9) can be split into three terms as follows,

$$\overline{W}(\text{st, ms}) = r_L CT + \sum_{i \in TDMA} \frac{A_i'(1)}{F'(1)} R_i T + \overline{W}^r. \quad (23.11)$$

The interpretation of Eq. (23.11) is as follows. The first terms concerns about the local traffic; CT is the distance in number of mini–slots between the end of the successful slot $\mathcal{C}$ for our tagged data packet and the end of the first available transmission slot $\mathcal{T}$ of our CH in the TDMA sub-frame. The second term of Eq. (23.11) deals with the exogenous traffic; $R_i T$ is the distance in number of mini-slots between the end of the reception slot $\mathcal{R}_i$ and the end of the transmission slot $\mathcal{T}$ of our CH (notice that the reception slot $\mathcal{R}_i$ is coincident with the transmission slot $\mathcal{T}_i$ of some CH in the neighboring outer ring). Finally $\overline{W}^r$ is the residual mean sojourn time in a given CH which is common to the local and to the exogenous traffic streams.

Therefore, for each CH we evaluate each term in Eq. (23.11) as follows. First, we obtain $\overline{W}(\text{st, ms})$, Eq. (23.9); second we obtain the fractions r_L and r_E, Eq. (23.10), i.e. the first two terms of Eq. (23.11) and finally we obtain $\overline{W}^r$ from the previous terms by simple arithmetic. In fact for a very low traffic load, $\overline{W}^r$ will be practically null, so only the first two terms of Eq. (23.11) will contribute to the mean sojourn time.

23.6.3 Delay of a Tagged Data Packet

The mean sojourn time of a given tagged data packet is defined as the time interval elapsed from the instant it is generated until it is delivered to the sink. For example, let $\overline{W}^L_{(3,2)}$ denote the sojourn time of a data packet from the moment it is generated by a mote in cluster $\langle 3, 2\rangle$ until it reaches the sink (L stand from local). Let us consider the CHs that belong to the set $R_3 \cap (A_0 \cup S_0 \cup A_1)$ (here ring 3 =R_3), i.e. $\langle 3, 0\rangle$, $\langle 3, 1\rangle$, $\langle 3, 2\rangle$, $\langle 3, 3\rangle$. In vector-matrix notation, we see that,

$$\begin{bmatrix} \overline{W}^L_{(3,3)} \\ \overline{W}^L_{(3,2)} \\ \overline{W}^L_{(3,1)} \\ \overline{W}^L_{(3,0)} \end{bmatrix} = \begin{bmatrix} \overline{AC}_{(3,3)} \\ \overline{AC}_{(3,2)} \\ \overline{AC}_{(3,1)} \\ \overline{AC}_{(3,0)} \end{bmatrix} + \begin{bmatrix} CT_{(3,3)} \\ CT_{(3,2)} \\ CT_{(3,1)} \\ CT_{(3,0)} \end{bmatrix} + \begin{bmatrix} \overline{RW}_{(3,3)} \\ \overline{RW}_{(3,2)} \\ \overline{RW}_{(3,1)} \\ \overline{RW}_{(3,0)} \end{bmatrix}$$

$$(23.12)$$

In a compact way we write previous equation as,

$$\mathbf{W}^L_{0,0,1}(3) = \mathbf{AC}_{0,0,1}(3) + \mathbf{CT}_{0,0,1}(3) + \mathbf{RW}_{0,0,1}(3) \quad (23.13)$$

with the short notation, $A_0, S_0, A_1 = 0, 0, 1$, and $R_3 = 3$.

In Eq. (23.13), $\overline{AC}_{\langle i,j\rangle}$, takes into account the delay of our packet in the contention process at CH $\langle i, j\rangle$. $CT_{\langle i,j\rangle}$, is the number of mini-slots between the end of the successful slot $\mathcal{C}$ (mode $\mathcal{CONT}$) and the end of the first available slot $\mathcal{T}$ in the TDMA sub-frame. $\overline{RW}_{\langle i,j\rangle}$ is the remaining sojourn time to reaches the sink. That is, $\overline{RW}_{\langle i,j\rangle}$ is the elapsed time between the end of the first available transmission slot $\mathcal{T}$ in CH $\langle i, j\rangle$ until our packet reaches the sink. In vector-matrix notation, $\overline{RW}_{\langle i,j\rangle}$ is expressed as,

$$\left[\overline{RW}_{(3,3)}, \overline{RW}_{(3,2)}, \overline{RW}_{(3,1)}, \overline{RW}_{(3,0)} \right]' =$$
$$\left[\overline{W}^r_{(3,3)}, \overline{W}^r_{(3,2)}, \overline{W}^r_{(3,1)}, \overline{W}^r_{(3,0)} \right]' +$$
$$+ \boldsymbol{PE}_{0,0,1}(3) \begin{bmatrix} TT_{(3,3),(2,2)} \\ TT_{(3,2),(2,2)} \\ TT_{(3,2),(2,1)} \\ TT_{(3,1),(2,1)} \\ TT_{(3,1),(2,0)} \\ TT_{(3,0),(2,0)} \end{bmatrix} + \boldsymbol{P}_{0,0,1}(3) \begin{bmatrix} \overline{RW}_{(2,2)} \\ \overline{RW}_{(2,1)} \\ \overline{RW}_{(2,0)} \end{bmatrix}$$

and writing previous expression in a compact way,

$$\mathbf{RW}_{0,0,1}(3) = \mathbf{W}^r_{0,0,1}(3) +$$
$$+ \boldsymbol{PE}_{0,0,1}(3)\mathbf{TT}_{0,0,1}(3) + \boldsymbol{P}_{0,0,1}(3)\mathbf{RW}_{0,0,1}(2) \quad (23.14)$$

In Eq. (23.14), $\boldsymbol{PE}_{0,0,1}(3)$ (stands from matrix P Extended) takes into account the routing probabilities between two neighboring sets of CH, in our example $R_3 \cap (A_0 \cup S_0 \cup A_1) \rightarrow R_2 \cap (A_0 \cup S_0 \cup A_1)$. They are obtained from the principle of load balancing, see Fig. 23.4,

$$\boldsymbol{PE}_{A_0,S_0,A_1}(R_3) = \boldsymbol{PE}_{0,0,1}(3) =$$
$$\begin{bmatrix} 1 & 0 & 0 & 0 & 0 & 0 \\ 0 & p_{(3,2),(2,2)} & p_{(3,2),(2,1)} & 0 & 0 & 0 \\ 0 & 0 & 0 & p_{(3,1),(2,1)} & p_{(3,1),(2,0)} & 0 \\ 0 & 0 & 0 & 0 & 0 & 1 \end{bmatrix}$$

$TT_{\langle i,j\rangle,\langle k,l\rangle}$ is the number of mini-slots between the transmission slot $\mathcal{T}$ of CH $\langle i, j\rangle$ and the transmission slot $\mathcal{T}$ of CH $\langle k, l\rangle$. Finally,

$$\boldsymbol{P}_{0,0,1}(3) = \boldsymbol{PE}_{0,0,1}(3) \begin{bmatrix} 1 & 0 & 0 \\ 1 & 0 & 0 \\ 0 & 1 & 0 \\ 0 & 1 & 0 \\ 0 & 0 & 1 \\ 0 & 0 & 1 \end{bmatrix}$$

As a resume, we evaluate $\mathbf{W}^L_{0,0,1}(k)$, the end-to-end transfer delay for each data packet generated at ring $k = 1, 2, \ldots, r_{max}$ as,

$$\mathbf{W}_{0,0,1}^{L}(k) = \mathbf{AC}_{0,0,1}(k) + \mathbf{CT}_{0,0,1}(k) + \mathbf{RW}_{0,0,1}(k) \tag{23.15}$$

with,

$$\mathbf{RW}_{0,0,1}(k) = \mathbf{W}_{0,0,1}^{r}(k) +$$
$$+ \boldsymbol{PE}_{0,0,1}(k)\mathbf{TT}_{0,0,1}(k) + \boldsymbol{P}_{0,0,1}(k)\mathbf{RW}_{0,0,1}(k-1)$$
$$1 < k \leq r_{max}$$
$$\mathbf{RW}_{0,0,1}(1) = \mathbf{W}_{0,0,1}^{r}(1) + \boldsymbol{PE}_{0,0,1}(1)\mathbf{TT}_{0,0,1}(1) \tag{23.16}$$

Then, the procedure is as follows. First, the local traffic at each cluster; we obtain the output and the delay of the contention process, $L(z)$ and as $AC(z)$, with mean values $L'(1) = \overline{L}$ and $AC'(1) = \overline{AC}$. Second, the ergodicity conditions given in Eq. (23.3) must be satisfied. Otherwise, the offered local traffic must be reduced until the ergodicity condition is met. Third, for each CHs of every ring we obtain the sojourn time, Eqs. (23.8) and (23.9); first for all the CH located in the outermost ring, second for all the CH located in the inner ring next to the previous one, and so on, until reaching the first neighbor ring of the sink. Fourth, from Eq. (23.11) we obtain $\overline{W}_{\langle x,y \rangle}^{r}$ for all CHs of every ring. Finally we evaluate the end-to-end delay using Eqs. (23.15) and (23.16).

23.7 Investigation of 4-Ring WSN

For illustration purposes we consider a 4-ring WSN, $r_{max} = 4$. The number of motes per cluster is $M_C = 8$ and each mote generates one data packet per mini-slot with probability $p_{act} = 0.001$. For the contention process we adopt the formulation given in [1], with permission probability 0.75. From the traffic load balance principle, see Fig. 23.4, the traffic carried by each CH (normalized to 1) is shown in Table 23.5, see Eq. (23.2).

We have computed $\overline{W}_{\langle x,y \rangle}^{L}$, Eq. (23.12), for all CHs. We do not show the access delay, $\overline{AC}_{\langle x,y \rangle}$ since it is common for all CHs; instead we focus on $CT_{\langle x,y \rangle}$ and $\overline{RW}_{\langle x,y \rangle}$. Figure 23.5 is for extremely low traffic, $\rho_i \approx 0$; for instance, for CH $\langle 3,0 \rangle_h$ we have $CT_{\langle 3,0 \rangle_h} = 26$ and $\overline{RW}_{\langle 3,0 \rangle_h} = 117$. When the offered traffic is as Table 23.5 shows, see Fig. 23.6, clearly $CT_{\langle 3,0 \rangle_h}$ does not change but $\overline{RW}_{\langle 3,0 \rangle_h}$ increase to $\overline{RW}_{\langle 3,0 \rangle_h} = 134, 58$.

In a comparative analysis we focus on three consecutive CHs on the A_1 axis, CH $\langle 1,1 \rangle_h$, CH $\langle 2,2 \rangle_h$ and CH $\langle 3,3 \rangle_h$. The differences between the values of $\overline{RW}_{\langle x,y \rangle_h}$ in Figs. 23.6

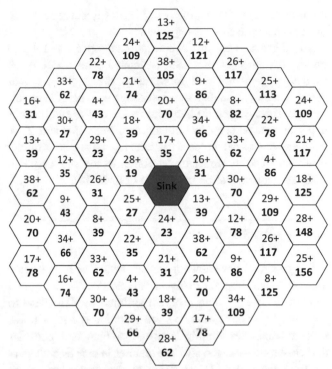

Fig. 23.5 $CT_{\langle x,y \rangle_h} + \overline{RW}_{\langle x,y \rangle_h}$, in mini-slots, with (N_{msC}, N_{intra}) =(5, 3), (N_{msT}, N_{inter})=(4, 7) and very low data traffic $p_{act} \approx 0$

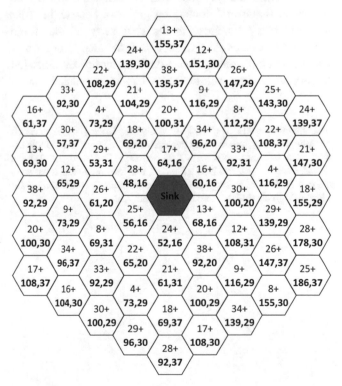

Fig. 23.6 $CT_{\langle x,y \rangle_h} + \overline{RW}_{\langle x,y \rangle_h}$, in mini-slots, with (N_{msC}, N_{intra}) =(5, 3), (N_{msT}, N_{inter})=(4, 7) with $p_{act} = 0.001$

and 23.5 are, respectively 29, 16; 30, 31 and 30, 37 mini-slots, i.e very similar. This fact manifests the bottleneck effect equivalent to the energy hole problem mentioned in

Table 23.5 Parameters, $(N_{msC}, N_{intra}, N_{msT}, N_{inter}) = (x, w, y, z)$; $r_{max} = 4$

(x, w, y, z)	N_{msCF}	p_{act}	ρ_1	ρ_2	ρ_3	ρ_4
(5, 3, 4, 7)	43	0.001	0.827	0.372	0.193	0.083

the introduction; that is, the delay is mostly concentrated in the CHs near the sink, as expected.

In addition, there are two important aspects to keep in mind; first, the set of tasks associated with a CH (such as data aggregation and forwarding) that entail a higher energy consumption than that associated with non-CH nodes. Second, the asymmetric behavior in the end-to-end transfer delay as can be seen in both figures, Figs. 23.5 and 23.6. Both drawbacks can be partially alleviated by some common solutions, such as direct transmission to the sink and also with the regular rotation of the role of CHs [14].

23.8 Conclusions

In this paper, we have develop a Markovian model to evaluate the end-to-end transfer delay in two tier WSN. The model capture the energy hole problem suffered by CHs close to the sink. In a near future, we are planning several actions, some of them are already in progress. First is to consider that clusters near to the sink are smaller in size than clusters far from the sink [13]. The size of the cluster impacts in the contention protocol to manage the local traffic; therefore a comparative analysis between several solution will be addressed for several contention protocol. Second, in order to avoid that CHs close to the sink carry all the traffic coming from outer ring, to face with the analytical models about direct transmission instead of hop-by-hop transmission (also some hybrid solutions) as has been pointed out in [14].

Acknowledgements The work of V. Casares-Giner (ITACA research institute) is partly supported by the Spanish national projects TIN2013-47272-C2-1-R and TEC2015-71932-REDT. The work of Tatiana Navas, Dolly Flórez, and Tito R. Vargas, and the collaboration between the two institutions, is supported by the Universidad Santo Tomás under Master Degree's research and academic projects.

References

1. V. Casares-Giner, V. Sempere-Payá, D.T. Ferrandis, Framed aloha protocol with FIFO-blocking and LIFO-push out discipline. Netw. Protocols Algoritm. **6**, 82–102 (2014)
2. V. Casares-Giner, P. Wüchner, D. Pacheco-Paramo, H. de Meer, Combined contention and TDMA-based communication in wireless sensor networks, in *Proceedings of the NGI'12 Conference* (2012)
3. L.M.P.L. de Brito, L.M.R. Peralta, An analysis of localization problems and solutions in wireless sensor networks. Tékhne - Revista de Estudos Politécnicos **6**(9), 1–27 (2008)
4. J.L. Hammond, P.J.P. O'Reilly, *Performance Analysis of Local Computer Networks* (Addison-Wesley, Boston, 1986)
5. A. Kusdaryono, K.O. Lee, A clustering protocol with mode selection for wireless sensor network. J. Inf. Process. Syst. **7**, 29–42 (2011)
6. V.H. MacDonald, Advanced mobile phone service: the cellular concept. Bell Syst. Tech. J. **58**(1), 15–41 (1979)
7. E. Martin, L. Liu, M. Covington, P. Pesti, M. Weber, Positioning technologies in location-based services, in *Location-Based Services Handbook—Applications, Technologies, and Security*, eds. by S.A. Ahson, M. Ilyas, (CRC Press, Boca Raton, 2010), pp. 1–45
8. A. Pal, Localization algorithms in wireless sensor networks: current approaches and future challenges. Netw. Protocols Algoritm. **2**(1), 45–74 (2010)
9. R. Rom, M. Sidi, *Multiple Access Protocols—Performance and Analysis* (Springer, New York, 1990)
10. A. Sari, Two-tier hierarchical cluster based topology in wireless sensor networks for contention based protocol suite. Int. J. Commun. Netw. Syst. Sci. **8**, 29–42 (2015)
11. L. Shi, A.O. Fapojuwo, TDMA scheduling with optimized energy efficiency and minimum delay in clustered wireless sensor networks. IEEE Trans. Mob. Comput. **9**(7), 927–940 (2010)
12. J.E. Wieelthier, A. Ephremides, L.A. Michaels, An exact analysis and performance evaluation of framed aloha with capture. IEEE Trans. Commun. **37**, 125–137 (1989)
13. D. Wu, J. He, H. Wang, C. Wang, R. Wang, A hierarchical packet forwarding mechanism for energy harvesting wireless sensor networks. IEEE Commun. Mag. **8**, 92–98 (2015)
14. H. Zhang, H. Shen, Balancing energy consumption to maximize net-work lifetime in data-gathering sensor networks. IEEE Trans. Parallel Distrib. Syst. **20**, 1526–1539 (2009)

Heleno Cardoso da Silva Filho, Glauco de Figueiredo Carneiro,
Ed Santana Martins Costa, and Miguel Monteiro

Abstract

The cloud computing paradigm represents a shift in the way companies deal with customizable and resourceful platforms to deploy software. It has been receiving increasing attention, partly due to its claimed financial and functional benefits. Cloud computing providers provide organizations with access to computing services without the need for those organizations to own the providing infrastructure. However, migration of legacy information systems to the cloud is not simple. This field is very dynamic and related technologies are rapidly evolving. For instance, Small and Medium Enterprises (SMEs) may not necessarily be well prepared to deal with issues such as multi-tenancy, elasticity, interoperability, and cloud services. With such issues in view, we searched for different types of tools referenced in the literature to support migration to the cloud and discussed related challenges and advantages of their use by SMEs.

Keywords

Cloud computing · Legacy systems · Cloud migration · Tools

24.1 Introduction

Cloud computing offers novel opportunities such as the economy of scale to SMEs. In exchange of having affordable access to sophisticated computers resources, SMEs must plan the migration of parts or the whole of their applications to the cloud. This entails expending efforts to understand existing legacy systems and in some cases redesign them. Considering that cloud related issues entail the analysis of various aspects such as economic, strategic risks and technological related issues [1], decision makers must have extensive judgment and insight to thoroughly comprehend the alternatives and the set of required choices towards the cloud adoption [2].

Migrating a legacy style application to the cloud is not a trivial task and arise several challenges. The size and the complexity of this task can be discouraging, especially in the cases of small and medium enterprises aiming at benefiting from the promised advantages of the cloud [3]. The issues to be addressed are still poorly understood and vary dynamically, due to the change of related technologies [3].

The cloud environment is characterized by a large amount of resources such as memory, CPU, network bandwidth and storage. These resources can be booked and released by service consumers, according to demand to optimize the usage in the case of workload variation[4].

Researchers have pointed out that empirical insights into cloud-sourcing decisions remains scarce [5]. For this reason, we decided to look for evidence in the literature about tools that have supported SMEs to migrate to the cloud.

The rest of this paper is organized as follows. The next section presents the context of this work. Section 24.3 describes the methodology of the study. Section 24.4 analyzes the results. Section 24.5 presents the conclusion and scope for future research.

24.2 Context of This Work

It is estimated that the worldwide cloud computing market will increase up to $241 billion by 2020 [6]. Academia and practitioners devoted research effort to this topic by focusing on technical solutions and also on the social and

H. C. da Silva Filho · G. de Figueiredo Carneiro (✉)
E. S. Martins Costa
Universidade Salvador (UNIFACS), Salvador, Bahia, Brazil
e-mail: Glauco.Carneiro@iscte-iul.pt

M. Monteiro
NOVA-LINCS, Universidade Nova de Lisboa (FCT/UNL), Lisbon, Portugal

non-technical consequences of the cloud as a paradigm [7]. Moving large-scale legacy systems to the cloud is not as straightforward as it might first appear [4] as systems often precede the cloud era and in most cases were developed without considering its unique characteristics [7, 8]. The complexity of migration is increased due to the development of legacy applications not considering requirements attributed to cloud environments such as elasticity, multi-tenancy, interoperability, and cloud service/platform selection [3,7]. Tools can support migration of legacy systems to the cloud, instead of carrying out such migrations in an ad-hoc manner. Such migrations may latter result in maintenance problems related to poor and non effective migrations [7].

The literature reports that SMEs have been facing challenges such as the classic lock-in effect towards the adoption of new cloud services [9]. Thus, before sourcing cloud services, companies have the option to use migration tools that account for various issues such as cost and risk factors.

Figure 24.1 was adapted from [7] and presents migration types from legacy systems to the cloud. We can identify types of tools that support activities related to each kind of migration presented as follows. **Type I** migration [7] relates to deploying the business logic tier of the legacy system in the cloud infrastructure through the *Infrastructure as a Service* (IaaS) model. In this case, the data tier remains in the local network of the company. Deploying an audio-processing component of an application in the cloud is an example of this type of migration. **Type II** migration [7] relates to the replacement of some components or the entire legacy application stack with a cloud service, by applying the service delivery model *Software as a Service* (SaaS). *Online Customer Relationship Management* (CRM) applications are a typical example of SaaS, which can be integrated with other applications via their available interfaces. **Type III** migration [7] relates to the deployment of a legacy database in a cloud data store provider through IaaS delivery service model. The components related to business logic tier are maintained in the local network of the company and the database is deployed in a public cloud data store. Amazon's Elastic Block Store (EBS), Amazon's *Simple Storage Service* (S3), and Dropbox are examples of public cloud data store serving this end. **Type IV** migration [7] relates to the conversion of the data, schema, and changing the data tier of the legacy application to a cloud native database such as e.g., Amazon DynamoDB[1] and Azure Cosmos DB.[2] Finally, **Type V** migration [7] relates to the deployment of the entire application stack in the cloud through IaaS. In this case, the legacy system is wrapped in a unique virtual machine (VM) to run in the cloud. Hosting a Web legacy system and the

corresponding Web server using a virtual machine on Digital Ocean[3] is an example of this type of migration.

In addition to migration type, the migration process is another relevant issue that can be used to contextualize the role tools play in the migration to the cloud. The migration process can be summarized by the following phases [4]. **Phase I** (Plan phase) comprises tasks such as context analysis, migration requirement analysis, legacy systems identification and plan definition. Examples of work products of this phase include the legacy system model, the migration requirements and the migration plan. **Phase II** (Design phase) comprises tasks such as design of the cloud solution, choose the cloud service/platform, identify incompatibilities, and design principles. Examples of work products of this phase include the cloud solution architecture and the virtual machine specification. **Phase III** (Enable phase) comprises tasks such as resolving incompatibilities, deploying system components, configuring network, deploying and testing system. This phase has as the main work product the system template.

24.3 The Semi Systematic Literature Review

To collect data for this paper, we conducted a semi-systematic literature review [10] to identify studies that report the use of tools to support the migration to the cloud and associated challenges as well as difficulties to perform the migration. The review fulfills just part of the criteria of a systematic literature review (SLR) [10]. For this reason, it is considered a semi-systematic literature review, since this seems to be the most accurate description [11]. The fulfilled criteria include: (1) search strings applied to a dedicated digital library, (2) analysis of number of hits, (3) documenting the included papers, and (4) usage of explicit inclusion/exclusion criteria [11]. The SLR criteria that are not met include: (a) evaluation of papers by multiple authors and (b) a more rigorous quality assessment of the study, data extraction and data synthesis. Additionally, we included papers that were not found via our search string, which is not part of SLR process.

The literature review assessed two research questions as follows. **Research Question 1 (RQ1):** Which tools support the migration of legacy systems to the cloud? The results of the semi-systematic literature review show that there are no tools that fully support the whole migration of a legacy system to the cloud. However, there are tools that provide a fully-automated support for specific tasks during the migration.

---

[1] https://aws.amazon.com/dynamodb/.

[2] https://goo.gl/BQUqBZ.

[3] https://www.digitalocean.com/.

Fig. 24.1 Migration types to the cloud. Adapted from [7]

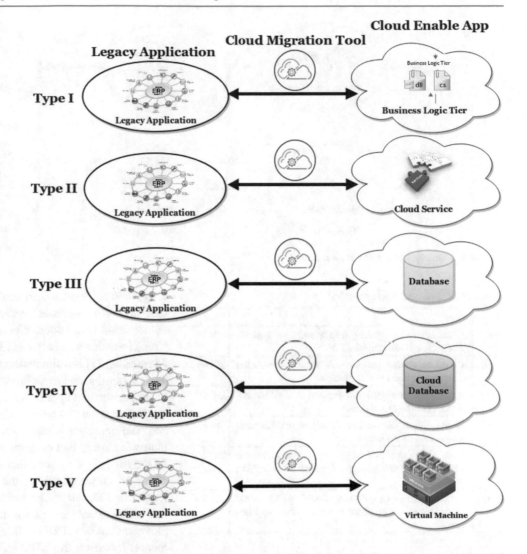

Research Question 2 (RQ2): What are the main challenges and opportunities reported in the literature related to the migration of legacy systems to the cloud? Studies from the literature show that difficulties are related to the understanding of the scope of the transition to the cloud as not only a technological improvement of existing legacy systems. Moreover, studies also reported that practitioners usually struggle in issues related to lack of standards for development of cloud services.

We applied the following search string to analyze the two research questions: *"cloud migration"* and *"tools"* and *"legacy systems"* for papers published between 2012 and 2017 (Fig. 24.2). The search string was executed on October 16th, 2017. We conducted the search queries in the Science Directory digital library and the number of papers returned was *six*. Once we obtained the results of these queries, we applied the inclusion and exclusion criteria. To be included, papers needed to fulfill at least one of the following criteria: *Inclusion Criteria 1 (IC1)*: papers that report empirical studies focusing on the study topic; *Inclusion Criteria 2*

(IC2): papers published from January 2012 to November 2017. *Exclusion Criteria 1 (EC1)*: papers that do not report empirical studies; *Exclusion Criteria 2 (EC2)*: papers not published from January 2012 to November 2017.

24.4 Analyzing Data from the Selected Papers

In this section, we present the findings of this study, together with the appropriate references. Table 24.1 presents a list of selected papers returned from the query of the search string in the *Science Direct* digital library. By analyzing these papers, we identified the tools presented in Table 24.2, as well as the migration phase they support.

Answers to RQ1: *Which tools support the migration of legacy systems to the cloud?*

Considering the tools listed in Table 24.2, the distribution of tools per phase is as follows: one tool to support Phase 1, twenty-two tools to support Phase 2, and two tools to support

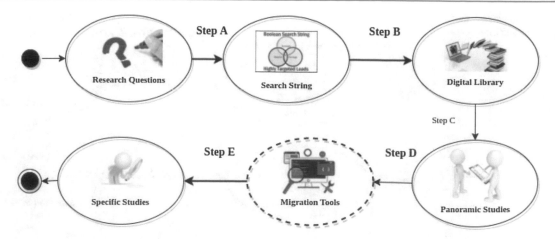

Fig. 24.2 Semi-systematic literature review

Table 24.1 Selected primary studies

ID	Title	Year
[4]	Challenges in migrating legacy software systems to the cloud—an empirical study	2017
[14]	Cloud migration process—A survey, evaluation framework, and open challenges	2016
[15]	Automated configuration support for infrastructure migration to the cloud	2016
[16]	White-box modernization of legacy applications: The oracle forms case study	2017
[17]	Understanding cloud-native applications after ten years of cloud computing—A systematic mapping study	2017
[18]	A framework to support selection of cloud providers based on security and privacy requirements	2013

Table 24.2 Tools to support the migration phases

Phase	Studies
1	CloudAdoption Toolkit [12]
2	CloudGenius [13], CDOSim [19], CloudSim [20], NetworkCloudSim [21], GreenCloud, iCanCloud, TeachCloud, GroudSim, CloudAnalyst, MDCSim, GDCSim, SPECI, Seagull, OPERA, Microsoft Migration Accelerator, SmartCloud, iCanCloud, CloudAnalyst, ContainerCloudSim, JCloudScale Midleware [22], CDOXplorer [23], CloudNetSim++ [24]
3	CloudMIG Xpress [19, 25, 26], Cloudify [27]

Phase 3. In the following paragraphs, we briefly describe these tools with their main features.

Cloud Adoption Toolkit [12] provides support for cloud migration decision making, including Energy Consumption Analysis, Technology Suitability Analysis, Responsibility Modeling, Stakeholder Impact Analysis, and Cost Modeling.
The CloudGenius Tool: also provides support to deal with the multi-criteria decision-making problems regarding the identification of an effective combination of a Cloud VM

image and a Cloud infrastructure service. For this end, the tool uses a model and methods to determine a suitable combination of a Cloud VM image and the corresponding Cloud infrastructure service [13].

CloudSim [21] is a simulation framework to support modeling, simulation, and experimentation in the Cloud computing infrastructure and application services. It enables evaluating the performance of a given application service in a controlled and heterogeneous Cloud environments (for example, combining the use of two or more different providers).

CDOSim [19] is a tool that can simulate cloud deployments of software systems that were reverse-engineered to Knowledge Discovery Meta-Model (KDM) models [28]. It can compare cost and performance of competing cloud deployment options (CDOs). It is compatible with application models based on the KDM of the OMG. This enables the simulation to be to some extent independent of programming languages for the cases that a corresponding KDM extractors is available for the target programming language. The tool incentives the use automated reverse-engineering techniques to create application models.

NetworkCloudSim [21] is a tool that extends CloudSim with modeling features of the application behavior as well as internal network of a data center.

GreenCloud [29] is an extension of the network simulator Ns2.[4] One of its relevant feature is the possibility to extract, aggregate, and provide information related to energy consumption of both computing and communication elements of the data center.

MDCSim [29] is a Multi-tier Data Center Simulation Platform is announced as a flexible and scalable simulation platform for in-depth analysis of multi-tier data centers. It was designed as a pluggable architecture aiming to capture the important design specifics of the underlying communi-

---
[4]http://www.isi.edu/nsnam/ns/.

cation paradigm, kernel level scheduling artifacts and the application level interactions among the tiers of a three-tier data center. The flexibility of the simulator is explained by its ability to experiment with different design alternatives in the three layers and in analyzing both performance and power consumption with realistic workloads.

The **iCanCloud** [30] tool is a simulation platform aimed at modeling and simulating cloud computing systems. iCanCloud was built to meet several requirements: (1) to be able conduct large experiments; (2) to provide a flexible and fully customizable global hypervisor, enabling users to implement any brokering policies; (3) to reproduce the instance types provided by a given cloud infrastructure; (4) to provide a user-friendly GUI for configuring and launching simulations, ranging from a single VM to large cloud computing systems comprising thousands of machines.

TeachCloud [31] is a modeling and simulation environment for cloud computing. It was developed an extension of CloudSim to experiment with different cloud components, namely processing elements, data centers, storage, networking, Service Level Agreement (SLA) constraints, web-based applications, Service Oriented Architecture, virtualization, management and automation, and Business Process Management. TeachCloud uses the Map-reduce processing model to handle "embarrassingly parallel" data processing tasks.

GroudSim [32] is a Grid and Cloud simulation toolkit for scientific applications based on a scalable simulation-independent discrete-event core. GroudSim aims to provide comprehensive support for complex simulation scenarios from simple job executions on leased computing resources. It enables calculation of costs and background load on resources. Simulations can be parameterised and are extendable on the basis of probability distribution packages to deal with failures that can occur in complex environments. To work, GroudSim requires one simulation thread only, instead of one separate thread per entity.

CloudAnalyst [33] is a tool built on top of CloudSim that aims to simulate large-scale cloud applications with the purpose of studying the behavior of such applications under various deployment configurations. CloudAnalyst aims to provide developers with insights on how to distribute applications among cloud infrastructures. It also provides services such as optimization of application performance. It supports visual modeling and simulation of large scale applications deployed on Cloud Infrastructures. CloudAnalyst also allows the description of application workloads, namely information of geographic location of users generating traffic, location of data centers and the number of resources in each data center.

GDCSim [34] is a simulation tool that unifies existing techniques to green data center management and aims to enable a holistic design and analysis prior to deployment. It is used to iteratively design green data centers. It analyses data center energy efficiency by studying and testing several factors such as: (1) different data center geometries, (2) workload characteristics, (3) platform power management schemes; (4) scheduling algorithms and (5) data center configurations.

SPECI (Simulation Program for Elastic Cloud Infrastructures) [35] is a simulation tool for the exploration of aspects of scaling as well as performance properties of future data centres.

OPERA (Optimization, Performance Evaluation and Resource Allocator) [36] is a layered queueing model used to evaluate the performance of web applications deployed on arbitrary infrastructures. OPERA serves to model an applications architecture and performance characteristics, perform operations on control points, estimate response time, throughput, and utilization of resources (i.e., CPU and disk).[5]

Microsoft Migration Accelerator (MA[6]) assists in the migration to the cloud [37]. MA is designed to seamlessly migrate physical, VMware, Amazon Web Services and Microsoft Hyper-V workloads into Azure. It automates all aspects of migration including discovery of source workloads, remote agent installation, network adaptation and endpoint configuration. It aims to reduce cost and risk of the migration project. It claims to change the cloud migration paradigm, by offering: *Heterogeneity*: MA enables migrate workloads running on a broad range of platforms such as VMware, Microsoft Hyper-V, Amazon Web Services and/or Physical servers within the environment. *Simple, Automated Migration*: the MA portal allows users to automatically discover their enterprise workloads, remotely from the cloud. It enables end-to-end configuration of migration scenarios. *Migrate Multi-tier Applications*: MA claims to have the unique ability to migrate multi-tier production system with application level consistency orchestrated across tiers. *Continuous Replication, Least Cutover Time:* MA for Azure provides full-system replication including the OS and application data.

SmartCloud iNotes [38] is a branded collection of Cloud products and solutions from IBM. It includes IaaS, SaaS, and Platform as a Service (PaaS) offered through public, private and hybrid cloud delivery models.[7]

ContainerCloudSim [39] was proposed for the study of resource management techniques in CaaS environments and was developed as an extension of CloudSim [21]. Its supports the modeling and simulation of "containerized" cloud computing environments. ContainerCloudSim provides an environment for evaluation of resource management techniques such as container scheduling, placement, and consolidation of containers.

---

[5]http://www.ceraslabs.com/technologies/opera.
[6]https://azure.microsoft.com/pt-br/blog/introducing-microsoft-migration-accelerator/.
[7]http://www.ibm.com/cloud-computing/us/en/.

JCloudScale Midleware [22] is a Java-based middleware supporting building elastic applications on top of a public or private IaaS cloud. It allows the migration of applications to the cloud, with minimal changes to the application code. It also takes over virtual machine management, application monitoring, load balancing, and code distribution. It aims to run on top of any IaaS cloud, making it a viable solution to implement applications for private or hybrid cloud settings.

CloudMIG Xpress [40] is a approach for supporting practitioners and researchers to semi-automatically migrate existing software systems to cloud-based applications. It incorporates usage patterns and varying resource demands in creating a target architecture candidate and concentrates on enterprise software systems offered by SaaS providers. The approach is composed of six major activities as follows. Extraction, Selection, Generation, Adaptation and Evaluation. It addresses challenges such as systematically comparing cloud environment candidates, checking the conformance with particular cloud environments, or simulating monitored workload for envisioned cloud-based target architectures to evaluate future costs and provides tool support for the comparison and planning phases to migrate software systems to PaaS or IaaS-based clouds [40].

Cloudify[8] and **Kubernetes**[9] are Open Source software projects that support the orchestration of Docker containers [41]. They can be used to automate the deployment and to scale applications in the cloud. Cloudify allows developers to model the application topology through YAML.

CloudNetSim++ [24] is a toolkit for modeling and simulation purposes to support the simulation of distributed data center architectures using the cloud. CloudNetSim++ was designed to enable the analysis of data center architectures regarding network traffic patterns through the use of custom protocols and applications. CloudNetSim++ claims to be the first cloud computing simulator that uses real network physical characteristics to model distributed data centers. The tool support users to define, among other features, a SLA policy, scheduling algorithms and modules for different components of data centers throughout the use of a generic framework.

Answers to RQ2: *What are the main challenges and opportunities reported in the literature related to the migration of legacy systems to the cloud?*

Studies from the literature reveal that the transition to the cloud is not limited to evolving existing legacy systems. It also results in modifying the way these systems operate, provide services, and are maintained [4]. For example, despite the ongoing advancements in the cloud computing, there is no common standard for the development of cloud services [42]. This leads to the challenge of integrating legacy systems to cloud services, since different providers offer cloud services with different underlying technologies and nonstandard proprietary APIs [4]. Moreover, evidence from the literature shows that many of the difficulties in the migration process are related to: (1) inappropriate understanding regarding cloud computing requirements, (2) inadequate or no planning [4]. In this context, many companies have concerns on how to avoid failure in cloud environment.

24.5 Conclusions and Future Research

In this paper, we presented an updated list of tools that support the migration of legacy systems to the cloud as follows: one tool to support the planning of the migration phase, 22 tools that support the design of the migration phase and finally two tools related to the enable phase. We briefly discussed the features of these tools and contextualized them in the migration process. To the best of our knowledge and based on the findings from this study, we did not identify in the literature reports from the use in the industry of tools that support the whole migration process to the cloud. Most of the tools focus on specific phases of the migration process.

As future work, we plan to evaluate the usage of the tools Cloudify as an open source cloud orchestration framework and the Open Tosca Container that is the TOSCA Runtime Environment to deploy and manage Cloud applications. It enables the automated provisioning of applications that are modeled using TOSCA and packaged as CSARs.

The first author of this paper thanks for the Scholarship (T.O.B)-No BOL0731/2016 provided by the Research Foundation State of Bahia (FAPESB).

References

1. B. Martens, F. Teuteberg, Decision-making in cloud computing environments: a cost and risk based approach. Inf. Syst. Front. **14**(4), 871–893 (2012)
2. B.A. Aubert, J.-F. Houde, M. Patry, S. Rivard, A multi-level investigation of information technology outsourcing. J. Strateg. Inf. Syst. **21**(3), 233–244 (2012)
3. A. Gunka, S. Seycek, H. Kühn, Moving an application to the cloud: an evolutionary approach, in *Proceedings of the 2013 International Workshop on Multi-Cloud Applications and Federated Clouds* (ACM, New York, 2013), pp. 35–42
4. M.F. Gholami, F. Daneshgar, G. Beydoun, F. Rabhi, Challenges in migrating legacy software systems to the cloud—an empirical study. Inf. Syst. **67**, 100–113 (2017)
5. H. Yang, M. Tate, A descriptive literature review and classification of cloud computing research, in *CAIS*, vol. 31 (2012), p. 2
6. H.K. Cheng, Z. Li, A. Naranjo, Research note—cloud computing spot pricing dynamics: latency and limits to arbitrage. Inf. Syst. Res. **27**(1), 145–165 (2016)
7. M.F. Gholami, F. Daneshgar, G. Low, G. Beydoun, Cloud migration process—a survey, evaluation framework, and open challenges. J. Syst. Softw. **120**, 31–69 (2016)

---

[8]http://getcloudify.org.

[9]kubernetes.io.

8. V. Andrikopoulos, T. Binz, F. Leymann, S. Strauch, How to adapt applications for the cloud environment. Computing **95**(6), 493–535 (2013)

9. S. Leimeister, M. Böhm, C. Riedl, H. Krcmar, The business perspective of cloud computing: actors, roles and value networks, in *ECIS* (2010), p. 56

10. B. Kitchenham, Procedures for performing systematic reviews, vol. 33, no. 2004 (Keele University, Keele, 2004), pp. 1–26

11. M.V. Mäntylä, B. Adams, F. Khomh, E. Engström, K. Petersen, On rapid releases and software testing: a case study and a semi-systematic literature review. Empir. Softw. Eng. **20**(5), 1384–1425 (2015)

12. A. Khajeh-Hosseini, D. Greenwood, J.W. Smith, I. Sommerville, The cloud adoption toolkit: supporting cloud adoption decisions in the enterprise. Softw. Pract. Exp. **42**(4), 447–465 (2012)

13. M. Menzel, R. Ranjan, Cloudgenius: decision support for web server cloud migration, in *Proceedings of the 21st International Conference on World Wide Web* (ACM, New York, 2012), pp. 979–988

14. M.F. Gholami, F. Daneshgar, G. Low, G. Beydoun, Cloud migration process—a survey, evaluation framework, and open challenges. J. Syst. Softw. **120**, 31–69 (2016)

15. J. García-Galán, P. Trinidad, O.F. Rana, A. Ruiz-Cortés, Automated configuration support for infrastructure migration to the cloud. Futur. Gener. Comput. Syst. **55**, 200–212 (2016)

16. K. Garcés, R. Casallas, C. Álvarez, E. Sandoval, A. Salamanca, F. Viera, F. Melo, J.M. Soto, White-box modernization of legacy applications: the oracle forms case study. Comput. Stand. Interf. **57**, 110–122 (2017)

17. N. Kratzke, P.-C. Quint, Understanding cloud-native applications after 10 years of cloud computing—a systematic mapping study. J. Syst. Softw. **126**, 1–16 (2017)

18. H. Mouratidis, S. Islam, C. Kalloniatis, S. Gritzalis, A framework to support selection of cloud providers based on security and privacy requirements. J. Syst. Softw. **86**(9), 2276–2293 (2013)

19. F. Fittkau, S. Frey, W. Hasselbring, Cdosim: simulating cloud deployment options for software migration support, in *2012 IEEE 6th International Workshop on the Maintenance and Evolution of Service-Oriented and Cloud-Based Systems (MESOCA)* (IEEE, Piscataway, 2012), pp. 37–46

20. R.N. Calheiros, R. Ranjan, A. Beloglazov, C.A. De Rose, R. Buyya, Cloudsim: a toolkit for modeling and simulation of cloud computing environments and evaluation of resource provisioning algorithms. Soft. Pract. Exp. **41**(1), 23–50 (2011)

21. S.K. Garg, R. Buyya, Networkcloudsim: modelling parallel applications in cloud simulations, in *2011 Fourth IEEE International Conference on Utility and Cloud Computing (UCC)* (IEEE, Piscataway, 2011), pp. 105–113

22. R. Zabolotnyi, P. Leitner, W. Hummer, S. Dustdar, Jcloudscale: closing the gap between IaaS and PaaS. ACM Trans. Internet Technol. (TOIT) **15**(3), 10 (2015)

23. S. Frey, F. Fittkau, W. Hasselbring, Optimizing the deployment of software in the cloud. ACM Trans. Internet Technol. (TOIT) **15**(3), 10 (2015)

24. A.W. Malik, K. Bilal, K. Aziz, D. Kliazovich, N. Ghani, S.U. Khan, R. Buyya, Cloudnetsim++: a toolkit for data center simulations in omnet++, in *2014 11th Annual High-Capacity Optical Networks and Emerging/Enabling Technologies (HONET)* (IEEE, Piscataway, 2014), pp. 104–108

25. S. Frey, W. Hasselbring, B. Schnoor, Automatic conformance checking for migrating software systems to cloud infrastructures and platforms. J. Softw. Evol. Process **25**(10), 1089–1115 (2013)

26. S. Frey, E. Schulz, M. Rau, K. Hesse, Cloudmig xpress 0.5 beta-user guide, in *CloudMIG XPress 0.5 Beta User Guide. Christian Albrechts Universität Kiel, Software Engineering* (2012), p. 3

27. R. Qasha, J. Cala, P. Watson, Towards automated workflow deployment in the cloud using tosca, in *2015 IEEE 8th International Conference on Cloud Computing (CLOUD)* (IEEE, Piscataway, 2015), pp. 1037–1040

28. R. Pérez-Castillo, I.G.-R. De Guzman, M. Piattini, Knowledge discovery metamodel-iso/iec 19506: a standard to modernize legacy systems. Comput. Stand. Interf. **33**(6), 519–532 (2011)

29. S.-H. Lim, B. Sharma, G. Nam, E.K. Kim, C.R. Das, Mdcsim: a multi-tier data center simulation, platform, in *IEEE International Conference on Cluster Computing and Workshops, 2009. CLUSTER'09* (IEEE, Piscataway, 2009), pp. 1–9

30. A. Núñez, J.L. Vázquez Poletti, C. Caminero, G.G. Castañé, J.C. Pérez, I.M. Llorente, iCanCloud: a flexible and scalable cloud infrastructure simulator. J. Grid Comput. **10**(1), 185–209 (2012)

31. Y. Jararweh, Z. Alshara, M. Jarrah, M. Kharbutli, M.N. Alsaleh, Teachcloud: a cloud computing educational toolkit. Int. J. Cloud Comput. 1 **2**(2–3), 237–257 (2013)

32. S. Ostermann, K. Plankensteiner, R. Prodan, T. Fahringer, Groudsim: an event-based simulation framework for computational grids and clouds, in *European Conference on Parallel Processing* (Springer, Cham, 2010), pp. 305–313

33. B. Wickremasinghe, R.N. Calheiros, R. Buyya, Cloudanalyst: a cloudsim-based visual modeller for analysing cloud computing environments and applications, in *2010 24th IEEE International Conference on Advanced Information Networking and Applications (AINA)* (IEEE, Piscataway, 2010), pp. 446–452

34. S.K. Gupta, R.R. Gilbert, A. Banerjee, Z. Abbasi, T. Mukherjee, G. Varsamopoulos, GDCSIM: a tool for analyzing green data center design and resource management techniques, in *2011 International Green Computing Conference and Workshops (IGCC)* (IEEE, Piscataway, 2011), pp. 1–8

35. I. Sriram, SPECI, a simulation tool exploring cloud-scale data centres, in *Cloud Computing* (2009), pp. 381–392

36. P. Zoghi, M. Shtern, M. Litoiu, H. Ghanbari, Designing adaptive applications deployed on cloud environments, ACM Trans. Auton. Adapt. Syst. (TAAS) **10**(4), 25 (2016)

37. P. Scandurra, G. Psaila, R. Capilla, R. Mirandola, Challenges and assessment in migrating it legacy applications to the cloud, in *2015 IEEE 9th International Symposium on the Maintenance and Evolution of Service-Oriented and Cloud-Based Environments (MESOCA)* (IEEE, Piscataway, 2015), pp. 7–14

38. M. Lynch, T. Cerqueus, C. Thorpe, Testing a cloud application: Ibm smartcloud inotes: methodologies and tools, in *Proceedings of the 2013 International Workshop on Testing the Cloud* (ACM, New York, 2013), pp. 13–17

39. S.F. Piraghaj, A.V. Dastjerdi, R.N. Calheiros, R. Buyya, Containercloudsim: an environment for modeling and simulation of containers in cloud data centers. Softw. Pract. Exp. **47**(4), 505–521 (2017)

40. S. Frey, W. Hasselbring, The cloudmig approach: model-based migration of software systems to cloud-optimized applications. Int. J. Adv. Softw. **4**(3 and 4), 342–353 (2011)

41. E. Casalicchio, Autonomic orchestration of containers: problem definition and research challenges, in *10th EAI International Conference on Performance Evaluation Methodologies and Tools. EAI* (2016)

42. A.N. Toosi, R.N. Calheiros, R. Buyya, Interconnected cloud computing environments: challenges, taxonomy, and survey. ACM Comput. Surv. (CSUR) **47**(1), 7 (2014)

A Dual Canister Medicine IoT Dispenser

Peter James Vial, James Sansom, David Stirling, Prashan Premaratne,
Le Chung Tran, and Montserrat Ros

Abstract

This study describes an automated medicine dispenser
that has enhanced functions provided by with the advent
of the Internet of Things (IoT) paradigm. The prototype
device outlined here is capable of delivering two different
medicines at approximately the same time. This work
describes the development of a medicine dispenser that
incorporates some of the features of IoT devices for the
home. It uses an Archimedes screw to deliver the tablets
and incorporates basic levels of visual communication
with the client, such as an LCD display and dispensing
push buttons. The prototype developed illustrates the
possible applications for the home that can be provided
by the IoT paradigm.

Keywords

Internet of things · Medicine dispenser · Arduino ·
ThingSpeak · Twilio

25.1 Introduction

Australia's aging population calls for more people requiring
particular medication on a daily basis. Studies have shown
that 60% of the population over 65 take at least four drugs every day [1]. As the number of drugs a person takes increases,
the more difficult it becomes to remember correct quantities
and timing for every single type of medication. Currently
there are basic devices that will help with providing the
correct doses, providing the user remembers to take them
and has correctly filled up the device at the start of the week.

As a result of these complexities there is a lot of medication
non adherence in society causing hospital admissions, large
costs to the community and in certain cases, fatal costs to
the patient. The Personal Medication Manager project seeks
to provide a solution that is simple for the user, however
comprehensive in all aspects of medication management,
sorting and dispensing.

This initial prototype begins the process of developing a
fully functional medication dispenser for those individuals
both young and old who regularly need medications to
live in the community and who may have their medication
monitored by medical personnel.

25.2 Literature Review

25.2.1 The Need for a Medicine Dispenser

Through the study of a large variety of literature a number of
issues have prevailed demonstrating the need for a personal
medication system. The primary concern is the current statistics surrounding medication management, non-adherence
and the negative effect on individuals as well as the greater
community as a result of non-adherence. Currently this issue
is provided with a 'band aid fix' with medication organisers,
that help organise which medicine to consume at a certain
time, however they neglect aspects including reminding the
user to take the medication, the sorting of the medication
and alerts to caregivers if the medication is not taken. These
issues and the effects they have require a complete and
effective solution.

25.2.2 Issues of Medication Management in the Home

The growing elderly population and the increase in medi-
cated diagnosis' in patients, means that medication management is now increasingly important. In Australia, on average,

P. J. Vial (✉) · J. Sansom · D. Stirling · P. Premaratne · L. C. Tran
M. Ros
University of Wollongong, Wollongong, NSW, Australia
e-mail: peter_vial@uow.edu.au

© Springer International Publishing AG, part of Springer Nature 2018
S. Latifi (ed.), *Information Technology – New Generations*, Advances in Intelligent Systems and Computing 738,
https://doi.org/10.1007/978-3-319-77028-4_25

two thirds of the population over the age of 60 take more than four pills for medical treatment [1]. This is commonly known as a polypharmacy and at this stage, problems for patients start to compound in terms of medication management. The issues surrounding medication management include consuming other than the prescribed quantities, consuming pills at the incorrect time and simply not adhering to their medical regime. International and local studies have found that medication non-compliance is common among the elderly and in some cases one fifth of patients have completely neglected to take one or more of their prescribed medicines [1]. Mentally ill patients are also known to refuse medication and require constant hospitalisation as a result. A medical dispenser that monitors and reports on such patients could potentially save on hospital admissions of the mentally ill and the extra social and monetary cost this inflicts on society. It is also noted that the effect of medicine non-compliance is accountable for approximately eight to eleven percent of all hospital admissions for elderly patients [2].

Current prescription packaging presents another concern for medication management in the home. Issues arise around the packaging in terms of being able to read the labels instructions, opening the lid and being able to take the required dose of the correct medicine from the container. In a study with a pool of 24 patients over the age of 65, whom 79.2% administered their own medication, 29.2% could not open the child resistant lid, 33% could not read the instructions and 37.5% were not able to differentiate certain coloured pills [3]. This illustrates a clear difficulty facing the older population as a result of polypharmacy.

25.2.3 Current Medication Organizers for the Home

There are a variety of medication organizers currently available, the most prominent being a manual weekly calendar organiser, a circular organizer with alarm and automatic dispensing with notifier. The most basic form of organizer provides the user with labelled compartments for up to 4 weeks supply of medicine. This removes the need of sorting through multiple medication containers at the time of taking the dose and finding the correct quantity for each one, as the medicine regime is organised into the container at the start of the program, with a caregiver if needed. This method has the benefit of removing the day to day task of sorting pills and is very simplistic in its design. The short comings are that the pills need to be sorted on a regular basis, it is easy to forget to take the medication at the right time and if medication is required to be taken multiple times throughout the day this greatly reduces the period of time the organiser lasts between top ups (see Fig. 25.1).

Slightly more advanced medication dispensers come with basic electronics to provide an alarm at the required time for

Fig. 25.1 Basic medication organizer [4]

Fig. 25.2 Partly automated medication organizer [5]

the medicine to be consumed and automatically rotates to the correct time slot. This reduces the risk of missing the correct time to take medication as well as alleviating the need for daily sorting of pills. Similarly to the basic organiser this type is required to be topped up on a weekly or fortnightly basis depending on the number of pills taken throughout the day. Another benefit of this format is that it will only allow the required dosage to be taken, it is not possible to accidentally take multiple dosages (see Fig. 25.2).

The most advanced medication organisers currently available hold high capacities of medication for a longer period of time as well notifying the user through a variety of ways, have low quantity warnings and have the ability to contact carers. Although the medication still needs to be sorted, these organisers have the capacity to hold a month's worth of medication. They have sophisticated inbuilt electrical systems with the ability to have visual and verbal notifications as

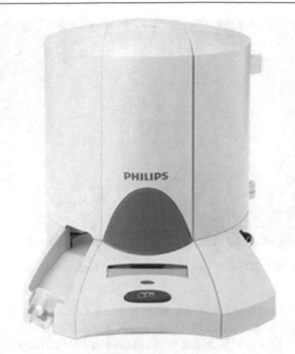

Fig. 25.3 Advanced medication dispenser [6]

well as text message notifications on the users phone. These advanced medication organisers have many great features making them reliable and precise yet remain simple for the user. The notable downfalls are the high cost and the need for the medication to be sorted at least once a month. The advanced medication dispenser shown in Fig. 25.3 has an ongoing monthly charge for service [6].

These medication dispensers are either expensive or have ongoing associated costs that make them inappropriate for many home situations where finances are an important factor. They also do not have all of the features that are possible with an Internet of Things (IoT) device connected to the internet and telephony via ThingSpeak [7] and Twilio [8].

25.3   Design of the Medicine Dispenser

This section outlines the design elements of the prototype IoT medicine dispenser. It incorporates hardware and software features. The device is designed to be modular in that the dispenser can be combined with additional dispensers in multiples of two (though this is not shown here in the original device). First we look at the design and prototyping of the method used to dispense a single type of tablet. We then examine the use of stepper motors, LCD message display panel and other physical (3D printed) and electrical components of the system. This is finally followed up with the development of the software and communications systems for the medicine dispenser.

25.3.1   Archimedes Screw for Tablet Dispensing

The Archimedes Screw is an important tool that has been used continuously for thousands of years [9]. It provides a means of transporting batches of materials up a gradient using a screw inside a cylinder. This method is often used for moving bulk loads of grain as an alternative to a conveyor and recently has been employed as a means to singulate homogenous units such as medication. For example, this method is often used in pharmaceutical medication dispensers [10, 11]. Configured in the right format the Archimedes screw is capable of both rapid movement of bulk materials and great separation [10]. The enclosed structure of the screw contains the transported material and reduces any waste through this progression. The resulting downside of the enclosed screw is that it can jam and damage the transported material and possibly require rebuilding to deem it useable again [11].

To overcome the inherent issues with the traditional Archimedes screw and its use with medication a design based on a similar concept has been reviewed. The design settled on here is different from traditional Archimedes screws by removing the central screw and attaching the helical thread to the inside wall of the cylinder and the complete cylinder is then rotated. This design is demonstrated in many patents for pharmaceutical medication dispensers [11–13] (Fig. 25.4).

The Archimedes screw for the medicine dispenser was incorporated into an STL file. The initial drawing for the canister design inside the medicine dispenser was as shown in Fig. 25.5. This shows the simple sketches with key parameters that were required for this device. The modelling step involves transferring the initial simple sketches and concepts into a comprehensive model with all the required detail ready for printing. This is a significant step and requires interpreting and adjusting the initial measurements and concepts to provide a working model. Figure 25.6 shows the

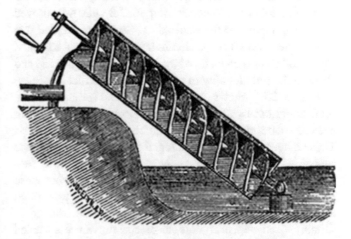

Fig. 25.4 Traditional Archimedes screw [14]

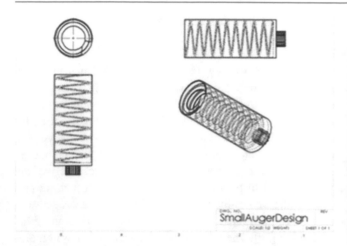

Fig. 25.5 Drawing of initial Canister design

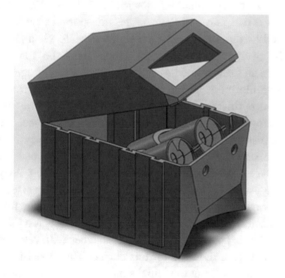

Fig. 25.6 3D printed case and canisters model

Fig. 25.7 3D printed half canister with scaffolding still attached

3D printing attempts did result in many failed print jobs as this was the authors first attempt at using 3D printing in a major project. It should be also noted that 3D printing does take a few hours to do even when successful, and often prints can fail and not be obvious until a long way into the print job.

25.3.2 Stepper Motors, 3D Casing and LCD Display

DC stepper motors provide a simplistic method to produce accurate rotational movements through a digital control system [15]. They are extensively used in industry due to the relative ease in achieving high performance with precise control [16]. The accuracy of stepper motors is attributed to their rotor and stator configuration [17]. The stator has coils positioned around the central rotor and when charged they provide an opposing field to the rotor's magnetic field which produces the required torque to spin the rotor a certain "step". This step is easily calculated depending on the specifications of the motor, therefore the rotation for each digital pulse is easily calculated. The accuracy of the motor to return to the same location is said to be approximately 3% of a single step size [15].

The two stepper motors used were as shown in Fig. 25.8. This device uses 5 V DC, has four phases, and a Torque of 34.4 milli-Nm. Each stepper motor was connected to a Motor Controller (UNL2003) Integrated Circuit. They were mechanically coupled to the canisters.

The design of the casing had a specific criteria based around being a suitable size for bench top storage, effective as a dispenser and aesthetically pleasing. The initial design was aiming for the size of a small coffee machine, with a similar shape and the dispenser at the front. The lid was designed with a cut out on an angled section on the front

completed two canister model STL diagram incorporating the two Archimedes screw based canisters and the lid with space for the LCD message screen. Initially the canisters were printed out as one canister model, but this proved difficult to clean out the scaffolding. So it was decided that the canisters would be printed in halves and glued together. This allowed the canisters to be properly cleaned, aligned and allowed the functionality of dispensing the medicine.

Figure 25.7 shows a half canister 3D print with the scaffolding left by the 3D printing process. This scaffolding needed to be cleaned away from the final half canisters. These halves were then glued together to form two complete canisters. There were some concern at creating a twin canister system using the 3D software and 3D printer but these were found to be minor in scale and scope and it was found to be easier than predicted. The canisters were coupled to suitably sized stepper motors for precise movements needed for dispensing medications. It should be noted that the initial

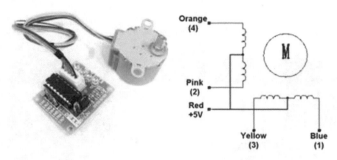

Orange
(4)

Pink
(2)

Red
+5V

Yellow   Blue
(3)   (1)

Fig. 25.8 Stepper motors and circuits

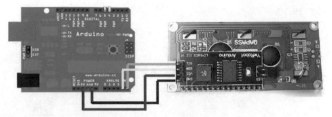

Fig. 25.10 Arduino Nano connection to LCD

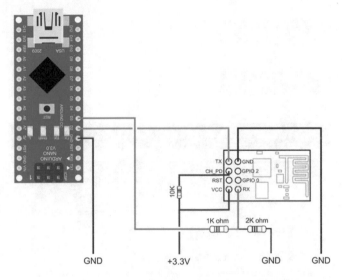

TX   GND
CH_PD   GPIO 2
RST   GPIO 0
VCC   RX

10K

1K ohm   2K ohm

GND   +3.3V   GND   GND

Fig. 25.9 Arduino Nano connection to WiFi module, ESP8266

Fig. 25.11 Completed unit with LCD display

to allow for an easy to see Graphic User Interface. Contours were designed vertically on the sides to provide the ability for multiple units to attach side by side. The overall design of the aesthetics was to give a slightly futuristic look as well as remaining functional. The front of the Medicine Dispenser was designed with a cut out and an overhang so a small collection cup could be placed underneath to capture the pills.

The Arduino Nano was used as the embedded microcontroller. This was interfaced to a Wi-Fi module ESP8266 to enabled WiFi communications with the local internet. The wiring connections are shown in Fig. 25.9.

A LCD display for messages was incorporated into the lid of the medicine dispenser. Figure 25.10 shows the connection between the Arduino Nano and the LCD display.

The electronics and canisters were enclosed into the 3D printed container and the lid had the LCD embedded in it. Figure 25.11 shows the completed unit as it appears with all components contained inside and the LCD display showing messages (the pushbuttons for starting the dispensing were added later and are not shown here).

25.3.3 Software and Communications

The microcontroller used was the Arduino Nano. This was programmed in C. In addition communication with the internet was performed using an interaction between the API for ThingSpeak [7] and the API for Twilio [8]. The Personal medication Manager was programmed to continually check if a command has been placed in the queue on the ThingSpeak Talkback application. At the scheduled time a certain specified command was sent to the Talkback application starting two processes, the dispense sequence on the Arduino and the SMS alert via Twilio.

Figure 25.12 shows the flow-chart of the programs set process, and demonstrates the basic outline of the procedure that the device goes through. The procedure can be broken into three major time frames of pre-dispensing, dispensing and post-dispensing. Prior to dispensing the online platform runs through a process from the TimeControl application to the TalkBack application. This is important to provide the schedule and store the data. The dispense period alerts the user, waits for the button press and dispenses the medication, verifying the quantity with break-beam sensors. The post-

Fig. 25.12 Flowchart of the program procedures

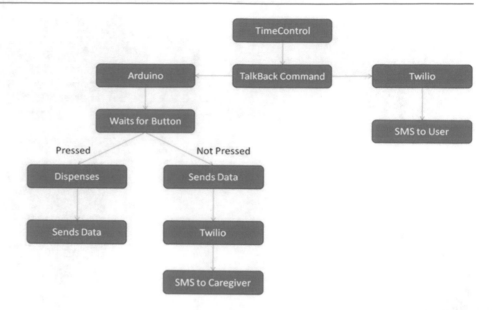

dispensing sends data back to ThingSpeak for storage and if the button has not been pressed it notifies a caregiver.

The internet platform works well employing two separate sites to communicate between the user's mobile phone and the medication dispensing device. The two web sites used are ThingSpeak [7] and Twilio [8], which work together to provide the communication and data storage for the system. ThingSpeak [7] was the major website used for communication and data storage. It provides a scheduling service, a command storing application and data collection and analysis. The most important feature is the TimeControl application, which provides the scheduling service. As can be seen in Fig. 25.13, using the TimeControl Application the process of adding to the schedule is simple and straight forward. The "add command" allows a phrase to be written which is stored in the TalkBack application at the scheduled time. The command is then stored until the Arduino requests the command, which is programmed for once every 30 s. Once the command is requested it is then removed from the queue. If two types of medication are needed at the one time the first command in the queue will be processed and then the second command.

Twilio [8] is an online program purely for communication for the IoT, providing messaging services, voice calls and cloud storage. The addition of Twilio provides the text messaging service simply through the addition of a command in the ThingSpeak TalkBack application. A predetermined message is sent to Twilio and the exact message is then sent through to any number of mobile phones. This is a basic but effective way to achieve mobile notifications and is ideal for the prototype.

Communication to and from the device is a vital component of the Personal Medication Manager as it allows for alerts and scheduling to be provided by an online platform.

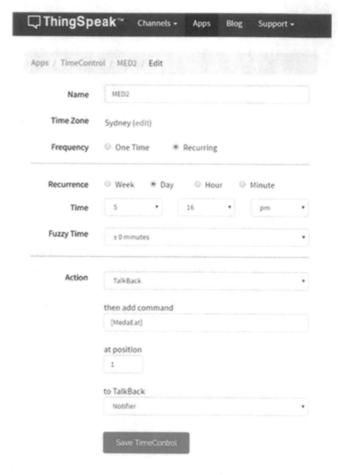

Fig. 25.13 ThingSpeak TimeControl web application

The communication set up between the device, the internet and the users' mobile phone works well and efficiently. The major communication link is between the internet platform

Got response from ESP8266:

busy s…

Recv 110 bytes

SEND OK

+IPD,0,132:{"id":2815886,"command_string"
    :"[MedaEat]","position":null,
        "executed_at":
            "2016-10-15T02:16:48Z"

Fig. 25.14 Response from GET request

and the Arduino device. This connection is made possible through the use of an ESP8266 module and AT commands sent through a serial connection from the Arduino. The ESP8266 connects to a specified Wi-Fi network and then sends a "GET" request every 20 s to ThingSpeak. If there is a command waiting in the TalkBack command queue, the "GET" request will return with a string of values including the pre-programmed command from the ThingSpeak application, TimeControl. Figure 25.14 shows the response from ThingSpeak that it receives on the serial monitor when generating a GET request. The first line shows that the Arduino is receiving data from the ESP8266 module, the fourth line (which has been extended over many lines for clarification purposes) provides the length of the string of data and the final row displays the string with the command positioned between the "[" and "]" (the final line was trimmed).

25.4   Conclusion and Future Work

Functionality testing of the device found that the features worked well together and the device completed the goal of precise medication dispensing. The final device successfully received commands at a specified time, alerted the user and successfully dispensed up to two medication types. The current medicine dispenser prototype device is estimated to cost about $120 Australian (about US$100) assuming that online websites used are free for home use.

Further developments of the system are in progress. These include facial recognition systems, embedding security into wireless and wired communications systems, pressure sensor for the tablets, touch screen controls and long range low data rate system incorporation (LoRaWan).

Acknowledgment   This work was funded by the Crown in Australia at the University of Wollongong.

References

1. R.A. Elliott, Problems with medication use in the elderly: an Australian perspective. J. Pharm. Pract. Res. **36**(1), 58–66 (2006)
2. S.A. Vik, C.J. Maxwell, D.B. Hogan, Measurement, correlates, and health outcomes of medication adherence among seniors. Ann. Pharmacother. **38**(2), 303–312 (2004)
3. R. Griffiths et al., A nursing intervention for the quality use of medicines by elderly community clients. Int. J. Nurs. Pract. **10**(4), 166–176 (2004)
4. Forgetting the Pill, website, visited, (2017), https://www.forgettingthepill.com/categories/pill-organizers
5. Medsmart, website, visited, (2017), http://alertutah.com/product/medsmart
6. Automated Medication Dispenser Service, website, visited, (2017), https://www.lifeline.philips.com/health-solutions/health-mdp
7. ThingSpeak, website, visited, (2017), https://thingspeak.com
8. Twilio, website, visited, (2017), https://www.twilio.com
9. C. Rorres, The turn of the screw: optimal design of an archimedes screw. J. Hydraul. Eng. **126**(1), 72 (2000)
10. W. Willemse, C.A. Willemse, W.W. Willemse, Pharmaceutical dispensing system for medicament and pre-packaged medication. Google Patents, (2010)
11. T.L. Kraft, et al., Rotating apparatus for dispensing single homogeneous units. Google Patents, (1993)
12. J.H. Boyer, J.P. Boyer, H. Gerlitz, Device that counts and dispenses pills. Google Patents, (1999)
13. J.H. Boyer, J.P. Boyer, Pharmaceutical dispensing system. Google Patents, (1999)
14. W.F. Inc, Archimedes' screw, website, visited, (2016), https://en.wikipedia.org/wiki/Archimedes%27_screw
15. T.L. Skvarenina, *The Power Electronics Handbook* (CRC Press, Boca Raton, FL, 2001)
16. M. Bodson, High-performance nonlinear feedback control of a permanent magnet stepper motor. IEEE Trans. Control Syst. Technol. **1**(1), 5–14 (1992)
17. Kiatronics, 28BYJ-48—5V Stepper Motor 2015 document on website, visited, (2017), http://robocraft.ru/files/datasheet/28BYJ-48.pdf

Ayako Arao and Hiroaki Higaki

Abstract

In wireless sensor networks, each wireless sensor node records events occurred in its observation area with their observation time. Each wireless sensor node possesses its own local clock whose drift and offset are generally different from the others. In conventional clock synchronization methods, wireless sensor nodes exchanges control messages with their local clock values and estimate their transmission delay. However, it is difficult to adjust their local clocks since transmission delay of control messages are difficult to estimate. By using observation records of the commonly observed events by neighbor wireless sensor nodes, this paper proposes a novel method to estimate the relative drift and offset between local clocks of the neighbor wireless sensor nodes. Here, each sensor node only detects the occurrences of events and cannot achieve the locations where the events occur. Hence, commonly observed events between neighbor wireless sensor nodes are required to be detected. Our proposed method applies a heuristic that multiple observation records in neighbor wireless sensor nodes whose intervals are the same are estimated to be commonly observed events.

Keywords

Wireless sensor networks · Observation time · Local clock synchronization · Relative drift estimation · Relative offset estimation

26.1 Introduction

A wireless sensor network consists of numerous number of wireless sensor nodes with their sensor modules for achieving environmental data and wireless communication

A. Arao · H. Higaki (✉)
Department of Robotics and Mechatronics, Tokyo Denki University, Tokyo, Japan
e-mail: arao@higlab.net; hig@higlab.net

modules for transmission of data messages containing the environmental data to one of stationary sink nodes by using wireless multihop communication based on wireless ad-hoc communication. Each wireless sensor node possesses its local clock and the sensor node records observed events with the clock value at that time [7]. Since the wireless sensor nodes work autonomously and their local clocks have individual differences, it is almost impossible for the local clocks in the wireless sensor nodes to be completely synchronized [3]. Especially due to individual differences in their crystal oscillators, incremented clock values in the same time duration are generally different one by one and networks with numerous number of nodes with their local clocks should be designed and managed on the assumption of the asynchronous local clocks [8]. Same as [10], this paper assumes that a local clock value $C_i(t)$ of a wireless sensor node S_i is represented with its offset O_i and drift dt_i/dt as $C_i(t) = (dt_i/dt)t + O_i$. Since each local clock of S_i has its own offset and drift, it is expected that a clock value difference $|C_i(t) - C_j(t)|$ between local clocks of S_i and S_j is required to be kept small by a certain clock synchronization procedure with a certain short interval. In addition, local clock values recorded when a wireless sensor node observes events are also required to be corrected according to the clock synchronization procedure.

In environments where GPS (Global Positioning System) or wave clocks are not available, relative offset and drift between two local clocks of wireless sensor nodes are required to be estimated. Various conventional methods for clock synchronization in wired networks have been proposed. Here, control messages carrying local clock values are exchanged among wired nodes and transmission delay for the messages are estimated for clock synchronization. However, in wireless networks, due to collision avoidance methods such as CSAM/CA and RTS/CTS control in wireless LAN protocols, dispersion of transmission delay of the control messages carrying local clock values is large and it becomes difficult to achieve precise synchronization of local clocks based on estimation of relative offset and drift between

© Springer International Publishing AG, part of Springer Nature 2018
S. Latifi (ed.), *Information Technology – New Generations*, Advances in Intelligent Systems and Computing 738,
https://doi.org/10.1007/978-3-319-77028-4_26

the local clocks of neighbor wireless sensor nodes. Hence, this paper proposes a novel clock synchronization method without control message transmissions with local clock values whose transmission delay is difficult to estimate. Our proposed method is based on the fact that observation areas of neighbor wireless sensor nodes are usually overlapped and events which occurs in the overlapped area are observed by the wireless sensor nodes simultaneously.

26.2 Related Works

The problem of synchronization among local clocks in a network has been discussed and various synchronization methods have been proposed. The most fundamental approach to solve the problem is the algorithm discussed in [1]. Here, between two computers, local clock value request and reply control messages are exchanged where these control messages carry local clock values of sender computers. However, since the receiver computer cannot achieve its local clock values when the received control message is transmitted, the transmission delay of the received control message is required to be estimated. Therefore, the methods for clock synchronization by exchange of local clock values require more precise estimation of transmission delay of control messages. Even with variation of transmission delay of control messages, it may be practically applicable for

proposed methods to wired networks whose variation of transmission delay is not so large.

For synchronization of local clocks of wireless nodes in wireless ad-hoc networks, RBS [2], FTSP [4] and TSPN [6] have been proposed. All these methods are based on the transmissions of control messages carrying local clock values as discussed before. Hence, for achieving highly precise synchronization among local clocks in wireless nodes, more precise estimation of transmission delay of control messages carrying local clock values are required. However, due to collision avoidance methods such as CSMA/CA and RTS/CTS control, it becomes much more difficult to estimate transmission delay of control messages for clock synchronization. The backoff timer for collision avoidance in CSMA/CA introduces unpredictable waiting time for data message transmissions and RTS/CTS control for avoiding collisions due to the hidden terminal problem requires much longer suspension of data message transmission procedure causing much higher unpredictability of total transmission delay as shown in Fig. 26.1. Especially in wireless sensor networks, high congestions of sensor data messages around the stationary wireless sink nodes are unavoidable so that prediction of transmission delay of control messages becomes difficult or almost impossible. In addition, burst traffic of data messages caused by some critical events also makes difficult to estimate transmission delay of control messages. In order to solve this problem, another approach without transmissions of control messages to which current local clock values are piggybacked are required to be considered.

Fig. 26.1 Unpredictable transmission delay of control messages for clock synchronization in wireless ad-hoc networks

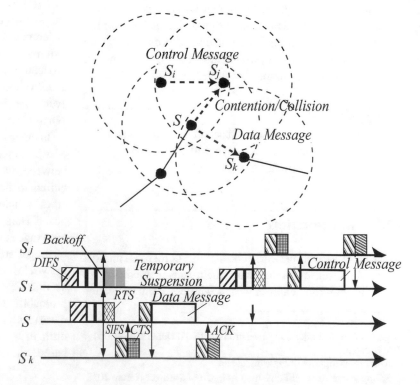

26.3 Proposal

26.3.1 Commonly Observed Events

Each wireless sensor node consists of a sensor module which detects events occurred within its observation area and a wireless communication module which transmits/receives wireless signals from/to its neighbor wireless nodes within its wireless signal transition area. A wireless sensor node S_i which detects an occurrence of an event within its observation area records kinds of the events with some additional related attributes including the clock value $C_i(t)$ of its local clock at the instance t when S_i observes the event. For simplicity, this paper assumes that each event is detected by all the wireless sensor nodes whose observation areas include the location of the event at that instance, i.e. without any observation delay. In reality, each sensor device requires its specific response time for an event observation and the effect of the delay is discussed in our future work. In addition, all events are assumed to be the same kind.[1] Hence, in accordance with the event observation records by a wireless sensor node S_i, a sequence $ESeq_i := |C_i(t_0), C_i(t_1), \ldots, C_i(t_{N_i})\rangle$ of the clock values at the instances when S_i observes the events is induced. Here, $C_i(t_j)$ is the value of the local clock of S_i at the instance t_j when S_i observes an occurrence of an event $e_i(t_j)$ in its observation area. On the other hand, each wireless sensor node S_i communicates with its neighbor wireless sensor nodes within its wireless signal transmission area. Thus, it is possible for S_i to exchange its clock value sequence $ESeq_i$ at occurrences of locally observed events with its neighbor wireless sensor nodes. Generally, the observation area of a wireless sensor node is included in its wireless signal transmission area. In addition, in a wireless sensor network, an observation area where all the event occurred are surely observed and recorded by at least one wireless sensor node is required to be covered by observation areas of multiple wireless sensor nodes as shown in Fig. 26.2 [5, 9]. Hence, observation areas of neighbor wireless sensor nodes usually overlap and the wireless sensor nodes whose observation area overlap can communicate directly by using wireless ad-hoc communication.

Suppose the case where observation areas of wireless sensor nodes S_i and S_j overlap as shown in Fig. 26.3. As mentioned, S_i and S_j can communicate directly by wireless ad-hoc communication since they are included in their wireless transmission areas one another. Here, all the events occurred in the overlapped observation area are observed by both S_i and S_j and recorded with clock values of their own

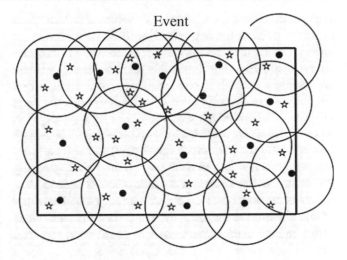

Fig. 26.2 Whole coverage of observation area by overlap observation areas of all sensor nodes

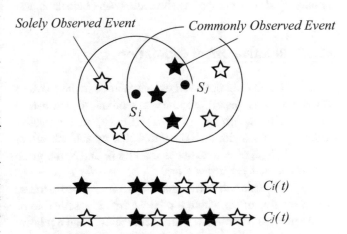

Fig. 26.3 Local clock values of observation time in S_i and S_j

local clocks. These events are called *commonly observed events* of S_i and S_j. The other events, i.e. events observed by only one of S_i and S_j, are called *solely observed events*.

Commonly/Solely Observed Events

An event which occurs at a certain instance t in an overlapped area of observation areas OA_i and OA_j of wireless sensor nodes S_i and S_j respectively and is observed and recorded with local clock values $C_i(t)$ and $C_j(t)$ into clock value sequences $ESeq_i$ and $Eseq_j$ by S_i and S_j respectively is called a commonly observed event of S_i and S_j. On the other hand, an event which occurs at a certain instance t in an area included by OA_i and excluded by OA_j and is observed and recorded with a clock value $C_i(t)$ into only a clock value sequence $ESeq_i$ by S_i is called a solely observed event of S_i against S_j. $\square$

Each wireless sensor node S_i assumes to observe all the events occur within an observation area OA_i of S_i. As various widely available sensor modules, S_i only identifies the occur-

---

[1]If various kinds of events are observed and identified by wireless sensor nodes, more precise estimation of commonly observed events is realized.

rence of the events and gets the clock values of its local clock at the instance of the occurrence of the events; however, it cannot identify the precise locations of the events in its observation area. Hence, it is impossible for S_i to identify whether an observed event is a commonly observed event with a neighbor wireless sensor node S_j or a solely observed event against S_j. Even though clock values at an instance when an event occurs are recorded by wireless sensor nodes which observe the event, since clock values $C_i(t)$ and $C_j(t)$ of wireless sensor nodes S_i and S_j at any instance t are generally different, it is impossible for a wireless sensor node to identify its commonly observed events with a specified neighbor wireless sensor nodes only by comparison of local clock values in their clock value sequences as shown in Fig. 26.3. Since clock values $C_i(t)$ and $C_j(t)$ of S_i and S_j for a commonly observed event at an instance t are different and it is impossible to identify commonly observed events of S_i and S_j only by simply comparing the sequences of clock values.

26.3.2 Relative Offset Estimation

By using commonly observed events defined in the previous subsection, this paper proposes a method to estimate a relative drift $dt_j/dt_i = (dt_j/dt)/(dt_i/dt)$ and a relative offset $O_j - O_i$ under an assumption that local clock values $C_i(t)$ and $C_j(t)$ of wireless sensor nodes S_i and S_j are given as $C_i(t) = (dt_i/dt)t + O_i$ and $C_j(t) = (dt_j/dt)t + O_j$, respectively. This subsection discusses a method to estimate only a relative offset where a relative drift is assumed to be 1. The method to estimate both a relative drift and a relative offset is discussed in the next subsection.

In case that a relative drift of $C_i(t)$ and $C_j(t)$ is 1, i.e. $dt_j/dt_i = 1$, $C_j(t) - C_i(t) = O_j - O_i$, i.e. a difference between clock values at any instance equals to their relative offset. Hence, if one of pairs of clock values of commonly observed events is identified, the difference between the clock values is their relative offset. However, it is difficult to identify a pair of clock values of a commonly observed event from local clock value sequences of neighbor wireless sensor node. This is because, as discussed in the previous section, even if wireless sensor nodes S_i and S_j observe the same event, i.e. their commonly observed event, at an instance t, their local clock values $C_i(t)$ and $C_j(t)$ at t are usually different, i.e. $C_i(t) \neq C_j(t)$. In addition, even if the instances t and t' of solely observed events observed by S_i and S_j respectively are different, i.e. $t \neq t'$, their local clock values $C_i(t)$ and $C_j(t')$ might be the same, i.e. $C_i(t) = C_j(t')$. Hence, the simple comparison between individual clock values $C_i(t)$ and $C_j(t')$ recorded in sequences $ESeq_i$ and $ESeq_j$ of local clock values of S_i and S_j does not result in correct estimation of the relative offset between their local clocks.

In order to solve this problem, this paper proposes a novel method to estimate the relative offset and drift between the local clocks of neighbor wireless sensor nodes by using multiple pairs of clock values recorded in the sequences of local clock values. As discussed, a clock value sequence $ESeq_i$ of local clock values of a wireless sensor node S_i when it observes events in its observation area OA_i includes local clock values of commonly observed events with its neighbor wireless node S_j. Though local clock values of S_j for the same commonly observed events are surely included in a clock value sequence $ESeq_j$ of local clock values of S_j when it observes them, it is impossible to detect the commonly observed events by simple comparison of local clock values in $ESeq_i$ and $ESeq_j$. However, since the commonly observed events, i.e. events which occurs in the overlapped area of observation areas OA_i and OA_i of S_i and S_j, are observed at the same instance t by S_i and S_j even though $C_i(t)$ and $C_j(t)$ may be different, intervals between the same pair of commonly observed events in S_i and S_j are the same. That is, suppose that clock values of S_i and S_j when they observe two commonly observed events occur at instances t and t' are $C_i(t), C_i(t'), C_j(t), C_j(t')$, respectively. Even if $C_i(t) \neq C_j(t)$ and $C_i(t') \neq C_j(t')$, $C_i(t') - C_i(t) = C_j(t') - C_j(t)$ is surely satisfied.

Since both locations where events occur and intervals between successive events contain a certain randomness, i.e. a certain unpredictability, this paper introduces a heuristic based on a reversed proposition of the above one into estimation of commonly observed events. Thus, if there exist local clock values $C_i(t_1)$ and $C_i(t_2)$ in $ESeq_i$ of S_i and $C_j(t_3)$ and $C_j(t_4)$ in $ESeq_j$ of S_j and $C_i(t_2) - C_i(t_1) = C_j(t_4) - C_j(t_3)$ is satisfied though $C_i(t_1) \neq C_j(t_3)$ and $C_i(t_2) \neq C_j(t_4)$, it is highly possible for S_i and S_j to have been observed two same events, i.e. there are two commonly observed events occurred at $t_1 = t_3$ and $t_2 = t_4$ respectively in the overlapped area of their observation areas. Needless to say, it might be possible for solely observed events whose recorded clock values are $C_i(t_1), C_i(t_2), C_j(t_3)$ and $C_j(t_4)$ to satisfy $C_i(t_2) - C_i(t_1) = C_j(t_4) - C_j(t_3)$ on accident. Hence, our heuristical method regards the possible relative offset that provides the maximum number of estimated commonly observed events which satisfies the above condition as an estimated relative offset.

Estimation of Relative Offset

Let $ESeq_i$ and $ESeq_j$ be sequences of local clock values $C_i(t)$ and $C_j(t)$ at instances when wireless sensor nodes S_i and S_j observe events. An estimated relative offset is what provides the maximum number of estimated commonly observed events where the transformed clock values with the estimated relative offset are the same. That is, with the estimated relative offset O, if the number of pairs of local

Fig. 26.4 Estimation of relative offset

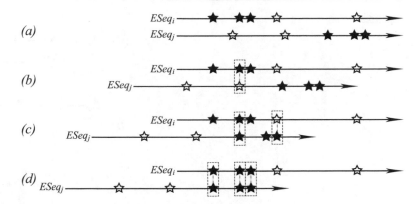

clock values satisfying $C_i(t) + O = C_j(t')$ where $C_i(t) \in ESeq_i$ and $C_j(t') \in ESeq_j$ is the maximum for all possible relative offsets, O is regarded as the estimated relative offset for S_i and S_j. □

For example, Fig. 26.4a shows two sequences of local clock values $ESeq_i$ and $ESeq_j$. Figure 26.4b,c and d show the results of parallel translation of $ESeq_j$ with possible relative offsets, i.e. where a pair of a local clock value $C_i(t)$ and a transformed local clock value with a possible relative offset $C_j(t') + O$ become the same value. There are one, two and three estimated commonly observed events with the same transformed local clock values. If the maximum number of estimated commonly observed events is 3, the relative offset in Fig. 26.4c is the estimation result in our method.

Now, we design an algorithm for estimation of a relative offset based on the heuristics. Here, for every pair of local clock values $C_i(t_k^i)$ and $C_j(t_l^j)$ in $ESeq_i$ and $ESeq_j$ respectively, it is assumed that these local clock values represents those at a certain commonly observed event, that is the difference $O = C_j(t_l^j) - C_i(t_k^i)$ is regarded as the estimated relative offset of S_i and S_j, and the number of estimated commonly observed events where $C_j(t_{l'}^j) = C_i(t_{k'}^i) + O$ is satisfied is counted. Here, the possible related offset is between the maximum $C_i(t_{N_i}^i) - C_j(t_0^j)$ and the minimum $C_i(t_0^i) - C_j(t_{N_j}^j)$ and the algorithm counts the estimated commonly observed events for every possible relative offset in this range. If there is an upper limit of relative offset between S_i and S_j, it is possible for the proposed algorithm to work with this limitation to reduce the time duration required for the proposed algorithm.

Relative Offset Estimation Algorithm

1. Initialize the maximum number of estimated commonly observed events of wireless sensor nodes S_i and S_j as 0 by $MCO_{iv} := 0$.
2. A temporary relative offset and the number of estimated commonly observed events are initialized as $Soff_{iv} := C_i(t_{N_i}^i) - C_j(t_0^j)$ and $CO_{ij} := 0$.

3. For each local clock value $C_i(t_k^i) \in ESeq_i = |C_i(t_0^i), C_i(t_1^i), \ldots, C_i(t_{N_i}^i)\rangle$, search events $C_j(t_l^j) \in ESeq_j = |C_j(t_0^j), C_j(t_1^j), \ldots, C_j(t_{N_j}^j)\rangle$ satisfying $C_i(t_k^i) = C_j(t_l^j) + Soff_{ij}$ and increments CO_{ij}.
4. If $CO_{ij} \geq MCO_{ij}$, $MCO_{ij} := CO_{ij}$ and an estimated relate offset $Eoff_{ij} := Soff_{ij}$.
5. If $Soff_{ij} = C_j(t_{N_j}^j) - C_i(t_0^i)$, jump to step 8).
6. Search a relative offset update $Uoff_{ij} := \min(C_j(t_l^j) + Soff_{ij} - C_i(t_k^i))$ where $C_j(t_l^j) + Soff_{ij} - C_i(t_k^i) > 0$.
7. $Soff_{ij} := Soff_{ij} - Uoff_{ij}$ and $CO_{ij} := 0$. Then, jump to step 3).
8. Return $Eoff_{ij}$ as the required estimated relative offset and the algorithm terminates. □

26.3.3 Relative Drift Estimation

This subsection proposes an extended algorithm for estimation of both the relative offset and the relative drift for recorded local clock values in two neighbor wireless sensor nodes whose observation areas overlap. Figure 26.5 shows the overview of our proposed method. Same as the method proposed in the previous subsection which supports only the cases with one relative drift, the number of estimated commonly observed events between local clock value sequences $ESeq_i$ and $ESeq_j$ for every possible relative offset $C_i(t_k^i) - C_j(t_l^j)$. In addition, for estimation of the relative drift, another pair of local clock values $C_i(t_{k'}^i) \in ESeq_i$ and $C_j(t_{l'}^j) \in ESeq_j$ ($k \neq k'$ and $l \neq l'$) is needed. Here, an estimated relative drift is $(C_i(t_{k'}^i) - C_i(t_k^i))/(C_j(t_{l'}^j) - C_j(t_l^j))$. After applying the transformation of local clock values with the estimated relative offset and the estimated relative drift, the number of estimated commonly observed events whose local clock values are the same is evaluated. Same as the previous subsection, according to a heuristic that the correct pair of relative offset and relative drift provides the maximum number of estimated commonly observed

Fig. 26.5 Estimation of relative drift

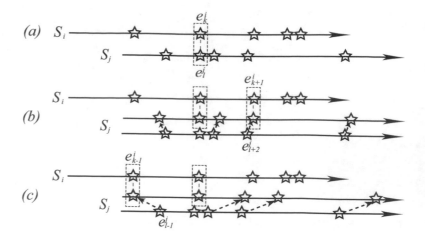

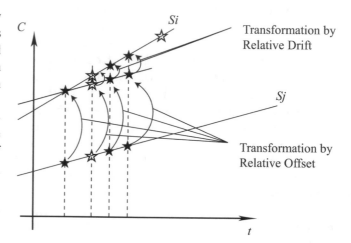

events, our proposed method estimate them. In order to apply our proposed method, for neighbor wireless sensor nodes to estimate relative offset and drifts to transform the local clock values for synchronization, there should be more than three commonly observed events. Hence, enough observation period to record local clock values are required.

Figure 26.6 shows a case of correct estimation of commonly observed events with correct estimation of a relative drift dt_j/dt_i and a relative offset $O_j - O_i$. Here, pairs of local clock values $C_i(t_1^i)$ and $C_j(t_1^j)$, $C_i(t_2^i)$ and $C_i(t_3^j)$, and $C_i(t_3^i)$ and $C_j(t_4^j)$ are those for commonly observed events, i.e., $t_1^i = t_1^j$, $t_2^i = t_3^j$ and $t_3^i = t_4^j$, respectively, and the rest $C_i(t_4^i)$ and $C_j(t_2^j)$ are local clock values for solely observed events in S_i and S_j, respectively. By consideration that $C_i(t_1^i)$ and $C_j(t_1^j)$ are local clock values in S_i and S_j when a commonly observed events of S_i and S_j occurs, the relative offset is estimated as $O_j - O_i = C_j(t_1^j) - C_i(t_1^i)$ and the line representing the local clock value in S_j is parallelly displaced as the points representing the local clock values $C_i(t_1^i)$ and $C_j(t_1^j)$ of the commonly observed event are overlapped. Then, by consideration that $C_i(t_2^i)$ and $C_j(t_3^j)$ are local clock values in S_i and S_j when a commonly observed events of S_i and S_j occurs, the relative drift is estimated as $dt_j/dt_i = (C_j(t_3^j) - C_j(t_1^j))/(C_i(t_2^i) - C_i(t_1^i))$ and the line representing the local clock value in S_j is rotated around the point representing the local clock value $C_i(t_1^i)$ as the points representing the local clock values $C_i(t_2^i)$ and $C_j(t_3^j)$ of the commonly observed event are overlapped. Now, the lines representing the local clock values of S_i and S_j are overlapped and all the commonly observed events including that for $C_i(t_3^i)$ and $C_j(t_4^j)$ are correctly estimated.

On the other hand, Figs. 26.7 and 26.8 show the cases when estimation of relative drift and/or offset is incorrect and estimation of commonly observed events is also incorrect as a result. In Fig. 26.7, same as in Fig. 26.6, $C_i(t_1^i)$ and $C_j(t_1^j)$ are considered to be local clock values in S_i and S_j when

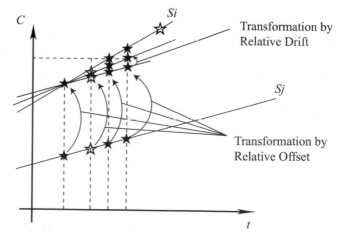

Fig. 26.6 Estimation of commonly observed events by offset and drift estimation (correct)

Fig. 26.7 Estimation of commonly observed events by offset and drift estimation (incorrect drift)

a commonly observed events of S_i and S_j occurs, and the relative offset is correctly estimated as $O_j - O_i = C_j(t_1^j) - C_i(t_1^i)$ and the line representing the local clock value in S_j

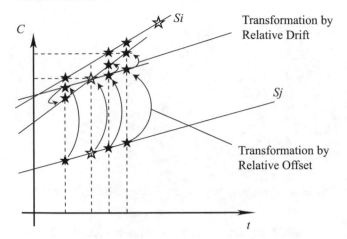

Fig. 26.8 Estimation of commonly observed events by offset and drift estimation (incorrect offset and drift)

is parallelly displaced as the points representing the local clock values $C_i(t_1^i)$ and $C_j(t_1^j)$ of the commonly observed event are overlapped. However, by incorrect consideration that $C_i(t_2^i)$ and $C_j(t_4^j)$ are local clock values in S_i and S_j when a commonly observed events of S_i and S_j occurs, the relative drift is incorrectly estimated as $dt_j/dt_i = (C_j(t_4^j) - C_j(t_1^j))/(C_i(t_2^i) - C_j(t_1^i))$ and the line representing the local clock value in S_j is rotated around the point representing the local clock value $C_i(t_1^i)$ as the points representing the local clock value $C_j(t_4^j)$ has the same C value (virtual axis) as $C_i(t_2^i)$. Here, pairs of points on the two lines representing the local clock values in S_i and S_j with the same C value (vertical axis) correspond to a commonly observed event of S_i and S_j. However, in Fig. 26.7, though pairs of $C_i(t_2^i)$ and $C_j(t_3^j)$, and $C_i(t_3^i)$ and $C_j(t_4^j)$ are those of local clock values for commonly observed events, their C values are not the same, i.e., these pairs of local clock values are not estimated to be those for commonly observed events.

Moreover, in Fig. 26.8, both relative offset and drift are incorrectly estimated. Here, $C_i(t_1^i)$ and $C_j(t_2^j)$ which is local clock value in S_j when its solely observed event occurs are considered to be local clock values in S_i and S_j when a commonly observed event of S_i and S_j occurs. A relative offset is incorrectly estimated as $O_j - O_i = C_j(t_2^j) - C_i(t_1^i)$ and the line representing the local clock value in S_i is parallelly displaced as the points representing the local clock values $C_i(t_1^i)$ and $C_j(t_2^j)$ have the same C value (vertical axis). Then, $C_i(t_2^i)$ and $C_j(t_4^j)$ are considered to be local clock values of the commonly observed event of S_i and S_j, that is, the relative drift is also incorrectly estimated as $De_j/dt_i = (C_j(t_4^j) - C_j(t_1^j))/(C_i(t_2^i) - C_i(t_1^i))$, and the line representing the local clock value in S_j is rotated around the point representing $C_j(t_1^j)$ which has already displaced from

the original position as the points representing the local clock value $C_j(t_4^j)$ has the same C value (vertical axis) as $C_i(t_2^i)$. Here, pairs of points on the two lines representing the local clock values in S_i and S_j with the same C value (vertical axis) correspond to a commonly observed event of S_i and S_j. In Fig. 26.8, no correct pairs of local clock values in S_i and S_j are estimated to be those of commonly observed events and two pairs of local clock values in S_i and S_j are incorrectly estimated to be those of commonly observed events.

As shown in these three examples in Figs. 26.6, 26.7 and 26.8, the number of estimated commonly observed events with incorrect estimation of relative offset and drift is usually smaller than that with correct estimation of them. It may be possible for pairs of local clock values of different events to be estimated as those of commonly observed events since the transformed C values are coincidentally the same. However, since the probability of such coincidental cases is low, the proposed heuristic that the correct relative drift and offset provides the maximum number of estimated commonly observed events is almost always applicable.

Relative Offset and Draft Estimation Algorithm

1. Initialize the maximum number of estimated commonly observed events of wireless sensor nodes S_i and S_j as 0 by $MCO_{iv} := 0$.
2. A temporary relative offset is initialized as $Soff_{iv} := C_i(t_{N_i}^i) - C_j(t_0^j)$.
3. For every possible temporary relative drift $Sdri_{iv} := (C_i(t_{k'}^i) - C_i(t_k^i))/(C_j(t_{l'}^j) - C_j(t_l^j)) > 0$, apply the following steps 4), 5) and 6).
4. The number of estimated commonly observed events is initialized as $CO_{ij} := 0$.
5. For each local clock value $C_i(t_k^i) \in ESeq_i = |C_i(t_0^i), C_i(t_1^i), \ldots, C_i(t_{N_i}^i)\rangle$, search events $C_j(t_l^j) \in ESeq_j = |C_j(t_0^j), C_j(t_1^j), \ldots, C_j(t_{N_j}^j)\rangle$ satisfying $(C_i(t_{k''}^i) - C_i(t_k^i))/(C_j(t_{l''}^j) - C_j(t_l^j)) = Sdri_{ij}$ and increments CO_{ij}.
6. If $CO_{ij} \geq MCO_{ij}$, $MCO_{ij} := CO_{ij}$, an estimated relate offset $Eoff_{ij} := Soff_{ij}$ and an estimated relative drift $Edri_{ij} := Sdri_{ij}$.
7. If $Soff_{ij} = C_j(t_{N_j}^j) - C_i(t_0^i)$, jump to step 10).
8. Search a relative offset update $Uoff_{ij} := \min(C_j(t_l^j) + Soff_{ij} - C_i(t_k^i))$ where $C_j(t_l^j) + Soff_{ij} - C_i(t_k^i) > 0$.
9. $Soff_{ij} := Soff_{ij} - Uoff_{ij}$ and $CO_{ij} := 0$. Then, jump to step 3).
10. Return $Eoff_{ij}$ and $Edri_{ij}$ as the required estimated relative offset and the required estimated relative drift and the algorithm terminates. $\square$

Fig. 26.9 Ratio of correct estimation of commonly observed events

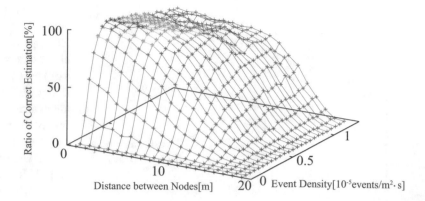

Figure 26.5 shows an example. According to the method proposed in the previous subsection, a pair of local clock values $C_i(t_k^i)$ and $C_j(t_l^j)$ is assumed to be for a possible commonly observed events. In addition, another pair of local clock values are also assumed to be for another possible commonly observed events and all the local clock values are transformed according to parallel translation. Then, the number of estimated commonly observed events with the same transformed local clock values are assigned is counted and the relative offset and drift that provide the maximum number of estimated commonly observed events is regarded as the correct ones.

26.4 Evaluation

Precision of our proposed method depends on the number of commonly observed events of neighbor wireless sensor nodes. Form this point of view, this section evaluates the performance of our proposed method by simulation experiments. Suppose two stationary wireless sensor nodes with 10 m observation ranges are located with their distance 0.5–19.5 m. Locations of events and intervals of two successive events are randomly determined according to the unique distribution and the exponential distribution,[2] respectively. With various event density, the ratio of correct estimation of commonly observed events, i.e. the ratio of correct estimation of relative offset and drift of their local clocks, is evaluated.

Figure 26.9 shows the simulation results. Red points represent correct estimation ratio higher than 99%, green points represent correct estimation ratio higher than 90%, and blue points represent others. Except for cases with extremely low event density and with extremely narrow overlapped observation area, our proposed method provides high correct estimation ratio. Less than $0.3 \times 10^{-5}/m^2s$ event occurrence density, too few commonly observed events occur. Hence, it is almost impossible to synchronize local clocks since

our method requires more them three commonly observed events for the drift and offset estimation. On the other hard, the authors have been afraid that the correct estimation ratio decreases as the event density becomes higher since incorrect estimation of the commonly observed events might be caused. However, the simulation result shows that no such degradation is observed even with event density higher than $20.0 \times 10^{-5}/m^2s$ (out of Fig. 26.9).

The performance is independent of the wireless transmission traffic of sensor data messages, e.g. around stationary wireless sink nodes, which is the most important advantage against the conventional method in which precise estimation of transmission delay of control messages are required.

26.5 Conclusion

This paper has proposed a novel clock synchronization method for wireless sensor networks. Different from the conventional methods by exchanging control messages with current local clock values and by estimation of transmission delay of the control messages, the proposed method estimates the relative offset and drift between two local clocks of neighbor wireless sensor nodes based on records of local clock values of event observations and estimation of commonly observed events of them. This paper has also designed estimation algorithms of relative offset and drift and evaluated their performance.

References

1. F. Cristian, Progabilistic clock synchronization. Distrib. Comput. **3**(3), 146–158 (1989)
2. E. Jeremy, G. Lewis, E. Deborah, Fine-grained network time synchronization using reference broadcasts, in *Proceedings of the 5th Symposium on Operating Systems Design and Implementation* (2002), pp. 147–163
3. H. Kopetz, W. Ochsenreiter, Clock synchronization in distributed real-time systems. IEICE Trans. Commun. **C-36**(8), 933–940 (1987)

---

[2]Events occur according to position arrivals.

4. M. Miklos, K. Branislav, S. Kayla, The flooding time synchroniza-tion protcol, in *Proceedings of the 2AD International Conference on Embedded Networked Sensor Systems* (2004), pp. 39–49

5. Y. Qu, S.V. Georgakopoulos, A distributed area coverage algorithm for maintenance of randomly distributed sensors with adjustable sensing range, in *ICE Global Communications Conference* (2013), pp. 286–291

6. G. Saurabh, K. Ram, B.S. Mani, Timing-sync protocol for sensor networks, in *Proceedings of the 1st International Conference on Embedded Networked Sensor Systems* (2003), pp. 138–149

7. L. Schick, W.L. Souza, A.F. Prado, Wireless body sensor network for monitoring and evaluating physical activity, in *Proceedings of the 14th ITNG* (2017)

8. A.S. Tanenbaum, M. Steen, *Distributed Systems Principles and Paradigms* (Prentice Hall, Upper Saddle River, 2002)

9. E. Tuba, M. Tuba, D. Simian, Wireless sensor network coverage problem using modified fireworks algorithm, in *Wireless Communications and Mobile Computing Conference* (2016), pp. 696–701

10. Y.-C. Wu, Q. Chaudhari, E. Serpedin, Clock synchronization of wireless sensor networks. ICE Signal Process. Mag. **28**(1), 124–138 (2011)

Ademola Philip Abidoye and Elisha Oketch Ochola

Abstract

A wireless sensor network (WSN) is a network consisting of small nodes with constrained capabilities to sense, collect, and transmit sensed data in many application areas such as the healthcare system, the automotive industry, sports, and open space surveillance. WSNs communicate through wireless mediums and are accessible to anyone, which makes sensor nodes vulnerable to various forms of attack. Considering the energy-constrained nature of sensor nodes, denial of service (DoS) attacks on these nodes are popular. This paper examines DoS attacks and proposes countermeasures based on use of the clustering technique. The method is compared with other related protocols, and the results show that our method is able to effectively detect and defend against DoS attacks in WSNs.

Keywords

Sensor networks · Security · Denial of service · Malicious node · Clustering · Integrity

27.1 Introduction

Recent improvement in micro-electromechanical systems (MEMs), wireless communications, highly integrated electronics, and low power devices have made the design of wireless sensor networks (WSNs) possible [1]. Sensor nodes are designed with the main aim of sensing physical quantities such as temperature, vibrations or humidity in the areas of interest. They communicate wirelessly with one another over a short distance. Generally, sensed data is transmitted

from sender nodes in a hop-by-hop fashion through each intermediate node until it reaches the final destination. WSNs currently have a large range of applications and they have been successfully applied in such wide ranging applications as ubiquitous web services, structural health monitoring, and smart parking systems [2]. They can be randomly or uniformly distributed in an environment and left unattended for long periods.

However, taken together, the characteristics listed below expose sensor nodes to various security attacks, as the wireless medium is open and accessible to anyone.

- The network topology changes constantly due to the dynamic nature of the network, and damage to or the death of some sensor nodes.
- Ad-hoc deployment of sensor nodes in WSNs helps attackers to launch attacks ranging from active interference to passive eavesdropping.

This makes it important to protect WSNs against attacks and, if there is an attack, measures should be taken to ensure that its effects on the network are insignificant. Security in the context of WSNs can thus be defined as the protection of legitimate sensor nodes against all known types of attacks. These attacks can be broadly divided into active and passive attacks. Denial of service (DoS) attacks are considered mainly because they target the limited sensor node energy in a WSN. DoS attacks aim to prevent an individual sensor node from sending its reading or from communicating with the network.

In this paper, an approach called Denial of Service Attacks and Countermeasures (DOSAC) is presented as a means to detect and prevent DoS attacks in WSNs. This approach is based on the clustering technique. An algorithm is used to uniformly distribute elected cluster heads within the network.

In the next section of the paper, we discuss related work. Section 27.3 presents the proposed system design. Proposed countermeasures against DoS attacks are discussed

A. P. Abidoye (✉) · E. O. Ochola
School of Computing, University of South Africa, Johannesburg, Gauteng, South Africa
e-mail: abidoap@unisa.ac.za; ocholeo@unisa.ac.za

© Springer International Publishing AG, part of Springer Nature 2018
S. Latifi (ed.), *Information Technology – New Generations*, Advances in Intelligent Systems and Computing 738,
https://doi.org/10.1007/978-3-319-77028-4_27

in Sect. 27.4. Section 27.5 presents performance evaluation, and Sect. 27.6 contains the conclusion.

27.2 Related Work

Wireless sensor nodes consist of different protocol layers of the Open Systems Interconnection (OSI) model. Each layer plays a specific role, such as framing, signalling, forwarding, reliable transportation and user interaction at both the sending as well as the receiving end. DoS attacks are identified at each layer of this model; these are purposeful, planned attacks intended to jeopardize the availability of service, thus restricting the WSN utility for application.

In [3], the authors analyse DoS attacks in WSNs. Their discussion includes the characteristics of WSNs, constraints and types of DoS attacks at different layers constituting obstacles to the smooth functioning of the networks. However, they do not provide countermeasures against the attacks.

Messai [4] divides possible attacks on WSNs into passive attacks and active attacks. The author discusses different attacks and security problems in each layer of the network's OSI model. However, he fails to provide a security measure against each attack discussed.

Han et al. [5] propose a security scheme against DoS attacks (SSAD) in cluster-based WSNs. The proposed method uses unique features to establish the trustworthiness of sensor nodes. The authors place all sensor nodes of a network into three domains: trusted, un-trusted, and uncertain. Cluster heads are selected from the trusted domain to ascertain their trustworthiness. These features allow the scheme to reduce the overhead involved in cluster head selection. In addition, it provides an efficient solution for detecting and defending against DoS attacks in a WSN.

Chen et al. [6] propose a novel method called path-based denial of service attacks (PDoS), which is operated at the base station to detect compromised sensor nodes within a network. The authors combined a Markov chain with triple exponential smoothing in order to make detection results more accurate. This approach is analytically presented; numerical representation of the model makes the approach scalable, and performance evaluation is well discussed. However, the approach is not flexible; it requires more computation, and more overhead is involved during computation.

27.3 Proposed System Design

The underlying network architecture for our proposed scheme consists of sensor nodes and a base station. With consideration for the resource-constrained nature of WSNs, we partition the network into finite clusters. Each cluster contains a cluster head (CH) and member nodes. The CHs

are periodically elected from among member nodes of each cluster in order to ensure a better energy balance while maintaining best detection coverage. An approach in [7] is used to divide the network into clusters, and each node is assigned an identification number (ID) to uniquely identify it in the network. An algorithm in [8] is adopted in order for the CHs to be uniformly distributed within the network.

27.3.1 Analysis of Denial of Service Attacks

Traffic pattern in WSNs is many-to-one: sensor nodes deployed in a target area for environmental monitoring need to transmit their readings to a data collection centre for further processing. In-network processing such as data compression or elimination of similar readings is needed for energy efficiency. This pre-processing requires high energy level sensor nodes such as CHs to receive and aggregate the content of the sensor readings and deliver the aggregated data packets to a final destination (base station). Based on this and other characteristics of WSNs mentioned above, end-to-end data packet transmission is susceptible to DoS attacks. If packet integrity is only verified at the base station, there is a high probability that the network may forward packets injected by an attacker many hops away from source nodes to the base station before the forged messages are identified in the network. This type of attack will dissipate the energy of sensor nodes and consume network bandwidth [9].

27.3.2 Legitimate Nodes and Malicious Nodes

Legitimate nodes: Legitimate nodes are nodes whose main functionalities have not been tampered with in the network; these include normal sensor nodes, cluster heads and the base station. Legitimate nodes are susceptible to a DoS attack launched by adversarial nodes in the network.

Malicious nodes: These nodes seek to deny service to legitimate sensor nodes in the network. Malicious nodes in WSNs include the following:

(a) Compromised nodes: These are legitimate sensor nodes whose responsibilities are taken over by the attackers for the purposes of disrupting normal network operations.

(b) Injected sensor nodes: These may be either legitimate nodes with normal sensing capability, or more powerful nodes with high processing capability such as the base station [9].

Legitimate sensor nodes and malicious nodes in a network are defined as follows:

The WSN model consists of a set of sensor nodes given by $N = \{n_1, n_2, n_3, \ldots, n_V\}$; $|N| = V$ are randomly distributed in an $M \times M$ m^2 network area. V represents the number of sensor nodes in a network.

Let $\{n_i\}$ denote set of nodes such that $1 \leq i \leq p$ denotes a set of normal nodes in a cluster $C_k \forall$ k $= 1, 2, \ldots, K$ with k being the number of clusters, and each node n_i a legitimate sensor node in the network where $p \in | C_k | \ll$ V.

Similarly, compromised nodes (A) in a network are expressed as follows:

$A = \left\{ n_i^| : n_1^|, n_2^|, \ldots, n_q^| \right\}$ such that $1 \leq i \leq q$, where $|A| = q \leq V$, q being the number of compromised nodes.

Thus, during network operation, legitimate nodes can transmit to themselves, to adversary nodes, and vice versa. The transmission can be expressed as follows:

1. $g(n_i: n_i \in C_k) \rightarrow g(n_j: n_j \in C_k)$; the expression shows that a normal sensor node transmits to a normal sensor node where g is a routing function.
2. $g(n_i: n_i \in C_k) \rightarrow g(n_j^|: n_j^| \in A)$; the expression shows that a normal sensor node transmits to a compromised node.
3. $g(n_i^|: n_i^| \in A) \rightarrow g(n_j: n_j \in C_k)$; the expression shows that a compromised node transmits to a normal sensor node.
4. $g(n_i^|: n_i^| \in A) \rightarrow g(n_j^|: n_j^| \in A)$; the expression shows that a compromised node transmits to a compromised node.

27.3.3 DoS Attacks Detection Mechanism

It is crucial to secure all sensor readings originating from the source nodes to the destination node without the possibility of the readings being forged by adversaries. However, if an adversary is able to launch an attack, data packets can be forged and sent to a receiver node. A good algorithm should be able to detect the sender of such packets, and remove its routing path from the network so that legitimate sensor nodes will not be able to communicate with the adversary node. In addition, the receiver node should be able to drop the packets sent by the adversary. We consider attacks on WSNs from the perspective of integrity and authentication attacks, and provide countermeasures against these.

Data Integrity Attack: During data transmission, an attacker can either intercept sensor readings that are not well encrypted or break the encryption, read everything in clear text, modify the content and either play back the message over the network or drop some or all of the messages. The attacker exploits the vulnerabilities of sensor nodes to set up a zombie army (bots). Once a zombie army has been set up within the network, the attacker is ready to attack the legitimate sensor nodes and modify the encrypted data. Similarly, en route data aggregation changes the representation of original sensor readings. Thus, it becomes difficult to authenticate the correctness of aggregated data. Therefore,

there is a need for a proper encryption and message integrity check algorithm to ensure that data packets received at the destination node have not been modified during transmission.

Data Authentication Attack: The intention of the attackers is to modify the content of the intercepted data packets and play back into the network. Forged and corrupted data packets could be a serious problem in a WSN, as any kind of forged data may lead to misinterpretation of a situation and be counter-productive to its own interest in military intelligence.

During communication, a sensor node relaying data packets uses its assigned code for transmission. A receiving node (CH or base station) with knowledge of the sender's personality expects a certain verification code in order to receive the packets. A man-in-the-middle adversary can perform an intercept, change the content of the sensor readings and replay the attack to pose as a sender node. This type of attack is an obstacle to the integrity of information, and deceives the receiver about the authenticity of messages from the sender.

Data integrity and authentication mechanisms are very important security measures in WSNs. The hash function is used to protect the authenticity and integrity of data packets between the sensor nodes and the base station. The hash function takes a message as input and produces an output referred to as a hash chain, or simply hash (h_C). A h_C is a set of values $\{x_0, x_1, \ldots, x_n\}$ that has length n for all n $\in$ $\mathfrak{Z}$ such that $x_i = $ h(x_{i+1}) for some hash function h, where $i \in [1, n]$ and x_0 is a valid input for h. Thus, x_n is the hash chain seed assumed to be randomly generated between 0 and 1. The length n of a hash chain is the number of hash function evaluations needed to generate the hash chain.

During network operation, the base station generates and distributes unique symmetric secret keys for all sensor nodes in the network, including the cluster heads (CHs), with the help of the elliptic curve Diffie-Hellman (ECDH) key exchange algorithm. Symmetric pre-shared keys are chosen because of low power consumption and speed compared with the asymmetric encryption technique. Individual sensor nodes receive the key and use it to encrypt their packets. A three-way-handshake connection protocol is established whenever a sensor node intends to transmit its readings to a CH node [10]. The cluster head in each cluster generates a code T_1 and sends it to a node that is given permission to transmit, while a copy of the code is kept as T_c. The code can be used to transmit only once, and it expires after 10 s. The sender node computes the hash value (H) of the message M to be transmitted, and encrypts the original message M with the shared key received from the base station. The node concatenates its *ID* with the encrypted M, $H(M)$ together with the code T_1 and sends it over the network to the corresponding CH for further processing.

27.4 Proposed Countermeasures AGAINST DoS Attacks

The message M in the proposed scheme can be of two types: either a legitimate message (LM) or a malicious message (MM).

Definition 1 Let LM be ξ and $\xi = \{lm_i: lm_1, lm_2, \ldots, lm_{|\xi|}\}$ and denote the set of legitimate messages which are successfully transmitted from normal nodes to the receiving node. lm_i is expressed by the tuple $lm_i = (ID, M, T_1, H)$ where ID is the unique number assigned to each sensor node, M indicates the original message, and H denotes the hash value of the message.

Definition 2 Let MM be $\wp$ and $\wp = \{mm_i: mm_1, mm_2, \ldots, mm_{|\wp|}\}$ and denote the set of messages which have been considered to be forged messages. mm_i is expressed by the tuple $mm_i = (ID, M^c, timestamp)$, where M^c indicates the content of the message that has been modified, and *timestamp* indicates the time at which M^c was considered to be a forged message.

Once a sensor node is given permission to transmit, the corresponding CH will be expecting to receive message from the node. However, if the CH was not able to receive the message from the sender node within the allocated time, it will assume the message to have been lost during transmission due to congestion. The CH will generate another code T_2, send it to the node, and update the copy of the code in its memory. During data transmission, attackers are able to intercept the concatenated message as shown in Fig. 27.1. The attackers can do two things to the message they intercept, and for each we provide a countermeasure.

27.4.1 First Layer Countermeasure

Sensor nodes communicate through a radio transceiver which is open to all neighbouring nodes, as a result of which the message transmitted during network operation is public and visible to attackers. It is possible for the attackers to know the secret key used by the sensor node to encrypt the message and to read the content of the sensor readings on the node. Alternatively, the attacker could intercept the message during transmission, modify the content, forward it to the CH and try to fool the CH into believing that the message came from a legitimate sender node. The proposed method is able to check the integrity of the message transmitted. Let us assume that an attacker is able to access and read the content on a sensor node or intercept the readings to achieve its aim during transmission. While the attacker is engaged in reading and modifying the content of the message it has intercepted, the lifetime of the code T_1 will expire. If the CH does not receive the message from the intended sender node within T_1, it generates T_2 and sends it to the node. When the CH finally receives the message, it compares the code that accompanied the message M (e.g. T_1) with stored copy T_c. If the values of T_1 and T_c are the same, then the CH will receive the message and assume that the integrity of the message M has been maintained, and that the message does indeed come from the legitimate sensor node. It is believed that an attacker cannot intercept a message, modify the content and retransmit the message within the T_1 lifetime. However, if the values of T_1 and T_c are not the same, the CH will suspect that the integrity of the message has been tampered with during transmission. It will announce the ID of the sender node to other member nodes, and mark the node as a potential attacker. A second security check is performed below in order to declare a sensor node to be an attacker.

Fig. 27.1 Proposed DoS attack model

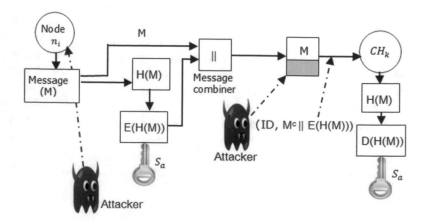

Algorithm 27.1 Malicious message detection

Begin

Given $\overline{A} = \frac{1}{|\lambda|} \sum_i^{new} H(M_i)$

Input $\left(M_i^{new}\right)$ and compute hash value

for $i = 1$ to $|\wp|$

if $T_1 \neq T_c$ and $D(H(M_i^c)) \neq E(H(M_i))$

$\forall i \subseteq |\wp|$ then

M_i are malicious messages

else

for $i = 1$ to c

if $(M_i^{new} \subseteq |\xi|$ and $H(M_i) > \overline{A})$ then

if $D(H(M_i)) = E(H(M_i))$ then

M_i^{new} are legitimate messages

end if

end if

end if

End

27.4.2 Second Layer Countermeasure

A second layer security check is performed in order for the CH node to authenticate the integrity of the message received from the sender node. First, the CH computes the hash value of the message and decrypts the encrypted message with the copy of the shared key (S_a). Thereafter, it compares the hash value of the encrypted message M with the decrypted hash value. If the decrypted hash value of M is the same as the encrypted value, i.e. $D(H(M)) = E(H(M))$, then it will accept the message, believing that there is no attack and that the content of the message has not been modified during transmission.

Alternatively, if the hash values are not the same, i.e. $D(H(M^c)) \neq E(H(M))$, then the CH will consider that there is an attack, and that the content of the message has been intercepted and modified during transmission. It will mark the sender node as a malicious node. It forwards the details of the malicious node to the base station, which will then update the attacker node details, and compute and distribute new keys to all the nodes in the network with the exception of the attacker node. Henceforth, the attacker is blocked from communicating with other nodes in the network. Algorithm 27.1 shows pseudo code for detecting malicious nodes in a network.

27.5 Performance Evaluation

We analysed the performance of our proposed method by means of simulation, and present our results comparatively. The results shown in the graphs are the average of 35 simulations. The network consists of 100 nodes randomly distributed over a 100 m × 100 m network area. NS-2 simulator was used to evaluate the performance of the proposed scheme and compare it with other related protocols. In our simulation, the following metrics were used for performance evaluation.

Energy consumption: We performed an experiment to simulate energy dissipation in the receiving nodes. The network was attacked at 300 s and the number of messages received by the nodes exceeded 4500 during transmission. Thereafter, the proposed method was implemented to defend against the DoS attack. Energy conservation of the proposed method was greater than the result obtained without countermeasures, as shown in Fig. 27.2a.

Figure 27.2b shows scenarios with and without attackers. When the number of attackers exceeded 25%, more than 175% forged packets were sent to cluster heads. This increased the energy consumption of the cluster heads, resulting in an increase in the rate of packet loss during transmission. The proposed approach is able to effectively detect and defend against all malicious nodes and remove forged messages from the network. The packet loss rate is very low during transmission. Thus, when DOSAC is not implemented, the packet loss rate increases as the number of attackers increases. However, when the countermeasure is implemented, the number of packets transmitted from sensor nodes to their corresponding cluster heads is constant, as shown in the figure.

End-to-end delay refers to the time taken for a packet to be transmitted over a network from source node to destination. The shorter the end-to-end delay, the better the performance of the protocol. The performance of end-to-end packet delay for PDoS, SSAD and DOSAC protocols during simulation time was analysed, as shown in Fig. 27.3c. In all three protocols, packet delay increases as the number of sensor nodes increases. DOSAC has minimal end-to-end packet delay compared with SSAD and PDoS protocols because our method is able to detect malicious nodes and remove all paths emanating from them, so that legitimate nodes will not transmit through them.

Figure 27.3d shows the expected packets, as well as abnormal packet transmission delays. By periodically generating the code for sensor nodes, the cluster head is able to detect abnormal data packets. This figure shows the ability of the cluster head to identify the data integrity attack. We observe varying packet delays by monitoring the network over different time intervals. The graph shows that the cluster head identifies abnormalities when the code and hash values are not the same as its copy.

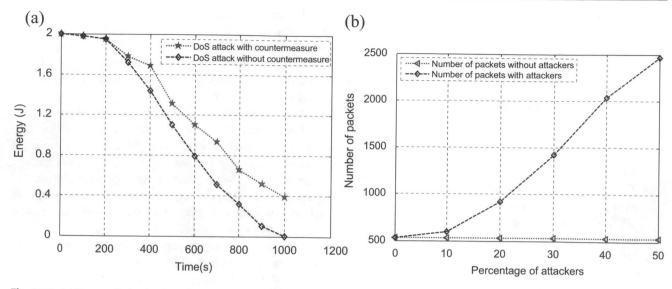

Fig. 27.2 (**a**) Energy dissipation varied with time. (**b**) Number of packets delivered versus percentage of attackers

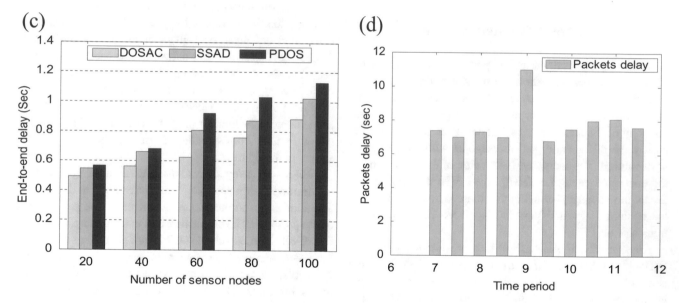

Fig. 27.3 (**c**) End-to-end delay versus number of sensor nodes. (**d**) Time period against packet delay

27.6   Conclusions

The communication patterns of sensor networks and their mode of deployment expose them to a variety of attacks. The privacy and security of data packets are the major issues of concern relating to WSNs. DoS attacks reduce the performance of the system. In this paper we present a unique method called DOSAC for detecting and defending against DoS attacks in WSNs. A hash function and encryption techniques are used to ensure data authenticity and integrity within the network. The DOSAC scheme generates unique codes and hash values to authenticate the transmission of data packets. Simulation results show that DOSAC is able to effectively detect and defend against DoS attacks in WSNs.

Acknowledgement Philip Abidoye acknowledges the support by University of South Africa, South Africa.

References

1. T. Amgoth, P.K. Jana, Energy-aware routing algorithm for wireless sensor networks. Comput. Electr. Eng. **41**, 357–367 (2015)
2. S.S. Iyengar, R.R. Brooks, *Distributed Sensor Networks: Sensor Networking and Applications*, 2nd edn. (CRC Press Taylor & Francis Group, Boca Raton, FL, 2016)
3. S. Ghildiyal, A.K. Mishra, A. Gupta, N. Garg, Analysis of Denial of Service (DOS) attacks in wireless sensor networks. IJRET. **3**, 2319–1163 (2014)
4. M.-L. Messai, Classification of attacks in wireless sensor networks, in *Proceedings of Telecommunication and Application*, (Bcjaia, Algeria, 2014)

5. G. Han, W. Shen, T.Q. Duong, M. Guizani, T. Hara, A proposed security scheme against DoS attacks in cluster-based wireless sensor networks. Secur. Commun. Netw. **7**, 2542–2554 (2014)
6. D. Chen, Z. Zhang, F.-H. Tseng, H.-C. Chao, L.-D. Chou, A novel method defends against the path-based DOS for wireless sensor network. Int. J. Distrib. Sens. Netw. **2014**, 205–216 (2014)
7. G. Kannan, T.S.R. Raja, Energy efficient distributed cluster head scheduling scheme for two tiered wireless sensor network. Egypt. Inf. J. **16**, 167–174 (2015)
8. A.P. Abidoye, N.A. Azeez, A.O. Adesina, K.K. Agbele, AN-CAEE: a novel clustering algorithm forenergy efficiency in wireless sensor networks. J. Wirel. Sens. Netw. **3**, 307–312 (2011)
9. C. Karlof, N. Sastry, D. Wagner, TinySec: a link layer security architecture for wireless sensor networks, in *Proceedings of the 2nd Int'l Conf. on Embedded Networked Sensor Systems*, 2004, pp. 162–175
10. W.R. Heinzelman, J. Kulik, H. Balakrishnan, Adaptive protocols for information dissemination in wireless sensor networks, in *Proceedings of ACM MobiCom'99* (Seattle, Washington USA, 1999), pp. 174–185

Part III

Education and Technology

João E. M. Rocha, Celso Olivete, Pedro H. A. Gomes, Rogério E. Garcia, Ronaldo C. M. Correia, Gabriel Spadon de Souza, and Danilo M. Eler

Abstract

This paper aims at introducing a methodology focused on student-centered learning and aided by an educational collaborative and graphical tool. Through it, we enable students to interact with abstract topics as well as interact with each other. Our motivation was the lack of capability to represent knowledge and abstractions faced by students that work alone. In this regard, we present as result a tool to be used in the whole educational processes, together with a teaching-learning methodology that is described from multiple points of view.

Keywords

Teaching methodology · Learning tool · Empirical analysis · Automata Theory · Formal Languages

28.1 Introduction

The computer science area has evolved on a large scale, becoming increasingly distinct. Such evolution, at such high rate, is responsible for the diversity and volume of information and learning challenges faced by students [1]. Consequently, researchers are constantly searching for educational tools that are capable of introducing highly complex topics in a more didactic method to improve the learning process. These tools act as facilitators when modeling the students' curricula [2], and they are, at the same time, innovative, reliable and handy.

J. E. M. Rocha · C. Olivete · P. H. A. Gomes
R. E. Garcia · R. C. M. Correia (✉) · G. S. de Souza · D. M. Eler
Sao Paulo State University (UNESP), Faculty of Science and Technology, Presidente Prudente, Brazil
e-mail: joao_edezio@outlook.com; olivete@fct.unesp.br; pdrogomes@live.com; garcia@fct.unesp.br; ronaldo@fct.unesp.br; spadon@fct.unesp.br; daniloeler@fct.unesp.br

Many courses that have an extensive theoretical background demand a high level of abstraction from students. Thus, teachers try to express the theory through examples and illustrations [3]. Such courses rely on educational tools to provide and facilitate knowledge exchange. That is the case of Formal Languages and Automata Theory (FLA), which introduces computational formalisms as automata, regular languages, and state machines to aspiring computer scientists.

For this reason, several educational tools have been used to represent formalisms and to aid the teaching-learning process [4–9]. They contribute to building a solid knowledge while dismantling incomprehension's barriers. However, it is clear that the tools by themselves are not enough [10], and from the perspective of the teacher, the interaction of students and formalisms must be real and collaborative, requiring novel methodological approaches and mechanisms to support the teaching and the learning [11].

This paper aims at introducing an educational methodology aided by a learning tool that is, at the same time, online, collaborative and graphical. With our methodology, we enable students to interact with the formalisms as the same way they interact with each other by building a common formalism. Our motivation was the lack of capability to represent knowledge and abstractions faced by students when they work alone. Our hypothesis is that *the knowledge inherent of formalisms is capable of being acquired when students work collaboratively*.

Through this methodology, students are exposed to formalism within an environment that promotes learning by collaboration among students; in which, they have the opportunity to work together in the task of discovering many facets of a common abstraction. By using our methodology, we contribute to the process of knowledge construction by enhancing the teaching process. Such contributions are summarized in:

- **Learning tool:** we present a novel tool that is capable of contributing to the knowledge representation process;
- **Teaching methodology:** we introduce a methodology that contributes to the knowledge transferring; and,
- **Case study:** we show how our methods and tool behaves in a real example, where students were exposed to the development and interaction of formalism by simulators.

The remainder of this paper is structured as follows: Sect. 28.2 presents the related work, discussing how our methodology contrasts the ones from the literature; Sect. 28.3 describes our methodology; Sect. 28.4 presents both teacher and student perspectives on using the proposed methodology during the discipline of Formal Language and Automata Theory; and, Sect. 28.5 presents the conclusions and remarks.

28.2 Literature Review

28.2.1 Related Simulators

The usage of computers to simulate complex models and formalisms abstractions have roots set by *M.W. Curtis* [12]. Considering the importance of such usage, along the years, after the first simulator, thousands of others have been developed to fill teaching and learning limitations. In this sense, our methodology relies on simulators, as an educational strategy, for this reason, the simulators described in this category are essential to contrast with the one of ours.

jFLAP [13] is one of the most traditional simulators used in theoretical computing courses. It supports a variety of formalism representation, from regular languages to state machines. Such broad support characterizes it as a teaching-learning framework. Regarding its design, it was built to simulate almost all variations of computing machines, being capable of several transformations from one formalism to another. However, the ability to be easy-to-use was lost because of its constant development. Such ability is derived from the way JFLAP organizes its information, and from the capacity of a user to reach that information.

jFAST [14] was developed to provide interactive visualization of several computer science formalisms. The aim of such tool is to improve the understanding of abstract concepts through "active learning" techniques—i.e. by involving students in the learning process. This tool is described as useful and handy for teachers and students. It is well known for its capability of representing finite state machines. Although, the simulator is limited to such formalism representation.

The literature is full of simulators, as so, they are not limited to the aforementioned ones. It is clear that all the tools can represent computer science formalisms—e.g. regular and irregular languages, regular expressions, finite state machines, along with others. Nonetheless, many of them have

focused on an icon-based interface to portray formalisms, while the desired result of a learning tool is to be able to aid the teaching-learning process. Therefore, by the fact that tools are not bound to a methodology, we identified a lack of an adequate methodological strategy to improve the knowledge exchange between students and teachers.

28.2.2 Related Teaching Methodologies

Here we report related works that proposed teaching methodologies. Such methodologies have the purpose of describing courses that are based on the development of simulators. In this sense, we discuss each one by presenting their contributions and limitations. In addition, we explain how our methods stand out from theirs.

In this regard, Souza et al. [3] described a methodology that follows the development of simulators as a way to evaluate the student's knowledge. The authors described the learning process as highly abstract and complex; because of it, they devised new technics to propagate their knowledge among students. Their results point positively to their proposal. However, there still is a lack of clear and precise methodology, which must be in-depth, defined in a step-by-step process to be validated as a whole. Besides, the authors report that they guide their classes through a closed-source simulator. Such simulator is presented through images, which limits the reproducibility of their work.

Further, other authors [11] introduced a methodology through grouping related courses and evaluating the students with a single and uniform method. Their methodology starts by merging the courses of Formal Languages and Automata Theory (FLA), Computer Science Theory (CST), and Theory of Compilers (TC) in a single one, which they called as Theoretical Computer Science (TCS) course. Through the analysis of the theoretical and practical test scores, the authors' results show an increase in the students' understanding. However, this bond between courses seems to be stronger for FLA and CST; this behavior can be derived from the fact that the correlation between the topics covered by FLA and CST are greater than any other pair of disciplines.

The last one [10] described a methodological approach to use technology to assist teaching-learning activities from data-structure courses. The authors also described the course topics as difficult to be understood, which is derived from the abstract concepts related to it. Consequently, they presented a learning tool, named as CADILAG, which was developed to support the understanding of abstract concepts. Their results were based on a 2-year evaluation, pointing positively to their findings. However, it does not seem they can scale the methodology to many students; also, it is not possible to intuitively adapt such methodology to other course types.

These works from above and others [15–17] depict the need for a methodology able to cover limitations that are constantly being reported and discovered during classes of different areas. As such, this work aims to serve as a guide to this process by presenting a new learning tool and a teaching methodology that we used to evaluate such tool.

28.3 Methodology

To understand the scenario where our methodology fits there is the need to explain where it was developed. We refer to the course of Formal Languages and Automata Theory (FLA) as the origin of our methodology. It is noteworthy that the methodology is not limited to this course. Our methods are abstractions from the procedures that we have followed in classes. Therefore, they can be extended or even repeated in any other computer science course, each one with its tool-set.

28.3.1 Formal Language and Automata Theory (FLA)

The course of FLA has the aim to provide the means for the understanding of procedures and computability. Such course is a combined version of the Formal Language together with Automata Theory. The first one focuses on the internal patterns and structures derived from syntactical languages, while the second one uses machines and automata to provide solutions for problems; both of them are characterized by the high level of complexity and abstraction. The purpose of FLA course is to improve the students' ability to solve problems. Such course is offered once a year with a 60-h workload. Half of it is reserved for teaching the theoretical concepts and the other half for practical activities. The main topics that are covered in such course are included in Chomsky's hierarchy [18].

This course has a large impact on the Computer Science curricula. It introduces topics that are required for the understanding of other theory-based courses. Given the importance of such course, our methodology describes a new learning approach that can contribute to the robustness of the knowledge acquiring process. We explored different ways of evaluating students, mainly by using theoretical and practical tests. The practical one is the development of a simulator, which must be capable of representing a computer formalism.

28.3.2 Teaching Methodology

Our teaching methodology is based on the premise that knowledge is obtained through the set: **Professor**; **Student**;

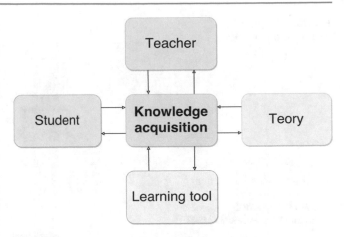

Fig. 28.1 Elements that provide knowledge acquisition

Theory; and **Learning Tool** as shown in Fig. 28.1. Hence, a learning tool was developed aiming to assist in the teaching process. The tool's purpose is to aid the learning by turning concepts into visual and interactive representations, which tends to facilitate the cognition during classes. The tool works as an oracle, showing how an arbitrary formalism behaves.

28.3.3 Learning Tool

Our learning-tool is a collaborative environment that was developed to aid in the teaching-learning of FLA. The tool by itself was developed using JavaScript, PHP, HTML5, and MySQL. As a consequence, any device that supports HTML5 and that has access to the internet can use it. This tool is structured in modules and submodules. The collaborative-environment and the tool-interface are the main ones; Fig. 28.2 depicts the hierarchy of the first one and Fig. 28.3 of the second one. Specifically, the collaborative-environment consists of four submodules, plus the tool-interface one. These submodules are the chat/log service and the user/file manager.

The chat service is responsible for the communication between the users of the environment, which can be between student-student or student-teacher. The user management is responsible for keeping track of which users are online in the environment, enabling more interactivity between them. Through the file management, the user is able to save their formalism locally or in the cloud, and also to share its work or keep it private. The log service performs the registration of all messages between teacher and student and also it stores all actions made in the development of a formalism; these logs are used by the teacher to detect possible difficulties in the student learning process. The tool interface is what enables the creation, simulation, and testing of all formalism mentioned up to here; specifically, these formalisms are the

Fig. 28.2 Diagram of
environment's modules

Fig. 28.3 Supported
abstractions by the learning tool

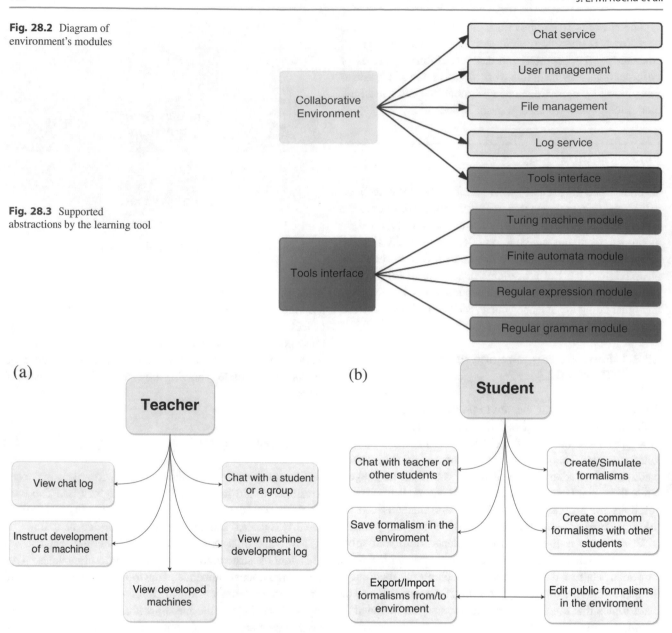

Fig. 28.4 Conceptual visions of the collaborative environment. (**a**) Teacher view of the collaborative environment. (**b**) Student view of the collaborative environment

finite automaton, Turing machine, regular expression and regular grammar. Finally, for collaboration purposes, our tool has the machine sharing option, that enables interaction between student-student or student-teacher; this feature is available only for the finite automaton and Turing machine. The main screen of the tool is depicted in Fig. 28.5, in which we show two students working together in collaboration.

Figure 28.4 described the tool's role to the student and the teacher. The figure says that the functions available to the teacher focus on ways to provide understanding about the students' difficulties and doubts. On the other hand, the ones made available to the student focus on collaborative learning (Fig. 28.5).

28.4   Results and Discussions

By applying our methodology and learning tool, we gathered reports from students and teachers. Both of them were submitted to the learning tool that we previously introduced; which was used in a single topic in the FLA discipline that was Finite Automata. During the time of the experiment, we made the tool completely available on a server provided by our university. The teacher used the tool during classes, aiming to demonstrate and simulate different formalisms.

Our experiment was not carried out during the whole course of FLA to avoid problems that could harm students'

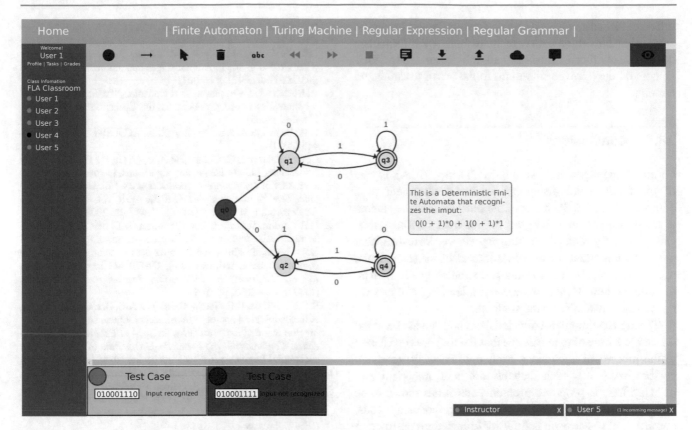

Fig. 28.5 A working proof of our learning tool. Such tool was developed to operate online, which allows students to interact through building a common formalism collaboratively. In the image, there is a stage where automata in currently being developed. The tool allows its creation by using a tool-set of circles and links. Notice that, other students and the instructor can observe in real-time the development of such formalisms. Also, the tool allows them to help in the building process

learning, also because of possible technical problems with the server or usability problems with the tool, since it had not been used yet. At the end of this study, we collected reports of the teacher and students about their experience in using the learning tool.

28.4.1 Student Report

The students reported that it was an advantage the possibility of exchanging messages during classes because it provided collaboration. They also reported that, by being taught by a simulator, their teacher was able to easily pass on the knowledge about the formalism. Another point mentioned by students is how easy was to study together (in a group) through the collaborative environment, even when they could not be at the college. As their final report, they said that by saving their formalism in the cloud they could easily study at home.

28.4.2 Teacher Report

The use of a platform for formalisms development and interaction is important. It enables the knowledge exchange between machine-and-users and between users-and-users through a machine, once it is collaborative. The idea behind the collaboration is to familiarize the knowledge exchange among different students once the act of learning is collective.

Considering the teacher view, the use of the platform for formalism development and interaction is of full importance, once it facilitates the understanding of regular, context-free and context-sensitive languages. The interaction helps by providing real-time results, which enables extensive and interactive tests, which are carried out considering a user's input.

We add to these advantages the web-chat facility, which allows user-to-user interaction during the development of different formalism. The annotation feature is also important since it enables the creation of notes during the formalism development. Not exclusively, all the features have their value, and they proved important to the act of teaching and learning.

28.5　Conclusions

Formal Languages and Automated Theory (FLA) is one of the fundamental disciplines in the development of a computer scientist. Such discipline introduces to the student a set of formalism belonging to the field of Theoretical Computing. By years of teaching experience, we realized that would be important for the development of the students the use of tools capable of building and simulating a formalism in collaboration. Hence, we created a learning tool and we have made it available to the students.

Through testimonials collected from both students and the teacher, we were able to observe that the tool has contributed to the process of knowledge exchange. From the teacher's perspective, it was clear that the tool is an important way of exploring the proposed problems and it has shown to be an efficient part of the teaching-learning methodology. Thus, our proposal was proved helpful for knowledge construction and exchanging; we also noticed that our learning tool motivated the students during the task of problem-solving.

Acknowledgements We are grateful to both Department of Mathematics and Computer Science (DMC) at Faculty of Science and Technology (FCT) in Sao Paulo State University (UNESP) and the students enrolled in Formal Language and Automata Theory course. We would like to thank Sao Paulo Research Foundation (FAPESP) that partially supported this research.

References

1. C.Y. Fook, G.K. Sidhu, Investigating learning challenges faced by students in higher education. Procedia Soc. Behav. Sci. **186**, 604–612 (2015)
2. A.B. Tucker, Strategic directions in computer science education. ACM Comput. Surv. **28**(4), 836–845 (1996)
3. G.S. de Souza, C. Olivete, R.C.M. Correia, R.E. Garcia, Teaching-learning methodology for formal languages and automata theory, in *2015 IEEE Frontiers in Education Conference (FIE)* (Institute of Electrical and Electronics Engineers (IEEE), Piscataway, 2015), pp. 1–7
4. M.T. Grinder, Animating automata. ACM SIGCSE Bull. **34**(1), 63 (2002)
5. C.I. Chesñevar, M.L. Cobo, W. Yurcik, Using theoretical computer simulators for formal languages and automata theory. ACM SIGCSE Bull. **35**(2), 33 (2003)
6. A. Esmoris, C.I. Chesñevar, M.P. González, TAGS: a software tool for simulating transducer automata. Int. J. Electr. Eng. Edu. **42**(4), 338–349 (2005)
7. C.W. Brown, E.A. Hardisty, RegeXeX. ACM SIGCSE Bull. **39**(1), 445 (2007)
8. C. García-Osorio, C. Gómez-Palacios, N. García-Pedrajas, A tool for teaching LL and LR parsing algorithms, in *Proceedings of the 13th Annual Conference on Innovation and Technology in Computer Science Education—ITiCSE'08*, April, vol. 40 (Association for Computing Machinery (ACM), New York, 2008), p. 317
9. G.P. Cardim, I. Marcal, C.M. de Sousa, D.L. de Campos, C.H.V. Marin, A.F.C. do Carmo, D.F. Toledo, A. Saito, R.C.M. Correia, R.E. Garcia, Teaching and learning data structures supported by computers: an experiment using CADILAG tool, in *2012 7th Iberian Conference on Information Systems and Technologies (CISTI)*, June 2012, pp. 1–5
10. R.C.M. Correia, R.E. Garcia, C. Olivete, A.C. Brandi, G.P. Cardim, A methodological approach to use technological support on teaching and learning data structures, in *2014 IEEE Frontiers in Education Conference (FIE) Proceedings* (Institute of Electrical and Electronics Engineers (IEEE), Piscataway, 2014), pp. 1–8
11. G.S. de Souza, P.H. de Andrade Gomes, R.C.M. Correia, C. Olivete, D.M. Eler, R.E. Garcia, Combined methodology for theoretical computing, in *2016 IEEE Frontiers in Education Conference (FIE)* (Institute of Electrical and Electronics Engineers (IEEE), Piscataway, 2016), pp. 1–7
12. M.W. Curtis, A turing machine simulator. J. ACM **12**(1), 1–13 (1965)
13. S.H. Rodger, H. Qin, J. Su, Changes to JFLAP to increase its use in courses, in *Proceedings of the 16th Annual Joint Conference on Innovation and Technology in Computer Science Education—ITiCSE'11*, March 2009 (Association for Computing Machinery (ACM), New York, 2011), p. 339
14. T.M. White, T.P. Way, jFAST, in *Proceedings of the 37th SIGCSE Technical Symposium on Computer Science Education—SIGCSE'06*, vol. 38, no. 1 (Association for Computing Machinery (ACM), New York, 2006), p. 384
15. M. Procopiuc, O. Procopiuc, S. Rodger, Visualization and interaction in the computer science formal languages course with JFLAP, in *Technology-Based Re-Engineering Engineering Education Proceedings of Frontiers in Education FIE'96 26th Annual Conference*, vol. 1 (Institute of Electrical and Electronics Engineers (IEEE), Piscataway, 1996), pp. 121–125
16. R. Cavalcante, T. Finley, S.H. Rodger, A visual and interactive automata theory course with JFLAP 4.0. ACM SIGCSE Bull. **36**(1), 140 (2004)
17. S. Rodger, Learning automata and formal languages interactively with JFLAP. ACM SIGCSE Bull. **38**(3), 360 (2006)
18. N. Chomsky, Three models for the description of language. IEEE Trans. Inf. Theory **2**(3), 113–124 (1956)

Teaching Communication Management in Software Projects Through Serious Educational Games

Rafaella Marchi Pellegrini, Carlos Eduardo Sanches da Silva, and Adler Diniz de Souza

Abstract

Companies that have been successful in implementing software project management, have focused efforts on people-oriented topics, for example, communication and teamwork. In order to effectively disseminate the attributes that the organization expects from a newly formed professional and what the university prepares, it is necessary to adopt ways of teaching that will encourage the involvement of these young people. It is in this context that active teaching methodologies, such as Game Based Learning, have emerged to include processes of experimentation and social interactivity. This work aims to identify and prioritize the practices inherent to Communication Management in Software Projects, that allow to perfect a game for teaching and learning. The steps of this research were: (1) identification of communication management practices and processes in the literature, (2) prioritization of practices and processes through the use of the AHP method, (3) conducting cycles of application of the object of study: an online board game and finally (4). The results allow to conclude that there was an improvement in the number of correct answers after the students played the game, especially in practices Communicate changes efficiently, Accurately collect requirements and Communicate frequently with interested parties. So, it is possible to prove statistically that the game increased students' knowledge about these practices.

Keywords

Game based learning · Communication management · Software projects management

R. M. Pellegrini · C. E. S. da Silva
Institute of Production Engineering and Management, Federal University of Itajuba, Itajuba, MG, Brazil

A. D. de Souza (✉)
Department of Computer Science, Federal University of Itajuba, Itajuba, MG, Brazil

29.1 Introduction

The complexity of the business environment has demanded companies to develop the capacity to coordinate, manage and control their activities. Several actions are being taken in order to pursue this adaptation, and one of the main pillars of these processes is using project management techniques that focus on organizational communication [1, 2]. Using precise information at the right time, and in the hands of the right person, is a rare differential that most project management teams lack [3].

Statistically, more than 65% of IT projects are not successfully. The main factor which contributes to their failure is the lack of communication or inefficient communication [4]. Therefore, it is crucial to plan how the communication will flow in the project [5].

It is important to identify how the professionals are being prepared, given that projects usually encompass professionals with different education levels, especially when dealing with software development projects. There is an increased interest in the utilization of games as educational instruments to assist students' learning and teachers' teaching procedures [6].

In this regard, the present study contributes toward better understanding of communication management in software development projects.

This article is organized in the following sections: Sect. 29.2 contains the research development methodology; Sect. 29.3 discusses the results obtained and, finally, Sect. 29.4 deals with the final considerations and premises for future research.

29.2 Method and Research Proposal

The research method used in this study is the Action Research, since it uses a research that classifies and prioritizes the Communication Management practices by applying them

Table 29.1 Research action cycle

Step	Research context
I	Identifying the gap between the market demands and what is taught regarding communication management in software projects
II	Literature review to identify the methods related to communication management in software projects
III	Interview with specialists and prioritization of the Communication Management practices using the *Analytics Hierarchy Process* (AHP)
IV	Development of a serious educational game that transmits the practices related to the Communication Management Process, prioritized by specialists
V	Previous measurement of the participants' knowledge in Communication Management
VI	Application of the game on undergraduate students of Computer Science, Administration and Information Systems courses
VII	Measurement of the Communication Management knowledge learned by the players
VIII	Evaluation and improvement of the serious educational game based on the students' reviews
IX	New round of game application

Table 29.2 Choice of specialists

Specialist	Position	Certifications	Hours of experience (h)
1	Engineering Director	No	>10,000
2	IT Project Manager	PMP, Prince2, SCRUM	>10,000
3	Professor	PMP	>10,000
4	Operations Director	No	>10,000
5	IT Manager	PMP, PMI-RMP, PSM	>10,000
6	IT Project Manager	No	>10,000

in a serious educational game. The participants are intentionally allowed to experience the management of communication in software projects. Table 29.1 shows the Research Action steps followed in this study.

The SCOPUS and ISI Web of Knowledge databases were used in steps I and II. The "Communication in Management of Software Projects" string was used, and filters related to Areas of Interest, Year of Publication, Language, and Type of Document were applied.

After applying these filters, 36 articles were selected based on how their objectives were aligned to the goals of this study, and 29 different Communication Management practices were identified.

In step III, 6 experts in Management of Software Projects from different Brazilian enterprises were interviewed. Table 29.2 shows the questions and answers of each specialist.

The specialists used the AHP method to prioritize the practices found in the step II. Data was collected using online questionnaires. The prioritization process is shown on Fig. 29.1.

The specialists prioritized the 29 practices according to their level of importance in Communication Management in software projects.

The most relevant Communication Management practices were detected using the Paretto Principle and are shown in Table 29.3.

Communication Management is composed of three processes: Planning the Communication Management, Managing Communication and Controlling Communication Management [7].

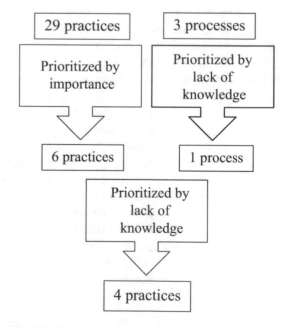

Fig. 29.1 Prioritization scheme of practices and processes

According to the interviewed specialists, Planning is the process where recent graduates usually have the highest deficit of knowledge.

The last prioritization concluded, with an 82.7% consensus rate between the specialists, which are the greatest knowledge deficits in the Communication Management Planning process regarding recent graduates (first four items in Table 29.3). These four practices were incorporated into the serious educational game.

Table 29.3 Important practices in communication management

ID	Communication management practices	Authors that reference these practices in steps I and II at Table 29.1
1	Communicate changes efficiently	[8, 9, 10, 11, 12, 13, 14, 15, 16]
2	Accurately collect requirements	[9]
3	Share information clearly	[15]
4	Communicate frequently with interested parties	[8, 17]
5	Have good communication and leadership skills	[18, 19, 20]
6	Communicate frequently with development team	[21, 22]

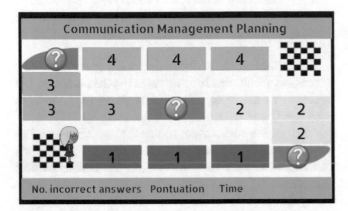

Fig. 29.2 Serious game design

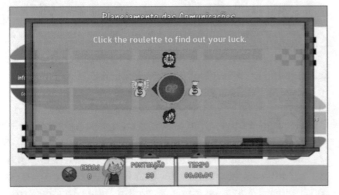

Fig. 29.3 Example of a random event

Step IV consisted of developing a serious electronic board game composed of questions and answers that aimed to present the practices prioritized by the specialists. The serious educational game was developed using the Unity3d platform.

The game was created based on the Game Based Learning (GBL) techniques, where the participants were submitted to a ludic environment [23]. The serious educational game was composed of twelve questions (three questions for each prioritized practices), as illustrated in Fig. 29.2.

Random events were included in order to increase Gamification, where participants won or lost points and/or time. The random events are shown in Fig. 29.3 and are represented by question marks in Fig. 29.2.

The participant had access to the number of incorrect answers, score, and time so he or she could track his performance. Only two students could win the game: The one with the highest score and the one that finished the game with the lowest time. Rewards, like chocolate, were given for their good performance.

An administrator panel was developed to store and access the following information for each participant:

- Score for each question.
- Time used to answer each question.
- Number of incorrect answers made by each player.
- Time gained or lost for each random event.
- Score gained or lost for each random event.
- Final score (Sum of score related to the questions and score gained or lost on random events);
- Final time (Sum of the time taken to answer the questions and time gained or lost through random events).

A questionnaire was used as a knowledge measurement instrument in steps V and VII. The questionnaire consisted of ten practical cases that the participants had to relate to each of the practices. The questionnaire was applied before and after the serious game, in order to detect any gain in knowledge.

Three application cycles of the serious game were performed, with students of the Information Systems, Computer Science, and Administration courses (step VI). At the end of each cycle, improvements were identified and implemented on the serious educational game (step VIII). Such advances were identified through observation, feedback and performance of the participants.

29.3 Results

The pared t hypothesis test was used to determine if there was a significant increase in the learning level of the participants after the serious educational game was applied. This test is useful to analyze the behavior of a sample that was submitted to two different treatments. The knowledge measurements were performed before and after the students played the serious educational game [24]. The t-hypothesis test was conducted using the following hypotheses:

Table 29.4 Performance of each application cycle

	Cycle 1	Cycle 2	Cycle 3
Number of participants	16	34	17
Mode of the number of correct answers before the game	4	3	3
Mode of the number of correct answers after the game	4	5	6
P-value	0.082	0.000	0.000
H0 Hypothesis	Not rejected	Rejected	Rejected

Table 29.5 Performance according to communication management practice

Practice ID	p-value Cycle 1	p-value Cycle 2	p-value Cycle 3
1	0.607	0.012	0.005
2	0.750	0.019	0.010
3	0.500	0.500	0.250
4	0.250	0.750	0.017

(H0) there was no knowledge gain after the students played the game:

- $StudentScore_{BeforePlay} - StudentScore_{AfterPlay} \geq 0$

(Ha) there was knowledge gain after the students played the serious game:

- $StudentScore_{BeforePlay} - StudenScore_{AfterPlay} < 0$

All samples considered a 95% confidence level (0.05 alpha). Table 29.4 shows a summary of each application cycle, as well as its respective p-value.

Table 29.5 summarizes each Communication Management practice approached by the serious educational game. This analysis was performed to determine which practices were improved in the participant's knowledge after the game. All values considered a 95% confidence level (0.05 alpha). Therefore, H0 is only rejected if its p-value is lower than 0.05.

The null hypothesis was not rejected when Cycle 1 was applied. There is no statistical evidence that there was an increase in the participants' knowledge.

When considering Cycle 2, there was statistical evidence that points toward the increase in the students' knowledge after playing the game. However, this increase was only seen in practices (1) Communicate changes efficiently, and (2) Accurately collect requirements.

The Cycle 3 had the best performance, and statistically showed improvements in three of the four considered practices: (1) Communicate changes efficiently, (2) Accurately collect requirements, and (4) Communicate frequently with interested parties.

It is believed that better results could have been obtained if the following aspects had been considered when planning the study object:

- The content of the serious educational game should be consistent with what is being taught by the professor. The game may not be capable of transmitting the knowledge by itself.
- Adapting the environment so that the game can be better implemented. A group with more than 20 participants demands a larger environment and the participation of moderators.
- Physical rewards for the game winners are not enough to make them feel engaged and involved. The students have to identify real value in the rewards. A good suggestion is to use their performance in the measurement questionnaire as part of their grade in the course.

The results suggest that the use of games can contribute to increase the knowledge of their participants.

However, serious educational games can also bring up questions and uncertainties about concepts that have already been learned, ratifying the need for the game to be properly planned.

The instrument chosen to evaluate the knowledge of the participants can be questioned. The combination of two or more measurement instruments would minimize the error rate.

Also, it is vital that the environment where the game is being applied is where the students can concentrate, so that they can be fully immersed and feel correctly motivated.

29.4 Conclusion

This study was able to identify which Communication Management practices recently-graduates most lack in the Computer Science, Administration and Information Systems courses, according to experts in the Communication Management for Software Projects context.

During the prioritization phase, 29 practices and three processes were analyzed. The practices a recent-graduate most lacks in the Communication Management Planning process are: Communicate changes efficiently; Accurately collect requirements; Share information clearly; and Communicate frequently with interested parties.

After the prioritization phase, a serious electronic board game was developed to disseminate knowledge in Communication Management for Software Projects, along with an online questionnaire used to measure the students' knowledge. The evaluation questionnaire was applied before and after the game, in order to verify the progress in the number of correct answers.

Improvement opportunities were detected in each application cycle and incorporated into the serious educational game, so that it could be reassessed in the next cycle, even if there was no statistical indication that the serious educational game did not improve the students' knowledge in the matter.

It is possible to prove statistically that the gasification contributes positively to the students' learning, since after the game, there was an improvement in the amount of correctness of these practices (1) Communicate changes efficiently, (2) Accurately collect requirements, and (4) Communicate frequently with interested parties.

This research proposed itself to: (1) Identify and prioritize practices in Communication Management for projects. (2) Elaborate a serious educational game to teach these practices, (3) Apply the serious game in classrooms to promote knowledge in the participants. The object of study can positively contribute towards the conceptual and practical formation of the students, since it allows students to simulate problems encountered on a daily basis in real enterprises in a safe and ludic environment.

References

1. T. Souza, C. Gomes, Bibliometric study of main maturity models in project management. Perspect. Manag. Knowl. **55**, 5–26 (2015)
2. D. Vargas Neto, L. Patah, Expanding the vision of indicators for projects: focus on virtual teams. Prod. Oper. Syst. Manag. São Paulo **9**(2), 17–33 (2014)
3. V. Brusamolin, The insertion of narrative discourse in the informational cycle and its impact on organizational learning. Ibero-Am. J. Inf. Sci. **8**(2), (2015)
4. M. Shah, R. Hasim, A. Shah, U. Khattak, Communication management guidelines for software organizations in Pakistan with clients from Afghanistan. IOP Conf. Ser. Mater. Sci. Eng. **160**, 012100 (2016)
5. H. Morais, L. Taconi, W. Mura, R. Barros, Solution for Communication Problems in Software Project Management, Londrina (2014)
6. S.S. Shabanah, et al., Designing computer games to teach algorithms, in *Information Technology: New Generations (ITNG), 2010 Seventh International Conference on. IEEE*, (2010), pp. 1119–1126
7. Project Management Institute, *A guide to the project management body of knowledge (PMBOK guide)*, 5th end edn. (Project Management Institute Inc., Newtown Square, PA, 2013)
8. M. Braglia, M. Frosolini, An integrated approach to implement project management information systems within the extended enterprise. Int. J. Proj. Manag. **32**, 18–29 (2014)
9. S. Ghobadi, L. Mathiassem, Perceived barriers to effective knowledge sharing in agile software teams. Inf. Syst. J. **26**(2), 95–125 (2016)
10. V. Turkulainen, I. Ruuska, T. Brady, K. Artto, Managing project-to-project and project-to-organization interfaces in programs: Organizational integration in a global operations expansion program. Int. J. Proj. Manag. **33**, 816–827 (2015)
11. J. García, A. Maldonado, A. Alvarado, D. Rivera, Human critical success factors for kaizen and its impacts in industrial performance. Int. J. Adv. Manuf. Technol. **70**(9–12), 2187–2198 (2014)
12. A. Brinkhoff, O. Ozer, G. Sargut, All you need is trust? An examination of inter-organizational supply chain projects. Prod. Oper. Manag. **24**(2), 181–200 (2015)
13. M. Battaglia, L. Bianchi, M. Frey, E. Passetti, Sustainability reporting and corporate identity: action research evidence in an Italian retailing cooperative. Bus. Ethics **24**(1), 52–72 (2015)
14. S. Shokri, S. Ahn, S. Lee, C. Haas, R. Haas, Current status of interface management in construction: drivers and effects of systematic interface management. J. Constr. Eng. Manag. **142**(2) (2016)
15. P. Wlazlak, G. Johansson, R&D in Sweden and manufacturing in China: a study of communication challenges. J. Manuf. Technol. Manag. **25**, 258–278 (2014)
16. W. Sun, S. Mollaoglu, V. Miller, B. Manata, Communication behaviors to implement innovations: how do AEC teams communicate in IPD projects? Proj. Manag. J. **46**(1), 84–96 (2015)
17. S. Xu, H. Lou, The information-related time loss on construction sites: a case study on two sites. Int. J. Adv. Robot. Syst. **11**, 128 (2014)
18. S. Dillon, H. Taylor, Employing grounded theory to uncover behavioral competencies of information technology project managers. Proj. Manag. J. **46**(4), 90–104 (2015)
19. J. Verner, M. Babar, N. Cerpa, T. Hall, S. Beecham, Factors that motivate software engineering teams: a four country empirical study. J. Syst. Softw. **92**, 115–127 (2014)
20. G. Cserhati, L. Szabo, The relationship between success criteria and success factors in organizational event projects. Int. J. Proj. Manag. **32**, 613–624 (2014)
21. A. Vollmer, P. Wolf, Adaption of conflict management styles during the encounter of cultures. Int. J. Cross. Cult. Manag. **15**, 151–166 (2015)
22. E. Papatheocharous, A. Andreou, Empirical evidence and state of practice of software agile teams. J. Softw. Evol. Process. **26**, 855–866 (2014)
23. V. Janarthanan, Serious video games: games for education and health, in *Information Technology: New Generations (ITNG), 2012 Ninth International Conference on. IEEE*, (2012), pp. 875–878
24. A. Chesire, Two P-values for a 2 Proportions Test? Am I Seeing Double? (2011), [Online]. http://blog.minitab.com/blog/quality-dataaanalysisand-statistics/two-p-values-for-a-2-proportions-test-am-i-seeing-double. Acessed 2 June 2017

Luiz Eduardo Guarino de Vasconcelos, Leandro Guarino de Vasconcelos, Leonardo B. Oliveira, Gabriel Guimarães, and Felipe Ayres

Abstract

The teaching of software development is not trivial, as it faces a great challenge that is to combine theory and practice of many concepts. Agile methodologies combined with active methodologies, such as Problem-based Learning (PBL), generate opportunities in the development of software projects in academic scenarios. However, some teams do not distribute activities evenly among members, hindering the learning and the project development. In this paper, we report a case study on the use of gamification as a motivating agent in the teaching-learning process of the agile Scrum methodology of software development combined with PBL. The gamification process was supported by a game called LevelLearn, that was created by the authors. At the end of the semester, a questionnaire about the influence of the game during the course was answered by the students. The results were satisfactory and showed that gamification motivated students and influenced the involvement with the developed project.

Keywords

Software engineering · Agile methodology · Gamification · Classroom

30.1 Introduction

In teaching software engineering, the educator usually has to combine theory and practice of many concepts. In addition, the educator needs to follow the rapid emergence of new technologies.

The methodology of software development has an impact on productivity and meeting deadlines during software development. According to Chaos [1], software applications developed through agile methodologies have a higher success rate and lower risk than the waterfall methodology.

Currently, the Scrum methodology (and its variations) is the agile methodology most used in software development projects [2].

Scrum can be taught in many ways, through books, articles, games, etc. Moreover, games to teach Scrum can be found on websites and blogs.

Nowadays, the interest in electronic games, that influenced the children and adolescents of the 80s has been increasing, because those children are adults today. The majority of Brazilian gamers [3] are between 25 and 34 years old (36.2%).

In this scenario, gamification, which is the application of principles and elements of game design in contexts that are not a game [4], has become relevant in several contexts, such as business [5] and education [6].

Applying gamification in the educational context and considering the lenses proposed by Schell [7], we developed a game called LevelLearn, whose objective is to transform a course of any academic level into a game, promoting competition between students and motivating them to comply the activities proposed by the educator.

We used LevelLearn during one semester in two Software Engineering courses, from an undergraduate course at a public college located in the countryside of Sao Paulo, Brazil. During the courses, students were organized into teams to design and develop a Web application using the Scrum methodology.

At the same time, the process of gamification of the activities of the courses was developed, supported by the game LevelLearn. In total, 45 students participated in the game and, at the end of the semester, they answered a questionnaire focused on the following research question:

The original version of this chapter was revised. An erratum to this chapter can be found at https://doi.org/10.1007/978-3-319-77028-4_102

L. E. G. de Vasconcelos (✉) · L. G. de Vasconcelos
Faculdade de Tecnologia de Guaratinguetá—FATEC, Guaratinguetá, Brazil

Centro Universitário Teresa D'Ávila—UNIFATEA, Lorena, Brazil

L. B. Oliveira · G. Guimarães · F. Ayres
Centro Universitário Teresa D'Ávila—UNIFATEA, Lorena, Brazil

Does the use of LevelLearn during the course motivate the students to carry out the learning activities?

The results presented in this paper show the positive influence of LevelLearn on the motivation of the students to fulfill the activities proposed by the professor, and they also show the greater involvement of them in the courses.

This paper is organized as follows: Sect. 30.2 presents the theoretical reference on gamification, agile methodologies and the work reported in the literature related to this research; Sect. 30.3 describes the method used in this research; Sect. 30.4 briefly presents the Level Learn game and the lenses proposed by Schell [7] that are addressed by the game; Sect. 30.5 discusses the results of the questionnaire; and Sect. 30.6 presents the final considerations on this research.

30.2   Theoretical

30.2.1 Scrum

Nowadays, there are dozens of agile methodologies for software development (e.g. Scrum [8], XP [9]), and all these methodologies are based on the Agile Manifesto [10].

Scrum is the most widely used agile methodology in the world. According to Cohn [11], some benefits of Scrum are: more than 80% increase in productivity; decrease of one-fourth of the cost; and improvement in approximately 40% of the quality of projects.

Recent work shows the use of Scrum in academic projects, such as those developed by [12, 13].

This methodology has three main roles: Product Owner (PO) who owns the product, Scrum Master (SM) who is the leader of the development team and team members [8].

The requirements (i.e. User Stories—US) should be identified, prioritized, and documented in the Product Backlog artifact [8].

After identifying the US, the development estimate can be defined by some estimation technique, for example Planning Poker. This technique has been used to increase the return on investment [14]. The development cycle is iterative and incremental, based on Sprints. It is recommended that each Sprint does not take more than 30 days [8].

Sprint planning is done at the beginning of each Sprint. This is a Scrum event where everyone involved in the project should attend. In this meeting, the PO—Product Owner (together with the team), establishes which US will be developed and delivered. Typically, User Stories are chosen according to the value to the business. During Sprint, short-term events of up to 15 minutes, called as Daily Scrum Meeting, occur so that the team can follow the development of the project. At the end of Sprint, the Sprint Review occurs, which is an event for the delivery of the US to the PO, that is, the US that were chosen in Sprint Planning are presented.

Then another event occurs, the Sprint Retrospective. At this meeting, the Scrum Master and the team can evaluate the progress of Sprint and they can suggest improvements to the next Sprint. The development progress monitoring is made through the Burndown chart.

Although the success rate of software delivery is greater with Scrum when compared to traditional methodologies, it is necessary to use software development techniques that allow the delivery of higher quality.

30.2.2 Gamification

Gamification is the application of the mechanics and typical elements of games, which can be used as a method to motivate the involvement, interest and problem solving [15]. When used correctly, it may still inspire the target audience to perform tasks that were previously uninteresting or undesirable [16].

This transforming capacity of gamification has made it attractive in different contexts. In education, there are a large number of researches that investigate the influence of gamification in the classroom [16–18].

Marasco et al. [17] applied the gamification in specific courses of an Electrical Engineering course, with the objective of evaluating the impact of the principles of games in the teaching of concepts considered difficult by the students. The results showed that the students who dedicated themselves to the game understood the concepts better.

Butler and Ahmed [18] applied the concepts of gamification in an undergraduate course of Computer Science. They have developed interactive and fun games to teach the concepts of the course. The research results show that subject concepts can be presented in interactive games to facilitate student understanding.

The literature reports researches with different purposes for the use of gamification in education, from the development of small interactive games to explain concepts to the creation of generic tools and games to gamify academic activities.

Section 30.3 presents the game LevelLearn, which was designed to assist the professor in the gamification of the teaching-learning process.

30.3   The LevelLearn Game

LevelLearn was designed by authors with the participation of first-semester students from a Pedagogy course. From the study of the lenses proposed by Schell [7], the students proposed characteristics of the teaching-learning process that should be considered in the game. Then, as it was the first contact of the students with gamification, the professor consolidated the different proposals in clear objectives and rules.

The game includes the following aspects of the teaching-learning process: attendance in class, punctuality, compliance with proposed activities, evaluation of proposed activities, individual and team work. LevelLearn does not limit the process of gamification that the professor wants to perform, but offers a core of rules and challenges for the professor to use gamification in their courses.

In the game, a student is a player, a group of students is a team, a class activity or extra class is a mission. The game can be used in one or more classes, this is flexible for the professor to define their group of students.

To assist the professor in the process of gamification, a Web application was implemented, available at http://www.levellearn.com.br, to manage the missions that the players must perform. In this web application, players respond the missions and the professor evaluates the answers. Automatically, the web application manages the rewards, rules and challenges. In this sense, the activities necessary to the professor performs in the web app are: the correction of the missions, the grading and the attendance record of the players.

It is important to note that the professor can disable rules and challenges in a class if he does not judge them as appropriate for his scenario.

The following lenses proposed by Schell [7] are supported by LevelLearn: 1 (essential experience), 16 (player), 25 (objectives), 26 (rules), 31 (challenge), 36 (competition), 37 (cooperation), 40 (reward), 41 (punishment), 49 (progress visible), 53 (control), 57 (feedback), 71 (freedom), 75 (avatar), 89 (time), 98 (responsibility) and 100 (secret purpose).

Since LevelLearn is a game that does not limit the process of gamification, the participation of the professor in the creation of the missions is fundamental to reach the benefits of the following lenses: 2 (surprise), 3 (fun), 5 (problem solving) and 39 (time).

Regarding the Web application, the access can be made from a computer or any mobile device, making it easier for players to follow the missions and follow the ranking.

30.4 Methodology

In this research, we observed the influence of gamification, through the game LevelLearn, on the motivation of students during the teaching of Scrum methodology. LevelLearn is a game that can be applied at any academic level by any professor, and it is supported by an online environment that assists the professor to manage activities and student attendance.

During the first semester of 2017, in a public college in the interior of Sao Paulo, Brazil, the game was used in two courses: Software Engineering and Applications (3rd semester) and Internet Programming (4th semester), respectively, called as Course 1 and Course 2 [19]. These two classes are part of the Information Technology Management undergraduate course, held during the evening, in which 45 students participated.

The graduated student of this course works in a segment of the area of computer science that covers the administration of the physical and logical infrastructure resources of the computerized environments. Thus, this professional has little time during the course to learn and practice software development because the focus is on IT management.

These two courses are based on the Scrum methodology, and the semester is divided into 4 sprints: Sprint 0, 1, 2 and 3.

Sprint 0 was created in order to reduce the effort of planning during other sprints. More details about this Sprint are presented in Table 30.1.

Sprints 1 and 2 are used for the development of Sprint Backlog. As it is an academic project, it is necessary to study the technologies involved and adaptations to the practice of Scrum. The Scrum event like Sprint Planning, Sprint Review and Sprint Retrospective are held in class with the participation of the professor, and if possible, with the participation of the PO.

In Sprint 3 students also implement a Sprint Backlog so they can deploy the software (in a local environment or the Internet) and so they can prepare for a final presentation.

The students of the courses are divided into teams with a maximum of 5 members. Each team must develop different software between them. During sprints, all students act as developers.

Although it isn't a Scrum practice, one student per group acts as a developer and Scrum Master. In each Sprint, the Scrum Master must be changed, so that the work overhead is for a limited time. This practice was adopted because all students need to practice development in the technologies adopted. As the Courses 1 and 2 are sequential, practice as a Scrum Master is also practiced by all students.

In Course 1, the PO is usually the business owner. In Course 2, the students themselves act as PO because they create some business. The Daily Scrum Meeting event is eventually held in class but is usually held online by students. This practice is encouraged by the professor.

All artifacts were available online in Google Drive and shared with team members, PO and professor.

Development monitoring was done through the Trello online tool. The software code was shared in Github. More details about the content of each Sprint can be seen in Table 30.1.

Course 1 aims to present the fundamental concepts about Software Engineering, software development methodologies, UML diagrams and the development of a web application with the data stored in database. Course 2 focuses on developing web-based software using Scrum and technologies such as persistence framework, Cascading Style Sheets Frameworks, Javascript Frameworks, API (Application Programming Interface) and MVC (Model

Table 30.1 Content of sprints in each course

Sprint	Course 1	Course 2	
#0	Software Engineering Concepts. Agile Methods. Focus on Scrum	Review about the Scrum Elevator Statement (Pitch) and Canvas	Study of technologies
#0	Division of teams		
#0	Specific Solution—Choosing a Real Company to Understand Problems and Determine Solution	General solution—Choose an idea that meets the real needs of society	
#0	Determining PO; Making project content available online: Google Drive, Trello and GitHub; Product Backlog - Preliminary Version; Development of UML and MER diagrams; Configuring the development environment		
#1	Sprint Backlog and Software Development		
#2	Sprint Backlog and Software Development		
#3	Sprint Backlog and Software Development		
#3	Software Deployment; Preparation for the final presentation; Final Presentation		

Table 30.2 Scrum events used in the courses

Stage	Activities
Sprint planning	They are determined: – Purpose of Sprint – Sprint Backlog – DoD—Definition of Done All artifacts are shared online with the teacher, PO and team members
Development	Software development
Sprint review	The purpose of Sprint is presented. Each User Story is read and displayed working The Acceptance Criteria are verified so that US can be accepted or not
Sprint retrospective	The team determines the percentage of each member's participation. Three questions are answered What worked? What went wrong? Suggestions for improvements?
Daily scrum meeting	The questions were adapted because it is not possible to make this event every class. Three questions are answered What have you done so far? What are you going to do in the next few days? What went wrong?

View Controller). Thus, Course 2 complements what was presented in Course 1, both of them are based on Sprints. The semester lasts 20 weeks. Each course has 80 lessons of 50 min, which are taught in 2 days of the week, each day having two classes. All classes are held in the laboratory with computer and Internet access.

Table 30.2 shows the details of what is covered in each Scrum event during the courses.

On the Sprint Planning and Sprint Review, is performed the presentation of N minutes per group, conducted in class with the professor, and if possible, with the PO.

The Sprint Retrospective stage, is an activity of N minutes per group, made in class with the professor.

The Daily Scrum Meeting is an activity of N minutes per group. This event was made in the class supported by professor, but it also performed outside of class time by students.

On the "Development" stage, it is important to note that many students work during the day and they study in the evening. Because it is an academic project, the amount of

hours of development is limited. The development time for each team member is combined in class. For both courses it was agreed that each student should work 2 h a day in the development of the project, considering only the working days.

In Scrum, the sprints help inexperienced students to conduct a more assertive project planning. However, when Kanban [20] is used, the more experienced student in software development produces more, and consequently the less experienced student participates less in code development. It is necessary that the professor proposes learning alternatives so that everyone can participate actively in the project.

In this research, gamification was the chosen learning methodology. During the semester, the professors created individual and group weekly missions in LevelLearn, determining the pace of the game. For Course 1, 23 missions were created, and 28 missions for Course 2. Each mission created has an associated reward that is managed in LevelLearn through notes and feedbacks that are given by the professor. Thus, the formative assessment (contiguous) was adopted in the courses. Formative assessment is characterized by Bloom, Hastings and Madaus [21], as "one that is held during the teaching-learning process, which aims to provide constant feedback to the student, assuring mastery of that learning module". With this type of assessment, the professor has the possibility to get more information to analyze the development of learning and the student has the information about his successes and failures.

At the end of the semester a structured questionnaire closed was applied to collect the perceptions of students about the habit that they have to play, motivation using the LevelLearn game in the courses, emotional and psychological pressure due to the participation in the game, and the influence of the rules of the game in the performance of academic activities.

The questionnaire was validated in advance at a pretest with six students randomly selected to evaluate possible inconsistencies and ambiguities in questions. After that, the model of the two multiple-choice questions was changed to multiple checkboxes.

All LevelLearn student players completed the questionnaire using an online form created in Google Forms. In Sect. 30.5, the questionnaire is presented and the data analysis is reported.

Section 30.5 details the questionnaire that was applied at the end of the semester and discusses the results found.

30.5   Results and Discussion

In the questionnaire, the questions were divided into four sections. The first section was used to identify the participant; the second section aimed to collect data about the participant's behavior and preferences related to games; the third section aimed to know the participants' perceptions regarding motivation and pressure when participating in the game; and the fourth section was intended to verify the participant's knowledge about the game.

For the answers obtained, the Cronbach's Alpha criterion [22] was applied for responses to non-demographic items and the factor 0.69 was obtained. According to Landis and Koch [23] this factor indicates that the questionnaire has substantial internal consistency.

Regarding demographic information, 75.5% of the students were aged up to 30 years, and 24.5% were 31 years old or older. As for the semester of the course, 60% were students of Course 1 and 40% of Course 2.

Concerning the behavior, when asked which types of games are in the habit of playing, between electronic games, cards and sports, only two participants reported that they do not usually play any game. 11.1% of the participants play some game every day; another 31.1% play once a week; 6.7% play from 5 to 6 times a week, and the majority (46.7%) play

from 2 to 4 times a week. In total, 64.4% of the participants have the habit of playing from 2 to 7 days a week, they are called gamers. 48.9% prefer to play on a team; 33.3% prefer to play alone and 17.8% like to play alone or in a team.

Regarding the students' perceptions about the game, 88.9% felt motivated to respond the activities. During the semester, each student participated in only one course that used LevelLearn. One question aimed to get the student to compare their motivation between the courses that used the game and the courses did not use it. 84.4% answered that they felt more motivated in the course in which LevelLearn was used, and 15.6% answered that the use of the game did not influence their motivation between the courses. It is worth noting that no one answered "In courses that did not use LevelLearn".

The act of participating in a game can put pressure on the participant for different reasons. Thus, some questions were intended to collect students' perceptions of the emotional and psychological pressure inherent in participating in the game. 82.2% answered that they felt more pressured (37 participants) and the others students did not feel pressured. Of those who felt pressured, 91.9% answered that the pressure was positive and 8.1% responded that the pressure was negative.

For those who felt negative pressure, the reason was the fear of being in the last positions of the ranking, according to questionnaire. For the 37 students who felt positively pressured, 59.5% said they did not want to be in the last ranking positions, 29.7% said that seeking the top ranking was the main reason; and the other 10.8% stated that the main reason was competition with other classmates, which shows the different ways that students deal with competition.

Regarding the influence of the aspects of the game on the behavior of the students, 66.7% stated that participation in the game influenced the decision to attend classes, and 84.4% felt influenced to arrive punctually at classes. This is an important behavior for the proper execution of the lesson planned by the professor. Regarding the activities, 82.2% felt influenced to fulfill the missions proposed by the professors due to the participation of the LevelLearn ranking; 80% were influenced by the participation in the game to deliver the activities on time.

An important factor for player engagement is knowledge of the rules. Regarding this, 88.9% of the students knew the rules, 8.9% were partially aware, and only one student was not aware of the rules and challenges to be achieved.

One of the concerns with the new generations is the difficulty in taking on commitments and responsibilities. The collected data revealed that LevelLearn was particularly interesting for the age group of 16–20 years (15 participants), since 86.7% of the participants of this age group stated that they were influenced to attend classes on time and to deliver activities in the deadline.

30.6 Conclusions

In this paper, we present the game LevelLearn, which is a proposal for gamification of the teaching-learning process. The game was designed from the perspectives proposed by Schell [7] on the concepts of game design. We used the game during a semester in a technological undergraduate course at a public college and we applied a questionnaire to collect data about students' perceptions.

The results are significantly positive, as they allow us to infer that LevelLearn increased the students' involvement in the courses and, although many felt pressured to participate in a game, the pressure was positive, as they stated that they felt more motivated to participate punctually of the classes and to fulfill the activities on time.

In the questionnaire, 100% of the students answered that they were motivated by the professors to get involved with the game.

In view of the significant results, it is important to highlight: (1) students' interest in games is a factor that motivates them to be involved with the gamification process; (2) the profile of students in an Information Technology course may facilitate engagement in a game; and (3) as Sepehr and Head [24] have observed, one of the main success aspects of the game is competition among participants.

In future works, we intend to apply the research in courses of other areas of knowledge, in general subjects, and with students of other age groups, such as elementary and high school. In addition, we aim to incorporate playful elements into the LevelLearn Web environment.

References

1. CHAOS. *The CHAOS Manifesto. Agile Succeeds Three Times More Often Than Waterfall* (The Standish Group, 2012)
2. Versionone, Survey: The 11th Annual State of Agile Development Survey, (2017)
3. PGB. Pesquisa Game Brasil. 2017. http://www.pesquisagame-brasil.com.br. Accessed 13 Oct 2017
4. K. Huotari, J. Hamari, Defining gamification: a service marketing perspective, in *Proceeding of the 16th International Academic MindTrek Conference (MindTrek'12)*, (ACM, New York, 2012), pp. 17–22. https://doi.org/10.1145/2393132.2393137
5. L.C. Stanculescu, A. Bozzon, R. Sips, G. Houben, Work and play: an experiment in enterprise gamification, in *Proceedings of the 19th ACM Conference on Computer-Supported Cooperative Work & Social Computing (CSCW '16)*, (ACM, New York, 2016), pp. 346–358. https://doi.org/10.1145/2818048.2820061
6. S.S. Borges, V.H.S. Durelli, H.M. Reis, S. Isotani, A systematic mapping on gamification applied to education, in *Proceedings of the 29th Annual ACM Symposium on Applied Computing (SAC '14)*, (ACM, New York, 2014), pp. 216–222. https://doi.org/10.1145/2554850.2554956
7. J. Schell, *The Art of Game Design: A Book of Lenses* (Morgan Kaufmann Publishers Inc., San Francisco, CA, 2008)
8. J. Sutherland, K. Schwaber, Scrum Guide, (2013). http://www.scrumguides.org/docs/scrumguide/v1/scrum-guide-us.pdf. Accessed 13 Oct 2017
9. EXTREME PROGRAMMING: A Gentle Introduction. http://www.extremeprogramming.org. Accessed 13 Oct 2017
10. Manifesto for Agile Software Development. http://agilemanifesto.org. Accessed 13 Oct 2017
11. M. Cohn, *Succeeding with Agile: Software Development Using Scrum* (AddisonWesley, Ann Arbor, 2010)
12. W. Phillips, S. Subramani, A. Gorantla, V. Phillips, Developing software in the academic environment, in *Information Technology: New Generations. Advances in Intelligent Systems and Computing*, vol 448, ed. By S. Latifi (Springer, Cham, 2016), https://doi.org/10.1007/978-3-319-32467-8_110
13. L.S. Siles, et al., An integrated academic system prototype using accidents and crises management as PBL, in *Information Technology—New Generations. Advances in Intelligent Systems and Computing*, vol 558, ed. By S. Latifi (Springer, Cham, 2018). https://doi.org/10.1007/978-3-319-54978-1_55
14. V. Sachdeva, Requirements prioritization in agile: use of planning poker for maximizing return on investment, in *Information Technology—New Generations. Advances in Intelligent Systems and Computing*, vol 558, ed. By S. Latifi (Springer, Cham, 2017). https://doi.org/10.1007/978-3-319-54978-1_53
15. G. Mehta, X. Luo, N. Parde, K. Patel, B. Rodgers, A. Sistla, Untangled—an interactive mapping game for engineering education, in *2013 IEEE International Conference on Microelectronics Systems Education*, (Austin, TX, 2013)
16. S. O'Donovan, J. Gain, P. Marais, A case study in the gamification of a university-level games development course, in *Proceedings of the South African Institute for Computer Scientists and Information Technologists Conference (SAICSIT '13)*, ed. By P. Machanick, M. Tsietsi (ACM, New York, 2013), pp. 242–251. https://doi.org/10.1145/2513456.2513469
17. E. Marasco, L. Behjat, M. Eggermont, W. Rosehart, M. Moshirpour, R. Hugo, Using gamification for engagement and learning in electrical and computer engineering classrooms, in *IEEE Frontiers in Education Conference (FIE)*, (Eire, PA, 2016), pp. 1–4. https://doi.org/10.1109/FIE.2016.7757352
18. S. Butler, D.T. Ahmed, Gamification to engage and motivate students to achieve computer science learning goals, in *International Conference on Computational Science and Computational Intelligence (CSCI)*, (Las Vegas, NV, 2016), pp. 237–240. https://doi.org/10.1109/CSCI.2016.0053
19. FATEC, http://www.fatecguaratingueta.edu.br/cursos_fatec/?p=14. Accessed 13 Oct 2017
20. D.J. Anderson, D. Reinertsen, G. Kanban, Successful Evolutionary Change for Your Technology Business, (2010)
21. B.S. Bloom, J.T. Hastings, G.F. Madaus, *Handbook on Formative and Sommative Evaluation of Student Learning* (McGrawHill, New York, 1971), p. 923
22. L.J. Cronbach, Coefficient alpha and the internal structure of tests. Psychometrika **16**(3), 297–334 (1951)
23. J.R. Landis, G.G. Koch, The measurement of observer agreement for categorical data. Biometrics. **33**(1), 159–174 (1977). Published by: International Biometric Society. http://www.jstor.org/stable/2529310
24. S. Sepehr, M. Head, Competition as an element of gamification for learning: an exploratory longitudinal investigation, in *Proceedings of the First International Conference on Gameful Design, Research, and Applications (Gamification '13)*, (ACM, New York, 2013), pp. 2–9. https://doi.org/10.1145/2583008.2583009

Adler Diniz de Souza, Rodrigo Duarte Seabra, Juliano Marinho Ribeiro, and Lucas Eduardo da Silva Rodrigues

Abstract

The use of serious games has emerged as a differentiated strategy to promote the teaching of essential concepts and techniques in several areas of knowledge. To contribute to the student's formation process of the Software Project Management, this research presents the development and validation of an electronic board serious game, named SCRUMI, to the teaching of concepts inherent to the SCRUM framework. The evaluation of the proposed game was carried out according to some criteria such as usability, quality of the question and presentation of the activities, applicability and motivation. The main results showed that the game is presented as a good alternative to be explored in the classroom.

Keywords

Serious games · Project management · SCRUM framework · SCRUMI

31.1 Introduction

The gaming market has grown significantly in Brazil. According to the Vice-President of the Brazilian Association of Game Developers, Fred Vasconcelos, in recent years, there has been an increase between 9 and 15% in the Brazilian video game industry. One of the most influential factors for this index is the popularization of tablets and smartphones, which allow interactivity anywhere [1].

Due to the accelerated expansion of the games industry, many researches have been developed aiming to generate knowledge about the engagement produced by this way of entertainment. In this context, the concept of gamification emerged, which concerns the use of games for various entertainment purposes [2]. In practice, the gamification is based on the use of mechanics observed in games in contexts that are not games [3]. The use of gamification in the educational field represents a valuable tool kindle the interest of students facing traditional methodologies, making learning more interesting [4, 5].

Among the various areas in which the use of gamification may provide interesting results, from the point of view of the teaching-learning process, is Software Project Management. Back in 2004, Dantas, Barros and Werner [6] argued that the use of games represented a different strategy to promote the teaching of the essential concepts and techniques of an area that, in some cases, is eventually forgotten because project management is an activity based on the knowledge acquired from the experience of the professionals having worked on several projects. In addition, games emerged as an innovative way, once they provided the feeling of a real environment, differently from traditional simulations. According to Werbach and Hunter [7], in the corporate environment, the use of gamification has presented good results regarding customer satisfaction and motivation of employees.

Because of the constant changes in the professional market, project managers often need to fit this scenario, having to reschedule their strategic decisions, reducing operational costs and adapting their processes and services in order to meet customers' demands. Based on this need, the importance of a more responsive way of project management and flexible to changes arises. In this case, the use of the SCRUM framework can represent a differential, because it prioritizes the iterative and incremental development and the flexibility required by the frequent changes in the labor market, in addition to maximizing the competitive advantage [8].

From the scenario above, this research aims to introduce the development of an electronic serious game, using some mechanics observed in board games, which can possibly

A. D. de Souza (✉) · R. D. Seabra · J. M. Ribeiro
L. E. da Silva Rodrigues
Institute of Mathematics and Computing, Federal University of Itajubá, Itajubá, Minas Gerais, Brazil
e-mail: rodrigo@unifei.edu.br

© Springer International Publishing AG, part of Springer Nature 2018
S. Latifi (ed.), *Information Technology – New Generations*, Advances in Intelligent Systems and Computing 738,
https://doi.org/10.1007/978-3-319-77028-4_31

support the teaching of concepts inherent to the SCRUM framework. The proposed educational game is expected to help students understand related contents for learning the discipline of Software Project Management. Moreover, the study investigates, from the students' perspective, the potential benefits provided due to the experienced use of the proposed game in that discipline lessons. The main contributions of the study are: (1) to help spread the idea of using educational serious games, so as to increase their use in education; (2) to qualitatively evaluate the students opinion involved in the study, verifying if the game developed met the expectations, as well as its degree of acceptance and contribution to the teaching process.

31.2   Theoretical Foundation

Project management comprises an area targeted in organizations, representing a differential factor in the success of a project. Brewer [9] considers that organizations are becoming increasingly geared to projects, and these are growing rapidly, which requires best managers. Given the increase in the degree of importance of good management, recruiting individuals with the required skills for the success of the project is made necessary. To exercise this function efficiently, besides the theoretical knowledge that is typically acquired in undergraduate courses, the project manager must be experienced in the area, which will influence the decision-making process required for the projects [6].

Despite the practical works, traditional education lacks effectively practical experiences, as observed in the universities or in specific training courses, in which classes are usually teacher-centered and the content is presented through lectures [10]. The lessons do not provide the practicality needed to the area and, consequently, fail to contribute to students' motivation. The lack of practical resources for classes is reflected in the corporate scenario. According to Brewer [9], in corporations, a large number of projects failed due to reasons related to mismanagement, caused by the absence of trained project managers.

This reality makes it essential to improve the educational process. To make the traditional teaching more enjoyable and fill in the blanks as to the practical experience required, according to Von Wangenheim and Prikladnicki [11], there is an emerging demand for new ways of teaching to improve project management classes.

Specifically regarding project management, the SCRUM framework has been intensively applied, to introduce best management practices. SCRUM is defined by its creators [12] as a structural framework used to manage complex products, which allows integrating multiple processes or techniques. SCRUM prescribes five events, also known as ceremonies, all of which have minimum and maximum lengths defined, and may be reduced or increased. One of the SCRUM events is the Sprint, considered the key point of the framework [12]. It is a cycle of 2–4 weeks, in which an incremental and potentially usable version of the product is created. Each Sprint has a list of specific features to be developed, called the Sprint backlog. Sprint is also composed of four other events in the SCRUM: Sprint Planning, Daily SCRUM, Sprint Review and Sprint Retrospective.

31.2.1   Related Researches

Developed to complement the teaching project management concepts, the Planager game focuses on the group of processes that involve the planning [13]. Focusing on the definition and simulation of Sprints, the Scrumming game aims to meet the needs related to teaching agile methods. The player assumes the role of Scrum Master in the simulator module, and his/her role is to set the Sprint and monitor his/her progress in the taskboard, visualize the burndown chart and manage the product backlog activities [13]. Paludo, Raabe and Benitti [10] developed RSKManager, an educational serious game focused on teaching risk management in software projects. The objective of the game is to exercise and to simulate situations involving software project risk and decision-making. The research by Campos et al. [14] offers a game based on simulations, named Kallango, which aims to give students the opportunity to analyze the impact of their choices in a controlled environment using the practices proposed in SCRUM. Several other studies consistently reported in the literature feature games developed exclusively for the teaching practices of the SCRUM framework: PlayScrum [15], The Scrum Game [16], Scrum from Hell [17], Ballpoint game [18], Scrum Game [19], Scrum Simulation with LEGO Bricks [20] and SCRUMIA [11]. Another approach can be found in the recent research by [21]. Still with regard to the use of games, other researches can be highlighted [22–25].

From the research presented, it is a fact that studies involving the use of games for teaching concepts linked to project management, especially in SCRUM, have raised the interest of researchers in the development of different projects that facilitate teaching and learning the theme. Similarly to the studies presented, the motivating factor involved in this opportunity is also to provide support to students who often demonstrate or report any kind of difficulty in learning the SCRUM framework. Thus, we here present another alternative in face of this challenge, offering a new opportunity for training concepts linked to the theme.

31.3 Method

31.3.1 The Game SCRUMI

SCRUMI is a board electronic game consisting of questions and answers, whose goal is to introduce key concepts of the SCRUM framework. The game was developed by the authors of this work. In its development, we used the activities that are part of the Sprint life cycle in a software project. The platform used for the game design was Unity. The game consists of two kinds of questions: (1) multiple choice or (2) drag and drop. The questions were distributed into five phases, namely: Preparation, Analysis, Execution, Monitoring and Control and Closing.

Figure 31.1 illustrates the activities of two phases of the life cycle and the game control panel. The player's progress occurs when he hits the question related to the activity in which he is on the board. The player who moves all the spaces within the stipulated time wins the game. Each question presents an estimated response period of 1 min, and the game total time consists of 44 min. The player who misses more than ten questions or spends more than 30% of the estimated time accumulated during the match loses the game. The player who spends less time on questions will have less time spent accumulated and, consequently, will have more time available to answer the next questions.

To facilitate monitoring the player status, there is a control panel (Fig. 31.2) that allows the activation and/or monitoring of the following actions: (1) to enable/disable the sound by the button indicated in 1; (2) to show the number of the player errors indicated in 2; (3) to control of the total time spent in the game indicated in 3; (4) time spent in current activity indicated in 4; (5) the clock (indicated in 5) display will flash in yellow when the player hits 50 s on the question, and will flash in red when the time exceeds the estimated duration of 60 s for the question.

Figure 31.3 shows a question example about a specific activity of the board. After the player answers it, the game provides a feedback stating whether he/she hit or missed the question, and if he/she spent more or less time than the estimated. Whenever a player misses a question, the player wasted the time spent on the question because he/she does not advance any board space. If the player sets the question, he/she may: (1) save time for the next questions, if answered in less than 60 s; (2) waste time, otherwise.

Since every project has a risk element involved, the spaces represented by an interrogation were added to the board. These spaces bring random events, positive or negative, to the time and cost of the project and are always related to phase activities of the life cycle in which the player is at the moment. The game can be accessed via the Internet at address: http://scrumigp.com.

31.3.2 Participants and Description of Method

An evaluation questionnaire, based on ISO/IEC 25010 standard, was developed to assess some attributes. This question-

Fig. 31.1 Game interface

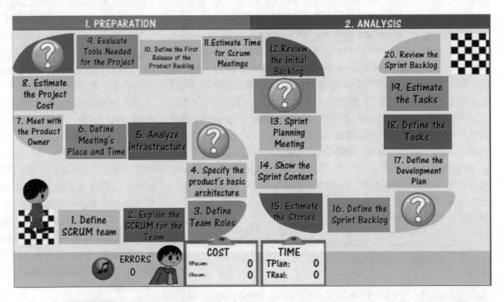

Fig. 31.2 SCRUMI control panel

Fig. 31.3 Example of drag and
drop question

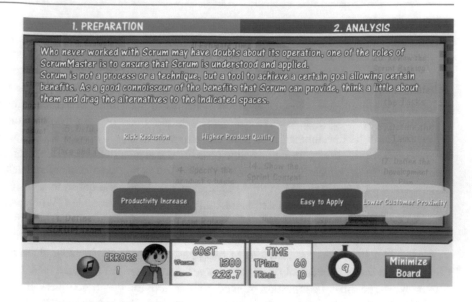

naire was reviewed by an expert researcher in ISO/IEC 25010
standard, who suggested improvements to be incorporated in
the questionnaire. Thereafter, game was released for a four
professionals' team who have been working with SCRUM
framework for 3 years. This team also suggested some
improvements, especially for the interface and for the score
panel. All the suggestions were fully incorporated into three
new versions of the game.

Students selected to participate in the study were at a stage
corresponding to the sixth period of the Information Systems
course of the Federal University of Itajubá—UNIFEI. The
lecturer responsible for the Software Management discipline
gave a theoretical lecture about the SCRUM framework
and, as a result, presented the SCRUMI game for students,
highlighting its functioning and its mechanics of progress.
Finally, the game was made available for use for 2 h.
The class was composed of 34 students who, after playing
the SCRUMI, answered a questionnaire composed of 27
questions (Table 31.1) based on the following attributes:
(1) **usability**, questions 1–8; (2) **questions quality and
activities presentation**, questions 9–15; (3) **applicability**,
questions 16–21; (4) **motivation**, questions 22–27. All the
questions presented answers based on Likert scale, whose
possibilities of response varied from 1 to 5, namely: 1—
strongly disagree, 2—partially disagree, 3—indifferent, 4—
partially agree and 5—totally agree.

31.4   Data Analysis

For discussing the results, the following feedbacks will be
considered: (1) positive—evaluated questions with answers
4 or 5; (2) indifferent—to the responses evaluated as 3;
(3) negative—in the case of answers 1 or 2. Conversely,
the incorrect classifications are represented as false positive
and false negative rates. Intuitively, false positives represent

incorrect class membership classification and false negatives
represent incorrect class non-membership.

Considering the positive assessments of the **usability** attribute, 77% of the students positively evaluated the attribute;
11% rated as indifferent and 12% disagreed with some
question. Through the boxplot chart depicted in Fig. 31.4,
it is possible to affirm that the students positively evaluated
questions Q1, Q2, Q3, Q5, Q6 and Q7. Regarding the game
design (Q5), despite having been positively evaluated, this
question showed the highest discrepancy as compared to
the previous result, with some indifferent reviews and only
a negative one. As to the game music (Q8), the student's
opinion majorly concentrated on the range 1–3, showing
certain rejection of this item. Because the SCRUMI is a game
that requires concentration, some students complained of the
sounds from the 34 computers performing the same song in
the classroom. Note that the player can turn off the game
sound during the match.

As to the **questions quality and activities presentation**
attribute, 89% of the participants positively validated this
attribute; only 8% assessed any questions as indifferent. Only
3% of the students negatively evaluated this attribute. A
certain discrepancy in the evaluation of the questions writing
quality (Q9) has been verified. This can be explained by the
fact that two questions of the kind "drag and drop" presented
a defect each. However, most of the values assigned to
this attribute were distributed between 3 and 5, assuming
a satisfactory result. The other questions (Q10–Q15) were
positively evaluated, with fewer students expressing to be
indifferent.

The evaluation of the **applicability** attribute showed an
increase in positive feedbacks, adding up to a total of 91%.
As for the negative results, only a few cases were observed in
which some student partially disagreed with some question.
For this attribute, no student completely disagreed of the

Table 31.1 Questions of qualitative assessment

Questions	
Q1.	Are the arrangement and distribution of items on the game screens clear and objective?
Q2.	Is the navigation in the game menus easy to understand and intuitive?
Q3.	Do the characters and animations of the game contribute to playful activity?
Q4.	Do the arrangement and the distribution of the colors not hinder reading the items contained in the board?
Q5.	Is the game design attractive?
Q6.	Are the game rules clear and objective?
Q7.	Was the understanding of the game and its use as study material easy?
Q8.	Is the game music pleasant?
Q9.	Are the questions well written?
Q10.	Are the questions well reputable?
Q11.	Are the questions appropriately challenging?
Q12.	Based on the proposed activities, is the present contextualization at the beginning of the questions well placed?
Q13.	Do the activities within each phase of the game match the phase to which they were assigned?
Q14.	Are the unforeseen events of the doubtful spaces adapted to the environment in which they are placed?
Q15.	Are the life cycle displayed in the game board and the activities contained therein easy to understand?
Q16.	Was the game content relevant to their interests?
Q17.	Does the SCRUMI allow a better understanding of the SCRUM concepts?
Q18.	Does the SCRUMI assist in studies for proof?
Q19.	Is it easier to study after playing the SCRUMI?
Q20.	Were the game mechanics suitable to your way of learning?
Q21.	Did you feel confident you were learning while going through the game stages?
Q22.	Did the game catch your attention while you were playing?
Q23.	Did you have a good time playing SCRUMI?
Q24.	Did you have positive feelings while you were playing the SCRUMI?
Q25.	Would you like to play this game again?
Q26.	Would you recommend this game to your friends?
Q27.	Based on the lectures, was the use of the game a different and enjoyable experience?

Fig. 31.4 Usability boxplot chart

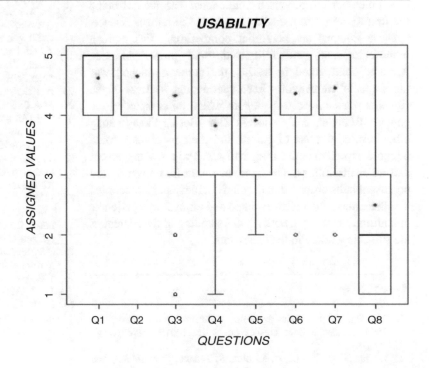

questions presented. In relation to this attribute, only a few students were indifferent and, on average, a single student partially disagreed with some question. The attribute applicability still showed positive comments by some students about the game, including: "*A great game to master the content in a different way*"; "*Very cool! With the game, I learned more about certain concepts of the SCRUM*"; "*Very well prepared, although with some rare bugs, but its interface is intuitive and easy gameplay*".

Considering the **motivation** attribute, the percentage of positive ratings focused in the range of 88%. The percentage of indifferent opinions in this attribute was 8% and the negative answers amounted to 4%, and in 1% of the questions there was total disagreement and 3% partial disagreement. In relation to the overall average, the students felt satisfied and had fun playing the SCRUMI. We can conclude that the SCRUMI was well evaluated in all questions, because most students positively assessed them and few were indifferent.

31.5 Final Considerations

Unlike the old conception that people had on the use of games, currently they are being increasingly used as learning tools, for marketing, for behavioral change and for entertainment purposes. In everyday life, most people play or have utilized some mechanics related to games for fun.

Based on the evaluation carried out from experienced usage of the SCRUMI game, we can notice that most of the students felt motivated to face the game questions, seeking to supplement the proposed challenges. The idea of being the first to complete a challenge shows the human essence, because humans are perennial competitors. This, among other features, adds credibility to the study presented herein. Another point noted in testing the game developed was the students' motivation after experiencing it. Most of the students proved keen to try again when not completing the game with the expected success. Considering these, among other results, the use of games and their mechanics could be more exploited in teaching Software Project Management and other disciplines. This statement can be proven by the positive results observed in the study, and it can be concluded that the games add a differentiated and enjoyable experience, in addition to allowing better understanding of the content of the subjects worked in the classroom.

References

1. G1—O portal de notícias da Globo, Mercado de games movimenta R$44 milhões e deve crescer em 2015, (2015), http://goo.gl/TCvpXy
2. Y. Vianna, M. Vianna, B. Medina, S. Tanaka, *Gamification, Inc: Como Reinventar Empresas a Partir De Jogos* (MJV Press, Rio de Janeiro, 2013)
3. V.M. Mastrocola, *Ludificador: Um Guia De Referências Para O Game Designer Brasileiro* (Edição do autor, São Paulo, 2011)
4. T.M. Bonetti, C.G. Von Wangenheim, Desenvolvimento de um repositório de jogos educacionais para o ensino de gerenciamento de projetos, in *Anais do XXIV Simpósio Brasileiro de Informática na Educação—SBIE*, (Campinas, 2013)
5. M.L. Fardo, A gamificação aplicada em ambientes de aprendizagem. RENOTE. **11**(1), (2013)
6. A. Dantas, M. Barros, C. Werner, Treinamento experimental com jogos de simulação para gerentes de projeto de software, in *Anais do XVIII Simpósio Brasileiro de Engenharia de Software*, (2004), pp. 23–28
7. K. Werbach, D. Hunter, *For the Win: How Game Thinking Can Revolutionize Your Business* (Wharton Digital Press, 2012)
8. R. Sabbagh, *Scrum: Gestão Ágil Para Projetos De Sucesso* (Editora Casa do Código, São Paulo, 2014)
9. J.L. Brewer, Project managers: can we make them or just make them better?, in *Proceedings of the 6th Conference on Information Technology Education*, (ACM, 2005), pp. 167–173
10. L. Paludo, A.L.A. Raabe, F.B.V. Benitti, RSKManager—um jogo para apoiar o ensino de gerência de riscos em projetos de software. RENOTE. **11**(3), (2013)
11. C.G. Von Wangenheim, R. Savi, A.F. Borgatto, SCRUMIA—an educational game for teaching SCRUM in computing courses. J. Syst. Softw. **86**(10), 2675–2687 (2013)
12. K. Schwaber, J. Sutherland, The Scrum Guide. Scrum.org, (2013)
13. C.G. Von Wangenheim, R. Prikladnicki, O uso de jogos educacionais para o ensino de gerência de projetos de software. Fórum de Educação em Engenharia de Software. **37**, (2007)
14. A.M. Campos, et al., Um jogo voltado à prática de gerenciamento de projetos, in *Anais do XXII Simpósio Brasileiro de Informática na Educação—SBIE*, (Aracaju, 2011)
15. J.M. Fernandes, S.M. Sousa, PlayScrum—a card game to learn the scrum agile method, in *Proceedings of Second International Conference on Games and Virtual Worlds for Serious Applications*, (Braga, Portugal, 2010)
16. W. Wake, M. Cohn, The Scrum Game, Mountaingoat, (2007), http://www.mountaingoatsoftware-.com/products/scrum-game
17. W. Wake, *SCRUM from Hell. Developed for the Scrum Gathering* (Denver/TX, 2004), http://xp123.com/articles/scrum-from-hell
18. B. Gloger, Ballpoint Game. (2008)
19. A. Gkritsi, ScrumGame: an agile software management game. *Master Thesis*, (University of Southampton, Eletronics and Computer Science, Great Britain, 2011)
20. A. Krivitsky, Scrum Simulation with LEGO Bricks, (2009)
21. M.A.C. Meireles, B.A. Bonifácio, Uso de métodos ágeis e aprendizagem baseada em problema no ensino de engenharia de software: um relato de experiência, in *Anais do XXVI Simpósio Brasileiro de Informática na Educação—SBIE*, (Maceió, 2015)
22. V. Janarthanan, Serious video games: games for education and health, in *Information Technology: New Generations (ITNG), 2012 Ninth International Conference on*. (IEEE, 2012), pp. 875–878
23. C.M. Kanode, H.M. Haddad, Software engineering challenges in game development, in *Information Technology: New Generations, 2009. ITNG'09. Sixth International Conference on*. (IEEE, 2009), pp. 260–265
24. S.S. Shabanah, et al., Designing computer games to teach algorithms, in *Information Technology: New Generations (ITNG), 2010 Seventh International Conference on*. (IEEE, 2010), pp. 1119–1126
25. E.P.P. Pe-than, D.H. Goh, C.S. Lee, A survey and typology of human computation games, in *Information Technology: New Generations (ITNG), 2012 Ninth International Conference on*. (IEEE, 2012), pp. 720–725

Part IV

Agile Software Testing and Development

Teaching Scrum by Doing Scrum in Internships in South Africa to Prepare Interns for Agile Projects

32

Laurie Butgereit

Abstract

Unemployment in South Africa is calculated to be approximately between 25 and 35% depending on whether or not one includes the number of people who are unemployed but not actively looking for a position. Even among people with some tertiary education, the unemployment rate is just under 20% and university graduates have an unemployment rate of approximately 7%. These high values have encouraged the South African Revenue Service to offer tax incentives to companies which maintain internships or learnerships. This paper looks specifically at how the Scrum Methodology can be introduced in internships in the IT industry to help prepare interns for Agile projects. Students who attend traditional programming courses are typically prepared for a Waterfall environment where the student is handed a specification and expected to write a program. Usually, students have never encountered an Agile environment during their training. This paper describes an internship which introduces Scrum during the internship by using Scrum in the internship itself.

Keywords

Scrum · Internships · Agile

Table 32.1 Unemployment rates by education level

Education level	Unemployment rate (%)
<Grade 12	33.1
Grade 12	27.5
Some tertiary	17.8
Univ graduate	7.3

32.1 Introduction

In first quarter 2017, the unemployment rate in South Africa was 27.7%. According to Stats SA (the official purveyor of statistics in South Africa), this was the highest rate of unemployment since September, 2003. The expanded unemployment rate which measures people who are unemployed but not actively looking for employment was 36.4% [1].

Education, however, does help to mitigate these values. Unemployment rates for different levels of education in South Africa can be seen in Table 32.1 [1].

To help alleviate this problem, the South African Revenue Service (SARS) offers various tax incentives to employers to hire and train entry level people [2]. Companies are encouraged to offer internships to unemployed or underemployed (people currently working at jobs below their level of training) people with the intention that the interns will become fully employable at the end of their internship.

Despite shortages in the Information Technology sector in South Africa, unemployment and underemployment does exist. These include people who have dropped out of university degrees because of financial reasons and people who have tertiary certificates from private educational organizations (as opposed to universities).

This paper looks at one such internship offered by Blue Label Telecoms in South Africa. Blue Label Telecoms is listed on the Johannesburg Stock Exchange. It is one of the largest distributors of secure tokens in South Africa. Blue Label Telecoms specializes in prepaid products and electronic distribution of virtual merchandise. Although the internship program was a general Information Technology internship and covered general topics such as Java programming, this paper specifically looks at how Scrum and other Agile methodologies were introduced into the internship to further prepare the interns for future employment.

L. Butgereit (✉)
Nelson Mandela University, Port Elizabeth, South Africa

Blue Label Telecoms, Sandton, South Africa
e-mail: laurie.butgereit@mandela.ac.za

© Springer International Publishing AG, part of Springer Nature 2018
S. Latifi (ed.), *Information Technology – New Generations*, Advances in Intelligent Systems and Computing 738,
https://doi.org/10.1007/978-3-319-77028-4_32

32.2   Research Methodology

Design Science Research was used for this research project. Design Science Research is often used in IS/IT projects to solve important, real-life problems. Design Science Research is an iterative methodology consisting of five steps: awareness, suggestion, development, evaluation, conclusion [3, 4]. These steps (especially the middle three steps—suggestion, development, and evaluation) are traversed numerous times until a satisfactory outcome is obtained.

The evaluation step of Design Science Research is extremely important. As is more fully explained in Sect. 32.9, anonymous surveys were sent to each intern weekly. These surveys were used to inform the next iteration of steps.

Design Science Research must create one or more artifacts. An artifact can be a construct, a method, a model, or an instantiation of a method or a model.

The research described in this paper produced a model for introducing Scrum in an internship by using Scrum to guide the internship itself. It also created an instantiation of that model by implementing the model in a specific internship.

32.3   Agile and Scrum

In 1970, Dr. Winston Royce developed the Waterfall Model for software development. The Waterfall Model was a non-iterative approach to software development which favored a number of discrete steps or phases such as requirements gathering, design, implementation, testing, and deployment. Using the Waterfall Model, each step had to be completed in full before the next step could be initiated; therefore, all requirements needed to be gathered before any design could take place and all design had to take place before any implementation could start [5]. This was the primary model for software development for many years.

In 2001, however, seventeen people met at a ski resort in Utah, United States, and drafted a document which came to be known as the *Agile Manifesto* [6, 7]. The manifesto clarified four values stating that the group valued: Individuals and interactions over processes and tools; Working software over comprehensive documentation; Customer collaboration over contract negotiation; Responding to change over following a plan. The manifesto also consisted of a number of guiding principles which emphasized frequent face-to-face meetings between business and development groups along with continuous software delivery.

These four values and 12 associated principles have become the basis of many Agile Methodologies including XP, Scrum, DSDM, and Lean Development.

The adoption of Agile Methodologies has grown worldwide although the research of how that adoption is measured

is beyond the scope of this paper. South African Master's student Vanker, however, has researched the adoption of Agile methodologies inside South Africa in his Master's dissertation *The Adoption of Agile Software Development Methodologies by Organisations in South Africa*. In his study, Vanker collected 85 responses from 25 software development companies in South Africa. Of those 85 responses, 71 (or 83.5%) used Scrum as their Agile methodology [8].

It was, therefore, decided that it would be important that interns learn how to work in a Scrum based Agile environment.

32.4   Brief Overview of Scrum

Jeff Sutherland was one of the original authors of the Agile Manifesto [6] and is usually attributed as the author or inventor of the Scrum Methodology. Sutherland himself, however, attributes many of the ideas basic to Scrum as coming from a 1986 article by Takeuchi and Nonaka in the Harvard Business Review entitled *The New New Product Development Game* [9, 10].

Regardless of the original authorship of the Scrum Methodology, Scrum teams are self-organizing teams which work together to do the planning, design, development, and testing of a software project in an iterative manner [9, 11]. Scrum defines a number of artifacts, a number of roles and a number of meetings or events. In any internship designed to introduce participants to Scrum, these artifacts, roles, and events need to be covered.

32.5   General Internship Format

The internship described in this paper is 1 year in duration. The first 6 months consist of formal training on (1) different ICT skills and products offered by the company under research and (2) Java Programming. The last 6 months consist of less formal training by working along side other experienced employees in the company under research.

The first 6 months was accompanied by formal course notes which covered products offered by the company under research and Java programming topics.

32.6   Scrum Artifacts in Internship

The Scrum Methodology consists of three important artifacts: Product backlog, Sprint backlog, and the produced Increment. These three artifacts are present in the internship described in this paper.

The specific topics covered by the course notes in the first 6 months of the internship became items in the product backlog. More specifically, one item for each topic was inserted into the product backlog for each intern. These items could easily be drawn from the table of contents of the course notes.

The sprint backlog consisted of the specific topics which were expected to be covered for the up-coming week.

The increment was defined as being produced and done if the intern had learned the topic specified.

32.7 Scrum Roles in Intership

For the scope of this internship, the facilitator took the role of the Product Owner. The interns initially took the role of the development team members. In addition, however, the role of scrum master rotated among the interns once they became more comfortable with the various events.

32.8 Scrum Events in Internship

The Scrum Methodology supports a number of events: (1) Sprint Planning, (2) Daily Stand-up (3) Sprint Review and (4) Sprint Retrospective. In addition, there is ongoing Backlog Grooming.

The morning of first day of the internship consisted of creating the Product Backlog. Each intern went through the table of contents of the course materials and created backlog items on a colored piece of paper and put them on the Scrum board.

After the product backlog was created, it was then explained that the interns needed to decide how much work they were going to do during this upcoming week. With strong guidance from the facilitator, the interns then moved a number of their product backlog items to the Sprint backlog column of the Scrum board.

As lecture and exercises progressed during the week, interns moved their Sprint backlog items into the In Progress and Done columns on the Scrum board.

Every morning, a Daily Standup was held before actual lecture. Initially the facilitator was the scrum master in these daily standups but as the interns learned the format of the event, that role was rotated amongst the interns. The three questions for each intern were slightly modified to (1) What did you learn yesterday? (2) What do you think you are going to learn today? (3) Is there anything that has been covered already that you don't yet understand?

Each Sprint was 1 week long and on Friday afternoons a Sprint Review was held in which participants could demonstrate what they had learned during the preceding week. Other people from the company under research were invited to the Sprint Reviews. This included representatives of the Human Resources department (who sponsored the internship).

Sprint Retrospectives were only introduced after the first month. They were held on Tuesday afternoons and gave the interns an opportunity to change the format of lectures, etc.

32.9 Results

On Mondays, the interns were emailed links to a survey on SurveyMonkey where they were asked various questions. Many of the questions were multiple choice and true/false whereas others elicited free format responses from the interns. Typical questions included:

1. Did you learn something last week?
2. Was the pace of the course too fast? Too slow? Just right?
3. What topic was the most interesting?
4. What topic was the easiest to learn?
5. What topic was the most difficult to learn?
6. Do you have any suggestions for upcoming weeks?
7. Do you have any outstanding questions from last week?

These questions helped insure that all the interns were actively learning new topics at a pace that was cost effective to all stakeholders.

Over the course of the 6 months, the comments from the interns obviously varied. During some weeks, some interns thought the course was too fast. During other weeks, some other interns thought the course was too slow. By doing weekly surveys, the pace of the course was varied depending on the difficulty of the topics.

In addition, the Sprint Retrospectives held within the internship itself helped elicit feedback from the interns and helped keep the course at a pace that was challenging to the interns.

During the later 6 months of the internship, the interns were assigned to various other teams in the company under research. Many of those teams were Agile teams and the interns were prepared to be active participants in those Agile teams.

32.10 Conclusion

Unemployment in South Africa is high enough that the South African Revenue Service offers tax incentives for companies to offer internships to people who may otherwise be unemployed. Even in the IT industry, unemployment exists among people who have not yet finished an IT related degree and, unfortunately, to a certain extent even among people who do have a tertiary certificate or degree.

Typically programming courses often prepare participants to take part in a Waterfall-type project where they are given a specification and expected to write a program to satisfy the specification. The industry, however, is becoming more and more Agile by following methodologies such as Scrum, XP, and Lean Development.

Any internship in the IT industry needs to introduce interns to Agile methodologies. The research described in this paper found that interns could easily learn Scrum by using Scrum in the internship itself.

References

1. K. Masiteng, Quarterly Labour Force Survey—QLFS Q1:2017, (Stats SA, Pretoria, South Africa, Tech. Rep. Statistical Release P0211, 2017)
2. Employment Tax Incentive (ETI), (2017), http://www.sars.gov.za/TaxTypes/PAYE/ETI/Pages/default.aspx
3. A.R. Hevner et al., Design science in information systems research. Manag. Inf. Syst. Q. **28**(1), 75–106 (2004)
4. Design Science research in information systems
5. J. Charvat, *Project Management Methodologies: Selecting, Implementing, and Supporting Methodologies and Processes for Projects* (Wiley, Hoboken, NJ, 2003)
6. M. Fowler, J. Highsmith, The agile manifesto. Softw. Dev. **9**(8), 28–35 (2001), http://andrey.hristov.com/fht-stuttgart/The_Agile_Manifesto_SDMagazine.pdf
7. Agile Alliance Website, (2017), https://www.agilealliance.org/
8. C. Vanker, The adoption of agile software development methodologies by organisations in South Africa, (2015)
9. J. Sutherland, *The Scrum Papers: Nuts, Bolts, and Origins of an Agile Framework* (Scrum, Inc., Cambridge, MA, 2012)
10. H. Takeuchi, I. Nonaka, The new new product development game. Harv. Bus. Rev. **64**(1), 321 (1998), https://hbr.org/1986/01/the-new-new-product-development-game
11. J. Sutherland, K. Schwaber, The scrum guide: the definitive guide to scrum: the rules of the game, (2013)

Alignment of Requirements and Testing in Agile: An Industrial Experience

Alessio Bucaioni, Antonio Cicchetti, Federico Ciccozzi, Manvisha Kodali, and Mikael Sjödin

Abstract

Agile development aims at switching the focus from processes to interactions between stakeholders, from heavy to minimalistic documentation, from contract negotiation and detailed plans to customer collaboration and prompt reaction to changes. With these premises, requirements traceability may appear to be an overly exigent activity, with little or no return-of-investment. However, since testing remains crucial even when going agile, the developers need to identify at a glance what to test and how to test it. That is why, even though requirements traceability has historically faced a firm resistance from the agile community, it can provide several benefits when promoting precise alignment of requirements with testing. This paper reports on our experience in promoting traceability of requirements and testing in the data communications for mission-critical systems in an industrial Scrum project. We define a semi-automated requirements tracing mechanism which coordinates four traceability techniques. We evaluate the solution by applying it to an industrial project aiming at enhancing the existing Virtual Router Redundancy Protocol by adding Simple Network Management Protocol support.

Keywords

Testing · Agile development · Requirements traceability · Scrum

A. Bucaioni · A. Cicchetti · F. Ciccozzi (✉) · M. Sjödin
Mälardalen University, Västerås, Sweden
e-mail: alessio.bucaioni@mdh.se; antonio.cicchetti@mdh.se;
federico.ciccozzi@mdh.se; mikael.sjodin@mdh.se

M. Kodali
Westermo, Västerås, Sweden
e-mail: manvisha.kodali@westermo.se

33.1 Introduction

Software is paramount in modern society as our lives are affected by, and in many cases rely on, it. Traditional and documentation-driven software development processes start with the elicitation and specification of functional and non-functional requirements. Thereafter, a high-level design is defined in terms of the architectural description of the software to be developed [1]. While the implementation is inspired by documented requirements and high-level design, the testing is driven by requirements. It is unquestionable that, within traditional development processes, requirements affect most of the development phases. Therefore, the ability to navigate back and forth from the requirements to any other development artefact is considered pivotal [2]. Requirements Traceability (RT) commonly refers to the ability to follow the life of a requirement, forwards and backwards, within the whole software life-cycle, that is to say from requirement to test case, across design and implementation artefacts [2]. From the early 1990s, elicitation and documentation of requirements and development artefacts started to incarnate strife and frustration for practitioners. On the one hand, technology and industry changed at an extraordinary pace making hard for the stakeholders to definitely identify requirements. On the other hand, stakeholders' expectations on the final software product increased. This triggered the need for new development processes which could be less bounded to heavy documentation and bootstrap phases: it was the dawn of Agile development [3]. For "agility", in this context, it is meant the ability to switch the focus from processes, comprehensive (but heavy) documentation, contract negotiation and detailed plans, to individuals and dense interaction among them, customer collaboration and prompt reaction to changes [4]. In this landscape, requirements engineering and especially RT may seem to be superfluous and burdensome, and to return little value to the development. However, when going agile, testing cannot be disregarded, but rather occupies a crucial position. In order to nimbly test a software system during its agile development, it is crucial to identify at a glance (1) what to test (e.g., requirements, code and development artefacts) and (2) how to test it (i.e., test cases). Although agile methods focus on face-to-face communication and continuous delivery, RT can come in handy for achieving agile testing thanks to precise mechanisms for relating requirements to test cases. The alignment between requirements and testing in terms of traceability can indeed provide several benefits among which progress checking, customer focus, resource savings, knowledge sharing and improved software quality [5–7]. However, there is evidence showing that RT has historically faced a firm resistance from the agile community since it is regarded as an activity that may introduce excessive overhead, hence standing in the way of the agile creed [8].

This paper reports on an industrial experience in promoting traceability of requirements and testing in data communications for mission-critical systems. We provide a semi-automated requirements tracing mechanism which coordinates four traceability techniques and apply it to an industrial project aiming at enhancing the existing Virtual Router Redundancy Protocol (VRRP[1]) by adding Simple Network Management Protocol (SNMP[2]) support. The mechanism can be considered as a necessary trade-off between a manual and an automated solution. In fact, on the one hand the overhead of a manual mechanism would not be compatible with the "agility" of the project. On the other hand, a fully automated mechanism would require a remarkably long bootstrap phase for being implemented in addition to an extensive and precise knowledge of requirements.

The scientific contribution of this paper are the definition of a lightweight approach for requirements tracing in agile software projects, and the results from its application to an industrial Scrum project.

The remainder of the paper is structured as follows. Section 33.2 presents a comparison between existing related approaches documented in the literature and our solution. Section 33.3 describes the proposed solution in all its constituents. Section 33.4 shows the application of the proposed solution in an industrial collaborative Scrum project. Sections 33.5 and 33.6 discuss the benefits and limitations of our solution and conclude the paper, respectively.

33.2   Related Work

This work deals with the problem of keeping track of requirements coverage and satisfaction through test cases in agile development. Generally, this problem is known as

alignment of requirements and verification & validation, and RT is considered as a possible solution [8, 9]. In general, RT is distinguished between horizontal, when tracing the evolution of requirements during the development process, and vertical, when considering the life of a requirement in terms of related artefacts, notably design decisions, source code, tests, and documentation [10]. In this respect, our solution supports vertical RT.

In traditional software development processes, requirements engineering encompasses a set of well defined preliminary phases dealing with analysis, planning, and documentation. Requirements are supposed to be largely known, and hence RT can be tackled as pertaining to requirements management stages. This allows, for instance, to configure and exploit traceability tools, or to adopt model-based/formal techniques for gaining some form of automation [8]. The work in [8] gives a broad overview of both solutions and challenges in realising the alignment between requirements and verification & validation in general, and by exploiting RT techniques in particular. As stated before in this paper, the basic principles of agile make traditional alignment solutions not suitable: requirements are very often only partially known, they evolve rapidly during the development process, and there is no space for preliminary analysis nor bootstrap activities. It is worth noting that, even if requirements are not subject to remarkable evolutionary pressure in traditional processes, RT is very often perceived as a time-consuming activity with poor ROI if not adequately supported [11, 12]. Notably, traces can be affected by "decay", that is the progressive loss of consistency between requirements and linked artefacts due to maintenance activities not reflected in the current traceability information [12]. This issue is exacerbated in agile processes, such that the lack of traceability is conceived as an intrinsic problem for this kind of development [13, 14]. We propose to alleviate the concerns related to requirements evolution by means of a semi-automated approach, which represents a trade-off between reliability of manual tracing and reduction of tedious and error-prone tasks through automation.

The recent work in [15] provides an extensive illustration of traceability in agile processes, coming from both academia and industry. Interestingly, several empirical observations they make and conclusions they draw are consistent with our industrial settings and suitability of the adopted solution. More specifically, when considering the types of relevant traceability, most companies chose "rationale" and "contribute", i.e. two vertical traces. In this respect, in our work requirements are the rationale to the creation of test cases. When it comes to traceability mechanisms, most companies exploit product/sprint backlogs and in some cases spreadsheets for implementing RT. It is not surprising that observations reveal a decrease of satisfaction proportional to the size of the company [15]. In other words, traceability-

---

[1]https://en.wikipedia.org/wiki/Virtual_Router_Redundancy_Protocol.
[2]https://en.wikipedia.org/wiki/Simple_Network_Management_Protocol.

matrix-like approaches, being largely manual, add too much overhead to be compatible with the agile vision. This aspect is also confirmed by checking the most relevant challenges expressed by interviewees: difficulty in identifying proper traceability links, difficulty in motivating the personnel to keep traces, and low ROI. In our scenario, tracing activity is simplified by the fact that it only addresses links between requirements and test cases. The solution is amalgamated with current used tools (both for requirements definition and test case specification) thus avoiding the need of additional knowledge. Moreover, the automated inspection can be a useful tool even for verifying the progress of the sprints. This last aspect is again confirmed by the conclusions made in [15] when discussing the potential benefits of RT mechanisms. Some approaches dealing with RT in agile development processes exist; notably, in [13] the authors define a set of requirements for RT support in agile and introduce a methodology based on Test-Driven Development and customisable roles (to provide multiple trace links semantics). The main difference with our proposal is that we were seeking a lightweight solution, requiring a negligible bootstrap effort in terms of implementation and adoption, due to the reasons mentioned above. A methodology forcing the adoption of test-driven development, or the preliminary definition of roles and links semantics project-by-project would have been considered as too much overhead and hence not acceptable. A heterogeneous solution for RT is suggested in [11]. In particular, the authors propose to exploit requirements layering with respect to different development process stages, project epics, and roles involved in their management. Then, they assign a different RT approach for each layer. Our approach shares with [11] the vision of adopting heterogenous strategies for supporting RT. However, we do not exploit requirements layering, mainly due to the volatility of project scenarios and the bootstrap costs of configuring RT support for each new project.

33.3 Proposed Solution

In this section we describe a mechanism introducing RT in the agile system development life cycle (SDLC) [16] for enhancing the alignment between requirements (REQs) and testing in terms of test cases (TCs). The goal is to show how the software development can be improved in terms of, e.g., resource savings, progress checking and improved software quality, while preserving its "agility". The proposed solution leverages four existing traceability techniques:

- Tagging. It is a technique which assigns a keyword to a piece of information for tracing the information throughout the development life-cycle [17]. The proposed solution uses tagging for assigning unique identifiers (IDs) to REQs and TCs and for tagging the TCs implementation with the IDs of REQs and TCs.
- Information retrieval. It is a technique which establishes traceability links among artefacts based on the similarity between their contained information [18]. The proposed solution uses information retrieval for retrieving all the elicited REQs and the TCs along with their relationships.
- Integrating documents. It is a technique which merges different information in a single document [19]. the proposed solution uses integrating documents for creating explicitly correspondences between REQs and TCs.
- Requirements traceability matrix (RTM). It is a technique which uses a two-dimensional grid for mapping REQs to other development artefacts [20]. The proposed solution uses RTM for collecting and displaying the traces information among REQs and TCs. In this respect, we extend the base RTM semantics with values for describing the relationships holding among REQs and TCs.

To the best of our knowledge, the proposed solution represents the first attempt in combining a set of generic RT techniques with the aim of providing an extensive RT mechanisms within the agile SDLC. Figure 33.1 shows the proposed solution in relation to the main phases of the agile SDLC as defined in [16]. The proposed solution comprises six tasks:

1. Assign IDs to REQs;
2. Assign IDs to TCs;
3. Match REQs and TCs;
4. Tag TCs implementation with IDs of REQs and TCs;
5. Build the RTM;
6. Populate the RTM.

1. Assign IDs to REQs The goal of this task is to associate IDs to the identified REQs. The input of this task is the list of the identified REQs. The output is a list $L_{REQ} = \{r_1, \ldots, r_n\}$ of records r_i. r_i is represented by the pair $< id, desc >$, where id is the REQ ID and $desc$ is the REQ description. This task should be performed during the inception phase (see phases in Fig. 33.1) and it can be automated by means of scripts.

2. Assign IDs to TCs The goal of this task is to associate IDs to the planned TCs. The input of this task is the list of the planned TCs. The output is a list $L_{TC} = \{t_1, \ldots, t_m\}$ of records t_i. t_i is represented by the pair $< id, desc >$ where id is the TC ID and $desc$ is the TC description. This task should be performed during the inception phase and it can be automated by means of scripts.

3. Match REQs and TCs This task should be performed prior the development occurring in each construction itera-

Fig. 33.1 Proposed solution

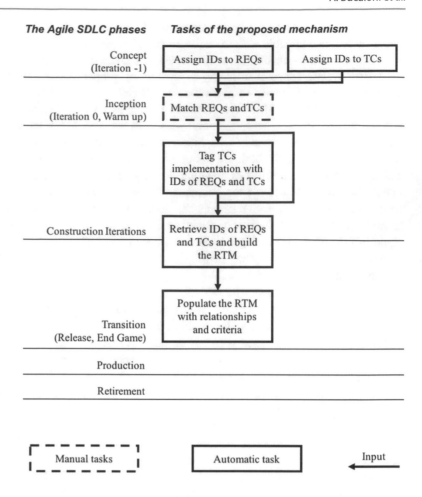

The Agile SDLC phases   Tasks of the proposed mechanism

tion phase and aims at formalising the relationships between REQs and TCs, which are typically identified during the concept phase (as TCs originate from the user stories derived from the REQs). The input of this tasks are the L_{REQ} and L_{TC} lists produced by the previous tasks. The output is a list $L_{REQ/TC} = \{r/t_1, \ldots, r/t_n\}$ of records r/t_i, where r/t_i is represented by the pair $< id, L_{TC_{ID}} >$ where id is the REQ ID and $L_{TC_{ID}}$ is the list of the IDs of the TCs verifying it.

4. Tag the TCs Implementation with IDs of REQs and TCs In the previous task, trace links between REQs and TCs are established. The goal of this task is to extend this links to the TCs implementation. To this end, each TCs implementation is tagged with the corresponding TC IDs and with the IDs of the REQs it verifies. The input of this task is the $L_{REQ/TC}$ list produced in the previous task. The output of this task is the TC implementation tagged with IDs of REQs and TCs. This task should be performed during the TCs design occurring in each construction iteration phase and it can be fully automated by scripts. It is important to note that in some development iterations TCs might not be defined prior the construction iteration or transition phases. When this happens, the task 2 and 3 of the proposed mechanism can not be performed. In this scenario, this task

provides the engineer with a further possibility for defining trace links between REQs and TCs, thus it enables more agility in the development process.

5. Retrieve IDs of REQs and TCs and Build the RTM The goal of this task is twofold. On the one hand, it builds the RTM. On the other hand, it verifies that all the trace links between REQs and TCs have been considered when tagging the TCs implementation. To this end, the IDs of REQs and TCs should be extracted from the TCs implementation and saved into a temporary list. Such a list is compared to the $L_{REQs/TCs}$ list produced in the task three with the aim of identifying and marking possible differences. Eventually, the two lists are merged and the RTM should be constructed accordingly. This task should be performed before the testing occurring in each construction iteration and transition phases and it can be fully automated by scripts.

6. Populate the RTM with Relations and Criteria The goal of this task is to populate the RTM with the test results. The input of this task is the RTM produced in the previous task. The output of this task is the populated RTM. More specifically, each entry e_i of the RTM is represented by a pair $<relation, status>$ where $relation$ describes the relationship between REQs and TCs while *status* describes the TC result. *relation* can have a value in the set {*planned, added, deleted*}, obtained from the comparison done in the previous task. *planned* indicates that the REQ is verified by the TC as planned during the tasks 1 and 2. *added* indicates that the decision to verify the REQ with the TC has been taken during the task 4. *deleted* indicates that the REQ has been deleted during the development process. *Status* can have two base values, *passed* and *failed*. However, depending on the adopted pass/fail criteria it can be extended with further values such as, e.g, blocked and not-run. This task should be performed after the testing occurring in the transition phase and it can be fully automated by scripts.

33.4 Applying the Solution to an Industrial Scrum Project

In this section we describe the application of our mechanism to the VRRP-MIB project. The VRRP-MIB project is an industrial project of Westermo[3] aiming at enhancing the existing VRRP protocol by adding SNMP support. It is defined as a Scrum project consisting of 34 REQs and 3 TCs grouping 22 tests. The project was run for 6 months by a team composed of 5 engineers from Westermo for a total of 253 man-hours. The elicitation phase required 10 man-hours. The development phase required 160 man-hours. The testing phase required 80 man-hours. Eventually, 2 man-hours were spent for checking that all the elicited REQs were tested. In the following, due to its verbosity and complexity, we will discuss a simplified version of the VRRP-MIB project corresponding to the first Scrum sprint and consisting of 10 REQs and 2 TCs.

Table 33.1 reports an example of two REQs considered in the first sprint and how they were described within West-

Table 33.1 Example of REQs for the VRRP-MIB project

REQs		
1	Name	vrrpOperVrId
	Description	Full OID description. The system should provide VRID as index into table
	Constraints	None
	Qualification	The test should verify that the OID within table entries match the VRID of a created instance (created via CLI)
2	Name	vrrpOperVirtualMacAdd
	Description	Full OID description (Our VRRP implementation VMAC meets VRRP standard)
	Constraints	None
	Qualification	Test should verify that VMAC matches VRRPv2 specification (i.e., VRRP/IETF-prex + VRID)

Table 33.2 Example of TCs for the VRRP-MIB project

TCs		
1	Name	verifyOperState
	Description	Verify that state changes the all supported oper-states are correct
2	Name	verifyVrrpAdvancedVrrpSetup
	Description	Verify that the values updated from VRRP are correct while having two VRRP instances and merging with a third instance

Table 33.3 Example of REQs description with IDs

REQs		
1	Name	vrrpOperVrId
	ID	r.weos.snmpmib.vrrpv2.ss1
	Description	Full OID description.The system should provide VRID as index into table
	Constraints	None
	Qualification	The test should verify that the OID within table entries match the VRID of a created instance (created via CLI)
2	Name	vrrpOperVirtualMacAdd
	ID	r.weos.snmpmib.vrrpv2.ss2
	Description	Full OID description (Our VRRP implementation VMAC meets VRRP standard)
	Constraints	None
	Qualification	Test should verify that VMAC matches VRRPv2 specication (i.e., VRRP/IETF-prex + VRID)

ermo. In particular, each REQ was described by means of a *name*, a *description*, a *qualification* and some *constraints*. The qualification gives basic information for testing while the constraints specify possible relationships with other REQs. Similarly, Table 33.2 shows an example of two TCs involved in the first sprint and how they were described within Westermo. Each TC was described by means of a *name* and a *description*. Within Westermo, REQs and TCs are represented and saved in separate files and organised in folders which are stored using the version control mechanism GIT.[4]

According to the first two tasks of the proposed mechanism, we assigned IDs to REQs and TCs. These assignments were automated by means of Python scripts. Tables 33.3 and 33.4 show the resulting descriptions containing IDs for REQs and TCs, respectively.

Table 33.5 shows the tabular representation of the formalised relationships between REQs and TCs as the result of the application of the third task of our proposed mechanism.

In particular, the TC *t.weos.snmpmib.vrrpv2.adv-test* tests the following REQs:

---

[3]http://www.westermo.com.

[4]https://git-scm.com.

Table 33.4 Example of TCs description with IDs

TCs		
1	Name	verifyOperState
	ID	t.weos.snmpmib.vrrpv2.ostate
	Description	Verify that state changes the all supported oper-states are correct
2	Name	verifyVrrpAdvancedVrrpSetup
	ID	t.weos.snmpmib.vrrpv2.adv-test
	Description	Verify that the values updated from VRRP are correct while having two VRRP instances and merging with a third instance

Table 33.5 Correspondence between REQs and TCs by IDs

REQs	TCs
r.weos.snmpmib.vrrpv2.ss1	t.weos.snmpmib.vrrpv2.adv-test
r.weos.snmpmib.vrrpv2.ss2	t.weos.snmpmib.vrrpv2.adv-test
r.weos.snmpmib.vrrpv2.ss3	t.weos.snmpmib.vrrpv2.adv-test
r.weos.snmpmib.vrrpv2.ss4	t.weos.snmpmib.vrrpv2.operState
r.weos.snmpmib.vrrpv2.ss5	t.weos.snmpmib.vrrpv2.operState
r.weos.snmpmib.vrrpv2.ss6	t.weos.snmpmib.vrrpv2.operState
r.weos.snmpmib.vrrpv2.ss7	t.weos.snmpmib.vrrpv2.adv-test
r.weos.snmpmib.vrrpv2.ss8	t.weos.snmpmib.vrrpv2.adv-test
r.weos.snmpmib.vrrpv2.ss9	t.weos.snmpmib.vrrpv2.adv-test
r.weos.snmpmib.vrrpv2.ss10	t.weos.snmpmib.vrrpv2.adv-test

- *r.weos.snmpmib.vrrpv2.ss1*
- *r.weos.snmpmib.vrrpv2.ss2*
- *r.weos.snmpmib.vrrpv2.ss3*
- *r.weos.snmpmib.vrrpv2.ss7*
- *r.weos.snmpmib.vrrpv2.ss8*
- *r.weos.snmpmib.vrrpv2.dss9*
- *r.weos.snmpmib.vrrpv2.ss10*

While the TC *t.weos.snmpmib.vrrpv2.operState* tests the following REQs:

- *r.weos.snmpmib.vrrpv2.ss4*
- *r.weos.snmpmib.vrrpv2.ss5*
- *r.weos.snmpmib.vrrpv2.ss6*

As aforementioned, the formalised relationships between REQs and TCs are stored in a textual file which is, in turn, and stored in the corresponding GIT folder. According to the fourth task of our proposed alignment mechanism, the TCs implementation must be tagged with the IDs of TCs and REQs. Within Westermo, TCs are implemented by means of Python scripts.[5] Those, were extended with two variables *testID* and *references*. *testID* is a string containing the ID of the TC whereas *references* is an array of strings

---

[5]Due to confidentiality we can not show the Python scripts implementing the TCs.

containing the IDs of the corresponding REQs. Such an extension was automatically performed by means of Python scripts. Moreover, we used Python scripts for automating the creation and the filling of the RTM, too. For the selected sprint, we performed unit and integration tests as well as impact analysis. Unit tests were run manually during the day, while integration tests were automatically run for nightly builds. Impact analysis was performed at the end of the test activities by counting the passed/failed tests. After the testing activities, a Python script collected the test results together with the information regarding the relationships among REQs and TCs.

Table 33.6 shows the final RTM filled with REQs, TCs, results and relationships. Within the VRRP-MIB project, Therefore, it was not necessary to extend the value of the variable status, as discussed in Sect. 33.3. During the testing activities, the Scrum team decided to exercise the *r.weos.snmpmib.vrrpv2.ss1* REQ with the *t.weos.snmpmib.vrrpv2.operState* TC too, despite during the sprint planning event the *r.weos.snmpmib.vrrpv2.ss1* REQ was associated with the *t.weos.snmpmib.vrrpv2.adv-test* TC only. This change was captured by the Python script which marked the relationship between *r.weos.snmpmib.vrrpv2.ss1* REQ and *t.weos.snmpmib.vrrpv2.operState* TC with the *added* value.

33.5 Discussion

Alignment between requirements and testing brings multiple benefits such as progress checking. This is especially true when such an alignment is achieved by means of semiautomatic mechanisms as the one presented in this paper. The proposed solution leverages the RTM and its newly extended semantics as the core artefacts for visualising traces between requirements and test cases as well as for checking the development progress. In fact, the information about correspondences between requirements, test cases and testing results allows the engineer to grasp the progress of the project at a glance without the use of additional tools as shown in the VRRP-MIB project. With respect to resource saving, in the VRRP-MIB project, we were able to achieve a 10% reduction of the required man-hours. In fact, the execution of a similar project required 253 man-hours, whereas within the VRRP-MIB project we were able to shorten the testing activities by 23 man-hours. Moreover, we did not need to spend additional 2 h for checking that the REQs were tested. Agile processes focus on the importance of customer involvement during the whole development process. Within the VRRP-MIB project, we observed an improved customer experience as the customer's decisions, and their fulfilment, could be easily recorded and trace throughout the development process. Moreover, we observed that after the first sprint, the

Table 33.6 RTM with REQs and TCs relations

		TCs	
		t.weos.snmpmib.vrrpv2.adv-test	*t.weos.snmpmib.vrrpv2.operState*
REQs	*r.weos.snmpmib.vrrpv2.ss1*	(planned,passed)	(added,passed)
	r.weos.snmpmib.vrrpv2.ss2	(planned,passed)	
	r.weos.snmpmib.vrrpv2.ss3	(planned,passed)	
	r.weos.snmpmib.vrrpv2.ss4		(planned,passed)
	r.weos.snmpmib.vrrpv2.ss5		(planned,passed)
	r.weos.snmpmib.vrrpv2.ss6		(planned,passed)
	r.weos.snmpmib.vrrpv2.ss7	(planned,passed)	
	r.weos.snmpmib.vrrpv2.ss8	(planned,passed)	
	r.weos.snmpmib.vrrpv2.ss9	(planned,passed)	
	r.weos.snmpmib.vrrpv2.ss10	(planned,passed)	

engineers involved in the project started to use the RTM as an effective progress tracking tool. Within the VRRP-MIB project, we did not observe any variation in the defects rate of the software. In fact, the proposed mechanism does not aim at improving the quality of testing. However, it improves the quality of the software development by supporting a more rational and traceable process. This, in turn, affects the quality of the software product during the production and retirement phases. Agile processes tend to cut down detailed documentation in order to minimise the overhead introduced by activities not related to the implementation. In this context, the artefacts produced within the proposed solution could serve as a base for the automatic generation of documentation. Doing so, documentation activities would not represent an unbearable burden and could seamlessly be included in the development without jeopardising agility. Concerning possible limitations of the mechanism, it can be argued that assigning identifiers to test cases, as a first step, could be unfeasible as test cases might be defined after the implementation phase. Although this could be a valid concern, it should be noted that the proposed mechanism allows the developer to enter the identifiers at later stages, when test cases are implemented, and the RTM is still generated, as described in Sect. 33.4. Our mechanism does not provide any support for assessing testing effectiveness and it at its best when applied to medium-small software projects. Although the work done in the collaborative project shows that the mechanism does not introduce any significant development and managerial overhead, it might require an initial effort in terms of scripting activities to provide automation, as discusses in Sect. 33.4. While this could be a valid concern, it should be noted that this is a one-time effort affecting only the first application of the mechanism as the scripts could be reused for the following projects, unless technology shifts.

The work reported in this paper was carried out in a tight collaborative fashion between academics and industrial practitioners. The project ran for 6 months with monthly meetings. Already from the beginning, both sides were actively involved in the definition of project goals, milestones and timeframe. Tight collaboration fostered new ideas and challenged our initial hypotheses making us to achieve a solution which was able to decrease the effort required for testing activities in a real world scenario. In this respect, the agile development process has to be considered as a key enabler of the collaboration, as it disclosed the opportunity of enacting quick develop-and-check iterations of the proposed mechanisms.

33.6 Conclusion

The Agile vision is to avoid monolithic development steps in order to promote flexibility. In this respect, traceability between requirements and test cases has been traditionally perceived as an accessory and time-consuming activity with low return-of-investment. In this paper we illustrated the activities aimed at introducing a traceability mechanism in an industrial agile development context. The proposed solution is necessarily pragmatic, as resulting from trading off fully manual and fully automated mechanisms. In fact, both of them would introduce excessive overhead and hence violate the fundaments of agile. The observations we conducted on an industrial Scrum project show encouraging results in terms of effectiveness. It is worth noting that the proposed technique does not assess how good are the tests, rather it keeps track of how requirements have been tested. As discussed throughout the work, these traces can provide useful feedbacks on how the verification & validation has been operated and its progress status in the sprints.

As future work, we plan to investigate additional automation to provide basic code documentation as derivable from the traceability between requirements and test cases. Moreover, we intend to study the application of our tracing technique in other suitable agile development scenarios, in order to better validate the proposed approach.

Acknowledgements The authors would like to thank Peter Johansson, Per Erik Strandberg, Jonas Nylander and Jon-Olov Vatn from Westermo Research and Development for their support through the VRRP-MIB project. This research is partially supported by the Knowledge Foundation through the MOMENTUM project (http://www.es.mdh.se/projects/458-MOMENTUM).

References

1. I. Jacobson, G. Booch, J. Rumbaugh, G. Booch, *The Unified Software Development Process*, vol. 1 (Addison-Wesley, Reading, 1999)
2. O.C.Z. Gotel, A.C.W. Finkelstein, An analysis of the requirements traceability problem, in *Proceedings of the First International Conference on Requirements Engineering, 1994* (IEEE, New York, 1994), pp. 94–101
3. A. De Lucia, A. Qusef, Requirements engineering in agile software development. J. Emerg. Technol. Web Intell. **2**(3), 212–220 (2010)
4. M. Fowler, J. Highsmith, The agile manifesto. Softw. Dev. **9**(8), 28–35 (2001)
5. C. Lee, L. Guadagno, X. Jia, An agile approach to capturing requirements and traceability, in *Proceedings of the 2nd International Workshop on Traceability in Emerging Forms of Software Engineering (TEFSE 2003)* (Citeseer, 2003)
6. V.E. Jyothi, K.N. Rao, Effective implementation of agile practices. Int. J. Adv. Comput. Sci. Appl. **2**(3), 41–48 pp. (2011)
7. J.H. Hayes, A. Dekhtyar, J. Osborne, Improving requirements tracing via information retrieval, in *Proceedings. 11th IEEE International Requirements Engineering Conference, 2003* (IEEE, New York, 2003), pp. 138–147
8. E. Bjarnason, P. Runeson, M. Borg, M. Unterkalmsteiner, E. Engström, B. Regnell, G. Sabaliauskaite, A. Loconsole, T. Gorschek, R. Feldt, Challenges and practices in aligning requirements with verification and validation: a case study of six companies. Empir. Softw. Eng. **19**(6), 1809–1855 (2014)
9. E.J. Uusitalo, M. Komssi, M. Kauppinen, A.M. Davis, Linking requirements and testing in practice, in *International Requirements Engineering, 2008 RE '08. 16th IEEE*, 2008, pp. 265–270
10. S.L. Pfleeger, S.A. Bohner, A framework for software maintenance metrics, in *Conference on Software Maintenance, 1990, Proceedings*, 1990, pp. 320–327
11. J. Cleland-Huang, G. Zemont, W. Lukasik, A heterogeneous solution for improving the return on investment of requirements traceability, in *Requirements Engineering Conference, 2004. Proceedings. 12th IEEE International*, 2004, pp. 230–239
12. G. Regan, F. McCaffery, K. McDaid, D. Flood, The barriers to traceability and their potential solutions: Towards a reference framework, in *2012 38th EUROMICRO Conference on Software Engineering and Advanced Applications (SEAA)* (2012), pp. 319–322
13. A. Espinoza, J. Garbajosa, A study to support agile methods more effectively through traceability. Innov. Syst. Softw. Eng. **7**(1), 53–69 (2011)
14. I. Inayat, L. Moraes, M. Daneva, S.S. Salim, A reflection on agile requirements engineering: Solutions brought and challenges posed, in *Scientific Workshop Proceedings of the XP2015*, XP '15 Workshops, New York, NY (ACM, New York, 2015), pp. 6:1–6:7
15. V.H. Duc, Traceability in agile software projects, 2013. Master's thesis, University of Gothenburg. http://hdl.handle.net/2077/38990
16. S.W. Ambler, The agile system development life cycle (sdlc) (2009). Ambysoft Inc., [Online]. Available: http://www.ambysoft.com/essays/agileLifecycle.html. Accessed 14 May 2014
17. M. Jakobsson, Implementing traceability in agile software development. Department of Computer Science, Lund University, 2009
18. J.H. Hayes, A. Dekhtyar, J. Osborne, Improving requirements tracing via information retrieval, in *Requirements Engineering Conference, 2003. Proceedings. 11th IEEE International* (IEEE, New York, 2003), pp. 138–147
19. M. Kolla, M. Banka, Merging functional requirements with test cases, Master Thesis Project, Malmö University, Department of Computer Science (2014)
20. G. Duraisamy, R. Atan, Requirement traceability matrix through documentation for scrum methodology. J. Theor. Appl. Inform. Technol. **52**(2), 154–159 (2013)

Health Care Information Systems: A Crisis Approach

34

Daniela America da Silva, Gildarcio Sousa Goncalves,
Samara Cardoso dos Santos, Victor Ulisses Pugliese,
Julhio Navas, Rodrigo Monteiro de Barros Santana,
Filipe Santiago Queiroz, Luiz Alberto Vieira Dias,
Adilson Marques da Cunha, and Paulo Marcelo Tasinaffo

Abstract

During the 1st Semester of 2017, at the BrazilianAeronautics Institute of Technology (Instituto Tecnologico de Aeronautica, ITA), a successful Interdisciplinary Problem-Based Learning (IPBL) experience took place. At that time, almost 30 undergraduate and graduate students from three different courses within just 17 academic weeks had the opportunity of conceptualizing, modeling, and developing a Computer System based on Big Data, Internet of Things, and other emerging technologies for governmental organizations and private sectors. The purpose of this system was to aggregate data and integrate actors, such as Patients, Hospitals, Physicians, and Suppliers for decision making processes related to crises management involving events of health systems, such as epidemics, that needs to manage data and information. Differently from other existing products from Universities, Research Centers, Governmental Agencies, Public and/or Private companies, this product was developed and tested in just 17 academic weeks, applying the Scrum agile method and its best practices available in the market. This experience was stored in a Google site and implemented as a Proof of Concept (PoC). It represents just one example of how to address the old problems of teaching, learning, and developing complex intelligent academic computer projects to solve health system problems, by collaboratively using the Scrum agile method with Python or Java, Spark, NoSQL databases, Kafka, and other technologies. The major contribution of this paper is the use of agile testing to verify and validate an academic health system case study.

Keywords

Health system · Big Data · Predictive models · Internet of Things (IoT) · Agile method · Problem-Based Learning (PBL) · Agile testing

34.1 Introduction

This paper focuses in an integration methodology applied to the project named TSA4HC, Technological Solutions Applicable in Health Care (in Portuguese, Solucoes Tecnologicas Aplicaveis a Midias e Produtos em Saude—STAMPS [13]), na academic computer project using Interdisciplinary ProblemBased Learning (IPBL) for the integration of three different courses.

Students from these three courses were divided into four teams: PATIENTS, PHYSICIANS, HOSPITALS, and SUPPLIERS, using the Scrum agile method and its best practices, high cohesion, and low coupling Software Engineering characteristics [1, 2].

The TSA4HC project was an academic computer system prototype developed and based on Big Data, Internet of Things (IoT), and other emerging Information Technologies (ITs) including the Scrum agile method with quality, reliability, safety, and testability requirements [3].

In addition, some aspects of certification, was taking into account using the ICD-10 [4] and the HL7 [5] standards. The host application was designed in Heroku and programming languages like Python, PHP, Java, and others, as shown in Fig. 34.1.

The integration strategy among groups of subsystems components has occurred by defining another architecture on top of those subsystems, named STAMPSNet.

The STAMPSNet is an intelligent system for defining the macro strategy of integration between the teams using as main steps events submitted by the subsystems processed according to the following stages: detection, screening, treatment, and response.

D. A. da Silva (✉) · G. S. Goncalves · S. C. dos Santos · V. U. Pugliese
J. Navas · R. M. de Barros Santana · F. S. Queiroz · L. A. V. Dias
A. M. da Cunha · P. M. Tasinaffo
Computer Science Department, Brazilian Aeronautics Institute of
Technology (Instituto Tecnológico de Aeronáutica—ITA), Sao Jose
dos Campos, Sao Paulo, Brazil
e-mail: vdias@ita.br; cunha@ita.br; tasinaffo@ita.br

© Springer International Publishing AG, part of Springer Nature 2018
S. Latifi (ed.), *Information Technology – New Generations*, Advances in Intelligent Systems and Computing 738,
https://doi.org/10.1007/978-3-319-77028-4_34

Fig. 34.1 The TSA4HC project technologies

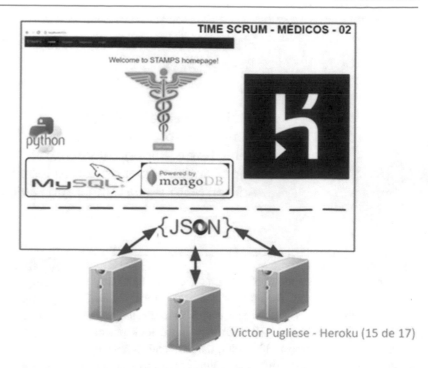

A peer-to-peer student evaluation method was used, considering the goals of each sprint defined in the Sprint Planning (SP). These goals have allowed the determination of what each two Development Team undertook to be delivered at the end of sprints.

During each SP, it was established a Definition of Done (DoD). At the end of each Sprint Review, some acceptance forms from developed user stories and team members were completed from interdisciplinary evaluations.

Thus, at the end of this STAMPS Academic Project, a case study simulation mission was assigned as a Proof of Concept (PoC) to demonstrate the STAMPS should be able to provide appropriate management and control of crises.

34.1.1 The Architecture Overview

The STAMPS application was developed in a cloud system and had each of the subsystems hosted in the Heroku Platform as a Service.

It has allowed source-code in PHP, Python, or Java programming language, by using: MySQL for the Relational Database and/or MongoDB for the Best of Relational; NoSQL; JSON, for data-interchange format; Apache Kafka, as a messaging system; Django, as a Python Web Framework for rapid development; and GitHub, as a development platform to review code, manage the project, and build software working in collaborations with remotely based developers and testers.

Each team was responsible to define its architecture, by identifying what was the more appropriate technology for the team. This has allowed team members to develop a product according to its best knowledge of technologies.

An integration of results through a common data bus was stablished operating according to the definitions of the STAMPSNet architecture.

Since the 1st Sprint, the architecture was developed thinking about the integration and interoperability of the subsystems PATIENT, PHYSICIAN, HOSPITAL, AND SUPPLIER.

34.1.2 The Testing Methods

The STAMPS Project was developed by using the Test Driven Development (TDD) technique having requirements turned into very specific test cases and it was prepared in the first week of the Sprint.

The development was done by taking into consideration test case specifications. The product was validated against those test cases every week of each Sprint, through an iterative development process, where requirements have evolved through collaboration among Team Developers (TDs), Product Owners (POs), Scrum Masters (SMs) and Stakeholders.

Teams were self-organized and have determined issues in advance, differently from conventional methods, when testing used to be performed only after implementations.

On the TDD scenario, testing is started before the implementation.

34.2 The Stamps Project Prototype

34.2.1 The TSA4HC Project Prototype Vision Artifact

Based upon the Scrum agile method, the following TSA4HC project vision artifact was defined:

"For public and/or private organizations involved in crisis management with health events (e.g. epidemics) which need to manage data and information for decision making, the TSA4HC academic project is a computer system based on big data, IoT, and other emerging technologies that aggregates data, integrating the actors of this scenario (PATIENTS, PHYSICIANS, HOSPITALS, AND SUPPLIERS), for decision making."

34.2.2 The TSA4HC Development Environment

Designed to host application systems using cloudcomputing resources, Heroku is a cloud service platform.

Some of its benefits are: abstraction of services configuration; support for various programming languages; practicality in application management—continuous deploy; and free to test cloud applications [6, 7].

Heroku runs on Amazon EC2, which is an Infrastructure as a Service (IaaS). It automates the creation of a new virtual machine named Dyno and configures the entire environment for development.

The TSA4HC project was developed, by using Git control version system, where each team stored their source-code on the GitHub.

The mLab Cloud MongoDB Hosting database was populated with over 100,000 MongoDB documents from the ICD-10 data collection standard, by adding symptoms of illness in English.

The ClearDB was used together with the MySQL database and had some tables and cadastral data implemented for physicians, screenings, and other operational and structured funtions, involving low volumes of data.

The data interchange to allow interoperability among TSA4HC project subsystems (PATIENT, PHYSICIAN, HOSPITAL, and SUPPLIER) was developed, by using Kafka, the HL7 Standard, and the JSON format. Kafka is a distributed streaming platform [8].

For the data interchange, it was also used the ZooKeeper, as part of Hadoop, and as a centralized service for maintaining configuration information, naming, and providing distributed synchronization and group services.

At this time, an important finding was that, for developing certifiable software, according to the HL7 standards, the use of a cloud service platform like Heroku can greatly reduce the wastage of time and other resources to build source-codes with high levels of quality, reliability, safety, and testability, as required nowadays by health care standards.

For software engineering developments, health care industries have become dependent on distant partners. Lately, they have been using geographically separated TDs from different countries. They need to employ more agile development methods, to integrate diverse areas of knowledge with different requirements.

They also need to manage the development of highly complex application systems using new technologies, processes, and methods, as the ones practiced during the 1st semester of 2017 at ITA, during the TSA4HC academic project prototype development.

34.2.3 The TSA4HC Academic Groups of Subsystems Structure

The TSA4HC academic project prototype was divided into four TDs composed by students from three different courses. Each Team had about five students and was responsible for developing a specific chosen group of subsystem components.

In order to satisfy the requirements of the TSA4HC, in a time frame of just 17 academic weeks, the project prototype was also divided into four groups of application subsystem components, based upon the Model View Controller (MVC) design pattern [9–11].

These four application subsystems were classified according to their high cohesion and low coupling characteristics as: (1) PATIENT, (2) PHYSICIAN, (3) HOSPITAL, and (4) SUPPLIER.

1. *The PATIENT Application Subsystem:* Within the PATIENT subsystem, it was implemented some digital component key features of the TSA4HC academic project to help patients to find health care information and also to benefit from the information made available from the project.

   Some of these key features were developed integrated with Facebook, allowing to reach around two billion users, reading statistics of utilization and also allowing information about geolocation, among others.

   The developed software for the PATIENT subsystem was successfully modeled, generated, tested, and verified, as shown in the geolocation map of Fig. 34.2.

2. *The PHYSICIAN Application Subsystem:* Within the PHYSICIAN subsystem, it was also implemented some digital component key features of the TSA4HC academic project to help the group PHYSICIAN in the

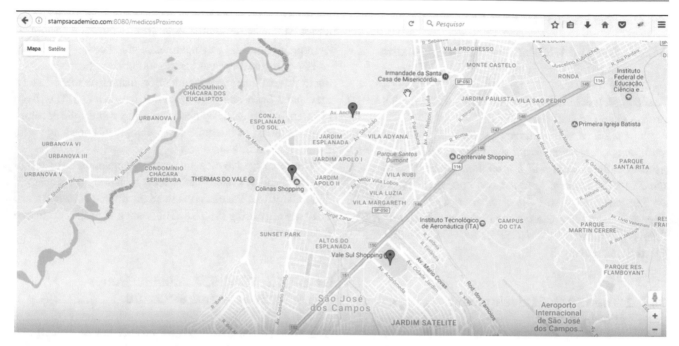

Fig. 34.2 The PATIENT finding the PHYSICIAN geolocation map

consultations/visits per patient, allowing benefits, such as identifying symptoms, diagnoses, and number of visits according to a geolocation and also benefiting every subsystem from this information made available by the project.

Some of these key features were developed by using the ICD-10 standard, which is the international "standard diagnostic tool for epidemiology, health management and clinical purposes", among other features.

This developed subsystem was also based on the HL7 data interchange standard, for the exchange, integration, sharing, and retrieval of electronic health information that supports clinical practice and management, delivery and evaluation of health services, allowing integration with the other TSA4HC subsystems, and also interoperability with any other health care subsystem.

The developed software for the PHYSICIAN subsystem was also successfully modeled, generated, tested, and verified, according to PATIENT application shown in Fig. 34.3.

3. *The HOSPITAL Application Subsystem:* Within the HOSPITAL subsystem, it was also implemented some digital component key features of the TSA4HC academic project to help hospitals to manage the progress of hospital treatments and manage resources per patient, allowing benefits, such as identifying patients location, medicines, prescriptions, and vital signs inside the hospital.

Some of these key features were developed by using also the ICD-10 standard, allowing to identify used rooms, according to a specific disease, among other features.

The developed software for the HOSPITAL subsystem was also successfully modeled, generated, tested, and verified, as shown in Fig. 34.4.

4. *The SUPPLIER Application Subsystem:* Within the SUPPLIER subsystem, it was also implemented some digital component key features of the TSA4HC academic project to help suppliers to be registered as the providers of various products and services needed by health care solutions, managed by the project.

It has allowed some benefits such as identifying necessary resources and purchase others, according to geolocations, among other features.

The developed software for the SUPPLIER subsystem was also successfully modeled, generated, tested, and verified as shown in Fig. 34.5.

5. *The STAMPSNet Intelligent System:* Within the STAMPSNet Intelligent System, it was implemented the integration capabilities to help each subsystem PATIENT, PHYSICIAN, HOSPITAL, and SUPPLIER to interchange data and send alerts for each subsystem to take action to respond to a crisis using health care solutions managed by the TSA4HC project, among other features.

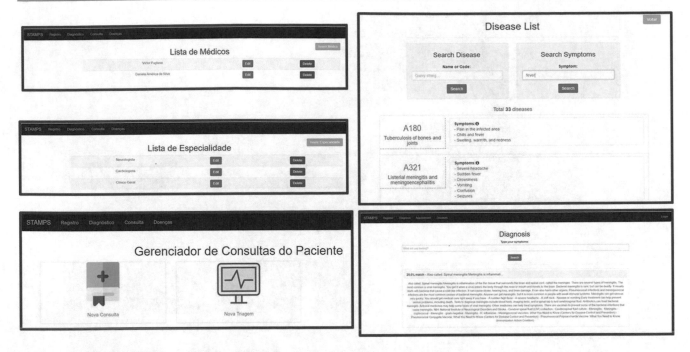

Fig. 34.3 The PATIENT finding PHYSICIAN, according to the application

Fig. 34.4 Managing hospital information per PATIENT

It also has allowed some benefits such as identifying the communication stages and actions to be taken by each subsystem, by using KAFKA, as the technology for data interchange, and also data based in the HL7 health care standard.

As a result, the STAMPSNet also allows a timeline describing every event and action involved in a health care crisis.

The STAMPSNet starts with an event, as shown in the following example:

1. A PATIENT arrives at the HOSPITAL;
2. A PHYSICIAN performs a diagnosis;
3. The Diagnosis is stored at the HOSPITAL database; and
4. The PHYSICIAN reports it to the STAMPS Net.

Then, the STAMPSNet operates according to the following the four stages of: *Detection, Screening, Treatment, and Response.*

– *Detection*—on this stage, data in social midia from PATIENT, PHYSICIAN and HOSPITAL subsystems will be monitored as source of information of social midia (e.g. Twitter, Google, and Facebook), city hall, hospitals, and others, as shown on the architecture details from Fig. 34.6.

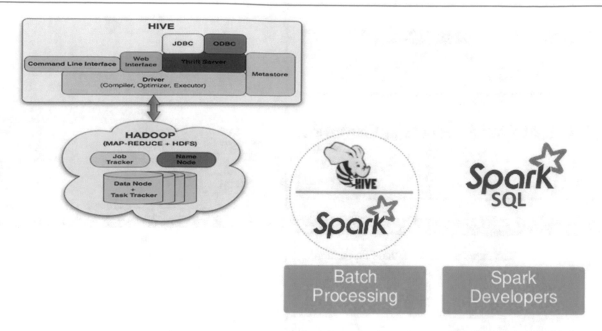

Fig. 34.5 Managing SUPPLIER data

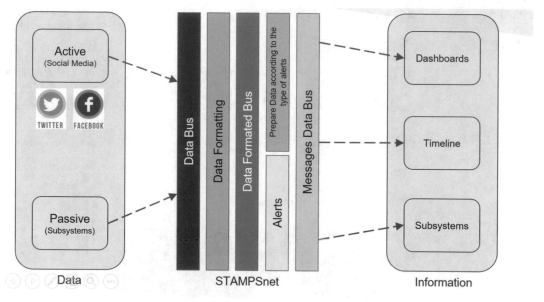

Fig. 34.6 The STAMPSNet detection stage

– *Screening*—on this stage, information will be received from the previous Detection stage and these information will be used to organize data on the intelligent system, allowing: the location of events, the identification of common symptoms and potential diseases, according to the ICD-10 standard, to forecast disease potential incidences, in order to alert the appropriate authorities to be involved, as shown on Fig. 34.7 the architecture details.

– *Treatment*—on this stage, according to the information identified and organized from the previous Screening stage, data will be processed and an alert will be sent, according to a calculated potential incidence.

This notification will be sent, considering a preventive action (e.g. 45% of the potential epidemic based upon statistical methods).

At this time, false/positive alerts will be also treated before being sent, as shown on the architecture details of Fig. 34.8.

– *Response*—on this stage, according to the event being treated, each subsystem, as shown on Table 34.1, PATIENT, PHYSICIAN, HOSPITAL, and SUPPLIER will be notified about what should be done (e.g. prevention, critical locations), what should be done in case of an epidemics, and what suppliers should provide in order to manage the crises.

This notification will be also sent to the appropriate authorities involved such as city hall and army, and after the situation is under control, the alert will be closed, as shown on the architecture details of Fig. 34.9.

34.3 The Proof of Concept Presentation as an Assigned Mission

This academic project was inspired by the needs of public and/or private organizations involved in crisis management involving health events (e.g. epidemics), which needs to manage data and information for decision making. At the end of 17 academic weeks, a simulated PoC was designed to demonstrate the use of the TSA4HC academic project in a fictitious epidemics for EBOLA.

To accomplish the simulated mission, the four subsystems PATIENT, PHYSICIAN, HOSPITAL, and SUPPLIER were integrated into the STAMPSNet Intelligent System to treat events according to the stages described as follows: Detection, Screening, Treatment, and Response.

34.3.1 The Detection Stage

During a national holiday, a Person (eventual patient) goes awry and faints in the middle of a Shopping. The security team at a Local Care Office or near hospital receives this patient, where a physician analyzes symptoms, such as very high fever, tremors, vomiting with blood, red eyes, and/or mental confusion.

The event is detected by the STAMPSNet and the patient 1 is identified by the system. In this Detection stage the STAMPSNet will receive information from the PATIENT subsystem informing the potential EBOLA events collected from social midia. And it will also receive information from the PHYSICIAN subsystem informing potential patients consultations/visits having EBOLA symptoms.

34.3.2 The Screening Stage

Considering also the reports of the patient about their severe joint pains and their recent work in an area affected by the EBOLA epidemic, a medical team reports that everything indicates that it is an EBOLA infection. From there, this patient can be considered as the first patient to start an epidemic in a region, if it is readily identified.

As a result, the patient 1 will be registered in the subsystem PHYSICIAN. And any new consultations/visits indicating an EBOLA infection will be also registered in the subsystem PHYSICIAN.

34.3.3 The Treatment Stage

A set of epidemiological events are managed in such way that:

- *those who have had contact with Ebola's patient(s) infection are promptly identified and/or cared for;*
- *the population/society has a computer system tool like the TSA4HC project capable of providing appropriate records, management, and controls, since the emergence could evolve into an epidemic;*
- *the tool must be capable of providing preventive management and controls of diagnoses of patients in hospitals, based upon at least one confirmed diagnosis, for example, of EBOLA, avoiding unnecessary panic and despair of the population/society;*
- *after that, to identify an EBOLA infection, the PHYSICIAN subsystem uses the Jaccard index [12] for measuring similarity for the two sets of data (ICD-10 and Patient Symptoms), with a range from 0 to 100%, also weighted by potential symptoms.*

Some symptoms are fever, headache, muscle pain, and chills. Later, a person may experience internal bleeding resulting in vomiting or coughing blood.

Based on the *screening* of consultations/visits by physicians and also on information shared by the PATIENT subsystem related to feeds coming from social media [14, 17, 18, 19], the PHYSICIAN subsystem also identifies when to send an epidemics alert based on statistical methods.

The criteria is described in the Fig. 34.10 and if there are more than four occurrences indicating EBOLA, then a YELLOW preventive alert is sent to the STAMPSNet, informing all subsystems PATIENT, PHYSICIAN, HOSPITAL, and SUPPLIER an ATTENTION STATE and preventively prepare for an EBOLA epidemics.

If occurrences evolve to above 5, then a CRITICAL STATE reactive alert is sent to the STAMPSNet informing all subsystems PATIENT, PHYSICIAN, HOSPITAL, and SUPPLIER to react to an EBOLA epidemics.

34.3.4 The Response Stage

A set of epidemiological events are managed in such way that:

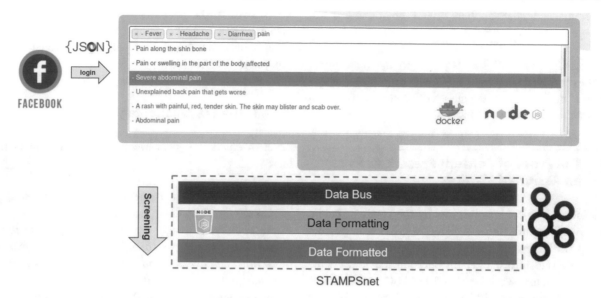

Fig. 34.7 The STAMPSNet screening stage

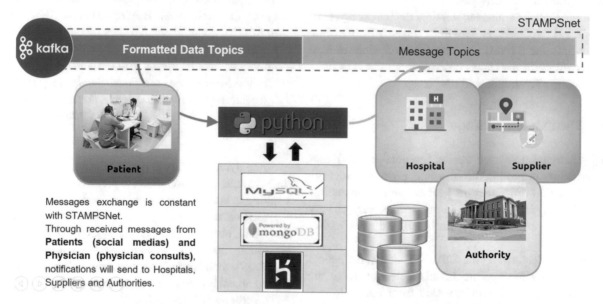

Fig. 34.8 The STAMPSNet treatment stage

Table 34.1 The STAMPSNet subsystem response

Subsystem	Response
PATIENT	Guidance about Prevention; Guidance to avoid risk areas; Guidance on crisis behavior
PHYSICIAN	Recommended medical treatment; Protocol for epidemic crisis
HOSPITAL	How to transport the PATIENT; Rooms available for the PATIENT and isolation if needed
SUPPLIER	Resources needed and SUPPLIERS available to provide it
ALERTS	Inform authorities (city hall, army and other); Inform SUPPLIERS (medicines and special clothes for healthcare professionals involved in the crisis; Isolate risk areas; Share alert for responsible authorities

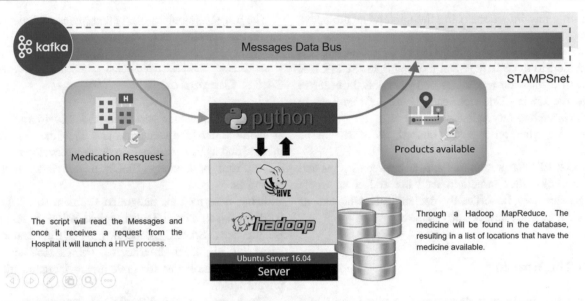

Fig. 34.9 The STAMPSNet response stage

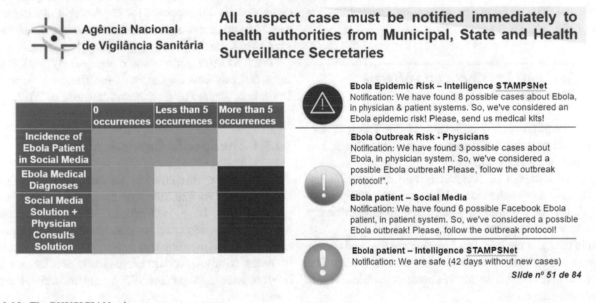

Fig. 34.10 The PHYSICIAN subsystem treatment stage

– *Hospital(s) must have the computational means to collaborate in the process of managing large flows of efficient patient care, using appropriate technologies and efficient screening methods [15, 16];*
– *The involved hospital(s) and their supplier(s) of medicines and devices also have appropriate tools to participate in an inventory management process of materials and medicines 6 (Remark: After all, not only Amoxicillin is important in a hospital, there are several consumer materials involved in a care to ensure the safety of health professionals (physicians) and the well-being of patients);*
– *Each confirmed case of patient can generate, within the inventory control of a hospital, the release of care kits, containing materials and medicines for the beginning*

of treatments. In these cases, in addition to medicines, protective equipment can also be considered important, given the rapid rate of contagion of diseases, such as EBOLA; and
– *Public administration has reliable data for decision-making in crisis situations.*

After that, the alert message from the treatment stage is sent to the STAMPSNet, and processed by the HOSPITAL subsystem in the response stage. The HOSPITAL subsystem will identify number of rooms available, and will start the medical treatment. The medical treatment is limited to supportive therapy, which consists of moisturizing the patient, maintaining their oxygen levels and blood pressure, and treating any infections using the appropriate protective clothing.

In the response stage, the HOSPITAL subsystem will send an alert to the STAMPSNet requesting the SUPPLIER subsystem to provide medicines and materials, in order to manage the crisis. This notification will be also sent to authorities, such as city hall and army.

After this situation is under control, the alert will be closed.

The first EBOLA symptoms appear between 2 days and up to 3 weeks after infection. And the end of an Ebola outbreak can only be officially declared after the end of 42 days without any new confirmed cases.

34.3.5 The Timeline

All the events in the assigned mission was presented in a dashboard, as a timeline, listing all actions taken in every stage of the STAMPSNet, as shown on the architecture details of Fig. 34.11.

34.4 The Learning Curve on Software Development Cycle

During the requirements specification of this TSA4HC academic project prototype, different design, development, and test activities were performed.

The project degree of complexity and the coordination among teams were evaluated. All groups had a real perception of this process complexity and the high level difficulty of the addressed integrated tasks.

Within the agile method, the development time and size of activities were reduced, and the focus was on activities. The main observable result from all this process participants was a steeper learning curve.

Usually, in projects where goals are achieved through iterative and incremental cycles, each team member has a small activity that can be quick and accurately performed, unlike on traditional methods, in which a member does not perform other tasks not belonging to him.

During the academic development of this TSA4HC project, all participants had the opportunity to carry out their tasks in an agile way. For some of them, it was the first time they had contact with the Scrum agile method, and also with different technologies, concepts, and standards. Nevertheless, they had a better performance than if they would be using other traditional methods of development.

According to TDs reports, the communication had a strong influence in accelerating the learning process, which occurred in conjunction with an increased productivity.

The project was successfully completed on time, suggesting that its learning curve was steeper.

34.5 Conclusion

This paper aimed to describe the development of an academic interdisciplinary project and the Scrum agile method and its best practices, in order to develop a prototype for a Proof of Concept (PoC), using cloud-computing resources.

It has described an Integrated Problem-Based Learning (IPBL) project, named Technological Solutions Applied for Health Care (TSA4HC) academic project, a computer system based on Big Data, Internet of Things (IoT) and other emerging technologies for governmental organizations and private sector.

The purpose of this TSA4HC system was to aggregate data and integrate actors, such as Patients, Hospitals, Physicians, and Health Suppliers for the decision making process related to crisis management of events in the health system, such as epidemics.

The TSA4HC project was developed by students from three different courses taught at the Brazilian Aeronautics Institute of Technology, on the 1st semester of 2017.

34.5.1 The Specific Conclusions

The use of interdisciplinarity on three Computer Science courses has worked as expected, since the students got to know how to work in teams to successfully develop a complex realtime embedded system. The cloud computing environment was extensively used by students, in order to allow collaborative work at distance, using hangout meetings, personal sites, and an official project website.

The Scrum framework was adapted to the reality of the ITA academic interdisciplinary environment, helping the whole team of around 30 students to deliver value to stakeholders, at the end of each sprint, and also at the end of this project.

The application of Test Driven Development (TDD) in this project was closely related to the adopted interdisciplinary approach, since the test and the development were created by students from all three courses.

Kafka, Spark, Python or Java, Django, and MongoDB technologies hosted in the Heroku cloud services were the tools applied for prototype modeling and automatic non structured data processing using the ICD-10 standard.

Results of this TSA4HC project prototype were successful and, at the end, students have presented the their academic final project as a PoC to professors, entrepreneurs, and some invited guests from industry and academia.

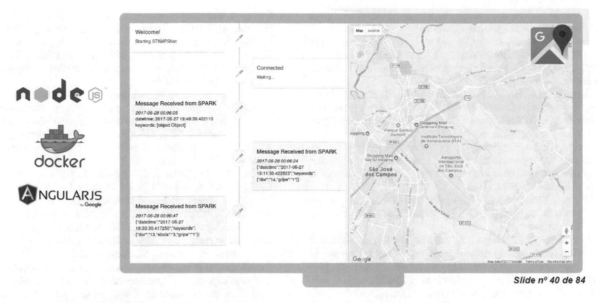

Fig. 34.11 The STAMPSNet application timeline

34.5.2 General Conclusions

According to the authors, the academic development of a critical intelligent system is a rewarding experience, which can be used in different undergrad and graduate courses.

The use of interdisciplinarity, cloud-computing, and agile methods appears to be a new interesting and motivational way of achieving academic goals in just one semester of 17 weeks and can be also extended to other knowledge domains.

34.5.3 Recommendations

The authors recommend that the assigned mission should be clearly defined at early stages of the project. In this project, its requirements specification took a few weeks to be defined.

For future projects, it is recommended that the assigned mission be defined on the first academic week. It is recommended that the integration of different layers be done as early as possible, using appropriate tools, allowing different teams to work on communication protocols, layouts refinements, and testing, also on the early stages of the project.

The authors also recommend the use of automated testing tools and procedures to accelerate the development process, while increasing the quality of the product. The automation testing tools with Python could be used, since it do provide some testing automation, but there were no time for students to take the full advantage of it in this project.

34.5.4 Future Work

It is suggested that the process used in this TSA4HC academic project can be extended to other embedded systems projects, as for example in the health domain, within the area of using wearables to collect and track personal health conditions. As future works, it is also suggested to extend cooperation with industry, in order to obtain academic projects selection aligned with up-to-date market needs.

Acknowledgment The authors would like to thank: the Brazilian Aeronautics Institute of Technology (ITA); the Casimiro Montenegro Filho Foundation (FCMF); the 2RP Net and the Ecossistema Enterprises for their infrastructure and financial support, during the development of this TSA4HC academic project prototype.

References

1. J. Sutherland, *CRUM Handbook* (Scrum Training Institute Press, 2010)
2. D. Cohen, et al., *An Introduction to Agile Methods, Fraunhofer Center for Experimental Software Engineering, Advances in Computers*, 62
3. K. Pugh, *Lean-Agile Acceptance Test-Driven Development: Better Software Through Collaboration* (Addison-Wesley, 2011, ISBN 978-0321714084)
4. ICD, International classification of diseases, (2017), http://www.who.int/classifications/icd/en
5. HL7, Health level seven international, (2017), http://www.hl7.org/documentcenter/public/training/IntroToHL7/player.html
6. IMasters, Development, creation and innovation, (2017), https://imasters.com.br/box/ferramenta/heroku. Accessed 11 June 2017
7. DevMedia, Codes for who develops codes, (2017), http://www.devmedia.com.br/primeiros-passos-em-paas-comheroku/29465. Accessed 11 June 2017

8. E. Freeman, B. Bates, K. Sierra, E. Robson, *Head First Design Patterns* (O'Reilly, Sebastopol, CA, 2004)

9. Model View Controller, http://c2.com/cgi/wiki?ModelViewController, Accessed 16 Aug 2013

10. MVC Pattern and Django, https://overiq.com/django/1.10/mvc-pattern-and-django. Accessed 15 June 2017

11. L. Han, S. Luo, H. Wang, L. Pan, X. Ma, T. Zhang, An intelligible risk stratification model based on pairwise and size constrained, JBHI Med. Inform. **21**(5), 1288–1296 (2017), http://ieeexplore.ieee.org/document/7762039

12. S. Niwattanakul, J. Singthongchai, E. Naenudorn, Using of Jaccard coefficient for keywords similarity, in *Proceedings of the International Multi Conference of Engineers and Computer Scientists 2013 Vol I, IMECS 2013*, (Hong Kong, 2013)

13. STAMPS, Technological solutions applicable to medias and products in health, (2017), https://sites.google.com/site/stampsacademico

14. M. Hoogendoorn, T. Berger, A. Schulz, T. Stolz, P. Szolovits, Predicting social anxiety treatment outcome based on therapeutic email conversations, JBHI Public Health Inform. **21**(5), 1449–1459 (2017), http://ieeexplore.ieee.org/document/7546552

15. J. Yoon, C. Davtyan, M. van der Schaar, Discovery and clinical decision support for personalized healthcare, JBHI Med. Inform. **21**(4), 1133–1145 (2017), http://ieeexplore.ieee.org/document/7482682

16. L. May, J. Karthikayen, S. Anita, W. Ruwan, W. Prasad, E. Kacey, F. Schubert, Lessons from the implementation of Mo-Buzz, a mobile pandemic surveillance system for dengue. JMIR Public Health Surveill. **3**(4), e65 (2017), https://publichealth.jmir.org/2017/4/e65/?utmsource = T rendMDutmmedium = cpcutmcampaign = JMIRT rendMD0

17. M. Michele, B. Tanvi, M. Roopteja, R. William, S. Amit, What are people tweeting about Zika? An exploratory study concerning its symptoms, treatment, transmission, and prevention. JMIR Public Health Surveill. **3**(2), e38, (2017), http://publichealth.jmir.org/2017/2/e38/?utmsource = T rendMDutmmedium = cpcutmcampaign = JMIRT rendMD0

18. S. Danielle, H. Richard, C. Robert, S. Catherine, Evaluating Google, Twitter, and Wikipedia as tools for influenza surveillance using Bayesian change point analysis: a comparative analysis. JMIR Public Health Surveill. **2**(2), e161, (2016), http://publichealth.jmir.org/2016/2/e161/?utmsource = T rendMDutmmedium = cpcutmcampaign = JMIRT rendMD1

19. M. Maimuna, S. Mauricio, M. Sumiko, M. Denise, K. Kamran, B. John, Utilizing nontraditional data sources for near real-time estimation of transmission dynamics during the 2015–2016 Colombian Zika virus disease outbreak. JMIR Public Health Surveill. **2**(1), e30, (2016), http://publichealth.jmir.org/2016/1/e30/?utmsource = T rendMDutmmedium = cpcutmcampaign = JMIRT rendMD1

Using Correct-by-Construction Software Agile Development

35

Rafael Augusto Lopes Shigemura, Gildarcio Sousa Goncalves,
Luiz Alberto Vieira Dias, Paulo Marcelo Tasinaffo, Adilson Marques da
Cunha, Luciana Sayuri Mizioka, Leticia Hissae Yanaguya,
and Victor Ulisses Pugliese

Abstract

Disasters and crises, whether climatic, economic, or social are undesirably frequent in everyday lives. In such situations, lives are lost mainly because of inadequate management, lack of qualified and accurate information, besides other factors that prevent full situational awareness, including software failures. The goal of this paper is to report the agile conceptualization, design, build, and demonstration of a computerized system, containing correct-by-construction software, to safely manage critical information, during alerts or crises situations. On this research, the following challenges and requirements were tackled: formal specifications, aerospatial-level reliability, agile development, embedded systems, controlled testability, and product assessment. An Interdisciplinary Problem-Based Learning (IPBL), involving a Scrum of Scrums Agile Framework was adapted for managing the cohesive, productive, and collaborative development team of around 100 undergrad and graduate students remotely working. In addition, the following hardware technologies, for supporting the software development were used: environment sensors, Radio Frequency Identification (RFID), and Unmanned Aerial Vehicles (UAVs). Other software technologies were also used, as well cloud-based web-responsive platforms and mobile applications to geographically manage resources at real-time. Finally, the ANSYS® SCADE (Safety-Critical Application Development Environment) was employed to support the embedded and correct-by-construction module of this system, according to Model-Driven Architecture (MDA) and Model-Driven Development (MDD).

Keywords

Agile software development · Correct-by-construction software · Model-Driven Architecture (MDA) · Model-Driven Development (MDD) · Scrum agile method · Interdisciplinarity

35.1 Introduction

According to the United Nations Office for Disaster Risk Reduction (UNISDR), a disaster is a serious disruption of community or society functions, involving widespread human, material, economic, or environmental losses and impacts, which exceeds the ability of the affected community or society to cope with, by using its own resources [1].

Only in 2016, there were 327 catastrophes worldwide, killing about 11,000 people and bringing an estimated total economic loss of USD 175 billion. Additionally, since the year 2000, there were three disasters with more than 100,000 victims each [2].

Given this huge global impact, several strategies are underway to mitigate its consequences, organized both national and internationally around the World [3].

However, a study published by the Swiss Reinsurance Company shows that the frequency of disasters, both natural and man-made, has been steadily increasing year by year, in the last 40 years, as summarized in Fig. 35.1 [2].

Information Technologies (ITs) can, undoubtedly, provide tools to manage critical information, during alerts and/or crises situations but high reliability is a must [4]. Even high-profile software systems, like the American 911, can suffer from dumb software defects [5]. Also, the ever-changing nature of occurrence demands for fast response and adaptation.

This scenario led some members of the Software Engineering Research Group (*Grupo de Pesquisa em Engenharia de Software*—GPES) of the Brazilian Aeronautics Institute

R. A. L. Shigemura (✉) · G. S. Goncalves · L. A. V. Dias
P. M. Tasinaffo · A. M. da Cunha · L. S. Mizioka · L. H. Yanaguya
V. U. Pugliese
Computer Science Department, Brazilian Aeronautics Institute of Technology (Instituto Tecnologico de Aeronautica—ITA), Sao Jose dos Campos, Sao Paulo, Brazil
e-mail: rafael@ita.br

© Springer International Publishing AG, part of Springer Nature 2018
S. Latifi (ed.), *Information Technology – New Generations*, Advances in Intelligent Systems and Computing 738,
https://doi.org/10.1007/978-3-319-77028-4_35

Fig. 35.1 The number of catastrophic events from 1970 to 2016 [2]

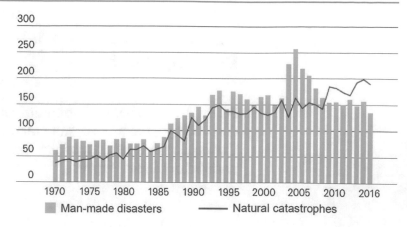

Man-made disasters   Natural catastrophes

Table 35.1 Standards partially used in the RT-ACMIS project, through SCADE KCG compiler

Standards	Descriptions
DO-330 TQL-1	Software tool qualification considerations
DO-331	Model-based development and verification supplement to DO-178C and DO-278A

of Technology (*Instituto Tecnologico de Aeronautica*—ITA) to raise the following essential research questions:

1. Is it possible to bring together and use, productively, the two supposedly divergent approaches: Agile Software Development and Formal Specifications?
2. Assuming agile development together with highly reliable software technologies, how could them be effectively applied to mitigate risks and/or increase community resilience?

Recent works and advances to answer the question 1 suggest that hybrid approaches, using Agile and Formal Methods, can bring 'the best of each' to the software engineering and/or system engineering fields [6].

Aiming to move forward in answering these two questions, this paper reports an academic capstone project of 17-weeks, during the second Semester of 2016, at the ITA, involving the following challenges and requirements: formal specifications, aero spatial-level of reliability, agile development, embedded systems, controlled testability, and product assessment.

An Interdisciplinary Problem-Based Learning (IPBL), involving a Scrum of Scrums Agile Framework [7, 8] was adapted, for managing the cohesive, productive, and collaborative development team of around 100 undergrad and graduate students remotely working and, applying knowledge gathered from the following courses (occurring paralleled to the project): CES-65 Embedded Systems Project; CE-235 Real-time Embedded Systems; CE-230 Software Quality, Reliability, and Safety; and CE-237 Advanced Topics in Software Testing.

35.2 Background

This section describes the following key concepts, methods, and techniques used in the development of the Real-Time Accident and Crises Management Integrated System (RT-ACMIS) project, named in Portuguese *Sistema Integrado de Gerenciamento em Tempo Real de Acidentes e Crises* (SIG-TRAC): Software Quality, Reliability, and Safety; Agile Scrum Method; Agile Testing; the ANSYS® SCADE; and also the involved hardware.

35.2.1 Software Quality, Reliability, and Safety

The RT-ACMIS project was developed, by following quality, reliability, safety, and testability requirements and also the DO-178C [9] and the DO-278A [10] standards.

Through the SCADE KCG compiler [11], other Standards were also partially applied, as shown in Table 35.1. The KCG is a C and Ada code generator from SCADE models. More detailed information will be presented in Sect. 35.2.4.

The software quality, reliability, and safety evaluation were performed throughout a systematic examination of activities during all the sprints. There was used an auditing process by checking the activities compliance with project and standards requirements, previously established, as shown in Fig. 35.2.

Quality never occurs by accident, it is always the result of high intention, sincere effort, intelligent direction, and skillful execution of expected planning [12].

Fig. 35.2 Example of DO-178C Compliance Matrix used in the RT-ACMIS

	Reference	Sprint 1			Sprint 2			Sprint 3			
		US01	US03	US06	US12	US17	US18	US12	US17	US13	US19
QUALITY	DO-178C A 3.6	S	S	S	S	S	S	S	S	S	S
	DO-178C A 3.5	S	S	S	S	S	S	S	S	S	S
	DO-178C A 2.4, A 4.1 e A 4.2	S	S	S	S	S	S	S	S	S	S
	DO-178C A 3.4 e A 4.4	S	S	S	S	S	S	S	S	S	S
	DO-178C A 2.4 e A 4.6	S	S	S	S	S	S	S	S	S	S
RELIABILITY	DO-178C A 2.3	S	S	S	S	S	S	S	S	S	S
	DO-178C A 2.7	S	S	S	S	S	S	S	S	S	S
	DO-178C A 6.1 e 6.3	S	S	S	S	S	S	S	S	S	S
	DO-178C A 2.1 e A 2.4	S	S	S	S	S	S	S	S	S	S
	DO-178C A 9.x	S	S	S	S	S	S	S	S	S	S
SAFETY	DO-178C A 2.2 e A 2.5	N/A	N/A	N/A	N/A	N/A	N/A	N/A	N/A	N/A	N/A
	DO-178C A 7.2	S	S	S	S	S	S	S	S	S	S

35.2.2 The Agile Scrum Method

According to the Scrum Alliance, Scrum is a framework within which people can address complex adaptive problems, while productive and creatively delivering products of the highest possible value [8].

Scrum has three pillars: transparency, inspection, and adaptation, involving team following roles, ceremonies, and artifacts, as presented in Fig. 35.3 [7]:

- Roles—Product Owner (PO), Scrum Master (SM), and Team Developer (TD);
- Ceremonies—Sprint Planning Meetings, Daily Sprints or Weekly Meetings, Sprint Reviews, and Sprint Retrospectives; and
- Artifacts—Product Backlog, Sprint Backlogs, Kanban, and Burndown Charts.

The roles are played by the Product Owners (POs), who represent interests of all stakeholders. They also provide requirements and funds and also accept deliverables; Development Teams (DTs) are responsible for developing and testing these deliverables. Finally, there are Scrum Masters (SMs) who are responsible for managing the Scrum process and the DT, solving any issue; in order to have deliverables complied with requirements, ensuring timely deadlines and high quality of products.

Sprint is a manageable short time period interaction. In general, it takes about 4 weeks. Its goal is to produce a tested and stable deliverable.

At the beginning of a Sprint, the team selects prioritized requirements of the Product Backlog to be developed and compiled in an artifact named Sprint Backlog.

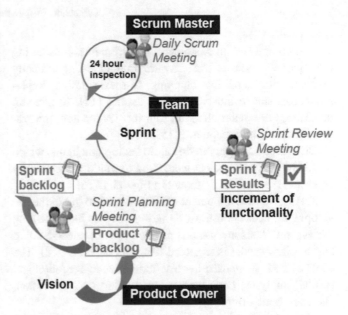

Fig. 35.3 The Scrum roles, ceremonies, and artifacts [13]

At the end of a Sprint, in the Sprint Review ceremony, the team presents Sprint results. The SM and the PO inspect and adapt the project and the product for the next Sprint. The DT and the SM hold a ceremony named Sprint Retrospective, to report any limitation or experience that could affect the team performance.

35.2.3 Agile Testing

Besides Formal Methods, software testing is used to identify possible defects in the software and to check whether the

Fig. 35.4 The agile testing
quadrants [16]

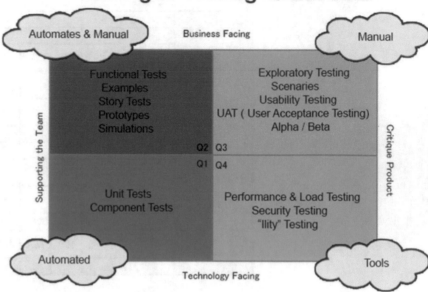

Fig. 35.4 The agile testing quadrants [16]

system complies with customers' requirements, considering effectiveness and use. The software product testing basically involves four steps: test planning, test case design, implementation, and evaluation of test results [14]. In general, these steps are materialized in four test levels: unit, integration, system, and acceptance [15].

Crispin and Gregory define agile testing quadrants, which in this RT-ACMIS project were used to guide the testability assessment activities, as shown in Fig. 35.4 [16].

Test Driven Development (TDD) is used to guide the development, because it must be written before implementing the system. Tests are used to provide project understanding and to clarify what is expected from the code [17, 18]. The TDD cycle is composed by: test adding, code execution and results' analyses, code writing, automated tests execution, and code refactoring.

The creation of unit or component testing is a crucial part of a project. Individual components are tested to ensure proper operations. Each hardware and software component must be independently tested. Components may be single entities such as functions or classes of objects or may be coherent groups of these entities. TDD is usually chosen for the following reasons [19, 20]:

- The programmer is the one who creates the test, while the software code is still very present in his mind;
- The test might be automated, ensuring greater frequency in implementation;
- It must also ensure that it runs with identical results, every time it is used; and

- Not only unit testing brings success to an application, but also it is necessary to test the system as a whole.

According to [21], components are integrated to compose the system. This process is related to the search for defects that result from interactions not provided between system components.

In this project, the agile software testing using Agile Test Quadrants aimed to help coding, significantly reducing problems from the development phase, as well to advance the study of applicability of this model in embedded, real-time and Internet of Things environment, as recommended in [22].

35.2.4 The ANSYS® SCADE

This section presents some theoretical overview of SCADE Suite® I-CASE-E tool and it's Synchronous Programming Model (SPM) of reactive systems. SPM is based on the synchronous concurrency model [23], in which concurrent processes can perform computation and exchange information instantly, at least at theoretical level.

This model is widely accepted and used by automatic control and engineering industry, ranging from hardware circuit design to large scale real-time process control, including embedded systems, drivers, communication protocols, aerospatial and automotive control, amongst others [23].

Reactive Systems Model (RSM), in turn, respond to stimuli from the environment, within a strictly defined period and safety standards, unlike interactive systems, which respond to users' stimuli according to the availability of resources [23]. This property of RSM is essential to safety-critical systems due of its behavioral determinism [23].

SPM and RSM form an ideal pair for development of embedded safety-critical systems, but can become a problem if they need to be coded by hand, reducing agility to change and flexibility. The SCADE Suite®, fully implements SPM and RSM, through a graphical Model-Driven Development (MDD) environment.

The MDD paradigm has been widely used to complex projects in various areas of science and engineering. The ability to perform computer simulations in abstract models can provide hundreds of million dollars savings, instead of generating a single physical prototype test [15].

It also provides the automatic generation of significant amount of source-code in C or Ada languages, through the implementation of native available components standardized according to DO-178C [24], as the SCADE KCG compiler.

SCADE Suite KCG is a C and Ada code generator from SCADE models that has been qualified as a development tool for DO-178B software up to Level A and DO-178C/DO-330 at TQL-1 [11].

This code generator saves verification effort in the coding phase, such as code reviews and low-level testing on the SCADE Suite KCG generated code. This productivity improvement shortens certification and/or modification time and effort. SCADE Suite KCG has successfully passed the qualification procedure on several large programs, and is currently used in production for several programs in Europe, Asia and the Americas [11].

Another highlight worth to mention is the fact that not only code, but all generated artifacts (including documentation) are readily certifiable by the DO-178C standard, and its use significantly reduces the waste of time and other resources in certification process [24].

Finally, SCADE developed models are formally guaranteed to accomplish the requisites, because is submitted to internal model checking formal verification. This check is performed using formal methods, namely Weak Bisimulation Reduction and Temporal Logic, over Finite State Machines [23].

35.2.5 Hardware

The following hardware were researched, implemented, and/or used in the RT-ACMIS project, as a Internet of Things Proof of Concept (PoC):

- Raspberry Pi, used as remote processing unit;
- Arduino, as sensors microcontroller;
- A high sensitive noise sensor;
- A temperature and humidity sensor;
- An inflammable gas and smoke sensor;

- A heartbeats sensor;
- A Radio Frequency Identification (RFID) transmitter/reader, used in this project to store serial numbers for personal, object, or information identifications on microchips;
- A RFID bracelet, a mix of a radio transmission device used to store and retain patient information, having a microchip and an antenna to allow communication to RFID transmitters/readers; and
- A drone Parrot 2.0, a quadcopter managed via WiFi connection, using a Software Development Kit (SDK) programmed with an Application Program Interface (API) in C language, and a Global Positioning System (GPS).

35.3 The Project Development

This section describes the usage of the Scrum method on a project management for academic purposes. It shows the product vision and the assigned mission project. At the end, it addresses the development and the main challenges faced on its four sprints. Figure 35.5 shows the RT-ACMIS project divided into segments and subsystems assigned from ST01 to ST08.

35.3.1 Tailoring the Scrum Agile Method

During the RT-ACMIS project, the Scrum of Scrums technique was adopted. It allowed STs to manage the development of products and services [19].

In this project, only for academic purposes, the following two new roles were created: General Product Owner (GPO) and General Scrum Master (GSM), in order to improve the RT-ACMIS project development management with students.

The project development was divided into eight STs listed below with their macro-functions:

- ST01—CIVIL DEFENSE/Collaboration and Coordination;
- ST02—HEALTH CARE/Medical and Ambulance First Aid;
- ST03—FIRE DEPARTMENT/Search and Rescue;
- ST04—POLICE DEPARTMENT/Police Report and Civilian Security;
- ST05—CIVIL DEFENSE/Communication and Cooperation;
- ST06—HEALTH CARE/Hospital and Intensive Care Unit (ICU);
- ST07—FIRE DEPARTMENT/Rescue and Aftermath; and
- ST08—POLICE DEPARTMENT/Preventive Security and Military Security.

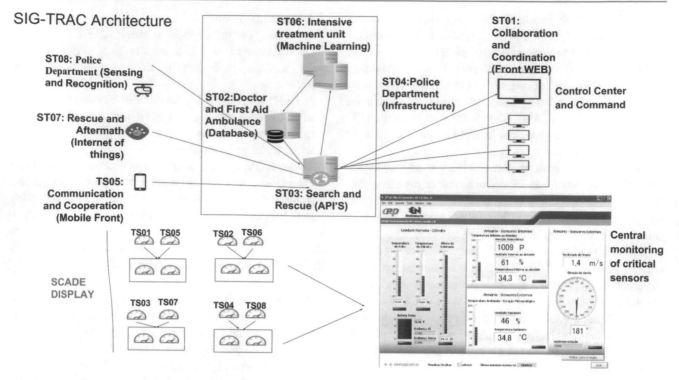

Fig. 35.5 The RT-ACMIS (SIG-TRAC) project architecture

35.3.2 The RT-ACMIS Project Pre-game Phase: Product Vision

During the preparation for Sprints, POs of each ST have created the product vision, as an important agile artifact, used to identify and describe the RT-ACMIS project focusing on the product to be developed, as follows:

> *"For public or private organizations involved in monitoring, warning, or accidents and/or crises preventions motivated by adverse events of any nature, including terrorist attacks, who require and/or wish to explore Real-time Embedded Systems, Big Data, Remote Sensing, Machine Learning, among other related emerging technologies, the RT-ACMIS project is a Real-time Computer System (involving Hardware and Software) for analysis and issuance of automatic alerts. Differently from existing products from Universities, Research Institutes, Government Agencies and/or Public or Private Enterprises, this product was developed in just 17 weeks in an academic environment, at a distance and as a part time project, using the best agile practices and cutting-edge technologies with quality, reliability, safety, and testability."*

35.3.2.1 The Assigned Mission

For the final analysis and evaluation of the RT-ACMIS project, the students had to show the accomplishment of a fictitious crisis assignment mission, demonstrating the management of it through a system operation Proof of Concept (PoC). This mission was composed by three main phases:

1. Preparation—Crisis alert and activation of firefighter segment;

2. Action—Segments acting on crisis; and

3. Reconstruction—Police acquiring images from the local of accident and closes the crisis.

35.3.3 The RT-ACMIS Project Development: Game Phase

This section tackles the academic project development and its challenges.

35.3.3.1 Sprint #0: Preparation for Sprints

The Sprint 0 was designed to provide basic training for all students in different subjects to enable their roles as TDs, POs and SMs, using the SCADE and several other tools.

The training was conducted in an agile, collaborative, and interdisciplinary way, through books, lectures, hands-on exercises, and classes. In the end, those involved were able to learn the embedded systems fundamentals in real-time.

35.3.3.2 Sprint #1

On this Sprint #1, both ST01 and ST05 (from the Civil Defense Segment) were able:

- To create a registration screen, named Civil Defense Community Centers (CDCC), with the ability to provide basic information about accidents and/or crises;
- To register and use the other segment resources; and

- To develop a service registration of accident and/or crisis report.

ST02 and ST06 (from the Health Segment) were able:

- To develop scripts, for calculating the number of doctors per ambulances;
- To develop the initial web portal layout;
- To develop a screen in SCADE for the ambulance;
- To develop some research on patient care protocols for crises and disasters; and
- To create an exhibition screen bed management for Intensive Care Unit (ICU) also using the SCADE.

ST03 and ST07 (from the Firefighter Segment) were able:

- To develop a victims layout classification;
- To establish constant contacts with real-life firemen to study, investigate, and better understand the used procedures of search and rescue and path location to the nearest firefighters; and also
- To study and investigate the integration of SCADE applications with some relevant database.

ST04 and ST08 (from the Police Segment) were able:

- To implement a preliminary modeling of the RT-ACMIS project database; and also
- To implement an agile software testing, applying TDD techniques in a prototype of a Cockpit Display System (CDS), aiming: to access the project database, by using the SCADE Suite; to define coordinates (latitude and longitude) and displacements of Drones; and also to create mechanisms for modeling and data availability.

35.3.3.3 Sprint #2

The Sprint #2 implementation has happened on the RT-ACMIS project, as hardware embedded software integration between STs.

ST01 and ST05 (from the Civil Defense Segment) were able:

- To make available the basic information about accidents and/or crises occurrence registrations in the RT-ACMIS project database from data obtained at SCADE, in a safety and reliable way.

ST02 and ST06 (from the Health Segment) were able:

- To perform scripts integration created from Sprint#1 with the web portal and the RT-ACMIS project database;

- To start the embedding software development in hardware;
- To acquire victims' vital signals from ambulances; and also
- To receive and maintain historical data from victims' vital signs to support the software development.

ST03 and ST07 (from the Firefighter Segment) were able:

- To define and integrate their data into a single screen;
- To process RFID bracelet data for victims' classification;
- To develop a mobile application, using a Simple Screening And Rapid Treatment Plan (START) method [25, 26];
- To register victims in the project database, by using a Raspberry Pi device connected to an RFID reader;
- To define a firefighter architecture;
- To develop an Application Program Interface (API) in Node.js; and also
- To create a CDS, for displaying signals obtained from noise sensors used to rescue victims from earthquakes, landslides, and/or debris.

ST04 and ST08 (from the Police Segment) were able:

- To implement an infrastructure for collecting sensor's data (like gases, fuel, smoke, temperature, and/or humidity);
- To develop a CDS for sensor data visualization;
- To control the Drone flight with a claw;
- To develop the Drone user-control interface connected on real-time to a mobile device; and
- To operate the Drone claw for delivering small packages, medicines, and/or supplies in inhospitable areas.

35.3.3.4 Sprint #3

On this Sprint #3, both ST01 and ST05 (from the Civil Defense Segment) were able:

- To finish the prototype implementation of a web portal for real-time crises management;
- To include on this accident and/or crises portal occurrences or resources (sensors, ambulances, operation bases, hospitals, among others); and
- To control a web map, involving a real-time monitoring and processing of historical data from alerts and/or crises in progress.

ST02 and ST06, (from the Health Segment) were able to develop and delivery the following working functionalities for the RT-ACMIS project web portal:

- A registration for recording historical data of occurrences in the project database;
- A management equipment module, for listing operational ambulances and its integrated embedded software functionalities;
- An integrated process for ambulances to receive, on real-time, the geographical position of accidents or crises, involving victim's vital signs (like temperature and heart beating);
- The total number of available beds and victims received by each hospital and also death notifications and released beds for receiving accident and/or crises new victims; and
- For the RT-ACMIS project architecture, the following devices and functionalities: two sensors (for temperature and heart beats) connected to an Arduino device capturing sensors' data, using C code; data sent, via network, to a Raspberry Pi microcomputer, running a server with Flask framework, using Python, to program data received from the cloud used by ST06—Hospitals, and to program data sent to the ambulances integrated screen, displaying on real-time, the embedded data, by using SCADE.

ST03 and ST07 (from the Firefighter Segment) were able:

- To implement a mobile application for the START method: by integrating ST03 with ST02, providing victims' data; by integrating ST03 with ST04, providing sensor data (light, gas, ethanol, and smoke) to aftermath functionalities; and also by integrating data on the RT-ACMIS project web portal; and
- To demonstrate the Raspberry Pi, as a PoC, for reading signals from noise sensors: by integrating with ST02 for reading vital signals and assigning victims with RFID bracelets.

ST04 and ST08 (from the Police Segment) were able:

- To implement the CDS and perform integration with hardware created from Sprint#2 for the persistent data collected from database and available to the firefighter segment; and also
- To implement a police report for crises monitoring, through the RT-ACMIS project web portal, integrating with all other project segments, the images taken by the Drone.

35.4 Conclusion

The goal of this paper was to report the agile conceptualization, design, build, and demonstration of a computerized system, containing correct-by-construction software, for safely managing critical information, during alerts or crises situations.

The implemented scenario has allowed students from 8 (eight) different Scrum Teams (STs) assigned to the 4 (four) segments of CIVIL DEFENSE, HEALTH CARE, FIRE DEPARTMENT, and POLICE DEPARTMENT of the Real-Time Accident and Crises Management Integrated System (RT-ACMIS) project to prove that: it is possible to use the two approaches, Agile Development and Formal Methods; and also it is possible to state that both approaches are able to be effectively applied to mitigate risks and/or increase community resilience.

The following challenges and requirements were successfully tackled on this research: formal specifications, aerospatial-level reliability, agile development, embedded systems, controlled testability, and product assessment.

An Interdisciplinary Problem-Based Learning (IPBL), involving a Scrum of Scrums Agile Framework was adapted for managing the cohesive, productive, and collaborative development team of around 100 undergrad and graduate students remotely working.

In addition, the following hardware technologies, for supporting the software development were used: environment sensors, Radio Frequency Identification (RFID), and Unmanned Aerial Vehicles (UAVs) as a Drone, together with other software technologies like cloud-based web-responsive platforms and mobile applications to geographically manage resources on real-time.

Finally, the ANSYS® SCADE (Safety-Critical Application Development Environment) was employed to support the embedded and correct-by-construction module of this system, according to Model-Driven Architecture (MDA) and Model-Driven Development (MDD).

The authors recommend that those implemented elements associated to different public agencies efforts be used to improve and speed up service quality on attendance to accidents and crises services in Brazil, thereby optimizing existing resources and contributing for saving lives.

35.5 Future Works

As a natural continuation of this research and due to its importance on the global context, the authors of this paper suggest the following works for further research, involving the expansion of the RT-ACMIS project:

- Its use in more complex scenarios of accident and crises management, incorporating new technologies;
- The use of new and emergent technologies to identify and predict accidents, disasters and/or crises, right after occurrences applying appropriate integrated actions like some of those already implemented; and
- Finally, the use the ANSYS® SCADE together with Model-Driven Architecture (MDA) and Model-Driven Development (MDD) to be expanded and applied to support the embedded and correct-by-construction modules of systems also in other knowledge domains.

Acknowledgment The authors would like to thank: the Brazilian Aeronautics Institute of Technology (*Instituto Tecnologico de Aeronautica—ITA*); the Casimiro Montenegro Filho Foundation (*Fundacao Casimiro Montenegro Filho—FCMF*); the Ecossistema Digital Business Ltd.; and the 2RP Net Ltd, for their infrastructure and financial support to the development of this research project, allowing its PoC in an academic and simulated real environment.

References

1. United Nations Office for Disaster Risk Reduction (UNISDR) Terminology. https://www.unisdr.org/we/inform/terminology. Accessed 18 Aug 2017
2. Swiss Re Institute, Natural catastrophes and man-made disasters in 2016: a year of widespread damages. http://www.preventionweb.net/publications/view/52534. Accessed 26 Aug 2017
3. UNISDR, International Strategy for Disaster Reduction. https://www.unisdr.org/who-we-are/international-strategy-for-disaster-reduction. Accessed 12 Nov 2016
4. UNISDR, Technology: the future of disaster risk reduction?. https://www.unisdr.org/archive/51043. Accessed 10 Jan 2017
5. Federal Communications Commission, April 2014 Multistate 911 outage: cause and impact. https://apps.fcc.gov/edocs_public/attachmatch/DOC-330012A1.pdf. Accessed 10 Aug 2017
6. W. Sunne, L. Hovmarken, Scrum goes formal: agile methods for safety-critical systems, in *Proceedings of the First International Workshop on Formal Methods in Software Engineering: Rigorous and Agile Approaches* (FormSERA, Zurich, Switzerland, 2012)
7. K.S. Rubin, *Essential SCRUM: A Practical Guide to the Most Popular Agile Process* (Addison-Wesley, New York, 2013)
8. J. Sutherland, K. Schwaber, The Definitive Guide to Scrum: The Rules of the Game. http://www.scrumguides.org/docs/scrumguide/v1/Scrum-Guide-US.pdf. Accessed 18 Mar 2016
9. RTCA DO-178C, *Software Considerations in Airborne Systems and Equipment Certification* (Radio Technical Commission for Aeronautics (RTCA), Washington, DC, 2011)
10. RTCA, *DO-278A. Software Integrity Assurance Considerations for Communication, Navigation, Surveillance and Air Traffic Management (CNS/ATM) Systems* (RTCA, Washington, DC, 2011)
11. Esterel Technologies Automatic Code Generation. http://www.ansys.com/products/embedded-software/ansys-scade-suite/scade-suite-capabilities#cap6. Accessed 20 Dec 2017
12. L. Rierson, *Developing Safety-Critical Software: A Practical Guide for Aviation Software and DO-178C Compliance* (CRC Press, New York, 2013)
13. T. Stober, U. Hansmann, *Agile Software Development Best Practices for Large Software Development Projects* (Springer, Heidelberg, 2010)
14. R.S. Pressman, *Software Engineering: A Practitioners Approach* (McGraw-Hill, New York, 1997)
15. L. Copeland, *A Practitioner's Guide to Software Test Design* (Artech House Publishers, Norwood, 2007)
16. L. Crispin, J. Gregory, *More Agile Testing* (Addison-Wesley, New York, 2015)
17. P. Jorgensen, C. Software, *Testing—A Craftsman's Approach* (CRC Press, Boca Raton, 2014)
18. G. Goncalves, et al., An agile developed interdisciplinary approach for safety-critical embedded system, in *14th International Conference on Information Technology: New Generations, vol 2017* (ITNG, Las Vegas, 2017)
19. D. Astels, *Test-Driven Development: A Pratical Guide* (Prentice Hall, Upper Saddle River, 2003)
20. K. Beck, *Test-Driven Development by Example* (Addison-Wesley, New York, 2002)
21. I. Sommerville, *Software Engineering*, 9th edn. (Addison-Wesley, Harlow, 2010)
22. J. Martins, et al., Agile testing quadrants on problem-based learning involving agile development, big data anda cloud computing, in *14th International Conference on Information Technology: New Generations (ITNG 2017)*, (Las Vegas, NV, 2017)
23. G. Berry, The foundations of Esterel, in *Proof, Language and Interaction: Essays in Honour of Robin Milner, Foundations of Computing Series*, ed. By G. Plotkin, C. Stirling, M. Tofte, (MIT Press, Cambridge, 2000)
24. Esterel Technologies. http://www.esterel-technologies.com/products/scade-arinc-661/. Accessed 26 Mar 2016
25. Esterel Technologies "SCADE Suite". http://www.esterel-technologies.com/products/scade-suite/. Accessed 22 Mar 2017
26. G. Super, S. Groth, R. Hook, et al., *START: Simple Triage and Rapid Treatment Plan* (Hoag Memorial Presbyterian Hospital, Newport Beach, 1994)

Service-Centered Operation Methodology (MOCA) Application Supported by Computer Science to Improve Continuously Care Quality in Public Services

Denis Avila Montini, Gustavo Ravanhani Matuck,
Danilo Douradinho Fernandes, Alessandra Avila Montini, Fernando Graton,
Plinio Ripari, and Flavia de Sousa Pinto

Abstract

The proposal of a Corporate Governance Model called Service-Focused Operation Methodology (MOCA) was carried out, applied in Public and Private Partnerships (PPP) to improve services quality offered by the Brazilian states. This PPP model enabled several Service Center (in portuguese *Central de Atendimento*—CA) implementation projects supported by several multidisciplinary knowledge areas that involve projects and governments. However, this article explored an aspect of how a MOCA's use with new technologies embedded in projects provide continuous improvements in results. In this case, for example, a demand study was applied to Planning and Control of Operations (PCO) in a use of Research and Development (R&D) to enable Artificial Intelligence algorithms for Planning Optimization in service production lines, aiming at improve citizen service aspects. In this CA PCO environment, a project outcomes set have been consolidated to demonstrate an impact that MOCA's use with new computational technologies can bring to society. The effective integration results for this R&D; MOCA applied in PCO; obtained from stabilized proof of concepts; providing data collection and more accurate performance information in each CA, collected directly by an ERP used. From these data, the design of service production lines was performed using the following methodologies: (1) Descriptive Statistics, (2) Temporal Series and (3) Temporal Underground Neural Networks (ANNT). A Temporal Neural Networks (ANNT) was obtained, using recursive corrections in demand balancing by attendant performance. Using these technologies, a more accurate performance forecast to estimates attendants work was achieved in order to obtain a more realistic operational planning.

Keywords

PPP · Public services · Corporate governance · IT approach

36.1 Introduction

Throughout its existence, Shopping do Cidadão (SC) has organized and developed around the following guidelines: (1) Constantly refined corporate governance; (2) Reduction of operating expenses through the efficiency of standardized and certified procedures; (3) Management based on quantitative and qualitative controls through service level indicators; (4) Reduction of deadlines and costs in an implantation and management of new plants; (5) Productivity optimization in the business operation; (6) Search for customer satisfaction [1], using his own methodology.

Therefore, it enabled the staff reallocation calculations and attendants exchange between service lines dynamically. As a side effect, these optimization calculations use an Installed Capacity identification of service rendering in the CA production lines, providing a smaller deviation between plans and realizations. In practice, with the same small number of people, using these methodologies, the same

D. A. Montini (✉) · G. R. Matuck
Brazilian Aeronautics Institute of Technology (ITA), São José dos Campos, Brazil

D. D. Fernandes
Federal Institute of Education, Science and Technology of São Paulo (IFSP), Campinas, Brazil

A. A. Montini
Department of Administration, University of São Paulo (USP), São Paulo, Brazil

F. Graton · P. Ripari
Shopping do Cidadão, São Paulo, Brazil

F. de Sousa Pinto
China Construction Bank, São Paulo, Brazil

© Springer International Publishing AG, part of Springer Nature 2018
S. Latifi (ed.), *Information Technology – New Generations*, Advances in Intelligent Systems and Computing 738,
https://doi.org/10.1007/978-3-319-77028-4_36

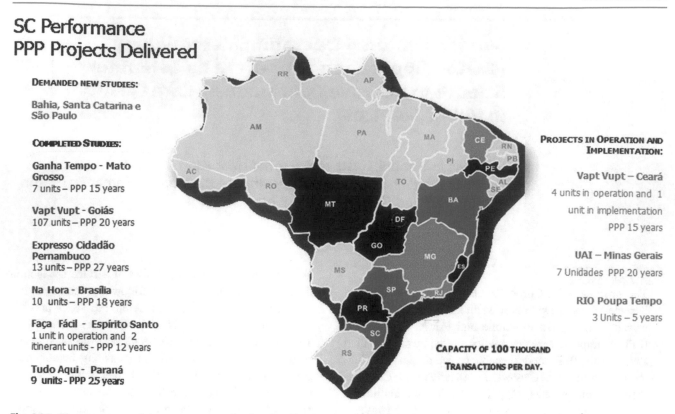

SC Performance PPP Projects Delivered

DEMANDED NEW STUDIES:

Bahia, Santa Catarina e São Paulo

COMPLETED STUDIES:

Ganha Tempo - Mato Grosso
7 units – PPP 15 years

Vapt Vupt - Goiás
107 units – PPP 20 years

Expresso Cidadão Pernambuco
13 units – PPP 27 years

Na Hora - Brasília
10 units – PPP 18 years

Faça Fácil - Espírito Santo
1 unit in operation and 2 itinerant units - PPP 12 years

Tudo Aqui - Paraná
9 units - PPP 25 years

PROJECTS IN OPERATION AND IMPLEMENTATION:

Vapt Vupt – Ceará
4 units in operation and 1 unit in implementation
PPP 15 years

UAI – Minas Gerais
7 Unidades PPP 20 years

RIO Poupa Tempo
3 Units – 5 years

CAPACITY OF 100 THOUSAND TRANSACTIONS PER DAY.

Fig. 36.1 The company performance map operating in a Brazil national territory [1]

demand decreasing was accomplished with a less Average Wait Time (TME) and Average Service Time (TMA) over operation than previous years. Therefore, a MOCA robustness by Shopping do Cidadão (SC) was verified through results achieved by PCO Optimization in CAs over last years.

36.1.1 The Company Shopping Do Cidadão

Founded in 2006, SC is a company specialized in: (1) developing, (2) deployment, and (3) operating Call Centers (CAs) for public citizen's services in Brazil. The Fig. 36.1 represents a performance verification in national territory.

The company's objective is to act with Government in public services evolution, providing to population with agile and quality structures, aiming a better approximation between State and each Citizen [1]. Based on these guidelines, in order to meet the needs of a citizen, new CA projects were developed to improve the progressive management model, aiming at a continuous improvement of service delivery by governments [1].

36.1.2 Operations Strategy

The managers guided and organized their resources for the company's objectives, as well as to meet the strategies

of the operation, using: (1) concepts, (2) models and (3) proven experiences in multinational companies, industry, and Brazilian third sector [1].

The feasibility and practical consistency of Planning and Control of Operations (PCO) strategy [2] was applied through a Service-Oriented Operation Methodology (MOCA) [2], being a basis for NBR ISO 9001:2008 certification [3].

The independent mechanism that verifies an implementation effectiveness of MOCA's strategic guidelines is a quality certification, for example ISO 9001:2008 [3]. This mechanism aims to identify whether contracts and agreements between the parties, for example: Public Private Partnership (PPP), are being: (1) maintained, (2) planned, (3) executed, (4) controlled, (5) corrected, and (6) adapted over time to meet customer needs [3].

36.1.3 Business Plan Templates

An adequate financial estimation is a fundamental tool, and practical application of this in administrative process determines how much each PPP can be more economical for; (1) Countries; (2) States; and (3) Cities; maintaining the same service level provided. Each PPP needs Business Plans with efficient and effective economic-financial fundamentals to enable products development or services effectively [1].

SC uses various business plan templates to support its PPP projects, containing: (1) Financial, (2) Accounting, (3) Tax, (4) Technological, (5) Management, and (6) Operational plans. These fundamentals application were integrated in their projects and it was a vital importance for an investment maintenance programs contracted by governments in short, medium, and long term [1].

36.1.4 Internal Communication Channels

The internal communication channels are the ways and means with instructions are transmitted to operation staff [3]. Each channel has its own definitions and purposes to enable a continuous alignment between PPP parts. In this context, MOCA's main internal communication channels are: (1) Internal satisfaction survey, (2) External satisfaction survey, (3) Monthly Accountability Meetings, (4) Results, and Performance Analysis meetings, (5) Ombudsman's office, (6) Internal, and (7) External Audits. The use of several communication channels makes possible a model improvement in a comprehensive and multidisciplinary way over time [1].

36.1.5 Constant New Opportunities Perceptions

Each new project has different characteristics. In each new partnership, MOCA provides support for PPPs elaboration with specific needs. In this case, this methodology was organized around some disciplines and technical projects bases, aiming to implement adjusted solutions for each new business demand [1].

With a society's evolution, each new project contains new business and technological challenges [1]. In this scenario, SC developed MOCA, content adaptive elements to meet new and more sophisticated CA demands. Therefore, this methodology is scalable and reconfigured in each new PPP project.

36.1.6 IT Tools for Operation Maintenance

Information technology (IT) is PPP management tool that incorporates new technologies, such as Enterprise Integrated Management Systems (SIGE), Enterprise Resource Planning (ERP) [2, 4]. SC's ERP provides a structured transaction logs catalog, organizing them into an information flow, making it possible to track any activity from its beginning to its completion [2].

Governance in the operation [1], transparency in operation, and evidence provision of a service rendered in ERP are a corporate governance guidelines applied foundation. However, a traceability is a normative requirement described by MOCA [1, 2]. At this point, SC used its ERP to follow the calls of attendance and make feasible a part of Corporate, shown in Fig. 36.2.

36.1.7 Maintaining a Quality Standard

A quality standard maintenance in PPP projects is envisaged by processes contained use in MOCA, as well as by experience acquired by SC in a development and CA deployment [1, 2]. In general, the MOCA macro processes for structuring new PPP projects are present in Fig. 36.2.

The quality MOCA standard has been applied successfully in several Brazilian states, such as: (1) São Paulo, (2) Rio de Janeiro, (3) Minas Gerais, and (4) Ceará. However, different solutions were developed for each of these projects.

36.1.8 R&D for Continuous Improvement

Research and Development (R&D) in Brazil exists. However, research is not widely practiced in this country because operation cost and his high tax rate, when compared with some of first world countries [5].

In this context, driven by market competition, in PPP public competitions, for this reason, a solution is a need to

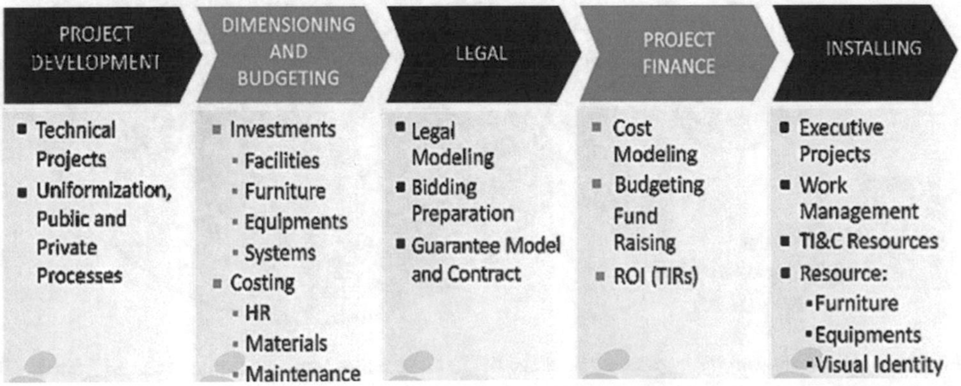

Fig. 36.2 PPP Projects structuring process. Adapted from Shopping do Cidadão Company [1]

applied a continuous improvement like ISO9001: 2008 [3]. In this case, an evolutionary methodology such as CMMI [4] that was used by SC, influenced SC that progressively refined its projects, aiming to improve its governance in PPPs through MOCA [1, 2].

The main investments sources in Brazil was made by public agencies and resources, being 83.64% public versus 16.36% financed by the business sector in 2009, according to data from the Ministry of Science and Technology [5]. Even in this environment, contrary to this trend of market context, SC makes continuous improvement in its public services provision could be made by R&D projects.

36.2   Business Model

The main governance players in SC's Business Model are: (1) Shareholders; (2) Senior management; (3) Directors board; (4) Government; and (5) Corporate Governance. In a Corporate Governance case, the main SC participants are: (1) Employees; (2) Suppliers; (3) Customers; (4) Banks; (5) Creditors; and (6) Regulatory Institutions such as Brazilian Securities and (7) Exchange Commission, Central Bank, and etc. [1].

Corporate Governance in SC was organized with Business Model supported by technological solution and a corporate ERP. In this context, this governance was supported and fed through data and information collection. The infrastructure required for this management was provided by an ERP

software, enabling a computerized governance operationalization system to meet the company's PCO [6].

In this context, this SC Business Model was implemented by an IT approach, using Information System (ERP) for Corporate Governance described in Fig. 36.3.

36.2.1 Corporate Governance

SC's Corporate Governance was defined and organized around a set of: (1) Processes; (2) Customs; (3) Policies; (4) Laws; (5) Regulations; and (6) Institutions. This set was created to regulate the way the company will attend to its projects [2].

In PPP environment, Corporate Governance is concerned with studying relationships among various actors involved. The SC's objectives and way in which these institutions work together to follow their guidelines and carry out their PCO [6].

36.2.2 Operation Model

The MOCA was inserted in an operation model, represented in Fig. 36.3, which defines for SC main decision operational points. These points required by MOCA were necessary to allow the operation dimensioning most precise, through the production lines of its service applications [1].

IT Approach

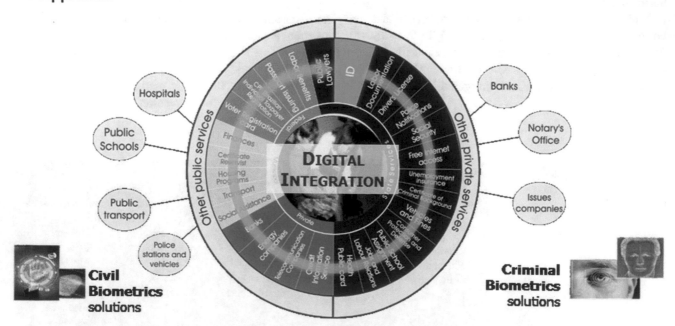

Fig. 36.3 Technological infrastructure to enable a PCO Governance implementation. Adapted from the Shopping do Cidadão [1]

In this case, the use of MOCA approach provides elements like (1) Statistical use for an Average data Time of Attendance (TMA), (2) Data classification by Artificial Neural Networks (ANNs) and (3) Time Series Analysis.

This set provides a daily sizing and a more precise for service units [1]. CA managers should calibrate configurations on their service production lines regularly to optimize their planning according to these more accurate scales.

36.2.2.1 Planning

O MOCA foi inserido em um Modelo de Operação, representado na Figura 3, que define um planejamento de demanda principal de SC. Esse planejamento é uma rotina mensal realizada por gerentes de unidade de cada CA [1]. This planning serves to prepare resources as (1) Inputs, (2) People, (3) Machines, (4) Equipment, (5) Processes, and (6) Service schedules to planning the CA operation to provide organized public services [1].

36.2.2.2 Sizing of Operational Demands

The monthly planning phase finalization work routines occurs from a daily sizing demand. Each sizing demand comes from each governmental service department in each CA. This dimensioning phase uses quantitative methods, containing those obtained by descriptive statistics, in order to establish means to enable estimated daily demands calculations for each CA [1].

36.2.2.3 MOCA Operational Control

Operational Control provides production data use from ERP databases. This use of data was fundamental for Indicators Time of Attendance (TMA) accounting and Average Time of Wait (TME).

In this case, these indicators were foreseen in contract and need to be monitored monthly in order to render accounts for the Federal Government [1].

36.2.3 MOCA Information Structure

A MOCA information structure is an ERP called Management Information Systems (SIGA) that provides information for databases supply and feeds PCO process [1].

36.2.4 MOCA

The Service-Focused Operation Methodology (MOCA) is a set of processes that relate the activities required to enable the Quality Management System (QMS), as recommended by ISO9001: 2008 [3]. The MOCA serves to make Operation Model feasible [2]. In this context, the relationships between MOCA processes was present in Fig. 36.4.

36.3 PCO Optimization

The SC defines Operational Planning and Control Optimization (PCO) in CA service production lines as identification for the best employee's composition, using human performance indicators obtained during the activities execution. Therefore, some errors between planned and realized of its activities converged to zero.

36.3.1 PCO Strategy for Customers Services

The OCP strategy was developed to apply demand PPP requirements for services through specialized computational algorithm implementation. From this point, data and information collection was performed to provide the calculations and estimates, using data stored in their ERP. These usage estimates served to provide a smaller deviation, between planned and realized, being identified at the end of this PCO estimation process [4]. In practice, this process serves to identify smaller error in people allocation versus daily services needs [1].

36.3.2 Methodology Developed

The research methodology developed in the SC was a systematic case studies application, reapplied in each new service production line. An application for this research methodology protocol needs was restarted in each new case study [4].

From scenario changes, the following goals need to be solved with each new round for success of this sizing protocol. Therefore, the following steps need to be redone:

1. Choose an application domain to be studied;
2. Restrict an action scope;
3. Choose some reference models for a domain;
4. Algorithmize a scope for chosen activities;
5. Standardize and stabilize development environment variables;
6. Formalize an Information System;
7. Develop a computational model for Planning Optimization;
8. Make an estimate based on the business system;
9. Perform simulations and tests.

36.3.2.1 PCO Algorithm

In order to systematize planning and control activities, the PCO area of the SC developed a PCO algorithm to perform these activities that each manager usually had to do in their daily life [4].

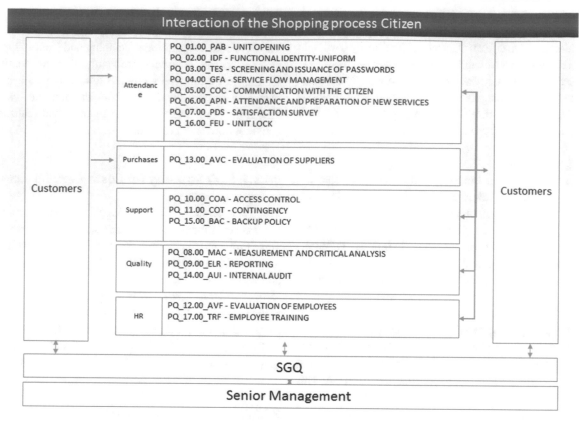

Fig. 36.4 The QMS processes relationship in MOCA, according to ISO9001:2008 criteria. Adapted from MOCA [2]

In this case, this PCO SC algorithm consists in performing activities set, being proposed as follows: (1) ERP parameterization in each government representative; (2) Data collection; (3) Tabulation; (4) Descriptive Statistics calculation; (5) SPC card calculation; (6) Time Series Neural Network to estimate demand for the period, (7) Services demand sizing; (8) Service production line sizing; (9) People allocation; (10) Adequacy the planning verification and validation; and (11) Correction. When deviation is greater than expected, this process must be restarted and resized.

36.3.3 New Concepts in PPP Projects Applications

New concepts and technologies application for PPP projects are a progressive way to use innovations and to improve citizens accessibility, satisfaction or citizen support [1]. For example, SC company in technological innovation dimension can use several quantitative methods to address this situation [2].

Quantitative methods are a fundamental part for knowledge acquisition process in large information volume database. In this context, a reality understanding was provided by data translation into information, and this methodology was supported by the descriptive statistics [7],

possible to be applied in SC's ERP software in a production environment.

MOCA aims to structure its processes to provide new Technologies' use, such as quantitative methods; to improve calculations and statistical reports, containing some studied phenomena results [5].

36.3.3.1 Quantitative Methods

Quantitative methods provide analyzes numerical, such as descriptive statistics of data performed, being frequently used during service rendering production. It happens using sampled or population data to present behavior patterns. At this point, managerial decisions about operation control can be made [2, 5].

36.3.3.2 Statistical Process Control

Statistical Process Control (SPC) provides an understanding in more structured and defined way than subjective impression [3]. Therefore, by graphical representations, the data consolidations and information provided by statistics facilitate understanding [5]. A Control Chart use example was done, and this analysis are present in Fig. 36.5.

Figure 36.5 shows SPC analysis where defined for each parameterized ERP server indicator, to enable that historical were collected in a central office, using following data parameters: (1) State; (2) City; (3) Customer Service Center;

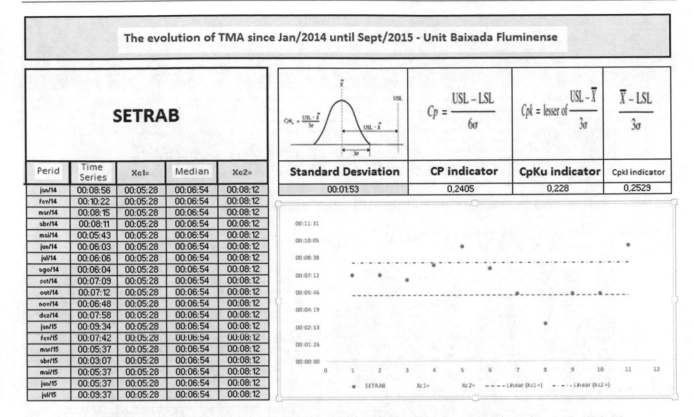

Fig. 36.5 CEP Chart for Attendance Time (TMA) from SETRAB Public Organ—Jan./14 to Sept./15—Baixada Fluminense Unit [1]

(4) Time period; (5) Indicators [1]. In this context, SC uses ERP data to supply the following TMA and TME indicators provided in contract [1] aiming to follow indicators oscillations [5].

The SPC needs Control Chart to make sense of the average data usage of all CA attendants who worked on that service [1]. According to Fig. 36.5, the parameters used to exemplify and illustrated in SPC Chart were: (1) Attendance Time Indicator (TMA); (2) SETRAB body; (3) Period Jan./14 to Sep./15; (4) Fluminense Baixada unit [1].

36.3.3.3 Times Series

The time series is realizations (observations) sequence for variable over time. Thus, this series are point's sequence (numerical data) in successive order, occurring generally at uniform intervals [7].

The SC has in its ERP several Times Series models for various governmental service department, containing many set of data sequences that were collected at regular intervals for several periods.

Therefore, Time Series techniques can be applied systematically and parameterized in automated classification and identification process [7], Therefore, these properties are presented in Fig. 36.6.

The data, sampled from this governmental service department in ERP, submitted to statistical analysis to identify

automatically: (1) SPC Control Chart; (2) Limits calculation; and (3) Database preparation for Time Series algorithms, in order to identify which series will return lowest Mean Absolute Deviation (MAD).

However, it is critical to see data behavior by example way. Figure 36.7 shows earlier selection Temporal Series phase example, containing TMA indicator for SETRAB public organ in Baixada Fluminense unit [1].

A ANN Times Series (ANNT) system has been developed, containing observations sequences over time for TMA indicator, being collected in uniform intervals over time series period. This system developed to find time series model that best fit phenomenon in question [8].

The identification process for best temporal model is data sampled was used obtained from ERP, after chosen public organ parameter and submit them to this Time Series system tabulation present in Fig. 36.6.

After obtaining structured data, and temporal ANN system preparation [8], a classification containing the month that is outside the CEP limits, the ANNT system automatically identifies, among a set of available algorithms, the algorithm that returns the lowest MAD [9].

Figure 36.7 presents the ANNT interface, containing these systematized automatic selection processes consolidated analysis to identify the most appropriate time series (TMA) scenario. In that case, an identification on SETRAB

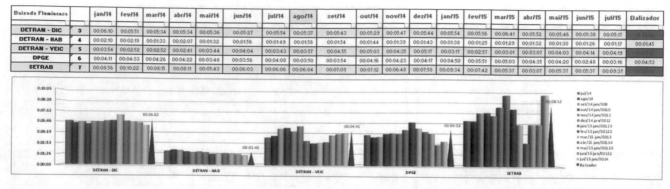

Baixada Fluminense		jan/14	fev/14	mar/14	abr/14	mai/14	jun/14	jul/14	ago/14	set/14	out/14	nov/14	dez/14	jan/15	fev/15	mar/15	abr/15	mai/15	jun/15	jul/15	Balizador
DETRAN - DIC	3	00:06:10	00:05:51	00:05:34	00:05:34	00:05:36	00:05:27	00:05:54	00:05:37	00:05:43	00:05:29	00:05:47	00:05:44	00:05:54	00:05:56	00:06:41	00:05:52	00:05:46	00:05:38	00:05:17	
DETRAN - HAB	4	00:02:10	00:02:19	00:01:33	00:02:07	00:01:32	00:01:56	00:01:43	00:01:58	00:01:54	00:01:44	00:01:39	00:01:43	00:01:38	00:01:25	00:01:23	00:01:32	00:01:30	00:01:26	00:01:17	00:01:45
DETRAN - VEIC	5	00:03:54	00:02:52	00:02:52	00:02:41	00:03:44	00:04:04	00:03:43	00:03:57	00:04:55	00:05:03	00:04:35	00:05:17	00:03:17	00:02:57	00:03:01	00:03:07	00:04:03	00:04:14	00:04:19	
DPGE	6	00:04:11	00:04:33	00:04:26	00:04:22	00:03:48	00:03:56	00:04:08	00:03:50	00:03:54	00:04:16	00:04:23	00:04:17	00:04:50	00:05:51	00:05:03	00:04:35	00:04:20	00:02:48	00:03:16	00:04:53
SETRAB	7	00:08:56	00:10:22	00:08:15	00:08:11	00:05:43	00:06:03	00:06:06	00:06:04	00:07:03	00:07:12	00:06:48	00:07:58	00:09:34	00:07:42	00:05:37	00:03:07	00:05:37	00:05:37	00:03:37	

Fig. 36.6 Average Attendance Evolution (TMA) in Time Series—1/14 to 7/15—Baixada Fluminense unit. Adapted from MOCA [1]

18.7.2 Forecasting methods for time series models: no trend and no seasonality:

Trend	Seasonality	Plan	Model	MAD 3 0,000000	Resuts 12 - Prediction model for Double exponential smoothing Method of H
No trend	No Seasonality	0-MMS	0 -Modelo de Média Móvel Simples (MMS)	0,000000	
No trend	No Seasonality	1-MME	1 - Enveloped moving average model (MMES)	0,000002	
No trend	No Seasonality	2-MMR	2 - Média Móvel Recorrente (MMR)	2,239939	
No trend	No Seasonality	3-MME	3 - Exponential Moving Average (MME)	0,827068	
No trend	No Seasonality	4-MMEP	4 - Pure Exponential Moving Average (MMEP)	0,000123	
No trend	No Seasonality	5-MMEV	5 - Exponential moving average with Volatility (MMEV)	0,015025	
No trend	No Seasonality	6-MMSES	6 - Moving average model with Simple Exponential Smoothing (MMSES)	0,999720	
No trend	No Seasonality	7-MMO	7 - Olympic moving average model (MMO)	0,000000	
No trend	No Seasonality	8-MMP	8 - Weighted Moving Average (MMP)	0,000026	
No trend	No Seasonality	9-MMPV	9 - Volume-Weighted moving average (MMPV)	0,000002	
No trend	No Seasonality	10-MMT	10 - Triangular Moving Average (MMT)	0,000005	

18.7.3 Forecasting methods for time series models with no trend and Seasonality

Com trend	No Seasonality	11-MMD	11 -Forecasting model with Double moving average (MPMMD)	0,000178	
Com trend	No Seasonality	12-MPAEDMH	12 - Prediction model for Double exponential smoothing Method of Holt (MPAEDMH)	0,000000	12 - Prediction model for Double exponential smoothing Method of Holt
Com trend	No Seasonality	13-MPAEDMB	13 - Prediction model for Double exponential smoothing (Brown method)	0,000085	

18.7.4 Forecasting methods for time series models without Trend and Seasonality

No trend	Com Seasonality	14-MMSM	14 - Moving average model with Multiplicative Seasonality (MMSM)	0,041435	
No trend	Com Seasonality	15-MPSA	15 - Forecast model with Additive Seasonal (MPSA)	100000,000000	

18.7.5 Forecasting methods for time series with Seasonality and Trend

Com trend	Com Seasonality	16-MMMSEH	16 - Moving average Exponential Smoothing method for HoltWinters (MMMSEH)	0,172248	
Com trend	Com Seasonality	17-MMMSET	17 - Moving average Method Triple Exponential Smoothing (MMMSET)	0,000000	
Com trend	Com Seasonality	18-MMEV	18 - Média Móvel Exponencial com Volatilidade (MMEV)	0,999704	
Com trend	Com Seasonality	19-MMSM	19 - Média Móvel com Sazonalidade Multiplicativo (HoltWinters) (MMSM)	43704,921417	
Com trend	Com Seasonality	20-MSAHW	20-MSAHW 20 - Modelo de Previsão com Sazonalidade Aditiva (HoltWinters) (MSAH	0,000001	

Fig. 36.7 The most appropriate Temporal Series (TMA) selection for SETRAB public service department for Jan./14 to Sept./15-time period scenario

public organ was done, using parameters like (1) data from January/2014 to September/2015; (2) Baixada Fluminense; (3) Rio de Janeiro estate [1].

An Jan./14 to Sept./15 period scenario was defined, after an identification of the best Time Series model for SETRAB governmental service department. After this fundamental definition, a PCO algorithm an automation program was run to identify the best time series [1], using mathematical model, present in Fig. 36.7.

To have a computational solution developed like this, it's critical to correct services demands to support allocation, predict and correct demand spikes in advance, in order to correct service production line capacity CA line. The proposed model result with Time Series and lowest MAD presented in Fig. 36.8, content a computational interface prototype.

36.3.3.4 Planning Optimization

Planning optimization in the CA was performed, using an estimation obtained through an automatic classification and ANNT system selection [10], being present in Fig. 36.8.

In this optimization stage, the average TMA sector data was used to enable an agile comparison. This method estimates a demand design, using a Planning Optimization system for a services production line.

After crossing information, CA manager simulates current employee's allocation in service production line to verify if current capacity will be sufficient to meet demand projected for the CA, using specified time period parameters.

In Fig. 36.9, a performance simulation example was shown to search in a Planning Optimization for service production line, content a report and some regularly parameters used. If manager notes that an allocated staff will not be able to meet demand, then managers can internally relocate resources to meet new service demands.

12 - Prediction model for Double exponential smoothing Method of Holt (MPAEDMH)

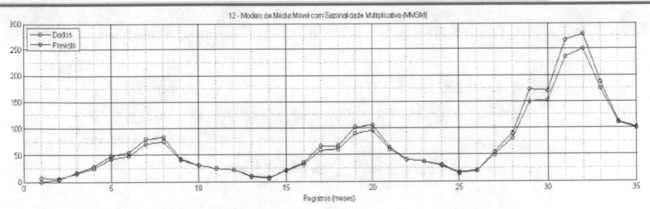

Fig. 36.8 Selection automation pilot and more appropriate automated Temporal Series (TMA) classification. Adapted from SC [1]

Fig. 36.9 The evolution of services managed by Shopping do Cidadão. Adapted from Shopping do Cidadão [1]

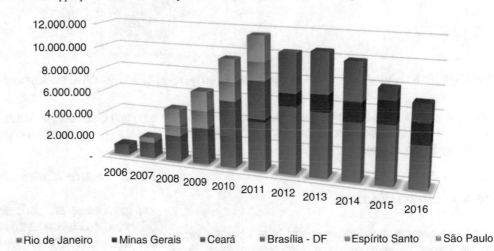

■ Rio de Janeiro ■ Minas Gerais ■ Ceará ■ Brasília - DF ■ Espírito Santo ■ São Paulo

36.4 Company's Program Evaluation

After new technologies use and his potential presentation, some advantages were described in this section. For example, the use of ERP data observed in PPP projects was accomplished, comparing public services among themselves.

36.4.1 Main Advantages in MOCA Implementation

With the MOCA application use, some advantages obtained during this process was described:

(a) New technologies incorporation.
(b) Integration between Public and Private Service, performing management and operation based on services level agreement.

(c) Training and continuing services provider's education, preserving functions in which public servant is indispensable.
(d) Expansion speed: private partner has greater flexibility for demands.
(e) Longer term for investment financing.
(f) Quality service duration with a maintenance and installed resources updating.
(g) Governance conducive to Research and Development (R&D) environment applied to business operation, such as Service Planning Optimization with dynamic resource allocations, aiming to reducing fixed operation costs.

36.4.2 Customer Service

The evolution of the results of the services managed by the SC was the summary of the consolidated activities; being carried out in the last decade [1]. The graph of Fig. 36.10

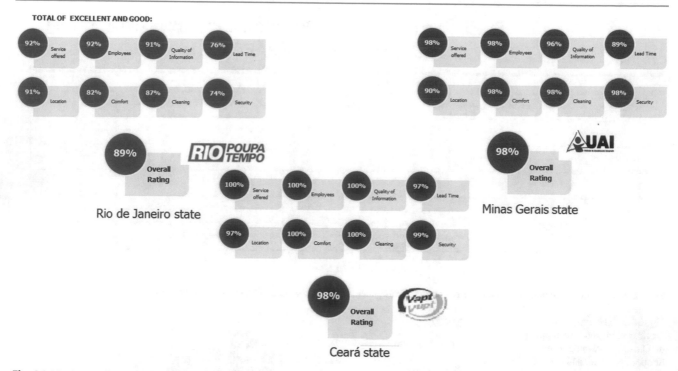

Fig. 36.10 Annual Consolidated 2016—Customer Satisfaction Survey in RJ, MG and CE states. Adapted from SC [1]

shows a volume of 81 million services performed, which demonstrates the robustness of the MOCA methodology, according to the integrated corporate solution applied.

36.4.3 Results Obtained

A way to observe quantitative results is to know the qualitative results, containing the client's vision about these services rendered. In this case, the satisfaction survey results in relation to services rendered in 2016 by the company Shopping do Cidadão are present in Fig. 36.10. This Figure presents a survey data that content consolidated result from MOCA activities and the several PPPs carried out in Brazilian national territory [1].

36.5 Conclusion

The Shopping do Cidadão company participates in more than 20 Citizen Assistance Center projects in different states with transparency, speed, and efficiency [1], providing an estimated saving for Brazilian state of 25%, maintaining a satisfaction pattern above of average for public service in general, over last 11 years.

The results obtained by MOCA use in PPP were obtained from constants results refinement for conducting its projects. A continuous effort to implement Optimization of its Plan-

ning and Operational Control occurred, being done by an internal Research and Development dedication of its teams [1].

36.5.1 Future Works

The governance of Public Service and Private Partnerships (PPP) projects use scientific and experimental research and development (R&D) to carry out Proof of concepts (PoC). Each new POC involves an integration with several technologies protocol [1] and this is a continuous movement.

However, research and development (R&D) in Brazil is still obscure matter and applied resources funding is not a well-resolved clear situation, needing to be more mature in order for the parties involved to make news quantitative and qualitative improvements leaps, as is already case in other countries.

The next development activities will follow in conception, formulation, modeling, algorithmization, Management Information Systems (IMS) prototyping, monitoring, analysis, training, deployment, evaluation, process inspection, final inspections, partnerships, project management review, and audit [4]. Even in an adverse Brazilian scenario, in order to reach continuously improve their quality standards in public and private services provision.

General Considerations Collaboration with Research institutes is an important point for foundation and continuous Research and Development (R&D) projects improvement.

Institutions and research groups such as Brazilian Technological Institute of Aeronautics, Technological Institute of Aeronautics (ITA), Brazilian Faculdade de Economia e Administração (FEA) of USP, and Fundação do Instituto de Administração (FIA) have contributed to specialized works advancement in this research field.

References

1. Shopping do Cidadão Ltda, Construindo exemplos na prestação de serviços públicos (2017) [Online], http://www.shopcidadao.com.br. Accessed 15 Apr 2017
2. N. Slack, S. Chambers, R. Johnston, *Operations Management* (Atlas, São Paulo, 1996)
3. ABNT, *NBR ISO 9001:2008 - Sistemas de Gestão da Qualidade: diretrizes para a melhoria de desempenho* (Rio de Janeiro, 2008)
4. D.A. Montini, *Modelo de Agente Inteligente para Otimização de Planejamento em Linhas de Produção de software* (São José dos Campos, Brazil, 2014)
5. BRASIL, Ministérios da Ciência e Tecnologia, "Principais Resultados" (2010) [Online], http://www.mct.gov.br/html/objects/_downloadblob.php?cod_blob=212232. Accessed 15 Apr 2017
6. IBGC, Governança Corporativa (2015) [Online], http://www.ibgc.org.br/index.php/governanca/governanca-corporativa. Accessed 28 Apr 2017
7. D.R. Anderson, D.J. Sweeney, T.A. Williams, *Statistics for Business and Economics*, 11th edn. (Cengage Learning, Cincinnati, 2011)
8. J.S. Oakland, R.R. Followell, *Statistical Process Control*, 5th edn. (Elsevier, Oxford, MA, 2003)
9. Shopping do Cidadão Ltda, Metodologia de Operação Centrada em Atendimento (MOCA) (2017) [Online], http://www.shopcidadao.com.br. Accessed 15 Apr 2017
10. S. Haykin, *Neural Networks: A Comprehensive Foundation* (Prentice Hall, 1999)

Improving Agile Software Development with Domain Ontologies

Pedro Lopes de Souza, Antonio Francisco do Prado, Wanderley Lopes de Souza, Sissi Marilia dos Santos Forghieri Pereira, and Luís Ferreira Pires

Abstract

In this paper we propose to apply domain ontologies in agile software development to reduce the ambiguity caused by using natural language as ubiquitous language to report user stories. To justify and demonstrate our approach, we present a case study that combines Scrum and Behaviour-Driven Development (BDD) in the development of an educational support system, which was built to support the activities of the Medicine Programme of Federal University of São Carlos (UFSCar) in Brazil. Starting from a reference ontology for the Higher Education domain, we gradually specialized this ontology for this programme. Since we selected the Evaluation Management module of this system for our case study, we applied the Evaluation Process Ontology to that programme, and defined user stories to identify the feature set to be implemented. For evaluation and validation purposes, we assessed the quality of all ontologies used in this work according to structural and functional dimensions.

Keywords

Ontology · PBL · LMS · Scrum · BDD

P. L. de Souza (✉) · A. F. do Prado · W. L. de Souza
Department of Computing, Federal University of São Carlos, São Paulo, Brazil

S. M. dos Santos Forghieri Pereira
Department of Medicine, Federal University of São Carlos, São Paulo, Brazil

L. F. Pires
Department of Electrical Engineering, Mathematics, and Computer Science, University of Twente, Enschede, The Netherlands

37.1 Introduction

Agile software development requires iterative development methodologies, like e.g., Scrum [1], in which requirements and solutions evolve through collaboration between clients and developers. Scrum prescribes *sprint reviews*, which are development team meetings, and the role of *Product Owner (PO)* to plan and evaluate sprints. A list of prioritised requirements, named *product backlog*, is created in a *sprint planning meeting*, and in each sprint the development team decide which requirements should be addressed, and then create a *sprint backlog* that contains the tasks to be performed during that sprint.

Behaviour-Driven Development (BDD) [2] is a development methodology based on the principle that "*stakeholders and developers should refer to the same system in the same way.*" This requires a ubiquitous language understandable by all developers, and that enables executable granular specifications of the system's behaviour and testing.

Ontologies are used in the design of Information Systems (IS) in several domains, with potential benefits due to their mathematical rigour. According to Guarino [3], an ontology can impact an IS both in the *temporal dimension*, depending whether it is used at design time and/or runtime, and in the *structural dimension* when it affects the main IS components.

The Medicine Programme of the Federal University of São Carlos (UFSCar) in Brazil follows a socio-constructivist educational approach, and employs active learning methodologies such as Problem-Based Learning (PBL) [4]. EAMS-CBALM (Educational and Academic Management System for Courses Based on Active Learning Methodologies, [5]) is a system developed to provide computational support for these learning methodologies. EAMS-CBALM was developed using Scrum, and during its development it was often necessary to redefine system behaviour scenarios, and consequently the product backlog items, due to misunderstanding of the stories reported by the PO. In addition, test suites defined for this system were incomplete and not always properly covered the system requirements.

Inspired by these problems, we defined the following research questions: (a) *"How to improve communication among PO and developers?"*, and (b) *"How to eliminate the ambiguities inherent to natural languages when reporting user stories?"* These questions led to two hypotheses: (1) combining BDD with Scrum can substantially improve communication, and (2) ontologies can eliminate natural language ambiguities. We validated hypothesis (1) in [6] with a case study using EAMS-CBALM, by proposing a ubiquitous language to define BDD scenarios and acceptance tests, allowing the PO to properly communicate with the development team members. This paper focuses on hypothesis (2), by employing domain ontologies as ubiquitous language for software development, and it is further structured as follows: Sect. 37.2 discusses related work; Sect. 37.3 introduces a reference ontology for the Higher Education domain; Sect. 37.4 presents the UFSCar ontology; Sect. 37.5 reports on our case study; and Sect. 37.6 presents some final remarks.

37.2 Related Work

In our systematic literature review of ontologies and agile software methodologies, we found some developments that combine these methodologies to improve software development.

In [7], the OntoSoft agile process is proposed, which associates practices of Software Engineering, Ontology Engineering and Scrum for improving the collaboration between software and ontology engineers. This process provides a set of guidelines for defining activities, tasks, roles, and artefacts to develop ontology-based software. OntoSoft was applied for developing an ontology-based application to map and recommend real estates.

An approach is presented in [8] to help team members perform more efficiently their daily tasks according to a specific process. This approach is based on the K-CRIO ontology for business processes modelling and on a multi-agent system for providing intelligent assistance to workers.

In [9], the Quality User Story (QUS) framework is proposed for ensuring the quality of agile requirements expressed as user stories. QUS contains 13 criteria that determine the quality of user stories in terms of syntax, semantics, and pragmatics. Based on QUS, the Automatic Quality User Story Artisan (AQUSA) tool was built to detect QUS quality criteria violations, and to improve user stories.

An ontological model is introduced in [10] to support scenario description and to test functional requirements of interactive systems. This model was developed based on BDD principles, describing user behaviours when interacting with User Interface (UI) elements in a scenario-based approach. Once described in the ontology, behaviours can be freely reused to write new scenarios in natural language, providing test automation. A case study is presented for the flight tickets e-commerce domain, where ontology-based tools were used to support the assessment of evolutionary prototypes and final UIs.

All these related developments employ ontologies for specific purposes: for boosting the collaboration among software and ontology engineers, for modelling the Scrum development process, for extracting semantic information to improve user stories, and to support test automation. In our work, in contrast, we use ontologies in a broader context, starting from a reference ontology for a given domain, and gradually specializing it to be used in the agile software development for that domain.

37.3 Ontologies

An ontology can be classified according to its generality and dependence levels in: (a) *Top-level ontology*, describes general concepts (e.g., Object, Property) that are independent of a particular domain; (b) *Domain ontology* describes the vocabulary related to a generic domain (e.g., Medicine, Programme) by specializing terms introduced in the top-level ontology; (c) *Task ontology* describes the vocabulary related to a generic task (e.g., Diagnosing, Lecturing), by specializing terms introduced in the top-level ontology; and (d) *Application ontology* describes concepts that depend on a particular domain and task (e.g., the *roles* played by domain entities while performing the activity of *given a lecture*), which are specializations of the related ontologies [3].

A top-level ontology aims at supporting semantic interoperability among domain ontologies. In some situations, domain ontologies may have to be merged, and if they are derived from the same top-level ontology this can be automated. Unfortunately, most of the available domain ontologies are not derived from the same top-level ontology, and different domain perceptions, usage intentions, and languages give rise to incompatible application ontologies in the same domain. To deal with these problems, application ontologies have to be defined based on a reference domain ontology.

Higher Education Reference Ontology (HERO) [11] was defined to provide consensual knowledge of the university domain. HERO describes several aspects of this domain, such as organizational structure, staff, and income. Based on HERO key concepts and according to the higher education areas described by Brazilian National Council for Scientific and Technological Development (CNPq), we extended this reference ontology to describe Brazilian universities, as shown in Fig. 37.1.

Fig. 37.1 HERO (from [11]) with CNPq areas

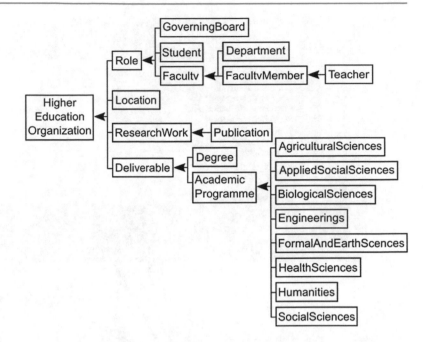

37.4 UFSCar Ontologies

We applied the concepts shown in Fig. 37.1 to define an ontology that represents all the UFSCar programmes. Figure 37.2 depicts an excerpt of this ontology in OWLViz/Protégé [12], showing the 8 CNPq large educational areas, and the 10 UFSCar programmes in the Health Sciences area.

37.4.1 UFSCar Medicine Programme

Most Brazilian universities employ teaching-learning methodologies based on classic frontal lectures, but some UFSCar programmes, like the Medicine Programme, employ active learning methodologies. Education in this programme is based on activities with no frontal lectures at all, organized in three educational units: Education Unit of Simulation of Professional Practice (EUSPP), Education Unit of Professional Practice (EUPP), and Education Unit of Elective Activities (EUEA) [13]. Figure 37.3 shows an excerpt of an ontology that describes the UFSCar Medicine Programme.

The UFSCar Medicine Programme learning methodology has several educational activities, such as Problem Situation (PS), Simulation Station (SS) and Team Based Learning (TBL). All of them have learning triggers, which are problems that simulate or portray the daily activities to be performed by the students. Each trigger makes the students traverse the constructivist spiral [13], starting by identifying the problem, formulating explanations, preparing learning questions, looking for new information, building new meanings, and evaluating the process. Figure 37.4 shows an excerpt

of the UFSCar Medicine Programme ontology, focusing on its learning methodology, showing some of its educational activities and the steps of the constructivist spiral.

37.5 Case Study

Our case study concentrates on one of the EAMS-CBALM modules. This system was developed using Scrum by the TokenLab commercial company, in collaboration with the Ubiquitous Computing Group (UCG) and Medicine Department (DMed) of UFSCar, and the Teaching and Research Institute (TRI) of the Sírio-Libanês Hospital (SLH).

During this development, weekly sprint meetings were held at TokenLab, and monthly sprint review meetings were held at TRI/SLH. During the TokenLab meetings, the PO (a teacher of the UFSCar Medicine Programme) reported user stories informally in Portuguese, describing activities to be performed by the EAMS-CBALM, and system requirements were also captured and specified in Portuguese. Using these specifications, the developers defined system behaviour scenarios and implemented screen pages, which were discussed at the next meeting. 109 hours have been spent with these meetings, in which the CBALM teaching-learning process was scrutinised, resulting in the definition of the functional and non-functional system requirements, and system architecture [6].

The Evaluation Management module of EAMS-CBALM generated the most controversies between PO and developers. This module had 14 functional requirements and although the scenarios of the "Evaluation Instrument Register" requirement have been redone several times, its final

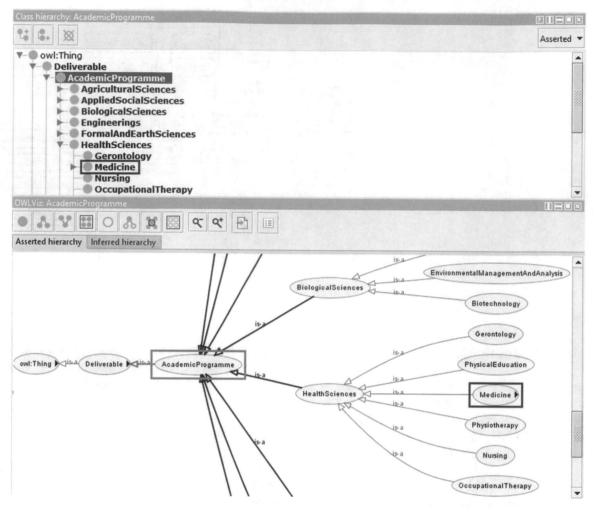

Fig. 37.2 UFSCar ontology (in OWLViz)

Fig. 37.3 UFSCar Medicine
Programme ontology

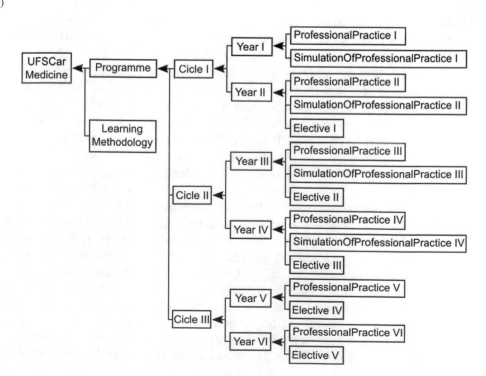

Fig. 37.4 Constructivist spiral steps and educational activities of UFSCar Medicine Programme ontology

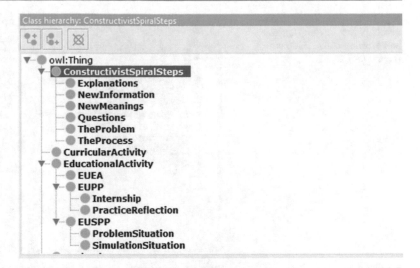

implementation did not fully satisfy the PO. This module was already selected in [6] to validate hypothesis (1) and is used here again to validate hypothesis (2).

37.5.1 Evaluation Process Ontology

The student evaluation process of the UFSCar Medicine Programme is quite peculiar and complex. Evaluations are performed by all people involved in the educational activities [13]. There are two evaluation types, formative and summative, and the results are "satisfactory," "unsatisfactory" or "needs improvement." In the latter case, the student must execute an improvement plan proposed by the teacher, and is then re-evaluated. Evaluations are consolidated by applying six instruments types:

(a) Performance Assessment of the Teaching-Learning Process (PATLP): teacher evaluates the student (formative) in three steps, teacher evaluation, classmate evaluation, and improvement plan;

(b) Reflective Portfolio (RP): teacher monitors each student's portfolio (formative), and students' present according to delivery dates (summative);

(c) Written Examination (WE): questions defined by the teacher, answered by the student, and then assigned by the teacher (summative). All questions must have a "satisfactory" result for the student to pass. Failed questions are considered as progress deficit and are worked out in the next WE;

(d) Progress Test (PT): multiple choice questions. Teacher monitors each student's performance (formative) and presence gives students a "satisfactory" result (summative);

(e) Objective and Structured Evaluation of Professional Performance (OSEPP): students act in clinical cases and are evaluated by the teacher similarly to WE (summative);

(f) Problems Based Exercise (PBE): assesses the student's individual ability to study and identify health needs, formulate patient and family problems, and propose a healthcare plan for a particular problem situation (formative).

Based on these instruments and [13], we defined the terminology (names, adjectives, and verbs) to be formally represented in the Evaluation Process. Figure 37.5 shows an excerpt of this ontology, where the *EducationalActivity* and *EvaluationProcess* classes model the concept of *CurricularActivity*.

Each *EducationalActivity* starts with one or more meetings, where a *Meeting* has the participation of students and teachers, each one with specific *Roles*, and triggers a *LearningTrigger*. Each *Learning Trigger* transverse the *ConstrutivistSpiralSteps*, and ends with an *EvaluationProcess*, which is consolidated by applying *EvaluationInstruments*.

Figure 37.6 shows an excerpt of the Evaluation Process ontology of the UFSCar Medicine Programme, focusing on its evaluation instruments types, and showing the PATLP instrument.

37.5.2 User Story and Scenario Ontology

In the BDD analysis phase the most expected system behaviours are identified from the business outcomes to be produced by the system. Based on them, feature sets are defined, where each feature indicates what should be accomplished to

Fig. 37.5 Evaluation Process ontology root classes (*left-side*) and *Meeting* class relations (*right-side*)

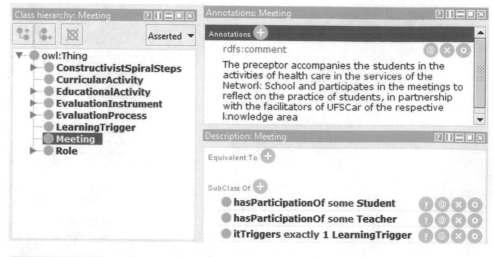

Fig. 37.6 Evaluation Process ontology with PATLP

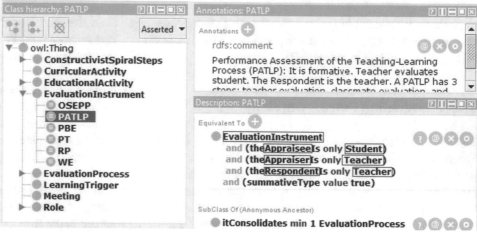

achieve a specific business outcome. When combining BDD with Scrum, the POs and developers should agree on the feature sets, and ideally define them together.

Features are expressed by user stories, describing the interactions between a user and the system. A user story should elucidate the user's role in this story, the feature desired by the user, and the benefit gained by the user if the system provides the desired feature. Due to different contexts, a user story may have different versions that will lead to different story instances (*scenarios*), which in turn should describe specific contexts and outcomes of this user story. For our case study, we have taken into account the following user story reported by the PO during the EAMS-CBALM development:

> In order for the programme coordinator to carry out a student evaluation, the six instrument types have to be previously registered. This requirement is needed because the evaluation form heading changes according to the employed instrument. When registering an instrument, the system must keep the following information: name, acronym and the relationship between who responds to the evaluation, who evaluates and who is evaluated. This last information is crucial since in conjunction with the curricular activity it defines which form type is applied when registering an evaluation.

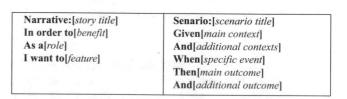

Narrative:[*story title*]	Senario:[*scenario title*]
In order to[*benefit*]	Given[*main context*]
As a[*role*]	And[*additional contexts*]
I want to[*feature*]	When[*specific event*]
	Then[*main outcome*]
	And[*additional outcome*]

Fig. 37.7 JBehave User Story and Scenario templates

BDD user stories and scenarios follow the templates described in [2], but BDD tools generally do not strictly follow these models. For example, JBehave [14] supports a slightly different user story template and the same scenario template, which are shown in Fig. 37.7. Since JBehave supports most of the BDD characteristics, it is well-accepted in the BDD community, it is open source software, and is frequently updated, we chose this tool to develop the case study reported in [6].

This scenario template is similar to an Extended Finite State Machine (EFSM) model, which was formally defined as an OWL ontology in [10]. We employed a similar EFSM model using the JBehave templates to build the User Story and Scenario ontology for our case study. There are six

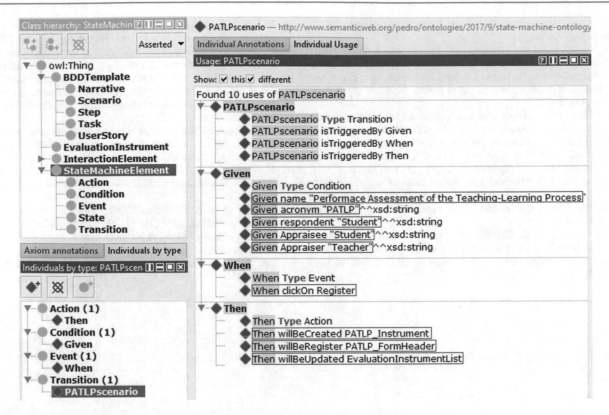

Fig. 37.8 User Story and Scenario ontology with PATLP

scenarios in our case study, one for each instrument type. Figure 37.8 shows an excerpt of this ontology for PATLP.

To validate our approach, we assessed the quality of our ontologies according to the structural and functional dimensions [15]. Structural validation considers the ontology logical structure, focusing on its syntax and formal semantics. Protégé [12] offers several ontology verification tools for detecting inconsistencies and redundancies in ontologies. For all ontologies we used the reasoners FaCT++, HermiT and Pellet, and we discovered neither inconsistencies nor redundancies on them.

Functional assessment focused on the ontologies usage. This assessment includes evaluation by domain experts, user satisfaction, task assessment, and topic assessment. Our ontologies were assessed in collaboration with our PO during development, aiming at verifying their structure, their restrictions, relations between concepts and the attributes of their concepts. The PO assessed how well these ontologies met predefined criteria, and they have been updated according to the PO suggestions.

37.6 Conclusion

In this paper, we proposed the use of domain ontologies to reduce the ambiguity introduced by using natural languages to report user stories. We validated this hypothesis by performing a case study in the context of the EAMS-

CBALM using a combination of Scrum and BDD. We started from a reference ontology, and we specialized it for the UFSCar Medicine Programme. We selected a module of this system, and used the Evaluation Process ontology of this programme with the user stories for determining the features to be developed.

This ontology provided the main terminology and its relations to the evaluation process that combined with PO user stories improved the communication between PO and developers. Furthermore, it facilitated the definition of scenarios, as well as the User Story and Scenario ontology.

The ontology presented in [10] is domain-free, and describes behaviours that report steps of scenarios performing actions on the UI. Although it is possible to reuse these steps in multiple testing scenarios, specific business behaviours of our case study had to be specified, and we had to map each term to a user interaction, and to write steps for these interactions. Since this ontology only covers UI testing, we intend to extend it to cover other aspects of software behaviour (e.g., persistence). We will also define a development process that combines Scrum, BDD, and Domain Ontologies.

References

1. K. Schwaber et al., *The Definitive Guide to Scrum: The Rules of the Game* (Scrum.Org and ScrumInc, 2016), 17 pp. https://goo.gl/SBsyUQ

2. D. North, *Introducing BDD* (Dan North & Associates, 2006). https://goo.gl/JBqmry

3. N. Guarino, Formal ontology and information systems. Front. Artif. Intell. Appl. **46**, 03–15 (1998)

4. J. Rhem, in *Problem Based Learning an Introduction*, vol. 8, no. 1 (National Teaching and Learning Forum, 1998), 07 pp. https://goo.gl/LckbVX

5. H.F. Santos et al., Augmented reality approach for knowledge visualization and production in educational and academic management system for courses based on active learning methodologies, in *Proceedings of ITNG 2016,* Advances in Intelligent Systems and Computing, vol. 448 (Springer, 2016), pp. 1113–1123

6. P.L. Souza et al., *Combining Behaviour-Driven Development with Scrum for Software Development in the Education Domain*, vol. 2 (SCITEPRESS–Science and Technology Publications Ltd, 2017), pp. 449–458

7. J.B. Machado et al., OntoSoft Process: Towards an agile process for ontology-based software, in *Proceedings of 49th Hawaii International Conference on System Sciences* (IEEE Computer Society, 2016), pp. 5813–5822

8. Y. Lin et al., Multi-Agent System for intelligent Scrum project management. Integr. Comput. Aided Eng. **22**(3), 281–296 (2015)

9. G. Lucassen et al., Improving agile requirements: the Quality User Story framework and tool. Requir. Eng. **21**(3), 283–403 (2016)

10. T. Silva et al., A behavior-based ontology for supporting automated assessment of interactive systems, in *Proceedings of 11th International Conference on Semantic Computing* (IEEE Computer Society, 2017), pp. 250–257

11. L. Zemmouchi-Ghomari et al., Process of building reference ontology for higher education, in *Proceedings of World Congress on Engineering*, vol. 3 (2013), 06 pp.

12. M. Horridge, *A Practical Guide to Building Owl Ontologies Using Protégé 4.0 and CODE Tools*, Edition 1.1 (University of Maryland, 2007)

13. UFSCar, *Curso de Medicina—CCBS Projeto Político Pedagógico* (Medicina UFSCar, 2007), 139 pp. https://goo.gl/NmWYi3

14. JBehave, *JBehave* (2015). http://jbehave.org/

15. A. Gangemi et al., in *Modelling ontology evaluation and validation*. Lecture Notes in Computer Science, vol. 4011 (2006), pp. 140–154

Danilo Douradinho Fernandes, Gustavo Ravanhani Matuck,
Denis Avila Montini, Luiz Alberto Vieira Dias, and Alessandra Avila Montini

Abstract

Artificial Neural Networks (ANN) MultiLayer Perceptron (MLP) are widely applied in a variety market segments to handle with real complex problems. The ability to deal with tasks in real time is essential in an environment that uses large volume do information available. In each new project, a decision-making system using ANN with time reduction and data processing is a key issue to test various learning algorithms; containing a variety of parameters when using this technology. From this starting point, the MLPs used data collected from a specific phenomenon and, based on statistical estimators, applied a data extraction algorithm for stratified sampling, aiming to reduce the time of ANN processing. In this context, this work proposes a Stratified Sampling algorithm (SSA), which was developed to minimize processing MLPs time without losing coverage and assertiveness, when comparing with training conducted on a population database. The case study consisted of a ANN performance influence with a population database and with its sample data obtained by the SSA model. This procedure with the RNAs aimed to evaluate the following properties: (1) meet the pre-established criteria of reliability of the model; (2) have a computer-automated procedure; (3) sort and select records more correlated, and (4) maintain sampling results within a track of assertiveness of total results obtained. From the realization of this case study, it was possible to identify the following gains made by the (1) reduction of ANN processing time by providing: (2) optimization of processing time; (3) automatic network selection; and (4) automatic parameters selection for training algorithms.

Keywords

Artificial Neural Network · Stratified Sampling Algorithm · Multilayer Perceptron

38.1 Introduction

There are several phenomena in nature that can only be explained by means of variables set. For example, the behavior of bank fraud in credit card use or credit risks analysis. For a wide range of making decision support situations, those behaviors can be monitored and classified through Artificial Intelligence (AI) techniques approaches. From this AI concepts, Artificial Neural Networks (ANN) MultiLayer Perceptron (MLP) [1] can be used to perform complex financial tasks.

Due to the databases size and the calculations amount required to reach the results, it has been possible to contextualize an inability to diagnose real time credit card risks analysis or detect frauds. In this context, to diagnose and improve results for this scenario, it was necessary to consider statistical approaches, providing a hybrid computational solution. However, was it possible to decrease data volume considering computational process and get the same performance rate? One possible way to handle this issue is the use of statistical concept called sampling.

The sampling approach aims to reduce the amount of data records from the database, obtaining a data sample with similar characteristics of the population database. However, there are some limitations that may occurs, such as the inability to deal with data mining without distorting behavior, as well as need to use a large data amount. This type of

D. D. Fernandes
Federal Institute of Education, Science and Technology of São Paulo (IFSP), Campinas, Brazil

G. R. Matuck · D. A. Montini (✉) · L. A. V. Dias
Computer Science Division, Brazilian Aeronautics Institute of Technology (ITA), São José dos Campos, Brazil

A. A. Montini
Department of Administration, University of São Paulo (USP), São Paulo, Brazil

© Springer International Publishing AG, part of Springer Nature 2018
S. Latifi (ed.), *Information Technology – New Generations*, Advances in Intelligent Systems and Computing 738,
https://doi.org/10.1007/978-3-319-77028-4_38

restrictions has been creating difficulties to apply real time computational models for financial segment [2].

Statistical sampling models can be applied in databases to be able to reproduce an original population pattern [8]. In ANN approaches conducted for finantial tasks, these models enable same detection performance level. However, in a shorter time interval [2].

There are some limitations when these techniques are used separately [2]. Due the high complexity of most non-linear real problems, some techniques applied alone have more difficulties to address some behaviors. For example, situations that have many variables, many input/output mapping and huge amount of available data. In order to overcome these model's limitations, there is a possibility to use statistical data sampling for the neural system optimization learning [3–5], a stratified sampling algorithm based on an index of reliability, producing low computational processing cost [2].

In this work, a sample extraction algorithm has been enhanced, using statistical fundamentals in an algorithm that traverses the vector of size N. Using a computer program developed with MATLAB® software [6], some results and comments are shown in the following sections.

This article is organized as follows: Sect. 38.1 Introduction discusses elements of a stratified sampling characterization to interact with an MLP ANN; Sect. 38.2 the Stratified sampling applied for real problems is described; Sect. 38.3 the SSA algorithm is described; Sect. 38.4 Artificial Networks; Sect. 38.5 describes Neural Networks and Sampling for Banking Credit Risks Analysis; Sect. 38.6 Computational Model Results evaluation; Sect. 38.7 presents the conclusion and future work and, we finsih with Acknowledgements and general considerations.

38.2 Stratified Sampling Applied for Real Problems

The stratified sampling used in this work belongs to probability samples family and consists of dividing the entire population or "study object" in different subgroups or different strata. So, that an individual can be part only of a single stratum or layer [3].

After the layers were defined, to create a data sample, the model selects individuals using any sampling technique in each layer separately [3].

A stratified sample is considered excellent, as this sampling that has a small standard deviation. This concept was fundamental to calculate: (1) layers size; (2) sample blocks size; as well as (3) sample size.

On the other hand, the extraction of the samples in each layer was progressively adjusted during the calculation of the standard deviation of the studied variables.

The program extracted from each layer only some data that met the population standard deviation, aiming that the final sample was obtained to obtain the best possible population representation [3].

The SSA developed was applied in a variety of real case studies, aiming to obtain representative samples, dealing with large volumes of data, in linear time "n". However, due the confidentiality context, in this article the case studies are explored to provide a better demonstration about the results and application possibilities.

Any population data can be divided into "n" subdata groups, or in "K" stratified cluster, with enough size to be processed by the available hardware used. For the experiments, the data cluster size was tested arbitrarily, exploring different scenarios. The data extraction process in the population database can be conducted just once, for each subdata cluster [3], Fig. 38.1 shows an overview.

38.3 SSA Algorithm

During the sampling process, the SSA model take decision based on statistical indicators. The algorithm was designed to identify which data records can statistically be selected for the sample database. The sample process stops after the criterias are reached, as well can also perform a swap of data records by another more appropriate between the sample and population databases.

The population database is divided in data cluster, with size "n" predefined by the user (n > 0). The input vector "V" of the data cluster is processed by the SSA to provide volume reduction of this vector "V" as the following steps:

SSA algorithm steps:
A- Plan (P) –Algorithm structuring:

1. Parameters definition for the algorithm execution.

B-Do (D) – Population Analysis

2. Get the data Cluster.
3. Parameters definition.
4. Correlation analysis (Cluster/Population).
5. Estimated population indicators calculations.

X1- Analysis and data visualization.

6. Cluster Indicators evaluation.
7. Outsiders analysis.
8. Indicators (cluster without Outsiders) evaluation.
9. Cluster Variances calculation sample size calculation.
10. Data analysis and visualization.
11. Sample extraction and Verification.
12. Implementation of Qualitative Sampling

Fig. 38.1 Data clusters process overview

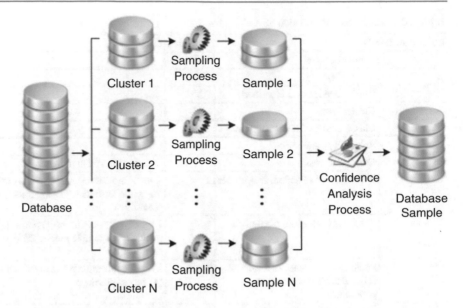

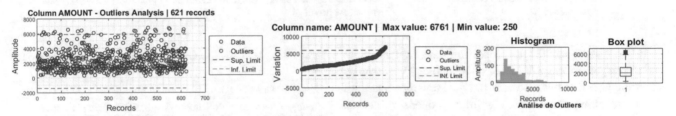

Fig. 38.2 Descriptive statistical indicators used in Algorithm AEN

C - Check (C) – Sapling consolidation

13. Final reconciliation of all clusters. Statistical indicators calculation and lower and upper limits of final sample.
14. X13 Data Visualization and Analysis

D – Act (A) - Corrective Actions and Results evaluation

15. Sample representativeness verification.

From line 1 to 14 of SSA algorithm steps, various statistical calculations are performed in sample obtained.

The algorithm AEN complexity is estimated as follows, being log (10 n), 10 (n), O (n) advance only indicators calculations are held, where n is data amount generated. If > and > n, being O (n) complexity order (Fig. 38.2).

From SSA explanation above, identified that an asymptotic order was estimated in O(n) for each cluster. Even so, N times (n), an estimated order is maintained, clusters number regardless.

38.3.1 Statistical Concepts Used

The SSA proposed algorithm uses statistical indicators, in order to assist in selection sampling procedure criteria. A unique feature of this algorithm consisted in fact that their parameters use is flexible, and need to be continuously defined [6, 7].

In other words, numerical parameters definition can be assigned arbitrarily on bookmarks each. However, each descriptive statistical indicator [3] may or may not participate in data extraction criteria of sampling SSA. In sampling integrated process with ANN.

This approach advantage could be established, considering fundamentally: (1) Descriptive data analysis use techniques in a program to sort the data, keeping your representativeness; (2) Processing time reduction; (3) Some quantitative properties maintenance in final sample. The SSA algorithm can be used in different applications [10].

Table 38.1, we have the SSA Algorithm insert containing some requirements applied to RNA training process [3, 4].

Table 38.1 Parameters identified in SSA algorithm

Parameter ID	ID	Valuation	Range
1	Population size	621	
2	Sample size	175	
3	Confidence interval identified	0.99	
4	Cluster size	200	
5	Classification of interest columns	C	Continuous data type = "C"
6	Reliability parameter	0.7	0.7
7	Correlation test	1	Selected to explain problem
8	Indicators set selection, set number	1	1 set of indicators uses: 'Arithmetic'; 'Weighted Average'; 'Median'; 'Variance'; 'Standard Deviation'; 'Amplitude', P; 'Quartile 1'; 'Quartile 2'; 'Quartile 3'; 'Quartile 4'
9	Graphs set selection, the number	1	1 set of indicators uses: (1) pizza; (2) bar; (3) points of the population; (4) population x sample points; (5) BoxPLot; (6) the confidence interval (CI); (7) convergence
10	Parâmetros de conexão a base de dados database connection parameters	1	1 set of connection parameters to the database: (1) path; (2) user; (3) password; (4) access privilege
11	Sample database connection parameters	1	1 set of connection parameters to the database: (1) path; (2) user; (3) password; (4) access privilege

In order to reduce: (1) the processing time, (2) bandwidth and (3) response time, a MLPs RNA technology was used by sampling aimed to reduce and avoid the large data amounts. After describing some SSA algorithm properties, then an introduction about this algorithm were presented.

This algorithm has several adjustable parameters to adjust the sampling performance in each new established phenomenon. A statistical parameterization analysis of SSA scores could be performed around a central concept (CI) confidence interval. Initially, each analyzed cluster is calculated, some indicators were described in Table 38.2.

The SSA algorithm calculates the values of the cluster, in other indicators [3], the values were accumulated to obtain a mean of all the multiple groupings, according to these data had to be processed as well as processed in the computer's memory.

38.3.2 Data Representativeness Evaluation

In this session, some graphs obtained during the process were presented. During the realization of the representation, the same calculation application filters were applied for both the population and the samples. In this context, in order to filter and remove the Outliers, an identified way to perform the confidence interval (CI) calculation was designed to test decrementally from 1 to 0.00. For this achievement, the population data were used in all indicators, being exemplified

Table 38.2 Descriptive statistical indicators used in the algorithm AEN

Confidence interval (CI)		0.99	0.01
Average values from "N" cluster-assumed to population values			
Statistical indicators	Lower bound	Indicated value r	Upper bound
'Arithmetic Mean'	2375.33	2387.26	2399.20
'Weighted Average'	2375.33	2387.26	2399.20
'Median'	2017.86	2028.00	2038.14
'Variance'	2,039,490.33	2,049,739.02	2,059,987.72
'Standard Deviation'	1424.53	1431.69	1438.85
'Interquartile Range'	6478.45	6511.00	6543.56
'Quartile 1'	1311.41	1318.00	1324.59
'Quartile 2'	2017.86	2028.00	2038.14
'Quartile 3'	3133.26	3149.00	3164.75
'Quartile 4'	6727.20	6761.00	6794.81

in Table 38.2 and in Fig. 38.3. In these cases, the same results obtained in sample were presented in Table 38.2.

This was a structured form that the SSA algorithm used to compare the Reliability Index (IC). This was one of tests performed to identify whether the sampling was within the confidence range obtained from the population.

The consolidated data from this SSA program processing was shown in Fig. 38.3. The SSA program recursively examined the NEA to refine and progressively improve and dynamize the IC.

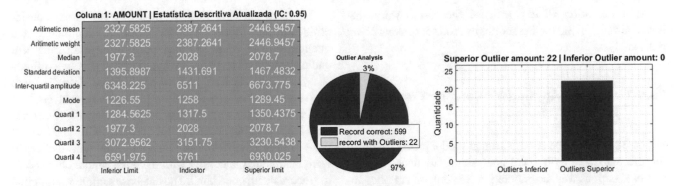

Fig. 38.3 Descriptive statistical indicators used in SSA Algorithm

By means of these parameterized tests, the algorithm recursively processed to the moment that SSA stop conditions program were satisfied and the final sample was obtained.

38.4   Artificial Neural Networks

Artificial Intelligence (AI) is a knowledge field that has being used in various market segments all around the world [4]. Nowadays AI can be experienced on market in a variety of services, products and business analysis. The Artificial Neural Networks (ANNs) is a specific AI subset that has a similar behavior as human brain natural network, both can analyze information, interpreting the data and making decisions [4, 7].

There are many types of ANNs in the scientific literature. A common neural network architecture is called MultiLayer Perceptron (MLP) [4, 7], widely applied in real complex problems. MLP network is structured by layers of neurons, an input layer, one or more hidden layers and the output layer, performing nonlinear interpolations for many problems. There are many learning algorithms that can be used to perform learning tasks, a common one used is called Backpropagation algorithm.

Financial Market attracts interest of many applications of AI, especially dealing with banking frauds detection, stock markets and bank credit risks analysis. Such issues have distinct characteristics like big data information available for analysis (non-structured) and many different variables involved. High computational power, complex computational algorithms and big data analysis capability, should support this kind of environment, providing real time effective solutions.

38.5   Neural Networks and Sampling for Banking Credit Risks Analysis

This work concentrates details only for the application with banking credit risk analysis. The computational model de-

veloped was also applied and evaluated in others real problems case studies. For example, applied for banking frauds detection and tax evaders identification, facing with millions of data, high power computed required and showing good performance results.

In this work, a sampling algorithm and ANN computational model were developed to perform a banking credit risk analysis.

This task is often done by finance specialist professionals, that analyze a variety amount of information, providing a score to allow or not financial credit for customers. To provide better analysis in real time, these companies are also using expert computational systems to handle this problem and reach good results.

For this study case, the data used have information about bank's customers, like age, profession, if have kids, if is employed or not, has car (new or used), education and so on. According with this information, 70% of customers were considered as good credit, with low risk. The other 30% of customers were labeled as bad credit, with high risk of compliance.

This unbalanced data proportion of good and bad credit profile can influence the neural network model performance during the learning phase. To avoid unwanted behavior to analyze credit risks by neural networks, some experiments performed data sampling process with good credit user profile.

An exploratory data analysis is performed in the database and the data behavior influence for credit risks was statistically studied. Some data variables can influence the neural networks learning performance and should be individually structured.

For this study, the neural network model was composed by a MLP neural network, its architecture was configured combining variety for strategies like, for example, with one and two hidden layers, different learning algorithm functions, momentum term, learning rate adaptive, different error thresholds, different data proportions for training, validation and test sets, different approaches for data normalization and so on.

After execution all experiments, the results were analyzed, aiming to find the best configuration for banking credit risks analysis.

38.5.1 Strategy Applied for Banking Credit Risk Analysis

Figure 38.4 shows the computational model process adopted for the banking credit risks analysis simulations. In each process step it was considered a variety of specific approaches. For a better comprehension about this study case simulation, four experiments were conducted, using or not the removing database's outliers and performing or not the sampling process.

This scenario provides a contextualization for understanding the ANN performance influence combining the sample process and data quality (without outliers). Figure 38.5 shows the experiments approaches.

The model works as follow. First the database (1) provides the data information used as an input for the computational model.

The next phase is to perform data analysis (2) considering different aspects like, for example, quantitative and qualitative data, missing data, performing data treatment and exploring some statistical approaches. This type of data analysis is required to produce a structured data (3), with useful information considered for banking risk analysis.

The stratified sampling algorithm developed (4) considered the following scenario: only records with good credit were sampled by SSA. The records labeled with bad credit were maintained integrally with the data sample obtained of the records with good label. The database sample was applied for the neural model learning process. Figure 38.6 shows the sampling process conducted for credit risks analysis.

Figure 38.7 shows de Neural network model (5) applied for experiments. The structured database was pre-processed by data normalization and division for training, validation and test sets. The MLP architecture was also configured according different strategies. The MLP network is trained to identify good and bad credit risks. After de MLP network training process, the post processing phase analyses the learning performance by the model.

Fig. 38.4 Computational model approach

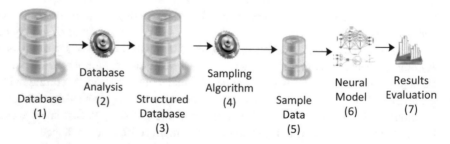

Fig. 38.5 Experiments approaches

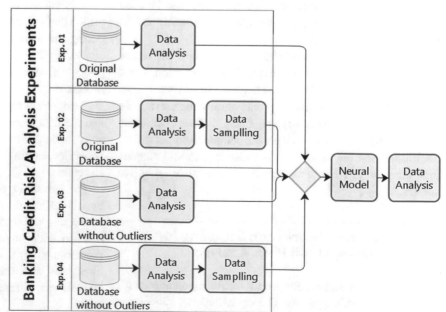

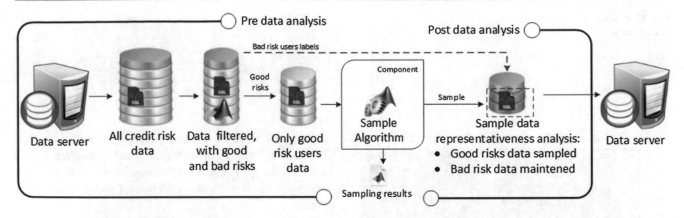

Fig. 38.6 Sampling process approach

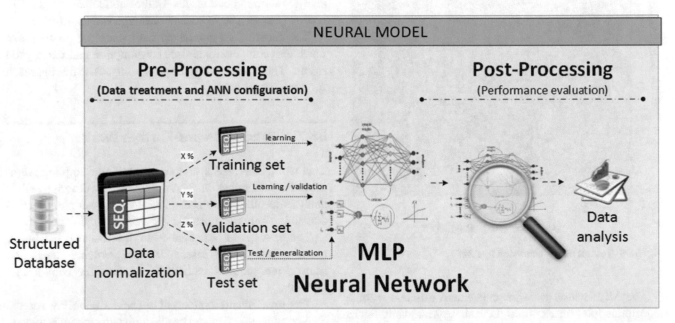

Fig. 38.7 Neural Network Model

38.5.2 Sampling Algorithm and MLP Neural Networks Application

The development computational model used MATLAB® software. Once implemented, the execution works automatically for each experiment, evaluating different neural networks configurations. An html report was produced with all simulation details.

38.6 Computational Model Results Evaluation

The database was composed by 1.000 registries and 30 different variables about costumer's information, 700 records labelled with good credit and 300 with bad credit of compliance. All data were analyzed and pre-processed, resulting a structured database to be used in the simulations experiments.

For the experiments conducted using data sampling process, only quantitative data variables were considered by the SSA. It was tested different parameterization aspects for the SSA sampling process. The best configuration found reduced the 700 registries labelled with good credit to 362 patterns, 51% of reduction. The model representativeness obtained 84% confidence interval. After the sampling process by SSA, the 300 registries labelled with bad credit were grouped with 362 registries sampled with good credit, totalizing 652 patterns for the neural model phase.

Before the neural model learning process, the data should be binaryzed and normalized between [0,1] range, considering quantitative and qualitative data aspects. Each normalized registry/pattern was composed by a vector with 39 data entries. All processed data were divided into training, validation and test sets, with different amount proportions for each group. For this study case, the sort data considered proportions like 70%, 80% and 90% for training set respectively, 15%, 10%, and 5% for validation and test set.

Fig. 38.8 MLP Neural Network
Architecture

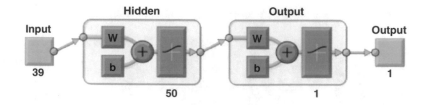

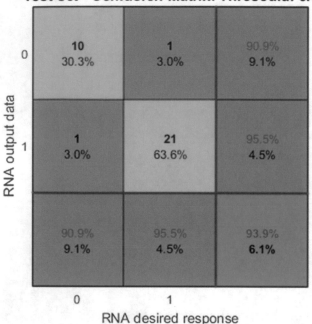

Fig. 38.9 Test set matrix confusion by ANN

The MLP neural network considered different learning algorithms like, for example, Levenberg-Marquardt, Scaled Conjugate Gradient, Bayesian Regularization, Conjugate Gradient, and Gradient Descent with Momentum. Random initial weights and bias values were used for the learning process [3].

After widely exploration of all experiments for banking credit risk analysis, the best ANN model found has only one hidden layer, with 50 neurons (Fig. 38.8). Logistic sigmoidal functions were applied for all neurons layers, Bayesian Regularization [9] training algorithm, adaptative momentum term and learning rate parameters were considered for this MLP network.

For the model learning performance evaluation, the test set was analyzed. Figure 38.9 shows the MLP network matrix confusion for the test set classification by ANN.

Other analysis carried out for this case study was to analyze the coverage and assertiveness of the neural model classification for unseen data (test set). Figure 38.10 shows set Coverage X Assertiveness and Test Set Alerts produced analysis.

Using 0.4 value for threshold, neural outputs more than this threshold value normalize to 1 and 0 instead, Figure 11 shows the MLP performance, considering coverage, assertiveness, alerts produced, with correct and wrong classification.

The four experiments conducted for banking credit risk analysis showed good results for the neural network generalization (test set), up to 90% of coverage and assertiveness.

The experiments conducted with sampling process take much less computational time consumption and reach good results. These results show de possibility of use this approach for real time problems.

38.7 Conclusion and Further Work

This work presented a sampling Stratified Sampling Algorithm for data reduction. SSA uses statistical descriptive data analysis techniques to sort data, allowing sample selection containing only the most relevant data for application.

The SSA model was applied in different real databases, reducing in same cases 90% of volume data and scoring the samples with 80% or more for confidence intervals.

The experiments conducted showed the ability for the SSA computational model handle with huge amounts of data, processing in linear time. All the samples extracted considering different databases (some databases with millions of data), producing samples with high confident intervals. The sampling results presented in this work, considering the banking risk credit analysis case study, showed the strategy for the sampling process, reducing the unbalanced data by good credit risk customers and reflecting a good neural network performance.

As a future work, extend the SSA algorithm to handle qualitative data, as well as performing an extra permutation data between sample and database, increasing the confidential interval for the data sample obtained by the model.

Acknowledgements and General Considerations The Research Group on Software Engineering thanks for institutions and research groups like the Brazilian Aeronautics Technological Institute (ITA) and Administration Institute Foundation (FIA), for the contributions, support and cooperation.

Fig. 38.10 Test set performance
Analysis

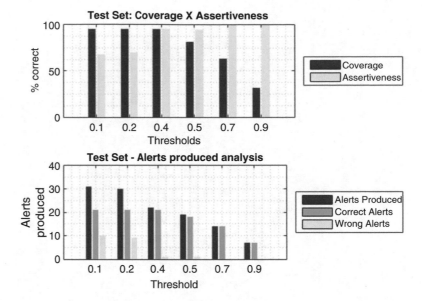

References

1. S. Haykin, *Neural Networks and Learning Machines* (Pearson Education, Inc., Upper Saddle River, NJ, 2009)
2. D.A. Montini, G.R. Matuck, A.M. da Cunha, L.A.V. Dias, A sampling diagnostics model for neural system training optimization, in *2013 10th International Conference on Information Technology: New Generations* (Las Vegas, 2013)
3. G.R. Matuck, J.R. Barbosa, C. Bringhenti, I. Lima, Multiple faults detection of gas turbine by MLP neural network, in *ASME Turbo Expo 2009, Power for Land, Sea, and Air* (Orlando, 2009)
4. S. Russell, P. Norvig, *Artificial Intelligence. A Modern Approach* (Prentice Hall, 2003)
5. D.A. Montini, P.M. Tasinaffo, A.A. Montini, L.A.V. Dias, A.M. Cunha, Um Meta-Algoritmo para Otimização de Planejamento em Linha de Produção de software, in *VIII International Conference on Engineering and Computer Education—ICECE 2013* (Luanda, 2003)
6. The MathWorks, Inc, MATLAB Software [Online], https://www.mathworks.com/products/matlab.html. Accessed 06 Apr 2017
7. W.J. Stevenson, B.J. Isselhardt, *Study Guide to Accompany Business Statistics: Concepts and Applications*, 2nd edn (Harper & Row, 1978)
8. C.M. Bishop, *Neural Networks for Pattern Recognition* (Clarendon Press, Oxford, 1995)
9. D.A. Montini, D. Battaglia, G.R. Matuck, A chi-square methodology applied in deviations control of project plan to support the RIMAM model, in *2014 11th International Conference on Information Technology: New Generations* (Las Vegas, 2014)
10. Z. Yue, Z. Songzheng, L. Tianshi, Bayesian regularization BP Neural Network model for predicting oil-gas drilling cost, in *2011 International Conference on Business Management and Electronic Information* (Guangzhou, China, 2011)

Part V

Data Mining/Machine Learning

Heloise Acco Tives Leão, Edna Dias Canedo, Marcelo Ladeira, and Fabiano Fagundes

Abstract

The National Institute of Educational Research and Studies (INEP) provides ENADE data for Higher Education Institutions (IES) from Brazil. This data is a rich source of support in improving the quality of education offered by these IES, but requires the application of data mining techniques to achieve the standards of the learning process and thus achieve improved academic performance of students in different courses. This paper aims to present the steps of mining the data provided by INEP, which will enable the identification of standards for the IES analyzed, as well as serve as a guide for other IES that wish to follow a similar process.

Keywords

Data mining · CRISP-DM · Association algorithm · Apriori

39.1 Introduction

The National Student Performance Exam (ENADE) is part of the National Higher Education Evaluation System (Sinaes) and the National Institute of Educational Studies Teixeira (INEP—http://portal.inep.gov.br/enade/) has conducted it annually since 2004.

The exam (ENADE) is carried out with a selected sample of first and last year undergraduate students from the Higher Education Institutions of Brazil in order to evaluate the

H. A. T. Leão (✉) · E. D. Canedo · M. Ladeira
Computer Science Department, University of Brasília (UnB), Brasília, Federal District, Brazil

F. Fagundes
Computer Science Department, Centro Universitário Luterano (ULBRA) de Palmas, Palmas, Tocantins, Brazil

quality of the higher education courses and to make a unique classification for undergraduate courses in Brazil.

Among the Enade steps are the Student Questionnaire, the Test and Courses Coordination Survey. This study will present the mining of collected data regarding the Student Questionnaire, organized and made available by INEP. The years from 2014 to 2016 were chosen for analysis and the Institutions linked to the Lutheran University of Brazil (ULBRA—http://www.ulbra.br/) chosen as the scope of the mining project, whose general objective is to identify the most relevant complaints of the students and, from these, propose alternatives of teaching process improvement.

The remainder of this paper is organized as follows. Section 39.2 presents the Literature Review. Section 39.3 presents the understanding of the business and an understanding of data. Section 39.4 presents data preparation and Modeling. Section 39.5 presents the evaluation. Section 39.6 presents an implementation. Section 39.7 presents the conclusions and future studies.

39.2 Literature Review

Data mining is a multidisciplinary research area, involving Database, Statistics and Machine Learning [1] and has been used for knowledge discovery in databases.

According to Jang et al. [2], identifying patterns in the mining patterns is one of the most important tasks in order to extract significant and useful information from raw data. This task aims to extract sets of items that represent some sort of homogeneity and/or regularity in data.

Among the techniques considered efficient for data mining, there are rules of association that seek to find links between attributes, that is, they assume that the presence of an attribute in an event implies the presence of another attribute in the same event [3].

The use of mining with association rules is appropriate to analyze educational data, which is intended to identify

© Springer International Publishing AG, part of Springer Nature 2018
S. Latifi (ed.), *Information Technology – New Generations*, Advances in Intelligent Systems and Computing 738,
https://doi.org/10.1007/978-3-319-77028-4_39

patterns of the learning process and improve the academic performance of students in different courses [4].

Kumar and Chadha [5] identifies the application of data association rules to improve the quality of management decisions to provide quality education. This is done to analyze the data and find out factors affecting academic achievement in order to increase chances of student success.

Among the association algorithms, Apriori was proposed by Agrawal et al. and Librelotto and Mozzaquatro [6, 7], and is the most widely used to discover association rules, since it thoroughly tests the attributes in search of expanded rules that represent the pattern of its society [2].

When using the Apriori algorithm, there are measures that influence the discovery of the rules: support, which is percentage of cases in which contains both A and B; confidence, which is the percentage of cases having A, and contains B; and lift, which is the confidence rate with the percentage of cases containing B [8].

39.3 Methods

Based on comparative research of data mining techniques [2, 9, 10] and data mining from the educational field: [4, 5, 11], the Apriori algorithm was chosen for the discovery of rules of association in this study.

The methodology used comes from the literature review and the choice of technique and algorithm. It consists in knowing the environment to which the data refer and using the CRISP-DM reference model to perform the mining steps, perform tests to evaluate the results found, present results and conclusions of the project as well as the suggestions of ways to implement improvements to increase academic satisfaction.

The CRISP-DM [12] reference model defines a set of sequential steps to guide the data mining and allows for the mining process to be fast, reliable and with more management control. It also comprehends the stages of business understanding, data comprehension, data preparation, modeling, evaluation and implementation [8]. The adoption of these phases help define the flows used to run the mining project.

39.3.1 Business Understanding

The IES Ulbra network consists of seven institutions, and their students take the ENADE exam since 2005, but to date there hasn't been a study about the information given by their students in mandatory ENADE questionnaires.

The main purpose of this study is to identify the most relevant student complaints through the evaluation of the student questionnaire responses, and from that to propose new ways to improve the quality of education provided by Ulbra network. It is also expect from the implementation of this project:

- To improve understanding of the socioeconomic profile of students in order to find ways to reduce absence [13];
- identify problems in physical infrastructure and services;
- To assess the didactic and pedagogical organization of the institutions from the perception of students for further study on process improvements;
- To expand academic and professional training opportunities in order to make them gradually more appropriate to the labor market.

The data used to carry out this mining project comes from the INEP bases, that is, public databases of free access. This way, other IES can replicate the models and standards identified in this project. Criteria for success of this project will be the identification of the factors with the highest index of dissatisfaction by academics and, based on this, to propose improvements or processes that contribute to the quality of the education offered as well as the increase of the students' satisfaction with the institution and with the undergraduate course they take.

The main tool used in this mining project is R-Studio, which has packages and tools to perform most of the mining steps.

39.3.2 Data Understanding

Initial data for the mining project was extracted from the INEP website (microdata http://portal.inep.gov.br/) and refers to a micro data file of each year, the variables dictionary and the student questionnaire. The period defined for the application of this mining was from 2014 to 2016.

From detailed analysis of data collected, understanding of attributes, and integrated database generation, a total of 9858 observations and 70 attributes was reached, as shown in Table 39.1.

Continuing the task of data comprehension, we identified the use of Likert scale with six points to the attributes of the Student Questionnaire. The process of attributes cleaning and the integration of some of them must be performed in the data preparation stage, with the objective of minimizing problems in the process of knowledge discovery, such as eliminating inconsistencies and adding value to the data.

Table 39.1 Attributes identified in the raw data

Attributes	Amount
Identifiers (year and institution)	2
Socioeconomic	26
Infrastructure and physical facilities	12
Didactic-pedagogical organization	23
Academic and professional training opportunities	7
Total	70

Table 39.2 Quantitative observations with at least 50% of missing data

	2014	2015	2016
Total gross	4165	3860	1833
Missing data	886	807	177
Frequency of absence	21.3%	20.9%	9.7%
Total refined	3279	3053	1656

39.4 Preparation of Data

The first activity performed in the data preparation was the cleaning of such data. As the evaluated data was extracted from questionnaires with predefined answer parameters, and were electronically answered, no outstanding values were identified.

Observations with more than 50% of blank attributes were considered missing values, and were often identified.

Table 39.2 shows the number of observations of each year which have been eliminated to avoid problems in the quality of analysis to be performed.

The process of evaluation of attributes was manual, as it was required to have an understanding of variables by consulting the data dictionary and checking the scale/pattern used in each one.

As all data was obtained from a single data source, just one transformation process was necessary to change the data value of 7 and 8 for "null" values, so as to not influence the process of merging of attributes. 6689 entries with value "7—I cannot answer" and 5818 observations with value "7—Not applicable" were identified, corresponding respectively to 2.07%, and 1.80% of 322.689 data entries on the Student Questionnaire.

With the support of a specialist, who is accompanying all phases of this project, it was possible to identify and exclude 16 attributes that represent socioeconomic variables from the project because they are not significant for the intended results. Example of excluded variables: q3, which deals with the nationality of the students, and q16, which stores State data on secondary education completion.

To identify correlation between the attributes of the Student Questionnaire, the Pearson correlation algorithm was applied in software R, which identified 5 attributes with correlation above 0.7 and could be deleted.

For analysis of other attributes of the Student Questionnaire, the histogram and the average of the other attributes were generated to help the individual analysis of each attribute. Thus, another 27 attributes were deleted, because all of them possess an average satisfaction of 5.18, and the maximum satisfaction score is 6.

The data set resulting from this preparation phase consists of 22 attributes, 7988 observations and 177,795 data entries. They are:

- Two attributes (year, IES) that will be used to make the separation of data and subsequent comparison of the results of each institution.
- Ten qualitative attributes that represent the socioeconomic data chosen by the expert to set the context for the inclusion of students.
- Ten remaining attributes of the Student Questionnaire which were filtered through the correlation and analysis of higher incidence of complaints by students.

From the study of data, cleaning, classification and analysis of attributes performed at this stage, it is possible to define models, select techniques and parameters to perform the mining process. The Modeling step of this project performs and presents these steps.

39.4.1 Modeling

In order to perform the attributes modeling of this project, variables association mechanisms will be used, together with the application of the Apriori algorithm.

As such algorithm is based on nominal or binary attributes, the values of the Student Questionnaire attributes had to be adapted. In accordance to the expert, it was defined that for 5 s and 6 s on the Likert scale, attributes would receive the "no" value, indicating no improvement pointed by students. For Likert scale values from 1 to 4, attributes would receive the "yes" value, indicating a need for analysis and evaluation of opportunities for improvement.

The data processing phase resulted in ten attributes of the Student Questionnaire. These were separated in five attributes for infrastructure and physical facilities, three attributes for the didactic and pedagogical organization, and two attributes for the academic and professional training opportunities. All these attributes have been adapted to the defined pattern.

The Apriori algorithm was applied and generated 69 association rules. Figure 39.1 presents the summary of statistics (Minimum, 1st Quartile, Median, Mean, value as average, Q1, Q3° Quartile and Maximum Value) to support parameters, confidence, lift and counter resulting from the application of Apriori algorithm.

The results generated by Apriori were filtered to identify just the rules that brought associations with the attributes derived from the Student Questionnaire. This filter generated a subset of 30 rules presented in Fig. 39.2, which will compose the result of the mining process.

With the definition of rulesets for mining, the modeling phase of the project is complete and it must move on to the evaluation of the generated rules, which will be held in Sect. 39.5.

```
> summary(r.g)
set of 69 rules

rule length distribution (lhs + rhs):sizes
 2  3  4  5
 1 32 32  4

   Min. 1st Qu. Median   Mean 3rd Qu.   Max.
  2.000   3.000  4.000  3.565   4.000  5.000

summary of quality measures:
     support           confidence          lift              count
 Min.   :0.1000   Min.   :0.9006   Min.   :1.206   Min.   : 799
 1st Qu.:0.1100   1st Qu.:0.9121   1st Qu.:1.221   1st Qu.: 879
 Median :0.1262   Median :0.9209   Median :1.233   Median :1008
 Mean   :0.1433   Mean   :0.9242   Mean   :1.238   Mean   :1145
 3rd Qu.:0.1589   3rd Qu.:0.9365   3rd Qu.:1.254   3rd Qu.:1269
 Max.   :0.3776   Max.   :0.9621   Max.   :1.288   Max.   :3016

mining info:
 data ntransactions support confidence
    g        7988    0.1        0.9
> |
```

Fig. 39.1 Statistics generated by applying the rules Apriori algorithm

39.5 Evaluation

The evaluation step is responsible for analyzing the model (or models) obtained in more detail, by reviewing the work done until this point to enable the validation of the final model.

In Fig. 39.3 it's possible to see the array of previous rules (LHS) with the successor attributes (RHS). The color intensity of the circles represents the scale of the **lift** parameter and the size of the circles indicate information on the support parameter.

Although most of the rules generated by Apriori point to the same successor attribute (q13 = A, indicating that students do not have a scholarship to finance their studies), the generated rules do not become invalid as this group of students represents the highest percentage (74.8%) of the students who answered the Student Questionnaire.

Figure 39.4 presents the list of 30 rules that are in analysis through color that indicate the **lift**, which has a minimum value of 1.208 and a maximum value of 1.278, and the size of the circles represent the support parameter, which has a minimum value of 0.1 and a maximum value of 0.174.

In the center of the graph lies the successor of the rules generated by Apriori. Around this attribute are the attributes that represent additional portions of the population (q17School = A, q21Family = A, q11FinanCourse = B, q2Color = A, q10Work = E, q23Hours = B).

In regards to other attributes, they are inferred to represent the greatest complaint indexes (Student Questionnaire responses with values from 1 to 4 on the Likert scale) where:

Fig. 39.2 Statement subset of mining rules

```
subrules <- subset(rules.g, subset = lhs %in% c("q27=yes", "q29=yes",
"q30=yes","q59=yes","q60=yes","q61=yes", "q62=yes","q64=yes","q46=yes
", "q52=yes" ))

> labels(subsultes)
 [1] "{q11Financing=B,q64=yes} => {q13Scholarship=A}"
 [2] "{q2Color=A,q64=yes} => {q13Scholarship=A}"
 [3] "{q10Job=E,q62=yes} => {q13Scholarship=A}"
 [4] "{q11Financing=B,q62=yes} => {q13Scholarship=A}"
 [5] "{q2Color=A,q62=yes} => {q13Scholarship=A}"
 [6] "{q23Hour=B,q61=yes} => {q13Scholarship=A}"
 [7] "{q10Job=E,q61=yes} => {q13Scholarship=A}"
 [8] "{q11Financing=B,q61=yes} => {q13Scholarship=A}"
 [9] "{q2Color=A,q61=yes} => {q13Scholarship=A}"
[10] "{q10Job=E,q60=yes} => {q13Scholarship=A}"
[11] "{q23Hour=B,q46=yes} => {q13Scholarship=A}"
[12] "{q10Job=E,q46=yes} => {q13Scholarship=A}"
[13] "{q11Financing=B,q46=yes} => {q13Scholarship=A}"
[14] "{q2Color=A,q46=yes} => {q13Scholarship=A}"
[15] "{q23Hour=B,q52=yes} => {q13Scholarship=A}"
[16] "{q10Job=E,q52=yes} => {q13Scholarship=A}"
[17] "{q11Financing=B,q52=yes} => {q13Scholarship=A}"
[18] "{q2Color=A,q61=yes,q62=yes} => {q13Scholarship=A}"
[19] "{q2Color=A,q60=yes,q61=yes} => {q13Scholarship=A}"
[20] "{q11Financing=B,q46=yes,q52=yes} => {q13Scholarship=A}"
[21] "{q2Color=A,q46=yes,q52=yes} => {q13Scholarship=A}"
[22] "{q17School=A,q46=yes,q52=yes} => {q13Scholarship=A}"
[23] "{q2Color=A,q11Financing=B,q46=yes} => {q13Scholarship=A}"
[24] "{q11Financing=B,q21Family=A,q46=yes} => {q13Scholarship=A}"
[25] "{q2Color=A,q17School=A,q46=yes} => {q13Scholarship=A}"
[26] "{q2Color=A,q21Family=A,q46=yes} => {q13Scholarship=A}"
[27] "{q10Job=E,q17School=A,q52=yes} => {q13Scholarship=A}"
[28] "{q2Color=A,q11Financing=B,q52=yes} => {q13Scholarship=A}"
[29] "{q11Financing=B,q17School=A,q52=yes} => {q13Scholarship=A}"
[30] "{q2Color=A,q17School=A,q52=yes} => {q13Scholarship=A}"
```

Grouped Matrix for 30 Rules
1 rules: {q11Financing=B, q46=yes, +1 items}
1 rules: {q11Financing=B, q52=yes, +1 items}
1 rules: {q17School=A, q11Financing=B, +1 items}
1 rules: {q10Job=E, q46=yes}
1 rules: {q17School=A, q46=yes, +1 items}
1 rules: {q17School=A, q10Job=E, +1 items}
1 rules: {q10Job=E, q61=yes}
1 rules: {q62=yes, q10Job=E}
1 rules: {q11Financing=B, q52=yes, +1 items}
1 rules: {q60=yes, q10Job=E}
1 rules: {q52=yes, q46=yes, +1 items}
1 rules: {q10Job=E, q52=yes}
1 rules: {q23Hour=B, q46=yes}
1 rules: {q62=yes, q61=yes, +1 items}
1 rules: {q46=yes, q2Color=A}
1 rules: {q11Financing=B, q46=yes}
1 rules: {q17School=A, q52=yes, +1 items}
1 rules: {q61=yes, q11Financing=B}
1 rules: {q21Family=A, q46=yes, +1 items}
1 rules: {q23Hour=B, q61=yes}
1 rules: {q60=yes, q61=yes, +1 items}
1 rules: {q11Financing=B, q52=yes}
1 rules: {q64=yes, q11Financing=B}
1 rules: {q62=yes, q2Color=A}
1 rules: {q64=yes, q2Color=A}
1 rules: {q21Family=A, q11Financing=B, +1 items}
1 rules: {q61=yes, q2Color=A}
1 rules: {q62=yes, q11Financing=B}
1 rules: {q17School=A, q52=yes, +1 items}
1 rules: {q23Hour=B, q52=yes}
Items in LHS Group
Size: support
Color: lift
RHS
{q13Scholarship=A}

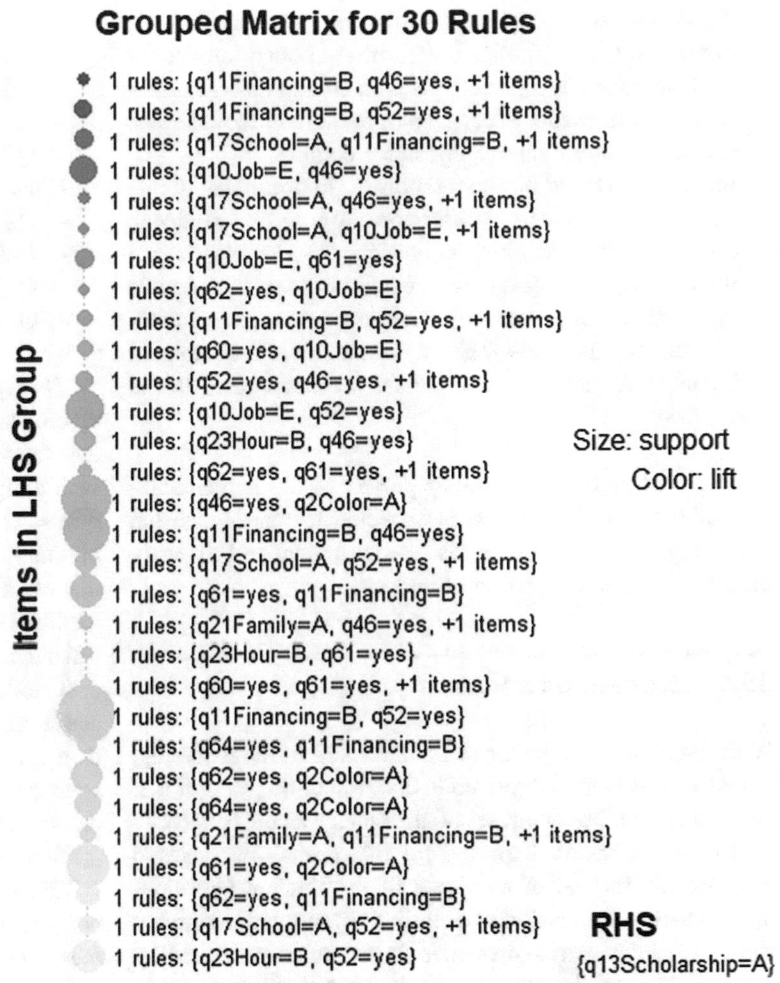

Fig. 39.3 Relationship matrix leading and succeeding rules

Graph for 30 rules
size: support (0.1 - 0.174)
color: lift (1.208 - 1.278)
q23Hour=B
q17School=A
q52=yes
q10Job=E
q46=yes
q61=yes q13Scholarship=A
q11Financing=B
q60=yes
q2Color=A
q21Family=A
q62=yes
q64=yes

Fig. 39.4 Graph interface 30 of the rules in question

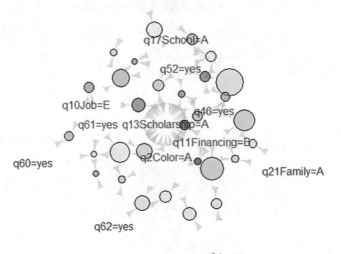

- Academic and professional training opportunities, in questions: Q46—The institution offered opportunities for students to act as representatives in collegiate organs and Q52—The students were given opportunities to undertake exchanges and/or internships in the country.
- Infrastructure and physical facilities, in questions: q60—The course provided monitors or tutors to help students; q61—The infrastructure conditions of the classrooms were adequate; q62—The equipment and materials available for class practices were adequate for the number of students and q64—The environments and equipment intended for the practical classes were adequate to the course.

The next step in the mining project is the implementation of the model, where it is expected to consolidate the knowledge discovered with the created model and to verify the fulfillment of the project objectives.

39.6   Implementation

With the confidence factor of 0.9 executed in the modeling, whose results were interpreted in the evaluation phase, it was verified that an important set of attributes was not covered.

To get the results expected for this project, we seek to evaluate the full set of attributes of the Student Questionnaire; tests were carried out until the complete identified set of attributes was represented in the rules generated by Apriori. The configuration made to meet this premise was with the use of the confidence parameter set to 0.6.

The result of new implementation of Apriori algorithm revealed the existence of 753 rules, and the amount of rules related to the attributes of the Student Questionnaire are:

- Academic and professional opportunities
  - Q46: 25 rules;
  - Q52: 50 rules;

- Physical infrastructure and facilities
  - Q60: 33 rules;
  - Q61: 31 rules;
  - Q62: 26 rules;
  - Q64: 6 rules;
- Didactic and pedagogical Organization
  - Q27: 8 rules;
  - Q29: 7 rules;
  - Q30: 5 rules;
  - Q59: 7 rules.

This quantify of generated rules can be seen Fig. 39.5, where it can be seen (by marking made with blue lines and the very thickness of the red lines) that the attributes with a higher incidence in rules are Q46 = yes, q52 = yes, q60 = yes, q61 = yes and q62 = yes. Based on this predominance, this set of attributes was determined as factors that can be better developed in the IES, and thus increase the quality of teaching offered and, consequently, the students' satisfaction.

The Analysis of two factors related to opportunities for academic and vocational training enabled the identification of a profile of students who were previously unknown to analyzed IES, regarding dissatisfaction with items of this nature. The identification of this profile is a starting point for defining improvements in the IES.

These are mostly white students (q2Cor = A), who do not use student financing mechanisms to pay the tuition fees (q11FinanCurso = B), who do not have scholarships to support their study (q13Bolsa = A), who went through high school in a public school (q17Escola = A) and have at least one family member who has completed higher education (q21Familia = yes).

The analysis of the items that refer to the Physical Infrastructure of IES resulted in the same pattern of students who present most of the complaints regarding the Institution. In addition, it was possible to highlight relevant factors for the identification of improvements in the institutions of the Ulbra network, and which are simple to implement. One example

Fig. 39.5 Attribute frequency in Apriori algorithm rules with reliable 0.6

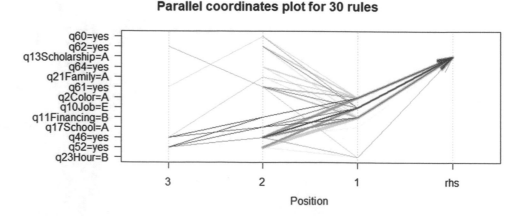

Parallel coordinates plot for 30 rules

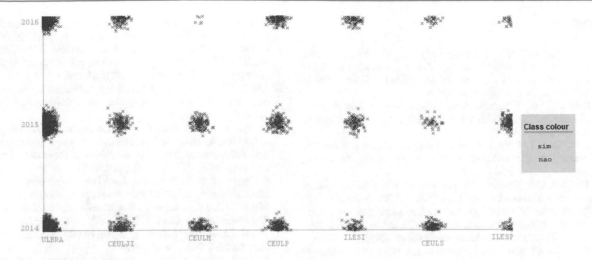

Fig. 39.6 Satisfaction of the representation of the students

of these factors is the increasing the availability of monitors or tutors for the students.

The mining assessment for these students also warranted the generation of Fig. 39.6, where the blue color showcases the amount of students who showed some dissatisfaction in regard to the items listed in the questionnaire. The graph shows the institutions of the Ulbra network in the "X axis" and the year of the evaluation in the "Y axis".

It can be seen from the evaluation of the image that, although the satisfaction index with the evaluation questions of IES is mostly positive (red x), there is a frequent occurrence of students' dissatisfaction (blue x).

This is proof that the data coming from the Student Questionnaire is relevant for proposing improvements in IES and thus trying to increase the level of academic satisfaction.

39.7   Conclusions and Future Work

With the execution of the steps of the CRISP-DM methodology with data provided by INEP to carry out this mining project, it was possible to display a large set of rules regarding the Student Questionnaire answered by students to take the Enade.

There was a need for cleaning, transforming, and adjusting the data to fit the Apriori algorithm chosen to perform the association task attributes.

The rules generated, together with the graphs executed in the software R, were easy to understand and of great value for the interpretation of the results, which led to the best

understanding and consequent attention to the main factors of students' dissatisfaction.

As a highlight of mining there is the identification that the factors that evaluate questions related to didactic-pedagogical, practices, despite being related by some students, do not represent the greatest factor of dissatisfaction.

The attributes that evaluate questions concerning the academic and professional training opportunities are the ones with the most dissatisfaction among students and require a specific study for bringing improvements.

For a better understanding of the questions related to Physical Infrastructure, it's recommended to apply specific questionnaires to survey the needs in each IES and thus set up an activity plan in order to meet the needs of the students. It is worth mentioning that some of these factors can have efficient solutions and simple implementation such as the increase in the number of tutors and monitors for the disciplines.

The conclusion is that this mining project has been of great value for analyzing the data mass that existed and saw no purpose. The rules generated by the application of the Apriori algorithm were satisfactory to the achievement of the project objectives.

As a continuation of this study, we expected the IES to use these results to implement factors that contribute to students' satisfaction and study environment. As a future research, the mining of the data provided by INEP every year is expected, in accordance to the rules modeled here.

It is important to inform that the data used to carry out this study is from public free access, making it so that the standards defined in this work can be replicated by other universities in Brazil.

References

1. U.M. Fayyad, G. Piatetsky-Shapiro, P. Smyth, The KDD process for extracting useful knowledge from volumes of data. Commun. ACM **39**(11), 27–34 (1996). https://doi.org/10.1145/240455.240464
2. S. Jang, K. Park, Y. Kim, H. Cho, T. Yoon, Comparison of h5n1, h5n8, and h3n2 using decision tree and apriori algorithm. J. Biosci. Med. **3**(06), 49 (2015)
3. L.A. da Silva, S.M. Peres, C. Boscarioli, *Introdução à mineração de dados: com aplicações em R* (Elsevier Brasil, Rio de Janeiro, 2017)
4. G. Mobasher, A. Shawish, O. Ibrahim, Educational data mining rule based recommender systems, in *CSEDU 2017—Proceedings of the 9th International Conference on Computer Supported Education*, vol. 1 (Porto, Portugal, April 21–23, 2017), pp. 292–299. [Online]. https://doi.org/10.5220/0006290902920299
5. V. Kumar, A. Chadha, Mining association rules in students assessment data. Int. J. Comput. Sci. Issues **9**(5), 211–216 (2012)
6. R. Agrawal, T. Imieliński, and A. Swami, Mining association rules between sets of items in large databases, in *93 Proceedings of the 1993 ACM SIGMOD international conference on Management of data*, vol. 22, no. 2 (ACM, 1993), pp. 207–216
7. S.R. Librelotto, P.M. Mozzaquatro, Análise dos algoritmos de mineração j48 e apriori aplicados na detecção de indicadores da qualidade de vida e saúde, Revista Interdisciplinar de Ensino, Pesquisa e Extensão, vol. 1, no. 1 (2014)
8. P. Kalgotra, R. Sharda, Progression analysis of signals: Extending CRISP-DM to stream analytics, in *2016 IEEE International Conference on Big Data, BigData 2016* (Washington, DC, USA, December 5–8, 2016), pp. 2880–2885 [Online]. https://doi.org/10.1109/BigData.2016.7840937
9. J.M. Luna, F. Padillo, M. Pechenizkiy, S. Ventura, Apriori versions based on mapreduce for mining frequent patterns on big data. IEEE Trans. Cybern. (2017)
10. C. Woo Kim, S.H. Ahn, T. Yoon, Comparison of flavivirus using datamining-apriori, k-means, and decision tree algorithm, in *2017 19th International Conference on Advanced Communication Technology (ICACT)* (IEEE, 2017), pp. 454–457
11. S. Ougiaroglou, G. Paschalis, Association rules mining from the educational data of ESOG web-based application, in *Artificial Intelligence Applications and Innovations—AIAI 2012 International Workshops: AIAB, AIeIA, CISE, COPA, IIVC, ISQL, MHDW, and WADTMB, Halkidiki, Greece, September 27–30, 2012, Proceedings, Part II* (2012), pp. 105–114
12. R. Wirth, J. Hipp, Crisp-dm: towards a standard process model for data mining, in *Proceedings of the 4th International Conference on the Practical Applications of Knowledge Discovery and Data Mining* (2000), pp. 29–39
13. R.M. Hoed, Análise da evasão em cursos superiores: o caso da evasão em cursos superiores da área de Computação, Dissertação, Universidade de Brasília, 2016. [Online], http://repositorio.unb.br/handle

Fault Diagnostic of Variance Shifts in Clinical Monitoring Using an Artificial Neural Network Input Gain Measurement Approximation (ANNIGMA)

Nadeera Gnan Tilshan Gunaratne, Mali Abdollahian, and Shamsul Huda

Abstract

Condition of a patient in an intensive care unit is assessed by monitoring multiple correlated variables with individual observations. Individual monitoring of variables leads to misdiagnosis. Therefore, variability of the correlated variables needs to be monitored simultaneously by deploying a multivariate control chart. Once the shift from the accepted range is detected, it is vital to identify the variables that are responsible for the variance shift detected by the chart. This will aid the medical practitioners to take the appropriate medical intervention to adjust the condition of the patient. In this paper, Multivariate Exponentially Weighted Moving Variance chart has been used as the variance shift identifier. Once the shift is detected, authors for the first time have used ANNIGMA to identify the variables responsible for variance shifts in the condition of the patient and rank the responsible variables in terms of the percentage of their contribution to the variance shift. The performance of the proposed ANNIGMA has been measured by computing average classification accuracy. A case study based on real data collected from ICU unit shows that ANNIGMA not only improve the diagnosis but also speed up the variable identification for the purpose of appropriate medical diagnosis.

Keywords

MEWMV chart · Neural networks · Clinical monitoring · Univariate moving range char · Multivariate variability

N. G. T. Gunaratne (✉) · M. Abdollahian
School of Science, RMIT University, Melbourne, VIC, Australia
e-mail: nadeera.gunaratne@rmit.edu.au;
mali.abdollahian@rmit.edu.au

S. Huda
School of Information Technology, Deakin University, Melbourne, VIC, Australia
e-mail: shamsul.huda@deakin.edu.au

40.1 Introduction

Patients are placed in an intensive care unit (ICU) following major surgery. Continuous monitoring is essential to the daily care of ICU patients. Ongoing and continuous monitoring is achieved by complex devices that require special training and experience to operate. If certain physiologic limits are exceeded, the devices set to generate alarms. Those alarms need to be investigated by following strict protocols. The measured observations are highly correlated for a given patient and the condition of the patient is assessed with individual observations. It is imperative to maintain overall variability of all the observations with respect to the accepted variability (target variance-covariance matrix) in order to achieve stable medical condition for the patient.

In this paper, Multivariate Exponentially Weighted Moving Variance (MEWMV) chart [1] has been used as the variance shift identifier for individual observations. The advantage of MEWMV chart is its ability to monitor variance while stabilizing mean of the process. The challenge in deploying multivariate control chart [2] is to identify variables responsible for the out-of-control (OOC) signals (fault diagnoses). Several machine learning approaches such as Artificial Neural Networks (ANN) and Support Vector Machines (SVM) have been proposed [3–12] for fault diagnoses. Hsu et al. [13] proposed an improved artificial neural networks called ANNIGMA approach. The method incorporates weights analysis based heuristic to direct the search in the wrapper model and allows effective feature selection for ANN.

This paper for the first time presents new strategy for fault diagnosis of variance shifts in multivariate clinical processes. The proposed approach integrates the deployment of MEWMV chart with ANNIGMA.

40.2 MEWMV Chart

MEWMV chart has the ability to monitor multivariate process variability while stabilizing the mean. Huwang et al. [1] has introduced the chart by estimating optimal control limits for up to 3 variables. Gunaratne et al. [14] have extended the charts ability to monitor high dimension multivariate processes by estimating control limits for up to 15 variables and introducing a mathematical model to estimate control limits beyond 15 variables.

Let $a = (a_1, \ldots a_p)^1$ be a random vector that represents p correlated quality characteristics from a multivariate process. Consider a transformation of a, $X = \sum_0^{-1/2} (a - \mu_0)$ such that X is distributed as $N(\mu, \Sigma)$, where $\mu = \sum_0^{-1/2} (\mu - \mu_0)$ and $\sum = \sum_0^{-1/2} \sum u \sum_0^{-1/2}$. Consequently, when the process is in-control, X is distributed as N $(0, I_p)$, where I_p is $p*p$ identity matrix.

The MEWMV statistic V_t [1] is defined by

$$\mathbf{V_t} = \omega\, (\mathbf{X}_t - \mathbf{Y}_t)\, (\mathbf{X}_t - \mathbf{Y}_t)' + (1 - \omega)\, \mathbf{V_{t-1}} \qquad (40.1)$$

Where Y_t is the predicted mean shift at sampling point t and its value is obtained by the multivariate exponentially moving average of X_t

$$\mathbf{Y_t} = \lambda\, \mathbf{X}_t + (1 - \lambda)\, \mathbf{Y_{t-1}} \qquad (40.2)$$

They have shown that for $0 < \omega < 1$, $0 < \lambda < 1$ and $t \le p$, the matrix V_t is positive definite with probability 1.

Defining I_t as the t*t identity matrix and X, Y, D and N as follows

$$\mathbf{X_t} = (\mathbf{X}_1, \mathbf{X}_2, \ldots \ldots \mathbf{X_t})'$$

$$\mathbf{Y_t} = (\mathbf{Y}_1, \mathbf{Y}_2, \ldots \ldots \mathbf{Y_t})'$$

$$D = \mathrm{diag}\ (D_1, D_2, \ldots \ldots D_t)$$

$$\mathbf{N} = \begin{pmatrix} \lambda & 0 & \cdots & 0 \\ \lambda(1-\lambda)\lambda & & \cdots & 0 \\ \vdots & \vdots & \ddots & \vdots \\ \lambda(1-\lambda)^{t-1} & \cdots & \lambda(1-\lambda) & \lambda \end{pmatrix}$$

Huwang et al. [1] showed that V_t can be written as

$$\mathbf{V_t} = (\mathbf{X} - \mathbf{Y})'\, D\ (\mathbf{X} - \mathbf{Y})$$

$$= \mathbf{X}'(\mathbf{I}_t - \mathbf{N})'\, D\ (\mathbf{I}_t - \mathbf{N})\, \mathbf{X}$$

$$\mathbf{V_t} = \mathbf{X}'\, \mathbf{RX}$$

$$\mathbf{E}\,[tr\,(\mathbf{V}_t)] = p^*tr\,(\mathbf{R}) \qquad (40.3)$$

$$\mathrm{Var}\,[tr\,(\mathbf{V_t})] \;=\; 2\,p \sum_{i=1}^{t}\sum_{j=1}^{t} r_{ij}^2 \qquad (40.4)$$

Therefore, the control limits for MEWMV chart are given by

$$E\,[tr\,(\mathbf{V_t})]\ \pm\ L\sqrt{\mathrm{Var}\,[tr\,(\mathbf{V_t})]}$$

$$= \; p\,tr\,(\mathbf{R}) \pm\ L\,\sqrt{2p\textstyle\sum_{i=1}^{t}\sum_{j=1}^{t} r_{ij}^2} \qquad (40.5)$$

The constant L depends on p, ω and λ. The value of L can be estimated by time consuming Monte Carlo simulations [15]. However, Gunaratne et al. [14] have developed predictive models to obtain the control limits for any high dimension multivariate process.

40.3 Annigma Approach

Hsu et al. [13] proposed a weights analysis based wrapper heuristic called ANNIGMA. It is a feature ranking approach which is mathematically derived from the back propagation training formulation of ANN. ANNIGMA also ranks the quality characteristics by the relevance which is based on the weight associated with the quality characteristic in a neural network based wrapper approach. Therefore, it is not necessary to train m neural nets for each branching point. Consequently, the speed of the fault diagnostic task using ANNIGMA would substantially increase.

For a two-layer neural network, if i, j and k are the input, hidden and output layer and F is a logistic activation linear function $F(x) = 1/(1 + exp(-x))$ then output of the network is given by Eq. (40.6).

$$O_k = \sum_j F\left(\sum_i A_i \times W_{ij}\right) \times W_{jk} \qquad (40.6)$$

where W_{ij} and W_{jk} are the network weights. The local gain can be defined as:

$$LG_{ik} = \left| \frac{\Delta O_k}{\Delta A_i} \right| \qquad (40.7)$$

According to [13], the local gain LG_{ik} can be defined in terms of network weights by

$$LG_{ik} = \sum_j |W_{ij} \times W_{jk}| \qquad (40.8)$$

The ANNIGMA score for ith input and kth node is defined as [13]

$$ANNIGMA_{ik} = \frac{LG_{ik}}{\max (LG_k)} \qquad (40.9)$$

Neural Network weights give an estimate of the relative importance of input features.

40.4 Case Study: Application of the Proposed Approach in Monitoring ICU Patients

Authors have used observations from 9 correlated variables that play a substantial role in assessing the condition of a patient after open heart surgery. This is usually achieved by screening Systolic Blood Pressure (SBP), Diastolic Blood Pressure (DBP), Mean Arterial Pressure (MAP), Systolic Pulmonary Artery Pressure (SPAP), Diastolic Pulmonary Artery Pressure (DPAP), Mean Pulmonary Artery Pressure (MPAP), Pulmonary Capillary Wedge Pressure (PCWP), Central Venous Pressure (CVP) and Heart Rate (HR). The characteristics indicate highly significant correlation (P-value $= 0.05$) among them. A total of 600 samples of size one with 9 characteristics in each sample were available. The data recording times were recommended by the medical practitioners. The study has used all the collected data.

The Time Series plots for 9 variables (Fig. 40.1) suggest that the most independent variables are CVP, DPAP and MAP. The Correlation analysis also confirms this.

40.4.1 MEWMV Chart for Monitoring the Variability of the Condition of a Patient After Heart Surgery

MEWMV chart has been used to monitor large variance shifts ($\omega = 0.9$) while mean is stabilized for small shift ($\lambda = 0.1$). Stabilizing mean is essential while monitoring variance of the process to avoid capturing mean changes. The control limits for the MEWMV charts are obtained using the predictive models developed by Gunaratne et al. [14]. Figure 40.2 shows 22 OOCs for MEWMV chart (out of 600 observations).

40.4.2 Fault Diagnostics to Identify the Responsible Characteristics Based on ANNIGMA Approach

The OOCs and in-control samples from MEWMV chart have been injected to ANNIGMA and other commonly used machine learning approaches to identify the group of variables responsible for in-controls and OOC signals and estimate the percentage of their individual contribution to the signals. The accuracy of ANNIGMA results have been investigated by deploying univariate Moving Range (UMR) charts.

Table 40.1 shows the ANNIGMA approach is superior to other commonly used approaches in selecting the minimum number of variables with higher accuracy. The accuracy computation starts with full variables set. The lowest ranked variable has been removed by utilizing Backword Elimination (BE) process. BE iteration continues until last variable in the subset. The subset with highest accuracy with minimum number of variables has been selected as the best subset. The

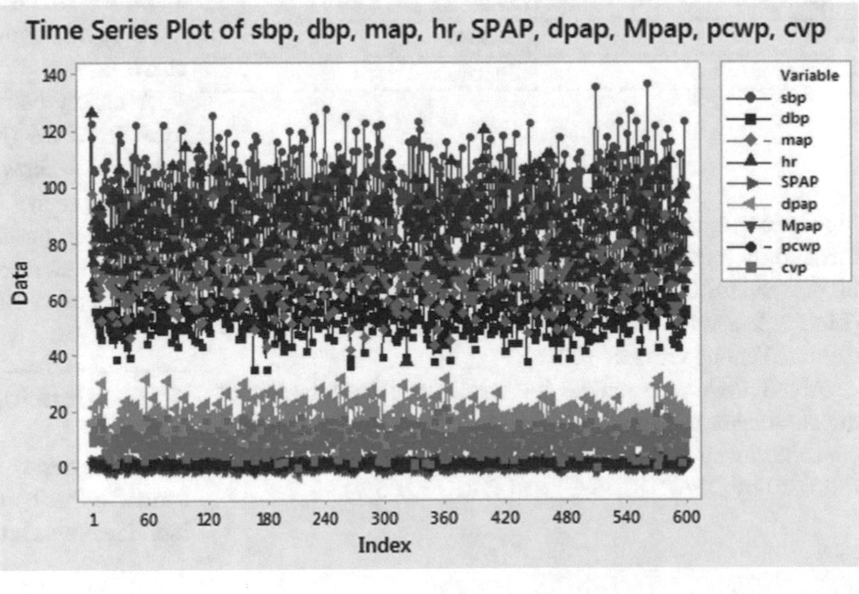

Fig. 40.1 Time series plot for 9 variables

Time Series Plot of sbp, dbp, map, hr, SPAP, dpap, Mpap, pcwp, cvp

Fig. 40.2 Out-of-controls for MEWMV chart

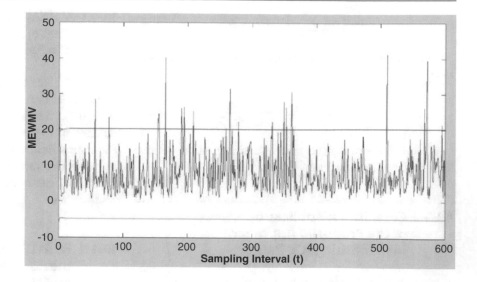

Table 40.1 Average accuracies for large variance shifts ($\omega = 0.9$) while mean is stabilized for small shifts ($\lambda = 0.1$)

Number of variables	ANNIGMA accuracy	Maximum relevance filter	SVM	Naïve-Bayes
9	96.53	96.58	96.33	94.83
8	96.96	96.58	96.33	94.83
7	96.43	96.16	96.33	96.00
6	96.26	**96.66**	96.33	96.16
5	96.53	95.66	96.33	96.66
4	96.60	95.83	96.33	**97.50**
3	**97.00**	95.83	96.33	97.33
2	96.53	95.91	96.33	96.83
1	96.86	96.33	96.33	96.83

Table 40.2 Percentage contribution of variables selected by ANNIGMA to fault signals

Variable name	% Contribution
MAP	37.96%
DPAP	31.99%
CVP	30.05%

highest accuracy (97%) achieved for ANNIGMA by monitoring only 3 characteristics, i.e., 97% of the total variability of the patient condition is due to Mean Arterial Pressure (MAP), Diastolic Pulmonary Artery Pressure (DPAP) and Central Venous Pressure (CVP).

ANNIGMA also ranked the percentage contribution of the significant variables as shown in Table 40.2. The highest contributing variable for the OOC signals is MAP (37.96%) followed by DPAP (31.99%) and CVP (30.05%).

40.5 Fault Diagnosis Using Univariate Moving Range (UMR) Charts

Traditional statistical approach for identifying variables responsible for the variance shift in multivariate chart is to deploy UMR charts for each individual variable and select the variables that produce OOC signals similar to MEWMV chart. However, this approach disregards the correlation among variables and may misdiagnosis the cause of the OOC signals (samples that are in control in multivariate chart may be OOC in UMR charts or vice versa).

UMR charts for SBP, DBP (Fig. 40.3a, b) and HR do not produce any OOC observations that matches OCCs produced by MEWMV chart. ANNIGMA removes SBP, DBP and HR variables as insignificant variables to process faults at early stage. The following UMR charts (Fig. 40.3c, d) show OOC signals for two of the responsible variables DPAP and CVP which have been identified by ANNIGMA. The OOC signals almost match those produced by the MEWMV chart.

Accuracy has been calculated for the variables selected by ANNIGMA (MAP, DPAP and CVP) using UMR charts. Table 40.3 shows the calculated accuracies are approximately close to 97% as indicated by ANNIGMA. Percentage contribution (around 33%) also in line with the ANNIGMA results. Therefore, UMR charts results further confirm the precision of results given by ANNIGMA.

40.6 Conclusion

Fault diagnostic in multivariate control chart can be performed either by deploying univariate control chart for each individual characteristics or deploying machine learning ap-

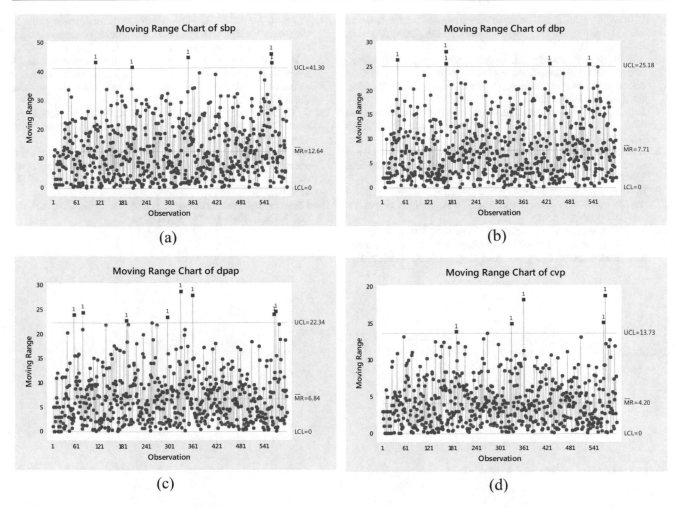

Fig. 40.3 UMR charts. (**a**) UMR charts for SBP (**b**) UMR charts for DBP (**c**) UMR charts show OOC signals for DPAP (**d**) UMR charts show OOC signals for CVP

Table 40.3 Accuracy and percentage contribution based on UMR charts

	MAP	DPAP	CVP
OOCs in MEWMV	22	22	22
OOCs in UMR	3	8	5
matching OOCs with UMR	1	5	4
matching in-controls with UMR	576	575	577
Accuracy for UMR (%)	96.1	96.6	96.8
Percentage contribution (%)	33.2	33.4	33.4

proaches such as ANNs, SVMs and ANNIGMA. However, univariate charts not only ignore the correlation among the variables but also are time consuming as the number of variables to be monitored increases. This paper for the first time deployed ANNIGMA to identify and rank the characteristics responsible for the multivariate variance shifts when monitoring ICU patients. Average classification accuracy has been used to select the most significant subset of variables. The comparison results show that ANNIGMA approach

select the responsible variables more effectively than other commonly used machine learning approaches. Information on the extent of the responsible variables' abnormal rates and rhythms to the patient condition can effectively aid the medical practitioners in their early diagnostics intervention tasks.

References

1. L. Huwang, A.B. Yeh, C. Wu, Monitoring multivariate process variabilty for individual observations. J. Qual. Technol. **39**(3), 258–278 (2007)
2. N.G.T. Gunaratne, M. Abdollahian, S. Huda, Monitoring multivariate progress variability after heart surgery, in *Innovative Trends in Multidisciplinary Academic Research,* Kuala Lumpur, 2014
3. C. Cheng, H. Cheng, Identifying the sources of variance shifts in the multivariate process using neural networks and support vector machines. Expert. Syst. Appl. **35**(1), 198–206 (2008)
4. S.T.A. Niaki, B. Abbasi, Fault diagnosis in multivariate control charts using artificial nueral networks. Qual. Reliab. Eng. **21**(8), 825–840 (2005)

5. C. IOW, C. Hsu, F. Yu, Analysis of variations in a multi-variate process using neural network. Int. J. Adv. Manuf. Technol. **22**(11), 911–121 (2003)

6. M.R. Maleki, A. Amiri, S.M. Mousavi, Step change point estimation in the multivarite-attribute process variabilty using artificial neural networks and maximum likelihood estimation. J. Ind. Eng. Int. **11**(4), 505–515 (2015)

7. S.X. Yin, H.R. Karimi, X. Zhu, Study on support vector machine based faulty detection in tennessee eastman process. Abstr. Appl. Anal. **2014**, 1–8 (2014)

8. S.R. Gunn, Support vector machines for classification and regression, Faculty of Engineering, Science and Mathematics, School of Electronics and Computer Science. 1–66 (1998)

9. R. Malhotra, Comparative analysis of statistical and machine learning methods for predicting faulty modules. Appl. Soft Comput. **21**, 286–297 (2014)

10. V. Venkatasubramanian, R. Rengaswamy, S.N. Kavuri, K. Yin, A review of process fault detection and diagnosis part III: process history based methods. Comput. Chem. Eng. **27**(3), 327–346 (2003)

11. S. Du, J. Lv, L. Xi, On-line classifying process mean shifts in multivariate control charts based on multicalss support vector machines. Int. J. Prod. Res. **50**(22), 6288–6310 (2012)

12. S. Huda, M. Abdollahian, M. Mammadav, J. Yearwood, S. Ahmed, I. Sultan, A hybrid wrapper-filter approach to detect the source(s) of out-of-control signals in multivariate manufacturing process. Eur. J. Oper. Res. **237**(3), 857–870 (2014)

13. C. Hsu, H. Huang, D. Schuschel, The ANNIGMA-Wrapper approach to fast feature selection for neural nets. IEEE Trans. Syst. Man Cybern. B Cybern. **32**(2), 207–212 (2002)

14. N.G.T. Gunaratne, M.A. Abdollahian, S. Huda, J. Yearwood, Exponentially weighted control charts to monitor multivariate process variability for high dimensions. Int. J. Prod. Res. **55**(17), 4948–4962 (2017)

15. J.S. Rosenthal, Parallel computing and Monte carlo algorithms. Far East J. Theor. Stat. **4**, 207–236 (2000)

Investigating Attribute Assessment for Credit Granting on a Brazilian Retail Enterprise

41

Strauss Carvalho Cunha, Emanuel Mineda Carneiro, Lineu Fernando Stege Mialaret, Luiz Alberto Vieira Dias, and Adilson Marques da Cunha

Abstract

In this article, we investigate which features are required to enhance a credit scoring model for a Brazilian retail enterprise. In order to find attributes that can improve the performance of classifier algorithms for credit granting, a national and an international survey were carried out. A logistic regression classifier was used and the main result has improved the performance of data mining classifiers. The main contribution of this article was the verification that additional financial and behavioral data increase defaulting prediction performance on credit granting.

Keywords

Credit granting · Attribute assessment · Classifier algorithms · Logistic regression · Receiver operating characteristic (ROC)

41.1 Introduction

On the last decades, the efficiency of management decisions has been representing an increase in the economic success of enterprises. Credit granting decisions became part of this scenario.

S. C. Cunha
Brazilian Federal Service of Data Processing - SERPRO, Brasilia, RJ, Brazil
e-mail: strauss.carvalho@serpro.gov.br

E. M. Carneiro · L. A. V. Dias · A. M. da Cunha
Federal Institute of Education, Science and Technology of Sao Paulo - IFSP, Jacarei, SP, Brazil
e-mail: mineda@ita.br; vdias@ita.br; cunha@ita.br

L. F. S. Mialaret (✉)
Computer Science Department, Brazilian Aeronautics Institute of Technology - ITA, Sao Jose dos Campos, Sao Paulo, Brazil
e-mail: lmialaret@ifsp.edu.br

The development and use of more efficient mechanisms for credit analysis and defaulting predictions have been representing fundamental issues for the commercial success of financial enterprises [2, 8, 9].

The use of predictive models for credit analysis has been implemented by the so-called credit scoring systems [1]. These systems, based upon recent customers' historical data in financial relationship with enterprises, can provide customers' different scores, allowing adequate analysis for credit decisions [10].

This research tackles the case study of a Brazilian retailer enterprise with hundreds of stores spread around the country, providing its customers with credit cards.

Typically, a credit-seeking candidate may go to a store and request a credit card, which can be used for shopping or acquiring services.

Once the credit is granted, a customer can then perform credit card transactions or obtain some personal loans, being limited to a predetermined credit profile.

The objective of the enterprise is to develop a system that allows to identify credit defaulting customers, among other available functionalities. The system uses data mining algorithms for customer defaulting predictions.

In order to improve the performance of several algorithms that presented unsatisfactory results, using demographic variables, with the Area Under Curve—Receiver Operating Characteristic (AUC-ROC) value = 0.9, we investigated which additional attributes must be used for better defaulting predictions.

The main contribution of this article was the verification that additional financial and behavioral data increase defaulting prediction performance on credit granting.

The rest of this article is organized as follows: Sect. 41.2 presents a survey on behavioral and financial attributes used for credit granting; Sect. 41.3 describes experiments using the logistic regression and others classifiers and its results; finally, Sect. 41.4 presents some conclusions, recommendations and suggestions for future work.

© Springer International Publishing AG, part of Springer Nature 2018
S. Latifi (ed.), *Information Technology – New Generations*, Advances in Intelligent Systems and Computing 738,
https://doi.org/10.1007/978-3-319-77028-4_41

41.2   Data Set Assessment

The choice and definition of data sets to be used in the defaulting prediction was a non-trivial process and the data quality has been influenced by the performance of the used algorithm. For this investigation, a sample of the data set was used and validated by the enterprise.

The initial data consisted of 6158 records, with 4461 related to the non-defaulting customers and 1696 related to defaulting customers.

The sample data set contains eight attributes: *income* (customer's income); *gender* (customer's gender); *mar_status* (customer's marital status); *dependents* (number of customer dependents); *residence* (customer residence type); *points* (customer's internal score value); *ext_credit_lim* (customer credit limit for external transactions); and *default* (the target class, classifying the customer as defaulting or non-defaulting).

41.2.1 Predictive Variables Used in Credit Scoring Systems from the International Literature

In the survey of the international specialized literature carried out by Hörkkö [7], involving 11 scientific articles, it was reported the predictive variables used for the development of theoretical and practical applications of credit scoring. Table 41.1 shows a tabulation by frequency of the variables identified within the research carried out.

In another survey of the international specialized literature, Delamaire [4] has elaborated a more in-depth research, involving 35 scientific articles, in which he has identified the predictive variables used for the development of credit scoring applications. Table 41.2 shows a frequency tabulation of the attributes identified in the investigation.

From this review, Delamaire [4] has concluded that the attributes used by researchers in credit scoring applications are different, depending upon the credit institution that provides the data.

However, socio demographic attributes such as income, age, marital status, type of housing, type of employment, number of dependents (children), or residence time at the current address are often mentioned.

Additional detailed banking information, electoral information, union membership information, nationality, and certain demographics and bank references are attributes that are not commonly used in credit scoring applications.

Table 41.1 List of variables discovered in the international specialized literature survey carried out by Hörkkö (2010), tabulated by frequency

Attribute name	#	%
Age	11	100
Income/change in income	9	82
Marital status	9	82
Residential status/housing	9	82
Occupation/type of employment	8	73
Loan size/credit limit	7	64
Current address/time in current address	6	55
Gender	6	55
Old loans/nr of other loans	6	55
Years of employment/time in present job	6	55
Zip code/region	5	45
Nr of children	4	36
Phone	4	36
Length of relationship	4	36
Maturity/duration of the loan	4	36
Credit card ownership	3	27
Education	3	27
Monthly expenses	3	27
Own resources/savings	3	27
Cosigner/guarantor	2	18
Credit type	2	18
Monthly payments	2	18
Score/points	2	18
Big city	1	9
Credit history	1	9
Foreign worker	1	9
Government assistance	1	9
Migrating out of state of birth	1	9
Nationality	1	9
Principal	1	9
Sector of employment	1	9
State of birth	1	9
Wealth	1	9
Working in private/public sector	1	9
Collateral type/value	1	9
Interest/interest rate	1	9
Loan to value ratio	1	9
Nr of payments	1	9
Payment performance	1	9

The review suggests that attributes such as age, for instance, are highly predictive.

Birth date has the advantage of being a fixed element and is generally a highly predictive attribute.

Table 41.2 List of variables discovered in the international specialized literature survey carried out by Delamaire (2012), tabulated by frequency

Attribute	#	%
Income	27	77
Age	26	74
Living status	24	69
Employment (title, class, place)	24	69
Time at present address	23	66
Marital status	22	63
Dependents-children number	20	57
Time with employer-previous	18	51
Bank accounts	16	46
Payments-outgoings	14	40
Sex	13	37
Telephone	13	37
Location	13	37
Debt	11	31
CC and other cards	11	31
CB information	11	31
Purpose of loan	9	26
Auto information	7	20
Wealth	7	20
Amount of loan	7	20
Education	6	17
Other loans 1	6	17
Spouse-family income	5	14
Race	5	14
Term of loan	5	14
Credit reference	4	11
Inquiries	4	11
Years at bank	4	11
Other reference	3	9
Insurance	3	9
Account opening	3	9
Bank reference	3	9
Age difference between man/wife	2	6
Location of relatives	2	6
Financial company reference	2	6
Electoral role	2	6
Trade union	2	6
Down payment	2	6
Account closing	2	6
Loan type	2	6
Nationality	2	6

It is possible to assume that the reason why certain attributes are recurrent in application forms is that they have a high explanatory power to identify defaulting customers.

Thus, for example, the 12 main variables surveyed (in terms of % of frequency) are often used in the development of credit granting systems, while some other attributes mentioned in these bibliographic reviews will be predictive or not, depending on the enterprise and also from the type of product for which the system was designed.

41.2.2 Predictive Variables Used in Credit Scoring Systems from the Brazilian Literature

It was carried out an investigation from the Brazilian specialized literature on the variables used in credit scoring applications, involving 36 articles, dissertations, and theses. The research results, describing the identified list of variables are presented in Table 41.3, in frequency tabulation mode.

The socio demographic variables are similar, with slight differences, from the revisions made. It is observed that the income and age variables appear in all articles. As already commented, these variables probably have a high predictive power. Other variables of this type also have intersections with the reviews carried out.

The so-called financial and behavioral variables, that contain information about customer's financial behavior, appear to be specific to the credit granting business and vary in application type.

In terms of number of variables to be used, in a research carried out by Aniceto [3], it was found that 53% of the surveyed articles used between 11 and 20 variables.

Finally, it has been observed that in the reviews, the socio demographic attributes are very similar, and attributes that characterize client's financial behavior are highly dependent on the business domain.

Behavioral variables provided by the Brazilian enterprise are presented in Table 41.4 that presents attributes, a small description, and the used aggregation function.

The provided sample data set correspond to a period of almost 2 years of financial activities.

However, for this investigation, it was considered an initial period of 13 months (10/2015 up to 10/2016). This

Table 41.3 List of variables resulting from the review of the Brazilian literature, tabulated by frequency

Attribute	#	%	Attribute	#	%
Customer age	32	89	Business net income	1	3
Gross Family Income	28	78	Total net income	1	3
Customer gender	27	75	Guarantor's gross revenue	1	3
Occupation	24	67	Guarantor's gross expense	1	3
Marital status	22	61	Guarantor's net income	1	3
Education	17	47	Last Loan Amount	1	3
Housing's type	13	36	Amount of the last loan amount	1	3
Time at present address	12	33	Nr of payments of last loan	1	3
Postal code	12	33	Indebtedness's Percentage	1	3
Financial dependents number	12	33	Nr of previous credits with the institution	1	3
Total amount of loan	12	33	Guarantor historic	1	3
Time in current address	11	31	Life insurance	1	3
Telephone	11	31	Health insurance	1	3
Nr parcels remaining	8	22	Credit card ownership	1	3
Commitment fee	8	22	Nr alienated goods	1	3
Length of relationship	7	19	Document's type	1	3
Equity situation	7	19	Investment	1	3
Credit reference	7	19	Salary	1	3
Payments value	6	17	First loan's acquisition	1	3
Wedding regime	5	14	Average card invoice	1	3
State	5	14	Nr years associated with card	1	3
Nationality	4	11	Average value of limits's excesses	1	3
Loan type	4	11	SELIC tax	1	3
Credit card quantity	4	11	SERASA register	1	3
Warranty type	4	11	Maximum delay	1	3
Age of spouse	3	8	Nr of paid parcels	1	3
Customer address	3	8	Monthly average balance	1	3
Business running time	3	8	Quarterly average balance	1	3
Average balance	3	8	Half-yearly average balance	1	3
Loans' term	3	8	CDB's balance	1	3
Nr of other loans	3	8	Investment funds balance	1	3
Financial constraints	3	8	Savings balance	1	3
Purpose of loan	3	8	Capitalization balance	1	3
Spouse income	2	6	Total reciprocity	1	3
Nature of business economic activity	2	6	Profitability	1	3
Neighborhood	2	6	Overdraft	1	3
City	2	6	Credit limit	1	3
Historic with financial institution	2	6	Alimony payment	1	3
Automotive insurance	2	6	Account balance	1	3
Residential insurance	2	6	Types of payments made	1	3
Returned check	2	6	Financial turnover	1	3
Amount accounts opening days	2	6	Utilization index	1	3
Payment's forms	2	6	Duration of the loan	1	3
Score	2	6	Contract percentage paid	1	3
Gross family expense	1	3	Payment's form (ticket or debit to account)	1	3
Familiar net income	1	3	Valor do Bem	1	3
Gross revenue	1	3	Interest rate	1	3
Expense gross	1	3	Invoice amount	1	3

Table 41.4 Additional behavioral attributes

Attribute	Description	Aggregate value
val-medio-encargo-12-ult-mes	Average value of charges in the last 12 months	Sum
qtd-bloqueio-ccred-band	Number of card locks from approval to reference date	Average
per-limite-utlz-ult-mes	Percentage use of limit in last month	Average
qtd-dia-maior-atrs-ult-3-mes	Maximum delay on card days in last 3 months	Average
per-financ-ccred-band-ult-mes	Percentage of funding in the last month	Average
qtd-ano-relc-cli	Time in years between the date of approval of the CDC and the reference date	Average
qtd-cont-ep-ult-12-mes	Number of contracts (personal loans) made in the last 12 months	Average
qtd-dia-maior-atrs-ccred-band	Maximum delay on card days, from approval to the reference date	Average
qtd-cpr-a-vista-ult-6-mes	Amount of sight purchases made in the last 6 months	Average
qtd-ftr-acima-lim-ult-6-mes	Amount of overlimit (invoice over the limit), made in the last 6 months	Average
num-idade-cliente	Age (in years) of the customer on the reference date	Average
qtd-ocor-spc-ult-24-mes-fech	Number of times the customer was denied or rehabilitated in the spc in the last 24 months	Sum
per-min-recb-fatura-ult-6-mes	Minimum percentage of invoice receipt in the last 6 months	Average
val-sld-dev-tot-ult-mes	Total debtor balance in the last month	Average
qtd-mes-atu-renda	Time in months between the reference date and the date of the last update of the rent	Average
qtd-pagto-acima-lim-ult-12-mes	Number of times the customer pays more than the minimum in the last 12 months	Sum
qtd-ocor-cobr-recd-ult-12-mes	Number of billing messages left for the customer in the last 12 months	Sum

sample data set has been stored in tables of a Data Base Management System (DBMS), in order to allow a more appropriate manipulation.

41.3 Experiments

The following experiments were performed using a different samples strategy for training and testing classifiers. The logistic regression classifier was chosen for these experiments, mainly because assessments have shown that it performs better, when compared to other classifiers.

One of the objectives of these experiments was to evaluate with past information, if it is possible to predict, with what performance and accuracy, future customer behaviors in terms of default patterns.

In order to implement these experiments, it was decided to use the Orange tool [5].

The created model is shown in Fig. 41.1, applying k-$fold$ cross-validation ($k = 10$), where the initial data set was randomly partitioned into k subsets (*folds*) k_1, k_2, ..., k_k of mutually exclusive sizes of approximately equal size. Training and testing were performed k times, and for each iteration i, the subset D_i was used as test set, and the other subsets were used for training the model [6, 11].

41.3.1 The Experiment Number 1

For the execution of this experiment 1, table *bhs-band-2015-10-12-cadast-behav* contains training samples and table *bhs-band-2016-10-01-cadast-behav* contains test samples.

In this experiment, it was used logistic regression classifier and gain ratio metric, to define the most important attributes for defaulting predictions.

After the classifier execution, the result of the AUC-ROC metric and other obtained measures, is shown in Fig. 41.2. It is observed that the value of the ROC Curve (AUC-ROC) is 0.986.

The confusion matrix obtained from this experiment has presented a percentage of false positives of 2.3% and of false negatives of 4.3%. As noticed, the classifier predicted 100 non-default customers as defaulting customers and predicted 36 defaulting customers as non-defaulting.

41.3.2 The Experiment Number 2

For the second experiment, the *bhs-band-2015-10-12-cadast-behav* and *bhs-band-adi-defaults-2016-not-2015* tables were used. The last table contains customers from the year 2016 data set who are not at the year 2015 data set. The metric gain ratio was used to define the most important attributes in prediction.

By executing the regressive model, the result of the AUC-ROC metric and other measures of classifier's performance used is shown in Fig. 41.3. The value of the ROC Curve (AUC-ROC) was equal to 0.987 in training.

As observed from the obtained confusion matrix, the classifier has predicted 20 non-defaulting customers as defaulting customers (about 3.0% of customers as false positives) and has predicted 5 defaulting customers as non-defaulting customers (about 2.8% of defaulting customers as false negatives). It is noticed that with this training, based on

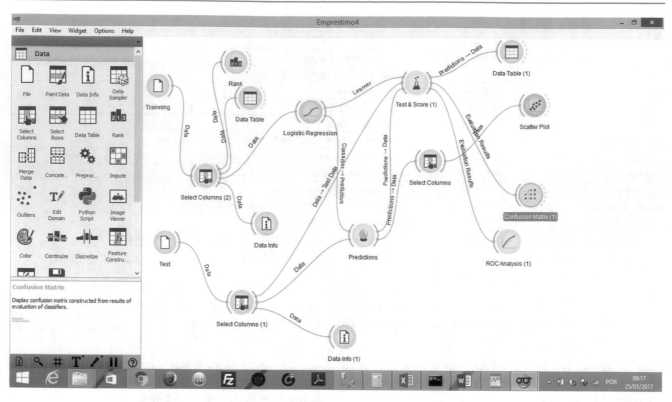

Fig. 41.1 The created model in the orange tool

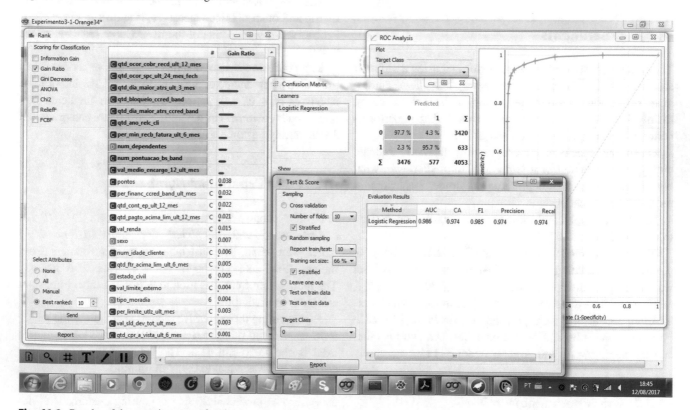

Fig. 41.2 Results of the experiment number 1

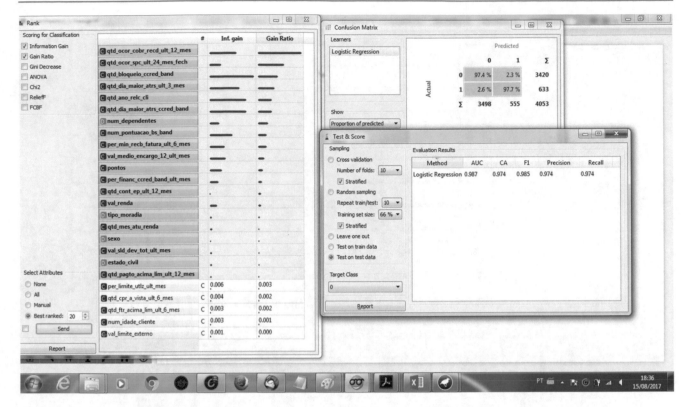

Fig. 41.3 Results of the experiment number 2

data from the year 2015, predictions were made about the defaulting customer in data from 2016, for customers who were not at the data set from the 2015 year.

41.3.3 The Experiment Number 3

For this experiment, two data sets were generated: one containing attributes characterized as demographics attributes and other containing attributes considered as financial/behavioral attributes. The performed analysis consisted of the evaluation of the performance of certain classifiers in the two data sets, in order to measure the improvement of the prediction with the use of these data sets.

From the specific case of the first data set, named *B1-Cadast*, which contains only demographics data, the following classifiers were used: Logistic Regression (LR), *k*-Nearest Neighbors (*k*NN), Decision Trees (DT), and Support Vector Machine (SVM). The Orange tool was used to perform the evaluation.

The assessment consisted of submitting the classifiers for several executions and, in each of them, a certain attribute was removed, based upon its value of the gain ratio metric (the attributes of smaller values were first removed).

Figure 41.4 presents the evaluation of the four classifiers mentioned, used in the *B1-Cadast* data set. It was observed

that the LR classifier has obtained the best performance in terms of AUC-ROC values, and the kNN classifier was the second best result in the evaluation. The DT and SVM classifiers obtained the worst results.

The next evaluation consisted of submitting the same classifiers to a new data set, called *B1-Cadast-Behav*, containing demographic data, together with the behavioral/financial data.

The four classifiers previously mentioned were used in this data set and Fig. 41.5 presents the evaluation of the classifiers. It is again observed that the LR classifier was the one that obtained the best performance, in terms of AUC-ROC values, and the DT classifier obtained the second best result in this evaluation. The *k*NN and SVM classifiers had the worst results.

It is observed that the junction of the two data sets, *B1-Cadast* and *B1-Cadast-Behav* significantly increases the predictive capacity of the LR classifier model, especially when only 19 variables are used, with an AUC-ROC value equal to 0.997.

Some observations obtained from these three experiments are necessary to state here:

- The use of behavioral variables significantly improves the prediction of defaulting customers, and classifiers get AUC-ROC values approximate from what was obtained in the specialized literature; and

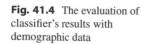

Fig. 41.4 The evaluation of classifier's results with demographic data

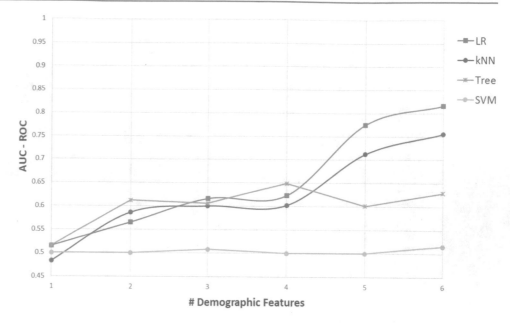

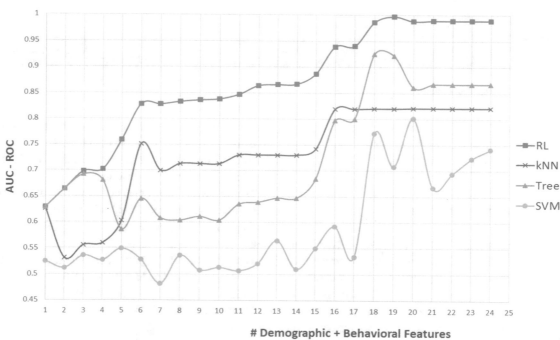

Fig. 41.5 Evaluation of classifier's results with demographic and behavioral data

- the data provided by the retail enterprise have allowed to confirm, based on performed tests, that high quality data (demographic and behavioral) were provided, which allows a significant accuracy in the classifier used.

41.4 Conclusion

This investigation was carried out on aspects inherent to data extraction from the development of the credit scoring system

prototype. Initial demographic data used were not adequate for defaulting predictions.

In order to improve accuracy on prediction, additional behavioral/finance data was investigated in specialized literature, to obtain also additional features to improve credit scoring. Real data was used and provided by a Brazilian retailer enterprise.

The Logistic Regression (LR) classifier was used and the results have shown that additional data have improved the classifier performance.

One area for further work is to use different classifiers and analyze their performance. Other area is getting more behavioral/finance attributes.

Acknowledgements The authors would like to thank: the Brazilian Aeronautics Institute of Technology (ITA); the Casimiro Montenegro Filho Foundation (FCMF); the Software Engineering Research Group (GPES) members; and the 2RP Net Enterprise for their infrastructure, assistance, advice, data set, and financial support for this work.

References

1. J. Abellán, G. Castellano, A comparative study on base classifiers in ensemble methods for credit scoring. Expert Syst. Appl. **73**, 1–10 (2017)
2. M. Ala'raj, M.F. Abbod, A new hybrid ensemble credit scoring model based on classifiers consensus system approach. Expert Syst. Appl. **64**, 36–55 (2016)
3. M.C. Aniceto, Estudo comparativo entre técnicas de aprendizado de máquina para estimação de risco de crédito. Dissertação (Mestrado em Administração). Universidade de Brasília, Brasília, 2016
4. L. Delamaire, Implementing a credit risk management system based on innovative scoring techniques, Ph.D. thesis, University of Birmingham, 2012
5. J. Demšar, T. Curk, A. Erjavec, Č. Gorup, T. Hočevar, M. Milutinovič, M. Možina, M. Polajnar, M. Toplak, A. Starič, M. Stajdohar, L. Umek, L. Zagar, J. Zbontar, M. Zitnik, B. Zupan, Orange: data mining toolbox in python. J. Mach. Learn. Res. **14**, 2349–2353 (2013)
6. J. Han, M. Kamber, J. Pei, *Data Mining - Concepts and Techniques*, 3rd edn. (Morgan Kaufmann, Amsterdam, 2012)
7. M. Hörkkö, The determinants of default in consumer credit market. Masters thesis, Aalto University School of Economics (2010). Retrived from http://epub.lib.aalto.fi/en/ethesis/pdf/12299/hse_ethesis_12299.pdf
8. M.B. Pascual, A.M. Martínez, A.M. Alamillos, Redes bayesianas aplicadas a problemas de credit scoring. Una aplicación práctica. Cuadernos de Economía **37**(104), 73–86 (2014)
9. R.M. Stein, The relationship between default prediction and lending profits: Integrating ROC analysis and loan pricing. J. Bank. Finance **29**, 1213–1236 (2005)
10. B. Waad, B.M. Ghazi, L. Mohamed, A three-stage feature selection using quadratic programming for credit scoring. Appl. Artif. Intell. Int. J. **27**, 8 (2013)
11. I. Witten, E. Frank, *Data Mining Practical Machine Learning Tools and Techniques*, 2nd edn. (Elsevier, Amsterdam, 2005)

Rafael P. da Silva, Flávio A. O. Santos, Filipe B. do Nascimento, and Hendrik T. Macedo

Abstract

Sentiment Analysis (SA) employs Natural Language Processing (NLP) techniques in order to infer emotional states and subjective information contained in texts. Generally, previously trained machine learning models are used to identify the polarity of an opinion concerning a given target (e.g. film, book, etc.). Therefore, engineering features in order to create the training set for the learning model is a central task in SA problems. Additionally, finding properly labeled datasets for NLP models containing non-English text is a big challenge. Thus, we aim to contribute to SA in texts written in Brazilian Portuguese (PtBR) by validating the use of ConvNet, a convolutional neural network (CNN) that works with character-level inputs, in analyzing the polarity of product reviews in PtBR. The results obtained from our experiments confirm the model's efficiency.

Keywords

Sentiment analysis · Natural language processing · Convolutional neural network · Character level representation · Linguistic corpus for PtBR

42.1 Introduction

Entrepreneurs, politicians, institutions and organizations are often interested in detailed information about their position in terms of public acceptance and opinion. The field of

R. P. da Silva · F. B. do Nascimento
Departamento de Computação, Universidade Federal de Sergipe, São Cristóvão, Brazil
e-mail: rafaelps@dcomp.ufs.br; filipe.nascimento@dcomp.ufs.br

F. A. O. Santos · H. T. Macedo (✉)
Programa de Pós-Graduação em Ciência da Computação, Universidade Federal de Sergipe, São Cristóvão, Brazil
e-mail: flavio.santos@dcomp.ufs.br; hendrik@dcomp.ufs.br

Artificial Intelligence that attempts to extract that kind of information from text sources is called Sentiment Analysis.

Performing SA is a challenging task because it is usually associated to extra preprocessing requirements [15]. However, according to [22], this task can be performed without preprocessing stages or embedded knowledge by ConvNet, a Convolutional Neural Network (CNN) with specific architecture that works with *character-level* inputs.

Motivated by the good results presented by CNNs in image processing tasks, researchers have started applying this model to Natural Language Processing (NLP), Text Classification and Sentiment Analysis in English and Chinese, among other languages. The ConvNet's behavior is still undocumented for texts in Brazilian Portuguese (PtBR) originated from automatic translation (English to PtBR). Therefore, we attempt to validate the use of this CNN in PtBR. We also train a CNN classifier for SA of product reviews written in PtBR.

This work is comprised of two main tasks: reproduction of the state-of-the-art work for cross-lingual SA by [22] and construction of a dataset containing reviews translated to PtBR from the Amazon-Review (AR) dataset, which contains product reviews written in English. As a collateral contribution, we have made the translated dataset available on line, contributing to the availability of labeled datasets in Portuguese that are as significant as the AR dataset for SA tasks.

The paper is organized as follows. In Sect. 42.2 we present the problem our project addresses and existing research results. In Sect. 42.3, it presents the input coding of the network, introduces the design [22] and describes dataset used to train the classifiers. Section 42.4 describes the experiments carried out in order to validate the proposal. Section 42.5 presents and discusses the results obtained through these experiments. Finally, Sect. 42.6 highlights the contributions, limitations, and ideas of future work.

42.2 Related Works

Most of the work performed in the AS task require that the training characteristics carry some kind of specific knowledge or that they have already been submitted to some pre-processing before even beginning the training of some classifier. Although there is still little embedded knowledge, works like [9, 10] introduce characteristics that come from characters. Already [22,23] shows that ConvNet with specific architecture can learn representations that are generated from words at level of characters without any additional knowledge.

The classification of cross-lingual sentiment seeks to transfer sentiments resources from one "rich" source language to another "poor" target language. This transfer is justified because making AS may require features such as sentiment dictionaries, labeled documents, or *labeled corpora*, and in many languages this is an almost inescapable problem in the face of the scarcity of such resources. For a subjectivity analysis task, which is a key subtask in sentence-level and entity-level AS, [6] proposes a method that transfers feeling resources from one source language to another target language using automatic translation systems (STAs). Prettenhofer and Stein [17] is based on cross-lingual structural matching (CL-SCL) learning to induce multilingual matches between source and target words in AS. Lu et al. [13] proposes the model called Join that consists of the union of an Entropy-based Maximun and a Likelihood model to adapt feeling resources. Pan et al. [16] designed model called BNMTF based on the NMTF model. While [19,20] it creates semi-labeled dictionaries labeled auto-level.

The integration of both distinct features (origin and target) is one of the paths that can be followed to improve classifier performance using labeled dataset that has its sentiment features transferred or projected from another source dataset (origin). In this point, [21] united characteristics of both languages in the Co-train approach. Banea et al. [7] integrates the characteristics to the multilingual classification with focus on a language. Balahur and Perea-Ortega [3] works with *unigrams* and *bigrams* features.

Works such as [4, 8] report the problems that may occur in the classification of sentiment when using target data that comes from a source language through STA in multilingual AS. In general, there may be an increase in the number of features, dispersion, addition of noise, change in word order, translation errors when taking context or different denial structures of each language. This can lead to loss of performance. Despite this, translated data is reliable. Balahur et al. [5], Balahur and Turchi [4] noted that the use of STA, which are widely used to obtain target data, brings significant improvement to the classifier.

In order to overcome these problems, there are approaches that combine models, introduce syntactic, lexical and semantic information [8]. Zhou et al. [24] already works with bilingual document representation learning (BiDRL). Mogadala and Rettinger [14] transfers knowledge from one source resource to another through the BRASE model. Finally, [12] proposes SCL learning based on distributed representations of words.

Already [1, 2] carries out a comprehensive evaluation of AS methods developed for the English language, applying them to the dataset translated into 9 different languages including portuguese. Santos et al. [11] analyzed which approach between use of lexicon of sentiment and machine learning, has better results for classification of emotions in multilingual texts and their translations to portuguese. The results show that machine learning is better.

Unlike the related works, we use the method [22] that does not require any kind of preprocessing, or embedded knowledge. Thus, it works directly with characters, on the entries of the polar and multi-class classifier. We focus on the portuguese language PtBR. Also the dataset labeled in PtBR created, is in scale of millions in quantity of samples in whereas others have hundreds or thousands of them.

42.3 Method

Given a discrete input function $g(x) \in [1, l] \rightarrow R$ and a discrete kernel function $f(x) \in [1, k] \rightarrow R$, a 1-D convolution, $h(y) \in [1, \lfloor \frac{(l-k)}{d} \rfloor + 1]$ is calculated between $f(x)$ and $g(x)$ with *stride d*:

$$h(y) = \sum_{x=1}^{k} f(x).g(y.d - x + c), \qquad (42.1)$$

where $c = k - d + 1$ is a constant *offset* [22]. Besides, is usual parametrize a convolution by a set of kernel function $f_{ij}(x)(i = 1, 2, \ldots, m$ e $n = 1, 2, \ldots, n)$, which we call weights, input set $g_i(x)$ and outputs $h_j(y)$ ($g_i(x)$ is input *frame* and $h_j(y)$ is output frame), m is the input frame length and n is the output frame length. Thus, the outputs $h_j(y)$ are formed by sum of convolutions between $g_i(x)$ and $f_{ij}(x)$ over index i. We generate features map after convolutions and calculate the 1-D max-pooling operation.

Therefore, given an discrete input function $g(x) \in [1, l]$, the function max-pooling $hh(y) \in [1, \lfloor \frac{(l-k)}{d} \rfloor + 1] \to R$ is defined as:

$$hh(y) = \max_{x=1}^{k} g(y.d - x + c), \qquad (42.2)$$

where $c = k - d + 1$ is a constant *offset*. We used the non-linear function $h(x) = \max(0, x)$ as activation function. It is similar to rectified linear units (ReLUs).

42.3.1 Character Quantization

The ConvNet [22] take the inputs as an character sequence of length l encode as *one-hot-code*. If some character to exceed l it is ignored. If the input character is not on character vocabulary or it is blank space, it is encoded as a vector of zeros. The alphabet M (with dimension m) to idiom english is formed by characters:

abcdefghijklmnopqrstuvwxyz0123456789−,; .!? :'''/|| @#$%ˆ& ∗˜`+− =<> ()[]

We included more 11 characters to idiom portuguese: "*áàãéêíóôõúç*", totalizing 81 *features*. That way, the input is a matrix X of dimension m x l. Although the model (ConvNet) be fed by sparse inputs (many zeros) and it do not use any normalization, there is not waste [22].

42.3.2 Model Architecture

The model is formed by nine deep layers, see Table 42.1. We used six convolutional layers and three fully-connected layers. Those layers use different hidden units number and different frame size (small frame). Table 42.1 show the model architecture and denote the configurations to dense and convolutional layers. We used two dropout layers between that dense layers.

Table 42.1 Model architecture configuration

Convolutional layers			
Layer	Small frame	Kernel (Filtro)	Pool
1	256	7	3
2	256	7	3
3	256	3	nda
4	256	3	nda
5	256	3	nda
6	256	3	3
Dense layers			
	Unit small output		
7	1024		
8	1024		
9	Depends on the problem		

42.4 Experiments

42.4.1 Dataset and Training Details

The Amazon-Review[1] (AR) is a dataset of 34,686,770 reviews from 6,643,669 users about 2,441,053 products whose opinions are labeled and listed in the five classes. This dataset was got from the Stanford Network Analysis Project (SNAP).

Table 42.2, in the Dataset AR lines, shows the number of samples after the selection of dataset AR reviews with lengths of 100–1014 characters and it is not repeated. The Multi-class and Polar datasets were generated through random sample selection by DatasMulti-class and DatasPolar class, with their amounts specified in the table.

Each review in the dataset has a title, a label and the message expressed by someone. The labels are enumeration 1 through 5, that are "very bad", "bad", "neutral", "good" and "very good". The labels 1 and 2 were mapped to the negative class and the 4 and 5 were mapped to the positive class in the polarity classification. The label 3 was not considered for this type of classification because a review of this class does not clearly state the opinion expressed in it.

The tool[2] uses for translation of AR in english into portuguese, in sentiment classification, was based Google Translate.

42.4.2 Settings

The experiment settings have their hyper-parameters configured such as the weights were randomly initialized using Gaussian Distribution with mean equal to zero and variance equal to 0.05, momentum is equal to 0.9. ReLU activation function and learning rate (lr) equal to 0.01 were used. In addition, the two layers of dropouts have a value of 0.5. Finally, each minibatch has 128 samples and the experiments were trained in 10 epochs, every three times the lr is reduce by halved.

Table 42.2 Amount of samples in datasets

	Total	Train	Test
Dataset AR (English and PtBR)			
DatasMulti-class	3,650,000	3,000,000	650,000
DatasPolar	4,000,000	3,600,000	400,000
Amount for each class (English and PtBR)			
Multi-class		600,000	130,000
Polar		1,800,000	200,000

---

[1] http://snap.stanford.edu/data/web-Amazon.html.
[2] https://github.com/rafaelps1/translate_from_csv.

Table 42.3 Description of the settings

Setting	Dataset	Language	Features amount
1	Multi-class	English	70
2	Multi-class	Portuguese	81
3	Polar	English	70
4	Polar	Portuguese	81

Table 42.3 show the setting of experiments performed in this work. First column named Setting identifies each setting via enumeration 1 through 4. The second column named Dataset informs which dataset is used for each setting. The Multi-class dataset has 5 classes and Polar dataset has 2 classes. The Language column informs the language of each dataset. The Features Amount column informs the number of features used in the ConvNet training process.

42.5 Results

42.5.1 Multi-class Classification

Figure 42.1 show accuracy and loss curve related to training and test dataset.

We choose epochs 5 and 6 because its presents better accuracy at test dataset and a lower loss compared to other epochs. To setting 1, follow the curve with label "En acc test", "En loss test". To setting 2, follow the curve with label "Pt acc test", "Pt loss test".

42.5.2 Polar Classification

Based on Fig. 42.2, we can see that epoch 4 and 5 has better results, according to adoted on Sect. 42.5.1 to classification. The curve with labels "En acc test" and "En loss test" represents setting 3. The curve with labels "Pt acc test" and "Pt loss test" represents setting 4.

42.5.3 Discussion

Tables 42.4 and 42.5 present the metric values and difference between accuracy, taking as reference the results of work [22].

From Table 42.4 we conclude which test accuracy of setting 1 is better than [22] in 1.99%. Setting 2 results is better than [22] in 1.45%. Its obtained results were expected, seeing that the dataset manages to transfer sentiment resources via STA. Table 42.5 show difference between their accuracy is 0.97%. The difference between accuracy of setting 4 and [22] is equal to 2.55%.

Thus, we consider that the objective was achieved because the minimum performance distance to polar classification is 2.5% between [22] and classifier at setting 4. The minimum performance difference to multi-class classification at setting 2 is 1.45%. Besides, when we compare the results of setting 2 and 4 with classifiers *Constituency Tree LSTM* [18], accuracy 88.1%, and *CNN-multichannel* [18], accuracy 50.6%, we note that classifiers are 7.52 and 3.85% better then setting 2 and 4 classifiers.

42.6 Conclusion

Through the creation of a dataset containing millions of properly labeled product reviews in PtBR (translated from AR in English), our work contributes to SA of texts written in PtBR. Our results confirm that the sentiment transfer process via automatic translation has proven to be effective: we have managed to analyse the sentiment of translated reviews with good accuracy, validating the use of CNNs with character-level inputs for this task.

We use the neural network architecture [22] because it allows learning directly from characters, the inputs do not require preprocessing or embedded knowledge. In addition, this architecture is robust as words outside the portuguese language, since there are many words that are not found in the classic embeddings.

As future work, we intend to use the dataset containing texts [4, 5, 21] in English and its PtBR translated version in order to train the same CNN.

Acknowledgements The authors thank CAPES and FAPITEC-SE for the financial support [Edital CAPES/FAPITEC/SE No 11/2016—PROEF, Processo 88887.160994/2017-00] and LCAD-UFS for providing a cluster for the execution of the experiments. The authors also thank FAPITEC-SE for granting a graduate scholarship to Flávio Santos, CNPq for granting a graduate scholarship to Filipe Nascimento and a productivity scholarship to Hendrik Macedo [DT-II, Processo 310446/2014-7]

Fig. 42.1 Evaluation of English and Portuguese multi-class classification to setting 1 and 2

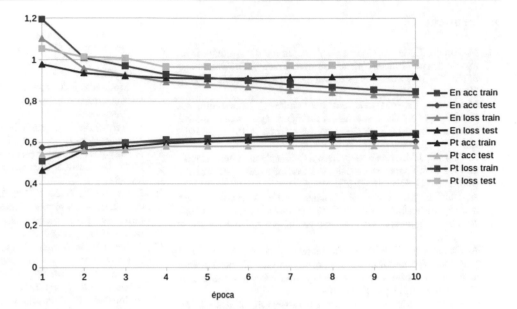

Fig. 42.2 Evaluation of English and Portuguese polar classification to setting 3 and 4

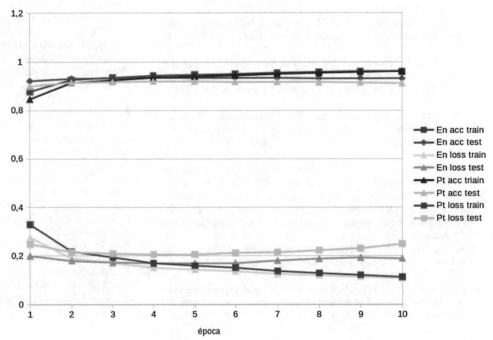

Table 42.4 Results of multi-class classification, small ConvNet model

	Language	Epoch	Acc/train (%)	Acc/test (%)
ConvNet [22]	English	–	69.24	59.57
Setting 1	English	6	62.29	60.56
Setting 2	Portuguese	5	60.32	58.12
ConvNet-Setting 1	–	–	6.95	−1.99
ConvNet-Setting 2	–	–	8.92	1.45

Table 42.5 Results of multi-class classification, small ConvNet model

	Language	Epoch	Acc/train (%)	Acc/test (%)
ConvNet [22]	English	–	96.03	94.50
Setting 3	English	4	94.33	93.53
Setting 4	Portuguese	5	93.96	91.95
ConvNet-Setting 3	–	–	1.7	0.97
ConvNet-Setting 4	–	–	2.07	2.55

References

1. M. Araújo, J. Reis, P. Gonçalves, A. Pereira, F. Benevenuto, Uma abordagem multilíngue para análise de sentimentos, in *Proceedings of the Brazilian Workshop on Social Network Analysis and Mining (BraSNAM)*, 2015
2. M. Araújo, J.C. dos Reis, A.C.M. Pereira, F. Benevenuto, An evaluation of machine translation for multilingual sentence-level sentiment analysis, in *SAC* (ACM, New York, 2016), pp. 1140–1145
3. A. Balahur, J.M. Perea-Ortega, Sentiment analysis system adaptation for multilingual processing: the case of tweets. Inf. Process. Manag. **51**(4), 547–556 (2015)
4. A. Balahur, M. Turchi, Multilingual sentiment analysis using machine translation? in *WASSA '12 Proceedings of the 3rd Workshop in Computational Approaches to Subjectivity and Sentiment Analysis*, 2012
5. A. Balahur, M. Turchi, R. Steinberger, Resource creation and evaluation for multilingual sentiment analysis in social media texts, in *Proceedings of the Language Resources and Evaluation Conference* (2001), pp. 4265–4269
6. C. Banea, R. Mihalcea, Multilingual subjectivity analysis using machine translation. Proceedings of EMNLP '08 Proceedings of the Conference on Empirical Methods in Natural Language Processing, Pages 127–135, Honolulu, Hawaii, USA, October 25–27, 2008
7. C. Banea, R. Mihalcea, J. Wiebe, Multilingual subjectivity: are more languages better? in *Proceedings of the 23rd International Conference on Computational Linguistics (Coling 2010)* (2010), pp. 28–36
8. S. Chitra, B. Madhusudhanan, G.R. Sakthidharan, P. Saravanan, Density based active self training for cross lingual sentiment classification. Lect. Notes Electr. Eng. **279**, 1225–1234 (2014)
9. C.N. dos Santos, M. Gatti, Deep convolutional neural networks for sentiment analysis of short texts, in *Coling-2014* (2014), pp. 69–78
10. C.N. Dos Santos, B. Zadrozny, Learning character-level representations for part-of-speech tagging, in *Proceedings of the 31st International Conference on International Conference on Machine Learning*, vol. 32 (2014)
11. A.G.L. dos Santos, K. Becker, V. Moreira, Mineração de emoções em textos multilíngues usando um corpus paralelo. SBBD Proc. **49**(79), 6–9 (2014)
12. N. Li, S. Zhai, Z. Zhang, B. Liu, Structural correspondence learning for cross-lingual sentiment classification with one-to-many mappings. CoRR (2016). abs/1611.0
13. B. Lu, C. Tan, C. Cardie, B.K. Tsou, Joint bilingual sentiment classification with unlabeled parallel corpora, in *Proceedings of the 49th Annual Meeting of the Association for Computational Linguistics: Human Language Technologies*, vol. 1(1) (2011), pp. 320–330
14. A. Mogadala, A. Rettinger, Bilingual word embeddings from parallel and non-parallel corpora for cross-language text classification, in *Proceedings of the 2016 Conference of the North American Chapter of the Association for Computational Linguistics: Human Language Technologies* (2016), pp. 692–702
15. P. Norvig, A unified theory of inference for text understanding, Ph.D. thesis, EECS Department, University of California, Berkeley, 1987
16. J. Pan, G.-R. Xue, Y. Yu, Y. Wang, Cross-lingual sentiment classification via bi-view non-negative matrix tri-factorization, in *Advances in Knowledge Discovery and Data Mining* (Springer, Berlin, 2011), pp. 289–290
17. P. Prettenhofer, B. Stein, Cross-language text classification using structural correspondence learning, in *ACL '10 Proceedings of the 48th Annual Meeting of the Association for Computational Linguistics* (2010), pp. 1118–1127
18. P. Singhal, P. Bhattacharyya, Sentiment analysis and deep learning: a survey (2016). Available online at: https://www.semanticscholar.org/paper/Sentiment-Analysis-and-Deep-Learning%3A-A-Survey-Singhal-Bhattacharyya/c60142358a3ff29a0b211673ccd74b6af14b7c85
19. J. Steinberger, P. Lenkova, M. Kabadjov, R. Steinberger, E. Van Der Goot, Multilingual entity-centered sentiment analysis evaluated by parallel corpora, in *Recent Advances in Natural Language Processing* (2011), pp. 770–775
20. J. Steinberger, M. Ebrahim, M. Ehrmann, A. Hurriyetoglu, M. Kabadjov, P. Lenkova, R. Steinberger, H. Tanev, S. Vázquez, V. Zavarella, Creating sentiment dictionaries via triangulation. Decis. Support Syst. **53**(4), 689–694 (2012)
21. X. Wan, Co-training for cross-lingual sentiment classification, in *ACL '09 Proceedings of the Joint Conference of the 47th Annual Meeting of the ACL and the 4th International Joint Conference on Natural Language* (2009), pp. 235–243
22. X. Zhang, Y. LeCun, Text understanding from scratch. APL Mater. **3**(5), 011102 (2016)
23. X. Zhang, J. Zhao, Y. LeCun, Character-level convolutional networks for text classification, in *NIPS Proceedings* (2015), pp. 1–9
24. X. Zhou, X. Wan, J. Xiao, Cross-lingual sentiment classification with bilingual document representation learning, in *Proceedings of the 54th Annual Meeting of the Association for Computational Linguistics (ACL 2016)* (2016), pp. 1403–1412

Thematic Spatiotemporal Association Rules to Track the Evolving of Visual Features and Their Meaning in Satellite Image Time Series

43

C. R. Silveira Jr., J. R. Cecatto, M. T. P. Santos, and M. X. Ribeiro

Abstract

Satellite Image Time Series (SITS) is a set of images taken from the same satellite scene at different times. The mining of SITS is challenging task because it requires spatiotemporal data analysis. An example of the need for SITS mining is the analysis of solar flares and their evolving. Thematic Spatiotemporal Association Rules (TSARs) are associations that show spatiotemporal relationships among the values of the thematics attributes. By employing TSARs, we propose an approach to track the evolving of visual features of SITS images and their meaning. Our approach, called Miner of Thematic Spatiotemporal Associations for Images (MiTSAI), considers the data extracting and transformation, the thematic spatiotemporal association rule mining (TSARs), and the post-processing of the mined TSARs, that relate the visual features and their meaning. Our experiment shows that the proposed approach improves the domain expert team understanding of Solar SITS. Moreover, MiTSAI presented an acceptable time performance being able of extracting and processing TSARs using a long period of historical data faster than the period needed for the arrival of new data in the database.

Keywords

Image classification · Spatiotemporal association classifier · Solar data · Thematic spatiotemporal association rules extraction · Temporal series of images · Temporal series of semantic data

C. R. Silveira Jr. (✉) · M. T. P. Santos · M. X. Ribeiro
Federal University of São Carlos (UFSCar), São Carlos, Brazil
e-mail: carlos.silveira@dc.ufscar.br; marilde@dc.ufscar.br; marcela@dc.ufscar.br

J. R. Cecatto
National Institute of Space Research, São José dos Campos, Brazil
e-mail: jr.cecatto@inpe.br

43.1 Introduction

A considerable amount of spatiotemporal data is daily generated by many different sources. Satellites are one of these sources that produce Satellite Image Time Series (SITS). In our work, the SITS are employed to analyze the solar data behavior. Solar SITSs are composed of solar images (acquired using different wavelengths)—collected along the time. The images can present sunspots (solar active regions) and they are enriched with textual data that classify the image sunspots. The textual data presents the sunspot's location (solar coordinates) and the date when the images were collected (spatiotemporal characteristics).

To enable a better understanding of Solar SITS behavior and to support the prediction of its behavior, we propose the Miner of Thematic Spatiotemporal Associations for Images (MiTSAI) algorithm. Our proposal is supported by the hypotheses: (1) it is possible to handle textual, spatiotemporal, and visual data, making the Solar SITS data manageable for data mining; (2) the extraction of Thematic Spatiotemporal Association Rules (TSAR) aids the analysis of the solar domain, and; (3) the TSAR can be post-processed to relate the visual sunspot features, their evolving and meaning, supporting its behavior analysis. TSARs consider the temporal evolution of the sunspots and also the relationship inside the sunspots that happen at the same time.

In our proposed method, a pre-processing access the Solar SITS, processing each image and the image's textual data in parallel. The result of this pre-processing is split according to the sunspots. MiTSAI extracts TSARs from the pre-processed solar SITS considering the visual features, their textual data, and their spatiotemporal features. The extracted TSARs are validated by the domain expert team. The domain expert team is the responsible for defining whether the mined rules are valid and also if the performance of the algorithm is acceptable. The TSARs are post-processed generating rules that relate the visual sunspots features, their evolving and their meaning, producing generalized rules are employed to analysis the sunspot behavior. The performance criterion is that MiTSAI must be able of extracting and processing TSARs using a long period of historical data, at least 8 years, faster than the period needed for the arrival of new data in the database.

This paper is organized as follows: Sect. 43.2 presents the concepts and background; Sect. 43.3 presents our proposed algorithm, the Miner of Thematic Spatiotemporal Associations for Images (MiTSAI); Sect. 43.4 presents the experiments performed to validate the MiTSAI and a discussion about their results; and Sect. 43.5 presents the conclusions and future works.

43.2 Concepts and Background

Satellite images are examples of sensor data, such as global position data, and their usage brings the necessity of processing huge volumes of data that are usually non-structured [1]. In several works in the literature, satellite images are processed using the Big Data concepts to handle those characteristics [2, 3].

The Hu et al. [4]-proposal uses the Hadoop Framework to store solar information (related to solar farms network) and manipulate it performing queries over this data. This approach allows the manipulation of a huge amount of data that also includes images. However, it does not perform any image processing, limiting its applicability. When working with Solar Satellite Images, the images demand pre-processing to separate the several sunspots that can occur in 1 day.

Cortés et al. [5] use high-resolution satellite images to detect patterns related to new/old ice coverage in different periods. That analysis does not require image pre-processing to extract feature vectors. That approach reduces the flexibility by not internally processing the images.

Spatiotemporal data are described by space and time properties [6, 7], supporting its behavior prediction. In a formal definition: the D-database is spatiotemporal only if its items have spatiotemporal characteristics. I.e., if i is an item of D-database then i is compose of tuples of the form $\{x, y, z, t, F\}$, where x, y and z are coordinations in a Cartesian space; t is a temporal coordination, and; F is a set of thematic attributes (non-spatiotemporal). Instances of spatiotemporal data are: meteorological data, sensor data, network traffic, among others [8, 9].

The spatiotemporal mining algorithms consider the space and time constraints. In this work, the constraints are applied during the mining process such as Pillai et al. [10] when the algorithm starts generating the itemset candidates. This step combines the frequent itemsets, generating itemset candidates that are larger than the seeds. If it is the first iteration, the frequent itemsets are the frequent items extracted from the database. The candidate itemsets are filtered using the spatial constraint (set by the user) resulting in spatial itemsets candidates. Those itemsets are filtered using the time constraints (set by the user) resulting in spatiotemporal itemsets candidates. The frequency of these candidates is calculated and the frequents are filtered. The frequent spatiotemporal itemsets are used as the seed to the candidate generation in the next iteration. If it is not possible to generate new frequent itemsets, the iterations stop and the algorithm generates the spatiotemporal rules.

This paper focuses on Thematic Spatiotemporal Association Rules (TSARs) that are association rules that involve space and time properties and attributes' values. TSARs usually have the following format: $a_1(R_1, t_1) \rightarrow a_2(R_2, t_2) < sup, con >$, where a_1 and a_2 are attributes of the domain to which the mining is being applied, and R_1 and R_2 are regions whose attributes are related to the t_1 and t_2 periods. Sup is support and conf is confidence. E.g., $Rainfall(New\ York,\ summer) \rightarrow Rainfall(New\ Jersey,\ autumn) < sup, con >$, it means that if it rains in New York in summer, it may rain in New Jersey in the autumn. An example of work that employs thematic rules is Landgrebe et al. [11].

Pillai et al. [10] present a new algorithm to extract spatiotemporal rules via the application of filters; these filters are used to restrict patterns that satisfy spatiotemporal constraints. The algorithm, based on Apriori, can handle a significant amount of data and is called FastSTCOPs-Miner. Pillai et al. [12] present an improvement of the previous work. In that, a framework for mining co-occurring patterns is presented, spatial events and their evolutions are modeled as 3D. Finally, an algorithm for the discovery of co-occurring rules based on the evolution of spatial relations is presented. The work is limited because it does not extract association rules, but rather sequential patterns for the evolution of an event, in this way, the work does not consider the influence that one event can have on another. In extension, none of the approaches consider thematic attributes: only images and spatiotemporal constraints.

43.3 Miner of Thematic Association Rules for Images

The Solar Satellite Image Time Series (Solar SITS) domain extracted from NOAA Satellites [13] is composed of Time Series of Solar Images and their Textual Data (Time Series of Textual Data). Our proposed approach is called Miner of Thematic Association Rules for Images (MiTSAI) and aims to extract knowledge from this Solar SITS. For the Solar SITS, each solar image has several sunspots and these sunspots are used during the knowledge extraction.

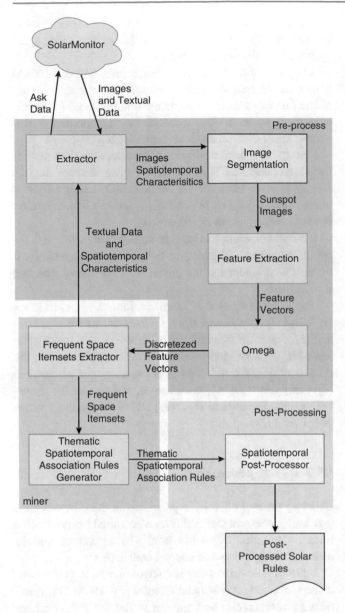

Fig. 43.1 Overview of the miner of thematic association rules for images (MiTSAI) approach

Figure 43.1 presents the MiTSAI overview. As it is shown, the approach is divided three parts: pre-processing (presented in Sect. 43.3.1), mining (presented in Sect. 43.3.2), and post-processing (presented in Sect. 43.3.3).

43.3.1 Pre-processing

The first step of MiTSAI approach consists in the extraction the Solar SITS from its data source (Satellite NOAA data—`solarmonitor.org`). The extraction process stores the images in a local folder, and the textual data in a JSON-format file. MiTSAI reads the images and the textual data;

the images proceed to the feature extraction process. Before enabling the feature extraction, MiTSAI requires image segmentation.

In the image segmentation, MiTSAI considers the spatiotemporal characteristics of each sunspot. Since the image resolution is constant, the conversion of solar coordinates (spatiotemporal characteristics) to image coordinates is performed by opposing the image with a fixed conversion grid.

At the end of the segmentation, each image segment has only one sunspot. After that, the segments proceed to the feature extraction process that aims to transform the image segments in the feature vectors. The feature extraction is done using SURF algorithm [14]. SURF is a form-based feature extractor; it is used in the work because the domain expert team designated that the sunspot form is an important indicator regarding the sunspot evolving.

The preprocessing of the data are organized as follows: a day with N sunspots results in a matrix $N \times M$, where M is the number of different wavelength images available in that day. For M different wavelength images, all image sunspots are found, and a feature vector for each sunspot is created. Usually, $M = 6$ but there are periods where some wavelength images are not available.

The last step of the pre-process is the feature vector discretization. In this step, the Omega algorithm [15] perform the discretization. Omega was chosen because it has been designed to minimize the number of intervals and the dataset entropy, what is desirable for the association rules mining. As a result of this step, each feature value in the feature vector becomes a feature interval. For instance, the feature vector $f = \{0.12, 0.15, 2.12, 0.4 \ldots\}$ is converted to $f^{\#} = \{[0.12-0.4), [0.12-0.4), [0.4-2.5), [0.4-2.5) \ldots\}$.

43.3.2 Mining

In the mining process, MiTSAI reads the discretized feature vectors and its textual data from the pre-processing step. During the Thematic Spatiotemporal Association Rules (TSARs) mining, MiTSAI considers the relationship between the sunspots that happen in the same moment and follow the spatial constraint (set by the user), and also, it considers the evolution of the sunspots according to a time constraint (set by the user).

The TSAR extraction has the following format:

$$r : i_{1\ldots n} \rightarrow j_{1\ldots m} \; < sup, \; conf, \; space, \; time >$$

where $i_{1\ldots n}$ is a set of items that happen at the same time and follow the spatial constraint. I.e., i_1 is close enough to the items $i_{2\ldots n}$, obeying the spatial constraint. The same is valid for $j_{1\ldots m}$ and *space* is the average of these space values between the items occurrences. From i to j, $time$ unit of time shows the evolution of the itemset in time variance.

sup and $conf$ are the support and confidence values for that rule. sup is calculated considering the spatial constraint: the $support(\{i_{1...n}\}) = \frac{|closeTo_{i_1}(i_{2...n})|}{|database|}$ where the is are thematic items and the function $closeTo_{i_1}(i_{2...n})$ returns the thematic items that are close enough of i_1; spatial constraint defined by the domain expert team. For example, consider the items i_1, i_2 and i_3 where i_1 and i_2 are never close enough but i_1 and i_3 are 5 times close enough. Calculating $support(\{i_1 i_2\})$, $|closeTo_{i_1}(i_2)|$ returns 0 because the items are never close enough in the database. Calculating $support(\{i_1 i_3\})$, $|closeTo_{i_1}(i_3)|$ returns 5 because the items are 5 times close enough in the database. $conf$ is calculated considering the time constraint: the $confidence(A \rightarrow b) = \frac{|timeClose(A,B)|}{|A|}$ where A and B are spatial itemsets and $timeClose(A, B)$ returns the occurrences of A and B that obey a time constraint defined by the domain expert team. For example, consider the itemsets I_1, I_2 and I_3 where I_1 and I_2 happens 3 times time-close enough but I_1 and I_3 never happens time-close enough. Calculating $confidence(I_1 \rightarrow I_2)$, the $|timeClose(I_1, I_2)|$ returns 3 times. Calculating $confidence(I_1 \rightarrow I_3)$, the $|timeClose(I_1, I_3)|$ returns 0 times due to they never happens time-close enough.

The MiTSAI algorithm is divided into two steps: (1) Find the frequent spatial itemsets in the database DB, and; (2) Generate the TSARs based on the frequent spatial itemsets generated at (1)-step.

An itemset I is a set of items, it is formally defined as $I = \{i_1 \dots i_n\}$ for $n \in Natural \mid n \geq 1$ and $i_a = i_b$ for $0 < a, b \leq n$ only if $a = b$. A spatial itemset $SI = si_1 \dots si_n$ is an itemset whose items have spatial characteristics such as $si_a.location$ and the items relate to each other obeying a spatial constraint.

An instance of a spatial constraint for the items $i_a, i_b \in SI$ can be stated using Euclidean distance among the items i_a, i_b. The spatial constraint is satisfied if the Euclidean distance is not greater than a parameter set by the domain expert team.

To find the spatial itemsets in the database DB, MiTSAI:

1. Extract frequent items;
2. Combine the items creating the candidate itemsets;
3. Remove the candidate itemsets that does not obey the spatial constraint, creating the spatial candidate itemsets;
4. Remove the non-frequent spatial candidate itemsets, creating the frequent spatial itemset, and;
5. Return to step 2 using the generated frequent spatial itemsets. It is performed until it is not possible to generate new larger itemsets.

The steps 3 and 4 are performed together; it consists in the itemset support calculation and, during this process, the spatial constraint is considered.

To generating the spatiotemporal rules-based, MiTSAI combines the frequent spatial itemsets generating the candidate rules $a \rightarrow b$. Each candidate rule is filtered by its rule confidence value. In other words, for each combination of i-itemset and j-itemset a rules r is created as $r = < i \rightarrow j >$.

During the rule's confidence calculation, the time restrictions are considered. It means that an occurrence of the rule $i \rightarrow j$ is considered for the confidence counting only if it obeys to $i.date < j.date \leq i.date + period$. Where $period$ is a time constraint set by the experts.

If rule's confidence values are higher than $minConf$, the rule is accepted and added to the result set; oppositely, if the rule's confidence is not higher than $minConf$, the rule is discarded.

The extracted TSARs have the format: $\{i_a \dots i_b\} \rightarrow \{i_x \dots i_y\} < sup, conf, time, spatial >$, where $\{i_a \dots i_b\}$ and $\{i_x \dots i_y\}$ are frequent spatial itemsets, sup is the average of $\{i_a \dots i_b\}$-support and $\{i_x \dots i_y\}$-support, $conf$ is the rules confidence value, $time$ is the average period between $\{i_a \dots i_b\}$ and $\{i_x \dots i_y\}$ occurrences, and $spatial$ is the spatial average in-between $\{i_a \dots i_b\}$ added the spatial average in-between $\{i_x \dots i_y\}$.

43.3.3 Post-processing

This step process all TSARs generated in the previous step, generating new summarized rules also called "classification rules". The rules relate low-level visual features and its meaning along the spatiotemporal constraints.

MiTSAI post-processing is composed by a loop over thematic spatiotemporal association rules and counts how many time a feature vector that appears in the rules' antecedents is associated with the same classification (McIntosh class) in the rules' consequents.

As a result, the feature vector values (low-level visual features) are associated with a class (high-level meaning). The spatiotemporal characteristics are considered, and at the end, the post-processing presents the average of the $time$ and $space$ of the summarized rule occurrences. The standard deviation for those values is also computed and presented to the user.

The MiTSAI post-processing aims to support solar image analysis, and because our rules present a time variation between antecedent and consequence, the analysis can be used to infer the future behavior of sunspots in Solar SITS.

For instance, if a sunspot presents a feature vector f and f is associated with a class X, and the time attribute is y

days. So, it is possible to say that f will be of class X in an average of y days, considering the support value chances.

Petitjean et al. [16] presented the obstacles of SITS's generalization. However, in the solar domain, the SITS's generalization allows predicting the sunspot behavior handling TSAR's spatiotemporal characteristic. MiTSAI postprocessing presented good results for solar domain as presented in the experiments.

43.4 Experiments

A computer with 8 GB of RAM, 500 GB of HD and processor Intel Due Core 2.53 GHz was used to perform the experiments. The operational system is an Arch Linux 64 bits. MiTSAI is implemented in Java version 8 and it is deployed using Docker container. The experiments were performed using Fist In First Out (FIFO) priority mode to reduce the number of external process interference.

The pre-processing was performed for 10,300 sunspots—for the period starting on August 25, 2007, and ending on August 24, 2016. The experiment took 10^4 s on average; to calculated it, the experiment was executed 7 times. The standard deviation for the measured time is $\pm3\%$. The pre-process phase used 20% of the time to the discretization process, the image segmentation and textual data processing used 10%, and the 70% left is used for feature extraction process. Figure 43.2 presents an example of pre-processing for 1 day of NOAA Satellite data.

Figure 43.3 shows the rules extracted from the Solar SITS. $R1$ presents a sunspot classified as Hsx that develops to Dso-McIntosh when it is associated with another sunspot with the presented visual feature. The distance separating the sunspots is in average 33.22 parts of the solar disk. The average time to that happens is 6.5 days. It happens in 16.4% of the data, and its confidence is 80%.

$R2$ presents two sunspots in the rule's antecedent. The distance separating them is 22.2 parts of the solar disk. The sunspot for the presented visual feature develops to a Dro-McIntosh in the average of 13 days. The rule's consequent shows the relation with a Bxo-McIntosh sunspot. It is possible to say that this association is required to the first sunspot develops itself to Dro-McIntosh. $R8$ occurs in 10.7% of the data and has a confidence of 79%.

$R3$ consequence presents two sunspots, and the distance between them is 30.248 parts of the solar disk. The sunspot with the presented visual characteristic in the rule antecedent develops to a Hsx-McIntosh in an approximately of 4 days. This rule represents two possible scenario: The Hsx-McIntosh sunspot can present one of the visual characteristics, or it can be from other sunspots close to it. The distance between the sunspots is an average of 30.248 parts of the

solar disk. By the rule's antecedent, it is possible to see that there is at least another sunspot associated with the first one. $R3$ is an important rule because it shows that a sunspot can directly be connected to the behavior of others.

Since the author had not found any work in the literature that was able to extract thematic spatiotemporal association rules from the solar domain; the mined patterns were new. Because of the association rule extraction is an explanatory search, the mined patterns tend to be valid for the Solar domain.

Figure 43.4 presents examples of "classification rules" produced by the postprocessing of TSARs. $C1$ shows an association of the feature vector $(784, 896; 785, 216)$, $(14, 534; 15, 198) \ldots$ of sunspots whose size is 20 parts of the solar disk with Axx-McIntosh. The average support for the rules that contributed to this association is 2.27% and the trust is 100%. The average of time between the occurrence of antecedent and the consequent is 1 day, and there is no variation in space. Since there is no space variation, the summarized rule indicates an evolution of the sunspot itself without the need to be associated with another sunspot.

$C2$ shows an association of the feature vector $(776, 995; 777, 279)$, $(14, 534; 15, 198) \ldots$ of a sunspot whose size is 10 parts of the solar disk with Dro-McIntosh. The average support for the rules that contributed to this association is 6.3%, and the confidence is 100%. The average of time is 2 days, and the variation in space is 23,005 parts of the solar disk on average. It means that when a sunspot has that feature vector, it may evolve to one sunspot that is classified as Dro-McIntosh in 2 days; however, it is necessary to have other sunspots close to it in 23,005 parts of the solar disk. Figure 43.5 presents a $R2$'s occurrence in the database and its post-processing $C2$.

$C3$ shows a feature vector that is $(664, 769; 665, 061)$, $(14, 534; 15, 198) \ldots$ associated with Axx-McIntosh. The average support for the rules that contributed to this association is 5.3%, and the confidence is 100%. The time and space variation are respectively 5.536 days, and the 42.423 parts of the solar disk.

By the variation in the time in-between the feature vector and the class, it is possible to predict that a sunspot that obeys a visual feature vector will present a given classification over an amount of time given by the post-processed rule.

43.5 Conclusion

Satellite Images Time Series (SITS) is a challenge for the knowledge discovery due to its multidisciplinary characteristics. Its analysis considers image processing, spatiotemporal characteristics, and textual data. Moreover, despite the vast amount of usage possibilities, its analysis is complex and

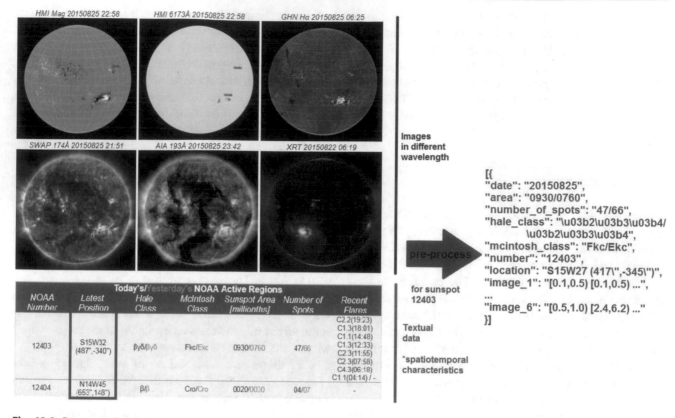

Fig. 43.2 Pre-processing the `SolarMonior.org` data. In the left slide, the data for a day with two sunspots. In the right side, the data for the sunspot 1203

```
(R1)
Hsx  <(665.847;666.469], (14.534;15.198],
(-0.428;8.490]... 0010> -> Dso
sup=0.164, conf=0.8, space=33.22, time=6.5

(R2)
<(776.995;777.279], (14.534;15.198],
(-0.428;8.490]... 0180> Bxo -> Dro
sup=0.107, conf=0.79, space=22.2, time=13$

(R3)
<(667.785;668.583], (14.534;15.198],
(-0.428;8.490]... 0040> Axx -> Hsx
<(406.643;407.087], (14.534;15.198],
(-0.428;8.490]... 0180> <(665.847;
666.469], (14.534;15.198], (-0.428;
8.490]... 0010> Axx
sup=0.028, conf=1, space=30.248, time=4
```

Fig. 43.3 Example of thematic spatiotemporal association rules (TSARs) extracted from the experiment database

```
C1:
(784.896;785.216], (14.534;15.198],
... 0020 : Axx
sup = 0.227 conf = 1 time = 1 space = 0

C2:
(776.995;777.279], (14.534;15.198],
... 0010 : Dro
sup = 0.063 conf = 1 time = 2 space = 23.005

C3:
(664.769;665.061], (14.534;15.198],
... 0030 : Axx
sup = 0.053 conf = 1 time = 5.536 space = 42.423
```

Fig. 43.4 Example of the summarized rules also called "classification rules" generated by MiTSAI post-processing

still limited, as the literature suggests. Helping to fulfill this gap, we proposed MiTSAI, an approach that aims to support the SITS analysis applied to Solar data domain. At pre-processing phase, MiTSAI performs image segmentation, feature extraction, and feature vector discretization. Feature vectors, textual description, and the spatiotemporal data are employed in the analysis of each sunspot. At data mining step, MiTSAI extracts Thematic Spatiotemporal Association

Rules (TSARs) that considers the relationship in-between events (sunspots) and their evolving. In our experiments, we show that MiTSAI was able to extract the TSARs from the Solar SITS. The domain expert team analyzed the results, judged them as new and relevant. At the post-processing step, MiTSAI produces summarized rules that relate visual features and semantics information about it. As a result, the summarized rules aid the Solar SITS behavior prediction.

A future work is to handle the visualization of the TSARs and usage of it for SITS classification.

Fig. 43.5 Example of $R2$'s occurrence in the database and its post-processed rules

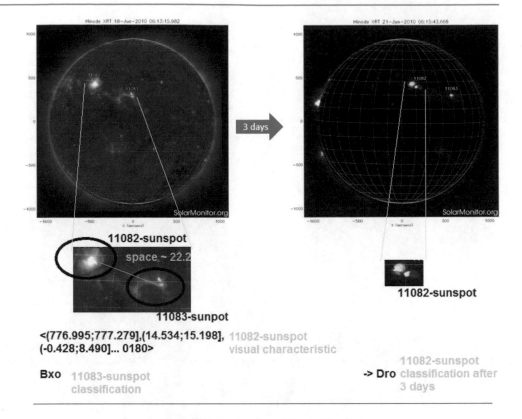

Acknowledgements The authors thank the SolarMonitor.org for free providing of the solar data used in this work. We also thank CAPES, CNPq and FAPESP for the financial support.

References

1. S.J. Ahmad, R.K. Jolly, Big data manipulation-a new concern to the ICT world (a massive survey/statistics along with the necessity) 1–51 (2015) International Journal of Engineering and Applied Sciences (IJEAS), **4**(5) (2017)

2. M. Ivanova, M. Kersten, S. Manegold, Y. Kargin, Data vaults: database technology for scientific file repositories. Comput. Sci. Eng. **15**(3), 32–42 (2013)

3. G. Feuerlicht, Database trends and directions: current challenges and opportunities, in *DATESO* (Citeseer, 2010), pp. 163–174

4. Y. Hu, V.Y. Gunapati, P. Zhao, D. Gordon, N.R. Wheeler, M.A. Hossain, T.J. Peshek, L.S. Bruckman, G.Q. Zhang, R.H. French, A nonrelational data warehouse for the analysis of field and laboratory data from multiple heterogeneous photovoltaic test sites. IEEE J. Photovoltaics **7**, 230–236 (2017)

5. G. Cortés, M. Girotto, S.A. Margulis, Analysis of sub-pixel snow and ice extent over the extratropical andes using spectral unmixing of historical landsat imagery. Remote Sens. Environ. **141**, 64–78 (2014)

6. A. Madraky, Z. Othman, A. Hamdan, Analytic methods for spatio-temporal data in a nature-inspired data model. Int. Rev. Comput. Softw. **9**(3), 547–556 (2014)

7. V. Radhakrishna, S.A. Aljawarneh, P. Kumar, V. Janaki, A novel fuzzy similarity measure and prevalence estimation approach for similarity profiled temporal association pattern mining. Futur. Gener. Comput. Syst. (2017)

8. C.R. Silveira-Junior, M.T.P. Santos, M.X. Ribeiro, Stretchy time pattern mining: a deeper analysis of environment sensor data, in *The Twenty-Sixth International FLAIRS Conference*, 2013

9. C.R. Silveira-Junior, D.C. Carvalho, M.T.P. Santos, M.X. Ribeiro, Incremental mining of frequent sequences in environmental sensor data, in *The Twenty-Sixth International FLAIRS Conference*, 2015

10. K. Pillai, R. Angryk, J. Banda, M. Schuh, T. Wylie, Spatio-temporal co-occurrence pattern mining in data sets with evolving regions, in *2012 IEEE 12th International Conference on Data Mining Workshops (ICDMW)*, 2012, pp. 805–812

11. T. Landgrebe, A. Merdith, A. Dutkiewicz, R. Mafaler, Relationships between palaeogeography and opal occurrence in Australia: a data-mining approach. Comput. Geosci. **56**, 76–82 (2013)

12. K. Pillai, R. Angryk, B. Aydin, A filter-and-refine approach to mine spatiotemporal co-occurrences, in *Proceedings of the 21st ACM SIGSPATIAL International Conference on Advances in Geographic Information Systems* (2013), pp. 104–113

13. NOAA, www.solarmonitor.org April 2016. Accessed 13 April 2016

14. H. Bay, T. Tuytelaars, L. Van Gool, Surf: speeded up robust features, in *European Conference on Computer Vision* (Springer, Berlin, 2006), pp. 404–417

15. M.X. Ribeiro, A.J.M. Traina, C. Traina Jr., A new algorithm for data discretization and feature selection, in *Proceedings of the 2008 ACM Symposium on Applied Computing*, SAC '08, New York, NY (ACM, New York, 2008), pp. 953–954

16. F. Petitjean, C. Kurtz, N. Passat, P. Gançarski, Spatio-temporal reasoning for the classification of satellite image time series. Pattern Recogn. Lett. **33**, 1805–1815 (2012)

Cláudio Augusto Silveira Lélis and André Luiz Silveira Lopardi

Abstract

The risk of default has grown as a concern for financial institutions. In a scenario of uncertainties, the correct decision is essential in the granting of credit. A predictive model of default risk and the linking of conflict management strategies can be critical in reducing financial losses and in decision-making doubts. This article presents an information system, called DeRis (Default Risk Information System), designed to support activities in the management of default risk in the context of a bank focused on the granting of credit. It covers a default prediction model based on conflict indicators, management, and financial indicators, a reasoner and visualization elements. Collecting historical data and sorting indicators is also possible. Through an experimental study, quantitative and qualitative data were collected. The feasibility of using DeRis was verified through an experimental study.

Keywords

Conflict indicators · Financial management ·
Knowledge-based decision-making · Default prediction
model · Data visualization

44.1 Introduction

Changes in the world financial scenario since the 1990s, such as deregulation of interest rates and exchange rates, increased liquidity and increased competitiveness, especially

C. A. S. Lélis (✉)
Scientific Initiation Program, IMES/Faculty ImesMercosur, Juiz de Fora, Brazil
e-mail: claudioaugustolelis@imes.org.br

A. L. S. Lopardi
Master's Program in Business Administration, FUMEC University, Belo Horizonte, Brazil

in the banking sector, have increased the concern of financial institutions with the risk of default. Although there are different concepts, default in the context of this research can be understood as a delay of more than 90 days in the liabilities assumed with a financial institution [1].

According to [2], credit risk is associated with the risk of a borrower or counterpart being defaulted. Thus, in the position of financial intermediaries, banks must act in a way that minimizes risk and enables fairer terms of credit acquisition. The difficulty of performing guarantees and recovering credit has led to uncertainty and instability in the market, making default the biggest cost of a bank's financial margin.

Over time, companies have been adapting to changes while remaining competitive and profitable in an increasingly crowded market. Applying constant investments in the area of Information Technology, financial institutions seek to offer products to their customers in a fast, safe and high technological value. Always attentive to high performance and information security, especially with the large volume of data. On the other hand, customers can count on the trust, performance and safety expected of a financial institution [3].

In this period, efficiency gained prominence and in companies where there were conflicts, there were also losses, impairing efficiency. According to the American Management Association (AMA), managers spend at least 24% of their time dealing with conflicts. Such conflicts represent, for example, a tension, a disagreement or polarization between two, or more people, or groups. It is part of the management and if it is treated in a constructive way, the conflict is considered as an opportunity [4].

The Bank Zak who became partner and offered their data for this research, for example, focuses its activities in generating resource and credit analysis. In addition, it fosters the consumption and investment needs of individuals and companies. Recognized the importance of the default risk has become important for the Bank Zak check if companies are shaping the economic environment, assessing their conflicts in business scope and influence on a possible default.

The use of default prediction models serves to measure, monitor and predict the financial situation of companies, reducing uncertainties and doubts in decision making [5]. The models are constructed with the support of statistical techniques and applied to analyze their dependent variables.

A financial institution should identify risks in lending situations, draw conclusions as to the borrower's ability to repay, and make recommendations regarding the best structuring and type of loan to be granted in the light of the applicant's financial needs [6]. In a scenario of uncertainties and incomplete information, risk analysis involves the ability to establish a decision rule to guide the granting of credit.

For the survival of financial institutions, the correct decision to grant credit is essential [7]. Any error in the decision to grant the credit may mean that the gain on other successful transactions is lost in a single transaction. Therefore, it is important to anticipate and reduce default [8], since the losses from unsuccessful credits should be covered by charging high interest rates on new concessions. Therefore, using a default risk forecasting model for a financial institution and linking management strategies to the reality of the borrower can be critical in assessing credit risk and reducing financial losses.

Considering that Zak Bank has management conflicts and the possibility of linking conflict reduction to efficiency and productivity gains, there is a need to evaluate possible organizational variables that impact the bank's course and its perpetuity. In addition, to verify the influence of conflict indicators in a default forecast model from Zak Bank's point of view.

For proper monitoring of the indicators involved, a significant amount of data must be collected, processed and stored over time. The process of discovering knowledge through these data may be associated with an information system that offers this information through interactive visualizations, aiming the recognition of new knowledge and assisting decision making. Visualizations enable the manager to interact and gain insight into the data they have, gaining new insight through distinct views across different perspectives. Such systems minimize the occurrence of misinterpretations when compared to analysis performed through a single view [9]. This demonstrates the importance of a support system in this context.

Therefore, this paper presents an information system, called DeRis, aimed to support activities in the management of default risk in the context of Zak Bank. It encompasses a default prediction model based on conflict indicators, management, and financial indicators, a reasoner and visualization elements. Through the storage of decisions a knowledge database is generated. Collecting historical data and sorting indicators is also possible.

This article is structured by this introduction and Sect. 44.2 shows the background in which the proposal is inserted and some related work. Section 44.3 details the components of the DeRis system. In Sect. 44.4, the experiment carried out and Sect. 44.5 the final considerations.

44.2 Background

Through a survey of the specialized technical literature, it was possible to perceive that the researchers' interest in default risk models dates back to the 1930s [10, 11]. Over the years, the pioneering work of Beaver [12] and especially Altman [13], boosted research in the 1970s with accounting indicators [14–18]. Since the mid-1990s, issues such as the emergence of new modeling techniques, the growing importance of credit risk management and the prevailing economic conditions, again aroused the interest in the area [19–22].

There are several techniques applied to credit risk forecasting models. They can be classified as discriminant analysis used in the model proposed by [13], neural networks, multiple linear regression, linear programming, genetic algorithms, decision tree, logistic regression used in the DeRis system model, and more recently the analysis of survival.

Bellovary et al. [23] investigated the main financial indicators used in studies to predict default and found the current liquidity present in 51 studies among those analyzed.

Bonfim [24] examined the determinants of corporate defaults in the banking sector in Portugal through the Logit or Probite Models of Survival Analysis. The study found that default is affected by specific characteristics of companies such as: capital structure, company size, profitability and liquidity, recent sales performance and investment policy. However, there was a significant improvement in the quality of the models, with the introduction of variables, especially the growth rate of all the riches produced in the country, the growth of lending, the average lending rate and the variation of stock market prices.

The model presented by [25] used the two most important macroeconomic factors that affect corporate default which are the nominal interest rate and the output gap. As financial variables specific to each company, the authors used the Earnings Before Interest, Taxes, Depreciation and Amortization (EBITDA) per Total Assets ratio, the interest coverage ratio, the leverage ratio, the total liability ratio and revenues, the ratio net assets and total liabilities and, finally, inventory turnover.

From the identified models, as well as the concepts of credit and risk, it should be noted that the default forecast models, mostly, have financial indicators as explanatory variables. Therefore, creating a model without taking such indicators into account would put its effectiveness in question.

However, the models identified in the survey conducted were not associated with information systems with visualizations capable of aiding decision making. In addition, indicators of conflicts in management have not been the object of study of the researchers, which justifies the interest for the present work.

44.3 DeRis System

The proposed DeRis system arose from the need to predict the financial situation of companies to avoid default, as well as support managers and financial institutions in making decisions regarding the granting of credit. Figure 44.1 shows an overview of the DeRis system architecture with its main components and the basic flow of information in the decision-making process.

The information flow while using the system starts in the repository that stores the historical data of the indicators. Additional information such as a brief description and the indicator classification are also stored. Indicator management is performed to determine which indicators will be used in the prediction model. This choice is made considering the possibility of calculating the indicator with the available data. Then, the default prediction model is triggered. Reasoner helps managers interpret the model results. Finally, the visualizations show the results and analyzes made by Reasoner and through interaction elements managers can associate preventive measures with the indicators. A knowledge database is also maintained as decisions are taken, that feeds the

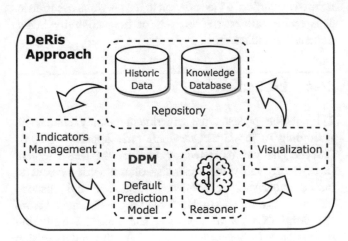

Fig. 44.1 DeRis architecture

system and this information is recorded to support future decisions. The other components of the system are detailed below.

44.3.1 Indicators Management

This is an important component of the system. It identifies the indicators whose data is stored, its additional information and mainly the classification that assists the Reasoner in the analyzes. These are the indicators that are candidates to participate in the model. It is necessary to make the selection of the indicators when starting the monitoring of a company, or through previous decisions, the own component preselects the indicators.

Another feature of this component is to relate the indicator to the way of collecting, or calculating, its value. For example, in the context of the Zak Bank considered in this study the indicators were classified between: conflict, management or financial as described below.

- **Number of analyzable business partners:** Represents the partners analyzed that have at least more than 1% of the company. **Acronym:** NABP. **Class:** Conflict.
- **Number of analyzable business partners by total:** Represents the ratio of partners who have at least more than 1% of the company by the total number of partners. **Acronym:** NABPT **Class:** Conflict
- **Age of oldest business partners:** Represents the age of the older partners over the age of 18. **Acronym:** AOBP **Class:** Conflict
- **Age of oldest leader business partners:** Represents the age of the older leaders over the age of 18. **Acronym:** AOLBP **Class:** Conflict
- **Gross Annual Revenue/1,000,000:** Represents all revenues earned by companies during the year. For scale purposes, it is divided by 1 million. **Acronym:** GAR/1,000,000 **Class:** Financial
- **Average balance in account and investment/Exposure in the last 12 months/1000:** Defined by the amount in cash and financial application with immediate liquidity that the company owns. It is divided by short-term obligations and represents current liquidity [23]. **Acronym:** (BAI/E)/1000 **Class:** Financial
- **Average balance in account and investment/GAR in the last 12 months:** Represents the amount in cash or financial application, divided by gross annual revenue. **Acronym:** BAI/GAR **Class:** Financial
- **Usage of Investment Lines Indicator:** Defined to indicate the management of the companies cash flow. **Acronym:** UIL(YES) **Class:** Financial

- **Account time in years:** It considers the time between the opening of the current account in the financial institution, until the current date. **Acronym:** ATY **Class:** Management
- **Activity time counted from the operation start:** Defined from the date on which the company actually started its operational activities. **Acronym:** ATOS **Class:** Management
- **Operating time at last address:** Defines the time of permanence in the last registered address. **Acronym:** OTLA **Class:** Management
- **Number of employees:** Defined by the number of employees informed to the financial institution when registering. For reasons of scale, the indicator is shown in the ratio of 10 employees. **Acronym:** NE/10 **Class:** Management

Although the indicators have been collected and are in the context of the Zak bank, the system is prepared to add new indicators and classifications, making it possible to adapt it to other contexts.

44.3.2 Prediction Model

The proposed model is based on conflict, management and financial indicators, classified in the indicators management stage.

The technique applied by the model is logistic regression [26] that allows analyzing the effect of one or more independent variables on a dichotomous dependent variable, representing the presence or absence of a characteristic. In this way, it describes the relationship between several independent variables. According to this theory, the model calculates the probability of default, given by Eq. (44.1):

$$ProbDefault(yes) = \frac{e^\eta}{1 + e^\eta} \qquad (44.1)$$

where η depends on the indicators and data available for the logistic regression calculation. In the next section, the two equations used for the η calculation during the evaluation are shown.

44.3.3 Reasoner Phase

Assuming that there are indicators A, B and C. However, only the data for indicators A and C are available. Given this, *would it be possible to replace B? Which indicator could replace it?* Questions like these that Reasoner tries to answer with their analysis.

These questions can be answered by the Reasoner due to information such as: the class to which the indicator belongs

(Conflict, Management or Financial), the unit of indicator measure, its degree of influence on the default and decisions taken previously after the exchange of indicators.

Another important function is to relate a moment of the past with a description of the decision made and what were the critical indicators for default, based on historical data and the knowledge base.

Although the review process is transparent to the user, the decision to replace an indicator is performed by the manager, when necessary, whenever a company's monitoring begins.

44.3.4 Visualization

The DeRis system provides two views developed from the JavaScript d3js library considering its flexibility of use and availability for editing. This library has been used successfully in the context of visualizations in information systems [27].

The Indicators Evolution View (Fig. 44.2) uses a line chart to represent the evolution of the default probability over time. Furthermore, it uses a gauge metaphor to highlight the influence percentage of each indicator considered on the probability of default. This decision was made since it would not make sense to compare its absolute values since the indicators are on different scales.

The view is generated after the user selects a range of days and a time period to be analyzed. As shown in Fig. 44.2, the line and the gauges are arranged as a dashboard for the decision maker.

Through interaction elements, it is possible to select a point in the line graph and obtain contextual information, such as: the future trend of the default probability, the values of each indicator, the model used and the decision taken at the time, if any. Moreover, the percentage of each indicator, colored according to the variation to the previous occurrence. This feature allows the analysis of the variability in the influence of indicators.

44.4 Evaluation

This section presents the experimental study conducted. According to the Goal/Question/Metric approach (GQM) [28] the goal can be stated as: **Analyze** the DeRis system **in order to** verify the feasibility of use **with respect to** the comprehension of conflict, management and financial indicators as a support tool to default prediction model **from the point of view of** managers and financial institution professionals **in the context of** Zak Bank through a decision support system.

In this sense, the metrics defined to verify the fit quality of the models were the result of the Hosmer-Lemeshow test

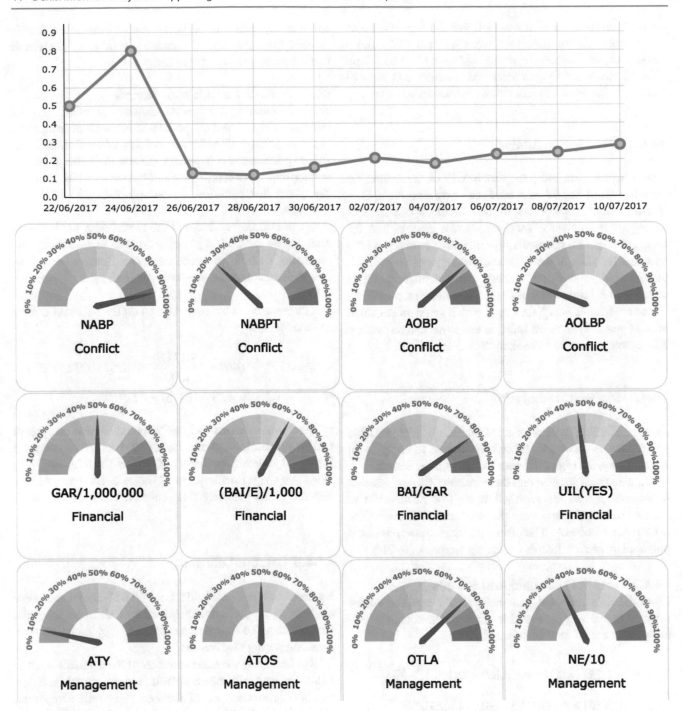

Fig. 44.2 Indicators evolution view

[26] based on *p*-value with significance level of 0.05. The sensitivity that is the ratio of true positives, assesses the ability of the model to classify that event occurred to an individual, since the event actually occurred. Finally, the specificity that is the ratio of true negatives, assesses the ability of the model to predict that the event did not occur.

The experiment was proposed based on a set of real data collected from documentary sources, from January to December 2015. The sample comprised 15,000 companies,

between defaulters and debt free companies, from various sectors of the economy located in the database of Zak Bank, intentionally selected, choosing management, conflict and financial indicators.

It is worth noting that there was a concern about the validity of the results found due to the fact that the sample was unbalanced, with 952 companies in default and 14,048 companies free of debt. Therefore, it was decided to repeat the process with a new sample that was balanced and thus obtain a revalidation of the model. For the construction of this sample, all the defaulters were selected (952) and a random sample was made in the 14,048 so that 952 were selected. In order to guarantee the external and internal validity of the results found, a cross validation was used.

44.4.1 Descriptive Analysis

The collected data indicates that 6.35% of the companies were in default and 28.65% used the investment lines. Considering family businesses, it was certified that 21.35% belong to the universe surveyed. It can be said that the companies had on average 1.48 analyzable partners, with a standard deviation of 0.63. It was observed that 48.09 years is the age of oldest business partners, with a standard deviation of 12.99. It is important to note that the average account time of the companies was 5.62 years, with a standard deviation of 5.02 years. The results indicate that firms had on average 7.05 employees, with a standard deviation of 11.93.

44.4.2 Statistical Analysis

The Logistic Regressions adjusted for each possible variable predicting the occurrence of default allowed to verify, in an isolated way, the impact of each variable on the default.

Data analysis showed that the variables: *Average balance in account and investment/GAR in the last 12 months* and *Number of employees* were potential risk factors for the occurrence of default. The other indicators were considered potential protection factors for the occurrence of default.

44.4.2.1 Model 1: Unbalanced Sample
From the data collected and analyzed, the equation of the selected model was presented to calculate the default probability, whose η value is calculated by:

$$\eta = -1.752 - 0.166 * NABP - 0.340 * \frac{(BAI/E)}{1000}$$
$$- 0.191 * UIL(YES) - 0.074 * ATY$$
$$- 0.019 * ATOS + 0.069 * NE/10$$

$$(44.2)$$

Considering the prevalence of default (6.35%), a sensitivity of 73.22%, a specificity value of 45.33%, was observed. Regarding the Hosmer-Lemeshow test, the *p*-value equals 0.085, which indicates a well-adjusted model.

The results show that the variable, "average balance in current account and investment/exposure in the last 12 months" was the most important to determine the default,

and then, account time in years, use of investment activity counted from the start of operation, number of analyzable members and number of employees.

44.4.2.2 Model 2: Balanced Sample
When considering a balanced sample, the model did not indicate as significant the variables: Number of analyzable business partners (NABP) and number of employees (NE). Other variables and interpretations were the same. Thus, the relationships between default and NABP and NE, found in the model that considers the sample unbalanced, are not validated.

It can also be verified that the model with the balanced sample was capable of pointing 78.18% of sensitivity and predicting 41.00% of specificity. The Hosmer-Lemeshow test indicates that the model is well-adjusted (*p*-value = 0.200).

The equation of the model based on the balanced sample has η calculated by:

$$\eta = 0.775 - 0.469 * \frac{(BAI/E)}{1000} - 0.263 * UIL(YES)$$
$$- 0.081 * ATY - 0.016 * ATOS$$

$$(44.3)$$

The results showed that the "Average balance in account and investment/Exposure in the last 12 months" was the most important to determine default. Then, are the following variables: "Account time in years", "Usage of Investment Lines indicator" and "activity time counted from the operation start".

44.4.3 Lessons Learned

By means of the data collection, 15,000 companies were analyzed, using indicators provided by Zak Bank. Once the companies to be searched are chosen, they come up with some interesting discoveries.

By identifying the main variables of the available conflict indicators that influence a default forecast model, such as: number of members, age of members and family companies, it was found, based on field research, that the larger the number of members the lower the probability that the company will default. One aspect that may have been captured by the model is that of divided responsibility, that is, with more partners there is more equity and subdivisions of the responsibilities assumed. Therefore, unlike the premise used in the research, conflicts related to the number of partners do not affect the risk of default by companies. The age of the partners also did not show enough influence to explain the default.

The family business indicator was not consistent to influence the risk of default. Thus, the fact that the company is familiar and having conflicts does not affect its default risk.

With regard to the influence of conflict indicators, it can be seen that, among the variables used in the default model of the research, only one (number of analyzable members) among the three in the conflict block was consistent to explain the default rate.

It was found that the higher the liquidity of the company, the lower its probability of default. The facilitating variable for the development of the model (use of investment lines) was efficient to explain the default, that is, the greater the use of these lines by the companies, the less likely they were to default.

The fact that all management variables are representative in the model is particularly significant. The variables (time of account in years and time of activity counted from the beginning of the operation) explained that the longer the company's experience in the market, the lower the probabilities of default. It should be noted that the variable (number of employees/10) showed an inverse relationship, that is, the higher the number of employees, the greater the probability of default. A more accurate analysis allows to infer a possible existence of conflicts within these companies.

44.5 Closing Remarks

This paper introduced the DeRis system to support predict the financial situation of companies to avoid default, as well as support managers and financial institutions in making decisions regarding the granting of credit. An experimental study was conducted and through the statistical analysis of the data, the system feasibility has been verified. Considering the results, it was concluded that the financial, management and conflict indicators are useful as an aid tool to the default prediction model.

As a contribution, this work offers financial institutions an approach to encourage the use of management, conflict and financial indicators, as a specification for the development of a default forecasting model, in the search for continuous improvement. A limitation of the study is associated to the universe of variables previously defined by the financial institution. It is also worth mentioning the impossibility of obtaining data from more than one financial institution. Thus, the results of the research are limited to the particularities of the financial institution under study. Its application in other institutions is subject to market conditions and may present different results.

As future work we intend to elaborate a study comparing other statistical techniques, such as: neural networks, discriminant analysis, among others. Moreover, integration with other visual tools to diversify the presented data possibilities.

References

1. J. Bessis, *Risk Management in Banking* (Wiley, New York, 2011)
2. S. Westgaard, N. Van der Wijst, Default probabilities in a corporate bank portfolio: a logistic model approach. Eur. J. Oper. Res. **135**(2), 338–349 (2001)
3. C.G. Bernardo, Loan system in Brazilian financial institution-a SOA application, in *2012 Ninth International Conference on Information Technology: New Generations (ITNG)* (IEEE, New York, 2012), pp. 293–298
4. G. Kohlrieser, Six essential skills for managing conflict. Perspect. Manag. **149**, 1–4 (2007)
5. M.T. Dugan, C.V. Zavgren, How a bankruptcy model could be incorporated as an analytic. CPA J. **59**(5), 64 (1989)
6. D. Duffie, K.J. Singleton, *Credit Risk: Pricing, Measurement, and Management* (Princeton University Press, Princeton, NJ, 2012)
7. L.J. Gitman, R. Juchau, J. Flanagan, *Principles of Managerial Finance* (Pearson Higher Education AU, Boston, MA, 2015)
8. M. Steiner, C. Carnieri, B. Kopittke, P.S. Neto, Probabilistic expert systems and neural networks in bank credit analysis. Int. J. Oper. Quant. Manag. **6**(4), 235–250 (2000)
9. S. Ainsworth, The functions of multiple representations. Comput. Educ. **33**(2), 131–152 (1999)
10. P.J. FitzPatrick, A comparison of the ratios of successful industrial enterprises with those of failed companies. Certif. Public Account. **12**, 598–605 (1932)
11. A. Winakor, R. Smith, Changes in the financial structure of unsuccessful industrial corporations. Bulletin **51**, 44 pp. (1935)
12. W. H. Beaver, Financial ratios as predictors of failure. J. Account. Res. **4**, 71–111 (1966)
13. E.I. Altman, Financial ratios, discriminant analysis and the prediction of corporate bankruptcy. J. Finance **23**(4), 589–609 (1968)
14. R.O. Edmister, An empirical test of financial ratio analysis for small business failure prediction. J. Financ. Quant. Anal. **7**(2), 1477–1493 (1972)
15. E.B. Deakin, A discriminant analysis of predictors of business failure. J. Account. Res. **10**, 167–179 (1972)
16. M. Blum, Failing company discriminant analysis. J. Account. Res. **12**, 1–25 (1974)
17. R. A. Eisenbeis, Pitfalls in the application of discriminant analysis in business, finance, and economics. J. Finance **32**(3), 875–900 (1977)
18. R.C. Moyer, Forecasting financial failure: a re-examination. Financ. Manag. **6**(1), 11 (1977)
19. E.I. Altman, G. Marco, F. Varetto, Corporate distress diagnosis: comparisons using linear discriminant analysis and neural networks (the Italian experience). J. Bank. Finance **18**(3), 505–529 (1994)
20. P. Brockett, W. Cooper, L. Golden, X. Xia, A case study in applying neural networks to predicting insolvency for property and casualty insurers. J. Oper. Res. Soc. **48**, 1153–1162 (1997)
21. C.Y. Shirata, Financial ratios as predictors of bankruptcy in Japan: an empirical research. Tsukuba College Technol. Jpn. **1**(1), 1–17 (1998)
22. C. Lennox, Identifying failing companies: a re-evaluation of the logit, probit and da approaches. J. Econ. Bus. **51**(4), 347–364 (1999)

23. J.L. Bellovary, D.E. Giacomino, M.D. Akers, A review of bankruptcy prediction studies: 1930 to present. J. Financ. Educ. **33**, 1–42 (2007)

24. D. Bonfim, Credit risk drivers: evaluating the contribution of firm level information and of macroeconomic dynamics. J. Bank. Finance **33**(2), 281–299 (2009)

25. T. Jacobson, J. Lindé, K. Roszbach, Firm default and aggregate fluctuations.J. Eur. Econ. Assoc. **11**(4), 945–972 (2013)

26. D.W. Hosmer Jr., S. Lemeshow, R.X. Sturdivant, *Applied Logistic Regression*, vol. 398 (Wiley, New York, 2014)

27. C.A. Lélis, M.A. Miguel, M.A.P. Araújo, J.M.N. David, R. Braga, Ad-reputation: a reputation-based approach to support effort estimation, in *Information Technology-New Generations* (Springer, Berlin, 2018), pp. 621–626

28. V.R. Basili, D.M. Weiss, A methodology for collecting valid software engineering data. IEEE Trans. Softw. Eng. **SE-10**(6), 728–738 (1984)

Taking a Steppe Towards Optimizing Note-Taking Software by Creation of a Note Classification Algorithm

45

Daniela Zieba, Wren Jenkins, Michael Galloway, and Jean-Luc Houle

Abstract

Note-taking software often far surpasses its paper-and-pencil counterpart when measured in metrics such as availability and reliability. However, there is ample opportunity relating to the analysis and organization of notes in structures often called folders, notebooks, or projects within various software. ShovelWare is a project designed for an ongoing field research project analyzing the Bronze and Iron Ages of Mongolia. Accessible through a web interface and cross-platform mobile application, it is a replacement for manual data collection on paper and excessive, error-ridden input into digital spreadsheets. We propose a machine learning algorithm that classifies notes using a variety of metrics, sorting them into graph structures to provide initial insights into the similarity of field notes. As a result, ShovelWare will allow archaeologists to more quickly and cleanly view and share their data. The algorithm, as well as the note-taking structure, are planned with hopes of scalability and applicability into more disciplines.

Keywords

Note-taking software · Archaeology-specific software · Machine learning-based classification · Data management software · Digital recording system

45.1 Introduction

Software intended for the replacement of paper has found a massive market, and everything is shifting to digital storage solutions—medical records, everyday notes, and mail are only a handful of examples of the vast amount of data stored and recorded digitally. The focus of our paper is on the development of our own note-taking software intended for use in academic field research projects. We explore a variety of algorithmic approaches to the optimization of data classification and analysis both generically and following discipline-specific analytical methods.

Our project finds application as a replacement to pencil-and-paper methods of recording archaeological field data, and is being developed with the overarching goal of deployment in the next field season of an ongoing project researching the sociopolitical changes of Mongolia in its Bronze and Iron Ages. The use of smart tablets for field archaeology has undergone initial experimentation, but would benefit from standardization and improvement of data recording methodologies.

45.2 Related Work

Similar smart tablet setups have been employed in various archaeological field research projects with moderate success [1, 2], and some attempts have been made at developing archaeology-specific software [3]. Although important to understanding the needs of field researchers, the most relevant works to our paper involve recent big data analytical methods and algorithm developments.

Machine learning is a well-documented and long-running success for various classification needs [4, 5]. Many different machine learning models are commonplace for researchers with different classification needs and methods, but our research currently emphasizes text-based analysis of notes using a neural network. Common methods of text analysis involve interpreting semantics and training machine learning algorithms to form ontologies for classification. Our project looks to build on the profusion of success in text-based analysis and tailor its use towards our specific needs.

D. Zieba (✉) · W. Jenkins · M. Galloway · J.-L. Houle
Western Kentucky University, Bowling Green, KY, USA
e-mail: daniela.zieba727@topper.wku.edu;
wren.jenkins685@topper.wku.edu; jeffrey.galloway@wku.edu;
jean-luc.houle@wku.edu

© Springer International Publishing AG, part of Springer Nature 2018
S. Latifi (ed.), *Information Technology – New Generations*, Advances in Intelligent Systems and Computing 738,
https://doi.org/10.1007/978-3-319-77028-4_45

Our project stands apart from previous archaeology software as well as classification algorithms by combining machine learning-based classification of data with a project structure and general note-taking software. Archaeology-specific software [3] is ill-supported and lacks in-depth analysis tools, and the same issue extends to the usage of generic data management software. The data referenced throughout the paper is from completed field seasons in Mongolia, and testing of algorithm analysis can be accomplished accordingly.

45.3 Project Architecture

45.3.1 Overview

The time it takes to record information, as well as likeliness of human error, prompted the initial creation of a digital archaeological project management and data storage system. This allows for more accuracy in data recording as well as a significant decrease in the time needed for menial work, allowing more time to be devoted to the analysis of results and further gathering of data. It has been dubbed ShovelWare as a pun on the typical software definition of shovelware (where quantity of software produced is valued over quality) and the archaeological component to this project.

Paper-and-pencil entries from different field researchers always have innate problems that digital recording can solve with ease. There is no danger of losing a pencil when using a tablet (though there is the same concern with using a stylus), and a common reason for inaccuracy in entries is in handwriting differences that a standard software font will not have. The technology currently used in the Mongolia project consists of personal cameras as well as a drone. Another danger lies in the use of personal cameras, which lack labels and allow for information to easily be deleted or lost by accident.

45.3.2 General Architecture

Figure 45.1 visualizes the project architecture and highlights data storage features, where clients can access ShovelWare through either its web interface or mobile application. Where users have internet connection, they can connect with cloud hosting features, and otherwise access local storage for their project data.

The overall ShovelWare software architecture is developed in a microservice-oriented fashion to best accommodate our future goals of expansion into other disciplines. Of course, limitations of offline capabilities mean that a typically network-based service-oriented architecture will be subject to modification. General design entails core features

necessary for note-taking software. Although, once again, core architectures must be slightly modified between the mobile application and web interface, the web-based components of this project will be deployed in a multitenant fashion. Web-based aspects to ShovelWare can be best classified as a Software-as-a-Service cloud.

45.3.3 Cross-Platform Capabilities

ShovelWare is accessible through its web interface and cross-platform mobile applications to ensure availability to as many research projects as possible. When tested for use in the 2018 Mongolia project field season, both Android and iOS devices will be used to document functionality. We will also determine the optimal hardware set-up to suggest for field research. One of our goals is to find the best balance for tightly-budgeted research projects between the cost and functionality of different platforms.

45.4 User Interfaces

Shown above in Fig. 45.2 are the login interfaces for Shovel-Ware. NativeScript [6] with Angular 2 and Typescript is used for mobile application development, primarily for cross-platform functionality, but also to accomplish a uniform look across platforms including that of the web interface. Design is an important part to the project, as other archaeological projects would claim [1, 2], in successful and simple data recording and display given the massive amounts of information. A contradiction some may notice is in the ShovelWare dinosaur logo, despite initial development towards archaeology projects, with no components specific to paleontology. As with our project name, the origami dinosaur is an intentional attempt at humoring users while providing the basis for our color palette and overarching design choices. Each future discipline that will be added will be designed around a corresponding animal.

Figure 45.3 shows the current home interface design, which aims to provide users with a central hub showing their projects and offering capabilities of creating or managing projects. The Western Mongolia project is displayed on the previous page, and tapping the project takes the user to another page with more project details. This page also houses the place where users can enter information relating to their project as well as view details such as the initial graph of Tsagaan Asgaa notes.

Fig. 45.1 Overall project architecture

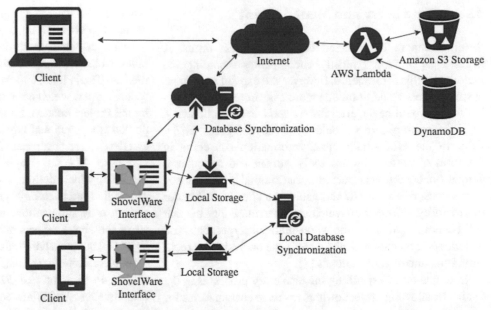

Fig. 45.2 (**a**) Android login page, (**b**) iOS login page. Two login screens on two different operating systems

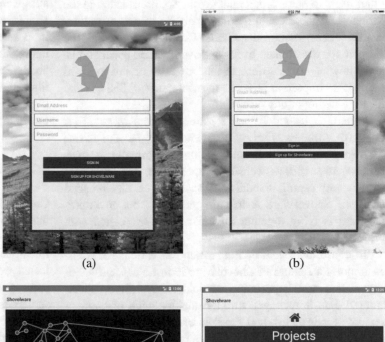

(a) (b)

Fig. 45.3 (**a**) Graph interface, (**b**) Home page interface. Two interfaces in ShovelWare, highlighting functionality of various components

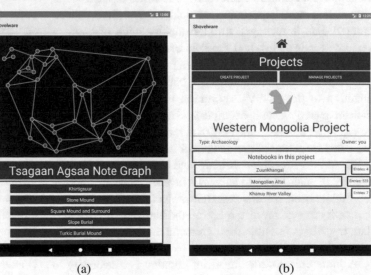

(a) (b)

45.5 Data Entry and Management

Specific data to be gathered comes in diverse forms. A generic paper form typically encompasses recording the majority of this information, however the capability of more custom forms would allow for more ease in recording. Digital forms would be superior for convenience and efficiency, as more custom forms would be disadvantageous in the field. In the Mongolia project, information can come in the form of pottery, bronze tools, human and agricultural animal bones, artifacts tied to burial mounds, monuments, deer stones, rich rock art, and habitation sites [7] fall under this majority. Information which may take more time but that still benefits from entry into a consolidated project database includes carbon dating of horse teeth and analysis of carbon, strontium, and oxygen isotopes [7].

One method of expediting the data entry process is in the feature of allowing project owners to create custom forms for other users to enter project data with. So, information in the Mongolia project could automatically be tagged as pottery shards, bones, or burial mounds. Custom forms would be simpler for researchers to fill out over generic paper forms, and allowing users to create custom text- or image-based fields is an important factor in the scalability of ShovelWare for note-taking of any discipline.

Data is managed between team members in countries in North America, Europe, and Mongolia, but the means of management are currently lacking. Information is parcelled across various websites, paper notes, and offline locations; no central database exists. Part of the intended usage of ShovelWare is in field recording, but an important part is tying together all information associated with projects.

To consolidate data floating around in various locations, an important feature of ShovelWare is in its capabilities of exportation and importation of field entries. Spreadsheet-entered data is managed through manipulation of comma-separated value files, and the data classification techniques used will organize the CSV entries most effectively. While the proposed graph structures are optimal for internal visualization of data, CSV exportation is a valued feature for data management and external backup. ShovelWare would be rendered useless if the new data recorded was completely alienated from that of previous field seasons.

In addition to cloud backup and data storage, Shovel-Ware will attempt to locally synchronize databases across the tablets used for one research project. The application's capability to synchronize relies on the hardware used, and if data transfer is possible through methods such as Bluetooth connectivity.

A hierarchical structure of information is a necessity to store projects in ShovelWare. Figure 45.4 shows the way projects are stored in ShovelWare. To accomplish this, the schemata for data is as following: a Project class consists of the properties ID, name, and notebooks. Notebooks hold the same metadata properties as Project but differ in holding notes. Notes are then further broken down into three types of media—Text, Photo, and Audio. Text can be made into more specific types, which are entirely reliant on the types defined by the Project created. Photos and audio can also be sorted; photos are tagged and labelled, while audio files can have a text description accompanying the recording.

Figure 45.4 is simple, especially in comparison to Fig. 45.5, which defines the project hierarchy used in the Mongolian archaeology project. The above structure is sectioned by sublocations needed to classify various notes; all of the above objects are field sites. So, every subset of Egiin Gol contains hundreds notes ranging from details about monumental sites to animal bones and the pottery discovered, adding up to a total of 523 notes. The Zuunkhangai and Khanuy River Valley are equally detailed, but their specific sites were omitted from Fig. 45.5 to make the diagram more legible. Being able to sort this data both by region and type—in its current state, the information is in one spreadsheet and unorganized—would be greatly beneficial to those analyzing and interpreting the data. The classification algorithm within ShovelWare is trained using a more detailed version of Fig. 45.5 that takes more factors into account than site location.

45.5.1 Cloud Hosting

Considerations with cloud storage were taken, and ultimately due to budgeting reasons, public cloud hosting with AWS services was decided upon to deploy web-based storage functionality of ShovelWare. AWS Lambda [8] was selected over other options for event-based pricing, and is most mature in support and features in comparison to its serverless competitors. Azure claims superiority over AWS in security, privacy, and compliance [9]. However, they have negligible differences, and pricing is nearly identical; both services offer one million free requests, then charge 0.20 dollars per subsequent one million requests. AWS then charges $0.00001667 per gigabyte-second compared to Azure's $0.000016 per gigabyte-second [8, 9]. The mobile application for ShovelWare works best with the serverless computing paradigm of charging by use because of the methods in which cloud storage and data synchronization occur. Instead of following an automatic, forced method of uploading locally-stored data, users are provided with the option of doing so.

One metric of comparison between private and public clouds lies in security features. Private clouds are arguably advantageous with regards to security because of the fact that public clouds can be accessible from anywhere where

Fig. 45.4 Generic project data structure

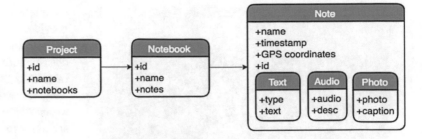

Fig. 45.5 Mongolia project structure

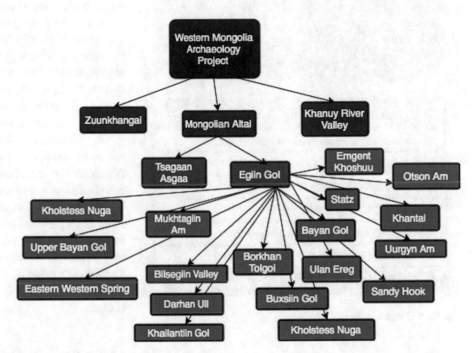

private clouds are not accessible on the same level. However, past that, public cloud vendors are more likely to ensure best security practices to retain large customers and protect confidential data. Any concerns regarding the security of AWS cloud hosting can be easily resolved by using ShovelWare and exclusively storing data locally.

Additionally, public clouds allow for freedom that private clouds lack—no hardware maintenance is necessary, and no costs, therefore, are associated with initial expenses or upkeep. Hardware is only a requirement for the clients accessing ShovelWare, and development time is shortened by removing the time otherwise needed for manual setup of a private cloud architecture.

45.6   Data Analysis

45.6.1 Reports

Entries for a particular project can be exported to CSV format, but another option is generation of a report. Also text-based, the report is not far off from the data in CSV

files. The reports double up in providing a general method of tracking project progress as well as information about the project. Increasing transparency internally regarding projects is arguably as important as external data sharing features with the aforementioned scope of team members from different continents. Project reports are available at any time as a log showing when and what changes are made to a project, as well as who is making changes. Of course, reports will be created locally if Internet connection is unavailable, and as with the other data, will synchronize with the rest of the project. As with CSV functionality, the log can be easily exported with the press of a button. Figure 45.6 shows the current log interface. Where the interface only shows titles of entries with the assumption that users would press for more details, exporting reports would provide all project details.

45.6.2 Graphs

To best serve the varying needs of projects, classification of project notes already initially contained in the ShovelWare Project data structure is performed by insertion into an

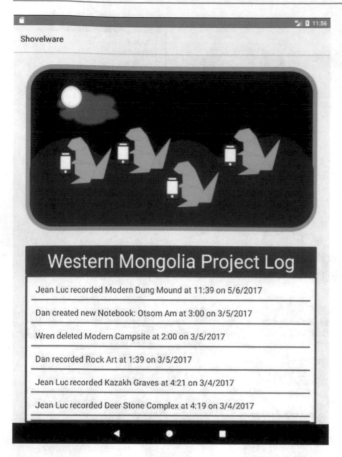

Fig. 45.6 Project log/report interface

overall project graph. Different graphs can be displayed, sorted, and filtered based on the metrics of classification, and the edges connecting graph nodes adjust accordingly. A clear indicator of closeness can be measured by distance from GPS coordinates, but beyond this, there are many more metrics with which to classify and rank closeness of specific notes or sites.

Internal and instant classification of notes would serve as a valuable tool in expediting the process of gathering data and drawing quantitative conclusions from field notes. For example, the Mongolia project could determine relationships across field sites such as the patterns of nomadic activity or similarities between tribes from different regions. Classification is a task best-suited for machine learning algorithms, and currently our focus is on text-based information over photos, though it will very likely become a topic of interest in the future.

Our machine learning algorithm utilizes TensorFlow [10] to classify notes, and is being trained using the notes from previous field seasons. In total, we are currently using 895 notes from the Tsagaan Agsaa field site, 237 notes from the Baga Gazaryn Chuluu field site, and 523 notes from the Egiin Gol field site. Once the most recent field season data entry is

complete, our dataset could more than double in entries and provide us with further testing material.

With the very open-ended generality of successful note classification, we must start with laying out our qualifications of related notes. The title of notes will be most strongly weighted when it comes to finding text-based similarities. Measuring and filtering parallels in entries gives priority to specified material. This feature will allow for greater ease when performing comprehensive studies of specific artifact types such as pottery shards or deer stones. So, for example, stone would go with stone, and bone would go with bone. Comment differences are ranked after this, and size of finds is kept separate as one offered method of sorted and displaying a project graph. Considerations for interpretation of parts of speech, for example, have shown to be unnecessary so far given the concise nature of comments where present.

One important question to answer with our datasets involves concerns of noise and how it is defined for our needs. Although the environment for our dataset is such that all entries follow a uniform language and format, this will not be the case come use in an actual project setting. Final field notes from previous field seasons came from many different students, but in the end were synthesized together and edited by one individual overseeing the entire project. This means that students using different semantic meanings could lead to inaccurate classification if our current dataset is not thorough enough.

45.6.3 Bioarchaeology

Another proposed application of our graph classification methods comes in its use towards bioarchaeological data. Protocol followed in the Mongolia project is as such: skeletal element data is chosen and identified according to the characteristics of potential for identification, survivability, ability to provide information about age and sex of animals, and ability to provide useful project measurements. Three database structures are used for classification of teeth, bones, and other fragments that cannot fall into the first two categories.

Figure 45.7 is a database diagram showing the classification methods used for bones found in the field. The need for storage of these structures in projects with similar setups is also enhanced by providing users with fill-in options. Most of the above fields would be most convenient if mapped to keys related to pre-determined classification possibilities. Taxonomic groups used, for example, are selected out of a pool of hundreds of groups expected and include more detailed fields to account for phylum, class, order, and family. More fields such as butchery have similar scales.

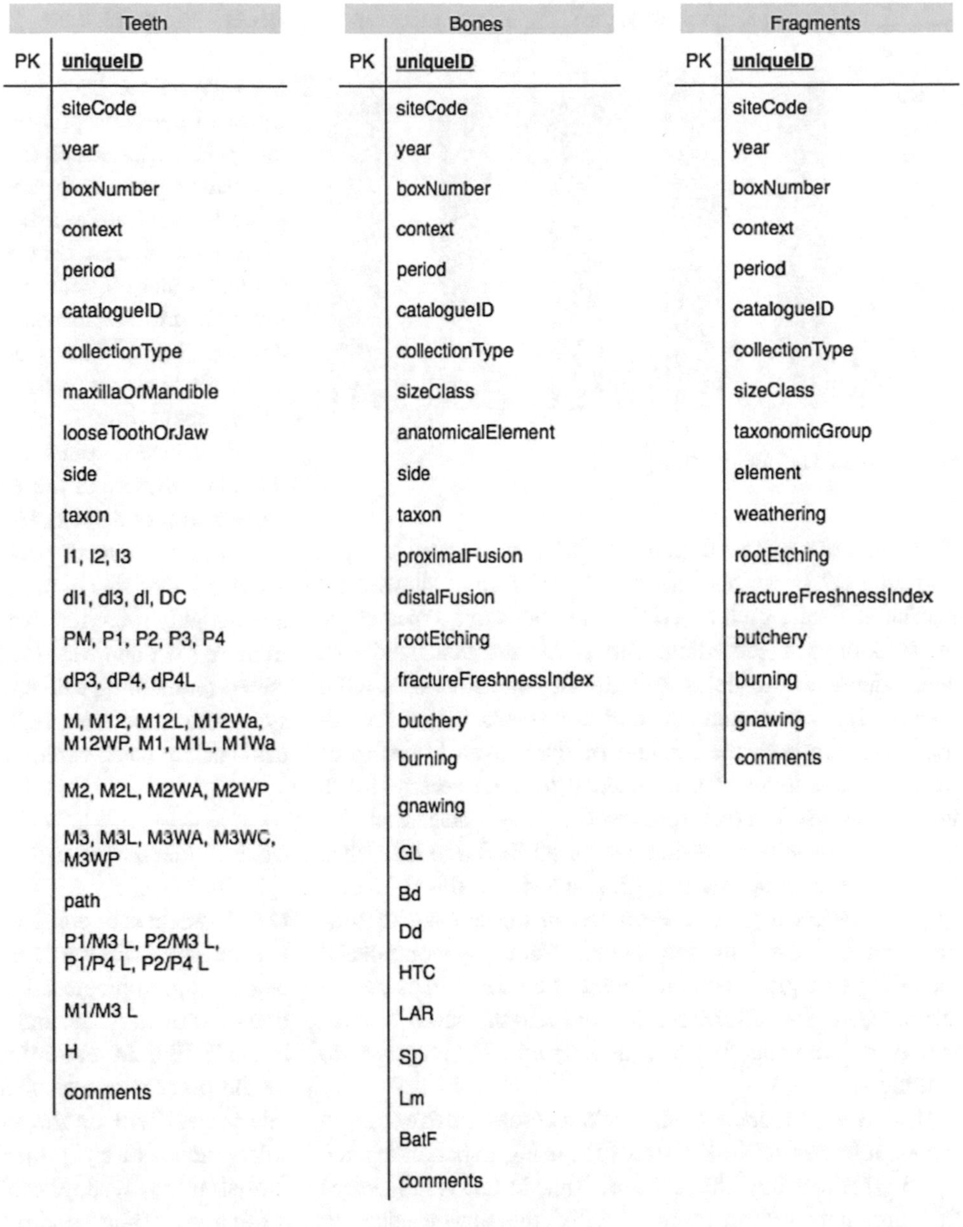

Fig. 45.7 Mongolian bioarchaeology database

Teeth		Bones		Fragments	
PK	**uniqueID**	PK	**uniqueID**	PK	**uniqueID**
	siteCode		siteCode		siteCode
	year		year		year
	boxNumber		boxNumber		boxNumber
	context		context		context
	period		period		period
	catalogueID		catalogueID		catalogueID
	collectionType		collectionType		collectionType
	maxillaOrMandible		sizeClass		sizeClass
	looseToothOrJaw		anatomicalElement		taxonomicGroup
	side		side		element
	taxon		taxon		weathering
	I1, I2, I3		proximalFusion		rootEtching
	dI1, dI3, dI, DC		distalFusion		fractureFreshnessIndex
	PM, P1, P2, P3, P4		rootEtching		butchery
	dP3, dP4, dP4L		fractureFreshnessIndex		burning
	M, M12, M12L, M12Wa, M12WP, M1, M1L, M1Wa		butchery		gnawing
	M2, M2L, M2WA, M2WP		burning		comments
	M3, M3L, M3WA, M3WC, M3WP		gnawing		
	path		GL		
	P1/M3 L, P2/M3 L, P1/P4 L, P2/P4 L		Bd		
	M1/M3 L		Dd		
	H		HTC		
	comments		LAR		
			SD		
			Lm		
			BatF		
			comments		

Bioinformatics tools available for genomic data processing have found immense success and popularity among researchers. ShovelWare takes on a different aspect to biology, aiming to find a middle ground between proper taxonomic information management and the disorganization of paper-and-pencil notes. We believe that our implementation of project structure storage combined with storage of pre-recorded fields will best serve the needs of a broad range of projects. This particular application provides an example of why such tools may be valuable in many different fields of research, and further application of such setup in the Mongolia project would also aid in the process of fauna identification.

45.7 Experiment

To quantify the amount of time needed for entry into digital spreadsheets as well as justify the needs for digital field recording systems in fields such as archaeology, data was collected to simulate recording methods in the field. The experiment was set up as follows: the same data was recorded using paper and pencil as well as our current digital entry capabilities. The pre-existing data from previous field seasons also used to train our machine learning algorithm was re-recorded by an individual who had not previously recorded or seen the information.

Figure 45.8 displays the results of the experiment. The data from five trials of 50 notes was recorded, showing significant time differences between digital recording and

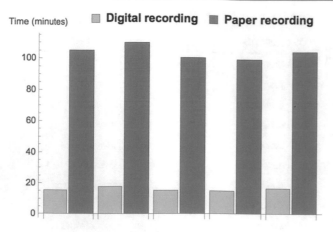

Fig. 45.8 Data recording results

paper recording. The digital recording was tested using a Samsung S7 Edge, and using a digital format allowed for particular fields, such as GPS coordinates and timestamps, to be skipped in recording. Otherwise, the fields and data were identical: the fields include the site, find, size, GPS coordinates, photo number, and comments. Paper recording factors in both the amount of time taken to record as well as the amount of time needed to enter recorded data into a Microsoft Excel spreadsheet. It is understood that large discrepancies in results can be attributed to individual writing speed compared to typing speed, but this data aims to give readers a general estimate on the amount of time that can be saved by the switch from paper-and-pencil recording to digital. Time differences between trials can be attributed to the differences in note length, which is most varied in comments that can range from full paragraphs to nothing.

The average amount of time taken across the five trials to record information was 104.20 min using paper, compared to 15.90 min using ShovelWare. This initial result means that digital recording takes 15 % of the time needed for paper recording. We hope to cut this down further by more extensive incorporation of custom form capabilities. A future experiment once our algorithms are more comprehensive will entail measuring the time reduction observed in analysis as well as in recording, and our beliefs based on this initial experiment are that we can lower recording time even further. Additionally, more information will be gathered to compare digital and paper recording experiences to gain further knowledge about particular demographics of field researchers and their inclinations towards certain recording methods. We would also like to gather data to break down what components of various recording methods specifically influence time taken to record. This will allow us to most accurately design our user interfaces to accommodate for our user preferences.

45.8 Conclusion

ShovelWare has been designed to accommodate for a multitude of common problems plaguing projects using paper-and-pencil approaches to data recording. As our experiment comparing paper-and-pencil to the time taken to record data using ShovelWare's current features shows, digital recording offers a massive advantage over paper. Our hopes are that the combination of digital recording and analysis greatly benefit research projects instead of hindering them as we further develop ShovelWare. Constructing a modular architecture is the best answer to our needs relating to deployment and development time.

One concern some may have for the move to a digital recording system is the ease with which data could potentially be lost or deleted. However, smart tablets are extremely reliable, and manually deleting information would require a series of steps that could not be unintentional. Smart tablets are arguably more reliable in the field than pencil-and-paper in more than one way, but if there are concerns of damaged tablets (something which would not result in data loss if local synchronization occurred), then the best solution is manual data backup on an external device.

45.9 Future Work

Development is ongoing with ShovelWare, and will continue in a variety of different forms: further maturation of features, bug testing, implementation of user feedback, and the addition of various forms and features are planned. Deployment in the 2018 field season for use in the Mongolia project will be the first major test of ShovelWare. Further extension of this project will be the use of ShovelWare for more than solely archaeology projects—the digital project/notebook format is easily applicable to research projects in other disciplines. If the opportunity of use in other disciplines is explored, then the microservice-oriented architecture will be highly valuable in accessibility to varied note-taking and data analysis options available through ShovelWare. In the future, features may be linked to the drone currently in use to record aerial images and comprehensively map out dig locations. If the scale of our project were raised, then development could come through making the drone more autonomous [11]. Such features could include enabling a visual connection between artifact discovery locations and the information gathered on said artifacts.

References

1. D. Sosna, L. Brunclkov, D. Henig, Testing iPad in the field: use of a relational database in garbological research. Anthropologie **51**, 421–430 (2013)
2. C. Motz, S. Carrier, *Paperless Recording at the Sangro Valley Project* (Amsterdam University Press, Amsterdam, 2012), pp. 1–2
3. Field acquired management information systems project. FAIMS Project (2017). Online Available: https://www.fedarch.org/
4. D. Michie, D.J. Spiegelhalter, C. Taylor, *Machine Learning, Neural and Statistical Classification* (Ellis Horwood, Upper Saddle River, 1994)
5. B. Pang, L. Lee, S. Vaithyanathan, Thumbs up?: sentiment classification using machine learning techniques, in *Proceedings of the ACL-02 Conference on Empirical Methods in Natural Language Processing - Volume 10*, Series EMNLP '02, Stroudsburg, PA (Association for Computational Linguistics, New York, 2002), pp. 79–86. Online Available: https://doi.org/10.3115/1118693.1118704
6. "NativeScript," NativeScript (2017). Online Available: https://www.nativescript.org/
7. J.-L. Houle, Bronze age mongolia (2017). Online Available: http://www.oxfordhandbooks.com/view/10.1093/oxfordhb/9780199935413.001.0001/oxfordhb-9780199935413-e-20
8. AWS Lambda, Amazon Web Services, Inc. (2017) Online Available: https://aws.amazon.com/lambda/
9. Microsoft Azure Functions, Microsoft (2017) Online Available: https://azure.microsoft.com/en-us/services/functions/
10. TensorFlow, Google (2017). Online Available: https://www.tensorflow.org/
11. C. Brooks, C. Goulet, M. Galloway, Toward indoor autonomous flight using a multi-rotor vehicle, in *International Conference on Information Technology: New Generations* (2016)

Pattern Recognition for Time Series Forecasting: A Case Study of a Helicopter's Flight Dynamics

Pedro Fernandes, Alexandre C. B. Ramos, Danilo Pereira Roque, and Marcelo Santiago de Sousa

Abstract

This paper presents a method for time series forecasting based on pattern recognition. As the system receives samples of time series, each of them representing one variable from the set of variables that describe the behavior of an application model, these samples are evaluated using a PCA algorithm, where each sample is represented by a feature vector. Different feature vectors (each of them representing a different sample of a particular case) are compared for pattern recognition. Once this sequence of steps is well performed, it's possible to estimate time series for different states between those represented by the previously analyzed samples. As an example for application of this method, a case study is presented for some variables under specific flight conditions. The chosen application for this case study, helicopter flight dynamics is a relevant study, for it can be used, for example, to provide precise data to a flight simulator, which implies in an important issue for pilot training, and subsequently, this type of application may help reducing the probability of pilot's faults in real flight missions. To demonstrate the applicability of the method, this paper shows results obtained when the system generated forecasts for flight dynamics variables in a specific scenario of initial conditions and while the helicopter performed a maneuver of response to collective command. Finally, some considerations are made about the work shown in this paper as the results, discussions and conclusions are presented.

Keywords

Helicopter flight dynamics · Pattern recognition · Flight simulator

46.1 Introduction

Due to the advances on the aviation's technology and the consequent increase in demand for the use of aircraft for different purposes, such as passenger transport, search and rescue missions, etc., safety of flight missions becomes even more relevant [1]. Among the main actions to improve it, advances in the quality of training provided to pilots can be cited, and in this context, the use of flight simulators is considered as one of these main activities [2]. Therefore, the development of more realistic flight simulators provides better quality training [3], which can contribute to minimize the risk of accidents.

Additionally, the modeling of a helicopter's flight dynamics is important to provide more realistic training, by its application in a flight simulator. This paper briefly presents fundamentals that are used for the computational model represented.

46.2 Flight Controls of a Helicopter

This section presents the helicopter flight controls as described by Cunha Jr, et al. [5]. The helicopter lift is generated by the resultant aerodynamic load applied on the blades of the main rotor. Helicopters have degree of freedom in the three spatial axes. The coordinate system used to study the dynamics of a helicopter is the rigid body system or system of the fuselage line reference. To operate it, there are three flight control instruments: *collective*, *cyclic* and *pedals*, which provide four controls: *longitudinal cyclic*, *lateral cyclic*, *collective* and *tail rotor*. These four controls

P. Fernandes · A. C. B. Ramos (✉)
Federal University of Itajubá, Mathematics and Computing Institute, Itajubá, MG, Brazil
e-mail: ramos@unifei.edu.br

D. P. Roque · M. S. de Sousa
Federal University of Itajubá, Mechanical Engineering Institute, Itajubá, MG, Brazil
e-mail: marcelo.santiago@unifei.edu.br

© Springer International Publishing AG, part of Springer Nature 2018
S. Latifi (ed.), *Information Technology – New Generations*, Advances in Intelligent Systems and Computing 738,
https://doi.org/10.1007/978-3-319-77028-4_46

allow the direct command of *pitch rate*, *roll rate*, *altitude* and *yaw rate*, respectively.

The use of the collective commands provide ascending and descending movements of the helicopter, changing the step of all main rotor's blades at the same time and at the deflection. For example, if the command to climb is given, the pilot must pull the collective and the resulting step is positive, otherwise the collective should be pushed, so the helicopter goes down.

The cyclic enables the pilot to make the longitudinal (pitch) and lateral (roll) movements of the helicopter, by changing the pitch of the main rotor blades differently, depending on the position where it is during the course of rotation. Examples: if a forward command is given, the pitch of the blades decreases when the blade is at the azimuth 90°, and increases when the blade at the azimuth 270°. If the command is given to the left, the pitch of the blades is decreased when the blade is at azimuth 0°, and increases if the blade is at azimuth 180°. Note that it's considered that the blades move anti-clockwise.

The pedals enable the pilot to control the rotations in the horizontal plane around the vertical z-axis (yaw) of the helicopter. They change the pitch of all tail rotor blades simultaneously and in the same pitch. The tail rotor is critical for the stability of the helicopter, for it is responsible for compensating the torque produced by the main rotor.

46.3 Modelling of a Helicopter's Flight Dynamics: A Conventional Method

The modeling and the information described in this section are mainly based on Cunha Jr, et al., Simplício and Padfield [4–6] and the presented application example is based on Simplício [5], who analyzed the *Bolkow Bo-105* model.

Initially, it can be said that a helicopter, as well as other aircraft, has its dynamic governed by the three laws of Newton: (1) if the body is in equilibrium, it will remain at rest or moving straight and with constant speed; (2) force equals the change of momentum; and (3) if a body A applies a force F on a body B, body B applies a force in the same module, and opposite direction to the body A (−F). From these laws, and knowledge of the forces (and moments) applied, it's possible to obtain the equations describing a helicopter's flight dynamics.

The forces acting on the main rotor and tail rotor are the weight and aerodynamic forces, similar to the forces acting on a wing. The difference is that the "aerodynamic surfaces", rotor blades, are in angular movement at a speed (approximately) constant. Each rotor blade airfoil section is subjected to a force that is proportional to both the dynamic pressure, the area of the unit section, the air density and the aerodynamic coefficients. The dynamic pressure is a function

Table 46.1 Description of some of the variables considered in a helicopter's flight dynamics—only the ones shown in the results section of this paper

Variable	Description
Time	Time instant (used as reference), [s]
Altitude	Helicopter's altitude during flight, [m]
α(**alpha**)	Angle of attack, [rad]
ϕ(**phi**)	Attitude roll angle, [rad]
q	Rotational rate around the body y-axis, [rad/s]
Speed	Helicopter's speed during flight, [m/s]
θ(**theta**)	Attitude pitch angle, [rad]

of helicopter's speed, angular speed of the blades, and blade position relative to the central axis that passes through the fuselage. The aerodynamic coefficients are function of the geometry of the section and of the rotor parameters, and the local angle of attack on the blade. This local angle of attack is dependent on different parameters, including fuselage angle of attack, pitch applied on the blades due to the collective and cyclic commands, inflow, pitch and roll rates and external disturbances. The angle of attack is calculated as function of the parameters described.

As it can be noticed, the conventional modelling of a helicopter's flight dynamics is a very complex task and requires the calculation of various parameters. The method shown in this paper, however, may be used for estimation of the flight dynamics over a time interval, and requires time series data samples of some variables that describe the flight dynamics of a specific helicopter model's flight under given conditions, which can be useful to provide quick initial information to help determining paths for further investigation.

For simplicity, the results of only some of the resulting variables are presented in this paper, as shown in Table 46.1.

46.4 A Brief Explanation of the Problem and About the Applied Concepts and Methods

As it was mentioned in the last section, there are different variables composing a helicopter's flight dynamics. Each of them can be analyzed in a time series context as there are available data relating the observed values at each instant within a given period (interval) of time. More formally, given a variable x, there are different x_t instants and each of them has a related x_{t_v} (value associated to a specific instant) within an observed time interval. It's also necessary to consider that each time series describing the behavior of a variable is related to some conditions. In this particular case, conditions as initial altitude and initial speed of the aircraft may be considered. Then, each x_t and its x_{t_v}, may be evaluated, in fact, as x_{t_c} and $x_{t_{v_c}}$, for there are different conditions related to each time series. So, for instance, considering a reference angle of the aircraft as the variable, let's calculate a forecast for a set of conditions, like 1000 m of initial altitude and 50 m/s of initial speed during 20 s of flight. To do so, the system already knows samples of how that same variable behaves when that same aircraft is flying in 1000 m of initial altitude and 30 m/s of initial speed and another sample when the initial altitude is 1000 and the initial speed is 60 m/s. So, if there is a way to identify the main features of each of the known samples and to recognize patterns between them, it's possible to make predictions based on this obtained knowledge. However, what makes more complicated to develop a model based on samples of time series in this particular case, is that the variables present a nonlinear behavior, so predicting a time series for a specific unknown condition based on few known samples that performs with a low error margin requires the usage of an efficient combination of techniques.

The first step is to ensure that the time series doesn't contain inconsistencies such as more than one value related to a given instant in time and it's also important that the time series be sequentially ordered, for example. So the first step is to remove inconsistencies off of the samples.

Once the first step was successfully performed, this paper suggests the use of some PCA (principal component analysis) algorithm to identify and determine a set composed by the more relevant valued instants within each sample. There are already some options available to analyze and determine which of them are the most important, but this paper presents a technique that considers the relevance of a given point of a time series based on a calculation of the angle of each point when related to its previous and its next point within the time series, applying the well-known law of cosines, as shown in the next equation.

$$p_{t_a} = \frac{\left(\Delta_t{}^2 + \Delta_v{}^2\right) + \left(\nabla_t{}^2 + \nabla_v{}^2\right) - \left((p_{t-1} - p_{t+1})^2 + (p_{t-1_v} - p_{t+1_v})^2\right)}{2 * \sqrt[2]{\left(\Delta_t{}^2 + \Delta_v{}^2\right)} {}^* \sqrt[2]{\left(\nabla_t{}^2 + \nabla_v{}^2\right)}}$$

Where p_{t_a} is the angle of the variable p at the instant t, $\Delta_t{}^2 = (p_t - p_{t-1})^2$, $\Delta_v{}^2 = \left(p_{t_v} - p_{t-1_v}\right)^2$, $\nabla_t{}^2 = (p_{t+1} - p_t)^2$, $\nabla_v{}^2 = \left(p_{t+1_v} - p_{t_v}\right)^2$, and p_{t_v} is the value of the variable p at the instant t. In this approach, the first and the last points of each time series always compose the relation of the selected points. Besides the values of the first and last instant, only the more relevant points are added to the selected points list—the criteria used is to add the n points with angle values more distant from the median of the angles of all the points to the list. Then each time series is now represented by a feature vector composed by the principal elements of the original time series.

Now the sequence of selected points may be paired to form a sequential set of linear functions. This approach enables the representation of the now simplified time series as a piecewise model [7] that describes the linear calculation of the values for a variable for instants between each range of initial and final instants.

Figure 46.1 is now presented as an example of a time series represented by a piecewise model, showing a sequence of commands relative to the longitudinal cyclic pitch of the main rotor (θ_{1s}) performing a maneuver of response to collective command.

Then it's necessary to check if this model is a good approximation to the original data, using a rule to calculate the error between the piecewise model and the original data. A suggestion is to use the square root of the mean squared error divided by the mean value of the variable in the interval.

The next step proposed in this paper is to search for similarities between different represented samples, to provide a way to establish relations between them. So, for instance, each "piece" of a piecewise model representing a sample may be compared to the pieces of another piecewise model representing another sample to determine which of them are the most similar to the one of the first sample. This process continues until all the pieces of a piecewise representation of a sample are already related to the pieces of the piecewise representation of the other compared sample. Different criteria may be used to compare the pieces, but this paper suggests using a weighted product of the terms described in the following equation.

$$s_a = \left(w_{a_a} {}^* s_{a_a}\right) + \left(w_{a_b} {}^* s_{a_b}\right) + \left(w_{a_c} {}^* s_{a_c}\right)$$

Where s_a is the score of the association between a piece from a model to a piece from another model, w_{a_i} is the

Fig. 46.1 Example of graphic representation of the longitudinal cyclic pitch of the main rotor command (θ_{1s}) while performing a maneuver of response to collective command, and its piecewise model, where $\theta 1s_t$ refers to the instant t in a time series of θ_{1s}

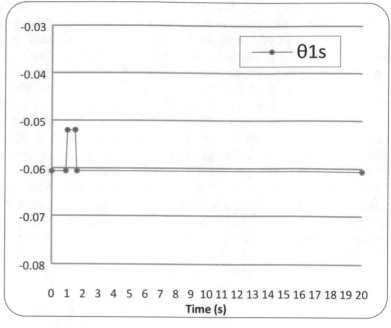

$$
f(\theta 1s_t)
= \begin{cases}
0.000018\ \theta 1s_t + (-0.060648\ ) & if\ 0 \leq \theta 1s_t \leq 0.9 \\
0.085898\ \theta 1s_t + (-0.137939\ ) & if\ 0.9 \leq \theta 1s_t \leq 1 \\
0.000074\ \theta 1s_t + (-0.052116\ ) & if\ 1 \leq \theta 1s_t \leq 1.5 \\
-0.085854\ \theta 1s_t + (0.076776\ ) & if\ 1.5 \leq \theta 1s_t \leq 1.6 \\
-0.000003\ \theta 1s_t + (-0.060585\ ) & if\ 1.6 \leq \theta 1s_t \leq 20
\end{cases}
$$

weight of the association of the term i and s_{a_i} is the score obtained by the association for the term i of the equation.

$$
s_{a_a} = \begin{cases}
\dfrac{m1_{q_m}}{m0_{p_m}} & if\ m0_{p_m} \geq m1_{q_m} \\[3mm]
\dfrac{m0_{p_m}}{m1_{q_m}} & if\ m0_{p_m} < m1_{q_m}
\end{cases}
$$

Where $m0_{p_m}$ is the multiplier value of the piece p from the piecewise model $m0$, and $m1_{q_m}$ is the multiplier value of the piece q from the piecewise model $m1$.

$$
s_{a_b} = \frac{(s_{ab1} + s_{ab2})}{2}
$$

The following equations explain the calculation of s_{ab1} and s_{ab2}.

$$
s_{ab1} = \begin{cases}
\dfrac{m1_{qax}}{m0_{pax}} & if\ m0_{pax} \geq m1_{qax} \\[3mm]
\dfrac{m0_{pax}}{m1_{qax}} & if\ m0_{pax} < m1_{qax}
\end{cases}
$$

Where $m0_{pax}$ is the average value of the x-axis range of the piece p from the piecewise model $m0$, and $m1_{qax}$ is the average value of the x-axis range of the piece q from the piecewise model $m1$.

$$
s_{ab2} = \begin{cases}
\dfrac{m1_{qay}}{m0_{pay}} & if\ m0_{pay} \geq m1_{qay} \\[3mm]
\dfrac{m0_{pay}}{m1_{qay}} & if\ m0_{pay} < m1_{qay}
\end{cases}
$$

Where $m0_{pay}$ is the average value of the y-axis range of the piece p from the piecewise model $m0$, and $m1_{qay}$ is the average value of the y-axis range of the piece p from the piecewise model $m1$.

$$
s_{a_c} = \frac{(s_{ac1} + s_{ac2})}{2}
$$

The following equations explain the calculation of s_{ac1} and s_{ac2}.

$$
s_{ac1} = \begin{cases}
\dfrac{m1_{qsx}}{m0_{psx}} & if\ m0_{psx} \geq m1_{qsx} \\[3mm]
\dfrac{m0_{psx}}{m1_{qsx}} & if\ m0_{psx} < m1_{qsx}
\end{cases}
$$

Where $m0_{p_{sx}}$ is the absolute value of the x-axis range of the piece p from the piecewise model $m0$, and $m1_{q_{sx}}$ is the absolute value of the x-axis range of the piece q from the piecewise model $m1$.

$$s_{a_{c2}} = \begin{cases} \dfrac{m1_{q_{sy}}}{m0_{p_{sy}}} & if\, m0_{p_{sy}} \geq m1_{q_{sy}} \\[3mm] \dfrac{m0_{p_{sy}}}{m1_{q_{sy}}} & if\, m0_{p_{sy}} < m1_{q_{sy}} \end{cases}$$

Where $m0_{p_{sy}}$ is the absolute value of the y-axis range of the piece p from the piecewise model $m0$, and $m1_{q_{sy}}$ is the absolute value of the y-axis range of the piece q from the piecewise model $m1$.

As it could be seen in the last equations, different combinations of weights may be used for the terms of the equation that calculates the scores s_a, and that's due to the fact that the best criteria to identify the best match between each piece of each model varies depending on the features of the models compared, so it's suggested to use some kind of search space algorithm to try different combination of weights for the terms to find the best one.

Now it makes sense that a weighted interpolation can be made between two modeled samples to generate a forecast representing a condition between them. But it isn't possible yet to determinate that this set of rules for generation of forecasts is good enough to be used. It's also necessary to have another sample, one that represents a condition between those of the modeled samples to check the applicability of the obtained set of rules. If this validation test succeeds, then it's possible to expect that another forecasts generated for that range of the considered conditions may be also a good approximation to the actual values. Else, it means that some adjustments have to be done and, only when the validation test is successful, it's minimally safe to use an obtained set of rules for forecasting. This may occur, since each specific case may present different features regarding, for example, level of complexity, similarity between samples, considered time interval of the samples, and so on, so it's suggested to use some kind of search space algorithm to try different adjustments in each step of the process to find a set of rules that generates forecasts with a satisfactory minimum error rate.

46.5 Results and Discussion

This section shows some results obtained with the use of a system developed as described in the previous section, comparing the actual values from validation samples to the forecast values obtained by the system for the same variables using two samples for each variable, one of them referring to the behavior of the helicopter starting in a stable flight at initial speed of 30 m/s and at 1000 m of altitude and the other with initial speed of 60 m/s and initial altitude of 1000 m also, and while performing a maneuver of response to the collective command. In this particular case, the next graphics presented in the Figs. 46.2, 46.3, 46.4, 46.5, 46.6 and 46.7 shows the behavior of six variables starting in a stable flight at initial speed of 45 m/s and at 1000 m of altitude and while performing a maneuver of response to the collective command (the same maneuver shown in Fig. 46.1).

Fig. 46.2 Comparison between actual and forecast data obtained by the system for the altitude variable, given initial speed of 45 m/s and 1000 m initial altitude, of the following 20 s

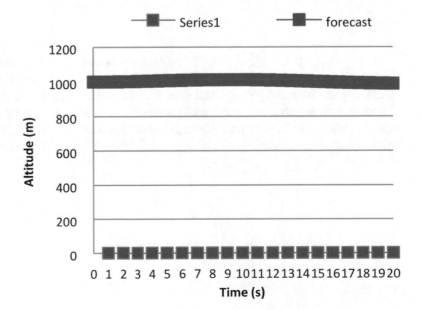

Fig. 46.3 Comparison between actual and forecast data obtained by the system for the alpha variable, given initial speed of 45 m/s and 1000 m initial altitude, of the following 20 s

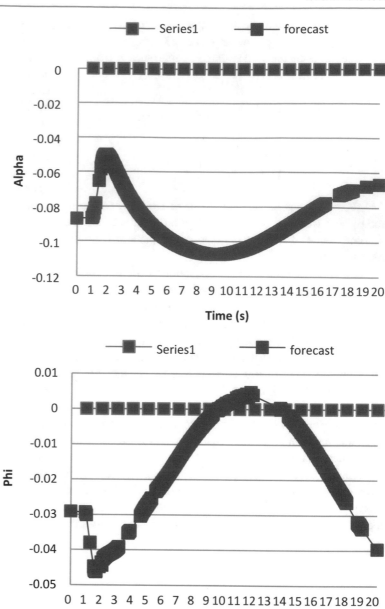

Fig. 46.4 Comparison between actual and forecast data obtained by the system for the phi variable, given initial speed of 45 m/s and 1000 m initial altitude, of the following 20 s

Figures 46.2, 46.3, 46.4, 46.5, 46.6 and 46.7 shows that, in general, the forecasts generated by the system present a similar aspect compared to the actual data used for validation, demonstrating that the system could detect the features from the samples and use its pattern recognition to make the predictions.

The results shown in Table 46.2, considering the rate between square root of MSE and the mean absolute values of the variables in the interval, indicate that the observed error is relatively low for the speed and altitude forecasts especially, but for the other variables there's still a need for improvements.

Fig. 46.5 Comparison between actual and forecast data obtained by the system for the q variable, given initial speed of 45 m/s and 1000 m initial altitude, of the following 20 s

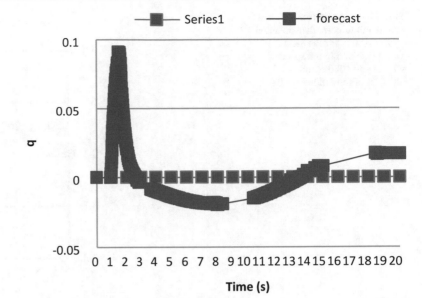

Fig. 46.6 Comparison between actual and forecast data obtained by the system for the speed variable, given initial speed of 45 m/s and 1000 m initial altitude, of the following 20 s

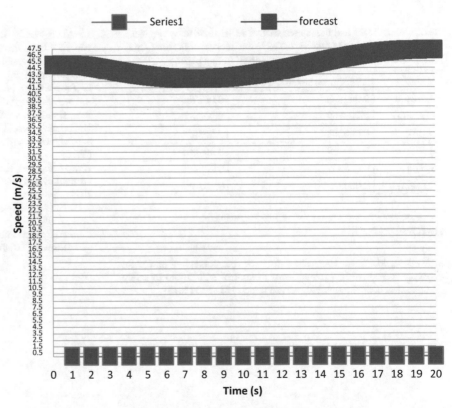

46.6   Conclusions

This paper presented a method used to develop a system able to generate time series predictions from time series samples used for training and validation. Also, it demonstrates the applicability of the method in this case study. The results show that improvements may be done to provide better approximation of values; however, it's noticeable that the system is already able to forecast the aspect of the behavior of the variables. Future work is planned to demonstrate how it's possible to achieve better results.

Acknowledgment We thank UNIFEI for research support and FAPEMIG for financial support.

Fig. 46.7 Comparison between actual and forecast data obtained by the system for the theta variable, given initial speed of 45 m/s and 1000 m initial altitude, of the following 20 s

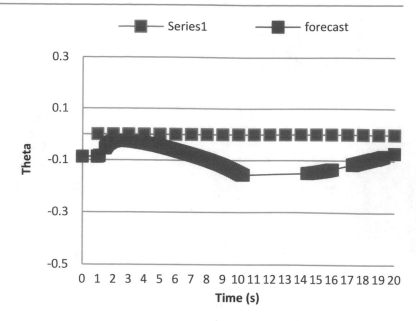

Table 46.2 MSE and the square root of MSE divided by the mean absolute value (MAV) of the variables in the interval of the time series obtained for each of the variables considered in this paper

Variable	MSE (mean squared error)	$\dfrac{\sqrt[2]{MSE}}{MAV \in theInterval}$
Altitude	2.902808	0.001700
α(**alpha**)	0.000269	0.227463
ϕ(**phi**)	0.000208	0.563060
q	0.000139	0.504985
Speed	0.026869	0.003680
θ(**theta**)	0.000873	0.453453

References

1. X. You, M. Ji, H. Han, The effects of risk perception and flight experience on airline pilots' locus of control with regard to safety operation behaviors. Accid. Anal. Prev. **9**, 131–139 (2013)

2. J.S. Melo, M.S.R. Tadeucci, A atividade aérea e uso de simulador de voo, XIV Encontro Latino Americano, 2010

3. J. Ryder, T. Santarelli, J. Scolaro, J. Hicinbothom, W. Zachary, Comparison of cognitive model uses in intelligent training systems, in *Proceedings of the Human Factors and Ergonomics Society Annual Meeting*, vol 4, 2000, pp. 374–377

4. S.S. Cunha Jr., M.S. de Sousa, D.P. Roque, A.C.B. Ramos, P. Fernandes Jr., Dynamic simulation of the flight behavior of a rotary-wing aircraft. Inf. Technol. N. Gener. **13**, 1087–1099 (2016)

5. P.V.M Simplício, Helicopter nonlinear flight control using incremental nonlinear dynamic inversion, Delft University of Technology, 2011

6. G.D. Padfield, *Helicopter Flight Dynamics*, 2nd edn. (Wiley, New York, 2008)

7. I. Lima, C.A.M. Pinheiro, F.A.O. Santos, *Inteligência Artificial*, 1st edn. (Elsevier, 2014)

A Model for Hour-Wise Prediction of Mobile Device Energy Availability

Mathias Longo, Cristian Mateos, and Alejandro Zunino

Abstract

Mobile devices have become so ubiquitous and their computational capabilities have increased so much that they have been deemed as first-class resource providers in modern computational paradigms. Particularly, novel Mobile Cloud Computing paradigms such as Dew Computing promote offloading heavy computations to nearby mobile devices. Not only this requires to produce resource allocators to take advantage of device resources, but also mechanisms to quantify current and future energy availability in target devices. We propose a model to produce hour-wise estimations of battery availability by inspecting past device owner's activity and relevant device state variables. The model includes a feature extraction approach to obtain representative features/variables, and a prediction approach, based on regression models and machine learning classifiers. Comparisons against a relevant related work in terms of the Mean Squared Error metric shows that our method provides more accurate battery availability predictions in the order of several hours ahead.

Keywords

Mobile cloud computing · Battery prediction · Feature selection · Time series · Android

47.1 Introduction

Mobile Cloud Computing (MCC) [1] is a computing paradigm that has been proposed as a way of augmenting mobile devices –and hence deal with their inherent

M. Longo
University of Southern California, Los Angeles, CA, USA
e-mail: mathiasl@usc.edu

C. Mateos (✉) · A. Zunino
ISISTAN-UNCPBA-CONICET, Tandil, Buenos Aires, Argentina
e-mail: cristian.mateos@isistan.unicen.edu.ar;
alejandro.zunino@isistan.unicen.edu.ar

limitations– with remote resources located in the Cloud. To this end, MCC combines advances from the areas of distributed architectures, mobile computing, cloud computing and wireless/fixed networks so that rich applications can be seamlessly and efficiently "executed" in mobile devices via the actual execution/processing of computations/data on remote Cloud resources. Examples of such applications are speech recognition and augmented reality. Moreover, moving computations and data from devices to remote resources while obtaining maximal benefit from the system in terms of application execution performance and energy saving is performed via offloading techniques [1–3].

Traditional MCC proved however insufficient to cope with many latency-sensitive applications and very large number of (mobile) client devices, such as critical IoT (Internet of Things) services [4]. In response, the Fog Computing paradigm [5] was proposed around 2012 by Cisco researchers to provide highly-scalable infrastructures for developing and deploying latency and location-aware applications, where geographical distribution, mobility and software/hardware heterogeneity are the rule. Fog Computing has the ability of augmenting mobile (e.g., laptops, smartphones, tablets, wearables) and wireless devices (e.g., sensors) with nearby fixed processing/storage resources. Moreover, motivated by the huge amount of mobile devices –there will be 1.5 mobile-connected devices per capita by 2021 (http://tinyurl.com/mokcut3)– with ever-growing software and hardware capabilities, recent research [6] has suggested the possibility of using nearby mobile devices as destination for offloading computations/data, paradigm which has been named Dew Computing [7, 8].

Among the many challenges this new computing paradigm intuitively poses is resource scheduling/allocation, i.e. the mechanism by which tasks or data to be run or processed, respectively, are placed in appropriate computational resources (mobile devices in this case). Compared to resource scheduling in conventional distributed computing environments, resource scheduling using a cluster of nearby mobile devices is challenging due to the highly dynamic and heterogeneous nature of resource availability [9]: mobile devices can change their location, they are non-dedicated by nature and have energy limitations. Quantifying resource availability, on the other hand, is of utmost importance for a Dew Computing scheduler to take good scheduling decisions, i.e. selecting the most appropriate nearby devices to execute some given computations. However, such quantification is difficult in light of Dew Computing high dynamism and heterogeneity.

In this context, we investigate in this paper a model to quantify resource availability in mobile devices that take into account the usage profile of device owner's, which is an open problem seldom explored in the literature [10]. The model produces ahead predictions of remaining battery in the order of hours, and it is built by analyzing relevant past owner's activity (charging state, application execution, activated radios, etc.). Both the model itself and the assessment of its predictive accuracy are based on real traces from the Device Analyzer data-set [11], which is at present the largest mobile device usage data-set and includes traces from more than 31,000 users worldwide and different Android-based mobile device brands.

The organization of this paper is as follows. The next section explain our model to predict energy availability in detail. Then, Sect. 47.3 evaluates the accuracy of the model in terms of the Mean Square Root Error metric. Finally, Sect. 47.4 summarizes the implications of our findings and delineates future works.

47.2 Approach

In this section, we present our approach for predicting mobile device battery lifetime based on owner's activity, i.e. device usage patterns. Based on the activity traces of an individual user, our approach relies on feature selection to select the most relevant activity types for building a prediction model. This is explained in detail in Sect. 47.2.1. Feature selection pursues two goals, namely reducing the number of features to reduce overfitting and improve the generalization of models, and gaining better understanding of the features and their relationship to the response variables [12]. Moreover, we also propose an ensemble of several Machine Learning algorithms, trained using the resulting features from previous steps, which is detailed in Sect. 47.2.2. For the sake of illustrating the proposal, values shown below correspond to applying the model to a user from the data-set, who has registered activity traces for over 6 weeks.

Lastly, the implementation of this approach, as well as the creation of the Machine Learning models, was done in Python using open-source libraries: Scikit-Learn, Pandas, Numpy and MatplotLib. The source code is available from a GitHub repository.[1]

47.2.1 Preliminary Data Analysis and Feature Selection

To come up with an approach to feature selection that is general enough in the problem domain at hand, we have as mentioned earlier focused our research in the Device Analyzer data-set.

Before analysing the data, we defined a structured format for it. To this end, the data-set that basically consists in plain logs is splitted into states, where each state has the value for each mobile sensor in a device. A mobile device state changes as a result of an event in time that changes the value of any sensor. For example, a change in the battery level can be defined as an event, which triggers a new state of the mobile device in which the battery level is modified and all other features remain the same. Initially, from the formatted data, the following combination of features were considered:

- Day of week: Day of week where the event occurred, numbered from 0 to 6. Type: Integer.
- Minute: Minute of the day in which the event took place. Type: Integer.
- External Supply: Whether the mobile device is plugged to an external energy supply, e.g. AC adapter or USB connection. Type: Boolean.
- Bright Level: Screen brightness intensity. Type: Integer.
- Screen on/off: Whether the mobile screen is active or inactive. Type: Boolean.
- Connected: Whether the mobile phone is connected to a 3G/4G network. Type: Boolean.
- Connected to Wifi: Whether the mobile phone is connected to a Wifi network or not. Type: Boolean.
- Temperature: Mobile phone's actual temperature. Type: Integer.
- Voltage: Current battery voltage. Type: Integer.
- Battery Level: Current battery level ranging between 0 and 100. Type: Integer.

The dataset itself contains several other features, such as those related to location and application usage. Nevertheless, these features were not considered as relevant to the battery level modelling as the ones previously listed. First of all, it is true that by knowing the location of a user in each state, it might be possible to infer if they are at home. If that is the case, the probability of charging the mobile phone increases.

---

[1]http://github.com/matlongo/battery-level-predictor.

Table 47.1 Extract from the formatted data-set for an individual user

Day of week	Minute	External supply	Bright level	Screen on/off	Connected	Connected to Wifi	Temperature	Voltage (mV)	Battery level
3	652	0	149	1	0	1	275	3686	31
3	653	0	149	1	0	1	286	3740	30
3	654	0	149	1	0	1	286	3740	30
3	655	0	149	1	0	1	286	3740	30

Cells in Boolean-typed columns contain either 0 (false) or 1 (true)

Fig. 47.1 Battery level overview of the sample user in the first 5 days

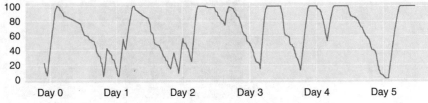

Fig. 47.2 Per-hour average battery level of the sample user: real (left) and sinus curve (right)

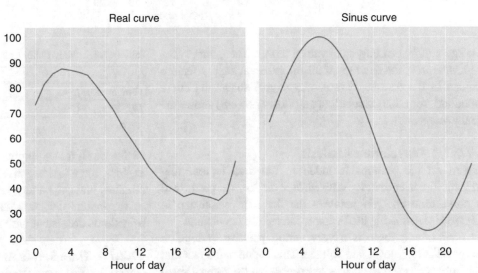

However, that information can also be obtained from the charging pattern using the Energy Supply feature. Secondly, application usage is highly seasonal, because applications tend to change in a short time, as well as the users might also change their applications periodically (e.g. replacements). Therefore, it is very difficult to generalize a model based on this feature, and it might incur in extra noise.

Table 47.1 shows an extract from the formatted data-set for one particular mobile device user. Furthermore, Fig. 47.1 depicts the battery level variation along time for this user (first 5 days of the sample). It is possible to see that the resulting curve is not exactly periodic since it takes different shapes, and it does not have a preset behavior. However, it is worth noting that there is a visual resemblance to a sinusoidal curve, because it continuously goes up and down. In fact, Fig. 47.2 (left) depicts a greater resemblance when the battery level is averaged per day. Considering this observation, which applied to many other users in the data-set as well, a new feature representing the sinus movement was added to the feature list: $Battery\,sinus = amplitude * sin(2 * pi * \frac{minute}{minsPerDay}) + batteryLevelMean$, where $amplitude$ de-

scribes how much the curve goes up and down, $minute$ is the minute of the day, $minsPerDay$ is the total number of minutes in a day (i.e., 1440), and $batteryLevelMean$ is the average battery level per day. The $batteryLevelMean$ is the mean per day battery level in the dataset. In addition, the maximum $amplitude$ is 50, since a bigger value makes the curve going above the maximum battery level or below the minimum battery level. Finally, it is worth pointing out that the only variable used to calculate the sinus is $minute$, which is easily accessible in every mobile device. Figure 47.2 (right) shows the resulting curve compared to the real one (in the left) we previously obtained using real battery level samples.

Likewise, from Fig. 47.1 it is possible to see that the battery level tends to go up during the night, due to the fact that the energy supply is connected. Therefore we can model the energy supply behavior with a cosine, getting the zenith during the night when it is usually connected, and going down during daytime. Concretely, we included the following extra feature: $Battery\,cosine = amplitude * cos(2 * pi * \frac{minute}{minsPerDay}) + batteryExternalMean$. In this case the $amplitude$ has a maximum value of 0.5, because the

Fig. 47.3 Per-hour average energy supply feature value on sample user dataset: real (left) and cosine curve (right)

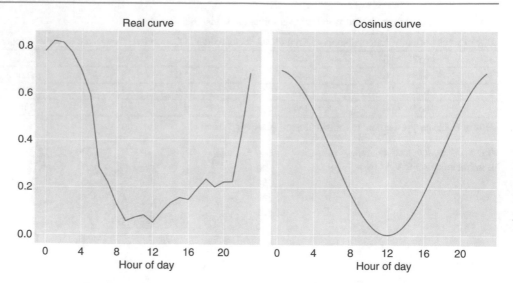

energy supply can only take values 0 or 1. Then, *batteryExternalMean* is the average of all the external supply feature values in the dataset. Figure 47.3 (right) shows the curve obtained from this calculation, and Fig. 47.3 (left) shows the real averaged curve.

47.2.1.1 Correlation Analysis

Based on the features included in the data representing any mobile user activity with his/her device, we performed a correlation analysis between the features established in previous steps, using the Pearson correlation coefficient.

First of all, there is a very strong positive correlation between battery level and voltage. This is due to the fact that the voltage is used as a variable to carry out the battery level. This means that voltage is not discriminant for our model and it will overfit any Machine Learning model, hence it should not be considered for the following steps. In addition to the voltage, the temperature should also be dismissed for future analysis, because it has a remarkable negative correlation with the battery level.

Secondly, we also obtained a very strong negative correlation between *Connected* and *Connected to Wifi*. That means, whenever the Wifi is connected, 3G/4G is not used, and vice versa. This might be because of the way Android works, since Android turns off 3G/4G connection when there is Wifi available so as to avoid incurring in monetary costs or wasting mobile data quota.

A more interesting relationship to point out is between the sinus, one of the last added features, and the battery level. This is a good symptom that the model can rely on this feature to predict the battery level for future states. Although slightly weaker, there is a noticeable positive correlation between the External Supply and the cosine which was also added as a new feature.

Another interesting point is that the screen tends to be off when the external supply is connected. Probably, the mobile

Table 47.2 Dickey-Fuller test: results

Test statistic	−13.37
Critical value (5%)	−2.86
Critical value (1%)	−3.43

device was left charging without so much interaction with it. Besides, there is a negative correlation between the hour (in minutes) and the battery level, meaning that as time passes by the mobile device tends to have less battery level. This behavior is consistent with the curve depicted in Fig. 47.1.

47.2.1.2 Time Series Analysis

Given the fact that the input data-set is a collection of data points gathered at constant time intervals -established by the Device Analyzer Android app that collects samples in a device- and that the battery level is time dependent, Time Series analysis can be used to determine how many *lag* intervals should be used to estimate a future battery level. For the purpose of this work, a *lag* is the number of previous states that are needed to come up with a good battery level estimation. Since intuitively estimations have a strong dependence on previous state's values, it is necessary to know how many previous states should be considered for the prediction.

We first checked if the time series is stationary. A time series is said to be stationary if its statistical properties such as mean and variance remain constant over time. Intuitively, it can be inferred that if a time series has a particular behavior over time, there is a very high probability that it will follow the same in the future. More formally, stationarity can be checked by using the Dickey-Fuller Test [13]. In this case, the null hypothesis is that a time series is non-stationary. Depending on the resulting critical value from the test, the level of confidence to say that the time series is stationary might be higher or lower. Table 47.2 shows the results for

Fig. 47.4 Autocorrelation and Partial Autocorrelation for battery level feature along the time

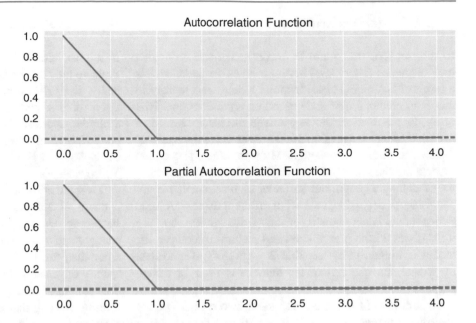

the Dickey-Fuller Test on the data-set. As we can see, the statistic test is less than the 1% critical value, meaning that there is a 99% of confidence to say that the time series is stationary.

Once proven its stationarity, we decided to apply an Auto-Correlation Function (ACF) and a Partial Auto-Correlation Function (PACF) to determine the number of lags that best represent the following state. Figure 47.4 shows the ACF and PACF applied to the dataset. It is possible to visually infer, according to the figure, that one lag is sufficient to estimate the following state. Therefore, a new feature is added to accomplish this relationship: Previous Battery Level.

47.2.1.3 Feature Selection

Once the dataset was preprocessed and the feature extraction steps is finished, we performed feature selection to obtain the minimal set of descriptive features. In this part of the process those features that are not influential in the battery level are filtered out. There exist many strategies that can be adopted for this part of the pipeline [12], and then, in this case, a combination of three different approaches have been considered.

First of all, two *Univariate Feature Selection* methods were considered: F-Test and Mutual Information. The former one is a statistical test for estimating the degree of linear dependency between two random variables, so it is performed for each feature against the battery level. On the other hand, the latter one is a non-parametric method that uses entropy to measure information content in data, in the sense that the higher the entropy the lower the information. Finally, the

Table 47.3 Feature selection using F-regression, mutual information and Lasso: scores

	F-Regression	Mutual Information	Lasso
Previous battery level	3.86E+09	3.995	0.9966
Minute	2.06E+05	0.599	0.0088
Day of week	5.25E+02	0.067	0.0002
External supply	1.28E+05	0.193	0.467
Connected	1.21E+03	0.028	0
Connected to Wifi	2.85E+03	0.024	0
Bright level	2.87E+04	0.002	0.0002
Screen on/off	3.22E+04	0.059	0.007
Sinus	2.61E+05	0.308	0.086
Cosine	6.39E+03	0.244	0

third approach considered is Lasso regression. Lasso regression is a regression model with $L_1 = |w_i|$, regularization term, where w_i is the coefficient used for x_i. Compared to the Ridge Regression regularization term, Lasso shrinks those "irrelevant" coefficients to zero instead of shrinking them to a small value. This model is parametrized by a meta-parameter called *alpha*. The larger the value of *alpha* the fewer the features selected.

Table 47.3 depicts the values obtained from the three mentioned techniques. The first column shows the F-Score calculated from the correlation between each feature and the target feature, ie, the battery level. The second column depicts the mutual information score calculated from the entropy of the dataset. Lastly, Lasso scores are the resultant coefficients associated for each feature after training the regression model with the regularization term.

47.2.2 Model Construction

In this section, to explain the proposed model to predict mobile phones battery level in future states. In particular, it is a result of combining classification models and a regression model to predict a new state based on a previous one. First of all, the selected model to estimate the battery level is a Multiple Linear Regression Model built using the resulting features from previous section. Multiple Linear Regression models are the most suitable Machine Learning algorithms for predicting a continuous variable, such as mobile phones battery level, depending on a set of different features. A Time Series model is not enough for this particular case, because it dismisses all the non-time related features. Moreover, the model is trained using the first 2 weeks of gathered data for a user, and the rest of the data-set is used for testing purposes.

In addition to the regression model, two complementary classification models were built to estimate the variability of external supply and screen on/off features. These models predict the state of both features in future states. The external supply classifier is a Random Forest classifier with ten estimators and its maximum depth is 3. It was trained using the cosine as well as the minute of the day that is being predicted and the previous state. The screen on/off estimator is a Decision Tree classifier built using the minute of day and the previous screen state.

The proposed mechanism to combine all the created models is an iterative method that estimates the following state based on the previous estimated states. The following is the pseudocode of the proposed method:

while current_state < desired_state:
  current_state[external_supply] =
    external_supply_classifier.estimate(current_state)
  current_state[screen] =
    screen_classifier.estimate(current_state)
  current_state =
    regression_model.estimate_following_state
    (current_state)

In this context, a *desired state* is a particular minute in the near future where we would like to know the battery level. This becomes pivotal in the context of mobile cloud scheduling, where the scheduler should consider, among several variables, how much available energy a mobile device has to execute specific tasks. By being able to know the device's future battery level, the scheduler is able to make more intelligent decisions, and avoiding assigning a task to a device that for example will run out of battery while executing.

47.3 Evaluation

In this section, we describe the experiments performed to evaluate the model proposed in the previous section. Specifically, the estimation model is trained using the activity traces of one particular user, and then it is compared to a similar approach from the literature [14]. To assess the prediction results and compare the approaches we used the Mean Squared Error metric, which is defined as $MSE = \sum_{i=1}^{N}(y_i - \hat{y}_i)^2$.

The method proposed in [14] to predict the battery level is based on defining all the possible combinations of sensor states, such as energy supply connected and Wifi connected, energy supply connected and Wifi disconnected, and so on. After that, the method figures out the average time a user spends on each state, and the average battery consumption per state. Finally, the method computes the battery level by feeding that information to the following formula: $BatteryLevel = T * \sum_{i=1}^{N} p_i * B_i$ where T is the number of minutes to be predicted, p_i is the average number of minutes spent on state i and B_i is the average battery consumption per minute.

Regarding the test setup, firstly, both models are trained using the first 2 weeks of the abovementioned user's traces. Then, for each of the following days in the dataset, specifically 30 days, we pick a particular hour of the day, 12 p.m., and each model is run to estimate the battery level along the next 6 h. After that, the MSE is calculated for each curve and averaged to get the MSE per day for each model. The hour 12 p.m. is chosen because it is the time of the day on which the mobile phone has more activity, and it is when schedulers might take more advantage of the model. Besides, 6 h is a good baseline for comparing both approaches, since [14]'s model does not return good estimations in the long run as it can be seen in Fig. 47.5.

The final result of this process can be found in Table 47.4. The first two columns show the average MSE per day for both methods. It is clear that our proposed method has a lower MSE considering every day. This outcome is due to the fact that [14] is based only in the average consumption, and it does not take into account time-related factors, such as when the battery is going to be charged. Our proposed method, instead, not only takes into account previous states by learning its behavior with a Regression Model, but also predicts whether the mobile phone is going to be connected to the energy supply or not in the future. That feature helps the model figure out if the series is going up or down at a specific time. Besides, by predicting whether the screen is going to be on, the model can adapt the fastness at which the battery level decreases or increases (depending on the energy supply).

Fig. 47.5 Predicted battery level for a period of 48 h using the proposed approach and [14]

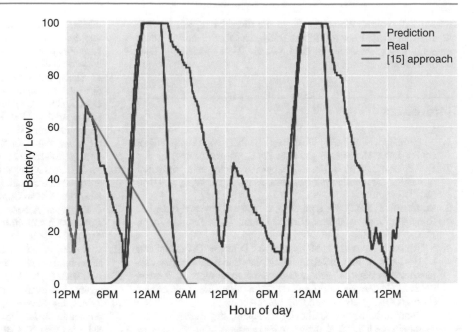

Table 47.4 Per-day average MSE of [14] and our approach

Day/approach	Average MSE		Minimum MSE		Maximum MSE	
	[14]	Ours	[14]	Ours	[14]	Ours
Sunday	33.26	18.82	9.89	1.96	55.29	44.34
Monday	35.44	21.09	24.82	6.47	50.09	49.79
Tuesday	31.99	24.44	16.93	7.20	48.69	36.58
Wednesday	38.36	26.10	18.29	4.87	55.90	47.73
Thursday	37.52	16.40	20.88	6.38	51.16	40.48
Friday	35.24	18.42	17.38	5.19	56.64	38.46
Saturday	33.59	17.58	11.42	7.28	52.53	39.68

Minimum and maximum MSE are also shown

In fact, the complementary models make our approach more precise for longer periods of times considering the test user. Figure 47.5 shows the predicted battery level for a period of 36 h using the proposed approach, i.e., from a given starting point it iteratively predicted, state by state, the final battery level after 48 h. It is clear that there is a significant visual resemblance between the real battery level and the estimated one. Moreover, the energy supply model had a very high influence in predicting the hour when the battery level is going to increase. For that particular case, [14]'s MSE is 57.67, while our approach obtained 27.86.

47.4   Conclusions

In this paper we have described a novel model to predict battery availability in mobile devices. The basic idea is to exploit past device owners activity and relevant device state

variables with a two-phase approach, which includes feature extraction/selection techniques on one hand and regression models and machine learning classifiers on the other hand.

Preliminary experiments performed using mobile phone usage data from the Device Analyzer data-set and comparisons against the estimation model published in [14] yielded encouraging results. Our model was able to reduce the MSE metric, and hence estimations are more accurate. This is in line with our utmost objective, which is quantifying future energy availability in mobile devices in order to consider them as first-class resource providers in state-of-the-art edge computing paradigms such as Dew Computing.

Future work involve generalizing our results with more test cases. Concretely, we need to test the per-user accuracy of our model using device activity from several device owners. Fortunately, the Device Analyzer data-set contains many users with activity data spanning several weeks and even months. As an aside, models to fill in the potential missing activity data must be developed (e.g. days for which activity data is missing due to the device is off). In addition, other Machine Learning models can be used in order better capture the intrinsic relationships between features, so as to come up with more accurate predictions. Specifically, we will analyze a recurrent neural network (NN) known as Long Short Term Memory (LSTM) [15]. As Recurrent NN predictions depend on previous states, LSTMs are very effective for predicting state sequences [16], hence all previous states can be taken into account. Finally, we could also compare our results against battery estimation models from the industry, such as those behind battery manager applications in the Google Play Store.

Acknowledgements We acknowledge the financial support by AN-PCyT through grant no. PICT-2013-0464. The first author acknowledges his MSc. scholarship in Data Science (USA) granted by Fundación Sadosky.

References

1. N. Fernando, S.W. Loke, W. Rahayu, Mobile cloud computing: a survey. Futur. Gener. Comput. Syst. **29**(1), 84–106 (2013)
2. K. Kumar, J. Liu, Y.-H. Lu, B. Bhargava, A survey of computation offloading for mobile systems. Mob. Netw. Appl. **18**(1), 129–140 (2013)
3. M. Sharifi, S. Kafaie, O. Kashefi, A survey and taxonomy of cyber foraging of mobile devices. IEEE Commun. Surv. Tutorials **14**(4), 1232–1243 (2012)
4. S. Nunna, A. Kousaridas, M. Ibrahim, M. Dillinger, C. Thuemmler, H. Feussner, A. Schneider, Enabling real-time context-aware collaboration through 5G and mobile edge computing, in *12th International Conference on Information Technology-New Generations (ITNG)* (IEEE, New York, 2015), pp. 601–605
5. F. Bonomi, R. Milito, J. Zhu, S. Addepalli, Fog computing and its role in the internet of things, in *Proceedings of the first edition of the workshop on Mobile Cloud Computing* (ACM, New York, 2012), pp. 13–16
6. P. Mach, Z. Becvar, Mobile edge computing: a survey on architecture and computation offloading. IEEE Commun. Surv. Tutorials **19**(3), 1628–1656 (2017)
7. M. Gusev, A dew computing solution for IoT streaming devices, in *40th International Convention on Information and Communication Technology, Electronics and Microelectronics (MIPRO)* (IEEE, New York, 2017), pp. 387–392
8. K. Skala, D. Davidovic, E. Afgan, I. Sovic, Z. Sojat, Scalable distributed computing hierarchy: cloud, fog and dew computing. Open J. Cloud Comput. **2**(1), 16–24 (2015)
9. C. Tapparello, C.F.B. Karaoglu, H. Ba, S. Hijazi, J. Shi, A. Aquino, W. Heinzelman, Volunteer computing on mobile devices: state of the art and future, in *Enabling Real-Time Mobile Cloud Computing through Emerging Technologies*, pp. 153–181 (2015)
10. M. Hirsch, J.M. Rodríguez, C. Mateos, A. Zunino, A two-phase energy-aware scheduling approach for CPU-intensive jobs in mobile grids. J. Grid Comput. **15**(1), 55–80 (2017)
11. D.T. Wagner, A. Rice, A.R. Beresford, Device analyzer: large-scale mobile data collection. ACM SIGMETRICS Perform. Eval. Rev. **41**(4), 53–56 (2014)
12. I. Guyon, A. Elisseeff, An introduction to variable and feature selection. J. Mach. Learn. Res. **3** 1157–1182 (2003)
13. F.X. Diebold, G.D. Rudebusch, On the power of dickey-fuller tests against fractional alternatives. Econ. Lett. **35**(2), 155–160 (1991)
14. J.-M. Kang, S.-S. Seo, J.W.-K. Hong, Personalized battery lifetime prediction for mobile devices based on usage patterns. J. Comput. Sci. Eng. **5**(4), 338–345 (2011)
15. S. Hochreiter, J. Schmidhuber, Long short-term memory. Neural Comput. **9**(8), 1735–1780 (1997)
16. H. Sak, A. Senior, F. Beaufays, Long short-term memory based recurrent neural network architectures for large vocabulary speech recognition (2014). arXiv preprint arXiv:1402.1128

Enhancing Lipstick Try-On with Augmented Reality and Color Prediction Model

48

Nuwee Wiwatwattana, Sirikarn Chareonnivassakul,
Noppon Maleerutmongkol, and Chavin Charoenvitvorakul

Abstract

One of the important tasks in purchasing cosmetics is the selection process. Swatching is the best way in shade-matching the look and feel of cosmetics. However, swatching the lipstick color on skins is far from being a good representation of the lips color. This paper aims to develop a virtual lipstick try-on application based on augmented reality and color prediction model. The goal of the color prediction model is to predict the RGB of the worn lips color given an undertone color of the lips and a lipstick shade. We have studied the performance of several learning models including simple and multiple linear regression, reduced-error pruning decision tree, M5P model tree, support vector regression, stacking technique, and random forests. We find that ensemble methods work best. However, since ensemble methods win only a small margin, our application is implemented with a simpler algorithm that is faster to train and to test, the M5P. The detection and tracking of lips are implemented using the OpenFace toolkit's facial landmark detection submodule. Measuring the prediction accuracy with MAE and RMSE, we have demonstrated that our approach that predicts worn lips colors performs better than without the prediction. Lipstick shades that resemble human skins have been shown to give more accurate results than dark shades or light pink shades.

Keywords

Virtual makeup · Lipstick color · Mobile augmented reality · M5P · Regression

N. Wiwatwattana (✉) · S. Chareonnivassakul · N. Maleerutmongkol · C. Charoenvitvorakul
Department of Computer Science, Faculty of Science, Srinakharinwirot University, Bangkok, Thailand
e-mail: nuwee@g.swu.ac.th; sirikarn.chareonnivassakul@g.swu.ac.th; noppon.maleerutmongkol@g.swu.ac.th; chavin.boat@g.swu.ac.th

48.1 Introduction

Cosmetics, especially makeup products, come in wide variety of colors, shades, and textures. Choosing the right cosmetics to match the skin color and tone is a cumbersome and confusing task for most ladies (and also gentlemen). On the other hand, cosmetics retailers would like to drive sales by improving the customer experience. One of the important tasks in purchasing cosmetics is the selection process. Trying the makeup directly on the face is rarely done due to hygienic issues. Sharing makeup is purposefully avoided, more seriously among the public. No one would want to be contagious to skin diseases because of trying on cosmetics at stores. The common solution employed by most is not to try the makeup on the face but on the wrist, the arm or the back of the hand, the so-called swatching. Swatching is the best shot in shade-matching the look and feel of cosmetics. However, swatching the lipstick color on skins is far from being a good representation of the lips color. It is definitely unrealistic. Since the emergence of smartphones just a little bit over 10 years ago, Augmented Reality (AR) has been making more progress in terms of adoption, not only in an entertainment industry but in serious applications as well. Virtual makeup is one such application that makes use of the augmented reality technology on smartphones handsomely. Sephora's Virtual Artist [1] and L'Oréal Paris's Makeup Genius [2] are among the famous applications.

Virtual makeup applications in the market usually apply a lipstick color directly according to the actual lipstick color, not considering the base color of the user's lips. We works on a different idea. Our assumption is that applying a lipstick color to different base lips colors should be (more or less) different. We simply prove our assumption by actually experimenting on people. The result, shown in Fig. 48.1, is quite obvious that applying the same lipstick shade to two people gives slightly different lips colors results. Looking into more details in the figure, readers should find that even on one person, the entire lips colors are not the same. The worn lips color is uneven. The application of lipstick colors are not universal due to the undertone of lips [3]. This article backups our assumption well. In additions, lighting in retail stores are usually set differently, this gives different effect on colors applied. Our assumption will be reaffirmed when we report results of the prediction model in subsequent sections.

This paper aims to develop a virtual lipstick try-on application based on augmented reality and color prediction model. Based on the lips undertone, the color prediction model is used to predict the lipstick color, the more accurate representation if the lipstick is indeed worn on the user's lips. The predicted lipstick color is overlayed on the lips of the user in an augmented reality style. Before we delve into the color prediction process, let us first describe the overall architecture of the system.

48.1.1 Overview of the System

Following the framework of the machine learning process, our research work consists of two main phases: the model construction phase and the application phase, as shown in Fig. 48.2. The model construction phase includes the lips color collection, color preparation, model training, and model evaluation and selection. The application phase is to put the color prediction model into real use in an augmented reality mobile application. The application first detects and tracks the lips of the user using the facial landmark detection framework. The lips color is sampled from the area of detected lips. The application then predicts the worn lips color according to the base lips color (the undertone) and the selected lipstick shade using the learned model. The predicted worn color is filled on the lips in the camera view of the user mobile device.

This paper is organized as follows. Section 48.2, discusses approaches used for predicting lips colors. Section 48.3 describes the module and framework used to detect and track lips as well as to overlay the lips color over the user's lips in real-time, the augmented reality section. Section 48.4 shows the experimental evaluation of our color prediction and the system overall. Lastly, the last two sections are related work and conclusion of the paper.

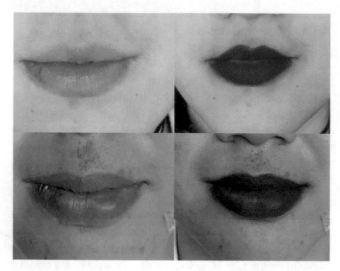

Fig. 48.1 Applying the same lipstick shade to two people gives different results: (left) before the application, (right) after the application

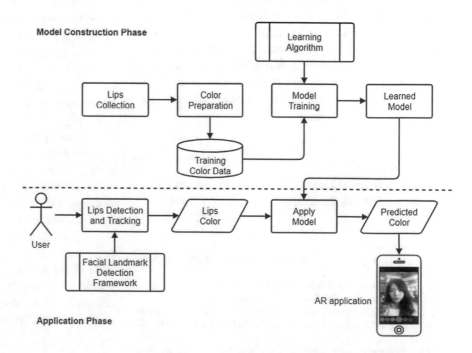

Fig. 48.2 Two processing phases of the system: the model construction phase and the application phase

48.2 Lips Color Prediction Approach

This section explains in details the construction of the color prediction model. Our problem statement is, given the user's undertone lips color in RGB, and given a lipstick color in RGB, we would like to predict the lips color in RGB after wearing the lipstick. We use numeric R, G, and B values, which are one of the most common representation of a color in computers throughout our whole process. We are sponsored six lipsticks shades to work on.

Let us define our prediction problem. As data values to be predicted are continuous, predicting a worn color is a regression problem and is solved by supervised learning algorithms. For each lipstick color, we use a learning algorithm to find three functions, each for the individual component of RGB.

$$\gamma_R : \langle RO, GO, BO \rangle \rightarrow \langle RN \rangle \qquad (48.1)$$

$$\gamma_G : \langle RO, GO, BO \rangle \rightarrow \langle GN \rangle \qquad (48.2)$$

$$\gamma_B : \langle RO, GO, BO \rangle \rightarrow \langle BN \rangle \qquad (48.3)$$

where RN, GN, and BN are target variables (N stands for the worn color), and RO, GO, and BO are predictors (O stands for the original undertone color). Once the functions

are learned, they can be applied to a test lips color. Hence, with six lipstick shades, there are 18 functions to learn.

48.2.1 Color Collection and Preparation

Since the training data for our research is not available anywhere, we need to collect them. We control the lighting environment of this process by recruiting 50 volunteers to wear the six lipstick colors in our laboratory, using only one camera during daytime with normal sunshine. Each volunteer is asked not to wear any makeup beforehand, and they will be photographed seven photos; the first one having no makeup, and the rest with the lipsticks worn. Next, lips photos are resized and cropped to 20×20 pixels. The color is sampled from the pixel. Thus, for each lipstick color, 20,000 records are collected, and totally 140,000 records are collected for one O and six N colors. We then combine each worn color record with the original undertone record to represent one training data record. For example, a record of the lipstick color no. 1 is:

$$\langle RO, GO, BO, RN, GN, BN \rangle = \langle 197, 144, 126, 206,$$
$$127, 122 \rangle$$

The scatter plots of attributes in the training data from the lipstick color no. 1 and no. 6 are illustrated in Figs. 48.3 and 48.4, respectively. It can be seen that RGB of the undertone

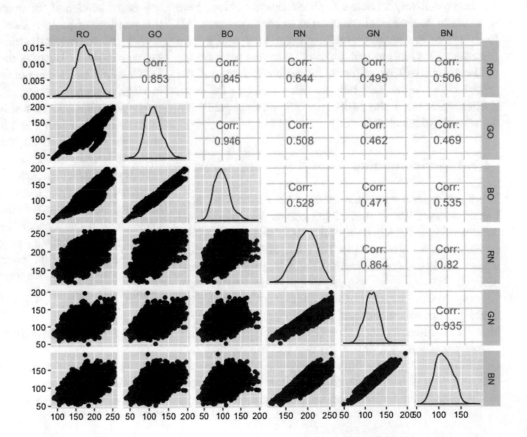

Fig. 48.3 The scatter plots of the training data from lipstick color no. 1. RO, GO, and BO are RGB of the undertone color. RN, GN, and BN are RGB of the observed worn color

Fig. 48.4 The scatter plots of the training data from lipstick color no. 6. *RO*, *GO*, and *BO* are RGB of the undertone color. *RN*, *GN*, and *BN* are RGB of the observed worn color

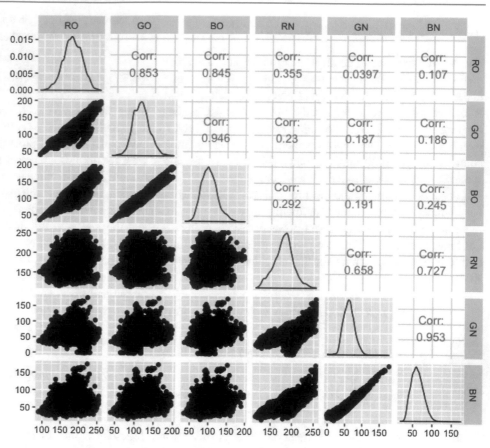

and RGB of the worn lipstick color no. 1 are moderately positively correlated, but for the lipstick color no. 6, they are less positively correlated. Other lipstick colors have numbers in between and are omitted to conserve space. All RGB values are roughly normally distributed with a little skewness. This hints us that the complexity and performance of the model will be different for different shades of the lipsticks. Exploring data tells us that predicting the worn lipstick color no. 1 should be less difficult than predicting the worn lipstick color no. 6.

48.2.2 Model Training

There are several candidate models, both linear and non-linear, that we use to predict the colors. We train all the models using WEKA, a data mining tool from the University of Waikato, New Zealand [4]. The (Simple/Multiple) Linear Regression is a statistical method that tries to find the linear model to fit training data values. For simple linear regression, we only use the matching RGB component to predict the target component, red for red, green for green, and blue for blue. Reduced-error pruning tree (REPTree) is a decision tree learner proposed by Quinlan [5] that use information gain as splitting criterion and prunes each node of the tree with backfitting. M5P [6] is a learning algorithm developed from the M5 algorithm for inducing trees of regression models.

M5P generates a decision tree with a linear functional model at each leaf. Support Vector Regression (SVR) [7] is the regression version of the support vector machines that finds a hyperplane or projects data to a higher dimension with a kernel trick to best fit the training data. For each algorithm, tuning parameters is part of the process. For example, setting M5P's minimum number of instances to allow at leaf nodes to 10 gives slightly better performance in predicting the blue color for the lipstick color no. 6 than setting to 50.

In addition to individual learner methods, we also use ensemble methods available in WEKA: Stacking and Random Forests. Multiple sub-models are constructed in Stacking [8] using multiple schemes, and a learned model combines results from them. In our paper, the stacking is an M5Rules model that combines M5P, REPTree, and multiple linear regression models together. Random Forests [9] creates multiple decision trees from random samplings of the training data and the prediction results are averaged on performance weights. We train all candidate models on full training data sets.

48.2.3 Model Evaluation and Selection

In order to select the right model to incorporate into the application in the latter phase, we use the tenfold cross-validation technique to evaluate the performance of the

Table 48.1 Mean Absolute Error (MAE) and Root Mean Squared Error (RMSE) of each learning method that learns to predict RN, GN, and BN for the lipstick color no. 1 and no. 6

| Learning method | Lipstick color no. 1 | | | | | | Lipstick color no. 6 | | | | | |
| | R | | G | | B | | R | | G | | B | |
	MAE	RMSE	MAE	RMSE	MAE	RMSE	MAE	RMSE	MAE	RMSE	MAE	RMSE
Simple linear regression	14.83	18.27	11.26	14.38	13.09	16.23	15.94	21.01	12.52	16.08	12.25	15.47
Multiple linear regression	14.64	18.13	10.89	13.99	12.74	15.85	15.60	20.45	12.27	15.55	12.03	15.11
REPTree	12.35	16.57	9.75	12.86	10.55	13.80	13.57	18.53	11.01	14.66	10.70	14.17
M5P	12.50	16.29	9.77	12.73	10.55	13.52	13.79	18.45	11.12	14.50	10.73	13.92
Support vector regression	14.55	18.21	10.74	13.86	12.56	15.83	15.52	20.51	12.19	15.55	11.91	15.17
Stacking	12.10	<u>15.85</u>	9.52	<u>12.46</u>	10.19	<u>13.13</u>	13.16	<u>17.81</u>	10.78	<u>14.16</u>	10.48	<u>13.67</u>
Random forests	<u>11.73</u>	15.92	<u>9.43</u>	12.64	<u>10.03</u>	13.23	<u>12.71</u>	17.83	<u>10.59</u>	14.41	<u>10.31</u>	13.96

Fig. 48.5 A set of examples from the M5P prediction

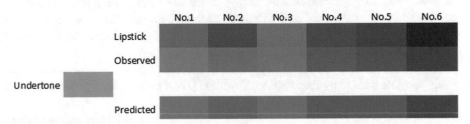

models. Good models are those that can predict the colors as close as possible to the observed worn colors. The difference between the predicted color (predicted RN, GN, BN) and the observed color (observed RN, GN, BN) is called an error (e). Two performance metrics considered are Mean Absolute Error (MAE), which measures the average of the error in the training set, and Root Mean Squared Error (RMSE) which penalizes more on large errors because errors are squared before they are averaged. Formally:

$$MAE = \frac{1}{n} \sum_{j=1}^{n} |e_j| \qquad (48.4)$$

$$RMSE = \sqrt{\frac{1}{n} \sum_{j=1}^{n} e_j{}^2} \qquad (48.5)$$

where n is the number of data values/records and e is the error.

Table 48.1 presents the prediction performance (MAE and RMSE) of our candidate models for each learning method that learns to predict RN, GN, and BN of the lipstick color no. 1 and no. 6. The underlined numbers are the best in each column. The linear regression models are considered baselines. Both the simple linear regression and the multiple linear regression are the worst from the pool. This is consistent with what we have seen in the scatter plots that we cannot easily fit the data with a line or a hyperplane. The performance of the support vector regressor is not any better than that of the linear regression even though we have tried to train using non-linear kernels. Unsurprisingly, the two ensemble methods always win, and REPTree and M5P are

the third or the fourth. However, in some functions, the win over REPTree and M5P methods is only marginal. Random forests produce the lowest MAE for each function; yet, the lowest RMSE belongs to Stacking. Errors of red are higher than errors of green and blue because red is the primary color of the lipstick shades. The exact numeric value of red is difficult to estimate.

Time is also the factor to ponder. Even though ensemble methods outperform individual learner methods, the win is small over REPTree and M5P. Ensemble algorithms take a longer time to train, and a longer time to apply. For example, it takes 14 s to train a stacking model, and 5 s to train a random forests model for the red color of the lipstick no. 1, but only 0.1 and 1 s for REPTree and M5P, respectively. The training time for support vector regression is also very slow due to a large number of training records we have. Offline training and testing are not problematic. However, instant interaction in an AR application is of significance. At last, we select M5P as our learning model in our implemented augmented reality application. This is because RMSE of M5P is a bit lower than RMSE of REPTree, although MAE of M5P is a bit higher than REPTree's. We would like to minimize the chance of getting a large deviation from our predicted color. Moreover, because the leaf node of REPTree model is a single number, while the leaf node of M5P is a linear regression model, M5P is more suitable for numeric prediction like in our problem.

Figure 48.5 illustrates a set of examples from the M5P prediction. The first row is the shade of the lipstick colors (no. 1–no 6). Given a user's undertone lips color on the left, the second row is the observed colors from the training data. The last row is the predicted colors from the M5P scheme.

This emphasizes our initial assumption that the worn color is not the lipstick color per se. The lipstick color acts as a complement to the undertone, not with a fixed degree but with varying degrees.

48.3 Detecting, Tracking and Augmenting Lips

In this section, we describe the application phase underlying the mobile iOS system that interacts with users. The tasks include detecting and tracking lips, drawing the contour of the lips, sampling lips color for prediction of the worn lips color, and layering the predicted color. All of these happen in real-time.

The toolkit we use for detecting and tracking lips is Open-Face [10] and its facial landmark detection sub-module [11], made possible for iOS by FaceAR/OpenFaceIOS [12]. Open-Face demonstrates that using the novel Constrained Lo-

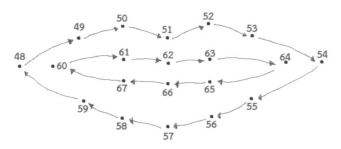

Fig. 48.6 Facial feature points no. 48–no. 68 are lips. The lips contour is drawn connecting these points

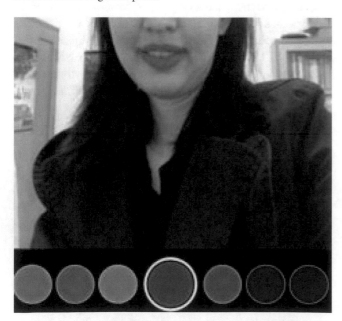

Fig. 48.7 The application interface (shown only the lower screen portion)

cal Neural Fields (CLNF), they are able to perform facial landmark detection in a variability of posing and lighting conditions. The facial landmark detector, in turn, utilizes OpenCV and Haar cascade classifier [13] for frontal face detection. The model marks 68 facial feature points, but we are particularly interested in the feature point no. 48 onwards because they are designated as lips. We then draw lips contour by connecting these points as seen in Fig. 48.6. The application gets the pixel color inside the lips area and sends the RGB information to the color prediction model together with the lipstick color number. The lips area is filled with the predicted worn lips color in the camera view. At last, we alpha-blend the color of the lipstick using the OpenCV functionality. Figure 48.7 captures the example of worn color and the application interface.

48.4 Application Results

In this section, we report the overall results for the implementation of six lipstick colors prediction on the augmented reality iOS application.

48.4.1 Comparative Evaluation

Figure 48.8 depicts MAE and RMSE of all the lipstick shades using the M5P algorithm. The number is an average of the RN, GN, and BN prediction errors. In addition to errors from the learned model alone, we calculate MAE and RMSE of the color if the lipstick color is put on without using the predicted color, a fixed color from the lipstick, denoted as "the fixed".

Apparently, putting on a fixed color deviates a lot from the actual observed color. Large errors are seen for the lipstick color no. 6, a dark reddish shade lipstick. For the predicted scheme, the lipstick color no. 3 incurs the highest errors with the lipstick color no. 6 the second highest. This shows that the learned model for no. 6 has already done a good job at predicting worn colors compared with no prediction at all. For no. 3, it is a light pink shade, and therefore, the green and blue components are more intensive. The undertone is not as good as a predictor compared to other shades.

48.4.2 Satisfaction Score

Aside from color deficiency, human vision may not imply the same RGB color as the same thing. Different people see different colors, and hence we conduct a user study as another way to evaluate our color prediction accuracy. We ask 50 volunteers how satisfied are they in terms of the accuracy of the predicted colors displayed in the application.

Fig. 48.8 Mean Absolute Error (MAE) and Root Mean Squared Error (RMSE) are averaged from the RGB components for the prediction of the lipstick color no. 1–no. 6 compared with the fixed color from the lipstick

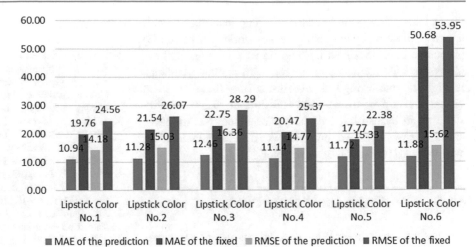

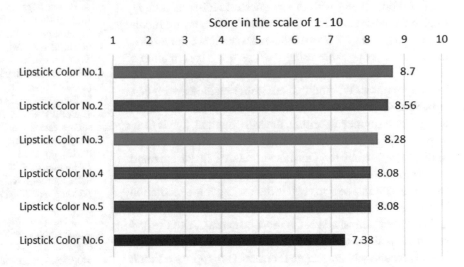

Fig. 48.9 Satisfaction scores from the user study

Volunteers give satisfaction scores for each of the lipstick shades based on a scale of 1–10. Figure 48.9 reports the mean of the satisfaction scores. The lipstick color no. 6 is perceptively less accurate than others, while no. 1 is the most accurate color. The deviation of the color displayed and the actual color may result from the different amount of pressure used when applying the lipstick. In fact, the sub-figures in Fig. 48.1 are people wearing the lipstick color no. 6. Consequently, the model performance is not as good as some light colors as can be seen earlier on. Since the color no. 6 is dark, a slight imprecision will be noticed easily. The lipstick color no. 1 and no. 2 are of shades that resemble human lips color more (somewhat warmer nude or brown), and so the blending of the color is less distorted, giving the perception that they are accurately predicted.

48.5   Related Work

Many famous cosmetics brands are powered by ModiFace [14], the most prominent AR start-up company specialized in the beauty industry. Its patent [15] describes a method to estimate skin color base tone, and simulate the lip coloring using a radial-gradient translucent colored mask. ModiFace AR application claims to shade-match lipsticks and lips colors. Jang et al. [16] reproduces facial skin colors after makeup using spectral reflectance data, considering characteristics of color equipment such as cameras and monitors. Rahman et al. [17] builds a smart mirror system using an IR camera to track faces which later augments and alpha-blends texture of the makeup on faces.

The popular aspect of virtual makeup is the recommendation of makeup from beauty model faces to ordinary users. Tong et al. [18] use a computer vision transfer of before and after image to modify base image layers with makeup texture. Improving Tong's technique, Guo and Sim [19] align the target face with an example makeup face, separates the image layers, and applies the transfer technique between the two faces. Xu et al. [20] work is similar to Guo and Sim with automatic landmark adjustment. Liu et al. [21] do not need an example image. They analyze and categorize user image attributes and use these attributes to recommend makeup from their beauty e-Experts database. Alashkar et al. [22] build a rule-based makeup recommendation system for different ethnic groups and occasions. Deep learning methods are currently employed in many recent works. Liu et al. [23] propose a deep localized makeup transfer network and exhibits good performance compared with shallow methods. It might be interesting to know further how these works on virtual makeup perform in the real-time augmented reality situation in terms of speed and performance. Nevertheless, unlike the works above, our work is not a recommendation system, but a prediction of worn color.

48.6 Conclusion and Future Work

The main contribution of this paper is the use of color prediction model along with the augmented reality technology to give the best experience to a virtual lipstick try-on mobile application. Our goal is to predict the worn lips color as close to the actual as possible using RGB as the representation of color. We have studied the performance of several candidate learning models. We find that ensemble methods work best. However, since ensemble methods win only a small margin, we opt for a simpler algorithm, the M5P method, that is faster to train and to test. The detection and tracking of lips are implemented using the OpenFace toolkit's facial landmark detection sub-module. Overall, our approach that predicts worn lips colors performs better than without the prediction. The shade of the lipstick also dictates how well the prediction do. The light pink shade is the most inaccurate, and the dark red shade is the second most inaccurate. The dark red shade is also perceptively inaccurate for users. Our approach should be able to apply to other makeup regions as well.

There are a few limitations in our framework. Firstly, if the color of the tested lips is out-of-normal-range, for example, in very low-light situations, the prediction will be conspicuously irregular as the range is not reflected in the model during the training phase. Secondly, glossy lipsticks cannot be modeled in the color representation, probably we need to add a different function. Thirdly, there always need be a training phase for a new lipstick color and that comes at a cost as opposed to using a fixed lipstick color. It might be worthwhile to try to use lab color space representation such as CIE L*a*b* (CIELAB) for model training instead of RGB, because the lab color space approximates more closely to human vision, and is device-independent.

Acknowledgements The work of the first author has been supported by Grant No. 533/2560 from Srinakharinwirot University, Thailand. Undergraduate research students have been supported by SSUP Group—Oriental Princess. The authors express our warmest thanks to SSUP Group—Oriental Princess for sponsoring the lipsticks, and Dr. Thitima Srivatanakul for invaluable comments. The authors would also like to thank Srinakharinwirot University for the travel grant to present and discuss the research with the community.

References

1. Sephora virtual artist | try on makeup virtually | sephora. Online Available: https://sephoravirtualartist.com
2. Makeup genius - virtual makeup application | loreal paris. Online Available: http://www.loreal-paris.co.uk/products/make-up/apps/make-up-genius
3. T. Shoneye, G. Mour Barrett, R. Patel, A. Malone, N. Lobanova. We tried the same lipsticks on different skin tones. Online Available: https://www.buzzfeed.com/tolanishoneye/heres-what-budget-lipstick-looks-like-on-different-skin
4. M. Hall, E. Frank, G. Holmes, B. Pfahringer, P. Reutemann, I.H. Witten, The weka data mining software: an update. SIGKDD Explor. **11**(1), 10–18 (2009)
5. J.R. Quinlan, *C4.5: Programs for Machine Learning* (Morgan Kaufmann Publishers Inc., San Francisco, CA, 1993)
6. Y. Wang, I. Witten, Inducing model trees for continuous classes, in *Proceedings of the Ninth European Conference on Machine Learning*, vol. 09 (1997)
7. S. Shevade, S. Keerthi, C. Bhattacharyya, K. Murthy, Improvements to the SMO algorithm for SVM regression. IEEE Trans. Neural Netw. **11**, 1188–1193 (1999)
8. D.H. Wolpert, Stacked generalization. Neural Netw. **5**, 241–259 (1992)
9. L. Breiman, Random forests. Mach. Learn. **45**(1), 5–32 (2001)
10. T. Baltrušaitis, P. Robinson, L.P. Morency, Openface: an open source facial behavior analysis toolkit, in *2016 IEEE Winter Conference on Applications of Computer Vision (WACV)*, March (2016), pp. 1–10
11. T. Baltrusaitis, P. Robinson, L.P. Morency, Constrained local neural fields for robust facial landmark detection in the wild, in *2013 IEEE International Conference on Computer Vision Workshops* (2013), pp. 354–361
12. K. Ren, Facear/openfaceios (2016). Online Available: https://github.com/FaceAR/OpenFaceIOS
13. Opencv library. Online Available: https://opencv.org/
14. Modiface - augmented reality. Online Available: http://modiface.com/
15. P. Aarabi, System and method for the indication of modification region boundaries on facial images, Sept 1 (2016), US Patent App. 15/056,748. Online Available: https://google.com/patents/US20160253713
16. I.S. Jang, J.W. Kim, J.S. Kim, Makeup color reproduction based on spectrum data, in *The 19th Korea-Japan Joint Workshop on Frontiers of Computer Vision*, Jan (2013), pp. 233–236
17. A.S.M.M. Rahman, T.T. Tran, S.A. Hossain, A.E. Saddik, Augmented rendering of makeup features in a smart interactive mirror system for decision support in cosmetic products selection, in *2010 IEEE/ACM 14th International Symposium on Distributed Simulation and Real Time Applications*, Oct (2010), pp. 203–206
18. W.-S. Tong, C.-K. Tang, M.S. Brown, Y.-Q. Xu, Example-based cosmetic transfer, in *Proceedings of the 15th Pacific Conference on Computer Graphics and Applications* (2007), pp. 211–218
19. D. Guo, T. Sim, Digital face makeup by example, in *2009 IEEE Conference on Computer Vision and Pattern Recognition*, June (2009), pp. 73–79
20. L. Xu, Y. Du, Y. Zhang, An automatic framework for example-based virtual makeup, in *2013 IEEE International Conference on Image Processing*, Sept (2013), pp. 3206–3210
21. L. Liu, H. Xu, J. Xing, S. Liu, X. Zhou, S. Yan, wow! you are so beautiful today!, in *Proceedings of the 21st ACM International Conference on Multimedia*, Series MM '13 (ACM, New York, NY, 2013), pp. 3–12

22. T. Alashkar, S. Jiang, Y. Fu, Rule-based facial makeup recommendation system, in *2017 12th IEEE International Conference on Automatic Face Gesture Recognition (FG 2017)*, May (2017), pp. 325–330

23. S. Liu, X. Ou, R. Qian, W. Wang, X. Cao, Makeup like a superstar: deep localized makeup transfer network. CoRR **abs/1604.07102** (2016) Online Available: http://arxiv.org/abs/1604.07102

Thiago Almeida, Hendrik Macedo, and Leonardo Matos

Abstract

Traffic lights detection and recognition research has grown every year. Time is coming when autonomous vehicle can navigate in urban roads and streets and intelligent systems aboard those cars would have to recognize traffic lights in real time. This article proposes a traffic light recognition (TLR) device prototype using a smartphone as camera and processing unit that can be used as a driver assistance. A TLR device has to be able to visualize the traffic scene from inside of a vehicle, generate stable images, and be protected from adverse conditions. To validate this layout prototype, a dataset was built and used to test an algorithm that uses an adaptive background suppression filter (AdaBSF) and Support Vector Machines (SVMs) to detect traffic lights. The application of AdaBSF and subsequent classification with SVM to the dataset achieved 100% precision rate and recall of 65%. Road testing shows that the TLR device prototype meets the requirements to be used as a driver assistance device.

Keywords

Traffic light detection and recognition · Support vector machines · Computer vision · Expert systems

49.1 Introduction

A study published by [1] shows that in August/2016, advancing the red sign in traffic light was the second main infraction associated with fatal accidents involving motorcycles, cars and bus in the city of São Paulo, Brazil.

Traffic lights are widely used as a traffic regulator device. Although it is a simple and logical device, drivers frequently cross the red light causing accidents with serious consequences as death to drivers, passengers, and pedestrians.

Some situations can be pointed as probable causes to these infractions:

- Poorly located traffic lights;
- Faulty/off traffic lights or in very dim light;
- Ambient light that disturbs the vision of the driver;
- Visual impairment of the driver;
- Doubt if there is enough time to cross the traffic light when the signal turns yellow;
- Number of traffic regulator items to be observed.

The first two listed items can be easily solved with the effort of the traffic regulator in arranging and maintaining traffic lights optimally on the streets. However, the problematic presented by the remaining items could be minimized by using a Traffic Light Recognition Device—TLR to assist the driver.

The main task of a TLR is to avoid accidents and save lives by informing the presence of a red or yellow traffic light to the driver in a non-intrusive way. In addition, an even more complex TLR can bring other information such as which is the main traffic light for a route when there is more than one and how far the traffic light is.

Another information that could be extracted from a more complex TLR is what speed the driver must maintain to advance the largest number of green signals in sequence on a given avenue.

A TLR would also be very useful for pedestrians who are visually impaired. Although several crossings for pedestrians have signaled adapted for visually impaired people, few adaptations include sound signaling. In addition, there are many crossings that do not have pedestrian traffic lights, thus

T. Almeida (✉) · H. Macedo · L. Matos
Programa de Pós-Graduação em Ciência da Computação - PROCC, Universidade Federal de Sergipe - UFS, São Cristóvão, Brazil
e-mail: thiagosa@dcomp.ufs.br; hendrik@dcomp.ufs.br; leonardo@dcomp.ufs.br

leaving the visually impaired dependent on others to cross the street in safety.

The device used to build a TLR and how it is positioned at the vehicle has a big influence in the TLR success. For example, if the device has a faulty camera the images may not reflect the scene reality. Also if the device can not see clearly the road, or it is not stable, the images can be blur or miss some important information from the real world.

In this paper we evaluate a TLR layout prototype using a detection and recognition method proposed by [2]. The proposed TLR uses a smartphone as camera and processing unit. The results shows that the proposed layout is valid and can be used to test TLRs, build traffic light datasets, and build other image datasets related to traffic and vehicles.

49.2 Related Work

An object recognition mechanism works in two phases in order to recognize objects from an image: (1) an initial phase to detect targets as possible objects, and (2) a second phase to classify the targets.

When working with object detection/recognition we need to define which object features shall be used to guide the algorithms. In traffic light recognition, features such as light, shape, and color are commonly used.

Concerned literature shows that Neural Networks, Saliency Map, and Blob Detection are the most common techniques used to detect traffic lights.

Weber et al. [3], John et al. [4–6] used Convolutional Neural Network—CNN to detect possible traffic lights, while [7] used a PCAnet NN.

Philipsen et al. [8] used a learning algorithm based on image feature channels and Histogram of Oriented Gradient—HOG to detection and recognition.

Saliency Maps was used as a detection tool by [9–12] and [5]. We also observed fine examples of Blob Detection use in [13–15].

Geometric transforms were used in detection phase by [16, 17] and [18], which applies the Hough Circular Transform and [19], which used the Radial Symmetry Fast Transform.

Some less common techniques used alone or in association with the ones cited before are Adaptive Filters [2], Template Matching [20], Gaussian Distribution [21], Probability Estimation with CNN [3], and Top Hat [22].

Processing image algorithms are also commonly used to detect traffic lights. Color or shape segmentation was used by [23] and [24]; and threshold was used by [25] and [26].

To recognize traffic lights, most works used Machine Learning algorithms, mainly CNN and variants, Support Vector Machines—SVMs, and Fuzzy systems. Chen and Huang [14] used CNN whereas [3] used a PCAnetwork, a NN that simulates a CNN using less layers. SVMs were used by [2, 7, 12–14, 27–31] to recognize traffic lights, sometimes along with a NN. Fuzzy was also used in [10] and [32].

Other techniques were used as ML substitutes, to improve false positives detection or to make the connection between detection output and recognition input. Zhou et al. [13], Michael and Schlipsing [28], Ji et al. [12], Almeida et al. [11], and Almagambetov et al. [33] used Histograms. Balcerek et al. [34], Cai [35], Omachi and Omachi [18] and [36] used Transforms. John et al. [5], Choi et al. [37], Fan [38], and de Charette and Nashashibi [39] used Template Matching. John et al. [6] used Saliency Map and [40] used Probability Histograms.

Normalized Cross Correlation was observed in [41] to recognize pedestrian traffic lights. Hidden Markov Models—HMM were used in [42] to recognize common traffic lights.

To highlight regions of interest—ROI at the image, [2] proposed an Adaptive Background Suppression Filter—AdaBSF. In the algorithm, a 4-channel feature map W_i, where i represent the 4-channel feature map index, are generated extracting R, G and B channels and calculating the normalized gradients of the input image.

To search for vertical and horizontal traffic lights, the window size for W_i is fixed as 16×8 pixels and 8×16 pixels, respectively. As each window is 4-dimensional the pixel amount is $D = 16 \times 8 \times 4$ per window. Each window is represented by a feature vector x of size $D = 512$. The multiscale problem was solved by down-sampling the original image to different scales while the window detection remains with fixed size.

The aim of AdaBSF algorithm is to design an Finite Impulse Response (FIR) filter specified by the vector $w = [w_1, w_2, \ldots, w_D]^T$ in a way that $y = w^T x$. The output y assigns a score to each detection window, which represents how likely the detection window covers a traffic light [2].

To classify the ROI found by AdaBSF, [2] used Support Vector Machines—SVM. The author created a cascade of SVM classifiers that begins classifying the ROI whether it is a traffic light or not. If it is a traffic light the next SVM classify the ROI into "red type" or "green type". After this the traffic light is classified in more specifics types considering if it has an arrow and its direction by the next SVM using a '1-vs-1' voting method.

In this paper, the method proposed by [2] was applied at images obtained by a TLR device that uses a smartphone as camera, and with possible use as a processing unit. The TLR follows a specific layout to use the TLR in real-time. This layout is specified in the following sections.

In order to validate the method presented in [2], the algorithm was reimplemented in Python language. SVMs and AdaBSF algorithm was trained with traffic light samples made available by the author and used in [2]. Negative samples, i.e. background samples, was extracted from four random test sequences also made available by the author, once the negative samples used in [2] was not accessible.

The algorithm was tested with the test sequences that was not used to generate the negative samples for training, obtaining a precision rate of 90%. In Fig. 49.5 it is possible to see the reproduction result in comparison with the original work result. There is little difference between the reproduction results and the original results, what validates the reproduction and the original work. Section 49.3.1 presents a detailed discussion over these result.

49.3   Traffic Light Recognition Device Prototype

A main question when prototyping a TLR Device is where it will be positioned at the vehicle, once it has to be in a position that allows it to observe the traffic clearly without compromising the vision of the driver. Another critical observation is that the device shall be protected from adverse meteorological conditions like rain, or be waterproof. The heat also might cause problems in some electronic devices, so the sunlight incidence at the device location may be considered as well.

As the vehicle moves, it is normal to observe some trepidation. However, this trepidation might have a negative influence in the device vision. Considering this, the device needs to be the most stabilized as possible. The device also has to be able to generate a warning sound to advise the driver, to see the traffic using a camera, and to have a computational unit to process the data. An accessible device that accomplishes these requirements and is commonly used to help drivers at traffic are the smartphones.

In this work, a smartphone was positioned inside a vehicle to capture real traffic scenes with and without traffic lights. Two kinds of supports are generally used to position a smartphone in a useful location to help the driver: air conditioning supports and windshield suction cups. Air conditioning supports can not be used to position a TLR Device because it has no outside view from the vehicle. Windshield suction cups supports are a possible choice, however, the support may fall down with or become very shaking if low quality suckers were used.

Fig. 49.1 TLR device support holding an iPhone 6

To overcome the smartphone supports problems and to meet the requirements specified previously we designed an stable device support using a two-sided tape and part of a windshield suction cup support. We remove the support part that holds the device from the cable with suction cup that is attached to the windshield. Then we fixed the first part centralized at the vehicle panel with the two-sided tape. This design allow the device to capture the traffic scene without a bias to the left or to the right. The proposed layout obligates the device to use the camera in landscape mode, minimizing the amount of sky captured and maximizing the traffic scene size obtained with more visible traffic lights (Fig. 49.1).

Three different smartphones was used to capture traffic videos containing traffic lights: Motorola G second generation, iPhone 6, and Galaxy S8+. All devices was configured to capture video with HD resolution. Figure 49.2 shows an example of images obtained with this devices. The images were extracted from videos at 5 frames per second (fps) rate.

49.3.1 Prototype Results

The images obtained by the TLR device using this support prototype were submitted to classification in a personal computer using the method applied in [2].

The images was obtained using three different smartphones. The first group obtained with Motorola G 2nd Generation did not present good results, for this reason it was not accounted in the results. The second group with images obtained by iPhone 6 contains 682 images, 209 negative samples and 473 traffic light samples. The third group is formed by 247 images obtained with Galaxy S8+, being 165 traffic light samples and 82 negative samples.

Fig. 49.2 Images obtained using the TLR Device support prototype with different smartphones. From top to bottom: image obtained by Motorola G 2nd Generation, by iPhone 6, and by Galaxy S8+

An amount of 929 traffic images were analyzed: 638 images containing green or red traffic lights and 291 images not containing traffic lights, the negative group.

Considering that most times there are two equal traffic lights for the same road, we account as one true positive for traffic light type when one or both of the traffic lights are recognized in image. So from each image we have one error or one hit. This also reflects the real life behavior when we just need to look at one traffic light to make a choice.

In Fig. 49.3 it is possible to see detailed results from each image group. The two groups achieved high precision rates, but the iPhone 6 group presented a low recall rate of 60%. This result can be can be explained by the fact that traffic lights samples used in training dataset are too different from some traffic lights present in the iPhone group dataset as shown in Fig. 49.4. If the training samples does not properly represent the real world some traffic lights can not be recognized.

Also the illumination condition in the dataset training are very different from the condition found in test dataset due to geographic/meteorological issues and possibly the device used to obtain it. These conditions have influence in the final result as well.

The distance from the TLR device to the traffic light is crucial to recognition. So far the device was able to correctly classify the traffic lights from second car line, considering the traffic stopped at red traffic light.

The iPhone group low recall rate influenced the final rates of TLR tests, as observed in Fig. 49.5. In comparison with the results obtained by [2] and by our reproduction using data from [2], the TLR result is valid to justify its use in future research.

49.4 Conclusion

This work presents a TLR device layout prototype used to capture road scenes. The tests achieved a 100% precision rate and 65% recall rate. The results demonstrate the prototype feasibility. The recall rate can be improved by training the applied algorithm with more representative samples, which will be done in the future along with cross-validation tests. The results also show that Galaxy S8+ and iPhone 6, two different mobile platforms, can be successfully used as TLR devices. Another future work includes real-time tests, investigating other detection and recognition models that could fit better with the obtained dataset, and expansion of the dataset itself.

Acknowledgements The authors thank CAPES and FAPITEC-SE for the financial support [Edital CAPES/FAPITEC/SE No 11/2016—PROEF, Processo 88887.160994/2017-00]. The authors also thank FAPITEC-SE for granting a graduate scholarship to Thiago Almeida and CNPq for granting a productivity scholarship to Hendrik Macedo [DT-II, Processo 310446/2014-7].

Fig. 49.3 Precision and recall rates by smartphone used to obtain the images

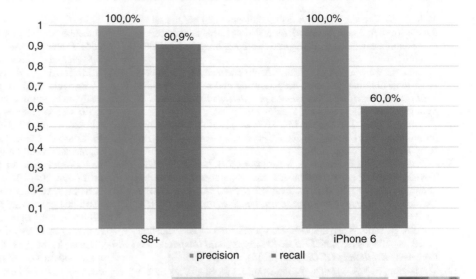

Fig. 49.4 From left to right: red and green traffic light sample used in training, red and green traffic light sample from the test dataset obtained with the TLR device prototype

Fig. 49.5 Precision and recall rates on our reproduction of [2], original work from [2], and tests using the images obtained with the TLR device prototype, respectively

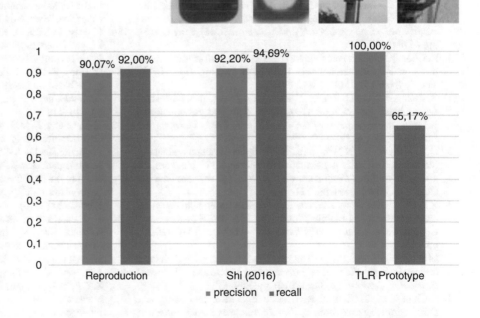

References

1. CET - Companhia de Engenharia de Tráfego. (2015) Análise da mortalidade ocorrida por acidentes de trânsito em agosto e setembro de 2016. Acesso em: 09 ago (2017). Online Available: http://www.cetsp.com.br/media/523410/parcial2016.pdf
2. Z. Shi, Z. Zou, C. Zhang, Real-time traffic light detection with adaptative background suppression filter. IEEE Trans. Intell. Transp. Syst. **17**(3), 690–700 (2016)
3. M. Weber, P. Wolf, J. M. Zöllner, Deeptlr: a single deep convolutional network for detection and classification of traffic lights, in *2016 IEEE Intelligent Vehicles Symposium (IV)*, June (2016), pp. 342–348
4. V. John, L. Zheming, S. Mita, Robust traffic light and arrow detection using optimal camera parameters and GPS-based priors, in *2016 Asia-Pacific Conference on Intelligent Robot Systems (ACIRS)*, July (2016), pp. 204–208

5. V. John, K. Yoneda, Z. Liu, S. Mita, Saliency map generation by the convolutional neural network for real-time traffic light detection using template matching. IEEE Trans. Comput. Imaging **1**(3), 159–173 (2015)

6. V. John, K. Yoneda, B. Qi, Z. Liu, S. Mita, Traffic light recognition in varying illumination using deep learning and saliency map, in *17th International IEEE Conference on Intelligent Transportation Systems (ITSC)*, Oct (2014), pp. 2286–2291

7. Z. Wang, Z. Bi, C. Wang, L. Lin, H. Wang, Traffic lights recognition based on PCANET, in *2015 Chinese Automation Congress (CAC)*, Nov (2015), pp. 559–564

8. M.P. Philipsen, M.B. Jensen, A. Møgelmose, T.B. Moeslund, M.M. Trivedi, Traffic light detection: a learning algorithm and evaluations on challenging dataset, in *2015 IEEE 18th International Conference on Intelligent Transportation Systems*, Sept (2015), pp. 2341–2345

9. S. Kim, E. Jang, S. Hyun, D.S. Han, Real time object detection based on saliency map, in *2016 IEEE International Conference on Consumer Electronics (ICCE)*, Jan (2016), pp. 534–535

10. T. Almeida, N. Vasconcelos, A. Benicasa, H. Macedo, Fuzzy model applied to the recognition of traffic lights signals, in *2016 8th Euro American Conference on Telematics and Information Systems (EATIS)*, April (2016), pp. 1–4

11. T. Almeida, N. Vasconcelos, A. Benicasa, Framework para detecção de semáforos baseado em atenção visual, in *Conference on Graphics, Patterns and Images, 28. (SIBGRAPI), Salvador* (2015)

12. Y. Ji, M. Yang, Z. Lu, C. Wang, Integrating visual selective attention model with hog features for traffic light detection and recognition, in *2015 IEEE Intelligent Vehicles Symposium (IV)*, June (2015), pp. 280–285

13. Y. Zhou, Z. Chen, X. Huang, A system-on-chip FPGA design for real-time traffic signal recognition system, in *2016 IEEE International Symposium on Circuits and Systems (ISCAS)*, May (2016), pp. 1778–1781

14. Z. Chen, X. Huang, Accurate and reliable detection of traffic lights using multiclass learning and multiobject tracking. IEEE Intell. Transp. Syst. Mag. **8**(4), 28–42 (2016)

15. Y. Zhang, J. Xue, G. Zhang, Y. Zhang, N. Zheng, A multi-feature fusion based traffic light recognition algorithm for intelligent vehicles, in *Proceedings of the 33rd Chinese Control Conference*, July (2014), pp. 4924–4929

16. D.H. Widyantoro, K.I. Saputra, Traffic lights detection and recognition based on color segmentation and circle hough transform, in *2015 International Conference on Data and Software Engineering (ICoDSE)*, Nov (2015), pp. 237–240

17. Y.T. Chiu, D.Y. Chen, J.W. Hsieh, Real-time traffic light detection on resource-limited mobile platform, in *2014 IEEE International Conference on Consumer Electronics - Taiwan*, May (2014), pp. 211–212

18. M. Omachi, S. Omachi, Detection of traffic light using structural information, in *IEEE 10th International Conference on Signal Processing Proceedings*, Oct (2010), pp. 809–812

19. S. Sooksatra, T. Kondo, Red traffic light detection using fast radial symmetry transform, in *2014 11th International Conference on Electrical Engineering/Electronics, Computer, Telecommunications and Information Technology (ECTI-CON)*, May (2014), pp. 1–6

20. G. Trehard, E. Pollard, B. Bradai, F. Nashashibi, Tracking both pose and status of a traffic light via an interacting multiple model filter, in *17th International Conference on Information Fusion (FUSION)*, July (2014), pp. 1–7

21. F. Oniga, S. Prodan, S. Nedevschi, Traffic light detection on mobile devices, in *2015 IEEE International Conference on Intelligent Computer Communication and Processing (ICCP)*, Sept (2015), pp. 287–292

22. Y. Jie, C. Xiaomin, G. Pengfei, X. Zhonglong, A new traffic light detection and recognition algorithm for electronic travel aid, in *2013 Fourth International Conference on Intelligent Control and Information Processing (ICICIP)*, June (2013), pp. 644–648

23. J. M. Borrmann, F. Haxel, D. Nienhüser, A. Viehl, J. M. Zöllner, O. Bringmann, W. Rosenstiel, Stellar - a case-study on systematically embedding a traffic light recognition, in *17th International IEEE Conference on Intelligent Transportation Systems (ITSC)*, Oct (2014), pp. 1258–1265

24. W. Zong, Q. Chen, Traffic light detection based on multi-feature segmentation and online selecting scheme, in *2014 IEEE International Conference on Systems, Man, and Cybernetics (SMC)*, Oct (2014), pp. 204–209

25. S. Sathiya, M. Balasubramanian, D.V. Priya, Real time recognition of traffic light and their signal count-down timings, in *International Conference on Information Communication and Embedded Systems (ICICES2014)*, Feb (2014), pp. 1–6

26. J. Gong, Y. Jiang, G. Xiong, C. Guan, G. Tao, H. Chen, The recognition and tracking of traffic lights based on color segmentation and camshift for intelligent vehicles, in *2010 IEEE Intelligent Vehicles Symposium*, June (2010), pp. 431–435

27. X. Shi, N. Zhao, Y. Xia, Detection and classification of traffic lights for automated setup of road surveillance systems. Multimed. Tools Appl. **75**(20), 12547–12562 (2016). Online Available: http://dx.doi.org/10.1007/s11042-014-2343-1

28. M. Michael, M. Schlipsing, Extending traffic light recognition: efficient classification of phase and pictogram, in *2015 International Joint Conference on Neural Networks (IJCNN)*, July (2015), pp. 1–8.

29. M. Salarian, A. Manavella, R. Ansari, A vision based system for traffic lights recognition, in *2015 SAI Intelligent Systems Conference (IntelliSys)*, Nov (2015), pp. 747–753

30. C. Jang, C. Kim, D. Kim, M. Lee, M. Sunwoo, Multiple exposure images based traffic light recognition, in *2014 IEEE Intelligent Vehicles Symposium Proceedings*, June (2014), pp. 1313–1318

31. Q. Chen, Z. Shi, Z. Zou, Robust and real-time traffic light recognition based on hierarchical vision architecture, in *2014 7th International Congress on Image and Signal Processing*, Oct (2014), pp. 114–119

32. Y.-C. Chung, J.-M. Wang, S.-W. Chen, A vision-based traffic light detection system at intersections. J. Natl. Taiwan Norm. Univ. Math. Sci. Technol. **47**, 67–86 (2002)

33. A. Almagambetov, S. Velipasalar, A. Baitassova, Mobile standards-based traffic light detection in assistive devices for individuals with color-vision deficiency. IEEE Trans. Intell. Transp. Syst. **16**(3), 1305–1320 (2015)

34. J. Balcerek, A. Konieczka, T. Marciniak, A. Dąbrowski, K. Maćkowiak, K. Piniarski, Automatic detection of traffic lights changes from red to green and car turn signals in order to improve urban traffic, in *2014 Signal Processing: Algorithms, Architectures, Arrangements, and Applications (SPA)*, Sept (2014), pp. 110–115.

35. Z. Cai, Y. Li, M. Gu, Real-time recognition system of traffic light in urban environment, in *2012 IEEE Symposium on Computational Intelligence for Security and Defence Applications*, July (2012), pp. 1–6

36. M. Omachi, S. Omachi, Traffic light detection with color and edge information, in *2009 2nd IEEE International Conference on Computer Science and Information Technology*, Aug (2009), pp. 284–287

37. J. Choi, B.T. Ahn, I.S. Kweon, Crosswalk and traffic light detection via integral framework, in *The 19th Korea-Japan Joint Workshop on Frontiers of Computer Vision*, Jan (2013), pp. 309–312

38. B. Fan, W. Lin, X. Yang, An efficient framework for recognizing traffic lights in night traffic images, in *2012 5th International Congress on Image and Signal Processing*, Oct (2012), pp. 832–835

39. R. de Charette, F. Nashashibi, Real time visual traffic lights recognition based on spot light detection and adaptive traffic lights templates, in *2009 IEEE Intelligent Vehicles Symposium*, June (2009), pp. 358–363

40. J. Levinson, J. Askeland, J. Dolson, S. Thrun, Traffic light mapping, localization, and state detection for autonomous vehicles, in *2011 IEEE International Conference on Robotics and Automation*, May (2011), pp. 5784–5791

41. S. Mascetti, D. Ahmetovic, A. Gerino, C. Bernareggi, M. Busso, A. Rizzi, Robust traffic lights detection on mobile devices for pedestrians with visual impairment. Comput. Vis. Image Underst. **148**(C), 123–135 (2016). Online Available: https://doi.org/10.1016/j.cviu.2015.11.017

42. A.E. Gomez, F.A.R. Alencar, P.V. Prado, F.S. Osório, D.F. Wolf, Traffic lights detection and state estimation using hidden Markov models, in *2014 IEEE Intelligent Vehicles Symposium Proceedings*, June (2014), pp. 750–755

An Approach to Prepare Data to Feed Visual Metaphors in a Multiple View Interactive Environment

50

Ronaldo de Matos Nascimento Filho, Glauco de Figueiredo Carneiro, and Miguel Monteiro

Abstract

This paper presents an approach to prepare data to feed visual metaphors in a multiple view interactive environment. We implemented a tool that supports programmers and users to prepare datasets from different domains to feed visual metaphors. To analyze the effectiveness of the approach, we conducted a case study with the data of the Brazilian National Health System (known as *SUS—Sistema Unico de Saude* in Portuguese). The results obtained are an initial evidence of the feasibility of the approach that support the preparation of data to a format suitable to the characteristics of visual metaphors. The case study illustrates scenarios in which both programmers and users are able to prepare datasets from different domains to feed visual metaphors that comprise a multiple view interactive visualization infrastructure.

Keywords

Cloud computing · Legacy systems · Cloud migration · Tools

50.1 Introduction

According to [1], data visualizations are algorithmically generated and can be easily regenerated with different data. Moreover, they are usually data-rich, and are often aesthetically shallow [1]. Popular tools for data visualization still have limitations, yielding visualizations of somewhat poor quality, with little or no interactivity with the tool user.

R. de Matos Nascimento Filho · G. de Figueiredo Carneiro (✉)
Universidade Salvador (UNIFACS), Salvador, Bahia, Brazil
e-mail: glauco.carneiro@unifacs.br

M. Monteiro
NOVA LINCS, Universidade Nova de Lisboa (FCT/UNL), Caparica, Portugal
e-mail: mtpm@fct.unl.pt

Practitioners have claimed that although the number of data file formats is unbounded, the structure of any data could be described using a small number of parameters [2]. The range of visualization algorithms applicable to a given type of data is narrow and the subset used within a given scientific discipline is even narrower. Thus, hardly all possible data structures need be covered, with the consequence that the solution space tailored to these activities should be relatively simple and easy to maintain. Researchers have also claimed that data visualization can point to new questions and to additional exploration directions, help identify sub-problems, show great volumes of data and leverage the human cognitive capabilities to identify patterns and communicate relationships and meaning [1]. Thus, it is desirable—and also feasible—to build a data visualization tool targeted for users that are not knowledgeable of these matters but need to deal with data in their daily activities.

The Problem To build graphical representations of data and make it available in the internet, tools such as HTML, CSS are usually used. Depending on the visualization metaphor, Scalable Vector Graphics (SVG) elements may also be required. Though preparation can be carried out manually, such a task would be laborious, time consuming and not scalable to large amounts of data. In addition, reuse requires considerable effort to be achieved. On the other hand, processes for building a graphical representation of data can be automated—with the aid of tools such as Javascript—thus facilitating the regeneration of the representation from different data sets (provided they are of similar structure). Automation makes it feasible to represent large quantities of data. These approaches are classified under *data visualization* [1]. The drawback is that build work will be larger, to prepare the whole dataset.

To tackle this problem, we decided to select tools, toolkits and frameworks that could aid in the aforementioned dataset preparation, so that users can focus on the problems and corresponding solutions. Taking this into account, we proposed an approach to prepare data to feed visual metaphors through the implementation of a multiple view interactive environment. Through it, users can explore and analyze the data by selecting the visual metaphors that best fit the tasks at hand.

The rest of this paper is organized as follows. The next section presents the research background. Section 50.3 describes the methodology of the study. Section 50.4 analyzes the results. Section 50.5 presents the conclusion and scope for future research.

50.2   Research Background

Regarding data visualization, unlike the traditional tree diagram, the *treemap* visual metaphor provides a graphical representation of nested (hierarchical) data and their respective values. These values can be represented by both the area of each rectangle and its color intensity. This visual metaphor provides an overview of all the data and their descendants, as well as their value [3]. On the other hand, the *sunburst* visual metaphor presents the same aspects of data as with the *treemap*, but with a different approach, facilitating the analysis of the hierarchical levels of the data, without one sub-level interfering in the visualization of another. It also provides a panoramic view of all levels [4].

The *circle packing* metaphor was designed for the visualization of data in categorized form, suitable for hierarchical data with many levels. It enables the recursive navigation through the various levels of a dataset structure.

Unlike the aforementioned views, which focus on hierarchical data, the *chord* view provides an alternative for representing relationships between entities, making it possible to see which entities are related to each other, as well as the direction of that relationship. Depending on the data, the understanding of this representation can be compromised, because if there are too many relations between the entities, some of the representations of the relations may overlap one another. For this reason, an interactive solution was adopted.

50.3   Proposed Solution

To perform the proposed approach, we implemented a multiple view interactive environment in which the visual metaphors are instantiated to represent data provided in JavaScript Object Notation (JSON). The graphical representations enable users to interact through filters, so as more detailed data display features.

Functional Requirements The environment should support the generation of interactive graphical representations, based on data that can be filtered according to users' needs. For this purpose, the data sent to the systems must be in a

structure, defined here as a characteristic of the data, to be exposed during the process. The environment should provide filters on the data sent by the user.

Non-functional Requirements For scalability purposes, propagation and ease of use, the system must be accessible through a web browser. Regarding the architecture of the environment, it should allow the processing and manipulation of data on the server. This targets a thin web browser client. The environment can be extended to support data manipulation, validation, and restructuring. Views should be built in SVG and the interface should be responsive. The environment should also support a large amount of data as input. Moreover, it should be extensible to enable the inclusion of new implementations of data characteristics, visual metaphors and their respective filters.

Steps to Prepare Data to Feed Visual Metaphors The activity diagram shown in Fig. 50.1 presents suggested steps to select and adjust the visual metaphors in the proposed multiple view interactive environment. As an initial requirement, the user select a dataset with the JSON format. Note the system was designed with the intention of adding future implementations, and the options shown here refer to just the visualization metaphors implemented so far. In Table 50.1, we present a short explanation of the suggested steps:

Proposed Solution The proposed architecture focus on the principle of the *thin client* architecture. This enables a minimal set of software requirement to function as a front-end user interface for a web application. On the other hand, this approach is limited to support an interactive real-time visual data manipulation and graphical visualization environment. Considering this scenario, we decided to implement the solution through a "thin" client. As a result, we needed to tailor the implementation of the visual metaphors to allow a thin client (i.e., any web browser) to send data and configurations for processing and instantiation of visualization metaphors, with the aid of filters and data treatments. This way, it is possible to transfer the heavier steps to the server whenever possible. Only the pre-processed data for rendering the visualization is returned to the client.

In order to meet the requirements of the proposed solution, we planned the architecture presented in Fig. 50.2. In the following paragraphs, we describe the components that comprise this architecture.

Python and Django The Python programming language was chosen for its scalability, support for productivity, simplicity and its open source nature. Django is an open source framework for Python, through which it is possible to focus directly on the solution. It offers us a whole structure for the creation of internet systems, in a simple and easy way,

Fig. 50.1 Steps to prepare data
to feed visual Metaphors

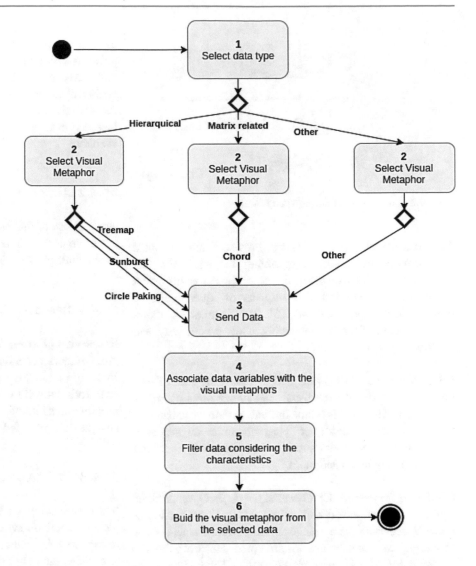

Table 50.1 Steps to prepare data to feed visual metaphors

Step	Description
1	Select the type of data
2	Select the visual metaphor
3	Provide data in the JSON format
4	Indicate which visual attributes will represent data real attributes in the selected visual metaphor [5]
5	Filter data to be presented in the visual metaphor
6	Build the visual metaphor

using an MVT (Model, View , Template), which resembles the well-known MVC (Model, View , Controller) pattern. The main differences can be found in the View layer. Django also brings an Object-relational mapping (ORM), allowing the creation of database-linked applications, simply and quickly, abstracting any SQL line of code. Another advantage of Django is its automatically generated administrative interface, which can be easily configured from the classes created in the Model layer. This interface allows us to

perform basic operations such as CRUD (Create, Read, Update, Delete), which may also be extended and/or modified separately.

MySql Considering that the proposed environment does not require specific database features, we decided to use MySql. It is a widely used database that provides all the basic requirements of a database, and it can be easily integrated with a Django application.

Fig. 50.2 Components of the proposed solution

Javascript and Jquery Current browsers have adopted Javascript as the main programming language. For this reason, we decided to adopt in the proposed environment JavaScript snippets and also snippets of Jquery code—a popular Javascript framework [6]. This framework allows for code simplification, enhancing code productivity and quality.

D3.js We selected the D3.js toolkit due to its ease of use, diversity and quality of visual metaphors already implemented [6] The toolkit is not limited to data visualization. It also includes facilities for object manipulation, requests, conversions, interactivity control, Document Object Model (DOM) manipulators and more.

CSS3 and Bootstrap CSS became the *de facto* standard for styling on the internet, despite minor differences in rendering between browsers. Its interface and important elements such as margins and spacing are not disrupted. However, the implementation of responsive elements via CSS are inherently verbose. For this reason, the most commonly used front-end framework—Bootstrap—was adopted. This tool supports the construction of responsive interfaces, besides many other possibilities of stylization.

50.4 The Case Study

In this section, we present a case study conducted to analyze the effectiveness of the solution proposed in this paper regarding the preparation of data to feed visual metaphors in a multiple view interactive environment.

50.4.1 Problems to be Addressed

One way to extract information from a large amount of data is by analyzing a graphical representation of the dataset that represent it. To tackle this problem, we implemented the proposed solution presented in Sect. 50.3.

The solution can be used by non-programmers as long as the visual metaphors they need were implemented prior to use and made available in the environment. In that case, the user just has to convert the data to be analyzed to an appropriate format (JSON). Considering that the environment is extensible, a visual metaphor can be included in the environment by a programmer, in case is not available.

50.4.2 Aims

The purpose of this case study is to illustrate the viability of use of an approach to prepare data to feed visual metaphors to in a multiple view interactive environment.

50.4.3 Research Questions

Research Question 1 (RQ1): To which extent can non-programmers generate a graphical representation of data in JSON format in the proposed multiple view environment?
Research Question 2 (RQ2): To which extent can non-programmers interact with the selected visual metaphors and analyze data provided to the environment in JSON format?

50.4.4 Tasks and Used Data

In this case study, we illustrated the viability of the multiple view interactive environment to prepare data to feed visual metaphors using data from the Brazilian Unified Health System (SUS) publicly available by the Brazilian government.[1] Public health plays an important role for citizens and has drawn attention of both policymakers and the public at large. Concerns about gaps in both the availability and quality of public health services have hit the headlines in response to both new and persistent health risks [7]. For this reason, decision makers and practitioners must be careful about the allocation, management, and administration of public health resources [8].

Brazil's citizens expect the public health system to make appropriate use of out-of-pocket health expenses. In 1988, within the new Constitution, the Brazilian Unified Health System (SUS) was created by the Brazilian Ministry of Health to offer free health care to the population, based on three pillars: universal coverage, integral health care and equity [9].

---

[1] datasus.saude.gov.br.

Fig. 50.3 Step 1: select the type of data

50.4.5 Strategy to Perform the Tasks

The activities executed in the case study followed the steps described in Table 50.1 and illustrated in Fig. 50.1. All the steps were previously tested by the first author, as well as the appropriateness of the data to instantiate and interact with the visual metaphors in the multiple view interactive environment.

1. **Step 1—Select Data Type:** According to Fig. 50.3, the user inform the type of data to feed the visual metaphors in the environment. The current version provides support for two types of data structure. The first is related to the relationship among data entities such as the one represented in a graph. For example, a graph that represent a standard graph of a social network. The second is related to hierarchical data as essentially a specialized form of network data. The difference from the first type of data structure is that in the second type they are all related to each other by the principle of containment. They, unlike standard data networks, do not use the principle of connection.

2. **Step 2—Select the Visual Metaphor:** the user selects the visual metaphor according to the data structure of the data he/she provided (Fig. 50.4). In this case, the treemap, sunburst and circle parking visual metaphors are related to hierarchical data representation. On the other hand, the network related data can be represented by the chord visual metaphor.

3. **Step 3—Provide Data in the JSON format:** the user select the path or url that contains the data to feed the selected visual metaphor in the environment (Fig. 50.5).

4. **Step 4—Indicate which Visual Attributes will Represent Data Real Attributes in the Selected Visual Metaphor [5]:** in this step the user indicates how entities from the data structure will be visually represented using the data attributes (Fig. 50.6).

5. **Step 5—Filter Data to be Represented in the Visual Metaphor:** in this step the user indicates the range of values to filter data to be visually represented (Figs. 50.7, 50.8 and 50.9).

6. **Step 6—Build the Visual Metaphor:** in this step the user requests the tool to carry out the build of the selected visual metaphor (Figs. 50.10 and 50.11).

Fig. 50.4 Step 2—select the visual metaphor

Fig. 50.5 Step 3—provide data in the JSON format

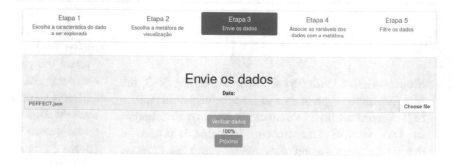

Fig. 50.6 Step 4—indicate which visual attributes will represent data real attributes in the selected visual metaphor

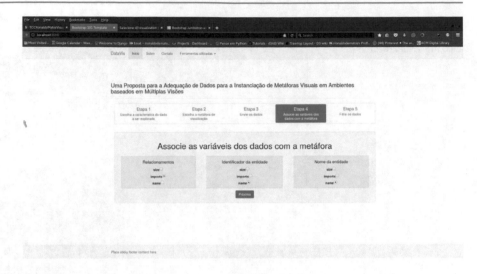

Fig. 50.7 Step 5—filter data to be represented in the chord visual metaphor

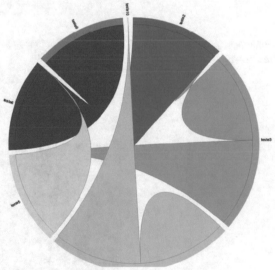

Fig. 50.8 Step 5—filter data to be represented in the circle packing visual metaphor

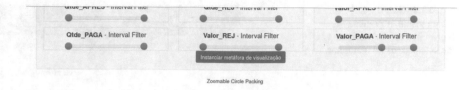

Fig. 50.9 Step 5—filter data to be represented in the treemap visual Metaphor

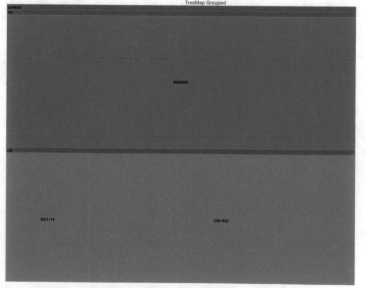

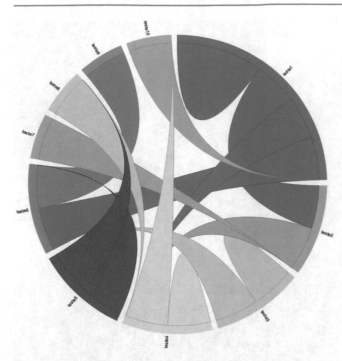

Fig. 50.10 Step 6—build the visual metaphor (the chord visual metaphor)

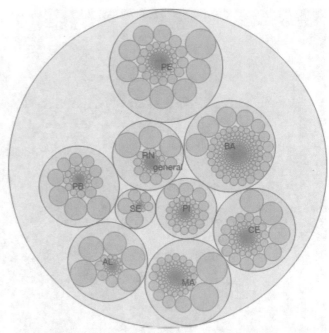

Fig. 50.11 Step 6—build the visual metaphor (the circlepaking visual metaphor)

50.4.6 Results

Considering the steps described before, we present the results using data from the Brazilian National Health System.

The participant combined the use of the available visual metaphors (treemap, chord, sunburst and circle packing) to accomplish the following tasks: **Task 1 (T1)**: *What are the top three Brazilian Northeast States in terms of highest approved values for performed procedures?* **Task 2 (T2)**:*Considering the States selected from Q1, which month had the highest approved value for performed procedures?*

The panoramic view provided by treemap (Fig. 50.12) can initially represent data related to the first level, i.e. the states in terms of approved accounts and the respective budget allocated for them. On the other hand, the circle packing visual metaphor not only provides a panoramic view of data (Fig. 50.11), but it also represents the subsequent levels at the same time. This helps the user to know to which extent the set of analyzed states, period of time (in this case, month), and health unit contribute in the amount of approved accounts.

To perform **Tasks 1 (T1) and 2 (T2)**, the participant identified the Brazilian Northeast States that had the highest approved values for performed procedures. In this version of treemap, the rectangle visual attribute is associated with the amount of approved accounts of a given State (Figs. 50.13 and 50.14).

50.5 Conclusion

With this case study with three visual metaphors, it was possible to analyze the adequacy of data for these models, as well as the approach to prepare data to feed visual metaphors in a multiple view interactive environment. It was also possible to check the interactivity with the filters, zoom, and highlighting for selected object.

With this approach, the process of understanding the data through graphic representation was summarized in six steps, using only the web interface, without the need to program a single line of code.

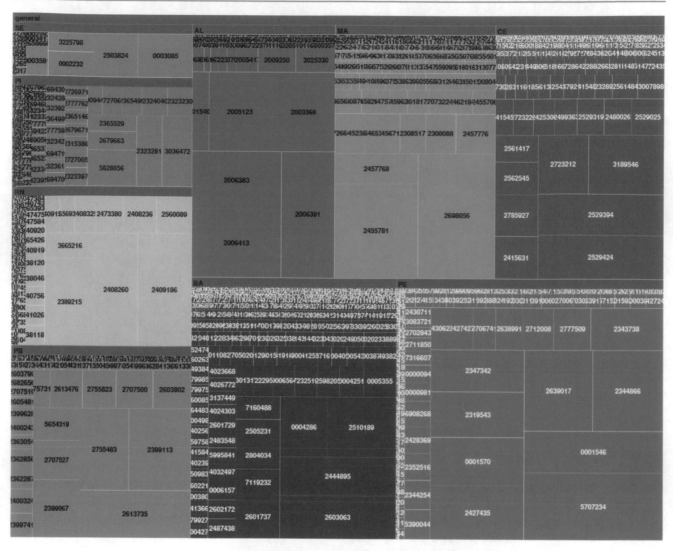

Fig. 50.12 Step 6—build the visual metaphor (the treemap visual metaphor)

Fig. 50.13 Estudo de caso da step 4

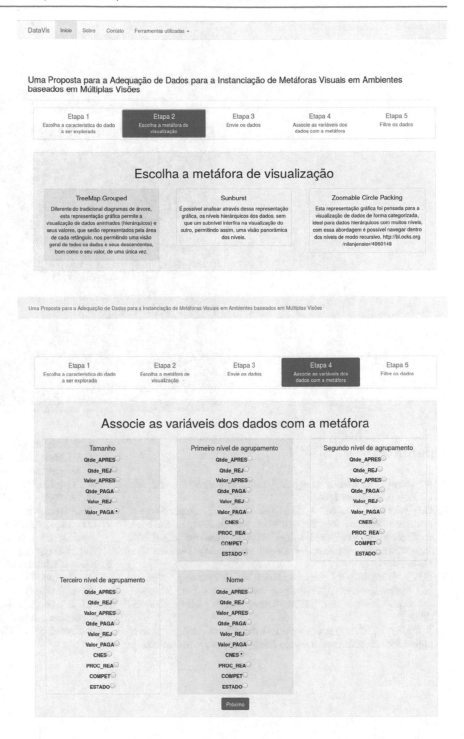

Fig. 50.14 Estudo de caso da step 5

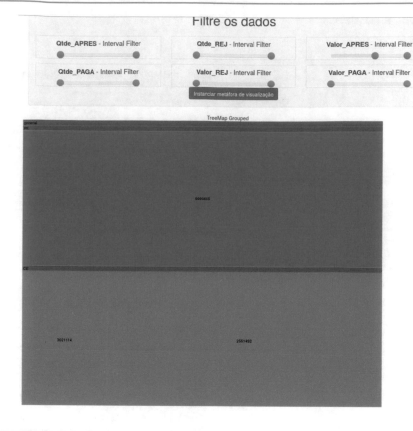

References

1. N. Iliinsky, J. Steele, *Designing Data Visualizations*, 1st edn. (O'Reilly, Sebastapol, 2011)
2. G.P Johnson, S.A. Mock, B.M. Westing, G.S. Johnson, Envision: a web-based tool for scientific visualization, in *EnVision: A Web-Based Tool for Scientific Visualization. 9th IEEE/ACM International Symposium on Cluster Computing and the Grid* (2009)
3. B.B. Bederson, B. Shneiderman, M. Wattenberg, Ordered and quantum treemaps: making effective use of 2d space to display hierarchies. ACM Trans. Graph. **21**(4), 833–854 (2002)
4. J. Stasko, E. Zhang, Focus+ context display and navigation techniques for enhancing radial, space-filling hierarchy visualizations, in *IEEE Symposium on Information Visualization, 2000. InfoVis 2000* (IEEE, New York, 2000), pp. 57–65
5. M. Carpendale, Considering visual variables as a basis for information visualisation (2003)
6. M. Bostock, V. Ogievetsky, J. Heer, D3 data-driven documents. IEEE Trans. Vis. Comput. Graph. **17**, 2301–2309 (2011)
7. G.P. Mays, F.D. Scutchfield, M.W. Bhandari, S.A. Smith, Understanding the organization of public health delivery systems: an empirical typology. Milbank Q. **88**(1), 81–111 (2010)
8. F.D. Scutchfield, M.W. Bhandari, N.A. Lawhorn, C.D. Lamberth, R.C. Ingram, Public health performance. Am. J. Prev. Med. **36**(3), 266–272 (2009)
9. A.J. Barros, A.D. Bertoldi, Out-of-pocket health expenditure in a population covered by the family health program in Brazil. Int. J. Epidemiol. **37**(4), 758–765 (2008)

Reproducible Research in Document Analysis and Recognition

51

Jorge Ramón Fonseca Cacho and Kazem Taghva

Abstract

With reproducible research becoming a de facto standard in computational sciences, many approaches have been explored to enable researchers in other disciplines to adopt this standard. In this paper, we explore the importance of reproducible research in the field of document analysis and recognition and in the Computer Science field as a whole. First, we report on the difficulties that one can face in trying to reproduce research in the current publication standards. These difficulties for a large percentage of research may include missing raw or original data, a lack of tidied up version of the data, no source code available, or lacking the software to run the experiment. Furthermore, even when we have all these tools available, we found it was not a trivial task to replicate the research due to lack of documentation and deprecated dependencies. In this paper, we offer a solution to these reproducible research issues by utilizing container technologies such as Docker. As an example, we revisit the installation and execution of OCRSpell which we reported on and implemented in 1994. While the code for OCRSpell is freely available on github, we continuously get emails from individuals who have difficulties compiling and using it in modern hardware platforms. We walk through the development of an OCRSpell Docker container for creating an image, uploading such an image, and enabling others to easily run this program by simply downloading the image and running the container.

Keywords

Reproducible research · Containers · Docker · OCRSpell · Document analysis and recognition

J. Ramón Fonseca Cacho (✉) · K. Taghva
Department of Computer Science, University of Nevada, Las Vegas, NV, USA
e-mail: Jorge.FonsecaCacho@unlv.edu; kazem.taghva@unlv.edu

51.1 Introduction

A key to advancing our field is to build and expand on previous work, namely cumulative science. The only way we can achieve this is if we understand the foundations and can replicate it. In this lies the importance of Reproducible Research, which means the ability to take a paper—code in many of our cases—and be able to run the experiment addressed in that paper so we can learn and expand on the paper's research or even refute it [1]. Knowing and having access to the raw, intermediate, and processed data is another important aspect as it is key in understanding how every result was produced [2].

Reproducible research should be more than the final data and product. The necessity to implement a gold standard for publications and conferences is ever increasing. A great deal can be learned from the steps it took to come up with an algorithm or solve a problem. Version control and the concept of *Git* is a great solution to increase transparency and see the evolution of code to its final form [3]. Reproducible research is also about how *TIDY* data is produced [4]. Recently, we wanted to revisit our research on post-processing of Optical Character Recognition (OCR) data. As a part of this work, we wanted to access some data which is referenced by some of the authors in the International Conference on Document Analysis and Recognition (ICDAR) proceedings. We were unsuccessful in obtaining the data since the download page produced errors. We contacted the university that had produced the OCR'd documents and ground truth, and never received a response. This is a common trend that is thoroughly documented by Christian Collberg et al. [5]. Collberg's group was in the pursuit of a project's source code that should have legally been available due to having been partially funded with federal grant money. After evasion from the university to release the code, Collberg threatened legal action which was met by lawyers' refusal and eventually avoiding his request by charging extreme retrieval fees. The exchange is well documented along with other examples of researchers giving reasons for not sharing the code such as it no longer existing or not being ready to publish it. Collberg ultimately found that only a quarter of the articles were reproducible [5].

People are usually criticized for unpolished or buggy code, and writing pristine code is usually time consuming and unnecessary. Authors may not want to be subject to that critique [6]. This creates an environment that encourages code that is not acceptable to not be released. There is no easy solution to this. Scientist must have confidence in that the *results* are what matters and not how the code is written as long as its reproducible. The code can always be cleaned up after the fact. Similarly, with the data used in experiments, many times researchers will not want to share it in order to avoid exposing potential bias in their research for False positive findings [7]. There is also the monetary potential that a project's code could bring [6]. In this case the researcher has hopes his new algorithm, or data set, could be monetized down the line giving no incentive to offer it for free initially.

Another difficulty in reproducible research lies in not all researchers having access to the same level of resources such as computing power required for certain resource-intensive projects. This makes it difficult to review or reproduce such research. There is no definite solution to that difficulty.

Roger D. Peng is known for his advocacy for Reproducible Research in several publications; as Peng mentions, requiring a reproducibility test when peer reviewing has helped computational sciences to only publish quality research. Peng clearly shows reproducible data is far more cited and of use to the scientific community [1]. Many others agree with the concept of creating a standard in the field of computer science that matches that of other sciences for reproducible research to the point of requiring mandatory data archiving policies [8]. Even the US Congress has shown interest and has had hearings on transparency [9], and while reproducible research helps, reproducibility of both data and code is insufficient to avoid problematic research in the first place [10]. Nevertheless, the benefits in transparency in the way data is handled will avoid potential risk of researchers being accused of skewing data to their advantage [11].

51.2   Docker

Docker is an open source project used to create images that run as Linux Containers with a virtualization of the OS level [12]. See *docs.docker.com* for more information.

Containers enable us to freeze the current state of a virtual operating system so that we can reload it and refer to it at any time. This enables us to store data and/or code that works at the time and be able to save with it any dependencies or requirements without worrying about deprecation or code-rot. They help to reduce the complexity of reproducing experiments [13]. The Dockerfile, which is what builds the

containers as a series of steps, enables one to see the steps used to create that container. This along with version control help to understand the history and steps used in research.

Docker does have limitations when it comes to rendering graphics, as it uses the host machine for that. Solutions to make this issue not be platform specific come in the form of GUIdock [14]. It is in this environment surrounding the Docker platform where the open source availability shines as most limitations have been removed with additional software ensuring it as a consistent solution to reproducible research.

Because containers are processes that have a lot of overhead, questions may arise as to the impact in terms of performance for larger projects with big data such as in bio-informatics; however, benchmarks prove that their fast start-up time along with negligible impact on execution performance has no negative effects on using them [15].

51.3   OCRSpell

OCRSpell is a spelling correction system designed for OCR generated text. Although the software was released in 1994, it continues to be relevant based on number of downloads and citations such as [16]. Making OCRSpell easily available for our own projects as well as others made it a good candidate for our work on reproducible research.

OCRSpell code is written as a mix of shell script commands in Linux and C code. It works by generating candidate words through different techniques including the use of ispell. For more information see [17] and [18]. At the time of writing, the source code is available at https://github.com/zw/ocrspell, and has a small *readme* file describing the steps to compile the source code. Several issues arise if one tries to build and run OCRspell using only these instructions:

1. Dependencies: to build, the readme says to `run` `autoconf` which means running a program of which no more information or version is given. Furthermore, no support is given for running that dependency.
2. Modifications by Hand: readme says:
   ```
   ./configure -prefix=/local/ocrspell
     -<version>
   ```
   and:
   ```
   in configure at line 685 change
   prefix=NONE to prefix=/home/graham
   /Downloads/ocrspell-1.0/src
   ```
   All these changes are manual changes that must be done in order to build and run the file which can be prone to mistakes due to lack of understanding what is happening.
3. Libraries and Guess Work: in order to build the program, several non-standard libraries must be included, programs like ispell must be installed. The only way to know what is required is to try and build, see the error, download that

program and try again. While in this case this works, it is a dangerous practice due to unknown changes in newer versions of dependencies.

4. Lack of Documentation: Aside from having documentation once the program is running, as is the case here, the readme is not very descriptive as to what is going on. Once the program runs with

```
./ocrspell -a -f ./ocr.freq <
quick_demo.txt
```

we have no confirmation that our output will be equal to what it was when the experiment was run years ago aside from one test file.

51.3.1 Docker as a Solution

Docker can resolve all of the above problems by creating an environment that is ready to go and is clearly defined to easily be replicated enabling researches to focus on the science instead of trying to glue different tools together [19]. Many have embraced Docker as a way to distribute easily reproducible raw and TIDY data along with several forms of code and even as a standardized way to share algorithms with AlgoRun [20].

51.4 Applying Docker to OCRSpell

51.4.1 Installing Docker

Docker will run in any of today's popular hardware platforms available and continued support due to its open-source nature ensures it will continue to do so. It can be downloaded and installed from the official website, which has step-by-step instructions on how to do so:

https://docs.docker.com/engine/installation/#platform-support-matrix

We recommend installation of Docker CE as this is the open-source community edition. For the remainder of this guide we will assume a Linux host system. However, the advantage of Docker means that the following commands will work in any platform the host system uses. To test the install make sure the docker service is running:

```
service docker start
```

and that we are connected to the docker repository by running a test container:

```
docker run hello-world
```

If it installed correctly it will pull the image from docker and display a message saying (among other things):

```
Hello from Docker.
```

This message shows that the installation appears to be working correctly.

If Docker was previously installed, we recommend deleting any existing images and containers before following this guide further. See Sect. 51.4.5 for instructions on how to do so.

51.4.2 Creating the Container

To create a Docker container, we must first create a Dockerfile. A Dockerfile contains the instructions needed to generate the appropriate image and includes all required dependencies. Each instruction in the Dockerfile creates an intermediary container that adds the change in that line. In that sense Docker is very modular; one can take other author's containers, add or remove a dependency or program, and publish their own version of the container for others to use. Using this concept we will begin to create our container by pulling a basic image of the Ubuntu OS as the base where OCRSpell will run. So we create a text file named Dockerfile and in the first line we add:

```
FROM ubuntu:14.04.2
```

This command pulls and installs the ubuntu:14.04.2 docker container. Next we add a maintainer line which adds a label to our container of who to contact in case of support.

```
MAINTAINER my@email.com
```

If we were to generate our container we would have a basic, non-gui working version of Ubuntu 14.04.2. However, OCRSpell requires certain dependencies that are not included in this basic version of Ubuntu to run. These dependencies may be acquirable today with the right install commands, but as they become deprecated with time, they may no longer be accessible. However, once we build our image, they will be saved permanently and never need to be reacquired again, enabling us to solve the issue of deprecated dependencies and code-rot. To install these dependencies we use the RUN command. First we will update the Ubuntu package list:

```
RUN apt-get -yqq update
```

Similarly we start to install the required libraries, software, and other dependencies we will need. We had to analyze the requirements of OCRSpell in order to determine these, but when a new author creates a container. They will be aware of what they need and easily include it:

```
RUN apt-get install unzip -yqq
RUN apt-get install autoconf -yqq
RUN apt-get install gcc -yqq
RUN apt-get install make -yqq
RUN apt-get install xutils-dev -yqq
RUN apt-get install nano -yqq
```

Notice we installed nano in order to be able to edit files within the container. The Ubuntu OS we have is as lightweight as possible and does not include basics like nano. Next we would normally want to install ispell, but instead we will do so while the container is running to show that option. Next we want to create our work directory before copying our source files. We use the WORKDIR command for that:

```
WORKDIR /home/ocrspell
```

This creates a folder in the virtual home folder called ocrspell. From now on whenever we start our container this will be the default starting directory. Next we want to download the source files from the github repository as a zip file. To do so we can use any web browser and copy the link in the quotes below or we can open a new terminal window and type:

wget "https://github.com/zw/ocrspell/archive/master.zip"

When finished downloading, place the zip file in the same directory as our Dockerfile. With this done we add the following command to copy the files into the image:

```
COPY master.zip ./
```

For our next line we want the container to unzip these files so we use RUN again:

```
RUN unzip master.zip
```

This prepares everything to start compiling the source files. As per the instructions in the readme, the first step is to run autoconf to generate a configure script. We can do this with a complex RUN command.

```
RUN cd ocrspell-master/src;autoconf;
  chmod +x configure.in ./
```

Because every RUN command is run on its own intermediary container we cannot create a run command to enter the folder src and another to run autoconf or chmod since each RUN command starts at the root folder which is our WORKDIR folder. To solve this semicolon is used to send multiple commands.

We could continue setting up the container from within the docker file by calling the makedepend and make commands as per the readme, but since we still need to install ispell and also do some manual modifications to get OCRSpell running due to its age, it is time to start up the container to do this.

51.4.3 Running the Container

So far we have a text file called Dockerfile with all of the above commands, but in order to create the container we have to feed this file to Docker. We do this by opening a new terminal in the same directory as the Dockerfile and OCRSpell zip source file(master.zip) and typing:

```
docker build -t ocrspell-master .
```

This will take some time as it downloads the Ubuntu image, runs it, downloads and install the dependencies (each on its own intermediate container), and then executes the remainder of the Dockerfile. When it is complete our image is ready to run. If there are any errors in any Dockerfile line the intermediate containers will remain in order to either run

those and find the problem or fix the problem and not have to start building from scratch. This is a great way to show with reproducible research the steps taken to reach a final version of a program. When ready, we start up our image by typing in the terminal:

```
docker run -it ocrspell-master /bin
  /bash
```

We are now running our container! Because the base is Ubuntu, any terminal command will work. A good way to test is to type in the terminal:

```
ls
```

It should show both our zip file source files and the unzipped directory. Now we can install ispell by running in our terminal:

```
apt-get install ispell -yqq
```

This is the same command we would do in a regular Linux machine. After it is done installing we can test it by running:

```
ispell -help
```

Now it is time to finish building the source. First, let's enter the src folder.

```
cd ocrspell-master/src/
```

As the readme on github points out, due to the age of OCRSpell and deprecated code, a few changes by hand must be made in order for the configure file to build correctly. First lets open the file in nano:

```
nano configure
```

Then go to line 712 and change:

```
prefix=NONE
```

to

```
prefix=/home/ocrspell/
  ocrspell-master/src
```

Next, go to lines 732 and 733 and change:

```
datarootdir='${prefix}/share'
datadir='${datarootdir}'
```

to

```
datarootdir='/home/ocrspell/
  ocrspell-master/src'
datadir='/home/ocrspell/
  ocrspell-master/src'
```

respectively. Save the file and close nano. Now we can run ./configure and then build as per the readme with makedepend and make:

```
./configure -prefix=/
  local/ocrspell-master
makedepend
make
```

OCRSpell is now fully compiled and we can test it with the included test file called quick_demo.txt:

```
./ocrspell -a -f ./ocr.freq < quick_d
  emo.txt
```

We have now successfully set up our container; however, due to the nature of the container. If we were to close the container we would lose all changes and the container would open in the same state as if he had just done the docker run command. So in order to save our final container we can use the `commit` command in a `different` terminal window than the one we are working with our container on. The syntax is:

```
docker commit <CONTAINER NAME FROM
    DOCKER PS> <file name>
```

In this case we type:

```
docker ps
```

to find our Container name and then use the commit command with those values and a name for our new container image. These names are randomly generated and change each time we run the container so we must pay special attention to selecting the right one; in this case it is `distracted_bardeen`:

```
docker commit distracted_bardeen
    ocrspell-final
```

We now have a saved version of our container and can close the running container and re-open it to the exact same state as it is now. To close it, in the terminal window where our container is active we type:

```
exit
```

If we want to save our docker image to share with other collaborators or publications we use the `save` command:

```
docker save -o <save image to
    path> <image name>
```

an example of this in our case is:

```
docker save -o /home/jfunlv/Desktop/
    test/ocrspell-final ocrspell-final
```

Be sure to modify the first part with the path where we will save the image. If there are any issues modifying the output image, use chmod and chown in linux to give rights to it or the equivalent in other platforms.

If we want to upload to the docker repository for other Docker users to collaborate or reproduce our research we need to create a free docker account at docker.com Once we have an account we have to tag and push the image. To do this we find the image id by typing:

```
docker images
```

Then, we tag the image by using:

```
docker tag 90e925195d6c username/
    ocrspell-final:latest
```

Replace username with one's docker user name and replace the image id with that of the appropriate image. Make sure one is logged in to docker by typing:

```
docker login
```

Finally we push by:

```
docker push username/ocrspell-final
```

For full details on tagging and pushing see:

https://docs.docker.com/engine/getstarted/step_six/

We have now uploaded a copy of our image for others to try, contribute and much more.

51.4.4 Downloading Our Version of the Container

The steps explained above should be done by the author of the research, but what if we want to download someone else's work and replicate it? In this case we will download the image that we created when writing this guide and run OCRSpell with a few simple commands.

We can download the image from an arbitrary location and load it up on docker, or download it from the official docker git repository:

1. Load image in Docker: Suppose we downloaded from the author's website an image with a container to the project of OCRSpell. The file name is 'ocrspell-image' To load this image we open up a terminal at the image location and type:

```
docker load -i ocrspell-image
```

Make sure one is in the directory of the image otherwise type the path to it such as:

```
docker load /home/user/
    Desktop/ocrspell-image
```

At this point we can type: `docker images` and verify that the entry was added. In our case, 'ocrspell-master'. As before we can now run it by typing:

```
docker run -it ocrspell-
    master /bin/bash
```

We now have a running container with OCRSpell that will not break or deprecate and includes all necessary source and software to run.

2. Download directly to Docker from Docker git repository: To search from the available images we use the 'docker search command' by typing the name of the image after the search keyword:

```
docker search ocrspell
```

A list of matching images will appear. In this case we want the ocrspell-master image from the unlvcs user, to download it we use the pull command:

```
docker pull unlvcs/ocrspell-master
```

If we check `docker images` we should see it listed under the repository and can now run it.

51.4.5 Deleting Old Images and Containers

Once we are done working with an image we can use the `docker rmi` command followed by the image ID which can be found next to the name of the image in `docker images`. In this case our Image id is: 90e925195d6c; therefore, we type in a terminal:

```
docker rmi 90e925195d6c
```

If there is a warning that the image is currently being used by a container. Make sure to first close the container and then delete the image. If we want to delete all containers stored in docker we can do so by typing in a terminal:

```
docker rm $(docker ps -a -q)
```

Similarly we can delete all images by typing:

```
docker rmi $(docker images -q)
```

51.4.6 Transferring Files In and Out of a Container

So far only when executing the Dockerfile did we copy data onto the container. Ideally we want to copy all of our data at this time and store it within the container to have everything in one place. But suppose that due to portability or projects with large file size we want to maintain the data in a separate docker container or repository in general. Docker communications within containers can easily achieve this with the `docker network` command. See for full details:

https://docs.docker.com/engine/userguide/networking/

If we want to instead transfer data from the container to and from the host machine we use the `docker cp` command.

51.4.7 Using the OCRSpell Container

Suppose we have an OCR document named `FR940104.0.clean` we would like to spell check with OCRSpell. The document is in our host machine and we have pulled the latest version of the OCRSpell container from the Docker repository. First we start our container by running in a new terminal:

```
docker run -it unlvcs/ocrspell
  -master /bin/bash
```

then we maneuver to the ocrspell program:

```
cd ocrspell-master/src
```

Next, we open a new terminal window at the location of our OCR document we will he running and type:

```
docker ps
```

We find and save our container name there for ocrspell-final. In this case it is `adoring_wescoff`, but it will be different each time. We are now ready to copy the file into the container. We run the following command:

```
docker cp FR940104.0.clean adoring_
  wescoff:/home/ocrspell/ocrspell-
  master/src/FR940104.0.clean
```

Note one will need to enter the correct name for one's container instead of 'adoring_wescoff'. The file should have copied successfully, so back in our container terminal we can type `ls` and verify it is there.

Now we run OCRSpell and rather than output to the terminal we will output to a file called `FR940104.0.output` which we will later copy back to the host machine. We use simple linux redirection to achieve this.

```
./ocrspell -a -f ./ocr.freq <
  FR940104.0.clean > FR940104.0.output
```

OCRSpell has now done its job for us. Now to copy the file back we open a terminal window where we wish to save our file and run the following command:

```
docker cp adoring_wescoff:/home/
  ocrspell/ocrspell-master/src/
  FR940104.0.output FR940104.0.output
```

The file is now saved in the host machine. We can now close the container with the `exit` command. Next time we open the container none of the files will exist in it as explained earlier. If we wish to retain this data in the container we use the commit and save message as mentioned previously.

51.5 Results

We have successfully used OCRSpell without having to go through the difficulties of tracking down source code and dependencies, compiling, or worrying about compatibility with hardware. We have made reproducible research in that anyone can take our data and run it through OCRSpell, modify the code without issues and publish their own version to improve on previous work.

As shown in this example, the steps taken to place OCRSpell into Docker are trivial and mechanical. The complicated part was finding the dependencies and by-hand modifications and making sure they were valid when first building the initial image. In new research this can be considered and easily stored in a Dockerfile making the added work to researchers minimal. The Dockerfile itself is a great way to view the construction of the image, and the container is a way to ensure that the reproducibility remains as it can be checked when trying to rebuild the image to see if it matches.

51.6 Conclusion

This paper reported on the state of reproducible research and its importance along with the challenges it brings. Docker containers are reviewed as a solution to consistent reproducible research and a complete application is shown with OCRSpell, a program that does not easily run in its current state, but after being placed in a container is now immortalized to be able to be tested anywhere and anytime with ease. Possible extensions to this project include parallel programming and complex GUI docker implementations examples, but more importantly a proposed standard for reproducible research for the ICDAR and other conferences in the hopes of a better future where we can all share and work together to create good reproducible research that benefits the scientific community.

References

1. R.D. Peng, Reproducible research in computational science. Science **334**(6060), 1226–1227 (2011)
2. G.K. Sandve, A. Nekrutenko, J. Taylor, E. Hovig, Ten simple rules for reproducible computational research. PLoS Comput. Biol. **9**(10), e1003285 (2013)
3. K. Ram, Git can facilitate greater reproducibility and increased transparency in science. Source Code Biol. Med. **8**(1) 7 (2013)
4. H. Wickham et al., Tidy data. J. Stat. Softw. **59**(10), 1–23 (2014)
5. C. Collberg, T. Proebsting, G. Moraila, A. Shankaran, Z. Shi, A.M. Warren, Measuring reproducibility in computer systems research, Technical report, 2014
6. N. Barnes, Publish your computer code: it is good enough. Nature **467**(7317), 753 (2010)
7. J.P. Ioannidis, Why most published research findings are false. PLos Med **2**(8), e124 (2005)
8. T.H. Vines, R.L. Andrew, D.G. Bock, M.T. Franklin, K.J. Gilbert, N.C. Kane, J.-S. Moore, B.T. Moyers, S. Renaut, D.J. Rennison et al., Mandated data archiving greatly improves access to research data. FASEB J **27**(4), 1304–1308 (2013)
9. Testimony on scientific integrity & transparency. https://www.gpo.gov/fdsys/pkg/CHRG-113hhrg79929/pdf/CHRG-113hhrg79929.pdf. Accessed 2017-03-01
10. J.T. Leek, R.D. Peng, Opinion: reproducible research can still be wrong: Adopting a prevention approach. Proc. Natl. Acad. Sci. **112**(6), 1645–1646 (2015)
11. G. Marcus, E. Davis, Eight (no, nine!) problems with big data. New York Times **6**(04), 2014 (2014)
12. C. Boettiger, An introduction to docker for reproducible research. ACM SIGOPS Oper. Syst. Rev. **49**(1), 71–79 (2015)
13. I. Jimenez, C. Maltzahn, A. Moody, K. Mohror, J. Lofstead, R. Arpaci-Dusseau, A. Arpaci-Dusseau, The role of container technology in reproducible computer systems research, in *2015 IEEE International Conference on Cloud Engineering (IC2E)* (IEEE, New York, 2015), pp. 379–385
14. L.-H. Hung, D. Kristiyanto, S.B. Lee, K.Y. Yeung, Guidock: using docker containers with a common graphics user interface to address the reproducibility of research. PloS One **11**(4), e0152686 (2016)
15. P. Di Tommaso, E. Palumbo, M. Chatzou, P. Prieto, M.L. Heuer, C. Notredame, The impact of docker containers on the performance of genomic pipelines. PeerJ **3**, e1273 (2015)
16. D. Hládek, J. Staš, S. Ondáš, J. Juhár, L. Kovács, Learning string distance with smoothing for OCR spelling correction. Multimedia Tools and Applications **76**(22), 24549–24567 (2017)
17. K. Taghva, E. Stofsky, Ocrspell: an interactive spelling correction system for OCR errors in text. Int. J. Doc. Anal. Recogn. **3**(3), 125–137 (2001)
18. K. Taghva, T. Nartker, J. Borsack, Information access in the presence of OCR errors, in *Proceedings of the 1st ACM Workshop on Hardcopy Document Processing* (ACM, New York, 2004), pp. 1–8
19. P. Belmann, J. Dröge, A. Bremges, A.C. McHardy, A. Sczyrba, M.D. Barton, Bioboxes: standardised containers for interchangeable bioinformatics software. Gigascience **4**(1), 47 (2015)
20. A. Hosny, P. Vera-Licona, R. Laubenbacher, T. Favre, Algorun, a docker-based packaging system for platform-agnostic implemented algorithms. Bioinformatics **32**, btw120 (2016)

Music Genre Classification Using Data Mining and Machine Learning

Nimesh Ramesh Prabhu, James Andro-Vasko, Doina Bein, and Wolfgang Bein

Abstract

With accelerated advances in internet technologies users make listen to a staggering amount of multimedia data available worldwide. Musical genres are descriptions that are used to characterize music in music stores, radio stations and now on the Internet. Music choices vary from person to person, even within the same geographical culture. Presently Apple's iTunes and Napster classify the genre of each song with the help of the listener, thus manually. We propose to develop an automatic genre classification technique for jazz, metal, pop and classical using neural networks using supervised training which will have high accuracy, efficiency and reliability, and can be used in media production house, radio stations etc. for a bulk categorization of music content.

Keywords

Automatic classification · Data mining · Machine learning · Music genre

52.1 Introduction

With accelerated advances in internet technologies users make listen to a staggering amount of multimedia data available worldwide. Apple's website iTunes, MP3.com, Napster.com, all boast millions of songs and over 15 genres

N. R. Prabhu · D. Bein (✉)
Department of Computer Science, California State University, Fullerton, Fullerton, CA, USA
e-mail: nimesh5@csu.fullerton.edu; dbein@fullerton.edu

J. Andro-Vasko · W. Bein
Department of Computer Science, University of Nevada, Las Vegas, NV, USA
e-mail: androvas@unlv.nevada.edu; wolfgang.bein@unlv.edu

Musical genres are descriptions that are used to characterize music in music stores, radio stations and now on the Internet. Music comes in many different types and styles ranging from traditional rock music to world pop, jazz, easy listening and bluegrass.

Data mining is a process of analyzing data from different perspectives and summarizing it into useful information that can be used to classify music samples. Basically data mining is the process of finding correlations or patterns among dozens of fields in large relational databases. Machine learning is a branch of artificial intelligence which works with construction and study of systems that can learn from data. The core of machine learning deals with representation and generalization. Representation of data instances and functions evaluated on these instances are part of all machine learning systems. Generalization is the property that the system will perform well on unseen data instances. Neural networks techniques will be used in this paper for classification.

Music choices vary from person to person, even within the same geographical culture. Presently Apple's iTunes and Napster classify the genre of each song with the help of the listener, thus manually. But manual classification is time consuming and classification is difficult when the song is in a language unknown to the listener. Classifying songs automatically into proper genres using machine learning rather than manual process which will save time and manpower and there is little research on this topic due to the difficulty to achieve low error rates [1].

We propose to develop an automatic genre classification technique for jazz, metal, pop and classical using neural networks using supervised training which will have high accuracy (between 80% and 90%), efficiency and reliability.

The paper is organized as follows. In Sect. 52.2 we present basic concepts, followed by related work in Sect. 52.3. A detailed description of our hardware-software system and what it achieves is given in Sect. 52.4. Experimental results are shown in Sect. 52.5. Concluding remarks and future work are presented in Sect. 52.6.

52.2   Basic Concepts

Machine learning is a subset of artificial intelligence where programs and systems are able to learn how to accomplish a task by learning through a training algorithm and a large amount of data. Supervised learning is a learning method where a program or model is trained with inputs that have target outputs. In other words, the input variables are mapped to output variables, allowing the system to learn in an assisted manner and be able to perform classification by adjusting for errors [2]. Regression and classification are the most common tasks for supervised learning, and it is also the most commonly used form of machine learning.

The robust capability of neural networks has made it a trending flavor of machine learning due to the complexity of modern classification and pattern matching problems, in addition to the rise in availability of large datasets [3].

Unlike other and older methods of classification, neural networks function as both a feature extractor and a classifier, providing both efficiency and capability in a range of machine learning tasks. A neural network is a system that is designed to model the way a human brain processes and performs a task, and it achieves this by employing a massive interconnection of simple computing cells that work as a parallel distributed processor [2]. These computing cells are referred to as "neurons" and are also regarded as "nodes" in the context of discussing the architecture of neural networks. Neural networks are visualized as consisting of multiple layers of nodes that are connected to each other. The basic structure of a simple neural network in modern applications consists of three layers: an input layer, hidden layer (or middle layer), and output layer. The input layers consist of the number of attributes or values, such as the 17 values of the five descriptors. The middle layer consists of one or more hidden layers, of which are responsible for the majority of the transformations on the input data into output signals, depending on their various synaptic weights and activation function [4]. The last layer, the output layer, combines all the signals or outputs from the last hidden layer and performs a classification or output transformation, such as the categorization of the song into the four genre. Most often, the output of the neural network does not match the actual (correct) result, so the error values acquired by comparing the output of the neural network against the actual target value for multiple such instances are then propagated backwards to each layer of the network to do adjustments to the weights. This process is called backpropagation and it is what gives the ability of neural networks to learn and improve from input data and solve problems beyond those that are only

linearly separable [5]. Thus, backpropagation provides a method of splitting the total output error backwards into error values per node in every layer. The amount of which to adjust the weights based on the error values is handled by the method called gradient descent. Gradient descent utilizes the error function realized from the training process of the neural network and selects adjustments to the synaptic weights that causes a decrease in the slope of the error function until it reaches the minimum [1]. The change in synaptic weights via these adjustments from gradient descent can be very small, especially if it is applied on a per input basis, but over time it will cause the error value to converge to the minimum of the error function after many training samples [4].

There has been work done in the area of automated categorization [6]. This involves labeling texts to a set of predefined categories, this is otherwise known as text categorization. Text categorization is applied to document indexing, document filtering, metadata generation, word sense disambiguation, and in any scenario where document organization is required. In the past, text categorization was based on knowledge engineering, which classified documents under a set of given categories by manually defining a set of rules to the expert knowledge engine to perform the classification. This method has become less popular and this mechanism has been applied by using a machine learning paradigm where a general inductive process automatically builds a text classifier by learning from a set of pre-classified documents.

Neural networks also provide a sound knowledge representation for information retrieval systems. In an information representation using a neural network, each node can be a keyword or an author and a link used as an association in the network. Information is retrieved using a parallel relaxation method where nodes are activated in parallel and are traversed until the network reaches a stable state using a single-layered interconnected neurons and weighted links. The strategy is explained in [7].

Symbolic learning has also been applied for information retrieval systems. In [8], the ID3 and ID5R algorithms were introduced. The ID3 is a decision tree based algorithm that used divide and conquer strategy to classify mixed objects into their associated classes based on the attribute values of the objects. Each node from the tree contains either a class name (leaf node) or contains an attribute test (a non-leaf node). Every training instance is an attribute-value pair. The ID3 strategy picks an attribute and categorizes to a list of objects based on this attribute. Using the divide and conquer approach, the ID3 method minimizes the number of expected tests to classify an object.

There has been work done in the area of genetic algorithms involving information retrieval. The method in which a genetic algorithm solves a problem is that given a problem, we apply a function on the input (normally known as a fitness function) and obtain a result from the fitness function.

Typically, we have a set of various inputs and we apply the fitness function onto each of the inputs. Once we generate the outputs we place them into a pool in which they are used again with the fitness function. When new solutions are added into the pool, certain solutions get discarded if they do not show improvement from previous generations. Then the idea is that the fitness functions generates new solutions from the pool and then inserts new solutions and/or discards new or old solutions (which is a generation), and this process continues until we obtain the desired solution.

Selecting a solution in the pool can be determined by applying a cross over which attempts to find the next best solution in the pool for the next generation and then we mutate the item to create a new generation. A genetic algorithm can be applied on NP problems to attempt to generate a solution quickly, or a quicker method than the brute force approach. The fitness function for a genetic algorithm can use some heuristic to speed up the process and try to obtain a solution without having too many generations.

Feature extraction is part of data mining technique in which set of features will be created by decomposing the original data. A feature is a combination of attributes that is of special interest and captures important characteristics of the data. A feature becomes a new attribute. Feature extraction make us describe data with a far smaller number of attributes than the original set. Feature extraction is an attribute reduction process which results in a much smaller and richer set of attributes.

52.3   Related Work

Genetic algorithms can be applied in information retrieval and document indexing, as in [9]. The keywords in a document are altered using genetic mutation and crossovers. The association of words with the documents are preserved in the chromosomes and each gene of the chromosome is a keyword associated to a document. After several generations and using a fitness function with the fitness score, the best population is generated which is a set of keywords that best describes the document. In [10] the authors extend the method to document clustering. Document clustering has been studied in [11, 12] where a genetic algorithm is applied on a weighted information retrieval system and a Boolean query was modified to improve recall and precision. In [13], a genetic algorithm approach is used for parallel information retrieval strategy.

Classifying songs automatically into proper genres using machine learning is a much needed but challenging task, due to the large rate of songs uploaded daily on Internet. Ujlambkar and Attar [14] analyzed various classification algorithms in order to learn, train and test the model for Indian music classification. Okuyucu et al. [15] performed a

feature and classifier analysis for the recognition of similar Environmental sound categories using MFCC along with Zero Crossing Rate as audio feature. Vyas and Dutta [16] used three set of features, namely MFCC, peak difference and frame energy, followed by the K-means algorithm to classify Indian music. Baniya et al. [17] combined the extreme learning machine (ELM) with bagging classifier; a majority score decided the final classification. Baniya et al. [18] uses various audio features of different weights to decide on the final score for genre classification.

52.4   Research Approach and Methodology

In this section, we first present the dataset of song fragments, the features chosen, and the neural network. We used the music dataset from GTZAN Genre Collection. Marsyas (Music Analysis, Retrieval, and Synthesis for Audio Signals) is an open source framework from which audio tracks, each 30 s long. It contains 10 genres, each represented by 100 tracks. The tracks are all 22,050 Hz Mono 16-bit audio files in .wav format. For this project we have chosen only four genre out of 10 genres as related past work has indicated that accuracy decreases when classification categories increases. The chosen genre are jazz, classical, metal and pop. The genre of a song is available under song's properties (Fig. 52.1).

Feature extraction is an attribute reduction process which results in a much smaller and richer set of attributes. We have chosen six features (with 16 values in total) which will be

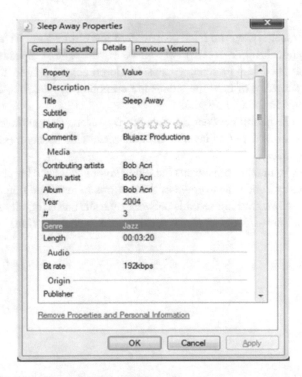

Fig. 52.1   Genre of a song, stored as a file

Fig. 52.2 Values of the 17-value features for the first 20 songs

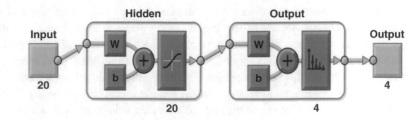

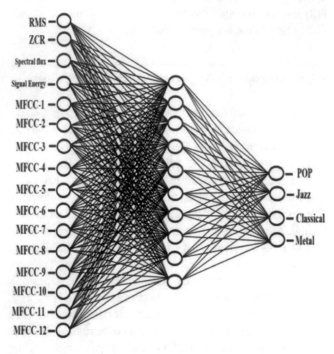

Fig. 52.3 Neural network used for classification of songs

extracted using the back propagation algorithm: Root Mean Square level, Zero Crossing Rate, Signal Energy, Spectral Flux, and Mel Frequency Cepstral Coefficients (12 in total). A snapshot of how the values are computed for the first 20 songs is shown in Fig. 52.2.

The neural network consists of 16 neurons in input layer, 4 neurons in output layer, and 10 neurons in hidden layer (see Fig. 52.3).

The number of neurons in hidden layer is not fixed but it is usually kept as an average of the neurons in input and output layer. We have chosen this network by trials and error, all the other networks gave worse performance in classification.

Since the neural network uses a supervised learning technique, out of 400 data samples, 300 data samples are used for training and validation, and remaining 100 are used for testing. The input to the neural network are the 16 values (from the five features) which are extracted during feature process (Fig. 52.4).

The network will give labels to the output neurons corresponding to a particular genre. The output for the first four songs is shown in Fig. 52.5.

52.5 Experimental Results

All experimental results were gathered in the MATLAB environment using the Signal Processing Toolbox to extract features and Neural Network Toolbox: used for training & classification. The performance of the neural network is shown in the confusion matrix. The confusion matrices produced by MATLAB show two green squares which represent correct classifications and two red squares representing incorrect classifications. Correct classifications on the confusion matrix are represented as true positive and true negative, where true positive refers to correct classifications of class membership and true negative refers to correct classifications of class non-membership. Conversely, the incorrect classifications are represented as false positive and false negative rates. Intuitively, false positives represent incorrect class membership classification and false negatives represent incorrect class non-membership.

The performance percentages are calculated by dividing the total number of correct classifications by the total number of classifications.

MATLAB also displays multiple instances of confusion matrices of each phase of the neural network: training, validation, and testing. These individual confusion

⊞ 20x400 double

	1	2	3	4	5	6	7	8	9	10	11	12	13	14	15	16	1
1	0.2051	0.0611	0.0392	0.1174	0.2894	0.0275	0.0331	0.0984	0.2300	0.0868	0.0460	0.1352	0.1362	0.0695	0.0350	0.1530	C
2	0.1268	0.0780	0.0980	0.1832	0.1495	0.0587	0.0874	0.1530	0.1190	0.0578	0.0899	0.1285	0.0854	0.0444	0.1084	0.1669	C
3	2.7836e...	2.4678e...	1.0156e...	9.1225e...	5.5419e...	502.0330	727.2428	6.4062e...	3.4996e...	4.9838e...	1.3996e...	1.2091e...	1.2278e...	3.1996e...	809.5040	1.5489e...	3.12
4	7.6987e...	3.4788e...	2.3570e...	2.5096e...	2.5925e...	7.7316e...	1.1948e...	1.6916e...	1.2713e...	9.6097e...	3.4844e...	3.3071e...	3.5701e...	5.0990e...	1.3080e...	4.1487e...	8.71
5	6.5146e...	5.7301e...	5.5644e...	5.6774e...	5.6182e...	4.5924e...	5.9597e...	5.1393e...	5.4874e...	5.7759e...	4.7080e...	5.3382e...	6.1805e...	3.9142e...	5.4754e...	5.4706e...	5.75
6	0.0167	0.0167	0.0167	9.3244e...	0.0167	9.3822e...	0.0167	0.0167	210.6487	27.1879	0.0167	0.0167	3.4194e...	0.0167	0.0167	0.0167	C
7	-8.2143	-4.5217	-8.7425	-11.5973	-7.9928	-5.3368	-9.8692	-12.2840	-9.1017	-7.1265	-10.2408	-11.9804	-9.9146	-5.9840	-6.1220	-12.2193	-11
8	35.4687	30.9685	39.9170	44.9884	32.3902	36.8329	39.9565	48.7262	36.2083	34.1696	42.8363	48.4994	44.0189	28.8191	33.5999	47.9522	48
9	0.9385	7.5633	9.6921	2.0263	0.5461	7.3513	10.2583	2.5402	1.3023	12.0238	9.5333	8.0412	8.0690	11.5123	9.9436	5.3372	3
10	4.0555	7.9410	7.9943	2.7909	3.9286	8.0429	9.3120	3.1493	4.3677	11.0557	8.0348	5.6745	7.8996	12.4086	7.8465	3.5418	5
11	0.5991	-3.0622	-6.1115	-2.7588	1.1923	-2.6842	-5.5482	-2.7677	1.0567	-5.7526	-5.5383	-6.9566	-4.9102	-2.6318	-7.2190	-6.6333	-C
12	1.3640	3.6191	5.7464	2.2433	2.0382	4.1102	6.0766	2.8001	2.2475	5.5387	6.0936	6.3081	2.7673	5.1395	6.2062	5.1626	1
13	0.8146	-1.8884	-3.5433	0.0277	0.1877	-1.7013	-3.9375	-0.6831	0.2875	-3.0893	-3.2671	-2.4464	-1.5026	-3.6140	-3.0221	-2.5558	-C
14	2.3025	1.8541	0.7995	1.6099	1.6491	2.0077	0.3506	1.4753	1.4524	2.6126	0.8312	0.5310	3.0137	2.3234	0.7903	0.1071	1
15	-0.2604	-0.9226	0.3648	0.2160	0.4354	-0.7279	-1.2284	1.3993	-0.3946	-1.1827	0.4903	1.4040	-0.8870	-1.3564	-0.2731	1.9989	-C
16	1.1550	1.0991	-0.7114	0.4334	0.6830	1.1796	-0.5922	0.3516	0.4711	1.2631	-0.7345	-1.1301	1.0256	1.6266	-0.5682	-1.5726	C
17	0.3141	-0.7082	-0.3629	0.5361	-0.4029	-0.6874	-0.9136	0.3716	-0.3128	-0.5729	-0.2090	0.3183	0.0473	-1.2585	0.0410	0.7623	-C
18	1.0805	0.8015	1.3607	0.6831	0.6812	1.0543	1.3995	0.7439	0.7757	1.5901	1.5627	0.7517	1.4920	1.7237	1.1708	1.3615	C
19	-0.5419	-0.5147	-1.1709	-0.2902	-0.6330	-0.4586	-0.8472	-0.6108	-0.4021	-1.1236	-1.2028	-1.3817	-0.3751	-1.9208	-0.5097	-1.1530	-C
20	0.4008	0.5337	1.1245	0.3748	0.2943	0.8428	1.2845	0.8654	0.5138	0.6290	1.2846	0.7997	0.2154	1.2191	0.9253	1.7034	C

Fig. 52.4 The five features with 16 coefficients for genre classification

⊞ 4x400 double

	1	2	3	4	5	6	7	8	9	10	11	12	13	14	15	16
1	1	0	0	0	1	0	0	0	1	0	0	0	1	0	0	0
2	0	1	0	0	0	1	0	0	0	1	0	0	0	1	0	0
3	0	0	1	0	0	0	1	0	0	0	1	0	0	0	1	0
4	0	0	0	1	0	0	0	1	0	0	0	1	0	0	0	1

Fig. 52.5 Output of the neural network for the first four songs

matrices offer a better glimpse into the performance of the network and insights onto possible improvements. The confusion matrix of the training sequence usually yields the highest performance rate and is normally regarded as the weakest indicator of true classification performance.

Validation and testing confusion matrices are the best indicators of true classification performance with validation performance usually being regarded as the indicator to be maximized when searching for the optimal number of hidden nodes in a network. The confusion matrix is shown in Fig. 52.6 the green squares represent correct classifications, the red squares represent incorrect classifications, and the blue square at the bottom right edge represents the total performance of the model's accuracy. The peak performance of the 10-hidden node neural network is for pop music at 91.7%, followed by metal at 90% (see Fig. 52.6).

52.6 Conclusions and Future Work

Music genre classification was achieved with 90% accuracy. Classification accuracy for pop (91.7%) and metal (90%) was higher while jazz (85%) and classical (89.5%) was lesser due to similarity in features. The adaptability and versatility of neural networks, along with the strong performance of classifying genre based on short music fragments, show a clear potential for the application of neural networks in automatic genre classification of songs. Addition of spectral features may further improve accuracy.

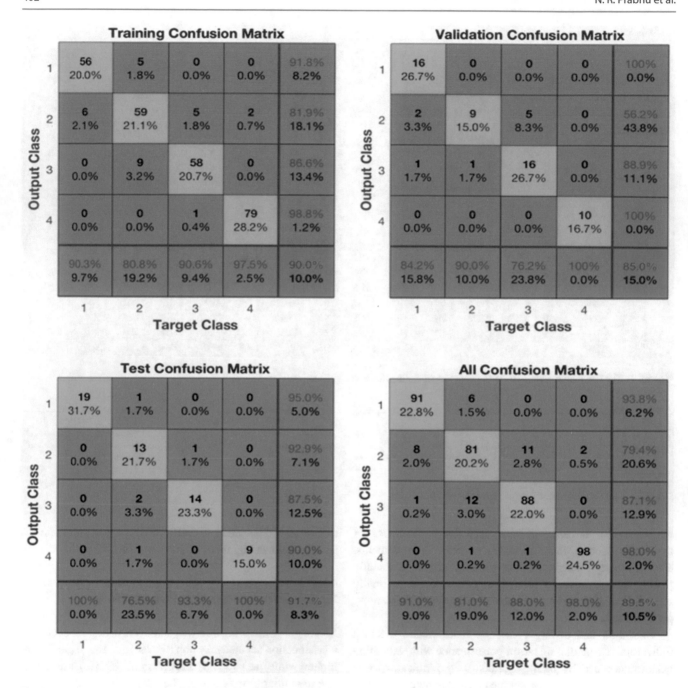

Fig. 52.6 Confusion matrix of the 400 songs (top left is metal, top right is jazz, bottom left is pop, and bottom right is classical)

It will be useful to test our algorithm for another available database provided by the Technical University Dortmund [19].

Acknowledgements Doina Bein acknowledges the support by Air Force Office of Scientific Research under award number FA9550–16–1-0257.

References

1. M.M. Panchwagh, V.D. Katkar, Music genre classification using data mining algorithm, in *2016 Conference on Advances in Signal Processing (CASP)*, Pune, India, 2016
2. S. Haykin, *Neural Networks and Learning Machines* (Pearson Education, Inc., Upper Saddle River, NJ, 2009)

3. M. Copeland, What's the difference between artificial intelligence, machine learning, and deep learning?, https://blogs.nvidia.com/blog/2016/07/29/whats-difference-artificial-intelligence-machine-learning-deep-learning-ai/. Accessed 22 Nov 2017

4. T. Rashid, *Make Your Own Neural Network: A Gentle Journey Through the Mathematics of Neural Networks, and Making Your Own Using the Python Computer Language* (CreateSpace Independent Publishing, San Bernardino, CA, 2016)

5. C.M. Bishop, *Neural Networks for Pattern Recognition* (Clarendon Press, Oxford, 1995)

6. F. Sebastiani, Machine learning in automated text categorization. ACM Comput. Surv. **34**(1), 1–47 (2002)

7. J.J. Hopfield, Neural network and physical systems with collective computational abilities, in *Proceedings of the National Academy of Science*, 1982

8. H. Chen, L. She, Inductive query by examples (IQBE): A machine learning approach, in *27th Annual Hawaii International Conference on System Sciences (HICSS-27)*, Los Alamitos, 1994

9. M. Gordon, Probabilistic and genetic algorithms for document retrieval. Commun. ACM **31**(10), 1208–1218 (1988)

10. M.D. Gordon, User-based document clustering by redescribing subject descriptions with a genetic algorithm. J. Assoc. Inf. Sci. Technol. **42**(5), 311–322 (1991)

11. V.V. Raghavan, B. Agarwal, Optimal determination of user-oriented clusters: An application for the reproductive plan, in *Proceedings of the Second International Conference on Genetic Algorithms on Genetic Algorithms and Their Application*, Cambridge, Massachusetts, USA, 1987

12. F.E. Petry, B.P. Buckles, D. Prabhu, D.H. Kraft, Fuzzy information retrieval using genetic algorithms and relevance feedback, in *Proceedings of the ASIS Annual Meeting*, Medford, NJ, 1993

13. O. Frieder, H.T. Siegelmann, On the allocation of documents in multiprocessor information retrieval systems, in *Proceedings of the Fourteenth Annual International ACM/SIGIR Conference on Research and Development in Information Retrieval*, NY, NY, 1991

14. A.M. Ujlambkar, V.Z. Attar, Automatic mood classification model for Indian popular music, in *Sixth Asia Modeling Symposium*, 2012

15. C. Okuyucu, M. Sert, A. Yazici, Audio feature and classifier analysis for efficient recognition of environmental sounds, in *International Symposium on Multimedia*, 2013

16. G. Vyas, M.K.K. Dutta, Automatic mood detection of Indian music using MFCCs and K-means Algorithm, in *Seventh International Conference on Contemporary Computing (IC3)*, 2014

17. B.K. Baniya, D. Ghimire, J. Lee, A novel approach of automatic music genre classification based on timbral texture and rhythmic content features, in *16th International Conference on Advanced Communication Technology (ICACT)*, 2014

18. B.K. Baniya, J. Lee, Z.-N. Li, Audio feature reduction and analysis for automatic music genre classification, in *International Conference on Systems Man and Cybernetics (SMC)*, 2014

Flávio Arthur O. Santos and Hendrik T. Macedo

Abstract

Recently, the NLP community has focused on finding methods for learning good vectorial word representations. These vectorial representations must be good enough to capture semantic relationships between words using simple vector arithmetic operations. Currently, two methods stand out: GloVe and word2vec. We argue that the proper usage of knowledge bases such as WordNet, Freebase and Paraphrase can improve even further the results of such methods. Although the attempt to incorporate information from knowledge bases in vectorial word representations is not new, results are not compared to that of GloVe nor word2vec. In this paper, we propose a method to incorporate the knowledge of Paraphrase knowledge base into GloVe. Results show that such incorporation improves GloVe's original results for at least three different benchmarks.

Keywords

GloVe · Paraphrase · Knowledge base · Word embeddings · Natural language processing

53.1 Introduction

Deep architectures of Multilayer Perceptron (MLP), Convolutional Neural Network (CNN) and Recurrent Neural Network (RNN) are the state-of-the-art for many NLP tasks, such as automatic translation [22], question & answering [23], named-entity recognition [15], automatic text summarization [19] and sentiment analysis [16]. Most NLP solutions involving Deep Learning use word embeddings, which are vectorial word representations. Word embeddings are vectors of real numbers that represent a word; in this way, each word has its own word embedding. There are three main techniques for learning word embeddings:

1. Context-window based methods;
2. Semantic Relationship based methods;
3. Graph distance based methods.

All three methods have disadvantages in their development. Some of the methods in (1), such as [9] and [17], use only the local context of each word instead of the global context for training. The methods in (2) and (3) use the WordNet [18] and Freebase [3] knowledge bases to learn the word embeddings. The main disadvantage of the methods in (2) is that they use only a subpart of the aforementioned knowledge bases and do not consider the Paraphrase dataset [12], which contains a set of word pairs that are written differently but share the same meaning. Methods in (3) use the Leacock-Chodorow [6] distance in order to capture the semantic information between two words; not considering other distance measures is a limitation.

In this work, we used the Paraphrase knowledge base to enrich our training base of word embeddings and trained them using GloVe [20], which considers the global context of words. The hypothesis to be tested is that such combination improves vectorial word representations.

In Sect. 53.2 we present some related works. In Sect. 53.3 we describe the method used to improve the training base using the Paraphrase knowledge base. Section 53.4 details the experiments and discusses the results. Finally, we conclude the work in Sect. 53.5.

F. A. O. Santos · H. T. Macedo (✉)
Computer Science Postgraduate Program, Federal University of Sergipe, São Cristóvão, Brazil
e-mail: flavio.santos@dcomp.ufs.br; hendrik@dcomp.ufs.br

© Springer International Publishing AG, part of Springer Nature 2018
S. Latifi (ed.), *Information Technology – New Generations*, Advances in Intelligent Systems and Computing 738,
https://doi.org/10.1007/978-3-319-77028-4_53

53.2   Related Work

53.2.1   Context-Window Based Methods

Collobert et al. [9] implemented a *Neural Language Model*
(NLM) where each vocabulary word i is related with a
vector $v_i \in R^n$ of dimension n, the word embedding of i.
A sentence s $= (s_1, s_2, s..., s_l)$ of size l is represented for a
vector x which is equal to concatenate vector of words em-
beddings from sentence s, $x = [v_{s_1} ; v_{s_2} ; \ldots; v_{s_l}]$, $x \in R^{ln}$.
After achieving x, it is propagated through a two layer
neural network to obtain a score assign of how real this
sentence is.

$$Score(x) = u^T(\sigma(Ax + b)) \qquad (53.1)$$

A is an weight matrix such that $A \in R^{h \times ln}$ and $b \in R^h$ is
the bias of first layer. The parameter h indicates how many
units are in the layer f. $u^T \in R^{1 \times h}$ is the weight vector of
output layer. The weight matrix and word embeddings of this
model are trained using *Noise Contrastive Estimation* (NCE)
[13], where, for each training sequence s, we build a noise
sequence s_c. To build s_c we choose a word from s and replace
it for a randomly selected word from vocabulary. Thus, we
have a vector x for s and a vector x_c for s_c. To train a neural
network able to achieve a high score on real sequences, we
minimized the function cost at Eq. (53.2).

$$cost = max(0, 1 - Score(x) + Score(x_c)) \qquad (53.2)$$

The word embeddings and parameters **A**, **b**, and **u** are
trained with backpropagation using Stochastic Gradient Descent (SGD) over a training *corpus*.

Mikolov et al. [17] presents two architectures to learn
word embeddings based on word context window inside an
sentence, the Skip-gram and bag-of-words (CBOW). The
skip-gram goal is: given a sentence s and a central word
c of s, predict the context words of c. The CBOW goal is
predict the central word c based on its context. Given an
word sequence $w_1, w_2, w_3, \cdots, w_T$, the Skip-gram goal is
maximize the E_{sk} function.

$$E_{sk} = \frac{1}{T} \sum_{t=1}^{T} \sum_{-c \leq j \geq c, j \neq 0} \log p(w_{t+j}|w_t), \qquad (53.3)$$

where c is the context window size used. The most simple
Skip-gram formula define $p(w_{t+j}|w_t)$ as:

$$p(w_{t+j}|w_t) = \frac{\exp(v'_{w_{t+1}}{}^T v_{w_t})}{\sum_{n=1}^{N} \exp(v'_{w_n}{}^T v_{w_t})} \qquad (53.4)$$

53.2.2   Semantic Relationship Based Methods

There are knowledge bases that present semantic information
about words, such as Freebase [3], WordNet [18], Dbpedia
[2], NELL [7]. Often, knowledge is represented by $t = (w_i, r, w_j)$, where r indicate an semantic relationship between words w_i e w_j. Some models, e.g. TransE [4], Neural
Tensor Network [21], try to learn word representations from
this semantic information: tuple t as input and the output is a
score indicating how real is the relationship r between words
w_i e w_j.

53.2.3   Graph Distance-Based Methods

Fried and Duh [11] proposes the *Graph Distance* (GD)
model. The goal of GD is to train the words embeddings
such that its similarity is equal to LCH distance between the
respective words in WordNet database. Its objective function
is:

$$L_{GD}(v_i, v_j) = (\frac{v_i v_j}{||v_i||^2 ||v_j||^2} - [a \times LCH(w_i, w_j) + b])^2, \qquad (53.5)$$

where v_i and v_j are word embeddings of w_i e w_j words,
respectively. The GD uses the parameters **a** and **b** to put the
LCH distance in the same scale as cosine similarity between
v_i e v_j

53.3   Model

Paraphrase is the task of rewrite an sentence p using different
words, but keeping the meaning of p. Word level Paraphrase
is when we rewrite an word w with different characters
but keep the w word meaning. Ganitkevitch et al. [12]
presents an database for Paraphrase (PPDB). This database
has around 73 million paraphrases at sentence level and 8
million paraphrases at word level. The PPDB is divided into
six sizes: S, M, L, XL, XXL, XXXL, in crescent order.
The subpart S, minor part, has a higher precision score.
In this work, we selected the PPDB subpart S and used
its 473 thousand word level paraphrases. We implemented
the *getparaphrase(word = w)* method which uses S; it
randomly selects one paraphrase of the word w.

In this work, we used the GloVe [20] model to train the
word embeddings. It is a context window based method. It
uses the word global context of training corpus. Over its
training, GloVe uses an word-to-word co-occurrence matrix
X, where X_{ij} indicates how many times the word j is
presented in word i context within the training corpus.

$$X_i = \sum_k X_{ik} \qquad (53.6)$$

After building the matrix X, the GloVe's goal is to minimize J loss function:

$$J = \sum_{i,j=1}^{V} f(X_{ij})(w_i^T \tilde{w}_j + b_i + \tilde{b}_j - log(X_{ij}))^2, \quad (53.7)$$

where V is the vocabulary size, w_i is the word embedding of central word i and $\tilde{w}_j$ is the word embedding of the context word j. Thus, we have two word embedding matrices, W and $\tilde{W}$. Equation (53.8) defines f(x) function.

$$f(x) = \begin{cases} (x/x_{max})^\alpha, & \text{if } x < x_{max} \\ 1, & \text{otherwise} \end{cases} \qquad (53.8)$$

At GloVe original work, the authors use $\alpha = 3/4$ and $x_{max} = 100$ to train the word embeddings and perform the experiments.

```
input : matrix X, int V
for i ← 1 to V do
    p = getparaphrase(i);
    for j ← 1 to V do
        if Xij == 0 and Xpj! = 0 then
            | Xij := Xpj
        end
    end
end
```
Algorithm 1: Algorithm used to enhance the X matrix

We use Algorithm 1 to enhance our X co-occurrence matrix and perform the GloVe's training. For each vocabulary word v, it randomly selects an paraphrase x and uses its context to fill the empty slots of v. In other words, it appends more information in our X matrix. This idea is valid because the words x and v have the same meaning, so the word v can be placed at the contexts of the word x.

53.4 Experiments

53.4.1 Evaluation Methods

We use three different benchmarks to evaluate the word embedding: (1) SimLex999 [14], (2) MEN [5] and (3) WordSimilarity-353 (WS353) [1]. They all measure the semantic similarity between two words. Each dataset has a set of tuples $t = (word1, word2)$, where each tuple has a score indicating how word1 and word2 are semantically

related. This score is defined by arithmetic mean of a score set defined by humans.

The great difference between the SimLex999 and the other two, is that it explicitly evaluates the semantic similarity between two words, whereas the MEN and WS353 also consider the relatedness between two words. For instance, the tuple (Freud, Psychology) has a low score in SimLex999 but has a high score in MEN and WS, since the name Freud has a high relation with psychology.

For each dataset, we compute the cosine similarity between the word embeddings of word1 and word2 of its tuple $t = (word1, word2)$, so we have the semantic similarity of its word embeddings. In the end, we calculate the Spearman correlation between word embeddings semantic similarity and humans semantic similarity to obtain how good is our word embeddings on that dataset.

53.4.2 Corpora and Training Details

To perform the experiment, we use the 1 Billion Word Language Model Benchmark [8] corpus. This corpus has approximately 1 billion tokens. We tokenize and lowercase every word in the corpus using the Stanford tokenizer. We build a vocabulary with the most 100 thousand frequent words and produce the X co-occurrence matrix. To build the X matrix, we use an context window of size 10.

For every experiment, we use a $x_{max} = 100, \alpha = 0.75$ and train the GloVe model using Adagrad [10] and stochastically select elements with values different of zero from X. The initial learning rate was 0.05. We execute 100 training iterations of each word embedding for every experiment. In this work, we use $W + \tilde{W}$ as our final word embedding matrix. We use the GloVe original implementation to train our word embeddings and keep its default settings.

53.4.3 Results

In Table 53.1 we present the best achieved accuracy values. It can be observed that using the Paraphrase dataset to improve GloVe's co-occurrence matrix X presents an improvement in every scenario. Another important aspect to be noted is the word embeddings' dimension: experiments with bigger word embeddings also present better results.

Table 53.1 Best results for each model

Model	Size	SimLex999	WS353	MEN
GloVe	100	21.85	25.95	44.00
GloVe-P	100	21.89	27.75	44.85
GloVe	200	22.74	27.60	46.87
GloVe-P	200	23.66	27.93	47.92

P paraphrase

Fig. 53.2 SimLex999 results

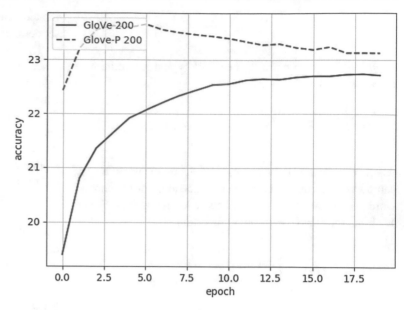

Fig. 53.3 MEN results

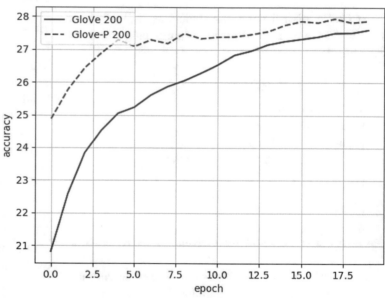

Figures 53.2, 53.3, and 53.4 present the accuracy evolution for Glove 200 and Glove-P 200 on the following benchmarks: SimLex999, MEN, and WS353, respectively. Aside from the fact that Glove-P 200 presents better results in every epoch and every evaluation, it is clear that during the first epochs, Glove-P shows a better improvement when compared to Glove 200. This is important due to the fact that high computational power is not always available to enable long-run training sessions.

53.5 Conclusion

Vectorial word representations are important for obtaining good results in NLP tasks using machine learning algorithms. Recently, some works have tried to incorporate information from knowledge bases in order to improve the learning of word embeddings. However, these works have not tried to achieve the state-of-the-art results in their methods. Also, they usually limit their experiments with the use of self-tailored datasets.

In this work, we have proposed a modification on the GloVe method, the state-of-the-art in word representation benchmarks. In particular, we presented a method to incorporate the knowledge of the Paraphrase dataset into GloVe's co-occurrence matrix. We have used an universal dataset to train the word embeddings and results have shown improved word embeddings if compared to GloVe" original approach.

As future work, we intend to come up with a method to incorporate similar knowledge into other relevant learning methods such as word2vec.

Fig. 53.4 WS353 results

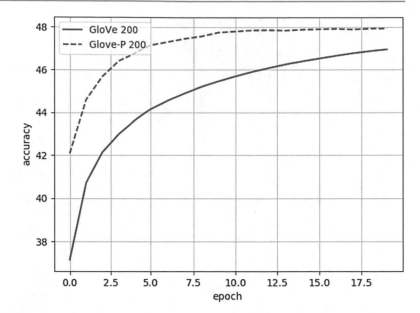

Acknowledgements The authors thank CAPES and FAPITEC-SE for the financial support [Edital CAPES/FAPITEC/SE No 11/2016 - PROEF, Processo 88887.160994/2017-00] and LCAD-UFS for providing a cluster for the execution of the experiments. The authors also thank FAPITEC-SE for granting a graduate scholarship to Flávio Santos, CNPq for granting an productivity scholarship to Hendrik Macedo [DT-II, Processo 310446/2014-7].

References

1. E. Agirre, E. Alfonseca, K. Hall, J. Kravalova, M. Paşca, A. Soroa, A study on similarity and relatedness using distributional and wordnet-based approaches, in *Proceedings of Human Language Technologies: The 2009 Annual Conference of the North American Chapter of the Association for Computational Linguistics*. Association for Computational Linguistics (2009), pp. 19–27

2. S. Auer, C. Bizer, G. Kobilarov, J. Lehmann, R. Cyganiak, Z. Ives, DBpedia: a nucleus for a web of open data, in *The semantic web* (Springer, Berlin, 2007), pp. 722–735

3. K. Bollacker, C. Evans, P. Paritosh, T. Sturge, J. Taylor, Freebase: a collaboratively created graph database for structuring human knowledge, in *Proceedings of the 2008 ACM SIGMOD International Conference on Management of Data* (ACM, New York, 2008), pp. 1247–1250

4. A. Bordes, N. Usunier, A. Garcia-Duran, J. Weston, O. Yakhnenko, Translating embeddings for modeling multi-relational data, in *Advances in Neural Information Processing Systems* (2013), pp. 2787–2795

5. E. Bruni, N.-K. Tran, M. Baroni, Multimodal distributional semantics. J. Artif. Intell. Res. **49**(2014), 1–47 (2014)

6. A. Budanitsky, G. Hirst, Semantic distance in wordnet: an experimental, application-oriented evaluation of five measures, in *Workshop on WordNet and Other Lexical Resources*, vol. 2 (2001), p. 2

7. A. Carlson, J. Betteridge, B. Kisiel, B. Settles, E.R. Hruschka Jr., T.M. Mitchell, Toward an architecture for never-ending language learning, in *AAAI*, vol. 5 (2010), p. 3

8. C. Chelba, T. Mikolov, M. Schuster, Q. Ge, T. Brants, P. Koehn, T. Robinson, One billion word benchmark for measuring progress in statistical language modeling (2013, preprint). arXiv:1312.3005

9. R. Collobert, J. Weston, L. Bottou, M. Karlen, K. Kavukcuoglu, P. Kuksa, Natural language processing (almost) from scratch. J. Mach. Learn. Res. **12**, 2493–2537 (2011)

10. J. Duchi, E. Hazan, Y. Singer, Adaptive subgradient methods for online learning and stochastic optimization. J. Mach. Learn. Res. **12**, 2121–2159 (2011)

11. D. Fried, K. Duh, Incorporating both distributional and relational semantics in word representations (2014, preprint). arXiv:1412.4369

12. J. Ganitkevitch, B. Van Durme, C. Callison-Burch, PPDB: the paraphrase database, in *Proceedings of NAACL-HLT*, Atlanta, GA, Association for Computational Linguistics (2013), pp. 758–764

13. M. Gutmann, A. Hyvärinen, Noise-contrastive estimation: a new estimation principle for unnormalized statistical models, in *Proceedings of the Thirteenth International Conference on Artificial Intelligence and Statistics* (2010), pp. 297–304

14. F. Hill, R. Reichart, A. Korhonen, Simlex-999: evaluating semantic models with (genuine) similarity estimation. Comput. Linguist. **41**, 665–695 (2016)

15. C. AEM Júnior, L.A. Barbosa, H.T. Macedo, S.E. Súo Cristóvão, Uma arquitetura híbrida lstm-cnn para reconhecimento de entidades nomeadas em textos naturais em língua portuguesa (2016)

16. H. Lakkaraju, R. Socher, C. Manning, Aspect specific sentiment analysis using hierarchical deep learning, in *NIPS Workshop on Deep Learning and Representation Learning* (2014)

17. T. Mikolov, I. Sutskever, K. Chen, G.S. Corrado, J. Dean, Distributed representations of words and phrases and their compositionality, in *Advances in Neural Information Processing Systems* (2013), pp. 3111–3119

18. G.A. Miller, Wordnet: a lexical database for english. Commun. ACM **38**(11): 39–41 (1995)

19. R. Paulus, C. Xiong, R. Socher, A deep reinforced model for abstractive summarization (2017, preprint). arXiv:1705.04304

20. J. Pennington, R. Socher, C.D. Manning, Glove: global vectors for word representation, in *EMNLP*, vol. 14 (2014), pp. 1532–1543

21. R. Socher, D. Chen, C.D. Manning, A. Ng, Reasoning with neural tensor networks for knowledge base completion, in *Advances in Neural Information Processing Systems* (2013), pp. 926–934

22. Y. Wu, M. Schuster, Z. Chen, Q.V. Le, M. Norouzi, W. Macherey, M. Krikun, Y. Cao, Q. Gao, K. Macherey, et al., Google's neural machine translation system: bridging the gap between human and machine translation (2016, preprint). arXiv:1609.08144

23. C. Xiong, V. Zhong, R. Socher, Dynamic coattention networks for question answering (2016, preprint). arXiv:1611.01604

A Initial Experimental Evaluation of the NeuroMessenger: A Collaborative Tool to Improve the Empathy of Text Interactions

Breno Santana Santos, Methanias Colaço Júnior, and Janisson Gois de Souza

Abstract

Empathy plays an important role in social interactions, such an effective teaching-learning process in a teacher-student relationship, and company-client or employee-customer relationship to retain potential clients and provide them with greater satisfaction. Increasingly, the Computer-Mediated Communication (CMC) support people in their interactions, especially when the interlocutors are geographically distant from one another. In CMC, there are different approaches to promote empathy in social or human-computer interactions. However, a little explored approach to gaining empathy in CMC is the use of the theory of Neurolinguistics that presents the possibility of developing a Preferred Representation System (PRS) for cognition in humans. This paper presents an initial experimental evaluation of the NeuroMessenger, a collaborative messenger library that uses the theory of Neurolinguistics to promote empathy by PRS identification and suggestion of textual matching based on the given PRS, using psychometry and text mining. The results showed that there was a difference between the means of grades in the empathy evaluation, in favor of NeuroMessenger. Although it is initial study, the results are encouraging, and more research on textual matching to gain empathy is needed.

Keywords

Text mining · Empathy · Rapport · Experimental evaluation · Collaborative systems

B. S. Santos (✉) · M. Colaço Júnior
Postgraduate Program in Computer Science (PROCC), Federal University of Sergipe (UFS), São Cristóvão, Sergipe, Brazil

J. G. de Souza
Competitive Intelligence Research and Practice Group (NUPIC), Federal University of Sergipe (UFS), Itabaiana, Sergipe, Brazil

54.1 Introduction

In a highly connected society, Computer-Mediated Communication (CMC) has become increasingly essential [1–4]. Various forms of interactions, such as audio, video and text, circumvent the barriers of distance between the interlocutors and allow activities in groups, without necessarily being in the same physical space [4–7].

In the context of Collaborative Systems, CMC tools are resources that allow greater interaction between individuals, thus contributing to the development of relationships and integration. In distance education systems, for example, these tools can contribute significantly to student retention [8–10].

One of the most commonly used CMC interaction types in Collaborative Systems is textual one. In this type of interaction, the resources of face-to-face communication, such as gestures and facial expression, are non-existent. However, individuals often use computer and hypermedia resources to create differentiated language codes, which demarcate their social presences [8, 11, 12] in the group and promote perception of the intentions of the interlocutors. Many researches have focused on perfecting this form of interaction, analyzing how an individual can establish a favorable social image to attract and hold attention to oneself, including using only the language itself [2, 13, 14]. In this line, an interesting perspective is the use of the language to increase the empathy of these interactions, promoting a well-being between the participants of the group.

According to previous studies [15], a little explored approach to gaining empathy in virtual environments is the use of the theory of Neurolinguistics that presents the possibility of developing a Preferred Representation System (PRS) for cognition in humans [16–18]. An PRS is the most commonly used representational system in a situation. For example, if the individual, at a given moment, uses more of the thought representation through images and diagrams, his current PRS, in the context in question, is the visual.

This is a widely discussed issue in the field of Psychology: different people, in different contexts, may have different representational preferences. In fact, this area accepts well these different forms of representation for cognition [19–21]. Internal mental processes, such as problem solving, memory usage, and language, are formed by visual representations (images and diagrams), auditory (sounds), and kinesthetic (physical and practical experiences). These are triggered when people think or engage in activities and daily tasks. Whether it is in a conversation, writing on a specific topic or reading a book, internal sensory representations are constantly formed and activated, directly impacting a person's performance in executing these activities.

The performance of people in the process of representation, cognition and communication is one of the main success factors in collaborative activities, which are influenced by the personality characteristics of each person [5, 7, 8, 14]. Thus, detecting representational preferences of interlocutors can increase empathy in their interactions. Empathy is a fundamental mutual understanding for the creation of affective bonds, be it with or without emotional contagion, as well as is essential for social interactions [22–24].

According to Psychology and Neurolinguistics, one of the ways to improve communication is to identify the Representational System (RS) that is most used by the individual and, through a process called matching, predominantly use the same system to construct empathy [16, 17, 25]. Matching consists of identifying the words that indicate a Representational System and using words from the same system for better communication with its interlocutor.

To evaluate the use of textual matching for gain of empathy, a collaborative messenger library, NeuroMessenger, was developed to identify the PRS of the interlocutors from their messages, as well as to recommend words belonging to this PRS in order to promote the empathy gain between those involved. The tool was used in an experiment with academic students of the Federal University of Sergipe (UFS). The results indicated that there was a difference between the means of grades in the empathy evaluation, in favor of NeuroMessenger, in other words, the use of the same text pattern (PRS) between interlocutors increases the empathy between them.

The rest of this paper is organized as follows. The next section introduces Neurolinguistics. Section 54.3 presents concepts related to empathy and its types. Section 54.4 describes our collaborative messenger library. In the Sect. 54.5, we detail the experimental evaluation of our approach. Section 54.6 discusses our results. In the Sect. 54.7, we detailed the threats to validity of our study. Section 54.8 describes related works. Finally, in the Sect. 54.9, we presented the conclusions and discussion of future work.

54.2 Neuro-Linguistic Programming

Neuro-linguistics (NLP) was developed by Richard Bandler and John Grinder. Bandler, whose experience was in mathematics and gestalt, developed a collaboration with John Grinder, a professor of linguistics, during his studies at the University of Santa Cruz [16, 17]. From this collaboration, his studies showed that people, in specific contexts, may prefer to communicate and/or learn in one of the basic systems of representation or through a combination of them.

The conception that there are different forms of representation for cognition, has already been accepted for a long time in the area of Psychology [19–21]. These representation systems are named according to the type of processing performed, receiving the following classification: (1) Visual, which involves the creation of internal images and the use of visions or observations of things, including photos, diagrams, demonstrations, expositions, leaflets, etc.; (2) Auditory, which involves memories of sounds and transfer of information through listening; and (3) Kinesthetic, which involves the internal sensations of touch, emotions, physical experiences, the execution to understand and the practice.

Because we use all three systems all the time, it is not possible to label a person as one type or another. In fact, what may occur is the predominance of one of them, being labeled PRS. Moreover, this predominance can be changeable depending on the emotional state and the environment in which the person is.

In addition to the use of a PRS, in specific contexts, NLP argues that people say words and phrases, also called verbal clues or sensory predicates, that indicate visual, auditory or kinesthetic processing [16–18, 25]. In other words, the phrases a person chooses to describe a situation may be specific to a sensory-based representational system and indicate how that person's consciousness is at that moment. The predicates indicate what portion of the internal representations the person has brought from consciousness. These clues can guide empathic and efficient communication or simply go unnoticed. In the next section, we will discuss the concept of empathy used in this paper.

54.3 Empathy in Social Interactions

Empathy can be understood as the ability to understand and express a deep understanding of another person's perspective and feelings, as well as experiencing feelings of compassion and concern for the other's well-being [22]. Although it is commonly known as "putting itself in the place of the other", empathy has been described as an uncertain and elusive concept with a long history marked by ambiguity and controversy [23, 24, 26]. Therefore, there is no precise and consensual definition of empathy. However, there are several discussions about empathy, in some cases described as a cognitive attribute characterized by the understanding of the internal experiences of others, and in others described as an emotional state allowing the sharing of emotions [22, 26, 27].

Therefore, its multidimensional perspectives are perceived, being classified in two types: cognitive and affective. Cognitive empathy refers to the taking of perspective, self-awareness, recognition and understanding of other people's mental states, without making it their own situation, i.e., without emotional contagion. Already affective empathy is considered an emotional response to another person by sharing their emotions, in other words, emotional contagion [22, 26, 27].

For both dimensions, empathy plays a key role for social interactions. According to Rodrigues and Ribeiro [24], empathy represents an important resource for a healthy and rewarding social interaction, as well as people who practice it are perceived as sensitive, warm and friendly, producing more positive results in relation to other interlocutors. Goleman [28] states that it is present in many aspects of life, in business practices, in administration, in courtship and paternity, in the doctor-patient relationship, in the teaching-learning process, in being pious and in political action.

According to Neurolinguistics, each of us has a very individual mental map (internal representation of thoughts and experiences) of our world, and to make communication easier is necessary to understand the internal reality or the map of the person with whom we are communicating [16, 17, 25]. One way to understand that map is to identify the PRS and, through a matching process, to use the same PRS for generating empathy. As previously seen, matching consists of identifying the sensory words that indicate a PRS and using predicates of the same PRS for a more harmonious interaction with its interlocutor [16, 17, 25].

Thus, our approach has automated matching to promote empathy in Collaborative Systems, but the evaluation was only of the cognitive empathy. Although the matching process may also suggest words that indicate affection, affective empathy depends on the emotional involvement of the interlocutor, making it difficult to propose this type of evaluation. However, it is worth emphasizing that in a textual interaction, the use of words may seem an emotional involvement, which can also be beneficial to empathy.

54.4 NeuroMessenger

As previously mentioned, in order to evaluate the viability of textual matching for gain of empathy, we developed a collaborative messenger library, NeuroMessenger, which allows the identification of the PRS of an interlocutor, from their messages, as well as recommends terms belonging to the obtained PRS, besides the possibility to recommend emojis previously used.

The process of identifying PRS occurs in two ways: (1) if the beginning of a new conversation or the sending of the last message of an interlocutor is more than 4 h, a general PRS is determined, based on the messages of all the conversations of this interlocutor; and (2) during an interaction, for each new message of the interlocutor (on moment), its PRS is specified, which it is based only on that message. It is noteworthy that during this process, it is possible to find more than one RS used, because a person is said to be multimodal when he/she expresses a thought by more than one RS [29, 30]. Thus, for more than one RS obtained, the preferred sequence (strategy) of using RSs for this individual is captured, the same approach adopted by Colaço Júnior [30].

Once with the determined PRS, NeuroMessenger presents recommendations for terms that can aid in the matching process. The suggestion of response follows the following restrictions: (1) only the emoji contained in the last message of the interlocutor are suggested; (2) for each captured RS, three sensory words are provided; and (3) the suggested terms are presented according to the strategy identified.

In order to support in the above mentioned tasks, firstly, the kernel of a text analysis tool based on Neurolinguistics, Neurominer, was improved in order to perform the processing of any textual information, including emojis [31, 32].

Neurominer uses Text Mining and Psychometry techniques to identify and classify PRSs of individuals based on loaded texts [31, 32]. This classification process is based on the counting of words contained in a LIWC (Linguistic Inquiry and Word Count) dictionary, which contains the psychological characteristics (in our context, neurolinguistic profile) of each term contained in it [33, 34].

Once with the improved Neurominer's kernel, as previously mentioned, NeuroMessenger was developed to evaluate the viability of textual matching for empathy gain through a controlled experiment (see next section).

54.5 Experiment

This section describes an experimental evaluation of our approach. The presented experimental process follows the guidelines by Wohlin et al. [35]. This section will focus on the experiment definition and planning. The following section present the obtained experimental results.

54.5.1 Goal Definition

The main goal of our study is to investigate the possibility of increase of empathy, using psychometry and Neurolinguistics in textual interactions via collaborative systems. This goal is formalized using the GQM Goal template proposed by Basili and Weiss [36] and presented by Solingen and Berghout [37]: **Analyze** the use of a psychometric analysis tool based on Neurolinguistics theory **with the purpose of** evaluation **with respect to** increased empathy **from the point of view of** project and marketing managers and users of collaborative systems and/or call center **in the context of** academic students of the Federal University of Sergipe (UFS).

54.5.2 Planning

This subsection details all experimental design.

54.5.2.1 Context Selection
The experiment will target academic students of the Itabaiana campus of the UFS.

54.5.2.2 Hypothesis Formulation
The issue we are trying to explorer is as follows: The use of the same text pattern (PRS) that your interlocutor, suggested by NeuroMessenger, in conversations via collaborative systems, increases empathy?

In order to evaluate this question, the mean of grades of the messages collected from an empathy evaluation questionnaire will be used.

For this issue, formally, the hypothesis that we are trying to confirm is:

Null hypothesis H_0: Textual messages that use the PRSs of the interlocutors obtain the same mean of the grades of the common messages in the empathy evaluation.
H_0: μ(Messages using PRS) = μ(Common Messages).
Alternative hypothesis H_1: Textual messages that use the PRSs of the interlocutors obtain the higher mean of the grades than the common messages in the empathy evaluation.
H_1: μ(Messages using PRS) > μ(Common Messages).

Note that H_0 is the hypothesis that we want to refute. Thus, to investigate which of the hypothesis are refuted, the following dependent, independent and intervening variables will be considered:

(a) *Independent variables*: NeuroMessenger tool and initial subject to conversation (see Instrumentation subsection).
(b) *Dependent variables*: PRS and mean of the grades of the messages collected from the questionnaire of empathy evaluation (see Instrumentation subsection).
(c) *Intervening variables*: Politeness, response time and "masked" behavior of the participants, i.e., the people pretend to be polite.

Table 54.1 Participants characterization

| Course | Information | | |
| | Quantity per gender | | |
	Man	Woman	Age group
Information systems	5	5	21–25
Biological sciences	1	2	19–21
Geography	1	0	22
Physics	1	0	19
Chemistry	2	2	19–21
Math	0	1	28

54.5.2.3 Participant and Artifact Selection
After the definition of the hypotheses and variables to be analyzed, the process of selecting participants and objects was started. Firstly, for convenience, it was determined that the Itabaiana campus would represent the population of this study, as well as the sample of individuals of this population would be chosen at random. Thus, a formal request was made to each department, inviting its students to voluntarily participate in such an experimental evaluation. Of the 2345 undergraduate students with active enrollment, according to the Integrated Academic Activities Management System (SIGAA) [38], only 20 showed interest in participating in the study, which were characterized according to the information presented in Table 54.1.

For legal reasons, we will not use the names of the participants in this work. Letters will be used to identify each individual.

54.5.2.4 Experimental Design
Based on the experimental designs of the studies of Bailenson and Yee [39], Hasler et al. [40], and Kummer et al. [41], the experiment was designed in a paired context, in which a group will evaluate both approaches: interaction without and with matching.

Firstly, the participants will be divided equally and classified as *Mediators*, who will use the two treatments (interaction without and with the use of matching), or as *Listeners Participants*, who will only interact without even knowing about the application of the intervention (the use of NeuroMessenger to matching).

The classification of the participants will use the following criteria: (1) the participants with the highest degree of affinity with the IT area will be the mediators, while those with less affinity will be allocated as listeners; and (2), if there is a homogeneity in relation to the criterion adopted, the distribution will be random.

Each class will be randomly divided into two subgroups, with the same number of members: S_1 and S_2, for the mediators; S_3 and S_4 for the listeners. Then, the paired groups will be defined, also randomly, that is, by raffle, where each will be composed of a subgroup of each class, for example, a group formed by S_1 and S_3 and another by S_2 and S_4. Thus, at the first moment, half of the listeners will interact with mediators who will use NeuroMessenger and the other half with mediators who will not use. In the second moment, the situation is inverted and paired for the listeners, with only these changing groups. It is worth emphasizing that, in the second moment, the subject will also be changed, to mitigate the learning.

The initial subjects were also determined to facilitate interaction among those involved (see subsection Instrumentation), because both subjects belong to their context.

Each moment will last for 1 h each and a 20-min break between them. It is worth mentioning that, in both moments, the pairs (mediator and listener), within the new groups formed with the inversion of the listeners, will be generated in a random way. In addition, participants will be allowed to interact only with their respective partners, as well as only with the use of the instant text messaging application, with or without use of NeuroMessenger.

54.5.2.5 Instrumentation

The instrumentation process will be done initially with the configuration of the environment for the experiment and planning of data collection. This will be held in a computer lab at the Itabaiana campus of the UFS.

Here are the resources to use.

(a) *NeuroMessenger tool:* It was shown in the Sect. 54.4.
(b) *Questionnaire of empathy evaluation:* Questionnaires have been a mechanism of data collection commonly used in studies that analyze empathy formation among individuals, as observed in the works of Bailenson and Yee [39], Hasler et al. [40], Tan et al. [42], Hojat [26] and Paro et al. [43]. Based on these studies, our questionnaire was designed to evaluate the increase of cognitive empathy among interlocutors. Some points were analyzed, such as understanding of the interlocutor's perspective, level of cohesiveness between partners, level of harmony of the interaction, how pleasant was the interlocutor during the interaction, among others.
(c) *Initial subject to conversation:* As previously mentioned, in order to facilite the interaction between the participants, two initial topics of conversation were determined, which are: "Report about the course" and "Report of experience in the discipline considered more difficult". It is noteworthy that, similarly to the studies of Bailenson and Yee [39] and Hasler et al. [40], such topics are part of the context of the participants, i.e., common themes of their conviviality and knowledge.

54.5.3 Operation

This subsection describes the experiment execution process.

54.5.3.1 Preparation

The following steps of preparation for the execution of the experiment were carried out.

(a) *Reception of the participants:* The volunteers were welcomed, as well as we presented what would be the experiment and its main objective, not explaining that it was an evaluation of empathy. In addition, they full filled the characterization and consent forms, which also not explaining that the experiment was an evaluation of empathy.
(b) *Training of the NeuroMessenger tool:* For ease of use, at different times before the experiment, a 30-min training with participants was conducted by a person not involved in the experiment, so that they could become familiar with the tool, as well as only the mediators received training related to textual matching.
(c) *Generation of interlocutors pairs and choice of the initial topic of conversation:* The pairs of interlocutors were formed as specified in the experimental design (see Experimental Design subsection), as well as the initial subjects for both moments were randomly selected, with theme "Report about the course" for the first and theme "Report of experience in the discipline considered more difficult" for the second.

In addition, the computers of the laboratory were prepared with the NeuroMessenger tool for the experiment.

54.5.3.2 Execution

After carrying out the previous steps, the experiment was started according to the design presented above.

(a) *Data Collection:* At the end of each moment, the listeners answered the questionnaire to assess the level of empathy of their partners (mediators). In addition, the exchanged messages between the interlocutors were stored in a database, in order to verify the occurrence of matching between their PRSs and emojis.

The result of these collected data will be presented in next section of this paper.

54.5.3.3 Data Validation

For the experiment, it was considered a factor, approach used to answer textual messages, and two treatments, without and with the use of textual matching. In this context, for both approaches, the grades of the interactions were collected from the questionnaire of empathy evaluation.

For the support in the analysis, interpretation and validation, two kind of statistic tests were used, Shapiro-Wilk test and t-test. The Shapiro-Wilk test were used to verify normality of the sample [35]. While t-test were used to compare the means of two paired groups [35]. In addition, all statistic tests were made from IBM SPSS tool [44]. We also performed a content analysis of the messages of the interlocutors who used the recommendation feature to validate the textual matching process.

54.6 Results and Discussion

In order to answer the research question, the following dependent variables were analyzed: PRS/strategy and mean of grades of the interactions collected from the empathy evaluation questionnaires.

Firstly, a content analysis was performed to validate the occurrence of matching in the conversations, in which the mediators used the feature of textual matching. The result of this analysis is presented in Table 54.2, where "Suggestions Provided" is the number of matching suggestions provided by NeuroMessenger; "Counter-Matching" is the number of situations in which the PRS or strategy were different for the interlocutors; "Matching" is the number of situations in which the mediator has effectively used the provided suggestion and; "Percentage of Use" is the percentage of use of matching recommendations.

According to Table 54.2, most of the participants used the textual matching recommendations, especially the interlocutors A, B, E, G and H, where the matching percentage was

Table 54.2 Results of the content analysis

| Participant | Numbers | | | |
	Suggestions provided	Counter-matching	Matching	Percentage of use (%)
A	24	5	17	70.83
B	25	3	14	56
C	12	2	2	16.67
D	44	5	21	47.73
E	29	4	15	51.72
F	21	3	9	42.86
G	12	0	6	50
H	10	0	8	80
I	20	3	9	45
J	21	3	10	47.62
Mean				50.84
Standard deviation				16.88

Table 54.3 Mediators' scores in the empathy evaluation

| Participant | Scores | | |
| | Non-matching | Matching | |
		Before	After
A	66	56	56
B	67	58	58
C	56	45	63
D	62	68	68
E	59	68	68
F	64	66	66
G	68	63	63
H	59	58	63
I	54	68	68
J	66	59	59
Mean	62.10	60.90	63.20

greater than or equal to 50% of the amount of suggestions provided by NeuroMessenger. On the other hand, user C had the lowest matching percentage (16.67%).

After the content analysis, the process of detection and treatment of outliers was carried out, in order to reduce its impact on the data set [45], as well as the score of each mediator was computed through the sum of its grades in the evaluation of empathy, for both treatments: with and without matching. The result can be seen in Table 54.3, where "Non-Matching" is general score for condition that the matching feature was not used; "Matching – Before" is general score for the use of textual matching before the treatment of the outliers and; "Matching – After" is general score for the use of the matching feature after the treatment of the outliers.

From the percentages of use, we determined the mean (50.84%) and the standard deviation (16.88%). With these values, we calculated the IQR (15.24%), upper (73.71%) and lower (27.98%) limits, and, based on them, we identified that the users C and H are outliers. Thus, for the use of the matching feature, the scores of the interlocutors C (45) and H (58) will be replaced by the score of the participant that has the percentage of use closest to the mean of that criterion [46]. Therefore, the score of user G (63) will replace the scores of the C and H interlocutors (see Table 54.3).

According to Table 54.3, for the matching feature, the mean of the scores was 63.20, while, without the use of the intervention, it was 62.10. These results suggest that the textual messages that use the PRSs of the interlocutors have a mean higher than the common messages in the evaluation of empathy. From this analysis, it is assumed that the answer to our research question would be "yes", which using the same text pattern suggested by NeuroMessenger may increase empathy between individuals. However, it is not possible to state without sufficiently conclusive statistical evidence.

Thus, we first defined a level of significance of 0.05 throughout the experiment and the Shapiro-Wilk test was applied for analysis of the normal distribution. For both treatments, with and without matching, the values of the variable Sig. (p-value) were, respectively, 0.198 and 0.391. As both values are greater than the level of significance adopted ($p > 0.05$), it is assumed that the data distribution is normal.

Due to the normality of the data, the hypothesis test applied in this context will be the t-test. From this, in the evaluation of empathy, it was verified that there was no statistically significant difference between the means of the grades of the messages that used the same text pattern and the ones of the common messages, because the Sig. obtained (p-value) of 0.686 is higher than the level of significance adopted. However, there was a difference between the means (1.100) in favor of NeuroMessenger, which is demonstrated by the positive value of the t statistic (0.417). It was also observed a moderate negative correlation between the empathy evaluation scores, with and without the use of matching, confirmed by the negative value of the Pearson Correlation ($r = -0.612$). This demonstrates that, for an empathy evaluation, as grades using matching increase, the grades without such a resource decrease.

Therefore, the null hypothesis (H_0) was not rejected, but, in front of the results, more research is needed on the use of textual matching to gain empathy among interlocutors.

54.7 Threats to Validity

The threats to validity for the present study were:

- **Construct validity:** For this type of threat, there are the choice of subject for conversation and training of tool. The first is related with the possibility of choosing of an unpleasant or unfamiliar subject to the interlocutors. In order to mitigate this threat, we choose subjects that are theoretically pleasant and familiar to the participants. Finally, the latter can be caused by inappropriate training about the use of matching suggestions. In order to mitigate this, before the experiment, a researcher who is not involved in the study conducted a training to the mediators in order to instruct them to use effectively the tool and matching suggestions.
- **Internal validity:** For this type of threat, there are the response time, boring subject for conversation, weariness and learning curve of tool. The first can be caused by the difficulty in formulating an adequate response through the suggestions provided by NeuroMessenger. In order to mitigate this threat, before the experiment, a researcher who is not involved in the study also conducted a training to the mediators in order to instruct them to use effectively

the tool and matching suggestions. The second threat can be caused by the choice of an unpleasant subject for the participants to interact with each other. In order to mitigate this, we choose two subjects very familiar to the participants, which are theoretically equally enjoyable. Already, the threat of weariness can be caused by the long interaction time (1 h) for each moment. In order to mitigate this threat, there was a 20-min pause between the moments, as well as, in both moments, the two treatments were used, thus not favoring one of the treatments. Finally, the latter is related to the possible unfamiliarity with the tool, since the interlocutors dot not have constant contact with it. In order to mitigate this, before the experiment, a researcher who is not involved in the study also conducted a training to the mediators in order to instruct them to use effectively the tool properly and matching suggestions. In addition, in order not to bias our study, the participants were not aware of the factor, metrics or research hypothesis, they only knew that it was a conversation assessment.
- **External validity:** The fact that it was realized in a period of academic recess resulted in a low number of participants to carry out the experiment. Despite the randomness, we cannot generalize our conclusions to the population analyzed in this study. However, our outcomes allow us to draw insights to guide further investigations.

54.8 Related Works

There are several studies on approaches to promoving empathy between individuals. Among these, we highlight the works of Bailenson and Yee [39], Hasler et al. [40] and Kummer et al. [41].

Bailenson and Yee [39] analyzed individuals who interacted with software based on artificial intelligence—an agent who imitated participants' movements (matching) was more convincing, receiving more positive ratings. It was the first virtual reality study that showed the effects of an automatic non-verbal imitator to gain empathy. These evidences provide an empirical basis for further investigation of empathy gain in virtual interactions.

Hasler et al. [40] developed a virtual agent that used the imitation of body posture (matching) to promote empathy between interlocutors from conflicting groups. To evaluate the agent's effectiveness, they conducted an experiment in which they used this agent in the context of the troubled relationship between Israelis and Palestinians. At the end of experiment, it was found that imitation allowed for increased empathy with the Palestinians, regardless of their previous feelings towards them prior to the experiment. The condition of imitation (matching) allowed the relationship to be more harmonious than in the condition of counter-imitation.

Kummer et al. [41] have created a prototype of an empathic facial expression recognition system, which identifies the emotional state of the partner involved in the interaction, as well as reproduces a song, that played in the background, corresponding to its emotional state, through the matching process with the identified emotional state. They also conducted a controlled experiment, in which participants watched a video of an interview of a mourning mother. At the end of the experiment, it was found that the test group was more empathic than the control group in relation to the mourning mother. The use of the matching process between emotional state and music corresponding to this state allows to identify/promote empathy between the interlocutors in social interactions.

54.9 Conclusion and Future Works

In Collaborative Systems, textual interaction is predominant, although this form of communication does not have social presence resources, such as gestures and facial expressions. However, it is common for individuals to use language as a demarcating of social presence, creating a social image, which favors the formation of empathy among the interlocutors.

In this context, this paper presented evidences regarding textual matching for gain of empathy among interlocutors, through the process of PRS identification and word recommendation related to obtained PRS, using Psychometry and Text Mining techniques.

Although it is an initial study, the results are encouraging. In this experiment, in an evaluation of empathy, we verified that there was a difference between the means, in favor of NeuroMessenger, i.e., the use of the same pattern of text between interlocutors increases the empathy between them. In addition, we have identified that, as the scores using matching increase, the scores without the use of NeuroMessenger decrease.

Thus, as future work, new investigations about the studied phenomenon are required, for example, new experiments, improvement of experimental design, use of other theories of Psychology to gain empathy, among others.

References

1. R. Ecker, Multiple-views analysis of computer-mediated discourses, in *Proceedings of the 17th International Conference on Information Integration and Web-based Applications & Services*, 2015, pp. 24:1–24:10
2. N. Liebman, D. Gergle, It's (not) simply a matter of time: the relationship between CMC cues and interpersonal affinity, in *Proceedings of the 19th ACM Conference on Computer-Supported Cooperative Work & Social Computing*, 2016, pp. 570–581
3. D.A. Morand, R.J. Ocker, Politeness theory and computer-mediated communication: a sociolinguistic approach to analyzing relational messages, in *Proceedings of the 36th Annual Hawaii International Conference on System Sciences*, 2003, pp. 1–10
4. R.T.Y. Hui, Coaching in computer-mediated communication at workplace, in *2015 IEEE International Conference on Teaching, Assessment, and Learning for Engineering (TALE)*, 2015, pp. 215–219
5. R.M. Fuller, C.M. Vician, S.A. Brown, Longitudinal effects of computer-mediated communication anxiety on interaction in virtual teams. IEEE Trans. Prof. Commun. **59**(3), 166–185 (2016)
6. R. Heckman, et al., Emergent decision-making practices in technology-supported self-organizing distributed teams, in *ICIS 2006—International Conference on Information Systems*, 2006, pp. 10–13
7. M. Pimentel, H. Fuks, *Sistemas Colaborativos* (Elsevier, Rio de Janeiro, 2012)
8. N.J.B. Jamil, Z. Tasir, Students' social presence in online learning system, in *2014 International Conference on Teaching and Learning in Computing and Engineering*, 2014, pp. 289–292
9. J. Khalfallah, J.B.H. Slama, Facial expression recognition for intelligent tutoring Systems in Remote Laboratories Platform. Procedia Comput. Sci. **73**, 274–281 (2015)
10. M. Martinez, High attrition rates in e-learning: challenges, predictors, and solutions. E-Learning Dev. J. **14**(1) (2003)
11. L. Rourke, T. Anderson, D.R. Garrison, W. Archer, Assessing social presence in asynchronous text-based computer conferencing. Int. J. E-Learning Distance Educ. **14**(2), 50–71 (2007)
12. M. Siitonen, M. Olbertz-Siitonen, I Am Right Here With You: constructing presence in distributed teams, in *Proceedings of International Conference on Making Sense of Converging Media*, 2013, pp. 11:11–11:16
13. A. Khawaji, F. Chen, N. Marcus, J. Zhou, Trust and cooperation in text-based computer-mediated communication, in *Proceedings of the 25th Australian Computer-Human Interaction Conference: Augmentation, Application, Innovation, Collaboration*, 2013, pp. 37–40
14. Y.R. Tausczik, J.W. Pennebaker, Improving teamwork using real-time language feedback, in *Proceedings of the SIGCHI Conference on Human Factors in Computing Systems*, 2013, pp. 459–468
15. B.S. Santos, M.C. Júnior, M.A.S.N. Nunes, Approaches for generating empathy: a systematic mapping, in *Information Technology—New Generations: 14th International Conference on Information Technology*, ed. By S. Latifi (Springer, Cham, 2018), pp. 715–722
16. R. Bandler, R. Dilts, J. DeLozier, J. Grinder, *Neuro-Linguistic Programming: The Study of the Structure of Subjective Experience*, 1st edn. (Meta, Capitola, 1980)
17. R. Ready, K. Burton, *Programação Neurolinguística para Leigos* (Alta Books, Rio de Janeiro, 2014)
18. J. Sturt et al., Neurolinguistic programming: a systematic review of the effects on health outcomes. Br. J. Gen. Pract. **62**(604), 757–764 (2012)
19. K.A. Dent, Cognitive Styles: Essence and Origins: Herman A. Witkin and Donald R. Goodenough, International Universities Press, New York, 1983. J. Am. Acad. Psychoanal. Dyn. Psychiatry **11**(4), 635–636 (1983)
20. M. Koć-Januchta, T. Höffler, G.-B. Thoma, H. Prechtl, D. Leutner, Visualizers versus verbalizers: Effects of cognitive style on learning with texts and pictures—an eye-tracking study. Comput. Human Behav. **68**, 170–179 (2017)
21. J. Simuth, I. Sarmany-Schuller, The preferences of cognitive style among university students from various study fields. Procedia **191**, 2537–2540 (2015)

22. R.R.B. Giaxa, *Tipos Psicológicos e Empatia: Contribuições da Psicologia para a Formação do (ser) Médico* (Universidade Autónoma de Lisboa, 2015)

23. J. Oxley, *The Moral Dimensions of Empathy* (Palgrave Macmillan, New York, 2011)

24. M.C. Rodrigues, N.N. Ribeiro, Avaliação da empatia em crianças participantes e não participantes de um programa de desenvolvimento sociocognitivo. Psicol. Teor. e prática **13**(2), 114–126 (2011)

25. A. Robbins, *Poder Sem Limites: o caminho do sucesso pessoal pela programação neurolinguística* (BestSeller, Rio de Janeiro, 2016)

26. M. Hojat, *Empathy in Patient Care: Antecedents, Development, Measurement, and Outcomes* (Springer Science & Business Media, Philadelphia, 2007)

27. A.R.M.S. Palhoco, *Estudo da empatia e da percepção de emoções em psicoterapeutas e estudantes de psicologia* (Universidade de Lisboa, 2011)

28. D. Goleman, *Inteligência emocional: a teoria revolucionária que redefine o que é ser inteligente* (Objetiva, Rio de Janeiro, 2012)

29. M. Colaço Júnior, *Identificação e Validação do Perfil Neurolinguístico de Programadores através da Mineração de Repositórios de Engenharia de Software* (Universidade Federal da Bahia, 2011)

30. M.C. Júnior, M. de Fátima Menezes, D. Corumba, M. Mendonça, B.S. Santos, Do software engineers have preferred representational systems? J. Res. Pract. Inf. Technol. **47**(1), 23 (2015)

31. M. Colaço Júnior, M. Mendonça, M.A.D.F. Farias, P. Henrique, D. Corumba, A neurolinguistic-based methodology for identifying OSS developers context-specific preferred representational systems, in *ICSEA 2012: The Seventh International Conference on Software Engineering Advances*, 2012, pp. 112–121

32. M. Colaço Júnior, M.A.D.F. Farias, I. Maciel, P.H. Dos Santos, M. Mendonca, Triangulating experiments in an industrial setting to evaluate preferred representational systems of software developers, in *2014 Brazilian Symposium on Software Engineering*, 2014, pp. 71–80

33. T.B. Kashdan et al., More than words: contemplating death enhances positive emotional word use. Pers. Individ. Dif. **71**, 171–175 (2014)

34. A.M. Katz, S.J. Czech, S.M. Orsillo, Putting values into words: an examination of the text characteristics of values articulation. J. Context. Behav. Sci. **3**(1), 16–20 (2014)

35. C. Wohlin, P. Runeson, M. Höst, M.C. Ohlsson, B. Regnell, A. Wesslen, *Experimentation in Software Engineering* (Springer, New York, 2012)

36. V.R. Basili, D.M. Weiss, A methodology for collecting valid software engineering data. IEEE Trans. Softw. Eng. **10**(6), 728–738 (1984)

37. R. Van Solingen, E. Berghout, *The Goal/Question/Metric Method: A Practical Guide for Quality Improvement of Software Development* (McGraw-Hill, London, 1999)

38. N. de Tec. da Inf. da UFS, SIGAA—Sistema Integrado de Gestão de Atividades Acadêmicas [Online], http://www.sigaa.ufs.br. Accessed 01 Oct 2017

39. J.N. Bailenson, N. Yee, Digital chameleons automatic assimilation of nonverbal gestures in immersive virtual environments. Psychol. Sci. **16**(10), 814–819 (2005)

40. B.S. Hasler, G. Hirschberger, T. Shani-Sherman, D.A. Friedman, Virtual peacemakers: mimicry increases empathy in simulated contact with virtual outgroup members. Cyberpsychol. Behav. Soc. Netw. **17**(12), 766–771 (2014)

41. N. Kummer, D. Kadish, A. Dulic, and H. Najjaran, The empathy machine, in *Conference Proceedings—IEEE International Conference on Systems, Man and Cybernetics*, 2012, pp. 2265–2271

42. C.S.S. Tan, K. Luyten, J. Van Den Bergh, J. Schöning, K. Coninx, The role of physiological cues during remote collaboration. Presence **23**(1), 90–107 (2014)

43. H.B.M.S. Paro, R.M. Daud-Gallotti, I.C. Tibério, R.M.C. Pinto, M.A. Martins, Brazilian version of the Jefferson Scale of Empathy: psychometric properties and factor analysis. BMC Med. Educ. **12**(1), 73 (2012)

44. IBM, IBM SPSS Software (2012)

45. M. Bramer, *Principles of Data Mining*, 3rd edn. (Springer, London, 2016)

46. T. Hastie, R. Tibshirani, J. Friedman, *The Elements of Statistical Learning: Data Mining, Inference, and Prediction*, 2nd edn. (Springer, New York, 2009)

Dual Long Short-Term Memory Networks for Sub-Character Representation Learning

Han He, Lei Wu, Xiaokun Yang, Hua Yan, Zhimin Gao, Yi Feng, and George Townsend

Abstract

Characters have commonly been regarded as the minimal processing unit in Natural Language Processing (NLP). But many non-latin languages have hieroglyphic writing systems, involving a big alphabet with thousands or millions of characters. Each character is composed of even smaller parts, which are often ignored by the previous work. In this paper, we propose a novel architecture employing two stacked Long Short-Term Memory Networks (LSTMs) to learn sub-character level representation and capture deeper level of semantic meanings. To build a concrete study and substantiate the efficiency of our neural architecture, we take Chinese Word Segmentation as a research case example. Among those languages, Chinese is a typical case, for which every character contains several components called radicals. Our networks employ a shared radical level embedding to solve both Simplified and Traditional Chinese Word Segmentation, without extra Traditional to Simplified Chinese conversion, in such a highly end-to-end way the word segmentation can be significantly simplified compared to the previous work. Radical level embeddings can also capture deeper semantic meaning below character level and improve the system performance of learning. By tying radical and character embeddings together, the parameter count is reduced whereas semantic knowledge is shared and transferred between two levels, boosting the performance largely. On 3 out of 4 Bakeoff 2005 datasets, our method surpassed state-of-the-art results by up to 0.4%. Our results are

H. He · L. Wu (✉) · X. Yang · H. Yan
University of Houston-Clear Lake, Houston, TX, USA
e-mail: heh1996@uhcl.edu; wul@uhcl.edu; yangxia@uhcl.edu; yan@uhcl.edu

Z. Gao
University of Houston, Houston, TX, USA
e-mail: zgao5@uh.edu

Y. Feng · G. Townsend
Algoma University, Sault Ste. Marie, ON, Canada
e-mail: feng@algomau.ca; townsend@algomau.ca

reproducible; source codes and corpora are available on GitHub (https://github.com/hankcs/sub-character-cws).

Keywords

AI algorithms and applications · Deep learning · Machine learning algorithms · Natural language processing · Neural networks · Pattern recognition

55.1 Introduction

Unlike English, the alphabet in many non-latin languages is often big and complex. In those hieroglyphic writing systems, every character can be decomposed into smaller parts or sub-characters, and each part has special meanings. But existing methods often follow common processing steps in latin flavor [1–5], and treat character as the minimal processing unit, leading to a neglecting of information inside non-latin characters. Early work exploiting sub-character information usually treat it as a separate level from character [6–9], ignoring the language phenomenon that some of those sub-characters themselves are often used as normal characters. From this phenomenon, we gained a new motivation to design a novel neural network architecture for learning character and sub-character representation jointly.

In linguists' view, Chinese writing system is such a highly hieroglyphic language, and it has a long history of character compositionality. Every Chinese character has several radicals ("部首"in Chinese), which serves as semantic component for encoding meaning, or phonetic component for representing pronouciation. For instance, we listed radicals of several Simplified and Traditional Chinese characters in Table 55.1. Chinese characters with same semantic component are closely correlated in semantic. As shown above, carp (鲤) and silverfish (鲢) are both fish (鱼). River (河) and gully (沟) are all filled with water (水). To catch (捞)

© Springer International Publishing AG, part of Springer Nature 2018
S. Latifi (ed.), *Information Technology – New Generations*, Advances in Intelligent Systems and Computing 738,
https://doi.org/10.1007/978-3-319-77028-4_55

Table 55.1 Illustration of semantic component (Sem.) and phonetic component (Pho.) in Simplified Chinese (SC) and Traditional Chinese (TC)

SC	Sem.	Pho.	TC	Sem.	Pho.
鲤	鱼	里	鯉	魚	里
鲢	鱼	连	鰱	魚	連
河	水	可	河	水	可
沟	水	勾	溝	水	冓
捞	手	劳	撈	手	勞
捡	手	金	撿	手	僉

or to pick up (捡) a fish, one needs to use hands (手). To exploit those semantic meanings under character embedding level, radical embedding emerged since 2014 [6, 8–10]. These early work treated sub-character and character as two separate levels, omitting that they can actually be unified as single minimal processing unit in language model. Instead of ignoring linguistic knowledge, we respect the divergence of human language, and propose a novel joint learning framework for both character and sub-character representations.

To verify the efficiency of our jointly learnt representations, we conducted extensive experiments on the Chinese Word Segmentation (CWS) task. As those languages often don't have explicit delimiters between words, making it hard to perform later NLP tasks like Information Retrieval or Question Answering. Chinese language is such a typical non-segmented language, which means unlike English language having spaces between every word, Chinese has no explicit word delimiters. Therefore, Chinese Word Segmentation is a preliminary pre-processing step for later Chinese language process tasks. Recently with the rapid rise of deep learning, neural word segmentation approaches arose to reduce efforts in feature engineering [11–16].

In this paper, we propose a novel model to dive deeper into character embeddings. In our framework, Simplified Chinese and Traditional Chinese corpora are unified via radical embedding, growing an end-to-end model. Every character is converted to a sequence of radicals with its original form. Character embeddings and radical embeddings are pretrained jointly in Bojanowski et al.'s [3] subword aware method. Finally, we conducted various experiments on corpora from SIGHAN bakeoff 2005. Results showed that our jointly learnt character embedding outperforms conventional character embedding training methods. Our models can improve performance by transfer learning between characters and radicals. The final scores surpassed previous work, and 3 out of 4 even surpassed previous preprocessing-heavy state-of-the-art learning work.

More specifically, the contributions of this paper could be summarized as:

- Explored a novel sub-character aware neural architecture and unified character and sub-character as one same level embedding.
- Released the first full Chinese character-radical conversion corpus along with pre-trained embeddings, which can be easily applied on other NLP tasks. Our codes and corpora are freely available for the public.

55.2 Related Work

In this section, we review the previous work from two directions—radical embedding and Chinese Word Segmentation.

55.2.1 Radical Embedding

To leverage the semantic meaning inside Chinese characters, Sun et al. [6] inaugurated radical information to enrich character embedding via softmax classification layer. In similar way, Li et al. [7] proposed charCBOW model taking concatenation of the character-level and component-level context embeddings as input. Making networks deeper, Shi et al. [8] proposed a deep CNN on top of radical embedding pre-trained via CBOW. Instead of utilizing CNNs, following Lample et al. [17], Dong et al. [9] used two level LSTMs taking character embedding and radical embedding as input respectively.

Our work is closely related to Dong et al. [9], but there are two major differences. In pre-training phase, their character embeddings were pre-trained separately, by utilizing conventional word2vec package, and the radical embeddings are randomly initialized. While we considered radical units as sub-characters (parts of one character) and trained the two level embeddings jointly, following Bojanowski et al.'s [3] approach. In training and testing phases, our two-level embeddings are tied up and unified as the sole minimal input unit of Chinese language.

55.2.2 Chinese Word Segmentation

Chinese Word Segmentation has been a well-known NLP task for decades [18]. After pioneer Xue et al. [19] transformed CWS into a character-based tagging problem, Peng et al. [20] adopted CRF as the sequence labeling model and showed its effectiveness. Following these pioneers, later sequence labeling based work [21–24] was proposed. Recent neural models [9, 11, 13, 14, 25, 26] also followed this sequence labeling fashion.

Our model is based on Bi-LSTM with CRF as top layer. Unlike previous approaches, the inputs to our model are both character and radical embeddings. Furthermore, we explored which embedding level is more tailored for Chinese language, either using both embeddings together, or even tying them up.

55.3 Joint Learning for Character Embedding and Radical Embedding

Previous work treated character and radical as two different levels, used them separately or used one to enhance the other. Although radicals are components of a character (belonging to a lower level), they can actually be learnt jointly. It is linguistically more reasonable to put radical embeddings and character embeddings in exactly the same vector space. We propose to train character vector representation being aware of its internal structure of radicals.

55.3.1 Character Decomposition

Every character can be decomposed into a list of radicals or components. To maintain character information in radical list, we simply add the raw form of character to its radical list. Taking the linguistic knowledge that semantic component contains richest meaning of one character into consideration, we append the semantic component to the end of its radical list, hence to make the semantic component appear more than once.

Formally, denote c as a character, r as a radical, $\mathcal{L}_c = [r_1, r_2 \cdots r_n]$ as the original radical list of c. Let $r_s \in \mathcal{L}_c$ be the semantic component of c. Our decomposition of c will be:

$$\mathcal{R}_c = [c, r_1, r_2 \cdots r_n, r_s] \tag{55.1}$$

55.3.2 General Continuous Skip-Gram (SG) Model

Take a brief review of the continuous skip-gram model introduced by Mikolov et al. [10], applied in character representation learning.

Given an alphabet, target is to learn a vectorial representation $\mathbf{v}_c$ for each character c. Let $c_1, ..., c_T$ be a large-scale corpus represented as a sequence of characters, the objective function of the skipgram model is to maximize the log-likelihood of correct prediction. The probability of a context character c_y given c_x is computed by a scoring function s which maps character and context to scores in $\mathbb{R}$.

The general SG model ignores the radical structure of characters, we propose a different scoring function s, in order to capture radical information.

Let all radicals form an alphabet of size R. Given a character c and the radical list $\mathcal{R}_c \subset \{1, \ldots, R\}$ of c, a vector representation $\mathbf{z}_r$ is associated to each radical r. Then a character is represented by the sum of the vector representations of its radicals. Thus the new scoring function will be:

$$s(c_x, c_y) = \sum_{r \in \mathcal{R}_{c_x}} \mathbf{z}_r^\top \mathbf{v}_{c_y}. \tag{55.2}$$

This simple model allows learning the representations of characters and radicals jointly.

55.4 Radical Aware Neural Architectures for General Chinese Word Segmentation

Once character and radical representations are learnt, one evaluation metric is how much it improves a NLP task. We choose the Chinese Word Segmentation task as a standard benchmark to examine their efficiency. One prevailing approach to CWS is casting it to character based sequence tagging problem, where our representations can be applied. A commonly used tagging set is $\mathcal{T} = \{B, M, E, S\}$, representing the **b**egin, **m**iddle, **e**nd of a word, or **s**ingle character forming a word.

Given a sequence $\mathbf{X}$ consisted of n features as $\mathbf{X} = (\mathbf{x}_1, \mathbf{x}_2, \ldots, \mathbf{x}_n)$, the goal of sequence tagging based CWS is to find the most possible tags $\mathbf{Y}^* = \{\mathbf{y}_1^*, \ldots, \mathbf{y}_n^*\}$:

$$\mathbf{Y}^* = \arg\max_{\mathbf{Y} \in \mathcal{T}^n} p(\mathbf{Y}|\mathbf{X}), \tag{55.3}$$

where $\mathcal{T} = \{B, M, E, S\}$.

Since tagging set restricts the order of adjacent tags, we model them jointly using a conditional random field, mostly following the architecture proposed by Lample et al. [17], via stacking two LSTMs with a CRF layer on top of them.

55.4.1 Radical LSTM Layer: Character Composition from Radicals

In this section, we'll review RNN with Bi-LSTM extension briefly, before introducing our character composition network.

55.4.1.1 LSTM

Long Short-Term Memory Networks (LSTMs) [27] are extensions of Recurrent Neural Networks (RNNs). They are designed to combat gradient vanishing issue via incorporating a memory-cell which enables long-range dependencies capturing.

55.4.1.2 Bi-LSTM

One LSTM can only produce the representation $\overrightarrow{\mathbf{h}_t}$ of the left context at every character t. To incorporate a representation of the right context $\overleftarrow{\mathbf{h}_t}$, a second LSTM which reads the same sequence in reverse order is used. Pair of this forward and backward LSTM is called bidirectional LSTM (Bi-LSTM) [28] in literature. By concatenating its left and right context representations, the final representation is produced as $\mathbf{h}_t = [\overrightarrow{\mathbf{h}_t}; \overleftarrow{\mathbf{h}_t}]$.

We apply a Bi-LSTM to compose character embeddings from radical embeddings in both directions. The raw character is inserted as the first radical, and the semantic component is appended as the last radical. The motivation behind this trick is to make use of LSTM's bias phenomena. In practice, LSTMs usually tend to be biased towards the most recent inputs of the sequence, thus the first one or last one depends on its direction.

As illustrated in Fig. 55.1, the character 明(bright) has the radical list of 日(sun) and 月(moon) with its raw form and duplicated semantic radical. Its compositional representation $\mathbf{h}_i^r \in \mathbb{R}^{2k}$ is agglomerated via a Bi-LSTM from these radical embeddings, where k is the dimension of radical embeddings.

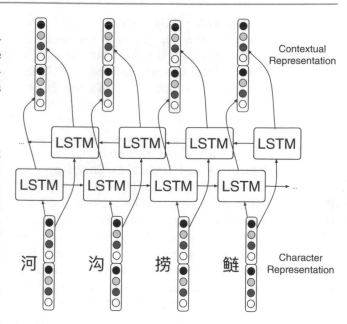

Fig. 55.2 Character LSTM Layer—capture contextual representation

55.4.2 Character Bi-LSTM Layer: Context Capturing

Once compositional character representation $\mathbf{h}_i^r$ is synthesized, the contextual representation $\mathbf{h}_t^c \in \mathbb{R}^{2d}$ at every character t in input sentence can be agglomerated by a second Bi-LSTM. The dimension d is a flexible hyper-parameter, which will be explored in later experiments.

Our architecture for contextual feature capturing is shown in Fig. 55.2. This contextual feature vector contains the meaning of a character, its radicals and its context.

55.4.3 CRF Layer: Tagging Inference

We employed a Conditional Random Fields(CRF) [29] layer as the inference layer. As first order linear chain CRFs only model bigram interactions between output tags, so the maximum of a posteriori sequence $\mathbf{Y}^*$ in Eq. (55.3) can be computed using dynamic programming, both in training and decoding phase. The training goal is to maximize the log-probability of the gold tag sequence.

55.5 Experiments

We conducted various experiments to verify the following questions:

1. Does radical embedding enhance character embedding in pre-training phase?

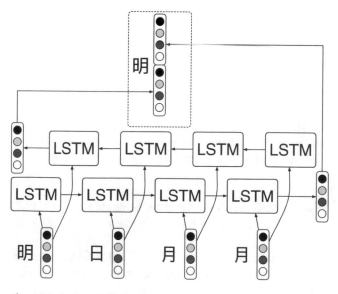

Fig. 55.1 Radical LSTM Layer—composition of character representation from radicals

2. Whether radical embedding helps character embedding in training phase and test phase (by using character embedding solely or using them both)?
3. Can radical embedding replace character embedding (by using radical embedding only)?
4. Should we tie up two level embeddings?

55.5.1 Datasets

To explore these questions, we experimented on the 4 prevalent CWS benchmark datasets from SIGHAN2005 [30]. Following conventions, the last 10% sentences of training set are used as development set.

55.5.2 Radical Decomposition

We obtained radical lists of character from the *online Xinhua Dictionary*,[1] which are included in our open-source project.

55.5.3 Pre-Training

Previous work have shown that pre-trained embeddings on large unlabeled corpus can improve performance. It usually involves lots of efforts to preprocess those corpus. Here we presented a novel solution.

The corpus used is Chinese Wikipedia of July 2017. Unlike most approaches, we don't perform Traditional Chinese to Simplified Chinese conversion. Our radical decomposition is sufficient of associate character to its similar variants. Not only traditional-simplified character pairs, those with similar radical decompositions will also share similar vectorial representations.

Further, instead of the commonly used word2vec [2], we utilized fastText[2] [3] to train character embeddings and radical embeddings jointly. We applied SG model, 100 dimension, and set both maximum and minimal n-gram length to 1, as the radical takes only one token.

55.5.4 Final Results on SIGHAN Bakeoff 2005

Our baseline model is Bi-LSTM-CRF trained on each datasets only with pre-trained character embedding (the conventional word2vec), no sub-character enhancement, no radical embeddings. Then we improved it with sub-character

Table 55.2 Comparison with previous state-of-the-art models of results on all four Bakeoff-2005 datasets

Models	PKU	MSR	CityU	AS
Tseng et al. [21]	95.0	96.4	–	–
Zhang and Clark [31]	95.0	96.4	–	–
Sun et al. [32]	95.2	97.3	–	–
Sun et al. [24]	95.4	**97.4**	–	–
Pei et al. [13]	95.2	97.2	–	–
Chen et al. [26]	94.3	96.0	95.6	94.8
Cai et al. [16]$^\diamond$	**95.8**	97.1	95.6	95.3
baseline	94.6	96.0	94.7	94.8
+subchar	95.0	96.0	94.9	94.9
+radical	94.6	96.7	95.3	95.2
+radical −char	94.4	96.5	95.0	95.1
+radical +tie	94.8	96.8	95.3	95.1
+radical +tie +bigram	95.3	**97.4**	**95.9**	**95.7**

The largest values in each column are bolded

information, adding radical embeddings, tying two level embeddings up. The final results are shown in Table 55.2.

All experiments are conducted with standard Bakeoff scoring program[3] calculating precision, recall, and F_1-score. Note that results with $\diamond$ expurgated long words in test set.

55.5.5 Model Analysis

Sub-character information enhances character embeddings. Previous work showed pre-trained character embeddings can improve performance. Our experiment showed with sub-character information (+subchar), performance can be further improved compared to no sub-character enhancement (baseline). By simply replacing the conventional word2vec embeddings to radical aware embeddings, the score can benefit an improvement as much as 0.4%.

Radical embeddings collaborate well with character embeddings. By building compositional embeddings from radical level (+radical), performance increased by up to 0.7% in comparison with model (baseline) on MSR dataset. But we also notice that: (1) On small dataset such as PKU, radical embeddings cause tiny performance drop. (2) With the additional bigram feature, performance can be further increased as much as 0.6%.

Radical embeddings can't fully replace character embeddings. Without character embeddings but use radical embeddings solely (+radical −char), performance drops a little (0.1–0.3%) compared to the model with character embeddings (+radical).

---

[1] http://tool.httpcn.com/Zi/.

[2] https://github.com/facebookresearch/fastText With tiny modification to output n-gram vectors.

[3] http://www.sighan.org/bakeoff2003/score This script rounds a score to one digit.

Tying two level embeddings up is a good idea. By tying radical embeddings and character embeddings together (+radical +tie), the raw feature is unified into the same vector space, knowledge is transferred between two levels, and performance is boosted up to 0.2%.

55.6 Conclusions and Future Work

In this paper, we proposed a novel neural network architecture with dedicated pre-training techniques to learn character and sub-character representations jointly. As an concrete application example, we unified Simplified and Traditional Chinese characters through sub-character or radical embeddings. We have utilized a practical way to train radical and character embeddings jointly. Our experiments showed that sub-character information can enhance character representations for a pictographic language like Chinese. By using both level embeddings and tying them up, our model has gained the most benefit and surpassed previous single criterial CWS systems on three datasets.

Our radical embeddings framework can be applied to extensive NLP tasks like POS-tagging and Named Entity Recognition (NER) for various hieroglyphic languages. These tasks will benefit from deeper level of semantic representations encoded with more linguistic knowledge.

References

1. T. Mikolov, M. Karafiát, L. Burget, J. Cernocký, S. Khudanpur, Recurrent neural network based language model, in *Interspeech*, vol. 2 (2010), p. 3
2. T. Mikolov, K. Chen, G. Corrado, J. Dean, Efficient estimation of word representations in vector space (2013). arXiv.org
3. P. Bojanowski, E. Grave, A. Joulin, T. Mikolov, Enriching word vectors with subword information (2016). arXiv.org. arXiv:1607.04606
4. Y. Kim, Y. Jernite, D. Sontag, A.M. Rush, Character-aware neural language models, in *AAAI* (2016), pp. 2741–2749
5. Y. Pinter, R. Guthrie, J. Eisenstein, Mimicking word embeddings using subword RNNs (2017, preprint). arXiv:1707.06961
6. Y. Sun, L. Lin, N. Yang, Z. Ji, X. Wang, Radical-enhanced Chinese character embedding, in *ICONIP*, vol. 8835, Chap. 34 (2014), pp. 279–286
7. Y. Li, W. Li, F. Sun, S. Li, Component-enhanced Chinese character embeddings, in *EMNLP* (2015)
8. X. Shi, J. Zhai, X. Yang, Z. Xie, C. Liu, Radical embedding - delving deeper to Chinese radicals, in *ACL* (2015)
9. C. Dong, J. Zhang, C. Zong, M. Hattori, H. Di, Character-based LSTM-CRF with radical-level features for Chinese named entity recognition, in *NLPCC/ICCPOL* (2016)
10. T. Mikolov, I. Sutskever, K. Chen, G. Corrado, J. Dean, Distributed representations of words and phrases and their compositionality, in *NIPS* (2013)
11. X. Zheng, H. Chen, T. Xu, Deep learning for Chinese word segmentation and POS tagging, in *EMNLP* (2013)
12. R. Collobert, J. Weston, L. Bottou, M. Karlen, K. Kavukcuoglu, P.P. Kuksa, Natural language processing (almost) from scratch. J. Mach. Learn. Res. **12**, 2493–2537 (2011)
13. W. Pei, T. Ge, B. Chang, Max-margin tensor neural network for Chinese word segmentation, in *ACL* (2014)
14. X. Chen, X. Qiu, C. Zhu, P. Liu, X. Huang, Long short-term memory neural networks for Chinese word segmentation, in *EMNLP* (2015)
15. D. Cai , H. Zhao, Neural word segmentation learning for Chinese, in *ACL* (2016)
16. D. Cai, H. Zhao, Z. Zhang, Y. Xin, Y. Wu, F. Huang, Fast and accurate neural word segmentation for Chinese (2017). arXiv.org. arXiv:1704.07047
17. G. Lample, M. Ballesteros, S. Subramanian, K. Kawakami, C. Dyer, Neural architectures for named entity recognition. *CoRR* (2016)
18. C. Huang, H. Zhao, Chinese word segmentation: a decade review. J. Chin. Inf. Process. **21**(3), 8–19 (2007)
19. N. Xue, Chinese word segmentation as character tagging, in *IJ-CLCLP* (2003)
20. F. Peng, F. Feng, A. Mccallum, Chinese segmentation and new word detection using conditional random fields, in *COLING* (2004), pp. 562–568
21. H. Tseng, P. Chang, G. Andrew, D. Jurafsky, C. Manning, A conditional random field word segmenter for sighan bakeoff 2005, in *SIGHAN Workshop on Chinese Language Processing* (2005), pp. 168–171
22. H. Zhao, C. Huang, M. Li, B.-L. Lu, Effective tag set selection in Chinese word segmentation via conditional random field modeling, in *PACLIC* (2006)
23. H. Zhao, C.N. Huang, M. Li, B.L. Lu, A unified character-based tagging framework for chinese word segmentation. ACM Trans. Asian Lang. Inf. Process. **9**(2), 1–32 (2010)
24. X. Sun, H. Wang, W. Li, Fast online training with frequency-adaptive learning rates for chinese word segmentation and new word detection, in *ACL* (2012), pp. 253–262
25. Y. Qi, S.G. Das, R. Collobert, J. Weston, Deep learning for character-based information extraction, in *ECIR* (2014)
26. X. Chen, Z. Shi, X. Qiu, X. Huang, Adversarial multi-criteria learning for Chinese word segmentation. vol. 1704 (2017). arXiv:1704.07556
27. S. Hochreiter, J. Schmidhuber, Long short-term memory. Neural Comput. **9**(8), 1735–1780 (1997)
28. A. Graves, J. Schmidhuber, Framewise phoneme classification with bidirectional LSTM and other neural network architectures. Neural Netw. **18**(5–6), 602–610 (2005)
29. J.D. Lafferty, A. Mccallum, F.C.N. Pereira, Conditional random fields: probabilistic models for segmenting and labeling sequence data, in *Eighteenth International Conference on Machine Learning* (2001), pp. 282–289
30. T. Emerson, The second international chinese word segmentation bakeoff, in *Proceedings of the Fourth SIGHAN Workshop on Chinese Language Processing*, Jeju Island (2005), pp. 123–133
31. Y. Zhang, S. Clark, *Chinese Segmentation with a Word-Based Perceptron Algorithm* (Association for Computational Linguistics, Prague, 2007), pp. 840–847. http://www.aclweb.org/anthology/P/P07/P07-1106
32. X. Sun, Y. Zhang, T. Matsuzaki, Y. Tsuruoka, J. Tsujii, A discriminative latent variable chinese segmenter with hybrid word/character information, in *NAACL* (2009), pp. 56–64

Business Intelligence Dashboard Application for Insurance Cross Selling

Jagan Mohan Narra, Doina Bein, and Vlad Popa

Abstract

Insurance Companies use Business Intelligence (BI) and Business Analytics (BA) to quantify their business and to predict their growth with the help of BI solutions. The primary objective of this paper is to build a software solution which provides a platform for insurance companies and ecommerce to find a set of tools and solutions that can be implemented for their business data analytics. The BI Dashboard application can be used by insurance companies to implement the concept of Cross-Selling and Up-selling of insurance products to their customers. The Ecommerce web based application is used to implement the concept of group-based collaborative marketing of products which internally uses data mining and clustering algorithms.

Keywords

Insurance cross-sell · Insurance up-sell · Data mining · Business intelligence · Group-based collaborative marketing · Ecommerce · BI dashboard

56.1 Introduction

Insurance Companies are making great efforts in turning the business data as a useful information source for the growth of their business using Business Intelligence (BI) and Business Analytics [1]. The technological advancements in Business Intelligence (BI) analytics provided the leverage to insurance companies to grow their business using a new concept called *Cross Selling(x-sell)* and *Up-selling(up-sell)*. Insurance Cross selling is a technique to sell insurance products to existing customers. It will provide the opportunity to increase the business at a quicker rate rather than selling the products to a new client [2]. In real-life scenario, there is a no readily available application to provide a complete BI and analytics of external and internal customer information for a generic insurance company.

The Business Intelligence (BI) includes architectures, tools, databases, applications, etc. aimed at obtaining current, historical, and predictive views(reports) of business operations for purposes of making better business decisions [3]. The BI tools allows us to transform the business data to information, then to decisions and predictions and finally into actions that implemented by business users [4]. We have encountered several growing BI tools that are currently available in the present market; each of these tools has made its own importance and sometimes it leads to confusion for developers to choose which tool for their business implementations. We note that currently:

- We have no proper tool to combine both external and internal customer information for prospecting the business growth.
- There is no readily available application/tool to analyze and create predictive model based on recent past trends of insurance companies' information.
- BI Dashboards are not mapped with the current analytical applications.

This paper focuses on identifying the possible scenarios to analyze and create a predictive model based on recent trends of data which can correctly visualize other product areas and customer segments in the insurance sector. This project aims at the development of an Innovative Dynamic dashboard that insurance companies can use it to visualize their business and predictions can be achieved through the

J. M. Narra · D. Bein (✉)
Department of Computer Science, California State University, Fullerton, Fullerton, CA, USA
e-mail: narra@csu.fullerton.edu; dbein@fullerton.edu

V. Popa
Liceul Tehnologic Petru Poni, Iasi, Romania

© Springer International Publishing AG, part of Springer Nature 2018
S. Latifi (ed.), *Information Technology – New Generations*, Advances in Intelligent Systems and Computing 738,
https://doi.org/10.1007/978-3-319-77028-4_56

key performance indicators (short KPIs) involved in it. We use the BI tool Tableau to generate dashboards and reports that contain the data analytics of an insurance company.

The paper is organized as follows. In Sect. 56.2 we present existing work. In Sect. 56.3 we present the system design, programming environments used for creating the software product, and the capabilities of the software product. We conclude in Section IV.

56.2   Related Work

Business Intelligence (BI) contains technologies such as Decision Support Systems (DSS), Executive Information Systems (EIS), On-Line Analytical Processing (OLAP), Relational OLAP (ROLAP), Multi-Dimensional OLAP (MOLAP), Hybrid OLAP (HOLAP, a combination of MOLAP and ROLAP), and more. BI can be broken down into four broad fields:

1. Multi-dimensional Analysis Tools: Tools that allow the user to look at the data from a number of different "angles". These tools often use a multi-dimensional database referred to as a "cube".
2. Query tools: Tools that allow the user to issue SQL (Structured Query Language) queries against the warehouse and get a result set back.
3. Data Mining Tools: Tools that automatically search for patterns in data. These tools are usually driven by complex statistical formulas. The easiest way to distinguish data mining from the various forms of OLAP is that OLAP can only answer questions you know to ask, data mining answers questions you didn't necessarily know to ask.
4. Data Visualization Tools: Tools that show graphical representations of data, including complex three-dimensional data pictures. The theory is that the user can "see" trends more effectively ogress in this area using the Virtual Reality Modeling Language (VRML)

Tableau is a data visualization tool that offers several features and functionalities which other data visualizations lack, such as bubble maps, world map based dashboards, word clouds, etc. Certainly, Tableau tool leads in the today's BI report generations and visualizations that are currently used in the present market. It is an American company that produces a family of interactive data visualization products focused on business Intelligence:

- Tableau desktop (Business analytics anyone can use) is based on breakthrough technology from Stanford University that lets you drag & drop to analyze data. You can connect to data in a few clicks, then visualize and create interactive dashboards with a few more.

- Tableau server is a business intelligence application that provides browser-based analytics anyone can use. It's a rapid-fire alternative to the slow pace of traditional business intelligence software
- Tableau online is a hosted version of Tableau Server. It makes rapid-fire business analytics easier than ever. Share dashboards with your whole company and with customers and partners—in minutes. Provide live, interactive views of data that let people answer their own questions, right in a web browser or on a tablet. And do it in a secure, hosted environment.
- Tableau Public is for anyone who wants to tell stories with interactive data on the web. It's delivered as a service that allows you to be up and running overnight. With Tableau Public, you can create amazing interactive visuals and publish them quickly, without the help of programmers or IT.

This project is an enterprise application using Tableau BI tool and MS SQL server (see Fig. 56.1).

This development project has two phases:

1. Developing XML data web service and Dataset:
2. Tableau Report Generation and database connections.

The database connections and its necessary code development is done in this phase of project. Once a successful data connection is code is developed, we can map data sources of our case study to Tableau tool to generate BI (business intelligence) reports.

56.3   Software Description

We need to write the necessary SQL, XML coding for this custom development component. The Tableau tool requires a XML Data Web service, the input data source is considered in the form of xml data files. To read the Xml data, we require a XML web service. We would develop a dataset for our application to supply the required KPI's for generating various visualizations.

The objectives of BI Dashboard are:

- An interactive prospecting visualization which provides insight into their customer information and what insurance products can they recommend as a part of cross-sell.
- Integrated third party data with the internal customers to give one customer information.
- Visual analytics so that customers can be prospected based on geography, industry classification, revenue and number of employees.
- Drill-down functionality for the product details

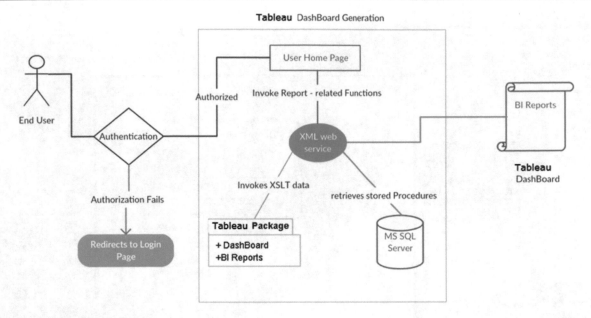

Fig. 56.1 Tableau dashboard architecture

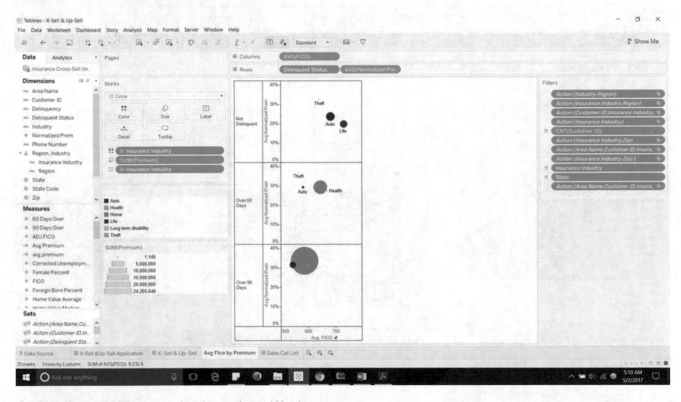

Fig. 56.2 Average FICO scores against the premium paid by the customer

We will provide the screenshots for every feature/functionality of the product we developed.

The tableau sheet in Fig. 56.2 shows the average FICO score of individual customers against the premium they pay. The KPI-filters applied can be viewed on right side of sheet.

The sheet in Fig. 56.3 shows the dynamic visuals of the customers that are spread across USA by using a Geo map feature of Tableau.

The sheet in Fig. 56.4 shows the dynamic visuals of the total count of customers by the industry type they belong to. The KPI's used are shown also.

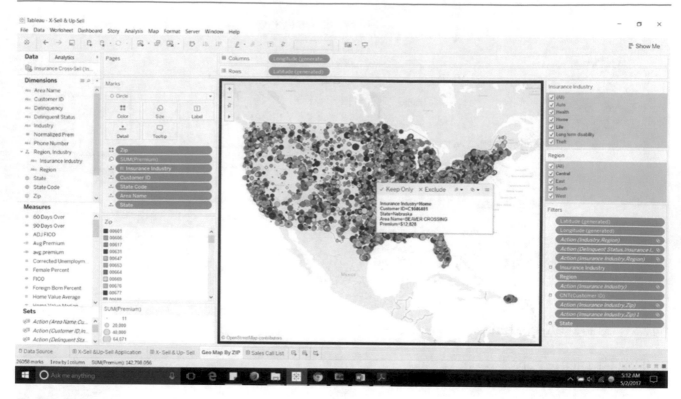

Fig. 56.3 Geo map sheet

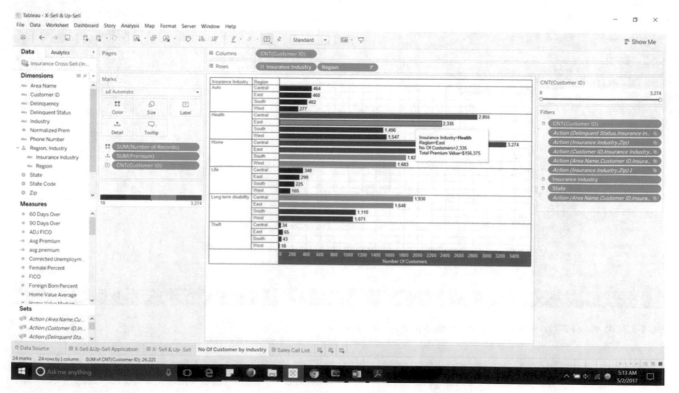

Fig. 56.4 Customers by industry

The sheet in Fig. 56.5 shows the visual chart of the total premium paid by customers, which are arranged according to their address/locations using zip code.

The dashboard in Fig. 56.6 combines all the four individual sheets to form an interactive dashboard. This dashboard is interactive and dynamic, i.e., if any changes are made in any

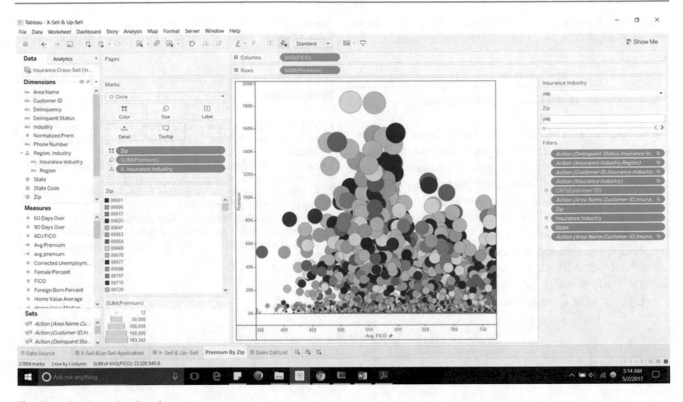

Fig. 56.5   Customers by zipcode

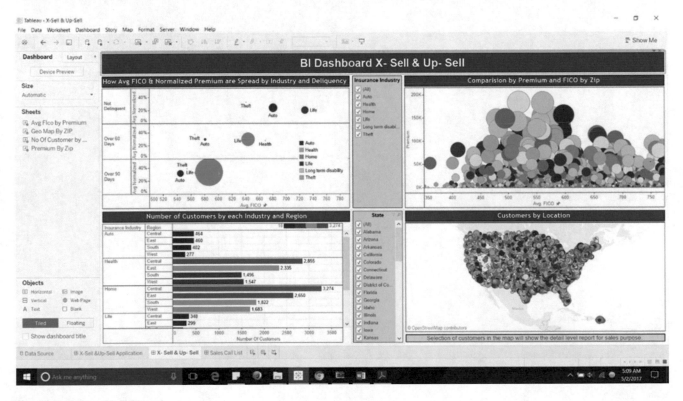

Fig. 56.6   Tableau BI dashboard

one of these four sheets, it will automatically create filters on the remaining sheets based on selection/changes made by the user.

56.4 Conclusions and Future Work

We believe our case study can be used to achieve different scenario results which mainly rely on BI tools used and based on the requirements of the customers. The Tableau dashboard application is developed using the dataset that we developed by combining multiple relevant data sources.

Our case study can also be extended to similar industries like banking, healthcare, and manufacturing, as they are similar to insurance and ecommerce industries. There are several other BI tools like Qlikview, Cognos, Crystal Reports, ABInito which can be alternatively used, based on the requirement of the customers.

Acknowledgment Doina Bein acknowledges the support by Air Force Office of Scientific Research under award number FA9550-16-1-0257.

References

1. H. Chen, R.H.L. Chiang, V.C. Storey, Business intelligence and analytics: from big data to big impact. MIS Q. **36**(4), 1165–1188 (2012)
2. M. Hilbert, P. López, *The World's Technological Capacity to Store, Communicate, and Compute Information* (2013)
3. R. Sherman, *Business Intelligence Guidebook: From Data Integration to Analytics* (Newnes, 2014)
4. M. Sarantopoulos, SVP, Insurance Practice and NTT Data, Inc, Explosive growth is no accident: driving digital transformation in the insurance industry, 19 Aug 2015 [Online]. Accessed 23 Nov 2017

Speech Features Analysis for Tone Language Speaker Discrimination Systems

57

Mercy Edoho, Moses Ekpenyong, and Udoinyang Inyang

Abstract

In this paper, a speech pattern analysis framework for tone language speaker discrimination systems is proposed. We hold the hypothesis that speech feature variability is an efficient means for discriminating speakers. To achieve this, we exploit prosody-related acoustic features (pitch, intensity and glottal pulse) of corpus recordings obtained from male and female speakers of varying age categories: children (0–15), youths (16–30), adults (31–50), seniors (above 50)—and captured under suboptimal conditions. The speaker dataset was segmented into three sets: train, validation and test set—in the ratio of 70%, 15% and 15%, respectively. A 41 × 14 self-organizing map (SOM) architecture was then used to model the speech features, thereby determining the relationship between the speech features, segments and patterns. Results of a speech pattern analysis indicated wide F0 variability amongst children speakers compared with other speakers. This gap however closes as the speaker ages. Further, the intensity variability among speakers was similar across all speaker classes/categories, while glottal pulse exhibited significant variation among the different speaker classes. Results of SOM feature visualization confirmed high inter-variability—between speakers, and low intra-variability—within speakers.

Keywords

Feature extraction · Pattern analysis · Self-organizing map · Speaker variability

M. Edoho · M. Ekpenyong (✉) · U. Inyang
Department of Computer Science, University of Uyo, Uyo, Nigeria
e-mail: mercyedoho@uniuyo.edu.ng;
mosesekpenyong@uniuyo.edu.ng; udoinyanginyang@uniuyo.edu.ng

57.1 Introduction

Human speech carries distinctive information about the speaker—to aid the process of recognition. Instances of this information include mood, manner and spoken words. But it has been argued that speech recognition also requires language ability [1]—as the human voice carries linguistic and paralinguistic information about the speaker's identity—and the auditory system has the capacity to decode both types of information. Hence, the formulation of an efficient discrimination framework depends on certain aspects of the human auditory system. Psychoacoustic studies have shown that the human ear discriminates acoustic features such as tones—based on its absolute relative frequency. Empirical evidence also suggests that the ear is more sensitive to low frequency signals, and the Mel-scale was formulated for sampling this important attribute using perceptual criteria [2]. Speech features extracted using the Mel-scale are known to produce superior speech recognition performance compared to linear-scale parameters [3]. Timing and control of speech signal remains one of the most intractable issues in speech processing, mainly due to the numerous contextual factors associated with timing, and the fact that most speech factors interact with themselves. Many statistical approaches such as regression—both linear and tree [4, 5]; Mean Squared Regression (MSR)—an extended linear and tree regressions [6]; sum-of-products model [7]; Hidden Markov Model (HMM) [8]; and neural networks [9, 10] have been used successfully for rhythm and tempo control. But, one most striking attribute of the human speech is feature variability and the key identity of speech usually lies in the variations that exist within the feature segments. Further, transition between each segment ensures the continuity of sounds for words and phrases, thereby improving the speech quality. This paper therefore focuses on the analysis of speech features required to discover pattern variability across speakers' gender (male, female) and age category (children (0–15), youths (16–30), adults (31–50), seniors (above 50)). We hypothesize that *speech feature variability is sufficient to discriminate a speaker.*

Speaker discrimination can therefore be regarded as a pattern recognition problem, and the problem statement can be formulated, thus: *Given a sequence of speaker utterances (where each speaker utterance is a sequence of unique speech feature vectors) of the speaker, output a decision on the speaker's category (gender or age).* Although, no unique features distinguishing between all speakers are known, it appears that inter-speaker variability can be explored between speakers at various levels, including temporal and spectral variability. Three basic classes of speech features (spectral, dynamic and prosodic features) have been described in [11]. Spectral features represent in entirety the physical characteristics of the vocal tract, while dynamic features are time variations of features other than spectral features. Prosodic features—the fundamental frequency (F0) and energy contours in speech are of three categories namely: source features—prosodic features within a single glottal period; supra-segmental features—prosodic features spanning a few glottal periods; and high-level features—long term features spanning the time duration of a word or phrase. Hence, prosody may vary from speaker to speaker and relies on long-term information of speech. In this paper, we exploit the following acoustic features: fundamental frequency (F0)—the acoustic correlate of tone, intensity—a measure of loudness, and glottal pulse—the acoustic correlate of respiration—as both pulse and respiration maintain an increasing ratio of approximately 1 breath for every 4 pulses or heartbeats. The tone language used in the study is Ibibio (New Benue Congo, Nigeria)—A West African language spoken in the southeast costal region of Nigeria—by about four million (4,000,000) speakers.

The paper is structured as follows: Sect. 57.2 presents the proposed system framework, discussing the methodological workflow. Section 57.3 discusses the results of speech feature pattern analysis, SOM quality evaluation and visualization. Section 57.4 concludes on the study and points to future research direction.

57.2 Methodology

The methodological workflow as shown in Fig. 57.1 begins with speech signal acquisition. Speech acquisition can be achieved through an audio recording device. In this paper, the speech recordings were captured using two devices: a mobile *iPhone*, and a *Zoom H4n* handy recorder. The recorded

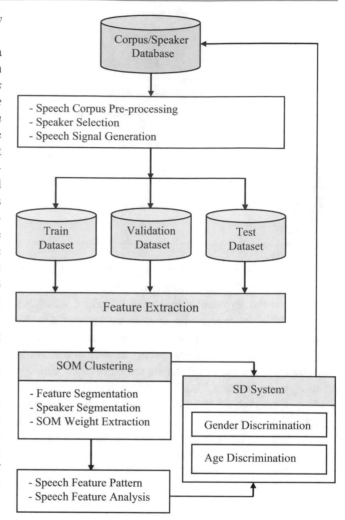

Fig. 57.1 Methodological framework for tone language speaker discrimination

utterance was the Ibibio sentence: 'fry groundnut blow its shell off'. Each speaker was recorded spontaneously after being told what to say. Our corpus/speaker database consists of recorded voice samples for male and female speakers according the following age category: 0–15 (children), 16–30 (youths), 31–50 (adults), above 50 (seniors)—a total of 8 classes of speakers. The selected speech features were pitch/F0, intensity and pulse. Hence, our speech database contained a 80 speakers (40 males and 40 females).

Figure 57.2 shows a *Praat* (speech processing and analysis software) sound file displaying the wave form and spectrogram of speech captured from a female child. Praat was used in the experiment to extract and generate the speech

Fig. 57.2 Praat sound file showing a captured speech

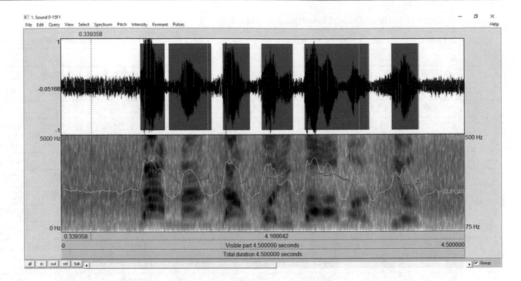

feature signals (see samples of generated features in Table 57.1). In Fig. 57.2, the F0 and intensity features are the blue and yellow curves that stretch across the centre of the spectrogram, while the pulse feature is the thick blue band covering the wave envelopes. We chose to perform the recordings under suboptimal conditions—that includes degradations caused either by the speaker, environment, channel, or a combination of these factors. For instance, the thick line running across the wave envelopes indicates heavy background noise due to rain.

The total (generated) dataset was divided into train, validation and test datasets in the ratio of 70%: 15%: 15%. Self-organizing Map (SOM) was then used to model the speech features and discover underlying relationship between the features, segments, and patterns. The SOM architecture on which our methodological framework rests is given in Fig. 57.3, and has a total of $4 \times 4 \times n$ weight connections. It is implemented using the following stages: (1) data structure construction, (2) data normalization, (3) map training, (4) map visualization and (5) feature analysis. In the data construction stage, the data structure is created with the *som_data_struct* function of MATLAB 2015a—and used to construct the map structure—using a 41 × 14 hexagonal grid. SOM n*ormalize* and *denormalize* functions were used to scale down the variables—as the Euclidean distance was adopted as the basis for determining the map. During training, the map prototypes were initialized randomly and training done using the sequential training function based on competitive and cooperative learning. The prototype vector and its neighbors that are most similar to a data vector were moved towards the data vector. First, with the large neighborhood radius and then fine-tuned with small radius. Visualization of the map was then provided in the U-matrix and SOM input planes. These visuals provided basis for similarity and variability analysis which output is required for speaker discrimination systems.

57.3 Results

57.3.1 Speech Pattern Analysis

Figures 57.4 and 57.5, show plots of F0 feature across the different age categories, for male and female speakers,

Table 57.1 Sample Features Dataset Generated from Praat

S/N.	F0 features for male speakers (Adult)					F0 features for female speakers (Adult)				
	m1	m2	m3	m4	m5	f1	f2	f3	f4	f5
1	98.5558	497.4887	173.0940	133.7036	171.6247	238.2796	197.0795	424.5775	265.5210	75.9271
2	109.6411	497.8139	172.3332	134.1659	172.6142	239.7103	194.1698	485.7897	271.3574	82.0483
3	113.9895	112.1117	172.7554	134.5621	175.1856	243.3563	192.9148	484.8395	258.3265	79.3058
4	115.8881	111.7933	173.0281	134.7068	176.1414	245.2204	190.4294	483.8177	252.4005	79.7060
5	116.8403	111.9033	179.7596	134.6359	180.7020	246.8022	191.6878	450.8297	251.7819	80.1223
6	117.2491	111.3808	184.4802	134.6459	182.2170	250.2702	192.3504	449.6640	247.5552	77.0751
7	117.3491	111.1474	187.4455	134.3871	183.6016	251.0139	196.9546	478.2303	249.0585	76.9830
8	117.0358	111.3700	189.0682	134.7542	184.3065	252.4351	200.3956	227.2484	248.5670	76.9940
9	117.3522	110.8549	189.6524	188.5831	185.0094	254.6155	199.2114	225.7937	249.0843	76.6743
10	117.4546	110.8631	190.3173	188.1681	184.5400	253.9582	198.1375	216.7308	248.9961	75.7503
S/N.	Intensity features for male speakers (Adult)					Intensity features for female speakers (Adult)				
	m1	m2	m3	m4	m5	f1	f2	f3	f4	f5
1	66.1410	70.4704	52.4520	70.0272	68.6173	58.6389	85.1853	54.2817	67.3221	59.3049
2	67.3352	74.1379	53.5415	70.9011	68.0168	59.4191	80.2720	54.8725	68.1054	58.1709
3	69.5176	73.7162	54.7622	71.6274	66.9298	58.8852	80.5123	58.9230	69.1992	58.8896
4	70.1385	72.6461	54.3097	71.9813	64.7642	58.4090	82.9598	61.3677	69.6819	60.1642
5	69.3748	75.6862	52.1648	72.1933	63.7987	58.6244	81.6141	60.6338	69.8889	60.6608
6	68.9586	77.9109	53.4827	72.0828	64.2934	60.2951	79.9555	60.7411	70.3774	61.4306
7	68.8292	77.5628	56.1590	72.0078	65.5724	62.4975	77.6855	62.5347	70.7705	61.5529
8	68.4343	77.4653	55.4623	72.2310	66.5777	63.1172	77.2605	63.2792	71.0914	60.6879
9	67.8689	78.6557	51.6701	72.3732	66.7889	65.7422	79.4234	63.2237	71.3975	60.3815
10	67.7595	78.2761	51.0957	72.5719	67.4040	67.0769	79.1504	61.3956	71.1904	60.1720
S/N.	Pulse features for male speakers (Adult)					Pulse features for female speakers (Adult)				
	m1	m2	m3	m4	m5	f1	f2	f3	f4	f5
1	1.2336	1.9694	1.5047	1.4662	1.0076	0.5358	0.9112	0.6192	0.1895	0.1874
2	1.2427	1.9719	1.5107	1.4737	1.0133	0.5397	0.9164	0.6216	0.1933	0.2000
3	1.2513	1.9739	1.5164	1.4811	1.0190	0.5439	0.9216	0.6233	0.1971	0.2130
4	1.2598	1.9760	1.5218	1.4885	1.0244	0.5480	0.9268	0.6251	0.2009	0.2254
5	1.2683	1.9779	1.5271	1.7805	1.0299	0.5520	0.9321	0.6270	0.2049	0.2397
6	1.2769	2.0882	1.5323	1.7857	1.0352	0.5560	0.9370	0.6291	0.2089	0.2563
7	1.2854	2.0971	1.5375	1.7911	1.0407	0.5600	0.9793	0.6307	0.2130	0.2688
8	1.2940	2.1060	1.5427	1.7966	1.0462	0.5640	0.9843	0.6326	0.2170	0.2813
9	1.3026	2.1151	1.5479	1.8020	1.0517	0.5678	0.9894	0.6342	0.2210	0.2943
10	1.3112	2.1241	1.5530	1.8073	1.0571	0.5718	0.9944	0.8842	0.2250	0.3068

respectively. The y-axis represents the F0 signal, while the x-axis represents the speech frame. The plots reveal that children exhibit wider variability in F0 pattern between speakers, compared to other age categories, and the variability gap closes as the speaker ages. Hence, F0 features are important for studying both inter- and intra- variability in speakers. The severe distortions noticed in plots of other age categories (i.e., youths (16–30), adults (31–50) and seniors (above 50)) indicate that F0 signals are easily prone to suboptimal conditions such as: environmental factors—background noise, channel defects—power degradation—as the distortions seem more severe in male and female speakers who have advanced in age. Thus, implying that higher F0 signals are not easily influenced by suboptimal conditions—as the environmental and channel defects tend to separate out during signal extraction, but are not easily separable for voices with lower F0 s. In Figs. 57.6 and 57.7, the *y*-axis represents intensity pattern, while the *x*-axis is the

speech-frame. The figures show that intensity features are not affected by suboptimal conditions—as the various plots indicate clean patterns, compared to the severe distortions experienced in the F0 signals (see Figs. 57.4 and 57.5). Also, variability in intensity pattern between speakers appears to be approximately the same across all the speaker categories—with few speakers in the children category producing a near linear (or leveled) intensity with insignificant pattern. The linear nature of the pattern may not be unconnected with the age of the child—as the pattern becomes more apparent as the Chile ages. In Figs. 57.8 and 57.9, the *y*-axis represents glottal pulse signal, while the *x*-axis represents the speech-frame. The figures indicate that all speakers showed variations in glottal pulse pattern, and this imply that glottal pulses are good candidates for speaker discrimination systems.

Fig. 57.3 SOM network architecture

57.3.2 SOM Quality

Self-organized learning enables the discovery of significant patterns or features in input data without expert knowledge. We assume that our input data contains an optimal map, and specify a cost function that explicitly defines the optimal

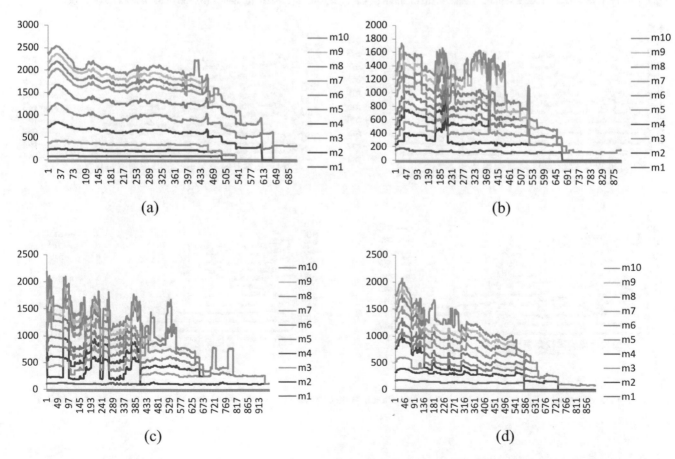

Fig. 57.4 Plots of F0 features for male speakers. (**a**) children (0–15), (**b**) youths (16–30), (**c**) adults (31–50), (**d**) seniors (above 50)

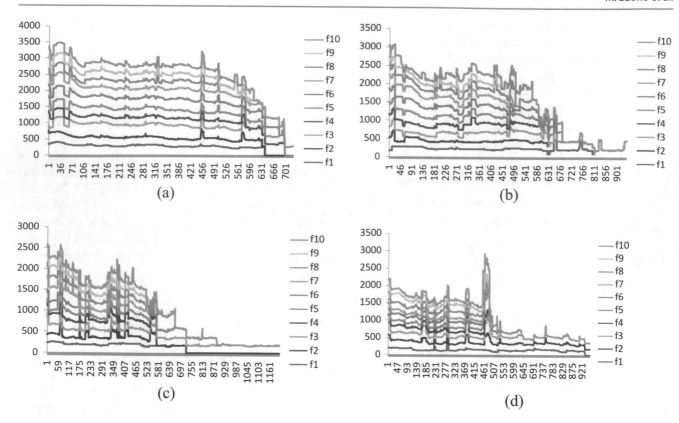

Fig. 57.5 Plots of F0 features for female speakers. (**a**) children (0–15), (**b**) youths (16–30), (**c**) adults (31–50), (**d**) seniors (above 50)

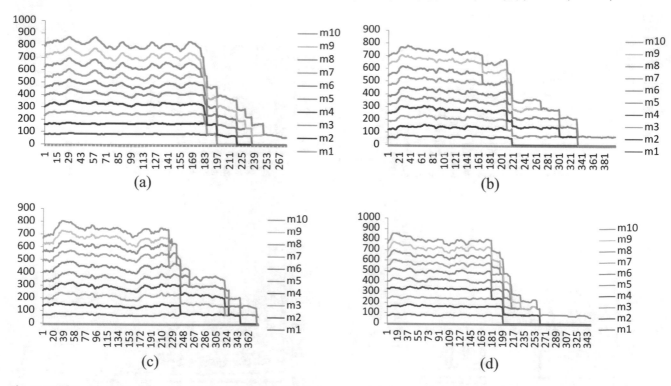

Fig. 57.6 Plots of intensity features for male speakers. (**a**) children (0–15), (**b**) youths (16–30), (**c**) adults (31–50), (**d**) seniors (above 50)

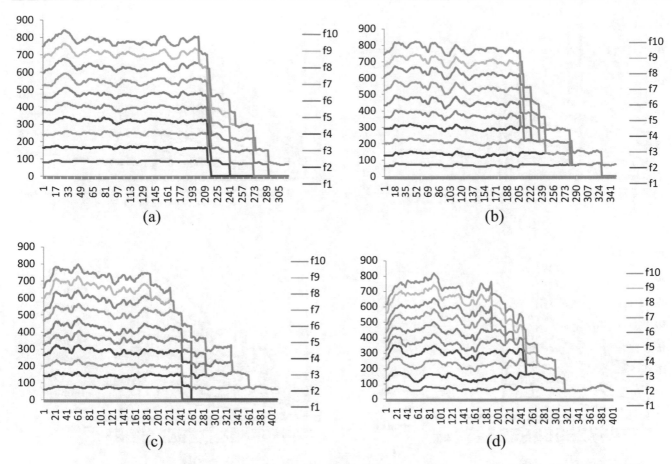

Fig. 57.7 Plots of intensity features for female speakers. (**a**) children (0–15), (**b**) youths (16–30), (**c**) adults (31–50), (**d**) seniors (above 50)

solution. The measures used in this paper to determine the map quality are the average quantization error and the topographic error, which formulas are given in Eqs. (57.1) and (57.2) [12], respectively,

$$E_q = \frac{1}{N} \sum_{i=1}^{N} \|x_i - m_i\| \qquad (57.1)$$

$$E_T = \frac{1}{N} \sum_{i=1}^{N} Nu\,(x_x) \qquad (57.2)$$

where N is the number of input vectors used to train the map, and $u(x_k)$ is 1—if the first and second best matching unit (BMU) of x_k are not direct neighbors of each other, otherwise $u(x_k)$ is 0. The average quantization and topographic errors after the SOM training were, 0.509 and 0.104, respectively.

A SOM with a lower average error is more accurate than a SOM with higher average error, and the quantization error declines as the map grows. Topographic error measures topographic preservation—the proportion of all data vectors for which the first and second adjacent units resides. The average quantization and topographic errors appear fair to guarantee robust map quality and preserve the map topology.

57.3.3 SOM Visualization

The U-matrix and component planes for the various speaker categories are presented in Table 57.2. The U-matrix is frequently used to illustrate the clustering of the reference vectors in the SOM. In the U-matrix, same color is assigned

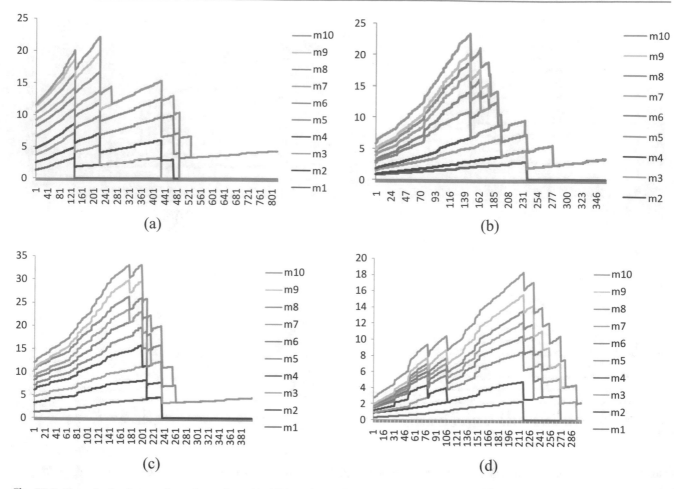

Fig. 57.8 Plots of pulse features for male speakers. (**a**) children (0–15), (**b**) youths (16–30), (**c**) adults (31–50), (**d**) seniors (above 50)

to similar nodes. A light coloring between nodes signifies that the reference vectors are close to each other in the input space, and a dark coloring between the nodes corresponds to larger distances or wide variability between the reference vectors of the input space. The component planes reveal the details concerning the spread of the component or feature values and are useful for correlation hunting—i.e., finding the feature planes with similar patterns. Concerning the individual component maps, most of the maps satisfied the properties of SOM, as their colors changed gradually from shades of red (high values) to shades of blue (low values). The SOM results confirm that there exists high inter-variability—between speakers—as the individual component maps showed weak correlation. Further, there seems to be low intra-variability—within speakers—as the osmosis from one color shade to another appears to be slow.

57.4 Conclusion and Future Work

In this paper, the analysis of speech features collected in suboptimal conditions was demonstrated. We have identified the existence of speaker variability for a possible discrimination of speaker category (gender, age) and clusters—based on the analysis of cascaded plots and SOM component planes. However, the cluster membership determination was subjective, as we relied on color coded distances between the estimated vectors of the map positions. The current paper represents work in progress and was aimed at proving the feasibility of the research. A more extensive research into the discovery and modeling of speaker variability with large corpus dataset is expected in an extended paper.

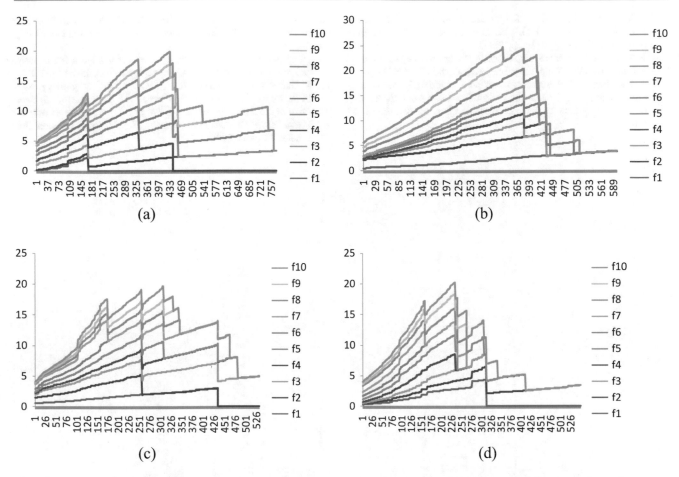

Fig. 57.9 Plots of pulse features for female speakers. (**a**) children (0–15), (**b**) youths (16–30), (**c**) adults (31–50), (**d**) seniors (above 50)

Table 57.2 Visualization result

Gender	Age category				U-matrix
	0-15	16-30	31-50	>50	
Male					
Female					

References

1. W. Koenig, A new frequency scale for acoustic measurements. Bell Telephone Lab. Rec. **27**, 299–301 (1949)
2. S.B. Davis, P. Ermelstein, Comparison of parametric representations for monosyllabic word recognition in continuously spoken sentences. IEEE Trans. Acoust. Speech Sig. Process. **28**(4), 357–366 (1980)
3. N. Kaiki, K. Takeda, Y. Sagisaka, Linguistic properties in the control of segmental duration for speech synthesis, in *Talking Machines: Theories, Models, and Designs*, ed. By G. Bailly, C. Benoit, T.R. Sawalis (Elsevier, Amsterdam, 1992), pp. 255–263
4. M. Riley, Tree-based modelling of segmental duration, in *Talking Machines: Theories, Models, and Designs*, ed. By G. Bailly, C. Benoit, T.R. Sawallis (Elsevier Science, Amsterdam, 1992), pp. 265–273
5. N. Iwahashi, Y. Sagisaka, Duration modeling with multiple split regression, in *Proceedings of the EUROSPEEC,* 1993, pp. 329–332
6. J.P.H. van Santen, C. Shih, B. Mobius, E. Tzoukermann, M. Tanenblatt, Multi-lingual duration modeling, in *Proceedings of the EUROSPEEC-97* vol. 5, 1997, pp. 2651–2654

7. T. Yoshimura, K. Tokuda, T. Masuko, T Kobayashi, T Kitamura, Duration modeling for HMM-based speech synthesis, in *Proceedings of the ICSLP 98*, 1998, pp. 29–31
8. K.S. Rao, B. Yegnanarayana, Modeling durations of syllables using neural networks. Comput. Speech Lang. **1**, 282–295 (2007)
9. T. Shreekantha, V. Udayashankarab, M. Chandrika, Duration modelling using neural networks for hindi TTS system considering position of syllable in a word. Procedia Comput. Sci. **46**, 60–67 (2015)
10. A.K. Jain, A. Ross, S. Prabhakar, An introduction to biometric recognition. IEEE Trans. Circuit. Syst. Video Technol. **14**(1), 4–20 (2004)
11. U. Bhattacharjee, K. Sarmah, Speaker verification using acoustic and prosodic features. Adv. Comput. Int. J. **4**(1), 45–51 (2013)
12. S. Gabrielsson, S. Gabrielsson. *The use of Self-Organizing Maps in Recommender Systems. A Survey of the Recommender Systems Field and a Presentation of a State of the Art Highly Interactive Visual Movie Recommender System*. M.Sc. Thesis, Uppsala Universitet, Sweden, 2006

Michael Chang, Rohan J. Dalpatadu, and Ashok K. Singh

Abstract

The binary logistic regression is a machine learning tool for classification and discrimination that is widely used in business analytics and medical research. Transforming continuous predictors to improve model performance of logistic regression is a common practice, but no systematic method for finding optimal transformations exists in the statistical or data mining literature. In this paper, the problem of selecting transformations of continuous predictors to improve the performance of logistic regression models is considered. The proposed method is based upon the point-biserial correlation coefficient between the binary response and a continuous predictor. Several examples are presented to illustrate the proposed method.

Keywords

Machine learning · Data mining · Precision · Recal · F1

58.1 Introduction

In fitting a regression model, continuous predictors are sometimes transformed to improve model fit [1]. The correlation coefficient between the continuous response variable and a continuous predictor can be used for this purpose. When the response is binary and the logistic regression (LR) is used to predict the response, predictor transformations are still used [2, 3], but no practical method seems to exist in the

M. Chang · R. J. Dalpatadu
Department of Mathematical Sciences, University of Nevada, Las Vegas, Las Vegas, NV, USA
e-mail: changm13@unlv.nevada.edu; rohan.dalpatadu@unlv.edu

A. K. Singh (✉)
William F. Harrah College of Hotel Administration, University of Nevada, Las Vegas, Las Vegas, NV, USA
e-mail: ashok.singh@unlv.nevada.edu

literature for improving the performance of prediction. In this article, we investigate the applicability of the point-biserial correlation [4, 5] in selection of predictor transformations for continuous predictors in order to improve the fit of an LR model. Pseudo R-square values, Precision, recall and F1-measure ([6–10]) are used to compare the LR models based on raw and optimally transformed predictors.

Examples from machine learning literature and also from big data analytics are presented in this paper to illustrate the proposed method. The model performance results based on optimally transformed predictors are found to be at least as good as those based on raw data.

58.2 Description of the Problem

Logistic regression (LR) is used to find a relationship between a binary dependent variable Y and a set of predictor variables $\{X_1, \ldots, X_P\}$. The predictor variables can be continuous or categorical; dummy variables are used in the latter case.

With π denoting the success probability $P(Y = 1)$ the LR model can be expressed as [8]

$$\frac{\pi}{1 - \pi} = e^{\beta_0 + \sum\limits_{j=1}^{P} \beta_j X_j}$$

or

$$\ln \left(\frac{\pi}{1 - \pi} \right) = \beta_0 + \sum_{j=1}^{P} \beta_j X_j$$

i.e., log-odds is a linear function of the predictors X_j, $j = 1, 2, \ldots, P$.

This article is concerned with determining transformations of all continuous predictors to improve the performance of the fitted LR model. The method for finding optimal transformations is based upon the point-biserial correlation coefficient, which is a correlation between a binary and a continuous variable; for creating optimal bins of a continuous predictor, the chi-square test of independence between the binary response and a binned predictor is used. Multicollinearity among predictors is handled as follows: one by one, any predictor with generalized variance inflation factor (GVIF) [11] above 5 is removed, and then any predictor which is insignificant at 5% significance level is removed to obtain the final LR model.

58.2.1 The Biserial and Point-biserial Correlation Coefficients

Given an independent random sample $\{(X_1, Y_1), \ldots, (X_n, Y_n)\}$ of n observations on a pair of random variables (rv) (X, Y), with X continuous and Y binary, the product-moment correlation coefficient between X and Y is called the biserial correlation coefficient if Y is a dichotomized version of a normally distributed rv Y^*; in case Y is a binary rv with no natural ordering (e.g., $Y = 1$ if subject survives, and 0 otherwise), the product-moment correlation coefficient between X and Y is called the point-biserial correlation coefficient [5]. The point-biserial coefficient can be calculated from the following expression [5]:

$$r_{PB} = \left(\frac{\overline{X}_1 - \overline{X}_0}{s_Y} \right) \sqrt{\frac{np_1(1-p_1)}{n-1}}$$

where

$$\overline{X}_j = \frac{\sum_{i=1}^{n_j} X_{ij}}{n_j} \text{ is the mean of continuous}$$

variable X when $Y = j$, $j = 0, 1$, and $P_1 = \sum_{i=1}^{n} Y_i / n$

The null hypothesis of 0 correlation between Y and X can be tested by using the t-statistic

$$t_{PB} = \frac{r_{PB}\sqrt{n-2}}{\sqrt{1 - r_{PB}^2}}$$

which has a t-distribution with degrees of freedom (df) $n-2$.

58.2.2 Determination of Optimal Transformation for a Continuous Predictor

We will demonstrate the proposed method with some of the commonly used transformations business analytics: natural log, square, square root, inverse, and binning.

In this article, we will consider the following continuous transformations for each continuous predictor X:

$$X_1 = \ln(X), X_2 = X^2, X_3 = \sqrt{X}, \text{ and } X_4 = 1/X.$$

The optimal continuous transformation can be determined as follows:

1. Compute the point-biserial correlation coefficient between the binary Y and X, $X_1, \ldots, X_4$.
2. Calculate the t-statistics t_{PB} for each version of the predictor in Step (i).
3. Use the predictor transformation that corresponds to $\max(|t_{PB}|)$; in case the predictor X yields the largest value, do not transform the predictor X.

In order to determine optimal bins for a continuous predictor, following steps are used:

1. Create k bins ($k \geq 2$) for the continuous predictor X.
2. Calculate the chi-square statistic and associated P-value for testing independence between Y and X.
3. Choose $k = k_0$ where k_0 yields the smallest P-value.

In the next section, the proposed method is illustrated with a few examples.

58.2.3 Performance Measures of Binary Classifiers

The commonly used performance measures for binary classifiers [9, 10] are calculated from the confusion matrix (Table 58.1) for each category {0,1} from the following formulas:

Table 58.1 Confusion matrix

		Predicted response	
		0	1
Actual response	0	$C_{0,0}$	$C_{0,1}$
	1	$C_{1,0}$	$C_{1,1}$

$$\text{Precision}_j = \frac{C_{j,j}}{\sum\limits_{k=0}^{1} C_{j,k}}$$

$$\text{Recall}_j = \frac{C_{j,j}}{\sum\limits_{k=0}^{1} C_{k,j}}$$

$$\text{F1}_j = \frac{2 \times \text{Precision}_j \times \text{Recall}_j}{(\text{Precision}_j + \text{Recall}_j)} \quad (j = 0, 1)$$

There are no multicollinearity issues in this model since all variance inflation values (VIF) values are less than 1.25. The pseudo-R^2 values (McFadden = 0.31, CoxSnell = 0.34, Nagelkerke = 0.46) suggest a good fit. Precision, recall, and F1 values for the two categories 1 and 0 for the above LR model are shown in Table 58.4.

58.3 Examples

In this section, we will present a few examples; for smaller data sets, instead of generating a training set, we will fit the LR model to the entire data set after casewise deletion of missing values.

Example 1: In this example, the well-known titanic data set [12] is used; titanic data set has following information on the 1309 passengers of Titanic:

The titanic data set has several missing values in the age column. Casewise deletion resulted in 1045 rows of data with no missing values in any column. The final LR model for the binary response Y (survived) fitted to this subset of data is shown in Table 58.2. Table 58.3 shows that being male reduces the log odds by 2.5 while a unit increase in age

Table 58.2 Description of the titanic data set

Name	Variable explanation
pclass	Passenger Class (1 = 1st; 2 = 2nd; 3 = 3rd)
Survived	Survival (0 = no, 1 = yes)
Name	Passenger name
Sex	Gender of passenger
Age	Age of passenger
Sibsp	(number of siblings/spouses aboard)
Parch	(number of parents/children aboard)
Ticket	Ticket number
Fare	Passenger fare (£)
Cabin	Cabin
Embarked	Port of Embarkation (C = Cherbourg; Q = Queenstown; S = Southampton)
Boat	Lifeboat
Body	Body Identification Number
Home.dest	Home/Destination

reduces the log odds by 0.03; moreover, log odds of survival are highest in pclass 1.

In the titanic data set, age is the only continuous predictor in the fitted LR model. The absolute t-values for the raw predictor age and each of the four transformations of age

$X_1 = ln(1 + X)$.
$X_2 = (age)^2$.
$X_3 = \sqrt{age}$.
$X_4 = 1/age$.

are above 3.1 (indicating highly significant point-biserial correlation) with the largest one corresponding to the log-transformation. The fitted LR model with age replaced by $\ln(1 + age)$ is shown in Table 58.5.

The pseudo-R^2 values for the model based on transformed predictors are same (McFadden = 0.31, CoxSnell = 0.34, Nagelkerke = 0.46) as before.

Precision, recall, and F1 values for both the categories 1 and 0 for the LR model using log-transformed age are slightly higher than those using age (Table 58.6).

Table 58.3 LR model fitted to titanic data with missing values removed

	Estimate	SE	z-value	P-value
(Intercept)	3.52	0.33	10.77	0.00
age	−0.03	0.01	−5.42	0.00
pclass 2	−1.28	0.23	−5.68	0.00
pclass 3	−2.29	0.23	−10.13	0.00
Male	−2.50	0.17	−15.04	0.00

Table 58.4 Precision, recall, and F1 values for the final LR model based on age

Category	Precision (%)	Recall (%)	F1 (%)
1	75	70	73
0	80	84	82

Table 58.5 LR model fitted to titanic data with age replaced by $\ln(1 + age)$

	Estimate	SE	z	P-value
(Intercept)	4.76	0.50	9.44	0
log(1 + Age)	−0.72	0.13	−5.74	0
pclass 2	−1.18	0.22	−5.41	0
pclass 3	−2.16	0.21	−10.20	0
Male	−2.51	0.17	−15.10	0

Table 58.6 Precision, recall, and F1 values for the final LR model based on ln(age)

Category	Precision	Recall	F1
1	0.78	0.71	0.74
0	0.81	0.86	0.83

Table 58.7 Values of abs(t) for predictor X and the transformations $\log(1 + X)$, X^2, $\sqrt{X}$, and $1/(1 + X)$ for the four predictors

	t.raw	t.log	t.sqr	t.sqrt	t.Inv
X1	31.8	23.7	22.5	27.9	29.3
X2	98.0	184.2	73.4	148.7	177.0
X3	83.1	128.7	72.2	108.3	294.3
X4	28.9	15.4	41.9	2.0	87.2

Table 58.8 Pseudo R-square for the transformed and untransformed predictors LR models

	McF	CS	N
Untransformed	0.26	0.17	0.34
Transformed	0.32	0.20	0.40

Example 2: The breast cancer survival data set used in this example is described in detail in [12]. The pre-processed data has 338,596 observations on the binary response variable (survivability) and 19 predictors; there are 38,381 cases (11.34%) of response 0 and 300,215 cases (88.66%) of response 1. Since this is a rather large data set, we split the data set into a training set and a test set by randomly selecting 25% of the observations for the test set.

In the final LR model for survivability based on the training set, there are five significant categorical predictors (Race, Marital status, Grade, Radiation, and csEODExtension) and four continuous predictors (X1 = ageAtDiagnosis, X2 = csEODTumorSize, X3 = regional NodesPositive, and X4 = NodesExamined). Maximum GVIF value for the fitted LR model is 1.2. The absolute values of the t-statistics, with the largest value shaded, for the 4 transformations for each of the 4 continuous predictors listed above are shown in Table 58.7.

Table 58.8 shows that X1 does not need to be transformed, and $\ln(1 + X2)$, $1/(1 + X3)$ and $1/(1 + X4)$ should replace X2, X3, and X4 respectively. The final LR model based on transformed predictors also has no multicollinearity issues as GVIF <1.2.

We will next compare the untransformed LR model to the transformed one. Table 58.8 shows that the transformed LR model performed slightly better than the untransformed one in terms of the pseudo R-square values.

Table 58.9 shows precision, recall and F1 values for categories 1 and 0, respectively. For category 1 (Table 58.9), there is hardly any difference in the two models, but slight gains in the transformed model are seen in for category 0 (Table 58.9).

Example 3: In the third example, we use a data set from credit scoring used in the credit and banking industries. After preprocessing and eliminating irrelevant variables, the data set had 122,763 observations on a total of 343 variables including the binary response Y which equals 1 for a high risk customer. After removing the set of continuous predictors

Table 58.9 Precision, recall and F1 measures for Categories 0 and 1

		Precision	Recall	F1
Category 1				
Untransformed	Training	0.92	0.99	0.95
Transformed	set	0.92	0.98	0.95
Untransformed	Test	0.92	0.99	0.95
Transformed	set	0.92	0.98	0.95
Category 0				
Untransformed	Training	0.72	0.29	0.42
Transformed	set	0.71	0.32	0.44
Untransformed	Test	0.72	0.29	0.42
Transformed	set	0.72	0.32	0.44

Table 58.10 Values of abs(t) for predictor X and the transformations $\log(1 + X)$, X^2, $\sqrt{X}$, and $1/(1 + X)$ for the top-20 predictors

	t.raw	t.log	t.Sqr	t.SqrT	t.Inv
var96	61.94	79.17	61.23	62.69	47.08
var93	57.18	69.67	56.54	57.25	38.34
var95	53.95	68.34	53.31	54.47	43.29
var73	49.87	74.22	16.99	57.28	52.12
var273	44.72	76.34	21.39	55.51	58.28
var113	42.39	74.84	30.19	51.74	57.39
var303	38.69	49.38	37.19	39.12	37.99
var97	32.47	47.79	10.63	39.57	32.28
var267	31.41	63.66	7.95	41.62	54.88
var92	30.18	35.38	30.41	29.61	24.28
var224	27.69	38.45	18.70	29.78	29.73
var22	25.93	35.02	23.20	27.14	27.59
var271	25.49	17.80	24.75	24.17	26.17
var53	26.44	36.33	18.43	28.24	28.03
var41	24.15	32.93	16.25	25.49	26.27
var272	22.78	19.13	11.20	20.67	10.32
var318	21.95	31.05	15.48	23.68	25.11
var99	19.97	2.14	15.27	16.34	33.16
var126	19.39	27.40	14.27	20.87	22.29
var89	21.16	64.01	0.80	42.52	53.17

which were perfectly correlated, and one which was constant, we were left with 319 continuous predictors. A model with 'top-20' predictors was needed for this data set; these were identified by computing the point-biserial correlations of these predictors with Y, and retaining the 20 predictors with the largest point-biserial correlations. In the final LR model, there were 18 significant predictors (P < 0.0004).

To determine best transformations of these predictors, the point-biserial correlations were calculated (Table 58.10).

All but var272 were transformed as indicated by the shaded cells in Table 58.10. We next compare the two models (untransformed and transformed predictors). Table 58.11 shows that the pseudo R-square values remained the same.

Table 58.11 Pseudo R-square values of the untransformed and transformed LR models

	McF	CS	N
Untransformed	0.07	0.09	0.13
Transformed	0.07	0.09	0.13

Table 58.12 Precision, recall and F1 measures for Category 1

		Precision	Recall	F1
Untransformed	Training	0.61	0.48	0.54
Transformed	set	0.62	0.51	0.56
Untransformed	Test	0.61	0.48	0.54
Transformed	set	0.62	0.50	0.56

Table 58.13 Values of abs(t) for predictor X and the transformations $\log(1 + X)$, X^2, $\sqrt{X}$, and $1/(1 + X)$

	t.raw	t.log	t.Sqr	t.SqrT	t.Inv
Pasthapp	4.70	2.41	5.65	2.57	1.53
Futurehapp	0.87	0.05	1.85	0.12	1.19
FTP	0.15	0.43	0.18	0.31	1.12

Table 58.14 Precision, recall and F1 measures for Category 1 for Example 4

	Precision	Recall	F1
Untransformed	0.71	0.57	0.63
Transformed	0.76	0.63	0.69

In the credit and banking applications, interest is only in predicting category 1, hence results for only category 1 are presented for this example. Table 58.12 shows precision, recall and F1 values for category 1 for the training and test data sets. Slight improvements are seen with transformed predictors.

Example 4: Data from this example is obtained from the University of Stanford website https://web.stanford.edu/class/psych252/tutorials/Tutorial_LogisticRegression.html. This data set has 63 observations on 9 potential predictors and a binary response variable 'complain'. In the final LR model, only the variable 'Responsible' was significant. The t-values for the point-biserial correlations for the remaining three continuous predictors are shown in Table 58.13.

The LR model with square-transformed Pasthapp and Futurehapp and 1/FTP resulted in precision, recall, F1 values that were similar to theLR model with untransformed

predictors [13–15]. We next used the method of binning on Pasthapp and found 3 bins to be optimal: $(-0.015,5]$, $(5,10]$, and $(10,15]$. The final LR model with binned Pasthapp, Responsible, Futurehapp^2 and 1/FTP turned out to be better than the LR model with untransformed predictors as shown in Table 58.14.

References

1. M.H. Kutner, C.J. Nachtsheim, J. Neter, *Applied Linear Regression Models*, 4th edn. (McGraw-Hill Higher Education, Boston, 2004), pp. 129–141
2. F.E. Harrell, *Regression Modeling Strategies: With Applications to Linear Models, Logistic Regression, and Survival Analysis* (Springer Science & Business Media, New York, 2001), pp. 7–10
3. E.W. Steyerberg, *Clinical Prediction Models: A Practical Approach to Development, Validation, and Updating* (Springer Science & Business Media, New York, 2008), pp. 57–58
4. R. Kay, S. Little, Transformations of the explanatory variables in the logistic regression model for binary data. Biomelrika **74**(3), 495–501 (1987)
5. H.C. Kraemer, Correlation coefficients in medical research: from product moment correlation to the odds ratio. Stat. Methods Med. Res. **15**, 525–545 (2006)
6. NCSS Statistical Software Manual, Chapter 302. Point-Biserial and Biserial Correlations. https://ncss-wpengine.netdna-ssl.com/wp-content/themes/ncss/pdf/Procedures/NCSS/Point-Biserial_and_Biserial_Correlations.pdf
7. F. Guillet, H. Hamilton, J. (eds.), *Quality Measures in Data Mining*, vol 43 (Springer, New York, 2007)
8. G. James, D. Witten, T. Hastie, R. Tibshirani, *An Introduction to Statistical Learning*, vol 6 (Springer, New York, 2013)
9. D.W. Hosmer Jr., H. Lemeshow, *Applied Logistic Regression* (Wiley, New York, 2004)
10. F. Cady, *The Data Science Handbook* (Wiley, New York, 2017), pp. 118–119
11. D.M.W. Powers, Evaluation: from precision, recall and F-measure to ROC, informedness, markedness and correlation. J. Mach. Learn. Technol. **2**(1), 37–63 (2011)
12. J. Fox, G. Monette, Generalized collinearity diagnostics. J. Am. Stat. Assoc. **87**, 178–183 (1992)
13. E.W. Steyerberg, A.J. Vickers, N.R. Cook, T. Gerds, M. Gonen, N. Obuchowski, M.J. Pencina, M.W. Kattan, Assessing the performance of prediction models: a framework for some traditional and novel measures. Epidemiology **21**(1), 128–138 (2010)
14. M. Bozorgi, K. Taghva, A.K. Singh, Cancer survivability with logistic regression, in *Computing Conference 2017*, London, July 2017, pp. 18–20
15. Y. Zhao, *R and Data Mining: Examples and Case Studies* (Academic Press, London, 2012), pp. 90–92

Part VI

Software Engineering

A Generic Approach to Efficiently Parallelize Legacy Sequential Software

Andreas Granholm and Federico Ciccozzi

Abstract

Multi-core processing units have been the answer to ever increasing demand of computational power of modern software. One of the main issues with the adoption of new hardware is portability of legacy software. In this specific case, in order for legacy sequential software to maximize the exploitation of the computational benefits brought by multi-core processors, it has to undergo a parallelization effort. Although there is a common agreement and well-specified support for parallelizing sequential algorithms, there is still a lack in supporting software engineers in identifying and assessing parallelization potentials in a legacy sequential application. In this work we provide a generic parallelization approach which supports the engineering in maximizing performance gain through parallelization while minimizing the cost of the parallelization effort. We evaluate the approach on an industrial use-case at ABB Robotics.

Keywords

Parallelization · Legacy · CUDA · OpenMP

59.1 Introduction

The greediness of modern software in terms of computational power has led to a wide industrial adoption of the so called multi-core processing units [1]. Besides multi-core Central Processing Units (CPUs), developers have an additional parallel computing platform for general-purpose programming at their disposal, namely Graphical Processing Unit (GPU). Initially designed for graphical computations, GPUs offer many more computational units than a multi-core CPU, with the drawback of a generally slower clock frequency.

In order to utilize the full potential of parallel hardware, existing sequential software needs to be re-engineered to exploit parallelization. Parallelizing sequential software mainly conceives two steps: (1) individuation of software portions with the best parallelization potentials in relation to a more or less fixed "parallelization budget".[1] While techniques for parallelizing sequential algorithms have been largely studied, there is lack of support for guiding the software engineering in identifying parallelization potentials [2].

Parallelizing software increases performance, but it can negatively affect other quality attributes, such as verifiability and maintainability [3]. Moreover, due to the intrinsic complexity of parallelizing software [4], introducing parallelization in existing sequential software can be a very costly task. In this study we are interested in finding out which software and process aspects shall be considered when parallelizing legacy sequential software and how to take them into account. Thus, we focus on providing a generic parallelization approach which aims at maximizing the increment of performance of existing software through parallelization while minimizing the cost of the parallelization effort. We consider both CPUs and GPUs as parallelization hardware targets to maximize the potential performance gain depending on the specific application type and we evaluate the parallelization approach on an industrial use-case.

The remainder of the paper is structured as follows. In Sect. 59.2, we provide a snapshot of the state-of-the-art in contraposition to our contribution. The parallelization approach and its details are unwound in Sect. 59.3, and its industrial evaluation is described in Sect. 59.4. The paper is

A. Granholm
ABB Robotics, Västerås, Sweden
e-mail: andreas.granholm@se.abb.com

F. Ciccozzi (✉)
Mälardalen University – IDT, Västerås, Sweden
e-mail: federico.ciccozzi@mdh.se

---

[1]The parallelization budget depends on several factors and it represents the budget in terms of maximum parallelization effort by which the parallelization itself is considered preferable to a re-implementation from scratch.

© Springer International Publishing AG, part of Springer Nature 2018
S. Latifi (ed.), *Information Technology – New Generations*, Advances in Intelligent Systems and Computing 738,
https://doi.org/10.1007/978-3-319-77028-4_59

concluded with a conclusive summary and identified future research directions in Sect. 59.5.

59.2   State-of-the-Art and Novelty

In 2003, Intel [5] presented a method to introduce threading in sequential software using a generic development lifecycle consisting of six different phases. This methods only targets developers using Intel threading tools and it only considers CPUs as target hardware. Tovinkere [6] presents an approach very similar to Intel's, also using threading to increase the performance of sequential software. Tovinkere's approach is less tool-dependent than Intel's, but focuses on CPUs only too. Jun-feng[7] provides an approach for parallelization, but without supporting the location of parallellization potentials and only targeting CPUs. Christmann et al. [8] present a method for porting existing sequential software to a parallel platform taking into account some financial aspects of the parallelization, but target CPUs only. The method proposed by Nvidia [9] is based upon an iterative approach able to deploy a parallelized portion as soon as possible to quickly create value for the users. However, it only considers GPUs. The method presented by Tinetti et al. [10] is iterative and focuses on parallelization of Fortran software using OpenMP on CPUs.

The novel aspect brought by our contribution is the provision and the interplay of the following four features:

1. consideration of effort estimation for the parallelization task;
2. support for identifying software portions with best parallelization potential;
3. consider both CPUs and GPUs as potential target parallel platforms;
4. not focus on specific languages or tools.

The combination of (1) and (2) gives the opportunity to prioritize software portions with parallelization potential that require lower effort and provide higher potential performance gain. With (3), we can maximize performance gains in case where both CPUs and GPUs are available. Through (4), we aim at providing a generic approach which can be instantiated using different technologies depending on the application scenario.

59.3   The Parallelization Approach

The parallelization approach that we propose consists of three phases and is depicted in Fig. 59.1. The first phase represents the definition of the goals of the parallelization as well as the tools to use. In the second phase, developers

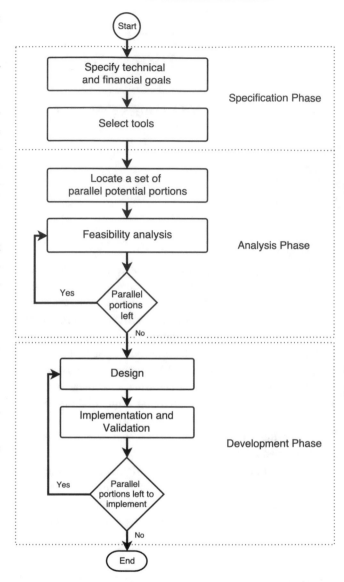

Fig. 59.1 Parallelization approach

analyze the software for individuating parallelization potential and perform a parallelization feasibility analysis. The third and last phase concerns the actual parallelization, where the selected software portions are further analyzed and a parallel solution is designed, implemented, and validated. In the following subsections we describe the three phases in more detail.

59.3.1 Specification Phase

In this phase, the engineer specifies the goals of the parallelization and decides on which tools to use. Goals are of two kinds: financial and technical. An example of financial goal is development effort introduced by the parallelization. An example of technical goal is the desired performance gain in terms of execution speedup as a result of the parallelization. In the industrial evaluation of our approach we focus on these two. Clearly, there are two ways to tradeoff them: either prioritizing cost over performance or the other way around [8]. In the first case, there is a fixed budget for carrying out the parallelization task and, once the budget is used, parallelization stops no matter how much performance has improved. In the second, we decide on a target level of performance to reach, and parallelization is carried on until that is reached, with looser constraints on cost.

Apart from goals, the engineer is supposed to select the tools to use for the parallelization, and this is usually very dependent on the characteristics of the software to parallelize. For instance, if the existing software is written in C++, then tools that support C++ need to be used. In some cases, it could be beneficial to first port the existing software in order for it to be used on a unsupported platform; this would require additional parallelization phases, and it is not in the scope of this work. A profiling tool, to be used during the identification of software portions with parallelization potential should be selected too, together with a monitoring tool to measure the software execution time to be used for feasibility analysis. Additionally, the engineer selects which parallel computing APIs to use, considering compatibility with the software to parallelize and the targeted parallel platform.

59.3.2 Analysis Phase

The purpose of this phase is to analyze the software to (1) find potential for parallelization, (2) estimation of maximum performance gain from parallelization, and (3) estimation of parallelization effort, in the given order. We address (2) and (3) as feasibility analysis.

59.3.2.1 Identification of Parallelization Potentials

Our approach indicates two complementary methods, to be exploited jointly, for carrying out this task: manual and automatic control flow analysis. Analyzing the control flow of the software to parallelize is needed to reveal parallelization potentials in the program flow. Manual analysis of an entire piece of software can be time-consuming, so automatic analysis can help in pointing out where in the software to look for parallelization potentials. The profiling tool selected in the specification phase can be used to search for pieces of the software where much of the execution time is spent, i.e. hot-spots. If these portions of the software are parallelized, the total gain of performance is greater than parallelizing "colder" portions. Once a set of hot-spots is identified, a manual inspection of their code needs to be performed to decide whether there is potential for parallelization. This is

done by looking for independent computations that can thus be performed in parallel.

59.3.2.2 Feasibility Analysis

Once portions with parallelization potential are found, we advise to run a feasibility analysis to find out whether it is worth parallelizing them. The first step is to measure how much code can be parallelized. Once this is defined, an estimation of the potential execution time speedup from parallelization can be calculated by using well-defined mathematical equations. In our approach we suggest the use of Amdahl's law[2] [12] to assess the potential speedup that can be achieved from parallel processing.

$$Speedup(N)_A = \frac{1}{(1 - P) + P/N + O_N} \qquad (59.1)$$

The formalization of Amdahl's law is depicted in Eq. (59.1), where P is the parallel portion of the process, N is the number of processors, and O_N the overhead introduced from using N, if any. The estimated speedup factor calculated by applying Amdahl's can then be used to calculate the actual speedup gain in time through Eq. (59.2), where $Speedup_{time}$ represents the speedup gain in time and $SeqET$ the total sequential execution time.

$$Speedup_{time} = SeqET - \frac{SeqET}{Speedup(N)_A} \qquad (59.2)$$

These equations can be applied to a piece of software in order to evaluate its parallel potential. The results can then be used to decide whether it is worth parallelizing the software or not. Since these laws expect a number of processors to apply the parallelization on, a decision of whether to utilize CPUs or GPUs (note that we suppose that both are available) for the parallelization must be taken beforehand. This decision can be taken looking at the type of parallelization we want to achieve: task parallelism, where the goal is to distribute task across processors running in parallel, or data parallelism, where data is supposed to be distributed. For task parallelism, CPUs are considered more suited due to higher clock frequencies and lower memory management overhead. For data parallelism, we suggest to make an estimation of the potential speedup in both the cases of targeting CPUs and GPUs. This is due to the fact that, besides varying processor's characteristics, such as clock frequency and memory clock frequency, the grain-size of the parallel task plays a role in the selection of the processing unit type too. Since GPUs often have several hundreds or

---

[2]An alternative to Amdahl's law is represented by Gustafson's law [11], which can be more suitable when parallelizing algorithms that can expand the amount of computation to fit the amount of parallelization available.

thousands of cores, the parallel task should be fine-grained enough to maximize the utilization of these cores; for coarse-grained tasks, it might be better to choose a CPU instead.

The second step of the feasibility analysis phase is to estimate the effort needed for the actual parallelization task in terms of time. There are three aspects that compose the total effort: (1) time to design a parallel implementation, (2) time to implement the parallelization, (3) time to validate the parallelized application.

Once estimated speedup is calculated for each candidate software portion, and depending on the set financial goals (i.e., maximize performance gain or minimize effort), the engineer decides whether to parallelize any of the candidates. The outcome of this step is a prioritized list of software portions to be parallelized within the given effort budget.

59.3.3 Development Phase

During this iterative phase, selected software portions are actually parallelized, in the prioritized order defined in the previous phase. The first step of the development phase is to design how the selected piece of software should be parallelized. In the analysis phase, an initial design decision was taken regarding which hardware platform to utilize. If the chosen hardware was CPU, we are facing either task or data parallelism. In the case of a task parallelism, we recommend to use a threading library, such as the C++ Thread Support Library.[3] For data parallelism on CPU, the recommendation is to use a compilation-based approach, such as OpenMP.[4] If parallelization targets a GPU, the engineer will use the parallel computing API selected in the specification phase, such as NVIDIA's CUDA.[5]

It is worth mentioning that further analysis of the software portion to parallelize is amenable since activities, such as refactoring of data, may be necessary to maximize parallelizability. Actual implementation and validation of the parallelization are decided by the engineer; our approach does not pose any limitation on them since they do not affect the expected gains, if properly carried out.

59.4 Industrial Evaluation

In order to evaluate our parallelization method, we set up an experiment exploiting a real-life industrial use case focusing on 3D sensors using structured light at ABB Robotics (site of Västerås, Sweden). The goal of the experiment was to answer the following set of research questions:

RC1 *What is the effort of the parallelization approach overall and the effort of its phases individually?*

RC2 *How much did the execution time of the parallelized software improve from the original?*

RC3 *Are there clearly perceived limitations in applying the parallelization approach?*

In order to answer RC1, the effort spent on each step of the approach was recorded so to track how much time was spent on preparation, planning, and implementation activities. Benchmarking was performed on the software portions selected for parallelization, before and after the application of the approach in order to answer RC2. Additionally, we kept track of the "sensations" of the engineers applying the approach so to have an informal understanding on clear limitations of the approach (RC3).

The parallelization approach was applied on a palletizer application, developed as a proof-of-concept for a 3D vision library at ABB Robotics. The application makes a robot arm to pick and place objects from point A to point B. The exact location of point B is unknown; only a larger area of where B's location is known beforehand. The same goes for the location of the objects, whose exact position is unknown. In order to identify the location of the placing area (point B) as well as position and orientation of the objects to be moved, the application uses the 3D vision library. The control flow of the application is shown in Fig. 59.2. Currently, the software running on the Palletizer is sequential, and the vision-related algorithms are so computational heavy that, once an image is taken, the application needs to wait for the vision algorithms to compute it before it can move the robot arm. This idle time increases the overall cycle time and limits throughput. The goal of the experiment was to apply the parallelization method to the sequential Palletizer application to improve its performance.

59.4.1 Specification Phase

The goal of the parallelization was to maximize performance gain in terms of execution time speedup; since the experiment's goal was to assess the parallelization method, we did not set any limit on parallelization effort, but rather measured it. Moreover, we aimed at providing parallelization for both targets (in case of data parallelism, where GPUs are favorable), CPU and GPU, in order (1) to compare results from the two, both in terms of effort and achieved speedup, and (2) to maximize portability (in case no GPUs are available). The development as well as the benchmarking was carried out using a Lenovo P50 laptop with Windows 7 as operating system. The laptop contains a CPU Intel Core i7-6820HQ vPro (8M Cache, up to 3.60 GHz) with a memory of 8 GB DDR4 2133 MHz, and a GPU Quadro M1000M,

---

[3]http://en.cppreference.com/w/cpp/thread.

[4]http://www.openmp.org/.

[5]https://developer.nvidia.com/cuda-zone.

Fig. 59.2 Control flow of the
Palletizer application

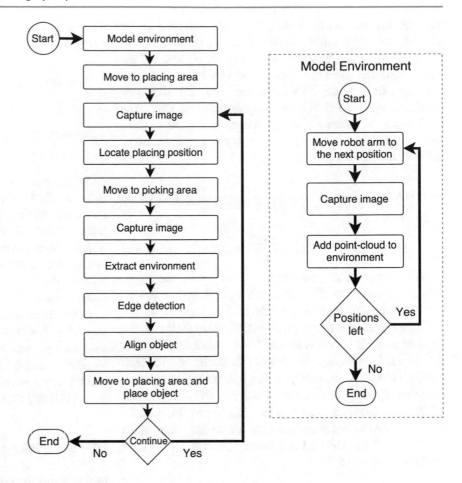

512 CUDA cores 993-1072 MHz with a memory of 4 GB GDDR5 5000 MHz and 128 Bit bus width.

The existing code base was developed in C++11 using Visual Studio 2015 (v140 platform toolset) and Microsofts VC++ compiler, and the code was compiled using the '-O2' optimization flag. The C++11 threading library and OpenMP were used in order to express concurrency on the CPU when applying the parallelization approach for task and data parallelism, respectively. To express concurrency on GPUs, we used NVIDIA's CUDA since the target system includes a CUDA-enabled GPU. Effort spent in this phase was 8 h.

59.4.2 Analysis Phase

The first step of the analysis phase is to locate a set of software portions that could potentially be parallelized. Based on the control flow of the Palletizer application and the dependencies between actions, there were two visible locations for parallelization. The first one was the Model environment procedure, where there were no dependencies between the robot moving and adding the point-cloud from the image to the point-cloud representing the environment. The two actions could be run in parallel. The

second one was when a picture of the placing area is taken and the placing position is calculated, after which a collision-free path to the picking area is planned. The two actions are again independent and could be run in parallel.

To systematically identify hot-spots, automatic (dynamic) analysis using Visual Studio Profiling Tools was run on the codebase. The result showed 13 functions that were accessed frequently and consumed much computational power. These functions were inspected and analyzed manually for parallelization potential. After the analysis, the following 4 functions were identified as parallelizable: Model environment, Extract environment, Align object, Edge detection. Once these locations of parallel potential software were located, we conducted a feasibility analysis on them. Model environment takes care of combining multiple images taken from the robot arms perspective. The robot arm moves to a set of positions and takes an image at each position. What we can do here is to add the previously taken image to the environment at the same time as moving the robot arm to the next position. The parallelization of this function would run on two parallel cores since only two tasks can run in parallel. Model environment's sequential execution time was 9822 ms. Then, the individual times of the two tasks that could run in parallel was 2816 ms for adding the image and 6635 ms for moving the robot arm. In theory, 5632 ms (2*2816, where 2816 ms is the shorter execution time), or 57.34%, of the total sequential execution time could run on two cores at the same time. Since we address task parallelism on two cores, we apply Amdahl's law only for a 2-core CPU. The application of Amdahl's law is shown in Eq. (59.3) gives an estimated speedup factor of 1.4, for a speedup time of 2806.29 ms (see Eq. (59.4)).

$$Speedup(2)_A = \frac{1}{(1 - 0.5734) + 0.5734/2} = 1.4 \quad (59.3)$$

$$Speedup_{time} = 9822 - \frac{9822}{1.4} = 2806.29 \quad (59.4)$$

The sequential execution time of Extract environment was 295.4 ms, with a parallelizable portion of 291.26 ms (98.6%). Since this is data parallelism, we estimate speedup on both CPU and GPU, using the maximum amount of available cores (4 for CPU and 512 for GPU). At this point, the speedup estimation was performed for both CPUs and GPUs according to the parallelization method. Absolute speedup factors for CPU and GPU are 3.83 and 62.79, respectively, as shown in Eqs. (59.5) and (59.6). Since the GPU used in this experiment has a core frequency which is 27.7% of the CPUs, the relative speedup for GPU is $62.79 * 0.277 = 16.5$.

$$Speedup(4)_A = \frac{1}{(1 - 0.986) + 0.986/4} = 3.83 \quad (59.5)$$

$$Speedup(512)_A = \frac{1}{(1 - 0.986) + 0.986/512} = 62.79$$
$$(59.6)$$

The reasoning is similar for the remaining functions, whose estimated speedup gains are as follows (for the sake of page limitation we do not provide all the details of the related parallelization rationale).

Aligning object has an execution time of 1548.54 ms, with 98.8% of it parallelizable through data parallelism. Absolute speedup factors for CPU and GPU are 3.86 and 71.79 respectively, as shown in Eqs. (59.7) and (59.8), with a relative GPU speedup factor of 19.88.

$$Speedup(4)_A = \frac{1}{(1 - 0.988) + 0.988/4} = 3.86 \quad (59.7)$$

$$Speedup(512)_A = \frac{1}{(1 - 0.988) + 0.988/512} = 71.79$$
$$(59.8)$$

Edge detection has an execution time was 32.73 ms, of which 92.6% parallelizable through data parallelism. Absolute speedup factors for CPU and GPU are 3.27 and

13.19 respectively, as shown in Eqs. (59.9) and (59.10), with a relative GPU speedup factor of 3.65.

$$Speedup(4)_A = \frac{1}{(1 - 0.926) + 0.926/4} = 3.27 \quad (59.9)$$

$$Speedup(512)_A = \frac{1}{(1 - 0.926) + 0.926/512} = 13.19$$
$$(59.10)$$

As we can see speedup factor for CPU (3.27) is slightly lower to the one for GPU (3.65). This would suggest to target GPU. Nevertheless, since the size of the point-clouds provided as input to Edge detection are normally up to 200 points, which would take up to 200 GPU cores, we will have a minimum of 312 cores always 'idling', thus severely under-utilizing the GPU. CPU is thereby a better candidate in this specific case.

In this experiment we prioritized the software portions to parallelize based on their estimated speedup factor achievable through parallelization. A summary of the estimated speedup factor, priority, type of target platform, and effort spent for the analysis of the specific software portion is shown in Table 59.1.

59.4.3 Development Phase

In this phase the selected software portions are parallelized from highest to lowest priority until the depletion of the available effort budget (no budget limits in our case since we wanted to measure the needed effort). Moreover, each parallelized code portion was validated through canonical unit testing. In the following we describe the results of this hand-crafted phase in terms of achieved speedup contra estimations done in the analysis phase.

The Align object procedure was parallelized both for CPU, using OpenMP, and for GPU, using CUDA. After further analysis of the related sequential code, we discovered that re-implementation of several mathematical functions had to be done for the CUDA implementation, since used third-party APIs did not provide native support for CUDA. Additionally, refactoring was needed to loosen up a number

Table 59.1 Estimated speedup, priority, platform, and analysis effort

Function	Estimated speedup	Priority	Target	Analysis effort
Align object	3.86	5	CPU	16
Align object	19.88	5	GPU	-
Extract env.	3.83	4	CPU	8
Extract env.	16.5	4	GPU	-
Edge det.	3.27	3	CPU	2
Model env.	1.4	2	CPU	4

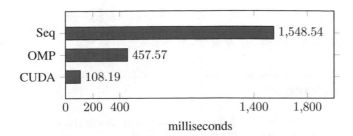

Fig. 59.3 Execution times of `Align Object`

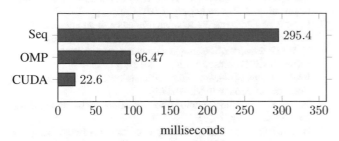

Fig. 59.4 Execution times of `Extract environment`

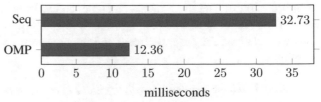

Fig. 59.5 Execution times of `Edge Detection`

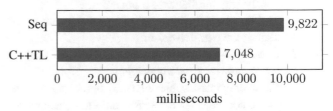

Fig. 59.6 Execution times of `Model environment`

Table 59.2 Experiment summary

Procedure	Estimated speedup	Actual speedup	Dev/val effort	Target
Align object	3.86	3.38	4	CPU
Align object	19.88	14.31	36	GPU
Extract env.	3.83	3.06	6	CPU
Extract env.	16.5	13.07	38	GPU
Edge det.	3.27	3.01	4	CPU
Model env.	1.4	1.39	6	CPU

of computation dependencies so that they could be performed in parallel. The results of the parallelization are shown in Fig. 59.3. Note that in Figs. 59.3, 59.4, 59.5, and 59.6, Seq, C++TL, OMP, and CUDA represent the execution times of the sequential application, the parallel application with C++ threading, with OpenMP, and with CUDA, respectively.

The achieved speedup factors were: 3.38 for CPU/ OpenMP (expected 3.86), and 14.31 for GPU/CUDA (expected 19.88), as shown in Fig. 59.3. Forty man-hours were spent on implementation and validation.

`Extract environment` was also parallelized for CPU, using OpenMP, and for GPU, using CUDA. From further code analysis, we identified a potential risk for race conditions due to reading and writing to a shared list. This was handled in different ways for the two implementations: for OpenMP, we added a critical section to protect from multiple access, while for CUDA, we added an array of booleans representing whether a point should be kept. The achieved speedup factors were: 3.06 for CPU/OpenMP (expected 3.83), and 13.07 for GPU/CUDA (expected 16.5), as shown in Fig. 59.4. Fort four man-hours were spent on implementation and validation.

`Edge detection` was parallelized for CPU using OpenMP problem in the analysis phase. Additionally, it was decided to parallelize it on the CPU using OpenMP. Also in this procedure we had to add a critical section to avoid race conditions. The achieved speedup factor was 3.01 for CPU/OpenMP (expected 3.27), as shown in Fig. 59.5. Four man-hours were spent on implementation and validation.

`Model environment` was identified as candidate for task parallelization, thus on CPU using C++ threading. To avoid race conditions, we add to protect some of the shared

data with a mutex. The achieved speedup factor was 1.39 for CPU/C++TL (expected 1.4), as shown in Fig. 59.6. Six man-hours were spent on implementation and validation.

A summary of the development activity results in relation to the estimations computed during the analysis phase is depicted in Table 59.2. In general we can observe that the actual speedup was indeed fairly close to the estimated one for all cases. As expected, speedups achieved targeting GPUs were higher than the one on CPUs. However, in all cases this came with an additional cost, since parallelization to GPU required additional much higher implementation effort. The overall recorded effort was 132 man-hours, of which 8 spent on the specification phase, 30 on the analysis, and 94 on development.

59.5   Conclusion

In this work we described and assessed a generic parallelization method for introducing parallelization in legacy sequential software. In the proposed method, automatic (dynamic) analysis in combination with manual analysis is used to locate parallelization potentials in existing software. Additionally, a feasibility analysis is used (1) to decide whether it is worth parallelizing a piece of software, and (2) to decide which hardware platform to target (CPU or GPU).

In order to evaluate the proposed method, an experiment was carried out in industrial settings. Three research questions were defined for the experiment and the outcomes are as follows:

RC1 *What is the effort of the parallelization approach overall and the effort of its phases individually?*

28.8% of the effort was spent preparing, locating and analyzing parallelization potential.

71.2% of the effort for designing, implementing and validating the parallelization.

RC2 *How much did the execution time of the parallelized software improve from the original?*

The average case achieved a 6.37 times faster execution time compared to the sequential implementation.

RC3 *Are there clearly perceived limitations in applying the parallelization approach?*

The parallelization method does not consider other hardware platforms than CPUs and GPUs.

Additionally, the experiment showed that parallelization using CPUs required less effort compared to parallelization using GPUs. However, the speedup gained from GPU parallelization was, expectedly, higher compared to what was achieved on a CPU. This resulted in the effort to speedup ratio being similar for both approaches. A possible future research work would be a study comparing existing parallel computation APIs in terms of achieved speedup and required development effort. The purpose of this would be to define suggestions regarding what API to choose depending on problem and goals.

Acknowledgements This research is partially supported by the Knowledge Foundation through the MOMENTUM project (http://www.es.mdh.se/projects/458-MOMENTUM).

References

1. E. Chovancova, J. Mihal'ov, Load balancing strategy for multicore systems, in *Proceedings of ICETA* (2015), pp. 1–6
2. M.A. Kiefer, K. Molitorisz, J. Bieler, W.F. Tichy, Parallelizing a real-time audio application – a case study in multithreaded software engineering, in *Proceedings of IPDPS* (2015), pp. 405–414
3. L. Bass, P. Clements, R. Kazman, *Software Architecture in Practice*, 3rd edn. (Addison-Wesley Professional, Reading, 2012)
4. H. Vandierendonck, T. Mens, Techniques and tools for parallelizing software. IEEE Softw. **29**, 22–25 (2012)
5. Intel, *Threading Methodology: Principles and Practices* (Intel Corporation, Mountain View, 2003)
6. V. Tovinkere, A methodology for threading serial applications. Intel White paper (2006)
7. B. Jun-feng, Application development methods based on multicore systems, in *2012 International Conference on Industrial Control and Electronics Engineering* (2012), pp. 858–862
8. C. Christmann, J. Falkner, A. Weisbecker, A methodology for porting sequential software to the multicore platform considering technical and economical aspects of software parallelization, in *Proceedings of ICSOFT-EA* (2014), pp. 551–559
9. Nvidia, CUDA C best practices guide. DG-05603-001_v8.0 (2017)
10. F.G. Tinetti, M. Méndez, A. De Giusti, Restructuring fortran legacy applications for parallel computing in multiprocessors. J. Supercomput. **64**(2), 638–659 (2013)
11. J.L. Gustafson, Reevaluating amdahl's law. Commun. ACM, **31**(5), 532–533 (1988). http://doi.acm.org/10.1145/42411.42415
12. G.M. Amdahl, Validity of the single processor approach to achieving large scale computing capabilities, in *Readings in Computer Architecture* (Morgan Kaufmann, San Francisco, 2000), pp. 79–81

Clustering and Combinatorial Methods for Test Suite Prioritization of GUI and Web Applications

60

Dmitry Nurmuradov, Renée Bryce, Shraddha Piparia, and Barrett Bryant

Abstract

This work introduces a novel test case prioritization method that combines clustering methods, dimensionality reduction techniques (DRTs), and combinatorial-based two-way prioritization for GUI and web applications. The use of clustering with interleaved cluster prioritization increases the diversity of the earliest selected test cases. The study applies four DRTs, four clustering algorithms, and three inter-cluster ranking methods to three GUI and one web applications in order to determine the best combination of methods. We compare the proposed clustering and dimensionality reduction approaches to random and two-way inter-window prioritization techniques. The outcome of the study indicates that the *Principal Component Analysis (PCA)* dimensionality reduction technique and *Mean Shift* clustering method outperform other techniques. There is no statistical difference between the three inter-cluster ranking criteria. In comparison to two-way inter-window prioritization, the *Mean Shift* clustering algorithm with *PCA* or *Independent Component Analysis (FICA)* generally produces faster rates of fault detection in the studies.

Keywords

Test suite prioritization · User session-based test · Cluster prioritization method · Inter-cluster ranking method · Graphical user interface · Dimensionality reduction approach

60.1 Introduction

A variety of software testing techniques exist to help developers to test their products [1–3]. One technique is that of test suite prioritization, a method of reordering test cases according to a given goal [4–7]. In this work, we focus on user session-based test suites [8] that are generated from the information recorded during user interactions with a system. Research has shown that user session-based test suites help testers to detect a complementary group of faults in a contrast to test suites that are traditionally produced by developers [8–10]. One study showed that two-way combinatorial prioritization increased the rate of fault detection for several applications and user-session-based test suites [6].

Different machine learning-based approaches improve software development processes [11–13]. Researchers in the software testing area also incorporate machine learning into their approaches [14–16].

In this paper we propose a novel technique that incorporates DRTs, clustering algorithms, and combinatorial-based prioritization for test suite prioritization of user session-based test suites for GUI and web applications. Clustering test cases and selecting one from each cluster iteratively allows for greater diversity in test case selection for test suite prioritization. The primary contributions of this work are (1) we propose a model for user session-based test cases that allows for the application of machine learning techniques (2) we use DRTs to reduce the number of features to overcome the curse of dimensionality, and (3) we conduct an empirical study comparing four clustering algorithms, four DRTs, and three inter-cluster ranking criteria to determine the best combination of three. For inter-cluster prioritization of test cases, we apply two-way inter-window prioritization [6].

Section 60.2 discusses the previous work. Section 60.3 describes our approach. Section 60.4 explains parameters of the experimental study. Section 60.5 provides results and gives guidance to testers. Section 60.6 gives the conclusion and future work.

D. Nurmuradov (✉) · R. Bryce · S. Piparia · B. Bryant
University of North Texas, Denton, TX, USA
e-mail: dmitrynurmuradov@my.unt.edu; renee.bryce@unt.edu; shraddhapiparia@my.unt.edu; barrett.bryant@unt.edu

© Springer International Publishing AG, part of Springer Nature 2018
S. Latifi (ed.), *Information Technology – New Generations*, Advances in Intelligent Systems and Computing 738,
https://doi.org/10.1007/978-3-319-77028-4_60

60.2 Related Work

Several papers apply machine learning techniques to test suite prioritization. Tonella et al. [17] utilize Case-Based Ranking (CBR) algorithm in order to gather pairwise comparison of test cases from testers. The algorithm uses a boosting technique that combines multiple learners into a more effective one. The results show that the algorithm performs better than traditional additional statement and total statement coverage methods. Our work, on the contrary, utilizes user-session based test suites and automatically uses criteria to cluster and prioritize test suites. Yoo et al. [16] propose clustering for test case prioritization, incorporating human tester knowledge. The authors use agglomerative hierarchical clustering applied to test suites in conjunction with Analytic Hierarchy Process (AHP) [18], which employs human testers. The authors use interleaved clustering prioritization that selects one test per cluster at a time for the prioritized test suite. The results show that the hybrid approach outperforms coverage-based approaches even when human input has a large number of errors. Our work differs as we use user session-based test cases and automate the test case clustering and prioritization process, so that human work is minimized. Carlson et al. [19] provide an industrial case study on Microsoft Dynamics Ax using agglomerative hierarchical clustering combined with multiple criteria such as code coverage, code complexity, fault history information, and their combinations. The authors employ the same approach as the previous work, adding one test case at a time to a prioritized test suite. They use the Euclidean distance as a distance metric to measure similarity of code coverage between test cases. The authors do not consider different metrics for inter-cluster ranking and use the original order of clusters. The results show noticeable improvements over non-clustered techniques. In our work, we use a black-box approach instead of the white-box. We extract information from user session-based test cases and use several clustering algorithms, as well as distance metrics to understand differences between the clustering approaches. Arafeen and Do [20] use requirements information and perform *K-means* clustering in addition to code complexity to prioritize test cases. They use a term-document matrix to determine similarity between requirements and use it for the *K-means* clustering. The *K-means* clustering algorithm employs the Euclidean distance metric. In addition, they use three metrics to prioritize a cluster: original ordering, random ordering and heuristic-based ordering. Heuristic-based ordering uses a proportional sum of each requirement weighted according to the developer's commitment level combined with code modification information. The work does not address the curse of dimensionality [21] or high dimensional data. Our study, on the other hand, employs dimensionality reduction techniques

to address the issue. We also compare different clustering algorithms as well as different distance metrics where possible.

60.3 The Proposed Method

Our hybrid test suite prioritization technique incorporates different clustering methods from machine learning with two-way inter-window prioritization method from combinatorial testing. Furthermore, different DRTs along with different inter-cluster ranking criteria are used in the proposed hybrid method. The proposed method includes the following steps:

1. Convert test cases into a format suitable for machine learning using window/parameter/value frequency count
2. Apply a dimensionality reduction technique to reduce the number of features
3. Apply a clustering algorithm to the results from step 2
4. Use two-way inter-window prioritization to prioritize test cases within clusters
5. Rank clusters using inter-cluster prioritization criteria
6. Use inter-leaved prioritization (one-at-a-time) to compile an ordered list of test suites

60.3.1 Clustering

The clustering process consists of four steps [22]: (1) Feature Selection, (2) Clustering Algorithm Selection, (3) Cluster Validation, and (4) Data Interpretation. This section explains each part of the clustering process.

60.3.1.1 Feature Selection

The feature selection process is one of the primary preprocessing techniques used in machine learning. The choice of features often determines how well a specific machine learning technique performs and whether the results are meaningful. For instance, the *K-means* clustering algorithm relies on the Euclidean distance, which makes it unsuitable choice for categorical features [23]. In addition, many machine learning algorithms suffer from the phenomenon called the curse of dimensionality, where the performance of an algorithm suffers with an increasing number of features [21]. These issues are usually addressed at the preprocessing stage. In our work, we split the feature selection process into two parts: feature extraction and dimensionality reduction. The feature extraction process converts existing test suites into a form that is acceptable by machine learning algorithms, while a DRT reduces the number of features in order to address the curse of dimensionality problem.

Feature Extraction

The conversion of user session-based test suites into a form suitable for machine learning algorithms requires preprocessing of test suites. Given that user session-based test suites contain various user interactions, some assumptions regarding the data are required. This work uses assumptions similar to ones that are used in the two-way inter-window prioritization method:

- The order of windows as they appear in a test case does not matter.
- If a window appears more than once in a test case and contains additional parameter/value tuples, those tuples are treated as in one window.

Using these assumptions, it is possible to convert a test case to a form that is readable by machine algorithm while representing **window/parameter/value** triples as features. Subsequently, test cases are represented as rows, whereas values for features are frequencies of an occurrence of a particular triple in a given test case.

To demonstrate the process, consider an example shown in Table 60.1. The example contains two test cases with three windows. Each window has a different number of **parameter-values**, and the number of **parameter-value** tuples is 11. Note that w_1pv_1 occurs twice in the t_2.

Table 60.2 shows a converted test suite from Table 60.1. Each feature represents a **window/parameter/value** triple and its value is the number of times the triple occurred in a test case.

Dimensionality Reduction

Test suites often have a large number of **window/parameter/value** triples. Such user session-based test suites converted using the proposed feature extraction method will suffer from the curse of dimensionality. To address the issue, we applied five different dimensionality reduction techniques:

- No Reduction (NR)
- Principal Component Analysis (PCA)
- Factor Analysis (FA)
- Non-negative Matrix Factorization (NMF)
- Independent Component Analysis (FICA)

No Reduction technique means that no reduction technique was applied. Each of the used techniques is widely known and used in statistics and machine learning and the detailed descriptions can be found in the corresponding literature [24–26]. The number of optimal target components may vary for each dataset and reduction technique. For this study, we decided to set the target components to 10, which is ten times less than the lowest number of test cases in the subject applications. In future work, we intend to explore a correlation between the number of components and the accuracy of representation of test case characteristics.

For each of the reduction techniques, with exception of non-negative matrix factorization, the data was standardized. Non-negative matrix factorization algorithm does not work with negative values and the data was not pre-processed.

60.3.1.2 Clustering Algorithm Selection

Many clustering techniques exists. To limit the number of choices, we concentrate on clustering techniques tha are available in scikit-learn library [27]. Four clustering methods were used in the study:

- K-Means (KMeans)
- Agglomerative Hierarchical Clustering (AHC)
- Mean Shift (MS)
- Affinity Propagation (AP)

Similarly to DRTs, the proposed clustering algorithms are well-studied [22, 28, 29]. Each of the clustering algorithms uses default settings provided by the scikit-learn library unless it requires the target number of clusters as an input parameter. *K-means* algorithm uses k-means++ seeding technique to increase the quality of clusters and speed up processing [30]. The next section provides the details regarding how our method chooses the number of clusters when an algorithm requires the target number of clusters.

60.3.1.3 Cluster Validation

Multiple cluster validation metrics are used in machine learning [31–34]. Many metrics rely on prior knowledge (datasets must contain target categories) in order to determine the

Table 60.1 An example of high-level representation of user session-based test suite

Test case	Windows	Tuples
t_1	$w_1 \rightarrow w_2 \rightarrow w_3$	$w_1pv_1, w_1pv_2, w_2pv_1, w_3pv_1, w_3pv_2, w_3pv_3$
t_2	$w_1 \rightarrow w_3 \rightarrow w_1 \rightarrow w_2$	$w_1pv_1, w_1pv_3, w_3pv_2, w_3pv_4, w_3pv_5, w_1pv_1, w_1pv_4, w_2pv_2$

Table 60.2 An example of converted test suite from Table 60.1 to a format suitable for machine learning algorithms

Test case	$f_{w_1pv_1}$	$f_{w_1pv_2}$	$f_{w_1pv_3}$	$f_{w_1pv_4}$	$f_{w_2pv_1}$	$f_{w_2pv_2}$	$f_{w_3pv_1}$	$f_{w_3pv_2}$	$f_{w_3pv_3}$	$f_{w_3pv_4}$	$f_{w_3pv_5}$
t_1	1	1	0	0	1	0	1	1	1	0	0
t_2	2	0	1	1	0	1	0	1	0	1	1

quality of a discovered clusters [31–33]. Given that clusters in the test suite are not known, the proposed approach relies on Silhouette coefficient [34] to evaluate the quality of discovered clusters.

If a clustering algorithm requires the number of clusters as an input, the proposed method iteratively evaluates the quality of the clusters by varying the number of target clusters from 10 to $\frac{1}{3}$ of the test suite size. The evaluation metric for cluster quality is the Silhouette coefficient. Once evaluation is completed, the number of clusters with the highest Silhouette coefficient score is used to proceed to the next phase.

60.3.1.4 Data Interpretation

To evaluate the effectiveness of our approach, we use the average percentage of faults detected (APFD) metric [35].

60.3.2 Two-Way Inter-Window Prioritization

The two-way inter-window prioritization is t-way combinatorial prioritization that combines inter-window pairs of **parameter-values**, i.e., pairs that have two unique windows [36].

60.3.3 Combining Clustering and Combinatorial Approaches

Previous work combines clustering approaches with test suite prioritization [16, 19]. The primary goal of clustering is to combine similar instances of data into clusters. Introducing additional test case diversity into existing test suite prioritization approaches may achieve a greater coverage sooner. To incorporate clustering into a prioritization process, we use *interleaved cluster prioritization* [16] when test cases are picked one test case per cluster at a time. This study compares several criteria for inter-cluster ranking:

- Original ranking
- The number of test cases in a cluster
- The number of unique parameter/values in a cluster

To prioritize test cases in clusters, the proposed method uses the two-way inter-window prioritization method inside a cluster. Once the prioritization process is complete, the clusters are ranked according to chosen criteria and interleaved cluster prioritization is performed to form an ordered test suite.

60.4 Empirical Study

To evaluate the proposed approach we conduct a series of experiments and present them in the empirical study. The study answers the following research questions:

RQ1. Which inter-cluster ranking criteria produces the fastest fault detection rate?

RQ2. Which dimensionality reduction method has the fastest fault detection rate?

RQ3. Which clustering algorithm yields the fastest fault detection rate?

RQ4. How does the proposed method compare to two-way inter-window prioritization and random ordering in terms of the fault detection rate?

60.4.1 Experimental Setup

The study uses the following applications under test for the experimental setup: TERP Word, TERP Paint, TERP Spreadsheet, and Open Journal Systems(OJS). TERP Office[1] applications were developed at the University of Maryland using the Java programming language. Previous work describes TERP Office and the test suites [6, 37]. Open Journal Systems is a web-based journal system that was developed by the Public Knowledge Project. OJS test suite was comprised of user sessions that were collected previously by the students at the University of North Texas. Multiple third-party frameworks such as CodeIgniter[2] and Smarty[3] are included in OJS, which explains a significantly larger number of lines, classes, and methods compared to other applications.

Test suite parameters for the subject applications are in Table 60.3. The number of lines of code for applications vary from 4893 to 364,290, the number of classes is between 104 and 1557, the number of methods is between 236 and 13,905. The test cases number varies from 105 to 274 with the number of faults varying from 29 to 118.

60.4.2 Evaluation Metrics

The average percentage of faults detected (APFD) metric [35], which measures the rate of fault detection is used as the target criterion.

The APFD metric is:

$$APFD = 1 - \frac{TF_1 + TF_2 + \ldots TF_m}{mn} + \frac{1}{2n} \qquad (60.1)$$

---

[1]https://www.cs.umd.edu/users/atif/TerpOffice/.
[2]https://codeigniter.com/.
[3]https://www.smarty.net/.

Table 60.3 Test suite parameters of applications

Description	Word	Ssheet	Paint	OJS
Lines of code	4893	12,791	18,376	364,290
Number of classes	104	125	219	1557
Number of methods	236	579	644	13,905
Number of test cases	105	268	274	109
Number of faults in a fault matrix	58	34	118	29
Number of test cases with at least 1 fault	87	40	68	106
Maximum number of non-unique windows per test case	13	9	11	74
Average number of non-unique windows per test case	4.03	2.54	2.59	16.75
Maximum number of faults found by a test case	9	7	17	5
Average number of faults found by a test case	3.65	0.24	1.18	2.27

In Eq. (60.1), n is a number of test cases in test suite TS that is ordered using some technique, m is a number of faults found by test suite TS, TF_i is the first test case in TS that finds fault i. APFD metric is the rate of fault detection, i.e., the area under the curve on the axis where x is the number of test cases executed and y is the total number of faults found.

60.4.3 Experiment Process

For each combination of inter-cluster ranking criteria, DRT, and clustering algorithm, the experiment was repeated 1000 times using random tie-breaking. The same procedure was performed for random ordering and two-way inter-window prioritization. As a result, 248,000 APFD values were obtained. APFD values for each subject application were normalized using minmax normalization to allow for the statistical analysis of the applications.

60.5 Results

60.5.1 Data Analysis

To answer RQ1, RQ2, and RQ3, we perform a nonparametric ANOVA statistical analysis [38] between each of the methods. We used Stats package from the SciPy[4] library to compute the H-statistic and p-values. Some of the resulting p-values were 0, which indicate that values were too small for the software to compute. Table 60.4 shows the results of the ANOVA analysis for inter-cluster ranking criteria. TERP Spreadsheet and TERP Word show the statistical difference between the results, while the total result for all applications shows no statistical difference. Given the statistical analysis, it is reasonable to conclude that the choice of inter-cluster ranking criteria depends on the application, but, on average, does not impact the outcome. The provided results give the answer for RQ1. Due to space limitations and a lack of the

Table 60.4 Results of ANOVA statistics for inter-cluster ranking methods (p-value < 0.01 indicates a significant statistical difference)

Application	H-statistic	p-value
Open journal systems	4.0408	1.3260e−001
TERP Paint	0.0679	9.6663e−001
TERP Spreadsheet	14.2476	8.0571e−004
TERP Word	35.7544	1.7220e−008
Total	0.3104	8.5623e−001

Table 60.5 Results of ANOVA statistics for dimensionality reduction methods (p-value < 0.01 indicates a very significant statistical difference)

Application	H-statistic	p-value
Open journal systems	6382.94	0.0000e−000
TERP paint	1167.14	2.1123e−251
TERP spreadsheet	4983.53	0.0000e−000
TERP word	3950.03	0.0000e−000
Total	9054.50	0.0000e−000

statistical difference in case of all applications, the answers for subsequent questions employ the original inter-cluster ranking only.

Table 60.5 shows the results of ANOVA analysis for the dimensionality reduction techniques. For all of the applications, p-values are below 0.01 that shows significant statistical differences. Means and standard deviations were compared to determine the technique that yields the highest result. Table 60.6 shows statistics of DRTs for all subject applications and provides the answer for RQ2. *PCA* has the highest APFD mean value and the second lowest standard deviation. *FICA* has a very close result to *PCA*. Other techniques have lower APFD values with differences of more than 1%.

Table 60.7 shows the results of ANOVA analysis for clustering algorithms. For all of the applications, p-values are too small to calculate and show significant statistical differences. Means and standard deviations were compared to determine the clustering algorithm that produces the highest APFD

---

[4]https://www.scipy.org/.

Table 60.6 Result statistics of dimensionality reduction techniques

Statistic	FA	FICA	NMF	NR	PCA
Mean value	0.7929	*0.8041*	0.7807	0.7971	0.8086
Standard deviation	0.0448	0.0421	0.0589	0.0380	0.0419
Minimum value	0.6876	0.7011	0.6032	0.7155	0.7073
25% percentile	0.7626	0.7866	0.7509	0.7699	0.7924
50% percentile	0.7967	0.8186	0.8060	0.8059	0.8205
75% percentile	0.8346	0.8300	0.8210	0.8246	0.8322
Maximum value	0.8626	0.8716	0.8596	0.8629	0.8766

FA factor analysis, *FICA* independent component analysis, *NMF* non-negative matrix factorization, *NR* no reduction, *PCA* principal component analysis

Table 60.7 Results of ANOVA statistics for clustering algorithms (*p*-value < 0.01 indicates a very significant statistical difference)

Application	H-statistic	*p*-value
Open journal systems	5340.73	0.0000e−000
TERP paint	16,197.89	0.0000e−000
TERP spreadsheet	5116.23	0.0000e−000
TERP word	6928.18	0.0000e−000
Total	9161.26	0.0000e−000

Table 60.8 Result statistics of clustering algorithms

Statistic	AHC	AP	KMeans	MS
Mean value	0.7912	0.7926	0.7926	0.8103
Standard deviation	0.0409	0.0560	0.0436	0.0422
Minimum value	0.6733	0.6032	0.6847	0.7221
25% percentile	0.7674	0.7594	0.7893	0.7662
50% percentile	0.7996	0.8075	0.8081	0.8227
75% percentile	0.8246	0.8334	0.8199	0.8379
Maximum value	0.8515	0.8626	0.8573	0.8766

AHC agglomerative hierarchical clustering, *AP* affinity propagation, *KMeans* k-means, *MS* mean shift

value. Table 60.8 shows statistics of clustering algorithms for all subject applications and gives the answer for RQ3. The mean value for *Mean Shift* clustering algorithm is about 2% higher than other tested algorithms. The results for *AHC* and *K-Means* algorithms may be affected by the target number of clusters that were determined by the Silhouette coefficient. To the extent of our knowledge, there is no other reliable metric to determine the quality of clusters without the prior information about the correct groups.

In order to answer RQ4, we compare the *Mean Shift* clustering algorithm with features processed by *FICA* and *PCA* dimensionality reduction techniques to the two-way inter-window prioritization and random ordering. Table 60.9 shows statistics for random, two-way inter-window, and a combination of *Mean Shift* with *FICA* and *PCA* for each application. Each application has different characteristics, as well as different faults and numbers of test cases, so it could be expected that the efficiency of approaches is application-

Table 60.9 Comparison of best clustering/dimensionality reduction combinations with two-way inter-window and random ordering.

Statistic	Random	2-Way	MS/FICA	MS/PCA
Open journal system				
Mean value	0.7587	*0.8037*	0.8003	0.8120
Standard deviation	0.0434	0.0090	0.0070	0.0064
TERP paint				
Mean value	0.6415	0.8534	*0.8677*	0.8733
Standard deviation	0.0574	0.0019	0.0015	0.0013
TERP spreadsheet				
Mean value	0.6009	0.7844	0.7532	*0.7583*
Standard deviation	0.0634	0.0103	0.0113	0.0087
TERP word				
Mean value	0.7943	*0.8288*	0.8328	*0.8259*
Standard deviation	0.0296	0.0036	0.0041	0.0021

dependent. The results in Table 60.9, however, show that in two out of four applications, the proposed clustering algorithm noticeably outperforms two-way inter-window prioritization with one of the dimensionality reduction techniques. The choice of a DRT seems to be application-dependent, with *PCA* performing slightly better than *FICA*. In future work, we plan to examine the correlation between dimensionality reduction techniques and application and test suite characteristics.

60.5.2 Guidance for Testers

The results demonstrate that *Mean Shift* clustering algorithm outperforms other clustering algorithms in this study. *PCA* generally produces better results compared to other techniques with *FICA* having slightly worse results. The dimensionality reduction techniques have been shown to be application-dependent, so testers should rely on the properties of their test suites and application to determine a better choice. There is no statistically significant difference between the inter-cluster ranking techniques, so using the original ranking order is encouraged as it does not require additional processing.

60.5.3 Threats To Validity

There are several threats to validity in this study. The use of GUI applications and faults that were written by students could affect the generalizability of the study. To minimize the threat, we also use an open-source web-based application. The number of target components for dimensionality reduction techniques may also affect the outcome of experiments. In this experiment we set the number to a constant. In future work, we plan to explore the correlation between the number of target components for dimensionality reduction techniques and application and test suite characteristics. Clustering algorithms require one or more input parameters. Each parameter may affect the outcome of experiments. Parameters are unique for each of the algorithms and testing all variations of the parameters is outside of the scope of the study. The default settings provided by the machine learning library were used in this study. The feature extraction process may affect the outcome. The use of frequencies as feature values may result in a loss of the information such as sequences of parameter/values and affect the fault detection rate. To minimize the threat, we use two-way inter-window prioritization within each cluster.

60.6 Conclusion and Future Work

The clustering of test cases and the subsequent interleaved cluster prioritization provide greater diversity of test cases in a prioritized test suite and yields better fault detection rates. Among the tested clustering algorithms, *Mean Shift* demonstrated consistently better results with mean APFD values higher by almost 2%. The use of dimensionality reduction techniques is encouraged as the difference in mean APFD values between *No Reduction* and *PCA* is more than 1%. *FICA* and *PCA* show very close results and the use of the either technique is application dependent. Finally, the proposed inter-cluster ranking criteria have no statistically significant effect on APFD values, so further research in the area is required.

In future work, we will adopt the proposed technique to test suites of other types, as well as, other software artifacts that may help in test suite prioritization. We will explore how the number of target components for dimensionality reduction techniques affect APFD values. We will incorporate cost-based techniques to the proposed method.

References

1. S. Anand, E.K. Burke, T.Y. Chen, J. Clark, M.B. Cohen, W. Grieskamp, M. Harman, M.J. Harrold, P. McMinn, An orchestrated survey of methodologies for automated software test case generation. J. Syst. Softw. **86**(8), 1978–2001 (2013)
2. S. Yoo, M. Harman, Regression testing minimization, selection and prioritization: a survey. Softw. Test. Verif. Reliab. **22**(2), 67–120 (2012)
3. A. Causevic, D. Sundmark, S. Punnekkat, An industrial survey on contemporary aspects of software testing, in *Proceedings of the International Conference on Software Testing, Verification and Validation* (IEEE, New York, 2010), pp. 393–401
4. G. Rothermel, R.H. Untch, C. Chu, M.J. Harrold, Test case prioritization: an empirical study, in *Proceedings of the international conference on software maintenance* (IEEE, New York, 1999), pp. 179–188
5. S. Elbaum, A.G. Malishevsky, G. Rothermel, Test case prioritization: a family of empirical studies. Trans. Softw. Eng. **28**(2), 159–182 (2002)
6. R.C. Bryce, S. Sampath, A.M. Memon, Developing a single model and test prioritization strategies for event-driven software. Trans. Softw. Eng. **37**(1), 48–64 (2011)
7. L. Zhang, D. Hao, L. Zhang, G. Rothermel, H. Mei, Bridging the gap between the total and additional test-case prioritization strategies, in *Proceedings of the International Conference on Software Engineering* (IEEE, New York, 2013), pp. 192–201
8. S. Elbaum, S. Karre, G. Rothermel, Improving web application testing with user session data, in *Proceedings of the international conference on software engineering* (IEEE Computer Society, Washington, 2003), pp. 49–59
9. S. Sampath, V. Mihaylov, A. Souter, L. Pollock, A scalable approach to user-session based testing of web applications through concept analysis, in *Proceedings of the International Conference on Automated Software Engineering* (IEEE, New York, 2004), pp. 132–141
10. S. Sampath, R.C. Bryce, Improving the effectiveness of test suite reduction for user-session-based testing of web applications. Inf. Softw. Technol. **54**(7), 724–738 (2012)
11. J. Cleland-Huang, A. Czauderna, M. Gibiec, J. Emenecker, A machine learning approach for tracing regulatory codes to product specific requirements, in *Proceedings of the International Conference on Software Engineering* (ACM, New York, 2010), pp. 155–164
12. J. Wen, S. Li, Z. Lin, Y. Hu, C. Huang, Systematic literature review of machine learning based software development effort estimation models. Inf. Softw. Technol. **54**(1), 41–59 (2012)
13. H.U. Asuncion, A.U. Asuncion, R.N. Taylor, Software traceability with topic modeling, in *Proceedings of the International Conference on Software Engineering* (ACM, New York, 2010), pp. 95–104
14. D. Leon, A. Podgurski, A comparison of coverage-based and distribution-based techniques for filtering and prioritizing test cases, in *Proceedings of the International Symposium on Software Reliability Engineering* (IEEE, New York, 2003), pp. 442–453
15. L.C. Briand, Y. Labiche, Z. Bawar, Using machine learning to refine black-box test specifications and test suites, in *International Conference on Quality Software* (IEEE, New York, 2008), pp. 135–144
16. S. Yoo, M. Harman, P. Tonella, A. Susi, Clustering test cases to achieve effective and scalable prioritisation incorporating expert knowledge, in *Proceedings of the International Symposium on Software Testing and Analysis* (ACM, New York, 2009), pp. 201–212
17. P. Tonella, P. Avesani, A. Susi, Using the case-based ranking methodology for test case prioritization, in *Proceedings of the International Conference on Software Maintenance* (IEEE, New York, 2006), pp. 123–133
18. T.L. Saaty, Decision making with the analytic hierarchy process. Int. J. Serv. Sci. **1**(1), 83–98 (2008)
19. R. Carlson, H. Do, A. Denton, A clustering approach to improving test case prioritization: an industrial case study, in *Proceedings of the International Conference on Software Maintenance* (IEEE, New York, 2011), pp. 382–391
20. M.J. Arafeen, H. Do, Test case prioritization using requirements-based clustering, in *Proceedings of the International Conference on Software Testing, Verification and Validation* (IEEE, New York, 2013), pp. 312–321
21. P. Domingos, A few useful things to know about machine learning. Commun. ACM **55**(10), 78–87 (2012)
22. R. Xu, D. Wunsch, Survey of clustering algorithms. IEEE Trans. Neural Netw. **16**(3), 645–678 (2005)

23. Z. Huang, Extensions to the k-means algorithm for clustering large data sets with categorical values. Data Min. Knowl. Disc. **2**(3), 283–304 (1998)

24. I. Jolliffe, *Principal Component Analysis*, 2nd edn. (Springer, Berlin, 2002)

25. D.D. Lee, H.S. Seung, Learning the parts of objects by non-negative matrix factorization. Nature **401**(6755), 788–791 (1999)

26. A. Hyvärinen, J. Karhunen, E. Oja, *Independent Component Analysis*, 1st edn. (Wiley-Interscience, London, 2001)

27. F. Pedregosa et al. Scikit-learn: machine learning in Python. J. Mach. Learn. Res. **12**, 2825–2830 (2011)

28. D. Comaniciu, P. Meer, Mean shift: a robust approach toward feature space analysis. IEEE Trans. Pattern Anal. Mach. Intell. **24**(5), 603–619 (2002)

29. D. Dueck, B.J. Frey, Non-metric affinity propagation for unsupervised image categorization, in *Proceedings of the International Conference on Computer Vision* (IEEE, New York, 2007), pp. 1–8

30. D. Arthur, S. Vassilvitskii, k-means++: the advantages of careful seeding, in *Proceedings of the Symposium on Discrete Algorithms* (Society for Industrial and Applied Mathematics, Philadelphia, 2007), pp. 1027–1035

31. L. Hubert, P. Arabie, Comparing partitions. J. Classif. **2**(1), 193–218 (1985)

32. N.X. Vinh, J. Epps, J. Bailey, Information theoretic measures for clusterings comparison: variants, properties, normalization and correction for chance. J. Mach. Learn. Res. **11**, 2837–2854 (2010)

33. A. Rosenberg, J. Hirschberg, V-Measure: a conditional entropy-based external cluster evaluation measure, in *Proceedings of the Joint Conference on Empirical Methods in Natural Language Processing and Computational Natural Language Learning* (2007), pp. 410–420

34. P.J. Rousseeuw, Silhouettes: a graphical aid to the interpretation and validation of cluster analysis. J. Comput. Appl. Math. **20**, 53–65 (1987)

35. G. Rothermel, R.H. Untch, C. Chu, M.J. Harrold, Prioritizing test cases for regression testing. Trans. Softw. Eng. **27**(10), 929–948 (2001)

36. R.C. Bryce, A.M. Memon, Test suite prioritization by interaction coverage, in *Proceedings of the Workshop on Domain-Specific Approaches to Software Test Automation* (ACM, New York, 2007), pp. 1–7

37. A. Memon, Q. Xie, Studying the fault-detection effectiveness of GUI test cases for rapidly evolving software. Trans. Softw. Eng. **31**(10), 884–896 (2005)

38. W.H. Kruskal, W.A. Wallis, Use of ranks in one-criterion variance analysis. J. Am. Stat. Assoc. **47**(260), 583–621 (1952)

Franciny M. Barreto, Joslaine Cristina Jeske de Freitas, and Stéphane Julia

Abstract

In this paper, an approach based on Petri nets for the design process of video games is presented. A WorkFlow net is used to represent the activities the player will perform in a video game. The main areas of the virtual world that the player will encounter during the game are modeled through a kind of Petri net named State Graph. A timed version of the WorkFlow net (that models the activities of the game) and of the State Graph (that models the topological map of the game) is presented in order to produce an estimated time that corresponds to the effective duration a player will need to complete a specific level of a game. The simulation software CPN Tools is used to simulate both models and show, through a kind of quantitative analysis, the influence that one model has over the other. The video game Silent Hill II is used to illustrate the proposed approach.

Keywords

Modeling · Petri nets · Video games · Timed petri nets · WorkFlow net

61.1 Introduction

A game is a closed and formal system that subjectively represents a subset of realities [1]. The study in [2], defines a video game as a synthesis of code, images, music, and animation that come together into a form of entertainment. A video game application differs from classical software due to a preproduction stage as well as of an extensive use and integration of multimedia assets. It is a difficult task to combine in software creation artistic and technical processes [3]. A game has to be interactive, entertaining and give controlled freedom to the player. According to [3], it is of fundamental importance to ensure that the game experience leads to a succession of goals within a reasonable time.

Over the years, video games have evolved and become more complex. The increasing complexity of game development highlights the need for tools to improve productivity in terms of time, cost, and quality [4]. A major issue leveled against the games industry is that most adopt a poor methodology for software creation [2]. In particular, it is important to adopt Software Engineering practices to address the challenges that game developers face. In [2], the authors state that game developers need to evolve Software Engineering methods and processes to meet their unique needs and to improve game development practices.

Formal methods have been used in game modeling, like the ones presented in [2, 5–7]. In [6] for example, a new approach based on WorkFlow nets was proposed to specify the scenarios existing at a quest level. In this approach, the sequent calculus of linear logic was used to prove the correctness of the scenarios a player can execute within a quest of a game. Such an approach only considers models based on the activities of the player and ignores completely the topological map vision of the game.

The study in [7] presents an approach where the scenarios of a video game are represented by the combination of a WorkFlow net and a State Graph. The WorkFlow net is used to represent the activities that exist at a game level. The topological map that represents the areas of the virtual world where the player can progress is represented by a State Graph. To specify the communication between both models, a synchronous communication mechanisms based on Colored Petri nets (CP-nets) was created. To verify the soundness of the model, an algorithm based on state space analysis was then automatically executed by some of the

F. M. Barreto (✉) · J. C. J. de Freitas
Federal University of Goiás, Jataí, GO, Brazil

S. Julia
Faculty of Computer Science, Federal University of Uberlândia, Uberlândia, MG, Brazil

© Springer International Publishing AG, part of Springer Nature 2018
S. Latifi (ed.), *Information Technology – New Generations*, Advances in Intelligent Systems and Computing 738,
https://doi.org/10.1007/978-3-319-77028-4_61

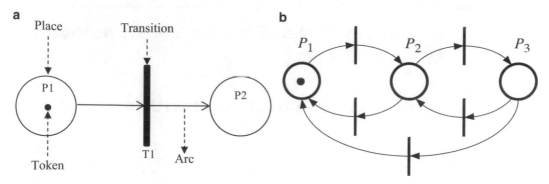

Fig. 61.1 (**a**) Elements of a Petri net. (**b**) Example of a State Graph with one token

existing functionalities of the CPN Tools. This approach only considers untimed models and, consequently, cannot be used to estimate the time duration of a video game.

In this article, an approach based on Petri nets for the modeling of video games is presented. The activities of the game will be modeled by a kind of timed WorkFlow net. A duration will be attached to each activity of the model. Such a duration will represent the execution time that a player will need to perform a specific activity. The areas of the virtual world will be represented by a State Graph. The passage from one area of the map to another area will also consider a duration associated to a transition of the model, which will represent the time a player will take to move from one area to another. Communication mechanisms will be added to formally join both models. Through the simulation of the global obtained model (timed activity model + timed topological model) it is possible then to show the interactions and influences a model has over the other. Thus, an estimated time that corresponds to the effective duration a player will need to complete a specific level of a game will be calculated. The proposed approach will be illustrated using a specific level of the video game Silent Hill II [8].

A brief presentation about the concepts used in this paper is given in section II. In section III, the approach is presented. The simulation of the models is produced in section IV. Finally, section V presents the conclusions and future work proposals.

61.2 Background

61.2.1 WorkFlow Net and State Graph

A Petri net is a graphical and mathematical modeling tool that allows one to model, analyze and control discrete event systems that involve parallel activities, concurrency between processes and asynchronous communication mechanisms [9]. Petri nets are formally defined as a directed bipartite graph with two types of nodes called places and transitions. Nodes are connected via directed arcs. Connections

between nodes of the same type are not allowed. Places are represented by circles and transitions by rectangles ([10, 11]). Figure 61.1a shows an example of a Petri net and its elements.

A Petri net that models a workflow process is called a WorkFlow net (WF-net) ([10, 12]). A WF-net satisfies the following properties [10]:

1. It has only one source place named i and only one sink place named o. These are special places, such that the place i has only outgoing arcs and the place o has only incoming arcs.
2. A token in i represents a case that needs to be handled and a token in o represents a case that has been handled.
3. Every task t (transition) and condition p (place) should be in a path from place i to place o.

An overview of WF-net can be found in [10]. An unmarked Petri net is a State Graph if, and only if, every transition has exactly one input and one output place [13]. A marked Petri net, known as a State Graph, will be equivalent to a State Graph in the classical sense (representing an automaton which is in only one state at a time) if, and only if, it contains exactly one token located in one of the places of the set P [13]. Figure 61.1b illustrates an example of a State Graph with one token.

61.2.2 CPN Tools

The Colored Petri Nets (CP-net) belong to the class of high-level Petri Nets. This class is characterized by the combination of Petri Nets and programming languages. In this way, a CP-net is a graphical modeling language that combines the strengths of Petri nets along with those of functional programming languages [14]. In a CP-net model, tokens can be coded as data values of a rich set of types (called color sets) and arc inscriptions can compute expressions and not just constants [15]. In this way, the CP-nets can be used to reduce the model size of simple Petri net models allowing in particular the individualization of tokens.

The practical application of CP-nets modeling and analysis relies heavily on the existence of computer tools supporting the creation and manipulation of the models. CPN Tools [16] is a tool suited to editing, simulating and providing state space analysis of CP-net models. In this paper, the CPN Tools is used to represent graphically the proposed model. For such, the game model was converted into a CP-net practically without semantic losses. Automatic simulation is one of the main functionalities provided by CPN Tools. The simulator of CPN Tools will be thus used to simulate the proposed model.

61.3   Approach

61.3.1   Timed Activity Model

It is possible to structure most video games into a group of levels. A level contains a group of activities that must be performed by the player. S.

Some of these activities must be executed sequentially or simultaneously, and some are obligatory or optional. After several activities from the same level have been performed, the goal of the level will be reached. Each activity of a game takes a duration to be performed. The duration depends on basically one factor: player experience. More experienced players tend to perform the game challenges more easily than the less experienced ones. The player's experience can come from experiences with previous games or obtained with the evolution of the game he is currently playing. Thus, the more a player executes the activities of the game, the more experience he will attain. In particular, when a player repeats a specific activity over the same game, they gain more playing experience. Consequently, it is more likely that they will perform the activity again in a shorter time than the first time.

WF-nets are very suitable to model the levels that a player must perform in order to win a game [6]. According to [7], a level is similar to the classical structure of a workflow process. In this way, the structure of a WF-net makes the modeling of levels possible. In a WF-net that models a level, the transitions represent the activities of the level and the places represent the conditions. Figure 61.2 shows the timed activity model of the first level of Silent Hill II.

In most of games, there exist activities based on finding objects, to solve puzzles or to interact with game characters (named NPC—Non-Player Character). Some specific interactions propose challenges where the player must win a competition against an NPC to perform the next task. In particular, this kind of activity allows the player to execute the activity more than one time. Figure 61.2 illustrates one of these situations. On the first level of the game Silent Hill II, it is necessary to execute the activity Kill creature where the player fights repeatedly against the same monster (an NPC).

If the player does not win the first time, they will be able to perform the activity over again until they manage to kill the monster. The activities Kill Creature and Take Radio form a parallel route. Thus, these activities can be executed in any sequence. In this specific case there exist four options:

1. the player successfully performs the activity Take Radio first, and then Kill Creature. After that, they move to the next tasks following the game flow;
2. the player successfully performs the activity Kill Creature first and then Take radio. After that, he moves to the next tasks following the game flow;
3. the player performs the activity Kill Creature and loses. As a consequence, the game is restarted to the checkpoint that corresponds to the conclusion of the activity Find map of Silent Hill;
4. the player successfully performs the activity Take Radio first, and then does not manage to complete the activity Kill Creature. As a consequence, the game is restarted to the checkpoint that corresponds to the conclusion of the activity Find map of Silent Hill.

In Fig. 61.2, the activities *Take Radio* and *Kill Creature* are represented by transitions of the same name. The transition L2 represents option 3 and the transition L1 represents option 4. L2 will be fired when there exists a token in place P2 and a token in place P3 (option 3). L1 will be fired if there exists a token in P3, if the transition L1 is fired, then L3 will be fired if there exists tokens in places P11 and P4 (option 4). This model produces a kind of an iterative route for the player when they fail to perform certain activities.

To represent the duration of the activities, an aleatory time function is associated to each transition of the activity model. These functions will simulate the duration a player needs to perform specific activities. The exponential function is used, as it is one of the most widely used random distribution functions for simulating interarrival times in most simulation problems [17]. The function is based on an exponential parameter r (real type). For $r > 0$, exponential(r) produces a value based on the distribution exponential with mean 1/r. In Fig. 61.2, the parameter of the exponential function is given by a real number e. e thus represents the experience of the player.

Initially, e has the value 0.5.[1] The inscription @++ exponential(e) then assigns a delay to the token used to fire the transition. When the player repeats an activity his experience increases. It is represented by the inscription of the outgoing arcs of transitions L3 and L2 $((p,e + 0.31))$. In that way, the duration (mean duration) to perform the activity again will be shorter.

---

[1]At first, these values were defined only for test purposes. As future work it will be interesting to consider a more accurate study to determine e with more precision.

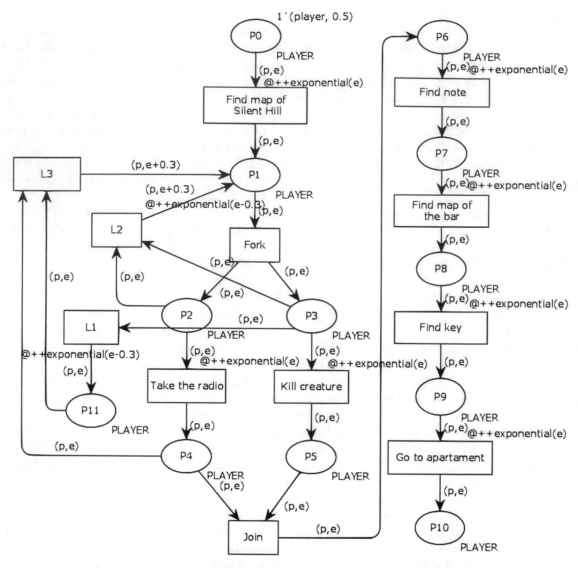

Fig. 61.2 Timed activity model of the first level of Silent Hill II

61.3.2 Timed Topological Model

It is also important to describe the topological properties of the virtual game world along with evolution of the player within it [3]. A game has a set of areas where the player has to fulfill specific tasks. These areas do not change during the game. To represent the formal definition of the topological map, a kind of Petri net named State Graph is used. The semantic of a State Graph makes the modeling of the topological map of a game easy. In the corresponding State Graph, a specific area of the virtual world is modeled by a specific place. The transitions represent the boundaries between adjacent areas. The arc orientation represents in which direction the player may go and a token in a specific place represents the location of the player on the map. In Fig. 61.3, each area is represented by a place with the same name.

The token in place Observation deck represents the current location of the player at the beginning of the game.

On the topological map a transition firing means that the player has moved from one area to another. The player can stay in a specific area for a short period of time or for a long period of time. So, they have a minimum and a maximum duration for passing from one area to another. Therefore, to simulate the duration of displacements over the map, a time function is added at each transition of the State Graph. The uniform function seems suitable to represent the duration that exists on the topological map as it has a minimum and maximum parameter. In Fig. 61.3, the inscription $@++Timer()$ is added at each transition. $@++Timer()$ is a function that includes the function $uniform(a,b)$ (both real type). For $b > a$, $uniform(a,b)$ produces a value from a uniform distribution with mean $(a + b)/2$ [17].

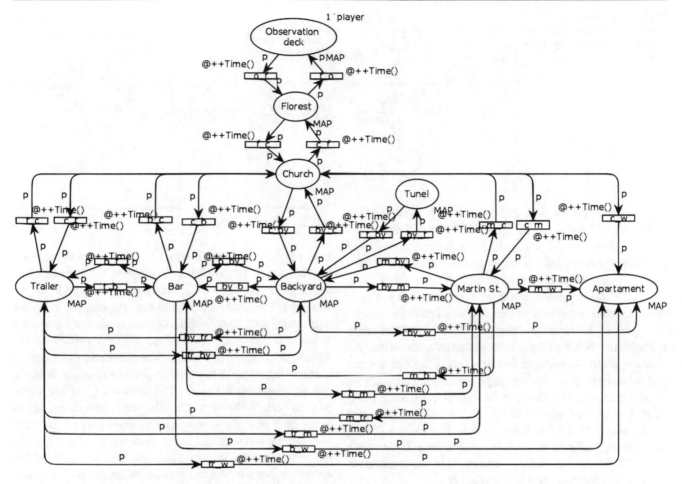

Fig. 61.3 Timed topological model of the first level of Silent Hill II

Initially, we defined $a = 0.1$ and $b = 1.0$ to represent the minimum and maximum duration, respectively. In that way, the player will take between 0.1 and 1.0 time units to move from one area to another.

61.4   Simulation

In order to simulate the models, the software CPN Tools was used. The CPN Tools simulator allows for interactive or automatic simulation. An interactive simulation provides a way to investigate different scenarios in detail and check how the model works. This kind of simulation is similar to single step debugging. During the simulation, the modeler is in charge and determines the next step by selecting between the enabled events, through a consideration of the current state [18]. On other hand, in an automatic simulation the token game is not displayed. Instead, a simulation report is produced.

In this paper, automatic simulation is performed in order to estimate the duration of a specific level of the game. The activity model presented in Fig. 61.2 shows all the

activities of the first level of Silent Hill II. This model is simulated automatically 10 times. Therefore, a replication functionality of CPN Tools, expressed by the inscription *CPN'Replications.nreplications10*, is used. The minimum duration for performing all tasks of the simulated level corresponds to approximately 4.94 time units. The maximum duration for performing all tasks corresponds to approximately 14.64 time units. The mean to performed all tasks of the level corresponds to approximately 9.40 time units.

The topological map presented in Fig. 61.3 shows all the areas of the first level of Silent Hill II. To estimate the duration of the map, the timed topological model is simulated 10 times. The inscription CPN 0 Replications.nreplications10 is used to make the replications and the replication report is generated automatically. According to the replication report, the minimum duration to cover all the areas of the map corresponds to approximately 1.17 time units. On the other hand, the maximum duration to cover all the areas of the map corresponds to approximately 10.50. The mean duration corresponds to approximately 5.01 time units.

In a game, the player can only perform a task if they are in the appropriate area. And some areas are accessed only after

Fig. 61.4 Communication between timed level and timed topological models using fusion places

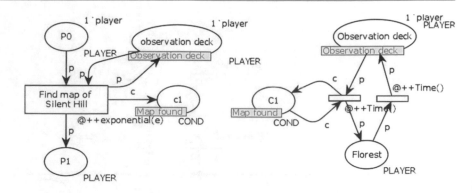

performing a specific task. A level is then composed of the tasks and the virtual space. Thus, the timed activity model and the timed topological model are interconnected, and together they formed the global model of the level. To implement the communication mechanisms between the activity model and the topological model, both models use a synchronous communication mechanism based on fusion places.

Figure 61.4 shows an example of the communication mechanisms. A fusion tag is represented by a blue rectangle. When a token is produced in one of the places of a same fusion set, the same token is then produced in all other places of the fusion set. For example, in Fig. 61.4, after the firing of transition *Find map of Silent Hill*, a token is produced in the place *c1* of the level model. The same token is then automatically reproduced (cloned) in the corresponding place *C1* of the topological model. This communication mechanisms are described in detail in [7].

To estimate the duration of the first level of the game, the timed global model is simulated 10 times. According to the replication report, the minimum duration of the level corresponds to approximately 59.13 time units, and the maximum duration corresponds to approximately 210.44. The mean duration of the level corresponds to approximately 87.16 time units.

When the models are simulated separately, the estimated duration refers only to the property of that specific model. This does not happen when considering the global model, since one model influences the other. For example, when the topological model is simulated alone all areas can be accessed, what is not possible when the global model is simulated, as a matter of fact, the player needs to perform some tasks to gain access to some areas. When the activity model is simulated alone all the activities can be performed almost immediately, which again is not possible when the global model is simulated, as a matter of fact, the player needs to be in a specific area of the map to perform a specific activity. In Fig. 61.3, for example, to execute the activity *Find the key*, the player has to be in *Martin St.* area. In this way, both models need to be considered in order to produce a realist simulation and obtain an accurate time estimate for the game level.

61.5 Conclusion

In this paper, an approach based on Petri nets was proposed for the design process of video games. To represent the activities of the level of a video game, a WorkFlow net was used. The areas of the game map (topological map) are represented by a State Graph. A timed version of the activity model was presented, as well as a timed version of the topological map. In particular, time functions were used to simulate the duration between activities and of the different passages between the areas. The software CPN Tools was used to present the approach. The automatic simulation is based on some of the existing functionalities of the CPN Tools, and it was used to simulate both models. By analyzing the simulation results, one notes the visible trends of the influences that a model has over the other, and through such, the possibility arose of producing an estimated time that corresponds to the effective duration a player will need to complete a specific game level.

As a future work proposal, it will be interesting to investigate how to obtain a realistic parameter that corresponds to the experience of the player. It will be interesting also to investigate multiplayer games and how to represent the interactions that exist between several players that collaborate to reach a common goal.

Acknowledgment The authors would like to thank FAPEMIG, FAPEG, CAPES and CNPq for financial support.

References

1. C. Crawford, *The Art of Computer Game Design*, 1982
2. C. M. Kanode, H. M Haddad, Software engineering challenges in game development, in *Information Technology: New Generations, 2009. ITNG'09. Sixth International Conference on*, ed. by S. Latifi (IEEE Computer Society, Washington, D.C, 2009), pp. 260–265
3. S. Natkin, L. Vega, S. Grünvogel, A new methodology for spatiotemporal game design, in *Proceedings of CGAIDE 2004, 5th Game-On International Conference on Computer Games: Artificial Intelligence, Design and Education*, 2004, ed. by Q. Mehdi and N. Gough, pp. 109–113

4. E.M. Reyno, J.C. Cubel, Automatic prototyping in model-driven game development. CIE **7**(2) (2009)

5. M. Araújo, L. Roque, Modeling games with petri nets, in *Breaking New Ground: Innovation in Games, Play, Practice and Theory. DIGRA2009* (Londres, Royaume Uni, 2009)

6. G.W. de Oliveira, S. Julia, L.M.S. Passos, Game modeling using workflow nets, in *SMC*, (IEEE, Washington, D.C, 2011), pp. 838–843

7. F.M. Barreto, S. Julia, Modeling and analysis of video games based on workflow nets and state graphs, in *Proceedings of 24th Annual International Conference on Computer Science and Software Engineering, Ser. CASCON '14*, (IBM Corp, Riverton, NJ, 2014), pp. 106–119

8. Konami, Silent hill 2, computer game, developed and published by konami (2001)

9. T. Murata, Petri nets: Properties, analysis and applications. Proc. IEEE **77**(4), 541–580 (1989)

10. W.M. van der Aalst, The application of petri nets to workflow management. JCSC **8**(1), 21–66 (1998)

11. W.M. van der Aalst, A.H. ter Hofstede, Verification of workflow task structures: a petri-net-baset approach. Inf. Syst. **25**(1), 43–69 (2000)

12. W. Van Der Aalst, K.M. Van Hee, *Workflow Management: Models, Methods, and Systems* (MIT Press, Cambridge, 2004)

13. D. René and A. Hassane, *Discrete, Continuous, and Hybrid Petri Nets* (Berlin, London, 2010)

14. R. Milner, R. Harper, M. Tofte, *The Definition of Standard ML* (MIT Press, Cambridge, 1990)

15. V. Gehlot and C. Nigro, An introduction to systems modeling and simulation with colored petri nets, in *Winter Simulation Conference* (WSC, 2010), pp. 104–118

16. K. Jensen, An introduction to the practical use of coloured petri nets, in *Lectures on Petri Nets II: Applications*, (Springer, Berlin, 1998), pp. 237–292

17. W.M. van der Aalst, C. Stahl, *Modeling Business Processes: A Petri Net-Oriented Approach* (MIT Press, Cambridge, 2011)

18. F. M. Barreto, J. C. Jeske de Freitas, M. S. Soares, and S. Julia, A straightforward introduction to formal methods using coloured petri nets, in *16th international conference on enterprise information systems, ser. ICEIS 2014*, vol. 2, 2014, pp. 145–152

Survey of Biometric Techniques for Automotive Applications

62

Maria Villa, Mikhail Gofman, and Sinjini Mitra

Abstract

Although significant research has been dedicated to developing biometric solutions for motorized vehicles, there are currently no survey works charting the progress in this field. This paper discusses a selection of biometrics research focusing on improving vehicle safety and protecting vehicles against theft. Specifically, we discuss research that focuses on detecting a driver's impaired ability to control the vehicle due to drowsiness, intoxication, or a medical emergency; developing techniques for identifying and preventing intrusions into the vehicle; and discovering driver distractions from within and without the vehicle. We also comment on the potential effectiveness, user-friendliness, privacy, security, and other aspects of the proposed approaches and identify directions for future research.

We supplement this paper with a comprehensive list of other works in the field, which is accessible from Gofman and Villa (Extended database of biometrics research for automotive applications, 2017. http://www.fullerton.edu/cybersecurity/research/Extended-Database-of-Biometrics-Research-for-Automotive-Applications.php).

Keywords

Biometrics · Machine learning · Vehicles · Automotive · Transportation

M. Villa · M. Gofman (✉)
Department of Computer Science, California State University, Fullerton, CA, USA
e-mail: ganymede527@csu.fullerton.edu; mgofman@fullerton.edu

S. Mitra
Department of Information Systems and Decision Sciences, California State University, Fullerton, CA, USA
e-mail: smitra@fullerton.edu

62.1 Introduction

Researchers and industry innovators have proposed biometric techniques for making vehicles safer to drive and protecting them against theft. This paper surveys a selection of salient research works on such techniques and concludes with a discussion of future directions for research in these areas. Section 62.2 focuses on road safety issues, while Sect. 62.3 discusses techniques for mitigating vehicle theft and intrusions, and Sect. 62.4 presents our conclusions.

62.2 Road Safety

The leading causes of death due to automobile accidents in the United States are adverse driving conditions, the driver's impaired physical and/or mental states (e.g., tiredness, intoxication, or stress) [40], and risky driving behaviors (e.g., speeding, following too closely, distractions from mobile devices, and violating traffic rules) [23]. Some researchers consider biometrics as an effective means of detecting a driver's impaired states and implementing corrective measures, if necessary.

62.2.1 Monitoring Psychological States

Gutmann et al. [20] proposed measuring drivers' psychological stress levels using neural networks to analyze drivers' brainwaves (through electroencephalography [EEG]), heart rhythm (through electrocardiography), breathing patterns (through respiratory inductance plethysmography), heart rate and inter-beat interval, body temperature, electro-dermal activity, blood oxygen levels (through photoplethysmography), and wrist and hip movements (e.g., 3-axis acceleration and angular velocity).

Brainwave data were gathered through wireless sensors embedded in headsets worn by the drivers. The remaining data were gathered through wired sensors attached to differ-

© Springer International Publishing AG, part of Springer Nature 2018
S. Latifi (ed.), *Information Technology – New Generations*, Advances in Intelligent Systems and Computing 738,
https://doi.org/10.1007/978-3-319-77028-4_62

ent parts of each driver's body. To evaluate the system, the researchers conducted experiments using a driving simulator in which human subjects had to drive in difficult conditions, such as bad weather and road obstacles. The findings from this simulation yielded promising results.

Monitoring biometrics such as electrocardiogram (ECG) can provide insights into driver's psychological state. This, however, may be inconvenient for the driver, requiring him/her to attach multiple sensors. Lee et al. [29] recognized this problem and proposed monitoring a driver's ECG signals using four dry electrodes in the form of 3M tape installed in the steering wheel. The ECG data, which are read when the driver puts his/her hands on the steering wheel, are analyzed for heart rate, waveform, ST segment, QT interval, heart rate variability (HRV), and RR interval. No significant differences were found between the ECG data collected using the proposed method and data collected using the traditional method, which uses wet electrodes, when simultaneously monitoring the same individual using both approaches.

The method of monitoring ECG by having the driver put his/her hands on the steering wheel can theoretically be more effective than the traditional method of attaching electrode sensors. However, like many other authors in the field of automotive biometrics, neither of the above works discuss drivers' (or passengers') concerns about their vehicles monitoring their state, which they may view as invasive to their privacy. These concerns are present in many biometric applications and will undoubtedly surface here as well. Potential research directions for addressing them can include designing systems whose operation is transparent to the driver, promoting relevant education, and developing cybersecurity solutions for protecting the collected data.

62.2.2 Detecting Medical Emergencies

During 2006–2016, an average of 10,000 people died every year in car accidents involving drunk driving and intoxication [42]; and an estimated 1.3% of all car crashes can be attributed to medical emergencies such as seizures, blackouts, and diabetic reactions [41]. Driver (and passenger) biometric data can be used to detect intoxication, common medical emergencies and other driving impairments.

Rathore and Gau [48] developed an Automotive Health-care and Safety (AHS) system that uses wearable biometric sensors to monitor the heart rate and body temperature of all vehicle occupants. It also includes a breath analyzer device located on the steering wheel to detect a driver's state of intoxication. Infrared cameras located on the dashboard are used to detect pupil dilation and facial symptoms of medical emergencies, such as high blood pressure and low or high glucose levels. Seat belts are equipped with an ECG monitor,

and seats have movement and weight sensors. If any of these biometric sensors indicate a medical urgency, emergency responders are notified.

The use of biometrics for detecting medical emergencies has also been explored by the automotive industry. Gestigon [18] created software using touch-less gesture recognition implementing body skeleton tracking, synthetic depth data, machine learning algorithms, and in real time, to monitor behavior and detect health problems for the driver and passenger(s). Sober Steering [56] embedded a breathalyzer on the steering wheel to detect alcohol levels and the system stops the vehicle if it detects that the driver's alcohol levels exceed a certain threshold; a similar idea was proposed by Chen et al. [11], who created a system in which the driver must prove sobriety with a breath alcohol detector prior to starting the car. Important concern with such approaches is ensuring that the individual performing the sobriety test is the actual driver.

62.2.3 Measuring Driver Distractions

Young et al. [61] studied in-vehicle driver distractions such as mobile phones, route guidance systems, and eating, smoking, or talking, which are responsible for nearly a quarter of all car accidents in the U.S. The biometric techniques proposed for measuring distractions include glance or eye movement monitoring.

Williams et al. [13] proposed detecting driver distractions caused by road conditions by studying the correlation between road conditions and biometric data collected through a body sensor network (BSN) [44] consisting of wearable sensors that monitor a driver's brainwaves, ECG signals, muscle activity (through electromyography [EMG]), galvanic skin response (GSR), and motion. Automotive sensors also record different aspects of driving behavior (e.g., aggressiveness and speed) http://www.scienceservingsociety.com/ts/text/ch09.htm. The data collected from five drivers driving during peak and non-peak traffic periods suggested that the theta and beta bands in the frontal cortex were correlated with the road conditions. The time-frequency dynamics of the drivers' brains provided useful features for the statistical measures of biometric indexes to detect early driving distractions.

The BSN and wearable sensors may, however, prove to be prohibitively invasive for the driver. Harman International Industries used a potentially less invasive approach in their system, which monitors the driver's pupil dilation with a camera to assess his/her cognitive load [39]. The system reacts when it recognizes a "high cognitive load", a possible indicator of distracted driving, by for example, switching the driver's mobile device to the do-not-disturb mode. Research comparing the accuracy of the less invasive approaches such as this one to more invasive approaches, such as that of Williams et al., is for establishing and optimizing the the convenience-accuracy tradeoff.

62.2.4 Detecting Drowsiness

Driving while sleep deprived is a common cause of car accidents. The Panasonic Corporation developed an early warning system to detect signs of drowsiness and keep the driver comfortably awake while driving (it will be available in 2018) [4]. The system first determines the level of drowsiness by continuously monitoring the driver's blinking rate, body heat loss, facial expressions, and degree of illuminance of the skin via cameras and sensors. After these data are processed with artificial intelligence algorithms, air conditioner settings and music volume are adjusted to keep the driver awake, or the driver is recommended to stop and rest.

Omron [30] is developing a system that uses an infrared camera attached to the vehicle's dashboard which monitors eye movements, gestures, blinking rate, and head movements that may be signs of drowsiness. If the driver is insufficiently alert to touch the steering wheel, the car is stopped.

Similar efforts in this area include those of Optalert [5], which implemented smart glasses to capture eyelid movements and sense drowsiness. Similarly, Vigo manufactures headsets that sense driver distractions, drowsiness, and slouching movements [59].

62.2.5 Driver Convenience

Agitation and inconvenient driving conditions can affect how people drive. For example, bright sunlight can cause discomfort for and impair the vision of the driver. Meschtscherjakov et al. [38] proposed an adaptive digital sunshade that tracks the driver's eye movements using low-cost webcams and uses the FreeFrame DShow9 node face-tracking algorithm to darken the area of the windshield on which the driver's gaze is fixed. All six drivers on whom the system was tested felt that it was effective.

Researchers such as Endres et al. [14] believe that the use of voice and body or hand gestures to control vehicle functions is more convenient and is less distracting for the driver. Endres et al. proposed an approach for controlling temperature, stereo, and other vehicle functions with finger gestures while the driver's hand rests on the steering wheel.

They monitored hand gestures using electric field sensing techniques and identified the gesture types using the

dynamic time warping (DTW) algorithm [55]; such an approach, the authors argued, is more robust in noisy settings than existing voice-based techniques [3]. The authors concluded that the recognition accuracy was not as high as that in similar studies because their model was trained on a single gesture that implemented only a one-dimensional "Geremin" (i.e., vertical antenna) for electromagnetic sensing, which could be improved by the use of two antennas and a hidden Markov model approach [8].

We believe that more research is needed comparing the accuracy and convenience of different approaches to gesture recognition (e.g., voice vs. hand movements), as these are not immediately clear from the existing research.

62.2.6 Miscellaneous Work

Reyes-Muñoz et al. [49] presented a system architecture in which a BSN was used to recognize impaired driving states, such as intoxicated, drowsy, emotional, or distracted. The system used EEG to monitor a driver's electrical brain activity; an ECG to monitor their heart activity; electrooculography to detect drowsiness; facial EMG to detect emotional states, such as fatigue; and plethysmography to measure intoxication. A monitoring station was used to receive biometric data from the BSN, which were processed via two modules: (1) feature extraction and (2) driver state recognition. The NeuroSky MindWave mobile sensor, a low-cost device for gathering EEG data (e.g., alpha, beta, gamma, delta and theta raw signals), is embedded in a headband worn by the driver. Measurements of attention, meditation, and eye blink are computed by proprietary NeuroSky algorithms. If an impaired state is detected, other nearby vehicles and pedestrians are notified through a vehicular ad-hoc network (VANET) and mobile devices.

62.3   Biometrics and Vehicle Security

From keyless vehicle access to detecting intruders in a car, biometrics-based authentication technology is a strong candidate for vehicle security. Whereas keys must be carried around and can be easily lost or stolen, biometrics can continuously verify the vehicle driver's identity and prevent access or disable the vehicle if the identity is not authorized. In our review of research on vehicle security using face recognition, voice, fingerprints, and other biometrics, most works adapted existing biometric recognition techniques. We expect this trend to continue in the future. In other works, an individual's driving patterns are characterized as a behavioral biometric useful for identity verification.

62.3.1 Facial Recognition-Based Authentication

Facial recognition for keyless access is already supported in Lexus, BMW, and Mercedes vehicles, [52] and other car companies have works in progress with this biometric technology.

Ishak et al. [22] proposed a system that verifies the driver's face to allow him/her to ignite the car. Their approach is designed to work efficiently in varying illumination conditions, as is common in automotive applications, and uses a low-cost 480×640 pixel webcam mounted on the driver's side. The image is processed using a combination of fast neural network [7] and classical neural network (CNN) approaches to detect the face. The detected face is recognized using an algorithm based on principal component analysis (PCA) [58] and linear discriminant analysis [6, 63]. General functionality is improved with a lightning illumination approach proposed by Rowley et al. [50], which employs a histogram equalization and a linear fit function to candidate regions before they are sent to the CNN. The scheme, which was tested using lightning normalization in typical automotive settings, showed a 91.4% recognition rate and a 0.75% false acceptance rate.

Liu [33] developed an embedded car theft detection and facial recognition scheme that uses an economical portable desktop camera (CCD). When the car starts up, the camera captures an image of the driver's face and analyzes it using the Eigenfaces algorithm [12, 45, 47, 58]. A near-infrared (NIR) illuminator and a narrow band-pass NIR filter (range 700–900 nm) are also implemented to minimize the impact of different light conditions and to constrict the pupil to help the face detection mechanism find the driver's eyes. If the driver is not authorized, a facial image will be sent to the owner or the police through general packet radio service (GPRS) networks. The results showed 96% accuracy in varying light and orientation conditions.

Performing facial recognition using infrared (IR) images of the face has also been proposed. These images are robust under uncontrolled conditions, such as varying illumination and shadows, in which vehicle-based face recognition systems are expected to operate. Liu et al. [34], for example, used an IR illuminator to cause the pupils to appear brighter against the face, making it easier to locate the eyes; the facial recognition method used was based on a PCA algorithm [12, 31, 47]. The test results of 55 drivers yielded a 100% rejection rate for unauthorized drivers and an 8% average rejection rate for authorized drivers.

Kang et al. [26] used a NIR camera (0.7 μm to 1.4 μm) and an artificial illuminator with NIR light emitting diodes (LEDs). A technique using Fisherfaces was implemented using test frames with 6, 18, and 24 NIR LEDs. In the resulting facial recognition rates, which used the CMU PIE database

for training [53], the highest percentage of difference in facial recognition accuracy between ambient and illuminated scenarios was 0.9619%.

Padmapriya et al. [46] proposed the optimization of facial recognition-based anti-theft systems for vehicles by using skin color information for face detection that uses the AdaBoost machine learning algorithm [16]. In their scheme, a camera on the car door captures a frame of the person's face, and a modified version of the AdaBoost algorithm optimized to take advantage of skin color features is then used to extract the face; finally, PCA via orthogonal transformation [9] is used to compare the input face to the known faces in the database. The MIT-CBCL database [10], which contained 2429 face samples with a 19×19 sample size, was used to train the AdaBoost algorithm. In the experiments, 95.91% face detection accuracy was achieved using the improved AdaBoost algorithm with skin color parameters, in comparison with the general AdaBoost algorithm, which achieved 84.50% accuracy.

62.3.2 Fingerprint-Based Biometric Authentication

Fingerprint-based authentication, if properly implemented, can be relatively secure and convenient as evidenced by its widespread use in high-security applications and its commercial success in consumer mobile devices. Therefore, researchers such as Zhu et al. [64] have recognized the potential of fingerprints in automotive security applications, such as keyless access, and other researchers have proposed concrete fingerprint verification-based schemes which we discuss next.

Sushmitha et al. [54] proposed a system that verifies the driver's fingerprint prior to starting the car. If the fingerprint does not match that of the authorized driver, the car will not start, and an SMS message will be dispatched to the owner and the police. The method is based on the R303A fingerprint verification hardware module developed by Apex Technologies [1]. The module includes an optical fingerprint scanner and is supported by the libfprint open source fingerprint processing library [32], which is used to match the minutia of the live fingerprint against the fingerprint templates of enrolled drivers. No performance results were reported.

Folorunso et al. [15] used the FPM20A fingerprint module to allow the driver to start the car using his/her fingerprint. Similar efforts have been undertaken by [25] and [27].

In contrast to previous works, Anjali et al. proposed a close integration of fingerprint verification with driving and vehicle ownership. In their system, the citizens of a country must submit their fingerprint images when receiving a driver's license, and these images will be stored in a smart card embedded in their driver's license. To start the car, the driver must use the car's fingerprint reader to verify his/her fingerprints against those stored in the driver's license.

62.3.3 Speech Recognition-Based Authentication

Speech recognition-based authentication, even if it is convenient, can prove challenging in an automotive context, as it must cope with highway, street, and other sonic interference. Various speech-based schemes proposed in the literature are discussed below.

In Kopparapu et al.'s system [28], a driver must simultaneously speak into his/her mobile phone as well as into the microphone mounted on the car to gain access to the vehicle. The system installed in the car verifies the user's voice using the DTW algorithm and linear prediction cepstral coefficient (LPCC) features. The mobile device also sends speech data to the remote server, which identifies the user through a more reliable verification system that implements mel frequency cepstral coefficient (MFCC) features and Gaussian mixture models (GMMs). The user is permitted entry into the vehicle if the remote server and the car both successfully verify the driver. These two means of authentication provide an extra level of security.

62.3.4 Seat Sensing Biometrics

Researchers at the Advanced Institute of Industrial Technology in Tokyo designed a car seat capable of accurately measuring the driver's buttocks, including its posterior contours [43]. The seat has 360 pressure sensors that measure the pressure points on the buttocks of the sitting driver and then uses these measurements to authenticate the driver. The researchers argued that this method is less invasive than other biometric methods of authentication, such as iris scanners. During testing, this method successfully identified drivers with 98% accuracy.

62.3.5 Behavioral Biometrics-Based Authentication

Driving behavior, which is believed to be unique to each driver, can be used to verify a driver's identity. The systems proposed in this area of research assume that the vehicle intruder has (1) already bypassed the car entry security mechanisms, such as car alarms and access approaches, which were discussed previously; (2) has entered into the vehicle; and (3) is able to drive it. If the driving behaviors of the intruder do not resemble those of the authorized driver(s), the owner or law enforcement can be notified.

Igarashi et al. [21] used GMMs to model driving preferences, such as the static and dynamic features of the accelerator and brake pedals as well as speed ranges, and verify whether the measured driving preferences of the driver likely represent those of an authorized driver. Their model was tested using data from 30 drivers. The resulting data of force on the accelerator and brake pedals showed a peak identification rate of 73%.

Markwood and Liu [36] proposed a technique for vehicle theft detection that continuously analyzes input data from negative and positive acceleration and braking to verify the driver's identity. First, the algorithm extracts features from authorized driver data and these features are computed into a series of probability distributions. The Kolmogorov–Smirnov (K-S) test, a non-parametric statistical test [57], and total variation distance [2] are used to check whether the data collected from the current driver represent that of the authorized driver(s) based on the distributions derived in the training phase. Results yielded 97% accuracy for authorized drivers and 91% for impostors.

Chen et al. [11] proposed a driver verification algorithm based on the recognition of hand-grip patterns on the steering wheel. The authors evaluated their scheme using a Tactilus pressure mapping mat less than 0.7-mm thick to record pressure loads; the map, which was installed on the steering wheel and connected to a computer, was used to gather hand-grip data from 21 subjects. The researchers applied quad-tree-based [51] multiresolution decomposition to the hand-grip images, used PCA-based dimension reduction, and classified drivers as either legitimate or illegitimate using a likelihood-ratio classifier. In Chen et al.'s experiments, the mean acceptance rate was between 78.15% and 78.22%, and the mean rejection rate was between 93.92% and 90.3%.

62.3.6 Multimodal Biometrics Authentication

Some schemes have been proposed that aim to improve vehicle security using multiple, or multimodal, biometrics. Jaguar Land Rover filed a patent [17, 24] for a "door access system for a vehicle" that can unlock a car using a camera connected to a biometric software system that identifies a driver approaching the car using facial and gait recognition. This system can also unlock car doors by recognizing hand gestures. Similarly, Ford was granted a patent in 2015 for a system that scans drivers' fingerprints, voice, and retina so that they can gain access to the vehicle and start the engine [37].

In [35], a scheme was proposed for identifying and verifying drivers based on fingerprint, iris, and voice recognition with sensors installed on the door and steering wheel and a camera installed on the front mirror. The captured biometric information can be sent to the authorities through a GPRS system and be matched against a police database to detect an unauthorized driver.

Yuan et al. [62] presented a vehicle anti-theft system based on palmprints and palm vein patterns, focusing on image acquisition methods and hardware architecture. The authors argue that their approach is convenient for in-vehicle use because it is non-invasive. No evaluation results were presented.

62.4 Conclusion

We have discussed a selection of academic and industry research focused on the integration of biometrics technologies with automotive vehicles. Although most works focused on making driving safer and safeguarding vehicles from theft and intrusion, many other subfields are likely to emerge in the near future. For example, VANETs present opportunities for novel biometric applications such as using biometrics for VANET security, privacy, and anonymity protocols (e.g., [60]). Emergence of self-driving cars also presents new research opportunities. We expect that even without a human driver, vehicles will still need to be protected from intrusions, unauthorized use, and hijackings. Hence, biometric research focusing on addressing these problems will remain relevant.

Innovative solutions that monitor the health and safety of passengers via biometrics and then leverage the self-driving capabilities of the vehicle to remove the passengers from danger are now possible. In addition, biometric identification can allow vehicles to automatically customize themselves for the comfort and needs of passengers, and wearable biometrics-enabled devices capable of communicating with vehicles also present untold research opportunities.

All future biometric techniques for vehicles will have to contend with the issues of user-friendliness, the privacy of collected data, and the social and legal implications of vehicles capable of biometrically monitoring their drivers and passengers. We expect these issues to become major topics of future research.

An interested reader can find our comprehensive list of works relevant to the field in [19].

References

1. 3pixelart.com. http://www.apexengineeringproject.com/display-product.php?id=AP106
2. J. Adell, P. Jodrá, Exact kolmogorov and total variation distances between some familiar discrete distributions. J. Inequal. Appl. **2006**(1), 64307 (2006)
3. F. Althoff, R. Lindl, L. Walchshausl, S. Hoch, Robust multimodal hand-and head gesture recognition for controlling automotive infotainment systems. VDI BERICHTE **1919**, 187 (2005)
4. Artificial intelligence helps to keep tired drivers awake (2017). http://www.digitaljournal.com/tech-and-science/technology/artificial-intelligence-helps-to-keep-tired-drivers-awake/article/499369
5. Automotive. http://www.optalert.com/automotive
6. P.N. Belhumeur, J.P. Hespanha, D.J. Kriegman, Eigenfaces vs. fisherfaces: recognition using class specific linear projection. IEEE Trans. Pattern Anal. Mach. Intell. **19**(7), 711–720 (1997)
7. S. Ben-Yacoub, B. Fasel, *Fast Multi-Scale Face Detection* (IDIAP, Martigny, 1998)
8. M. Billinghurst, B. Buxton, Gesture based interaction, in *Haptic Input*, 24 (2011)
9. K.W. Bowyer, K. Chang, P. Flynn, A survey of approaches and challenges in 3D and multi-modal 3D+ 2D face recognition. Comput. Vis. Image Underst. **101**(1), 1–15 (2006)
10. CBCL face recognition database. http://cbcl.mit.edu/software-datasets/heisele/facerecognition-database.html
11. R. Chen, M. She, J. Wang, X. Sun, L. Kong, Driver verification based on handgrip recognition on steering wheel, in *2011 IEEE International Conference on Systems, Man, and Cybernetics (SMC)* (IEEE, New York, 2011), pp. 1645–1651
12. X. Chen, P.J. Flynn, K.W. Bowyer, PCA-based face recognition in infrared imagery: baseline and comparative studies, in *IEEE International Workshop on Analysis and Modeling of Faces and Gestures, AMFG 2003* (IEEE, New York, 2003), pp. 127–134
13. O. Dehzangi, C. Williams, Towards multi-modal wearable driver monitoring: impact of road condition on driver distraction, in *2015 IEEE 12th International Conference on Wearable and Implantable Body Sensor Networks (BSN)* (IEEE, New York, 2015), pp. 1–6
14. C. Endres, T. Schwartz, C.A. Müller, Geremin: 2D microgestures for drivers based on electric field sensing, in *Proceedings of the 16th International Conference on Intelligent User Interfaces* (ACM, New York, 2011), pp. 327–330
15. C.O. Folorunso, L.A. Akinyemi, A.A. Ajasa, K. Oladipupo, Design and development of fingerprint based car starting system, in Presentation made at *16th International Conference on Electronic Packaging Technology (ICEPT 2015), Exhibition on Power and Telecommunications.* http://nieee.org.ng/portfolio/papers/view/Design_and_ Development_of_Fingerprint_based_Car_Starting_System_(Folorunsho_C_et_al.pdf
16. Y. Freund, R.E. Schapire, A desicion-theoretic generalization of on-line learning and an application to boosting, in *European Conference on Computational Learning Theory* (Springer, Berlin, 1995), pp. 23–37
17. Future jaguar cars may recognize approaching drivers (2016). http://findbiometrics.com/jaguar-cars-face-biometrics-311247/
18. Gestigon, The future of mobility is not about cars. http://www.gestigon.com/automotive-industry/
19. M. Gofman, M. Villa, Extended database of biometrics research for automotive applications. (2017) http://www.fullerton.edu/cybersecurity/research/Extended-Database-of-Biometrics-Research-for-Automotive-Applications.php
20. M. Gutmann, P. Grausberg, K. Kyamakya, Detecting human driver's physiological stress and emotions using sophisticated one-person cockpit vehicle simulator, in *Information Technologies in Innovation Business Conference (ITIB)* (IEEE, New York, 2015), pp. 15–18
21. K. Igarashi, C. Miyajima, K. Itou, K. Takeda, F. Itakura, H. Abut, Biometric identification using driving behavioral signals, in *2004 IEEE International Conference on Multimedia and Expo, 2004. ICME'04*, vol. 1 (IEEE, New York, 2004), pp. 65–68
22. K.A. Ishak, S.A. Samad, A. Hussain, A face detection and recognition system for intelligent vehicles. Inf. Technol. J. **5**(3), 507–515 (2006)
23. R. Ivers, T. Senserrick, S. Boufous, M. Stevenson, H.-Y. Chen, M. Woodward, R. Norton, Novice drivers' risky driving behavior, risk perception, and crash risk findings from the drive study (2009). https://www.ncbi.nlm.nih.gov/pmc/articles/PMC2724457/
24. HYPERLINK "https://www.biometricupdate.com/author/justin-lee" J. Lee, Jaguar files patent for vehicle access system with facial

recognition and gait analysis (2016). http://www.biometricupdate.com/201611/jaguar-files-patent-for-vehicle-access-system-with-facial-recognition-and-gait-analysis

25. J.B. Jadav, K.H. Wandra, R. Dabhi, Innovative automobile security system using various security modules. Int. J. Sci. Prog. Res. **8**(1), 24–27 (2015)

26. J. Kang, D.V. Anderson, M.H. Hayes, Face recognition in vehicles with near infrared frame differencing, in *IEEE Signal Processing and Signal Processing Education Workshop (SP/SPE)* (IEEE, New York, 2015), pp. 358–363

27. N. Kiruthiga, S. Thangasamy, et al., Real time biometrics based vehicle security system with GPS and GSM technology. Proc. Comput. Sci. **47**, 471–479 (2015)

28. S.K. Kopparapu, A robust speech biometric system for vehicle access, in *2009 IEEE International Conference on Vehicular Electronics and Safety (ICVES)* (IEEE, New York, 2009), pp. 174–177

29. H.B. Lee, J.M. Choi, J.S. Kim, Y.S. Kim, H.J. Baek, M.S. Ryu, R.H. Sohn, K.S. Park, Nonintrusive biosignal measurement system in a vehicle, in *29th Annual International Conference of the IEEE Engineering in Medicine and Biology Society, EMBS 2007* (IEEE, New York, 2007), pp. 2303–2306

30. J. Lee, Omron integrating facial recognition into autonomous driving system (2016). http://www.biometricupdate.com/201610/omron-integrating-facial-recognition-into-autonomous-driving-system

31. A. Leonardis, H. Bischof, Dealing with occlusions in the eigenspace approach, in *1996 IEEE Computer Society Conference on Computer Vision and Pattern Recognition, 1996. Proceedings CVPR'96* (IEEE, New York, 1996), pp. 453–458

32. libfprint API reference. http://www.reactivated.net/fprint/api/

33. Z. Liu, A new embedded car theft detection system, in *Second International Conference Onembedded Software and Systems, 2005* (IEEE, New York, 2005), 6 pp.

34. Z. Liu, G. He, Research on vehicle anti-theft and alarm system using facing recognition, in *International Conference on Neural Networks and Brain, 2005. ICNN&B'05*, vol. 2 (IEEE, New York, 2005), pp. 925–929

35. C. Lupu, V. Lupu, Multimodal biometrics for access control in an intelligent car, in *International Symposium on Computational Intelligence and Intelligent Informatics, 2007. ISCIII'07* (IEEE, New York, 2007), pp. 261–267

36. I.D. Markwood, Y. Liu, Vehicle self-surveillance: sensor-enabled automatic driver recognition, in *Proceedings of the 11th ACM on Asia Conference on Computer and Communications Security* (ACM, New York, 2016), pp. 425–436

37. S. Mayhew, Ford granted patent for keyless biometric system for vehicles (2015). http://www.biometricupdate.com/201502/ford-granted-patent-for-keyless-biometric-system-for-vehicles

38. A. Meschtscherjakov, H. Scharfetter, S.P. Kernjak, N.M. Kratzer, J. Stadon, Adaptive digital sunshade: blocking the sun from blinding the driver, in *Adjunct Proceedings of the 7th International Conference on Automotive User Interfaces and Interactive Vehicular Applications* (ACM, New York, 2015), pp. 78–83

39. Mobile ID World, Keeping drivers safe with pupil biometrics (2016). https://findbiometrics.com/keeping-drivers-safe-with-pupil-biometrics-301058/

40. National Highway Traffic Safety Administration et al., Early estimate of motor vehicle traffic fatalities for the first 9 months of 2016 (2017). https://crashstats.nhtsa.dot.gov/Api/Public/ViewPublication/812358

41. NHTSA, Contribution of medical conditions to passenger vehicle crashes (2009). https://crashstats.nhtsa.dot.gov/Api/Public/ViewPublication/811219

42. NHTSA, Drunk driving (2017). https://www.nhtsa.gov/risky-driving/drunk-driving

43. D. Nosowitz, A car seat that authenticates the driver with butt recognition (2011). https://www.popsci.com/cars/article/2011-12/car-seat-recognizes-your-butt-security-and-fun

44. O. Omeni, A.C. Wai Wong, A.J. Burdett, C. Toumazou, Energy efficient medium access protocol for wireless medical body area sensor networks. IEEE Trans. Biomed. Circuits Syst. **2**(4), 251–259 (2008)

45. M. Oravec, J. Pavlovicova, Face recognition methods based on principal component analysis and feedforward neural networks, in *Proceedings of 2004 IEEE International Joint Conference on Neural Networks*, vol. 1 (IEEE, New York, 2004), pp. 437–441

46. S. Padmapriya, E.A. KalaJames, Real time smart car lock security system using face detection and recognition, in *International Conference on Computer Communication and Informatics (ICCCI)* (IEEE, New York, 2012), pp. 1–6

47. A. Pentland, B. Moghaddam, T. Starner, et al., View-based and modular eigenspaces for face recognition, in *CVPR*, vol. 94 (1994), pp. 84–91

48. R. Rathore, C. Gau, Integrating biometric sensors into automotive internet of things, in *International Conference on Cloud Computing and Internet of Things (CCIOT)* (2014), pp. 178–181

49. A. Reyes-Muñoz, M.C. Domingo, M.A. López-Trinidad, J.L. Delgado, Integration of body sensor networks and vehicular ad-hoc networks for traffic safety. Sensors **16**(1), 107 (2016)

50. H.A. Rowley, S. Baluja, T. Kanade, Human face detection in visual scenes, in *Advances in Neural Information Processing Systems* (1996), pp. 875–881

51. H. Samet, The quadtree and related hierarchical data structures. ACM Comput. Surv.(CSUR) **16**(2), 187–260 (1984)

52. Sense holdings acquires exclusive sales, marketing and purchase rights for biometric patent to secure vehicles. http://www.theautochannel.com/news/2004/03/18/185331.html

53. T. Sim, S. Baker, M. Bsat, The CMU pose, illumination, and expression (PIE) database, in *Proceedings Fifth IEEE International Conference on Automatic Face and Gesture Recognition* (IEEE, New York, 2002), pp. 53–58

54. N. Sushmitha, B. Supriya, R. Prajeeshan, Bio-metric automobile security. Int. J. Sci. Eng. Technol. Res. **4**(19), 3550–3554 (2015)

55. G.A. ten Holt, M.J.T. Reinders, E.A. Hendriks, Multi-dimensional dynamic time warping for gesture recognition, in *Thirteenth Annual Conference of the Advanced School for Computing and Imaging*, vol. 300 (2007)

56. The power to stop drunk driving is now in the palm of your hand. http://sobersteering.com/how-it-works/

57. H.C. Tijms, *Stochastic Models: An Algorithmic Approach*, vol. 303 (Wiley, London, 1994)

58. M. Turk, A. Pentland, Eigenfaces for recognition. J. Cogn. Neurosci. **3**(1), 71–86 (1991)

59. Vigo the science. https://www.wearvigo.com/science

60. L. Yao, C. Lin, J. Deng, F. Deng, J. Miao, K. Yim, G. Wu, Biometrics-based data link layer anonymous authentication in vanets, in *2013 Seventh International Conference on Innovative Mobile and Internet Services in Ubiquitous Computing (IMIS)* (IEEE, New York, 2013), pp. 182–187

61. K. Young, M. Regan, M. Hammer, Driver distraction: a review of the literature, in *Distracted Driving*, ed. by I.J. Faulks, M. Regan, M. Stevenson, J. Brown, A. Porter, J.D. Irwin (Australasian College of Road Safety, Sydney, 2007), pp. 379–405

62. W. Yuan, Y. Tang, The driver authentication device based on the characteristics of palmprint and palm vein, in *2011 International Conference on Hand-Based Biometrics (ICHB)* (IEEE, New York, 2011), pp. 1–5

63. W. Zhao, R. Chellappa, A. Krishnaswamy, Discriminant analysis of principal components for face recognition, in *Proceedings of third IEEE International Conference on Automatic Face and Gesture Recognition, 1998* (IEEE, New York, 1998), pp. 336–341

64. Z. Zhu, F. Chen, Fingerprint recognition-based access controlling system for automobiles, in *2011 4th International Congress on Image and Signal Processing (CISP)*, vol. 4 (IEEE, New York, 2011), pp. 1899–1902

A Survey on Adoption Good Practices for ICT Governance at Enhanced Organizations

63

Marianne Batista Diniz da Silva, Alef Menezes dos Santos, Michel dos Santos Soares, Rogério Patrício Chagas do Nascimento, and Isabel Dillmann Nunes

Abstract

Governance in Information and Communication Technology (ICT) is a relevant area of research and practice. The Audit Court of the Union (ACU) periodically evaluates all Brazilian Federal Public Organizations in order to disseminate the importance of implementing good governance system and raising awareness of positive contribution of adopting Good Practices. As a result of these evaluations, it is clear that evolution of ICT Governance in Federal Public Administration (FPA) in Brazil is growing slowly. The number of organizations that effectively adopt good governance practices is low when compared to all other FPAs. This article presents results of a survey conducted at Public Organizations that have improved capability (iGovTI) stages according to the ACU. The iGovTI is the index of governance in which the organization is inserted, it can be (initial, basic, intermediate and enhanced). Knowing this, this survey collected used practices and identifies the profiles of organizations and their interviewees. As main results, we recognize that the Good Practices used in Enhanced Organizations are the same known in academia as well as in industry (for instance, COBIT, ITIL, CMMI, MPS.Br, PMBOK). Another relevant result is the evidence that even Enhanced Organizations do not adopt practices in topics considered relevant, including project management, information security and risk management.

ICT governance · Public · Enhanced Organization · Good practices · Survey

Keywords

M. B. D. da Silva (✉) · A. M. dos Santos · M. dos Santos Soares · R. P. C. do Nascimento
Postgraduate Program in Computer Science (PROCC), Federal University of Sergipe (UFS), São Cristóvão, Sergipe, Brazil
e-mail: rogerio@ufs.br

I. D. Nunes
Instituto de Metrópole Digital (IMD), Federal University of Rio Grande do Norte (UFRN), Natal, Rio Grande do Norte, Brazil
e-mail: bel@imd.ufrn.br

63.1 Introduction

Recently, Information and Communication Technology (ICT) has been playing a key role in public and private organizations, especially because most organizational transactions are becoming computerized. ICT is a resource capable of supporting the organization's end-activity, providing agility, mobility and support for decision-making [1, 2]. Importance of ICT is increasing and it has lead to reflection and greater attention on issues related to growth of ICT investments. It is a value that ICT adds to the organization, its products and services.

These factors make ICT decision-making and ICT governance issues more frequent in academic and corporate environments, as well as in the public organizations environment, because of diffusion of Public Administration principles [3].

Within this context, ICT Governance in Brazil's Federal Public Administration (FPA) has been facing an unfavorable scenario. Low investments in Governance policies have lead to an increase in project failures, waste of resources, services with low quality among other issues. Adoption of Good Practices (COBIT, ITIL, CMMI, MPS.Br, PMBOK) can be a way to extinguish or mitigate such problems [4–7].

Considering this unfavorable scenario (ungovernance), the Audit Court of the Union (ACU) realizes an evaluation every 2 years, which is a survey of the organizational capability. This capability is measured by the Information Technology Governance Index (iGovTI). This evaluation is performed through six dimensions (Leadership, Information, People, Processes, Outcomes and Strategy and Plans), which

© Springer International Publishing AG, part of Springer Nature 2018
S. Latifi (ed.), *Information Technology – New Generations*, Advances in Intelligent Systems and Computing 738,
https://doi.org/10.1007/978-3-319-77028-4_63

defines the stage of capability of organizations. These stages are ordered from initial, then basic, intermediate and improved.

IGovTI is calculated by consolidating the answers to the questionnaire prepared by the Information Technology Inspection Secretariat (ITIS). The general equation is defined as $iGovTI = d1p1 + d2p2 + ... + dnpn$, where each "d" (ranging from 0 to 1) represents the dimension degree and each "p" parameter (ranging from 0 to 1) represents the weight of that dimension in the iGovTI calculation. As a result, organizations can be classified as: (a) initial if it has index of less than 0.30; (b) basic if the index is between 0.30 and 0.50; (c) intermediate, between 0.50 and 0.70; and (d) enhanced with an index greater than 0.70.

The objective of this evaluation is to identify how organizations are adopting Good Practices, aimed to an improvement of ICT governance and, consequently, in population services rendering in general [8].

Based on the last survey developed by ACU in 2016, it was found that only (11%) of FPA's relevant Organizations present an Improved Governance level. In contrast, (51%) of them are in lower levels, being beginning (14%) and basic (37%), in a total of 368 organizations [9]. These data indicate the low level of governance of FPA organizations. Therefore, ICTs will hardly contribute efficiently to generate value to business.

In this article, we present a survey, specific to public organizations at improved capability stage, in order to collect their Good Practices that are commonly used. A questionnaire consisting of 20 questions divided into three blocks was applied. First one deals with the organization's profile, the second is about the interviewee profile, and finally the third block consists of Good Practices adopted on the basis of the themes: ICT Committee, Strategic Planning, Project Management, Services Management, Personnel Hiring, Software Processes, Information Security and Risk Management. The questionnaire was made available on the Internet. Organizational Improvement Managers were invited to respond. A sample of 11 responses was obtained.

Results indicate that Good Practices used in Enhanced Organizations are the same known in academia as in industry (COBIT, ITIL, CMMI, MPS.Br and PMBOK).

63.2   Related Works

To the best of our knowledge, there are no scientific surveys with the same research objective of this article, including dealing with Good ICT Governance Practices adopted in public organizations with the enhanced capability stage. However, similar works were published before, and are briefly mentioned as below.

Ramos [10] identified and verified issues through statistical analysis that can be considered critical success factors (CCF) in ICT Governance for FPA bodies. Interviews were conducted with ICT Managers to classify the Critical Success Factors. Results of this interview showed that 66.66% of variables were classified in the same way as the CCF previously identified through qualitative research, classifying them as High Impact Critical Success Factors in ICT Governance.

Luciano and Wiedenhoft [11] identified and validated a list of mechanisms that can meet the objectives and principles of ICT Governance in Public Organizations and that can be selected by Public Organizations to implement their Governance model. The study was able to refine 25 mechanisms through the survey with 98 public administration servers resulting in a list of 11 IT Governance mechanisms to meet the objectives and principles of Governance in Public Administration.

Al Qassimi and Rusu [12] carried out an analysis of ICT Governance practices based on Van Grembergen's De Haes framework, which aims to identify some problems and restraints faced by the IT department in budgeting and decision-making. In addition, research has revealed that there is a lower level of knowledge regarding ICT governance in the government organization and therefore there is a need to improve the structures, processes, and mechanisms of relationships that will promote accountability of ICT projects and contribute to an effective implementation of ICT Governance in the organization.

Subsermsri et al. [13] have developed a formal set of IT Governance practices based on the sufficiency economy philosophy (SEP) to support a generic context for Thai universities. To do this, they conducted interviews with 20 Chief Information Officer (CIOs) from universities, five IT specialists, and five SEP specialists. The study provided two findings: the set of SEP-based practices for Thai Universities, and the mapping of IT governance practices based on SEP and ISO/IEC 38500, in a total of 65 practices that can be used as a guide for Thai universities.

These works encourage the research of how Public Organizations are addressing this issue and whether they adopt or have Good Practices. In addition, they stimulate creation of hypotheses about the need for a framework to direct organizations. The following section details the steps involved for conducting the survey.

63.3   Survey

This section presents all steps related to the research (survey), from its objective, passing through selection of participants, instrumentation, operation, to the analysis and interpretation of collected answers.

63.3.1 Objective

The overall objective of this survey is to collect Good ICT Governance Practices with managers of Enhanced Organizations in the Federal Public Administration. This goal is formalized using the Goal, Question, Metric (GQM) model proposed in [14], as presented in [15]:

To analyze Good ICT Governance Practices with the purpose to characterize, with respect to the use of tools and techniques according to the dimensions defined by the ACU, from the point of view of managers or technicians, in the context of FPA organizations with enhanced capability stages.

Based on this objective, the following research questions were formulated:

Q1. Are there specific employees for the area of ICT Governance?

Q2. Does Good ICT Governance control practices used by the enhanced capability training organizations differs from those used in the industry and/or academia?

Q3. What are the practices by mechanisms (Leadership and Strategy)?

These research questions were used to derive the questions of the questionnaire, analyzed in the following sections.

63.3.2 Planning

This section presents the phases for planning the survey.

63.3.2.1 Formulation of Hypothesis

To evaluate the research questions we used frequency-based metrics, making up the number of employees working in the area of ICT Governance (Q1), defined practices (Q2), and mechanisms (Q3).

Once the objective and metrics are defined, it will still be considered the hypothesis related to the relationship between the improved capability stage and adoption of good known practices. In this way, the hypothesis to be tested is:

H0: Organizations with enhanced capability stage adopt unknown Good Practices.

H1: Organizations with enhanced capability stage adopt best-known practices.

63.3.2.2 Selection of Participants and Sample

Selection of participants considered a ranking of the organizations that participated in the audit/survey of ACU in 2014. The ranking was defined based on the iGovTI notes of each organization, and then a population of 28 organizations is obtained, all of them part of the Enhanced Capability Stage.

The sampling was non-probabilistic and collected for convenience.

63.3.2.3 Methodology

A pilot study was designed with IT professionals and IT Governance Experts that had had direct relationship with the ICT Governance in the FPA in the accomplishment of their daily tasks.

The sample of the pilot study should be small, in order to identify possible problems and inconsistencies in questions. This pre-test is necessary and aims to improve the research instrument, being executed in the same way as it will be applied. The selection of pretest participants is flexible. However, it is recommended that people should be reasonably adequate for the questions [16].

In order to guarantee the answers of all organizations, some additional care was taken. Due to the research being performed on the Internet [17], the time spent by the respondent should not be more than 10 min, the navigation time between one page and another should not exceed 8 (eight) s, and clear language and openness in any browser.

63.3.2.4 Instrumentation

The questionnaire was Developed in Google Forms and distributed via the Internet. It contains an initial presentation, followed by questions about the profile of the organization and the interviewee, and finally, the last step, in which the questions are related to Good Practices of ICT Governance in the FPA.

63.3.3 Operation

This section explains the phases for Operation of the survey.

63.3.3.1 Application

Initially, a pilot of the questionnaire was applied to 5 (five) professionals defined in the methodology and selected by trial, who did not participate in the survey, but contributed to modifications, making the questionnaire clearer, cohesive and objective.

The organizations were then listed as indicated in the participant selection (Sect. 63.3.2.2).

63.3.3.2 Data Collection and Validation

Despite the fact that we used a specialized tool for the construction of surveys, it was verified whether the results were really consistent with those indicated by the survey, as well as the total responses. In addition, as a form of validation, the participants' capability stages were investigated.

63.3.4 Data Analysis and Interpretation

This section addresses the results obtained in the survey.

63.3.4.1 Gross Results

Eleven questions were elaborated to identify the profile of the organization and the interviewees. Seven questions are about the profile of the organization and four (four) about the profile of the interviewee. Regarding the position that the interviewees occupy in the companies (Fig. 63.1), we had in the first place position Coordinator (28%), followed by Secretary and Director each with (18%), Chief, Systems Analyst, Superintendent and Pro-Rector both with (9%). This diversity of positions may indicate the management policy of each organization since they are public organizations.

Figure 63.2 shows how long the respondents are in the previous position. This indicates that in public organizations there is a lot of turnover, mainly for positions such as Coordinator and Director.

The majority of the interviewed has between 3 and 5 years (38%) of activity in the area of ICT Governance. This is an important fact for the reliability and ownership of the answers. Only 10% have less than 1 year. Figure 63.3 shows the other distributions.

The ACU classifies organizations into six types: EXE-SISP (Universities, Institutes), EXE-DEST (Public and Federal Enterprises), JUD (Organizations that are part of the Judiciary), LEG (of the Legislative Power), MPU (Organizations that are part of the Public Ministry of the Union) and Third Sector (Organizations that are not part of the previous classifications).

Knowing this category of Organizations (Fig. 63.4), we had first the EXE-SISP organizations (46%), followed by JUD (27%), MPU (18%) and EXE-DEST (9%). It did not appear in our survey the type LEG and Third Sector organizations. The high index of EXE-SISP type organizations is justified because it is the category that most contemplates organizations in the 2014 and 2016 survey realized per ACU intervention.

Answer to the research question 1 (Q1), is that the number of employees that work with dedication in the area is still small, which can be observed that between 1 to 5 employees in total (55%), followed by 6 to 12 employees (27%), 12 to 20 and 21 to 50 both with (9%). Figure 63.5 illustrates the data.

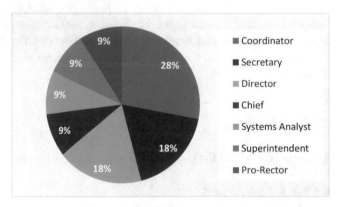

Fig. 63.1 Position of interviewees

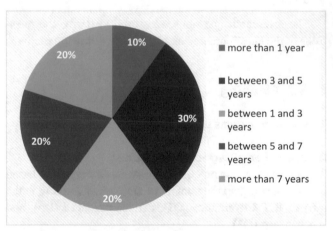

Fig. 63.3 Experience of the Interviewees

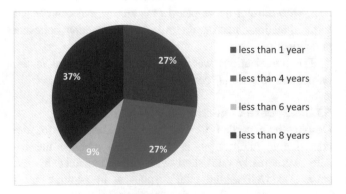

Fig. 63.2 Acting time in charge

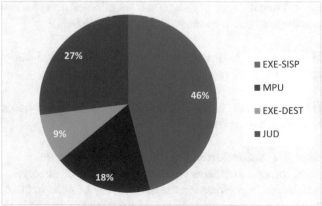

Fig. 63.4 Organization Category

63.3.4.2 Analysis of Results

The research question 1 (Q1), as presented previously, showed that (55%) of the sample had between 1 and 5 employees with dedication in ICT Governance. Therefore, it was clear that most come from organizations with fewer than 80 ICT workers, as depicted in Fig. 63.6, which describes the average distribution of employees with exclusive dedication in ICT Governance based on the total number of employees, respectively.

Figure 63.6 shows that organizations that presents less than 20 employees only have 1 exclusive collaborator in ICT Governance, and for organizations of up to 80 employees there is an average of 4 employees.

For a better characterization, an interception was made of the number of employees with an exclusive dedication to the audit time that the organization has already participated. Figure 63.7 shows this relationship. It is noticed that organizations with more than 12 employees with exclusive dedication in ICT Governance have already participated in the 5 surveys (audits) carried out by ACU. This is an interesting fact as it is clear that organizations are investing

in employees to improve their maturity (iGovTI). This fact can be a differential point of the improved organizations in respect to the initial and basic.

Answer to research question 2 (Q2), indicates that (37%) of organizations point out that they use Control Objectives for Information and Related Technology (COBIT) as Good Practice. (27%) declared they use ISO/IEC 38500, own and Hybrid Methodology, both with (18%). Hybrid Methodology refers to COBIT, Information Technology Infrastructure Library (ITIL), Improvement in the Brazilian Software Process (MPS.Br) and Project Management Body of Knowledge (PMBOK).

Therefore, it can be seen that the practices used in organizations are the same ones used in industry and/or academia, according to [18, 19].

In order to answer research question 3 (Q3), 8 questions were elaborated, in which they will be separated by mechanisms such as Leadership and Strategy.

For the Leadership mechanism, we have two themes, IT Committee and Personnel Hiring. In the mechanism IT Committee there are Good Practices used illustrated in Fig. 63.8, (46%) use the SISP Guide as good practice, (27%) that use their own methodology, (18%) that do not use any practice and (9%) that use a hybrid practice in which it is composed by the SISP Guide. Even organizations that are not part of the EXE-SISP category also adopt the Guide.

As for the process of Hiring Professionals (45.5%) of organizations do not adopt any practice, (18.2%) use Resolution 182/2013 of the CNJ and (36.4%) defines the use of Contests.

In the Strategy mechanism, we have the following themes: Strategic Planning, Project Management, Service Management, Software Process, Information Security and Risk Management. The Good Practices for each of the themes is highlighted as follows.

Regarding Strategic Planning, Good Practices adopted are (55%) Information Technology Master Plan (PDTI) sug-

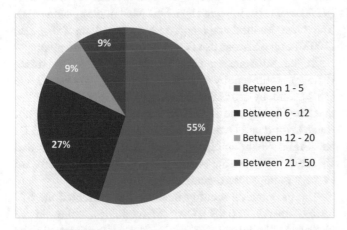

Fig. 63.5 Number of employees with dedication to ICT Governance

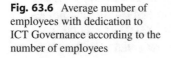

Fig. 63.6 Average number of employees with dedication to ICT Governance according to the number of employees

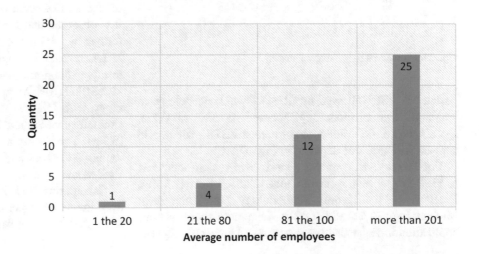

Fig. 63.7 Exclusive Dedication versus Audit Participation Officers

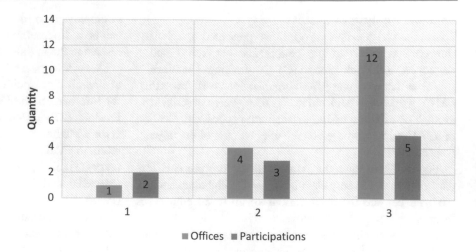

■ Offices ■ Participations

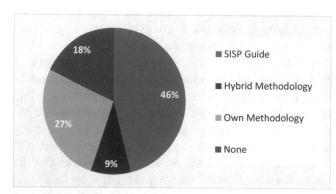

Fig. 63.8 Practices for IT Committee

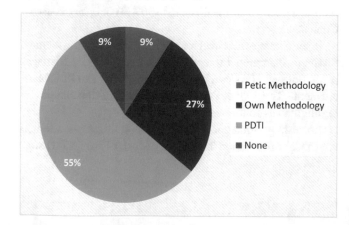

Fig. 63.9 Practices for Strategic Planning

gested by SISP, followed by (27%) Own Methodology, in which its own methodology is based on SISP of PDTI, and a specific ICT Methodology named PETIC, which also appears with (9%), as depicted in Fig. 63.9.

For Project Management, Good Practices are identified as SISP Project Management Guide (27.5%), None (27.5%), PMBOK (18%), Hybrid Methodology (18%) and Own Methodology (9%). PMBOK is the practice with greater application in Enhanced organizations. Another highlight is

also the percentage of non-adoption of any practice, which is reflected precisely in what the Tribunal de Contas da União (a government control department) (2017) reports, that only (24%) of the Organizations, in general, executes Project Management process. Even improved organizations do not adopt this practice.

In ICT Service Management the practice adopted with (91%) was ITIL, followed by a Self-Methodology with (9%). The Own Methodology approach is based on ITIL, i.e., (100%) organizations use ITIL for Service Management.

In the Software Process, the results were diversified. (27.5%), followed by the SISP Software Process Guide (18%), and by MPS.Br, Capability Maturity Model Integration (CMMI) and Hybrid Methodology, both with (9%). Since Hybrid and Own Methodologies are based on MPS.Br and Agile Methodologies. Noting that both MPS.Br and ISO/IEC 15504 are the practices that dominate the Software Process in improved organizations.

The information security thematic has presented the following results. (36.4%) Own Methodology, followed by Hybrid Methodology, ISO/IEC 27001 (Requirements for Implementing Information Security Management) and none, both with (18.2%). And finally, ISO/IEC 27002 (Practices for the Management of Information Security) with (9.1%). It is observed that the Own and Hybrid Methodologies are formed by joining the two ISOs (27,001 and 27,002).

Lastly, Risk Management is reflected with the following results. Adoption of No Practice with (36.4%), followed by ISO 31000 (Risk Management) with (27.3%), Own Methodology with (18.2%) and, lastly, Hybrid Methodology and Committee of Sponsoring Organizations (COSO) both with (9.1%). The Hybrid and Own methodologies are formed by joining ISO 31000 and ISO/IEC 27005 (Information Systems Risk Management).

Considering Risk Management, it is also observed that even improved organizations are not giving a certain value to the Risk Management policy, since approximately (9%) of organizations, in general, adopt Risk Management process [9]. This can prevent the IT Management from fulfilling its mission of helping the organization achieving its institutional goals.

Questions elaborated to answer the research question 3 (Q3) also allow answering the test of the hypothesis presented in the planning. A null hypothesis is raised and tested "organizations adopt Good Practices unknown" (see H0, in planning). If different results are found, then the null hypothesis must be rejected in favor of the alternative hypothesis: "organizations adopt Good Practices known" (see H1, in planning).

Based on the responses of the Good Practices of the thematic on mechanisms, we perceive that the practices adopted in the organizations are known, that is, they are the same ones used in organizations and/or the academy as described [18, 19]. As a matter of fact, we should reject the null hypothesis.

63.4 Threats to Validity

Different problems can occur during the individuals' participation in the questionnaire:

- Adequately prepared instrumentation (**internal validity**): the participants answered the questionnaire without any supervision, so there is a probability that they did not understand a specific question. To mitigate this type of problem, a pilot was accomplished.
- Representative population (**external validity**): the ranking that determines the population was constructed based on information provided by the organizations themselves. Variety of participants who answered the questionnaire was significant, however, there are categories of organizations that did not respond.
- Distribution of participants (**conclusion validity**): Experience of professionals or their actual job functions' can affect the results, however, both the more experienced and the positions of greater interest occupied by the participants are distributed.

63.5 Conclusion

This work presented results of a quantitative and qualitative lifting that can be used by managers of FPA Organizations for decision-making, as well as by researchers in the area to direct their research according to the observed demand.

It was found that (37%) of organizations point that they use COBIT as a Good IT Governance Practice, followed by ISO/IEC 38500 (27%), and that (36%) use Own and Hybrid Methodology. Considered Good Practices are the same known in the industry and/or academy.

Another factor to consider is that even organizations that have improved capability stages do not adopt some relevant thematic practices for iGovTi, such as Project Management, Information Security and Risk Management.

The main difficulty in this work was the task of applying a field survey, taking into account the constant concern with the veracity of answers given by participants. In addition, it is worth noting the need to expand field research in the area, with the aim of finding gaps such as those identified here.

As for future work, it is suggested the creation of a repository of knowledge of Good Practices of ICT Governance for FPA Organization. The knowledge repository will contain identified practices for each dimension defined by the ACU.

Another possible contribution is to evaluate the perception of managers of organizations with initial and basic capability stages, the reason for not adopting Good Practices since they (ITIL, COBIT and ISO/IEC 38500) are known.

This scientific research does not guarantee that only the adoption of any Good Practice listed here will improve iGovTI, and it does not ensure that other Practices cannot meet similar needs considering specific contexts. However, it does suggest the horizon for organizations about which practices are being adopted.

Finally, a tool is in phase of development with three intentions: (1) to support organizations assessed by the ACU that have initial and basic capability stages (iGovTI); (2) to monitor organizations based on their deficits in the dimensions defined by the ACU; and (3) to direct the ICT managers in how to implement Good ICT Governance Practices considered relevant for ACU evaluation.

Acknowledgments Acknowledgement to the development agencies: CAPES (Coordination for the Improvement of Higher Education Personnel), for granting a scholarship to and to INES (National Institute for Software Engineering), as well as the institutional collaboration of the various FPA Organizations.

References

1. F.S. Affeldt, A.A. Vanti, Information Technology strategic alignment: analysis of alignment models and proposals for future research. J. Inf. Syst. Technol. Manag. **6**(2), 203–226 (2009)
2. I.D.S. Batista et al., Information Technology Governance Today the Importance of Adopting Best Practice Models in Organizations, in *II World Congress on Systems Engineering and Information Technology*, Vigo, Spain, 2015. pp. 109–113
3. Y. Arshad, A.R. Ahlan, B.A. Ajayi, Intelligent IT governance decision-making support framework for a developing country's public university. Int. Dec. Tech. **8**(2), 131–146 (2014)
4. F. Lampathaki et al., Paving the way for future research in ICT for governance and policy modelling, in *Electronic Government. EGOV 2011. Lecture Notes in Computer Science*, vol. 6846, ed. By M. Janssen, H.J. Scholl, M.A. Wimmer, Y. Tan (Springer, Berlin,2011)

5. Jansen A, The Understanding of ICTs in Public Sector and Its Impact on Governance, in *Electronic Government. EGOV 2012. Lecture Notes in Computer Science*, vol. 7443, ed. By H.J. Scholl, M. Janssen, M.A. Wimmer, C.E. Moe, L.S. Flak (Springer, Berlin, 2012)

6. K. Jairak, P. Praneetpolgrang, Applying IT governance balanced scorecard and importance-performance analysis for providing IT governance strategy in university. Inf. Manag. Comput. Security **21**(4), 228–249 (2013)

7. G.C. Borges, J.B. Simao, R.S. Miani, Exploratory Analysis of ICT Best Practices for Brazilian Federal Universities, in *2016 35th International Conference of the Chilean Computer Science Society (SCCC)*, ValParaíso, 2016, pp. 1–12

8. Tribunal de Contas da União—TCU, Referencial Básico de Governança, 2014b, p. 80

9. Tribunal de Contas da União—TCU, Acórdão 882/2017

10. K.H.C. Ramos, Multidimensional analysis of critical success factors for IT Governance within the Brazilian Federal Public Administration, in *The Light of External Auditing Data. 12th International CONTECSI*, 2015

11. E.M. Luciano, G.C. Wiedenhoft, Identification of mechanisms to meet objectives and principles of Governance of Information Technology in Public Organizations, in *V International Symposium on Project Management, Innovation and Sustainability*, vol. 14, issue no. 1, 2016. pp. 69–87

12. N. Al Qassimi, L. Rusu, IT Governance in a public organization in a developing country: a case study of a governmental organization. Procedia Comp. Sci. **64**, 450–456 (2015)

13. P. Subsermsri, K. Jairak, P. Praneetpolgrang, Information technology governance practices based on sufficiency economy philosophy in the Thai University sector. Inform. Technol. People **28**(1), 195–223 (2015)

14. V.R. Basili, D.M. Weiss, A methodology for collecting valid software engineering data. IEEE Trans. Software Eng. **10**, 728–738 (1984). (Capítulo 14)

15. R.Van Solingen et al., Goal question metric (GQM) approach, in *Encyclopedia of Software Engineering,* (Sage, Publications, Inc. 1995) 200 pages

16. F.J. Fowler Junior, *Improving Survey Questions: Design and Evaluation, Applied Social Research Methods Series*, vol 38 (Sage, Thousand Oaks, CA, 1995)

17. F.M. Wolf, *Meta-Analysis: Quantitative Methods for Research Synthesis* (Sage, Thousand Oaks, CA, 1986)

18. G.L. Lunardi et al., The impact of adopting IT governance on financial performance: An empirical analysis among Brazilian firms. Int. J. Account. Inf. Syst. **15**(1), 66–81 (2014)

19. M.B.D. Da Silva et al., Public ICT governance: a quasi-systematic review. ICEIS **2**, 351–359 (2017)

Rui Wu, Jose Painumkal, Sergiu M. Dascalu, and Frederick C. Harris Jr.

Abstract

The Precipitation-Runoff Modeling System (PRMS) is used to study and simulate hydrological environment systems. It is common for an environmental scientist to execute hundreds of PRMS model runs to learn different scenarios in a study field. If the study case is complex, this procedure can be very time-consuming. Also, it is very hard to create different scenarios without an efficient method. In this paper, we propose a PRMS scenario web application. It can execute multiple model runs in parallel and automatically rent extra servers based on needs. The control strategy introduced in the paper guarantees that the expense is within the planned budget and can remind a system manager if the quantified user feedback score crosses the predefined threshold. The application has user-friendly interfaces and any user can create and execute different PRMS model scenarios by simply clicking buttons. The application can support other environmental models besides PRMS by filling the blueprint file.

Keywords

PRMS · Budget control · User feedback · Web application

64.1 Introduction

The U.S. Geological Survey developed the Precipitation-Runoff Modeling System (PRMS) in the 1980s [8–10]. The model is widely used in hydrological research. PRMS can consume a very long time to finish a model run with a regular personal computer, especially if a user chooses to generate a PRMS animation file. This problem becomes worse if a user builds a different scenario and start multiple PRMS model runs. There are some similar works already done. However, most of them do not consider how to change a server size based on the needs. Another problem is that PRMS is executed only in a terminal without friendly user interfaces and all the input data is stored with the text files. A new user can spend a very long time to study how to start a model run and modify the input parameters.

To solve these problems, we built a web-based PRMS scenario tool. It executes PRMS models in parallel, changes service size based on budget, takes into account user opinions, and provides user-friendly interfaces. The tool contains two parts: server and client. The server contains multiple Docker workers [2] to finish the PRMS model run requests. These workers contain execution files and are independent. Usually, a server has better hardware than a normal personal computer. Therefore, the performance is guaranteed. If there are many PRMS model run requests and more than the owned server capability, the server can automatically rent machines to increase the server power. It can also quantify the user feedback and warn the system manager if users are not satisfied with the system. The client provides user-friendly interfaces. A user can execute model runs, check modifications, and create different scenarios by clicking mouse buttons.

Our proposed method controls the system from the budget and user feedback. Budget to set up a server is crucial. Unlike industry companies, the academia always has limited funding and the budget should be controlled by the plan. User feedback can be used to test if the users are satisfied. However, if there is a huge amount of the user feedback it can be hard to process them. In our opinion, the user feedback should be quantified and this can simplify the analysis procedure. The prototype system is set up and running in [16].

In the rest of the paper, Sect. 64.2 introduces some related work; Sect. 64.3 shows the system design and how

R. Wu (✉) · J. Painumkal · S. M. Dascalu · F. C. Harris Jr.
Department of Computer Science and Engineering, University of Nevada, Reno, NV, USA
e-mail: rui@cse.unr.edu; josepainumkal@nevada.unr.edu; dascalu@cse.unr.edu; fred.harris@cse.unr.edu

© Springer International Publishing AG, part of Springer Nature 2018
S. Latifi (ed.), *Information Technology – New Generations*, Advances in Intelligent Systems and Computing 738,
https://doi.org/10.1007/978-3-319-77028-4_64

the components are connected; Sect. 64.4 presents how the system changes its size automatically based on the budget and quantify the user opinion; Sect. 64.5 explains how to create a PRMS scenario and other services.

64.2 Related Work

There are numerous studies conducted in the field of dynamic provisioning of computing resources in a cloud environment. Some of the successful works are briefly discussed in this section.

Rodrigo et al. [1] proposed an adaptive provisioning of computing resources based on workload information and analytical performance to offer end users the guaranteed Quality of Services (QoS). The QoS targets were application specific and were based on requests service time, the rejection rate of requests and utilization of available resources. The proposed model could estimate the number of VM instances that are to be allocated for each application by analyzing the observed system performance and the predicted load information. The efficiency of the proposed provisioning approach was tested using application-specific workloads, and the model could dynamically provision resources to meet the predefined QoS targets by analyzing the variations in the workload intensity. However, the approach offers no control over the expenses as it does not consider budget constraints and user feedback while provisioning resources to ensure guaranteed QoS.

Qian Zhu et al. [18] proposed a dynamic resource provisioning algorithm based on feedback control and budget constraints to allocate computational resources. The goal of the study was to maximize the application QoS by meeting both time and budget constraints. The CPU cycles and memory were dynamically provisioned between multiple virtual machines inside a cluster to meet the application QoS targets. The proposed approach worked better than the static scheduling methods and conserving strategies on resource provisioning. The flaw with this approach was that it requires the reconfiguration of computing resources within the machine instances, which is not well recommended in the current cloud environment where resources could be efficiently managed by the addition and removal of virtual machines from the cloud host providers. Moreover, the dynamic allocation of resources based on CPU cycle and memory usage could go inaccurate more often, as the parameters cannot truly indicate the need for more resources. There are chances that, the virtual machine is just busy with some low-CPU or low network jobs. In this paper, we propose an innovative server-usage optimization approach to facilitate on-demand provisioning of computing resources to ensure reduced waiting time for jobs consistently over a predefined period of time within the allocated budget constraints. The proposed approach uses a modified queuing model to provide estimations on waiting time and queue length based on the budget amount which is very relevant as it helps the admin in making budget decisions more easily. The user feedbacks are continuously monitored in the system and auto alert emails are generated to notify the admin of experiencing severe performance issues.

There have been many types of research going on in the field of environmental modeling by different interdisciplinary research groups. Consortium of Universities for the Advancement of Hydrologic Science, Inc (CUASHI) [6] is a research organization comprising the universities in America to develop services and infrastructure for understanding and exploring the mysteries related to water science. Hydroshare [14] is one of their projects aimed at providing cyberinfrastructure to facilitate an online collaborative environment for sharing hydrological models and data. Hydroshare offers various web apps to share, visualize, analyze and run hydrological models. The goal of Hydroshare is to enhance the collaboration in the research community by helping in the discovery and access of data models published by other researchers. Geographic Storage, Transformation and Retrieval Engine (GSToRE) [15] is a data management framework to support the storage, management, discovery and sharing of scientific and geographic data. It was developed at Earth Data Analysis Center, the University of New Mexico with a goal to offer a flexible and scalable data management platform for scientific research. GSToRE offers a REST API to facilitate the storage, retrieval, and removal of geospatial data and associated metadata.

64.3 System Design

The system mainly has three services: PRMS scenario tool, Data conversion, and authentication. The system is designed as Fig. 64.1 shows.

64.3.1 Queue Master

To arrange resources reasonably and in order, our system has a queue component. All the user requests are handled by a docker container named "Queue Master" (see Fig. 64.1). This container classifies the requests into different groups based on the required service types, Then different requests go into different queues. For example, if a user wants to run a PRMS scenario, the request is handled by the PRMS scenario service. Therefore, it will enter the corresponding queue. The system can offer an estimated waiting time based on a proposed method introduced in this thesis and the user can choose which queue based on their needs.

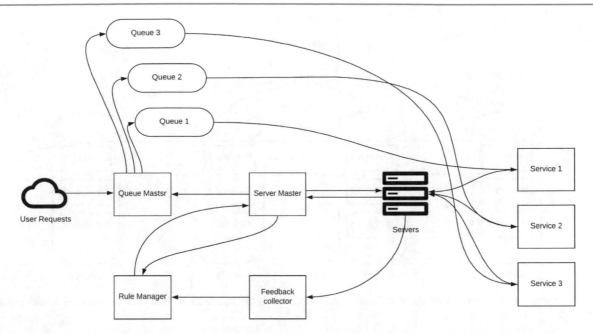

Fig. 64.1 Architecture design. The system contains queue master, queues, server master, servers, rule master, and feedback collector

64.3.2 Server Master

The server master is used to inspect all the host machines health information, such as server failures and budget information. For example, the CPU, memory, and network usage percentages. It can automatically rent another host machine based on the control strategy. The rent host machine event can be triggered based on the rules stored in Rule Manager container.

In each host machine, there are worker containers. These worker containers are arranged into different groups based on the service. For example, Container 1, Container 4, Container 7, and Container 10 are in the same group in Fig. 64.2. All the workers in this group are created with the same Docker image and they know how to finish the job based on the input files. For example, the users can run PRMS scenarios in the system. They need to upload input files to start a model run. The workers in PRMS service group obtain the input files from the database based on the job ID and store the model output files into the database after the job is finished.

To connect different docker containers in different host machines, we set up a key-value store node. If docker containers are on the same host machine they can ping each other directly without any further operations. However, docker containers cannot ping each other if they are on different host machines. The key-value store node is used to store different host machine IPs, networks, and endpoints. After the node is setup, different host machines can view each other. Then, it is easy to create a docker overlay network across different host machines.

For each group, there should be a task manager node and a feedback collector. The task manager node is used to create worker containers in different host machines and delete the worker container after the job is finished. We did not use any orchestration tool, such as Docker swarm [3] and Apache Mesos [11], because it is not possible to stop a container in a certain machine with these tools based on our knowledge. These tools can change the server size based on some events, such as CPU and memory usage percentages. However, it is at a high level (server as a whole). Based on our experiences, only the worker container itself knows what happens inside. It is not reasonable to shrink the server size based on CPU usage or time. Sometimes, the CPU usage is low and the container is busy. For example, file transportation jobs mainly use I/O bandwidth instead of CPU or memory. In our opinion, we can stop the container, only when the container finishes the last line of the script. Therefore, each worker in our prototype system sends a termination request to the task manager after it finishes the job and then the task manager will stop the container. For a large cluster, it is possible that many containers report termination events to the server master container at the same time. It can cause problems if the network bandwidth is not big enough. There are two solutions for this problem: (1) more than one server master containers are set up in the system to process the reports. Each master container is only in charge a group of containers and this method reduces the burden. (2) Jittering APIs can be applied. Each container does not send the termination information to the server master through the API directly after the container finish the job. The worker container waits a random time and then send the information.

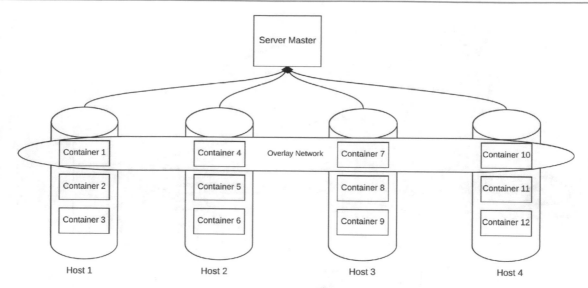

Fig. 64.2 Server master. The server master is in charge of all the host machines. It inspects all the host machine information, such as CPU and memory usage

This avoids too much information occupies the network at the same time. The relationships between the server master node, host machines, and worker container are displayed in Fig. 64.2.

64.3.3 Servers

Servers are physical machines in the system. These machines are set into different groups based on the needs of different services. For example, there are more PRMS scenario requests than other requests. Therefore, more machines are in PRMS scenario group than other service groups. The server master runs docker configuration files to download docker images and setup services in different machines. The server master may rent more machines automatically based on the rules stored in the rule manager.

64.3.4 Feedback Collector

The user feedback is very important for the project manager to set up reasonable rules. The survey is used to collect the user feedback in our prototype system. The system can turn the survey results into a feedback score and change the server size automatically or offer suggestions to the project manager based on the feedback score.

The feedback collector can send a survey invitation to the user after he/she uses the service. Each question has different weights and the options of different questions have different points. The project manager can setup a threshold for each question. If the point passes the threshold, it means the

project manager needs to do something. Here is an example: the project manager wants to know the user's opinion about the service performance. Therefore, he puts two questions in the survey: (1) What's your opinion about the waiting time? (question weight 0.8). Options: A. Too long (2 points), B. Long (1 point), C. Not Sure (0 point), D. Short (−1 point), E. Very short (−2 points). (2) Do you want to pay more to have a faster service? (question weight 1.2). Options: A. Strongly Agree (2 points). B. Agree (1 point). C. Not Sure (0 point). D. Disagree (−1 point). E. Strongly disagree (−2 points). If a user chooses A for the first question and D for the second question, then it contributes $0.8*2 + 1.2*(−1)=0.4$ to the global feedback score. If the global feedback score passes the threshold it means the users believe the server is slow and they want to pay more for a faster service. Therefore, the project manager may need to allow the server master to rent more machines from the third party companies. Each service has a feedback collector. The feedback collector contains a survey predefined by the project manager. Based on the feedback score, the feedback collector can affect rules stored in the rule manager.

64.3.5 Rule Manager

Queue master and server master follow rules stored in the rule manager. The rules are applied to these two masters through RESTful APIs. When the project managers want to add a new rule, they may also need to modify RESTful APIs in the queue master and server master. This is because the RESTful APIs may not include the functions required in the rules. For example, there is a rule requiring average job waiting time in Service 1 queue should be 10 s. However, the queue master does not have a RESTful API to change the average job waiting time. Then, the project managers should work on the API first.

64.4 Control Strategy

The control strategy is stored in the rule manager of the prototype system (introduced in Sect. 64.3.5). The strategy includes how the service requests are handled in a queue and how to manage the server based on user feedback. This section introduces brief ideas. More details on the algorithm and validation can be found in our previous work [5, 17].

The $M/M/1/1/\infty/\infty$ [7] queuing model was modified and used in the proposed self-managed elastic scale hybrid server to estimate the queue length and job waiting time in the modelling environment. The modified queuing model includes the allocated budget amount (B), budget period (T_b), cost of rented instances ($\$P$/hour), the average time for the job execution in rented instance (T_{rent}) and the average job execution time in owned instance (T_{own}). The maximum of number of jobs that can be processed with owned servers would be ($N_0 * T_b)/T_{own}$, where N_0 is the number of owned severs in the hybrid cluster. $B/ (P * T_{rent})$ would be the total number of jobs that can be processed with rented servers for the allocated budget amount B. Hence, the total number of jobs processed by the hybrid cluster during the budget period T_b would be the sum of ($N_0 * T_b)/T_{own}$ and $B/ (P * T_{rent})$. On incorporating the above details into the queuing model, the expected average queue length (L_H) and the expected average wait time of job (T_H) in the queue would be estimated as follows:

$$L_H = \frac{\lambda^2}{(\frac{N_0}{T_{own}} + \frac{B}{P*T_{rent}})^2 - \lambda(\frac{N_0}{T_{own}} + \frac{B}{P*T_{rent}})} \quad (64.1)$$

$$T_H = \frac{\lambda}{(\frac{N_0}{T_{own}} + \frac{B}{P*T_{rent}})^2 - \lambda(\frac{N_0}{T_{own}} + \frac{B}{P*T_{rent}})} \quad (64.2)$$

Algorithm 1 illustrates the logic for the creation of new rented workers in the proposed system. On inputting the budget amount (B) and the cost of rented instances ($\$P$/hr), the system estimates the total available rented time (T) from the cloud provider. The average execution time of the job (T_{rent}) is already available in the system from previous job execution details. Then the total number of jobs that could be processed with rented workers is $N = T/T_{rent}$. The counter variable RW (Rented Workers) would keep track of the total number of jobs rented. To utilize the rented resources judiciously, the usage of rented workers is distributed uniformly across the budget time period T_b. To achieve this, the manager should

---

Algorithm 1 Create rent worker

1 function rented_worker_creation (RW, UR, N, T_{int});
   Input : RW denotes number of rented workers; UR denotes unused rentals; N denotes maximum number of models processed with rented workers for the input budget; T_{int} denotes the time interval
2 **if** $RW < N$ **then**
3   **if** $Jobs\ in\ queue$ **then**
4   Create Worker;
5         $RW = RW + 1$;
6   **while** $UR > 0\ AND\ RW < N\ AND\ Jobs\ in\ queue$ **do**
7   Create Worker;
8             $RW = RW + 1$;
9             $UR = UR - 1$;
10   **end**
11   Sleep T_{int} and go to line 2
12   **else**
13         $UR = UR + 1$;
14   **end**
15 **else**
16   No more rented workers available;
17 **end**

---

rent a job at every time interval, $T_{int} = (T_b * T_{rent} * P)/B$, if the owned servers are not available at T_{int} to process the job. At every T_{int} interval, the system would inspect whether there is a necessity for new workers. At T_{int}, if owned workers are not available (i.e. there are jobs waiting in the queue), then the system will create a new worker in one of the rented machines in the worker pool and increments the counter variable RW by one. If at T_{int}, an owned worker is available, then the system would record such occasions on to a counter variable UR (Unused Rentals), so that later, if a job comes in and the owned workers are not available, the system could immediately create a new worker to handle the job instead of waiting for the next T_{int} interval. The project manager can increase or decrease the budget amount in the middle of the execution and the system updates N accordingly with the changes in the budget amount. The execution time of the job varies with the workload on the host machine. The value of N is constantly updated on completion of each job based on the actual running time each job has taken for its execution. This process will be repeated until the number of jobs rented equals N, i.e. the maximum number of jobs that could be processed with rented containers for the given budget. More details about the budget control strategy can be found in our previous work [17].

The system also includes a dashboard where the user can view the details of the finished jobs in real time. On finishing a model simulation job, the dashboard will display the details of the job such as the task id, the cost for the job execution, run-time of the job, waiting time in the queue, the name of the worker that processed the job and the category to which the worker belongs (owned or rented). The dashboard also shows the total number of jobs finished, the number of jobs processed with rented and owned workers, and also the remaining amount available to spend. The prototype has a feedback survey form, where the user can provide feedbacks on the performance of the service. The manager can also view the results of the feedback survey from the users in Survey Results page. The page displays separate bar graphs for each question in the survey questionnaire. The bar graphs show the total votes obtained for each option of the question. This will help the manager to easily understand how efficiently the system can serve its users and help in taking decisions on increasing or decreasing the budget amount.

64.5 PRMS Scenario Tool

PRMS Model Scenario component enables researchers to modify existing model simulations and re-run models with modified input files to analyze user-defined model scenarios. It also provides data conversion service. This allows a user to modify model input and output files format. The user does not need to be required any programming skills to use our model modification component. The user interface is intuitive and user-friendly so that the user can perform the model modification activities through simple mouse clicks.

To create a user-defined simulation scenario, the user has to choose one of the existing model simulations or a default simulation for modification. Then, the user determines to modify which parameters to get the desired model scenario. For example, the user can change the vegetation types of the study area from "forest" into "bare ground" to study what can happen if people cut too many trees in the field. Once the parameters are decided, the user needs to specify Hydrologic Response Units (HRUs) of the study area that should be changed. Then, the system knows where and what to modify.

64.5.1 HRU Selection Methods

PRMS divides the model area into discrete HRUs, where each HRU is composed either of land, lake, swale or other types. The PRMS modification component offers two different ways to select the HRUs for parameter modification. They are parameter selection and manual selection. In parameter selection, the HRUs can be selected based on its parameter values and in the manual selection, the user can manually choose the desired HRUs from a 2D HRU grid map. After finishing the modification of HRUs, the user can re-run the model with the modified inputs. Figure 64.3 shows a screenshot of the model modification component in PRMS Scenarios Tool. The modification component of PRMS scenarios tool has a tabbed interface, where the user can choose the desired HRU selection method by clicking on the corresponding tab.

64.5.1.1 Manual Selection

Using manual selection, the user could select the HRU cells directly on the 2D grid map through simple drag and drop mouse click operation. To select an HRU, place the mouse cursor over the desired HRU cell on the 2D grip map and then perform a left click. To select multiple HRUs, left click on the HRU cell, drag along the desired direction, and then release the mouse button. The chosen HRUs will be then highlighted with yellow color. On clicking 'Apply to Grid' button, the underlying HRU grid map will get updated with the new value for the selected HRUs. on clicking 'Save To File' button, the chosen parameter value of the selected HRUs would be updated with the new value in the underlying model input file. Figure 64.4 shows a screenshot of model modification using manual selection, where the user is changing the vegetation type of selected HRUs to shrubs (Type 2) and grass (Type 1) and trees (Type 3). The model modification component of PRMS Scenarios Tool is very convenient and intuitive. It allows users to modify different parameters at the same time and avoids the unnecessary rerunning of the model. The tool also gives instant alerts while making a modification to the parameters. On selecting the parameter, an alert box would be displayed with the details of the chosen parameter. The displayed details include the name of the parameter, description, and the allowed minimum/maximum value for the parameter. This alert mechanism is very helpful and effective, as it warns the user on inputting wrong value for the modifying parameter and thereby saves the time and effort of the researchers while performing scenario-based studies.

64.5.1.2 Parameter Selection

Using parameter selection, the user can specify the parameter constraints for the HRUs to be filtered out from HRU set. To define a parameter constraint, the user needs to specify the name of the parameter, the operator (greater than, less than or between), and the parameter value. For example, Fig. 64.5 displays the scenario where the user wants to change the vegetation type to trees (Type 3) for HRUs whose elevation is between 2000 and 4000 and whose vegetation type is grass (Type 1). Here, the parameter to be modified would be 'cov_type' (i.e. vegetation), and the modified value is '3'. To define the parameter constraint that elevation should be between 2000 and 4000, the user needs to choose the parameter name as 'hru_elev' (i.e. elevation), the operator as 'between', and then input the values 2000 and 4000. Multiple parameter constraints can be defined to fine-tune the selection of HRUs. 'Add' button can be used to add more parameter constraints and 'Delete' button can be used

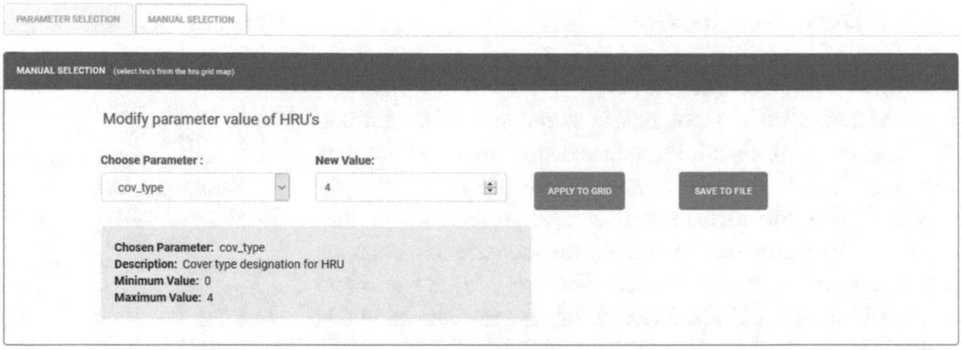

Fig. 64.3 Screenshot of the model modification component in PRMS scenarios tool

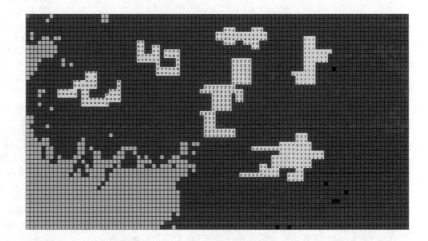

Fig. 64.4 Model modification using manual selection. Modified the vegetation type of chosen HRUs to bare soil (0), shrubs (2), grasses (1), trees (3) and coniferous (4)

Fig. 64.5 Model modification using parameter selection of the HRUs

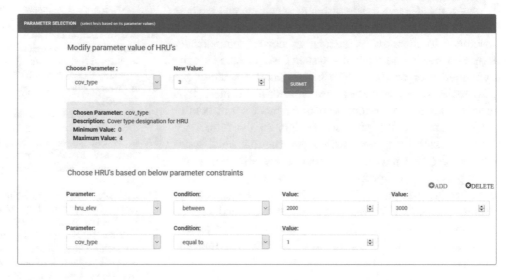

to remove an unwanted parameter constraint from the HRU selection process. Here, to define the second parameter constraint that the vegetation type should be grass, choose 'cov_type' as the parameter name, the condition should be 'equal' and the value should be given as '1'. On clicking 'Submit' button, the system would filter out HRU's that satisfies all the given parameter constraints and then update the parameter which is to be modified with the new given value. The modifications could be visualized in real time on a

2D HRU grid map. On the HRU grid map, the color intensity of the HRU cells varies with the values of the parameter. The higher and lower values of the parameter are represented using dark and light colors respectively. The final modified 2D grid map is overlapped on a Google map. Google Map gives the user geological information, which can be used to verify the data veracity. The user can add/remove the 2D grid map overlay and change the 2D grid map transparency by clicking on the respective buttons.

64.5.2 Other Services

64.5.2.1 Data Convertor

In the PRMS Scenario tool, data is stored in NetCDF format. NetCDF is a self-describing and machine-independent data format [12]. It is widely used in climate data research. However, this file formats may not be supported by other tools used by a modeler. Therefore, the scenario tool contains a data convertor. It can convert NetCDF file into text and text file into NetCDF file. More details are introduced in this paper [13].

64.5.2.2 Authentication

The system offers the one-time authentication service. This means a user only needs to login once and the user can use all the services in the system. This is done by using JWT (JSON Web Token). It is safer Because the system uses JWT instead of passing the user's username and password. More details can be found in our previous work [4].

64.6 Conclusion and Future Work

In this paper, we have proposed a PRMS scenario web application and a budget and user feedback control framework. It allows a modeler to create different scenarios and execute them in parallel. The application's server can rent extra machines to increase its computing power automatically based on needs and warn the system manger based on the quantified user feedback. The budget control strategy can also make sure the renting cost is within the plan. It is easy to extend the system with other models and control rules because of the proposed design. In the future, we want to extend the tools with more environmental models and also add payment component. We also would like to improve the proposed queuing model by considering a server starting time. This can be a challenge because usually the server starting time is not fixed and can be very long. Last but not least, the proposed tools should be validated by different programs besides environmental models.

Acknowledgements This material is based upon work supported by the National Science Foundation under grant numbers IIA-1329469 and IIA-1301726. Any opinions, findings, and conclusions or recommendations expressed in this material are those of the authors and do not necessarily reflect the views of the National Science Foundation.

References

1. R.N. Calheiros, R. Ranjan, R. Buyya, Virtual machine provisioning based on analytical performance and QoS in cloud computing environments, in *Proceedings of the 2011 International Conference on Parallel Processing*. ICPP '11 (IEEE Computer Society, Washington, DC, 2011), pp. 295–304
2. Docker, Docker - build, ship and run any app. https://www.docker.com/. Accessed 18 July 2017
3. Docker, Docker Swarm | Docker. https://www.docker.com/products/dockerswarm. Accessed 18 July 2017
4. M.M. Hossain et al., Web-service framework for environmental models, in *Seventh International Conference on Internet Technologies & Applications (ITA)* (IEEE, New York, 2017)
5. M. Hossain et al., Becoming dataone tier-4 member node: steps taken by the nevada research data center, in *2017 International Conference on Optimization of Electrical and Electronic Equipment (OPTIM) & 2017 International Aegean Conference on Electrical Machines and Power Electronics (ACEMP)*(IEEE, New York, 2017), pp. 1089–1094
6. In Consortium of universities for the advancement of hydrologic science. *CUAHSI*. https://www.cuahsi.org/. Accessed 18 July 2017
7. S. Karlin, J. McGregor, Many server queueing processes with Poisson input and exponential service times. Pacific J. Math. **8**(1), 87–118 (1958)
8. G.H. Leavesley et al., Precipitaion-runoff modeling system: user's manual. Water-Resources Investigations Report (1983), pp. 83–4238
9. S.L. Markstrom, R.G. Niswonger et al., GSFLOW – coupled ground-water and surface-water flow model based on the integration of the precipitation-runoff modeling system (PRMS) and the modular ground-water flow model. Water-Resources Investigations Report (2005)
10. S.L. Markstrom et al., *The Precipitation-Runoff Modeling System*. Version 4. U.S. Geological Survey Techniques and Methods, Book 6 (chap. B7) (Clarendon Press, Oxford, 2015), p. 158. http://doi.org/http://dx.doi.org/10.3133/tm6B7
11. A. Mesos, Apache Mesos. http://mesos.apache.org/. Accessed 18 July 2017
12. Open Geospatial Consortium, OGC network common data form (netCDF) standards suite (2014)
13. L. Palathingal et al., Data processing toolset for the virtual watershed, in *2016 International Conference on Collaboration Technologies and Systems (CTS)* (IEEE, New York, 2016), pp. 281–287
14. D.G. Tarboton et al., HydroShare: an online, collaborative environment for the sharing of hydrologic data and models (Invited). AGU Fall Meeting Abstracts (2013)
15. J. Wheeler, K. Benedict, Functional requirements specification for archival asset management: identification and integration of essential properties of services-oriented architecture products. J. Map Geogr. Libr. **11**(2), 155–179 (2015)
16. R. Wu, Virtual watershed platform. https://virtualwatershed.org/. Accessed 18 May 2017
17. R. Wu et al., Self-managed elastic scale hybrid server using budget input and user feedback, in *12th FC: Workshop on Feedback Computing. ICAC 2017*, Columbus, OH (2017)
18. Q. Zhu, G. Agrawal, Resource provisioning with budget constraints for adaptive applications in cloud environments, in *Proceedings of the 19th ACM International Symposium on High Performance Distributed Computing* (ACM, New York, 2010), pp. 304–307

A Controlled Natural Language Editor for Semantic of Business Vocabulary and Rules

65

Carlos Eugênio P. da Purificação and Paulo Caetano da Silva

Abstract

Defining system business models and rules using conceptual schemas is not an easy task. The Object Management Group's standard SBVR—Semantics of Business Vocabulary and Rules, define semantics for expressing business focused vocabularies and rules. It is based on a metamodel with roots on formal first-order logic. In order to create valid business vocabulary and rules, based on this standard, business analysts need tools that can facilitate modeling efforts using the standard. In this work, we contribute with a proposed tool that would allow business analyst designers to define the keywords that represent each of the Logical Formulation Concepts in the SBVR Meta-model. Therefore, this approach would enable the creation of Controlled Natural Language Libraries based on the SBVR meta-model that can be dynamically included in SBVR Modeling projects. These Language Libraries can then be used to model business rules and vocabularies in the tool. As a result, one can support multiple controlled natural languages and represent the SBVR metamodel using the tool. Examples of different controlled natural languages using the proposed SBVR editor tool are provided.

Keywords

Business rules editor · Semantic of business rules and vocabulary · Business rule editing · Controlled natural languages

65.1 Introduction

The Semantics of Business Vocabulary and Business Rules Standard—SBVR, provides a metamodel capable of modeling business concepts using Controlled Natural Languages and recently reached version 1.4 [1]. This metamodel can be used to define Conceptual Schemas—CS [2] by using Controlled Natural Languages—CNL. Conceptual Schemas are very important in system design. It can be used to represent business concepts through business models. Unfortunately, it can be difficult to business practitioners to create correct CS business models to define system concepts. Due to its sound formal logic foundation, SBVR provides the necessary formalism to enable the SBVR-based rules and vocabulary, expressed in CNL, to represent valid CS business models amenable to machine processing.

The SBVR Structured English—SBVR-SE is defined in the SBVR Standard as an example of how SBVR concepts can be represented by means of a CNL. Although the standard itself notice that there is not only one possible representation form of SBVR concepts, SBVR-SE became the most used notation to model SBVR-based business concepts using a textual form of vocabulary. Nevertheless, the SBVR Standard is based on formal logic, and is not tied to any particular representation. Although the SBVR Standard does not define any specific language for expressing SBVR concepts, the SBVR-SE, presented as an example in the standard, defines group of keywords to represent SBVR modalities concepts such as the obligation claim—"**It is obligatory that**", or necessity claim—"**It is necessary that**" or yet universal quantifications—"**each**". As most of the current SBVR related tools and editors use SBVR-SE as a base for the tool-modeling infrastructure, the produced artifacts are usually tied to this language. Moreover, most of these SBVR-based editors and tools do not present features capable of representing business rules and vocabularies in other formats or switching between them.

C. E. P. da Purificação · P. C. da Silva (✉)
Universidade Salvador (UNIFACS), Salvador, BA, Brazil
e-mail: paulo.caetano@unifacs.br

© Springer International Publishing AG, part of Springer Nature 2018
S. Latifi (ed.), *Information Technology – New Generations*, Advances in Intelligent Systems and Computing 738,
https://doi.org/10.1007/978-3-319-77028-4_65

To support the writing of SBVR-based business vocabulary and rules in a multi-language environment, there must exist tools to enable the easy definition, storage, manipulation and transformation of these business artifacts in whatever language format business analysts need. Currently, there are tools that do give some support for maintaining SBVR-based vocabulary and business rules, however the support to create new SBVR-based CNL using the tool itself could not be found. Indeed, *RuleSpeak* [3] is a tool where SBVR related concepts could be expressed in a language other than SBVR-SE. Even in this tool, this alternate notation requires a translation effort in the tool itself to support languages other than *RuleSpeak*.

With these problems in perspective, in this work we propose a tool capable of expressing SBVR business rules and vocabulary using the standard SBVR-SE, which is the most used notation in SBVR research area, but also capable of defining Controlled Natural Languages based on SBVR standard. Using the proposed toolset, these models can be exported to other formats such as XMI, consumed by other tools or rule processing engines, capable to process SBVR metamodel-based concepts. The rest of this paper is organized as follows. Section 65.2 presents basic concepts. Section 65.3 presents related work. Section 65.4 shows the editor and its capabilities with examples of its usage. Section 65.5 draws conclusions and future work.

65.2   Concepts and Background

Conceptual schemas are very important in system design and are widely used in industry to formally represent the system knowledge [2]. Therefore, CS can be used to represent the Business knowledge through Business Models. However, these CS are very complex to be directly used and maintained by business stakeholders.

The SBVR standard [1] provides a metamodel for modeling business concepts and statements that can be used to define a CS [2] by using a Controlled Natural Language—CNL. Such language resembles natural language but provides the necessary formalism to enable the SBVR based rules and vocabulary to be amenable to machine processing, due to its formal logic foundation. The SBVR Standard provides a meta-model that contains conceptual model elements that are needed to define business-oriented vocabulary and rules. In the standard, the proposition statements about business rules—BR, are defined in a Structured English format—SBVR-SE, which enables direct validation of these rules by business stakeholders since they are written using business defined concepts. Such approach has several advantages including: (1) the use of business vocabulary instead of some specific business rule engine or framework language;

(2) easy storage and manipulation due to the textual format; (3) machine processing of rules are a key objective in SBVR that is based on formal logic propositions. Besides, as the standard is heavily based on ontologies and conceptual models, it allows defining conceptual business structure contributing to solve business rule verbalization and data model problems [4].

SBVR defines two high level concepts that introduce meaning in a SBVR-based model: *Meanings and Representations Vocabulary* and *Vocabulary for Describing Business Rules*. While the former defines the basic domain concepts used by business stakeholders in the course of its daily activities, the later represents propositions that provide structure or constraints business activities. The *Meanings and Representations Vocabulary* is composed of *Concepts* that can be either *Noun Concepts* and *Verb Concepts*. For example, the terms "order", "product" and "customer" would all be part of a Retail Online Store business domain vocabulary and are *Noun Concepts*. The *Verb Concepts* are verb phrases that have one or more *Roles*. These *Roles* are represented in the *Verb Concept* by *Noun Concepts*. For example, the *Verb Concept* "customer *places* order" has one verb—*places*, and two *Roles* played by *Noun Concepts* customer and order. As each of these *Concepts* can be represented by various representations such as text, images and sound, among others. SBVR separation of meanings from representation, allows that the same *Concept* to be expressed in different ways and languages [5].

The *Business Rule Vocabulary* conversely uses the meaning vocabulary, along with *Logical Formulations*, to create propositions that formulate necessity or obligation. Rules are of two generic types: *definitional* or *structural rules*, which are used to define the business structure, and *operative rules*, which govern the conduct of business activity [6]. The rules are built posing different restrictions to *Verb Concepts* such as quantifiers and logical operators. Another aspect of SBVR Standard is the semantic formulations: the SBVR specification has defined a set of *Logical Formulations* (LF) used to provide the conceptualization of business rules propositions formal logic. These *Logical Formulations* define a language independent model, to represent the meaning of a rule in a set of logic structures, so that it can be machine processed. It includes concepts prevenient from first-order logic (conjunction, disjunction, etc.), quantifications (universal, existential, etc.), and modal operators (necessity, obligation, etc.). The general model for these formulations, as defined in the SBVR metamodel is shown in Fig. 65.1. The main objective of this metamodel is to depict intent from the set of propositions described using this logical formulation model and formulate meaning from it. The main aspects of the logical formulation model related to this work are the possibility of definition of keywords for *"modal formulation"*, *"logical operation"*

Fig. 65.1 SBVR Logical
Formulations

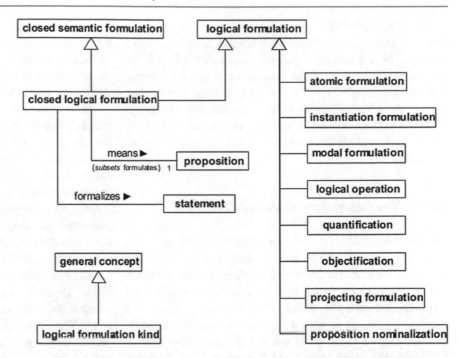

and *"quantification"* modalities. Those cover a great range of possibilities in the definition of business rules using an SBVR-based tool.

The SBVR-SE in the standard includes modal formulation keywords for obligation modalities in the form: "**It is obligatory that** …", and for quantification such as "… **exactly one** …". This group of keywords introduces an obligation formulation and quantification restrictions respectively in an SBVR-SE based business rule definition such as in: "**It is obligatory that each** <u>order</u> *has* **exactly one** payment method". This rule is defined in SBVR as an *obligation formulation*, constraining the possible set of "<u>orders</u>" concept in a business rule to have a quantification modality set to "**exactly one**" element for the concept "payment method".

65.3   Related Work

Some effort has been made towards SBVR rules and vocabulary editing using natural language. The Eclipse plugin called SBeaVeR [7] was probably the first effort towards this goal. That tool had some highlighting functionalities but had shortcomings with the provided support for concepts modeling languages with SBVR, since it required dash to connect nouns and verbs with multiple words. Therefore, when trying to state the rule that a course is obligatory for a student, it would need to be stated in the following form: "student must-be-registered-for course". Business analysts would arguably disagree on having to clutter their requirement documents with a dash-like representation for every compound word concept. While this notation may facilitate the tool parsing implementation, it is not business friendly.

VetisTool [7, 8] was an effort to provide an editor for SBVR based rules and vocabulary. It was based on SBeaVeR and added some features like UML exporting and integration with MagicDraw UML Case Tool [9], with UML OCL based constraints to represent rules, and exporting to SBVR 1.0 XMI Schema. The tool still had the same problems mentioned above at it had an underscore-style verbs concept wording notation. The language predefined verb concepts *"is_property_of"* and *"is_category_of"* are examples. Furthermore, the tool does not have a clear way of creating other representation than SBVR-SE style notations or languages other than English. RuleXpress [10] is a tool for creating business vocabularies and rules based on RuleSpeak format that can be also used to create SBVR like vocabularies and rules. It also has visualization capabilities but we could not find support for multiple languages. The work in [11] showed an SBVR Editor capable of auto-completion and syntax highlighting. The tool adds support for more SBVR concepts aside those provided by VetisTool and SBeaVer but does not allow for representations other than SBVR-SE. Moreover, as the authors highlighted, the tool would not be able highlight vocabulary attribute definitions.

65.4   The SBVR Editor

The SBVR editor is based on the XText Framework [12], which allows the creation of a DSL metamodel that is then transformed into a EMF model [13] and used thereafter to provide various features. These include the possibility to check language syntax, semantic validations, content assist and content highlighting. While not covering yet the entire SBVR Meta-model, the editor is capable of syntax highlighting of SBVR *Noun Concepts*, *Verb Concepts* and *Business Rules*, and their attributes, using a complete configurable color and font style (initially set to match SBVR-SE representation color schema), content assist based on syntax and semantic analysis and real-time graphical parsing tree visualization. The following sections explain these language elements and features along with the created editor components and an explanation about the SBVR Editor DSL design decisions.

65.4.1 The Compound Keywords Problem

The metamodel defined in the created DSL is largely based on SBVR concepts which can be directly mapped to SBVR core model elements. For example, there are terms (*Noun Concepts*), *Verb Concepts*, *Verbs*, *Logical Formulation* and other elements in the language model. Nevertheless, we have found that defining all SBVR *Logical Formulation* elements as keywords in the DSL is not the recommended way to implement the editor, since the SBVR vocabulary is intended to be used and understood by business people. Therefore, for example, the standard SBVR-SE, used by many related work, defines keywords to represent logical modalities formulations such as *"It is obligatory that"* or *"It is not permitted that"*. Defining this kind of character sequence as a keyword for the language would raise a problem in the DSL parser created by XText. This kind of expressions will make the parser always look for the *"obligatory"* keyword after the sequence of characters *"It is"*. This problem may generate false alerts or parser errors in the tool. This may be the reason why other approaches used dashes or underscores to define keywords that would rather need spaces like in *"It_is_obligatory_that"* [14].

Therefore, we have opted to map only the basic SBVR standard elements in the DSL and let the identification of *Logical Formulation* elements not to happen in lexer and parser analysis phases, but to postpone the syntax validation of these keywords to the model validation phase. One of the advantages of this approach is the possibility to represent the model keywords with any textual representation, which brings a real possibility to create new CLN using the editor. Nevertheless, a possible disadvantage of this modeling approach would be the complexity of parser and validation implementation, and the necessity to include libraries containing the language definition keyword in every project.

65.4.2 The Language Model

For the presented SBVR editor, a metamodel was created for the syntax definition, which represents some concepts present in SBVR standard. In addition, other concepts necessary to allow the definition of controlled natural languages based on SBVR standard were provided, such as *Logical Formulation Sets*. The Fig. 65.2 shows the partial EMF eCore model from the Editor DSL definition, which is representative for the language understanding.

As can be noticed by the Fig. 65.2, the SBVR vocabulary model is composed of elements represented by the concept *SbvrVocabularyElementDef*. These elements do not represent vocabulary entries—section A.4 of SBVR-SE language example [1]. Nonetheless, they represent a vocabulary entry group, in which each vocabulary entry belongs to a category, in contrast to a disconnected element presented randomly on the SBVR document. These groups are equivalent to the *Rule Entry Set* concept in SBVR specification (SBVR standard section A.5), but represent a generic concept to group more specific concepts. They group *Terms*, *Verbal Concepts* and *SBVR Keywords*. All project's group definitions contribute to the business vocabulary and rules. Therefore, all definitions inside a group, within a project, even when those definitions appear in separated files, will contribute to the language business vocabulary. Each of these concept groups—*SbvrXXXGroupDef*, has an entry named—*SbvrXXXDef*. They represent a SBVR vocabulary entry for the corresponding group—SBVR standard [1]. The entries are composed of sentences—*SbvrXXXStatementDef*. Statement definitions starts with a dash symbol "-", followed by the concept representation in the target language, which defines the primary representation for the concept and a set of attributes—*SbvrCaptionAttributeDef*, which will further detail the concept that is being defined. For example, the *Definition* attribute describes the concept being defined. This is consistent with SBVR-SE term captions. Figure 65.3 shows a representation in the editor for a minimal SBVR Vocabulary in a fictitious online sales system that will serve as the example for the following sections.

65.4.3 SBVR Terms Definition

In the proposed tool, the SBVR *Terms* concepts are represented in a set of term definition statements, which will be used later by *Verb Concepts* and *Rules*. In SBVR standard, these *Terms* are SBVR *Nouns Concepts* elements, which are used to express a unique meaning about a business concept. These *Terms* may be generic concepts about something (analogous to the Class concept in Object-Oriented models) or individual concepts, which represents an individual instance of an entity (analogous to the Object instance in Object-Oriented models). In our SBVR editor, a *Term* is defined in a section introduced by the keyword *TermSet*. Beyond the *Terms* definition, it is possible, similarly as in the SBVR-SE language, to define associated attributes for further refine the *Term*. The Fig. 65.3 shows attributes definitions to the

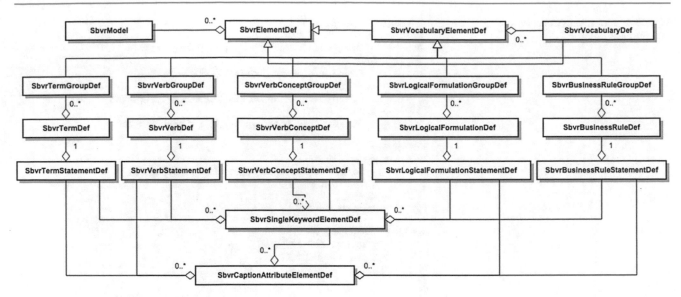

Fig. 65.2 The SBVR Editor Language Meta-model

Term **"order"**. As shown in Fig. 65.3, the tool uses a similar representation as in the SBVR-SE specification. Underlined font style represents *Terms*, *Verbs* are in italic and *keywords* are in bold, while all other elements are in regular font style. After their definition in the editor, these terms are used to create SBVR *Verbal Concepts* and SBVR *Business Rules*.

65.4.4 SBVR Verb Concepts Definition

According to the SBVR standard, *Verb Concepts* usually define some relation between vocabulary terms. The *Verb Concepts* definitions in the editor are defined within a *Verb-ConceptsSet* group. These *Verb Concepts* can them be used in *Business Rules* definitions. Figure 65.3 already showed *VerbConcepts* defined in the *VerbConceptsSet*. Since in SBVR *Verb Concepts* defines either a characteristic, if one *Term* is provided, or a relation, in case of two or more *Terms*, and a *Verb* connecting them, the parser will identify the *Verb Concepts* and relate them to *Terms*. Moreover, they are associated with *Logical Formulations*, in *Business Rules* case. The editor is not yet capable of parsing ternary *Verb Concepts*.

65.4.5 SBVR Business Rules

The SBVR standard enables the business analyst designer to express business rules through controlled natural languages based on the standard. This should be realized by a set of textual business rules using business standard concepts. The *Business Rules* are defined in a section called *RuleSet*. Once *Terms* (*Noun Concepts*), *Verb Concepts* and *Logical*

Formulation elements for the target language are defined, them the business rules can be drawn from those definitions. Each business rule may have a name, as can be seen from the first rule in Fig. 65.3. In the example, the Rule name is specified in square brackets—R1. The rules are composed of *FormulationElements*, which the parser will try to match. The model in the *SBVR Editor* for those elements is compatible with SBVR original metamodel and has elements for *Noun Concepts*, *Verb Concepts*, *Roles*, *Rules* and *Logical Formulations*. The parser will try to match these elements against the so called—SBVR Global Registry in the tool, as the user enters new information in files with the "sbvr" extension. Then, the model is updated automatically and presented to the user, as shown in Fig. 65.4. In Fig. 65.3, the textual representation for the model was shown. In Fig. 65.4, the *SBVR Editor Registry View* shows the current *Global Registry* contents. The *SBVR Editor Global Registry View* (right pane) shows the *Global Registry* produced by the SBVR *Editor Logical Formulation* Parser and the *SBVR Editor Xtext Validation* components.

65.4.6 SBVR Parsing Approach

To support the previously mentioned features, this work uses a similar approach as presented in [5] to parse textual representation of business rules requirements in SBVR through a set of components, each having a specific responsibility. In addition, we do allow the definition of SBVR *Logical Formulation* keywords mapping to textual representation. The parser will consider this mapping to discover *Formulation Elements* defined in all *Business Rules* for the enclosing

Fig. 65.3 Terms, Verb Concepts and Business Rules

```
 1  LogicalFormulationSet {
 2      - It is obligatory that
 3          Formulation_Kind: obligation_formulation
 4      - each
 5          Formulation_Kind: universal_quantification
 6      - at least one
 7          Formulation_Kind: at_least_one_quantification
 8      - exactly one
 9          Formulation_Kind: exactly_one_quantification
10  }
11  TermSet {
12      - order
13          Definition: A instruction for supply goods
14          Synonym: orders
15      - product
16      - payment method
17  }
18  VerbConceptsSet {
19      - order is for product
20      - order has product
21      - order has payment method
22  }
23
24  RuleSet {
25      - [R1] It is obligatory that each order has at least one product
26      - It is obligatory that each order has at least one payment method
27  }
```

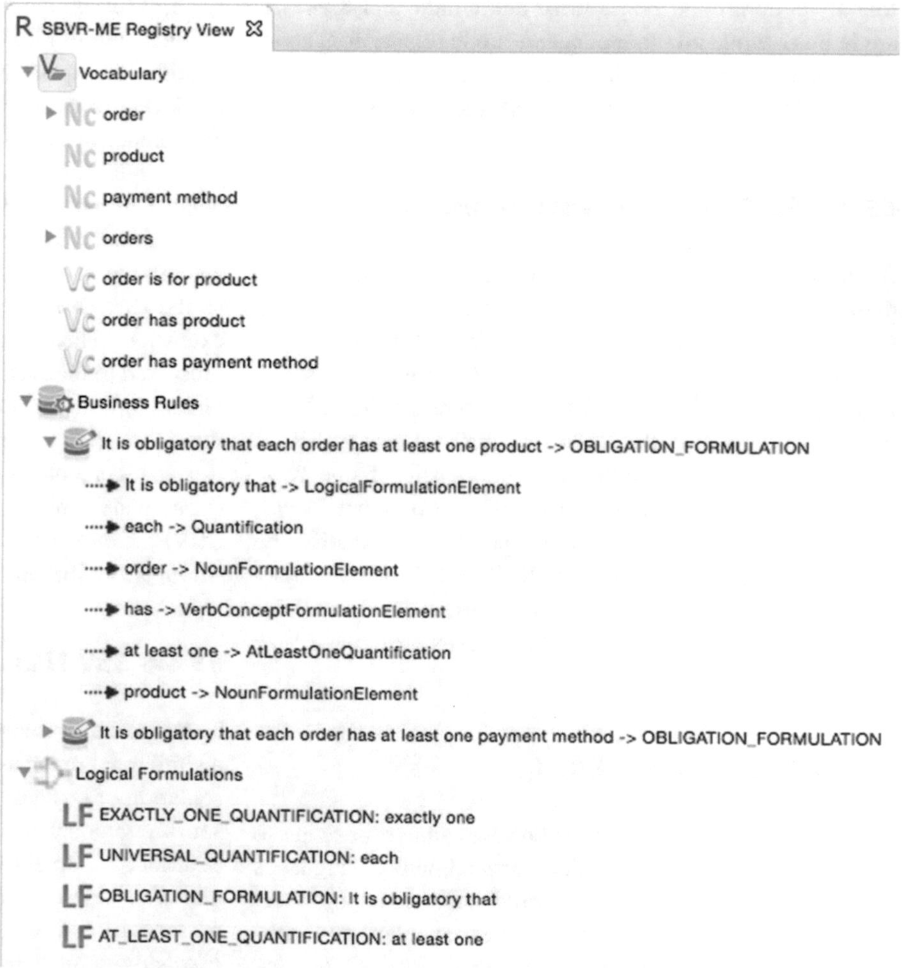

Fig. 65.4 An English Vocabulary and SBVR Rules

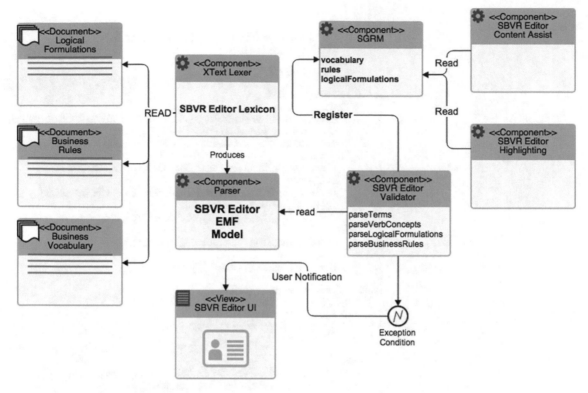

Fig. 65.5 The SBVR Editor Parsing Architecture

project. As shown in Fig. 65.5, the parsing architecture of textual SBVR model in the proposed editor is subdivided into components. The first one is the *XText Lexer and Parser Component* that parses and tokenizes the textual representation, and produces an EMF Model that corresponds to model elements previously shown in Fig. 65.2, such as *SbvrStatements* and *SbvrSingleKeywords*. These elements will form the *SBVR Editor Lexicon* for the model. The *XText Lexer and Parser Module* then pass this EMF model to the *SBVR Editor Validator Component*. The *SBVR Editor Validator Component* is responsible to analyze the semantic of the various statements for correctness. It is the *grammar*. Then it will store the defined *SBVR Language Logical Formulation Keywords*, *Terms* and *Verbs Concepts*, and *Business Rules*, as elements of the SBVR Model into the *SBVR Global Concepts Registry Module—SGRM*.

The entries in the SGRM are lexical elements for the model and can be of three types: *Vocabulary*—entries corresponding to terms and verb concepts of SBVR Model; *Rules*—entries corresponding to Business Rules after the parsing phase and the *Formulation Phrases,* which correspond to the output of the *Logical Formulation Mapping* module. We can visualize these elements in the *SBVR Registry Editor View* window in the Fig. 65.3, which shows the graphical parser result that is generated in real-time, as the user enters information about the SBVR Model.

65.4.7 Syntax Highlighting

The XText generated infrastructure is open for customization in various aspects, and one of them is the syntax highlighting. We have implemented in the proposed editor a syntax-highlighting infrastructure that respects the parsing algorithm already discussed. The recognition of Terms, Verbs and Keywords use the information stored in SGRM. The configuration is initially defined to use the same style schema used in SBVR-SE, but can be customized.

65.5 SBVR Editor Logical Formulations Representation Language Independency

One of the key objectives of this work is to be able to handle **SBVR Vocabularies** in multiple Controlled Natural Languages. To enable the definition of controlled natural languages such as SBVR-SE, and other controlled natural languages using the SBVR standard, in the proposed editor implementation, it became necessary to allow the language definition to express the *Logical Formulation* keywords in a configurable way. Therefore, a group of elements was defined in the language called *LogicalFormualtionSet*, which groups definitions of *Logical Formulations* and the *Logical-Formulation_Kind* caption using SBVR way of defining new

Fig. 65.6 RuleSpeak style example for the Vocabulary and SBVR Rules

```
TermSet {
    - order
        Definition: A instruction for supply goods
        Synonym: orders
    - product
    - payment method
}
LogicalFormulationSet {
    - Each
        Definition: A universal quantification stating that the formulation
        apply to all the following term instances
        Formulation_Kind: universal_quantification
    - at least one
        Formulation_Kind: at_least_one_quantification
    - exactly one
        Definition: A quantification stating that the cardinality of the
        following term is exactly one
        Formulation_Kind: exactly_one_quantification
    - must
        Formulation_Kind: obligation_formulation
    - that
        Formulation_Kind: other_keyword
}
VerbConceptsSet verbsconcepts1 {
    - order is for product
    - order has product
        Synonym: order have product
    - order has payment method
}
RuleSet {
    - [R1] Each order must have at least one product
    - Each order has exactly one payment method
}
```

representations for a concept. In the proposed implementation, not only the business language itself is defined by business *Noun Concepts*, *Verb Concepts* and *Business Rules*, but also the SBVR *Logical Formulation* elements must be defined before a single SBVR business model can be created. There are not predefined language keywords for expressing *Business Rules*. The language keywords corresponding to the *Logical Formulation* elements must be included in the vocabulary, as well all *Terms*, *Verb Concepts* and *Business Rules* would. This vocabulary can then be easily shared between projects by just adding a *LogicalFormulationSet* definitions file in another project.

As already stated, the identification of concepts in the proposed editor implementation is not done by the SBVR DSL lexer or parser, but in the validation and suggestion complete phases, where the set of *Logical Formulation* elements defined by the project can be verified. Each *LogicalFormulationSet* have **statement** entries. These entries are statements that specify the *keywords* that should be used to express the *Logical Formulations* concept. Along with the *LogicalFormulation_Kind* for the entry, which maps to SBVR Meta-model elements such as model logic formulations (obligation, necessity, etc.), quantifications and other keywords, they compose the infrastructure necessary to allow these elements to be used later in the *Business Rules* definitions. Figure 65.3 shows the logical formulation examples defined in the proposed toolset using the standard SBVR-SE,

with obligation formulation semantics, areas the Fig. 65.6 shows the same *Logical Formulations* defined using a *RuleSpeak* style idiom for the same semantics, and the following Fig. 65.7 shows the respondent *SBVR Registry Editor View* for the *RuleSpeak* style version. These same semantics can even be represented in another spoken language like French, as can be seen in Fig. 65.8.

65.6 Conclusion and Future Work

An SBVR Editor is proposed which, while does not yet cover the entire SBVR Meta-model, is capable of recognize SBVR *Noun Concepts*, *Verb Concepts* and *Business Rules* and their captions, and allows the definition, visualization and manipulation of SBVR Business Vocabularies and Rules directly by business analysts in a textual form. It was demonstrated that not only predefined Controlled Natural Languages like SBVR-SE can be used but also other language based on SBVR meta-model can be defined. Other features include syntax highlighting, content assist based on syntax and semantic analysis and real-time graphical parsing tree visualization. The proposed tool allows the representation of SBVR-based models in any language, without the need to recompile and reassemble the tool. The parsing strategy for Business Rules was also covered, while insight on how the internal components work was provided. We are looking

Fig. 65.7 RuleSpeak style
output in the SBVR Global
Registry View

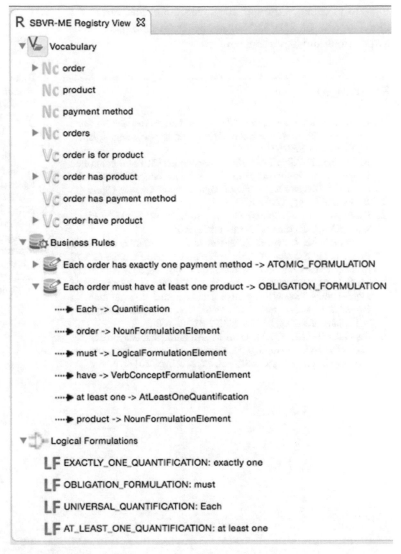

Fig. 65.8 French example for
the Vocabulary and SBVR Rules

```
LogicalFormulationSet {
    - Il est obligatoire que
        Formulation_Kind: obligation_formulation
    - chaque
        Formulation_Kind: universal_quantification
    - au moins un
        Formulation_Kind: at_least_one_quantification
}
TermSet {
    - ordre
    - produit
    - mode de paiement
}
VerbConceptsSet {
    - ordre a produit
        Synonym: ordre a un produit
    - ordre a au moins un mode de paiement
        Synonym: ordre a mode de paiement
}

RuleSet {
    - [R1] Il est obligatoire que chaque ordre a au moins un produit
    - Il est obligatoire que chaque ordre
        a au moins un mode de paiement
}
```

forward to enhance the tool to provide more features, cover more aspects of SBVR Meta-model such as ternary or n-associations and export capabilities.

References

1. OMG, *About the Semantics of Business Vocabulary and Business Rules—SBVR*. OMG Standard (2017). http://www.omg.org/spec/SBVR/About-SBVR/
2. M. Kleiner, P. Albert, J. Bézivin, Parsing SBVR-based controlled languages, in *Proceedings of the 12th International Conference on Model Driven Engineering Languages and Systems*, (Springer, Berlin, 2009), pp. 122–136
3. Business Rules Solutions L, RuleSpeak (2015). http://www.rulespeak.com/en/. Accessed 2 Jan 2015
4. J. vom Brocke, J. Becker, A.M. Braccini, et al., Current and future issues in BPM research: a European perspective from the ERCIS meeting 2010. Commun. Assoc. Inform. Syst. **28**, 394–414 (2011)
5. M. Selway, W. Mayer, M. Stumptner, Semantic interpretation of requirements through cognitive grammar and configuration, in *Pacific Rim International Conference on Artificial Intelligence*, 2014. https://doi.org/10.1007/978-3-319-13560-1
6. Reynares E, Caliusco M, Galli M, An automatable approach for SBVR to OWL 2 mappings, in *XVI Ibero-American Conference on Software Engineering|CIbSE*, vol. 17, 2013, pp. 201–214
7. L. Nemuraite, T. Skersys, VETIS tool for editing and transforming SBVR business vocabularies and business rules into UML&OCL models ... and software ..., 2010, pp. 377–384
8. L. Nemuraite, T. Skersys, A. Sukys, et al., VETIS Tool for Editing and Transforming SBVR Business Vocabularies and Business Rules into UML and OCL Models, in *Proceedings of the 16th International Conference on Information and Software Technologies (IT 2010)*, (Kaunas, Lithuania, 2010), pp. 377–384
9. Magic Draw., https://www.magicdraw.com/main.php. Accessed 2 Jan 2015
10. RuleArts, LLC RuleXpress: The business tool for expressing and communicating business rule, http://rulexpress.com
11. A. Marinos, P. Gazzard, P. Krause, An SBVR Editor with Highlighting and Auto-completion. RuleML2011@ BRF Challenge 1–8, 2011.
12. XText, http:// www.xtext. org. Accessed 2 Jan 2015
13. A. Natali, Introduction to EMF, Ecore and XText, 2012
14. A. Agrawal, S. Singh, *OPAALS—Graphical Editor for Knowledge Representation Based on SBVR. Open Philosophies for Associative Autopoietic Digital Ecosystems. Semantics of Business Process Vocabulary and Process Rules and a Visual Editor of SBVR, 36*, 2009, https://www.cse.iitk.ac.in/users/agrawala/thesis.pdf

An Approach Based on Possibilistic WorkFlow Nets to Model Multiplayer Video Games

Franciny M. Barreto, Leiliane Pereira de Rezende, and Stéphane Julia

Abstract

In this paper, an approach based on Possibilistic Work-Flow nets is proposed to model mutiplayer game scenarios. In a multiplayer game scenario, the actions of a player may influence, directly or indirectly, the actions of other players. This type of interaction may change the normal flow of activities in the game causing eventually then an uncertain behavior. In this work, the routing structure of WorkFlow nets to model the activities of a multiplayer video game is used. The uncertain reasoning of a possibilistic Petri net is then used to represent the possible interactions between the players. The resulting model (Multiplayer Game activity Model) can then simulate and analyze (qualitatively and quantitatively) the game's behavior in terms of its gameplay. The video game Tom Clancy's Ghost Recon: Wildlands is used to illustrate the proposed approach.

Keywords

Petri Nets · Possibilistic workflow net · Game design · Multiplayer games · Video games

66.1 Introduction

A game is a closed, formal system that subjectively represents a subset of reality. By closed it means that the game is complete and self-sufficient in its structure. By formal it means only that the game has explicit rules. The term system

F. M. Barreto (✉)
Federal University of Goiás, Jataí, GO, Brazil

L. P. de Rezende · S. Julia
Faculty of Computer Science, Federal University of Uberlândia, Uberlândia, MG, Brazil

is used due to the fact that a game is a collection of parts that interact with each other, often in complex ways [1].

A video game application differs from classical software because of a preproduction stage and because of an extensive use and integration of multimedia assets. Video game creation involves several specific activities that do not necessarily exist when considering more traditional software development processes [2]. Some of these activities are the game design and the level design. Game design defines the main aspects concerning the universe of the game: epoch and style, context of the game, goal to be reached, types of objects involved, user perception of the game, etc. It is at the level design that the main actions and objects of the game are defined [2].

In general, there are two game categories: singleplayer and multiplayer. In the singleplayer category, the player is the only one to perform all activities and interact with the game objects. On the other hand, in the multiplayer category, activities as well as game objects are shared among all the players. In addition, in shared game environments, player's actions have an impact on the actions of other players. For example, if a single game object (such as a key) is recovered by a player, this implies that other players will not be able to retrieve the same object and consequently will not be able to perform a specific game activity (such as opening a door, for example).

According to [3], the vast majority of games played all over the world are collective in nature. Despite this, the early years of electronic game development have targeted the individual player because of the high costs associated with technology. However, with the popularization of the Internet, there was a massification of online play environments.

A multiplayer game is different from an individual one. Thus, it becomes important to explain and understand the fundamental characteristics of multiplayer games. These are attributes that are not always present in individual games and it is important to understand how these elements relate to each other and to the game itself [3]. According to [4], the representation and simulation of multiplayer scenarios present an interesting challenge in the creation of video games. The authors also affirm that in games with more than one player, the complexity of competing events in the game may represent very complex scenario models. They state in particular that modeling based on Petri nets may be especially important for simulating multiplayer game, because Petri Nets can be expressive, easy to understand and have capability of modeling concurrent operations.

In this article, Petri nets will be explored for modeling the activities existing in a multiplayer game. In particular, a kind of possibilistic WorkFlow net will be used to represent the activities of the game as well as the interactions between several players. With the presented approach, it will be possible to show the activities that each player performs during the game and the consequences of such actions in terms of gameplay. Besides that, a possibilistic WorkFlow net makes possible the representation of the expected behavior of a player in a game as well as the unexpected behavior generated by the individual choices of distinct players.

In Sect. 66.2, the definition of a WorkFlow net is provided. In Sect. 66.3, the concept of possibilistic reasoning in Petri net is given. In Sect. 66.4, a new approach to model multiplayer video game scenarios is defined. Finally, the last section concludes this work.

66.2 WorkFlow Net

A Petri net that models a Workflow Process is called a WorkFlow net [5]. According to [6], a WorkFlow net satisfies the following properties:

- It has only one source place, named Start and only one sink place, named End. These are special places such that the place Start has only outgoing arcs and the place End has only incoming arcs.
- A token in Start represents a case that needs to be handled and a token in End represents a case that has been handled.
- Every task t (transition) and condition p (place) should be on a path from place Start to place End.

A process defines which tasks need to be executed and in which order [6]. Modeling a Workflow Process in terms of a WorkFlow net is rather straightforward: transitions are active components and model the tasks, places are passive components and model conditions and tokens model cases [5, 6]. Four basic constructions for routing are presented in [5, 6]: sequential, parallel, conditional and iterative.

66.3 Possibilistic Petri Net

Possibilistic Petri nets are derived from Object Petri nets [7]. According to [8], a possibilistic Petri net is a model where a marked place corresponds to a possible partial state, a transition to a possible state change, and a firing sequence to a possible behavior. A possibilistic Petri net model associates a possibility distribution $\Pi_o(p)$ to the location of an object o, p being a place of a Petri net.

Formally, a marking in a possibilistic Petri net is then a mapping:

$$M : O \times P \to 0, 1 \qquad (66.1)$$

where O is a set of objects and P a set of places. A marking M of the net allows one to represent a precise marking and an imprecise marking:

- A precise marking: $M(o,p) = 1$ and $\forall p_i \neq p, M(o,p_i) = 0$.
- An imprecise marking: if there exists a possibility at a certain time to have the same object o in two different places them $M(o,p_1) = M(o,p_2) = 1$.

In a possibilistic Petri net, the firing of a transition t is decomposed into beginning and end of a firing. In the beginning of a firing, the objects are put into output places of t but are not removed from its input places. The end of a firing can be a firing cancellation or a firing achievement. In a firing cancellation tokens are removed from the output places of t. In a firing achievement tokens are removed from the input places of t. A certain firing consists then of a beginning of a firing and an immediate firing achievement. A pseudo-firing that will increase the uncertainty of the marking corresponds only to the beginning of a firing.

The interpretation of a possibilistic Petri net is defined by attaching to each transition an authorization function defined as followed:

$$\eta x_1, \ldots, x_n : T \to \{\text{False, Uncertain, True}\} \qquad (66.2)$$

Petri net models can be directly executed using a specialized inference mechanism called token player algorithm that allows for a simplified monitoring of the represented processes. Figure 66.1(a) illustrates a classical token player algorithm depicted by an activity diagram. This algorithm is only based on normal expected events. However, in complex systems, unexpected events can happen introducing then

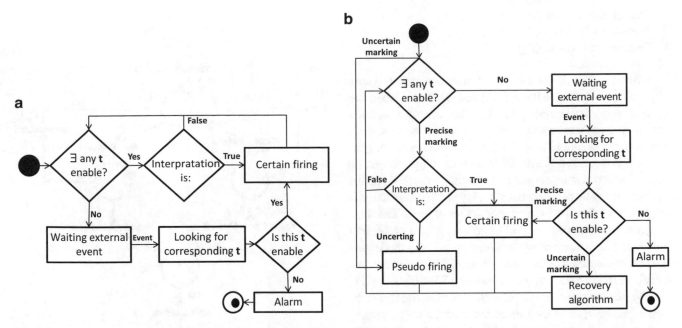

Fig. 66.1 (a) Classical token player of Petri net. (b) Token player of possibilistic Petri net

some degree of uncertainty and should be taken into account in the model of a process [9]. Thus, when an unexpected event has to be taken into account in a process, the token player algorithm illustrated in Fig. 66.1(b) (presented in [9]) is considered.

66.4   Multiplayer Game Activity Model

According to [3], the vast majority of games played all over the world are collective in nature, that is, they involve the participation of more than one player. These kind of games, are called multiplayer games. A multiplayer game has a high degree of social interaction where the main goal can be achieved only if there is social interaction among the participants at one time or another [3].

In general, a multiplayer game is characterized by the existence of human opponents or cooperators. Competition refers to the fact that the participants (opponents) of the game are struggling towards a goal that will result in the declaration of a winner. On the other hand, in cooperative games the participants strive towards a common goal [3]. In this kind of game, mutual assistance is sometimes the way for the players to reach the objective.

According to [1], successful video games are more than software because they should enthrall a user. A game has to capture the full attention of a gamer. The environment and narrative that many games present have the ability to submerge the player and motivate them to fulfill all the tasks proposed by the game. Thus, every game must have a narrative that moves the player.

A narrative is an ordered sequence of events. A set of ordered sequence of events is named scenarios. The study in [2] states that there is always a scenario in a game. The authors also affirm that a scenario may be reduced to a sequence of goals to be reached or a path which must be followed. In this way, it is important to consider the logic sequence of the actions in the game. The logical sequence of the game activities will depend on the objectives that the players shall achieve. To achieve a specific goal, it is necessary that the player performs a certain sequence of activities (tasks). In a multiplayer game, some of these activities can (or must) be performed in partnership with other players.

The video game *Tom Clancy's Ghost Recon: Wildlands* [10] will be used to illustrate the approach presented in this paper. *Tom Clancy's Ghost Recon: Wildlands* is a multiplayer game that takes place in Bolivia, South America. The players are sent behind the enemy lines to create chaos that will destabilize and break the alliance between the *Santa Blanca Mexican drug Cartel* and the corrupted government. The game has a variety of quests that can be executed in any order by the players. Each mission has a specific goal. The completion of the quests will contribute to the goal of the game, which is to destroy the *Santa Blanca cartel*.

The game *Tom Clancy's Ghost Recon: Wildlands* has a quest named The Chemist. The activities that the players must execute to complete the quest are the following ones:

- Enter the area (T0);
- Fight enemies (T1);
- Use strategy (T2);
- Find the chemist (T5);

- Capture the chemist (T6);
- Transport to prison (T7);
- Finalize the mission (T8).

With only one player the execution of the activities usually occurs according to the defined flow. However, when two or more players are running the same flow of activities, interactions between them can make changes in the execution. For example, activity *T6* of *The Chemist* mission can only be performed once. If this activity is performed by a player, no other player active in the game at that time can run *T6* again. Therefore, when performed by a player, the *T6* activity is implicitly performed by all other active players. This type of game behavior can be seen as an unexpected event, thus generating an inconsistency between the activity model and the actual execution of the game. A model based on a possibilistic Petri net the routing structure of a WorkFlow net [11] is proposed in this work to deal with such behavior that is the direct consequence of the interaction between the players.

The possibilistic Petri net with objects that respects the routing structure of a workflow net presented in Fig. 66.2 represents the multiplayer game activity model for the quest *The Chemist*. C1 and C2 in place *P0* corresponds to objects belonging to the class *PLAYER* as well as variables *x* and *y* (attached to the arcs of the model) and all the places of the model. The objects *C1* and *C2* represent two players in the game. The place *P0* indicates the beginning of the quest and place *P8* indicates the end of the quest. Transitions from *T0* to *T8* represent the activities of the quest. The activities *T1* and *T2* belong to a selective routing, i.e., the players can choose which activity they want to perform. *T1* and *T2* represent an OR-split in a Workflow net structure; *T3* and *T4* represent an OR-join [5]. Transitions from *T5* to *T8* belong to a sequential routine, which means that these have to be performed one after another. Transitions from *T9* to *T11* represent possible player failures when performing a specific activity. For example, if the activity *Fight enemies* (transition *T1*) is successfully executed, transition *T3* is fired and the player can move forward. Otherwise, transition *T10* is fired and the player return to the beginning of the quest. In a WorkFlow net, such transitions correspond then to iterative routing structures.

The class *PLAYER* is composed of the boolean attributes *dead1*, *dead2*, *seen* and *end*. *Dead1* and *seen*, when true, represent the fact that the player has failed an activity and will have to return to previous point. *Dead2* is true when the player has failed to complete the mission. Finally, when attribute *end* is true, it means the quest was successfully completed.

To simulate a possible scenario which shows how the game works with more than one player, the following facts can be stated:

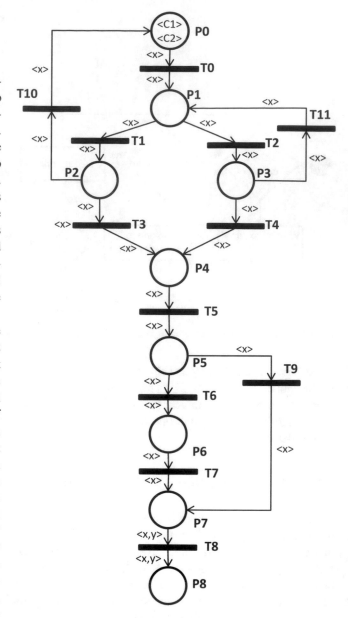

Fig. 66.2 Multiplayer game activity model

- *T0* must be executed by all players;
- *T1* and *T2* represent challenges and they can be executed by one or more players at the same time;
- *T6*, *T7* and *T8* should be performed only once;
- for example, if one player has performed *T6*, the other players will no longer be able to execute the corresponding activity;
- *T6*, *T7* and *T8* can be executed by one or more players;
- *T8* represents the end of the quest.

The interpretations associated to transitions T0 to T11 are given by the following distributions:

$$\eta_x(T0) = \begin{cases} \text{true if (x.end)} \\ \text{uncertain if (x.end)} \end{cases} \qquad (66.3)$$

$$\eta_x(T1) = \begin{cases} \text{true if (x.end)} \\ \text{uncertain if (x.end)} \end{cases} \qquad (66.4)$$

$$\eta_x(T2) = \begin{cases} \text{true if (x.end)} \\ \text{uncertain if (x.end)} \end{cases} \qquad (66.5)$$

$$\eta_x(T3) = \begin{cases} \text{true if (x.dead1)} \\ \text{uncertain if (x.end)} \end{cases} \qquad (66.6)$$

$$\eta_x(T4) = \begin{cases} \text{true if (x.seen)} \\ \text{uncertain if (x.end)} \end{cases} \qquad (66.7)$$

$$\eta_x(T5) = \begin{cases} \text{true if (x.end)} \\ \text{uncertain if (x.end)} \end{cases} \qquad (66.8)$$

$$\eta_x(T6) = \begin{cases} \text{true if (x.dead2)} \\ \text{uncertain if (x.end)} \end{cases} \qquad (66.9)$$

$$\eta_x(T7) = \begin{cases} \text{true if (x.end)} \\ \text{uncertain if (x.end)} \end{cases} \qquad (66.10)$$

$$\eta_x(T8) = \{\text{true if (x.end} \wedge \text{y.end)} \qquad (66.11)$$

$$\eta_x(T9) = \begin{cases} \text{true if (x.dead2)} \\ \text{uncertain if (x.end)} \end{cases} \qquad (66.12)$$

$$\eta_x(T10) = \begin{cases} \text{true if (x.dead1)} \\ \text{uncertain if (x.end)} \end{cases} \qquad (66.13)$$

$$\eta_x(T11) = \begin{cases} \text{true if (x.seen)} \\ \text{uncertain if (x.end)} \end{cases} \qquad (66.14)$$

For simulation purposes, it can be assumed that the players $C1$ and $C2$ have already executed the activity $T0$. After that, each player performs a different activity. Thus, $C1$ will perform activity $T1$ and $C2$ will perform activity $T2$. In both activities, the players can execute them successfully or not. Consider that the player $C1$ failed to execute $T1$, therefore the attribute *dead1* becomes true. Then, $T10$ is fired and $C1$ returns to the start of the quest (place $P0$). Considering that $C2$ completed $T2$ successfully, $T4$ is then fired and $C2$ follows with the other activities of the game (place $P4$). While the player $C1$ tries to go through the activity $T1$, $C2$ performs the activities $T5$, $T6$ and $T7$ successfully. When $T7$

is fired, the attribute end becomes true, indicating that the quest has been completed successfully, although $C1$ did not already perform all activities.

The expected behavior of a multiplayer game is to performed the activities in group. When a player ends a quest, but there exists still players evolve with some of the activities of the same quest, from the point of view of the formal model of representation of the activities, an inconsistency may occur. This will happen in particular when one of the players manage to complete the activities of the quest; as a direct consequence, the other player will have to cancel the execution of some of the activities the other player have already completed. In the specific case of the example presented in this work, the activities are $T3$, $T5$, $T6$ and $T7$. A way of solving such a problem is to use the concept of cancelation of activities presented in [11]; in this work, the authors manage to cancel some activities of a business process using the concept of transition pseudo-firing of a possibilistic WorkFlow net.

Considering that the player $C2$ performed all activities successfully and supposing that the player $C1$ is in place $P2$. Considering a non-possibilistic Petri net model (an ordinary place/transition net), the player $C1$, in order to respect the control structure of the model in Fig. 66.2, should still complete the activities $T3$, $T5$, $T6$ and $T7$ to reach the end of the quest. But because the player $C2$ has already managed to finalize such activities, the main goal of the player $C1$ is simply to reach the player $C2$ at the end of the quest for initiating the next quest. The following scenario (illustrate in Fig. 66.3(a)) will show how the existence of transition pseudo-firing in a possibilistic Petri net model can manage to maintain correct the semantic of a multiplayer game modeled by a Petri net:

- if *end* = true, then $\eta_x(T3)$ = uncertain and $T3$ is pseudo-fired for object $C1$;
- if *end* = true, then $\eta_x(T5)$ = uncertain and $T5$ is pseudo-fired for object $C1$;
- if *end* = true, then $\eta_x(T6)$ = uncertain and $T6$ is pseudo-fired for object $C1$;
- if *end* = true, then $\eta_x(T7)$ = uncertain and $T7$ is pseudo-fired for object $C1$;
- if *end* = true and $C1$ and $C2$ are in place $P7$, then $\eta_x(T8)$ = true. $T8$ is then enabled by an uncertain marking with a true interpretation. Consequently the recovery algorithm, presented in [12] is called to go back to the certain marking corresponding to Fig. 66.3(b).

The activity model of the quest The Chemist is then finalized (all the players in place P8), only when all the players are in place P7.

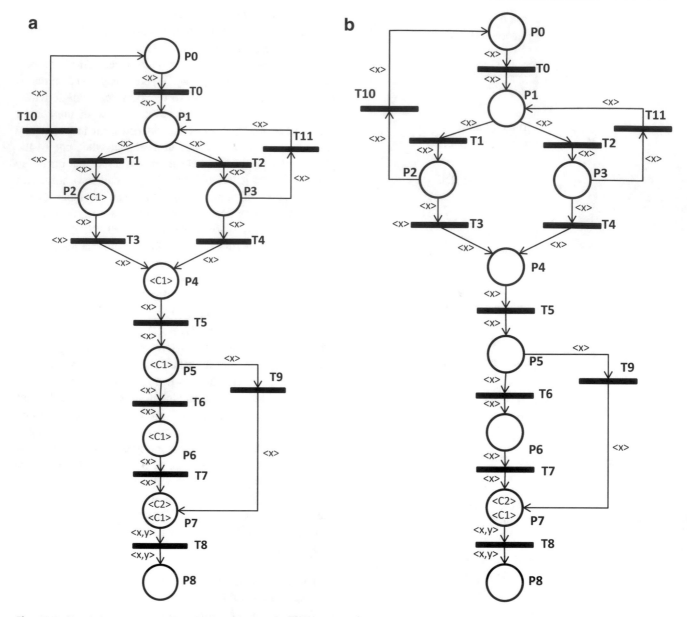

Fig. 66.3 Simulation results. (**a**) Uncertain marking to C1. (**b**) Certain marking to C1 and C2

If all the activities represented on the Petri net activities were to be performed by all the players, the beginning to the end of the quest, all the transitions of the model would have to be fired with certainty. However, since each player has the autonomy to do whatever he wants in the game and because in case of multiplayer game it exists a certain degree of collaboration to reach a common goal, unexpected behaviors generated by the individual choices of each player have to be allowed by the model.

66.5 Conclusions

In this article, a new approach to model multiplayer video games was presented. In particular, a specific kind of possibilistic Petri net with the routing structure of a Workflow net, was used. The routing structure of WorkFlow nets made possible the modeling of activities at a game level. The uncertain reasoning of possibilistic Petri nets made possible the explicit representation of the interactions that exist between players collaborating to reach a common goal. Furthermore, through an uncertain marking, several execution options can be created without the need to pollute the model. Thus, using a kind of possibilistic WorkFlow net was a suitable way to represent the distinct actions of each player during a multiplayer game and to formally understand the consequences of such actions in terms of gameplay. In particular, through a multiplayer activity model will be possible to track the actions that each player will perform during the game as well as the consequences of such actions on the other players. Thus, it will be possible to conduct a type of qualitative analysis to evaluate the game's behavior in terms of gameplay before its development.

As a future work proposal, it will be interesting to consider a timed version of the multiplayer activity model, in order to perform a kind of quantitative analysis to estimate the average length of multiplayer video games.

References

1. C. Crawford, *The Art of Computer Game Design*, 1982
2. V. Gal, C. Le Prado, S. Natkin, and L. Vega, Writing for video games, in *Proceedings Laval Virtual (IVRC)*, 2002
3. J.P. Zagal, M. Nussbaum, R. Rosas, A model to support the design of multiplayer games. Presence Teleop. Virt. **9**(5), 448–462 (2000)
4. M. Araújo and L. Roque, Modeling games with petri nets, in *Breaking New Ground: Innovation in Games, Play, Practice and Theory. DIGRA2009*. (Londres, Royaume Uni, 2009)
5. W. Van Der Aalst, K.M. Van Hee, *Workflow Management: Models, Methods, and Systems* (MIT press, Cambridge, 2004)
6. W.M. van der Aalst, The application of petri nets to workflow management. JCSC **8**(01), 21–66 (1998)
7. C. Sibertin-Blanc, Cooperative objects: Principles, use and implementation, Concurrent object-oriented programming and petri nets, pp. 216–246, 2001
8. J. Cardoso, H. Camargo, Time fuzzy petri nets. Fuzziness in Petri Nets **22**, 115–145 (1999)
9. L. P. de Rezende, S. Julia, and J. Cardoso, Possibilistic workflow nets to deal with non-conformance in process execution, in *Systems, Man, and Cybernetics (SMC)*, 2012 *IEEE International Conference on*, (IEEE, New Jersey, 2012), pp. 1219–1224
10. Ubisoft. (2017) Tom clancy's ghost recon: Wildlands, developed by ubisoft
11. L. P. d. Rezende, S. Julia, and J. Cardoso, Possibilistic workflow nets for dealing with cancellation regions in business processes, in *Proceedings of the 18th International Conference on Enterprise Information Systems, ser.* ICEIS 2016, pp. 126–133
12. J. Cardoso, R. Valette, D. Dubois, Petri nets with uncertain markings, in *International Conference on Application and Theory of Petri Nets*, (Springer, Berlin, 1989), pp. 64–78

A Requirements Engineering-Based Approach for Evaluating Security Requirements Engineering Methodologies

Sravani Teja Bulusu, Romain Laborde, Ahmad Samer Wazan, Francois Barrère, and Abdelmalek Benzekri

Abstract

The significance of security requirements in building safety and security critical systems is widely acknowledged. However, given the multitude of security requirements engineering methodologies that exists today, selecting the best suitable methodology remains challenging. In a previous work, we proposed a generic evaluation methodology to elicit and evaluate the anticipated characteristics of a security requirements engineering methodology with regards to the stakeholders' working context. In this article, we provide the empirical evaluation of three security requirements engineering methodologies KAOS, STS and SEPP with respect to the evaluation criteria elicited for network SRE context. The study show that none of them provide good support to derive network security requirements.

Keywords

Security requirements engineering · Evaluation methodology

67.1 Introduction

Security requirements engineering (SRE) deals with the process of eliciting, evaluating and documenting security requirements. Several SRE methodologies have been proposed to improve this process [1–3]. However, selecting one best suitable SRE methodology still stands as a challenging task to requirement engineers. Although many comparative and evaluation studies of SRE methodologies were made in the past, their evaluation results were not reusable due to various issues such as: ad-hoc criteria, lack of consideration of all the phases of the RE process; and finally non-consideration of the working context of the security requirement engineers [4]. To address this issue, in our previous work [4] we have proposed a generic evaluation methodology using a requirements engineering based approach. This methodology facilitates to elicit the characteristics of good SRE methodology specific to a known SRE context. These characteristics are considered as evaluation criteria for evaluating the SRE methodologies. In the next following work [5] we have briefed on the instantiation of our evaluation methodology to the context of network security requirements engineering. In this article, we discuss in detail the empirical evaluation of three widely recognized SRE: KAOS [1], STS [2] and SEPP [3] with the help of the evaluation criteria for network SRE context. The study show that none of them provide good support to derive network security requirements.

The rest of the article is structured as follows. Sect. 67.2 introduces our evaluation methodology and the example use case for network SRE context. Sect. 67.3 provide the elicited evaluation criteria specific to the given network SRE context. In Sect. 67.4 we discuss the performance of the SRE methodologies in network SRE context. Finally, we conclude our work in Sect. 67.5.

67.2 Presentation of Our Work

67.2.1 Our Context of SRE Methodologies Evaluation

Our work is part of the research project IREHDO2 and concerns the aircraft network security engineering. In this project, the security experts of an aircraft company want to improve their security process in order to increase the assurance on the final security solution enforced on their aircraft networks. More precisely, they are interested in enhancing their security requirement practices. This group of security experts includes the security requirement engineers,

S. T. Bulusu (✉) · R. Laborde · A. S. Wazan · F. Barrère · A. Benzekri
IRIT/Université Paul Sabatier, Toulouse, France
e-mail: Sravani-Teja.Bulusu@irit.fr

© Springer International Publishing AG, part of Springer Nature 2018
S. Latifi (ed.), *Information Technology – New Generations*, Advances in Intelligent Systems and Computing 738,
https://doi.org/10.1007/978-3-319-77028-4_67

risks analysts as well as the security testing experts who are involved at different levels of the security process. Our task in this project consists in proposing the best SRE methodology which will help them in writing good security requirements. However, each security expert had a different point of view on what could be a good SRE methodology. As a first attempt, they provided us with a use case scenario summarizing their SRE problem context.

This scenario in Fig. 67.1 depicts a situation related to the maintenance of the aircraft in order to anticipate its health of the on-board aircraft system by verifying specific parameters. The On-board aircraft system is integrated the aircraft monitoring application and the aircraft control application which are connected to each other via an internal avionic bus network. The maintenance people are allowed to connect their laptops to the monitoring application in order to fetch the monitored parameters. The security goals are expressed in terms of protecting the integrity and availability of the monitored parameters. Security experts needed to derive good network security requirements which can drive them to identify right design solutions i.e., maintenance people can potentially connect to the aircraft using an Ethernet cable or a wireless connection.

Overall, this scenario gathers network security requirements engineering context information in an unstructured format. It provides some insights on what kind of network security requirements can be elicited. However, the question of SRE methodology goodness from the point of view of the security experts is still open. Without this information it will difficult to anticipate what kind of SRE methodology would be interesting to the security experts.

67.2.2 Our SRE Evaluation Methodology Strategy

Our proposed SRE evaluation methodology is built on the classical idea of requirements engineering approach by assuming the target system-to-be as the ideal SRE-methodology-to-be that best fits the SRE context. It differs its strategy from previous comparative studies for two reasons. Firstly, it considers the security experts who are the SRE end-users in the whole process. Secondly, it allows the elicitation of SRE evaluation criteria in regards with the anticipated characteristics of a good SRE methodology. Figure 67.2 depicts an overview of our approach. It subsumes three steps: (1) identifying the problem context and eliciting initial high-level characteristic goals. This is done by coupling the stakeholder's working SRE context as well as the quality criteria of good security requirements; (2) refining the high-level characteristic goals into final requirements of the SRE methodology-to-be (R^M); (3) evaluating the existing SRE methodologies using the elicited requirements (R^M).

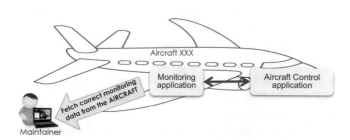

Fig. 67.1 Example scenario context

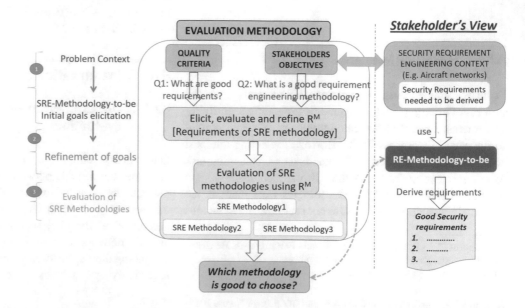

Fig. 67.2 Our evaluation methodology

67.3 Step 1 and Step 2: Elicitation of Evaluation Criteria

In [5] we have illustrated the elicitation process in the given scenario context which concerns the first two steps of our evaluation methodology. We used the brainstorming technique to encourage the people to exchange ideas on the "best suitable SRE methodology" befitting their needs. Ideally, the ultimate goal of the security experts is to derive good security requirements. The SRE-methodology-to-be is a way to achieve this goal. They are refined into sub-goals that ultimately represent the anticipated characteristics of SRE-methodology-to-be. We represent the elicited goals using KAOS goal modelling notation, see Fig. 67.3. The root goals represent the characteristics of good security requirements. The refinement uses the AND-construct and it is continued until the final refined goals are realized as verifiable. The leaf goal nodes are realized as verifiable eventually become the evaluation criteria R^M. The verification method reflects the suggested way used for evaluating the performance of the SRE methodology against the evaluation criteria. Respectively, the type of verification and expected performance metrics differs with respect to the type of evaluation criteria. For instance, if we consider the evaluation criterion $R^M6.2$. The verification method must facilitate to evaluate the supportability of the SRE-methodology-to-be in capturing risk attributes related to environmental constraints and interaction dependency constraints, risk priority information. Respectively, the performance metrics to measure the evaluation of this criterion is given in Table 67.1. The qualitative scale used for performance measure expresses the degree of supportability, i.e., *high*—highly supportable, *medium*—partially supportable, *low*—less likely supportable and *nil*—not supportable.

67.4 Step 3: Evaluation of SRE Methodologies

The goal of step3 is to test the performance of the SRE methodologies using the elicited evaluation criteria from previous steps. For evaluation, we choose three widely recognized methodologies: Secure KAOS (a goal-oriented methodology—noted KAOS) [1], Secure Socio-Technical System (an agent-oriented methodology—noted STS) [2] and Security Engineering Process using Patterns (a problem-oriented methodology—noted SEPP) [3].

The practical experimentation was carried out as follows. First, a description of the system-to-be is presented to three different persons whose initial knowledge fits the aforementioned methodologies the best. Then, each one of them has been asked to elaborate the system to-be using the

methodology that he is familiar with. In end, each of them has come up with a different list of security requirements for the system-to-be with respect to the example scenario. The results of their works have been presented during a meeting that involved the security experts. The evaluation of each work was based on the elicited requirements R^M of the *SRE-methodology-to-be* and the discussions with the security experts of our research project.

In Fig. 67.4, we resumed the evaluation results of the SRE methodologies (in tabular format). From our experimentation we observed that each of these three SRE methodologies exhibit different capabilities with respect to the evaluation criteria. However, when seen from network SRE context, none of the methodologies provides good support. The criteria $R^M3.2$, $R^M6.1$ and $R^M6.4$ are related to the network security requirements engineering context. In the following we discuss our observations on the performance of the SRE methodologies with respect to the evaluation criteria.

67.4.1 Secure KAOS Methodology

Secure KAOS, mainly focuses on eliciting goals and refining them in to sub-goals until they are atomic. Goal refinements are realized via the AND/OR constructs. When a goal cannot be refined further, it is called as the *security requirement* of the system-to-be and is assigned to an agent represented. If a security requirement is assigned to an environment agent (e.g., human), it is called an expectation. The link between a security requirements and a risk is explicitly expressed by the concepts of *obstacles/anti-goals*. In addition, KAOS defines some based goal refinement patterns based on a temporal logic in order to introduce formalism. Figure 67.5 depicts a sample goal model specified in our example scenario context.

We used the KAOS free trial version tool known as *Objectiver* [6]. It took some time and effort to get familiar with the tool and its terminology with the help of available references ($R^M2.1.1$, $R^M2.1.2$ and $R^M2.1.3$). Since KAOS drives RE analyst to define *agents* later in the RE process, it does not help in expressing the relation between the agents and their interaction dependencies. While defining the network agents in our scenario context, we had an issue when we needed to add a new device to the network ($R^M3.2$). In the other hand, KAOS notation provides good support to achieve traceability ($R^M4.1$). *Anti-goals* can be refined like 'normal' goals resulting in the specification of attack trees. Obstacles include two risk attributes *likelihood* and *criticality*. However, there is no explicit relationship defined between the priority of a security goal and the risk of an associated obstacle ($R^M6.3$). In addition, it helps in observing the environmental constraints upon the goals through specifying domain properties. (e.g., physical laws), see Fig. 67.5.

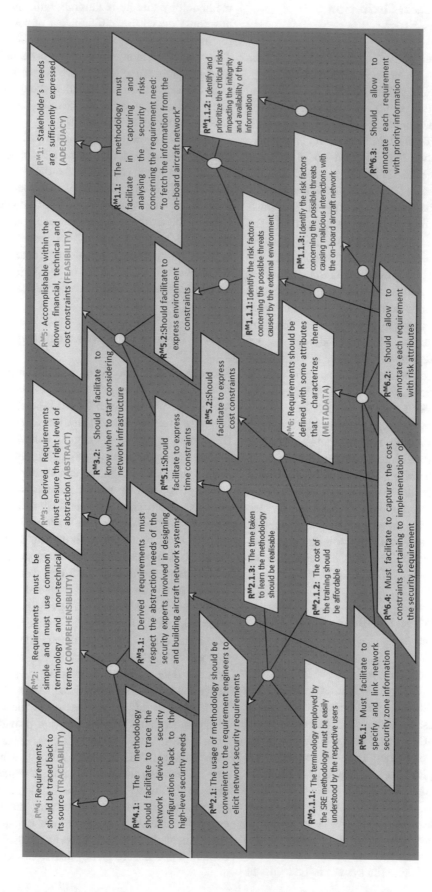

Fig. 67.3 R^M refinement (sample)

Table 67.1 Verification method for $R^M 6.2$

Verification method	Performance measure
Requirement cannot be annotated with any risk information	Nil
Requirements can be annotated with at least one of the attributes	Low
Requirements can be annotated with risk priority and threat events	Medium
The annotation feature is extensible. Requirements can be annotated with multiple risk attributes	High

Elicited evaluation criteria list (R^M)	STS	Secure KAOS	SEPP
$R^M 2.1.1$: The terminology employed by the SRE-Methodology-to-be must be easily understood by respective users	high	medium	low
$R^M 2.1.2$: The cost of the training should be affordable	high	medium	low
$R^M 2.1.3$: The time taken to learn th emethodology approach should be realisable	high	medium	low
$R^M 3.2$: Should facilitate to know when to start considering network infrastructure	nil	nil	nil
$R^M 4.1$: should facilitate to trace the network device security configurations back to the high-level security needs	medium	high	low
$R^M 6.1$: Must facilitate to specify and link network security zone information	nil	nil	nil
$R^M 6.2$: Should allow to annotate each requirement with risk attributes	low	medium	nil
$R^M 6.3$: Should allow to annotate each requirement with priority information	nil	high	nil
$R^M 6.4$: Must facilitate to capture the cost constraints pertaining to implementation of the security requirement	nil	nil	nil

Fig. 67.4 Sample of the evaluation results

67.4.2 STS Methodology

STS mainly focuses on early elicitation of security requirements based on the social interactions between the agents. Similar to KAOS, STS framework offers the possibility to create composite goals via the AND/OR constructs. However, the respective goals and sub-goals are determined in the scope of each actor. An *actor* can be either a *role* or an *agent*. The social relationships between actors are manifested by the relationships such as *goal delegation* and *resource provision*. This is modelled in the *social view*. Delegated goal

implies that an actor depends on another actor to achieve a goal. In addition, the social relationships between actors may also include the exchange of *documents* that contain necessary information for the achievement of a goal. Figure 67.6 depicts a sample social view of the scenario.

We used STS tool [7] that is freely available ($R^M 2.1.2$). Simple terminology as well the user friendly tool took less effort to get used to the overall concepts and terminology ($R^M 2.1.2$ and $R^M 2.1.3$). However, we had issue in handling the dependencies between the multiple network actors/agents. At some point, the social view became too complex and complicated to express the security interaction needs between the network agents. Furthermore, agent modelling approach defined by STS does not respect abstraction needs of the security experts and it became almost impossible to know when to start considering the network security agents ($R^M 3.2$). In addition, STS does not help to achieve traceability in a full-fledged manner like in KAOS ($R^M 4.1$). This is because, the *security needs* in STS are expressed implicitly in form of security constraints on the agents' interactions (see Fig. 67.6). Furthermore, in STS, the *threat analysis* is used to show the effects over goal trees and goal/resource relationships that may have a threating event, see Fig. 67.5. Also, it defines attributes (implicit) to link countermeasures to threat events ($R^M 6.2$). However, the threat analysis is limited to threat event propagation.

67.4.3 SEPP Methodology

SEPP extends the concepts and terminology of problem frames approach to the security context. A *problem frame* is a problem pattern representing the common characteristics of a recognized class of problem. Respectively, SEPP guides the RE analyst to define security problem patterns, called as security *problem frames* (SPF). The security solution patterns, called as *concertized security problem frames* (CSPF) are defined separately. The security problems (security goals) are identified using the what-if analysis technique similar to the Hazard analysis [8]. Figure 67.6 depicts an example of secure problem frames specification.

The non-availability of a tool for SEPP made our experimentation very hard. As a consequence, in our experimentation we have manually modelled the SPF and CSPF patterns manually. A comprehensive training is must in order

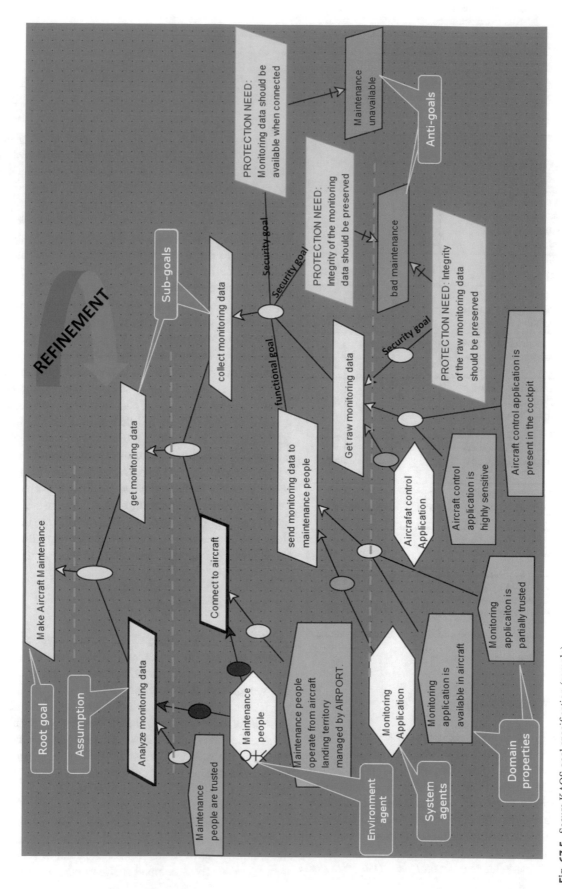

Fig. 67.5 Secure KAOS goal specification (sample)

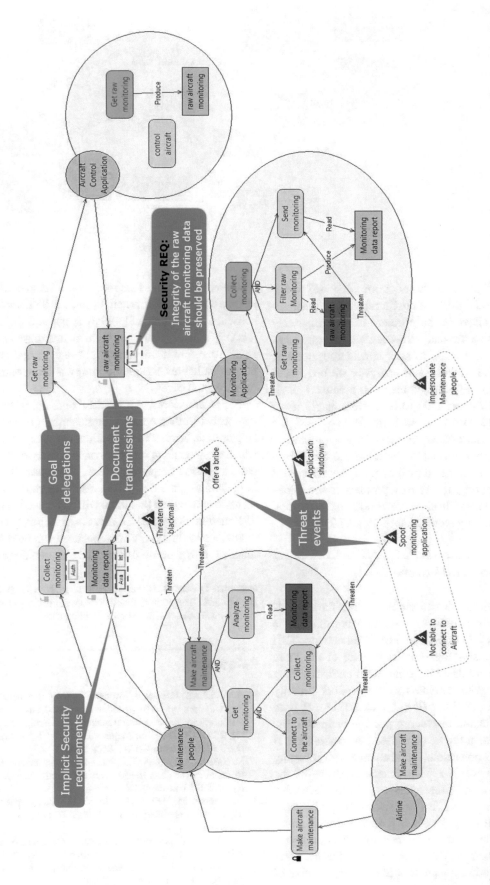

Fig. 67.6 STS social view specification (sample)

Fig. 67.7 SEPP SPF diagram (sample)

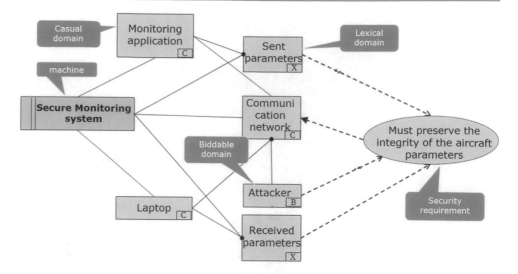

to get thorough with its concepts and terminology ($R^M2.1.2$, $R^M2.1.2$ and $R^M2.1.3$). SEPP supports reusability these security patterns, by allowing the problem frames separately from security solution frames. However, this feature does not facilitate to specify when to start considering network infrastructure ($R^M3.2$). During our analysis, we had issues in identifying the all the acting domains in a network environment. This approach seemed to be more suitable if we had known the network design in hand. Furthermore, the constraints on the security requirements are expressed in terms of *pre-conditions* attribute. These are the formalized conditions that must be satisfied by the problem environment on prior, before applying the security problem frame. Similarly, the *post-conditions* attribute correspond to the formal expression of the security requirements (Fig. 67.7).

67.5   Conclusion and Future Work

The principle objective of this article is illustrate the instantiation of our evaluation approach to compare and study three SRE methodologies KAOS, STS and SEPP in network SRE context. Our empirical study show that none of the three SRE methodologies fulfils all the criteria. In particular, they did not satisfy any criteria related to the network security requirement analysis ($R^M3.2$, $R^M6.1$ and $R^M6.4$). It is to note that these evaluation results are purely confined to the context and therefore not to be considered as generalized. It means that the evaluation results could change with changing SRE context. Likewise, the performance measure of the criteria verification also differs with regards to the preferences of the security experts. However, there might be some generic characteristics (e.g., *feasibility*, *abstraction*, *comprehensibility*) that hold common interest of the requirement engineers despite their varying SRE context. Furthermore, our evaluation methodology can be applied to any number of

SRE methodologies. This might raise some concerns related to time and costs. In practice, once a SRE methodology is chosen, a lot of time and money is put to train the users and it is very unlikely that one would switch to new methodology soon. Therefore, from industrial usage perspective choosing the best suitable SRE methodology at earlier stages reduces overhead and saves time.

For future works, we would like to apply our evaluation approach to other security engineering contexts. This will help us to determine which evaluation criteria are generic and which are specific to security context. In the end, we intend to build a common repository (e.g., cloud based) that can help in maintaining the evaluation results carried out in different scenario contexts so that there will be no need to re-evaluate a SRE methodology for a similar context already considered in a previous evaluation. This repository can help build a solid foundation to propose future SRE research directions.

Acknowledgment This work is part of project IREHDO2 funded by DGA/DGAC. The authors thank the security experts at Airbus and the anonymous reviewers for their useful comments.

References

1. A. Van Lamsweerde, S. Brohez, R. De Landtsheer, D. Janssens, From system goals to intruder anti-goals: attack generation and resolution for security requirements engineering, in *Proceedings of the RE'03 Workshop on Requirements for High Assurance Systems (RHAS'03)*, Monterey (CA), Sept. 2003
2. M. Salnitri, E. Paja, P. Giorgini, From socio-technical requirements to technical security design: an sts-based framework, Technical report, DISI-University of Trento
3. D. Hatebur, M. Heisel, H. Schmidt, A pattern system for security requirements engineering, in *ARES 2007, the Second International Conference*
4. S.T. Bulusu, R. Laborde, F. Barrère, A. Benzekri, A. Samer Wazan, Which security requirements engineering methodology should I choose? Towards a requirements engineering-based evaluation approach, presented at the ARES'2017

5. S.T. Bulusu, R. Laborde, F. Barrère, A. Benzekri, A. Samer Wazan, Applying a requirement engineering based approach to evaluate the security requirements engineering methodologies, in *ACM SAC'2018 (To appear)* (Pau, France, 2018)
6. KAOS Tool—Objectiver: HomePage, http://www.objectiver.com/index.php?id=4
7. E. Paja, F. Dalpiaz, P. Giorgini, Sts-tool: Security requirements engineering for socio-technical systems, in *Engineering Secure Future Internet Services and Systems* (Springer, 2014), pp. 65–96
8. T.A. Kletz, *Hazop and Hazan: Identifying and Assessing Process Industry Hazards* (IChemE, 1999)

Alexandre Moreira Nascimento, Vinícius Veloso de Melo, Luiz Alberto Vieira Dias, and Adilson Marques da Cunha

Abstract

This paper reviews the main concepts related to software testing, its difficulties and the impossibility of a complete software test. Then, it proposes an approach to predict which module is defective, aiming to assure the usually limited software test resources will be wisely distributed to maximize the coverage of the modules most prone to defects. The used approach employs the recently proposed Kaizen Programming (KP) to automatically discover high-quality nonlinear combinations of the original features of a database to be used by the classification technique, replacing a human in the feature engineering process. Using a NASA open dataset with Software metrics of over 9500 modules, the experimental analysis shows that the new features can significantly boost the detection of detective modules, allowing testers to find 216% more defects than with a random module selection; this is also an improvement of 1% when compared to the original features.

Keywords

Machine learning · Feature engineering · Software defect prediction · Test effort · Software test

A. M. Nascimento (✉)
Department of Computer Science, Aeronautics Institute of Technology (ITA), Sao Jose dos Campos, Sao Paulo, Brazil

Institute of Science and Technology, Federal University of Sao Paulo (ICT-UNIFESP), Sao Jose dos Campos, Sao Paulo, Brazil

V. V. de Melo
Institute of Science and Technology, Federal University of Sao Paulo (ICT-UNIFESP), Sao Jose dos Campos, Sao Paulo, Brazil

L. A. V. Dias · A. M. da Cunha
Department of Computer Science, Aeronautics Institute of Technology (ITA), Sao Jose dos Campos, Sao Paulo, Brazil

68.1 Introduction

Over the years, software has been assuming a central role in our lives. In all verticals (industry sectors), software importance has been growing. Moreover, it is a core piece of the product quality and companies' productivity [1].

However, most of the released software has a considerable number of defects which affect their usability, security, and reliability. Those issues impact business and sometimes result in significant losses [2]. In fact, it is practically impossible to develop a first-time-right complex system based on software [1].

Any software, regardless of the testing [3] technologies used, has bugs. Some are detected and removed at development time. Others are found and repaired during formal testing. All software producers know that bugs remain in the software and that some of them will have to be fixed later [4]. Testing is a prerequisite for successful software implementation, but with the currently available testing technologies, it is often considered difficult, tedious, time-consuming, and inadequate. One study reported that bugs in end products cost the United States economy $ 59.2 billion per year [5], according to a study by the US Department of Commerce's Institute of Standards and Technology (NIST) [5].

Although the tests and the quality of the software are not synonymous, indeed the test quality level of software is a critical factor, among others, to define the quality of the final product, that depends on the process of development of this software [2].

Thus, a series of analytical measures should be made to evaluate the results of the different stages of development and detect the errors as early as possible. The test is the most important analytical technique, along with revisions and inspections. It is, however, a very sophisticated and time-consuming task, particularly in the field of embedded systems [1].

During the software development process, some activities seek to ensure the quality of the final product. Still, despite the methods, techniques, and tools used, product failures may occur. Thus, the test step, which represents one of the quality assurance activities, is of great importance for the identification and elimination of failures. Testing is an area of software engineering and aims to improve productivity and provide evidence of software reliability and quality in addition to other quality assurance activities throughout the software development process [6].

Tests consume 25–50% of the total budget on many development projects [7]. A test team consists of engineers who act as manual testers, tool users, and tool developers. Both the budget and the staff are important because the product under development must be tested as entirely as possible [7].

The big problem that exists is that maintenance performed on software already in production is performed within very tight time windows and under an intense pressure to update the version in operation. Accordingly, the time and resources required for a system regression test are often insufficient to ensure an adequate level of reliability to get the software up and running. In practice—and due to lack of a decision-making criterion to select the most relevant test cases—the tests performed are only the exploratory tests on the functionalities directly related to the maintenance performed, or even a structured test, more still considering only such functionalities. This scenario results in the use of an application with inadequate levels of reliability, generating an increasing frequency of errors and reducing the mean time between failures (MTBF). Finally, this scenario leads to an increasing volume of corrective maintenance, with even longer terms of pressures, what contributes more and more to accentuate such situation, results in a decreasing reliability of the software in question, and potential losses on the businesses supported by this system.

In order to improve software reliability, one may use software defect prediction to assist developers in the modules with the highest potential of defects so the testing efforts can be wisely and more efficiently allocated [8–10]. In fact, these predictors are useful for prioritizing a resource-bound exploration of code that has yet to be inspected [11] and to devote extra resources to faulty system parts [12]. Thus, the software defect prediction is an important decision support activity in software quality assurance for large and complex software systems, especially considering these defects usually behave according to the Pareto principle: the majority of defects, approximately 80%, are concentrated in a small proportion of system components (approximately 20%) [13, 14].

A software defect predictor can be a classifier induced by a machine learning (ML) algorithm on a set of metrics [15, 16] extracted from the source code [7, 8, 10]. These metrics are considered independent from each other, but they may be related. In [11], the authors state that researchers should not seek "best" subsets of static code attributes. Instead, they

should concentrate their efforts in combining multiple partial defect indicators. Hence, a researcher should investigate the metrics and propose new features to be used by the classifier. This is an expensive and time-consuming task that should be automated.

This paper proposes a method for defect prediction based on the recently proposed Kaizen Programming (KP) approach [17] to automatically discover high-quality nonlinear combinations of the original features of a database to be used by the classification technique, replacing a human in the feature engineering process. KP is an iterative approach focused on efficient problem-solving techniques that could come from Statistics, ML, Classical Artificial Intelligence (AI), Econometrics, or other related areas. For instance, KP has been used for predicting continuous values (regression task) with Ordinary Least Squares [18, 19] and categorical values (classification task) with Logistic Regression [20, 21], CART decision tree [22], and Random Forests [23]. Also, a greedy approach was developed for solving a control problem known as the virtual Lawn Mower [24]. KP is a valuable tool for helping to solve different machine learning problems, but it is the first time it is employed in the software testing topic.

This paper is organized as follows: Sect. 68.2 presents a background of software testing. Section 68.3 has the Materials and Methods. Results and discussion on the experimental analysis are presented in Sect. 68.4. Section 68.5 concludes the paper.

68.2 Background

68.2.1 Defects

Burnstein [1] states that errors are created even under the best development conditions, resulting in defects injected during the software life cycle phases. The defects come from the following sources: education, communication, carelessness, transcription, or process [1].

In this work, although the various definitions and differences are presented in the view of some authors, we consider the terms error, failure, defect, and bug, as synonymous for the same reasons stated by Beizer [25]. Another reason is that, because all of them, regardless of their taxonomy, lead the software to an undesired behavior.

Beizer [4] states that bugs are always more incidental than expected and that their importance depends on frequency, cost of repair, cost of installation, and consequences. The cost of correction is the sum of two factors, the cost of discovery and the cost of correction. This cost, according to Beizer [4], grows dramatically throughout the development cycle. Correction costs also depend on the size of the system, since the larger its cost, the higher the cost of correcting a single bug. The installation cost depends on the number of installations. Beizer [4] points out the possibility of the cost of fixing a single bug along with the distribution of this fix to exceed the cost of all system development. The consequences of the bug, according to Beizer [4] can be measured by the mean size of concessions made by juries to the victims of their error [4].

Frequency, according to Beizer [4], generally does not depend on the application or the environment; however, the costs of correction, installation, and consequences do. Consequences can be of 10 levels, from mild to infectious [4]: mild, moderate, annoying, disturbing, serious, very serious, extreme, intolerable, catastrophic, and infectious.

68.2.2 The Barrier of the Impossibility of the Complete Test

Several authors argue that it is impossible to test all possible conditions of a piece of software [4, 26]. Robert Binder [27] provides a good example that points to this impossibility. A simple 4-line program, shown below, contains only one wrong line, as shown next to it. This simple software on a 16-bit computer can accept 65,536 entries and, therefore, it would be possible to delineate 65,536 test cases [26].

```
int blech (int j) {
    j = j -1; // the correct code
        would be j = j + 1
    j = j / 30000;
    return j;
}
```

Table 68.1 shows 4 randomly selected test cases, the expected result if the software was correct, and the actual result obtained with its incorrect implementation [26].

Note that none of the test cases revealed the problem, and, as Copeland [26] states, only four test cases out of 65,536 can reveal the discrepancy. Given that in software of this size and complexity, 65,536 tests are unlikely to be performed, how likely is it to select one or more of the 4 correct test cases out of 65,536 possible? Myers [28], in his classic "The art of software testing", illustrates the impossibility of a complete test with another example. The author analyzes a supposedly simple application with 11 states and 15 transitions, where the transition from state X to A can occur no more than 20 times. In the analysis, this simple application has $5^1 + 5^2 + \ldots + 5^{19} + 5^{20} = 10^{14}$,

or rather 100 trillion paths through the program to be tested. If, according to the author, someone can write, run and check a test case every 5 min, this test would take around a billion years.

According to Beizer [4], there are three different approaches that can be used to demonstrate that a program is correct: function-based, structure-based, and formal compliance tests. Each one of them allows concluding that the complete test, in the philosophy of proving that the software is totally correct, is neither theoretically nor practically possible.

A complete functional test consists of subjecting the program to all possible inputs producing correct or incorrect behaviors or outputs. A simple 10-character input has 280 possible input combinations, which if each is tested in a microsecond time interval, the test will last twice the estimated age of the universe. Though, when it comes to structural testing, the idea is to exercise at least once each possible path through software routines. A small software routine can have millions or billions of possible paths, so a test of all paths is impractical [4].

Proof of compliance is based on a combination of functional and structural concepts. In this approach, an inductive proof examines each instruction of the program to verify that the routine will produce the correct output for any sequence of inputs, according to the specifications. However, notwithstanding the fact that such tests are very expensive and their application restricts to only numerical cases, Beizer [4] raises a more fundamental question: how can one know if the specification can be proved correctly? Even if one considers that this is possible, the mechanism used to prove the software, the steps in the test, the logic used, and so on, must be proven. Mathematicians and logicians are as error-free as programmers and testers. This leads to an endless sequence of unverifiable considerations [4].

Beizer [4] summarized the theoretical barriers to complete testing in (1) it is impossible to be sure that the specifications are correct; (2) no verification system can check the entire program; and (3) it is impossible to be sure that the verification system is correct.

Thus, Beizer [4] states that the goal is to provide sufficient testing to ensure that the probability of failure due to hibernating bugs is low enough to make the software acceptable. Nevertheless, what is acceptable for a computer game is insufficient for a control software of a nuclear reactor; therefore, each type of application has a different demand for tests due to the level of reliability required [4].

Broekman and Notenboom [1] recognize the existence of a universal rule that states that it is impossible to find all software defects, since there are never enough resources, such as time, people and money to test a software completely. In this way, Broekman and Notenboom [1] states that choices

Table 68.1 Inputs × actual outputs × expected outputs

Input (j)	Expected result	Actual result
1	0	0
42	0	0
40,000	1	1
−64,000	−2	−2

Source: Copeland [26]

should be made about how to distribute available resources intelligently.

De Young and Rätzmann [29] mention that for a long time the basis for the generation of test plans and metrics was the coverage of the functional properties and the coverage of the specifications. However, when researchers realized that these metrics could not be entirely tested, subsequent methods have been developed to discover redundancies in test cases and test data.

68.2.3 Paradoxes of Software Testing

Beizer [4] presents two paradoxes of software testing. The first is an analogy made to the farmer who uses different pesticides every year, because each pesticide used becomes inefficient next year, as the remaining pests are resistant to its effects. Similarly, the author states that each method used to prevent or find errors leaves a set of residual bugs against which these methods are inefficient and to combat it a variety of methods must be used. Still, he points out that this is not so bad since software is becoming increasingly better [4].

The other paradox is the barrier of complexity. Beizer [4] argues that the complexity of both software and bugs grows to the limit of our ability to deal with it. Beizer [4] explains that eliminating the easiest bugs moves to another scale of features and complexity, but this time there are more subtle bugs to deal with, just to maintain the reliability one had before.

Users always push development to the complexity barrier. How closely one can approach it is determined by the strengths of the techniques and the ability to use them against the most complex and subtle bugs [4].

A fundamental principle that can help guide test efforts is pointed out by Burnstein [30]. This principle states that the likelihood of additional defects in a software component is proportional to the number of defects already detected in this component.

68.2.4 The Reasons for the Difficulty of Software Testing

Fewster and Graham [31] affirm that software testing nowadays is more difficult. This is due to the variety of operating systems, programming languages and machine platforms, as well as the fact that, in the present times, most activities are supported in some way in the use of computers, unlike in the 1970s.

According to Craig and Jaskiel [32], other problems that make software testing so tricky are the incorrect and ambigu-

ous requirements in addition to the tight schedules, not to mention that often the testers are not adequately trained.

Hutcheson [33] presents the results of a study that quantifies this difficulty and describes two main reasons, in his view, of this situation. According to the results of this study, conducted in 1993 and 1994, 80–90% of the bugs found in production were found during the test and that approximately 60% of these errors were considered "hard to reproduce." The coverage of the tests was sufficient, but the test effort was not, since there were not enough resources to track these errors and correct them. The author also states that testing efforts usually do not fail because the bugs were not discovered, but instead because an unacceptable number of bugs remain in the product. The author affirms that one of the reasons some bugs are difficult to reproduce is that they exist only in specific environments, that may not be present in the software being tested, but rather in other environmentally friendly software such as the operating system or a database management system.

Another reason presented in [33], for which some bugs are difficult to reproduce, is that the systems where the software is running are large and with many users, hence, they cannot be considered a finite state machine. While the tester is performing the tests, other applications may be being used simultaneously, for example, a CD may be being played, an internet search for some document may be being performed, a word processor may be open for making notes, among other applications, all at the same time. When an error occurs, it is impossible to recreate the exact states in which the system was at the time the failure occurred [33].

68.2.5 Related Studies

Many different defect prediction models have been published [9–13, 34–52]. Size and complexity metrics are largely used in defect prediction models [34]. According to [35], the performances are reported to be similar, rarely performing above 80% of recall. A survey study found the fuzzy logic and McCabe based metrics to be better in handling the software fault prediction [36]. A systematic literature review including 106 papers (1991–2011) found the Object-oriented metrics (49%) were used nearly twice as often compared to traditional source code metrics (27%) or process metrics (24%), and they also have been reported to be more successful in finding faults compared to traditional size and complexity metrics [37].

In [38], NaiveBayes learners are better than entropy-based decision-tree learners when learning defect detectors from static code measures with the additional advantage of not needing more than 200–300 examples to learn adequate detectors. Rodriguez et al. [41] found in a literature review study that the main usage of the Bayesian concepts in the software testing field is through the application of Bayesian networks for software defect prediction based on static software metrics and Bayesian classifiers [41].

Other study's results indicate that the prediction performance of Support Vector Machine (SVM) is generally better than, or at least, is competitive against eight statistical and machine learning models in the context of four NASA datasets [9]. An investigation found ensemble methods produced improved performance for the prediction of number of software faults when compared to the single fault prediction technique [43].

Finally, [53] affirms that "size" and "complexity" metrics are not sufficient for accurately predicting real-time software defects while [11] states the debate about which feature is better is irrelevant since how the features are used to build predictors is much more important than which features are used, suggesting that researchers should combine the metrics. Thus, these are relevant finding to support the research done in this paper, which employs a computational technique to construct features.

68.2.6 Kaizen Programming

Kaizen Programming [17] is a recent algorithm based on the concepts of the Kaizen methodology [54], partially implementing a Kaizen event with Plan-Do-Check-Act (PDCA [55]) methodology to guide the continuous improvement process. PDCA is largely employed in industry and business to solve specific process issues.

In the Kaizen methodology, a team of experts is put together to investigate a standard procedure of performing a task and optimize it. During a kaizen event, modifications to solve the issue are planned, executed, checked, and new actions are taken based on the results obtained with the modifications. The cycle is repeated until the optimization the desired target result is obtained [54].

In this methodology, every action taken can be evaluated according to its effectiveness in helping to solve the issue [54]. Therefore, the team can acquire more knowledge on the problem at each cycle, which is used to avoid poor decisions and guide the search towards an increasingly better solution.

KP is a computational implementation of that cycle to solve a problem that can have its solution split into partial solutions [17]. KP has a set of procedures (the experts) with different strategies to generate more partial solutions that compose the standard. High-quality and high-efficiency statistical and machine learning methods are employed to measure the importance of each partial solution, considering both the current and the newly generated ones [17]. Finally, the most important solutions are chosen to be the new trial

standard. If the trial is better than the current standard, according to a quality measure, then the first replaces the later and a new cycle begins.

In this paper, partial solutions generated by KP are automatically engineered features. Each new feature is a formula using functions from a function set and the available original features (terminal set). For instance, supposing the function set F = {+, −} and the terminal set T = {A, B}, one could have a new feature X = (A + A) − B. Then, the classifier will use X, instead of A and B, to predict the response. The objective is to generate a new set of features that can have fewer features than the original dataset (dimensionality reduction) or more features (feature expansion). Because KP is stochastic, each run gives a different set of features.

68.3 Materials and Methods

This section presents experimental results of KP coupled with Logistic Regression to perform automatic feature engineering for classification. Later, we evaluate the new features with three popular classifiers: Logistic Regression, J48 (decision tree), and Random Forest (ensemble of decision trees).

68.3.1 Dataset

In this work, we investigate the well-known cleaned version of the NASA JM1 [56] dataset, because the data sets require significant pre-processing in order to be suitable for defect prediction [57]. It is a real-time predictive ground system which uses simulations to generate predictions. The source codes of the software are in C programming language, with 9593 modules and 18.33% of defects. There are 21 numerical features that come from McCabe and Halstead features extractors of source code (see Table 68.2). These features are an attempt to characterize code features that are associated with software quality: 5 different lines of code measure, 3 McCabe metrics, 4 base Halstead measures, 8 derived Halstead measures, a branch-count [58–61]. There are no missing values.

68.3.2 Implementation and Configuration of the Algorithms

KP was implemented in Python using DEAP (Distributed Evolutionary Algorithms in Python) [62] and the statsmodels package [63]. Multicollinearity is treated by first calculating the Pearson correlation coefficient among the new features and then looping over them. The loop keeps the first feature and drops the following ones that are highly correlated (>=0.8, empirically chosen) with the former.

Table 68.2 Descriptive statistics of the features in the dataset

Feature	Min	Mean	Median	Max	Std-dev
LOC_BLANK	0	5.05	3	447	10.13
BRANCH_COUNT	1	10.27	5	826	21.96
LOC_CODE_AND_COMMENT	0	0.41	0	108	2.01
LOC_COMMENTS	0	3.03	0	344	9.45
CYCLOMATIC_COMPLEXITY	1	5.83	3	470	12.86
DESIGN_COMPLEXITY	1	3.77	2	402	9
ESSENTIAL_COMPLEXITY	1	3.06	1	165	6.48
LOC_EXECUTABLE	0	28.39	15	2824	59.37
HALSTEAD_CONTENT	0	32.58	24.1	569.78	34.42
HALSTEAD_DIFFICULTY	0	15.54	10.42	418.2	18.72
HALSTEAD_EFFORT	0	38,736.2	2808.48	31,079,780	450,858
HALSTEAD_ERROR_EST	0	0.24	0.09	26.95	0.65
HALSTEAD_LENGTH	0	123.92	57	8441	251.05
HALSTEAD_LEVEL	0	0.15	0.09	1	0.16
HALSTEAD_PROG_TIME	0	2152.01	156.03	1,726,655	25047.67
HALSTEAD_VOLUME	0	725.09	263.64	80,843.08	1954.74
NUM_OPERANDS	0	50.18	23	3021	100.59
NUM_OPERATORS	0	73.74	34	5420	152.15
NUM_UNIQUE_OPERANDS	0	18.35	12	1026	26.91
NUM_UNIQUE_OPERATORS	0	12.36	11	411	9.74
LOC_TOTAL	1	39.28	21	3442	74.12

KP fits a regularized logistic regression model on the low-correlated features and the p-value gives the importance of each one. Then, KP fits another regularized logistic regression model on the most important features and evaluates it using the area under the ROC curve (AUC). We did run KP for a few times to optimize 50 features (we chose this amount empirically) during 100 cycles and selected the best run for analysis.

We evaluated the new features using the machine learning software Weka [64–66] to run the experiments in a $10\times$ ten-fold cross-validation approach, resulting in 100 validations. We tested the Logistic Regression (regularized), J48, and Random Forest algorithms with their default configuration and used a paired t-test (with correction) to compare the averages of three different quality measures: precision [44], recall [44], and AUC.

Table 68.3 Results of precision

Method	New data		Original data		Sig
	Mean	Std-dev	Mean	Std-dev	
Logistic regression	0.787	0.0166	0.781	0.0168	=
J48	0.769	0.0142	0.7703	0.014	=
Random forest	0.8053	0.0145	0.8007	0.0145	=

For the significance test, symbol "=" means that the results using both datasets are equivalent, ">" means that New data is better than Original data, and "<" means that original data is better than new data

Table 68.4 Results of recall

Method	New data		Original Data		Sig
	Mean	Std-dev	Mean	Std-dev	
Logistic regression	0.8228	0.0057	0.8207	0.0052	=
J48	0.8032	0.0112	0.8021	0.0099	=
Random forest	0.8319	0.0074	0.8295	0.0081	=

68.4 Results and Discussion

Tables 68.3, 68.4, and 68.5 show the results for Precision, Recall, and AUC, respectively. Recall is the ratio of the number of modules correctly predicted as defective (true positives) divided by the actual number of defective modules. Precision is the ratio of the number of modules correctly predicted as defective (true positives) divided by the total number of mod-

ules predicted as defective (true positives + false positives). Each table also presents the result of the significance test at a 5% level.

Although the methods achieve better performance with the new dataset generated by KP, the t-test shows no significant difference for the Precision and Recall measures. It is interesting that J48 had better Precision and AUC with the Original data, probably because of the default configuration.

Table 68.5 Results of AUC

Method	New data		Original data		Sig
	Mean	Std-dev	Mean	Std-dev	
Logistic regression	0.7266	0.0219	0.7052	0.0238	>
J48	0.6306	0.0318	0.6622	0.0307	<
Random forest	0.7667	0.0176	0.7595	0.0172	>

One could try to tune J48 parameters to obtain better performance in a future work.

As KP was configured to use Logistic Regression to optimize the AUC, it was expected that this configuration showed the larger improvement, which can be verified in Table 68.5. However, the best overall method was the Random Forest, confirming what is argued in [43].

In summary, the results demonstrate that the KP technique works as expected, i.e., KP can automatically discover features to improve the performance of classifiers.

Below, we show the five most important features of the dataset generated by KP (F_1 to F_5) out of 50 features. One may notice that most operations are algebraic, with a few constants. Features F_2 and F_3 are very similar, but F_3 has "NUM_OPERATORS –" in the denominator. Features F_4 and F_5 are much simpler than the previous ones, showing that KP can find high-quality features with different levels of complexity. It is important to remember that KP is unable to interpret equations; therefore, this task belongs to software engineers. For instance, the most important feature in this dataset uses no information about number of lines of code (LOC), which is in consonance with the results found in [11].

$$F_1 = \frac{\frac{CYCLOMATIC\_COMPLEXITY}{\frac{(-16.41 + BRANCH\_COUNT + NUM\_OPERANDS)}{3.0}} * \tanh(HALSTEAD\_CONTENT)}{NUM\_UNIQUE\_OPERATORS}$$

$$F_2 = \frac{(BRANCH\_COUNT + ESSENTIAL\_COMPLEXITY) * HALSTEAD\_LEVEL}{\left(\frac{\left(\frac{\frac{LOC\_TOTAL}{LOC\_CODE\_AND\_COMMENT}}{LOC\_COMMENTS - 60.77}\right) + \left(\frac{\tanh(NUM\_UNIQUE\_OPERANDS)}{\frac{HALSTEAD\_EFFORT}{CYCLOMATIC\_COMPLEXITY}}\right)}{3.0} + (\log(LOC\_CODE\_AND\_COMMENT))\right)}$$

$$F_3 = \frac{(BRANCH\_COUNT + ESSENTIAL\_COMPLEXITY) * HALSTEAD\_LEVEL}{NUM\_OPERATORS - \left(\frac{\left(\frac{\frac{LOC\_TOTAL}{LOC\_CODE\_AND\_COMMENT}}{LOC\_COMMENTS - 60.77}\right) + \left(\frac{\tanh(NUM\_UNIQUE\_OPERANDS)}{\frac{HALSTEAD\_EFFORT}{CYCLOMATIC\_COMPLEXITY}}\right)}{3.0} + (\log(LOC\_CODE\_AND\_COMMENT))\right)}$$

$$F_4 = \frac{(DESIGN\_COMPLEXITY - LOC\_COMMENTS)}{NUM\_UNIQUE\_OPERATORS} \qquad F_5 = \frac{\tanh(LOC\_BLANK)}{DESIGN\_COMPLEXITY}$$

The results indicate the proposed model could improve significantly the results of the available software test resources by suggesting a wiser allocation of the test effort. Here, the test effort is the ratio of the total number of modules predicted as defective (true positives + false positives) divided by the total number of modules in the dataset. So, using the same hypothetical scenario proposed

by Myers [28] where the whole test cycle for each test case would take 5 min, and considering each module requires only 1 test case for its validation, the total time required to test the 9593 modules would be 47,965 min or around 800 h. A tester working a journey of 8 h a day would need 100 days for executing it. So, considering the available resources are two testers for 10 days to execute the tests, they would be able to test only 1920 modules (20%). If the testers select the modules randomly, they would probably find around 352 modules with defect (18.33% of 1920 modules tested with defect). On the other hand, if they used the approach proposed in this paper, they would test 899 modules suggested by the model (KP + Random Forest), taking only 4.7 days (47% of the original available time). As a result, they would find 761 defective modules or 216% more than a random module selection. Therefore, the testers would spend half the resources to find twice the number of defective modules, what indicates the proposed approach can enhance the test effort distribution. If the testers did not use KP to prepare the data, but used Random Forest with the original data, they would spend 4.6 days to find 756 defective modules, which outperforms the random modules selection approach by 215%. Finally, considering this simple example, KP helped to find additional seven defective modules.

68.5   Conclusion and Future Works

Software has been taking an important role in our lives over the last decades. However, it has defects which impact business and result in significant losses. To reduce those issues, many software testing approaches have been developed using metrics and classifiers to identify potential defects in source codes. Researchers suggested combining these metrics in some way to improve the performance of classifiers. To do that, we investigated Kaizen Programming (KP) coupled with Logistic Regression to automatically extract useful combination of features from a widely studied software defect prediction dataset, aiming to improve the prediction performance of different classifiers.

The results presented in this paper show that KP works as expected, improving the performance of two popular classifiers with respect to the AUC metric. In fact, the proposed approach applied for test effort allocation outperformed the defect discovery rate of a test based on a random module selection by 216% requiring less than half the testing time.

This work contributes for the prediction of software defective modules research topic on achieving the level of metrics combination required by the software engineering community.

The authors recommend the use of metrics combination to improve the performance of classifiers instead of using metrics in an independent way.

As future work, it is intended to extend the analysis to other datasets and evaluate other classifiers. Also, it is important to verify whether the features generated for the JM1 dataset can improve the performance of classifiers on related datasets, meaning the discovered features are not dataset-specific.

References

1. B. Broekman, E. Notenboom, *Testing embedded software* (Pearson Education, 2003)
2. T.R. Moreira Filho, E. Rios, *Projeto & engenharia de software: teste de software* (Alta Books, Rio de Janeiro, 2003)
3. H. Reza, K. Ogaard, A. Malge, A model based testing technique to test web applications using statecharts, in *Fifth International Conference on Information Technology: New Generations (ITNG)* (2008), pp. 183–188
4. B. Beizer, *Software testing techniques* (New York, 1990)
5. S. Planning, *The economic impacts of inadequate infrastructure for software testing* (2002)
6. C. Inthurn, Qualidade & teste de software. Florianóp. Vis. (2001)
7. K. Li, M. Wu, *Effective Software Test Automation: Developing an Automated Software Testing Tool* (Wiley, 2006)
8. J. Li, P. He, J. Zhu, M.R. Lyu, Software Defect Prediction via Convolutional Neural Network, in *2017 IEEE International Conference on Software Quality, Reliability and Security (QRS)* (2017), pp. 318–328
9. K.O. Elish, M.O. Elish, Predicting defect-prone software modules using support vector machines. J. Syst. Softw. **81**, 649–660 (2008)
10. H. Zhang, X. Zhang, M. Gu, Predicting defective software components from code complexity measures, in *13th Pacific Rim International Symposium on Dependable Computing (PRDC)* (2007), pp. 93–96
11. T. Menzies, J. Greenwald, A. Frank, Data mining static code attributes to learn defect predictors. IEEE Trans. Softw. Eng. **33**(1), 2–13 (2007)
12. E. Arisholm, L.C. Briand, E.B. Johannessen, A systematic and comprehensive investigation of methods to build and evaluate fault prediction models. J. Syst. Softw. **83**(1), 2–17 (2010)
13. G. Mauša, T.G. Grbac, Co-evolutionary multi-population genetic programming for classification in software defect prediction: An empirical case study. Appl. Soft Comput. **55**, 331–351 (2017)
14. T.G. Grbac, P. Runeson, D. Huljenić, A second replicated quantitative analysis of fault distributions in complex software systems. IEEE Trans. Softw. Eng. **39**(4), 462–476 (2013)
15. M.J. Ordonez, H.M. Haddad, The state of metrics in software industry, in *Fifth International Conference on Information Technology: New Generations (ITNG)* (2008), pp. 453–458
16. S.G. Shiva, L.A. Shala, Software reuse: Research and practice, in *Fourth International Conference on Information Technology (ITNG'07)* (2007), pp. 603–609
17. V.V. De Melo, Kaizen Programming, in *Proceedings of the 2014 Conference on Genetic and Evolutionary Computation* (2014), pp. 895–902
18. V.V. de Melo, W. Banzhaf, Automatic feature engineering for regression models with machine learning: An evolutionary computation and statistics hybrid. Inf. Sci. **430**, 287–313 (2018)
19. V.V. de Melo, W. Banzhaf, Improving the prediction of material properties of concrete using kaizen programming with simulated annealing. Neurocomputing **246**, 25–44 (2017)
20. V.V. de Melo, Breast cancer detection with logistic regression improved by features constructed by Kaizen programming in a hybrid approach, in *2016 IEEE Congress on Evolutionary Computation (CEC)* (2016), pp. 16–23
21. V.V. de Melo, W. Banzhaf, Improving Logistic Regression Classification of Credit Approval with Features Constructed by Kaizen Programming, in *Proceedings of the 2016 on Genetic and Evolutionary Computation Conference Companion* (2016), pp. 61–62
22. V.V. de Melo, W. Banzhaf, Kaizen Programming for Feature Construction for Classification, in *Genetic Programming Theory and Practice XIII* (Springer, 2016), pp. 39–57

23. L.F.D.P. Sotto, R.C. Coelho, V.V de Melo, Classification of Cardiac Arrhythmia by Random Forests with Features Constructed by Kaizen Programming with Linear Genetic Programming, in *Proceedings of the 2016 on Genetic and Evolutionary Computation Conference* (2016), pp. 813–820

24. L.F.D.P. Sotto, V.V. de Melo, Solving the Lawn Mower problem with Kaizen Programming and λ-Linear Genetic Programming for Module Acquisition, in *Proceedings of the 2016 on Genetic and Evolutionary Computation Conference Companion* (2016), pp. 113–114

25. B. Beizer, Software is different. Ann. Softw. Eng. **10**(1), 293–310 (2000)

26. L. Copeland, *A practitioner's guide to software test design* (Artech House, 2004)

27. R.V. Binder, *Testing object-oriented systems: models, patterns, and tools* (Addison-Wesley Professional, 2000)

28. G.J. Myers, C. Sandler, T. Badgett, *The art of software testing* (Wiley, 2011)

29. M. Rätzmann, C. De Young, *Software testing and internationalization* (Lemoine International, Incorporated, 2003)

30. I. Burnstein, *Practical software testing: A process-oriented approach* (Springer Science & Business Media, 2006)

31. M. Fewster, D. Graham, *Software test automation* (Addison-Wesley Professional, 1999)

32. R.D. Craig, S.P. Jaskiel, *Systematic software testing* (Artech House, 2002)

33. M.L. Hutcheson, *Software testing fundamentals: Methods and metrics* (Wiley, 2003)

34. N.E. Fenton, M. Neil, A critique of software defect prediction models. IEEE Trans. Softw. Eng. **25**(5), 675–689 (1999)

35. D. Bowes, T. Hall, J. Petrić, Software defect prediction: Do different classifiers find the same defects? Softw. Qual. J., 1–28 (2017)

36. P. Ranjan, S. Kumar, U. Kumar, Software fault prediction using computational intelligence techniques: A survey. Indian J. Sci. Technol. **10**(18), 1–9 (2017)

37. D. Radjenović, M. Heričko, R. Torkar, A. Živkovič, D. Radjenovic, Software fault prediction metrics: A systematic literature review. Inf. Softw. Technol. **55**(8), 1397–1418 (2013)

38. T. Menzies, J. DiStefano, A. Orrego, R. Chapman, Assessing predictors of software defects, in *Proceedings of Workshop on Predictive Software Models* (2004)

39. Y. Zhou, H. Leung, Predicting object-oriented software maintainability using multivariate adaptive regression splines. J. Syst. Softw. **80**(8), 1349–1361 (2007)

40. C. Chang, C. Chu, Y. Yeh, Integrating in-process software defect prediction with association mining to discover defect pattern. Inf. Softw. Technol. **51**(2), 375–384 (2009)

41. D. Rodriguez, J. Dolado, J. Tuya, Bayesian concepts in software testing: An initial review, in *Proceedings of the 6th International Workshop on Automating Test Case Design, Selection and Evaluation* (2015), pp. 41–46

42. Z. Ali, M.A. Mian, S. Shamail, Knowledge-based systems improving recall of software defect prediction models using association mining. Knowl. Based Syst. **90**, 1–13 (2015)

43. S.S. Rathore, S. Kumar, Towards an ensemble based system for predicting the number of software faults. Expert Syst. Appl. **82**, 357–382 (2017)

44. T. Menzies, J.S. Di Stefano, How good is your blind spot sampling policy, in *Proceedings, Eighth IEEE International Symposium on High Assurance Systems Engineering* (2004), pp. 129–138

45. L. Kumar, S. Misra, S. Ku, An empirical analysis of the effectiveness of software metrics and fault prediction model for identifying faulty classes. Comput. Stand. Interfaces **53**(December 2016), 1–32 (2017)

46. R. Moussa, D. Azar, A PSO-GA approach targeting fault-prone software modules. J. Syst. Softw. **132**, 41–49 (2017)

47. S.S. Rathore, S. Kumar, Knowledge-based systems linear and nonlinear heterogeneous ensemble methods to predict the number of faults in software systems. Knowl. Based Syst. **119**, 232–256 (2017)

48. M.J. Siers, Z. Islam, Software defect prediction using a cost sensitive decision forest and voting, and a potential solution to the class imbalance problem. Inf. Syst. **51**, 62–71 (2015)

49. L. Tian, A. Noore, Evolutionary neural network modeling for software cumulative failure time prediction. Reliab. Eng. Syst. Saf. **87**(1), 45–51 (2005)

50. C. Catal, B. Diri, Investigating the effect of dataset size, metrics sets, and feature selection techniques on software fault prediction problem. Inf. Sci. **179**(8), 1040–1058 (2009)

51. C. Andersson, P. Runeson, A replicated quantitative analysis of fault distributions in complex software systems. IEEE Trans. Softw. Eng. **33**(5), 273 (2007)

52. C. Catal, B. Diri, A systematic review of software fault prediction studies. Expert Syst. Appl. **36**(4), 7346–7354 (2009)

53. V.U.B. Challagulla, F.B. Bastani, I. Yen, R.A. Paul, Empirical assessment of machine learning based software defect prediction techniques, in *10th IEEE International Workshop on Object-Oriented Real-Time Dependable Systems (WORDS)* (2005), pp. 263–270

54. M. Imai, *Kaizen (Ky'zen), the Key to Japan's Competitive Success* (McGraw-Hill, 1986)

55. H. Gitlow, S. Gitlow, A. Oppenheim, R. Oppenheim, *Tools and Methods for the Improvement of Quality* (Taylor & Francis, 1989)

56. T. Menzies, M. Shepperd et al., "jm1." Dec 2004

57. D. Gray, D. Bowes, N. Davey, Y. Sun, B. Christianson, The misuse of the NASA metrics data program data sets for automated software defect prediction, in *15th Annual Conference on Evaluation & Assessment in Software Engineering (EASE)* (2011), pp. 96–103

58. T.J. McCabe, A complexity measure. *IEEE Trans. Softw. Eng.* **2**(4), 308–320 (1976)

59. T.J. McCabe, C.W. Butler, Design complexity measurement and testing. Commun. ACM **32**(12), 1415–1425 (1989)

60. M.H. Halstead, Toward a theoretical basis for estimating programming effort, in *Proceedings of the 1975 Annual Conference* (1975), pp. 222–224

61. J.E. Gaffney Jr, Metrics in software quality assurance, in *Proceedings of the ACM'81 Conference* (1981), pp. 126–130

62. F.-A. Fortin, F.-M. De Rainville, M.-A. Gardner, M. Parizeau, C. Gagné, {DEAP}: Evolutionary algorithms made easy. J. Mach. Learn. Res. **13**, 2171–2175 (2012)

63. S. Seabold, J. Perktold, Statsmodels: Econometric and statistical modeling with python, in *Proceedings of the 9th Python in Science Conference*, vol. 57 (2010), p. 61

64. Weka Machine Learning Project, Weka. University of Waikato

65. G. Holmes, A. Donkin, I.H. Witten, Weka: A machine learning workbench, in *Proceedings of the 1994 Second Australian and New Zealand Conference on Intelligent Information Systems* (1994), pp. 357–361

66. M. Hall, E. Frank, G. Holmes, B. Pfahringer, P. Reutemann, I.H. Witten, The WEKA data mining software: An update. SIGKDD Explor. Newsl. **11**(1), 10–18 (2009)

Part VII

High Performance Computing Architectures

NSF Noyce Recruitment and Mentorship

Fangyang Shen, Janine Roccosalvo, Jun Zhang, Yanqing Ji, Yang Yi, and Lieselle Trinidad

Abstract

This research discusses the detailed experiences of recruitment and training of Noyce interns to become qualified STEM teachers. In this paper, both successful experiences and challenges in the first 4 years of a NSF Noyce project are discussed with the three-tier model. In addition, this model has proven to be effective by using two types of evidences. First, the survey data collected from over 25 STEM teacher candidates is described. Secondly, the actual interview data and student feedback are reported.

Keywords

Noyce · STEM · STEM Teacher Education

69.1 Introduction

In 2011, President Obama stressed the importance of acquiring more Science, Technology, Engineering and Mathematics (STEM) teachers across the nation. One of President Obama's objectives was to train 100,000 new STEM teachers over the next decade [3]. The National Science Foundation

F. Shen (✉) · J. Roccosalvo
Department of CST, NYC College of Technology (CUNY), Brooklyn, NY, USA
e-mail: fshen@citytech.cuny.edu

J. Zhang
Department of Math and CS, University of Maryland, Eastern Shore, Princess Anne, MD, USA

Y. Ji
Department of ECE, Gonzaga University, Spokane, WA, USA

Y. Yi
Department of ECE, Virginia Tech, Blacksburg, VA, USA

L. Trinidad
Department of MAE, University at Buffalo, Buffalo, NY, USA

along with 28 other organizations have funded programs to recruit and train more STEM educators. The National Science Foundation created the Robert Noyce Teacher Scholarship Program to recruit highly talented Science, Technology, Engineering and Mathematics major students and train them to become STEM teachers in K-12 grades, especially for high-need schools and communities. Both New York City College of Technology (City Tech) and Borough of Manhattan Community College (BMCC) collaborated to implement this project.

The goals of the NSF Noyce Project (NEST Project) at City Tech and BMCC in 5 years are to create a new STEM teacher preparation pathway and to produce a total of 600 Noyce interns and summer program students and 25 STEM teachers. In the past few years, the Noyce project continued to use a variety of strategies to recruit highly qualified and dedicated students and provide training and mentorships. Multiple recruitment activities were conducted to motivate new applicants to pursue a career in STEM teaching and facilitate the transition of BMCC Noyce students to City Tech. This consisted of a year-round effort with mini workshops at both colleges with guest speakers, monthly information sessions about the program and advertisement of the Noyce project. Information sessions featured an overview of the project's objectives along with several other recruitment activities. New York State teacher certification requirements were discussed with applications and flyers readily available for students. Other recruitment techniques included the use of the digital-platform Open Lab on City Tech's web page, emails, computer labs, STEM clubs and student-teaching oriented workshops.

The Noyce internship program served as an effective scholar production mechanism. The three-tiered recruitment strategy helped identify and train the best interns to proceed to become qualified Noyce scholars. One of the main objectives of the Noyce scholarship is to mentor students who are interested in teaching STEM and for them to complete observation and fieldwork hours which will give them the

© Springer International Publishing AG, part of Springer Nature 2018
S. Latifi (ed.), *Information Technology – New Generations*, Advances in Intelligent Systems and Computing 738,
https://doi.org/10.1007/978-3-319-77028-4_69

necessary experience to become successful STEM teachers. Scholarship candidates were those City Tech and BMCC interns who demonstrated a zeal for STEM education, determination and high academic achievement. As interns are in the process of transitioning to scholars, they are carefully evaluated by a set of selection criteria. Upon acceptance, scholars are closely mentored toward their induction into the teaching workforce.

The rest of this paper is organized as follows: Sect. 69.2 reviews the literature for this topic; Sect. 69.3 introduces the detailed experiences of recruitment and training of interns to become successful STEM teachers during the phases of the Robert Noyce Teacher Scholarship Program; Sect. 69.4 presents the survey results, Noyce scholar interview data and student feedback; Sect. 69.5 summarizes the findings of this study and discusses possible directions for future research.

69.2 Literature Review

According to [1, 2], one of the main challenges facing STEM education today in the United States is to recruit and retain more STEM teachers. Therefore, it is significant to develop strong STEM teacher preparation programs throughout the nation.

In [3], the White House made an effort to dramatically change this situation in STEM education. The Obama Administration announced an aggressive plan to prepare 100,000 excellent Math and Science teachers by 2020.

On the federal level, such as with the National Science Foundation, there is a reputable program called the NSF Noyce Program [4] which will also contribute to the White House's teacher training goal by 2020. The National Science Foundation's Robert Noyce Teacher Scholarship Program seeks to encourage talented Science, Technology, Engineering and Mathematics majors and professionals to become K-12 STEM teachers.

There are some existing examples of STEM teacher recruitment and retention programs such as [5]. It describes a STEM teacher recruiting and training practice developed through the Talented Teachers in Training for Texas (T4) program.

In [6], this paper discusses the foundation built to better prepare teachers in STEM, specifically in Science and Math. Students participated in fieldwork internships at a school which integrated content learned from their university as well. As a result, students gained experience and confidence from their internships which effectively prepared them to become future STEM teachers.

Craig et al. [7] focused on the methods of training in one of the Noyce projects. As part of their training, students interned as camp counselors and teaching assistants in the summer for a high-needs middle school. Students also participated in professional development and an interactive physics course. This paper overall stresses the significance of both formal and informal education to train and retain STEM teachers.

In [8], this research presents the implementation details of a Noyce project that has been successful in STEM teacher education. The results of the project proved that the project management applied was effective. Over ten Noyce scholars who participated in the program resulted in becoming qualified STEM educators.

As a result of the above methods taken from [5–7], none were able to provide a complete and comprehensive solution to efficiently recruit and train students interested in STEM education to becoming effective STEM teachers.

Based on [8], the three-tiered structure was further investigated and proved to be effective in recruiting and training STEM major students to become STEM teachers. New research in this paper specifically describes the detailed experiences of recruitment and training of interns during the phases of the Robert Noyce Teacher Scholarship Program. After applying the three-tier model, a high percentage of qualified Noyce scholars were successfully retained to become STEM teachers.

69.3 Noyce Recruitent and Mentorship

STEM teacher shortages persist throughout the nation, especially in high-needs schools and communities. The Robert Noyce Teacher Scholarship Program at City Tech and BMCC has designed a three-tier model that designates potential scholars as Noyce Explorers, continues to support a selected cohort as Noyce Scholars and continues to give professional support as they become Noyce Teachers. The Noyce project team includes five faculty members from STEM fields, three faculty members from education fields and a professional external Noyce program evaluator. To supply the growing demand and reduce turnover, the Noyce project will specifically foster the development of Mathematics and Technology teachers and learners in New York City.

The experience of recruitment and training of interns to become successful STEM teachers during the phases of the Robert Noyce Teacher Scholarship Program has had several positive outcomes from implementing the Noyce project at City Tech and BMCC.

First, a solid framework was established which consists of a three-tiered Noyce model. This is an efficient recruitment strategy to recruit and retain high quality STEM teachers.

Tier I is designated for Noyce Explorers. Students enrolled in associate degree STEM programs who have a passion for teaching are encouraged to apply to become Noyce Explorers. Noyce Explorers participate in paid internship placements, the Noyce Explorers Summer Program and various workshop seminars. For the internships, students are placed in New York City high schools, middle schools and/or with City Tech and BMCC faculty mentors. Strong partnerships were built and maintained among local schools and college faculty mentors to accommodate our interns.

In the Noyce Explorers Summer Program, students are provided with experiential-based learning and enrichment activities that include both STEM and Education training.

Tier II is designated for Noyce Scholars. Noyce Scholars are mostly selected from current Noyce Explorers. Noyce Scholars are third and fourth year undergraduates enrolled in a STEM baccalaureate program at City Tech and take courses in the Mathematics Education or Career and Technical Teacher Education program. Scholars receive a scholarship of $16K per year. The main goal in this phase is to train scholars to become qualified STEM teachers. They participate in teaching internships and mentorships. For mentorship, the Noyce project team members worked collaboratively to guide and facilitate the learning of Noyce scholars. Scholars are involved in a teaching-oriented project in a STEM discipline under the supervision of their mentors. Scholars are required to attend several Noyce activities such as information sessions, individual mentorship meetings, STEM workshops, peer tutoring, STEM research project presentations and Noyce social events.

Tier III is the final phase where Noyce Scholars become Noyce Teachers. After graduating from a baccalaureate program, Noyce Scholars are qualified to apply for an initial teacher certificate in New York State which will allow them to teach in a STEM field. After receiving initial certification, Scholars are required to teach for 2 years in a high-needs school district for each year of support from the Robert Noyce Teacher Scholarship Program.

Second, there is a solid filtering system for recruitment where only the top students from both City Tech and BMCC are chosen for this program. Students are selected not solely based on high GPAs, but also by further looking at the complete profile of each candidate. Most importantly, students must display a genuine interest in STEM teaching. As a result of great efforts made by the project team, BMCC Noyce interns who demonstrated excellence are in the process of being transferred to City Tech and will participate in City Tech's Noyce Scholarship Program. During the Noyce Scholarship application process, students were evaluated and interviewed by the Noyce recruitment committee from both BMCC and City Tech. Multiple faculty members form a Noyce recruitment committee and collaborate to make a final decision on each scholarship and intern candidate. Faculty members are from highly diverse backgrounds in both STEM and Education. As a result, two of the Noyce students were impressively selected as the City Tech's Salutatorians in June 2015 and June 2017.

Third, management is systematic and effective. The quality of the Noyce scholarship program has continued to develop and improve. The harmonious collaboration between City Tech, BMCC and local school districts created a solid administrative environment and maximized the efficiency of the project management. Overall, a strong foundation was built for the continued growth and improvement of the Noyce project.

Fourth, the Noyce project at City Tech and BMCC is well-known. This conveys that advertisement is effective which allows more elite students to be recruited. Various recruitment activities were conducted to facilitate the transition of BMCC Noyce students to City Tech. The recruitment process of interns and scholars consisted of a year-round open application process which helped acquire a larger pool of candidates. Mini workshops and information sessions were held to motivate new applicants to pursue a career in STEM teaching. Each Fall and Spring semester, more than four information sessions were hosted at City Tech and BMCC, featuring an overview of the project's objectives along with recruitment activities, flyers and applications. During the information sessions, PowerPoint presentations and motivational speeches were given by professors which resulted in hundreds of applicants per year. Teacher certification requirements in Technology Education and Math Education were reviewed. Noyce interns and scholars were also invited as guest speakers to share and reflect upon their classroom experiences. After the information sessions, attendees received follow-up emails which confirmed their participation and provided guidance and support on how to proceed.

Fifth, in the last few years, the program has continued to be modified by making necessary minor changes to resolve problems that have arisen. For example, interns used to only participate for one semester before applying for the Noyce scholarship. Now, interns participate for more than one semester to be better trained for the Noyce scholarship. In addition, the best practices of other Noyce projects have been adopted from annual NSF Noyce Summits.

Moreover, feedback from the students and program evaluator are used to make any adjustments needed to improve the program management. Specifically, feedback is obtained from surveys and student interviews from the program evaluator. The feedback conveys that students are gaining knowledge from the internships and summer programs which has allowed them to become better Noyce scholars.

Finally, high-quality Noyce scholars have successfully been retained and committed to the Technology Teacher Education and Math Education program. The number of Noyce scholars grew from 1 to 5 in the second year and from 5 to 8 in the third year and from 8 to 13 in the fourth year.

There have also been some challenges while implementing the Noyce project.

First, it would be useful to extend the mentorship. The budget is limited, there is not enough professors to contribute enough hours to help mentor students. A solution could be finding more professors who would like to volunteer their extra time to mentor students or asking existing professors to add more hours to virtually mentor students. If professors were able to mentor a couple of hours more per week via Skype, this would help students to better reach their teaching potential.

Secondly, the use of timesheets by the students has not been effective, to maintain accuracy of the reported hours, an electronic software system may need to be established instead. An electronic software system such as Doodle can provide teachers a way to give feedback about the students to the Noyce project. One of the challenges of the handwritten timesheets has been that students may be able to alter the timesheets by themselves. In addition, an evaluation report for teachers to fill out about interns can help the Noyce project be more involved with the internships provided.

Third, there is much competition with several other internship programs to recruit top students. There has been some difficulty to recruit and retain high-quality Noyce scholars to become STEM educators. Some Noyce scholar candidates may change their minds about teaching and pursue other careers instead. One successful strategy has been having Noyce scholars referred from other current students in the program, so they have a clearer understanding of the program as a whole. In the process of Noyce scholars to become Noyce teachers, they need to be provided with a stronger support network which will increase their confidence in the teaching workforce.

69.4 Survey and Interview Results

The Noyce Explorers and Scholars were surveyed at the end of each semester. The survey consisted of about 20 questions. The overall feedback about the Noyce program and the students' personal experiences with the program continues to remain positive. Figures 69.1 and 69.2 below illustrate three vital questions of the survey from Spring 2017 that reflect the content of this paper.

The survey results of the questions in Figs. 69.1 and 69.2 show that most of the interns are confident and inspired about teaching and learning. The internship experiences along with the individual mentorships have prepared them with essential skills that will greatly help for their future teaching careers in STEM.

To sustain the excellence of the Noyce program, some direct feedback has been collected about the program implementation from the students in the survey. Some of the direct quotes from student surveys were as follows. "I am very happy for the opportunity and experience I gained." "It was great having an opportunity to actually help students understand and learn and make a difference." "I learned a lot by working with students and gained insights of pedagogical

Fig. 69.1 Assisting student learning. Question—After completing my internship, I am more comfortable presenting topics to students

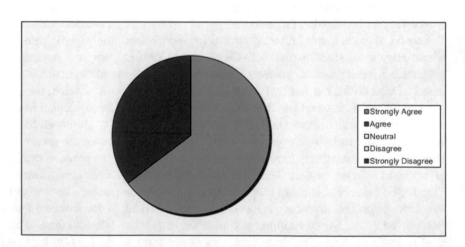

Answer Options	Response Percent	Response Count
Strongly Agree	64.7%	11
Agree	35.3%	6
Neutral	0.0%	0
Disagree	0.0%	0
Strongly Disagree	0.0%	0
	answered question	17
	skipped question	1

Fig. 69.2 Motivating student learning. Question—After completing my internship, I have more confidence in my ability to help motivate students to learn

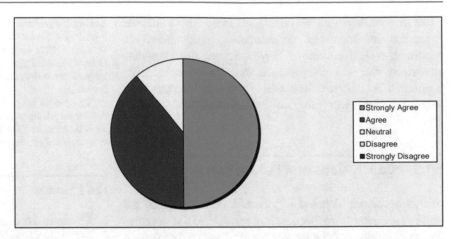

Answer Options	Response Percent	Response Count
Strongly Agree	50.0%	9
Agree	38.9%	7
Neutral	11.1%	2
Disagree	0.0%	0
Strongly Disagree	0.0%	0
	answered question	18
	skipped question	0

ways that we can use for the students. Students obtain knowledge in different ways that we need to pay a lot of attention to in keeping them at the same pace." "What a wonderful experience." "I enjoyed this program and I hope that future students will have this opportunity." "Thank you for the opportunity. I learned a lot from both the professor and students."

The above quotes further convey that the students of the Noyce program are impressed and excited to be a part of the experience. Students expressed that this program was both highly motivating and educational. They acquired knowledge about STEM education not only from observations, but from working collaboratively with their peers, mentors and students in middle school and high school classrooms, too.

Overall, students strongly agreed that they have benefitted greatly from this program. They have improved both their teaching and learning skills of students. They have been given the opportunity to critique and reflect upon their own learning as well. After completing the internships, students gained a significant amount of instructional experience and were better able to have a positive impact on student learning.

In June 2017, three Noyce students were interviewed by the external program evaluator during the summer program. The student interviews were reported as follows.

Noyce Student 1 was a female Noyce intern. She started the Noyce program in 2014 and graduated from BMCC with an Associate's Degree in Mathematics in 2015. She was referred to the program by a BMCC professor. She worked at City Polytechnic High School for three semesters tutoring students in Algebra 1, Algebra 2 and Geometry.

Her goal is to teach high school students in New York City and start on a Master's degree in education. With regards to the Noyce summer program, she thought the material was excellent and would recommend it to other students. She already influenced one friend to participate. She liked the assignments, group work and discussions. These activities are all helping her to become a better listener. She wants to be the kind of teacher that makes her students enjoy working hard.

Noyce Student 2 was a female Noyce intern. She started at BMCC taking ESL classes and was referred to the program by a friend. She wants to be a teacher and will also transfer this year from BMCC to City Tech. She would like to teach Algebra at a middle school or high school. With regards to the Noyce summer program, she loved the passion of the instructors and students. She learned how to see the core of a problem, and she understood that teaching is harder than learning and would enhance learning. What she liked most about it were the summer program topics and the passion of the instructors.

Noyce Student 3 was a female Noyce scholar. She wanted to teach computer courses in the United States, but financial aid has been an issue. Noyce along with the scholarship provided her salvation. She will look for a teaching job after she graduates. With regards to the Noyce summer program, she learned to give students time to process questions and enjoyed the opportunity to work with other students. The workshops have increased her interest in becoming a STEM teacher. This student was extremely grateful for the opportunity the program has provided.

After completing the workshop, all three Noyce students expressed an increased understanding and interest in becoming STEM educators. Noyce student interview data confirmed the effectiveness of the Noyce scholarship program and Noyce internship program which were based on the solid program management and strong mentorship.

69.5 Conclusions and Future Work

In this paper, the detailed experiences of recruitment and training of interns to become successful STEM teachers during the phases of the Robert Noyce Teacher Scholarship Program were discussed. There have been several positive outcomes along with some challenges from implementing the Noyce project at City Tech and BMCC. In addition, survey results, interview data and student feedback and experiences about the Noyce project were presented and conducted. The results conveyed that the program is highly effective and could be applied to many other similar projects nationwide. For future work, we plan to continue to improve the three-tiered model structure and continue to modify and collect more experiences and meaningful results for the Noyce project which could greatly contribute to future STEM education research.

Acknowledgments This work is supported by the National Science Foundation (Grant Number: NSF 1340007, $1,418,976, Jan. 2014-Dec. 2018, PI: Fangyang Shen; Co-PI: Mete Kok, Annie Han, Andrew Douglas, Estela Rojas, Lieselle Trinidad, Hon Jie Teo, Project Manager: Janine Roccosalvo, Program Assistant: Kendra Guo, Nanase Akagami, Ivy Mei).

The Noyce project team would also like to thank Prof. Gordon Snyder for his help on the project's evaluation. We also want to thank all faculty and staffs at both City Tech and BMCC who have helped and supported our Noyce project in the past 5 years.

References

1. J. Rothwell, Short on STEM Talent, US NEWS, Sept 2014
2. The STEM Crisis, https://www.nms.org
3. R. Weiss, Obama Administration Announces New Steps to Meet President's Goal of Preparing 100,000 STEM Teachers, Office of Science and Technology Policy Executive Office of the President, Mar 2013
4. Robert Noyce Teacher Scholarship Program Solicitation NSF 16-559, National Science Foundation, Sept 2016
5. H. Keith et al., A university approach to improving STEM teacher recruitment and retention. Kappa Delta Pi Record **51**(2), 69–74 (2015)
6. E. Eckman, M. Silver-Thorn, M. Williams, An integrated model for STEM teacher preparation: the value of a teaching cooperative educational experience. J. STEM Teach. Educ. **51**(I) (2016)
7. C. Craig, P. Evans, D. Stokes, *Developing STEM Teachers through both Informal and Formal Learning Experiences* (Ediciones Universidad de Salamanca, 2017)
8. F. Shen, J. Roccosalvo et al., *A New Approach for STEM Teacher Scholarship Implementation*, vol. 558 (Springer, 2017), pp. 659–666

Mining Associations Between Two Categories Using Unstructured Text Data in Cloud

Yanqing Ji, Yun Tian, Fangyang Shen, and John Tran

Abstract

Finding associations between itemsets within two categories (e.g., drugs and adverse effects, genes and diseases) are very important in many domains. However, these association mining tasks often involve computation-intensive algorithms and a large amount of data. This paper investigates how to leverage MapReduce to effectively mine the associations between itemsets within two categories using a large set of unstructured data. While existing MapReduce-based association mining algorithms focus on frequent itemset mining (i.e., finding itemsets whose frequencies are higher than a threshold), we proposed a MapReduce algorithm that could be used to compute all the interestingness measures defined on the basis of a 2×2 contingency table. The algorithm was applied to mine the associations between drugs and diseases using 33,959 full-text biomedical articles on the Amazon Elastic MapReduce (EMR) platform. Experiment results indicate that the proposed algorithm exhibits linear scalability.

Keywords

Association mining · MapReduce · Cloud computing

Y. Ji (✉)
Department of Electrical and Computer Engineering, Gonzaga University, Spokane, WA, USA
e-mail: ji@gonzaga.edu

Y. Tian
Department of Computer Science, Eastern Washington University, Cheney, WA, USA

F. Shen
Department of Computer System Technology, New York City College of Technology, Brooklyn, NY, USA

J. Tran
Frontier Behavioral Health, Spokane, WA, USA
e-mail: jtran@smhca.org

70.1 Introduction

Investigating the associations between itemsets within two categories (e.g., drugs and diseases) is often a fundamental research objective in many domains such as biomedicine. That is, researchers are interested in the strength of association between an itemset belonging to one category and a different itemset belonging to another category. Various interestingness measures and algorithms have been developed to find the associations between any two itemsets [1, 2]. Apriori [3] and FP-growth [4] represent the two most well known association mining algorithms in the literature.

Association mining tasks are computation-intensive. Given d items, 2^d number of itemsets could be generated, which is the sum of the number of combinations of d items, $d - 1$ items, $d - 2$ items, ... 2 items, and 1 item (i.e., $\sum_{i=1}^{d} C_d^i$). Association mining is also data-intensive as it often involves large amount of data. We are interested in mining associations using biomedical articles. Pubmed [5] represents the most influential database in the biomedical field. It contains more than 24 million articles and approximately 10,000 articles are added to the database every week.

Parallel programming becomes a necessity to deal with computation-intensive and data-intensive problems. MapReduce represents a parallel programming paradigm proposed for processing large-scale datasets on clusters of computers [6]. There are several studies that attempt to adapt MapReduce to association mining tasks [7–10]. These studies focus on mining frequent itemsets whose frequencies are larger than a threshold. All of them use k MapReduce phases where k depends on applications and can be large. Most of them scan the database by k times. In addition, none of them deals with unstructured data and examines associations between itemsets within two categories.

MapReduce has been utilized to process large volume of data in different application domains [11]. However, there exist few works on the application of MapReduce in

© Springer International Publishing AG, part of Springer Nature 2018
S. Latifi (ed.), *Information Technology – New Generations*, Advances in Intelligent Systems and Computing 738,
https://doi.org/10.1007/978-3-319-77028-4_70

biomedical association mining. In this study, we attempted to mine the associations between biomedically meaningful items from unstructured texts in biomedical literatures, even though our algorithm can also be easily adapted to unstructured texts in other areas.

We have developed a MapReduce algorithm to mine the associations between any two biomedically meaningful concepts based on massive amount of free-text data [12, 13]. Our previous work focuses on associations between two single items (i.e., itemset size is equal to 1). Finding the associations between items within two categories relies on post-processing after obtaining all the associations. In this study, we handle itemsets with any size. In addition, categorizing items is integrated into the algorithm and make the association mining results relate to two categories only.

The uniqueness and advantages of this study are summarized below:

- Our implementation can be applied to any interesting measures defined on the basis of a 2×2 contingency table.
- Our algorithm only scans the dataset one time instead of k times.
- We employ a stripes approach to reduce the number of MapReduce phases. More details about this approach will be discussed in Sect. 70.3.
- We deal with large-scale unstructured text data in documents or articles and are interested in the finding the associations between itemsets within two categories.

70.2 Problem Formalization

We are interested in finding association rules within two categories from unstructured text data. Let $S = \{d_1, d_2, \cdots, d_m\}$ be a set of documents or articles and $T = \{t_1, t_2, \cdots, t_n\}$ be a set of unique terms found in the documents in S, where each term can be a word or phase in a sentence. We consider each term as an item and use term and item interchangeably in the following discussions. In the context of this study, an association rule is an implication expression in the form of $X \rightarrow Y$, where $X \subset I$, $Y \subset I$, $X \in C_X$, $Y \in C_Y$, and $X \cap Y = \varnothing$. X and Y represent two itemsets, each of which may contain one or more items. C_X and C_Y indicate two categories in a particular domain. An association rule indicates that the presence of X implies the presence of Y.

Most existing MapReduce algorithms proposed for association mining focus on finding frequent itemsets whose support is larger than a threshold, where support is defined as the fraction of transactions that contain an itemset. To more effectively assess the degree of association between X and Y, researchers have proposed dozens of interestingness measures [1]. Most of them are based on the frequency

Table 70.1 A 2×2 contingency table for X and Y

	X	$\overline{X}$	
Y	f_{XY}	$f_{\overline{X}Y}$	f_Y
$\overline{Y}$	$f_{X\overline{Y}}$	$f_{\overline{X}\overline{Y}}$	$f_{\overline{Y}}$
	f_X	$f_{\overline{X}}$	N

counts tabulated in a 2×2 contingency table as shown in Table 70.1. In this study, we attempt to develop a MapReduce algorithm for association mining where the associations are evaluated by this group of interestingness measures whose computations depend on the 2×2 contingency table.

In Table 70.1, we use the notation $\overline{X}\left(\overline{Y}\right)$ to specify that $X(Y)$ is absent from a document. Each entry f indicates a frequency count. For example, $f_{X\overline{Y}}$ is the number of documents that contain X but not Y. In this table, $f_X = f_{XY} + f_{X\overline{Y}}$ and $f_Y = f_{XY} + f_{\overline{X}Y}$, which represent the number of documents that contain X and Y, respectively. N represents the total number of documents in a dataset S. Our task is to efficiently find the values of four entries f_{XY}, $f_{X\overline{Y}}$ and $f_{\overline{X}\,\overline{Y}}$ using the MapReduce paradigm given a large set of documents S.

70.3 MapReduce Algorithm Design

The MapReduce model simplifies the parallel and distributed programming into two phases: map and reduce, where two methods Map ( ) and Reduce ( ) need to be defined, respectively. Figure 70.1 presents the pseudo-code of our Map ( ) method. To assist the following descriptions of our algorithm, we assume the input is an example dataset that only contains two small documents, d_1 and d_2. The MapReduce framework guarantees that each document is processed by one mapper, a worker that is assigned a map task. Figure 70.2 gives the input (i.e., the two documents) and output of the Map ( ) method. We use x_i and y_j to represent an item in a document that belongs to category C_X and C_Y, respectively. The notation z_k represents an item that does not belong to category C_X or C_Y. The first loop (lines 4–10) in the Map ( ) reads each item in a document, checks whether it belongs to category C_X or C_Y, and, for each category, generates a list of itemsets, where each itemset only have one item (i.e., itemset size is 1). That is, $<x_2\,x_1>$ and $<y_1>$ will be generated for document d_1. Line 12 and 13 lexicographically sorts the two lists. Thus, the two lists will be transformed to $<x_1\,x_2>$ and $<y_1>$, assuming that the subscript of an item represents its lexicographical order. This step makes sure that, when itemsets with size $k + 1$ are generated on the basis of itemsets with size k by calling the *createNewItemsets* ( ) method, the items with lower lexicographical order will always precede the items with higher order. This avoids the possibility of generating duplicate itemsets whose items simply have

```
1: method MAP(docid id, doc d)
2:     ItemsetsOfSize1_X ⟵ new ArrayList;
3:     ItemsetsOfSize1_Y ⟵ new ArrayList;
4:     for each item t ∈ d
5:         if( t ∈ C_X)
6:             if(ItemsetsOfSize1_X.contains(t) = false)
7:                 ItemsetsOfSize1_X.add(t);
8:         else if( t ∈ C_Y)
9:             if(ItemsetsOfSize1_Y.contains(t) = false)
10:                ItemsetsOfSize1_Y.add(t);
11:    end for
12:    SORT(ItemsetsOfSize1_X);
13:    SORT(ItemsetsOfSize1_Y);
14:    AllItemSets_X ⟵ new ArrayList;
15:    NewItemSets ⟵ new ArrayList;
16:    OldItemSets ⟵ new ArrayList;
17:    NewItemSets = ItemSetsOfSize1_X
18:    while (NewItemsets.size() > 0)
19:        AllItemSets_X = AllItemSets_X ∪ NewItemSets
20:        OldItemSets = NewItemSets
21:        NewItemSets = createNewItemsets(OldItemSets)
22:    end while
23:    AllItemSets_Y ⟵ new ArrayList;
24:    NewItemSets = ItemSetsOfSize1_Y
25:    while (NewItemSets.size() > 0)
26:        AllItemSets_Y = AllItemSets_Y ∪ NewItemSets
27:        OldItemSets = NewItemSets
28:        NewItemSets = createNewItemsets(OldItemSets)
29:    end while
30:    for ItemSet_i ∈ AllItemSets_X, 1 ≤ i ≤ AllItemSets_X.size()
31:        H ⟵ new HashMap;
32:        H{ItemSet_i} ⟵ 1;
33:        for ItemSet_j ∈ AllItemSets_Y, 1 ≤ j ≤ AllItemSets_Y.size()
34:            H{ItemSet_i : ItemSet_j} ⟵ 1;
35:        end for
36:        EMIT(ItemSet_i, hashmap H);
37:    end for
38:    for ItemSet_j ∈ AllItemSets_Y, 1 ≤ j ≤ AllItemSets_Y.size()
39:        H ⟵ new HashMap;
40:        H{ItemSet_j} ⟵ 1;
41:        EMIT(ItemSet_j, hashmap H);
42:    end for
43: end method
```

Fig. 70.1 Pseudo-Code for the Map () method

input *Mapper 1:* $x_2\ z_1\ y_1\ x_1\ z_3\ z_2\ x_2$ *(document d1)*

Mapper 2: $y_1\ z_5\ z_1\ y_1\ x_1\ z_4\ y_3$ *(document d2)*

output *Mapper 1:* $\{x_1, [(x_1\ 1)\ (x_1y_1\ 1)]\}$
$\{x_2, [(x_2\ 1)\ (x_2y_1\ 1)]\}$
$\{x_1x_2, [(x_1x_2,\ 1)\ (x_1x_2y_1\ 1)]\}$
$\{y_1, [(y_1\ 1)]\}$

Mapper 2: $\{x_1, [(x_1\ 1)\ (x_1y_1\ 1)\ (x_1y_3\ 1)\ (x_1y_1y_3\ 1)]\}$
$\{y_1, [(y_1\ 1)]\}$
$\{y_3, [(y_3\ 1)]\}$
$\{y_1y_3, [(y_1y_3\ 1)]\}$

Fig. 70.2 Input and output of the Map () method given the example dataset

different orders. The next loop (lines 18–22) generates all the possible itemsets containing items that belong to category C_X in a document. We call them X itemsets. It starts with itemsets with size 1 and continuously generates itemsets with size $k + 1$ based on itemsets with size k by calling the *createNewItemsets* ( ) method until no more itemsets are generated. The algorithm of the *createNewItemsets* ( ) is same as the one used in the serial version of the well-known Apriori Algorithm. Similarly, lines 25–29 generate all the possible itemsets with items belonging to category C_Y in a document. We call them Y itemsets. The next (nested) loop (lines 30–37) generates all the XY itemset pairs, where each pair represents a $X \rightarrow Y$ association rule. As we use a *one occurrence per document* counting scheme, the count for each X itemset and each of the XY pairs is 1. In the pseudo code, each X itemset (i.e., $ItemSet_i$) is used as a hash key and $H\{ItemSet_i\}$ represents the hash value for the hash key $ItemSet_i$. Similarly, each itemset pair (i.e., $ItemSet_i : ItemSet_j$) is also used as a hash key and its corresponding count is the hash value of $H\{ItemSet_i : ItemSet_j\}$. The last loop (lines 38–42) simply emits each Y itemset.

As shown in Figs. 70.1 and 70.2, a "stripes" approach is employed in our algorithm. That is, each X itemset and the associated itemset pairs are stored in a hashmap H, and the whole H is considered as a value emitted together with the itemset, which is the key. Please note that, in Fig. 70.2, a bracket [...] represents a hashmap which may contain one or more itemset-frequency count pairs. Given the example dataset, *mapper 1* emits four key-value pairs where the keys are the three X itemsets x_1, x_2, x_1x_2 and one Y itemset y_1. The value of a pair may include the X itemset and its count, the Y itemset and its count as well as each XY pair associated with the X itemset and its count. This approach generates fewer intermediate key-value pairs and reduces network traffics. The potential limitation of a "stripes" approach is that the memory may be used up if the size of a hashmap is too large. However, in our application, each mapper is assigned to process only one document and thus the size of each emitted hashmap is moderate.

Figure 70.3 shows the pseudo-code of our Reduce ( ) method. This method conducts an element-wise sum of all hashmaps associated with the same key where the key is either a X itemset or a Y itemset. The MapReduce framework guarantees that all hashmaps with the same key will be sent to the same reducer for processing. Given the example dataset, the input and output of the Reduce ( ) method is provided in Fig. 70.4. As three X itemsets (i.e., x_1, x_2 and x_1x_2) and three Y itemsets (i.e., y_1, y_2 and y_1y_2) are generated from the dataset and each itemset is a key, the intermediate outputs from the Map( ) method are automatically partitioned into six groups by the MapReduce framework and each group is processed by one reducer. In our Reduce ( ) method, the frequency counts associated with the same itemset or itemset pairs in different hashmaps are accumulated and the results are stored in a new hashmap in each reducer. The final hashmap is emitted using the same key. Each reducer saves

```
1:  method REDUCE(itemset ItemSet_i, hashmaps[H_1, H_2 ... H_m])
2:      H ⟵ new HashMap;
3:      for each hashmap H_i ∈ hashmaps[H_1, H_2 ... H_m]
4:          for each key k ∈ H_i
5:              if(H.contains(k))
6:                  H{k} ⟵ H{k} + H_i{k};
7:              else
8:                  H.add(k, H_i{k});
9:          end for
10:     end for
11:     EMIT(itemset ItemSet_i, hashmap H);
12: end method
```

Fig. 70.3 Pseudo-Code for the Reduce () method

input   *Reducer 1:* $\{x_1, [(x_1\ 1)\ (x_1 y_1\ 1)]$
$[(x_1\ 1)\ (x_1 y_1\ 1)\ (x_1 y_3\ 1)\ (x_1 y_1 y_3\ 1)]\}$
Reducer 2: $\{x_2, [(x_2\ 1)\ (x_2 y_1\ 1)]\}$
Reducer 3: $\{x_1 x_2, [(x_1 x_2\ 1)\ (x_1 x_2 y_1\ 1)\}$
Reducer 4: $\{y_1, [(y_1\ 1)]\ [(y_1\ 1)]\}$
Reducer 5: $\{y_3, [(y_3\ 1)]\}$
Reducer 6: $\{y_1 y_3, [(y_1 y_3\ 1)]\}$

output *Reducer 1:* $\{x_1, [(x_1\ 2)\ (x_1 y_1\ 2)\ (x_1 y_3\ 1)\ (x_1 y_1 y_3\ 1)]\}$
Reducer 2: $\{x_2, [(x_2\ 1)\ (x_2 y_1\ 1)]\}$
Reducer 3: $\{x_1 x_2, [(x_1 x_2\ 1)\ (x_1 x_2 y_1\ 1)]\}$
Reducer 4: $\{y_1, [(y_1\ 2)]\}$
Reducer 5: $\{y_3, [(y_3\ 1)]\}$
Reducer 6: $\{y_1 y_3, [(y_1 y_3\ 1)]\}$

Fig. 70.4 Input and output of the Reduce () method given the example dataset

its emitted hashmaps in a separate file on the hard drives of the cluster that runs the MapReduce platform.

With the results from the above MapReduce job, there is still not enough information to compute the values of interestingness measures defined based on the 2×2 contingency table shown in Table 70.1. The final hashmaps generated by different reducers contain three pieces of information: the frequency count of each itemset pair XY, the frequency count of each X itemset and the frequency count of each Y itemset. The former two pieces of information are always in the same file, while the frequency count of a Y itemset associated with a pair XY is in a different file. That is, given an itemset pair (X, Y), (f_{XY}) and f_X are known and stored together after the above MapReduce job. In order to get all the frequency counts shown in Table 70.1, f_Y must be brought to the same worker (i.e., either a mapper or a reducer) with f_{XY} and f_X. After that, the following equations can be used to find $f_{X\overline{Y}}$, $f_{\overline{X}Y}$ and $f_{\overline{X}\ \overline{Y}}$ within the same worker:

$$f_{X\overline{Y}} = f_X - f_{XY} \qquad (70.1)$$

$$f_{\overline{X}Y} = f_Y - f_{XY} \qquad (70.2)$$

input   *Mapper 1:* $\{x_1, [(x_1\ 2)\ (x_1 y_1\ 2)\ (x_1 y_3\ 1)\ (x_1 y_1 y_3\ 1)]\}$
Mapper 2: $\{x_2, [(x_2\ 1)\ (x_2 y_1\ 1)]\}$
Mapper 3: $\{x_1 x_2, [(x_1 x_2\ 1)\ (x_1 x_2 y_1\ 1)]\}$
Mapper 4: $\{y_1, [(y_1\ 2)]\}$
Mapper 5: $\{y_3, [(y_3\ 1)]\}$
Mapper 6: $\{y_1 y_3, [(y_1 y_3\ 1)]\}$

output *Mapper 1:* $\{y_1, [(x_1 y_1\ 2\ 2)]\}\ \{y_3, [(x_1 y_3\ 1\ 2)]\}$
$\{y_1 y_3, [(x_1 y_1 y_3\ 1\ 2)]\}$
Mapper 2: $\{y_1, [(x_2 y_1\ 1\ 1)]\}$
Mapper 3: $\{x_1 x_2, [(x_1 x_2 y_1\ 1\ 1)]\}$
Mapper 4: $\{y_1, [(y_1\ 2)]\}$
Mapper 5: $\{y_3, [(y_3\ 1)]\}$
Mapper 6: $\{y_1 y_3, [(y_1 y_3\ 1)]\}$

Fig. 70.5 Input and output of the Map 2 () method given the example dataset

$$f_{\overline{X}\ \overline{Y}} = N - f_{XY} - f_{X\overline{Y}} - f_{\overline{X}Y} \qquad (70.3)$$

where N is the total number of documents in the dataset.

To put f_{XY}, f_X, and f_Y in the same worker, we designed another MapReduce job. We use Map 2 ( ) and Reduce2 ( ) to represent the map and reduce methods, respectively, in this second MapReduce job. The input of the Map 2 ( ) method are the final hashmaps emitted by the Reduce ( ) method from the preveous MapReduce job. Each mapper will read one hashmap at a time. It processes the hashmap one after another. The Map 2 ( ) method reads the contents of each hashmap. If the hashmap is associated with an X itemset and then the frequency count of the X itemset is appended to each itemset pair entry in the hashmap. After that, each new pair entry is emitted using the Y itemset of the pair as the key. That is, for an entry $(XY f_{XY})$, $\{Y, [(XY f_{XY} f_X)]\}$ is emitted. If the Map 2 ( ) method reads a hashmap associated with a Y itemset, it simply re-emits the hashmap using the Y itemset as the key. Figure 70.5 shows the input and output of the Map 2 ( ) method for the example dataset.

In the reduce phase of the second MapReduce job, each reducer receives f_Y and the information of all itemset pairs whose second itemset is Y since they have the same key. That is, for a itemset pair XY, $\{Y, [(XY f_{XY} f_X)]\}$ and $\{Y, [(Y f_Y)]\}$ are sent into the same reducer. As f_X is already attached to the itemset pair XY, the reducer has all the three values f_{XY}, f_X, and f_Y. With these values, $f_{X\overline{Y}}$, $f_{\overline{X}Y}$ and $f_{\overline{X}\ \overline{Y}}$ can be computed using Eqs. (70.1)–(70.3). The reducer now has enough information to compute the value of any interestingness measure defined on the basis of the 2×2 contingency table. We use $V(XY)$ to represent the value of an interestingness measure for an itemset pair XY. This value is emitted by the reducer with the pair as the key. The input and output of the Reduce2 ( ) method is given in Fig. 70.6. As the pseudo codes for Map 2 ( ) and Reduce2 ( ) are straightforward, they are not provided in the text.

input	*Reducer 1:*	$\{y_1, [(y_1\ 2)]\ [(x_1y_1\ 2\ 2)]\ [(x_2y_1\ 1\ 1)]\ [(x_1x_2y_1\ 1\ 1)]\}$
	Reducer 2:	$\{y_3, [(y_3\ 1)]\ [(x_1y_3\ 1\ 2)]\}$
	Reducer 3:	$\{y_1y_3, [(y_1y_3\ 1)]\ [(x_1y_1y_3\ 1\ 2)]\}$
output	*Reducer 1:*	$\{x_1y_1, [V(x_1y_1)]\}\ \{x_2y_1, [V(x_2y_1)]\}\ \{x_1x_2y_1, [V(x_1x_2y_1)]\}$
	Reducer 2:	$\{x_1y_3, [V(x_1y_3)]\}$
	Reducer 3:	$\{x_1y_1y_3, [V(x_1y_1y_3\ )]\}$

Fig. 70.6 Input and output of the Reduce2 () method given the example dataset

We already described one advantage of the stripes approach—it emits much fewer key-value pairs since all itemset pairs starting with the same X itemset are packaged into one hashmap. Another advantage of this approach is that it reduces the total number MapReduce jobs needed to get the final results as both f_{XY} and f_X are obtained for an itemset pair XY in only one MapReduce job.

70.4 Experiments

70.4.1 Experiment Data and Platform

To test our MapReduce algorithm, we obtained 33,959 articles from the TREC 2006 Genomics Track [14]. These data files were retrieved from various biomedical journal publishers by the track. Before applying our MapReduce algorithm, the data were preprocessed using Unified Medical Language System (UMLS) and MetaMap [15]. UMLS is a large vocabulary and standard database containing health and biomedical concepts. MetaMap is a lexical tool that breaks text into phrases and then maps each phrase to a standard concept defined in UMLS. The total size of all the preprocessed files is 15.8G. These files are the input of our MapReduce algorithm.

Our experiments were conducted using the Amazon Elastic MapReduce (EMR) platform, a web-based service provided by Amazon. EMR uses Hadoop to manage a cluster of virtual nodes maintained by Amazon. Each node is an Amazon Elastic Compute Cloud (EC2) instance, a virtual machine that has CPU, memory, storage and networking capacity. As MapReduce was primarily designed to utilize less powerful computing nodes to process a massive volume of data in parallel, a moderate instance type (named as *m3.xlarge* by Amazon) was chosen in this study. This instance type has 4 virtual CPUs and 15 GB memory. The most recent Hadoop version (i.e., 5.9.0) supported by Amazon EMR was selected. The input and output data were stored in the Hadoop Distributed File System (HDFS) on the created cluster. HDFS represents the standard data storage layer for a Hadoop system.

Table 70.2 Execution time of our algorithm using Amazon EMR (s)

Jobs \ Worker nodes	4	8	12	16
MapReduce job 1	4864	2767	1891	1486
MapReduce job 2	99	77	73	69
Total time	4963	2844	1964	1555

70.4.2 Experiment Results

Table 70.2 presents the execution time of our MapReduce algorithm using different number of worker nodes. The results indicate that the total execution time has significant decrease as the number of worker nodes increases. As our algorithm consists of two MapReduce jobs, the execution time for each job is provided in the table separately. One can see that the first MapReduce job consumes most of the execution time because reading the input data, generating all the itemset pairs and finding their counts take a lot of time.

Speedup rates for different number of worker nodes are computed and provided in Fig. 70.7. The speedup rate for n number of worker nodes is defined as the total execution time for 4 worker nodes divided by the total execution time for n worker nodes. The figure indicates that our algorithm has linear scalability. One can observe that the computation power of all worker nodes is not fully utilized when the cluster includes more nodes. For example, when the number of worker nodes is increased from 4 to 8 (i.e, the number of nodes doubles), the speedup rate is 1.75. This is reasonable because, no matter how many worker nodes are included, there exist unavoidable overheads that cannot be reduced by parallelism, such as JVM startup, scheduling, disk I/O, etc.

70.5 Conclusion

A MapReduce algorithm has been developed to evaluate the degrees of associations between itemsets that belong to two different categories in large unstructured text datasets. The algorithm scans the dataset only one time and uses a stripes approach to reduce the number of MapReduce phases. In addition, it can be applied to any interestingness measure that is based on a 2 × 2 contingency table. The scalability of the proposed algorithm were investigated using 33,959 documents retrieved from the TREC 2006 Genomics Track on the Amazon EMR platform. The experiment results indicate that our algorithm is linearly scalable in terms of the number of worker nodes in the cluster.

Fig. 70.7 Scalability of our algorithm in terms of the number of slave nodes

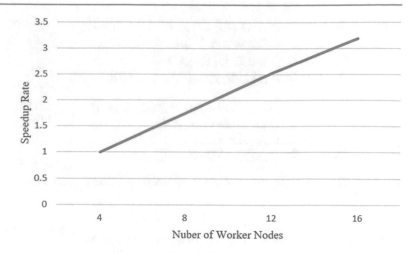

References

1. L. Geng, H.J. Hamilton, Interestingness measures for data mining: a survey, ACM. Comput. Surv. **38**, (2006)
2. P.-N. Tan, M. Steinbach, V. Kumar, *Introduction to Data Mining*, 1st edn. (Addison Wesley, Boston, 2005)
3. R. Agrawal, R. Srikant, Fast algorithms for mining association rules. Presented at the proceedings of the 20th international conference on very large databases, Santiago, Chile, 1994
4. J. Han, J. Pei, Y. Yin, Mining frequent patterns without candidate generation. SIGMOD. Rec. **29**, 1–12 (2000)
5. N.C.f.B. Information, *PubMed*, 2017. http://www.ncbi.nlm.nih.gov/pubmed.
6. J. Dean, S. Ghemawat, MapReduce: simplified data processing on large clusters. Commun. ACM. **51**, 107–113 (2008)
7. F. Kovács, J. Illés, Frequent itemset mining on hadoop, in *2013 IEEE 9th International Conference on Computational Cybernetics (ICCC)*, 2013, pp. 241–245
8. X.Y. Yang, Z. Liu, Y. Fu, MapReduce as a programming model for association rules algorithm on Hadoop, in *The 3rd International Conference on Information Sciences and Interaction Sciences*, 2010, pp. 99–102
9. K. Chavan, P. Kulkarni, P. Ghodekar, S.N. Patil, Frequent itemset mining for Big data, in *2015 International Conference On Green Computing and Internet of Things (ICGCIoT)*, 2015, pp. 1365–1368
10. N. Li, L. Zeng, Q. He, Z. Shi, Parallel implementation of apriori algorithm based on MapReduce, in *2012 13th ACIS International Conference on Software Engineering, Artificial Intelligence, Networking and Parallel/Distributed Computing*, 2012, pp. 236–241
11. C. Doulkeridis, K. Nørvåg, A survey of large-scale analytical query processing in MapReduce. *VLDB J.* **23**, 355–380 (2014)
12. Y. Ji, Y. Tian, F. Shen, J. Tran, Leveraging MapReduce to efficiently extract associations between biomedical concepts from large text data. Microprocess. Microsyst. **46**, 202–210 (2016)
13. Y. Ji, Y. Tian, F. Shen, J. Tran, High-performance biomedical association mining with MapReduce, in *2015 12th International Conference on Information Technology—New Generations*, 2015, pp. 465–470
14. T.R. Conference, TREC 2006 Genomics Track. http://skynet.ohsu.edu/trec-gen/.
15. A.R. Aronson, F.M. Lang, An overview of MetaMap: historical perspective and recent advances. J. Am. Med. Inform. Assoc. **17**, 229–236 (2010)

A Note on Computational Science Curriculum

Jun Zhang and Fangyang Shen

Abstract

Computational science is simply the application of computing capabilities to the solution of problems in the real-world. It is considered as one of the five college majors on the rise. Computational science is officially listed as a new study area in the Computer Science Curricula 2013 (CS2013), by the Joint Task Force on Computing Curricula Association for Computing Machinery (ACM) and IEEE Computer Society. The authors introduced Binomial Simulation Method (BSM) as a new algorithm in the study of Computer Science. BSM is a simple and effective method to model real-world phenomena that involve up and down movements, and has been successfully used in many financial calculations. This work extends the previous study significantly with comparison with Black-Sholes and Monte Carlo simulation; it is intended to help the study of computational science in order to realize the potential power to solve more and more challenging real-world problems. We believe that it is very important to incorporate BSM into computational science education.

Keywords

Computational science · Binomial simulation method · Black-Sholes · Monte Carlo simulation · Education

71.1 Introduction

Computational science is not only important itself, as it is considered as the third pillar for scientific research, but also drives to advance all of sciences and technologies. It is even believed that the most scientifically important and economically promising research frontiers in this century will be conquered by those most skilled with advanced computing technologies and computational science applications. Computational science is considered as one of the five college majors on the rise. Even in the traditional study of computer science, computational science is officially listed as a new area of study, and "computational science topics are extremely valuable components of an undergraduate program in computer science (CS2013)." Computational science is so important since it provides a unique window through which researchers can investigate problems that are otherwise impractical or impossible to address; it is very important in interdisciplinary research between computer scientists and researchers in other areas such as finance, geography, and biology. "However, only a small fraction of the potential of computational science is being realized [5]." This work is intended to help the study of computational science, to realize the potential power to solve more and more challenging real-world problems facing us.

More and more colleges and universities offer computational science courses in the undergraduate or graduate computing related science programs. What should we introduce in such kind of courses? The authors studied computational science education [7, 9, 10]. This work extends the study in [7] significantly with a new goal by introducing BSM in comparison with Black-Sholes and Monte Carlo Simulation. Not only can BSM be served as a method in algorithm related courses, but also in computational science related courses. We believe that it is very important to incorporate BSM into computational science education.

The BSM plays an important role in the financial industry. It is widely and successfully used in option pricing and related calculation by the name of binomial tree. In computer science, binomial tree is defined differently. For example, it was introduced as part of binomial heaps in [1]. Since the differences in the definition between finance and computer

J. Zhang (✉)
Department of Mathematics and Computer Science, University of Maryland Eastern Shore, Princess Anne, MD, USA
e-mail: jzhang@umes.edu

F. Shen
Department of Computer Systems Technology, New York City College of Technology/CUNY, Brooklyn, NY, USA

© Springer International Publishing AG, part of Springer Nature 2018
S. Latifi (ed.), *Information Technology – New Generations*, Advances in Intelligent Systems and Computing 738,
https://doi.org/10.1007/978-3-319-77028-4_71

science, we call the binomial tree method in finance as Binomial Simulation Method. For financial application, we still keep the name as binomial tree but please be aware that the tree is not the same as defined in computer science [1]. Unfortunately, so far, there is no textbook for undergraduate algorithms courses or computational science courses that introduce the BSM as an algorithm for calculation or simulation purposes. Based on our industrial working experience and professional teaching experience, we think it is a good idea to introduce the BSM as an algorithm for calculation and simulation for computational science course works.

Doing so can give many benefits to computational science education, especially for undergraduate students. For examples: (1) This method is relatively easy to introduce to undergraduate and graduate students. (2) It involves many basic algorithmic techniques in computational science. (3) It promotes computational thinking for students, which is critical in modern education. (4) It can be used to solve many applications in the real-world.

71.2 The Option Pricing Problem

We shall introduce options in this section. The first options were used in ancient Greece to speculate on the olive harvest; however, modern option contracts commonly refer to equities. Options play a crucial role in current financial industry. They can be used as an incentive to retain company employees, or a tool of investment. Now, let's introduce some basic terminologies regarding to options.

1. A call option gives the holder the right to buy an asset by a certain date at a certain price.
2. A put option gives the holder the right to sell an asset by a certain date at a certain price.
3. A European option can be excised only at its expiration.
3. An American option can by excised at any time on or before its expiration.

Determining the price of options is an important task of the financial institutions and investors. Suppose a stock is currently sold at $50 per share, and a European call option is to buy the stock at $52 per share (strike price) after 3 months. If at the end of the 3 months the stock price becomes $55, then the fair value of the option will be 55 − 52 = $3. If the stock price becomes $45, the option price will be $0, because the option holder would not exercise the option to buy the stock at $52 when the stock price is $45.

However, the options are sold and bought when the future is not known. Financial institutions and investors need to determine the price of options based on simulation of the stock market (Fig. 71.1).

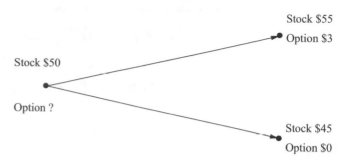

Fig. 71.1 A European call option, strike price $52, maturity 3 months

Generally, the European option pricing problem can be formulated as follows. Assume a stock currently sold at S, how to value a European call option F to buy the stock at the strike price of X at the end of a period of time T?

71.3 The Binomial Simulation Method for Option Pricing

Binomial tree was introduced by Cox, Ross and Rubinstein in an important paper [2]. Many financial institutions use a "binomial tree" method to calculate the option price [3]. Instead of tracing the infinite number of paths of that the stock price may take over the lifetime of the option, the binomial tree method models the changes of stock price with two movements: an up move from the current price of S to Su (where $u > 1$) with a probability p and a down move from the current price of S to Sd (where $0 < d < 1$) with a probability $1 - p$. The numbers u, d and p are determined by a mathematics model. This is a one-step binomial tree and can be used to determine the price of the option (Fig. 71.2).

If we use symbol F_u to denote the option price after the period of time T when the stock price is Su, and F_d to denote the option price after the period of time T when the stock price is Sd, then

$$F_u = max\{Su - X, 0\}, \quad F_d = max\{Sd - X, 0\} \quad (71.1)$$

The risk-free evaluation is a widely used principle to determine the price of financial derivatives [4]. It states that if a portfolio has no uncertainty, then the rate of return of the portfolio is the risk-free interest rate. Consider a risk-free portfolio that includes a long position of buying D shares of the stock, and a short position of selling one European call option. The value of the portfolio would be $DSu - F_u$ if stock price moves up to Su, or $DSd - F_d$ if stock price moves down to Sd. From the risk-free valuation,

$$DSu - F_u = DSd - F_d \quad (71.2)$$

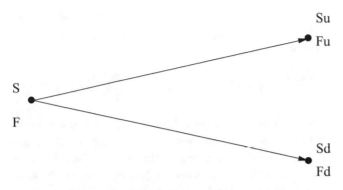

Fig. 71.2 A European call option, strike price X, maturity T

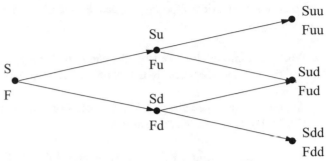

Fig. 71.3 Two-step tree. There are 3 one-step trees

Therefore,

$$D = \frac{F_u - F_d}{Su - Sd} \qquad (71.3)$$

Assume r is the risk-free interest rate, and the interest is continuously compounded, then the present value of the portfolio must be $(DSu - F_u)e^{-rT}$. If the price of the option is F, then the cost of setting up the portfolio is $SD - F$. So

$$SD - F = (DSu - F_u)e^{-rT} \qquad (71.4)$$

Solving Eqs. (71.3) and (71.4), we have

$$F = (pF_u + (1 - p)F_d)e^{-rT} \qquad (71.5)$$

where

$$p = \frac{e^{rT} - d}{u - d} \qquad (71.6)$$

and can be interpreted as the probability of the up move, while $1 - p$ as the probability of the down move.

Using formulas (71.1), (71.6) and (71.5), the option price F can be determined.

This procedure is called a one-step binomial tree. In actual practice, the one-step binomial tree is too simple to model the complicated changes in stock price. In order to model the changes of stock price more closely, the maturity time T is divided into many periods and the option price is calculated backward using one-step binomial trees for each period. The result is a multiple-step tree.

To calculate the option price F with a two-step tree, the option prices are calculated backward. The option prices at the expiration of the option are first calculated at three stock price levels, then the option prices at the midpoints, and finally the current option price, as shown in Fig. 71.3.

$$F_u = (pF_{uu} + (1 - p)F_{ud})e^{-rT/2}$$
$$F_d = (pF_{ud} + (1 - p)F_{dd})e^{-rT/2}$$
$$F = (pF_u + (1 - p)F_d)e^{-rT/2}$$

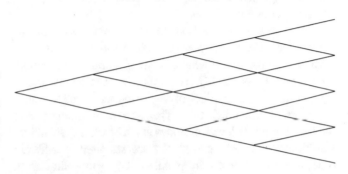

Fig. 71.4 Binomial tree

Note that F_u and F_d can be calculated in parallel. Since the three formulas are actually the same formula with different values, so the calculation of F can be implemented recursively.

It is generally accepted that the values of u and d are determined by the stock price volatility, σ. Using ΔT as the length of each mini-step, one choice of determining u, d and p is [3]:

$$u = e^{\sigma\sqrt{\Delta T}}$$
$$d = e^{-\sigma\sqrt{\Delta T}}$$
$$p = \frac{e^{r\Delta T} - d}{u - d}$$

In practice, a binomial tree is typically divided into 30 or more steps. There is a binomial stock price movement corresponding to each time step. A 30-step binomial tree has 31 terminal stock prices and corresponds to 2^{30} possible paths for stock movement. The basic idea about the calculation is straightforward, but it involves a lot of works as the step size is large. So calculation manually is impractical (Fig. 71.4).

A binomial tree with n steps is equivalent to a one-step tree and two $n - 1$ step trees. So the problem can be divided to two $n - 1$ step trees and conquered later with a one step tree. The calculation of these two $n - 1$ step trees can be done recursively and (or) in parallel. Furthermore, a binomial tree with n steps ends up with $n+1$ terminal possible stock values. So we can check if one of the terminal values matches our expected value.

To evaluate American Options, we can use the BSM with some changes:

1. Work back through the tree from the end to beginning.
2. For final nodes, the value is the same as European Options.
3. At earlier nodes, the values is: Max{Values from formula (71.5) above; Payoff of early exercise}.

As a result, by nature, BSM can be used for the study of parallel, recursion, simulation, modeling, divide-and-conquer, pattern matching, economic forecasting, and computational finance.

BSM is a good method to study high performance calculation. It can be implemented in parallel in many ways with variations, so students can study parallel computing. One example is as [8]: it studied a parallel algorithm that computes the price of an American option on a recombining binomial tree. The tree is partitioned into blocks of multiple levels of nodes and a block is divided into sub-blocks and these sub-blocks are assigned to different processors to process in parallel. The processing of a block by multiple processors consists of two phases. In phase one, the processing is carried out on the nodes at which the computation has no external dependency, and in phase two, the nodes are processed where such dependency exists and has been resolved in phase one. The parallel algorithm dynamically adjusts the assignment of sub-blocks to processors since the level of parallelism decreases as the computation proceeds from the leaf nodes to the root. It also discussed the performances for such computation.

A similar method is called trinomial tree method. This modifies the binomial model by allowing a stock price to move up, down or stay the same with certain probabilities. Here is a good question for students: to compare binomial to trinomial.

71.4 The Black-Scholes Method for Option Pricing

Now, let's take a another look at the formula (71.5) from above:

$$F = (pF_u + (1 - p)F_d)e^{-rT} \qquad (71.7)$$

Suppose we consider the continuous Black-Scholes model as the "exact" model. Since the option price depends on the underline stock price S and the time t, by continuous analog this formula, for small Δt, we have

$$F(S, t - \Delta t) = (pF(Su, t) + (1 - p)F(Sd, t))e^{-r\Delta t}$$
$$0 = F(S, t - \Delta t) - (pF(Su, t) - (1 - p)F(Sd, t))e^{-r\Delta t}$$

Assuming $F(S, t)$ is smooth function of two variables, we perform the Taylor expansion in the above equation, and take limit. We have:

$$\frac{\partial F(S, t)}{\partial t} + rS\frac{\partial F(S, t)}{\partial S} + \frac{\sigma^2}{2}S^2\frac{\partial^2 F(S, t)}{\partial S^2} = rF(S, t) \qquad (71.8)$$

The above formula is the famous Black-Scholes formula. In recognition of the pioneering fundamental contribution to financial world, Scholes and Merton received Nobel Prize in Economic Sciences "for a new method to determine the value of derivatives" in 1997. Unfortunately, Black was unable to receive the same award since he had already passed away at that time.

The Black-Scholes formula calculates the price of European put and call options. This price is consistent with the Black-Scholes equation as above; this follows since the formula can be obtained by solving the equation for the corresponding terminal and boundary conditions. The value of a call option for a non-dividend-paying underlying stock in terms of the Black-Scholes parameters is:

$$F(S, t) = N(d_1)S - N(d_2)Xe^{-r(T-t)}$$
$$d_1 = \frac{1}{\sigma\sqrt{T-t}}(ln(\frac{S}{X}) + (r + \frac{\sigma^2}{2})(T - t))$$
$$d_2 = d_1 - \sigma\sqrt{T-t}$$

The price of a corresponding put option based on put − call parity is:

$$P(S, t) = Xe^{-r(T-t)} - S + F(S, t)$$
$$= N(-d_2)Xe^{-r(T-t)} - N(-d_1)S$$

For both as above:

- $N(\cdot)$ is the cumulative distribution function of the standard normal distribution
- $T - t$ is the time to maturity (expressed in years)
- S is the stock spot price
- X is the strike price
- r is the risk free rate (annual rate, expressed in terms of continuous compounding)
- σ is the volatility of returns of the underlying asset

The Black-Scholes model is widely used in practice for some regular options. It is very easy to calculate with the closed form formula. There are some online calculators one can use easily. For these regular European options, using a Black-Scholes model is pretty good. The Black-Scholes model can be extended for variable (but deterministic) rates and volatilities. The model may also be used to value European options on instruments paying dividends. In this case, closed-form solutions are available if the dividend is a known proportion of the stock price.

The BSM approach has also been widely used since it is able to handle a variety of conditions for which other models cannot easily be applied. This is largely because the BSM is based on the description of an underlying instrument over a period of time rather than a single time point, so it is used to value American options that are exercisable at any time in a given interval as well as Bermudan options that are exercisable at specific instances of time, and Black-Scholes simply doesn't work for these options. For Black-Scholes, that idea is not simple, but the calculation is simple with such closed form formula. On the contrary, the idea for BSM is very simple, at each step, the model predicts two possible moves for the stock price, one up and one down, by an amount calculated using volatility and time to expiration. But the total time of the BSM calculation may be long if the step size is large. Although computationally slower than the Black-Scholes formula, it is more accurate, particularly for longer-dated options on securities with dividend payments. For these reasons, various versions of the binomial model are widely used by practitioners in the option markets.

The BSM provides a discrete time approximation to the continuous process underlying the Black-Scholes model. For European options without dividends, the value from BSM converges on the value from Black-Scholes formula as the number of time steps increases. However, the binomial model also offers more flexibility because the user can modify the inputs at each step in the process to account for differences in the ability to exercise a particular option that shows non-standard features. The downside is that binomial models are complex to construct and depending on the number of steps used in the model, the calculation may be time-consuming.

71.5   Monte Carlo Simulation

A Monte Carlo simulation is a probabilistic model involving an element of chances [6]. Monte Carlo methods are computational algorithms that are based on repeated computation and random sampling. The first application to option pricing was by Phelim Boyle in 1977 for European options. In 1996, M. Broadie and P. Glasserman showed how to price Asian options by Monte Carlo. In 2001 F. A. Longstaff and E.S. Schwartz developed a practical Monte Carlo method for pricing American-style options.

As for option pricing by Monte Carlo simulation. First, the price of the underlying asset is simulated by random number generation for a number of paths. Then, the value of the option is found by calculating the average of discounted re-

turns over all paths. Since option is priced under risk-neutral measure, according to risk-neutral valuation principle, the discount rate is the risk-free interest rate. In order to get a good estimate from simulation, the variance of the estimator must go to zero and the number of samples should go to infinity, which is computationally impractical. But the job can be done with variance reduction techniques.

American Option Pricing can be done by Least Square Monte Carlo Method. At maturity, the optimal exercise strategy for an American option is to exercise the option if it is in-the-money. Prior to maturity, the optimal strategy is to compare the immediate exercise value with the expected cash flows from continuing to hold the option, and then exercise if immediate exercise is more valuable. Thus, the key to optimally exercising an American option is identifying the conditional expected value of continuation. In the Least Square Monte Carlo approach, use the cross-sectional information in the simulated paths to identify the conditional expectation function. This is done by regressing the subsequently realized cash flows from continuation on a set of basis functions of the values of the relevant state variables.

As can be seen, Monte Carlo Methods are particularly useful in the valuation of options with multiple sources of uncertainty or with complicated features, which would make them difficult to value through a straight-forward BlackScholes-style or BSM based computation. The technique is thus widely used in valuing path dependent structures like Asian options and in real options analysis.

However, if an analytical technique for valuing the option exists, or even a numeric technique, such as a BSM is valid, Monte Carlo method is less valuable since it is usually too slow to be competitive.

In general, Black-Scholes is less flexible than BSM, and Monte Carlo Methods are even more flexible than BSM. However the calculations in Monte Carlo Methods are much slower and expensive.

71.6   The Binomial Simulation Method in General

BSM can be used beyond the scope of finance in other computation related applications. Many phenomena in the real world involve up and down movements, for examples: temperature, gas price, the number of software companies, the number of students enrolled in a university, the number of foreclosure houses in a month. The binomial simulation method can be used to simulate these phenomena.

The binomial simulation method is very flexible, and can be used in different manners to solve different problems. The above example in option pricing shows the method can be used for derivative related calculation.

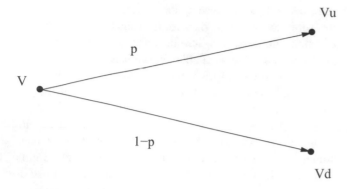

Fig. 71.5 Expected value of Q

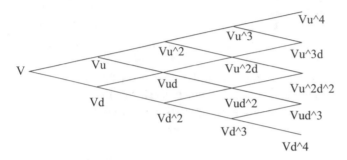

Fig. 71.6 Terminal values of Q

The following are a few more examples where the binomial simulation method can be used.

1. Assume that there is a quantity Q and the current value of Q is V, at the end of time T the value will be either Vu or Vd, where $u > 1$ and $0 < d < 1$. Assume the probability to move up is p and move down is $1 - p$, then the expected value of Q can be calculated as $pVu + (1 - p)Vd$ (Fig. 71.5).

2. Assume that there is a quantity Q, the current value of Q is V, and at the end of each day the value will move up with a factor u or down with a factor d, where $u > 1$ and $0 < d < 1$. We can use the binomial simulation method to calculate the $n + 1$ possible terminal values at the end of n days (Fig. 71.6).

3. Similar to (2), assume that there is a quantity Q, the current value of Q is V, and at the end of each day the value will move up with a factor u or down with a factor d, where $u > 1$ and $0 < d < 1$. Is it possible for Q to be E at the end of n days?

A good question is to ask students to solve a real-world problem by using BSM method.

71.7 Meeting ACM/IEEE CS2013 Curriculum Requirements

The ACM/IEEE CS2013 Curriculum is the single most important guidance for any computer science program all over the world. Since the BSM can be used in many different areas, in this section, we explain why introducing this method in the undergraduate computational science course meets the requirements of such a computer science curriculum.

In the year of 2013, the ACM/IEEE computer society made an update in the computer science curriculum (CS2013). In the following, we show that BSM is fundamental and useful to the principles in CS2013.

Principle 1 in CS2013 Computer science curricula should be designed to provide students with the flexibility to work across many disciplines

Principle 2 in CS2013 Computer science curricula should be designed to prepare graduates for a variety of professions, attracting the full range of talent to the field.

Comments Black-Scholes is a very famous differential mathematical equation that provides a closed form for option pricing. It can be used for European options and American call options, but not American put options. As one can see in Sect. 71.3, the BSM can be used for option pricing simulation. In fact, the BSM can be used for both European and American options, for both call and put, and the results by the BSM converge to these by Black-Scholes. This is a very good example to show to students such that discrete method and continuous method converge to each other. The above option pricing examples involve mathematics, computer science and finance. Some universities even provide programs in financial engineering or computational finance. The BSM is a very useful method to apply math and computer science for financial applications. So BSM is an important method for computational finance, which is explicitly listed in Principle 2 of CS2013. So BSM is very useful for Principles 1 and 2 in CS2013.

Principle 8 in CS 2013 CS2013 should identify the fundamental skills and knowledge that all computer science graduates should possess while providing the greatest flexibility in selecting topics.

Comments The BSM provides a very useful method for simulation. It is already widely used to simulate stock price movements and other financial phenomena. There are a lot of phenomena in the real world involving up and down movements, we think the BSM can be used to simulate these phenomena. Of course, for different problems, the method should be used somewhat differently. We can use this method to study many topics in CS2013, including but not limited to: parallelism, recurrence, simulation, modeling, divide-and-conquer, pattern matching, computational finance and economic forecasting, etc.

71.8   Conclusions

Computational science is incorporated as a new area in the traditional computer science program on a small scale in CS2013. The only reference book listed in CS2013 for Computational Science is [6]. While [6] is a good book containing rich contents regarding Computational Science, BSM is not introduced in that book. BSM is a great method for algorithms in computational science course works, as it was discussed in the above section. Computers are widely used for calculation and simulation in real-world, but algorithms are needed in the calculation and simulation. BSM is a very powerful algorithm for calculation and simulation, and it is relatively simple to understand and suitable to introduce to students, especially undergraduate students.

Computational science is a new discipline itself on a large scale, and one of the five college majors on the rise. According to [5]: "While it is itself a discipline, computational science serves to advance all of science". It is believed that most scientifically important and economically promising research frontiers in the twenty-first century will be conquered by those most skilled with advanced computing technologies and computational science applications. BSM is important in computational finance, but the basic idea and techniques involved are useful beyond the scope of financial applications. It is good to incorporate into computational science study.

References

1. T. Cormen, C. Leiserson, R. Riverst, C. Stein, *Introduction to Algorithms*, 2nd edn. (McGraw-Hill, New York, NY, 2003)
2. J.C. Cox, S.A. Ross, M. Rubinstein, Option pricing: a simplified approach. J. Financ. Econ. **7**(3), 229–263 (1979)
3. J. Hull, *Introduction to Futures & Options Markets* (Prentice-Hall, Upper Saddle River, NJ, 1995)
4. Y. Kwok, *Mathematical Models of Financial Derivatives* (Springer, Berlin, 1998)
5. Presidents Information Technology Advisory Committee, Computational science: ensuring America's competitiveness. Online document (2005)
6. A.B. Shiflet, G.W. Shiflet, *Introduction to Computational Science: Modeling and Simulation for the Sciences* (Princeton University Press, Princeton, NJ, 2006)
7. J. Zhang, C. Liu, Introducing the binomial simulation method in the undergraduate algorithms course, in *The Proceedings of the 4th International Conference on Computer Science and Education (ICCSE 2009)* (IEEE, Piscataway, NJ, 2009)
8. N. Zhang, E.G. Lim, K.L. Man, C.U. Le, CPU-GPU hybrid parallel binomial American option pricing, in *IMECS 2012*, Hong Kong (2012)
9. J. Zhang, F. Shen, Y. Waguespack, Incorporating generating functions to computational science education, in *The Proceedings of the 2016 International Conference on Computational Science and Computational Intelligence* (IEEE, Piscataway, NJ, 2016)
10. J. Zhang, F. Shen, C. Liu, A computational approach to introduce Sumudu Transform to students, in *The Proceedings of the 12th International Conference on Frontiers in Education: Computer Science and Computer Engineering* (CSREA Press, Las vegas, 2016)

Development of a Local Cloud-Based Bioinformatics Architecture

Chandler Staggs and Michael Galloway

Abstract

Cloud computing has become increasingly popular as a means of providing computational resources to ubiquitous computing tasks. Our research specifically defines computing resource needs while developing an architecture for processing and analyzing microbiome data sets. We propose a specialized cloud architecture with processing capabilities defined by various toolchains and bioinformatics scripts. This "Bioinformatics-as-a-Service" cloud architecture, named BioCloud, is in the optimization stage for processing bioinformatic requests, and allowing multi-tenant access of resources through a simple to use web-based graphical user interface. We'll be compiling a list of Bioinformatics tools, some of which will be discussed in this paper, that will be optional components in our Biocloud platform. These tools will become apart of the plug-and-play system envisioned by the BioCloud team.

Keywords

Bioinformatics · Biology · Cloud architectures · Docker containers · Virtualization · Cross-disciplinary

72.1 Introduction

Bioinformatics is the study of biology, specifically molecular biology, integrated with informatics derived by mathematics and computer science to understand and organize large amounts of molecular and genomic information. We introduce BioCloud, a private customized local cloud architecture optimized for processing and analyzing microbiome data

C. Staggs (✉) · M. Galloway
Computer Science, Western Kentucky University, Bowling Green, KY, USA
e-mail: chandler.staggs945@topper.wku.edu;
jeffrey.galloway@.wku.edu

sets. During initial designs of the cloud architecture, the development team considered attributes common to non-profit organizations, such as university research laboratories. Since these groups cannot always afford to purchase access to licensed software and public vendor-based computing resources such as Amazon's EC2 and Google's Compute Engine, we propose that these organizations should maintain their own private cloud.

While an organization has many options for open source cloud architectures, these are often general purpose cloud architectures and may not suit the needs of an individual research group. Disadvantages of these general purpose architectures are the lack of intuitive and/or graphical user interface, and generally comes with a somewhat complicated installation and deployment process. Many of these architectures, such as Eucalyputs [1], OpenStack [2], and OpenNebula [3] require sophisticated configuration scripts and rely heavily on command line interfacing to software features provided by the cloud architecture. These are not desirable traits for organizations wanting to maintain their own specialized cloud cluster.

A cloud architecture designed for these specific markets must have the following attributes: ease of deployment, user friendly interface, energy efficiency, and cost effectiveness. In consideration of these qualities we have designed a new specialized cloud architecture tailored to the microbial data science field, called BioCloud. The BioCloud software architecture is designed to run within a traditional server cluster architecture. BioCloud development is composed of all three layers of cloud architectures: Infrastructure-as-a-Service (Iaas), Platform-as-a-Service (PaaS), and Software-as-a-Service (SaaS). The IaaS attributes of BioCloud include the deployment of virtual appliances (special purpose virtual machines), Docker containers, and communication protocols between these environments and physical compute and storage nodes in the BioCloud cluster. The PaaS implementation includes a persistent file system developed using GlusterFS [4] as a network attached storage (NAS). The PaaS of BioCloud also includes interfaces between virtual

© Springer International Publishing AG, part of Springer Nature 2018
S. Latifi (ed.), *Information Technology – New Generations*, Advances in Intelligent Systems and Computing 738,
https://doi.org/10.1007/978-3-319-77028-4_72

appliances, Docker containers, databases, and the web-based graphical user interface (GUI) provided by BioCloud SaaS components. BioCloud provides an easy-to-use, web-based GUI to biologists. Users are able to upload data sets to BioCloud, select specific jobs to run against their data sets and retrieve the results of these jobs. BioCloud also provides a multi-tenant architecture that differs from traditional bioinformatics software. This allows many users to utilize BioCloud remotely without having to install software locally. BioCloud also provides means in which users can share their results and data sets among each other, for collaborative purposes.

This paper focuses on the environment development for processing microbiome data sets. The work flow environments, discussed in more detail in Sect. 72.4, include physical (non-virtualized, non-containerized) machines, Docker containers [5], and virtual appliances. Docker containers are environments that decouple the underlying operating system (Linux) from applications. This allows migrations of "packages" of software needed to perform specific processes. Virtual machines are replicas of entire operating systems hosted by a hypervisor. A hypervisor can be classified as type 1, guest operating systems are executed directly on the host physical hardware, or type 2, guest operating systems are executed on top of the physical hardware's host operating system. BioCloud makes use of the type 2 KVM [6] hypervisor.

Section 72.2 presents a list of open source bioinformatics tools to be offered within the proposed BioCloud platform. Section 72.3 presents related work on bioinformatics software pipelines. Section 72.4 describes the QIIME [7] architecture used for handling microbiome data sets. We give the hardware and software architecture of BioCloud in Sect. 72.4. Section 72.5 gives final thoughts and future work efforts for the BioCloud project.

72.2 A Survey of Bioinformatics Tools

A thorough examination of various bioinformatics tools will be given treatise to utilize in the BioCloud platform. A number of open source bioinformatics utilities exists that haven't been given a proper analysis in the Computer Science field. This paper will give a survey of these utilities. Ultimately, these tools will be implemented as plugins in BioCloud as additional options for researchers using this cloud architecture.

Properties such as usability, performance, I/O, and purpose will be discussed for each of these utilities. Usability represents how the user might interact with the program and its ease of use, we'll also be discussing the what sort of interaction is offered with this tool such as if it is GUI or CLI. Performance will offer various metrics on how the

this tool performs under certain conditions and ran with in a docker container on Ubuntu 16.04 . These metrics include its physical limitations if they exist, the run-time given certain input, and potentially a comparison to other tools. I/O merely discusses the variety of inputs the pipeline can take and also it's output after processing the input. Finally, purpose is the description of the software, what it's intended to accomplish, how it can be integrated into particular pipelines.

72.2.1 FastQC

Our first Bioinformatics tool to be examined will be FastQC. This tool performs extraneous error checking after the DNA/RNA sequencer tool has finished. Sequencer's often provide their own quality check, but often only identify errors it created. FastQC aims to identify problems in the sequencer or the starting material. It offers two ways to interact with it: a GUI or CLI. The tool generates an html file with the plotting of various statistics that can be analyzed by the researcher. these are listed in Table 72.1

FastQC is compatible with most major sequence file formats. Accepted standard formats include FastQ, Casava FastQ, Colorspace FastQ, GZip compressed FastQ, SAM, BAM, SAM/BAM Mapped only (normally used for colorspace data). All these accepted file inputs can be analyzed for quality control, and they are supported across many Biological services.

FastQC comes packaged with two methods of use: a GUI or CLI. The GUI of course comes with a limited number of parameters to work with, but might be easier for the user. The trade off though is a loss to flexibility, customization, and piping to other commands that's offered by the CLI.

FastQC performance is hard to establish in reference to other utilities yet. It performed an average of 15 s on about 594,434,430 base count DNA sequence. This was performed on a fastq sequence file inside of a docker container running on Ubuntu 16.04. Internally, there is a command line option

Table 72.1 Statistics supplied

Basic statistics
Per base sequence quality
Per base sequence quality scores
Per base sequence content
Per sequence GC content
Per base N content
Sequence length distribution
Duplicate sequences
Overrepresented sequences
Adapter content
Kmer content
Per tile sequence quality

to run it in parallel or in a single thread. For more performance metrics we'll be measuring within Docker container and maybe looking at it's accuracy of flagging incorrect sequences

72.2.2 Cruzdb

Cruzdb is a python-based utility for interacting with the UCSC genome MySQL database. It provides several command line options to mirror the remote database to your own local storage. You can also annotate certain gene sequences based on queries. This utility provides an easier way to download certain tables then run annotation from annotation.py on your local instance and also add to the existing table in your local database.leveraging the sql-alchemy module to accomplish its querying needs to the database, Cruzdb seems to simplify some other harder tasks.

Performance has obviously been examined to handle lots of queries to a remote database of large DNA sequences as this. They implemented their own interval tree to handle searching for overlap intervals from the gene sequence. There are additional options present in the code to run certain segments in parallel which is an option when performing annotations. Test cases for performance of retrieval from database are being generated, but won't make it into the paper here. This tool could prove invaluable and potentially adaptable to other genomic databases that exist. And we could extend its application to work with other databases as well or improve our inhouse database sequencing system [8].

72.2.3 Bowtie2

Bowtie2, successor to Bowtie, is a long sequence aligner aiming to improve upon where its successor falters. Bowtie2 can handle long sequence alignments much more efficiently than Bowtie can. Bowtie2 is also implemented in Python. It comes packaged in the original source, via the BioConda environment, or from a docker container. Some improvements over Bowtie was the ability to handle some gaps in the sequence strands, where bowtie could only handle continuous sequences. There is also no read end length in Bowtie2; in Bowtie there was a limit of a 1000 base-pairs. Bowtie2 can handle reads of longer than 50 bp faster, more sensitively, and with less memory than bowtie could. We can use the tool in conjunction with the other 2 to analyze a particular sequence of a genome [9].

The BioCloud team will be generating performance test cases and metrics for analytical purposes. This will be necessary for the local environments they'll be running on and also to give statistical information for use in the BioCloud toolchain later. We'll be testing the run time and

also how it can handle gaps with the sequences being cross-referenced with. We could also compare this with its previous predecessor, Bowtie.

72.3 Related Work

Authors of [10] state the issues surrounding bioinformatics and the progress of computational efficiency. Sequence data sets are being generated more quickly every year, although raw performance of computing equipment follows the trend of Moore's Law. This trend of computing performance (in terms of density, and throughput) has slowed to roughly every 18–24 months. The authors recommend taking a distributed approach to increase throughput of microbiome data sets. BioCloud uses a multi-tenant approach for processing and analyzing these data sets allowing users to share resources in the cluster in order to increase throughput. BioCloud development also includes current trends for source code parallelization, when possible, to increase throughput.

A comparison of three bioinformatics pipelines is reviewed by Plummer et al. [11]. The authors compare mothur [12], MetaGenome Rapid Annotation using Subsystem Technology (MG-RAST) [13], and Qualitative Insight into Microbial Ecology (QIIME) [7] in terms of usability and performance. MG-RAST provides a web based interface for user interactions, QIIME primarily uses a command-line approach for appending multiple external and internal bioinformatics processes, and Mothur is similar to QIIME with reduced external dependencies making it easier to manage and install. Based on the performance metrics given in [11], the BioCloud development team chose the QIIME environment for handling requests generated by users.

QIIME is a bioinformatics application written in Python that performs microbial ecology analysis [7]. QIIME 2, the latest version of the QIIME software, analyzes and interprets nucleic acid sequence data. It takes the sequence data from one of the sequence source producing programs such as Illumina, Roche/454 and Sanger [7]. Plugins allows developers and users to build and incorporate new functional modules into QIIME 2. The original QIIME graphical user interface QIITA [14] offers limited functionality. In addition to the QIIME 2 GUI, the development community also works on interfaces that provide better functionality to the software, such as q2d2 [7]. QIIME 2 also offers a database independent approach to assess the quality of operational taxonomic units [15]. QIIME2 is the bioinformatics tool that the BioCloud started with, and what we eventually modeled our BioCloud platform after. Our BioCloud seeks to offer an all inclusive environment that includes all the tools that researchers would

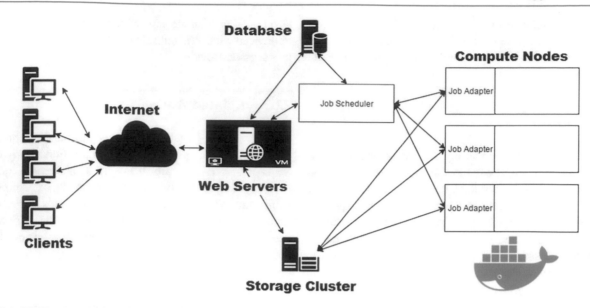

Fig. 72.1 BioCloud architecture

desire to use, much like how QIIME2 has a plugin system to include a multitude of utilities and options.

72.4 BioCloud Architecture

The BioCloud architecture, seen in Fig. 72.1, aims to provide on-demand compute and storage resources to biology research groups with little technical experience in system administration. Our primary focus is to provide research groups with the means to facilitate their computing needs in a cost effective manner while also supporting their needs with dynamic and scalable local cloud services. The BioCloud architecture is composed of a special purpose private cloud stack, which can be leveraged using traditional thick-client devices, as well as low power thin-client devices.

BioCloud utilizes a number of compute nodes, in addition to persistent storage nodes with a redundant backup, as well as a custom DHCP service, MySQL database, and a system administration interface. The BioCloud software architecture is developed and optimized for deployment on commodity hardware typically found in biology research laboratories. No special equipment is needed. It is worth mentioning here that a future work effort for BioCloud is the augmentation of bioinformatics algorithms with Nvidia's CUDA architecture [16]. Execution of massively parallelable algorithms will benefit from this enhancement to the BioCloud architecture, although having a CUDA processing environment is not mandatory.

72.4.1 Compute Nodes

The compute nodes hold environments for microbiome jobs requested by users. These environments include Docker containers and virtual appliances specialized for executing different stages of the QIIME 2 pipeline. Many instances of the environments may exit at once to handle dynamic workloads from multiple users. The middleware assists in managing the launch of these environments, and passing of jobs to and from the running environments. Compute nodes in the BioCloud architecture are made of x86_64 CPUs such as the Intel iSeries and AMD FX series CPUs. Compute nodes are connected with 1 Gbps copper Ethernet to a private local area network.

72.4.2 Database Virtual Appliance

The database server stores information about the state of multiple BioCloud components and their data sources in a well formed database schema. The database is manipulated to accurately portray the state of BioCloud using the web interfaces. Information regarding what processes are running, the estimated completion time of a process, and if the results have been returned are stored in the database and are accessible by users.

Figure 72.2 shows the current state of the BioCloud database. The schema shows information about users connecting to BioCloud resources, The state of jobs submitted by those users, results of those jobs, and states of physical resources in the cluster.

Fig. 72.2 Database schema for BioCloud

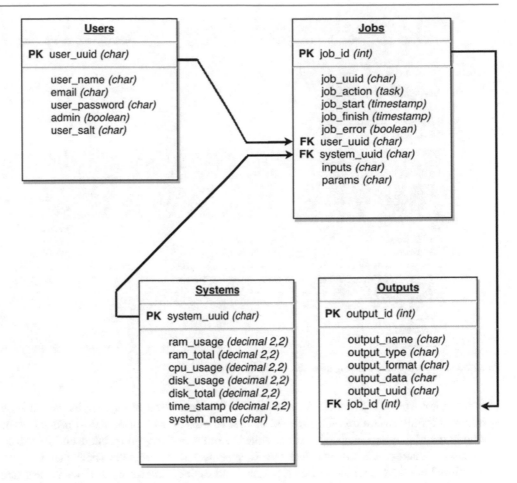

72.4.3 Middleware

Development of a cloud architecture revolves around resource communication and management. A major goal of BioCloud is to improve the quality of service by focusing on efficient resource management and increasing software component reliability. The middleware solution for BioCloud is designed for management of compute and storage resources, including instantiation of virtual appliances and Docker containers, construction and mapping of network attached storage, metadata aggregation, and administrative tasks.

The load balancer assists in job submission and job run time management. When jobs are submitted to BioCloud, the middleware is able to call on the job adapter interfaces on each compute node, and request an optimal node for handling a given request. Any given compute node with the available resources can retrieve the job, and process the job accordingly. The job adapters communicate current environment states with the middleware. Once a job is complete, the middleware receives a notification about the finished job. The middleware updates the database with the changes, and notifies the client.

72.4.4 Data Storage

Distributed storage is a primary goal in cloud computing systems. The BioCloud storage cluster uses a model that allows all nodes connected on the cloud to store data on what would be considered one logical volume. BioCloud uses Gluster File System (GlusterFS) a Network Attached Storage solution [4]. However, the current implementation of BioCloud utilizes GlusterFS on a dedicated storage server, which connects to all nodes on the cloud. This limits data storage to one location.

72.4.5 User Interface

The web server virtual appliance hosts web interfaces, which provides a pathway for users to access BioCloud resources. The web interface allows clients to upload their data sets to be processed, run jobs against those data sets, and see the results produced. The web interface also allows clients to access existing data sources produced by other clients, and review prior results. Additionally, the web interface notifies clients on the states of their jobs, whether a job is currently running, or has completed. The web server can determine

Fig. 72.3 BioCloud job scheduling interface

whether or not a node is available for processing a job. This is achieved through *system polling*. Based on system polls, one node may be determined to be better suited to run one job instead of another job. The web interface is implemented into a virtual appliance, which makes it portable and easier to maintain. Scalability is also available because the virtual appliance can be duplicated many times, and spread across multiple nodes, in case of high traffic conditions.

The web interfaces also provide a means of multi-tenancy for users. Where QIIME 2 is generally restricted to one user and one time on one machine, BioCloud introduces a way for many users to access bioinformatics resources at one time, potentially on a single physical machine. The web interface, coupled with QIIME 2 instances running in isolated environments achieve this goal. Figure 72.3 gives the interface for submitting job requests to BioCloud. This job scheduling interface is where researchers would select specific utilities to run in.

72.5 Conclusions and Future Work

We have introduced a specialized cloud computing architecture called BioCloud that is focused on increasing the efficiency of processing and analyzing microbiome data sets. Current bioinformatics software can be cumbersome to use, especially if the user is not trained on command-line interactions. The overall goals of BioCloud are to make efficient use of commodity hardware typically found in university research environments, increase the efficiency of

the researcher by creating an easy to use graphical user interface, and to provide a multi-tenant architecture that is easy to maintain and scale based on current needs.

Results show that Docker containers execute bioinformatics work flows in near native speed. We combine these results with the fact that containers are easy to deploy and maintain to use this environment for handling microbiome processing and analyzing requests from BioCloud users. Current research aims to deploy various bioinformatics tools to containers where they can be used as plug-and-play scripts for researcher's desired pipelines.

Once these tools have been examined, they'll be fully integrated into the BioCloud architecture as options to be run in a pipeline with the full accompaniment of available arguments. Ultimately, the aim is to compile as many Bioinformatics tools into BioCloud environment as possible so researchers have a plethora of options to choose from and a central tool that can fulfill their research demands. We'll be deploying these tools with docker creating separate images for each and spawning new containers when they're needed. There will be middleware of could to handle the spawning of these containers and also ensure proper consolidation in the physical machine environment. Considerations will have to be considered when running a compute intensive cluster such as this to ensure that resources are maximized as much as possible. So proper migration of these containers will have to be accounted for once spawned.

Future extensions will include fully configurable pipeline toolchains where researchers will have more flexibility than they've ever had before and all in central location. In addition, there will be potential performance improvements for these toolsets with the use of GPU's to improve computational performance. Also maybe include tutorials for beginners to understand these toolchains which is why it's helpful now to be performing a survey of them inorder to get a better understanding. These tutorials will show how to use the BioCloud architecture and also provide an introduction to the particular toolset that will be included in the Biocloud architecture.

The BioCloud research project is ongoing, with many future enhancements scheduled. A current research area for BioCloud is the augmentation of bioinformatics algorithms with Nvidia's CUDA architecture. Many processes in the pipeline used for the experiments in this paper have potential to be massively parallelized. Another future goal of BioCloud is to generate turn-key solutions for cluster deployment and scaling. This can be accomplished with PXE booting and network subnet isolation, and integration of publicly available cluster control suites such at Canonical's Metal-as-a-Service (MaaS).

We believe that development of a local cloud based architecture tailored to solving bioinformatics problems will be beneficial for university research environments. Further studies and efforts in development of new features will validate the effectiveness of this architecture.

References

1. E.E. Cloud, Available: http://eucalyptus.com/
2. OpenStack, Available: http://openstack.org/
3. OpenNebula, Available: https://opennebula.org
4. R. Hat, Storage for your cloud? gluster (2016). Available: https://www.gluster.org/
5. D. Merkel, Docker: lightweight linux containers for consistent development and deployment. Linux J. **2014**(239), 2 (2014)
6. R. Hat, Kvm - kernel-based virtual machine (2016). Available: https://www.redhat.com/en/resources/kvm-%E2%80%93-kernel-based-virtual-machine
7. J.G. Caporaso, et al., QIIME allows analysis of high-throughput community sequencing data. Nat. Methods **7**, 335–336 (2010)
8. S. De, B.S. Pedersen, I.V. Yang, CruzDB: software for annotation of genomic intervals with UCSC genome-browser database. Bioinformatics **29**(23), 3003–3006 (2013)
9. B. Langmead, C. Trapnell, M. Pop, S.L. Salzberg, Ultrafast and memory-efficient alignment of short DNA sequences to the human genome. Genome Biol. **10**, R25 (2009). https://genomebiology.biomedcentral.com/articles/10.1186/gb-2009-10-3-r25
10. M.C. Schatz, B. Langmead, S.L. Salzberg, Cloud computing and the dna data race. Nat. Biotechnol. **28**, 691–693 (2010)
11. E. Plummer, J. Twin, D.M. Bulach, S.M. Garland, S. Tabrizi, A comparison of three bioinformatics pipelines for the analysis of preterm gut microbiota using 16S rRNA gene sequencing data. J. Proteomics Bioinform. **8**, 283–291 (2015)
12. P. Schloss, et al., Introducing mothur: open-source, platform-independent, community-supported software for describing and comparing microbial communities. Appl. Environ. Microbiol. **75**(23), 7537–7541 (2009)
13. F. Meyer, D. Paarmann, M. D'Souza, R. Olson, E. Glass, et al., The metagenomics rast server - a public resource for the automatic phylogenetic and functional analysis of metagenomes. BMC Bioinform. **9**, 386 (2008)
14. Q.D. Team, Qiita: report of progress towards an open access microbiome data analysis and visualization platform (2015)
15. Q. News and Announcements, Toward QIIME 2, Online (2015). Available: https://qiime.wordpress.com/2015/10/30/toward-qiime-2/
16. J. Nickolls, I. Buck, M. Garland, K. Skadron, Scalable parallel programming with cuda. Queue **6**(2), 40–53 (2008). http://doi.acm.org/10.1145/1365490.1365500

Part VIII

Computer Vision, Image Processing/Analysis

A Computer Vision Based Algorithm for Obstacle Avoidance

Wander Mendes Martins, Rafael Gomes Braga,
Alexandre Carlos Brandaõ Ramos, and Felix Mora-Camino

Abstract

This paper presents the implementation of an algorithm based on elementary computer vision techniques that allow an UAV (Unmanned Aerial Vehicle) to identify obstacles (including another UAV) and to avoid them, using only a trivial 5MP camera and applying six mathematical treatments on image. The proposed algorithm of this paper was applied in a drone in real flight. The algorithm proved to be quite efficient both in identifying obstacles ahead and in transposing the same obstacles. Another interesting result is that the algorithm can identify small mobile obstacles and avoid collisions, for example other drones.

Keywords

Canny edge detector · Embedded systems · Image processing · Obstacle detection · Unmanned aerial vehicles

73.1 Introduction

In the last 50 years, machine vision has evolved into a mature field embracing a wide range of applications including surveillance, automated inspection, robot assembly, vehicle guidance, traffic monitoring and control, signature verification, biometric measurement and analysis of remotely sensed images [1], detecting change using aerial images obtained by satellite [2], etc. Computational vision is the study of the extraction of information from an image [3, 4]. More specifically, it is the construction of explicit and clear descriptions of objects in an image [5]. Computational-based navigation of autonomous mobile robots has been the subject of more than three decades of research and it has been intensively studied [6, 7]. Processing images in real time is critical for decision making during flight [8] or driving of autonomous vehicle because they require continuous path generation [9].

Another technology that is gaining great popularity are the Unmanned Aerial Vehicles (UAVs), commonly known as drones. Since the technology to build them today is inexpensive and well understood, they are already being used in many researches and applications. Among the proposed applications in the civil area are fire monitoring and extinguishing, inspection of bridges and buildings, crop dusting and even search an rescue of survivors after a disaster. In the military area the applications are surveillance, defense and even air strikes.

There are many ways to make a drone perceive obstacles in their path and deviate from them, such as using monocular or stereo camera and sensors [10] such as sonars, GPS (global position system), previously known routes, LIDAR (LIght Detecting And Ranging) [9], etc. In this work only was used computer vision through the treatment of images collected in real time from a trivial embedded camera. The advantage of this solution is to be simple and to have a low cost, proving to be efficient in the tests performed of outdoor flight.

Low-cost solutions to drones are very interesting for use their in large-scale global projects [11] and to popularize their application [12].

In this work the images are captured in real time during the drone flight, providing a ready-to-run solution.

The platform considered is a quadrotor micro aerial vehicle (MAV) which is similar to a helicopter, but has four

W. M. Martins (✉) · R. G. Braga
Federal University of Itajubá, Itajubá, Minas Gerais, Brazil
e-mail: wandermendes@unifei.edu.br; rafaelbraga@unifei.edu.br

A. C. B. Ramos
Federal University of Itajubá, Mathematics and Computation's Institute, Itajubá, Minas Gerais, Brazil
e-mail: ramos@unifei.edu.br

F. Mora-Camino
Ecole Nationale de l'Aviation Civile, Toulouse, France
e-mail: felix.mora@enac.fr

rotors [13]. The quadrotor platform is appealing because of its mechanical simplicity, agility, and well understood dynamics [14]. The rest of the paper is structured as follows. In Sect. 73.2, we present the resources, hardware, software and we detail the technique used. The Sect. 73.3 presents some considerations for use of this algorithm in outdoor flights. Section 73.4 shows and discusses the experimental results obtained. Section 73.5 presents the conclusion of the work and an evaluation as to its applicability.

73.2 Materials and Methods

We combine hardware and software to acquire, treat and interpret images in real time during flight, and embedded the developed algorithm into a drone.

73.2.1 Software

For development we used Linux operating system (OS) Ubuntu Desktop 14.04 LTS [15]. The code was written in C++ language using OpenCV 3.2 open source graphic library [16, 17]. We used ROS Indigo (Robot Operating System) firmware [18] embedded into a Raspiberry PI board on the drone.

Fig. 73.1 Captured photo—a drone flying

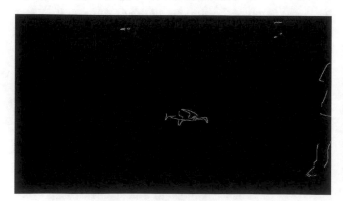

Fig. 73.2 Canny1986

73.2.2 Hardware—UAV Platform

The proposed algorithm was intended to be run on a 250 mm quadrotor using a Pixhawk [19] as the main controller board. The Pixhawk is an open-source flight controller board responsible for the low-level control of the quadrotor. It is equipped with gyroscope, accelerometers, magnetometer, barometer and can also be connected to an external GPS module and has a powerful embedded software that implements the basic control functions. An useful feature of the Pixhawk is the ability to communicate with other devices through a protocol called MAVLink [20], which was developed specifically for UAV applications. This can be used to achieve autonomous control of the UAV, by running the control algorithms in a small portable computer, such as a Raspberry Pi [21], which is carried by the UAV and sends commands to the Pixhawk by MAVLink messages. The UAV is also equipped with a web camera, mounted on its front, to capture the images of the path it is moving into.

73.2.3 Technique

The technique consists (1) image capturing; (2) apply gray scale to the captured image; (3) blur the image; (4) detect edges; (5) find contours; (6) draw contours; (7) identify obstacles and free areas; (8) command the UAV moves to the freer area; and (9) to repeat the process. The Figs. 73.1, 73.2, 73.3, 73.4 and 73.5 show the result of this process. The images shown in these pictures were taken by the embedded camera. The diagram of the Fig. 73.6 shows this sequence.

1. Image Capturing: Capturing frame by frame the image of the front camera (Fig. 73.1).
2. Apply Grey Scale to the captured image: The first mathematical treatment that the primitive image receives is to have reduced the number of colors to a narrower band, limited to tones or degrees or scales of gray, using the

Fig. 73.3 Suzuki2005

Fig. 73.4 Obstacle detecting

Fig. 73.7 Gray scale

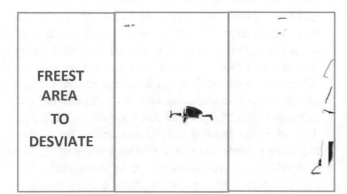

Fig. 73.5 Freest area to deviate

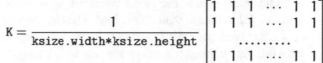

Fig. 73.8 Kernel used by the Blur open CV library function

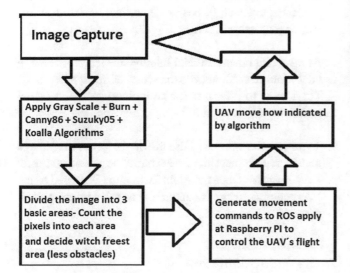

Fig. 73.6 Process's diagram

Fig. 73.9 Blurred image

toCvShare cvbridge library function with the "mono8" parameter [22]. The Fig. 73.7 shows the original image converted into a gray scale image.

3. Blur the image: The "blur" openCV library function is used to blur the image. This function blurs an image using both the normalized box filter and the following kernel K (Fig. 73.8) [23]. The Fig. 73.9 shows the gray scale image after applied the blur process.

4. Detect Edges: The "Canny" openCV library function is used to apply the Canny Algorithm to detect edges into image. The Canny Edge detector was developed by John F. Canny in 1986. Also known to many as the optimal detector, Canny algorithm aims to satisfy three main criteria: (a) Low error rate: Meaning a good detection of only existent edges. (b) Good localization: The distance between edge pixels detected and real edge pixels have to be minimized. (c) Minimal response: Only one detector response per edge [24]. The Fig. 73.2 shows the blur image after applied the Canny86 algorithm.

5. Find Contours: The "findContours" openCV library function is used to find object limits into image. The function retrieves contours from the binary image using the algorithm [Suzuki85]. The contours are a useful tool for shape analysis and object detection and recognition [25].

6. Draw Contours: The "Scalar" and "drawContours" opencv functions are used to draw the object's contours into the image."Scalar" represents a 4-element vector. The type Scalar is widely used in OpenCV for passing pixel values. We define a BGR color such as: Blue = a, Green = b and Red = c, Scalar (a, b, c) [26]. The "drawContours" function draws contours outlines or filled contours [27]. The Fig. 73.3 shows the last result after applied the Suzuky05 algorithm and Scalar function.

7. Identify obstacles and free areas: In this point the image has two kinds of basic pixels (dots): the black pixels (RGB 0,0,0, called OFF dots) and the non-black pixels. Our algorithm converts the black pixels into white pixels (RGB 255,255,255, called ON dots) and it converts all non-black pixels into black-pixels, except the pixels belonging to the contours that will have their colors held. The black pixels within the contours will have their colors unchanged. After this, the white pixels represents free spaces and the black pixels represents obstacles (Fig. 73.4). Dividing the area into nine (or more) subareas, we interpret as the most appropriate way for the UAV to advance: the area with more white dots. The Fig. 73.5 shows the image divided into three horizontal areas (or segments). In this example the left area is the freest area. The UAV must deviates using this area.

  (a) Scanning the image: The process of identifying freest area and obstacles consists scanning the image from the outermost pixels to the inner ones (from the outside to the inside) (Algorithm 73.1). As this is an external flight, we consider the entire free area until the edge contour points of the figure are found (non-white pixels). From there, what is inside the contour is considered an obstacle and what is out of the contour is considered free area where there is some chance of the drone passing through the obstacles.

  (b) Count the amount of white pixels in each area: Defined the three areas, the Algorithm 73.2 counts the number of "ON" points in each area, represented by $S(n)$, where S means area ("segment") and n is the segment, $0 \leq n \leq 2$.

  (c) Suggest that the UAV moves to the segment with the more amount of white pixels (totally 255): The algorithm interprets as the most appropriate way for the UAV to advance, the segment $S(n)$ with smaller amount of black dots. Here it interprets black pixel as obstacle and white pixel as free area. In the first step the algorithm divides the image into three areas: left $S(0)$, center $S(1)$ and right $S(2)$.

The decision table is:

When two or more segments have the same amount of pixels ON—RGB (255,255,255), the following decision table is applied:

If	And	Action
$S(0) > S(1)$	$S(0) > S(2)$	Turn left
$S(1) > S(0)$	$S(1) > S(2)$	Go center
$S(2) > S(0)$	$S(2) > S(1)$	Turn right

If	Action
$S(n) = S(1)$	Go center
$S(0) = S(1)$	Turn right

8. Command the UAV moves to the freer area: Once it is determined that the UAV has a chance to advance from the some free space and that there is sufficient amount of free space for this advance, it should be assessed whether the free space is arranged in such a way as to allow the UAV to pass through the segment chosen. Lighted points being scattered may indicate that their sum is greater than the dimensions of the UAV but that their arrangement in space prevents their advance. Commands witch control the UAV movement, as ROLL, PITCH and YAW (Fig. 73.10) [28]. The movement decision is translated neither flying command and transmitted to the UAV that will execute it. The Algorithm 73.3 commands the drone movements. The msg.channels(0..3) simulate the radio control channels. Channel(0) is the roll movement. Channel(1) is the pitch movement, channel(2) is the rotors throttle. The YAW guidance, channel(3), has not been implemented in this work, so its value is zero.

At this point other Artificial Intelligence features come in and decisions that fall outside the scope of this work.

The idea is to offer a quick preliminary decision on the direction the UAV should follow.

9. To repeat the process: Discard of the processed image and its replacement by a new frame, now with the new UAV position. Once the flight instruction is passed to the UAV, another image is captured at a $(t + 1)$ time, and all processing is repeated.

73.2.4 Implementation

This algorithm was implemented in C++ and runs on the ROS platform. ROS (Robot Operational System) is an open source technology created to aid researchers in developing robotic applications. ROS provides us with many tools and facilities that were very useful in our work.

A ROS application is a network of nodes that communicate with each other. Each node is an independent program in the system and a Master node also exists to manage the network. Nodes that generate data publish this information

for *Each row of the image. (from 0 to maxrow)* **do**
  for *Each column of the row. (from 0 to maxcolumn)*
    do
      while *not found a pixel non-black* **do**
        | Turn white the color pixel;
      end
    end
end
for *Each row of the image. (from 0 to maxrow)* **do**
  for *Each column of the row. (from maxcolumn
    downto 0)* **do**
      while *not found a pixel non-black* **do**
        | Turn white the color pixel;
      end
    end
end
for *Each column of the image. (from 0 to maxColumn)*
  do
    for *Each row of the column. (from 0 to maxrow)* **do**
      while *not found a pixel non-black* **do**
        | Turn white the color pixel;
      end
    end
end
for *Each column of the image. (from 0 to maxColumn)*
  do
    for *Each row of the column. (from maxrow downto
    0)* **do**
      while *not found a pixel non-black* **do**
        | Turn white the color pixel;
      end
    end
end
for *Each pixel of the image. (row x column)* **do**
  | if color pixel is non-white
  | Turn black the color pixel;
end

Algorithm 73.1 Scan the contour image

for *each segment n* **do**
  | Count the number of "ON" pixels (Sn);
end

Algorithm 73.2 Count pixels ON

in topics as messages, while nodes that need that data subscribe to the corresponding topics and receive the published messages.

In this application was created a node called image subscriber, which subscribes to the topic where the image messages from the camera are being published and is responsible for processing the images and decide where the UAV should move. The image messages come from a node connected directly to the camera hardware. Another node, called Mavros, is responsible for communicating with the Pixhawk. When

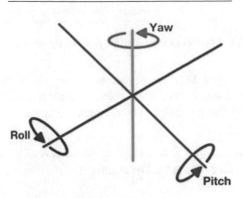

Fig. 73.10 Quadcopter's orientation

```
//Define Constants
#define FACTOR 0.6
#define BASERC 1500
//Preset No Movement - The UAV Stop
rollAction = 0;
pitchAction = 0;
if decision is turn left then
 | rollAction = 100;
end
if decision is to go ahead then
 | pitchAction = 200;
end
if decision is turn right then
 | rollAction = -100;
end
Roll = BASERC - rollAction * FACTOR;
Pitch = BASERC - pitchAction * FACTOR;
msg.channels[0] = Roll;
msg.channels[1] = Pitch;
msg.channels[2] = BASERC; //Throttle
msg.channels[3] = 0; //Yaw(Not implemented)
```

Algorithm 73.3 Command the UAV movements

the image subscriber node decides where to move the UAV, it creates a message of type mavros_msgs/OverrideRCIn, which represents a command from a radio controller, fills it with the corresponding values to cause the desired movement and publishes it to a topic where Mavros is subscribed. Mavros creates a MAVLink message containing that information and sends to the Pixhawk via a serial connection. The Fig. 73.11 shows a diagram generated by a ROS tool called rqt_graph showing the nodes and the relevant topics.

73.3 The Experiment

The experiments were carried out on the campus of the Federal University of Itajubá. The video which contains the images showed here can be seen in [29]. The images was

Fig. 73.11 Diagram generated by the program rqt graph showing the relevant nodes and topics in the application

captured by a 5MP (mega pixels) camera in 1280×720 pixels resolution. We used a Parrot Bebop 2 drone [30], weighing 500 g controlled by a human operator.

73.4 Results and Discussion

The tests show that the algorithm is efficient and diverted the drone from all the obstacles it encountered in its path in a outdoor flight. However this work limited itself to diverting the drone and not executing a flight plan. In this context, it is possible to say that the goal of the algorithm was successfully achieved. Getting the drone back on its original route after it veers off an obstacle is not the scope of this algorithm and there are other codes to do this. Also we do not include the calculation of the distance between the obstacle sighted and the drone in flight. Again the reason is the existence of other algorithms to perform this task. The initial focus is for outdoor flight, and was not implemented deviations over or under obstacles. Deviations to the sides, to the center, up and down were contemplated. Although the algorithm was efficient in detecting obstacles and free spaces in indoor images, no tests were performed in this sense.

73.5 Conclusion

The algorithm was proved efficient in driving the drones through obstacles in outdoor flight without causing collisions. There is a limitation related to the lighting in the environment. It is known that computer vision solutions are very sensitive to changes in lighting, so it would be interesting in future works to test our algorithm in different conditions.

Acknowledgement We thank the Black Bee team of the Federal University of Itabubá that made the drones available and operated during the experiments.

This work was funded by Capes—Coordination of Improvement of Higher Level Personnel [31].

References

1. E.R. Davies, *Machine Vision: Theory, Algorithms, Practicalities, 2005*, ISBN 012206092X, 9780122060922. (2005).
2. M.D.L. Santos, E.H. Shiguemori, R.L.M. Mota, A.C.B. Ramos, Change detection in satellite images using self-organizing maps, in *12th International Conference on Information Technology—New Generations (ITNG 2015), Las Vegas, Nevada, USA* (2015), pp. 662–667
3. R.C. Gonzales, E.R. Woods, *Processamento de Imagens Digitais (in Portuguese)* (São Paulo, Brazil, 2000)
4. A. Bueno, *Fundamentos da Computacão Gráfica (in Portuguese)* (Pontifícia Universidade Catolica, Brasil, Rio de Janeiro, 2011)
5. D.H. Ballard, C.M. Brown, *Computer Vision* (Prentice Hall, New Jersey, 1982)
6. A.M. Waxman, J.J. LeMoigne, B. Scinvasan, A visual navigation system for autonomous land vehicles. IEEE J. Robot. Autom. **RA-3**(2), 124–141 (1987)
7. C. Thrope, M.H. Hebert, T. Kanade, S.A. Shafer, Vision and navigation for the Carnegie-Mellon Navilab. IEEE Trans. Pattern. Anal. Mach. Intell. **PAM1-10**(3), 362–373 (1988)
8. A. Davison, Real-time simultaneous localization and mapping with a single camera. IEEE ICCV **2**, 1403–1410 (2003)
9. M. Lee, S. Hur, Y. Park, An obstacle classification method using multi feature comparison based on 2D LIDAR database, 2015, Information Technology—New Generations (ITNG 2015), in *12th International Conference on, Las Vegas, Nevada, USA* (2015), pp. 674–679
10. S. Garćia, M.E. Lopez, R. Barea, L.M. Bergasa, A. Gomez, E.J. Molinos, *International Conference on Indoor SLAM for Micro Aerial Vehicles Control Using Monocular Camera and Sensor Fusion, Autonomous Robot Systems and Competitions* (ICARSC 2016) (2016)
11. J.T. Amenyo, D. Phelps, O. Oladipo, F. Sewovoe-Ekuoe, S. Jadoo-nanan, S. Jadoonanan, T. Tabassum, S. Gnabode, T.D. Sherpa, M. Falzone, A. Hossain, A. Kublal, MedizDroids Project: ultra-low cost, low-altitude, affordable and sustainable UAV multicopter drones for mosquito vector control in malaria disease management, in *IEEE Global Humanitarian Technology Conference (GHTC 2014)* (2014)
12. M.F.A. Rahman, A.I.C. Ani, S.Z. Yahaya, Z. Hussain, R. Boudville, A. Ahmad, Implementation of Quadcopter as a teaching tool to enhance engineering courses, in *IEEE 8th International Conference on Engineering Education (ICEED 2016)* (2016)
13. Ascending Technologies, GmbH, http://www.asctec.de. Accessed 13 March 2017
14. K. Sreenath, T. Lee, V. Kumar, geometric control and differential flatness of a quadrotor UAV with a cable-suspended load, in *IEEE Conference on Decision and Control (CDC)* (Florence, Italy, 2013), pp. 2269–2274
15. Ubuntu Desktop 14.04 LT, https://www.ubuntu.com, Accessed 13 March 2017
16. OpenCV 3.2, http://opencv.org. Accessed 13 March 2017
17. G. Bradski, A. Kaehler, *Learning OpenCV: Computer Vision with the Open CV Library* (O'Reilly)
18. ROS Indigo (Robot Operation System), http://www.ros.org. Accessed 13 March 2017
19. Pixhawk, https://pixhawk.org/. Accessed 13 March 2017
20. MavLink, http://www.mavlink.org/. Accessed 13 March 2017
21. Raspberry pi, https://www.raspberrypi.org. Accessed 13 March 2017
22. L.F. Lima (2010), https://lazarolima.wordpress.com/2010/08/19/proces-sando-imagens-em-grayscale-e-negativo-em-c/(in Portuguese). Accessed 13 March 2017
23. OpenCV 2.4.13.2 documentation, *Blur*, http://docs.opencv.org/2.4/modules/imgproc/doc/filtering.html?highlight=blurcv2.blur. Accessed 27 April 2017

24. OpenCV 2.4.13.2 documentation (imgproc module), *Image Processing, Canny Edge Detector*, http://docs.opencv.org/2.4/doc/tutorials/imgproc/imgtrans/canny_detector/cannydetector.html?highlight=canny. Accessed 27 April 2017

25. OpenCV 2.4.13.2 documentation, *Structural Analysis and Shape De-scriptors*, http://docs.opencv.org/2.4/modules/imgproc/doc/structural_analysis_and_shapedescriptors.html?highlight=findcontourscv2.findConto.urs. Accessed 27 April 2017

26. OpenCV 2.4.13.2 documentation, *Basic Drawing*, http://docs.opencv.org/2.4/doc/tutorials/core/basic_geometric_drawing/basic_geometric_drawing.html?highlight=scalar. Accessed 27 April 2017

27. OpenCV 2.4.13.2 documentation, *drawContours*, http://docs.opencv.org/2.4/modules/imgproc/doc/structural_analysis_and_shape_descriptors.html?highlight=drawcontoursdrawcontours. Accessed 27 April 2017

28. The Bored Engineers (https://theboredengineers.com/), *The Quadcopter: Control the Orientation*, https://theboredengineers.com/2012/05/30/the-quadcopter-basics/. Accessed 11 April 2017

29. Experiment, *Drone Flight*, https://youtube/JA_oQORdcjs. Accessed 27 April 2017

30. The Bebop Parrot Drone website, https://www.parrot.com/us/drones/parrotbebop2. Accessed 05 May 2017

31. CAPES, http://www.capes.gov.br. Accessed 13 March 2017

The ST-Vis Tool for SpatioTemporal Visualization

Ana Paula S. Braatz Vieira, Rafael S. João, Luciana A. S. Romani, and Marcela X. Ribeiro

Abstract

Analyzing and understanding spatial data that vary over time is a complex task. Usually, the data is arranged in a tabular or text forms. We develop the ST-Vis (SpatioTemporal Visualization) tool to provide a visual representation of spatiotemporal data, which must help users to understand a temporal variation in a region when combining the parallel coordinates graph with a geographic map, a temporal texture, and a table. The temporal texture maps the linear form of the variation of the Normalized Difference Vegetation Index (NDVI), resulting in a representation of colors texture, and each texture cell refers to a period. ST-Vis provides a simultaneous spatiotemporal representation of data, and the visualizations interact with each other through animations. We evaluated ST-Vis by interviewing some domain experts, computer science, and other field students, who experienced ST-Vis tool. The results show that ST-Vis allows the understanding of spatiotemporal data through the generated visualizations. This tool simultaneously displays visualizations, which have interactions with each other through animations.

Keywords

NDVI · Parallel coordinates · Spatial data · Temporal data · Temporal texture

74.1 Introduction

The analysis of complex data such as spatiotemporal data is a hard and complex task since interpreting and understanding information from tables and texts is a task that demands time and attention. Thus, it is necessary to develop spatiotemporal models to represent visually data that varies both in time and in space. As for example the analysis and monitoring of data on multitemporal coverages, in which the soil cover for crop, forest, and environmental monitoring analyzes is highlighted [16]. That way, the user can understand the data with lesser cognitive effort since it is simpler to interpret the information through images instead of sequential text. This is due to the fact that an image contains extensive information on a small space, which may be analyzed in parallel. In contrast, the sequential text is sequentially analyzed line by line, which demands more time.

In this context, we developed the first version of the ST-Vis tool. The main objective of this tool is to support the specialist in the analysis of spatiotemporal data, representing them through a spatiotemporal visualization. In order to reach this goal, ST-Vis represents the variation of NDVI data, made available by an agricultural company. That way, ST-Vis aims to assist the specialist in the data analysis by providing visual representations that combine a parallel coordinate graph with a map and a temporal texture to provide a spatiotemporal representation on a single screen.

To evaluate ST-Vis, we released a multiple-choice form on the web to find out whether the visualization provided by ST-Vis helps the user in the interpretation of spatiotemporal data. The form was made released to some experts in NDVI analysis and also to some students and teachers in the computing area.

A. P. S. Braatz Vieira (✉) · R. S. João · M. X. Ribeiro
Federal University of São Carlos (UFSCar), São Carlos, Brazil
e-mail: ana.vieira@dc.ufscar.br; rafael.joao@dc.ufscar.br; marcela@dc.ufscar.br

L. A. S. Romani
Embrapa Agricultural Informatics, Campinas, SP, Brazil
e-mail: luciana.romani@embrapa.br

© Springer International Publishing AG, part of Springer Nature 2018
S. Latifi (ed.), *Information Technology – New Generations*, Advances in Intelligent Systems and Computing 738,
https://doi.org/10.1007/978-3-319-77028-4_74

74.2 Related Work

There are currently few tools that treat spatiotemporal data and provide a space-time visualization. The tools that deal with this data have different focuses and areas, such as economic data, areas with crime rate, and fires. In this context, the VIS-STAMP (Visualization System for Spacing-Time and Multivariate Patterns) tool [7] that focuses on the analysis of patterns visualization through the clustering of spatiotemporal data, two-dimensional visualization techniques.

The VIS-STAMP tool provides a temporal representation through a MapMatrix, a color representation associated with a cluster, the Space-Time Matrix that organizes the multivariate data patterns into a temporal matrix, which in each cell (associated with a year) contains a cartographic map with colors associated with the clustering. Moreover, it uses a Parallel Coordinate the technique, for the visualization of multivariate patterns.

The GeoSTAT (Geographic SpatioTemporal Analysis Tool) tool [4] presents spatial and temporal visualization techniques and data mining capabilities through Weka based on fire outbreaks and fault events in power transmission lines. The tool aims to find evidence to prove the hypothesis that fires occurring near the transmission lines could be the cause of failures in the energy system. GeoSTAT has a spatial view through an interactive map of Google Maps and a two-dimensional ScatterPlot chart for the temporal representation.

The GE-based Visualization tool [3] provides a spatial-temporal view to perform an exploratory data mining (K-means) analysis. This tool uses the animated 3D Google Earth map for spatial representation. Also, it has a dimensional panel that allows controlling the time by using a sliding bar (time bar). In visual representation, data is organized in some layers with different colors.

The GeoVISTA CrimeViz tool [12] makes a spatial representation through a map possible by using the Google Maps service. This tool analyzes crime data and highlights outbreaks in the regions by types of crime, such as arson, homicide, and sexual abuse. Its temporal representation is carried through the use of a frequency histogram.

The InfoScope tool [10] is a commercial software developed by Macrofocus InfoScope, which comprises: a cartographic map for spatial representation; a graph of Parallel Coordinates for multidimensional views (with economic data on gross and net purchase value, years of inflation, among others); and, a representation through ScatterPlot graph to analyze similarities (by name of cities). The tool accepts own files with .mis extension (Macrofocus InfoScope).

Among the tools that analyze time-varying spatial data, once focus on the NDVI analysis (this work focus): the SATVeg [5] tool. The SATVeg (Temporal Vegetation Analysis System) tool shows the variation of NDVI by employing a two-dimensional line chart. However, SATVeg does not allow to track spatiotemporal evolution in a single visualization. Hence, the goal of ST-Vis is to allow that the user sees in a single visualization spatiotemporal thematic attribute evolving.

74.3 ST-Vis: The Proposed Tool

Our approach aims to represent the spatiotemporal data using a simultaneous visualization. To perform it, the user can view the map, the Parallel Coordinates graph, and a Temporal Texture in a single view when using ST-Vis. The spatial information is displayed in parallel with the temporal information. It results in a spatiotemporal visualization with just a single interactive representation, more comprehensible to the user.

Visualization techniques such as the map and the Parallel Coordinates graph were used to generate the spatiotemporal visualization. Thus, ST-Vis is a web tool composed of an architecture (Fig. 74.1) with the visualizations: (1) spatial, represented by means of a map, (2) temporal, represented by Temporal Texture consisting of colors, and (3) space-time represented by the combination of a Parallel Coordinate graph, a Map, and a Temporal Texture. The views generated by ST-Vis interact with each other, making the visualization more intuitive to the user.

Simply, the user, through the web tool, loads the file separated by commas that he wants to see, the information is loaded in ST-Vis (Fig. 74.1-1). The latitude and the longitude variables are manipulated for map generation, which represents spatial visualization.

In parallel (Fig. 74.1-2) the latitude, longitude, date and NDVI variables are manipulated for the generation of a Parallel Coordinates graph. Finally, (Fig. 74.1-3) the date and NDVI variables are manipulated for Temporal Texture generation, which is a color texture.

Thus, the upload view has events (Fig. 74.1-4) like the interaction[1] and the events change the information in the visual representations. The simple move of the mouse in the instances of the table or click on the map markers, enable interaction events between views.

74.3.1 Spatiotemporal Data

Spatiotemporal data files were made available by an agricultural company containing the NDVI variation of a Country region. The NDVI is an index for analysis of the vegetation condition proposed in [13, 14] that can be collected through

---

[1]Highlight instances in different visualizations.

Fig. 74.1 ST-Vis architecture

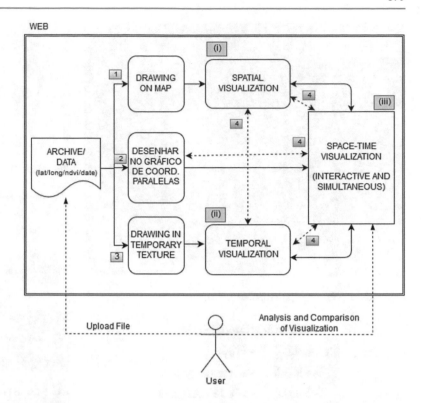

The value of NDVI varies from −1 to 1, so that the closer to 1, the higher the indication of the presence of vegetation and the closer to −1, the higher the evidence of the presence of discovered soils, rocks or water. Theoretically, the value 0 refers to vegetation without leaves, submitted to the water stress condition due to soil water deficit [8].

Fig. 74.2 Example of natural color comparison and NDVI in an agricultural area. Source: [6]

remote sensing, and it is applied to crop monitoring, and mapping, drought detection, pest damage detection, agricultural estimation productivity, hydrological modeling and mapping of agricultural areas [15].

NDVI allows performing analyzes at various scales on the vegetation cover of a given region. It is generated by images provided by sensors of onboard satellites such as the AVHRR/NOAA[2] and the MODIS/Terra.[3] The NDVI is the bidirectional reflectance factors of the near red and infrared bands [11], according to Fig. 74.2.

74.3.2 ST-Vis: Spatial Visualization

The ST-Vis uses the map to assist in spatial visualization. This map is generated by a Google maps API. In this map, some markers can be plotted referring to the spatial data (latitude and longitude).The green dots presented in Fig. 74.3 are samples of this marking step.

74.3.3 ST-Vis: Temporal Visualization

To represent the temporality of the NDVI in ST-Vis a Temporal Texture was implemented, a temporal representation of the variation of the NDVI over time. This texture maps the data evolving of a single latitude and longitude (marker on the map of Fig. 74.3) linearly, associating the numerical values in color proportional to the variation of the NDVI class, according to the colors used by the experts in the field (Fig. 74.4) and by means of the article [1].

---

[2]Advanced Very High-Resolution Radiometer (AVHRR) sensor, onboard the National Oceanic and Atmospheric Administration (NOAA) satellite series.

[3]MODerate Imaging Spectroradiometer aboard the Terra platform.

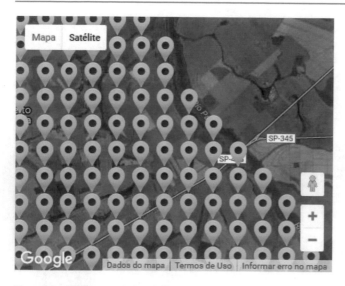

Fig. 74.3 ST-Vis—spatial visualization—map

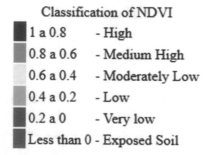

Fig. 74.4 Variation of NDVI. Adapted from [1]

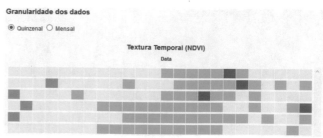

Fig. 74.5 Temporal visualization—temporal texture (1)

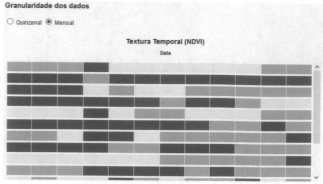

Fig. 74.6 ST-Vis—temporal visualization—temporal texture (2)

74.3.4 ST-Vis: Temporal Visualization

Because of this association of NDVI values with colors, ST-Vis represents the temporal data in a linear form, where each row represents 1 year, and the columns represent fortnights or months. In this way, the expert can choose the granularity of the data to be loaded, being biweekly or monthly. Thus, when choosing the fortnightly granularity, ST-Vis displays a Temporal Texture with n lines, where each row contains 24 columns, and each row represents 1 year (Fig. 74.5). If the user chooses the monthly granularity, the tool will display a Temporal Texture with n lines containing 12 columns (Fig. 74.6).

74.3.5 Visualization Using a Parallel Coordinates Graph

An approach incorporated in ST-Vis to obtain a visual representation of the data (latitude, longitude, NDVI, and date) is the Parallel Coordinates. Inselberg [9] introduced this chart and provided a possibility to represent multidimensional

data[4] using vertical lines called axes and horizontal lines, displaying their dimensions parallel to each other in a two-dimensional plane.

The Parallel Coordinates graph allows the user to relate the data information using horizontal blue lines in Fig. 74.7 that pass through all the parallel axes in the visual representation. Each axis is a dimension so that each vertical line can be a different attribute of an object. The code of the Parallel Coordinates graph obtained was reused through the GitHub source code hosting platform, in which the code used was created by Kai Chang [2] and collaborators, so it was modified and adapted for ST-Vis.

The graph provides a simultaneous view of the data as well as associates parallel axes to different dimensions in a single view. The graph shows the temporal dimensions (dates) in their vertical axes, the spatial information (latitude and longitude) and the dimensions of thematic data (non-spatial and non-temporal data, for example, city name, crop classification or areas, id, among others). Figure 74.8 shows an example of Parallel Coordinate Graph of the ST-Vis tool, where the data dimensions are interconnected by horizontal lines.

This graph aims to help the exploration and understanding of spatiotemporal data, representing in a single visualization

---

[4]Data with more than one dimension, such as the NDVI variation, which has temporal, spatial and thematic dimensions.

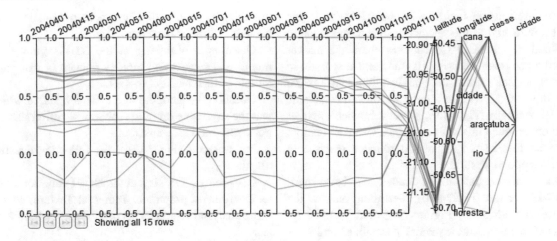

Fig. 74.7 Parallel coordinate graph view

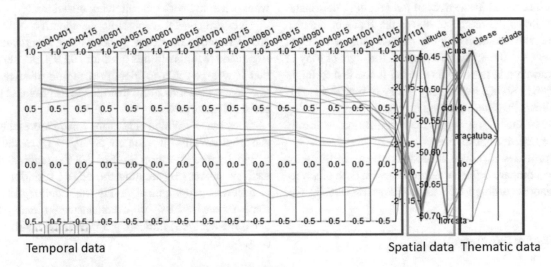

Temporal data   Spatial data Thematic data

Fig. 74.8 Parallel coordinates graph (spatial, temporal, and thematic data)

both the spatial, temporal and thematic data simultaneously (Fig. 74.8).

74.3.6 ST-Vis: Spatiotemporal Visualization

For a space-time view, ST-Vis displays all views (map, Parallel Coordinate graph, and Temporal Texture) in a set of views displayed in a single presentation (in the display). In this way, it supports the user to understanding the information through the set of visualizations such as a map, a Temporal Texture, and a Parallel Coordinates graph.

The available views are associated with a table, which displays all the data loaded from the file (loaded by the user). Thus, when traversing the table with the mouse cursor, a horizontal line is highlighted in a Parallel Coordinates graph, a map marker begins to skip and is generated a Temporal Texture (Fig. 74.9).

74.4 Results

ST-Vis, unlike the tools mentioned in the related works, provides a simultaneous visualization, since the user can observe several visual representations in a single display, and interactive as it provides a link between them visualizations. The ST-Vis represents Temporal Texture (color variation) the variations of NDVI over time in points (markers) loaded in the file.

The loaded file has the CSV format (Comma-Separated Values), separated by commas. This file, when loaded, plots the data on the map, the Parallel Coordinates graph, the table, and the Temporal Texture simultaneously. So when the user puts the mouse over the instances of the table, animated events are enabled in the visualizations, and when the user selects a marker on the map, the instance in the parallel coordinates plot is highlighted, and a new temporal texture is generated.

When the user interacts with an instance in the table, the horizontal row related to the selected instance (in the table) is highlighted in a Parallel Coordinates chart, the marker related to the geographical point (latitude and longitude) in the map starts a visual animation. Finally, a Temporal Texture is generated, where each color represents the variation value of the NDVI over time (Fig. 74.9). Moreover, when a marker is selected on the map, this marker starts a visual animation, highlights the line in a Parallel Coordinates graph, and generates a Temporal Texture.

The values of the data to be loaded can be normalized (Fig. 74.9) or not (Fig. 74.10), depending on how the user requires visualization. Figures 74.9 and 74.10 show the difference between the instances normalized and nonnormalized (referring to the same latitude and longitude)

There is a function in the axes of the Parallel Coordinates graph that allows the expert to select the focus of interest. For example, the selection of the instances with the variation of NDVI between 0.6 and 0.8 in the first fortnight of May of 2003 and variation between 0.55 and 0.7 in the first fortnight of November, as shown by the gray square in Fig. 74.11. This selection allows the filtering of the instances, thus facilitating the analysis of the data through the visualization, as it only displays the instances of interest.

ST-Vis provides two simultaneous analyzes. In this way, the user can compare different regions to with each other, relating the data according to the focus of interest (Fig. 74.12).

74.4.1 ST-Vis: Evaluation

To evaluate the first version of the ST-Vis, a web form was generated, describing a brief explanation of how the user can analyze the NDVI in a spatiotemporal view, explaining the behavior of a region with sugarcane plantation area, the area with water (river) and urban area (city). This form was answered by 30 people, being 3 specialists of agricultural area, 23 people from the computer science area, and 4 people from other areas.

To evaluate the first version of the ST-Vis, we elaborated a web form with a brief explanation of how the user can analyze the NDVI in a spatiotemporal visualization. This form also exhibits the NDVI range for three different regions: a sugarcane plantation area, an area with water (river) and an urban area (city). Thirty people answered this form, three of them are specialists, 23 from the area computer science, and 4 from other areas.

The form granted some images for the user to analyze and answer the following questions about the images provided, for Image 1 (Fig. 74.13) the following questions were asked:

Question 1—Looking at the variation of NDVI in the Parallel Coordinates graph and the Temporal Texture, is it possible to identify this region as a sugarcane producing behavior? 96.4% answered Yes.

Question 2—Looking at the ST-Vis graphs, in which month was sugarcane probably planted in that region? The hit rate of this question was 89.3%.

Question 3—Looking at ST-Vis graphs, in which month was the sugarcane pruning probably occurred? This question got a 75% hit on the answers.

For Image 2 (Fig. 74.14), the following questions were asked:

Question 1—Looking at the NDVI variation in the Parallel Coordinates graph and Temporal Texture, which culture is the analyzed region? This question got a 92.9% hit on the answers.

For Image 3 (Fig. 74.15), two views of different regions were presented with the following questions:

Question 1—Is it possible to identify differences in NDVI variation over time by comparing sugarcane and non-sugarcane regions? In this question, 92.9% of users reported that it was possible to identify a region of sugarcane and non-sugarcane, indicating that the views provided by ST-Vis assist data analysis.

Question 2—Which side of the image represents the non-cane region? This question got an 89.3% hit on the answers.

Finally, the Question 3—Has ST-Vis facilitated the data analysis process by treating the NDVI variation over time at different geographical points (latitude/longitude) on the same screen? 92.9% of users answered that the ST-Vis aided the analysis, indicating a promising result for ST-Vis (Fig. 74.16).

74.5   Conclusions and Future Works

The simultaneous visualization of spatiotemporal data is still a challenge in the visualization area because of the difficult task of adding temporal variation to spatial data. In this context, this work presents the ST-Vis tool, which provides a visual representation of textual and tabular data, combining a map with a parallel coordinates graph and a temporal texture. The initial ST-Vis visualizations aid the users to understand the spatiotemporal information. That is confirmed by the results of the evaluation form applied to students and specialists in the area. ST-Vis simultaneously displays visualizations, which have interactions with each other through animations. The domain expert utilizes the spatiotemporal visualization to identify areas of land and crops.

Future directions of this work involve the improvement of ST-Vis by adding more options for visualization and analysis, such as temperature, soil precipitation, humidity, among others.

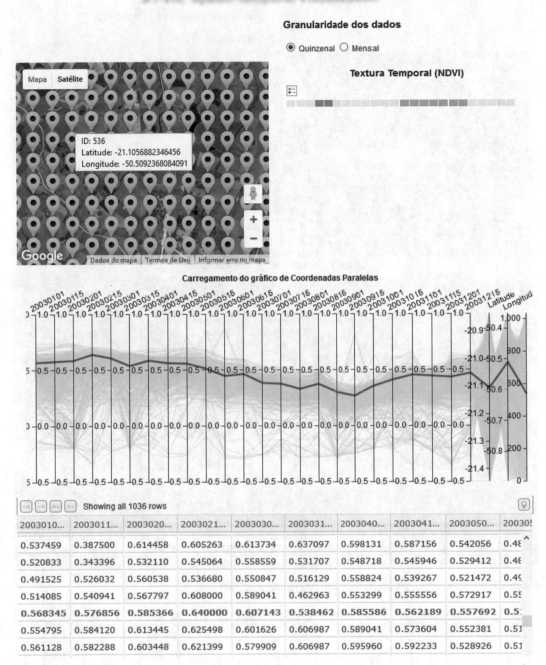

Fig. 74.9 An example of a spatiotemporal visualization—ST-Vis (normalized)

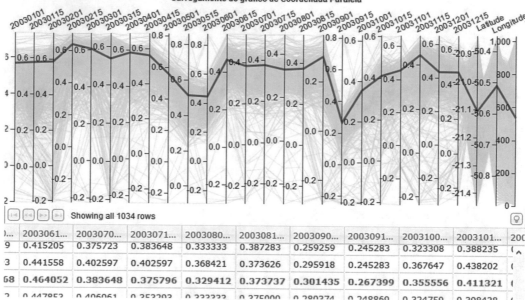

Fig. 74.10 An example of a spatiotemporal visualization—ST-Vis (non-normalized)

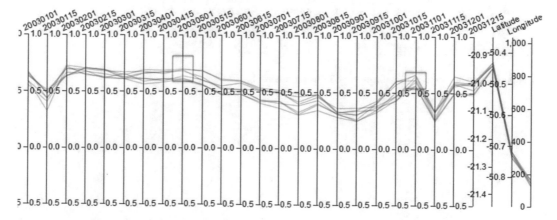

Fig. 74.11 Parallel coordinates graph—selection of the focus of interest

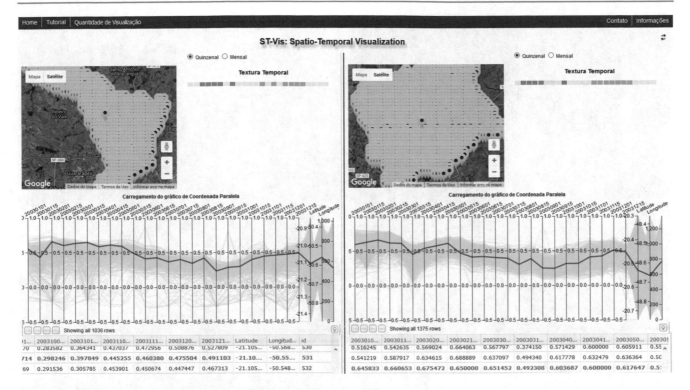

Fig. 74.12 Simultaneous consultation through ST-Vis (visualization in two different areas)

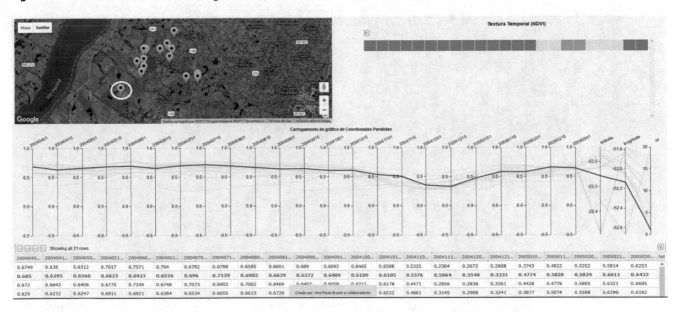

Fig. 74.13 Form—Image 1

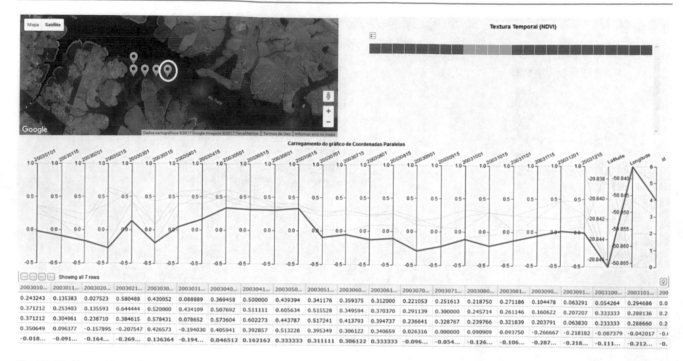

Fig. 74.14 Form—Image 2

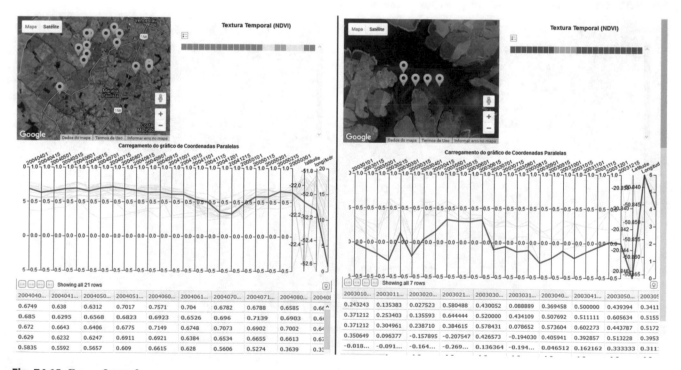

Fig. 74.15 Form—Image 3

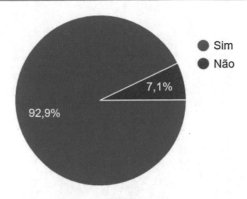

Fig. 74.16 Percentage of respondents that ST-Vis facilitates data analysis

References

1. C.M.S. Aquino, J.G.B. Oliveira, Estudo da dinâmica do Índice de Vegetação por Diferença Normalizada (NDVI) no núcleo de São Raimundo Nonato-PI. GEOUSP: Espaço e Tempo (Online) **31**, 157–168 (2012)

2. K. Chang, Parallel coordinates (2012), https://github.com/syntagmatic/parallel-coordinates

3. P. Compieta et al., Exploratory spatio-temporal data mining and visualization. J. Vis. Lang. Comput. **18**(3), 255–279 (2007)

4. M.G. de Oliveira, C. de Souza Baptista, GeoSTAT - a system for visualization, analysis and clustering of distributed spatiotemporal data, in *GeoInfo* (2012), pp. 108–119

5. EMBRAPA, SATVeg (2014). https://www.satveg.cnptia.embrapa.br/satveg/login.html

6. ENGESAT, NDVI - Criando ìndice de vegetação no global mapper (2017). http://www.engesat.com.br/softwares/global-mapper/calculo-do-indice-de-vegetacao-ndvi-no-global-mapper

7. D. Guo, J. Chen, A.M. Maceachren, K. Liao, A visualization system for spacetime and multivariate patterns (VIS-STAMP). IEEE Trans. Vis. Comput. Graph. **12**(6), 1461–1474 (2006)

8. INSA, NDVI - Índice de Vegetação por Diferença Normalizada (2014). http://www.insa.gov.br/ndvi/n#.V6fKRTWWmTA

9. A. Inselberg, The plane with parallel coordinates. Vis. Comput. **1**(2), 69–91 (1985)

10. MACROFOCUS, Infoscope (2015). https://www.macrofocus.com/public/products/infoscope/

11. A. Maria, C. Petrini, C. Arraes, V. Jansle, J. Rocha, Comparação entre perfis temporais de NDVI e NDVI ponderado em relação ao uso da terra, in *Anais XV Simpósio Brasileiro de Sensoriamento Remoto - SBSR*, Curitiba - PR, INPE (2017), p. 0452

12. R.E. Roth, K.S. Ross, B.G. Finch, W. Luo, A.M. Maceachren, A user-centered approach for designing and developing spatiotemporal crime analysis tools, in *Proceedings of GIScience*, [S.l.: s.n.], vol. 15 (2010)

13. J.W. Rouse et al., *Monitoring the Vernal Advancement and Retrogradation (Green Wave Effect) of Natural Vegetation* (Texas A&M University, Texas, 1974)

14. J. Rouse Jr., R. Haas, J. Schell, D. Deering, Monitoring vegetation systems in the great plains with ERTS, 1974

15. L.S. Shiratsuchi et al., *Sensoriamento remoto: conceitos básicos e aplicações na agricultura de precisão* (Embrapa Solos-Capítulo em livro técnico (INFOTECA-E), 2014)

16. R.R. Vatsavai et al., *Miner: a suit of classifiers for spatial, temporal, ancillary, and remote sensing data mining, in *Information Technology: New Generations, 2008. ITNG 2008. Fifth International Conference on* (IEEE, Piscataway, NJ, 2008), pp. 801–806

Detection of Early Gastric Cancer from Endoscopic Images Using Wavelet Transform Modulus Maxima

Yuya Tanaka and Teruya Minamoto

Abstract

It is said that the overlooking rate of early gastric cancer in endoscopic examination reaches 20–25% in Japan, and it is desirable to develop a detection method for early gastric cancer from endoscopic images to reduce the overlooking rate. We propose a new method for detecting early gastric cancer from endoscopic images using the wavelet transform modulus maxima (WTMM). First, our method converts the original image into the CIE L*a*b* color space. Next, we apply the dyadic wavelet transform (DYWT) to the a* component image and compute the WTMM of the high frequency component. It is shown that the WTMM of the abnormal parts tends to become smaller than the WTMM of the normal parts. We describe the method detecting the abnormal parts based on these features in detail, we show experimental results demonstrating that the proposed method are able to detect the regions suspected of being early gastric cancer from endoscopic images.

Keywords

Image analysis · Frequency analysis · Early gastric cancer · Dyadic wavelet transform · Wavelet transform modulus maxima

75.1 Introduction

As shown in Ref. [1], about 953 thousand new cases of gastric cancer were estimated to have occurred in 2012 in the world. Most types of cancer have four stages, numbered from 1 to 4. The different stages of cancer describe how far the cancer has grown and spread at diagnosis. According to

Ref. [2], the 5-year survival rate of the patients with stage 2 or 3 gastric cancer is 64.9% in patients under 70 years old, and 33.1% at those over 70 years old, while the patients with stage 1 gastric cancer almost completely recovered. Treating early gastric cancer, the 5-year survival rate reaches 96% as shown in Ref. [3]. Therefore, it is very important to discover gastric cancer in early stage.

However, it is difficult for doctors to find abnormal parts, that is, early gastric cancer parts from the endoscopic image obtained by usual white light endoscopy in general Because, the abnormal region and the other region called "normal region" in this paper are visually very similar to each other. In fact, according to Ref. [4], the overlooking rate of early gastric cancer in a medical examination using endoscopic reaches 20–25% in Japan. Moreover, diagnostic criteria for early gastric cancer based on endoscopic images does not establish, and the endoscope diagnosis depends on the subjective diagnosis of each doctor and their skills or experiences. Therefore, it is desired to develop a method for detecting early gastric cancer from an endoscopic image and to reduce the overlooking rate.

The aim of this paper is to develop a method for detecting early gastric cancer from endoscopic images. Recently, many methods for detecting early gastric cancer from endoscopic images have been proposed as in Refs. [3, 4], and [5]. However, all of these studies have detected early gastric cancer from endoscopic images taken in NBI (Narrow Band Imaging) mode. According to Ref. [6], the NBI mode is the shooting mode installed in the Olympus endoscope system. On the other hand, there are few studies that detect early gastric cancer from images taken with white light compared ones with NBI mode.

There are also many methods for detecting early cancer based on wavelet transforms, as in Refs. [7, 11] and [8]. The detection methods of early gastric and esophageal cancer using discrete wavelet transforms (DWT) have been proposed in Refs. [7] and [8], respectively. In Ref. [11], the detection method of early esophageal cancer based on

Y. Tanaka (✉) · T. Minamoto
Department of Information Science, Saga University, Saga, Japan
e-mail: tanakay@ma.is.saga-u.ac.jp; minamoto@ma.is.saga-u.ac.jp

© Springer International Publishing AG, part of Springer Nature 2018
S. Latifi (ed.), *Information Technology – New Generations*, Advances in Intelligent Systems and Computing 738,
https://doi.org/10.1007/978-3-319-77028-4_75

the dyadic wavelet transform (DYWT) was proposed and it seems that the detection accuracy of this method is superior to the method based on the DWT. However, the authors have not considered esophageal cancer. Based on these findings, we develop a new method based on the DYWT for detecting early gastric cancer from endoscopic images taken with white light. We also use the wavelet transform modulus maxima (WTMM) to extract the image features.

The rest of this paper is organized as follows. We give a brief introduction to the DYWT in Sect. 75.2 and then describe the WTMM in Sect. 75.3 in Sect. 75.4, we explain the features of normal and abnormal regions based on the WTMM. In Sect. 75.5, we propose a new detection method for early gastric cancer from endoscopic images. We present the experimental results in Sect. 75.6 and conclude this paper in Sect. 75.7.

75.2 Dyadic Wavelet Transform

The DYWT is one of the most famous frequency analysis methods.The DYWT is shift-invariant, and the size of each frequency component is the same as in the original image, and it is utilized to perform tasks such as feature extraction, denoising and digital watermarking [9–11].

It is known from Refs. [11, 12] that the DYWT for images is given by

$$C^{m+1}[i,j] = \sum_{l=-\infty}^{+\infty} \sum_{k=-\infty}^{+\infty} h[l]h[k]C^m[i+2^m l, j+2^m k],$$

$$D^{m+1}[i,j] = \sum_{l=-\infty}^{+\infty} \sum_{k=-\infty}^{+\infty} g[l]h[k]C^m[i+2^m l, j+2^m k],$$

$$E^{m+1}[i,j] = \sum_{l=-\infty}^{+\infty} \sum_{k=-\infty}^{+\infty} h[l]g[k]C^m[i+2^m l, j+2^m k],$$

$$F^{m+1}[i,j] = \sum_{l=-\infty}^{+\infty} \sum_{k=-\infty}^{+\infty} g[l]g[k]C^m[i+2^m l, j+2^m k].$$

For $m \geq 0$, where $C^0[i,j]$ is the original image, h is a low-pass filter, and g is a high-pass filter. As a result, $C[i,j]$, $D[i,j]$, $E[i,j]$, and $F[i,j]$ are the low frequency component, the horizontal high frequency component, the vertical high frequency component, and the high frequency component in both directions, respectively. The indices i and j indicate the locations in the horizontal and vertical directions, respectively.

Figure 75.1 displays an example of the DYWT. As can be seen from Fig. 75.1, the low frequency component is the smoothed image, the three high frequency components are the edge information.

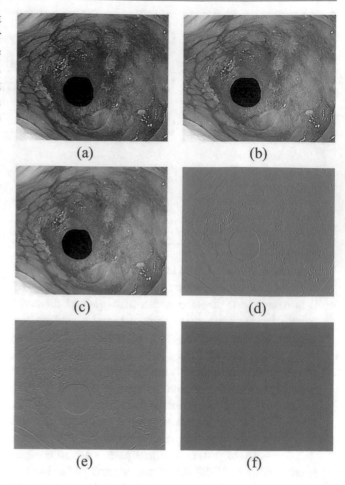

(a)   (b)   (c)   (d)   (e)   (f)

Fig. 75.1 The original image and its frequency components decomposed by the DYWT. (**a**) Original image. (**b**) Grey scale image. (**c**) C component. (**d**) D component. (**e**) E component. (**f**) F component

75.3 Wavelet Transform Modulus Maxima

The WTMM was developed by Mallat et al. [12, 13], and the wavelet transform modulus (WTM) is originally defined by

$$M_o^m[i,j] = \sqrt{|D^m[i,j]|^2 + |E^m[i,j]|^2},$$

which are multiscale edge maps of the original image. The WTMM are defined as locations $[i,j]$ where the modulus image $M_o^m[i,j]$ is locally maximum, along the gradient direction given by

$$A_o^m[i,j] = \begin{cases} \alpha_o^m[i,j] & \text{if} D^m[i,j] \geq 0 \\ \pi + \alpha_o^m[i,j] & \text{if} D^m[i,j] < 0 \end{cases}$$

with

$$\alpha_o^m[i,j] = \tan^{-1}\left(\frac{E^m[i,j]}{D^m[i,j]}\right).$$

In contrast, we define the wavelet transform modulus by the following:

$$WM^m[i, j] = \sqrt{|D^m[i, j]|^2 + |E^m[i, j]|^2 + |F^m[i, j]|^2}.$$

We also define the WTMM as locations $[i, j]$ where the modulus image $WM^m[i, j]$ is locally maximum, along the gradient direction given by $A_o^m[i, j]$.

Figure 75.2 shows the modulus image WM^1 of the grayscaled image at the top right of Fig. 75.1. As we can see in Fig. 75.2, it seems that the WTM detects edges in all directions in image.

Figure 75.3 shows the modulus maxima image of the grayscaled image at the top right of Fig. 75.1.

Since local maxima corresponding to light texture variations can be removed by the thresholding, we define the WTMM image W^m using the thresholding as follows:

Fig. 75.4 The WTMM image W^1 using the thresholding

$$W^m[i, j] = \begin{cases} 1 & \text{if} WM^m[i, j] \text{ is locally maximum} \\ & \text{and} WM^m[i, j] \geq \mu + \sigma \\ 0 & \text{otherwise.} \end{cases}$$

Here, μ and σ are the mean value and standard deviation of the WTM image WM^m, respectively.

Figure 75.4 shows the WTMM image W^1 of the grayscaled image at the top right of Fig. 75.1. As we can see in Fig. 75.4, the intensity variation corresponding to the edge points with the high modulus of the WTMM image is sharper than the one of the WTM image.

From now on, we assume that WTMM means the threshold processed WTMM.

Fig. 75.2 The WTM image WM^1 of the grayscaled image at the top right of Fig. 75.1

75.4 Preliminary Experiment

We compared the features obtained from the WTMM for normal and abnormal regions to distinguish these two regions.

The procedure of the preliminary experiment is as follows.

1. Convert the endoscopic image to the CIE L*a*b* color space. In this experiment, we use the a* component.
2. Clip the a* component to 640×640 pixels, and normalize its mean value and variance to 0 and 1, respectively.
3. Applying the DYWT twice to the image obtained by the previous step, the high frequency components are obtained and the WTMM is computed by using these components. In this experiment, we use the DYWT with the coefficients of filters computed from the quadratic spline wavelets and the scaling functions as described in Ref. [12].

Fig. 75.3 The WTMM image of the grayscaled image at the top right of Fig. 75.1

Table 75.1 The average pixel values of two normal and abnormal regions

	Average value
Normal regions 1	0.0188
Normal regions 2	0.0110
Abnormal regions 1	0.0066
Abnormal regions 2	0.0009

4. Divide the WTMM image into non-overlapping blocks with a size of 64 × 64 pixels.
5. Compare representative values at blocks including normal and abnormal parts.

We selected two blocks from normal and abnormal regions, respectively. Table 75.1 shows the average WTMM value.

As we can see in Table 75.1, the WTMM values of the abnormal regions tend to be smaller than the ones of the normal regions. This fact means that there is a certain threshold which are able to distinguish the abnormal and normal regions.

75.5 Algorithm for Early Gastric Cancer Detection

Based on the preliminary experiment, we present an algorithm for detecting abnormal regions as follows :

1. Convert the endoscopic image into the CIE L*a*b* color space. In this experiment, we use the a* component.
2. Clip the a* component to 640 × 640 pixels, and normalize its mean value and variance to zero and one, respectively.
3. Apply the DYWT twice to the image obtained by the previous step, and compute the WTMM. In this experiment, we use the DYWT with the coefficients of filters computed from the quadratic spline wavelets and the scaling functions as described in Ref. [12].
4. Divide the binary image into non-overlapping blocks with a size of 64 × 64 pixels, as shown in Fig. 75.5. In this experiment, the image will be divided into 100 blocks.
5. Compute the representative value $R[i, j]$ of each block which is the average pixel value of the block. Figure 75.6 shows an example of computing a representative value when the size of the block is 4 × 4 pixels. In this study, we set the block size to 64 × 64 pixels. Here, the indices i and j are the block locations in the vertical and horizontal directions, respectively.
6. Compute the average pixel value μ and the standard deviation σ of the representative values of all blocks.
7. Generate the enhanced image O_{bin} using the following relations:

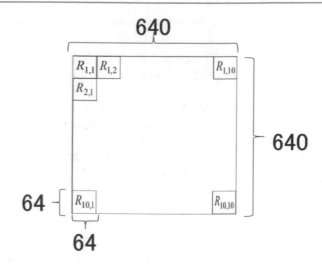

Fig. 75.5 Example of the block configuration in the image

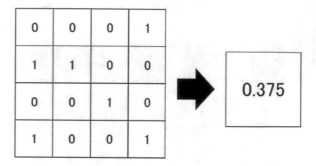

Fig. 75.6 An example of a representative value when the size of the block is 4 × 4 pixels

$$O_{bin}[i, j] = \begin{cases} 1 & \text{if} R[i, j] \leq \mu - \sigma \\ 0 & \text{otherwise.} \end{cases}$$

75.6 Experimental Results

We conducted experiments using endoscopic images provided by the department of internal medicine, Saga University, Japan. The experiment results are shown in Figs. 75.7, 75.8, 75.9, 75.10, 75.11, and 75.12.

The areas which are detected as the abnormal regions by our method is displayed in white. As shown in Figs. 75.7, 75.8, 75.9, 75.10, 75.11, and 75.12, we found that some areas in white of the images obtained by our method include the region of early gastric cancer marked by a doctor.

On the other hand, the areas detected as the abnormal regions are wider than the region of the early gastric cancer marked by a doctor. This means that the WTMM is very useful to distinguish the abnormal and normal regions of the endoscopic image, however, we need to adjust the parameters such as a block size and a dynamic threshold more appropriate to detect the abnormal ones more accurate.

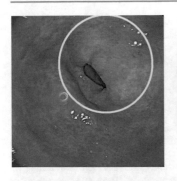

Fig. 75.7 An endoscopic image with the region of the early gastric cancer marked by a doctor (left) and the detection result with our method (right)

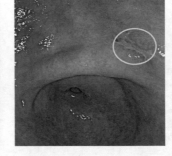

Fig. 75.10 An endoscopic image with the region of the early gastric cancer marked by a doctor (left) and the detection result with our method (right)

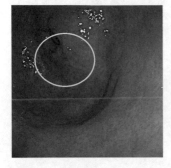

Fig. 75.8 An endoscopic image with the region of the early gastric cancer marked by a doctor (left) and the detection result with our method (right)

Fig. 75.11 An endoscopic image with the region of the early gastric cancer marked by a doctor (left) and the detection result with our method (right)

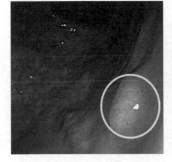

Fig. 75.9 An endoscopic image with the region of the early gastric cancer marked by a doctor (left) and the detection result with our method (right)

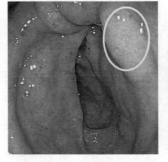

Fig. 75.12 An endoscopic image with the region of the early gastric cancer marked by a doctor (left) and the detection result with our method (right)

75.7   Conclusion

We propose a new method for detecting early gastric cancer from endoscopic images using the WTMM. Experimental results show that it is possible to detect areas containing abnormal areas corresponding to the early gastric cancer, and our method will help inexperienced doctors to detect the region of suspected of being gastric cancer from endoscopic images. This would lead to a reduction of overlooking rate of early gastric cancer in endoscopic examination. Finding more appropriate parameters such as a block size and a dynamic threshold to detect the abnormal regions with higher accuracy and using other wavelets remain the topics of a future study.

References

1. IARC, Stomach cancer estimated incidence, mortality and prevalence worldwide in 2012. http://globocan.iarc.fr/old/FactSheets/cancers/stomach-new.asp

2. T. Aoyama, T. Yoshikawa, T. Watanabe, T. Hayashi, T. Ogata, H. Cho, A. Tsuburaya, Macroscopic tumor size as an independent prognostic factor for stage II/III gastric cancer patients who underwent D2 gastrectomy followed by adjuvant chemotherapy with S-1. Gastric Cancer **14**, 274–278 (2011)

3. M. Serrano, I. Kikuste, M. Dinis-Ribeiro, Advanced endoscopic imaging for gastric cancer assessment: new insights with new optics? Best Pract. Res. Clin. Gastroenterol. **28**, 1079–1091 (2014)

4. M. Kaise, Advanced endoscopic imaging for early gastric cancer. Best Pract. Res. Clin. Gastroenterol. **29**, 575–587 (2015)

5. M. Song, T.L. Ang, Early detection of early gastric cancer using image-enhanced endoscopy: current trends. Gastrointest. Interv. **3**, 1–7 (2014)

6. Y. Morimoto, M. Kubo, M. Kuramoto, H. Yamaguchi, T. Kaku, Development of a New Generation Endoscope System with Lasers "LASEREO". Fujifilm Res. Dev. **58**, 6 pp. (2013)

7. T. Hu, Y.H. Lu, C.G. Cheng, X.C. Sun, Study on the early detection of gastric cancer based on discrete wavelet transformation feature extraction of FT-IR spectra combined with probability neural network. Spectroscopy **26**(3), 155–165 (2011)

8. H. Matsunaga, H. Omura, R. Ohura, T. Minamoto, Daubechies wavelet-based method for early esophageal cancer detection from flexible spectral imaging color enhancement image. Adv. Intell. Syst. Comput. **448**, 939–948 (2016)

9. T. Minamoto, K. Tsuruta, S. Fujii, Edge-preserving image denoising method based on dyadic lifting schemes. IPSJ Trans. Comput. Vis. Appl. **2**, 48–58 (2010)

10. T. Minamoto, R. Ohura, A blind digital image watermarking method based on the dyadic wavelet transform and interval arithmetic. Appl. Math. Comput. **226**, 306–319 (2014)

11. R. Ohura, H. Omura, Y. Sakata, T. Minamoto, Computer-aided diagnosis method for detecting early esophageal cancer from endoscopic image by using dyadic wavelet transform and fractal dimension. Adv. Intell. Syst. Comput. **448**, 929–938 (2016)

12. S. Mallat, *A Wavelet Tour of Signal Processing: The Sparse Way*, 3rd edn. (Academic, Burlington, MA, 2008)

13. S. Mallat, S. Zhong, Characterization of signals from multiscale edges. IEEE Trans. Pattern Anal. Mach. Intell. **14**(7), 710–732 (1992)

Detection Method of Early Esophageal Cancer from Endoscopic Image Using Dyadic Wavelet Transform and Four-Layer Neural Network

76

Hajime Omura and Teruya Minamoto

Abstract

We propose a new detection method of early esophageal cancer from endoscopic image by using the dyadic wavelet transform (DYWT) and the four-layered neural network (NN). We prepare 6500 appropriate training images to make a NN classifier for early esophageal cancer. Each training image is converted into HSV and CIEL*a*b* color spaces, and each fusion image is made from the S (saturation), a* (complementary color), and b* (complementary color) components. The fusion image is enhanced contrast so as to emphasize the difference of the pixel values between the normal and abnormal regions, and we use only high pixel values of this image for learning in the neural network. We can obtain the important image features by applying the inverse DYWT to processed image. We describe our proposed method in detail and present experimental results demonstrating that the detection result of the proposed method is superior to that of the deep learning technique utilizing the endoscopic image marked an early esophageal cancer by a doctor.

Keywords

Early esophageal cancer · Endoscopic image · Image enhancement · Dyadic wavelet transform · Layered neural network classifier

76.1 Introduction

The number of esophageal cancer patients and deaths has been increasing year by year in Japan. To avoid the risk of esophageal cancer and improve the recovery rate, it is important to find cancer as early as possible and concentrate on treatment. In the present, endoscopic examination is widely used for the diagnosis of esophageal cancer. However, as shown in Fig. 76.1, since the normal region and the abnormal region which is suspected of being early cancer are very similar in the endoscopic images, it is difficult to find early cancer. In addition, there is no diagnostic criteria for diagnosing early cancer based on endoscopic images at the present.

There are some methods to detect early esophageal cancer by emphasizing the visual difference between normal and abnormal regions of the image obtained by the endoscopic imaging system. For example, it is to perform the Lugol's iodine dye-enhanced endoscopy or to use a endoscope system that uses lasers with different wavelengths as light source. It is widely accepted by doctors that chromoendoscopy using Lugol's iodine solution is effective for the detection of esophageal cancer. However, many patients have side effects such as heartburn and chest pain, and their symptoms continue from several hours to 1 day. In order to alleviate the burden on such patients, new endoscopic systems adopting laser light source have been developed for diagnosing without the dyeing, such as the LASEREO [5] series of Fujifilm Corp. This endoscope system is available to use four modes by changing the ratio of emission intensity in two types of the laser. The four modes are Normal (White light), FICE (Flexible spectral Imaging Color Enhancement), BLI (Blue LASER Imaging), and BLI-bright. This endoscope system can emphasize minute changes in the mucosal surface layer of normal and abnormal regions. However, since diagnostic criteria for early esophageal cancer based on endoscopic images does not establishes, the endoscope diagnosis depends on subjective judgments of each doctor. Therefore, a method for detecting early esophageal cancer that does not depend on the subjective judgments of each doctor is required.

In recent years, the application of deep learning (DL) to medical image analysis has been actively studied. Litjens et al. [2] review major DL techniques associated with

H. Omura (✉) · T. Minamoto
Department of Information Science, Saga University, Saga, Japan
e-mail: ohmurah@ma.is.saga-u.ac.jp; minamoto@ma.is.saga-u.ac.jp

© Springer International Publishing AG, part of Springer Nature 2018
S. Latifi (ed.), *Information Technology – New Generations*, Advances in Intelligent Systems and Computing 738,
https://doi.org/10.1007/978-3-319-77028-4_76

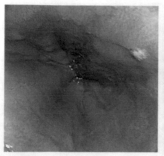

Fig. 76.1 Endoscopic image and the region of early esophageal cancer marked by a doctor

medical image analysis, and summarize some papers in this field. In Ref. [8], a patch based system with a hybrid convolutional neural network and support vector machine (SVM) model is proposed for intraepithelial papillary capillary loops recognition to aid clinical diagnosis, though, this method does not deal with early cancer. DL is a multi-layered neural network (NN) composed of dozens of hidden layers for performing nonlinear processing combining convolution and pooling layers. The merit of the DL technique can be performed the feature extraction automatically from the training data. However, as the number of layers of the DL technique increases, the number of parameters required for learning becomes enormous, and moreover, the number of layers has to be decided by trial and error. In addition, high quality training data is needed to increase the accuracy of the classifier obtained by the DL technique, and collection of these data takes considerable time and effort. Hence, it is desirable that the detection method is constituted by a small number of NNs to avoid the problem of the DL technique.

The proposed method in Ref. [1] detects the ulcer region using NN, SVM, and texture extraction scheme from the endoscopic image obtained by the capsule endoscopy. The detection for esophageal cancer is proposed in Ref. [7], however, it does not deal with the endoscopic image and early cancer.

The aim of this paper is to present a new method to detect early esophageal cancer f rom endoscopic image based on NN constructed using a small number of layers. In order to classify early esophageal cancer with a small number of layers, it is necessary to devise a feature extraction method of the training images. Since the nonlinear processing is performed in the feature extraction of the DL, the feature extraction method of the proposed method is also designed to be nonlinear. In Ref. [6], an abnormal region from the endoscopic image is highlighted by computing the fractal dimension of the image obtained by applying low-gradation processing to the enhanced image based on the low frequency component of the DYWT. We employ the images to which the inverse DYWT is applied for the pixel values within the specific range of the enhanced image as the training images

to be used for the NN classifier. Here, we set all pixel values of the high frequency component used in the inverse DYWT to 0. The proposed detection method is constructed using the NN classifier.

The remainder of this paper is organized as follows. In Sect. 76.2, we briefly describe the basics of the DYWT. In Sect. 76.3, we describe a classifier used for the proposed detection method. In Sect. 76.4, we present a new method to detect early esophageal cancer from an endoscopic image. We present experimental results in Sect. 76.5 and conclude the paper in Sect. 76.6.

76.2 Dyadic Wavelet Transform (DYWT)

Let us represent the original image by $C^0[m, n]$, which are samples of a normalized discrete image defined on a two-dimensional lattice of finite extent. It is well-known from Refs. [3, 4] that the dyadic wavelet transform (DYWT) for this image based on "algorithme à trous" is given by:

$$
\begin{aligned}
C^{j+1}[m, n] &= \sum_k \sum_l h[k]h[l]C_{k,l}^j[m, n], \\
D^{j+1}[m, n] &= \sum_k \sum_l g[k]h[l]C_{k,l}^j[m, n], \\
E^{j+1}[m, n] &= \sum_k \sum_l h[k]g[l]C_{k,l}^j[m, n], \\
F^{j+1}[m, n] &= \sum_k \sum_l g[k]g[l]C_{k,l}^j[m, n].
\end{aligned}
\tag{76.1}
$$

Here, $C_{k,l}^j[m, n] = C^j[m + 2^j k, n + 2^j l]$, h is a low-pass filter, and g is a high-pass filter. More precisely, $C^j[m, n]$, $D^j[m, n]$, $E^j[m, n]$, and $F^j[m, n]$ are the low-frequency components, the horizontal high-frequency components, the vertical high-frequency components, and the high-frequency components in both directions, respectively. The indices m and n indicate the locations in the horizontal and vertical directions, respectively.

The inverse DYWT is calculated by the following reconstruction algorithm:

$$
\begin{aligned}
C^j[m, n] = \frac{1}{4} \sum_k \sum_l (&\hat{C}_{\tilde{h}_k, \tilde{h}_l}^{j+1}[m, n] + \hat{D}_{\tilde{g}_k, \tilde{h}_l}^{j+1}[m, n] \\
&+ \hat{E}_{\tilde{h}_k, \tilde{g}_l}^{j+1}[m, n] + \hat{F}_{\tilde{g}_k, \tilde{g}_l}^{j+1}[m, n]),
\end{aligned}
\tag{76.2}
$$

where, $\hat{C}_{\tilde{h}_k, \tilde{g}_l}^{j+1}[m, n] = \tilde{h}[k]\tilde{g}[l]C^{j+1}[m - 2^j k, n - 2^j l]$, $\tilde{h}$ is a dual low-pass filter, and $\tilde{g}$ is a dual high-pass filter. Using the relations (76.1) and (76.2), the original discrete image C^0 is obtained.

76.3   Neural Network (NN) Classifier

In this section, we describe how to make the NN classifier for classifying an input image into normal, abnormal, and border region. Here, the border region includes both normal and abnormal region.

76.3.1   Preparation for Learning Image

In this subsection, we explain the feature extraction method for training images which are used to make the NN classifier. The purpose of this processing is to prepare appropriate training images for making better NN classifier. We apply the following processing to four endoscopic images in Fig. 76.2.

A-1.   Convert the RGB image to HSV and CIEL*a*b* color space, and obtain the H (hue), S (saturation), V (value), L (luminance), a^* (complementary color), and b^* (complementary color) components.

A-2.   Normalize the pixel values of S, a^* and b^* components in the range between 0 and 255.

A-3.   Compute the fusion image Sa^*b^* using normalized S, a^* and b^* components as follows:

$$Sa^*b^*[i, j] = \sqrt{(S[i, j])^2 + (a^*[i, j])^2 + (b^*[i, j])^2}$$

A-4.   Apply contrast enhancement to the fusion image Sa^*b^*, and obtain the image $Sa^*b^*_{hist}$.

Next, we prepared 52 images in total by cropping 30 normal, 10 abnormal or 12 border images from the four images in Fig. 76.3. Here, we explain the data augmentation processing used to increase the training images. The data augmentation employs the processing of the cropping and flipping in the same manner as Ref. [8]. We crop all 52 images of arbitrary sizes, and then fold the upper half or the lower half of these images in the vertical direction and the left half and the right half in the horizontal direction. Figure 76.4 shows an example of applying data augmentation to images of size 4 × 4 to produce the images of size 3 × 3. After all, we are able to make 20 images (4 × 5) from an image of size 4 × 4 in this example.

And, we obtained 6500 training images (3750 normal images, 1250 abnormal images, 1500 border images) of size 64 × 64 by applying data augmentation processing to 52 images. We perform the following procedures to each 6500 training images.

B-1.   Compute $EI[i, j]$ by using $Sa^*b^*_{hist}$ and the following relation:

$$EI[i, j] = \begin{cases} 0 & Sa^*b^*_{hist}[i, j] \leq 223 \\ Sa^*b^*_{hist}[i, j] & otherwise. \end{cases}$$

According to our preliminary experiments, the pixel values of the abnormal region in Fig. 76.3 tend to be higher, and we set the threshold to 223.

B-2.   Apply the DYWT three times to EI, and obtain the low frequency component C^3.

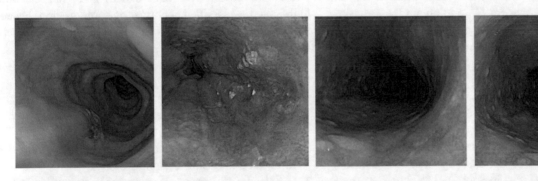

Fig. 76.2 Endoscopic images used for learning

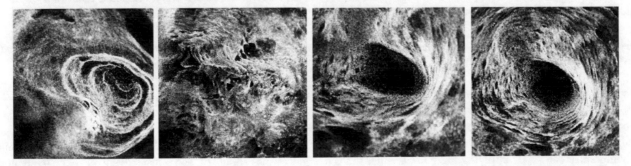

Fig. 76.3 The images obtained by applying the processing (A-1–A-4) to the images in Fig. 76.2

Fig. 76.4 Procedure of data augmentation

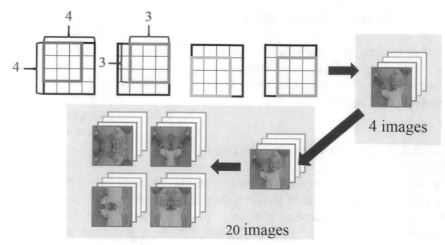

Fig. 76.5 Architecture of the classifier

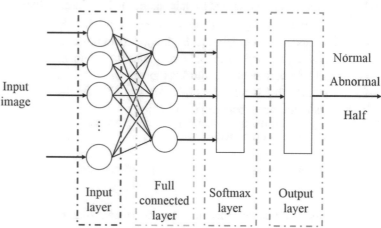

B-3. Apply the inverse DYWT three times to the low frequency component C^3, and obtain the reconstruct image. Here, we set the pixel values of all the high frequency components to 0 and apply the inverse DYWT.

76.3.2 Architecture of the NN Classifier

Figure 76.5 shows the architecture of the classifier. We have this NN classifier learn the training images obtained by performing the procedures in Sect. 76.3 to classify correctly normal, abnormal, and border region. We use the Stochastic gradient descent with momentum in the learning algorithm.

76.4 Detecting Procedure

It seems that doctors look for all regions where early esophageal cancer is suspected from endoscopic images. Hence, the proposed method divides the input endoscopic image into small blocks, and highlights the blocks suspected of being early cancer by applying the NN classifier to each

blocks. Moreover, we would like to note that the block highlighted is classified abnormal or border region, because we consider border region as abnormal region by the idea of false positives.

The procedure of our proposed detection method is as follow.

1. Apply all the procedures described in Sect. 76.3 to an input endoscopic image.
2. Divide the image obtained by the previous step 1 into 64×64 pixel non-overlapping blocks.
3. Apply the NN classifier to each blocks and set all the pixel values of the block classified abnormal or border to 0.

Figure 76.6 shows the example of our experimental results obtained by the proposed detection method.

76.5 Experimental Results

In the experiment, we used 35 endoscopic images obtained in Normal mode of early esophageal cancer. To evaluate the performance of the proposed method, we compared the

Fig. 76.6 Example of the detection result (*No* Normal region, *Ab* Abnormal region, *Bo* Border region)

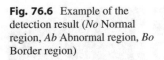
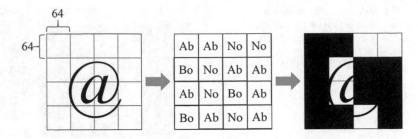

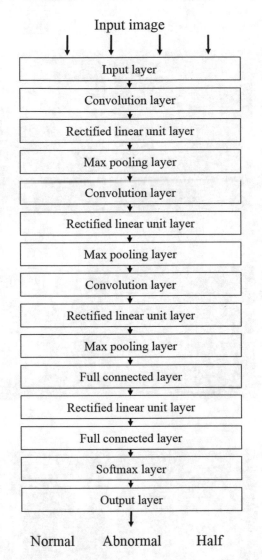

Fig. 76.7 Architecture of the DL technique

region detected by the proposed method with the region detected using the DL technique using the early esophageal cancer region marked by a doctor.

Figure 76.7 shows the architecture of the DL technique used to compare with the proposed method. We briefly describe the detection procedure using the DL technique. We made the DL classifier of the deep learning using the training images obtained by applying the processing from A-1 to A-4 in Sect. 76.3.

Detection procedure using the DL classifier is the same manner as Sect. 76.4. Figures 76.8, 76.9, 76.10, 76.11, and 76.12 show the results obtained by using the proposed method and the DL technique.

As shown in Fig. 76.8, the proposed method detects the region of esophageal cancer marked by a doctor. On the other hand, the DL technique does not detect the region of esophageal cancer marked by a doctor.

As shown in Fig. 76.9, the detection results of the proposed method and the DL technique are the small number of the blocks suspected of being early cancer in comparison with the region of esophageal cancer marked by a doctor.

As shown in Figs. 76.10, 76.11, 76.12, and 76.13, the detection results of the proposed method and the DL technique are the large number of the blocks suspected of being early cancer in comparison with the region of esophageal cancer marked by a doctor. However, as shown in Figs. 76.8, 76.9, 76.10, 76.11, 76.12, and 76.13, the detection results of the proposed method and the DL technique are the large number of the blocks detected the normal region as the abnormal or border region.

76.6 Conclusion

We propose a detection method of early esophageal cancer from endoscopic image using the dyadic wavelet transform and four-layered neural network. Our experimental results demonstrated that the proposed method is better than the DL technique with respect to the performance. In Fig. 76.8, the proposed method detected the region of esophageal cancer marked by a doctor. On the other hand, the DL technique did not detect this region. In addition, the detection accuracy of the proposed method is the same as one of the DL technique when both methods detected the regions marked by a doctor. Therefore, it is found that the feature extraction method of the proposed method described in Sect. 76.3 is more useful than the one of the DL technique, such as the convolution and pooling.

However, as indicated by the detection results of both the proposed method and the DL technique, there were many blocks classifying the normal region as abnormal or border region.

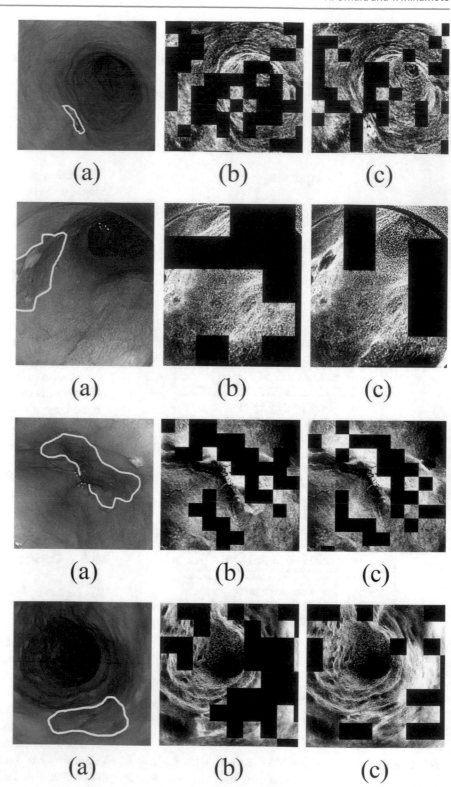

Fig. 76.8 (**a**) is the regions of early esophageal cancer marked by a doctor. (**b**) is the detection result obtained by the proposed method. (**c**) is the detection result obtained by the DL technique

Fig. 76.9 (**a**) is the regions of early esophageal cancer marked by a doctor. (**b**) is the detection result obtained by the proposed method. (**c**) is the detection result obtained by the DL technique

Fig. 76.10 (**a**) is the regions of early esophageal cancer marked by a doctor. (**b**) is the detection result obtained by the proposed method. (**c**) is the detection result obtained by the DL technique

Fig. 76.11 (**a**) is the regions of early esophageal cancer marked by a doctor. (**b**) is the detection result obtained by the proposed method. (**c**) is the detection result obtained by the DL technique

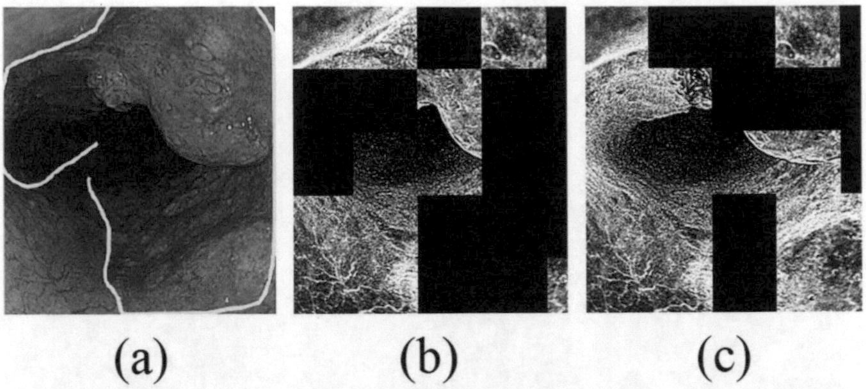

Fig. 76.12 (**a**) is the regions of early esophageal cancer marked by a doctor. (**b**) is the detection result obtained by the proposed method. (**c**) is the detection result obtained by the DL technique

(a)   (b)   (c)

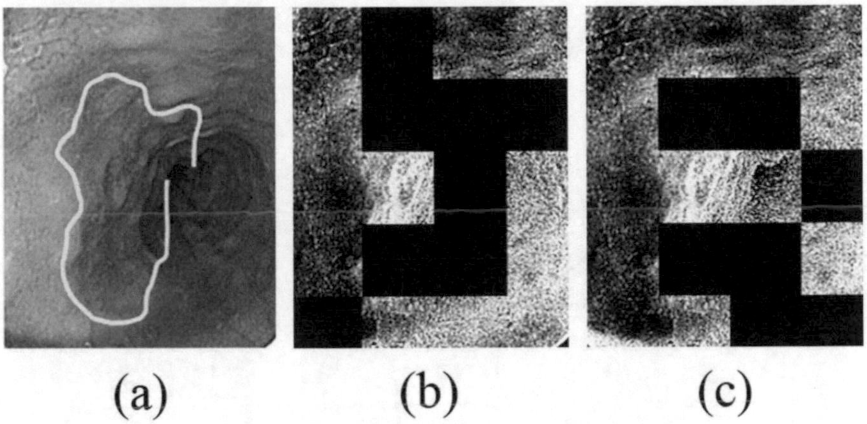

Fig. 76.13 (**a**) is the regions of early esophageal cancer marked by a doctor. (**b**) is the detection result obtained by the proposed method. (**c**) is the detection result obtained by the DL technique

(a)   (b)   (c)

In future work, we will attempt to improve the detection accuracy of our method, and develop a detection method based on the NN classifier using the features extracted from the high frequency components which were not used in the proposed method.

References

1. B. Li, M.Q.-H. Meng, Texture analysis for ulcer detection in capsule endoscopy images. Image Vis. Comput. **27**(9), 1336–1342 (2009)
2. G. Litjens, T. Kooi, B. Bejnordi, A. Setio, F. Ciompi, M. Ghafoorian, J. van der Laak, B. van Ginneken, C. Sanchez, A survey on deep learning in medical image analysis. Med. Image Anal. **42**, 60–88 (2017)
3. S. Mallat, *A Wavelet Tour of Signal Processing* (Academic, New York, NY, 2009)
4. T. Minamoto, R. Ohura, A blind digital image watermarking method based on the dyadic wavelet transform and interval arithmetic. Appl. Math. Comput. **226**, 306–319 (2014)
5. Y. Morimoto, M. Kubo, M. Kuramoto, H. Yamaguchi, T. Kaku, Development of a new generation endoscope system with lasers "LASEREO". Fujifilm Res. Dev. **58**, 6 pp. (2013)
6. R. Ohura, H. Omura, Y. Sakata, T. Minamoto, Computer-aided diagnosis method for detecting early esophageal cancer from endoscopic image by using dyadic wavelet transform and fractal dimension. Adv. Intell. Syst. Comput. **448**, 929–934 (2016)
7. Y. Xu, F.M. Selaru, J. Yin, T.T. Zou, V. Shustova, Y. Mori, F. Sato, T.C. Liu, A. Olaru, S. Wang, M.C. Kimos, K. Perry, K. Desai, B.D. Greenwald, M.J. Krasna, D. Shibata, J.M. Abraham, S.J. Meltzer, Artificial Neural Networks and gene filtering distinguish between global gene expression profiles of Barrett's esophagus and esophageal cancer. Cancer Res. **62**(12), 3493–3497 (2002)
8. D.-X. Xue, R. Zhang, H. Feng, Y.-L. Wang, CNN-SVM For microvascular morphological type recognition with data augmentation. J. Med. Biol. Eng. **36**(6), 755–764 (2016)

Study of Specific Location of Exhaustive Matching in Order to Improve the Optical Flow Estimation

77

Vanel Lazcano

Abstract

Optical flow is defined as pixel motion between two images. Hence, in order to estimate optical flow, an energy model is proposed. This model considers: a data term and a regularization term. Data term is an optical flow error estimation and regularization term imposes spatial smoothness. Most of traditional variational models use a linearized version of data term, which fails when the displacement of the object is larger than their own size. Last years the precision of optical flow method has been increased due to the use of additional information, which comes from correspondences computed between two images obtained by: SIFT, Deep-matching or exhaustive search. This paper presents an experimental study to evaluate strategies for locating exhaustive correspondences improving flow estimation. We considered different location for matching: random location, uniform location, maximum of the gradient and maximum error of the optical flow estimation. Best performance (minimum EPE and AAE error) was obtained by the Uniform Location which outperforms reported results in the literature.

Keywords

Motion estimation · Large displacement · Variational model · Gradient constancy constraint · Color constancy constraint

77.1 Introduction

Optical flow is the apparent motion pattern of the objects in a video sequence. Optical flow methods consider two consecutive images: reference image (current image) and target image (next image). In order to estimate motion in a sequence of images optical flow methods propose an energy model depending on an argument u. The argument u that minimizes the proposed energy model is the optical flow of the video sequence. This energy model considers two terms: a data term and a regularization term [4]. The data term aims to find corresponding pixels (of the reference image) of similar gray/color value in the target image and the regularization term imposes spatial smoothness of the optical flow. Normally optical flow methods use a linear approximation of the data term. Models that consider this linear approximation fail to estimate the optical flow whether the displacements of the object are larger than their own size. Last years a new term that considers correspondences between two images have been added to these approximated models [2, 5, 9, 13]. The inclusion of this additional information (as a prior) has improved the performance of the optical flow estimation giving the model the capability of getting large displacements.

In [13] a model to handle large displacement is proposed. This model proposed an energy that considers a data term, a regularization term and a term for additional information. The additional information term used in this model comes from correspondences computed by SIFT. With each computed correspondence a constant candidate flow is proposed as a possible motion present in the image. Authors select the optimal flow among the constant candidates for each pixel in the image sequence as a labeling problem. The authors solve this problem using discrete optimization QPBO (Quadratic Pseudo-Boolean Optimization).

In [3] is presented a model for estimating the optical flow that utilizes a robust data term, a regularization term and a term that considers additional matching. Additional matching is obtained using HoG (Histograms of Gradients). The incorporation of additional matching is weighted by a confidence value which is not simple to compute. This weight depends on the distance to the second best candidate

The original version of this chapter was revised. An erratum to this chapter can be found at https://doi.org/10.1007/978-3-319-77028-4_102

V. Lazcano (✉)
Núcleo de Matemáticas, Física y Estadística, Facultad de Ciencias, Universidad Mayor, Chile
e-mail: vanel.lazcano@umayor.cl

© Springer International Publishing AG, part of Springer Nature 2018
S. Latifi (ed.), *Information Technology – New Generations*, Advances in Intelligent Systems and Computing 738, https://doi.org/10.1007/978-3-319-77028-4_77

of the matching. The location of the matching depends on the texture of the image and also on the error of the optical flow estimation.

Deep-flow presented in [11] is an optical flow method inspired by (1) deep convolution neural networks and (2) the work of [2]. Deep-flow is an optical flow estimation method to handle large displacements. This method computes dense correspondences between the actual image and the next image. These correspondences are estimated using small patches (of 4×4 pixels). A patch of 8×8 is interpreted as composed by 4 patches of 4×4 pixels, each small patch is called a quadrant. The matching score of an 8×8 patch is formed by averaging the max-pooled scores of the quadrants[11] . This process is repeated recursively for 16×16, 32×32 and 64×64 pixels becoming a more discriminant virtual patch. Computed matching are considered a prior term in an energy model. Deep-flow uses an uniform grid to locate the correspondences.

In [7] the motion estimation is performed segmenting the sequence of images in meaningful objects using color and texture. Then, an object tracking algorithm is applied between consecutive images.

In [10] is presented an application of block matching in order to determine integrity and authenticity of digital images.

We present an experimental study to evaluate different strategies to locate additional correspondences (coming from exhaustive search) to improve the precision of the optical flow estimation. In our opinion none of above revised works has answered precisely the question "where do we locate additional correspondences in order to improve the performance of the optical flow estimation?". We considered four possible locations of matching: (1) uniform locations, (2) random locations, (3) location in the maximum gradients of the reference image and (4) location in the maximum error of optical flow.

This document presents the following structure. In Sect. 77.2 we present the model we use to estimate the optical flow. In Sect. 77.3 the implementation of the methods is presented and also the pseudo-code of the algorithm. In Sect. 77.4 we present performed experiments and the database used and in Sect. 77.5 obtained results are presented. Finally, in Sect. 77.6 we present our conclusions.

77.2   Proposed Model

Inspired by models presented in [8, 12, 13] and [9] we propose a variational model to estimate the optical flow. Those considered models use the L^1 norm (a data term which is robust to illumination changes) and an additional term that incorporate additional information coming from exhaustive search.

Let $I_0, I_1 : \Omega \subset \mathbb{R}^2 \to \mathbb{R}$ be two consecutive images. Let $\mathbf{u} = (u_1, u_2) : \Omega \subset \mathbb{R}^2 \to \mathbb{R}^2$ the optical flow between the images:

$$J(\mathbf{u}) = J_d(\mathbf{u}) + J_r(\mathbf{u}),$$

where $J_d(\mathbf{u})$ is the data term and is given by:

$$J_d(\mathbf{u}) = \int_\Omega \lambda \, |I_0(\mathbf{x}) - I_1(\mathbf{x} + \mathbf{u})| . \qquad (77.1)$$

where λ is a real constant and $J_r(\mathbf{u})$ is given by:

$$J_r(\mathbf{u}) = \int_\Omega \sqrt{|\nabla u_1|^2 + |\nabla u_2|^2} .$$

77.2.1 Linearization

The model presented in [12] considers a linearization of the data term in Eq. (77.1), $I_1(\mathbf{x})$ is linearized around $\mathbf{x} + \mathbf{u_0}$:

$$I_1(\mathbf{x} + \mathbf{u}) = I_1(\mathbf{x} + \mathbf{u_0}) + < \mathbf{u} - \mathbf{u_0}, \nabla I_1(\mathbf{x} + \mathbf{u_0}) >,$$

where $\mathbf{u_0}$ is a known optical flow and $\nabla I_1(\mathbf{x} + \mathbf{u_0})$ is the gradient of the warped image $I_1(\mathbf{x} + \mathbf{u_0})$. Considering this linearization we obtain a new data term that can be written as:

$$\tilde{J}_d(\mathbf{u}) = \int_\Omega \lambda |I_1(\mathbf{x} + \mathbf{u_0}) \\ + < \mathbf{u} - \mathbf{u_0}, \nabla I_1(\mathbf{x} + \mathbf{u_0}) > - I_0(\mathbf{x})| d\mathbf{x}. \qquad (77.2)$$

77.2.2 Data Term Robust to Illumination Changes

Data term in Eq. (77.2) is based on the brightness constancy assumption, which states that the intensity of the pixels in the image keeps constant along the sequence. In most of the cases, this assumption does not hold due to shadows, reflections or illumination changes. The gradient constancy assumption appears as an alternative that can handle pixels intensity changes.

We define a weight map $\alpha(x) : \mathbb{R}^2 \to [0, 1]$ to switch between the brightness and gradient constancy assumption as in [13]. We construct a new data term:

$$J_d(\mathbf{u}) = \lambda \int_\Omega \alpha(x) D_I(\mathbf{u}, \mathbf{x}) \\ + \lambda \int_\Omega \tau_d (1 - \alpha(\mathbf{x})) D_{\nabla I}(\mathbf{u}, \mathbf{x}). \qquad (77.3)$$

where,

$$D_I(\mathbf{u}, \mathbf{x}) = |I_1(\mathbf{x} + \mathbf{u_0}) +$$
$$< \mathbf{u} - \mathbf{u_0}, \nabla I_1(\mathbf{x} + \mathbf{u_0}) > -I_0(\mathbf{x})|. \quad (77.4)$$

Equation (77.4) represents a linearized version of the brightness constancy assumption and,

$$D_{\nabla I}(\mathbf{x}, \mathbf{u}) = |\partial_x I_1(\mathbf{x} + \mathbf{u_0}) + < \mathbf{u} - \mathbf{u_0}, \nabla \partial_x I_1(\mathbf{x} + \mathbf{u_0}) >$$
$$- \partial_x I_0(\mathbf{x})| + |\partial_y I_1(\mathbf{x} + \mathbf{u_0}) + < \mathbf{u} - \mathbf{u_0}, \nabla \partial_y I_1(\mathbf{x} + \mathbf{u_0}) >$$
$$- \partial_y I_0(\mathbf{x})|, \quad (77.5)$$

represents the gradient constancy assumption, where τ_d is a positive constant. In Eq. (77.5) the terms $\partial_x I_0$, $\partial_x I_1$ and $\partial_y I_0$, $\partial_y I_1$ are the partial derivatives w.r.t. x and y of I_0 and I_1 respectively.

Considering Eqs. (77.4) and (77.5), we follow [13] and we state the adaptive weight map $\alpha(x)$:

$$\alpha(\mathbf{x}) = \frac{1}{1 + e^{\beta(D_I(\mathbf{x}) - \tau_d D_{\nabla I}(\mathbf{x}))}},$$

where β is a positive constant real value.

The computation of $\alpha(\mathbf{x})$ depends on the difference of two terms: D_I and D_∇. In one hand if D_I is larger than D_∇, the data term will be more confident in the gradient constancy constrain. In the other hand if D_I less than D_∇, the data term will be more confident on the color constancy constrain [5, 13].

In order to minimize the proposed functional in Eq. (77.1) we propose to use three decoupling variables ($\mathbf{v_1}$, $\mathbf{v_2}$, $\mathbf{v_3}$) and we penalize its deviation from $\mathbf{u}$, then, the functional become:

$$J(\mathbf{u}, \mathbf{v_1}, \mathbf{v_2}, \mathbf{v_3}) = J_d(\mathbf{u}, \mathbf{v_1}, \mathbf{v_2}, \mathbf{v_3}) + J_r(\mathbf{u})$$
$$+ \frac{1}{2\theta} \int_\Omega \sum_{i=1}^{3} \bar{\alpha}_i (\mathbf{u} - \mathbf{v_i})^2, \quad (77.6)$$

where, $\bar{\alpha} \in \mathbb{R}^3$ and is defined as : $\bar{\alpha}(\mathbf{x}) = \big(\alpha(\mathbf{x}), 1 - \alpha(\mathbf{x}), 1 - \alpha(\mathbf{x})\big)^T$.

77.2.3 Color Model

Considering color images in RGB space ($I = \{I_1, I_2, I_3\}$ which correspond to red, blue and green components respectively) we define five decoupling variables $\mathbf{v_1}$, $\mathbf{v_2}$, $\mathbf{v_3}$ for color component and $\mathbf{v_3}$, $\mathbf{v_4}$ for gradients, thus the functional became:

$$J(\mathbf{u}, \bar{\mathbf{v}}) = J_d(\mathbf{u}, \bar{\mathbf{v}}) + J_r(\mathbf{u}) + \frac{1}{2\theta} \int_\Omega \sum_{i=1}^{5} \bar{\alpha}_i (\mathbf{u} - \mathbf{v_i})^2, \quad (77.7)$$

where we have defined $\bar{\mathbf{v}} = \{\mathbf{v_1}, \mathbf{v_2}, \mathbf{v_3}, \mathbf{v_4}, \mathbf{v_5}\}$ and $\bar{\alpha} \in \mathbb{R}^5$ and defined as : $\bar{\alpha}(\mathbf{x}) = \big(\alpha(\mathbf{x}), \alpha(\mathbf{x}), \alpha(\mathbf{x}), 1 - \alpha(\mathbf{x}), 1 - \alpha(\mathbf{x})\big)^T$.

77.2.4 Optical Flow to Handle Large Displacements

In order to cope with large displacements, we use additional information coming from exhaustive matchings computed between images of video sequence used as a precomputed sparse vector field (a prior). The main idea is that this vector field guides the optical flow estimation in regions where the approximated linearized model fails [9].

Let $\mathbf{u_e}$ be this sparse vector field. We added to our model a term to enforce the solution $\mathbf{u}$ to be similar to the sparse flow $\mathbf{u_e}$ as in [9], and our model became:

$$J(\mathbf{u}, \bar{\mathbf{v}}, \mathbf{u_e}) = \tilde{J}_d(\mathbf{u}, \bar{\mathbf{v}}) + J_r(\mathbf{u}) + \frac{1}{2\theta} \int_\Omega \sum_{i=1}^{5} \bar{\alpha}_i (\mathbf{u} - \mathbf{v_i})^2$$
$$+ \int_\Omega \kappa \chi(\mathbf{x})(\mathbf{u} - \mathbf{u_e})^2,$$

where $\chi(\mathbf{x})$ is binary mask indicating where the matching was computed, κ is a decreasing weight for each scale. Following [9] the κ is updated for each iteration $\kappa = \kappa_0 = (0.5)^n$, where $\kappa_0 = 300$ and n is the iteration number.

The binary $\chi(\mathbf{x})$ value indicates where $\mathbf{u_e}$ was computed. We use this $\chi(\mathbf{x})$ value to test different location of $\mathbf{u_e}$ to evaluate the influence of additional matchings in the performance.

77.2.5 solving the Model

For a fixed $\mathbf{u_0}$ and following the notation in [12] we define: $\rho_i(\mathbf{u})$. Let $\rho_i(\mathbf{u}) = I_i(\mathbf{x} + \mathbf{u_0}) + \langle \mathbf{u} - \mathbf{u_0}, \nabla I_i \rangle - I_0$ with $i = 1, .., 3$. $\rho_4(\mathbf{u}) = \partial_x I_1(\mathbf{x} + \mathbf{u_0}) + \langle \mathbf{u} - \mathbf{u_0}, \nabla \partial_x I_1 \rangle - \partial_x I_0$ and $\rho_5(\mathbf{u}) = \partial_y I_1(\mathbf{x} + \mathbf{u_0}) + \langle \mathbf{u} - \mathbf{u_0}, \nabla \partial_y I_1 \rangle - \partial_y I_0$. If θ is a small constant, then $\mathbf{v_1}$, $\mathbf{v_2}$, $\mathbf{v_3}$, $\mathbf{v_4}$ and $\mathbf{v_5}$ are close to $\mathbf{u}$. This convex problem can be minimized by alternating steps as in [12]:

1. Solve exhaustively

$$J_d(\mathbf{u_e}) = \min_{\mathbf{u_e}} \int_\Omega |I_0(\mathbf{x}) - I_1(\mathbf{x} + \mathbf{u_e})|. \quad (77.8)$$

2. Let us fix $\mathbf{v_1}$, $\mathbf{v_2}$, $\mathbf{v_3}$, $\mathbf{v_4}$, $\mathbf{v_5}$ and then solve for $\mathbf{u}$:

$$\min_{\mathbf{u}} \left\{ \int_{\Omega} \sum_{i=1}^{5} \frac{\bar{\alpha}_i (\mathbf{u} - \mathbf{v_i})^2}{2\theta} + \int_{\Omega} \kappa \chi (\mathbf{u} - \mathbf{u_e}) + \int_{\Omega} \|\nabla u\| \right\} \tag{77.9}$$

3. Let us fix $\mathbf{u}$ and solve the problem for $\mathbf{v_1}$, $\mathbf{v_2}$, $\mathbf{v_3}$, $\mathbf{v_4}$, $\mathbf{v_5}$:

$$\min_{\mathbf{v_i}} \left\{ \int_{\Omega} \sum_{i=1}^{5} (\mathbf{u} - \mathbf{v_i})^2 + \int_{\Omega} |\rho_i(\mathbf{v_i})| \right\}. \tag{77.10}$$

This minimization problem for $\mathbf{v_1}$ $\mathbf{v_2}$, $\mathbf{v_3}$, $\mathbf{v_4}$, $\mathbf{v_5}$ can be solved point-wise.

Due that the propositions in [12] are fundamentals for our work we adapted them to our model.

Proposition 1 *The solution of Eq. (77.9) is given by:*

$$u = \frac{\alpha \frac{v_1 + v_2 + v_3}{3} + (1 - \alpha)\left(\frac{v_4 + v_5}{2}\right) + \theta \, div(g\xi) + \kappa \chi u_e}{1 + \kappa \chi} \tag{77.11}$$

The dual variable $\xi = (\xi_1, \xi_2)^T$ is defines as:

$$\xi_1 = \frac{\xi_1 + \frac{\tau}{\theta} \nabla u_1}{1 + \frac{\tau}{\theta} \sqrt{|\nabla u_1|^2 + |\nabla u_2|^2}}, \tag{77.12}$$

$$\xi_2 = \frac{\xi_2 + \frac{\tau}{\theta} \nabla u_2}{1 + \frac{\tau}{\theta} \sqrt{|\nabla u_1|^2 + |\nabla u_2|^2}}, \tag{77.13}$$

where $\tau < \frac{1}{4}$.

Proposition 2 *The solution of the minimizing problem in Eq. (77.10) is given by:*

$$\mathbf{v_i} = u + \begin{cases} 3\lambda\theta\nabla I_i(\mathbf{x} + \mathbf{u_0}) & \text{if } \rho_i(\mathbf{u}) < -3\lambda\theta\mathbf{m_i} \\ -\frac{\rho_i(u)}{|\nabla I_i|}\nabla I_i(\mathbf{x} + \mathbf{u_0}) & \text{if } |\rho_i(\mathbf{u})| < 3\lambda\theta\mathbf{m_i} \\ -3\lambda\theta\nabla I_i(\mathbf{x} + \mathbf{u_0}) & \text{if } \rho_i(\mathbf{u}) > 3\lambda\theta\mathbf{m_i} \end{cases} \tag{77.14}$$

For $i = 1, 2, 3$ and $\mathbf{m_i} = |\nabla I_i(\mathbf{x} + \mathbf{u_0})|^2$.

$$\mathbf{v_i} = u + \begin{cases} 2\lambda\theta\tau_d\nabla\partial_i I_1(\mathbf{x} + \mathbf{u_0}) & \text{if } \rho_i(\mathbf{u}) < -2\lambda\theta\tau_d\mathbf{md_i} \\ -\frac{\rho_i(u)}{|\nabla\partial_i I_1|}\nabla\partial_i I_1(\mathbf{x} + \mathbf{u_0}) & \text{if } |\rho_i(\mathbf{u})| < 2\lambda\theta\tau_d\mathbf{md_i} \\ -2\lambda\theta\tau_d\nabla\partial_i I_1(\mathbf{x} + \mathbf{u_0}) & \text{if } \rho_i(\mathbf{u}) > 2\lambda\theta\tau_d\mathbf{md_i} \end{cases} \tag{77.15}$$

For $i = 4, 5$ and $\partial_4 = \partial_x$ and $\partial_5 = \partial_y$ and $\mathbf{md_i} = |\nabla\partial_i I_1(\mathbf{x} + \mathbf{u_0})|^2$.

77.3　Implementation and Pseudo-Code

The model was solved by a sequence of optimization steps. First, we performed the exhaustive search in specific locations obtaining $\mathbf{u_e}$ flow, then we fixed $\mathbf{u}$ to estimate $\bar{\mathbf{v}}$, finally we estimate the $\mathbf{u}$ and the dual variable ξ. All those steps where performed iteratively. Our implementation is based on [6] which consider a coarse to fine multiscale approach.

77.3.1　Exhaustive Search

The parameter P defines the size of a neighborhood in the reference image, i.e. a neighborhood of $(2P + 1) \times (2P + 1)$ pixels. For each patch in (I_0) we computed:

$$J_d(\mathbf{u_e}) = \int_{\Omega} |I_0(\mathbf{x}) - I_1(\mathbf{x} + \mathbf{u_e})|, \tag{77.16}$$

we search for the argument $\mathbf{u_e}$ that minimizes the cost value.

77.3.2　Matching Confidence Value

Let $c(x)$ be the confidence measure given to each exhaustive matching. The proposed model for $C(x)$ is based on the distance between the first-second and second-third best candidates of the exhaustive search.

$$c(x) = \left(\frac{d_1 - d_2}{d_1}\right), \tag{77.17}$$

where d_1 is the distance between the first and second candidate and d_2 is the distance between the second and the third candidate.

77.3.3　Pseudo Code

The model was implemented based on the available code in IPOL [6] for the TVL1 model. The model was programmed in C in a Laptop with i7 processor and 16 GB RAM. The pseudo code is presented in Algorithm 2.

Algorithm to compute optical flow using additional information:

77.4　Experiments and Database

77.4.1　Database

The proposed model has been tested in the available Middlebury database [1] and ground truth is available for sequences with small displacements. We have divided the Middlebury

Algorithm 2 Optical flow with additional matching

Input
Two consecutives color images I_0, I_1
Parameters α, λ, P, θ_0, τ_d, β, $MaxIter$, β, κ, $Number_{scales}$, $Number_{warpings}$.

Output
optical flow $u = (u_1, u_2)$

$Down - scale I_0$, $I_1 for scale = 1, ..., Number_{scales}$
Inicialize
Scale images I_{-1}, I_0, I_1.

Initialization $u = v = w = 0$.

for $scales \leftarrow Number_{scales}$ to 1 **do**
  Construct ψ
  In locations defined by ψ, compute $\mathbf{u_e}$ using Eq. (77.7).
  for $w \leftarrow 1$ to $Number_{warpings}$ **do**
    Compute $\alpha(\mathbf{x})$.
    Compute $\mathbf{v_i}$, Eqs. (77.13) and (77.14).
    Compute $\mathbf{u}$, Eq. (77.10).
    Compute ξ Eqs. (77.11) and (77.12).
    update $\kappa_n = \kappa(0.5)^{scales}$
  end for
  up-sample $\mathbf{u}$
end for
Out $\mathbf{u}$.

sequences in two groups: (1) those sequences where the displacements are smaller than the size of the objects in the scene and having no major illumination changes (see Fig. 77.1), (2) sequences containing displacements larger than the size of the object itself, shadows or reflections (Fig. 77.2).

Figure 77.1 shows two consecutive frames, namely, frame 10, frame 11. In our model, I_0 corresponds to frame 10, I_1 to frame 11. In the Fig. 77.1a, b correspond to Grove2 sequence. In (c) and (d), Grove3 sequence. In (e) and (f), Rubberwhale. In (g) and (h), Hydra sequence. In (i) and (j), Urban2 sequence. In (k) and (l), Urban3 sequence. In all those sequences displacements are smaller than the size of the corresponding moving scene objects.

In Fig. 77.2a, b, we present Dogdance sequence. In (c) and (d), Beanbags sequence.

77.5 Results

In this section we present quantitative results obtained by the optical flow estimation model presented above. We have divided the data base in training set and validation set. For small displacement we used the sequences Grove3 and Rubberwhale as training set (TRAINING_SMALL) and for large displacement we used the sequences Dogdance and Beanbags as training set(TRAINING_LARGE). The other sequences are used to validate the method.

77.5.1 Parameter Estimation

Initially, we estimated the best parameters in our TRAIN-ING_SMALL set considering $\kappa = 0.0$ i.e, the model cannot handle large displacements. We scan the parameter θ, λ fixing $\tau = 1.0$, $\beta = 0.0$ estimating EPE (End Point Error) and AAE (Average Angular Error) error. we show the average EPE in Fig. 77.3

We observe in Fig. 77.3 that the minimum value for both EPE and AAE error is located in $\theta = 0.1$ and $\lambda = 0.1$. We selected these parameter value. In Fig. 77.4 we show the obtained optical flow for fixed θ and λ parameters.

With these parameters we obtained an average EPE = 0.1547, AAE = 3.7764.

We fixed the value of θ and λ and then we varied the value of τ_d and β parameters obtaining EPE and AAE as we show in Fig. 77.5.

We have the obtained result varying τ_d form 0.1 to 2.3 and β from 1 to 8. We obtained a minimum in $\tau_d = 1.9$ and $\beta = 2.0$. With these parameters we obtained and average EPE = 0.1369, AAE = 3.1186. In Fig. 77.6 we show the optical flow and the weight map $\alpha(x)$.

We observe in Fig. 77.6 in (a) and (d) the obtained optical flow using weight map $\alpha(x)$. we observe an improvement for both estimated optical flow. In (c) and (d) we present the α function for both sequences. Low gray levels represent low values of $alpha(x)$ i.e. the uses the gradient constancy assumption. Higher gray level means that the model uses the brightness constancy assumption. As we see in (d) the model uses gradients on shadows in the right side of the whale and left side of the wheel. In most location $\alpha(x) = 0.5$.

77.5.2 Reported Results

We show in Table 77.1 the reported values for TV-L1 in [6] using gray level images of the Middlebury database.
In Table 77.2 we present our results obtained using the set of parameters above determined.

In Table 77.2 we observe that in most of the cases the obtained result are similar to the one reported in [6]. For real sequences Dime and Hydra our model outperform the model in [6]. In the sequence Urban3 our method present larger error (AAE) than the one obtained in Table 77.1.

77.5.3 Specific Location of Matching $\kappa \neq 0$

Considering the integration of exhaustive matching to our variational model we perform an empirical evaluation to determine the best location of exhaustive matching in order to improve the optical flow estimation. We compare four strategies to locate exhaustive matching: (1) uniform location

Fig. 77.1 Images of Middlebury database containing small displacements. (**a**) Grove2 sequence, (**b**) Grove2 sequence, (**c**) Grove3 sequence, (**d**) Grove3 sequence, (**e**) Rubberwhale, (**f**) Rubberwhale, (**g**) Hydra sequence, (**h**) Hydra sequence, (**i**) Urban2 sequence, (**j**) Urban2 sequence, (**k**) Urban3 sequence, (**i**) Urban3 sequence

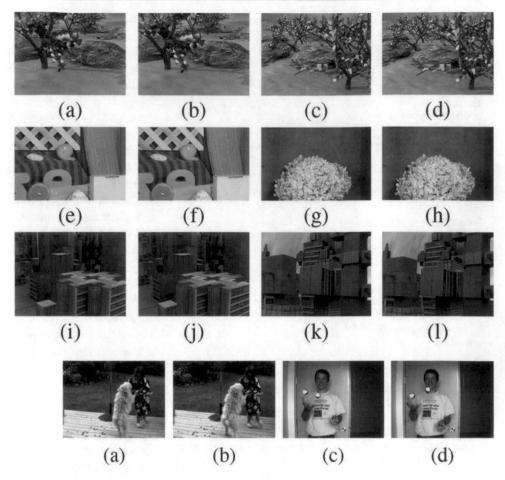

Fig. 77.2 Images of Middlebury database containing large displacements. (**a**) Dogdance sequence, (**b**) Dogdance sequence, (**c**) Beanbags sequence, (**d**) Beanbags sequence

Fig. 77.3 EPE and AEE average error for Grove2 and RubberWhale sequence. (**a**) AAE error. (**b**) EPE error

Fig. 77.4 Color coded optical flow. (**a**) Color coded optical flow for Grove2. (**b**) Color coded optical flow for Rubberwhale. (**c**) Color code

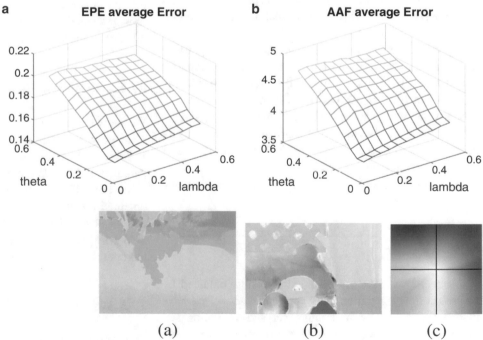

Fig. 77.5 EPE and AEE average error for Grove2 and RubberWhale sequence varying τ and β. (**a**) AAE error. (**b**) EPE error

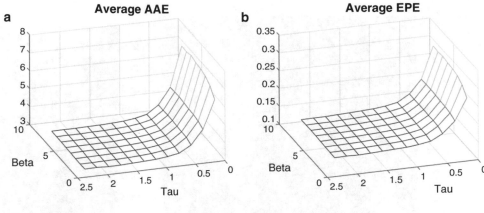

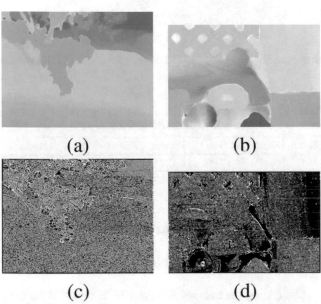

(a)   (b)

(c)   (d)

Fig. 77.6 Color coded optical flow. (**a**) Color coded optical flow for Grove2. (**b**) Color coded optical flow for Rubberwhale. (**c**) Weight map $\alpha(x)$ for Grove2. (**d**) Weight map $\alpha(x)$ for Urban2

Table 77.1 Reported performance of TV-L1 in Middelbury [6]

Error	Dime	Grove3	Hydra	Urban3	Venus	Average
EPE	0.162	0.721	0.258	0.711	0.394	0.4492
AAE	2.888	6.590	2.814	6.631	6.831	5.1508

Table 77.2 Obtained results of our model in Middlebury with $\kappa = 0.0$

Error	Dime	Grove3	Hydra	Urban3	Venus	Average
EPE	0.0925	0.7090	0.1729	0.7078	0.3492	0.4063
AAE	1.8248	6.5913	2.0626	6.9080	6.0818	4.6937

in a grid $\mathcal{G} \subset \Omega$, (2) random location of matchings, (3) matchings located in maximum of the magnitude of the gradient and (4) maximum of the optical flow estimation error $= \sum_{i=1}^{3} \rho_i(u)$.

77.5.3.1 Uniform Locations

This is the most simple strategy to locate exhaustive matching. Location depends on the size of the Grid $\mathcal{G}$. Let us represent the grid $\mathcal{G}$ with the D parameter i.e. we locate the exhaustive matching every other D pixel. We represent the size of a patch with the parameter P. It means that we have two parameter to define the Uniform locations of the matching.

In Fig. 77.7 we present exhaustive correspondences computed in a uniform grid. We present a zoomed area for Grove2 and Rubberwhale sequences.

We vary these parameters P and D from 2 to 10 and from 2 to 18, respectively. We show our results in Fig. 77.8.

We observe that the minimum of the error is obtained for large values of the D due to frequently the exhaustive search gives some false matching as we see in Fig. 77.7b. Increasing the Grid D parameter produces a more confident matching. Thus, we select $P = 4$ and $D = 16$. With these parameters we include in the model around 900 matching. Considering these selected parameters we obtained an average EPE $= 0.1332$ and AAE $= 3.0080$ in TRAINING_SMALL set. In VALIDATION_SMALL we obtained the results showed in Table 77.3.

For sequence Urban3 we used $P = 24$ and $\alpha(x) = 1.0$. Due to this image is produce by cgi and it presents autosimilarities.

77.5.3.2 Random Locations

We performed the experiments locating the matching and using a grid created randomly. We computed around 900 matching in each experiment. We performed three realization for each experiment obtaining the result in Table 77.4.

77.5.3.3 Locations for Maximum Optical Flow Error

We performed our experiments locating the exhaustive matching in points where the maximum optical flow error was obtained. The obtained performance is presented in Table 77.5.

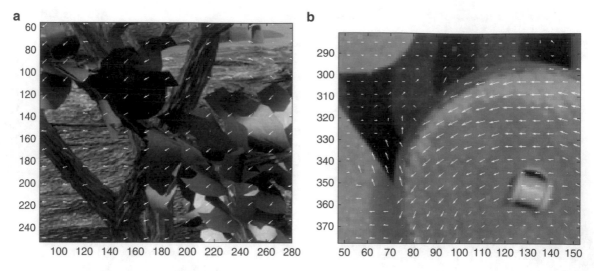

Fig. 77.7 Exhaustive matching represented with white arrows. (**a**) Exhaustive matching using $D = 18$ and $P = 10$ for Grove2. (**b**) Exhaustive matching using $D = 6$ and $p = 8$ for Rubberwhale

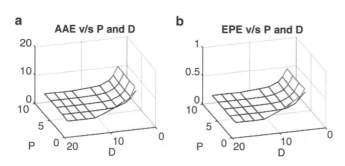

Fig. 77.8 EPE and AAE obtained with the addition of exhaustive matching for different parameters P and D considering uniform matching location. (**a**) EPE error. (**b**) AAE Error

Table 77.3 Results obtained by uniform matching location strategy in VALIDATION_SMALL using

Error	Dime	Grove3	Hydra	Urban3	Venus	Average
EPE	0.0975	0.6924	0.1672	0.4811	0.3034	0.3485
AAE	1.8739	6.4759	2.0160	4.334	4.2259	3.7872

Table 77.4 Average EPE and AAE obtained by random location strategy in VALIDATION_SMALL set

Error	Dime	Grove3	Hydra	Urban3	Venus	Average
EPE	0.0967	0.6798	0.1666	0.5446	0.2988	0.3573
AAE	1.8876	6.3781	2.0214	4.8060	4.1977	3.8581

Table 77.5 Average EPE and AAE obtained by maximum optical flow error location strategy in VALIDATION_SMALL set

Error	Dime	Grove3	Hydra	Urban3	Venus	Average
EPE	0.0942	0.8083	0.177	0.8039	0.3304	0.4428
AAE	1.853	7.8037	2.1368	5.2347	4.7152	4.387

Table 77.6 Average EPE and AAE obtained by maximum gradient error location strategy in VALIDATION_SMALL set

Error	Dime	Grove3	Hydra	Urban3	Venus	Average
EPE	0.0938	0.7147	0.1772	0.7338	0.3014	0.4042
AAE	1.8596	6.5793	2.1159	5.9172	4.3285	4.1601

77.5.3.4 Locations for Maximum Magnitudes of the Gradient

We present in Table 77.6 our results using maximum gradient.

Comparing the average EPE and AAE obtained for each strategy we observe that the best performance was obtained by Uniform Location Strategy, second best performance was obtained by Random Location, third is by Maximum Gradient and Finally obtained by Maximum Optical Flow error.

As proof of concept we present in Fig. 77.9 results for Beanbags sequence considering $P = 4$, $D = 16$ and $P4$, $D = 4$ and $\alpha(x) = 1.0$ for both cases. We represent the estimated flow using white arrows. For Large displacement better results were obtained for smaller D parameter.

77.6 Conclusions

We proposed a model to estimate the optical flow which can incorporate additional matching in order to improve the optical flow estimation. We have evaluated empirically four different strategies to locate these additional matching. Our results show that the best strategy to locate these matching is

Fig. 77.9 Estimated optical flow for Beanbags sequence using uniform location. (**a**) results using $P = 4$ and $D = 16$. (**b**) results using $P = 4$ and $D = 4$

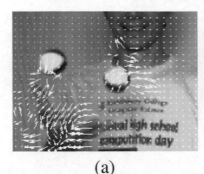 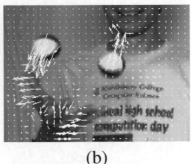

(a)   (b)

the Uniform Location(EPE $= 0.3485$ and AAE $= 3.7872$), outperforming the strategy to locate matching in Maximum Errors of the Optical Flow estimation. As future work is necessary to develop a methodology in order to validate the exhaustive matching. The exhaustive matching frequently gives false matching and this error is propagated to the estimation. The exhaustive search can be computed in a parallel way using GPU.

References

1. S. Baker, D. Scharstein, J. Lewis, S. Roth, M. Black, R. Szelinsky, A database and evaluation methodology for optical flow. Int. J. Comput. Vis. **92**, 1–31 (2011)
2. T. Brox, C. Bregler, J. Malik, Large displacement optical flow, in *IEEE conference on Computer Vision and Pattern Recognition* (2009)
3. A. Bruhn, J. Weickert, C. Feddern, T. Kohlberger, C. Schnoerr, Real-time optical flow computation with variational methods, in *International Conference on Computer Analysis of Images and Patterns 2003*, The Netherlands (2003), pp. 222–229
4. B.K.P Horn, B.G. Schunck, Determining optical flow. Artif. Intell. **17**, 185–204 (1981)
5. V. Lazcano, Some problems in depth enhanced video processing, Ph.D. thesis, 2016. http://www.tdx.cat/handle/10803/373917
6. J. Sánchez, E. Meinhardt-Llopis, G. Facciolo, TV-L1 optical flow estimation. Image Process. Line **3**, 137–150 (2013). https://doi.org/10.5201/ipol.2013.26
7. M. Smith, R. Hashemi, L. Sears, Classification of movies and television shows using motion, in *6th International Conference on Information Technology: New Generations*, Las Vegas, Nevada (2009)
8. F. Steinbruecker, T. Pock, D. Cremers, Large displacement optical flow computation without warping, in *IEEE International Conference on Computer Vision (ICCV)*, Kyoto (2009), pp. 185–203
9. M. Stoll, S. Volz, A. Bruhn, Adaptive integration of features matches into variational optical flow methods, in *Asian Conference on Computer Vision - ACIP2012* (2012)
10. Y. Wang, K. Gurule, J. Wise, J. Zheng, Wavelet based region duplication forgery detection, in *12th International Conference on Information Technology: New Generations*, Las Vegas, Nevada (2012)
11. P. Weinzaepfel, J. Revaud, Z. Harchaoui, C. Schmid, DeepFlow: large displacement optical flow with deep matching, in *IEEE International Conference on Computer Vision (ICCV)*, Sydney (2013)
12. A. Wedel, T. Pock, C. Zach, H. Bischof, D. Cremers, An improved algorithm for TV-L1 optical flow, in *Statistical and Geometrical Approaches to Visual Motion Analysis*. Lecture Notes in Computer Science, vol. 5604 (Springer, Berlin, 2009)
13. L. Xu, J. Jia, Y. Matsushita, *IEEE Conference on Computer Vision and Pattern Recognition (CVPR)*, San Francisco, CA, 13–18 June 2010

Solar-Powered UAV Platform System: A Case Study for Ground ChangeDetection in BRIC Countries

Alexandre C. B. Ramos, Elcio H. Shiguemori, Sergey Serokhvostov, P. K. Gupta, Lunlong Zhong, and Xiao Bing Hu

Abstract

This paper aims to present some applications in Geospatial Technology area, from the use of UAV, Communication, IT and High Performance Computing tools. Important research topics in this area are the detection of changes in multiple images of a soil region to security, deforestation identification and changes in plantations, river courses, shorelines and glaciers. Students, teachers and researchers from four BRIC countries: Brazil, Russia, India and China are conducting joint research in low-cost systems involving aircraft powered by solar energy (Russian team), communication systems over long distances (Chinese team), change detection algorithms in the soil (Brazilian team) and cloud based distributed systems for identification of the type of change detected (Indian team). Some intermediate results already achieved individually by each team are also presented and discussed in this study.

Keywords

Change detection · Solar powered airplanes · Cloud based systems

A. C. B. Ramos · E. H. Shiguemori (✉)
Federal University of Itajubá, Itajubá, Brazil

Advanced Studies Institute, São Paulo, Brazil
e-mail: ramos@unifei.edu.br; elcio@ieav.cta.br

S. Serokhvostov
Moscow Institute of Physics and Technology, Dolgoprudny, Moscow, Russia

P. K. Gupta (✉)
Jaypee University of Information Technology, Solan, Himachal Pradesh, India
e-mail: pkgupta@ieee.org

L. Zhong · X. B. Hu
Civil Aviation University of China, Tianjin, China

78.1 Introduction

This paper presents an International Cooperation Project that aims at joining collective efforts of research groups of BRICS countries (Brazil, Russia, India and China) to develop Unmanned Aerial Vehicles—UAV (or Remotely Piloted Aircraft—RPA as used in this paper) solar-powered, equipped with electronic systems to ensure, precisely, its position and trajectory control and collect ground images to be transmitted to a control station at a distance for cloud storage and subsequent digital processing.

Currently, capture images of the earth are gaining a lot of importance, in particular for ground change analysis for several purposes, such as geospatial studies, forest fires, natural disasters, agriculture etc. In most cases, images are needed not only of a region but images of huge tracts of land, such as forests, large farms etc., can also be used for analyzing the ground change detection. In this case, it is necessary to comply with a wide range of requirements. In order to cheapen the process of acquiring photos, satellite photos can be replaced by photos taken from sensors installed in proposed RPA, which uses technology that allows its flight practically in automatic way.

78.2 Objective

Tasks are divided among BRICS countries team members for designing and implementation of proposed RPA, communication model and digital processing techniques to find ground change detection. The Russian researcher's team is responsible for the specification, design, and construction of the solar-powered RPA, as the members of team have deep and strong knowledge about RPAs aerodynamic research, and the field of electric power-plant design for this type of aircraft, combined with the research of solar receiver systems as well as extensive experience in the design, manufacture, piloting, and conducting various RPA tests. Also, studies are investigating the peculiarities of the airflow around the wing as well as the stability and control of aircraft designed. Thorough knowledge and expertise about these skills can be find from the various referenced articles worked out by Russian team members [1–4].

The role of Brazilian researcher's team involves the analysis, design, implementation, testing and integration of Artificial Neural Network—ANN algorithms to identify deviations in the trajectory of the RPA and the resulting chain of command necessary for the aircraft route correction. The expertise and strong knowledge of Brazilian team member can be found from referenced articles [5–12] including the partnership with the Chinese team to carry out joint studies related to flight dynamics of the aircraft built by the Russian team.

The role of Indian researcher's team is to develop studies related to Artificial Intelligence applied to identify the type of change occurred in the soil from various obtained images and videos provided by sensors embedded in the RPA. Team will also develop the various studies related to data mining and machine learning for analyzing and comparing the captured images as well as developing the human computer interface related to the presentation of obtained information to the users of the developed system. Strong technical knowledge of the Indian team members in relation to the above mentioned tasks can be found from referenced articles [13–15].

The problems relating to long distance communication will be addressed by the researcher's team from China. The strong point of Chinese team is the knowledge in the application and implementation of signal processing techniques and design, construction, and communication systems tests. Since 2010, Chinese team has implemented various devices, for example voice air-ground communication system with a noise suppression system, as well as GPS receivers. Various studies conducted by the Chinese team can be found from referenced articles [16–26].

78.3 Intermediate Results

Due to its dimensions, UAV fixed-wing electrical aircraft are very susceptible to atmospheric disturbances and also have less flight range. Thus, to get good pictures, it is necessary to find good flight plans and aircraft parameters. In particular, to optimize stability and autonomy one should optimize the aircraft's shape, in particular a wing whose shape leads to different types of flow and the specific Reynolds number as shown in Fig. 78.1.

To extend the time and flight distance, the Russian researchers of this project, led by Dr. Sergey Serokhvostov of the Moscow Institute of Physics and Technology—MIPT, have studied various strategies [1–4], two of the most promising are: (a) the use of solar cells on the upper surface of the wing, which influences in various problems due to the physical and mechanical properties of solar cells that can change the shape of the wing causing deformations that can influent the wing shape and possible deformations; and (b) use special surfaces with the changing orientation.

Despite its limitations the use of UAV, powered by electric motors, is quite growing about to become indispensable in many applications where human intervention is dull, dangerous, risky or expensive, for example border surveillance, forests monitoring, inspection of large plantations or extensive electric transmission lines among others.

Due to its vast territorial area Brazil, Russia, India, and China are among the seven largest countries in the world, for these countries border surveillance is a major problem, whose solution can be supported from the use of RPA using navigation based on the Global Positioning System—GPS.

Fig. 78.1 An UAV solar powered prototype. Source: Authors

Fig. 78.2 Different techniques for RPA estimated position (yellow) and real position (red). Source: Authors

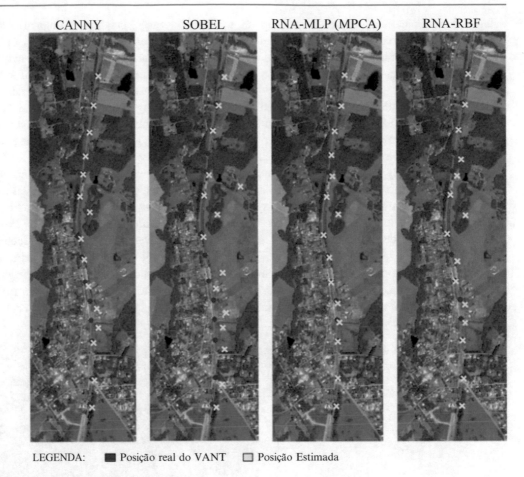

CANNY   SOBEL   RNA-MLP (MPCA)   RNA-RBF

LEGENDA: ■ Posição real do VANT   □ Posição Estimada

However, there might be several problems with the use of GPS derived instrument defects, or antennas, or problems as the South Atlantic Anomaly—SAA, a change in the Earth's magnetic field that makes inaccurate for autonomous navigation of the RPA. In this context, several works evolving RPA [5–12], have been conducted by Brazilian team coordinated by Prof. Dr. Alexandre C.B. Ramos at the Federal University of Itajubá—UNIFEI, to develop more accurate navigation systems using from the ground recognition of milestones comparing Geo-referenced images (provided by satellite or by RPA in previous flights) with images collected by the RPA in real-time and subsequent trajectory correction of the aircraft as shown in Fig. 78.2.

Currently, most of the image transmission systems for RPA employ direct line of sight communication (LOS) or wireless mobile networks. The distance of effective communication LOS is limited. The relaying mobile communication is limited by the position of the base station, also the transmission quality of mobile communication is problematic because the signal intensity around the base station which can be changed randomly. To ensure the working distance and quality of transmitted images, Chinese researchers coordinated by Prof. Dr. Xiao Bing Hu from Civil Aviation University of China—CAUC, are working on developing

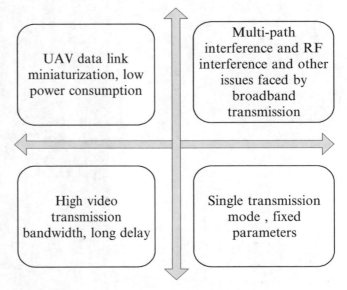

Fig. 78.3 Existing problems for RPA datalink. Source: Authors

a long-range communication system [16–26], as shown in Fig. 78.3.

Considering the long-range and robustness coverage requirements on the quality of communication signal, the satellite communication becomes a good option, to ensure low power dissipation, the light weight and small size of the external communication terminal for use in embedded systems implementing board communication terminals and earth.

Different information will be transmitted via the communication system, for example, ground images, the RPA control commands, movies from camcorder to the ground station, the RPA telemetry, trajectory correction commands for both is currently a communication protocol. Taking into account real-time transmission and communication bandwidth limitation, a video compression system is being implemented to be embedded in the RPA and a decompression system is designed to operate at ground control station.

Humans are promoting an accelerated modification of the earth's landscape, these changes lead even the climate changes that are profoundly altering the Earth surface pro-

cesses, creating ecological challenges. It is expected that the environmental impacts of human activities encourage an increase in temperature will continue growing and generating global warming the extent to which the planet becomes increasingly populated, industrialized and urbanized. A key example to recognize the degree of destruction is the ground erosion. Soil erosion is a natural process, but it has been greatly accelerated due to deforestation, cultivation and wrong land use practices.

Incidents such as drought, pests, forest fires, melting ice caps, displacement of coastal lines and change of riverbeds are now reported worldwide every day. In this context, the Indian team coordinated by Prof. Dr. P. K. Gupta of Jaypee University of Information Technology [13–15] proposes the development of machine learning algorithms based on computational cloud to perform geospatial image comparisons captured from RPA to identify changes patterns in Earth structure, as shown in Fig. 78.4.

Fig. 78.4 Colored maps to change detection

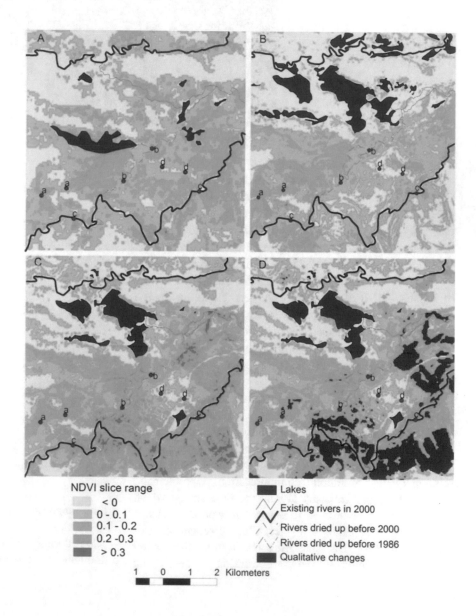

Proposed system, under study also helps to identify and track the pollutants moving waterways, such as canals, rivers and oceans. Initially the algorithm will identify changes in the Earth's structure (rivers, forests, farms, glaciers, etc.) using digital image processing and then predict the extent of the changes in the next months and years using various machine learning algorithms.

78.4   Methodology

Proposed system will be deployed using cloud based technology that will allow users to get results and share their findings on a common platform. Among the various subareas of Geo-sciences, this research study will focus on many important issues and is currently in discussion with the scientific communities, namely:

- A solar powered RPA.
- Trajectory control from the pattern matching with known images.
- Detection of changes in the environment from the ground pictures patterns.
- Detection of pests in crops.
- Monitoring changes in coastlines, rivers and lakes.
- Automatic control of RPA trajectories.

The approach of the subareas above, allows to develop research projects focusing on different areas of human knowledge that are integrated to solve the problems addressed by the different project teams.

In order to obtain satisfactory results, it is necessary interaction with researchers who have prior knowledge of the described sub-areas and are conducting advanced research in the area and are willing to join forces. In this context, it is carried out several work missions among team members initially to set goals, in a second time for monitoring aimed at assessing the work carried out during the 36 months of the project duration and finally project completion meetings.

With the development of this work we can see great opportunities among the team members of the BRICS countries, for example, the Brazilian team: (a) allowing students attending training courses that are not offered by UNIFEI (b) Realization of stages of 30 days for graduate students, (c) Conducting Postdoctoral stages 30 days, (d) Interaction with members of foreign teams in the laboratories of foreign universities, (e)Scientific publications in magazines/ international events, (f) Opportunity to improve foreign language and insert into another culture.

In terms of activities and opportunities for other teams from BRICS countries are: (a) allowing researchers to take courses/training seminars that are offered by the Graduate UNIFEI programs, (b) perform numerical simulations and experimental tests using UNIFEI laboratory, (c) realization

PhD stage, (d) Postdoctoral training and short visits to develop or learn new techniques and apply them to the project sub-areas, (f) scientific publications in journals/international conferences) Opportunity to improve foreign language and enter in our culture.

In the academic area, the integration and cooperation favored by the internationalization of the institutions involved in the project process will bring great benefits to Graduate programs of the different countries that will allow teachers and foreign researchers will teach courses and conduct joint research. This process will increase the quality of work done in the context of contributing Graduate programs for the development of scientific technology parks of different countries.

In the industrial area, there are great prospects in the realization of products and services favored by this project especially, in Brazil, with the Airbus Helicopters Company, the only one helicopters factory in the southern hemisphere, leading member an aeronautical park in the city of Itajubá (MG) which is headquartered UNIFEI. The development of trajectories of control algorithms, digital algorithm processing and solar powered aircraft are certainly of interest from Airbus Helicopters which has been developing joint projects with members of the Brazilian team.

78.5   Conclusion

With reference to the products and results as shown in Sect. 78.4, schedules can represent that this joint research project study has four main results:

1. The development of a RPAS, low cost, driven by an electric motor provided with a solar cell system, with payload of approximately 10 kg, and cameras with electronic systems that operate in the visual spectrum (below may also operate in infra-red spectrum).
2. The development of a software system that allows the identification of differences between RPA $\times$ Satellite photos and images to identify changes, such as plagues, invasions, deforestation, etc.
3. Developing a cloud-based system for distributed capture and identification of anomalies made by man, such as deforestation, fires, changes in river courses and changes in coastal and glaciers.
4. The development of a signal processing system for long distance communication, provided with specific antennae systems, electronic, mechanical and computer algorithms in communication protocols.

Acknowledgement Prof. Ramos acknowledges the support by National Council for Scientific and Technological Development-CNPq under award number 301263/2016-7.

References

1. S. Serokhvostov, T.E. Churkina, Optimization of the trajectory and accumulator mass for the solar-powered airplane, in *Proc. of 3rd. Congress of the International Council of the Aeronautical Sciences* (ICA, Daejeon, Korea, 2016)

2. S. Serokhvostov, T.E. Churkina, Optimal control for the sun-powered airplane with taking into account efficiency of on-board accumulator charging discharging and chage limits, in *Proc. of 6th. European conference for Aeronautics and Space Sciences* (EUCASS, kraków, Poland, 2015)

3. S. Serokhvostov, T.E. Churkina, Estimation of main parameters for solar-powered long endurance airplane at preliminary design stage, in *Proc. of European Conf. Aeronautics and Space Sciences* (EUCASS, Munich, Germany, 2013)

4. S. Serokhvostov, Optimization of flight regime and performance for the aircraft with electrical powerplant for flight on the fixed distance with the wind presence, in *Polish Society of Theoretical and Applied Mechanics*. Scientific aspects of unmanned aerial vehicle (Poland, 2015)

5. F. Felizardo Luiz, R.L.M. Mota, E.H. Shiguemori, M.T. Neves, A.C.B. Ramos, Embedding ANN in UAV for surveillance a case study for urban areas observation. JIAS **9**, 1 (2014)

6. L.F. Felizardo, R.L. Mota, E.H. Shiguemori, M.T. Neves, A.B. Ramos, F. Mora-Camino . Using ANN and UAV for terrain surveillance, in *Proc. of 2013 13th International Conference on Hybrid Intelligent Systems (HIS2013)*, vol. 1 (Gammarth, 2013), p. 1

7. R.L.M. Mota, L.F. Felzardo, E.H. Shguemori, A.B. Ramos, F. Mora-Camino, Expanding small UAV capabilities with ANN: a case study for urban areas observation, in *2013 IEEE Second International Conference on Image Information Processing (ICIIP)* (India, 2013), p. 516

8. R.L. Mota, L.F. Felizardo, E.H. Shiguemori, A.C.B. Ramos, F. Mora-Camino, Expanding small UAV capabilities with ANN: a case study for urban areas inspection. Br. J. Appl. Sci. Technol. **4**, 387–398 (2014)

9. Santos, M.D.M., Mota, R.L.M., Shiguemori, E.H., Ramos, A.C.B., Uso de mapas auto-organizáveis de Kohonen na detecção automática de mudanças na Represa de Paraibuna, in *XVII Simpósio Brasileiro de Sensoriamento Remoto—SBSR,* vol. 1 (João Pessoa, 2015). pp. 7169-7176

10. R.L.M. Mota, E.H. Shiguemori, A.C.B. Ramos, Application of self-organizing maps at change detection in Amazon forest, in *2014 Eleventh International Conference on Information Technology: New Generations (ITNG)* (Las Vegas, 2014), pp. 371–376

11. L. Zhong, A.C.B. Ramos, F. Mora-Camino, A two stages approach for fault tolerant control, in *2014 33rd Chinese Control Conference CCC2014* (Nanjing, China, 2014)

12. S.S. Cunha, M.S. de Sousa, D.P. Roque, A.C.B. Ramos, P. Fernandes, Dynamic simulation of the flight behavior of a rotary-wing aircraft, in *Advances in Intelligent Systems and Computing*, 448th edn., (Springer International Publishing, Berlin, 2016), pp. 1087–1099

13. P.K. Gupta, G. Singh, A novel human computer interaction aware algorithm to minimize energy consumption. Wireless Pers Commun **81**(2), 661–683 (2015)

14. P.K. Gupta, A.F. Kavishe, et al., Smart vehicle navigation sustem using hidden markov model and RFID technology. Wireless Pers Commun **90**(4), 1717–1742 (2016)

15. Pattanaik, V., Suran, S. Prabakaran, S., *Inducing Human-like Motion in Robots*,I-Care 2014, Bangalore. https://doi.org/10.1145/2662117.2662118

16. T. Hu, Y. Wu, Q. Shi, X. Wang, Design and Implement of bi-channel constant modulus anti-interference VHF receiver. J. Civ. Aviat. Univ. China **33**(1), 13–18 (2015)

17. T. Hu, T. Meng, Design for fast acquiring of high dynamic GPS signal based on FPGA. J. Civ. Aviat. Univ. China **31**(2), 27–31 (2013)

18. L. Zhong, R. Wu, T. Hu, Q. Shi, *Bi-channels Continuous Interference Suppression Method and System used in Civil Aviation Air-Ground Communication*, CN201410534749.4, Chinese Patent-CP, 2013

19. R. Wu, L. Zhong, T. Hu, S. Wang, Q. Shi, *Robust Bi-Channels Interference Suppression Method and System used in Civil Aviation Air-Ground Communication*, CN200810052084, CP, 2012

20. R. Wu, L. Zhong, T. Hu, S. Wang, et al, *Single-Channel Optimal Constant Modulus Algorithm and System used in Civil Aviation Air-Ground Communication*, CN200710059767, CP, 2011

21. Q. Shi, R. Wu, L. Zhong, D. Lu, et al, *Smart Antenna Adaptive Interference Suppression Method Based on LS-LMS Algorithm*, CN200910069090, CP, 2012

22. R. Wu, Q. Shi, S. Wang, T. Hu, L. Zhong, *A Novel Bi-Channels Constant Modulus Interference Suppression Method and System used in Civil Aviation Air-Ground Communication*, CN200810052085, CP, 2011

23. D. Lu, R. Wu, Q. Shi, W. Lei, L. Zhong, *Blind Adaptive GPS Interference Suppression Method Based on Code Structure*, CN200910069091, CP, 2012

24. R. Wu, J. Huang, L. Zhong, T. Hu, et al, *Single-Channel Signal Suppression Algorithm and System used in Civil Aviation Air-Ground Communication*, CN200710057266, CP, 2010

25. R. Wu, Q. Shi, S. Wang, J. Ma, T. Hu, L. Zhong, et al, *Blind Interference Suppression Method and System Used in Civil Aviation Air-Ground Communication*, CN200710057267, CP, 2010

26. R. Wu, J. Ma, L. Zhong et al, *Constant Modulus Interference Suppression Method and System used in Civil Aviation Air-Ground Communication*, CN200710057268, CP, 2010

Benefits of Establishing Makerspaces in Distributed Development Environment

Basit Shahzad and Kashif Saleem

Abstract

Makerspace is an innovative concept of working in a community based, semi-organized groups working to tinker, design, fabricate or develop, and market the ideas. The involvement of the community is vital to the success of every application of the makerspace concept. Some areas, like Science, Technology, Engineering, and Management (STEM) are among the extremely popular areas in the makerspace, while other popular areas include programming, and curriculum development. In such areas, where the community involvement is expected to be high, it is possible that the makerspace can't accommodate all the individuals along with their equipment, at one place. Since the cost to develop the makerspace is high, we will be interested to see that how the small makerspaces can interact with the central makerspace to share the ideas and resources. In this paper, we investigate the popular areas of community involvement, opportunities and challenges in forming the distributed makerspaces, and also provide the analyses of their productivity in terms of problems solving, fabrication of small components, and software development. A model is proposed that provides a framework of conducting activities in distributed makerspaces and integrating the activities (project components) to form a product.

Keywords

Distributed makerspace model · Franchise makerspace · Concept commercialization

B. Shahzad (✉)
Faculty of Engineering & CS, National University of Modern Languages, Islamabad, Pakistan

K. Saleem
Center of Excellence in Information Assurance, King Saud University, Riyadh, Saudi Arabia

79.1 Introduction

A makerspace is a place where individuals can gather to create, invent, tinker, explore and discover using a variety of tools and materials [1]. There are different concepts and thoughts that where the makerspace should be operated? Among the most common places, are the community centers and the libraries [2]. The makerspace provides learning, technology manufacturing, software development, and may other creative opportunities to the general public [3, 4]. The greatest advantage of the makerspace is that it allows the community to use the expensive tools, like 3-D printers, to manufacture or fabricate the required items [5]. Such tools are not easily available at home or for localized use, since they are expensive and require customized environment [6]. The construction of a makerspace is at least as expensive as developing a software house or a hi-tech learning environment [7, 8]. The expenses on the makerspace are typically funded either by the non-governmental organizations or through the membership fees, that the members pay on the monthly basis. Each makerspace is custom built to maximize the output in the area of its specialization. This allows the individuals to improve their experience in inter-disciplinary expertise.

The establishment of the new makerspace is a healthy activity as it brings a utility of the time for the individuals living in a community. It allows the people to utilize their time more constructively and be productive at the same time. For the large cities and towns, it is very easily possible to develop a makerspace that can be customized to specific environment and productive in the way that it generates some profit from the commercialization of the products, fabricated or developed in the makerspace [9]. But the small localities, like villages, may not be that much privileged to have a large makerspace that may be productive as the same time. These new and small setups can he helped by the well-known makerspaces to establish small setup in the rural areas. These small community centers can help work as the outlets or a franchise office of the makerspace [2].

The idea of the franchise makerspace can be brought in-place very easily. The small makerspaces and the main makerspace are connected in sharing the virtual resources, immersive learning and any other fabrication [10]. The small makerspace work both as an independent makerspace where they can do localized research and development while they can work as outlet of a large makerspace when they provide service to a large setup. This model helps in growing the small setups to grow in resources, ideas, development, and fabrication while at the same time it eliminates the financial liabilities from the small setup, until they small makerspace can afford to bear its burden of being operational [11]. The distributed makerspace model has many advantages, as some of them have been discussed. This research is focused to identify the challenges that may arise in establishing the distributed development environment in the makerspace. The main objective of this research is to observe the following:

1. To identify the challenges in establishing in the communities and makerspace.
2. To identify the commercialization aspect of the products being developed in the distributed makerspaces.

This research will address the following research question:

RQ. 1   What are the fundamental challenges in establishing the communities and makerspaces?
RQ. 2   How the commercialization objectives can be achieved in distributed makerspace?

79.2   Literature Review

The technology is gaining control in the world for the technological advancements to become realities to help prosper the human life. National growth now ad days, largely depends on the development of new methodologies and strategies for participation in global standard and for enhancement of capabilities by providing new educational opportunities. Makerspace's concept, therefore is very consistent with such tasks, as it focusses on the community based development.

Makerspaces are reliable instrument for creating and innovative designing where student and engineers rediscover new ideas with innovation and creation of finding a new solution regarding problems. Hira [12] works about the similarities of theories related to the knowledge is a self-made activity that a person constructs. However, as Piaget [13] identifies that the focus of development should be on the students, while Papert's [14] theory depends upon using of tools

and methodologies. Our concept of maker spaces is more innovative by using these two theories.

Makerspaces is basically an infrastructure related to designing, adaptation and repairing of the concepts, tools, software, and items that can be fabricated [15]. The study evaluates that how the makerspaces concept is challenging normative understandings of civic participation in adhering alternative thinking and responsible action in Northern Ireland's. The study evaluates different things like availability of information, network accessibility, software development. McCosker [15] has focused to identify the technological challenges in developing the makerspaces by addressing the availability, copyright, and development issues in the makerspace formulation.

Makerspaces in different geographic locations share commonalities [16], such as governance guidelines, accounting software, or machine operation manuals in contextual of makerspace. Adrian Smith [17] highlighted the philosophies of the 'Movement for Socially Useful Production' of 1981 which emphasis on learning by doing in live collaboration for material projects. The Chaos Computer Club is widely considered to be the first grassroots organization in Europe to call itself a hackerspace which serve a civil society organization. However, makerspace is a "fringe phenomena" that have marginal social impact [18–24].

Makerspace cannot signally provide a service but also provide a physical space and informal education. The structures and dynamics of makerspaces have even been situated as somewhat replicating those of online communities who use commons-based production methods [25]. Apart from other issues in formation of the makerspaces, the community involvement is also a major problem that varies in its importance in different parts of the world.

There are three spaces in Northern Ireland whose making practices focus on digital technologies: Farset Labs, Fab Lab Belfast, Fab Lab Nerve Centre in Derry [15]. Farset Labs is a non-profit company people pay monthly to use the spaces its machines and network of people. In contrast, Fab Lab Belfast and Fab Lab Nerve Centre Derry—collectively known as Fab Labs NI—focus their energies on peacebuilding initiatives. Fab Labs NI are supported by the European Union's Peace III.

The list of Fab Lab equipment includes, a laser cutter for making 3D structures from 2D design, a large CNC mill for making furniture and housing, a NC knife and smaller mini-mill for making circuits and molds for casting, 3D printers, an electronics workbench, and a suite of tooling and materials. In 2014, Fab Lab Nerve Centre undertook an ambitious civic engagement project called Temple.

Turning our attention to Farset Lab, we see a rather different way of operating as civic activity in Northern Ireland. While Fab Labs NI are concerned with nurturing maker agents through community development projects,

Farset Labs primarily facilitates the activities of self-directed maker agents. NESTA describes four main technological for working in a specific maker spaces, open hardware, open networks, open data, and open knowledge. By applying all these ideas, we make makerspace related to humanize the civic participation. There are difficulties associated with recommending better practices and resources for makerspaces as they serve diverse communities with different needs.

79.3 Challenges in Makerspace Formation

While considering the cost of makerspaces, it is noted that makerspaces takes extra expenditure due to specific resources and equipment. For example, makerspace in public or private library featured with 3-D printers, would involve the extra budget for making extra innovative work. Along with the cost, staffing and scheduling are also important to be considered for making better makerspace. Moorefield-Lang [26] reports, library, classes need to get creative and this cannot be done without having the specified staff. Extra staffing is also required for testing new equipment at proper schedule time.

Makerspace also require trained staff for making participatory working of all the members. Makerspaces, by their very nature, can invite "creative mess". For example, carpet and furniture can be damaged due to use of equipment in maker spaces. Furthermore, Burke [27] asserts that some makerspace equipment is loud and may require a dedicated space with added noise reduction features. Safety is also a basic prompt because it's a compulsory consideration to safe our makerspace with emphasis on proper liabilities.

Within a school library makerspace, the responsibility to ensure that students are respecting copyright and intellectual property would most likely rest with the teacher-librarian, who may also ensure that the students don't make dangerous things and make their own design without copying the others [28]. It can be observed that the challenges faced by the makerspace development are diversified in nature. The challenges in forming the makerspace are multidirectional in nature. The challenges about the space, cost, community involvement, safety, noise reduction, copyrights, protection of the team, fund raising for the makerspace, and distributed resource planning are among the major challenges faced by the makerspaces [29, 30].

1. *Cost oriented:* There are a number of challenges in makerspace development that are related to cost. They include but are not limited to the initial setup-cost, running cost, equipment purchasing cost, space management, and financial loss elimination. Since the makerspaces are not setup with large budgets, it is important that the new setup can work and grow gradually and improve in resources

and deliverables. The member's financial contribution is important in making the things running in the beginning. A developing makerspace, may well be in position to start working on the break-even cost in less than five years' time. Pilot makerspaces, are important to establish as they work as the success stories.

2. *Community oriented:* Among the community oriented challenges, most prominent are: interest development, safety, responsibility, working as a team, and identifying the volunteers to perform the tasks of emergent needs. All these tasks need the deep community involvement to work as a team to develop the makerspace and to accomplish the tasks that are oriented in the work environment. The makerspaces, may charge a nominal membership fee to keep the setup running.

3. *Technology oriented:* There are some challenges that are oriented to technology in makerspaces. The technological challenges of the makerspaces include: computational setup, network maintenance, team structure, and lack of skill etc.

In Sect. 79.4, we discuss that how the challenges can be addressed in developing makerspaces.

79.4 Distributed Makerspaces and Commercialization

The makerspaces are a community based development concept and the chances for successful development can be improved by composing a successful model of development. Each makerspace may face number of challenges as mentioned in Sect. 79.3, in order to avoid the challenges to a larger extent, the concept of distributed makerspaces is introduced. A distributed model of the makerspaces can decrease the cost of operations and can help in taking full benefits from the existing computational power by not only optimizing the resource utilization but also by improving the community involvement in the makerspace development.

The concept of distributed makerspaces comes from the concept of distributed computing [31, 32]. The rationale behind considering the distributed setup of the makerspaces is to decrease or eliminate the cost of developing the new makerspaces, the concept is demonstrated in Fig. 79.1.

The concept revolves around forming one larger and (initially) funded makerspace that can establish itself and can earn to run itself in some years. Once the makerspace is completely operational, and it starts getting good business opportunities, in science, technology, engineering, and management, the makerspace's administration may think of developing a new makerspace in another area of socio-economic viability. In the new makerspace, the computational power, task assignments, and administration is governed by the main

Fig. 79.1 Formation of
makerspaces and new setups

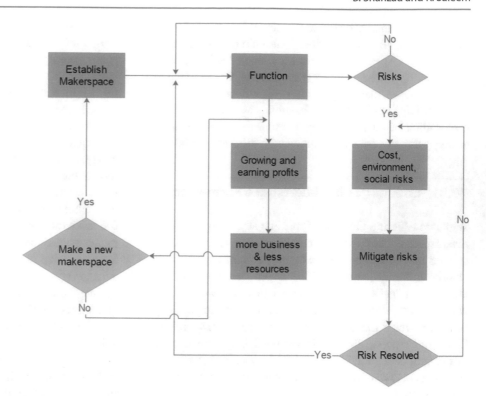

makerspace or by the designated representatives of the main makerspace. Thus the distribution cycle continues and yields only those setups that are economically, technologically, and socially workable and can help in the commercialization process.

79.5 Conclusion

The concept of developing the makerspace that have multi-purpose involvement in developing and fabricating diversified items, is very prominent. The makerspace, when formulated, have their own challenges along with the features that they possess. The challenges vary from the social, financial, and technological. Much of these challenges arise if the making of makerspace is not well scheduled. The concept of the distributed makerspace helps in developing the small setups being governed by the large setups, and established only when they are needed. The challenges about the space, cost, community involvement, safety, noise reduction, copyrights, protection of the team, fund raising for the makerspace, and distributed resource planning are among the major challenges faced by the makerspaces, and can well be resolved by applying the distributed development approach. This approach reduces the chances of failure, and helps in dealing with many social, financial, and technical challenges.

References

1. R.S. Kurti, D. Kurti, L. Fleming, Practical implementation of an educational makerspace. Teach. Libr. **42**, 20 (2014)
2. T. Colegrove, Editorial board thoughts: libraries as makerspace? Inf. Technol. Libr. **32**, 2 (2013)
3. R.S. Kurti, D.L. Kurti, L. Fleming, The philosophy of educational makerspaces part 1 of making an educational makerspace. Teach. Libr. **41**, 8 (2014)
4. H.N. Okpala, D. Baker, Making a makerspace case for academic libraries in Nigeria. New Libr. World **117**, 568–586 (2016)
5. S. Pryor, Implementing a 3D printing service in an academic library. J. Libr. Adm. **54**, 1–10 (2014)
6. T. Brady, C. Salas, A. Nuriddin, W. Rodgers, M. Subramaniam, MakeAbility: Creating accessible makerspace events in a public library. Public Libr. Q. **33**, 330–347 (2014)
7. I.L. Craddock, Makers on the move: a mobile makerspace at a comprehensive public high school. Libr. Hi Tech **33**, 497–504 (2015)
8. K. Fontichiaro, Sustaining a makerspace. Teach. Libr. **43**, 39 (2016)
9. M. Gaved, I. Jowers, D. Dallison, G. Elliott-Cirigottis, A. Rochead,M. Craig, *Online Distributed Prototyping Through a University-Makerspace Collaboration* (2016)
10. M. Krebs, Manufacturing expertise for the people: the open-source hardware movement in Japan, in *Ethnographic Praxis in Industry Conference Proceedings* (2014), pp. 20–35
11. E. Boyle, M. Collins, R. Kinsey, C. Noonan, A. Pocock, Making the case for creative spaces in Australian libraries. Aust. Libr. J. **65**, 30–40 (2016)
12. A. Hira, C.H. Joslyn, M.M. Hynes, Classroom makerspaces: identifying the opportunities and challenges, in *2014 IEEE Frontiers in Education Conference (FIE) Proceedings* (2014), pp. 1–5

13. J. Piaget, *To Understand is to Invent: The Future of Education* (1973)
14. S. Papert, *The Connected Family: Bridging the Digital Generation Gap Longstreet Press* (1996)
15. A. McCosker, S. Vivienne, A. Johns, *Civic Practices, Design, and Makerspaces*
16. A. Sleigh, H. Stewart, K. Stokes, *Open Dataset of UK Makerspaces: a User's Guide* (Nesta, London, 2015)
17. A. Smith, M. Fressoli, H. Thomas, Grassroots innovation movements: challenges and contributions. J. Clean. Prod. **63**, 114–124 (2014)
18. J. Söderberg, A. Delfanti, Hacking hacked! The life cycles of digital innovation. Sci. Technol. Hum. Values **40**, 793 (2015)
19. B. Shahzad, E. Alwagait, Best and the worst times to tweet: an experimental study, in *15th International Conference on Mathematics and Computers in Business and Economics (MCBE '14)* (2014), pp. 122–126
20. E. Alwagait, B. Shahzad, Maximization of Tweet's viewership with respect to time, in *2014 World Symposium on Computer Applications & Research (WSCAR)* (2014), pp. 1–5
21. E. Alwagait, B. Shahzad, When are tweets better valued? An empirical study. J. Univers. Comput. Sci. **20**, 1511–1521 (2014)
22. B. Shahzad, E. Alwagait, S. Alim, Impact of change in weekend days on social networking culture in Saudi Arabia, in *2014 International Conference on Future Internet of Things and Cloud (FiCloud)* (2014), pp. 553–558
23. B. Shahzad, E. Alwagait, S. Alim, I. Resaercher, Investigating the relationship between social media usage and students' grades in Saudi Arabia: a mixed method approach, in *Recent Advances in Electrical Engineering and Educational Technologies* (2015), pp. 211–214
24. E. Alwagait, B. Shahzad, S. Alim, Impact of social media usage on students academic performance in Saudi Arabia. Comput. Hum. Behav. **51**, 1092–1097 (2015)
25. V. Kostakis, V. Niaros, G. Dafermos, M. Bauwens, Design global, manufacture local: exploring the contours of an emerging productive model. Futures **73**, 126–135 (2015)
26. H. Moorefield-Lang, Change in the making: makerspaces and the ever-changing landscape of libraries. TechTrends **59**, 107–112 (2015)
27. J.J. Burke, *Makerspaces: A practical guide for librarians*, vol vol. 8 (Rowman & Littlefield, Lanham, 2014)
28. A. Simons, The LA Makerspace and the role of citizen science in education. Bull. South. Calif. Acad. Sci. **113**, 114–115 (2014)
29. D. Slatter, Z. Howard, A place to make, hack, and learn: makerspaces in Australian public libraries. Aust. Libr. J. **62**, 272–284 (2013)
30. N. Taylor, U. Hurley, P. Connolly, Making community: the wider role of makerspaces in public life, in *Proceedings of the 2016 CHI Conference on Human Factors in Computing Systems* (2016), pp. 1415–1425
31. T.A. Faruquie, H.P. Karanam, M.K. Mohania, L.V. Subramaniam, G. Venkatachaliah, *Resources Management in Distributed Computing Environment*, Google Patents, 2015
32. W.M. Wong, M.C. Hui, *Method and System for Modeling and Analyzing Computing Resource Requirements of Software Applications in a Shared and Distributed Computing Environment*, Google Patents, 2016

Antonella Carbonaro, Filippo Piccinini, and Roberto Reda

Abstract

With the blooming of data created for example by IoT
devices, the possibility to handle all information coming
from healthcare applications is becoming increasingly
challenging. Cognitive computing systems can be used to
analyse large information volume by providing insights
and recommendations to represent, access, integrate, and
investigate data in order to improve outcomes across many
domains, including healthcare. This paper presents an
ontology-based system for the eHealth domain. It provides semantic interoperability among heterogeneous IoT
devices and facilitates data integration and sharing. The
novelty of the proposed approach lies in exploiting semantic web technologies to explicitly describe the meaning of
sensor data and define a common communication strategy
for information representation and exchange.

Keywords

eHealth · Semantic web technologies · Ontology-based
representation · IoT · Cognitive computing

80.1   Introduction

eHealth is referred to as the system with different applications of information and communications technology that
can support healthcare, wellness and fitness industry services. The increasing usage of wearable and mobile tech-

nologies is creating the next milestone advancement for
assisted eHealth. For example, typically worn on the wrist
devices such as *Fitbit* or *Jawbone*, track physical activities
of the wearer, including steps taken, stairs climbed, distance
travelled, and sleep hours, on a continuous real-time basis.
More sophisticated models can also monitor heart rate,
body temperature, and other basic physiological parameters,
resulting in this case an important means also for monitoring
people with health problems, for instance cardiologic and
oncologic patients [1]. Due to these reasons, within the health
and fitness domain, Internet of Things (IoT) technology is becoming one of the most popular trends [2, 3]. The estimation
of digital healthcare data from all over the world was almost
500 petabytes (10^{15}) in 2012, and it is expected to increase
and reach 25 exabytes (10^{18}) in 2020 [4]. Nevertheless, with
the ubiquitous utilization of modern network technologies,
data are usually incompletely located in separate sources and
in complex disorder. Basically, they cannot directly represent
the whole knowledge.

A cognitive computer eHealth system could be fed with
all the data available and redirected to a certain specific
subject [5], such as ascertain the sources of the data, combine
that data with context regarding the patient symptoms and
environmental information to provide contextual insights and
more informed medical care. Moreover, a cognitive computer
approach can be also exploited when eHealth services and
applications use different vocabularies, concepts and models,
which lead to problems of interoperability and knowledge
sharing [6, 7]. By offering a strategy to deal with the diversities in eHealth knowledge systems, a shared ontology helps
to deal with these problems. Ontology, from a Semantic Web
(SW) aspect, is defined as: "an explicit machine-readable
specification of a shared conceptualization". Ontologies offer
a generic infrastructure for interchange, integration and creative reuse of structured data, which can help to cross some of
the boundaries that the eHealth systems are facing nowadays.

The goal of applying ontologies in eHealth is to establish
a common semantic for addressing domain concepts by

A. Carbonaro (✉) · R. Reda
Department of Computer Science and Engineering, University of
Bologna, Bologna, Italy
e-mail: antonella.carbonaro@unibo.it; roberto.reda@unibo.it

F. Piccinini
Istituto Scientifico Romagnolo per lo Studio e la Cura dei Tumori
(IRST) S.r.l., IRCCS, Oncology Research Hospital, Meldola, FC, Italy
e-mail: filippo.piccinini@irst.emr.it

proposing a cognitive computing approach to better access the knowledge. IoT data can also be collected in the form of images, in this case it is necessary to use computer vision techniques [8, 9] and specific imaging ontologies. By mapping low-level image features to high-level ontology concepts, a semantic technology as the ontology offers promising approaches also to image analysis.

In this paper, we propose a cognitive computing system based on an ontology representation to provide semantic interoperability among heterogeneous IoT fitness and wellness devices to facilitate data integration and sharing. The novelty of the proposed approach lies in exploiting SW technologies to explicitly describe the meaning of sensor data, and to facilitate interoperability and data integration among different devices.

The paper is organized as follows: the next Section introduces the main previous works in the Literature describing SW technologies used in the healthcare context and explores research efforts related to manage different IoT data, highlighting the main open-issues in the field. Section 80.3 describes the technological aspects of the context and shows the overall architecture of the proposed framework. Section 80.4 reviews our development process in order to design the ontology and describes its main characteristics. Section 80.5 introduces the mapping process by which data are semantically annotated according to our ontology. Finally, Sect. 80.6 provides some considerations on a representative case study.

80.2 Related Works

In [10] is provided an extensive overview of computational methods of big data in medical and eHealth, focused on the "4Vs" model (volume, variety, velocity, and veracity) and its challenges. The problem is how to deal with large volumes of healthcare data from diverse sources preserving the speed for generating and processing those data. For example, data are classified according to the variety of sources and the complexity of different forms of data into unstructured, structured, and semi-structured. The survey lists approaches widely used for analyzing healthcare data, including preprocessing, feature extraction/selection, and machine learning. Despite several opportunities and approaches have been presented, there are many other directions to be explored, concerning various aspects of healthcare data. For example, the integration and fusion of multisource healthcare data with increasing scale constitutes a great challenge. In addition, one of the main open issues connected with the existing IoT applications is that devices are not (or little) interoperable with each other since their data are based on proprietary formats and do not use common terms or vocabularies. Moreover, promote interoperability, reusability, and resource sharing among IoT applications is more complicated if IoT

solutions are designed by considering only a single domain. SW technologies can be employed in IoT (SWoT) to overcome these challenges. Recently, Patel *et al.* created *SWoT-Suite* [11], which is an infrastructure that enables SWoT applications. It takes high-level specifications as input, parses them and generates code that can be deployed on IoT systems to manage sensors, actuators and user interface devices.

From the above-mentioned papers, it is possible to underline some main issues: the semantic interoperability of eHealth connected objects and their data is crucial but still poorly widespread. Often, data concerning the connected objects (*e.g.* devices characteristics, state and properties) and data concerning the patient (*e.g.* vital signs, activity) are represented in a disjointed context resulting into a vertical application development.

80.3 The Problem Context

SW can help to cross some of the boundaries that *Web 2.0* is facing. In fact, *Web 2.0* offers just basic query possibilities like browsing by keywords or tags. Semantic-based systems can facilitate knowledge representation, extraction and content integration [12–15]. We can implement semantic systems to efficiently manipulate and represent knowledge [16]. Through the ontologies, systems express key entities and relationships describing resources in a formal machine-processable representation.

In eHealth domain, there are massive information resources in which the knowledge formation process is associated with multiple data sources. However, the systems, grammar, structure and semantics of resources are heterogeneous. The idea behind the SW approach is to use the Web for exposing, connecting and sharing data through dereferenceable Uniform Resource Identifiers (URIs). The goal of SW is to extend the Web by publishing various open datasets as Resource Description Framework (RDF) triples and by setting RDF links between data items among several sources. Using URIs, RDF language and Ontology Web Language (OWL), SW technologies easily allow users to connect pieces of data, share information and knowledge on the Web. Ontologies are a mean to express concepts of a given domain and the relationships among the concepts; they specify complex constraints on the types of resources and their properties.

Semantic data annotation is the key step for every SW project. Our framework aims to semantically annotate heterogeneous IoT fitness and life logging data collected by wearable devices and wellness appliances in order to make them integrated and machine-understandable.

Figure 80.1 shows the overall architecture of the proposed framework. The two core components of the entire system are the IoT Fitness Ontology (IFO) and the mapping process (*i.e.* the RML processor and the mapping specifications).

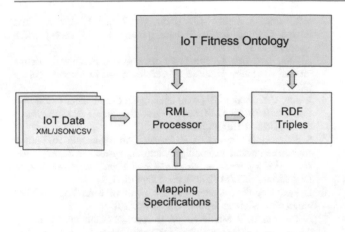

Fig. 80.1 Proposed system architecture: how to semantically annotate IoT raw data according to the IFO ontology to produce an RDF graph

The primary role of the IFO ontology is to provide a formal representation of the main concepts within the IoT fitness domain. The RML processor, supplied with the mapping specifications for the various sources, consumes the IoT raw data and transforms it into an RDF graph, which represent the same input data semantically annotated according to the IFO ontology.

80.4 Proposed Ontology

The proposed IFO ontology is a lightweight extensible domain-specific ontology which aims to provide a formal representation of the most common concepts and their relationships within the IoT fitness and wellness devices, including mobile health applications.

For the development process of the IFO ontology, we followed the well-known methodology proposed by Noy and McGuiness which is a quick but complete approach for building ontologies [17]. We wrote the IFO ontology in OWL, a W3C recommendation and the *de facto* standard language for publishing and sharing ontologies in the SW. Finally, to check for inconsistencies we validated it using the ontology reasoner *HermiT* [18].

To identify the concepts described in the IFO ontology we considered and carefully analysed the characteristics and functionalities provided by several IoT wearable devices and wellness appliances as well as health mobile applications available in the market. The list of products and vendors that were taken in consideration during the design process includes: *Apple HealthKit, Microsoft HealthVault, Google Fit, Fitbit, Jawbone, Strava, Runtastic, iHealth* and *Nokia Health*. The result is a harmonised ontology of the most important common concepts in the considered domain. The first version of the IFO ontology consists of 93 classes, 16 object properties, 7 data properties, and 47 individuals.

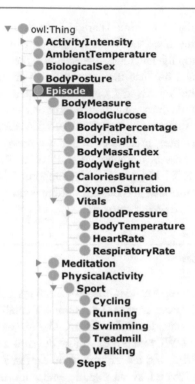

Fig. 80.2 Developed ontology structure in *Protégé* editor

To achieve a better integration with other systems and better specify the meaning of each class, we referred to other standardized ontologies such as *SNOMED-CT*. Personal information (*e.g.* date of birth) are based on *FOAF* ontology and the *Basic geo* (WGS84 lat/long) vocabulary was used for the geospatial locations. Figure 80.2 shows IFO ontology classes hierarchy as it can be seen within the *Protégé* editor.

80.5 Mapping

Mapping is the process by which values within the data sources are semantically annotated according to an ontology [19]. The mapping process constitutes the second core component of our framework. Essentially, a map processor consumes the input sources along with the mapping specifications to produce the RDF graph. It is important that the semantic annotation process adheres to a common standard to guarantee interoperability between different systems. RDF, the cornerstone of the SW, provides a standardized mean for adding metadata annotations to resources [20] in order to reach semantic interoperability and integration, and querying of data having heterogeneous formats. Therefore, generating RDF triples from sources having various formats is a key step for our system.

We defined the mapping specifications for three IoT systems among the ones we used to construct the ontology (*i.e.* Fitbit, *Apple Health* and *Nokia Health*). In particular, the mapping rules are relative to some shared concepts among these systems (*e.g.* the heart rate). As an evidence of the flexibility of the mapping language, we selected the IoTs devices aforementioned because they use different formats to store the data collected. Even though we mapped only a limited number of devices, mapping definitions can be easily reused across different sources that provide similar information. As a mapping process executor, we opted for RML Mapper which is a Java implementation of an RML mapping processor. RDF Mapper already supports XML, JSON and CSV data formats, and therefore there is no need to extend or modify the existing software.

80.6 Conclusion

Our system is able to support classification findings using ontology-represented measurements about temporal relationships, vital signs and statistical information. The reasoning tests performed using OWL and SWRL allow the automatic classification of classes using description logic expressions. The inferences were revised by an expert, who confirmed that they were valid based on his analysis of the episode annotation information. We are carrying out some more tests to verify that our model can efficiently implement the process of episode classification.

In this paper, we proposed an ontology representation of heterogeneous IoT fitness and life log data collected by wearable fitness devices and wellness appliances. The system addresses the issue of the dimension and heterogeneity in source and format of data captured by eHealth IoT devices by representing the semantics of both the domain of the connected objects and their relationships. Two are the main contributions of this work. First, we proposed a semantic-based approach that starts with data collection, followed by knowledge extraction and semantic modelling of the knowledge, in order to explicitly describe the meaning of the sensors data. Second, we described an eHealth system that integrates ontologies to facilitate the interoperability and data integration among different devices by illustrating the effectiveness of the proposed approach for ontology building and evaluation.

References

1. J.A. Mendoza, K.S. Baker, M.A. Moreno, K. Whitlock, M. Abbey-Lambertz, A. Waite, T. Colburn, E.J. Chow, Fitbit and Facebook mHealth intervention for promoting physical activity among adolescent and young adult childhood cancer survivors: a pilot study. Pediatr. Blood Cancer **64**(12) (2017)

2. S.R. Islam, D. Kwak, M.H. Kabir, M. Hossain, K.-S. Kwak, The internet of things for health care: a comprehensive survey. IEEE Access **3**, 678–708 (2015)

3. J. Kim, J.W. Lee, OpenIoT: an open service framework for the internet of things, in *IEEE World Forum on Internet of Things* (2014)

4. J. Sun, C.K. Reddy, Big data analytics for healthcare, in *Tutorial Presentation at the SIAM International Conference on Data Mining* (Texas, USA, 2013), p. 327

5. S. Riccucci, A. Carbonaro, G. Casadei, An architecture for knowledge management in intelligent tutoring system, in *IADIS International Conference on Cognition and Exploratory Learning in Digital Age, CELDA* (2005), pp. 473–476

6. J. Fox, Cognitive systems at the point of care: The CREDO program. J. Biomed. Inform. **68**, 83–95 (2017)

7. A. Carbonaro, V. Maniezzo, M. Roccetti, P. Salomoni, Modelling the student in Pitagora 2.0. User Model. User-Adap. Inter. **4**(4), 233–251 (1994)

8. A. Carbonaro, P. Zingaretti, Object tracking in a varying environment, in *IEEE Conference Publication Issue* 443 pt 1. (1997), pp. 229–233

9. A. Carbonaro, P. Zingaretti, A comprehensive approach to image-contrast enhancement, in *Proceedings—International Conference on Image Analysis and Processing*, Article number 797602 (1999), pp. 241–246

10. R. Fang, S. Pouyanfar, Y. Yang, S.-C. Chen, S.S. Iyengar, Computational health informatics in the Big Data Age: a survey. ACM Comput. Surv **49**(1), Article 12 (2016)

11. A.G. Patel, S.K. Datta, M.I. Ali, SWoTSuite: a toolkit for prototyping end-to-end semantic web of things applications, in *Proceedings of the 26th International Conference on World Wide Web Companion* (2017), pp. 263–267

12. A. Carbonaro, Towards an automatic forum summarization to support tutoring, in *Technology Enhanced Learning: Quality of Teaching and Educational Reform*, (Springer, Berlin, Heidelberg, 2010), pp. 141–147

13. N. Henze, P. Dolog, W. Nejdl, Reasoning and ontologies for personalized e-learning in the semantic web. Educ. Technol. Soc. **7**(4), 82–97 (2004)

14. A. Andronico, A. Carbonaro, L. Colazzo, A. Molinari, M. Ronchetti, A. Trifonova, Designing models and services for learning management systems in mobile settings, in *Workshop on Mobile and Ubiquitous Information Access*, (Springer, Berlin, 2003)

15. A. Andronico, A. Carbonaro, L. Colazzo, A. Molinari, Personalisation services for learning management systems in mobile settings. Int. J. Contin. Eng. Educ. Life Long Learn **14**(4–5), 353–369 (2004)

16. Carbonaro A., Defining personalized learning views of relevant learning objects in a collaborative bookmark management system, in *Web-Based Intelligent ELearning Systems: Technologies and Applications*, ed. by Z. Ma (Information Science Publishing, Hershey, PA), 2006, pp. 139–155

17. N.F. Noy, D.L. McGuinness, Ontology development 101: a guide to creating your first ontology. *Stanford Knowledge Systems Laboratory Technical Report KSL-01-05* (2001)

18. Shearer R., B. Motik, I. Horrocks, Hermit: a highly-efficient owl reasoner, in *OWLED*, vol. 432 (2008), p 91

19. F. Amardeilh, Semantic annotation and ontology population, in *Semantic Web Engineering in the Knowledge Society* (2008), p. 424

20. F. Manola, E. Miller, B. McBride, RDF primer. W3C Recommend. **10**(1–107), 6 (2004)

Applying Transfer Learning to QSAR Regression Models

Rodolfo S. Simões, Patrícia R. Oliveira, Káthia M. Honório,
and Clodoaldo A. M. Lima

Abstract

Aiming at avoiding high costs in the production and analysis of new drug candidates, databases containing molecular information have been generated, and thus, computational models can be constructed from these data. The quantitative study of structure-activity relationships (QSAR) involves building predictive models that relate chemical descriptors for a compound set and biological activity with respect to one or more targets in the human body. Datasets manipulated by researchers in QSAR analyses are generally characterized by a small number of instances, which can affect the accuracy of the resulting models. In this context, transfer learning techniques that take information from other QSAR models to the same biological target would be desirable, reducing efforts and costs for evaluating new chemical compounds. This article presents a novel transfer learning method that can be applied to build QSAR regression models by Support Vectors Regression (SVR). The SVR-Adapted method for Transfer Learning (ATL) was compared with standard SVR method regarding values of mean squared error. From experimental studies, the performance of both methods was evaluated for different proportions of the original training set. The obtained results show that transfer learning is capable to exploit knowledge from models built from other datasets, which is effective primarily for small target training datasets.

Keywords

Transfer learning · Support-vector regression ·
Cheminformatics · QSAR models · Medicinal chemistry

81.1 Introduction

Studies in Medicinal Chemistry aim at understanding the main mechanisms related to evolution of diseases in order to suggest new chemicals as drug candidates. To develop a new drug, researchers must analyze the biological targets of a certain disease, for discovering and developing drug candidates for these targets. Next, biological tests must be carried out to validate the efficiency and the side effects of those candidates.

In order to avoid high costs for the development and analysis of these chemical compounds, databases are generated, containing a huge amount of molecular information, and, consequently, computational models can be constructed from these data. Among the existing activities in the process of drug discovery, there is a data analysis strategy that proposes the establishment of relationships between chemical structures and biological activity (SAR) of a series of molecules. The quantitative study of the structure-activity relationship (QSAR) involves the construction of models that quantitatively describe a set of descriptors of a chemical compound and its biological activity in relation to one or more targets in the organism [1].

QSAR analyses are widely used to study the chemical properties of a compound group in order to predict the corresponding biological activity levels. For this analysis, machine learning techniques can be applied to estimate values that quantify the biological activity (using regression techniques) or class values (from classification techniques).

Ning and Karypis [2] argue that many of chemical compounds do not have pre-defined labels and the number of labeled instances are very small, which can generate an inefficient model. In addition to the small number of instances and the little information available, others challenges related to machine learning methods, which are constantly found in issues related to cheminformatics, require special attention in an attempt to solve them [3]. More specifically, machine learning algorithms assume that both training and test data

R. S. Simões (✉) · P. R. Oliveira · K. M. Honório · C. A. M. Lima
School of Arts, Sciences, and Humanities, University of Sao Paulo
(USP), Ermelino Matarazzo, Sao Paulo, Brazil
e-mail: simoesrodolfo@usp.br

© Springer International Publishing AG, part of Springer Nature 2018
S. Latifi (ed.), *Information Technology – New Generations*, Advances in Intelligent Systems and Computing 738,
https://doi.org/10.1007/978-3-319-77028-4_81

derive from the same probability distribution, which is not the usual situation for the medicinal chemistry data, since the synthesized compounds to be tested can easily move away from the probability distribution of the instances used in training, considerably reducing the model performance in the evaluation stage.

In scenarios like these, transfer learning techniques could be applied to reduce the effort of researchers and the cost of the process to generate new sets of chemical descriptors. Thus, it is possible to utilize the knowledge of a related dataset to help build a model for a target dataset, where the available data are scarce [4].

In this article, a novel transfer learning method is introduced and applied to build QSAR regression models by Support Vectors Regression (SVR). Experimental results show that using previous knowledge, obtained by a related (source) task, can make a model for a new (target) task to increase its performance, specially when the dataset available for the target is small. This paper is organized as follows. In Sect. 81.2, transfer learning fundamentals are presented. In Sect. 81.3, a brief introduction to SVR method and its adapted version for transfer learning proposed in this work are described. The datasets and experimental results are presented in Sect. 81.4. Finally, conclusions and future work are addressed in Sect. 81.5.

81.2 Transfer Learning

Data mining and machine learning approaches, including classification, regression and clustering methods have achieved significant success in several knowledge areas. However, many of these techniques work well only under the assumption that the training and test data are drawn from the same feature space and follow the same probability distribution [5]. If changes in data distribution are observed, most of predictive models need to be rebuilt from the beginning using newly collected training data, which can be expensive or even impossible in many real-world applications. In such cases, knowledge transfer or transfer learning between related tasks or domains would be desirable since this approach allows that domains, tasks and probability distributions considered in training and testing phases to be different [6].

The development of transfer learning techniques was motivated by the assumption that is possible to apply the previously acquired knowledge in a certain task to solve new related problems more quickly and with better solutions. In special, transfer learning approaches can save a significant amount of collecting and labeling effort [5].

Many examples in knowledge engineering can be found where transfer learning can be truly beneficial [6]. In particular, researches in medicinal chemistry area for the discovery

of new drugs have taken advantage of transfer learning techniques, as it can be seen in [4, 7] and [8]. Aiming at contributing to the advance of such application, this is also the focus of this work.

81.3 Methods

The transfer learning approach proposed in this work is based on the standard SVR method, which is briefly described in the next section. Subsequently, we present a related study that makes use of knowledge obtained from related tasks in a multitask learning approach. Finally, the proposed version for transfer learning approach is presented, considering single-target QSAR models.

81.3.1 Support Vector Regression (SVR)

A single-target QSAR problem encompasses a dataset $\mathbf{X} = \{(\mathbf{x_i}, y_i), i = 1, \cdots, l\}$, where $\mathbf{x_i} \in \mathcal{R}^n$ and $y_i \in \mathcal{R}$ is a biological activity value. Given such a dataset, SVR solves a constrained optimization problem by the following primal problem:

$$\min_{\mathbf{w}, \xi^*, \xi} = \frac{1}{2}(\mathbf{w}^T \mathbf{w}) + C \left(\sum_{i=1}^{l} \xi_i + \sum_{i=1}^{l} \xi_i^* \right), \quad (81.1)$$

where the term $(\mathbf{w}^T \mathbf{w})$ regularizes the model complexity, $C > 0$ is a parameter defined by the user, and ξ and ξ_i^* are slack variables, introduced to cope with otherwise infeasible constraints of the optimization problem. As presented in Eq. (81.2). Figure 81.1 presents the gap variables on both sides of the hyperplane. The complete formulation of SVR is stated by [9].

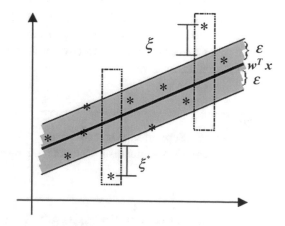

Fig. 81.1 Illustration of support vector for a regression problem with the gap variables ξ and ξ^* in two sides of the hyperplane [10]

$$\begin{cases} y_i - (\mathbf{w} \cdot \mathbf{x_i}) - b \le \epsilon + \xi_i \\ (\mathbf{w} \cdot \mathbf{x_i}) + b - y_i \le \epsilon + \xi_i^* \\ \xi_i, \xi_i^* \ge 0, i = 1, \cdots, l. \end{cases} \quad (81.2)$$

The ϵ-quadratic loss function for SVR, associated with $(\mathbf{x_i}, y_i)$ is defined by:

$$L_{\epsilon-\text{quadratic}}(f(\mathbf{x}) - y) = \begin{cases} 0 & \text{if} |f(\mathbf{x}) - y| < \epsilon \\ (|f(\mathbf{x}) - y| - \epsilon)^2 & \text{otherwise.} \end{cases} \quad (81.3)$$

The loss function ensures that the loss is zero if $|\mathbf{w}^T \mathbf{x_i} - y_i| = |f(\mathbf{x_i}) - y_i| \le \epsilon$. This means that the actual target value y_i is within an expected interval. Using the loss function ϵ-quadratic, the dual formulation assumes the following configuration:

$$\max_{\alpha, \alpha^*} \left[-\frac{1}{2} \sum_{i=1}^{l} \sum_{j=1}^{l} (\alpha_i^* - \alpha_i)(\alpha_j^* - \alpha_j)(\mathbf{x_i} \cdot \mathbf{x_j}) \right.$$
$$\left. + \sum_{i=1}^{l} \alpha_i^*(y_i - \epsilon) - \alpha_i(y_i + \epsilon) \right] - \frac{1}{2C} \sum_{i=1}^{l} (\alpha_i^2 + (\alpha_i^*)^2). \quad (81.4)$$

Making the substitution $\beta_i = \alpha_i - \alpha_i^*$, in formulation (81.4), a simplification is achieved by KKT conditions, where:

$$\alpha_i \alpha_i^* = 0, \quad i = 1, \cdots, l, \quad (81.5)$$

which implies that: $\beta_i^2 = \alpha_i^2 + (\alpha_i^*)^2$ the $|\beta_i| = |\alpha_i - \alpha_i^*| = \alpha_i + \alpha_i^*$. Now, the dual problem considering the loss function ϵ-quadratic can be defined as follows:

$$\min_{\beta} = \frac{1}{2} \sum_{i=1}^{l} \sum_{j=1}^{l} \beta_i \beta_j (\mathbf{x_i} \cdot \mathbf{x_j}) - \sum_{i=1}^{l} \beta_i y_i + \frac{1}{2C} \sum_{i=1}^{l} \beta_i^2$$
$$+ \sum_{i=1}^{l} \epsilon |\beta_i|, \quad (81.6)$$

$$\sum_{i=1}^{l} \beta_i = 0. \quad (81.7)$$

Next, the adaptation of SVR for transfer learning from a source task s to a target task t, which is named by SVR-ATL, is described.

81.3.2 SVR-Adapted for Transfer Learning (SVR-ATL)

In a pioneer study, Evgeniou and Pontil [11] introduced a multitask learning approach for the SVR optimization problem based on graphs. In their approach, each task corresponds to a node in a graph and the similarities among the tasks are encoded by weighted edges summarized in an adjacency matrix A, where $A_{st} \ge 0$. These authors additioned a regularization term $J(\mathbf{w_1}, \cdots, \mathbf{w_T})$ to the primal optimization problem (81.1). They argue that this addition makes the T models, obtained by the T tasks, to be more similar to each other, and consequently, a model with a good generalization power, obtained from a training set with a large number of instances, can assist inefficient models built from not enough data. The regularization term is given by:

$$J(\mathbf{w_1}, \cdots, \mathbf{w_t}) = \frac{1}{4} \sum_{s=1}^{T} \sum_{t=1}^{T} A_{st} ||\mathbf{w_s} - \mathbf{w_t}||^2. \quad (81.8)$$

Following similar ideas, as in [11] and [7], and combining Eqs. (81.1) and (81.8), the primal optimization problem for the SVR-ATL is formulated by:

$$\min_{\mathbf{w_s}, \mathbf{w_t}, \xi_s^*, \xi_t^*, \xi_s, \xi_t} = \frac{1}{2}(\mathbf{w_s}^T \mathbf{w_s}) + \frac{1}{2}(\mathbf{w_t}^T \mathbf{w_t}) + J(\mathbf{w_s}, \mathbf{w_t}) +$$
$$\frac{C}{2} \left(\sum_{i=1}^{l} (\xi_{si})^2 + \sum_{i=1}^{l} (\xi_{si}^*)^2 \right) + \frac{C}{2} \left(\sum_{i=1}^{l} (\xi_{ti})^2 + \sum_{i=1}^{l} (\xi_{ti}^*)^2 \right),$$

$$\text{s.t.} \quad J(\mathbf{w_s}, \mathbf{w_t}) = \frac{1}{4} ||\mathbf{w_s} - \mathbf{w_t}||^2. \quad (81.9)$$

As in Eq. (81.1), the terms $||\mathbf{w_s}||^2, ||\mathbf{w_t}||^2$ control the complexity of the specific task model, $C > 0$ is a parameter defined by the user, $\xi_{si}, \xi_{ti}, \xi_{si}^*$ and ξ_{ti}^* are the slack variables introduced to cope with otherwise infeasible constraints of the optimization problem, representing the model constraints for source and target task, respectively. As also show in Eq. (81.2). Additionally, the function $J(\mathbf{w_s}, \mathbf{w_t})$ represents a regularization term that increases the similarity of the weight vectors for source and target tasks. The transfer of knowledge is achieved by imposing that the function f_t is more similar to the function f_s as possible. Figure 81.2 illustrates the

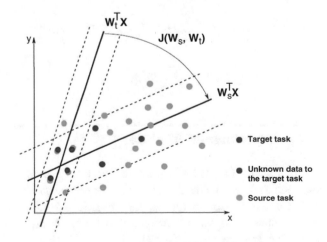

Fig. 81.2 Knowledge transfer from source task, which comprises a lot of training data (green), to a similar target task, containing little training data (blue). The term $J(\mathbf{w_s}, \mathbf{w_T})$ forces the source model ($\mathbf{w_s}$) to be more similar to the target model ($\mathbf{w_t}$). Figure adapted from [7]

knowledge transfer between source and target tasks by using a regularization term.

As in Eq. (81.4) using the loss function ϵ-quadratic, the dual formulation assumes the following configuration:

$$
\begin{aligned}
\min_{\mathbf{w_s},\mathbf{w_t},\xi_s^*,\xi_t^*,\xi_s,\xi_t} &= \frac{1}{2}(\mathbf{w_s}^T\mathbf{w_s}) + \frac{1}{2}(\mathbf{w_t}^T\mathbf{w_t}) \\
&+ \frac{1}{4}(\mathbf{w_s}^T - \mathbf{w_t}^T)(\mathbf{w_s} - \mathbf{w_t}) \\
&+ \frac{c}{2}(\sum_{i=1}^{l}(\xi_{si})^2 + \sum_{i=1}^{l}(\xi_{si}^*)^2) + \frac{c}{2}(\sum_{i=1}^{l}(\xi_{ti})^2 + \sum_{i=1}^{l}(\xi_{ti}^*)^2) \\
&+ \sum_{i=1}^{l}\alpha_{si}(y_{si} - \mathbf{w_s}^T\mathbf{x_{si}} - \epsilon_s - \xi_{si}) \\
&+ \sum_{i=1}^{l}\alpha_{ti}(y_{ti} - \mathbf{w_t}^T\mathbf{x_{ti}} - \epsilon_t - \xi_{ti}) \\
&+ \sum_{i=1}^{l}\alpha_{si}^*(\mathbf{w_s}^T\mathbf{x_{si}} - y_{si} - \epsilon_s - \xi_{si}^*) \\
&+ \sum_{i=1}^{l}\alpha_{ti}^*(\mathbf{w_t}^T\mathbf{x_{ti}} - y_{ti} - \epsilon_t - \xi_{ti}^*).
\end{aligned} \tag{81.10}
$$

Making a substitution as in Eq. (81.5) and using the derivatives in respect to $\mathbf{w_s}, \mathbf{w_t}, \xi_{si}^*, \xi_{ti}^*, \xi_{si}, \xi_{ti}$, the following dual formulation of the primal in (81.9) is obtained:

$$
\begin{aligned}
\min_{\beta_s,\beta_t} &= -\frac{3}{8}\sum_{i=1}^{l}\beta_{si}\beta_{sj}(\mathbf{x_{si}} \cdot \mathbf{x_{sj}}) \\
&- \frac{1}{4}\sum_{i=1}^{l}\beta_{si}\beta_{tj}(\mathbf{x_{si}} \cdot \mathbf{x_{tj}}) - \frac{3}{8}\sum_{i=1}^{l}\beta_{ti}\beta_{tj} \\
(\mathbf{x_{ti}} \cdot \mathbf{x_{tj}}) &- \sum_{i=1}^{l}\frac{\beta_{si}^2}{2C} - \sum_{i=1}^{l}\frac{\beta_{ti}^2}{2C} + \sum_{i=1}^{l}\beta_{si}y_{si} - \sum_{i=1}^{l}|\beta_{si}|\epsilon_s \\
&+ \sum_{i=1}^{l}\beta_{ti}y_{ti} - \sum_{i=1}^{l}|\beta_{ti}|\epsilon_t.
\end{aligned} \tag{81.11}
$$

81.4 Experimental Analyses

In this section, the datasets used in our experiments are described, followed by the discussion on the obtained results. First, for comparison purposes, the investigated methods were evaluated on three benchmark datasets. Next, five chemical datasets were considered.

81.4.1 Benchmark Data

The first pair of datasets considered in this paper was taken from *kin family* database, which was generated from a realistic simulation of the forward dynamics of an 8 link all-revolute robot arm.[1] In the experiments of this work, a dataset formed by nonlinear medium variance data in *kin family* was considered as source data and other dataset consisting of non linear high variance data was used as target dataset. The second database analyzed here is named by *Earthquake* [12], with observations on earthquakes occurred in different countries. On a first sight, one can think that a predictive model generated from data measured in California, for instance, is only suitable for making future forecasts of earthquakes in that location and it may not be appropriate for forecasts in other countries. However, if data collected in Japan are very scarce, a model generated from such data may not have a good generalization power. Thus, although the probability distributions of data from California and from Japan differ, it is generally reasonable to assume that it is possible to use the model generated for the first country to improve the model built for the second one. Therefore, the transfer learning experiment consisted on using the data collected in California as the origin set and the data collected in Japan as the destination set.

The third database describes arrival and departure details for all commercial flights[2] in United States, containing flight records from October 1987 to April 2008. In this case, the value to be predicted is the delay of a particular flight. For the experiments of this work, the data of 2007 flights were considered as origin set and the data of 2008 as destination set.

81.4.2 Chemical Data

Due to the large amount of data produced in all areas of science and industry today, there are possibly many datasets related to the task at hand. Therefore, the six dataset pairs used in the experiments of this work are only a selection from a wider range of possibilities. Here, it is assumed that similar datasets are available for applying transfer learning techniques.

Unlike other studies, the compounds that are categorized as inactive were not discarded, i.e. all structures of chemical compounds available in the datasets were considered in the experiments. In this context, the main goal of medicinal chemistry researches is to predict the inhibition value presented by compounds as measured by $IC50$ values that indicate how much of a given substance is needed to block a biological activity by half.

---

[1] Kin datasets are part of the delve dataset repository, available in: http://www.cs.toronto.edu/~delve/data/kin/desc.html.

[2] Dataset available in: http://stat-computing.org/dataexpo/2009/.

The first pair of datasets represents data on activin receptor-like kinase 5 (ALK-5) [13, 14], which is an attractive target to treat cancer. The second and third pair of datasets contains bioactive compounds that activate peroxisome proliferator-activated receptors (PPARs) [15], which constitute a class of nuclear receptors whose main function is to regulate gene transcription related to lipid and carbohydrate metabolism. The second pair correspond to the PPAR α receptor that is the major responsible for lipid metabolism and is mostly expressed in the liver. The third pair corresponds to PPAR-δ, which regulates lipid metabolism (including lipid absorption and transport), insulin resistance and weight reduction and is mostly expressed in several tissues and cells. To form the second and third pairs of datasets, one selected data available in Pubchem database[3] as source datasets (AID 279988 and 279989). In general, the goal of QSAR models using PPAR ligands is to predict the $EC50$ values.

For the fourth pair of datasets, abbreviated by DHFR 4q and DHFR-S [16, 17], the goal is to predict the dihydrofolate reductase inhibition of compounds as measured by $IC50$. The fifth pair of datasets [16, 17], called as COX2-4q and COX2-S, were used to predict the cyclooxygenase-2 inhibition of compounds as measured by the $IC50$ values. For the sixth and last pair of datasets, data on ER-TOX and ER-LIT [17] were selected, with values of the logarithmized relative binding affinities of compounds in relation to the estrogen receptor with respect to β-estradiol. Summarized information on the above described chemical datasets are presented in Table 81.1.

81.4.3 Description of Experiments

The choice of source datasets used in the experiments of this work was mainly based on the number of instances available for training. In all cases, the largest dataset in the

Table 81.1 Details on the selected chemical datasets

Dataset	Number of instances	Source/target
ALK5 [13]	59	Target
ALK5 [14]	117	Source
PPARα [15]	70	Target
PPARα (AID 279988)	89	Source
PPARδ [15]	70	Target
PPARδ (AID 279989)	89	Source
DHFR [16]	391	Target
DHFR [17]	739	Source
COX2 [16]	317	Target
COX2 [17]	431	Source
ER-TOX [16]	323	Target
ER-LIT [16]	380	Source

[3]https://pubchem.ncbi.nlm.nih.gov/.

pair was selected as source. This decision was motivated by the assumption that transfer learning is generally beneficial if applied from a dataset with a greater number of instances to a dataset with fewer instances [7].

In order to obtain a baseline criterion of performance, the SVR method was evaluated for the target chemical datasets with variable sizes, i.e., considering the proportions as 100%, 75%, 50% and 25% of their original sizes, aiming also at analyzing the impact of transfer learning. Each run consisted of a fivefold cross-validation process and the Mean Square Error (MSE) values were calculated as a performance measure. The SVR method was implemented by the *e1071* library of R software,[4] with the following parameter values: SVM-Type: eps-regression, SVM-Kernel: linear, cost=100, 10 and 0.1.

For applying the SVR-ATL method, it is necessary previously to generate the source and target models. For building the target model, the target datasets generated for the SVR method experiments were also considered. For obtaining the source model, the complete source datasets (without any instance removal) were used. The resulting models obtained by the SVR-ATL method were evaluated considering the unknown data (not used in the training phase) in target set. Such implementation used the quadprog function[5] of Matlab for the dual optimization problem in Eq. (81.11), where the matrix in Eq. (81.12) was given as input to the quadprog function, also varying the values for parameter C, as 100, 10 and 0.1.

$$\begin{bmatrix} -3/4 * Xs * Xs' - eye(N) * 1/C & -1/4 * Xs * Xt' \\ -1/4 * Xt * Xs' & -3/4 * Xt * Xt' - eye(M) * 1/C \end{bmatrix}.$$
(81.12)

81.4.4 Discussion of Results

The goal, here, is to investigate in which situations the transfer learning improves the predictive performance in target tasks. Therefore, the results obtained by SVR method was compared to those obtained by the proposed approach considering the trade-off between performance and amount of training data from target tasks. In this sense, these methods were evaluated in different scenarios, drawn by varying the proportion of target data used in the training phase.

The results obtained in the experiments with benchmark datasets are presented in Table 81.2, considering target datasets with different sizes (n values). The results of experiments with chemical datasets are shown in Table 81.3. As can be seen in Tables, the transfer learning approach overperformed the SVR method for most of the scenarios

[4]https://www.r-project.org/.

[5]https://www.mathworks.com/help/optim/ug/quadprog.html.

Table 81.2 Experimental results obtained by the methods considering benchmark datasets

Target dataset	n	SVR			SVR-ATL		
		cost=0.1	cost=10	cost=100	C=0.1	C=10	C=100
Kin-family nh	50	7.36E-01	8.54E-01	8.53E-01	6.86E-01	7.92E-01	7.94E-01
	100	8.05E-01	8.06E-01	8.06E-01	6.88E-01	7.06E-01	7.06E-01
	150	6.76E-01	6.95E-01	6.95E-01	6.07E-01	6.17E-01	6.17E-01
	200	6.34E-01	6.44E-01	6.44E-01	6.09E-01	6.10E-01	6.10E-01
Earthquake Japan	20	1.54E+00	9.05E-01	1.01E+01	1.36E+00	1.26E+00	1.26E+00
	30	1.52E+00	1.01E+00	1.08E+01	1.13E+00	9.33E-01	9.55E-01
	50	7.00E-01	7.35E-01	5.13E+00	7.17E-01	5.47E-01	5.52E-01
	70	7.99E-01	9.35E-01	4.87E+00	7.09E-01	7.34E-01	7.59E-01
Flight 2008	50	5.14E-02	5.14E-02	5.14E-02	1.20E-02	1.23E-06	2.40E-08
	200	4.96E-03	4.96E-03	4.96E-03	1.84E-04	1.89E-08	2.49E-09
	400	5.82E-02	5.82E-02	5.82E-02	8.75E-03	1.06E-06	1.32E-08
	800	2.97E-03	2.97E-03	2.97E-03	2.89E-03	3.20E-07	4.98E-09

Table 81.3 Experimental results obtained by the methods considering chemical datasets

Target dataset	n	SVR			SVR-ATL		
		cost=0.1	cost=10	cost=100	C=0.1	C=10	C=100
ALK5-S	25%	4.69E+00	8.89E+00	5.86E+00	1.01E+00	4.59E+00	1.12E+01
	50%	1.02E+00	1.31E+00	8.39E+00	7.22E-01	1.17E+00	2.05E+00
	75%	8.05E-01	7.53E-01	7.60E-01	7.23E-01	8.38E-01	9.09E-01
	100%	1.08E+00	1.09E+00	1.05E+00	7.71E-01	7.99E-01	9.14E-01
PPARα	25%	1.34E+00	8.59E+00	6.81E+00	6.48E-01	4.44E+00	5.97E+00
	50%	8.83E-01	1.41E+00	1.26E+00	6.80E-01	1.25E+00	1.31E+00
	75%	5.60E-01	6.63E-01	6.94E-01	4.93E-01	5.52E-01	5.85E-01
	100%	5.36E-01	4.84E-01	4.85E-01	5.49E-01	6.34E-01	6.38E-01
PPARδ	25%	1.09E+00	1.42E+00	1.87E+00	8.51E-01	1.41E+00	1.58E+00
	50%	1.00E+00	1.16E+00	1.19E+00	9.63E-01	1.20E+00	1.22E+00
	75%	1.09E+00	1.10E+00	1.10E+00	1.04E+00	1.21E+00	1.21E+00
	100%	9.32E-01	9.72E-01	9.73E-01	8.90E-01	9.63E-01	9.67E-01
DHFR-S	25%	1.35E+00	1.36E+00	1.42E+00	1.27E+00	1.19E+00	1.19E+00
	50%	1.47E+00	1.45E+00	1.45E+00	1.38E+00	1.37E+00	1.37E+00
	75%	1.29E+00	1.28E+00	1.29E+00	1.29E+00	1.28E+00	1.28E+00
	100%	1.22E+00	1.26E+00	1.26E+00	1.23E+00	1.23E+00	1.23E+00
COX2-S	25%	1.44E+00	1.79E+00	1.82E+00	1.41E+00	1.44E+00	1.44E+00
	50%	1.96E+00	2.03E+00	2.02E+00	1.76E+00	1.78E+00	1.78E+00
	75%	1.80E+00	1.83E+00	1.83E+00	1.68E+00	1.69E+00	1.69E+00
	100%	1.87E+00	1.88E+00	1.89E+00	1.75E+00	1.74E+00	1.74E+00
ER-TOX	25%	7.26E-01	8.07E-01	8.23-01	7.09E-01	7.20E-01	7.330E-01
	50%	9.10E-01	8.90E-01	8.56E-01	8.35E-01	1.27E+00	1.72E+00
	75%	9.06E-01	9.18E-01	9.04E-01	8.56E-01	8.52E-01	8.63E-01
	100%	7.94E-01	7.72E-01	7.63E-01	7.79E-01	7.57E-01	7.53E-01

analyzed, especially when there is less training data available in the target datasets.

Analyzing Table 81.3, the SVR-ATL method achieved better results for all scenarios with 25% and 50% of information available for training; five scenarios with 75%, and four scenarios with the complete set available for training. These results indicate that transfer learning was more effective for tasks with very few training instances, in comparison to those that used more data in their training phase.

81.5 Conclusions and Future Work

Chemical data used in QSAR studies are characterized by generally missing biological activity values and, even when such values are available, the number of instances in dataset is small. This makes the construction of predictive models for molecular phenomena that constitute the chemical processes a very complex task. In this context, transfer learning approaches take advantage over traditional methods by using information from other related domains with more instances available for the same biological target.

In this paper, an adapted SVR method for transfer learning was proposed and evaluated in experiments involving benchmark data and QSAR regression models. A comparative analysis between the proposed approach and the standard SVR method showed promising results, especially when applied for datasets with few training instances. One can also say that besides improving the performance in the target task, such method can be applied to reduce efforts and costs related to the construction of new models from chemical descriptors.

Acknowledgements The authors thank to the Brazilian funding agencies CAPES and FAPESP, and to IBM for financial support.

References

1. J. Devillers, A.T. Balaban, *Topological Indices and Related Descriptors in QSAR and QSPAR* (CRC Press, Boca Raton, 2000)
2. X. Ning, G. Karypis, In silico structure-activity-relationship (SAR) models from machine learning: a review. Drug Dev. Res. **72**(2), 138–146 (2011)
3. A. Varnek, I. Baskin, Machine learning methods for property prediction in chemoinformatics: Quo Vadis? J. Chem. Inf. Model. **52**(6), 1413–1437 (2012)
4. T. Turki, Z. Wei, J.T. Wang, Transfer learning approaches to improve drug sensitivity prediction in multiple myeloma patients. IEEE Access **5**, 7381–7393 (2017)
5. S. Wang, Z. Li, A new transfer learning boosting approach based on distribution measure with an application on facial expression recognition, in *2014 International Joint Conference on Neural Networks (IJCNN)* (IEEE, 2014), pp. 432–439
6. S.J. Pan, Q. Yang, A survey on transfer learning. IEEE Trans. Knowl. Data Eng. **22**(10), 1345–1359 (2010)
7. L. Rosenbaum, A. Dörr, M.R. Bauer, F.M. Boeckler, A. Zell, Inferring multi-target QSAR models with taxonomy-based multi-task learning. J. Cheminformatics **5**(1–2), 33 (2013)
8. T. Girschick, U. Rückert, S. Kramer, Adapted transfer of distance measures for quantitative structure-activity relationships and data-driven selection of source datasets. Comput. J. bxs092 **56**(3), 274–288 (2013)
9. V.N. Vapnik, *The Nature of Statistical Learning Theory* (Springer, New York, 1995)
10. C.A. de Moraes Lima, Comitê de máquinas: uma abordagem unificada empregando máquinas de vetores-suporte, Ph.D. Dissertation, Universidade Estadual de Campinas, 2004
11. T. Evgeniou, M. Pontil, Regularized multi-task learning, in *Proceedings of the Tenth ACM SIGKDD International Conference on Knowledge Discovery and Data Mining* (ACM, 2004), pp. 109–117
12. J. Garcke, T. Vanck, Importance weighted inductive transfer learning for regression, in *Joint European Conference on Machine Learning and Knowledge Discovery in Databases* (Springer, Berlin, 2014), pp. 466–481
13. S.C. Araujo, V.G. Maltarollo, D.C. Silva, J.C. Gertrudes, K.M. Honorio, ALK-5 inhibition: a molecular interpretation of the main physicochemical properties related to bioactive ligands. J. Braz. Chem. Soc. **26**(9), 1936–1946 (2015)
14. M.O. Almeida, G.H. Trossini, V.G. Maltarollo, D.d.C. Silva, K.M. Honorio, In silico studies on the interaction between bioactive ligands and ALK5, a biological target related to the cancer treatment. J. Biomol. Struct. Dyn. **34**(9), 2045–2053 (2016)
15. V.G. Maltarollo, K.M. Honorio, Ligand-and structure-based drug design strategies and PPARδ/α selectivity. Chem. Biol. Drug Des. **80**(4), 533–544 (2012)
16. J.J. Sutherland, L.A. O'brien, D.F. Weaver, Spline-fitting with a genetic algorithm: a method for developing classification structure-activity relationships. J. Chem. Inf. Comput. Sci. **43**(6), 1906–1915 (2003)
17. J.J. Sutherland, L.A. O'Brien, D.F. Weaver, A comparison of methods for modeling quantitative structure-activity relationships. J. Med. Chem. **47**(22), 5541–5554 (2004)

Investigating the Recognition of Non-articulatory Sounds by Using Statistical Tests and Support Vector Machine

Francisco Carlos M. Souza, Alinne C. Corrêa Souza, Gilberto M. Nakamura, M. D. Soares, Patrícia Pupin Mandrá, and Alessandra A. Macedo

Abstract

People with articulation and phonological disorders need training to plan and to execute sounds of speech. Compared to other children, children with Down Syndrome have significantly delayed speech development because they present developmental disabilities, mainly apraxia of speech. In practice, speech therapists plan and perform trainings of articulatory and non-articulatory sounds such as blow production and popping lips in order to assist speech production. Mobile applications can be integrated into the clinical treatment to transcend the boundaries of clinics and schedules and therefore reach more people at any time. The use of artificial intelligence and machine learning techniques can improve this kind of application. The aim of this pilot study is to assess speech recognition methods prioritizing the training of sounds for speech production, particularly the non-articulatory sounds. These methods apply Mel-Frequency Cepstrum Coefficients and Laplace transform to extract features, as well as traditional statistical tests and Support Vector Machine (SVM) to recognize sounds. This study also reports experimental results regarding the effectiveness of the methods on a set of 197 sounds. Overall, SVM provides higher accuracy.

Keywords

Delayed speech development · Speech recognition methods · Machine learning · Automatic speech recognition

F. C. M. Souza · A. C. C. Souza · G. M. Nakamura · P. P. Mandrá · A. A. Macedo (✉)
USP, Ribeirão Preto, SP, Brazil
e-mail: fcarlos@icmc.usp.br; alinne@icmc.usp.br; gmnakamura@usp.br; ppmandra@fmrp.usp.br; ale.alaniz@usp.br

M. D. Soares
National Institute for Space Research, São José dos Campos, SP, Brazil

82.1 Introduction

Speech disorder occurs when a person cannot produce the sounds of speech correctly. This disorder may be related to neurological, myofunctional, and/or congenital-linguistic alterations and has different levels of severity. Speech disorders appear as phonological disability in children with apraxia of speech, such as children with Down Syndrome (DS). DS is a genetic disorder caused by the presence of a third chromosome 21. It is often associated with intellectual deficiency and developmental disabilities like hearing impairment, muscle hypotonia, and vocal tract abnormalities that can interfere in speech production [1]. In the world, one baby, in every seven hundred, is born with DS.[1] In Brazil, one in every six-eight hundred babies is born with DS.[2] This number highlights the need for initiatives to overcome barriers and to improve the quality of life of children with DS.

In general, children with DS develop speech with significant delay as compared to other children: children with DS perceive the articulatory properties of consonants and plan and execute articulatory gestures differently. The delay is due neuromuscular control issues associated with hypotonia and somatosensory alterations [2]. Consequently, children with DS, or even any children with disorders of the sounds of speech, need rigorous training to plan and to execute motor acts of speech. Speech training starts with facial motor praxia activities and oral myofunctional exercises during which non-articulatory sounds such as blow production and kisses (lip protrusion) are produced. When it comes to producing phonemes and words, non-articulatory sounds can be considered precursors.

The production of speech involves a complex coordination between selection, organization, planning and execu-

[1] https://www.cdc.gov/ncbddd/birthdefects/downsyndrome/data.html.
[2] http://www.sdh.gov.br/noticias/2014/marco/21-de-marco-dia-internacional-da-sindrome-de-down.

tion of movements for the production of the articulatory gesture. Learning new words may be associated with oral motor skills. The training of face motor praxis and oral myofunctional skills for the adequacy of muscle strength and function can be used to improve the production of the articulatory gesture, and the production of phonemes, syllables and words. Exercises with the muscles of the lips, cheeks, tongue, among others can be emphasized since they are related to the articulatory gesture for the production of words [3]. Considering the articulatory (perceptual and motor) properties of Brazilian Portuguese phonemes, it is possible to perform myofunctional, preparatory exercises, with the production of blowing and popping of lips (kiss), among others. These kind of exercises are considered as nonspeech orofacial movement.

For several years, great effort of multimedia processing has been devoted to addressing the recognition of different types of articulatory sounds. In terms of Speech Recognition (SR),[3] phonemes and words have been manipulated by traditional techniques [4, 5] that analyze, extract features and recognize information about speeches and voices [6]. By applying the same traditional techniques of sound recognition, non-articulatory sounds like blows and kisses can be treated as noise sounds. One challenge in Automatic SR (ASR) is to face the variable speech signal input. For example, each individual has a different vocal tract and collaterally produces a wide range of signals in regard to themselves and to others. Another challenge is to manipulate sounds that resemble noises. When two challenges occur simultaneously, Speech Recognition may be less to recognize non-articulatory sounds.

Here, we present an Automated Approach for Non-Articulatory sound recognition (ANA) that combines feature extractors and two different techniques to recognize the signals. The first technique is based on statistics and uses classic statistical tests, followed by Support Vector Machine (SVM). The proposed approach employs a very popular method called Mel-Frequency Cepstrum Coefficients (MFCC) and a Laplace Transform to characterize a speech signal. To test ANA, we conduct a pilot study involving participants with and without DS. ANA is part of a large project that is being developed at the University of São Paulo (USP) and which being funded by CNPq (Conselho Nacional de Pesquisa—National Counsel of Technological and Scientific Development). The large project, called SofiaFala (Sistema Inteligente de Apoio a Fala—Intelligent Speech Training System), intends to assist children with DS to produce speech. SofiaFala relies on extensive collaboration among members of a multidisciplinary team (computer scientists, physicists, speech therapist, physician, and psychologists). Whereas ANA just manipulates non-

articulatory sounds of speech, the new approaches that are being currently developed address other types of sounds and image processing of lips and cheeks during the speech of speech therapists and children.

Overall, the contributions of the present work can be summarized into: (1) an automated approach to support the recognition of the speech produced by individuals with DS; (2) an automated approach to assist speech production by individuals with DS; (3) recognition of non-articulatory sounds by means of classic statistical tests and machine learning; and (4) an exploratory investigation and an empirical assessment of the effectiveness of the proposed approach. Contrary to traditional investigations that have focused on articulatory sounds, this paper aims to recognize noisy sounds and to find out how traditional techniques can support this activity.

The remainder sections are organized as follows: Sect. 82.2 depicts the background. Section 82.3 details the automated SR approach. Section 82.4 reports the experimental study conducted herein. Section 82.5 presents the results and discusses the proposal benefits and relevance. Section 82.6 shows related study. Section 82.7 shows the conclusions and proposes future works.

82.2 Background

Speech recognition techniques have been widely investigated over the past years. Most studies have concentrated on articulatory speech sounds (words and phonemes). Some techniques like MFCC, Laplace transform, statistical methods, and SVM have been used to recognize these types of sounds. In this section, we show how these techniques are used to focus on non-articulatory sounds.

82.2.1 Mel-Frequency Cepstrum Coefficients

Sound waves are mechanical waves that propagate through continuous media, including air and water. Sound waves can interact with thin surfaces and membranes, such as membranes in general purpose microphones, to produce local oscillations in the material. The oscillation amplitudes along time are converted to numbers, whereas the time-ordered sequence formed by them generates the audio signal $\psi(t)$. For human speech, the corresponding audio signal may lack uniform or simple oscillatory patterns, which demands for additional audio analysis techniques. Speech recognition shares deep ties with sound waves spectral analysis, in which sound waves are decomposed into several simpler waves with characteristic lengths and oscillation frequency. The most common way to decompose a given audio signal $\psi(t)$ is to employ the Fourier transform [7]:

$$\psi(t) = \frac{1}{\sqrt{2\pi}} \int d\nu \, \Psi(\nu) e^{2\pi i \nu t}, \qquad (82.1)$$

---

[3]Speech Recognition is defined as a process in which an algorithm or technique converts human speech to a sequence of features that can be identified by a computer.

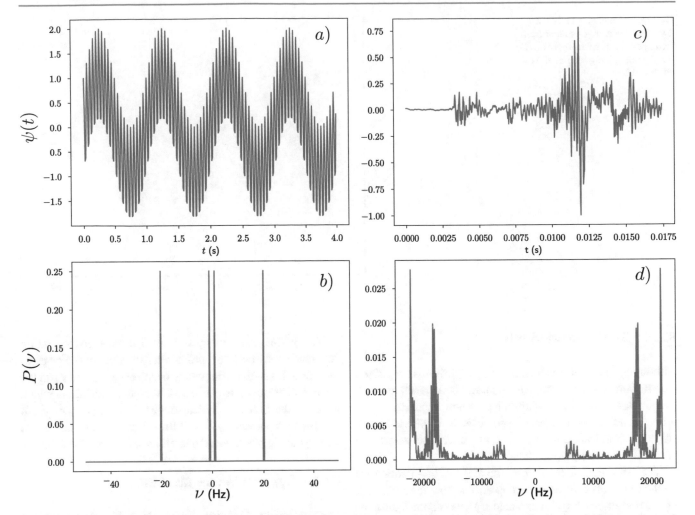

Fig. 82.1 Signals and spectrograms. (**a**) The signal $\psi(t) = \sin(2\pi t) + \cos(40\pi t)$ emerges from the combination of $\nu = 1$ and 20 Hz, respectively, and (**b**) the corresponding spectrogram (frequency centered).

(**c**) A non-articulatory sound (kiss) audio signal and (**d**) the corresponding spectrogram

where $\Psi(\nu)$ are complex valued coefficients that correspond to monochromatic planar waves with frequency ν. The Fourier transform is an invertible linear transform, which means that the original signal can be transformed and recovered. The audio signal spectrogram $P(\nu)$ complements the Fourier decomposition by informing each frequency contribution to the signal. For the Discrete Fourier Transform,

$$P(\nu) = |\Psi(\nu)|^2 / \sum_{\xi} |\Psi(\xi)|^2, \qquad (82.2)$$

which plays the role of a likelihood estimator for the frequency ν. For real valued signals, contributions from positive and negative frequencies mirror each other, so negative frequencies are usually discarded. Figure 82.1 exemplifies two spectrograms: one derived from harmonic signal and another derived from one non-articulatory sound (kiss). For simpler signals, the spectrogram provides enough information. As

sound complexity increases, as in the case of sounds produced by human speech, the number of modes available in a given signal also increases. Class intervals, or *bins*, circumvent this issue by breaking the spectrogram down into fewer frequency groups. The selection of class intervals depends on which frequency domain region or behavior one intends to highlight. The human auditory system perceives relative changes better than absolute changes, which suggests a logarithmic scale transformation for frequencies. The Mel scale satisfies this requirement $\nu_m = 2595 \log_{10}(1 + \nu/700)$. Accordingly, uniform Mel-frequency domain division provides the desired class intervals. Finally, the Mel-frequency Cepstrum (MFC) summarizes $P(\nu_m)$ within a given class interval, and its numerical value follows from centroid or another average evaluation. The MFC coefficients (MFCC) are the main features for speech recognition and classification [8]. They are evaluated by taking the log of MFCs, followed by the Cosine-DFT.

Fig. 82.2 Linear separability. Two features were extracted from the experiments by using MFCC for kissing and blowing sounds produced by t_2

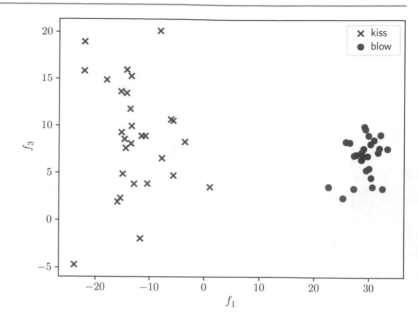

82.2.2 Statistical Methods

Although the use of machine learning algorithms for pattern recognition has increased, statistical methods (such as t-test and χ^2-test) are viable alternatives when specifics of the problem are known. These hypothesis tests provide cost-effective solutions and can be quite useful to assess the prediction of other approaches.

The t-test evaluates whether the average of a continuous random variable x from one group differs from the average μ of a different group (with variance $\hat{s}^2$) by random chance, or if it emerges from distinct probability distributions. In other words, the method relies on the statistical $t = (x - \mu)/\hat{s}$ and t-probability density function to evaluate whether the difference between groups is statistically significant for a given significance level α [9].

The χ^2-test verifies whether a collection of N categorical random variables x_k are distributed according to N independent normal distributions $\mathcal{N}(y_k, \hat{s}^2)$, centered around y_k with standard deviation $\hat{s}_k$ for $k = 1, 2, \ldots, N$. In this case, the relevant statistical $\chi^2 = \sum_{k=1}^{N} (x_k - y_k)^2/\hat{s}_k \geqslant 0$ follows the χ^2-distribution with $N - 1$ degrees of freedom.

From the χ^2-distribution, it is possible to see the chance of observing an χ^2 value can be evaluated. After that, a decision about accepting (or not) of the hypothesis of N independent normal distributions can be taken by considering a given significance level (α).

The χ^2-test has several uses in data analysis, including adherence tests between probability distributions. For positive variables such as frequency occurrence, one may use the Poisson distribution to estimate the standard deviation, which produces the well-known Pearson-$\chi^2 = \sum_k (x_k - y_k)^2/y_k$. In this paper, however, we retain the original definition so that we can handle positive and negative valued random variables.

82.2.3 Support Vector Machine

Support Vector Machine (SVM) is a Machine Learning technique that is based on the statistical learning theory [10]. The main SVM procedure is to find an optimal hyperplane in order to maximize the margin between it and the data. The optimal hyperplane can be considered as a line that separates the classes. It is mainly determined by the support vectors which are data points in the boundary region. For non-linearly separable problems, SVM uses kernel functions to transform the inputs into a high dimensionality features vector. The goal of this vector is to enable linear separation [11]. Therefore, starting from a training set, the goal is to find the optimal hyperplane, i.e., the hyperplane with the greatest feasible margin between the hyperplane and any sample in the training set. Hence, it is possible to classify new data not used in the training phase correctly [12].

In this paper, we treat the speech dataset as being linearly separable into two categories (Fig. 82.2). This interpretation is based on the training phase and on two features extracted from the plot. For linearly separable problems, different hyperplanes that can correctly separate the training dataset may exist. However, the optimal hyperplane is the one with the maximum correct classification for all the training.

82.3 Approach for Non-articulatory Sound Recognition

This paper presents an automated Approach for Non-Articulatory sound recognition (ANA). ANA is a project that has been specially designed for individuals with DS, but it can also be used by anyone training non-articulatory sounds. ANA consists of three steps: (1) Sound recording; (2) Feature extraction; and (3) Speech recognition. Figure 82.3 depicts an overview of this approach.

The first step (see "Sound recording" in Fig. 82.3.1) records the sounds. Next, MFCC and Laplace Transform methods help to extract a set of features by using the individual's speech signal. Many investigators usually consider "Sound recording" as one of the most important task to achieve high recognition accuracy. The "Feature extraction" step (see Fig. 82.3.2) represents the recorded sound by a set of features. The last step (see Fig. 82.3.3) explores two sound recognition methods to recognize the characterized sounds. The first method combines the T-test and the Chi-square test, whilst the second method uses SVM. The goal is to verify whether a given sound (represented by a set of features) is in the same category the sounds produced by the speech therapist. Each step is detailed in the following sections.

82.3.1 Sound Recording

ANA has been designed to record words and non-articulatory sounds by using conventional smartphones placed 15 cm away from the participants' mouth. Non-articulatory sounds such as blow and popping lips are the selected sounds because they are myofunctional and serve as preparatory activities to produce speech.

Smartphones have been adopted because (1) they are present in most Brazilian homes, and (2) the SofiaFala project intends to assist the speech of children with DS. Consequently, the approaches employed in this experiment should work as close as possible to the final application. For example, speech therapists or relatives of individuals with DS assist recording on the smartphone.

82.3.2 Feature Extraction

82.3.2.1 MFCC

The recorded sounds are input data for the feature extraction process if we consider MFCC and Laplace. MFCCs exhibits a high degree of linear separability for non-articulatory sounds. This observation adds up to well-known evidence that suggests MFCCs as viable for featuring audio signals. Therefore, for a given audio signal $\psi(t)$, ANA extracts MFCC corresponding to $n = 13$ Mel-frequency spectra, processes them, and assigns them to a feature factor with $N = 14$ entries. The last entry of the feature vector is set by the Laplace transform of the signal and includes a feature that improves separation of non-articulatory sounds.

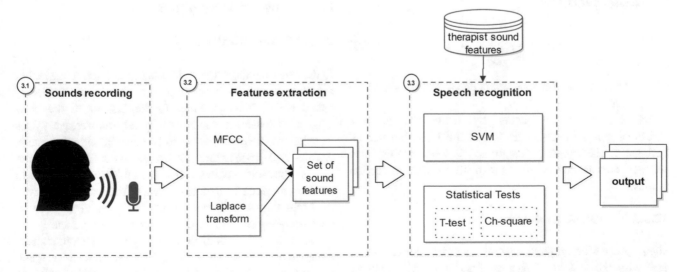

Fig. 82.3 Non-articulatory sound processing

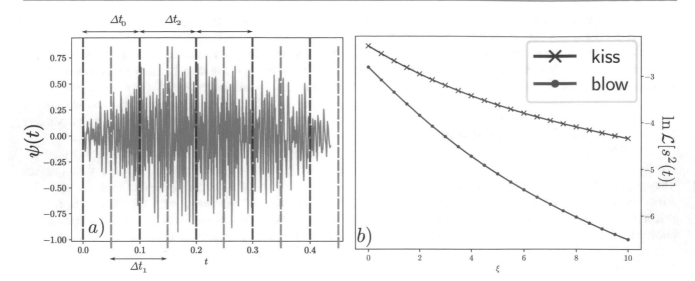

Fig. 82.4 (**a**) Frames and (**b**) Laplace transform

The general procedure used to extract MFCCs follows the guidelines detailed in Sect. 82.2. However, during spectrogram $P(\nu)$ evaluation, the frequency resolution $\Delta\nu$ in accordance to the uncertainty principle $\Delta t \Delta \nu \propto (4\pi)^{-2}$ must be considered. In short, the principle asserts the impossibility to achieve fixed resolution $\Delta\nu$ for arbitrary signal duration Δt. Instead, the signal $\psi(t)$ is subdivided into smaller frames with fixed duration Δt (see Fig. 82.4a), and Fourier analysis is conducted with fixed resolution $\Delta\nu = 1/(44,100 \times 512)$ Hz.

After the signal is partitioned into shorter frames, each frame produces a sequence of MFCCs. Let $\phi_\ell(\tau)$ be the ℓ-th MFC coefficient corresponding to the τ-th frame. Because signals with different time duration would also produce MFCC collections with different sizes, it is necessary to process them further. ANA intends to recognize non-articulatory sounds, which are naturally short-lived, so we consider the time-averaged MFCCs:

$$\langle\phi_\ell\rangle = \frac{1}{M}\sum_{\tau=0}^{M-1}\phi_\ell(\tau), \qquad (82.3)$$

where $M > 0$ is the total number of frames and $\ell = 0, 1, \ldots, n-1$.

MFCCs extraction occurs by using the package `python-speech-features` and the following default settings: frame duration length $\Delta t = 20$ ms; time step between two frames = 10 ms; and 13 MFCCs extraction frames.

82.3.2.2 Laplace Transform

Signal processing employs several linear transformations to deal with the variety of signals. Fourier analysis features among the most popular because it is useful during oscil-

lating signal analysis. Another popular linear transformation is the Laplace transform, which exploits the behavior of signal amplitude growth and decay. ANA applies the Laplace transform to the signal squared amplitudes (always positive)

$$\mathcal{L}[\psi^2(t)] = \int_0^\infty dt\, e^{-\xi t}\psi^2(t), \qquad (82.4)$$

to classify signals depending on how they evolve along time. We take the logarithm of the Laplace transform to produce more pronounced signal separation. Figure 82.4b depicts the log of Laplace transform for various parameters $\xi > 0$ for two non-articulatory sounds, in which the class separation increases for increasing ξ values. To avoid introduction of spurious correlations, we include $\ln \mathcal{L}[\psi^2(t)]$ with parameter $\xi = 10$ as the 14-th entry of the feature vector.

82.3.3 Speech Recognition

82.3.3.1 Statistical Test

In the experiments, Statistical Tests (STs) determine whether a feature vector corresponding to a given non-articulatory sound and it belongs either to the kiss or to the blow classes. Statistical methods usually rely on average values and their standard deviation to produce significant results. Both t- and χ^2-tests are not exceptions to this rule: both require that relevant descriptive variables be evaluated to produce meaningful hypothesis tests. This can be achieved by evaluating a reference vector for each class and the corresponding standard deviation for each component.

Each class consists of $m = 30$ segmented audio signals, recorded by t_2. Features are extracted from each audio signal, to produce a collection of feature vectors. Minimization of the Euclidean distance among the vectors in the collection *via* conjugate gradient results in a single reference vector $\Phi^{(\ell)}$ for the ℓ-th class, which in turn can be used in statistical tests. In addition, the standard deviation $\sigma_k^{(\ell)}$ among the collection associated with the k-th feature in class ℓ is recorded, with $k = 0, 1, \ldots, 13$.

For the t-tests, we check whether the k-th component of the feature vector is compatible with the value $\Phi_k^{(\ell)}$ of class ℓ within a significance level $\alpha = 0.05$. Each test results in a binary value, 1 for success and 0, otherwise. The average success rate of t-tests against a given class ℓ produces the t-score $0 \leqslant s_t(\ell) \leqslant 1$. The χ^2-test requires every component of the feature vector and produces the score $s_\chi(\ell) = 1$ for success and vanishes otherwise. The class score for the ℓ-th class is the summation $s(\ell) = s_t(\ell) + s_\chi(\ell)$.

The process is repeated for the remaining class. The probability that the audio signal belongs to the ℓ-th class reads $p(\ell) = s(\ell)/[s(0) + s(1)]$. Based on these numbers, we assert that the class of the audio signal under investigation exhibits the largest likelihood value as well. As a final note, we highlight that the choice regarding the weights in class scores follows the maximum entropy principle.

82.3.3.2 Support Vector Machine

Automatic sound recognition by SVM comprises a training phase and a prediction phase. In both phases, ANA uses the well-documented python package `scikit-learn` [13].

In the training phase, SVM fit with linear kernel uses datasets consisting of feature vectors from segmented audio signals recorded by speech therapist. Linear kernels appropriateness depends mostly on the feature linear separability, which justifies the choice of MFCCs and Laplace coefficients. After the fit, the dataset is partitioned into distinct classes. During the prediction phase, the SVM predicts the classes of feature vectors derived from target sound signals. The correct classification of each target sound signal is known a priori, which allows the evaluation of the accuracy corresponding to the SVM predictions.

82.4   Experiments

ANA experiments constitute an piloty study because they intend to discover whether well-known speech recognition techniques (MFCC, STs and SVM can effectively recognize non-articulatory sounds. For the experiments a small number of DS individuals was utilized due to some difficulties faced such as identification participants with DS, invalid audio collection and ethical issues. The experiments focused on the non-articulatory sounds since they are considered as precursors to produce phonemes, and words recognition. The methodology used to conduct the experiments is based on [14].

82.4.1 Goals

To reach the goals of the experiments, Research Questions (RQ_i) must be formulated. Specifically, two RQs are considered. **RQ$_1$** enquires about the effectiveness of the techniques when they manipulate words through sound "articulation". **RQ$_1$** was:

Which Method Recognizes the Words More Effectively?

To answer RQ_1, ANA manipulates the Portuguese words "churrasco" and "baba"[4] by using (1) MFCC, Laplace transform, T-test and Chi-Square statistical tests; and (2) MFCC, Laplace transform and SVM. Method effectiveness is evaluated by considering the accuracy rates. After we experiment the techniques, they apply them to recognize non-articulatory sounds on the basis of **RQ$_2$**:

Which Method More Efficiently Recognizes Non-articulatory Sounds Produced by Individuals with DS?

To answer RQ_2, ANA analyzes the non-articulatory blowing and kissing sounds by using (1) MFCC, Laplace transform, T-test and Chi-Square; and (2) MFCC, Laplace transform and SVM. Method effectiveness is also evaluated by considering the accuracy rates.

82.4.2 Experiment Design

The experiments involved nine participants: five participants without DS ($P = p_1, p_2, p_3, p_4, p_5$), two participants with DS ($P = p_6, p_7$) and two speech therapists ($T = t_1, t_2$). The participants were separated into two groups ($G = g_1, g_2$) as follows: (1) a group of participants without DS (g_1) and (2) a group of participants with DS (g_2). Participants belonging to g_1, were 22–35 years old; the two participants in g_2 were 3 and 18 years old.

This pilot study comprises three different experiments ($E = (e_1; e_2; e_3)$). In all the experiments, MFCC and Laplace transform extract sounds features, and the STs and SVM help to verify the effectiveness of these methods for speech recognition. The first experiment (e_1) answers RQ_1 by comparing the production of the two words, "churrasco" and "baba" by g_1 and by t_1. This experiment verifies the recognition efficacy of the STs and SVM methods. Confirmation that both methods are effective enables their use to recognize non-articulatory sounds produced by individuals with DS.

The second (e_2) and the third (e_3) experiments answer RQ_2. Experiment e_2 analyzes the similarity (or the difference) in the non-articulatory sounds (blow and kiss) pro-

---

[4]Churrasco barbecue and baba babysitter means, in English.

Table 82.1 Experimental design

Activity	Participant	Description
Sound recording	p_1, p_2, p_3, p_4, p_5, t_1, t_2	For experiment e_1 the words "churrasco" and "baba" were produced 11 times by g_1 and 30 times by t_1 and $t_2 = 71$ sounds
	p_1, p_2, p_3, p_4, p_5, p_6, p_7, t_2	The non-articulatory sound (blow and kiss) was produced 10 times by g_1, in the experiment e_2; 56 times by g_2 in the experiment e_3; and 60 times by $t_2 = 126$ sounds in the experiments e_2 and e_3
Sound segmentation	p_1, p_2, p_3, p_4, p_5, p_6, p_7, t_1, t_2	Each sound was segmented because (1) it is necessary to capture a unique temporal dynamics within speech and (2) the feature extraction step is based on each framed speech segment
Feature extraction	–	MFCC and Laplace transform extracted 14 sound features
Sound recognition	–	STs sand SVM recognized sounds. It was possible to assess the effectiveness and accuracy of both methods
Analysis	–	STs and SVM were compared to verify and to select the most adequate method to recognize words and non-articulatory sounds

duced by g_1 and by t_2. Experiment e_3 examines the same sounds analyzed by e_2. However, the focus is to compare the sounds produced by g_2 with the sounds produced by t_2. Table 82.1 list the activities followed to perform the experiments and the number of words and non-articulatory sounds recorded for all the participants.

82.5 Results and Discussion

The results of the three experiments (e_1, e_2, and e_3) answer the RQ_1 and RQ_2 research questions in terms of effectiveness. This section analyses the outcomes and indicates which technique is more suitable to recognize non-articulatory sounds, mainly for individuals with DS.

To address RQ_1, we use two datasets of segmented articulatory signals: one dataset corresponds to the class *churrasco*, recorded by t_1 with $n_2 = 30$ samples; the other dataset corresponds to the class *baba*, recorded by t_2 with $n_2 = 30$ samples. These datasets allowed us to evaluate the reference feature vectors required by STs, and to execute the SVM training phase. Figure 82.5 depicts the g_1 feature vectors represented by k on the x-axis. The shaded gray in Fig. 82.5a represents the 95% confidence interval. Except for four MFCCs sets (4, 6, 7, and 10), the data falls mostly under the confidence interval. In Fig. 82.5b, the data exhibit severe spreading, producing inaccurate predictions.

The test dataset includes the segmented sounds produced by participants in g_1, with $n = 11$ samples. The true class label for each datum is stored in order to estimate the classification method accuracy. Figure 82.6 illustrates the classification accuracy for each class. SVM correctly classifies every signal (100%). On the other hand, the ST mis-classifies 40% of the signals.

To answer RQ_2, audio signals emitted by participants in g_1 and g_2 have been classified by using both STs and SVM. As in the case of RQ_1, reference feature vectors (STs) and training phase (SVM) have been performed by considering the two segmented non-articulatory audio signals datasets of t_2. One dataset corresponds to sounds from the class *kiss*,

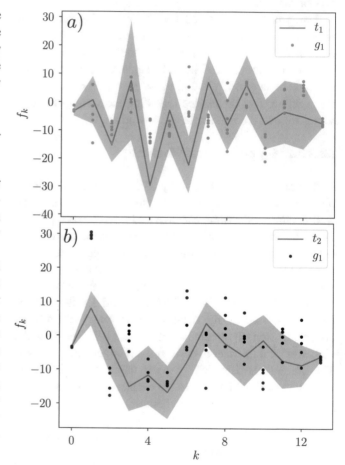

Fig. 82.5 Feature distribution for words produced by g_1. (**a**) Features extracted from the Portuguese word *churrasco* for participants in g_1 (dots) and the reference feature vector derived from t_1 (solid gray line). (**b**) Features extracted from the Portuguese word *baba* and the reference features from t_2

recorded by t_2 with $n_2 = 30$ samples. The other dataset corresponds to signals from the class *blow*, with $n_2 = 30$ samples. Figure 82.7 displays the typical distribution of the feature vectors values of g_2 (the target group). The participants p_6, p_7, and t_2 differ in age. This paper does not

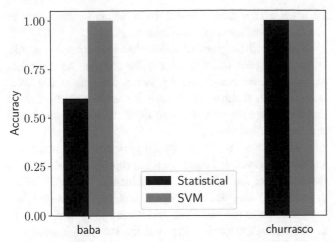

Fig. 82.6 Accuracy for "churrasco" and "baba" produced by t_1 and g_1 by using ST and SVM

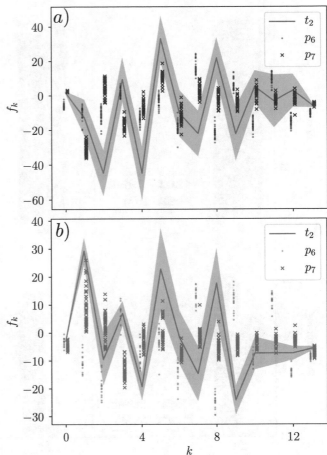

Fig. 82.7 Feature distribution for non-articulatory sounds produced by g_2. (**a**) Features extracted from kiss sound for participants in g_1 (dots) in relation to t_1 (solid gray line). The shaded gray area represents the 95% confidence interval. (**b**) Similar experiment for the blow sound

consider age effects on the sound recognition. The data in Fig. 82.7b reveals large deviations in the features of p_6 in relation to the features of t_2 in both experiments. However, accuracy is significantly worse than in Fig. 82.7a, which increases the chance of blow signals misclassification.

The test dataset for g_1 contains $n_1 = 10$ samples, whereas g_2 includes $n_2 = 56$ samples. Again, the true class label is stored. Figure 82.8 depicts the accuracy of each method and group for each non-articulatory sound.

SVM correctly classifies all the kissing sounds, whereas STs misclassify one instance for participants with DS. However, classification by using STs is significantly less effective for blow sounds, specially for participants with DS. In this case, STs misclassify 52 out of 56 audio signals from g_2. This accuracy is much lower than the accuracy produced by SVM for g_2, the target group. Thus, RQ_2 indicates STs are not viable to classify non-articulatory sounds of children with DS, at least when the current methodology is used.

82.6 Related Work

The speech produced by individuals with DS is limited due to their anatomical and motor specificities. Although some of these limitations of DS cannot be overcome, early speech training can improve the quality with which individuals with DS communicate. In this context, some studies have examined speech production by focusing on articulatory sounds made by children with DS [2, 15–17]. In [15], a system supports speech training with the aid of a virtual speech tutor, which uses three-dimensional animations of the face and internal mouth parts (tongue, palate, jaw etc.) to give feedback on the difference between the user's deviation and the correct pronunciation.

Kuan et al. analyzed a system to assess and practice sounds aiming to improve the language ability of children with DS [16]. This system uses the language ability of children with DS as input to generate graphs and to provide each child with suitable training. Moreover, the system acts as a DS information provider and a child data manager for parents and trainers.

Hennequin et al. [2] analyzed whether the addition of vision to audition can improve the intelligibility of speech produced by individuals with DS. Felix et al. [17] presented a computer-assisted learning tool for children with DS that uses mobile computing, multimedia design, and computer speech recognition to improve reading and writting abilities in Spanish through speech and drawing activities like letter identification, reading, spelling and handwriting.

Some efforts have been directed toward improving the speech produced by children with DS. However, the most of these efforts focus on systems for articulatory sounds that address phoneme and word production. These sounds are easier to recognize than non-articulatory sounds. Therefore,

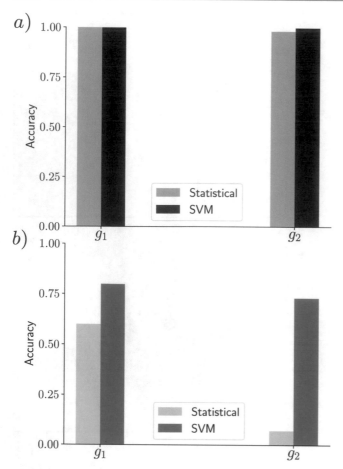

Fig. 82.8 Accuracy for non-articulatory sounds using STs and SVM produced by t_2, g_1 and g_2. (**a**) Data regarding the kiss and (**b**) data regarding the blow sound

systems to deal with non-articulatory sound recognition are fundamental because they must serve as preparatory activities for speech production by children with speech disorder, justifying the importance of our study.

82.7 Final Remarks

The present paper presents the results of a piloty and an exploratory study of methods for automatic speech recognition of non-conventional sounds described as non-articulatory sounds. First, we presented a different applications of statistical tests and their combination. Next, we applied and analyzed SVM. In both methods, we exploited two feature extraction algorithms for speech recognition: Mel Frequency Cepstral Coefficients (MFCC) and Laplace transform.

According to the outcomes of the experiments, the overall performance of SVM based on speech recognition for non-articulatory sounds ($RQ2$) was always better than the statistical tests when the same dataset was used. Moreover, the results for words showed that the statistical tests based

on speech recognition could be a suitable alternative to recognize words and non-articulatory sounds.

To deal with the particularities of non-articulatory sounds, especially their similarity with noise sounds like blow and kiss sounds, we performed a previous analysis of the spectrograms and features to observe the audio signal behavior and the features distribution into the classification space, and then we handled them.

SVM proved to be an excellent method to recognize speech. However, it requires an appropriate set of features that represent the type of sound addressed by the SofiaFala project. For many decades, MFCC has been the most effective extractor in the literature, and it has been combined with the Laplace transform to increase the recognition accuracy and to decrease the generalization errors.

As future work, we will conduct: (1) a new experiment that considers a protocol to collect the sounds and which involves a larger number of participants with DS; (2) an investigation of articulatory and non-articulatory sound recognition in the same classification space; (3) a new module to improve recognition speech based on image processing; and (4) the development of a mobile speech recognition prototype for children with DS.

Acknowledgements Authors are grateful to CNPq (442533/2016-0) and FAPESP (2016/13206-4) for the funding. We would also to thank Maria Roberta Cantarelli, Myrian Neves, Thais Moretti, Aline Camargo, and the individuals with DS by their participation.

References

1. B. Dodd, L. Thompson, Speech disorder in children with down's syndrome. J. Intellect. Disabil. Res. **4**, 308–316 (2001)
2. A. Hennequin, A. Rochet-Capellan, M. Dohen, Auditory-visual perception of VCVs produced by people with down syndrome: preliminary results, in *17th Annual Conference of the International Speech Communication Association (Interspeech 2016)*, San Francisco, Sept. 2016
3. R.D. Kent, Nonspeech oral movements and oral motor disorders: a narrative review. Am. J. Speech Lang. Pathol. **24**, 763–789 (2015)
4. H. Sakoe, S. Chiba, Dynamic programming algorithm optimization for spoken word recognition, in *Readings in Speech Recognition*, ed. by A. Waibel, K.-F. Lee (Morgan Kaufmann Publishers Inc., San Francisco, CA, 1990), pp. 159–165. Available: http://dl.acm.org/citation.cfm?id=108235.108244
5. A. Alatwi, S. So, K.K. Paliwal, Perceptually motivated linear prediction cepstral features for network speech recognition, in *10th International Conference on Signal Processing and Communication Systems, ICSPCS 2016, Surfers Paradise, Gold Coast, Australia, December 19–21, 2016* (2016), pp. 1–5
6. D. Yu, L. Deng, *Automatic Speech Recognition: A Deep Learning Approach* (Springer, Berlin, 2014)
7. R. Courant, D. Hilbert, *Methods of Mathematical Physics*, vol. 1 (Interscience, New York, 1953)
8. S. Jothilakshmi, V. Ramalingam, S. Palanivel, Unsupervised speaker segmentation with residual phase and MFCC features. Expert Syst. Appl. **36**(6), 9799–9804 (2009)

9. D. Kremelberg, *Practical Statistics: A Quick and Easy Guide to IBM SPSS Statistics, STATA, and Other Statistical Software* (Sage Publications, Inc., Thousand Oaks, 2010)

10. V.N. Vapnik, *The Nature of Statistical Learning Theory* (Springer, Inc., New York, 1995)

11. S. Haykin, *Neural Networks: A Comprehensive Foundation*, 2nd edn. (Prentice Hall PTR, Upper Saddle River, 1998)

12. B.E. Boser, I.M. Guyon, V.N. Vapnik, A training algorithm for optimal margin classifiers, in *Proceedings of the Fifth Annual Workshop on Computational Learning Theory* (ACM, New York, 1992), pp. 144–152

13. F. Pedregosa, G. Varoquaux, A. Gramfort, V. Michel, B. Thirion, O. Grisel, M. Blondel, P. Prettenhofer, R. Weiss, V. Dubourg, J. Vanderplas, A. Passos, D. Cournapeau, M. Brucher, M. Perrot, E. Duchesnay, Scikit-learn: machine learning in Python. J. Mach. Learn. Res. **12**, 2825–2830 (2011)

14. C. Wohlin, P. Runeson, M. Höst, M.C. Ohlsson, B. Regnell, A. Wesslén, *Experimentation in Software Engineering: An Introduction*, 1st edn. (Springer, Berlin, 2012)

15. O. Bälter, O. Engwall, A.-M. Öster, H. Kjellström, Wizard-of-Oz test of ARTUR: a computer-based speech training system with articulation correction, in *Proceedings of the 7th International ACM SIGACCESS Conference on Computers and Accessibility*, ser. Assets '05 (ACM, New York, 2005), pp. 36–43

16. T.M. Kuan, Y.K. Jiar, E. Supriyanto, Language assessment and training support system (LATSS) for down syndrome children under 6 years old. WSEAS Trans. Inf. Sci. Appl. **7**(8), 1058–1067 (2010)

17. V.G. Felix, L.J. Mena, R. Ostos, G. Maestre, A pilot study of the use of emerging computer technologies to improve the effectiveness of reading and writing therapies in children with down syndrome. Br. J. Educ. Technol. **48**(2), 611–624 (2017)

A Complete Diabetes Management and Care System

83

Cláudio Augusto Silveira Lélis and Renan Motta

Abstract

Diabetes has become a serious health concern. The development of highly evolved blood glucose measurement devices have led to tremendous improvements in glucose monitoring and diabetic management. Tracking and maintaining traceability between glucose measurements, insulin doses and carbohydrate intake can provide useful information to physicians, health professionals, and patients. This paper presents an information system, called GLUMIS (GLUcose Management Information System), aimed to support diabetes management activities. It encompasses a rule-based method for predicting future glucose values, a reasoner and visualization elements. Through integration with glucose measurement devices it is possible to collect historical treatment data and with REALI system insulin doses and dietary habits can be processed. Through an experimental study, quantitative and qualitative data was collected. An analysis was applied and shown that GLUMIS is feasible and capable of resulting interesting rules that can help diabetics.

Keywords

Knowledge-based systems · Diabetes management · Glucose monitoring · Decision tree · Continuous domain · Data visualization

C. A. S. Lélis (✉)
Scientific Initiation Program, IMES/Faculty ImesMercosur, Juiz de Fora, Brazil
e-mail: claudioaugustolelis@imes.org.br

R. Motta
Universidade Federal de Juiz de Fora (PGCC/UFJF), Juiz de Fora, Brazil
e-mail: renan.motta@ice.ufjf.br

83.1 Introduction

Diabetes Mellitus (DM) is increasing worldwide at an unprecedented pace and has become a serious health concern during the last two decades. It is a major cause of mortality in the age group of 20–79 years. The total number of diabetics was 171 million in 2000 and grew to 372 million in 2012, it has been declared a global epidemic [1–3]. Type I diabetes mellitus refers to the juvenile offset stage when the pancreas cannot produce sufficient insulin, while type II diabetes mellitus reflects the inability of the body to use the secreted insulin.

The frequent monitoring of blood glucose is critical for diabetic management, as the maintenance of physiological glucose level is the only way that a diabetic can lead a healthy lifestyle by avoiding life-threatening diabetic complications, such as diabetic retinopathy, kidney damage, heart diseases, stroke, neuropathy and birth defects [4]. For long-term glycemic control, the determination of glycated hemoglobin, or HbA1c, is used to evaluate the quality of care provided to diabetics [5]. Blood glucose levels are controlled by infusion of insulin and attention to diet and carbohydrate intake, depending on type of diabetes. The assessment of glycemic control in type 2 diabetics is usually done by monitoring HbA1c, fasting plasma glucose and postprandial glucose. However, the glucose variability is also equally important [6].

The most widely used glucose monitoring devices are Blood Glucose Meters (BGM) [7] based on minimally-invasive fingerstick tests. However, the recent trend is shifting towards non-invasive glucose monitoring (NGM) [8], as it alleviates the pain and suffering of diabetics, who have to frequently prick their skin, but it lacks the precision and specificity of blood glucose meters. The Continuous Glucose Monitoring Systems (CGMS), provides a large number of glucose measurements, which are highly useful to determine the fasting and postprandial blood glucose levels for better adjustment of the insulin dose and the detection of unrecognized hypo- or hyper-glycemia [9, 10]. In this way, it offers more extensive information regarding the glucose profile than blood glucose meters. However, the main limitation is their extremely high cost, which is beyond the reach of most diabetics.

In view of this, there is an immense need for Systems that provides health care professionals and patients with useful information pertaining to the trends in glucose concentration throughout the day [11–13]. Moreover, tracking and maintaining traceability between glucose measurements, insulin doses and carbohydrate intake can provide useful information to physicians, health professionals, and patients. This enables the prevention of hypoglycemic episodes and enables the diabetic to maintain the physiological glucose concentration level with reduced glycemic variability.

Therefore, this paper presents an information system, called GLUMIS, aimed to support diabetes management activities. It encompasses a prediction rule-based method for glucose measurement, a reasoner and visualization elements. Through integration with BGM and NGM devices and CGMS it is possible to collect historical treatment data and with REALI system, insulin doses and dietary habits can be processed.

This article is structured by this introduction and Sect. 83.2 shows the background in which the proposal is inserted and some related work. Section 83.3 details the components of the GLUMIS system. In Sect. 83.4, the experiment carried out and Sect. 83.5 the final considerations.

83.2 Background

Although helpful on providing information about the current state of the glucose, devices such as BGMs and CGMs do not allow the register of additional information such as insulin dosage and food intake that could be used to generate information and discovery of knowledge about the current treatment, which could be used to give an insight about future glucose values. This opens an opportunity for an integration between a system that records information on physical activity, food consumption and insulin doses, with another system that maintains the records of glucose measurements, with the possibility of analyzing through more elaborate visualizations. Moreover, such system could use this information to find rules to model a patient's profile and thus derive relevant knowledge to both patients and physicians.

Prediction models and classifiers have already been used in the context of diabetes management. However, with a different focus from that applied in this study, such as detect incorrect readings from CGMS [14]. Most previous work on glucose prediction trough computational means focus solely on the use of CGMS [15]. Due to CGMS's higher measurement rate predicting future glucose can be more precise than with the use of BGMs. Since BGMs are more commonly used than CGMS, a prediction model that also works with the input of a BGM could have a more widespread use by diabetes patients than current prediction algorithms that rely only on CGMS's data.

Thus, the GLUMIS system innovates by integrating data from the three types of glucose metering devices with a system that records food consumption and insulin doses. In addition to a model for glucose prediction. The lack of an approach that brings together all the characteristics analyzed shows the importance of the GLUMIS system.

83.3 GLUMIS System

The proposed GLUMIS system arose from the need to maintain traceability between diabetes management data to support physicians and health professionals on decision making regarding patient care as well as characteristics that influence treatment such as eating habits, for example. Figure 83.1 shows the GLUMIS system architecture with its main components and integration with the REALI system.

The REALI System is a tool developed to support the monitoring of diets with a focus on carbohydrate counting therapy. Its main objective is to record the value of carbohydrates ingested each time the patient feeds, in

Fig. 83.1 GLUMIS architecture

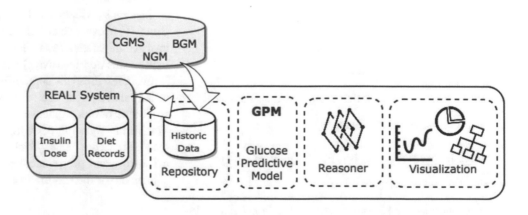

Fig. 83.2 Process to create the tree

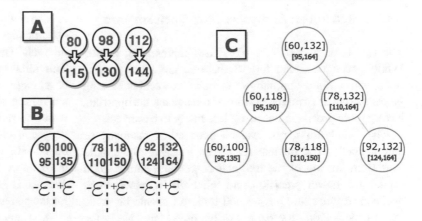

addition to the time the meal is made and the amount of insulin applied to neutralize the carbohydrate. The tool allows the registration of partial carbohydrate values for each item ingested, maintaining greater control over the type of food ingested and its main properties. In addition, the user can export reports and send them by e-mail. Through the integration between the REALI and the GLUMIS system, the data recorded by the tool becomes available and composes the data repository, being consumed by the GLUMIS system in the traceability process.

In addition to integrating with the REALI tool, the GLUMIS system is capable of integrating data from three different sources: CGMS systems, NGM devices or importing data from glycemic meters (BGM). There is also the possibility of manually entering the glucose level data, the date and time of the measurement. The data is uploaded regularly to the GLUMIS system forming a repository of historical data. A knowledge database is also maintained as decisions are taken, treatment is changed and this information is recorded to support future decisions. The other components of the system are detailed below.

83.3.1 Glucose Prediction

The presented prediction method is based on Fuzzy ART [16] which has inspired methods that have already been used on other medical areas [17].

The prediction method uses a tree created from data taken from a BGM, CGM or even a NGM device, consisting of the glucose value as well as the day and the time period when it was measured (*before breakfast*, *before lunch*, etc.). The tree outputs rules consisting of two sets, each consisting of: an interval of glucose values and a time period. The rules can be interpreted as: if the patient's current glucose is on the first set, then it is expected that his future glucose will be on the second set. Each node from the tree has one interval of glucose from one time period and a second interval from another time period, thus each node represents a different rule. An example of a rule can be seen below:

if(glucose *before lunch* ∈ [80, 120]) then (glucose *before dinner* ∈ [130, 170])

The process of creating a tree is bottom-up. Each terminal node is created from a different glucose measure for a given period of time and the measure of another time period that is related to the first one. For example, if it is sought to predict how the patient's glucose will be *before lunch* based on measurements done *before breakfast*, then each node of the tree should have the glucose measurement of *before breakfast* and the measurement of *before lunch*, both from the same day. These values are then each transformed into intervals of size ε where the measured value is in the center.

The nodes are then sorted by the value of their first set. For each pair of neighbour nodes of the same level, a parent node is created if there is an intersection on theirs first intervals. The intervals of the parent node are the union of the intervals of both child nodes. This process is repeated until no more parent nodes can be created. Figure 83.2 illustrates the process, highlighted in A, B, and C, in which the prediction tree is created. The numbers in black represent the value of glucose at the time period *before breakfast*, and red numbers represent blood glucose at *before lunch*.

An example of raw data collected from a BGM is highlighted in A. Each pair of circles represents measurements taken from the BGM on different days. Circles with black numbers show the value of blood glucose at *before breakfast* and the circles they point represent the glucose value at the *before lunch* period from each respective day.

Each measurement from *before breakfast* with it's related *before lunch* is highlighted in B, as terminal nodes. Each value from A was transformed into an interval using ε = 20. Each circle is a rule that can be interpreted as: if the a glucose measured at *before breakfast* is in the black interval, then it will be in the red interval at *before lunch* time.

Finally, it is highlighted in C, the tree after being completely built. Parent nodes were created by joining the intervals of it's child nodes if they had an intersection.

83.3.2 Reasoner: Analysis of the Decision Tree

The tree is composed of nodes, each representing a rule. While nodes from the top of the tree are more generic rules, with a higher probability of being correct but lacking precision, nodes from the bottom of the tree are the opposite, having more precision but being less likely to be correct.

The search for a rule can be done either manually or automatically. The manual search for a usable rule should start from the top of the tree and descending until a good trade-off between precision and reliability is found. Such decision of what rule has a good trade-off should be made by an expert, either the patient or his physician. Due to the nature of the way the tree is built, every non-terminal node is connected to it's two child nodes, the left one always having it's center with a smaller value than the center of the right child, making the tree similar to a binary search tree. Thus, the search for a good rule can be done in an efficient way.

An automatic search for a rule can be done by the GLU-MIS system. The user inputs his/her latest measured glucose, the time period of the measurement, the time period for the future value to be predicted and how reliable the rule should be. The reliability of a rule is given by the number of terminal nodes used to create it. Next, the GLUMIS system searches for nodes whose first range contains the inputted glycemia with reliability higher than, or equal, to the desired one. Finally, nodes meeting these criteria are displayed, sorted by reliability and by the distance from the center of it's first interval to the indicated blood glucose. The Prediction Tree view, presented in the next section, supports this search process.

83.3.2.1 Advantages of Predicting on a Continuous Domain

The problem of predicting future glucose values differs from traditional classification problems because while the latter has a discrete number of target classes, glucose values are a continuous domain. Clustering the glucose values into an arbitrary number of classes presents a serious problem in case the patient's glucose values are clustered around the boundary between two classes. For example, if the class *good* is defined with values ranging from 80 to 120 and the class *medium* has values from 121 to 160, then if the measured values vary from 110 to 130, part of them will be classified as *good* and the other part as *medium*. This making the prediction difficult since part of his glucose is classified as *medium*, which would call for a raise on insulin dosage, while the other part, classified as *good*, poses a risk of hypoglycemia in case the raise is applied. Because of this problem, most well known classifiers are unable to present rules with enough precision for a change on the treatment since they require the use of discrete target classes.

The main advantage of the proposed method over other classification algorithms lies in its ability to produce rules as intervals. Thus, there is no need for the data to be discretized. This allows for a more realistic overview of the behavior of glucose changes over time. In the example presented above, the algorithm would indicate a range of 110–130, which correctly models the patient, thus facilitating a correct treatment change. If a prediction turns out to be wrong, outside the range that should be, the error is calculated as the distance between the measurement to the interval. If the distance is small, this error may not prove to be a problem for the patient's health.

A secondary advantage of this method is its ability to only predict glucose from measurements that do not differ by more than the ϵ interval chosen during the training. This feature serves as a safety device, especially in applications such as this one which deals with a health application. For example, if a very different measure from those used in training appears, the algorithm will not give a prediction, instead it will indicate the possible existence of a new glycemic profile of the patient. Which is safer than giving a prediction with high probability of error which may result in hypoglycemia.

83.3.3 Visualization

The GLUMIS system provides three views arranged as a dashboard for the decision maker. They were developed from the JavaScript d3js library. This library was previously used with success in another information system [18].

The Profile View (Fig. 83.3) uses a radar chart to represent different types of information about the glycemic profiles identified through the repository and the knowledge base. Values closer to the center indicate a better profile and thus, more adjusted glycemic control. The identification of the profiles takes into account the average glucose measurements for each of the time periods configured by the user. The user can also add tags that describe the profile, for example, "vacation", or the range of days to which it belongs.

Through interaction elements it is possible to select a specific profile and highlight the average of each time period, using it to compare with other profiles. In Fig. 83.3 the last identified profiles are displayed and the best one is the Profile C associated to the last 3 months.

The Prediction Tree View (Fig. 83.4) uses a graph to represent, at each node, the information about the identified rule and the analyzes made by Reasoner. This view is the user interface to configure the prediction tree creation. The user can define, for example, the epsilon value and the number of measurements to be considered.

Through interaction elements it is possible to select the rule that will guide the decision-making process. In addi-

Fig. 83.3 Profile view

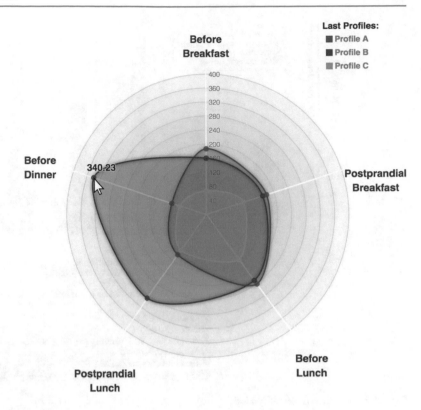

tion, obtain information such as the rule outlining the measurement intervals, the number of occurrences considered to generate the rule and the epsilon value considered, as well as the date of measurement and which time period is associated. The dosage of insulin applied and the amount of total carbohydrate ingested are also highlighted, with the possibility of showing a detailed description. In Fig. 83.4 the rules and the reasoner analysis are displayed for the example given in the previous subsection. The Historical Traceability View (Fig. 83.5) uses a combined bar and line chart to represent traceability information between glucose measurements, carbohydrate intake, and insulin doses.

The view is generated after the user selects a range of days and a time period to be analyzed. As shown in Fig. 83.5, the line represents the evolution of glucose measurements in the chosen period. The line color is associated with the measurements mean against a normality scale for glucose levels. This scale can be changed by the physician or health care professional, although it has a set pattern. Bars represent the amounts of insulin and carbohydrate, respectively.

Through interaction elements it is possible to obtain contextual information such as the average glucose measurements in the period, with a reference to the range of values considered "normal", the average carbohydrate intake in the period, as well as the average insulin applied. The ratio of carbohydrate to insulin is also highlighted. Regarding the

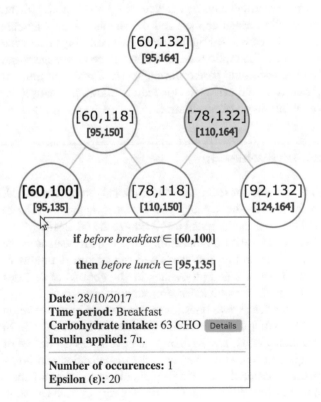

Fig. 83.4 Prediction tree view

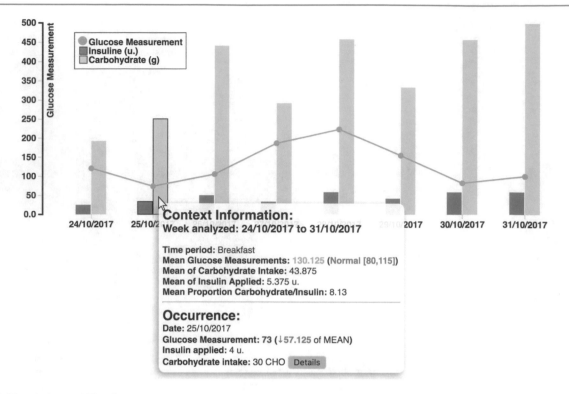

Fig. 83.5 Historical traceability view

current occurrence under analysis, the date of measurement, the insulin dosage applied and the amount of carbohydrate ingested are also highlighted, with the possibility of showing a detailed description. In addition, glucose measurement, colored according to the normality scale and how much it varied from the average. This feature allows the analysis of variability in glycemic control.

83.4 Evaluation

This section presents the experimental study conducted. According to the Goal/Question/Metric approach (GQM) [19] the goal can be stated as: "**Analyze** the GLUMIS system **in order to** verify the feasibility of use **with respect to** the task of interpreting the views and rules **from the point of view of** patients and physicians **in the context of** diabetes management through a decision support system".

In this sense, two questions were defined to be answered by the participants, for each visualization of the system. In Question 1 (Q1), the participant should assess the degree of comprehension associated with the visualization and information presented. For this they should use a scale where 1 indicates very difficult and 5 indicates very easy. In Question 2 (Q2), if the participant agreed that the view supported the understanding of the rules and the analysis made by Reasoner. Using for this a scale where 1 indicates totally disagree and 5 indicates totally agree.

The experiment was proposed based on a set of real data collected from two consecutive months taken from measurements done by BGM and CGMS. A database was considered with the glucose measurements of a patient that agreed to partake on this study. The time periods used were *before breakfast, before lunch* and *before dinner* and for each one was collected at least 25 measurements.

This experiment included 10 participants, being 9 patients and 1 specialist. After filling out a form characterization, it was observed that the patients had age between 21 and 62 years, most of them with diabetes mellitus type 1 and 2 with diabetes mellitus type 2. Among patients with type 2 diabetes, one use BGM and the other a CGMS. Among patients with type 1 diabetes, 3 stated that they use a CGMS and the other 4 make use of a BGM as a glucose meter. For characterization reasons, two questions were answered by the 10 participants. It was possible to identify that with respect to the participant's ease of dealing with new technologies, 20% of interviewees said they had a very high level of ease, another 40% said they had high ease, 30% regular and 10% indicate that they have low ease in dealing with new technologies. In addition, about the ease of interpreting charts, 30% of respondents said that they had a very high level of ease, 20% said they had high ease, 40% say they have a regular facility, and 10% say they have low ease in interpreting charts. This diversity shows the GLUMIS system's ability to assist people with different skill levels in dealing with new technologies or in interpreting charts.

The participants were submitted to online training where the preliminary doubts were answered. Then, during the conduction of the experiment, the evaluation environment and participants were observed by the authors of this study. Also the participants were encouraged to comment and describe their impressions.

During the analysis and decision-making process, the Prediction Tree View was displayed with the rules identified. In addition, the Profile View and the Historical Traceability View were presented, showing the new glycemic profiles identified and the historical traceability data between diet information and carbohydrates ingested, the amount of insulin applied and glucose measurements through time. Through interaction elements the visualizations were analyzed by a specialist to find relevant rules for a change on the patient's treatment.

The GLUMIS system was able to provide many interesting rules which helped to provide valuable information about each patient. Some rules found with the data of one patient are shown bellow.

Rule 1: if glucose *before breakfast* ∈ [47, 89] then glucose at *afternoon break in* [160, 306]

Rule 2: if glucose at *afternoon break* ∈ [58, 92] then glucose *before dinner* ∈ [56, 160]

Rule 3: if glucose *before dinner* ∈ [184, 214] then glucose *before breakfast* of the next day ∈ [53, 131]

These three rules were able to aid the specialist on changing this specific patient's treatment by providing a more precise view of his condition. Bellow is the reasoner's interpretation of the rules, why they are relevant in this context, and the association with diet data and insulin dosages.

The Rule 1 indicates that if there is a hypoglycemia *before breakfast*, then the glucose will be high in the *afternoon break*. By identifying the patient's glycemic profile and eating habits, it was possible to identify that due to the low glucose in the *morning*, the patient increased carbohydrate intake during *lunch* and decreased the dose of insulin. This resulted in an increase of glucose at *after lunch*.

The Rule 2 indicates that if glucose is low *after lunch*, then glucose may show normal value *before dinner*. This fact shows signs that the current dose of insulin and food intake, in this case, are already adjusted.

The Rule 3 indicates that if glucose is high *before dinner*, then glucose may be low by the *morning* of the next day. This fact showed that the proportion of insulin ingested at *night* was high resulting on hypoglycemia in the next *morning*.

83.4.1 Results and Lessons Learned

Responses and considerations were collected and organized. Table 83.1 shows the averages received by each visualization in the Q1 and Q2 survey questions.

Table 83.1 Research questions average

Visualization	Q1 average	Q2 average
Prediction tree view	4.6	4.8
Profile view	4.6	4.4
Historical traceability view	4.8	3.8

In general, the views were considered by participants with easy or very easy comprehension. Although the Prediction Tree View received a high rating for Q1, some participants considered it to be very simple and could be improved to show, for example, the path that originated the rule in the automated search. Regarding Q2, participants indicated that they agreed or fully agreed that the "Profile View" and "Prediction Tree View" supported the understanding of the rules and the analysis made by Reasoner.

It was possible to note that four participants stated that Historical Traceability View would be indifferent in understanding the rules, and Reasoner analyzes. This may have happened because the Prediction Tree View shows, through a tooltip, the insulin-related data and the carbohydrates ingested specifically from that time period. Thus the participant did not realize the need to also use the contextual data of the other days shown by Historical Traceability View. In spite of this, the average of the classifications received is superior to 3 (three), therefore above the area of indifference proposed by the scale. Thus, according to participants, Historical Traceability View also supports the understanding of the rules and the analysis made by Reasoner.

Through a textual report, one of the participants suggested that the system offer the user the possibility of defining a desirable or ideal profile. From this, change the treatment and follow up if the current profile approaches what is established as desirable.

As threats to validity, we can mention the reduced number of participants containing 1 specialist. To minimize the effect of this threat, it was possible to observe that the participants can represent different profiles.

Throughout the experiment, the generated database had balanced amounts of measurements of glucose, insulin and carbohydrates ingested for the periods of time considered. The application of this study on databases concentrated in specific periods of the day, can reach different results.

83.5 Closing Remarks

It is common for patients with diabetes to periodically measure their glucose level as part of their treatment. The presented system, GLUMIS, is able to predict future glucose values based on measurements obtained from a Blood Glucose Meter (BGM), or a Continuous Glucose Measurement

System (CGMS), or even a Non-invasive Glucose Monitoring (NGM) device. Prediction produces rules that would otherwise not be found by traditional methods of glucose monitoring.

The GLUMIS system is not intended to replace the health professional or physician. Rather, it provides users with information enriched by visualizations which helps to create a grand image of the current treatment.

Among the contributions of this study it is possible to cite the GLUMIS system itself, the method of prediction applied, the creation of a patient's own knowledge database and the possibility of maintaining traceability between different information, at the same time as it stores the new decisions made at every change in treatment. This helps in obtaining a historical view of the patient as well as a future perspective.

An experimental study was carried out to analyze the system, prediction method and visualizations in a decision-making context and resulted in interesting rules that have helped to improve patient care.

As future works, seeking new partnerships and conducting new experiments in order to draw a parallel between the use of the system by patients with type 1 diabetes and type 2 patients. In addition, making improvements for the system to become a recommendation system, indicating possible changes in the insulin application schedule to favor glycemic control.

References

1. D.R. Whiting, L. Guariguata, C. Weil, J. Shaw, IDF diabetes atlas: global estimates of the prevalence of diabetes for 2011 and 2030. Diabetes Res. Clin. Pract. **94**(3), 311–321 (2011)
2. L. Guariguata, D. Whiting, C. Weil, N. Unwin, The international diabetes federation diabetes atlas methodology for estimating global and national prevalence of diabetes in adults. Diabetes Res. Clin. Pract. **94**(3), 322–332 (2011)
3. K. Ogurtsova, J. da Rocha Fernandes, Y. Huang, U. Linnenkamp, L. Guariguata, N. Cho, D. Cavan, J. Shaw, L. Makaroff, IDF diabetes atlas: global estimates for the prevalence of diabetes for 2015 and 2040. Diabetes Res. Clin. Pract. **128**, 40–50 (2017)
4. D. Aronson, Hyperglycemia and the pathobiology of diabetic complications, in *Cardiovascular Diabetology: Clinical, Metabolic and Inflammatory Facets*, vol. 45 (Karger Publishers, Basel, 2008), pp. 1–16
5. S. Rahbar, The discovery of glycated hemoglobin: a major event in the study of nonenzymatic chemistry in biological systems. Ann. N. Y. Acad. Sci. **1043**(1), 9–19 (2005)
6. S.K. Vashist, Continuous glucose monitoring systems: a review. Diagnostics 3(4), 385–412 (2013)
7. S.K. Vashist, D. Zheng, K. Al-Rubeaan, J.H. Luong, F.-S. Sheu, Technology behind commercial devices for blood glucose monitoring in diabetes management: a review. Anal. Chim. Acta **703**(2), 124–136 (2011)
8. S.K. Vashist, Non-invasive glucose monitoring technology in diabetes management: a review. Anal. Chim. Acta **750**, 16–27 (2012)
9. L. Guillod, S. Comte-Perret, D. Monbaron, R.C. Gaillard, J. Ruiz, Nocturnal hypoglycemias in type 1 diabetic patients: what we can learn with continuous glucose monitoring? Diabetes Metab. **33**, 360–365 (2007)
10. F. Maia, L. Araujo, Effect of continuous glucose monitoring system (CGMS) to detect postprandial hyperglycemia and unrecognized hypoglycemia in type 1 diabetic patients. Diabetes Res. Clin. Pract. **75**, 30–34 (2007)
11. A. Vazeou, Continuous blood glucose monitoring in diabetes treatment. Diabetes Res. Clin. Pract. **93**, S125–S130 (2011)
12. A. Sola-Gazagnes, C. Vigeral, Emergent technologies applied to diabetes: What do we need to integrate continuous glucose monitoring into daily practice? Where the long-term use of continuous glucose monitoring stands in 2011. Diabetes Metab. **37**, S65–S70 (2011)
13. E.G. Moser, A.A. Morris, S.K. Garg, Emerging diabetes therapies and technologies. Diabetes Res. Clin. Pract. **97**(1), 16–26 (2012)
14. J. Bondia, C. Tarín, W. García-Gabin, E. Esteve, J.M. Fernández-Real, W. Ricart, J. Vehí, Using support vector machines to detect therapeutically incorrect measurements by the MiniMed CGMS®. J. Diabetes Sci. Technol. **2**(4), 622–629 (2008)
15. K.S. Eljil, G. Qadah, M. Pasquier, Predicting hypoglycemia in diabetic patients using data mining techniques, in *2013 9th International Conference on Innovations in Information Technology (IIT)* (IEEE, 2013), pp. 130–135
16. G. Carpenter, S. Grossberg, D. Rosen, Fuzzy art: fast stable learning and categorization of analog patterns by an adaptive resonance system. Neural Netw. **4**, 759, 771 (1991)
17. R. Xu, G. Anagnostopoulos, D. Wunsch, Multiclass cancer classification using semisupervised ellipsoid artmap and particle swarm optimization with gene expression data. IEEE/ACM Trans. Comput. Biol. Bioinform. **4**, 65–77 (2007)
18. C.A. Lélis, M.A. Miguel, M.A.P. Araújo, J.M.N. David, R. Braga, AD-reputation: a reputation-based approach to support effort estimation, in *Information Technology-New Generations* (Springer, Berlin, 2018), pp. 621 626
19. V.R. Basili, D.M. Weiss, A methodology for collecting valid software engineering data. IEEE Trans. Softw. Eng. **SE-10**(6), 728–738 (1984)

On the Use of van der Pauw Technique to Monitor Skin Burning in Patients Undergoing Interferential Current Therapy (IFC) with Extension to Other E-Stim Monitoring

Lawrence V. Hmurcik, Sarosh Patel, and Navarun Gupta

Abstract

Interferential Current (IFC) therapy is routinely used on patients in order to reduce pain, to speed up the healing of wounds in muscles, and to strengthen muscles and bodily structure. The van der Pauw (vdP) technique is a process used to measure a material's sheet resistance when the material has a geometric shape that has a uniform thickness, but whose other two dimensions are arbitrary. By combining these techniques, the skin's sheet resistance can be measured before, after, and during IFC therapy, and this will show a disturbance in skin sheet resistance caused by accidental burning. This technique can also be extended to monitoring TENS (transcutaneous electrical nerve stimulation) and other types of e-stim monitoring.

Keywords

Interferential current · van der Pauw · Skin resistance · Electrical burns

84.1 Introduction

The human body has a very complex geometry. For electrical impedance measurements of the layers of human skin, there are many complex electrical models [1], but we can often approximate the skin's complex geometry as something much simpler [2, 3]. In Fig. 84.1, the contact resistance of the electrodes applied to the patient is a simple resistor. This resistance is called the ESR (equivalent series resistance).

L. V. Hmurcik · S. Patel (✉) · N. Gupta
Department of Electrical Engineering, University of Bridgeport, Bridgeport, CT, USA
e-mail: hmurcik@bridgeport.edu; saroshp@bridgeport.edu; navarung@bridgeport.edu

The skin is a parallel combination of a resistor/capacitor. The internal organs/muscles/fluid are also a parallel combination of a resistor and capacitor. In Fig. 84.2, the human's internal organs and muscles and fluids are represented as a white square. There is a power source with voltage V1 that causes current to travel from left to right through contacts (shaded in black) and skin (shaded with diagonal lines) and internal organs and fluids and muscles (shown as un-shaded or white). A similar source V2 causes current to flow through the same flesh from top to bottom. This model of the human skin and internal body is sufficient for us to introduce two concepts in this paper: interferential current therapy (IFC) which is caused by the 2 V sources shown in Fig. 84.2 and the measurement of surface skin sheet resistance by the 4-probe van der Pauw technique (vdP). NOTE: sheet resistance (R) is the value of the skin's resistivity divided by the skin's effective thickness: $R = (\rho/d)$.

Consider, first, the two voltage sources in Fig. 84.2. Both are AC sources with frequencies of typically 5000 and 4800 Hz. These power sources do NOT interact with each other electrically, providing they are built as truly independent power sources, i.e. there are no points that are electrically in common between them. Each voltage is independent of the other, and each current is independent of the other. But both voltages and currents are dependent on the person's skin and on the internal fluids beneath the skin. The reaction of the skin and muscles beneath the skin is very different from the electrical stimulation they receive. Muscles cannot react to frequencies above 200 Hz. But they can react to the beat frequency of 200 Hz (5000–4800) or even less, down to a few tens of Hz. Beat frequencies are produced in the muscle because the flesh and tissue tends to mix the higher frequencies in order to react to the much lower beat frequency. Mathematically, the two sine wave sources add their signals together and produce new signals that are the sum and difference of their two frequencies. It is the difference frequency or beats to which the muscles are capable of responding.

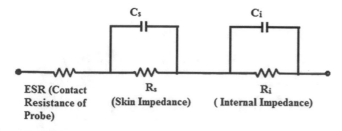

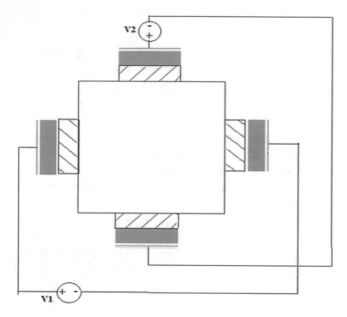

Fig. 84.1 Shows the electrical model of the human skin and internal muscles/fluids. It also shows the applied electrode (aka electric probe) as an equivalent series resistor (ESR)

Fig. 84.2 shows the IFC probes applied to a small area of the human skin. Two sine wave power sources of different high frequencies are used to produce "beats" that penetrate through the skin and massage the muscle tissue beneath

In Fig. 84.2, the contact resistance is small (generally 0.1 Ω or less), and the reactance to the skin is very small at the frequencies listed. If the IFC's two power sources were to operate at the muscles' natural frequency (50–200 Hz), there would be a problem with the delivery of this power to the muscles. Skin has a much higher impedance at 10–200 Hz than it does at 5000 Hz. Referring to Fig. 84.1, skin can have a resistance (Rs) of the order of hundreds of thousands of ohms. By contrast, the skin's capacitive impedance is much lower. It can be of the order of 10s of ohms for frequencies of the order of 5000 Hz, and this number changes in a linear and predictable manner with the applied frequency. For example, if the skin impedance is 200 Ω at 5 kHz, then it is $200 \times 100 = 20{,}000$ Ω when the power source frequency is 50 Hz = 5000/100 [4–6]. High frequency AC is needed to deliver the power to the muscles beneath the skin, but it is the signal at the electrical beat frequency that is absorbed and does the actual massaging of the muscles. Typical values

for the skin resistance and capacitance for a standard contact area of 4 cm-sq would be 10 kΩ and 200 nF [7].

The vdP technique is well known in the fields of semiconductors and superconductors [8–11]. This process is useful in measuring the sheet resistance of a material that has a uniform thickness and an arbitrary shape in the remaining two dimensions. In simple terms, the material can be a square or a circle or even a "pancake" of arbitrary shape. So long as the sample has a uniform thickness, the shape of the sample can be completely arbitrary, and it may or may not have a shape that is geometrically simple. A very good and simple teaching primer for the van der Pauw technique can be found on Wikipedia.

The vdP technique is well known in the fields of semiconductors and superconductors [8–11]. This process is useful in measuring the sheet resistance of a material that has a uniform thickness and an arbitrary shape in the remaining two dimensions. In simple terms, the material can be a square or a circle or even a "pancake" of arbitrary shape. So long as the sample has a uniform thickness, the shape of the sample can be completely arbitrary, and it may or may not have a shape that is geometrically simple. A very good and simple teaching primer for the van der Pauw technique can be found on Wikipedia.

The IFC process already lends itself to placing four electrodes on the human body in positions that are relatively arbitrary, i.e. the positions are different relative to the placement on the body by different medical personnel. The placement of these electrodes generally defines the corners of a rectangle, but with differing patients and differing medical personnel, the defined shape is only approximately rectangular. Also, the IFC technique uses voltage sources that have a large frequency (typically 5000 Hz). But the vdP technique works best with a DC source or very low frequency AC. The vdP's DC voltage has a very difficult time penetrating the skin surface. Hence the skin appears to be of 2-dimensional geometry, i.e. it is shaped like a rectangle/pancake. By contrast, the power sources at around 5 kHz penetrate through the skin deep into the patient's muscles and internal tissue. The vdP measurement only measures surface effects of the skin.

Our idea is to use the vdP technique as a monitor to prevent the burning of a patient by the IFC technique. NOTE: the vdP monitoring system that we propose can also be applied to a TENS with four electrodes. TENS is transcutaneous electric nerve stimulator, which uses a pulse frequency of the order of 100 Hz, but these pulses can be modulated with an AC frequency of 5 kHz if desired, i.e. 2 TENS sources can mimic the massaging ability of the IFC. For the IFC monitor, the monitoring process would begin at the start of the therapy session: At the beginning of a therapy session, a baseline measurement is taken of the skin's sheet resistance using the vdP method. This measurement becomes the standard for the therapy session and thus it is immune to changes in skin from person to person—for example, if one person's skin is dry and the other's is oily, they both produce the same "relative" reading according to vdP. A machine can monitor the van der Pauw readings from the beginning to the end of the session, and it can sound an alarm if the readings become dangerous, i.e. they change by 10% or more, as we will discuss later in this paper. As the session proceeds, there will, of course, be minor changes in resistivity, but major changes do not occur unless there is a major change in the material properties of the skin (due to burning). Most notably, when burning occurs at an electrode, the electrode resistance (ESR) becomes large. This is caused by the electrode being dirty if it is used more than once or from bad skin preparation before the electrode's application. A bad electrode contact in the vdP method would incur an error of 10% or more [12], and we will discuss this later.

84.2   Analysis

First, confirm that you have the correct template for your paper size. This template has been tailored for output on the A4 paper size. If you are using US letter-sized paper, please close this file and d Start with the ideal case in order to identify the electronic model that characterizes the process of IFC therapy. See Fig. 84.1. The current from the 2 AC power sources enters at each contact and traverses the contacts/the skin/the interior of the body. The skin acts as a lossy capacitor, i.e. it behaves as a perfect capacitor with a shunt resistance. The internal body also behaves as a lossy capacitor. In both of these cases, the capacitance dominates, the impedance is low, and current passes through the skin and internal body quite easily, and it is absorbed in the muscles. The contacts can each be represented by a small ESR, generally 0.1 Ω or less.

If the contacts get dirty there is NO change in the value of the capacitance of the lossy capacitors of the skin and the internal body. But there is a very large change in the ESR. With a constant current, the power dissipated at the contact/skin interface is heat loss aka the I-squared-R loss, and hence the amount of burning damage increases with the increase in the degree of degradation of the contacts. The ESR and the skin resistivity/sheet resistance are directly proportional, and hence monitoring one can tell us the quality of the other.

Monitoring the quality of the contacts to the patient's skin is (at present) based on a wait-and-see approach, with feedback coming from the patient. The medical attendant places the four IFC contacts on the patient's skin with an idea of the time the machine needs for the therapy to be effective. For example, the attendant may set the machine's timer for 5 min (for a new patient) or 15 min for someone with whom the attendant is familiar. For the new patient, the attendant

may ask the usual questions about how the therapy feels, or is there any pain, or should the dosage (electric current) be increased or decreased or is there anything making the patient un-comfortable. But the overall comfort and health of the patient would not be in the hands of the machine but rather in the hands of the attendant's ability to react to the input from the patient. This is NOT a bad way to monitor IFC therapy, but it can invite problems. What if the attendant is distracted and leaves the patient. There are many cases where this resulted in the patient receiving third degree burns and muscle damage [13, 14]. The first and most obvious solution to this problem is to enforce upon the medical attendant that they must be present to monitor the patient's every minute of therapy—if they leave the patient for any reason, then the therapy must end, or at least the electric power to the patient must be turned off.

But there is another approach which may work as well. What if the machine can detect burning or other problems at each of the electrodes EARLY? Severe burning from IFC therapy requires a minute of time (or possibly more). An electronic monitor can measure and process data in one second or less. Monitor the sheet resistance of the skin, and use the vdP technique. The speed of electronic machines and microprocessors is so fast (micro-seconds) compared to the time it takes to burn a person via IFC (minutes), that the time needed to perform a complex mathematical solution is trivial. Also, the vdP technique has the advantage that there is NO need to put the contacts into a simple arrangement. Other 4-probes often require the four contacts to be placed along a straight line and equally spaced, similar to four soldiers marching, or they may require the probes to be placed on a "square" with exact measurements defined for this "square". In the vdP-4-probe arrangement, the four probes (in this case, the IFC electrodes which do double duty as vdP electrodes) are placed in any pattern that is very roughly 2-dimensional. In layman's terms, place the four probes on the edge of a pancake.

The vdP technique generally uses a DC power source or low frequency AC, and thus the impedance measured is purely resistive and not reactive. In the case of IFC measurements, this works well. The two medium frequency power sources used in IFC are generally at values of about 4–5 kHz. This value of frequency allows for easy penetration of the human skin. The DC power or low frequency AC used to supply the vdP readings will penetrate the skin very little, since the resistance is generally large. Skin resistances vary greatly, from a few ohms for wet skin to millions of ohms for very dry skin. A good rule to remember is that a DC voltage will be noticeable to a human at 50 V or more. DC at 50 V will hurt but not harm a person; it is like a bad mosquito bite.

The equations that govern the use of the vdP technique are very well known. As a basic teaching primer, we would encourage those interested to go to Wikipedia and look up the topic "van der Pauw". The treatment in Wikipedia is well written and clear even to the novice. If we place four electric probes around a confined 2-D sample of any shape (ugly-pancake) and if we number these probes in a clockwise fashion as 1, 2, 3, and 4, then a current is applied through nodes 1, 2 while the voltage is measured at 3, 4. Divide voltage by current to get the trans-resistance R (1234). Then, apply current through nodes 2, 3 and measure voltage at nodes 1, 4. Again, divide voltage by current to get the trans-resistance R (2341). These two sets of readings are sufficient to solve the vdP equation for the skin's sheet resistance R.

$$F(R) = 0 = \exp(-\pi R(1234)/R) + \exp(-\pi R(2341)/R)$$
$$(84.1)$$

There are 2 things to mention about Eq. (84.1). First, it cannot be solved in closed form; it requires a solution generated by a computer or microprocessor. The simplest way to come up with this solution is to assume that R = 0.000001, plug this value into Eq. (84.1) and find F(R) which does not, of course, equal zero, as it should if it fit the vdP equation exactly. Then, assume that R = 0.000002, and find F(R) again. Then, let R = 0.000003, etc. The value for R where F(R) changes from negative to positive (i.e. it passes through F(R) = 0) is the value of R that satisfies the vdP equation in its original form, i.e. for F(R) = 0. This method of computation is sometimes called the "brute force" method of solution for finding R. A more elegant and quicker solution can be achieved if one uses standard techniques for the computer solution of a transcendental equation: Newton-Raphson or Bisection are just two of many techniques.

But what is the projected range of values that R can have? The values measured for R are very different for the many different kinds of human skin tested—dry, oily, soft, hard, etc. Also, even if we were only to measure R for a single patient, the values for R can be quite different on different days of IFC treatment. Additionally, what if the same patient on the same day has two sets of IFC electrodes placed on them— four electrodes per set, with each set placed some distance from the other set. Values for R can be very different. To sum up: for many humans, on many different days, with electrodes placed on many different parts of their body, the values recorded for R will be very, very different. However, these values typically fall into a range given by $0.001 < R < 1000\ \Omega$. Even though the "brute force" method is not the most elegant way to solve Eq. (84.1), the incredibly fast speed of modern computers and microprocessors can output the value for R in a fraction of a second.

The second thing to note about Eq. (84.1) is that we can come up with different experimental measurements for our sample that also satisfy Eq. (84.1). For example, run the current through nodes 2, 3 while measuring voltage at 1, 4, and then run current through 3, 4 while measuring voltage at

1, 2. In fact, we can come up with 4 different sets of values for the trans-resistance R (abcd), and each of these sets can give us to the sheet resistance R. Also, if we use DC for our vdP measurements, we can come up with eight sets of data to solve Eq. (84.1) by simply reversing the polarity of each of the four sets of measurements that we take. In normal applications, all eight sets of data are collected, and from this an average value for R plus its error (one standard deviation) are calculated. If any of the values for R deviate from the average by 10% or more, then we would have a problem with at least one of the contacts [12]. The "bad" contact is the one that would be part of the measured data for both values of trans-resistance listed in Eq. (84.1). This is a very strong point, and we will discuss this later. For now, we need to address two other points. Given that there is a 10% change in R, it can be shown from Eq. (84.1) and simple calculus that there must be a 10% change in R (ab2d), where a, b, d are any numbers not equal to 2, and we are assuming that contact "2" is the bad contact. Also, the vdP technique is a 4-probe technique. In theory and practice, a bad contact should not effect a 4-probe measurement. A sample (skin) measured with four good contacts should produce the same value for R as the same sample measured with one bad contact. The reason that the bad contact effects the 4-probe measurement is that with the skin burning, it is not the contact per se that is effecting the measurement, but rather it is the change in the uniformity of the sample. A skin sample with no burn is fairly uniform, but a skin sample where part of the skin is burned (the part under the bad contact) is not uniform. To a first approximation, we assume that the burnt skin is thin enough (relative to the thickness of the unburnt skin) that the bad contact plus the burned skin plus the clean skin is approximated as a clean contact with clean skin and an extra resistor (as a model for the burnt skin). This changes the trans-resistances and ultimately the sheet resistance [12], and it changes these by the same percentage.

There are some other problems with the measurement of R via the vdP technique. The contacts must be "points" with a geometrical dimension of zero. Finite contacts require a correction factor to our solution of R via Eq. (84.1). See [15]. Also, the vdP technique is derived for application to a finite sample. When the IFC contacts are placed on to a patient's skin, there are areas of conduction outside the perimeter defined by these contacts. How can we measure the resistivity for the bounded area of skin when electricity travels through all of the skin? One solution to this problem is to assume that the human skin is infinite in size (or at least very large) when compared to the area contained by the four electrodes. In this case, the value measured for R is actually half the true value [16]. Furthermore, given that the human body is not infinite (even approximately) and given also that the 2-D geometry of the skin is effected by the fact that it does not lie in a simple plane but rather is spread over a 3-D frame (skeleton), we can still use Eq. (84.1) if we apply a correction factor to our measurements [17, 18]. Despite the fact that these two correction factors (and possibly others) are required to force Eq. (84.1) to give us the true value for R, we do NOT need to find these factors since we do not need the exact value for R. It is not an absolute value for R that makes our innovation work, but rather it is the measurement of the relative value of R as the conditions of therapy change the biology of the skin: find R before therapy begins, and use this as a basis. Changes in R during therapy that are 5–10% or greater would need to be addressed, and the therapy process would need to cease immediately in order to preclude burning the patient. Also, before therapy, measure eight values for R, and if any trans-resistance reading differs frin the others by approximately 10% or more, than it is safe to say that the contact which forms part of this reading is a bad contact, and this should be analyzed further.

As the process of therapy begins, there will be noticeable changes in the values of trans-resistances R (1234) and R (2341) etc. If the electrodes used are cleaned properly and if they are of the high conducting quality demanded of IFC therapy, then we can still expect to measure R from eight sets of readings and within a small percentage of error. If one electrode is dirty or if it is not applied properly, there will be a noticeable change in R, and the percentage error can increase dramatically. Suppose for the sake of argument, that all of the electrodes are good except for one of them— choose electrode #2 as the bad electrode. We illustrate this in Fig. 84.3. All four points of contact to our sample have a value of ESR or contact resistance. In our example, the contact resistance is 0.1 Ω or less, except for contact #2. We can calculate R and a percentage error in R in the usual manner from eight sets of readings as discussed already. The percentage error will be large (>10% typically). This result alone will teach us that one of the electrodes is bad, but it will not tell us the bad electrode (#2 for our example). To find the bad electrode, note that all of our measurements are the same except for the contact made by this bad electrode. We can then say that our vdP measurements are for an "ideal" sample with the addition of a resistor in series with electrode #2 and the patient's skin. This extra resistor is the ESR of the dirty electrode. Let us consider two cases. First, ESR (node # 2) = 0.1 or less. The contact at node # 2 is good. The trans-resistance: R (1234) = R (3412), assuming we restrict our sample geometry to a rectangle. See Fig. 84.3. Second, let the ESR (node # 2) be large (greater than 0.1 Ω). Normally, the ESR is much less than 0.1 Ω. But due to dirt on the electrode or poor sticking quality, the ESR can be much greater than 0.1, and typically 10 or 100 Ω or more. With no calculations, this electrode could be identified by the fact that using a constant current source, the current values used in Fig. 84.3, do NOT change when passing through node # 2. But the voltage values for nodes # 1, 2 are higher than the voltages

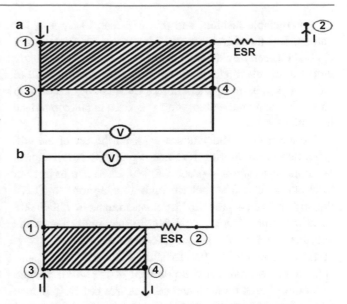

Fig. 84.3 (**a**) A typical van der Pauw trans-resistance is found by measuring the voltage of a rectangular sample at nodes 3, 4 while sending a constant current through nodes 1, 2. All four nodes have a contact resistance (ESR). Assuming that node 2 is bad, the ESR is large, but the vdP measurement is un-effected. (**b**) Assuming that node 2 is bad and its ESR is large, the voltage used to calculate the trans-resistance R (3412) is greater than the true value of the measured sample (skin)

measured for nodes 3, 4. The voltage values (and hence the trans-resistances) are higher by 10% or more, though even a small difference (2%) can be the predictor of a bad contact at # 2. Node # 2 has a large ESR due to the dirt on the electrode, this would come from the re-use of disposable electrodes or the improper cleaning of non-disposable electrodes or even improper skin preparation.

84.3   Conclusion

There are a number of cases of patients undergoing IFC therapy that get severely burned. Besides those reported in the literature, there are at least sic cases this year alone that have been reported to us privately. Monitoring the vdP sheet resistance can show a marked change in the non-uniformity of the skin caused by burning, and this can set off an alarm to warn of the danger of burning the patient. Burning of human skin by IFC malfunction takes some time (at least a minute in most cases). By contrast the shift in skin resistivity is very fast and can alert both patient and attendant in time to reduce the chance of a third degree burn to a first degree burn or to no burn at all.

Furthermore, raw data used to calculate the vdP sheet resistance has the ability to tell the attendant at an IFC therapy session the exact electrode that is causing trouble. It is always true that IFC therapy must be undertaken with clean electrodes. The re-use of electrodes builds up the ESR in a predictable fashion, and this will lead to harming the patient. But there are cases where a clean electrode is not applied correctly by the attendant or where there is a factory defect in the electrode even before its first use. Given all of these ways to harm a patient during IFC therapy, it is good to have a fast and predictable "alarm" system in place to reduce the patient's risk.

We are excited about future work on the use of the vdP technique in monitoring IFC and 4-probe TENS therapies. We note that even a 2-probe TENS system can have each electrode split and so behave both as a 2-probe to TENS therapy and as a 4-probe to vdP measurement of TENS/skin sheet resistance. We are confident in the application of the vdP technique to the random placement of probes that each of these therapies entails. To add further evidence to our application, we ran a live experiment of the vdP technique to monitor burns on a human subject. We did NOT induce a burn beyond a simple first degree burn—similar to a bad sunburn. The burn was under the "bad" contact—we used contact #2. We first ran a set of four clean contacts and measured the skin's sheet resistance (about 700 Ω for our particular test subject). We then pulled up contact #2 off the skin, cleaned the skin underneath, and re-attached the contact to the skin. Its ability to stick to the skin was compromised by our action. The skin's sheet resistance increased. We did this three times. The skin's sheet resistance increased by a total of 16%, as did the trans-resistance values that included contact 2. We repeated this process of pulling up the contact probe and re-attaching it three more times until the sheet resistance was 20% above the starting value. We also noted the development of a red mark or burn on the human subject under electrode #2. In the interests of safety, we stopped the experiment—we did NOT induce a second degree or third degree burn in any human subject. In each case, we allowed the electric current to burn our subject for 30 s, and this also precluded our burn becoming second or third degree.

Our results for first degree burns on a human subject prove the ability of the vdP technique to spot a problem in skin burning before it becomes serious. To verify these results for second and third degree burns, pig skin can be used. Published lab experiments have shown that the burning of a pig's skin mimics the burning of human skin.

References

1. W. Hart, A five-part resistor-capacitor network for measurement of voltage and current levels related to electric shock and burns, in *Proceedings of the First International Symposium on electrical Shock Safety Criteria*, (Pergamon Press, New York, 1985)
2. J. G. Webster (ed.), *Electrical Impedance Tomography* (Taylor & Francis Group, Milton Park, 1990)
3. J.R. Macdonald, *Impedance Spectroscopy*, vol vol. 11 (Wiley, New York, 1987)
4. G.C. Goats, Interferential current therapy. Br. J. Sports Med. **24**(2), 87 (1990)
5. M.I. Johnson, G. Tabasam, An investigation into the analgesic effects of interferental currents and transcutaneous electrical nerve stimulation on experimentally induced ischemic pain in otherwise pain-free volunteers. Phys. Ther. **83**(3), 208 (2003)
6. L. Snyder-Mackler, A.J. Robinson, *Clinical Electrophysiology: Electrotherapy and Electrophysiologic Testing* (Williams & Wilkins, Philadelphia, 1995)
7. E.A. White, M.E. Orazem, A.L. Bunge, Single-frequency LCR databridge impedance measurements as surrogate measures for the integrity of human skin. J. Electrochem. Soc. **159**(12), G161–G165 (2012)
8. L. van der Pauyv, A method of measuring specific resistivity and Hall effect of discs of arbitrary shape. Philips Res. Rep. **13**, 1–9 (1958)
9. L.J. van der Pauw, A method of measuring the resistivity and Hall coefficient on lamellae of arbitrary shape. Philips Res. Rep. **20**, 220–224 (1959)
10. L.V. Hmurcik, A. Bidarian, B. Ibarra, L.D. Matthews, A technique for measuring the 3-dimensional to 2-dimensional conductivity change of YBCO superconductors at the normal-to-superconducting phase change. J. Mater. Sci. **33**(23), 5653–5659 (1998)
11. J.G. Webster, *Electrical Measurement, Signal Processing, and Displays* (CRC Press, Boca Raton, 2003)
12. K.S. Ford, M.W. Shrader, J. Smith, T.J. Mclean, D.L. Dahm, Full-thickness burn formation after the use of electrical stimulation for rehabilitation of unicompartmental knee arthroplasty. J. Arthroplast. **20**(7), 950–953 (2005)
13. E.K. Satter, Third-degree burns incurred as a result of interferential current therapy. Am. J. Dermatopathol. **30**(3), 281–283 (2008)
14. J.D. Wasscher, Note on four-point resistivity measurements on anisotropic conductors. Philips Res. Rep. **16**, 301–306 (1961)
15. I. Miccoli, F. Edler, H. Pfnür, C. Tegenkamp, The 100th anniversary of the four-point probe technique: the role of probe geometries in isotropic and anisotropic systems. J. Phys. Condens. Matter **27**(22), 223201 (2015)
16. S.H.N. Lim, D.R. McKenzie, M.M.M. Bilek, Van der Pauw method for measuring resistivity of a plane sample with distant boundaries. Rev. Sci. Instrum. **80**(7), 075109 (2009)
17. D.K. De Vries, A.D. Wieck, Potential distribution in the van der Pauw technique. Am. J. Phys. **63**(12), 1074–1078 (1995)
18. L.A. Geddes, *Handbook of Electrical Hazards and Accidents* (CRC Press, Boca Raton, 1995)

Part X

Potpourri

Smart Lighting Controlling System: Case Study of Yarmouk University Museum

Mohammed Akour, Ziad Al Saad, Abdel Rahman Alasmar, and Abdulraheem Aljarrah

Abstract

In museum, the light plays important role in viewing the value of the collections, but light might cause gradual objects damage. The light damages are permanent and cumulative. No object can be recovered from light damage. Resting objects from the effects of light does not mean that they could handle more light; the object will not "heal". Typically, it is visible light that fades (or bleaches) colors. This light would come from the sun shining directly into museum. UV light will not only fade colors but it will cause "yellowing, chalking, weakening, and/or disintegration" of objects. UV light not only comes from the sun but also comes from some sources of artificial lighting, such as fluorescent. IR light heats the surface of objects, which then leads to the same conditions as Incorrect Temperature IR light comes from the sun as well as Incandescent lighting. In this paper, smart system is built to control the lights in the museum. The system is mainly consisting of thermal sensors that detect the presence of humans, DC LED spotlights, Arduino boards and Zigbee modules for a wireless communication to send data to a server. Once the visitor stops by the display, the thermal sensors will be able to detect that visitor and prepare to calculate several measurements. The system is already installed to be working in the Main Museum in the college of Archaeology and Anthropology as a prototype in Yarmouk University. The measurements show how the system is reliable and effective.

Keywords

Sensor network · Lighting system · Smart museum · Arduino

85.1 Introduction

In museum, the light plays important role in viewing the value of the collections, but light might cause gradual objects damage. The light damages are permanent and cumulative. No object can be recovered from light damage. Resting objects from the effects of light does not mean that they could handle more light; the object will not "heal". Typically, it is visible light that fades (or bleaches) colors. This light would come from the sun shining directly into museum. UV light will not only fade colors but it will cause "yellowing, chalking, weakening, and/or disintegration" of objects. UV light not only comes from the sun but also comes from some sources of artificial lighting such as fluorescent. IR light heats the surface of objects, which then leads to the same conditions as Incorrect Temperature IR light comes from the sun as well as Incandescent lighting.

It is true that museum collections might be guarded in a vault, keep in very dark place, but that leads to kill the spirit and the mission of the museum. Museum lighting is considered as one of the most complicated environmental factor surrounding museum collections. Researches proof that how light could cause severe damage of cultural artifacts through fading and other visible changes. Indeed, museums cannot get rid of lighting. The propagation of oxygen can be restricted into microenvironments, the temperatures can be controlled and kept within required levels, also the limits for other factors can be managed—but still the gradual damage from light exposure must be accepted. However, these risk management processes would not make museum lighting any more noticeable than other environmental threaten parame-

The original version of this chapter was revised.
An erratum to this chapter can be found at
https://doi.org/10.1007/978-3-319-77028-4_102

M. Akour (✉) · A. R. Alasmar
Computer Information Systems Department, Yarmouk University, Irbid, Jordan
e-mail: mohammed.akour@yu.edu.jo

Z. Al Saad
Archaeology and Anthropology Department, Yarmouk University, Irbid, Jordan

A. Aljarrah
Electrical and Computer Engineering Department, Oakland University, Rochester, MI, USA

ters if computer wise sensory and cognitive were introduce to be part of the museum collection protector equation.

The main contributions of this paper are as follows:

- Avoid unnecessary light exposure for sensitive artifacts.
- Minimize light damage by minimizing the energy absorbed by artifacts.
- Address how much exposure to light sources will consume a significant or unacceptable portion of the total display lifetime of the museum artifact.
- Design a lighting computer controlled system to lower the overall light levels.
- Provides maximum preservation while allowing the artifacts to be easily viewed.
- Better display way (attract the visitor attention to what he is looking to, without any distraction).
- Power saving.
- Generate some statistics about:
  - The time duration for each artifact while it exposed to the light.
  - Most viewed artifacts in the museum + the time duration of view for each.

These statistics are helpful for the periodically conservation and preservation for the shown object in the museum. Knowing how much light face each of the objects might help to know the damage amount.

85.2 Literature Review

Museum objects could be affected by several factors; light is considered as one of prevalent damage source to these objects. Organic materials based are very susceptible to light (i.e. paper, cloth, leather, photographs, and media [1, 2]. Fading might be brought with damage to the physical and chemical components of objects. Light and ultraviolet radiation plays important roles in the damage of objects as they supply power to fuel the photochemical reactions which eventually cause the damage. In spite of that UV is the main reason behind of this destruction, still light is a dilemma [3, 4]. Objects color might be changed in dyes and colorants as a consequence of Intensity and long exposure times. Ultraviolet radiation causes many more problems such as weakening, bleaching, and yellowing of paper and other organic materials [5]. All of these changes can diminish readability, affect the aesthetic appreciation of artwork, and impact access to the information contained therein [6].

Objects damage is incremental and irreparable. Therefore, protecting these objects is important and how to save them in a priority. It is well known that UV radiation is one of the most cause of destructive, and the thought of reducing

this energetic source may cease the damage is not right unfortunately. Although UV damage can be eliminated or diminished in the exhibit and stores areas, decreasing visible light needs specialized action plans [7–9]. The color lifetime of museum collection can be managed explicitly. Offering high visibility of museum collections on display even with low or zero vulnerability requires expert knowledge and will provoke custodial anxiety due to uncertainty [10]. Tracing light exposure by using Lux may supply helpful information on how bright exhibition lighting can be by clearly showing that the same amount of expected damage occurs with brighter light and short time as dimmer light and long time. This strategy will be effective if exhibition durations and actual light levels are recorded and studied [11].

Museums has to determine the favorable maximum limit of exposure (lux hours per year) for exhibited collections, taking into account that it may varied upon on the different museum collections [12, 13]. It is important to take in the mind how to achieve trade off in terms of lighting risk management, the value of artifact may be reduced because of the poor visual access or permanent damage may happen because of high visual. The two key dimensions' visual access and the ethics, so that thinking about the rights of the future generations should take a place not only the rights of exist people. Practically, diverse decision might be produced as different artifacts have different degree of sensitivity to light and their visibility [14].

85.3 Research Methodology

One of the well-known causes of increasing the risk of the artifacts damage is exhibition. More visual and accessible artifacts mean higher susceptible for damage. Exhibition raises the risk of light damage, the talk here about photochemical photomechanical damage. It is true that museum collections might be guarded in a vault, keep in very dark place, but that leads to kill the spirit and the mission of the museum.

85.3.1 Smart Lighting System

A system was built to control the lights in the museum. Briefly, the produced system is mainly consisting of thermal sensors that detect the presence of humans, DC LED spotlights, Arduino boards and Zigbee modules for a wireless communication to send data to a server. Schick et al. [15], built wireless Body Sensor Network for Monitoring and Evaluating Physical Activity. Their system is used to real-time monitoring individuals during their physical activity. The wireless sensor network in this paper is built monitor the displays in the museum and detect that visitor then prepare to calculate several measurements.

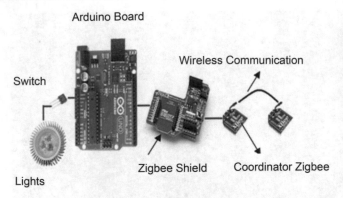

Fig. 85.1 Smart System main artifacts

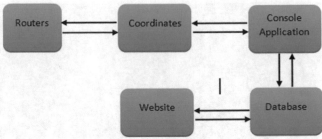

Fig. 85.2 Smart System framework

After detecting the visitor, Arduino which is controlling all the hardware system will turn on the DC LED spotlight and start calculating the duration time in seconds while the LED spotlight is turned on, the Arduino board is storing the durations of the visits with their counts in the memory of the processor. In case the museum display was wide, all the surrounding area can be covered by using multiple thermal sensors, each additional sensor is connected to additional axillaries Arduino board; these axillaries boards are connected to the main Arduino board. The main board has a router Zigbee module to receive and send data wirelessly. In server side there is a coordinate Arduino board is connected to the server using a serial port, this board has a coordinate Zigbee module to communicate with all the museum display's routers to send a data request message and receive the durations and view counts for each museum display. Figure 85.1 shows the main parts of our system.

85.3.2 Software Side

Console application is programmed by using C# programming language, the application is able to:

1. Read some attribute from the database (COM Port used by the Arduino coordinate, client objects ID's, timeout ... etc.).
2. Send data request message using the Serial port to the router of each museum object.
3. Read the returned data (durations with the checksum) from each router.
4. Validate the returned data to make sure it's from the same required router without any missing or corruption.
5. Convert the data from the hexadecimal format to the decimal format.
6. Store the data (Durations) to the database with a timestamp for each record.

In the Web programming side, a website is built to:

1. Show the museum object's information (name, type, location).
2. Show the number of the views and the total duration for each museum object.
3. Show all the durations with the timestamp for each museum object.
4. Illustrate all the data for each museum object in a graphical representation using graphs which facilitates the monitoring of the daily, weekly, monthly and yearly visits in a graphical interface.
5. Show some information regarding the number of views for the entire museum objects (most viewed object, less viewed object ... etc.).
6. Show some information regarding the advantage of using our system in a graphical representation (percentage of saved power, percentage of reduced damage for the museum objects ... etc.).

Programming languages and tools:

1. C#.
2. PHP.
3. HTML with (JavaScript, JQuery, CSS and Bootstrap Library).
4. MySQL Database.

Figure 85.2 shows the platform of how the proposed system works.

85.4 Experimental Results

In this section, several screenshots are taken where each one presents different view point of statistical measurements result. Figures 85.3, 85.4, 85.5, 85.6, 85.7, and 85.8 presents some of captured result.

The daily number of views for each display in the museum, including the date of each day.

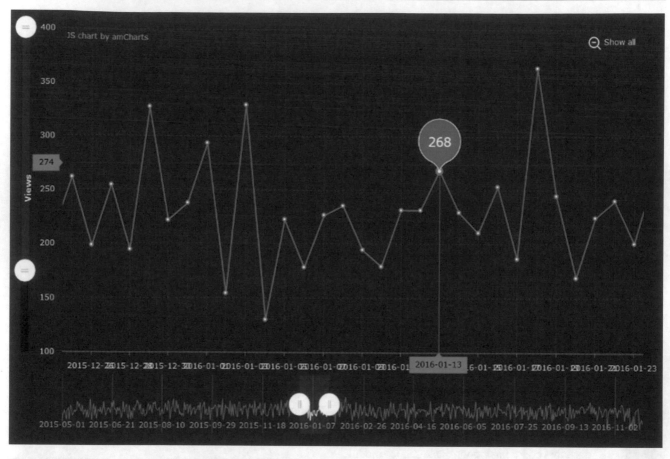

Fig. 85.3 Statistical measurements result in December 2015–January 2016

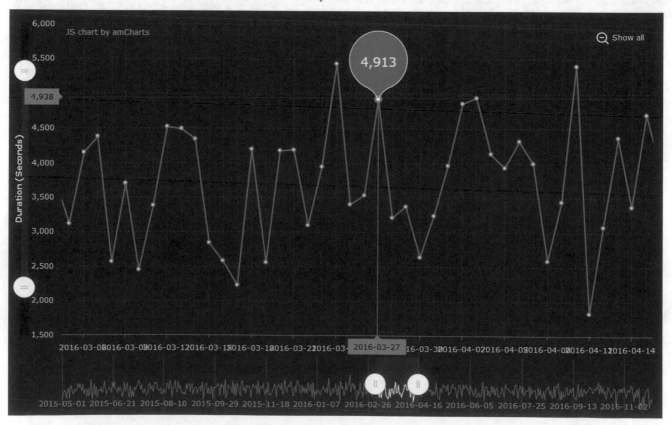

Fig. 85.4 Statistical measurements result in March–April 2016

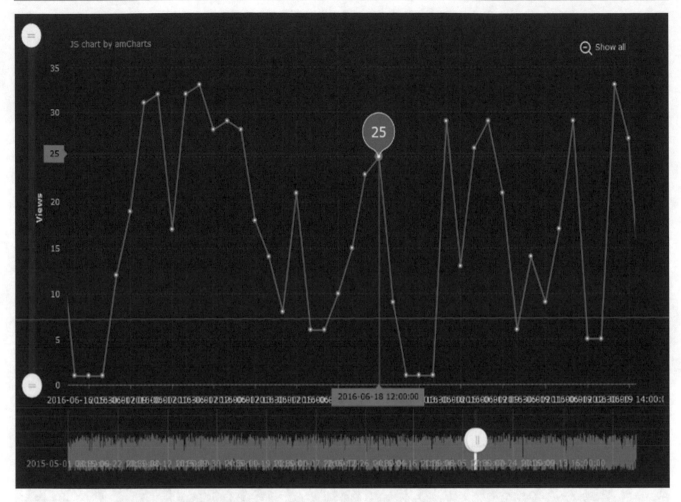

Fig. 85.5 Statistical measurements result in June 2016

The daily total durations (in seconds) of views for each display in the museum, including the date of each day.

The number of views during a smaller time unit (in this example our time unit is every half hour), including the time and date.

The total number of views during daily working hours, along with options to choose a specific day, month and year.

The total number of views for the week days, including a filtration option to choose a time range between two selected dates.

The total number of views for each display in the museum, in every month for a specific year or a specific time range between two selected dates.

85.5 Conclusion

Since the light is the most dangerous deterioration agent that affects the artifacts, this paper presents smart lighting system for the museum using some devices (sensors, motion detectors and adjustable led lights) and a central server that control those devices. This system was able to reduce the lighting as much as possible by avoid unnecessary light exposure for sensitive artifacts. The system addressed how much exposure to light sources will consume a significant or unacceptable portion of the total display lifetime of the museum artifact. The system provides maximum preservation while allowing the artifacts to be easily viewed, and better display way

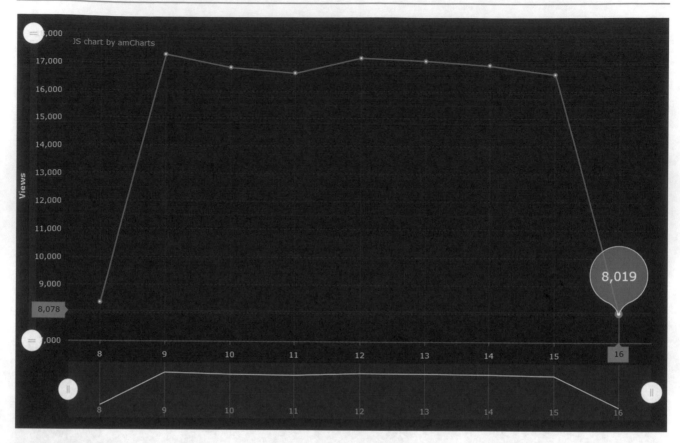

Fig. 85.6 Total number of views during daily working hours

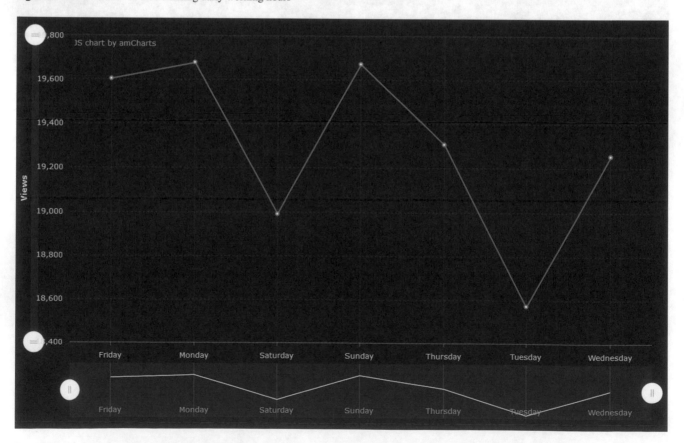

Fig. 85.7 Total number of views for the week days

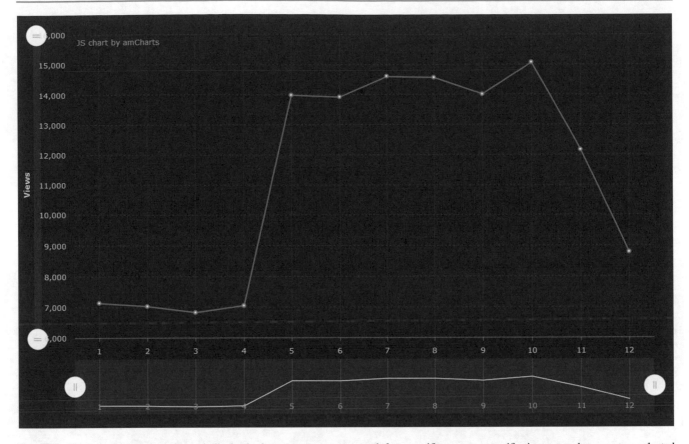

Fig. 85.8 Total number of views for each display in the museum, *n* every month for a specific year or a specific time range, between two selected dates

(attract the visitor attention to what he is looking to, without any distraction). Finally, the statistics are measured by the systems are helpful for the periodically conservation and preservation for the shown object in the museum. Knowing how much light face each of the objects might help to know the damage amount.

Acknowledgement This project is funded by Yarmouk University under project number 2015/24.

References

1. C. Boye, F. Preusser, T. Schaeffer, UV-blocking window films for use in museums—revisited. WAAC Newslett. **32**(1), 13–18 (2010)
2. J. Druzik, Illuminating alternatives: research in museum lighting. Getty Conservation Institute Newslett. **19**(1) (2004)
3. R.L. Feller, *The Deteriorating Effect of Light on Museum Objects*, Museum News Technical Supplement No. 3 (American Association of Museums, Washington, DC, 1964)
4. W.P. Lull, with the assistance of Paul N. Banks, *Conservation Environment Guidelines for Libraries and Archives* (Canadian Council of Archives, Ottawa, ON, 1995)
5. S. Michalski, Light, ultraviolet and infrared, in *Canadian Conservation Institute Caring for Collections*, (2011)
6. Museum exhibit lighting, an interdisciplinary approach: conservation, design, and technology, in *Proceedings of a workshop presented by the National Park Service and the American Institute for Conservation at the AIC Annual Meeting* (1997)
7. J. Miller, *Optics and Physiology of Human Vision in a Museum Environment* (NoUVIR Research, Seaford, 1994)
8. T.T. Schaeffer, *Effects of Light on Materials in Collections Data on Photoflash and Related Sources* (2001)
9. National Park Service, Chapter 4: museum collections environment, in Museum Handbook, Part I: Museum Collections. Accessed 29 April 2014
10. S. Staniforth, Agents of deterioration, in *Manual of Housekeeping: The Care of Collections in Historic Houses Open to the Public*, (Elsevier, Amsterdam, 2006), p. 51
11. S. Staniforth, 10: relative humidity as an agent of deterioration, in *Manual of housekeeping: the care of collections in historic houses open to the public*, (Elsevier, Amsterdam, 2006)
12. L. Bullock, 9: light as an agent of deterioration, in *Manual of Housekeeping: The Care of Collections in Historic Houses Open to the Public*, (Elsevier, Amsterdam, 2006), p. 93
13. K. Bachmann, Principles of storage, in *Conservation Concerns: A Guide for Collectors and Curators*, (Smithsonian Books, Washington, DC, 1992)
14. Stefan Michalski, *Agent of Deterioration: Light, Ultraviolet and Infrared* (2016), http://canada.pch.gc.ca/eng/1444925073140
15. L. Schick, W.L. de Souza, A.F. do Prado, Wireless body sensor network for monitoring and evaluating physical activity, in *Information Technology –New Generations*, (Springer, Cham, 2018), pp. 81–86

Pedro Fernandes, Jr., Alexandre C. B. Ramos, Danilo Pereira Roque, and Marcelo Santiago de Sousa

Abstract

This paper presents a method for the development of artificial neural networks (ANN) that consists in the use of a search space algorithm to adjust the components of an ANN's initial structure, based on the performance obtained by different network configurations. Also, it is possible to represent an ANN's structure as a genetic sequence, which enables directly loading a corresponding genetic sequence to instantly generate and run a previously trained ANN. This paper also shows some results obtained by different ANNs developed by this method, which demonstrate its features by analyzing its accuracy and trueness. As an example for application of this method, a case study is presented for a specific flight simulation, using data obtained from a helicopter's flight dynamics simulator for ANN training. Helicopter flight dynamics is a relevant study, for it can be used, for example, to provide precise data to a flight simulator, which implies in an important issue for pilot training, and subsequently, this type of application may help reducing the probability of pilot's faults in a real flight mission. Finally, some considerations are made about the work shown in this paper as the results, discussions and conclusions are presented.

Keywords

ANN · Artificial Intelligence · Helicopter

P. Fernandes, Jr. · A. C. B. Ramos (✉)
Federal University of Itajubá, Mathematics and Computng Institute, Itajubá, MG, Brazil
e-mail: ramos@unifei.edu.br

D. P. Roque · M. S. de Sousa
Federal University of Itajubá, Mechanical Engineering Institute, Itajubá, MG, Brazil
e-mail: marcelo.santiago@unifei.edu.br

86.1 Introduction

Due to the advances on the aviation's technology and the consequent increase in demand for the use of aircraft for different purposes, such as passenger transport, search and rescue missions, etc., safety of flight missions becomes even more relevant [1]. Among the main actions to improve it, advances in the quality of training provided to pilots can be cited, and in this context, the use of simulators is considered as one of these main activities [2]. Therefore, the development of more realistic flight simulators provides better quality training [3], which can contribute to minimize the risk of accidents.

Additionally, the modeling of flight dynamics is important to provide more realistic training, by its application in a flight simulator. This paper briefly presents fundamentals that arc used for the computational model represented. It is important to mention that, despite of the availability of advanced flight simulators, there are at least two advantages when a customized system is developed: (1) it is specifically designed for a particular aircraft (eventually one that is not yet available in a commercial simulator), which provides added realism to the simulation and (2) even the possibility of the development of an autopilot for a particular aircraft [4]. Also, as an ANN (Artificial Neural Network) can be successfully used to reproduce causal relations, even for complex systems, it is an interesting solution for this kind of application [5–7].

There are several methods for the development, training and validation of ANN [5, 8]. This paper presents a method that is based on some concepts, such as evolutionary development [8], incremental development made by mutations [9] and the representation of an ANN with a corresponding genetic sequence [10].

86.2 Flight Controls of a Helicopter

This section presents the helicopter flight controls as described by Cunha Jr. [11]. The helicopter lift is generated by the resultant force of the air passage (relative wind) into the blades. Helicopters have degree of freedom in the three spatial axes. The coordinate system used to study the dynamics of a helicopter is the rigid body system or system of the fuselage line reference. To operate it, there are three flight control instruments: *collective*, *cyclic* and *pedals*, which provide four degrees of control freedom: pitch, roll, yaw and flight.

The use of the collective commands provide ascending and descending movements of the helicopter, changing the step of all main rotor's blades at the same time and at the same angle of attack. For example, if given the command to go up, the pilot must pull the collective and the resulting step is positive, otherwise the collective should be pushed, so the helicopter goes down.

The cyclic enables the pilot to make the longitudinal (pitch) and lateral (roll) movements of the helicopter, by changing the pitch of the main rotor blades differently, depending on the position where it is during the course of rotation. Examples: if given a forward command, the pitch of the blades decreases when they are going ahead and increases when they pass through the back of the helicopter. If the command is given to the left, the pitch of the blades is reduced when passing the left side and increases when they pass the right side.

The pedals enable the pilot to control the rotations in the horizontal plane around the vertical z-axis (yaw) of the helicopter. They change the pitch of all tail rotor blades simultaneously and in the same angle of attack. The tail rotor is critical for the stability of the helicopter, for it is responsible for neutralizing or not the torque generated by the main rotor on the fuselage.

86.3 Modeling of a Helicopter's Flight Dynamics

The modeling and the information described in this section are based mainly on [11–13] and the presented application example is based on [12], who analyzed the *Bolkow Bo-105* model.

Initially, it can be said that a helicopter, as well as other aircraft, has its dynamic governed by the three laws of Newton: (1) a balance in the body (sum of zero forces) tends to remain at rest or moving straight and with constant speed; (2) force equals the change of momentum; and (3) if a body A applies a force F on a body B, body B applies a force in the same module, the same direction and the opposite way to the body A (-F). From these laws, and knowledge of the forces

(and moments) applied, it is possible to obtain the equations describing a helicopter's flight dynamics.

The forces acting on the main rotor and tail rotor are the weight force and aerodynamic forces, similar to the forces acting on a wing. The difference is that the "aerodynamic surface", rotor blades, are in angular movement at a speed (approximately) constant. Each rotor blade airfoil section is subjected to a force that is proportional to both the dynamic pressure, the area of the unit section, the air density and the aerodynamic coefficients. The dynamic pressure is a function of helicopter's speed, angular velocity of the blades, and blade position relative to the central axis that passes through the fuselage. The aerodynamic coefficients are a function of the geometry of the section and the rotor as a whole and the local angle of attack on the blade. This local attack angle is dependent on different parameters, including the fuselage angle of attack orientation of the main rotor shaft, twist in the rotor blade due to cyclic controls and collective inflow, angular velocity and rate, and external disturbances. The attack angle of the rotor blades is a function that is calculated using these variables: beat, inflow, helicopter controls, and angular velocities.

Now it is presented the conceptual description of the implemented modeling. Initially, the forces are calculated in each section, and these may be integrated along the length of the blades of both rotors so that the total forces and moments acting on the main rotor and the tail rotor are obtained. Then, those values are used to calculate aerodynamic coefficients by their respective equations. To solve the differential equations, it is important to make a numerical integration, which requires the equations of motion, data relative to the helicopter and the initial conditions of simulation.

The initial conditions are obtained by a trimming process (obtaining equilibrium conditions). On balance, the resulting force and moment are zero. In this case, the differential equations become algebraic equations. And an optimization process is used to obtain the values of states and controls to ensure the achievement of the equilibrium condition. It requires equations to be used, helicopter data and some parameters required for the initial condition: speed, altitude, slip angle, curve speed and climb speed (or gamma angle). The equilibrium condition requires minimizing various equations. It wasn't possible to minimize all the equations simultaneously, so it was initially supposed inflow equals to zero, and thus obtained the states and controls of the helicopter (without inflow). Then, the obtained states are used as initial conditions to find the inflow value. So it is made the trimming again with the new inflow parameters. This sequence is repeated until convergence of values. Finally, having the initial conditions, numerical integration is made, which enables calculation of flight parameters that provide reference data for the ANN's development as input and output values.

86.4   A Brief Review on Artificial Neural Networks and Explanation on the Method

The content presented in this section is mainly based on [14]. An ANN, as its name suggests, is basically a computer application that simulates a biological neural network's functioning. This is done by creating a virtual structure composed by interconnected neurons. Each neuron's structure is basically similar to the following description (Fig. 86.1).

Where: X_1, X_2, ..., X_n give the input values; W_1, W_2 ..., W_n are the weights respectively applied to the input values; Σ is the sum of the input values after they were multiplied by their respective weights, and outputs a value a, then processed by an activation function $f(a)$, that generates an output value according to its function; and y is the output value that will be sent to another neuron or given as result.

There are different ways to implement an ANN. For example, regarding to the activation function of a neuron, it can be linear or semi-linear, the connections between neurons may or not compose cycles, different learning rules can be applied, etc. Learning rules consist in the method used to modify an ANN's topology, in a way that these changes tend to generate a new and more accurate topology for the network, which means that the error (difference between expected output values and resulted output values obtained by the use of an ANN) must decrease. In general, an ANN can "learn" patterns, by gradually adapting, according to the data received during training, until it is capable to perform the intended functions with previously specified goal parameters. During training, it is necessary to make tests as validation, to check ANN's generalization capability, so it must provide correct output data when given inputs that are different from those used for adapting in training. If the ANN still performs well, it can be tested with different data to be evaluated, and if approved it's then used for that specific application for which it was developed.

The proposed method can be described as following: once both the quantity of inputs and outputs for a given ANN are known, it can be generated an initial topology for the ANN consisting in the input and output layers as expected and also a hidden layer that has the same number of neurons as the number of outputs of the ANN. Each of the inputs is connected to each of the hidden layer's neurons, and each of the hidden layer's neurons is connected to only one

of the outputs (in a way that each of the hidden layer's neurons is connected to one different output). This basic initial structure is then optimized by applying a first round of training. Whenever the predetermined performance goals are achieved by the developed ANN, training is interrupted. If it doesn't occur after this first step of adaptation, that initial structure is updated by the addition of a new set of neurons in the hidden layer, exactly as that initial hidden layer, that is, with the same arrangement of connections between inputs and outputs. The previously trained neurons and connections are maintained as they were, and only the new components are trained. After the training, the ANN is evaluated again. This process continues until it is obtained the best tested ANN topology for that application. By applying this method, it is possible to represent an ANN's topology as a genetic sequence, which may be composed, for example, by predefined ranges of values for each of the ANN's topology components: connection weights, neuron's activation functions, etc., enabling to encode from an ANN's topology to its genetic sequence and also to decode from a genetic sequence to an ANN's topology, which allows the system to load a specific ANN's genetic sequence, generate its respective ANN and make it promptly available to be used.

Using the topology shown in Fig. 86.2, one way to represent this ANN's topology as a genetic sequence is: *4. 5. 2. abcdefghijklmnopqrst. vwxyz. ABCDEFGHIJKLMNOPQRST. VWXYZ*, where each character respectively refers to: *inputs amount. outputs amount. hidden layers amount. weight of each connection between inputs and hidden layer's neurons by order. weight of each connection between hidden layer's neurons and outputs by order*. Note that the characters are related to their actual values shown in Table 86.1.

This is only a conceptual simplified example; there are other topological characteristics that should be represented, like each neuron's activation function. It is important to men-

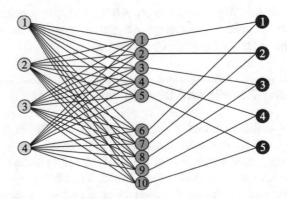

Fig. 86.1 Basic representation of an ANN's artificial neuron

Fig. 86.2 example of an ANN topology. Each neuron is numbered by its position in its respective layer, for clearer identification related to its respective genetic representation

Table 86.1 Values from different magnitudes (T1)

Table T1

Actual value	Reference	Char	Actual value	Reference	Char
−9	63	?	0.005000	95	_
−8	64	@	0.006000	96	`
−7	65	A	0.007000	97	a
−6	66	B	0.008000	98	b
−5	67	C	0.009000	99	c
−4	68	D	0.010000	100	d
−3	69	E	0.020000	101	e
−2	70	F	0.030000	102	f
−1	71	G	0.040000	103	g
−0.900000	72	H	0.050000	104	h
−0.800000	73	I	0.060000	105	i
−0.700000	74	J	0.070000	106	j
−0.600000	75	K	0.080000	107	k
−0.500000	76	L	0.090000	108	l
−0.400000	77	M	0.100000	109	m
−0.300000	78	N	0.200000	110	n
−0.200000	79	O	0.300000	111	o
−0.100000	80	P	0.400000	112	p
−0.090000	81	Q	0.500000	113	q
−0.080000	82	R	0.600000	114	r
−0.070000	83	S	0.700000	115	s
−0.060000	84	T	0.800000	116	t
−0.050000	85	U	0.900000	117	u
−0.040000	86	V	1	118	v
−0.030000	87	W	2	119	w
−0.020000	88	X	3	120	x
−0.010000	89	Y	4	121	y
0	90	Z	5	122	z
0.001000	91	[	6	123	{
0.002000	92	\	7	124		
0.003000	93	]	8	125	}
0.004000	94	^	9	126	~

tion that, in this method, every ANN's mutation performed is set by running a search space algorithm that finds the best tested value for each ANN's component.

86.5 Results and Discussion

This section shows sample results obtained by different ANN generated by this work's method. In this case study, as an simple example for testing the method, let's consider the helicopter flying at 3200 m of altitude, both slip angle, curve speed and climb speed valued as zero and speed varying from 1 to 56 m/s (meters per second) as initial conditions, and as result the ANN must give the correct values used as

Table 86.2 Summarized results

Type	Best perf. (%)	Time (s)	Mutations
1 (random, T1, custom)	91.317	406	79
2 (random, T1, naive)	91.699	295	47
3 (random, T2, custom)	26.012	318	79
4 (random, T2, naive)	72.902	205	41
5 (0, T1, custom)	69.474	233	68
6 (0, T1, naive)	67.601	345	49
7 (0, T2, custom)	−98.822	593	99
8 (0, T2, naive)	−9.126	0	2
9 (1, T1, custom)	83.974	156	61
10 (1, T1, naive)	77.541	381	51
11 (1, T2, custom)	−98.822	592	99
12 (1, T2, naive)	62.871	551	59

reference for each of the respective helicopter commands, totalizing five input parameters (speed, altitude, slip angle, curve speed and climb speed) and four output parameters (collective, cyclic pitch, cyclic roll and pedals).

Some different adjustments were tried as a way to compare their results, also to find the best combination between the tried adjustments and to provide a general behavior view of the ANN generated. For a comparison between different ways to define initial values for the links' weights, the following three tries were made: each weight was initialized by receiving a different random value; all weights were initialized set to 1, and all weights were initialized set to 0. Other comparison made is between two different value's tables used as reference for the link's weights: table T1, mentioned in the previous section and table T2, which has the same reference and char values as table T1, but has different actual values, real values obtained by two divisions, the first one gives 28 values, calculated by x/3, where x varies by 1, from −27 to 0, and another gives the last 36 values, calculated by y/4, where y varies by 1, from 1 to 36. And finally, comparing two different 1D (one dimensional) search space algorithms, used to set the best found value to each link's weight: a customized search based on the concept of search used in the golden section search algorithm and naive search. Each combination of initial set value, referenced table and search space algorithm gives a different type of test. Each type of test was performed at a total time of 600 s and the summarized results are presented in Table 86.2, that shows how much time was elapsed and how many mutations occurred to the ANN until it has reached its best performance (regarding trueness).

Other results presented in this section are related to the generalization capability of the ANN along its training, by comparing results obtained by the ANN with both training and validation datasets.

Each case of the ANN's performance was calculated by the following rules:

Computing Range 1 and calculating trueness:
If (error $\leq$ output$_{[x]}$.amplitude/6): Range1++

$$Trueness = 100 - \left(\left(\frac{error}{\frac{output[x].amplitude}{6}} \right) * 33.333333 \right)$$

Computing Range 2 and calculating trueness:
Else If (error $\leq$ output$_{[x]}$.amplitude/3): Range2++

$$Trueness = 100 - \left(\left(\frac{error}{\frac{output[x].amplitude}{3}} \right) * 66.666666 \right)$$

Computing Range 3 and calculating trueness:
Else If (error $\leq$ output$_{[x]}$.amplitude/2): Range3++

$$Trueness = 100 - \left(\left(\frac{error}{\frac{output[x].amplitude}{2}} \right) * 100 \right)$$

Computing Range 4 and calculating trueness:
Else: Range4++

$$Trueness = \left(\left(\frac{\frac{output[x].amplitude}{2}}{error} \right) - 1 \right) * 100$$

Where:
output$_{[x]}$.amplitude = Output$_{[x]}$.max$-$Output$_{[x]}$.min.
error = |output$_{[x]}$.obtained$-$output$_{[x]}$.expected|.

Accuracy is given by the sum of the obtained results by each range of closeness. Trueness is calculated as average of the obtained outputs' closeness in each epoch (mutation) of the ANN.

The next table shows the summarized results obtained by each of the 12 before mentioned tests.

Even those summarized results already show some information to discuss about. It's noticeable that the ANNs developed using table T1 had, in general, best results than those that used table T2. The custom search method showed poor results when using table T2, especially when the links' weights are initialized set to 0 or 1. In general, when the links' weights are initialized with random values, the developed ANNs have best performance. The next table shows the average results by each adjustment applied to the developed ANNs.

The results presented in Table 86.3 show the importance of the correct adjustments—as this method is very limited in values to be used as links' weights—for example, table T1 that has values from different magnitudes, have provided to its developed ANNs much better results than those obtained

Table 86.3 Average results by adjustment

Adjustment	Best perf. (%)	Time (s)	Mutations
Initial random values	50.248	307	38
Initial value is 0	7.282	293	55
Initial value is 1	31.391	420	68
Table T1	80.268	303	59
Table T2	−7.498	377	63
Custom search method	12.189	383	81
Naive search method	60.581	296	42

by the ANNs trained using table T2. Also, the initial values' setting is relevant, as the results have shown. And finally, about the search method, although naïve search is the most expensive, considering a very restrict search space, it can be even a good option, for it will set the very best values for each ANN's component, so the best topology may be found within less mutations. Although the average performance of the naïve search was better than that obtained by the custom method, both had similar performances in best conditions (using table T1 and random initial values), as it can be seen in Table 86.2.

As it can be seen in the Figs. 86.3 and 86.4, as the mutations occur, they generally provide enhancements in the ANN's performance, and also considering the over fit effect, the ANN tends to keep a performance par, being capable to maintain or recover performance with a larger topology.

The next figure shows a detailed comparison between obtained and expected values for one of the outputs, when the ANN is already trained and performing with trueness above 90% (Fig. 86.5).

86.6 Conclusions

This paper presented a method for the development of an ANN using search space algorithms to adjust each of the ANN's components, and it also enables genetic representation of an ANN's topology, which can provide benefits like promptly load and run an already generated ANN by its topology's description. Different adjustments were tested and their results shown for comparison, providing analysis about the method such as its general performance along its incremental development. It's important to notice that the presented results only constitute a very specific scenario within this case study, as a sample to show and discuss some of this method's characteristics.

Acknowledgment The author thank UNIFEI for research support, and CAPES and FAPEMIG for financial support. Confirmation number: 270.

Fig. 86.3 obtained trueness in each mutation (new running of type 2)

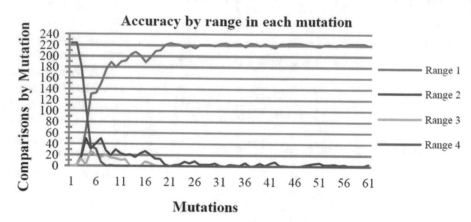

Fig. 86.4 obtained accuracy by range of closeness in each mutation (new running of type 2)

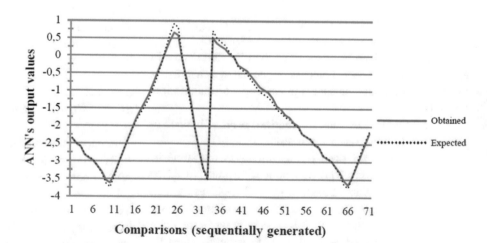

Fig. 86.5 Comparison between expected and obtained values by the ANN after training for longitudinal cyclic (pitch) in the proposed scenario

References

1. X. You, M. Ji, H. Han, The effects of risk perception and flight experience on airline pilots' locus of control with regard to safety operation behaviors. Accid. Anal. Prev. **9**, 131–139 (2013)
2. J.S. Melo, M.S.R. Tadeucci. *A atividade aérea e uso de simulador de voo*, XIV Encontro Latino Americano, (2010)
3. J. Ryder, T. Santarelli, J. Scolaro, J. Hicinbothom, W. Zachary, Comparison of cognitive model uses in intelligent training systems. Proc. Hum. Factors Ergon. Soc. Annu. Meet. **4**, 374–377 (2000)
4. L.R. Ribeiro, *Plataforma de Testes para Sistemas de Piloto Automático Utilizando Matlab/Simulink e Simulador de voo X-Plane* (Instituto Tecnológico de Aeronáutica, São José dos Campos, 2011)
5. W.C. Lu, R.M. Faye, A.C.B. Ramos, J. Slama, F. Mora-Camino, Neural inversion of flight guidance dynamics. ISDA 2007 **6**, 190–195 (2007)
6. A.K. Ghosh, S.C. Raisinghani, Frequency-domain estimation of parameters from flight data using neural networks. J. Guid. Control. Dyn. **6**, 525–530 (2001)

7. D.J. Linse, R.F. Stengel, Identification of aerodynamic coefficients using computational neural networks. J. Guid. Control. Dyn. **8**, 1018–1025 (1993)

8. X. Yao, Evolving artificial neural networks. Proc. IEEE **25**, 1423–1447 (1999)

9. K.O. Stanley, R. Miikkulainen, Efficient evolution of neural network topologies. Proc. 2002 Cong. Evol. Comput. **6**, 1757–1762 (2002)

10. S. Cussat-Blanc, K. Harrington, J. Pollack, Gene regulatory network evolution through augmenting topologies. IEEE Trans. Evol. Comput. **15**, 823–837 (2015)

11. S.S. Cunha Jr., M.S. de Sousa, D.P. Roque, A.C.B. Ramos, P. Fernandes Jr., Dynamic simulation of the flight behavior of a rotary-wing aircraft. Inf. Tech. N. Gener. **13**, 1087–1099 (2016)

12. P.V.M. Simplício, *Helicopter Nonlinear Flight Control Using Incremental Nonlinear Dynamic Inversion* (Delft University of Technology, Delft, 2011)

13. G.D. Padfield, *Helicopter Flight Dynamics*, 2nd edn. (John Wiley & Sons, Hoboken, 2008)

14. I. Lima, C.A.M. Pinheiro, F.A.O. Santos, *Inteligência Artificial*, 1st edn. (Elsevier, Brasil, 2014)

Laxmi P. Gewali and Bhaikaji Gurung

Abstract

Generating constrained triangulation of point sites distributed in the plane is an important problem in computational geometry. We present theoretical and experimental investigation results for generating triangulations for polygons and point sites that address node degree constraints. We characterize point sites that have almost all vertices of odd degree. We present experimental results on the node degree distribution of Delaunay triangulation of point sites generated randomly. Additionally, we present a heuristic algorithm for triangulating a given normal annular region with increased number of even degree vertices.

Keywords

Triangulation · Degree-constrained triangulation ·
Annular region triangulation

87.1 Introduction

Triangulation of a given set of point sites in the plane is the process of connecting them by line segments so that the region populated by point sites is tiled by triangles. Each triangle of the triangulation is also called face. The line segments connecting point sites are called edges. In a triangulated mesh, no two edges can intersect in their interior. The problem of composing triangulation for a given set of point sites has been extensively investigated in computational geometry literature [1, 2].

Triangulation algorithms have been applied widely in several scientific and engineering disciplines including:

(i) geographic information system (GIS), (ii) computer graphics, (iii) image processing, (iv) finite element method, and (v) robotics. In Geographic Information System (GIS), the surface of the terrain is modeled by using triangles whose vertices are located close together in regions of rapid slope change and sparse in regions where slope change is minimal. In finite element method (FEM), computational domain is partitioned into a triangular mesh to obtain an approximate solution for heat flow and fluid flow problems. In computer graphics and image processing, the surface of a 3D object is modeled by triangular mesh which is processed in streamline form to construct and transmit an image of the object model.

The notion of 'quality' has been considered in triangulation networks. A triangulation is said to be of better quality if it has a large proportion of triangles with an aspect ratio close to one. It is remarked that the aspect ratio $asp(t)$ of a triangle t is defined in terms of the smallest enclosing rectangle $er(t)$. Specifically, $asp(t)$ is the ratio of the width (smaller side) to length (larger side) of $er(t)$. If the aspect ratio is one then the smallest enclosing rectangle is a square. When a triangular mesh has a large proportion of triangles with a high aspect ratio then such mesh can lead to increased accuracy in the approximate solution of a partial differential equation in finite element methods.

Triangulation networks are used in computer graphics and image processing for rendering (generating an image from a geometric model) and transmission (transferring object model). In such applications, it is necessary to construct a sequence of adjacent (edge sharing) triangles to form a "strip" [3]. Such strips can be transmitted and rendered very efficiently. Triangulation mesh whose triangles can be arranged in one strip is called Hamiltonian triangulation. Generating Hamiltonian triangulation of a given set of point sites is a challenging problem and some noticeable results are reported in [3, 10].

Another interesting problem in triangulation is the generation of minimum weight triangulation which is a triangulation that minimizes the total length of triangle edges [11].

L. P. Gewali (✉) · B. Gurung
Department of Computer Science, University of Nevada, Las Vegas, NV, USA
e-mail: Laxmi.gewali@unlv.edu; gurunb1@unlv.nevada.edu

© Springer International Publishing AG, part of Springer Nature 2018
S. Latifi (ed.), *Information Technology – New Generations*, Advances in Intelligent Systems and Computing 738,
https://doi.org/10.1007/978-3-319-77028-4_87

Minimum weight triangulation was a long standing problem in computational geometry area. In 2008, Mulzer and Rote [4] established that this problem is NP-Hard. An interesting variation of a triangulation problem is the degree-constrained triangulation which seeks to construct a triangulated mesh with a high proportion of even-degree nodes [5].

An overview of this paper is as follows. In Sect. 87.2, we present a brief review of characterization and algorithm development in relation to the problem of generating triangulated mesh with a large proportion of even degree nodes. In Sect. 87.3, we introduce one of the main contributions of this paper and describe the characterization of even degree triangulation of an annular region. We point out an $O(n^2)$ time algorithm for triangulating of an annular region with a large proportion of even degree vertices. we report an experimental investigation of degree distribution in Delaunay triangulation whose point sites are randomly generated. Finally, in Sect. 87.4, we present: (i) discussions on the results obtained from experimental investigation, (ii) remarks on the algorithms developed in Sect. 87.3, and (iii) possible extensions and scope for future investigation on degree constrained triangulation.

87.2 Constrained Triangulation

In this section, we first present an overview of algorithms for generating triangulation mesh for point sites distributed in the plane. We then review important results on the generating triangulations satisfying node-degree constraints.

87.2.1 Triangulation

Given a set S of n point sites $p_0, p_1, \ldots, p_{n-1}$, a triangulation formed by these sites is a partitioning of its convex hull such that: (i) the region inside the convex hull is partitioned into triangles and (ii) only the given point sites can be the vertices of the triangles (Fig. 87.1).

It is known that a given set S of n point sites admits exponentially many triangulations [1, 2]. While there are so many ways to triangulate a given set of points in 2D, a special type of triangulation called Delaunay triangulation [2], has been considered extensively for many practical application [1].

Delaunay triangulation satisfies many interesting properties that include: (i) empty circle property, (ii) closest pair property, (iii) smallest angle property, and (iv) minimum spanning tree property. Specifically, the empty circle property states that the circle passing through any two/three point sites of a Delaunay triangle does not contain any other site. The closest pair are neighbors in the Delaunay triangulation. The minimum spanning tree of a set of points is a subgraph of the Delaunay triangulation (see Fig. 87.2).

A triangulation of n point sites in the plane is called *even triangulation* if all vertices are of even degree. Figure 87.3 shows an example of even triangulation.

Remark 1: When considering even triangulation most authors [2] consider the triangulation inside the convex hull of given point sites.

Some of the recent results on even degree triangulation were reported in [5–7]. It has been established that any bipartite 2-connected planar graph can be modified to a triangulation which is 3-colorable. This result can be applied for guard placement in orthogonal polygons [7]. A notable result on even triangulation with a large proportion of even degree vertices was reported by Pelaez et al. [5]. In this paper, it is shown that any given points can be triangulated to have at least *floor(2n/3)-3* vertices with even degree. The

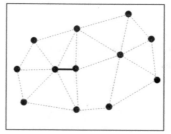

Fig. 87.2 Closest pair and minimum spanning tree

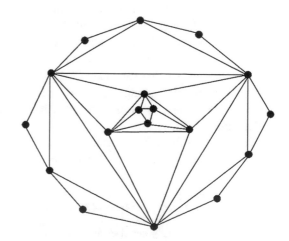

Fig. 87.3 Illustrating even-degree triangulation

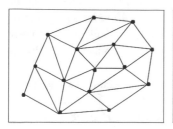

Fig. 87.1 Many triangulations

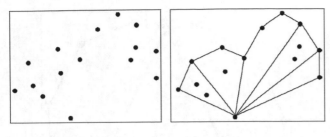

Fig. 87.4 Sector Partitioning

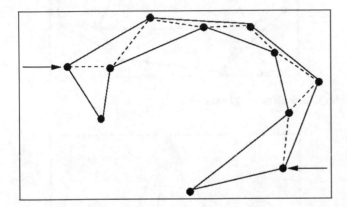

Fig. 87.5 A polygon that does not admit even triangulation

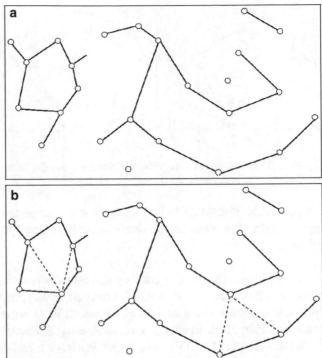

Fig. 87.6 (**a**) A planar straight line graph (pslg). (**b**) Adding edges to planar straight line graph

method essentially partitions n input point sets into disjoint sectors $S1, S2, \ldots Sk$ originating at the point with the lowest y-coordinate. These sector partitioning is such that each sector except the last one (Sk) contains exactly four points (not including sector source point). An example of sector partitioning is shown in Fig. 87.4.

The method presented in [5] processes points in each sector in the order $S_1, S_2, \ldots, S_k$. During each sector processing, edges are added to obtain triangulation that tends to increase the number of even degree vertices. When processing points in sector Si, the connectivity for the points in all sectors $S_1, S_2, \ldots, S_i$ are examined. By arguing complicated case analysis, it is shown that the resulting triangulation contain at least *floor(2n/3)-3* vertices with an even degree.

Not all polygon can be even triangulated [8]. In fact, there are polygon whose triangulation does not have any node of even degree [12]. A long spiral polygon can be constructed in such a way that it admits only one triangulation and not all vertices are of even-degree [13–17]. Figure 87.5 shows an example polygon that does not admit even triangulation.

87.3   Generating Even Triangulation

In this section a new approach for developing efficient algorithms for generating triangulations that tend to have a large proportion of even-degree nodes is presented.

87.3.1   Preliminaries

Consider a set S of n point sites $p_1, p_2, \ldots, p_n$ in 2D plane some of which are connected to form a planar straight line graph (**pslg**) as shown in Fig. 87.6a.

We characterize a pslg in term of degree potential which is defined as follows.

Definition 3.1: The *even potential* of a pslg is the total number of even degree vertices.

A triangulation of high *even potential* will have high proportion of even degree vertices.

Definition 3.2: (*Valid chain*) A chain $p_{i1}, p_{i2}, \ldots, p_{ik}$ formed by connecting k vertices of pslg is called *valid* if none of the edges of the chain intersect with the existing edges of the pslg.

Now we examine the requirements that do not decrease the even potential when valid chains are added to given pslg.

Property 3.1: Let $ch1 = p_{i1}, p_{i2}, \ldots, p_{ik}$ be a sequence of non-consecutive vertices of the pslg. Adding $ch1$ to pslg increases the even potential of new pslg if the degrees of both extreme vertices (before adding the chain) are odd. If only one of the p_{i1} or p_{ik} vertex is of odd degree then the even potential stays the same.

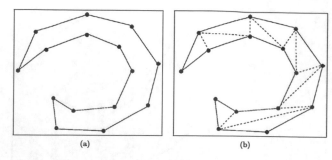

Fig. 87.7 Triangulating spiral polygon. (**a**) Spiral polygon (**b**) Triangulation based on back and forth approach

Property 3.2: If the degrees of both vertices p_{il} and p_{ik} are even then the even potential will decrease as ch1 is added to the pslg.

A polygon whose boundary consists of exactly one convex chain and one concave chain is referred to as spiral polygon. Note that a convex chain of a polygon has all its internal angle less than 180°. Similarly, a concave chain's internal angles are greater than 180°. Figure 87.7a shows a spiral polygon in which the size of its convex chain and concave chain are comparable. It is remarked that when we use the term 'concave chain' or 'convex chain' of a spiral polygon it is understood to be maximal chains.

A spiral polygon having convex and concave chains of comparable size can be triangulated in a "*back and forth*" manner to have most vertices of even degree. In back and forth approach for triangulation concave chain and convex chain are connected by a chain by picking vertices from each alternatively so that (except for start and end vertices) all vertices are of even degrees. Figure 87.7b shows the triangulation based on back and forth approach.

87.3.2 Triangulating Annular Region

An annular region is formed by two closed circular chains. We can also think an annular region as a polygon with one hole. We now consider the problem of triangulating an annular region to maximize the number of even degree vertices [18–20]. We first examine some extreme instances of an annular region. Consider the situation when the interior chain is just a triangle and the outside chain consists of many vertices. In our investigation, we consider both interior and outside chains to be convex. This is illustrated in Fig. 87.8. The annular region can be partitioned into six convex regions by using two diagonals emanating from the vertices of the triangle, which are shown by dashed lines in Fig. 87.8. Out of the seven regions, four are triangles and the other three are convex shapes. The convex regions can be triangulated to have all vertices of an even degree by using algorithm described in [8]. In the resulting triangulation, except for six vertices in the outer chain, all vertices are of even degree. This is stated in Lemma 3.1.

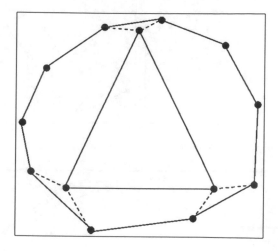

Fig. 87.8 Illustrating Lemma 3.1

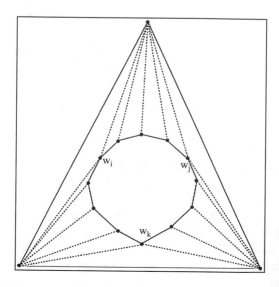

Fig. 87.9 Illustrating Lemma 3.2

Lemma 3.1: If inner chain is just a triangle then the annular region can be triangulated to have at most six vertices of odd degrees.

Remark 3.1: If the outer chain is also triangle then the triangulation becomes such that all six triangles are of even degree. Next, we examine the situation when the outside chain is a triangle and the inside chain has many vertices. This is illustrated in Fig. 87.9. Any triangulation of such an annular region is such that only three vertices in the inner chain are of even degree. The degree parity of the vertices of the outer chain depends on the visibility relationship between inner and outer chain. This is stated in Lemma 3.2.

Lemma 3.2: For any given $n > 3$, we can always construct an annular region that admits triangulation with no more than six vertices with of even degree.

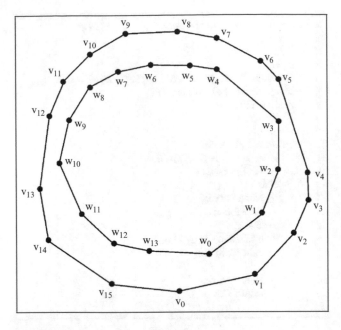

Fig. 87.10 A normal annular region

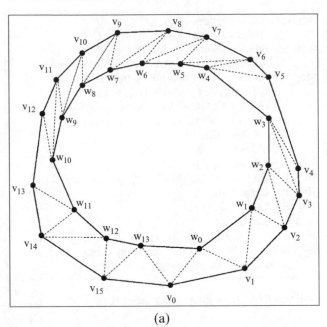

(a)

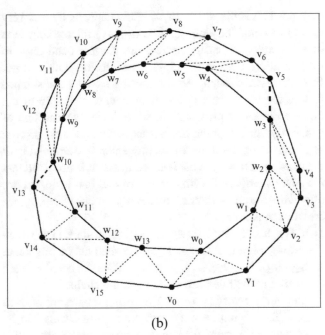

(b)

Fig. 87.11 Triangulation of annular region. (**a**) the next alternating chain starts at v_5 (**b**) the next alternating chain starts at v_{13}

Proof: Construct a big enclosing triangle that encloses a convex polygon with *n-3* vertices. Observe that any triangulation of the annular region must have edges with one vertex in an outer triangle and one vertex in an inner convex polygon [21, 22]. Furthermore, at most two diagonals can be incident upon a vertex of the inner chain. Let w_i, w_j, and w_k be the vertices of the inner chain where two diagonals are incident as shown in Fig. 87.9. On all other vertices of the inner chain, exactly one diagonal will be incident—making all of them of odd degree. Hence at most three vertices of outer chain and only three vertices of the inner chain can be of even degree which implies that no more than six vertices are of even degree.

The annular region formed by two convex chains of a comparable number of vertices in each chain is referred to as a **normal annular region**. An example of normal annular region is illustrated in Fig. 87.10, where the outer chain has 16 vertices and the inner chain has 14 vertices. An efficient heuristic algorithm for triangulating normal annular region with increased number of even degree vertices is described next.

87.3.3 Development of Alternate Marching Algorithm

Let v_0, v_1, v_2, $\ldots$, v_{n1} be the vertices in the outer boundary (counterclockwise order). Similarly, let w_0, w_1, w_2, $\ldots$, w_{n2} be the vertices in the inner boundary in counterclockwise order. In the **Alternate Marching algorithm (AM algorithm)**

we propose, a chain is constructed connecting vertices of outer and inner boundary alternately as far as possible to obtain triangles whose vertices, except the first triangle and the last triangle, will be of even degree. Such a chain is referred to as Alternating Max Chain (*AM-Chain* (v_i)), where v_i is the starting vertex of the chain. This is illustrated in Fig. 87.11, where AM-Chain (v_0) is the chain <v_0, w_0, v_1, w_2, $\ldots$, w_3, v_4>. The chain cannot proceed beyond w_3 as (v_4, w_4) intersects with inner boundary. The next connecting chain is AM-Chain (v_5). In some unusual cases, vertex v_5

Input: (i) Outer vertices $v_0, v_1, \ldots, v_{n1} = CH_O$
(ii) Inner vertices $w_0, w_1, \ldots, w_{n2} = CH_I$
Output: Triangulation of Annual Region R with
With increased number of even degree vertices
Step 1: (i) Let $v_{s,o}$ be the start vertex in boundary CH_O
(ii) Let $w_{r,o}$ be the vertex in CH_I closest to $v_{s,o}$
(iii) Ch = ConstructAM-Chain($v_{s,0}$, CH_I, CH_O)
(iv) Let Ch be: $v_{(s,0)}$, $w_{(r,0)}$, $v_{(s,0)+1}$, $\ldots$, $v_{(s,0)+t0}$
(v) Output Ch
(vi) $i = 0; j = 0;$
Step 2: while $v_{(s,i)+t(i)} \neq v_{(s,0)}$ **do**
Step 3:   Ch = ConstructAM-Chain($v_{(s,i)+t(i+1)}$, CH_I, CH_O);
Step 4:   Output Ch;
Step 5: $i = i+1; j = j+1;$
Step 6:   Let Ch be:
$v_{(s,i)}$, $w_{(r,j)}$, $v_{(s,i)+1}$, $w_{(r,j)+1}$, $\ldots$, $v_{(s,i)+(t,i)}$, $w_{(r,j)+(t,i)}$
Step 7: Triangulate squeezed regions by using
standard polygon triangulation algorithm

Algorithm 87.1 Triangulate annular region R

```
1  Function ConstructAM-Chain (v_a, CH_I, CH_O)
2     Ch = φ;
3     Add v_a to Ch;
4     s = a;
5     Let w_b be the unprocessed vertex of CH_I closest to v_a
6     if w_b is null then  return Ch;
7     Add w_b to Ch;
8     Done = false;
9     s = s + 1;
10    while not Done do
11       if w_b is visible to v_s then
12          Add v_s to Ch;
13       else
14          Done = true;
15          return Ch;
16       b = b + 1;
17       if v_s is visible to w_b then
18          Add w_b to Ch;
19       else
20          Done = true;
21          return Ch;
22
```

Fig. 87.12 Alternate merging function

may not be visible to vertex w_4. This happens if v_5 is very close to v_4 making line segment (v_5, w_4) intersecting with inner boundary. If many vertices are clustered and close to v_4 then all vertices in the cluster may not be visible to w_4. In such cases, enough vertices starting from v_4 are skipped to find the first vertex in the outer boundary visible to w_4. For the clarity of presentation, we assume, without loss of generality, that skipping one vertex is enough. This process of constructing maximal alternating chain is continued until the starting vertex v_0 is not reached again. It is observed that for AM-Chain(v_0), the first vertex v_0 and last vertex v_4 are of odd degree and all other vertices $w_0, v_1, w_1, v_2, w_2, v_3, w_3$ are of even degree.

In Fig. 87.11a, the next alternating chain starts at v_5 which is $<v_5, w_4, v_6, w_5, \ldots, w_{10}, v_{12}>$. The next alternating chain is $<v_{13}, w_{11}, v_{14}, w_{12}, \ldots, w_{13}, v_0>$. Thus the annular chain is covered with three maximal alternating chains.

The interior vertices of all alternating chains are of even degree. The region between two alternating chains can be a polygon with more than three vertices which we call a **squeezed region**. In the example (Fig. 87.11a) there are two squeezed regions each with four vertices. The squeezed regions are triangulated by using any polygon triangulation algorithms [2]. The algorithm can be formally sketched as listed in Algorithm 87.1. Algorithm 87.1 invokes function ConstructAM-Chain (v_a, CH_I, CH_O) which triangulates the region between two chains CHO and CHI starting at v_a by constructing AM-Chain(v_0). It is noted that AM-Chain(v_0) is maximal (Fig. 87.12).

Once the triangulation is available in dcel data structure, it is very convenient to compute several properties of faces,

vertices, and edges [23–25]. For example, we can find the degree of a node in time proportional to the value of the degree. We performed several executions of the program to count the number of even/odd degree nodes on the Delaunay triangulation of randomly generated nodes. The number n of randomly generated nodes is taken as $n = 50, 100, 200, 300, 400, 500, 600, 700$, and 800. For each value of n we generated randomly located nodes five times. The even/odd node degree count values for each five set of nodes are averaged. To generate a randomly located node nd_i, its x-coordinate and y-coordinate are generated by using rand function of Java in the range of the size of the canvas. The results are shown in Table 87.1.

87.4 Discussion

We presented a cursory review of noteworthy results on node degree aware triangulation of polygonal shapes and point sites in two dimensional Euclidean planes. Most results on node degree aware triangulation deal with the characterization and development of efficient algorithms [26]. No algorithmic result has been reported that generates a triangulation that maximizes the number of even degree nodes for input point sites. It is known that the problem of generating degree constrained spanning tree is NP-Hard [9]. This means that it may be worth to explore whether the triangulation problem that maximizes the number of even degree is NP-Hard. Some other constrained triangulations are known to be NP-Hard.

Table 87.1 Tabulation of degree distribution

No of nodes	Odd degree count	Even degree count	Odd percentage	Even percentage
400	206	194	51.5	48.5
400	192	208	48	52
400	196	204	49	51
400	212	188	53	47
400	204	196	51	49
Average	**202**	**198**	**50.5**	**49.5**
500	246	254	49.2	50.8
500	222	278	44.4	55.6
500	242	258	48.4	51.6
500	252	248	50.4	49.6
500	260	240	52	48
Average	**244.4**	**255.6**	**48.88**	**51.12**
600	286	314	47.67	52.33
600	296	304	49.33	50.67
600	292	308	48.67	51.33
600	308	292	51.33	48.67
600	312	288	52	48
Average	**298.8**	**301.2**	**49.8**	**50.2**

As pointed in Sect. 87.2, the minimum weight triangulation problem is NP-Hard [4]. This further gives us hint that the triangulation problem that maximizes the total number of even degree nodes is not easy.

Some structural insight on degree constrained triangulation is needed to settle the problem. The first result we presented is the characterization of node distribution that admits even-degree triangulation. By constructing nested structure we characterize the distribution of point sites that indeed admits even-degree triangulation. The second result we presented is the characterization of the annular region whose triangulation will have most nodes with odd degree. Specifically, we showed that the annular region with an outer chain with (relatively) a large number of vertices and inner chain just a triangle will have a triangulation of which most vertices are of odd degree. We presented an efficient heuristic algorithm (Alternate Marching Algorithm) that triangulates a normal annular region with most vertices of even-degree. The time complexity is $O(n^2)$, where n is the number of vertices in the region. We performed an experimental investigation of node degree distribution on Delaunay triangulation of points generated randomly. The experimental results (Table 87.1) reveal that the average count of even-degree and odd-degree nodes are almost equal—the range is [48–50%].

References

1. M. de Berg, M. van Kreveld, M. Overmars, O. Schwarzkopf, *Computational Geometry: Algorithms and Applications* (Springer-Verlag New York, Inc., Secaucus, NJ, 1997)
2. J. O'Rourke, *Art Gallery Theorems and Algorithms* (Oxford University Press Inc, New York, NY, 1987)
3. T. Auer, M. Held, Heuristics for the generation of random polygons, in *Proceedings of the 28th Canadian Conference on Computational Geometry, CCCG 2016*, (Carleton University, Ottawa, 1996), pp. 38–43
4. W. Mulzer, G. Rote, Minimum-weight triangulation is np-hard. J. ACM **55**(2), 11:1–11:29 (2008)
5. C. Pelaez, A. Ramrez-Vigueras, and J. Urrutia. Triangulations with many points of even degree, in *Proceedings of the 22nd Annual Canadian Conference on Computational Geometry* (2010), pp. 103–106
6. O. Aichholzer, T. Hackl, M. Homann, A. Pilz, G. Rote, B. Speckmann, and B. Vogtenhuber. Plane graphs with parity constraints, in *Algorithms and Data Structures, 11th International Symposium, WADS 2009, Ban, Canada, August 21–23, 2009. Proceedings* (2009), pp. 13–24
7. F. Homann, K. Kriegel, A graph-coloring result and its consequences for polygon-guarding problems. SIAM J. Discret. Math. **9**(2), 210–224 (May 1996)
8. R. Gyawali, *Degree Constrained Triangulation*. Master's thesis (University of Nevada, Las Vegas, 2012)
9. M.R. Garey, D.S. Johnson, *Computers and Intractability: A Guide to the Theory of NP-Completeness* (W. H. Freeman & Co., New York, NY, 1979)

10. E.M. Arkin, M. Held, J.S.B. Mitchell, S.S. Skiena, Hamiltonian triangulations for fast rendering. Vis. Comput. **12**(9), 429–444 (1996)

11. M. Bern, H. Edelsbrunner, D. Eppstein, S. Mitchell, T.S. Tan, Edge insertion for optimal triangulations. Discrete Comput. Geom. **10**(1), 47–65 (1993)

12. T.C. Biedl, A. Lubiw, S. Mehrabi, S. Verdonschot, Rectangle of influence triangulations, in *Proceedings of the 28th Canadian Conference on Com-putational Geometry, CCCG 2016, August 3–5, 2016*, (Simon Fraser University, Vancouver, British Columbia, 2016), pp. 237–243

13. C. Burnikel, K. Mehlhorn, S. Schirra, On degeneracy in geometric computations, in *Proceedings of the Fifth Annual ACM-SIAM Symposium on Dis-crete Algorithms, SODA '94*, (Society for Industrial and Applied Mathematics, Philadelphia, PA, 1994), pp. 16–23

14. B. Chazelle, Triangulating a simple polygon in linear time. Discrete Comput. Geom. **6**(3), 485–524 (1991)

15. S. Fortune, A sweepline algorithm for voronoi diagrams. Algorithmica **2**, 153–174 (1987)

16. L.J. Guibas, D.E. Knuth, M. Sharir, Randomized incremental construction of delaunay and voronoi diagrams. Algorithmica **7**(4), 381–413 (1992)

17. S.K. Ghosh, D.M. Mount, An output-sensitive algorithm for computing visibility graphs. SIAM J. Comput. **20**(5), 888–910 (1991)

18. L. Guibas, J. Stol, Primitives for the manipulation of general subdivisions and the computations of voronoi diagrams. ACM Trans. Graph **4**, 74–123 (1985)

19. S. Hertel, K. Mehlhorn, Fast triangulation of simple polygons, in *Proceedings of the 1983 International FCT-Conference on Fundamentals of Computation Theory*, (Springer-Verlag, London, UK, 1983), pp. 207–218

20. F. Hurtado, M. Noy, The graph of triangulations of a convex polygon, in *Proceedings of the Twelfth Annual Symposium on Computational Geometry, SCG '96*, (ACM, New York, NY, 1996), pp. 407–408

21. F. Hurtado, M. Noy, J. Urrutia, Flipping edges in triangulations, in *Proceedings of the Twelfth Annual Symposium on Computational Geometry, SCG '96*, (ACM, New York, NY, 1996), pp. 214–223

22. D.V. Hutton, Fundamentals of finite element analysis, in *Mcgraw-Hill Series in Mechanical Engineering*, (McGraw-Hill, New York, 2004)

23. C.L. Lawson. Software for c1 surface interpolation, in *Mathematical Software III* (1977), pp. 161–194

24. G.H. Meisters, Polygon have ears. Am. Math. Mon. **82**, 648–651 (1975)

25. D.E. Muller, F.P. Preparata, Finding the intersection of two convex polyhedra. Theor. Comput. Sci. **7**, 217–236 (1978)

26. E. Osherovich, A.M. Bruckstein, All triangulations are reachable via sequences of edge-ips: an elementary proof. Comput. Aided Geom. Des. **25**, 157–161 (2008)

Heuristic Approaches for the Open-Shop Scheduling Problem

Wissam Marrouche and Haidar M. Harmanani

Abstract

The *open-shop scheduling problem* is concerned with the allocation of tasks to resources, especially when resources are scarce. The problem has many practical applications in the production, manufacturing, testing, and telecommunication domains. In this paper, we study the non-preemptive open-shop scheduling problem with more than two machines using two *metaheuristic* algorithms: *cuckoo search* and *ant colony optimization*. The proposed algorithms are implemented using `Python`, and tested on the `Taillard` benchmarks. Favorable results comparisons are reported.

Keywords

Non-preemptive open-shop scheduling · Cuckoo search and ant colony system

88.1 Introduction

Scheduling is an optimization problem that determines when activities are to start and finish especially when resources are scarce. Various scheduling problems have been studied in the literature including, among others, the *shop scheduling* problem which has been classified into *job shop*, *flow shop* and *open-shop scheduling*. Baker et al. [1] provide an extensive review of scheduling problems emerging theory.

A scheduling algorithm maybe classified as *preemptive* or *non-preemptive*. In *preemptive scheduling models* a job maybe interrupted one or more time and resumed later on the same or on another machine. In *non-preemptive* models, once

W. Marrouche · H. M. Harmanani (✉)
Department of Computer Science and Mathematics, Lebanese American University, Byblos, Lebanon
e-mail: haidar@lau.edu.lb

the execution of a job starts on a machine, it must complete on that machine without interruption.

The open-shop scheduling problem (OSSP) was first studied by Gonzalez et al. [11] who showed that the problem of obtaining minimum finish time non-preemptive schedules when the open-shop has more than two machines is $\mathcal{NP}$-hard. The problem was reduced to the partition problem, and shown to have a polynomial time complexity in the case of preemptive schedules [11]. Garey and Johnson [9] formally define the open-shop problem as follows:

Given a number $m \in Z^+$ of processors, a set $\mathcal{J}$ of jobs, each $j \in \mathcal{J}$ consisting of m operations $O_{i,j}$ with $1 \leq i \leq m$ (with $O_{i,j}$ to be executed by processor i), and for each operation a length $l_{i,j} \in N$, find a collection of one-processor schedules $f_i : \mathcal{J} \to N, 1 \leq i \leq m$, such that $f_i(j) > f_i(j')$ implies $f_i(j) > f_i(j') + l_{i,j'}$ such that for each $j \in \mathcal{J}$ the intervals $[f_i(j), f_i(j) + l_{i,j})$ are all disjoint and the completion time of the schedule is minimized:

$$\max_{1 \leq i \leq m, j \in \mathcal{J}} f_i(j) + l_{i,j}$$

Pineda [23] established a lower bound which is valid for all shop problems:

$$\mathcal{LP} = \max \left\{ \max_i \sum_{j=1}^{m} p_{ij}, \max_j \sum_{i=1}^{n} p_{ij} \right\} \quad (88.1)$$

The first part in Eq. (88.1) is concerned with the length of job J_i while the second part is concerned with the total time needed on machine M_j. Although a schedule that achieves $\mathcal{LP}$ must be optimal, the *makespan* for the open-shop scheduling problem is not necessarily equal to $\mathcal{LP}$. In fact, the optimal *makespan* is equal to $\mathcal{LP}$ in the preemptive case as well as in all relaxations that can be solved in polynomial time [13].

Consider the 4×4 Taillard benchmark instance in Table 88.1 which consists of 4 jobs and 4 machines. Obviously, each job is composed of four operations. The ith operation of the jth job requires p_{ij} units of processing time to be

© Springer International Publishing AG, part of Springer Nature 2018
S. Latifi (ed.), *Information Technology – New Generations*, Advances in Intelligent Systems and Computing 738,
https://doi.org/10.1007/978-3-319-77028-4_88

Table 88.1 A 4×4 *Taillard* benchmark instance for the OSSP

	M_1	M_2	M_3	M_4	p_i
J_1	37	46	91	11	185
J_2	91	1	10	76	178
J_3	7	91	4	61	163
J_4	50	36	42	30	158
Z_j	185	174	147	178	185

completed on the ith machine. Any feasible schedule would last for at least 185 units, the $\mathcal{LP}$ value in this case. No two operations of the same job may be processed concurrently, nor may any single machine process two jobs simultaneously. Figure 88.1 shows a graphical representation of a possible solution with an optimal *makespan* of 189. One can easily observe inactivity periods, mostly on M_3.

In this work, we propose two heuristic non-preemptive scheduling algorithms based on *Ant Colony Optimization (ACO)* and *Cuckoo Search (CS)* for solving the non-preemptive *open-shop scheduling problem (OSSP)*. The rest of this paper is organized as follows. Section 88.2 reviews the current literature related to the open-shop-scheduling problem. Section 88.3 presents the open-shop problem implementation using cuckoo search while Sect. 88.4 presents the ant colony optimization formulation. Experimental results are provided in Sect. 88.5, and concluding remarks are presented in Sect. 88.6.

88.2   Related Work

Early solutions for the open-shop scheduling problem focused mostly on *branch and bound* approaches [3, 4, 12]. However, these approaches were not efficient when dealing with the problem's large search space. Other researchers proposed *metaheuristic techniques*. For example, Yamada et al. [28] proposed the first serious approach for solving the job shop scheduling problem based on genetic algorithms. Liaw [17] introduced an iterative improvement approach based on decomposition for solving the open-shop scheduling problem. The same author proposed heuristic approaches based on simulated annealing [19], tabu search [18], and genetic algorithms [20]. Prins [24] presented a genetic algorithm that uses problem-specific heuristics in order to minimize the *makespan*. Khuri et al. [16] compared three different genetic algorithm implementations: permutation-based, hybrid, and selfish-gene. Chen et al. [5] proposed an ant colony optimization algorithm for solving the flow shop scheduling. Blum [2] introduced a new approach, Beam-ACO, which hybridizes the solution construction mechanism of ant colony optimization with beam search while

Shaa et al. [25] proposed a particle swarm optimization algorithm. Yu et al. [31] proposed a solution for the open-shop and flow shop scheduling problems based on routing. Recently, Chen et al. [6] introduced an algorithm for solving the parallel open-shop scheduling problem. Van et al. [26] presented an adaptive open-shop scheduling problem for solving the optical resource scheduling problem. Hassan et al. [15] proposed a mathematical model for solving the open-shop scheduling problem based on the derivation of classes of valid inequalities. However, the method can optimally solve only small size instances. Bou Ghosn et al. [10] proposed a parallel genetic algorithm with genetic operators that combine *deterministic* and *random moves*. The method is implemented using MPI on a Beowulf cluster. Harmanani et al. [14] proposed a simulated annealing algorithm in order to solve the non-preemptive open-shop scheduling problem.

88.3   Cuckoo Search OSSP

Cuckoo Search is a nature-inspired *metaheuristic* algorithm that was proposed by Yang et al. [29]. The algorithm is inspired by the cuckoo bird aggressive breeding behavior. Cuckoo birds are *brood* parasites who place their eggs in the nest of other host species. If the host discovers that an egg is not its own, it may either throw it away, or abandon the nest and build a new one at a different location. Otherwise, it would take care of the egg presuming it is its own.

88.3.1 Cuckoo Search Algorithm

The cuckoo brood behavior is used to develop an effective optimization algorithm. The algorithm iterates for a number of generations where each generation is represented by a set of nests whose number is fixed. A cuckoo lays one egg (schedule) at a time in a randomly selected nest. All nests are evaluated based on their fitness, and the most fit nest will survive to the next generation. The fitness of the solution is improved during each generation by generating a candidate solution using a Lévy flight from the current solution. If the candidate solution is found to be better than a randomly chosen existing solution then the least fit solution is replaced with the new one. Since the host bird may discover the cuckoo *egg* with a probability $p_a \in [0, 1]$, the algorithm replaces the least fit $p_a\%$ solutions during every generation. This efficiently deals with the problem of convergence on local sub-optimal solutions. The algorithm is typically improved using Lévy flights since they are more efficient in exploring the search space than simple random walks.

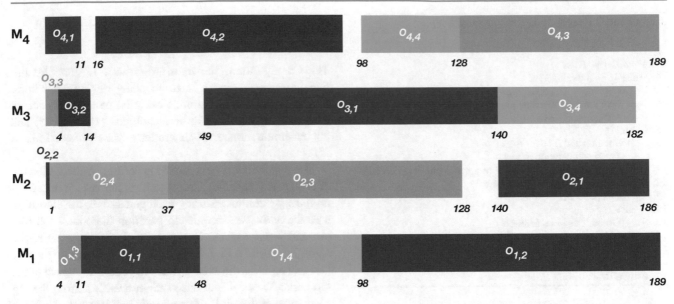

Fig. 88.1 Optimal schedule for Taillard 4 × 4-6 (Table 88.1)

Algorithm 1 Modified open-shop cuckoo search algorithm [27]

1: $p_a \leftarrow 0.75$ ▷ Percentage of the least fit nests to be abandoned
2: *MaxGenerations* $\leftarrow 350$ ▷ Number of generations
3: *popSize* $\leftarrow 15$ ▷ Population size
4: Create a random population
5: Rank the population according to *makespan*
6: **for** g = 1 to MaxGenerations **do**
7:     Partition the population into *top* and *bottom* nests based on p_a
8:     **for all** $X_i \in \{$bottom nests$\}$ **do**   ▷ Abandon the least fit nests
9:         Use Lévy flight to create a new nest X_k
10:         Replace X_i with X_k
11:     **end for**
12:     Rank the population according to *fitness*
13:     **for all** $X_i \in \{$top nests$\}$ **do**
14:         Select a random top nest X_j
15:         **if** $(X_i = X_j)$ **then**
16:             Use Lévy flight to create a new nest X_k
17:             Select a random nest X_l
18:             **if** $($Cost $(X_k) <$ Cost $(X_l))$ **then**
19:                 Replace X_l with X_k
20:             **end if**
21:         **else**
22:             Move a distance from X_i to create a new nest X_k
23:             Select a random nest X_l
24:             **if** Cost $(X_k) <$ Cost (X_l) **then**
25:                 Replace X_l with X_k
26:             **end if**
27:         **end if**
28:     **end for**
29: **end for**
30: Return the best schedule and its *makespan*

88.3.2 Initial Solution

The initial solutions are generated based on random permutations between 0 and $(\mathcal{J} \times \mathcal{M}) - 1$, where $\mathcal{J}$ is the number of jobs and $\mathcal{M}$ is the number of machines. The schedules are feasible by construction, and the algorithm ensures that the gaps between the jobs are minimized using the rescheduling transformation (Algorithm 2).

88.3.3 Lévy Flight(X_i)

A Lévy flight is a random walk that represents a probability distribution that is self-similar, but with infinite variance, and features scale-invariant fractals [22]. Lévy flights are essential in cuckoo search as they help exploring the neighborhood of existing solutions. Thus, the algorithm selects a nest X_i from either the upper or bottom nests where the bottom nests are the nests to be abandoned. Next, the algorithm randomly selects a machine, and permutes all its allocated operations. Since the transformation may result in an unfeasible solution, the algorithm reschedules all the operations in order to ensure that we get a new valid nest, X_k.

88.3.4 Move Distance

While the *Lévy flight* transformation ensures local search, the *move distance* transformation ensures hill-climbing by migrating one-machine schedules from one nest to another. Thus, the algorithm selects two random nests X_i and X_j and migrates one-machine schedule from nests X_i in the direction of X_j with a probability $P_d = 50\%$ in order to form a new nest X_k. In fact, X_k is simply a random combination of distinct one-machine schedules selected from X_i and X_j. The algorithm next reschedules X_k in order to ensure a valid new nest.

Algorithm 2 Rescheduling transformation

1: $U \leftarrow \{O_{1k}, O_{2k}, ..., O_{mk}\}$ ▷ Operations orderings
2: $i = 1$
3: $Violation \leftarrow False$
4: **while** $U \neq \emptyset$ **do**
5:     Get operation O_{ik} and assign it to machine k
6:     **if** there are inter-machine job dependencies **then**
7:         $Violation \leftarrow True$
8:     **end if**
9:     **if** violation and (i != m) **then**
10:         Get next operation in List
11:         Put back the operation in U in order to preserve the order
12:     **else if** violation and (i == m) **then**
13:         Postpone O_{ik}
14:     **else**
15:         Commit O_{ik} to machine k
16:     **end if**
17:     i++
18: **end while**
19: **return** Best

88.3.5 Rescheduling Transformation

Creating initial random schedules, permuting operations in schedules, or migrating one-machine schedules from one schedule to another may result in either large idle times in the machine schedules or violations across machines since (1) no operation can be processed on more than one machine at a time, (2) nor may a single machine process two jobs simultaneously.

The rescheduling transformation determines the start times of the operations assigned to a specific machine in a greedy fashion. The transformation iterates over the operations and dispatches one operation O_{ik} at a time, and checks for the above two constraints before committing the operation. If there are any violations then the algorithm postpones the current operation and attempts to schedule operation $i + 1$ in a rotating manner, i.e. returning to O_{ik}; thus, preserving as much as possible the ordering of the operations. Once all operations have been scheduled, the algorithm delays the operations that are causing violations by x cycles so that to resolve all dependencies and violations.

88.3.6 Fitness Function

The objective of the open-shop scheduling problem is to determine a sequence of operations for each job so that the makespan, C_{max}, is minimized. Thus, the problem reduces to finding a set of minimal one-machine schedules. The fitness function is given by:

$$F = \frac{1}{C_{max}} \qquad (88.2)$$

88.3.7 Cuckoo Search Open-Shop Scheduling Algorithm

The CS algorithm, shown in Algorithm 1, starts by initializing a population of size 15 using random schedules, and by setting the algorithm's essential parameters such as the percentage of eggs to be abandoned ($P_a = 0.75$) and the maximum number of generations, $MaxGenerations = 350$.

The population is next ranked according to the *makespan* of each nest (schedule). The algorithm iterates for *MaxGenerations* generations. During each generation, the algorithm uses the *makespan* in order to partition the population into *top* and *bottom* nests. For each of the bottom nests, the algorithm performs a *Lévy flight* in order to generate a new nest that replaces the existing nest. In contrast, for each of the top nests, X_i, we select one random nest, X_j, from the top nests to be replaced. If the randomly selected nest X_j is the same as the present top nest, then a *Lévy flight* is performed from X_i to generate a new nest X_k. Finally, another nest, X_l, is randomly selected from the entire population. If the *makespan* of X_k is less than that of X_l, then the nest X_l is replaced with X_k (Fig. 88.2).

88.4 Ant Colony Optimization OSSP

Ant colony optimization (ACO) is a recent *metaheuristic* approach that is used to approximate solutions for complex combinatorial optimization problems [8]. The algorithm is inspired by the behavior of real ants foraging behavior where ants communicate with each others using a chemical substance called *pheromone* in order to find the shortest path from the nest to the food source. By sensing pheromone trails, foragers can follow the path to food discovered by other ants. Thus, the shortest routes will have a high concentration of pheromones as almost all ants end up using this path. In other words, the main difference between the ACO and the CS implementations is that schedules in the case of the ACO are not solely selected based on the *makespan* but also based on the pheromones values.

88.4.1 Pheromones Updates

There has been various improvements for the ACO algorithm since it was first proposed [7]. In this work, we implement an *exploitative* version that uses an elitist approach to update the pheromones where we only increase the pheromones of the best discovered trails so far [21]. The algorithm uses a learning approach based on the following:

$$(1 - \alpha)p_i + \alpha \times \text{Fitness}(\text{Best}) \qquad (88.3)$$

Fig. 88.2 Illustrating the ACO algorithm

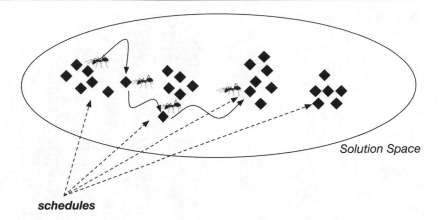

Solution Space

schedules

88.4.2 Initial Trails Generation

The ACO algorithm starts by constructing a disjunctive graph from all the jobs. The algorithm generates next a population of 2500 trails or feasible candidate schedules. The fitness of each trail is next evaluated. Initially, all pheromones are set to $\gamma = 1$.

88.4.3 Trails Selection

During each iteration, we select, subject to a probability $(p = 0.5)$, a trail that has the highest desirability, combining values and pheromones, with a probability q where desirability is equal to:

$$p_i^\delta \times \left(\frac{1}{\text{makespan(schedule}_i))} \right)^\epsilon \qquad (88.4)$$

Otherwise, we select a trail in a desirability-proportionate way, in a similar way to spinning a *roulette wheel* where the probability of each possible trail, q_i, determines a slice on the wheel. Thus, the algorithm computes the cumulative probability. The wheel is next spun, and a random number r, $0 < r < q$ is drawn, and a wedge on the wheel is selected by ensuring that r falls in the interval $q_{i-1} < r \le q_i$ on the wheel.

88.4.4 OSSP ACO Algorithm

The proposed method simulates the ant colony search using two types of *population:* the *jobs* that make up the schedules, and the candidate schedules or *trails* with the best *fitness* and *pheromone* values. The algorithm starts by building 2500 trails or candidate solutions. The algorithm next improves the trails using the steepest ascent hill-climbing with replacement approach, shown in Algorithm 4. Thus, the algorithm iterates for 40 times over the trails, selecting a random trail in every iteration and permuting the order of execution of two randomly selected operations on a one-machine schedule. The algorithm reschedules the one-machine schedule in order to ensure that the solution is valid. During each generation, the algorithm selects a trail in an elitist fashion and assesses its fitness. The pheromone value is updated accordingly.

88.5 Results

We implemented the proposed algorithms, *Cuckoo Search* as well as *Ant Colony Optimization*, using `Python` on a Linux machine. We verified both algorithms using the `Taillard Benchmark` instances. The first 20 `Taillard Benchmark` instances correspond to small size problems (4×4) and (5×5) while the next 20 instances correspond to medium size problems (7×7) and (10×10). The last 20 instances are large size problems (15×15) and (20×20). For each problem we provide the lower bound $(\mathcal{LP})$, the known best, and the *makespans* that were generated by our methods.

In order to tune the cuckoo search parameters, we varied the number of nests as well as the probability p_a. We have used $n = 15, 20, 25, 30$, and 35 as these ranges were suggested in the literature [30]. As for the probability, $p_a = 0.75$ was determined based on our simulation to be sufficient for our problem. As for the ACO parameters shown in Table 88.3, they were determined based on a combination of best practices and empirical analysis. Thus, we determined that a population size of 100 and 2500 initial trails were sufficient for our problem.

Figures 88.3, 88.4, and 88.5 illustrate the problem complexity through three optimal schedules that were derived by our system: 10×10, 15×15, and 20×20. The system also generated a graphical representation of the schedule. Table 88.2 illustrates the results obtained by our systems, compared to the lower bound as well as to the best known optimal answers in each case of the benchmark instances.

Table 88.2 Taillard benchmark results

Instance	$\mathcal{LP}$	Known best	ACS	CS	Instance	$\mathcal{LP}$	Known best	ACS	CS
4×4-1	186	193	193	193	10×10-1	637	637	638	639
4×4-2	229	236	236	236	10×10-2	588	588	588	688
4×4-3	262	271	271	271	10×10-3	598	598	599	600
4×4-4	245	250	245	252	10×10-4	577	577	577	577
4×4-5	287	295	295	295	10×10-5	640	640	640	640
4×4-6	185	189	189	189	10×10-6	538	538	538	538
4×4-7	197	201	201	201	10×10-7	616	616	616	616
4×4-8	212	217	217	217	10×10-8	595	595	595	595
4×4-9	258	261	261	261	10×10-9	595	595	595	595
4×4-10	213	217	217	217	10×10-10	596	596	596	596
5×5-1	295	300	301	301	15×15-1	937	937	937	937
5×5-2	255	262	262	262	15×15-2	918	918	918	918
5×5-3	321	323	331	335	15×15-3	871	871	871	871
5×5-4	306	310	315	314	15×15-4	934	934	934	934
5×5-5	321	326	331	329	15×15-5	946	946	946	946
5×5-6	307	312	317	318	15×15-6	933	933	933	933
5×5-7	298	303	308	305	15×15-7	891	891	891	891
5×5-8	292	300	304	303	15×15-8	893	893	893	893
5×5-9	349	353	358	358	15×15-9	899	899	902	904
5×5-10	321	326	329	329	15×15-10	902	902	902	902
7×7-1	435	435	435	436	20×20-1	1155	1155	1155	1155
7×7-2	443	443	445	447	20×20-2	1241	1242	1242	1243
7×7-3	468	468	479	472	20×20-3	1257	1257	1257	1257
7×7-4	463	463	467	466	20×20-4	1248	1248	1248	1248
7×7-5	416	416	419	416	20×20-5	1256	1256	1256	1256
7×7-6	451	451	460	454	20×20-6	1204	1204	1204	1204
7×7-7	422	422	435	425	20×20-7	1294	1294	1295	1294
7×7-8	424	423	424	424	20×20-8	1169	1169	1176	1175
7×7-0	458	458	458	458	20×20-9	1289	1289	1289	1289
7×7-10	397	398	398	399	20×20-10	1241	1241	1241	1241

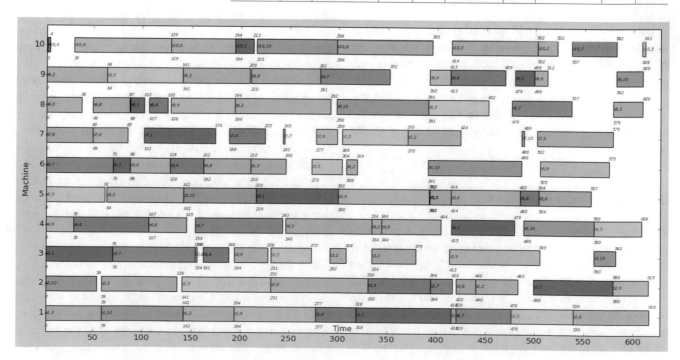

Fig. 88.3 Solution for the 10×10 *Taillard* benchmark, instance 7

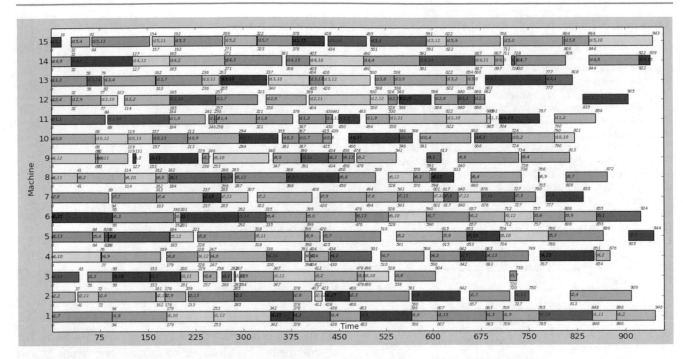

Fig. 88.4 Solution for the 15×15 *Taillard* benchmark, instance 5

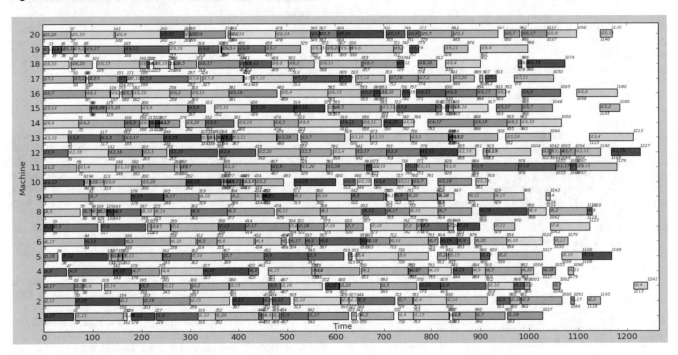

Fig. 88.5 Solution for the 20×20 *Taillard* benchmark, instance 10

Algorithm 3 The ant colony system (ACS)

```
1:  C ← {C₁, C₂, ..., Cₙ} Components
2:  popsize ← number of trails to construct at once
3:  α ← elitist learning rate
4:  β ← evaporation rate
5:  γ ← initial value for pheromones
6:  δ ← Tuning parameter for heuristics in component selection
7:  ε ← tuning parameter for pheromones in component selection
8:  t ← iterations to Hill-Climb
9:  q ← probability of selecting components in an elitist way
10: p ← [p₁, .., pₙ] pheromones of the components, all set to γ
11: Generate random valid solutions
12: Best ← Best randomly generated solution so far
13: repeat
14:     P ← ∅                              ▷ Candidate solutions
15:     for i = 1 to popsize do
16:         S ← ∅                          ▷ Build some trails
17:         if a relatively small probability (15 %) then
18:             S ← Valid solutions selected randomly in an elitist way
19:         else
20:             repeat
21:                 if C' ← component in C − S then
22:                     if C' is empty then
23:                         S ← ∅
24:                     else
25:                         S ← S ∪ {Component selected from C'}
26:                     end if
27:                 end if
28:             until S is a complete trail
29:         end if
30:     end for
31:     S ← Hill-Climb(S) for t iterations
32:     AssessFitness(S)
33:     if Fitness(S) > Fitness(Best) then
34:         Best ← S
35:     end if
36:     for each pᵢ ∈ p do do        ▷ Decrease pheromones (evaporation)
37:         pᵢ ← (1 − β)pᵢ + βγ
38:     end for
39:     for each component Sᵢ do
40:         if Sᵢ was used in Best then
41:             pᵢ ← (1 − α)pᵢ + α Fitness(Best);
42:         end if
43:     end for
44: until Best is the desired sub-optimal solution or we have run out of
    time
45: return Best
```

Table 88.3 Parameters settings of ACO for our simulation

Parameter	γ	α	β	t	Pop size	Schedules	MaxTime
Value	0.05	0.75	0.5	40	100	2500	10

It is clear from the results that although both algorithms achieved mostly optimum answers, the results from the ACO slightly outperformed the Cuckoo search results. However, the running time for CS was much faster than ACO. Also, it was much easier to tune CS since we only had to deal with three parameters (Table 88.3).

Algorithm 4 Steepest ascent hill-climbing

```
1:  n ← 40                  ▷ Number of attempts to sample the gradient
2:  CurrentSch ← Randomly selected one-machine schedule
3:  repeat
4:      NewSch ← Permute(CurrentSch)
5:      for i = 0 to n − 1 do
6:          Temp ← Permute(CurrentSch)
7:          if fitness(Temp) > fitness(NewSch) then
8:              NewSch ← Temp
9:          end if
10:     end for
11:     if fitness(NewSch) > fitness(CurrentSch) then
12:         CurrentSch ← NewSch
13:     end if
14: until CurrentSch is the desired schedule or we have run out of time
15: return CurrentSch
```

88.6 Conclusion

This paper presented two *metaheuristic* algorithms for solving the non-preemptive open-shop scheduling problem. The algorithms are based on cuckoo search and dynamic ants optimization, and yielded optimal solutions in almost all attempted benchmarks.

References

1. K. Baker, D. Trietsch, *Principles to Sequencing and Scheduling* (Wiley, London, 2009)
2. C. Blum, Beam-ACO—hybridizing ant colony optimization with beam search: an application to open shop scheduling. Comput. Oper. Res. **32**(6), 1565–1591 (2005)
3. P. Brucker, J. Huring, B. Wostmann, A branch and bound algorithm for the open shop problem. Discret. Appl. Math. **76**, 43–59 (1997)
4. J. Carlier, E. Pinson, An algorithm for solving the job shop problem. Manag. Sci. **35**(2), 164–176 (1989)
5. R. Chen, S. Lo, C. Wu, T. Lin, An effective ant colony optimization-based algorithm for flow shop scheduling, in *IEEE Conference on Soft Computing in Industrial Applications* (2008), pp. 101–106
6. Y. Chen, A. Zhang, G. Chen, J. Dong, Approximation algorithms for parallel open shop scheduling. Inf. Process. Lett. **113**(7), 220–224 (2013)
7. M. Dorigo, Optimization, learning and natural algorithms, Ph.D. thesis, Politecnico di Milano, 1992
8. M. Dorigo, T. Stützle, *Ant Colony Optimization* (MIT Press, Cambridge, MA, 2004)
9. M.R. Garey, D.S. Johnson, *Computers and Intractability: A Guide to the Theory of NP-Completeness* (W. H. Freeman, San Francisco, CA, 1979)
10. S.B. Ghosn, F. Drouby, H. Harmanani, A parallel genetic algorithm for the open-shop scheduling problem using deterministic and random moves. Int. J. Artif. Intell. **14**(1), 130–144 (2016)
11. T. Gonzalez, S. Sahni, Open shop scheduling to minimize finish time. J. Assoc. Comput. Mach. **23**(4), 665–679 (1976)

12. C. Gueret, C. Prins, Classical and new heuristics for the open-shop problem: a computational evaluation. Eur. J. Oper. Res. **107**, 306–314 (1998)
13. C. Guéret, C. Prins, A new lower bound for the open-shop problem. Ann. Oper. Res. **92**, 165–183 (1999)
14. H. Harmanani, S. Bou Ghosn, An efficient method for the open-shop scheduling problem using simulated annealing, in *Information Technology: New Generations: 13th International Conference on Information Technology* (Springer, Cham, 2016), pp. 1183–1193
15. M. Hassan, I. Kacem, S. Martin, I.M. Osman, Mathematical formulation for open shop scheduling problem, in *International Conference on Control, Decision and Information Technologies (CoDIT)* (2017), pp. 803–808
16. S. Khuri, S. Miryala, Genetic algorithms for solving open shop scheduling problems, in *Proceedings of the Portuguese Conference on Artificial Intelligence* (1999), pp. 357–368
17. C.-F. Liaw, An iterative improvement approach for the nonpreemptive open shop scheduling problem. Eur. J. Oper. Res. **111**, 509–517 (1998)
18. C.-F. Liaw, A tabu search algorithm or the open shop scheduling problem. Comput. Oper. Res. **26**(2), 109–126 (1999)
19. C.-F. Liaw, Applying simulated annealing to the open shop scheduling problem. IIE Trans. Schedul. Logist. **31**(5), 457–465 (1999)
20. C.-F. Liaw, A hybrid genetic algorithm for the open shop scheduling problem. Eur. J. Oper. Res. **124**, 28–42 (2000)
21. S. Luke, *Essentials of Metaheuristics* (Lulu, Morrisville, NC, 2013)
22. I. Pavlyukevich, Lévy flights, non-local search and simulated annealing. J. Comput. Phys. **226**, 1830–1844 (2007)
23. M. Pineda, *Scheduling: Theory, Algorithms, and Systems* (Prentice Hall, Englewood Cliffs, NJ, 1995)
24. C. Prins, Competitive genetic algorithms for the open-shop scheduling problem. Math. Meth. Oper. Res. **52**(3), 389–411 (2000)
25. D.Y. Shaa, C.-Y. Hsu, A new particle swarm optimization for the open shop scheduling problem. Comput. Oper. Res. **35**, 3243–3261 (2008)
26. D.P. Van, M. Fiorani, L. Wosinska, J. Chen, Adaptive open-shop scheduling for optical interconnection networks. J. Lightwave Technol. **35**(13), 2503–2513 (2017)
27. S. Walton, O. Hassan, K. Morgan, M.R. Brown, Modified cuckoo search: a new gradient free optimisation algorithm. Chaos, Solitons Fractals **44**, 710–718 (2011)
28. T. Yamada, R. Nakano, A genetic algorithm applicable to large-scale job-shop problems, in *Parallel Problem Solving from Nature* (1992), pp. 281–290
29. X.-S. Yang, S. Deb, Cuckoo search via Lévy flights, in *World Congress on Nature and Biologically Inspired Computing NaBIC* (2009), pp. 210–214
30. X.-S. Yang, S. Deb, Engineering optimisation by cuckoo search. Int. J. Math. Model. Numer. Optim. **1**(4), 330–343 (2010)
31. W. Yu, Z. Liu, L. Wanga, T. Fan, Routing open shop and flow shop scheduling problems. Discret. Optim. **213**, 24–36 (2011)

James Andro-Vasko, Surya Ravali Avasarala, and Wolfgang Bein

Abstract

In the continuous power-down problem one considers a device, which has states OFF, ON, and an infinite number of intermediate states. The state of the device can be switched at any time. In the OFF state the device consumes zero energy and in the ON state it works at its full power consumption. The intermediate states consume only some fraction of energy proportional to usage time but switching back to the ON state has various switch up cost depending on the state. Requests for service, i.e. for when the device has to be in the ON state, are not known in advance; power-down problems are thus studied in the framework of online competitive analysis. Power-down can be used to model the control of traditional power generation in an electrical grid predominantly supplied by renewable energy. We analyze a number of systems, namely "linear", "optimal-following", "progressive", "logarithmic" as well as "exponential", and give competitive ratios for these systems. We show that highly competitive systems must have schedules which are accelerated from the offline solution.

Keywords

Green computing · Power-down systems · Online competitive analysis · Renewable energy · Game theory

89.1 Introduction

We consider a device which has two states, called ON, OFF, and additionally a continuous set of intermediate states. The

J. Andro-Vasko · S. R. Avasarala · W. Bein (✉)
Department of Computer Science, University of Nevada, Las Vegas, NV, USA
e-mail: androvas@unlv.nevada.edu; avasaral@unlv.nevada.edu; wolfgang.bein@unlv.edu

set of states is $r \in [0, 1]$, where the value 0 is mapped to the ON-state and the value 1 is mapped to the OFF state and the interval $(0, 1)$ is mapped to the intermediate states. The running cost of the device in the ON state is proportional to the time of usage and the device in the OFF state consumes zero amount of energy; the intermediate states serve as sleep states, where the running cost is also proportional to time, but at smaller cost $0 < a(r) < 1$. There is no cost to switching from ON to OFF or any of the intermediate states, but a fixed cost $0 < d(r) < c$ occurs to switching from any of the intermediate states to ON.

To manage power usage, power-down mechanisms are widely used: for background on algorithmic approaches to power down see [6, 7]. Power-down is also related to "speed-scaling" of CPUs [3]. In earlier papers [4, 5] we have considered the case where there are a finite number of $(k - 2)$ intermediate states $1, \ldots, k - 2$, which are called k state systems (i.e., there are $(k - 2)$ states plus states ON and OFF for a total of k states.) Finite state systems are common in electronic control, such as power optimization for hand-held devices, laptop computers, work stations and data centers [1, 2, 13, 14]. Continuous system are useful to model power-down phenomena in the electrical grid [9]. When renewables produce a surplus of energy, such surplus generally does not affect the operation of traditional power plants. Instead, renewables are throttled down or the surplus is simply ignored. But when a majority of power is generated by renewables this is not tenable. Instead traditional power plant output needs be throttled down or switched off.

Power-down problems are studied in the framework of online competitive analysis, see [4, 6, 7]. In online computation, an algorithm must make decisions without knowledge of future inputs. Onli orithms can be analyzed in terms of competitiveness, a measure of performance that compares the solution obtained online with the optimal offline solution for the same problem, where the lowest possible competitiveness is best. Online competitive models have the advantage that no statistical insights are needed, instead a worst case view is taken: this is appropriate as, for example, short term gaps in renewable energy supply are hard to predict. It be could argued that a game-theoretic approach which assumes an omniscient adversary may not be so realistic for modeling the grid. However, worst case analysis gives a performance guarantee in the absence of reliable forecasting. To add to this, there have been unusual weather patterns in recent years suspected by some climate scientists [12] as related to a change in the Arctic Oscillation (OA) and North Atlantic Oscillation (NAO). In order to construct a truly resilient grid, worst case assumptions should thus be taken into account.

Our Contribution In this paper we study power-down problems with an infinite number of states. Such systems have not been the focus of extensive research as the algorithm community is generally more interested in general results with a finite number of states. We develop here the continuous model in the framework of online competitive analysis. We give a closed form solution for the offline problem and analyze five different online power-down schemes: linear, optimal-following, progressive, Logarithmic and exponential. The paper is organized as follows: In Sect. 89.2 we further develop the online model and Sect. 89.3 defines the continuous system together with five online strategies. Section 89.4 gives all simulation results and in Sect. 89.5 we give concluding remarks.

89.2 Online Computation and the Smart Grid

Models which employ queuing theory, Markov chains or Petri nets often rely on assumptions as to when the system may be more active or idle. For example in the traditional power grid, it is assumed that at night the demand for power is lower than during the day. During different seasons of the year, the power demand changes and thus scheduling power demand can be more easily predicted [10]. With renewable, decentralized power production such predictions are much more precarious. Here the competitive ratio for an online algorithm acts as a guarantee no matter how unusual the configuration becomes.

An online algorithm makes its decisions without knowledge of future input. For the power-down problem this means that an online algorithm has to decide whether to switch states without knowing what the next request will be. This is in contrast to on offline algorithm which operates on full

knowledge of the entire request sequence in advance. We say that algorithm A has competitive ratio C for a given request sequence σ, if

$$Cost_A(\sigma) \leq c \cdot Cost_{opt}(\sigma)$$

where $Cost_A(\sigma)$ is the cost of A to serve σ and $Cost_{opt}(\sigma)$ is the cost of the optimal offline algorithm on that same request sequence. If the inequality holds for all possible input sequences, then we say that the online algorithm is C-competitive; furthermore the competitive ratio for a given algorithm A is defined as the smallest such C possible. The goal is thus to find the best online algorithm possible, i.e. the online algorithm with the smallest competitive ratio—that ratio is also referred to as the competitive ratio of the problem. For a comprehensive overview on online competitive analysis see [11].

Returning now to the formulation of the power-down problem, at any time the device may be in any state but it must be turned to the ON state when service is requested. Let $t_1^s, \ldots, t_n^s$ and $t_1^e, \ldots, t_n^e$ be non-negative real values that represent requests for service between start of service times t_i^s and end of the service times t_i^e, $(i = 1, 2, \ldots, n)$. The sequence satisfies $0 \leq t_1^s < t_1^e < t_2^s < t_2^e < \cdots < t_n^s < t_n^e$. Thus, at time t_i^s the state of device must be in ON until time t_i^e. In between requests the device can remain in the ON state or go to the OFF state or any of the intermediate states. Note that if t_{i+1}^s is shortly after t_i^e it may be wasteful to turn the device off and it could instead be better to leave the machine on or perhaps keep the device in any of the intermediate states. We note that during usage, the device must be kept on; this is true for the offline as well the online algorithm. Thus from the standpoint of competitive analysis the length of the service $t_i^e - t_i^s$ is irrelevant—the issue is only whether the machine switches to a new state at time t_i^e—and we can thus assume without loss of generality that usage times of the device are infinitesimal. Therefore, we redefine the input sequence as where $t_i := t_i^s = t_i^e$ and define a request sequence in terms of the arrival time of request i.

89.3 The Continuous State Problem

In the continuous state problem, we choose continuous functions for the idle costs and for the power up costs, namely the idle cost curve is given as $a(r) = 1 - r^a$ and a power up cost curve is given as $d(r) = cr^d$ where $r \in [0, 1]$ is the power state and $a, d, c > 0$ are control parameters. In Fig. 89.1 these curves are shown for $a = 3, d = 5, c = 1.5$.

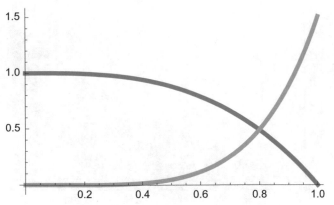

Fig. 89.1 $a(r)$ and $d(r)$ curves

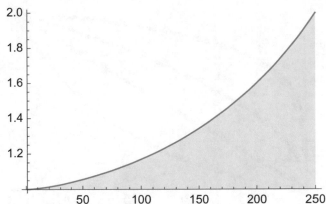

Fig. 89.3 Competitive ratio

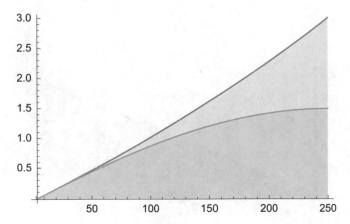

Fig. 89.2 Cost of OPT and ONLINE

$$\frac{ax_m}{C \cdot d} = 1$$

$$x_m = \frac{c \cdot d}{a}$$

The online algorithm starts from its initial state and transitions to lower power states until the next request arrives. In systems with finite states one considers the "Lower Envelope Algorithm (LEA)" [7] where the online algorithms mimics the behavior of the optimal offline algorithm. The first strategy considered in this paper is a continuous version of LEA, we have $\text{Strategy}_{\text{ONLINE}}(r) = \text{Strategy}_{\text{OFF}}(r)$, and thus

$$\text{Cost}_{\text{OFF}}(r) = r \cdot a(\text{Strategy}_{\text{OFF}}(r)) + d(\text{Strategy}_{\text{OFF}}(r))$$

and the cost of the online algorithm will be

$$\text{Cost}_{\text{ONLINE}}(r) = \int_0^r a(\text{Strategy}_{\text{ONLINE}}(r))dr$$
$$+ d(\text{Strategy}_{\text{ONLINE}}(r)).$$

The cost curves and competitive ratio curve from Figs. 89.2 and 89.3, show similar behavior to the LEA, the competitive ratio grows as the idle duration increases and once the idle duration reaches the value of x_m, the competitive ratio is maximized, and thus this strategy is 2-competitive. This behavior occurs due to the fact that the strategy used by the online algorithm is identical to the offline algorithm.

Thus it is of interest to see what would be required of strategies with "better than 2" competitiveness. In what follows we have experimented with the a number of online strategies—mainly based on decelerated or accelerated schedules when compared to the power-down behavior of the offline algorithm. Specifically we have analyzed the following functions:

Using the two curves, we will develop a strategy for the online and offline model as to when to switch to lower power states while idling.

As with the discrete model, the power state of the offline algorithm can determine the idle period length ahead of time; we simply take the derivative of $a(r) + d(r)$ and obtain the function $\text{Stategy}_{\text{OFF}}(r) = (\frac{a \cdot r}{d \cdot c})^{\frac{1}{d-a}}$. Since the offline model chooses the state to minimize the cost from the start of the idle period to when the job arrives, the curve $\text{Stategy}_{\text{OFF}}(r)$ is the optimal cost for this system. In the offline model the idle duration is known in advance, thus we compute a threshold value x_m, which denotes the time when the machine powers down. In effect, if a request arrives after time x_m the machine will be in the lowest power state (the OFF state), before processing the request, which means the machine will have to do a complete power up from OFF state to the ON state before processing the request. We derive this result by determining the time length needed in the idle duration to reach state 1. The calculation can be seen below.

$$\left(\frac{a \cdot x_m}{d \cdot c}\right)^{\frac{1}{d-a}} = 1$$

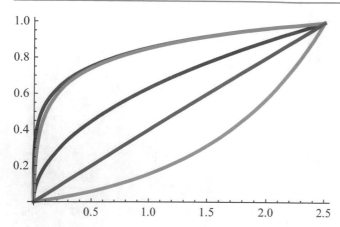

Fig. 89.4 Linear, Logarithmic$(200, r)$, Exp$(1, r)$, Progressive$_{0.312, 0.1}(r)$ Strategy curves

$$\text{Linear}(r) = r/x_m \tag{89.1}$$

$$\text{Logarithmic}(C, r) = \ln(Cr)/\ln(Cx_m + 1) \tag{89.2}$$

$$\text{Exp}(C, r) = (e^{Cr} - 1)/(e^{Cx_m} - 1) \tag{89.3}$$

$$\text{Progressive}_{t,z}(r) = \text{Strategy}_{\text{OFF}}(r)(1 + r^{t+z} - r^{1+z}) \tag{89.4}$$

The values C, t, and z are parameters controlling acceleration and deceleration of the online strategies.

In Fig. 89.4, we show how the strategies change states during the idle duration. We see that the curves for the Linear strategy and Exp$(1, r)$ are both below Strategy$_{\text{OFF}}$, i.e. they are changing to lower power states at a slower rate. The curves for strategies Logarithmic$(200, r)$ and Progressive$_{0.312, 0.1}(r)$ are both above the curve of Strategy$_{\text{OFF}}$, which indicates that these two curves are transitioning to lower power states at faster rates than the optimal offline curve.

89.4 Simulation Results

We now analyze the three strategies "Linear", "Exp", and "Logarithmic", as well as "Progressive".

Figures 89.5, 89.6, and 89.7 show the costs for algorithms which use the strategies that transition to lower states less aggressively ("Linear", "Exp") and more aggressively ("Logarithmic"). The Exp and Linear strategies have better costs when compared to the Logarithmic strategy if the idle duration is short. However, if the idle duration is longer, e.g. the request arrives closely before x_m, then the cost of the Logarithmic strategy has the smallest cost among the three strategies. The costs of Exp and Linear are worse in this situation as they stay in a higher power state longer than the Logarithmic strategy which causes energy waste.

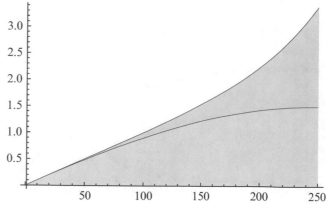

Fig. 89.5 Cost linear(r)

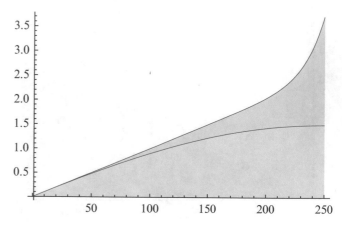

Fig. 89.6 Cost Strategy$_e(1, r)$

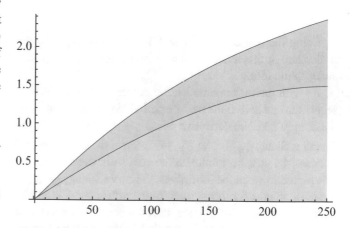

Fig. 89.7 Cost Strategy$_{\ln}(200, r)$

Figures 89.8, 89.9, and 89.10 show the competitive ratios for the online algorithms that use Linear, Exp, and Logarithmic strategies. The competitive ratios bear out what was described above. The Linear and Exp strategies have better competitive ratios at the start of the idle duration compared to the Logarithmic strategy but only for a small duration are better than the Logarithmic strategy and then they rapidly increase as the idle duration increases. From our analysis,

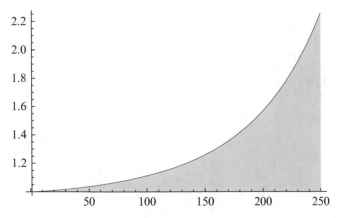

Fig. 89.8 Competitive ratio linear function

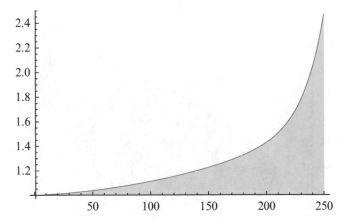

Fig. 89.9 Competitive ratio Strategy$_e(1, r)$

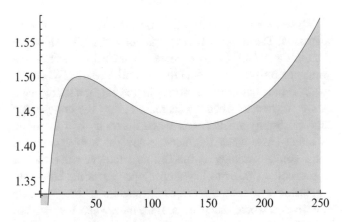

Fig. 89.10 Competitive ratio Strategy$_{\ln}(200, r)$

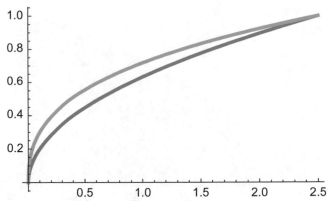

Fig. 89.11 OPT and online strategies for $t = 0.712, z = 0.1$

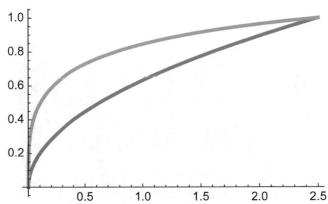

Fig. 89.12 OPT and online strategies for $t = 0.312, z = 0.2$

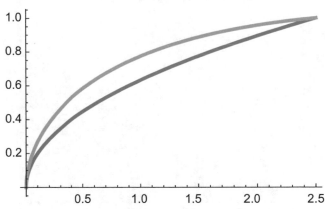

Fig. 89.13 OPT and online strategies for $t = 0.312, z = 1.1$

the better strategy is when we power down to lower power states at a faster rate than the offline strategy.

We now show turn to examples of Progressive$_{t,z}(r)$.

Figures 89.11, 89.12, and 89.13 show Progressive$_{t,z}(r)$ for different t and z parameters. For small values of t and z the online algorithm transitions to the lower power state at an accelerated rate. Indeed, the control parameters t and z adjust the rate at which the online strategy Progressive$_{t,z}(r)$

transitions to lower power states. The value of t causes a more rapid impact on the curve than the value of z since we only increased t by a smaller amount than z to obtain similar strategies. Our simulations show analyze the competitive ratios for various t and z values.

Figures 89.14 and 89.17 show the cost and the competitive ratio for an online algorithm using the Progressive strategy, using a smaller t (Fig. 89.15). As we saw with "Linear", "Exp", and "Logarithmic" strategies, the competitive ratio

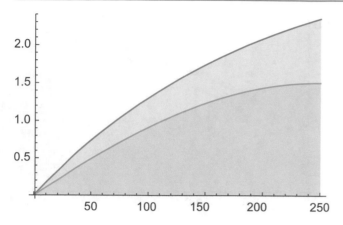

Fig. 89.14 Costs Progressive$_{t,z}(r)$ for $t = 0.312$, $z = 0.1$

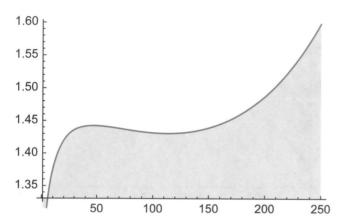

Fig. 89.15 Competitive ratio $t = 0.312$, $z = 0.2$

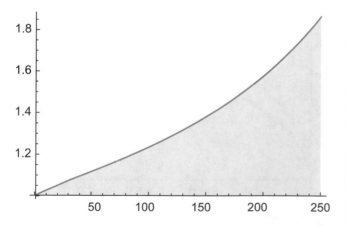

Fig. 89.16 Competitive ratio $t = 0.712$, $z = 0.1$

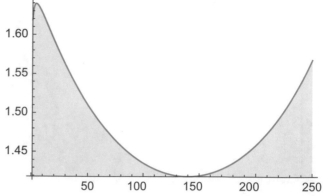

Fig. 89.17 Competitive ratio $t = 0.312$, $z = 0.1$

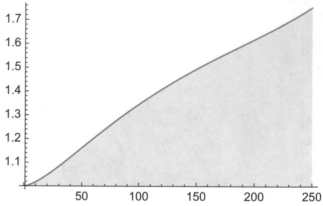

Fig. 89.18 Competitive ratio $t = 0.312$, $z = 1.1$

We see similar pattern when we increase z as when we increase t. The competitive ratio shown in Fig. 89.18 is worse than in Fig. 89.15. However, here we needed to increase the value of z by a larger amount to see similar results. When z is increased the competitive ratio is increasing at a more linear rate compared to when we increase t, also the competitive ratio is slightly smaller than when the value of t is larger. In either case, when we increase the value of t or z, we get a similar strategy as the offline strategy which causes it to become similar to lower envelope algorithm. However, increasing t causes a more rapid change to the schedule and gives a worse competitive ratio than when we increase the value of z, although there is a long period during the idle duration where the competitive ratio is better for higher t values, but overall competitive ratio is worse for higher t values. Table 89.1 summarizes the competitive ratios by applying several test values for t and z.

89.5 Conclusions

As society transitions to the smart grid models online competitive analysis is seen as a realistic framework to study power down mechanisms. In this paper, we studied the online

is smaller when the online strategy changes to a lower state more aggressively, in Fig. 89.16 we see the competitive ratio is larger since it is changing states less aggressively. As we saw in Figs. 89.17 and 89.11, when we increase t the Progressive and offline strategy curves behave similarly which causes the strategy to become similar to the lower envelope algorithm. Now we consider the strategy for increased values of z.

Table 89.1 Competitive ratios for progressive$_{t,z}$

t value	z value	Competitive ratio
0.32	0.1	1.58
0.39	0.1	1.63
0.50	0.1	1.73
0.40	0.2	1.67
0.60	0.2	1.81

power down problem with infinite states, whereas previous work has mainly focused on the discrete model for the power down problem. The purpose of this work was to analyze an example system and show several strategies to find the best strategy that yields the best competitive ratio. It can be seen that in order to obtain a better competitive ratio, the online strategy needs to switch to lower power states at a faster rate than the offline model. This insights can be useful in general for constructing new strategies for idle and power up costs other than the ones considered in this paper. For discrete power down problems, Bein et al. [4, 8] have introduced the Decrease and Reset Algorithm (DRA), which decreases the standby time gradually when the frequency of the device usage becomes low. Such an approach may also be useful in the continuous case.

Acknowledgements Discussions with Rüdiger Reischuk of Universität Lübeck during his sabbatical visit are acknowledged. The work of author Wolfgang Bein was supported by National Science Foundation grant IIA 1427584.

References

1. Y. Agarwal, S. Hodges, R. Chandra, J. Scott, P. Bahl, R. Gupta, Somniloquy: augmenting network interfaces to reduce PC energy usage, in *Proceedings of the 6th USENIX Symposium on Networked Systems Design and Implementation*, Berkeley, CA, pp. 365–380 (USENIX Association, Berkeley, 2009)
2. Y. Agarwal, S. Savage, R. Gupta, Sleepserver: a software-only approach for reducing the energy consumption of PCs within enterprise environments, in *Proceedings of the 2010 USENIX Conference on USENIX Annual Technical Conference*, Berkeley, CA, pp. 22–22 (USENIX Association, Berkeley, 2010)
3. S. Albers, Energy-efficient algorithms. Commun. ACM **53**(5), 86–96 (2010)
4. J. Andro-Vasko, W. Bein, D. Nyknahad, H. Ito, Evaluation of online power-down algorithms, in *Proceedings of the 12th International Conference on Information Technology – New Generations*, pp. 473–478 (IEEE Conference Publications, 2015)
5. J. Andro-Vasko, W. Bein, H. Ito, G. Pathak, A heuristic for state power down systems with few states, in *Information Technology – New Generations: 14th International Conference on Information Technology*, ed. by S. Latifi, pp. 877–882 (Springer International Publishing, Heidelberg, 2018)
6. J. Augustine, S. Irani, C. Swamy, Optimal power-down strategies, in *IEEE Symposium on Foundations of Computer Science*, pp. 530–539 (Cambridge University Press, Cambridge, 2004)
7. J. Augustine, S. Irani, C. Swamy, Optimal power-down strategies. SIAM J. Comput. **37**(5), 1499–1516 (2008)
8. W. Bein, N. Hatta, N. Hernandez-Cons, H. Ito, S. Kasahara, J. Kawahara, An online algorithm optimally self-tuning to congestion for power management problems, in *Proceedings of the 9th International Conference on Approximation and Online Algorithms*, pp. 35–48 (Springer, New York, 2012)
9. W. Bein, B.B. Madan, D. Bein, D. Nyknahad, Algorithmic approaches for a dependable smart grid, in *Information Technology: New Generations: 13th International Conference on Information Technology*, ed. by S. Latifi, pp. 677–687 (Springer International Publishing, Heidelberg, 2016)
10. C.E. Borges, Y.K. Penya, I. Fernández, Evaluating combined load forecasting in large power systems and smart grids. IEEE Trans. Ind. Inf. **9**(3), 1570–1577 (2013)
11. A. Borodin, R. El-Yaniv, *Online Computation and Competitive Analysis* (Cambridge University Press, Cambridge, 1998)
12. R. Hall, R. Erdélyi, E. Hanna, J.M. Jones, A.A. Scaife, Drivers of North Atlantic polar front jet stream variability. Int. J. Climatol. **35**, 1697–1720 (2015)
13. S. Nedevschi, J. Chandrashekar, J. Liu, B. Nordman, S. Ratnasamy, N. Taft, Skilled in the art of being idle: reducing energy waste in networked systems, in *Proceedings of the 6th USENIX Symposium on Networked Systems Design and Implementation*, Berkeley, CA, pp. 381–394 (USENIX Association, Berkeley, 2009)
14. J. Reich, M. Goraczko, A. Kansal, J. Padhye, Sleepless in Seattle no longer, in *Proceedings of the 2010 USENIX Conference on USENIX Annual Technical Conference*, Berkeley, CA, p. 17 (USENIX Association, Berkeley, 2010)

Extracting Timing Models from Component-Based Multi-Criticality Vehicular Embedded Systems

90

Saad Mubeen, Mattias Gålnander, John Lundbäck,
and Kurt-Lennart Lundbäck

Abstract

Timing models include crucial information that is required by the timing analysis engines to verify timing behavior of vehicular embedded systems. The extraction of this information from these systems is challenging due to the software complexity, distribution of functionality and multiple criticality levels. To meet this challenge, this paper presents a comprehensive end-to-end timing model for multi-criticality vehicular distributed embedded systems. The model is comprehensive, in the sense that it captures detailed timing information and supports various types of real-time network protocols used in the vehicular domain. Moreover, the paper provides a method to extract these models from the software architectures of these systems. The proposed model is aligned with the component models and standards in the vehicular domain that support the pipe-and-filter communication among their basic building elements.

Keywords

End-to-end timing model · Vehicular distributed embedded system · Real-time requirement · Mixed criticality model · Software component

S. Mubeen (✉)
Mälardalen University, Västerås, Sweden
e-mail: saad.mubeen@mdh.se

M. Gålnander · J. Lundbäck · K.-L. Lundbäck
Arcticus Systems AB, Järfälla, Sweden
e-mail: mattias.galnander@arcticus-systems.com;
john.lundback@arcticus-systems.com;
kurt.lundback@arcticus-systems.com

90.1 Introduction

Many vehicular embedded systems are real-time systems. This means, the times at which these systems provide their responses are as important as functional correctness of the responses. The manufacturer of such a system is required to ensure that logically correct response by the system will be provided at the time that is appropriate for the system and its environment. This is often mandated by the certification bodies in the case of safety-critical vehicular embedded systems. The appropriate time for response delivery is defined by the timing requirements that are specified on the system. Note that not all functions in modern vehicles have real-time requirements. In fact, the vehicle software consists of functions with different criticality levels, e.g., some functions are safety-critical with stringent real-time requirements, some are not safety-critical but have real-time requirements, and the rest are non-critical functions. As a result, the vehicle software has multiple criticality levels. The main challenge for the developers of these systems is to support the development of multi-criticality software in a reliable and cost-effective manner.

Model- and component-based software development has emerged as a promising approach to handle the complexity of vehicle software [1]. This approach allows to use models throughout the development process, raises the level of abstraction during the software development, supports separation of concerns, allows to build large software systems from pre-existing and reusable software components and their architectures, and supports automation. One remarkable advantage of this approach is that it allows to extract the end-to-end timing information from the software architectures and use the extracted information to populate the end-to-end timing models earlier during the development of these systems. The end-to-end timing models are vital in performing the end-to-end timing analysis [2, 3] of the systems.

There are several component models in the vehicular domain that support development of vehicular distributed

© Springer International Publishing AG, part of Springer Nature 2018
S. Latifi (ed.), *Information Technology – New Generations*, Advances in Intelligent Systems and Computing 738,
https://doi.org/10.1007/978-3-319-77028-4_90

embedded systems, following the model- and component-based software development approach, e.g., AUTOSAR [4], Rubus Component Model (RCM) [5], ProCom [6], COMDES [7], CORBA [8], just to name a few. The end-to-end timing model and the model extraction method presented in this paper conform to any component model that supports a pipe and filter style for communication. Hence, the presented model is aligned with the above mentioned component models.

Mixed-criticality is becoming a well-studied topic in the real-time systems community [9]. The mixed-criticality model is based on the work by Vestal [10], where a task (a run-time entity corresponding to a software component) is assumed to have more than one criticality level. In comparison, the multi-criticality model, which is part of the end-to-end timing model presented in this paper, associates a unique criticality level to the application software and not to individual components (or tasks). The presented model is inspired by the functional safety standard for road vehicles ISO26262 [11] and the aerospace standard DO178C [12]. Timing model for the AUTOSAR standard was developed in the TIMMO2USE project [13] using the TADL2 [14] language. The timing requirements model, part of the presented end-to-end timing model, is aligned with the timing constraints in TADL2. There are a few works that extract timing models from distributed embedded systems such as [15, 16]. Unlike the model presented in this paper, these models are limited to single-criticality systems.

This paper presents a comprehensive end-to-end timing model for multi-criticality distributed vehicular embedded systems. The model incorporates several real-time network protocols that are used in the vehicle industry today. The paper also presents a method for the extraction of the end-to-end timing models from the software architectures of the systems that are developed using the model- and component-based software development approach. Moreover, the paper discusses the consequences of extracting unambiguous timing model from the software architecture with a concrete example. The proposed model and method are generally applicable to any component model for distributed embedded real-time systems that supports a pipe-and-filter communication style for interaction among the software components.

90.2 End-to-End Timing Model in Vehicular Systems

An end-to-end timing model contains all the information that is required by analysis engines to perform the end-to-end timing analysis of a distributed embedded system. This information includes timing properties, requirements and dependencies in the system. The relationship among the software architecture, the end-to-end timing model and the timing analysis engines is depicted in Fig. 90.1. The end-to-end timing model consists of three models: (1) timing model, (2) linking model and (3) timing requirements model, as shown in Fig. 90.1.

90.2.1 Timing Model

A distributed embedded system, denoted by $\mathcal{S}$, consists of two or more nodes and one or more networks. A node or an ECU can be denoted by $\mathcal{E}$, whereas a network is denoted by $\mathcal{N}$. Hence, the system can be represented as follows.

$$\mathcal{S} := \langle \{\mathcal{E}_1, \ldots, \mathcal{E}_n\}, \{\mathcal{N}_1, \ldots, \mathcal{N}_m\} \rangle \qquad (90.1)$$

That is, the system consists of n number of nodes and m number of networks. This paper considers the node and network timing models separately. Together these two models comprise the system timing model.

90.2.1.1 Node Timing Model

This model contains all the timing information within a node. This model is based on the transactional task model [16–19]. The most important aspect of the transactional task model is that it models tasks with offsets, externally imposed time intervals between the arrivals of the triggering events and release (for execution) of the corresponding tasks.

A node, $\mathcal{E}_i$, consists of one or more *partitions*. A partition is denoted by $\mathfrak{P}_{ij}$. The first subscript, i, represents the node to which this partition belongs, whereas the second subscript, j, represents the index of the partition within the node. The number of partitions in node $\mathcal{E}_i$ is represented by $|\mathcal{E}_i|$. The node $\mathcal{E}_i$ can be represented as follows.

$$\mathcal{E}_i := \{\mathfrak{P}_{i1}, \ldots, \mathfrak{P}_{i|\mathcal{E}_i|}\} \qquad (90.2)$$

The partition represents the logical division of a node into multiple execution resources. The partition provides a mechanism to isolate the software within a node in both time and space. Separation in time means that each partition gets a reserved share of the node's processing time for the execution of the software allocated to it. Separation in space means that the memory available to each node is divided among its partitions. Each partition executes a part of the system with specific criticality. Hence, a criticality level, denoted by $\mathfrak{C}_{ij}$, is associated to each partition. The criticality levels conform to the four Automotive Safety Integrity Levels (ASIL A, ASIL B, ASIL C and ASIL D) that are defined in the ISO 26262 functional safety standard for road vehicle [11]. According to the standard, ASIL D is the highest safety integrity level, whereas ASIL A is the lowest safety integrity level. Note that the presented timingmodel can be easily

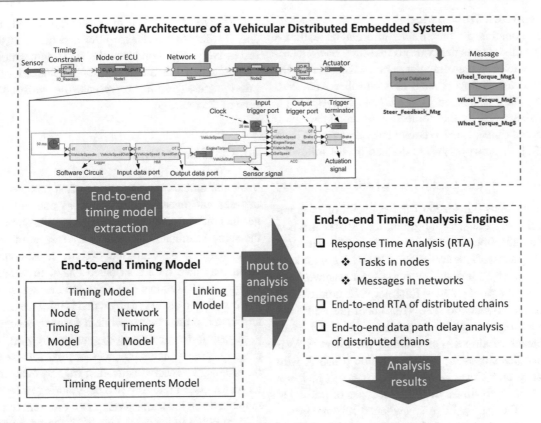

Fig. 90.1 Relationship among the software architecture, end-to-end timing model and timing analysis engines

adapted to the multi-criticality aerospace embedded systems by considering the five criticality levels (A-E) specified in the DO-178C standard [12].

A partition, $\mathfrak{P}_{ij}$, consists of a set of $|\mathfrak{P}_{ij}|$ transactions. Let a transaction be denoted by Γ_{ijk}. The first and second subscripts, i and j, represent IDs of the node and partition to which this transaction belongs respectively. The third subscript, k, denotes the index of the transaction within the partition. Hence, the partition $\mathfrak{P}_{ij}$ can be represented by the following tuple.

$$\mathfrak{P}_{ij} := \langle \{\Gamma_{ij1}, \ldots, \Gamma_{ij|\mathcal{E}_k|}\}, \mathfrak{C}_{ij}\rangle \quad (90.3)$$

Each transaction Γ_{ijk} is assumed to be activated by mutually independent events with arbitrary phasing. This means, the activating events can be periodic with a periodicity of T_{ijk} or sporadic with T_{ijk} representing the minimum inter-arrival time between two consecutive events. The transaction Γ_{ijk} contains $|\Gamma_{ijk}|$ number of tasks. Each task in Γ_{ijk} may not be activated until a certain time, known as the *offset*, elapses after the arrival of the event. An offset also specifies temporal dependency among releases of tasks within the transaction.

A task is denoted by τ_{ijkl}. The first, second and third subscripts, i, j and k, denote the IDs of the node, partition and transaction to which the task belongs. The fourth subscript, l, specifies the ID the task within the transaction. A transaction

belonging to partition $\mathfrak{P}_{ij}$ can be represented as follows.

$$\Gamma_{ijk} := \langle \{\tau_{ijk1}, \ldots, \tau_{ijk|\Gamma_{ijk}|}\}, T_{ijk}\rangle \quad (90.4)$$

A task, τ_{ijk}, is defined by the following tuple.

$$\tau_{ijkl} := \langle C_{ijkl}, T_{ijkl}, O_{ijkl}, P_{ijkl}, J_{ijkl}, B_{ijkl},$$
$$R_{ijkl}, D_{ijkl}\rangle \quad (90.5)$$

Where, C_{ijkl} denotes the worst-case execution time of the task. O_{ijkl} and P_{ijkl} represent the offset and priority of the task respectively. J_{ijkl} denotes the maximum release *jitter* of the task. Jitter is the difference between the earliest and the latest point in time a task starts to execute (relative to its nominal start time). B_{ijkl} denotes the maximum blocking time for the task. B_{ijkl} is defined as the maximum amount of time the task has to wait for a shared resource that is already locked by a lower priority task. The upper bound on the blocking time for a task can be obtained by using a resource sharing (synchronization) protocol such as Stack Resource Policy (SRP) [20] and Priority Ceiling Protocol (PCP) [21]. R_{ijkl} represents the worst-case response time of the task. D_{ij} denotes the deadline of the task. In this model, there are no restrictions on the offset, deadline or jitter. This means that each of these parameters can each be smaller that, equal to or greater than the task corresponding period.

90.2.1.2 Network Timing Model

This model contains all the timing information within a network. The model considers various real-time network protocols that are used in the vehicular domain. These networks include broadcast protocols such as Controller Area Network (CAN) [22], CANopen [23], HCAN [24] AUTOSAR COMM [25] as well as the point-to-point communication protocols based on switched Ethernet such as AVB [26] and HaRTES [27]. A network, $\mathcal{N}_i$, is defined by the following tuple.

$$\mathcal{N}_i := \langle \mathfrak{Z}_i, \mathfrak{S}_i, \mathcal{L}_i, \mathfrak{T}_i, \mathcal{W}_i, \mathcal{M}_i \rangle \qquad (90.6)$$

Where $\mathfrak{Z}_i$ represents the speed of the network, often represented in Kbit/s or Mbit/s. $\mathfrak{S}_i$ represents the set of switches in the case of a multi-hop network, for example Ethernet AVB. In a multi-hop network, a switch is connected to a node or to another switch by a link. All such links in the network are represented by the set $\mathcal{L}_i$. In the Ethernet AVB protocol and the Time Sensitive Network (TSN) protocol [28], different types of traffic can be specified a portion of the total bandwidth by means of slopes. For example the Ethernet AVB protocol specifies slopes for real-time traffic (Class A with higher priority and Class B with lower priority) and non real-time traffic. The slopes of different types of traffic are represented in the set $\mathfrak{T}_i$. In some switched Ethernet protocols like HaRTES, the transmission is performed within pre-configured fixed-duration time slot called Elementary Cycle (EC). The EC consists of two windows that are dedicated to synchronous and asynchronous traffic. The size of the EC and the two windows is represented in the set $\mathcal{W}_i$. Finally, $\mathcal{M}_i$ denotes the set of messages that are communicated over the network. $\mathcal{M}_i$ is represented by the following tuple.

$$\mathcal{M}_i := \langle \mathcal{X}_{ij}, \mathcal{F}_{ij}, P_{ij}, C_{ij}, s_{ij}, T_{ij}^P, T_{ij}^S,$$
$$J_{ij}, O_{ij}, B_{ij}, R_{ij} \rangle \qquad (90.7)$$

There are two subscripts associated to each term in the above tuple. The first subscript, i, represents the network to which the message set belongs. The second subscript, j, specifies a unique identifier for each message in the message set. $\mathcal{X}_{ij}$ specifies the type of the message. A message can be periodic, sporadic or mixed (both periodic and sporadic) [29]. $\mathcal{F}_{ij}$ specifies the frame type, i.e., whether the frame is a Standard or an Extended frame in the case of CAN and its higher-level protocols. P_{ij} denotes the message priority. C_{ij} represents the worst-case transmission time of the message (considering no interferences). s_{ij} denotes the data payload in the message. If the transmission type of the message is periodic, T_{ij}^P denotes the period of the message. If the transmission type of the message is sporadic, T_{ij}^S represents the minimum time that should elapse between the transmission of any two consecutive instances of the message. Whereas, both T_{ij}^P

and T_{ij}^S are specified in the case of a mixed message. J_{ij} and O_{ij} denote the release jitter and offset of the message respectively. B_{ij} represents the maximum amount of time during which the message can be blocked by the lower priority messages. R_{ij} represents the worst-case response time of the message.

90.2.2 Linking Model

Vehicular embedded systems are often modeled with chains of tasks and messages. A chain has one initiator and one terminator. Different chains may have the same initiator or the same terminator. A chain may reside on one node, in which case it is composed of only a sequence tasks. A chain may also be a distributed chain, in which case it is composed of a sequence of tasks and messages. An example of a distributed chain is a chain that is initiated at a sensor and terminated at an actuator, while it spans over several nodes.

A task in the chain may be activated by an independent trigger source or by its predecessor task. Moreover, a task in the chain may receive activation trigger, data or both from its predecessor task. Any two neighboring tasks in the chain may reside on the same node or two different nodes.

A message in the chain may be triggered for transmission by the predecessor task (also called sending task) in the case of passive networks like CAN or Ethernet AVB. Whereas, in the case of active networks like the HaRTES protocol, a message in the chain can be triggered for transmission by the network itself (regardless of the sending task). In the case of multi-hop networks, a message in the chain may traverse through several links and switches between the predecessor and successor tasks in the chain.

All this information regarding activations, trigger flows, data flows, mapping and linking within the chains constitute the system linking model. This information is crucial for the analysis engines to perform the end-to-end timing analysis.

90.2.3 Timing Requirements Model

Timing requirements in vehicular embedded systems are specified by means of timing constraints. The timing requirements model includes information regarding the specified constraints on all chains in the system. Note that the timing requirements on individual tasks and messages (e.g., deadlines of tasks and messages) are not part of this model as they are already included in the node and network timing models respectively. The set of all specified timing requirements in the system is denoted by $\mathfrak{R}$. The set $\mathfrak{R}$ contains n number of timing requirements as represented below.

$$\mathfrak{R} := \langle \{\mathfrak{R}_1, \ldots, \mathfrak{R}_n\} \rangle \qquad (90.8)$$

Each timing requirement $\mathfrak{R}_i$ has three attributes: (1) *Type*, (2) minimum value of the constraint, denoted by *MIN*, and (3) maximum value of the constraint, denoted by *MAX*.

$$\mathfrak{R}_i := \{Type, MIN, MAX\} \qquad (90.9)$$

There are eighteen timing constraints that are included in the AUTOSAR standard [4]. However, most of these constraints are specific to single or pair of events. That is, they are specific to individual tasks or a set of independent tasks that are not part of the same chain. In this model, we consider only four of these constraints, which are applicable to the chains. Hence, $\mathfrak{R}_i(Type)$ can be one of the four constraints that are defined in the timing model of the AUTOSAR standard.

$$\mathfrak{R}_i(Type) := \{Age, Reaction, Output\ Synchronization,$$
$$Input\ Synchronization\}$$
$$(90.10)$$

The *Age* constraint constrains the maximum age of the data from the input to the output of the chain. The *Reaction* constraint constrains the first output (reaction) of the chain corresponding to the data at the input of the chain, considering the new data "just missed" the read access at the initiator element of the chain. If two chains have the same initiator but different terminators, the *OutputSynchronization* constraint restricts the closeness of the occurrences of outputs of the two chains. In other words, this constraint defines how far apart the outputs of the two chains can occur corresponding to the same input of the chains. On the other hand, if two chains have the same terminator but different initiators, the *InputSynchronization* constraint restricts the closeness of the occurrences of inputs of the two chains. That is, this constraint defines how far apart the inputs of the two chains can occur corresponding to the same output of the chains.

90.3 End-to-End Timing Model Extraction Method

In a model- and component-based software development process, the end-to-end timing model is extracted from the software architecture of the modeled system as shown in Fig. 90.1. There are two types of information that are extracted in the end-to-end timing model. The first type of information is explicitly specified by the user on the software architecture. This information is rather easy to extract from the properties of structural elements in the software architecture. The second type of information is not explicitly provided by the user. This information has to be extracted from the software architecture. If some of this information cannot be extracted unambiguously then assumptions are made about the missing information for the purpose of providing the complete end-to-end timing model to the analysis engines.

90.3.1 Extracting the Node Timing Model

Majority of the information in the node timing model falls into the first type of timing information (user-defined). For instance, most of the information in relations (90.2)–(90.5) is extracted from the user-defined properties of corresponding structural elements in the software architecture.

The criticality levels associated to partitions in relation (90.3) are not user-specified. The user can only specify a unique criticality level on each part of the complete software architecture, called the application. The application can reside on one or more partitions in the node. Since the main purpose of the partition element is to provide separation in time space, a partition is not allowed to host multiple applications with different criticality levels. Note that any inter-partition interference is prevented by using memory protection mechanisms. A node can host multiple applications with different criticality levels. Hence, the criticality level of a partition is extracted from the criticality level of the hosted application.

The transaction period in relation (90.4) is not user-specified. The user can only specify periods (or minimum inter-arrival times) of individual software components by means of clocks (or events or interrupts) as shown in Fig. 90.2. The corresponding task inherits the period or minimum inter-arrival time (depicted in relation (90.5)) from the software component. Each event- or interrupt-triggered task forms a transaction of its own. The transaction inherits the minimum inter-arrival time from the task. In the case of clock-triggered tasks, the transaction period is derived by calculating the least common multiple of the extracted periods of all tasks in the transaction (chain).

The individual deadlines of the tasks in relation (90.5) are not user-specified. In the case of time-triggered software component with no explicit release jitter, we assume implicit deadlines, i.e., the deadline of each task is equal to its period. Otherwise, the corresponding jitter and trigger information is sent to the analysis engines to make appropriate assumptions about the missing information.

90.3.2 Extracting the Network Timing Model

All network-level timing information shown in relation (90.6) and some of message timing information (including frame type, priority, offset and data payload) shown in relation (90.7) are user-specified. This information

Fig. 90.2 A two-node multi-criticality vehicular system

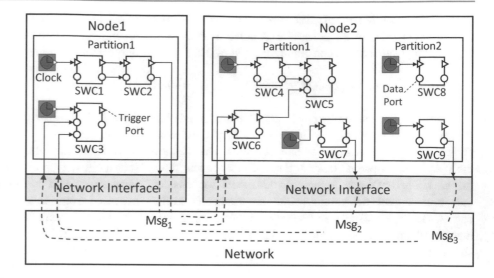

is extracted from the properties of the corresponding structural elements in the network and message models of the software architecture. Whereas, the worst-case transmission time, message priority, message type, period or minimum inter-transmission time, release jitter and message blocking time are not explicitly specified by the user; these properties are extracted from the software architecture.

The worst-case transmission time of a message is calculated using the data payload and network speed. In the case of CAN and its higher-level protocols, the priority of a message is extracted from its ID. Unlike the other protocols, the priority of a message is unique in CAN. Whereas, in the case of the other protocols, the priority of a message is a user-defined attribute, which is extracted from the message model in the software architecture. The blocking time of message is derived by considering the maximum value among the worst-case transmission times of all lower priority messages. Whereas, the release jitter of a message is derived by subtracting the sender task's (sender software component's) best-case response time from the worst-case response time.

The information regarding the message type is extracted from the sender software component. If the sender is triggered by a periodic clock, the message type becomes periodic. If the sender is triggered by a sporadic event or an interrupt, the message type becomes sporadic. Whereas, if the sender is triggered by both periodic clock and a sporadic event or an interrupt, the message type becomes mixed. Depending upon the message type, the message inherits the period, minimum transmission time or both from the sender. This information is crucial for the analysis engines as different analysis profiles are used to analysis different message types [29].

90.3.3 Extracting the Linking Model

The linking information for all distributed chains in the software architecture are extracted in the system linking model. Consider an example of the software architecture of a two-node multi-criticality vehicular distributed embedded system depicted in Fig. 90.2. There are three distributed chains in the system as follows.

$Chain_1$: SWC1 $\rightarrow$ SWC2 $\rightarrow$ Msg$_1$ $\rightarrow$ SWC6 $\rightarrow$ SWC5
$Chain_2$: SWC7 $\rightarrow$ Msg$_2$ $\rightarrow$ SWC3
$Chain_3$: SWC9 $\rightarrow$ Msg$_3$ $\rightarrow$ SWC3

The linking information for each chain is captured in a reference set. This set contains references to the data and trigger ports of each software component along the distributed chain. The ordering of references within this set corresponds to the ordering of software components and messages within the distributed chain. For example, the reference set for $Chain_2$ includes references to the trigger and data input and input ports of SWC7 and SWC8 together with the reference to Msg$_2$.

In order to extract control flows along the chains, each task τ_{ijk1} is assigned a trigger dependency attribute, denoted by $\mathfrak{TD}_{\tau_{ijk1}}$. The domain of this attribute is defined as follows.

$$\mathfrak{TD}_{\tau_{ijk1}} := \{Independent, Dependent\}$$

where, $\mathfrak{TD}_{\tau_{ijk1}}$ is assigned *Independent* if the software component corresponding to task τ_{ijk1} is activated by an independent triggering source, e.g, SWC1, SWC3, SWC4, SWC7, SWC8 and SWC9 in Fig. 90.2. Whereas, $\mathfrak{TD}_{\tau_{ijk1}}$ is assigned *Dependent* if the software component corresponding to task τ_{ijk1} is activated by its predecessor software component, e.g, SWC2, SWC5 and SWC6 in Fig. 90.2. A precedence constraint is implicitly included between the two tasks in the case of *Dependent* triggering. This constraint restricts the activation of successor task before the completion of the predecessor task. Note that SWC2 and SWC 5 are triggered by their predecessors within the same partitions, whereas SWC6 is triggered by its predecessor via the network.

In CAN and its higher-level protocols, a message can traverse through only one link (i.e., the bus or network) between the sender and receiver software components. However, in the multi-hop switched Ethernet protocols (e.g., AVB, HaRTES), a message may traverse through several links between the sender and receiver software components. These links are extracted for every message in a dedicated set as follows.

$$\mathcal{L}_{\mathcal{M}_{ij}} := \langle \mathcal{L}_1, \ldots, \mathcal{L}_k \rangle$$

Where, $\mathcal{L}_{\mathcal{M}_{ij}}$ represents the set of k links through which the message $\mathcal{M}_{ij}$ traverses between the sender and receiver software components. In the case of CAN and its higher-level protocols, this set is equal to one link.

90.3.4 Extracting the Timing Requirements Model

The information in the timing requirements model represented with relations (90.8)–(90.10) is user-defined. The user specifies the timing requirements on the chains within the software architecture by means of the "start" and "end" objects for each constraint. This means, the timing constraints can be specified on a complete chain or part of the chain. The *MAX* value of each constraint extracted from the corresponding property of the "end" object. If *MIN* value of the constraint is not specified, it is extracted in the model as zero.

90.4 Discussion

It is important that the extracted information in the end-to-end timing model should be unambiguous, otherwise the timing analysis results can be under- or over-estimated. Under-estimated analysis results can have severe (or even catastrophic) consequences. For example, analysis results verify that the task responsible for the deployment of airbag will meet its deadline in the case of a crash. If the analysis results are under-estimated then the task can actually miss its deadline and may lead to catastrophe. Whereas, over-estimated analysis results can lead to underutilization of the system resources. In order to elaborate on this, consider an example of a system consisting of one distributed transaction (chain of tasks and messages) corresponding to the software architecture of a distributed chain (chain of software components and messages) as shown in Fig. 90.3. The chain is distributed over two nodes connected by a CAN network. There are three tasks (one in Node1 and two in Node2) and one message in the chain. The timing information about the chain is also depicted in Fig. 90.3. The calculations for the *Age* and *Reaction* delays depend upon several parameters including the trigger dependency attribute. This attribute for the receiving task τ_2, denoted by $\mathfrak{TD}_{\tau_2}$, can be *Independent* or *Dependent*, meaning that the receiving task implements the interrupt-based or polling-based policy to receive the message, respectively. The *Age* and *Reaction* delays for the system in Fig. 90.3 are shown in Figs. 90.4 and 90.5 if the receiving task implements the interrupt-based policy or the polling-based policy for receiving Msg$_1$, respectively. By comparing the values of the *Age* and *Reaction* delays in Figs. 90.4 and 90.5, it is clear that if the value of $\mathfrak{TD}_{\tau_2}$ is not extracted or wrongly extracted then the analysis results can be either under-estimated or over-estimated.

Fig. 90.3 Example of a distributed transaction corresponding to the software architecture of a distributed chain

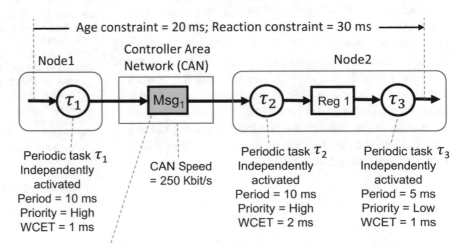

Msg$_1$: Number of data bytes = 8; Calculated transmission time = 540 us

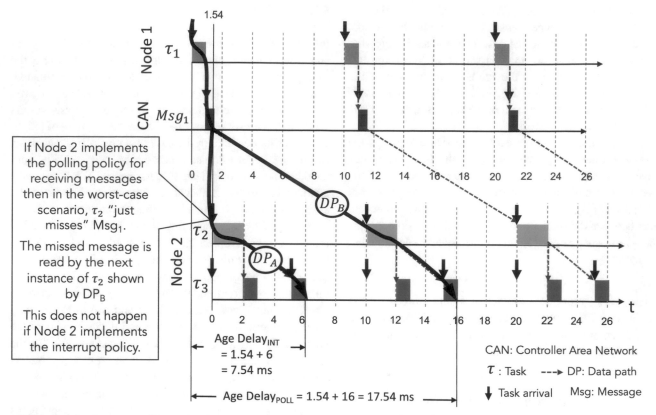

If Node 2 implements the polling policy for receiving messages then in the worst-case scenario, τ_2 "just misses" Msg_1.

The missed message is read by the next instance of τ_2 shown by DP_B

This does not happen if Node 2 implements the interrupt policy.

Age Delay$_{INT}$ = 1.54 + 6 = 7.54 ms

Age Delay$_{POLL}$ = 1.54 + 16 = 17.54 ms

CAN: Controller Area Network
τ : Task   ---▸ DP: Data path
↓ Task arrival   Msg: Message

POLL: Task implements polling policy for receiving message   INT: Task implements interrupt-based policy for receiving message

Fig. 90.4 Different *Age* delays in the system in Fig. 90.3 if Node2 uses the interrupt or polling policy for receiving messages

90.5   Summary and Conclusion

This paper has presented a comprehensive end-to-end timing model for multi-criticality vehicular distributed embedded systems. Such a model is required by the end-to-end timing analysis engines for pre-runtime verification of timing behavior of the systems (i.e., verifying the specified timing requirements before running the system). The paper takes the leverage of the principles of model- and component-based software development in providing a method to extract the end-to-end timing models from software architectures of these systems. The proposed model conforms to the component models and standards in the vehicular domain that support a pipe-and-filter communication among their software components. In the future, we plan to transfer the results to the industry by implementing the proposed model and method in the analysis framework of an existing industrial tool suite (Rubus-ICE).

Acknowledgements The work in this paper is supported by the KKS foundation through the project PreVeiw. We thank our industrial partners Arcticus Systems, Volvo CE and BAE Systems Hägglunds.

References

1. I. Crnkovic, M. Larsson, *Building Reliable Component-Based Software Systems* (Artech House, Norwood, MA, 2002)
2. S. Mubeen, J. Mäki-Turja, M. Sjödin, Support for end-to-end response-time and delay analysis in the industrial tool suite: issues, experiences and a case study. Comput. Sci. Inf. Syst. **10**(1), 453–482 (2013)
3. N. Feiertag, K. Richter, J. Nordlander, J. Jonsson, A compositional framework for end-to-end path delay calculation of automotive systems under different path semantics, in *CRTS Workshop* (2008)
4. AUTOSAR Techincal Overview, Release 4.1, Rev.2, Ver.1.1.0. http://autosar.org
5. K. Hänninen et al., The rubus component model for resource constrained real-time systems, in *IEEE Symposium on Industrial Embedded Systems* (2008)
6. S. Sentilles, A. Vulgarakis, T. Bures, J. Carlson, I. Crnkovic, A component model for control-intensive distributed embedded systems, in *CBSE* (2008)

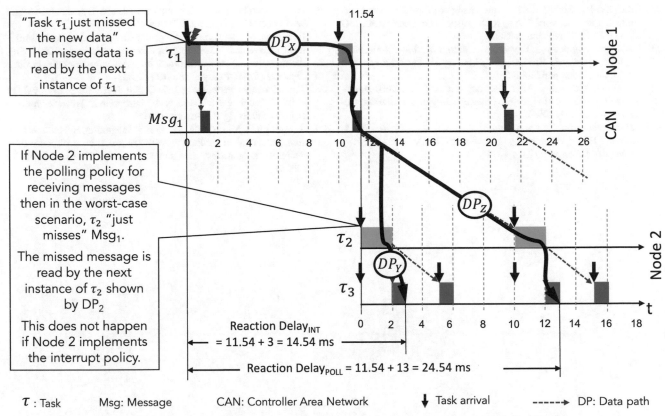

Fig. 90.5 Different *Reaction* delays in the system in Fig. 90.3 if Node2 uses interrupt or polling policy for receiving messages

7. X. Ke, K. Sierszecki, C. Angelov, COMDES-II: a component-based framework for generative development of distributed real-time control systems, in *13th IEEE International Conference on Embedded and Real-Time Computing Systems and Applications, RTCSA 2007*, pp. 199–208 (2007)
8. D. Schmidt, F. Kuhns, An overview of the real-time CORBA specification. Computer **33**(6), 56–63 (2000)
9. A. Burns, R. Davis, Mixed criticality systems – a review, ninth edition, Technical report, Department of Computer Science, University of York, 2017. https://www-users.cs.york.ac.uk/burns/review.pdf.
10. S. Vestal, Preemptive scheduling of multi-criticality systems with varying degrees of execution time assurance, in *28th IEEE International Symposium on Real-Time Systems*, pp. 239–243 (2007)
11. International Organization for Standardization (ISO), ISO 26262-1:2011: Road vehicles – Functional safety. http://www.\discretionary-iso.\discretionary-org/
12. Special C. of RTCA. DO-178C, software considerations in airborne systems and equipment certification (2011)
13. TIMMO-2-USE. https://itea3.\discretionary-org/project/timmo-2-use.\discretionary-html
14. Timing Augmented Description Language (TADL2) syntax, semantics, metamodel Ver. 2, Deliverable 11, August 2012
15. S. Mubeen, J. Mäki-Turja, M. Sjödin, Extraction of end-to-end timing model from component-based distributed real-time embedded systems, in *Time Analysis and Model-Based Design, from Functional Models to Distributed Deployments (TiMoBD) Workshop Located at Embedded Systems Week* (Springer, Berlin, 2011), pp. 1–6
16. S. Mubeen, J. Mäki-Turja, M. Sjödin, Communications-oriented development of component- based vehicular distributed real-time embedded systems. J. Syst. Archit. **60**(2), 207–220 (2014)
17. K. Tindell, Adding time-offsets to schedulability analysis, Technical report, Department of Computer Science, University of York, England, 1994
18. J. Palencia, M.G. Harbour, Schedulability analysis for tasks with static and dynamic offsets, in *IEEE International Real-Time Systems Symposium*, p. 26 (1998)
19. J. Mäki-Turja, M. Nolin, Efficient implementation of tight response-times for tasks with offsets. Real-Time Syst. **40**(1), 77–116 (2008)
20. T.P. Baker, Stack-based scheduling for realtime processes. Real-Time Syst. **3**(1), 67–99 (1991) [Online]. Available: http://dx.doi.org/10.1007/BF00365393
21. L. Sha, R. Rajkumar, J. Lehoczky, Priority inheritance protocols: an approach to real-time synchronization. IEEE Trans. Comput. **39**(9), 1175–1185 (1990)

22. ISO 11898-1, Road Vehicles? interchange of digital information? controller area network (CAN) for high-speed communication, ISO Standard-11898, November 1993

23. CANopen Application Layer and Communication Profile. CiA Draft Standard 301. Version 4.02. February 13, 2002. http://www.can-cia.org/index.php?id=440

24. Hägglunds Controller Area Network (HCAN), Network Implementation Specification, in *BAE Systems Hägglunds, Sweden (Internal Document)* (2009)

25. Requirements on Communication, Rel. 4.1, Rev. 3, Ver. 3.3.1, March, 2014. www.autosar.org/download/R4.1/AUTOSAR_SRS_COM.pdf. Accessed 05 May 2014

26. Audio/video bridging task group of IEEE 802.1, available at http://www.ieee802.org/1/pages/avbridges.html

27. R. Santos, M. Behnam, T. Nolte, P. Pedreiras, L. Almeida, Multilevel hierarchical scheduling in ethernet switches, in *2011 Proceedings of the Ninth ACM International Conference on Embedded Software (EMSOFT)*, pp. 185–194 (2011)

28. Time-Sensitive Networking Task Group, IEEE Std 802.1Qbv-2015 – IEEE Standard for Local and Metropolitan Area Networks – Bridges and Bridged Networks (2015)

29. S. Mubeen, J. Mäki-Turja, M. Sjödin, Integrating mixed transmission and practical limitations with the worst-case response-time analysis for controller area network. J. Syst. Softw. **99**, 66–84 (2015)

Part XI

Short Papers

Thomas Jell, Claudia Baumgartner, Arne Bröring, and Jelena Mitic

Abstract

The Internet of Things (IoT) is today separated by different vertically oriented platforms for integration of all the different devices. Developers who aim to access other platforms and access that data are forced to manually adapt their interfaces to the specific platform API and data models.

This paper highlights the work of the BIG IoT project that aims at launching an IoT marketplace and ecosystem as part of the European Platform Initiative (IoT EPI).

We will present the setup of and the results of integration of the use cases that have been implemented in Northern Germany and Barcelona.

Please refer to www.big-iot.eu for further details.

Keywords

BigIoT · IoT · Interconnecting IoT platforms · Northern German UseCase

91.1 The Problem of Missing IoT Interoperability

The idea of the IoT is in widespread use since the last years, collecting sensor data from various application domains. However, so far, these IoT platforms do not form a vibrant ecosystem. There have been lots of research and innovation projects in the context of the IoT. Nonetheless, no broadly used professional ecosystems for the IoT exist today.

One reason for this is the large number of stakeholders who are involved in IoT ecosystems. Among these are

T. Jell (✉) · A. Bröring · J. Mitic
Siemens AG, Munich, Germany
e-mail: Thomas.jell@siemens.com

C. Baumgartner
VMZ Berlin, Berlin, Germany

providers of platforms and things, as well as application developers, and end users. Another reason for this issue are the high entry barriers for developers of services and applications. This is cased by the heterogeneity of all known IoT platforms. Developers who want to access things and additional data from different platforms need to manually access them by implementing specific adapters. Also, incentives are missing for platform providers to open their systems to third parties.

These different issues all relate to one particular challenge: the missing interoperability on the IoT. Today, various protocols and standards are available on the IoT [1]. This heterogeneity ranges from basic communication protocols such as CoAP [2] and MQTT [3], to focused standard families, such as oneM2M [4] or OGC SWE [5].

91.2 The BIG IoT Approach

Bridging the Interoperability Gap of the IoT (BIG IoT) [6] is the project that aims at enabling the access of services and applications from multiple IoT platforms, standards and domains towards building IoT ecosystems.

Previous EC-funded projects that address such enablement of IoT ecosystems are, e.g., IoT-A [http://www.iot-a.eu], by providing a common architecture, FIWARE [http://www.fiware.org] that offers Generic Enablers as building blocks, or projects such as compose [http://www.compose-project.eu] and OpenIoT [http://openiot.eu], which offer dedicated IoT platforms to aggregate other platforms and systems. BIG IoT will not develop yet another platform in order to enable cross-platform IoT applications.

Instead, to reach the above outlined goal, BIG IoT builds up on three key pillars for an interoperable IoT ecosystem: (1) a common BIG IoT API, (2) well-defined information models, and (3) a marketplace to monetize access to resources. This approach is illustrated in Fig. 91.1. Of central importance is the BIG IoT API, which includes functionali-

© Springer International Publishing AG, part of Springer Nature 2018
S. Latifi (ed.), *Information Technology – New Generations*, Advances in Intelligent Systems and Computing 738,
https://doi.org/10.1007/978-3-319-77028-4_91

Fig. 91.1 Overview of the BIG
IoT approach (Icons made by
Freepik from www.flaticon.com).
(Source: [7])

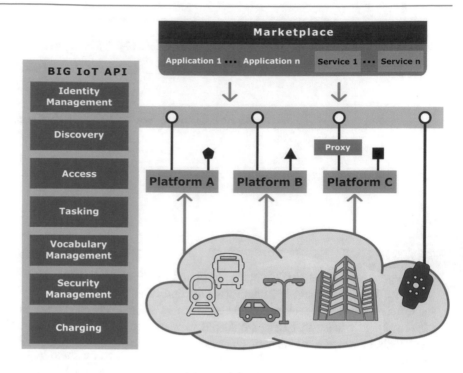

ties such as ID management and discovery of things, access
to things on platforms, tasking of things to send commands,
as well as vocabulary management for handling semantics
and security management. In order to interact with the
marketplace, the API implemented by IoT platforms supports
charging for access to things. The generic BIG IoT API as
well as the underlying information models have been defined
in conjunction with the Web of Things Interest Group at the
W3C for standardization.

The details of this technical baseline have already been
specified [8] in a comprehensive architectural design.
Thereby, particular importance has been given to specific
security and privacy requirements [9]. While these technical
considerations build the foundation for the ecosystem to
function, a crucial aspect to growing an ecosystem is the
underlying business model. Therefore, the BIG IoT project
has analyzed various business cases and value networks.

91.3   Use Cases: Overview and Example

The BIG IoT project has developed a first prototype of
an IoT ecosystem with overall eight IoT platforms using
all the common BIG IoT API. Among them are platforms
from most of the partners: Bosch, CSI, Siemens, VMZ, and
WorldSensing. The use cases to verify the interoperability
span the mobility domain and include smart parking, bike
sharing and traffic management.

They are demonstrated and verified in pilots in Barcelona
(Spain), Piedmont (Italy) and Berlin/Wolfsburg (NG,
Northern-Germany).

Main focus is put on specifying services integrated and
offered via the BIG IoT Marketplace. Additionally, applications based on the services that are showcased are specified.
The work is executed for all three pilots, taking into account
the specific characteristics of the infrastructure as well as
pilot-specific requirements.

The Northern Germany Pilot focuses in Berlin on the
already installed network of parking sensors (Siemens) in
dedicated areas as well as a variety of sensors throughout
the city (VMZ).

Additional a semi public parking area at VMZ's premises
will be equipped with radar sensors to detect parking vehicles. Provided services and apps will be:

- Smart parking
- Smart charging
- Public transport optimization
- Multimodal route optimization
- Parking and charging info and
- Reservation.

The smart objects are charging stations, parking detectors
and Wi-Fi probes as well as location sensors on buses,
which deliver their data to availability services for further
provision to the BIG IoT ecosystem. The data from those
smart objects provided by the availability services are used
by other services or by the end user applications directly.

- The services are
- Parking spot availability
- Parking spot WMS

- People density estimation on bus
- People density estimation in area
- Live bus location
- Charging station availability and
- Charging station WMS.

The services support the different applications with offerings in terms of raw and aggregated data and functionalities.

We will present the first success story showing the integration of parking data from different sources (Berlin, Munich, Barcelona, . . .) via the already existing Marketplace into integrated end user applications.

91.4   Northern Germany Pilot

This BIG IoT Pilot makes use of innovative solutions already in place in the mobility innovation labs Berlin and Wolfsburg, the Northern Germany headquarter of automotive industry. The pilot shows how BIG IoT can contribute to mobility innovation in metropolitan areas, middle-sized towns and the connected commuter traffic, addressing the future needs of urban and rural mobility. The pilots´ main target is to enable solutions for efficient parking, optimized public transport, better usage of e-mobility infrastructure and multimodal mobility information to support an efficient and sustainable mobility and a better environment. This is done by providing services and apps for.

Smart Parking: Making use of on street Siemens parking radar sensors in Berlin and parking detectors in public car parks in Wolfsburg. BIG IoT provides a Smart Parking App to inform car drivers on location and availability of parking spots. Thus, car drivers find the closest parking spots and parking search traffic—a major cause for urban traffic stress—is reduced. The sensor data are provided by BIG IoT-enabled platforms such as Siemens APM (Advanced Parking Management) platform and BOSCH Bezirk platform. In addition to parking availability, reservation of parking spots will be provided as a service. Being BIG-IoTized enables Siemens Smart Parking App to consume any BIG IoT parking offerings, helps to extend the geographical coverage of parking information and increases business opportunities for service providers. Step one on the way to a European solution has already been done with the integration of WorldSensing parking data of our co-pilot Barcelona—enabled by: BIG IoT.

Public Transport Optimization: Based on wifi-sensors on connected buses Wolfsburg public transport operators get better information on bus occupancy and people waiting at bus stations. Wifi-sensor data is integrated in BIG IoT enabled BOSCH Smart City Platform. This helps to optimize vehicle usage and bus line planning to get more customer demand oriented public transport services.

E-Mobility: Where can I find the next free charging station to charge my e-car, e-scooter, e-van? By providing this crucial information to e-mobility users BIG IoT contributes to the success of e-mobility. E-Mobility in Berlin picked up speed in 2012 with first charging stations on public ground and has been continuously extended to presently more than 350 charging points. Location and status of more than 350 charging stations in Berlin are currently provided via BIG IoT enabled VMZ multimodal mobility platform. With higher numbers of e-vehicles the need to reserve a charging station will increase in the future. Thus BIG IoT reservation service for charging stations is an appreciated Open Call contribution.

Multimodal Commuter App: This App consumes sensor and mobility data coming from various BIG IoT enabled platforms to inform Commuters on the route between Berlin and Wolfsburg. The App provides car and public transport routing functionalities and guides car drivers to available parking spots and charging stations, includes BIG IoT offerings for real time traffic information such as traffic detectors data, incidents and traffic messages for car and public transport. Incorporating diverse data offerings of the BIG IoT Marketplace offering collection the App bridges the interoperability gap of various platforms to provide a multimodal real-time based information system for mobility end users.

91.5   Conclusions and Outlook

BIG IoT provides the common base for enabling different IoT platforms to access their sensors, data and services by a common BIG IoT API and the marketplace behind to orchestrate exchange.

Acknowledgments This work is supported by the BIG IoT project that has received funding from the European Commission's Horizon 2020 research and innovation program under grant agreement No 688038. This article presents the current status of work in the project. We thank the consortium partners for their feedback and fruitful discussions. The work will be further evolved as part of the ongoing architecture development in the project.

References

1. A. Bröring, S.K. Datta, C. Bonnet, A categorization of discovery technologies for the internet of things, in *6th International Conference on the Internet of Things (IoT 2016)*, (ACM, Stuttgart, 2016). ISBN 978-1-4503-4814-0. http://dl.acm.org/citation.cfm?doid=2991561.2991570
2. C. Bormann, A.P. Castellani, Z. Shelby, CoAP: an application protocol for billions of tiny internet nodes. IEEE Internet Comput. **16**(2), 62–67 (Mar. 2012)
3. IBM and Eurotech, *MQTT V3.1 Protocol Specification*. [Online]. http://public.dhe.ibm.com/software/dw/webservices/ws-mqtt/mqtt-v3r1.html. Accessed 24 April 2014

4. J. Swetina, G. Lu, P. Jacobs, F. Ennesser, J. Song, Toward a standardized common M2M service layer platform: introduction to oneM2M. Wirel. Commun. IEEE **21**(3), 20–26 (2014)

5. A. Bröring, J. Echterhoff, S. Jirka, I. Simonis, T. Everding, C. Stasch, S. Liang, R. Lemmens, New generation sensor web enablement. Sensors **11**(3), 2652–2699 (2011)

6. A. Bröring, S. Schmid, C.-K.Schindhelm, A. Khelil, S. Kaebisch, D. Kramer, D. Le Phuoc, J. Mitic, D. Anicic, E. Teniente, *Enabling IoT Ecosystems through Platform Interoperability*. IEEE Software, special issue on: Software Engineering for the Internet of Things **34**(1), 54–61 (2017)

7. Kubler, S., K. Främling, A. Zaslavsky, C. Doukas, E. Olivares, G. Fortino, C. E. Palau, S. Soursos, I. Podnar Zarko, Y. Fang, S. Krco, C. Heinz, C. Grimm, A. Bröring, J. Mitic, K. Olstedt O. Vermesan (2016): IoT platforms initiative. Vermesan, O. & P. Friess, Digitising the Industry - Internet of Things Connecting the Physical, Digital and Virtual World. 265–292. River Publishers, Houston 978-87-93379-82-4

8. S. Schmid, A. Bröring, D. Kramer, S. Kaebisch, A. Zappa, M. Lorenz, Y. Wang, L. Gioppo, An architecture for interoperable IoT Ecosystems, in *2nd International Workshop on Interoperability & Open Source Solutions for the Internet of Things (InterOSS-IoT 2016) at 6th International Conference on the Internet of Things (IoT 2016), vol. 10218, 39–55, 7. November 2016*, (Springer, LNCS, Stuttgart, Germany, 2017)

9. J. Hernandez-Serrano, J.L. Munoz, A. Bröring, O. Esparza, L. Mikkelsen, W. Schwarzott, O. Leon, On the road to secure and privacy-preserving IoT Ecosystems, in *2nd International Workshop on Interoperability & Open Source Solutions for the Internet of Things (InterOSS-IoT 2016) at 6th International Conference on the Internet of Things (IoT 2016), vol. 10218, 107–122, 7. November 2016*, (Springer, LNCS, Stuttgart, Germany, 2017)

Cross-Cultural Perspective of E-Commerce Website Usability Requirements: Through the Lens of Individual's Perception

Jay Jung, Jae Min Jung, and Sonya Zhang

Abstract

Although website usability is one of the prominent factors that determine the success of web-based businesses, extant research on website usability does not focus on the diversity of the users who actually use the website. Drawing on Hofstede's cultural values and Nisbett's cognitive style framework, this study proposes that individuals perceive website usability differently. The results from our online survey suggest that users who are more exposed to Western culture are more responsive to personalized and customizable features in B2C fashion websites, since their level of individualism is strongly associated with all aspects of the MUG usability requirements.

Keywords

Cross-cultural usability and user experience ·
E-commerce personalization · Microsoft usability
guidelines

92.1 Introduction

Since the evolution of the web has accelerated the globalization of the world, it is more challenging for firms to understand diverse online user behavior as they come from all around the world. Although it has been known that usability of the website's interface is one of the prominent factors that are able to determine the success of a website [1, 2], previous studies do not focus on the diversity of the users who actually use a website. There has been limited research examining how website's usability is perceived differently by individuals. Hence, the purpose of this study is to examine the associations between individuals' different cultural values and their cognitive style with website's usability requirements.

92.2 Literature Review

The definition of usability by ISO 9241-11 is "the extent to which a product can be used by specified users to achieve specified goals with effectiveness, efficiency and satisfaction in a specified context of use" [3]. The 'effectiveness' and 'efficiency' are related to the specific tasks that users perform toward achieving their goals, and the 'satisfaction' is perceived quality of the users. Because measuring usability is not intrinsically objective in nature, but rather depends upon the personal interpretation and interaction of an evaluator [4], it is required to have a set of guidelines that can be comprehensively deployed. The Microsoft Usability Guidelines (MUG), as shown in Table 92.1, is a heuristic evaluation of usability requirement that are compatible with the definition of usability by ISO [5]. Marcus and Gould (2000) analyzed cross-cultural websites' design and mapped Social Psychologist Hofstede's five cultural dimensions (Table 92.2) into five user interface components; however, their guideline is not exactly based on cultures, but rather on user's country or nationality [6]. Furthermore, cognitive psychologists view behavioral diversity as being produced by not only cultural traits, but also formed by cognitive processes [7]. As Nisbett (2001) explains Eastern Asians and Westerners have developed distinctive thinking styles (Table 92.3); how they perceive information on websites are also different.

J. Jung (✉) · S. Zhang
Department of Computer Information Systems, California State Polytechnic University, Pomona, CA, USA
e-mail: jyjung@cpp.edu; xszhang@cpp.edu

J. M. Jung
Department of International Business and Marketing, California State Polytechnic University, Pomona, CA, USA
e-mail: jmjung@cpp.edu

© Springer International Publishing AG, part of Springer Nature 2018
S. Latifi (ed.), *Information Technology – New Generations*, Advances in Intelligent Systems and Computing 738,
https://doi.org/10.1007/978-3-319-77028-4_92

Table 92.1 Microsoft usability guidelines (MUG)

Category	Description
Content	• Extent to which a website offers informational and transactional capability.
Ease of use	• Extent to which a website is free of effort.
Made-for-medium	• Extent to which a website can be tailored to fit your specific needs.
Emotion	• Extent to which a website evokes emotional reactions from you.
Promotion	• Extent to which Web site is well promoted on Web and other media

Table 92.2 Hofstede's cultural value

Dimension	Description
Individualism vs. collectivism	• Personal independence and goal (Ind.) vs. Group goals and harmony (Col.)
Power distance	• Degree to which hierarchy and unequal power distributions are accepted. (high vs. low)
Masculinity vs. femininity	• Distribution of roles between genders (mas. vs. fem.)
Uncertainty avoidance	• Prefer the known systems and rules (High) vs. Comfortable with ambiguous situations and risk (low)

Table 92.3 Nisbett's cognitive style

Analytic: Westerners (European culture)	Holistic: Easterners (East Asian culture)
• Detachment of the object from its context • A tendency to focus on attributes of the object • A preference for using rules	• An orientation to the background and contextual of field as a whole. • A preference for explaining and predicting events on the basis of such relationships between the objects and its context

92.3   Methodology

Based on the literature review presented, this study proposes that usability evaluation is influenced by individuals' cultural values and their cognitive styles. A conceptual model is presented in Fig. 92.1. To test the hypotheses, a web-based survey was conducted. Participants were asked to complete given usability tasks on two fashion business-to-consumer (B2C) websites (www.yesstyle.com, us.riverisland.com); one reflects Eastern culture and the other reflects Western culture. Then the participants were asked to complete a web-based survey regarding their background, experience and perceptions. All the constructs were measured on a 7-point Likert-type scale. Five website usability requirements based on MUG was measured using a scale adapted from the usability instrument and served as a dependent variable. Each of the five cultural value dimensions were measured with four items, adopted from cultural value scale. Participants' cognitive style was measured with six items per each four dimensions and it was adapted from Choi's analysis-holism scale.

92.4   Results

A total of 217 usable responses were received. Fifty three percent are female participants. The average age is 22, ranging from 18 to 44 years old. Most participants reported their ethnicity either as Hispanic/Latino (35.8%) or Asian (35.4%) following by White (19.8%). The majority of participants were born in the U.S. (77.9%), speak English as their primary language (72.6%), and identify with American culture (73.7%). We ran five multiple regression models with

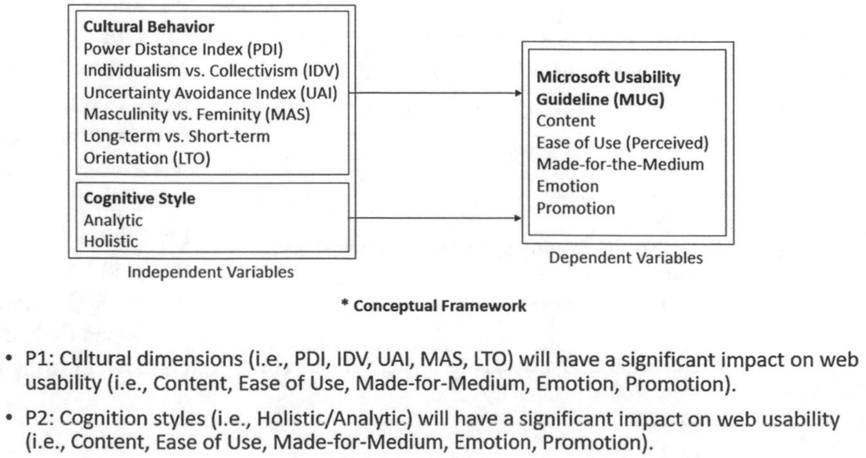

Fig. 92.1 Conceptual framework

* **Conceptual Framework**

- P1: Cultural dimensions (i.e., PDI, IDV, UAI, MAS, LTO) will have a significant impact on web usability (i.e., Content, Ease of Use, Made-for-Medium, Emotion, Promotion).

- P2: Cognition styles (i.e., Holistic/Analytic) will have a significant impact on web usability (i.e., Content, Ease of Use, Made-for-Medium, Emotion, Promotion).

each of the five dimensions of the website usability as a dependent variable one at a time and with all the cultural value dimensions (IND, COL, PD, MAS, and UA) and cognitive style (CS) as independent variables consistently in all the models. The results show that users' level of individualism is strongly associated with the content and made-for-medium dimension of the usability requirements, as well as their level of masculinity is associated with the emotion dimension of usability requirements. The results also show that analytic thinkers are more critical of their assessment of the content, made-for-medium, and emotion aspects of the usability requirements.

92.5 Conclusion and Discussion

This study examined the associations between individuals' cultural values and their cognitive style with website usability requirements. As the results show, users' level of individualism is strongly associated with all aspects of the MUG usability requirements in B2C fashion websites. Practitioners should be aware that users' cultural background, as well as their cognitive style hugely affect how users experience the website when they perform usability testing. Particularly, e-commerce websites should be able to provide personalized and customizable features for users who have more exposed to Western culture to make the website more usable. However, it is unclear if the results would be the same when testing different websites other than e-commerce, such as news, travel or forum websites. Future studies can also examine alternate usability requirements other than MUG, with varying types of websites. Furthermore, usability testing on various devices such as mobile phones or tablets will result in exciting and useful findings in cross-cultural research.

References

1. C. Downing, C. Liu, Does web site usability correlate with web site usage? JITIM **18**(3/4), 443–454 (2009)
2. Y. Lee, A.K. Kozar, Understanding of website usability-specifying and measuring constructs and their relationships. Decis. Support. Syst. **52**, 450–463 (2012)
3. J. Karat, User-centered software evaluation methodologies, in *Handbook of Human-Computer Interaction*. ed. by M. Helander, T.K. Landauer, P. Prabhu, (Elsevier, Amsterdam, 1997), pp. 689–704
4. R. Agarwal, V. Venkatesh, Assessing a firm's web presence—a heuristic evaluation procedure for the measurement of usability. Inf. Syst. Res. **13**(2), 168–186 (2002)
5. R. Agarwal, V. Venkatesh, Turning visitor into customers—a usability-centric perspective on purchase behavior in electronic channels. Manag. Sci. **52**(3), 367–382 (2006)
6. Z. Ishak, A. Jaafar, A. Ahmad, Interface design for cultural differences. Soc. Behav. Sci. **65**(3), 793–801 (2012)
7. A. Faiola, S.A. Matei, Cultural cognitive style and web design: beyond a behavioral inquiry into computer-mediated communication. J. Comput.-Mediat. Commun. **11**(1), 375–394 (2005)

Methods of Ensuring the Reliability and Fault Tolerance of Information Systems

Askar Boranbayev, Seilkhan Boranbayev, Kuanysh Yersakhanov, Assel Nurusheva, and Roman Taberkhan

Abstract

This article is devoted to ensuring the reliability of information systems. An approach based on risk assessment and neutralization is used to increase the reliability of information systems. This approach allows for early risk assessment of the software development process and determines the most effective mitigation strategies.

Keywords

Method · Reliability · Software · Application · Design

93.1 Introduction

This article considers an approach based on risk assessment and neutralization to increase the reliability of information systems. The approach is based on the adaptation of the RED [1, 2] and GREEN methods to assess the risks of information systems. It is shown that the RED method can be used in the early stages of the software development process to identify and analyze the risk represented by potential software errors. For the first time, the RED method was used in the field of electromechanical design. The GREEN method is a tool that helps in reducing risk by using risk assessment and mitigation strategies based on historical data [3]. This article shows that the RED and GREEN methods can be adapted and used in the field of information systems to provide the risk assessment based on its functionality.

A. Boranbayev (✉)
Department of Computer Science, Nazarbayev University, Astana, Kazakhstan
e-mail: aboranbayev@nu.edu.kz

S. Boranbayev · K. Yersakhanov · A. Nurusheva · R. Taberkhan
Department of Information Systems, L.N. Gumilyov Eurasian National University, Astana, Kazakhstan
e-mail: sboranba@yandex.kz

93.2 Methods RED and GREEN

RED provides an important information about the product, showing the exact status of the risk of the test product [4]. This method provides valuable historical information on the likelihood of occurrence and the consequences of specific product risks. In order to perform the analysis, it is necessary to collect data that contains information about components, functions, failure modes and the severity of registered failures.

To obtain the final result about the product risk, three matrices must be filled with important data. One of these Matrices is the Function-Component Matrix (EC), which has information about the functions and components of a test product. In case of Information Systems, we may consider modules as components of the product. Next, there is a matrix called the Component-Failure (CF). Here is the information about failures and components of the test product. The two matrices are multiplied together to get the resulting Function-Failure matrix (EF) that forms the failure knowledge base [5].

93.3 Ensuring Reliability and Fault Tolerance of Information Systems

The RED method was used in engineering design. In this paper we show how the RED method can be used in the field of Information system reliability assessment.

When developing an information system, especially if it is a complex system, there is always a possibility that an error will occur. To describe the situation and the sequence of actions that led to the incorrect operation of the system, a document called "bug report" [6] is created. In each bug report such attributes as severity and priority are indicated. Severity—indicates how serious the failure is and how it can affect the software performance. Priority—indicates the priority for each task to fix the problem. Thus, the first in the queue is a failure with the highest priority. The severity of the failure is usually identified by five types.

Thus, the data that is presented in the bug report can be used to determine the reliability of information systems using the RED method.

To automate the calculation of reliability and fault tolerance of Information systems a special prototype based on RED and GREEN methods was developed. This prototype may have changes in the future. Loading of initial data into the prototype software is done in two ways: manually and using Excel.

Thus, the prototype software solves the following tasks:

1. Forecasting of potential software failures. Risk assessment.
2. Sorting the bug reports.
3. Use of mitigation strategies.

To prevent (mitigate) failures, it is required to have a database with mitigation strategies. To build such a database, information from bug reports is used. Also, it is possible to find a suitable (close) strategy in created database. Mitigation strategies can improve the reliability of certain parts of the software product, or the whole product. Most of these strategies are created on the basis of expert knowledge. The software system allows you to determine which strategies should be used to reduce the risks of the information system.

4. Getting a detailed bug report

The software allows you to review and evaluate the risk of the whole product or each risk individually. It allows you to assess the reliability of the product, improve the product quality in the future, find suitable strategies for mitigating failures.

93.4 Conclusion

In this paper, an approach for assessing risks and ensuring the reliability of information system was considered and the prototype software based on the RED and GREEN methods was presented. Risk assessment plays an important role in ensuring the reliability of the information system,

especially if it provides automation of the operation of critical systems. Having a good tool for risk assessment can prevent threats that can negatively affect the operation of the system. Modern tools for risk assessment require expert knowledge in order to predict possible failures, the likelihood of their occurrence and consequences. The data used for risk assessment should be well cataloged and correctly used, as incorrect filling of information can lead to a great damage and losses. The software system provides information in a format that is understandable to any user. The end result is information about the Information system risks. Further, based on the received information on risks, the software system generates data on strategies for certain failures and allows you to choose the best way to eliminate them. The proposed approach can be used in further development of the research presented in [7, 8].

References

1. K. Grantham Lough, R. Stone, and I. Tumer. Prescribing and implementing the Risk in Early Design (RED) method, in *Proceedings of DETC'06*, number DETC2006-99374, (Philadelphia, PA, 2006), pp. 431–439
2. K. Grantham Lough, R. Stone, and I. Tumer. The Risk in Early Design (RED) method: likelihood and consequence formulations, in *Proceedings of DETC'06,* number DETC2006-99375 (Philadelphia, PA, 2006), pp. 1119–1129
3. D.A. Krus, *The Risk Mitigation Strategy Taxonomy and Generated Risk Event Effect Neutralization method.* Doctoral Dissertations, 2012, p. 176
4. K.G. Lough, R. Stone, I.Y. Tumer, The risk in early design method. J. Eng. Des. **20**(2), 155–173 (2009). https://doi.org/10.1080/09544820701684271
5. J.P. Vucovich et al., Risk assessment in early software design based on the software function-failure design method, in *Proceedings of the 31st Annual International Computer Software and Applications Conference*, (Institute of Electrical and Electronics Engineers (IEEE), 2007), pp. 405–412
6. Main fields of bug/defect report [Online source]/Website Pro Testing—Software Testing. http://www.protesting.ru/testing/bugstructure.html
7. S. Boranbayev, S. Altayev, A. Boranbayev. Applying the method of diverse redundancy in cloud based systems for increasing reliability, in *Proceedings of the 12th International Conference on Information Technology: New Generations (ITNG 2015)* (Las Vegas, Nevada, 2015), pp. 796–799
8. S. Boranbayev, A. Boranbayev, S. Altayev, A. Nurbekov. Mathematical model for optimal designing of reliable information systems, in *Proceedings of the 2014 IEEE 8th International Conference on Application of Information and Communication Technologies-AICT2014*, (Astana, 2014), pp. 123–127

Applying a Method for Credit Limit Reviews in a Brazilian Retail Enterprise

Strauss Carvalho Cunha, Emanuel Mineda Carneiro,
Lineu Fernando Stege Mialaret, Luiz Alberto Vieira Dias,
and Adilson Marques da Cunha

Abstract

In this article, we investigate an approach for credit limit revision for a Brazilian retail company, using real data. The Linear Regression classifier was used and the results show that there was an improvement in the company's profit using the proposed approach.

Keywords

Management decisions · Credit granting · Classification · Credit limit · Linear regression

94.1 Introduction

In recent years, credit demands have increased. Within the credit granting context, in addition to identify defaulting customers, other relevant issue refers to granting credit limits.

The credit limit assignment problem has been addressed on different approaches: dynamic programming [1]; Markovian decision processes [2]; dynamic system modeling [3]; Compound Poisson process [4]; fuzzy logic [5]; and linear programming [6].

In this paper, a heuristic approach developed by Selau [7] and Costa [8] was used for applying a method for credit

S. C. Cunha
Brazilian Federal Service of Data Processing – SERPRO, Rio de Janeiro, Brazil
e-mail: strauss.carvalho@serpro.gov.br

E. M. Carneiro · L. A. V. Dias · A. M. da Cunha
Computer Science Department, Brazilian Aeronautics Institute of Technology – ITA, Sao Jose dos Campos, SP, Brazil
e-mail: mineda@ita.br; vdias@ita.br; cunha@ita.br

L. F. S. Mialaret (✉)
Federal Institute of Education, Science and Technology of Sao Paulo – IFSP, Jacarei, SP, Brazil
e-mail: lmialaret@ifsp.edu.br

limit reviews in a Brazilian retail enterprise. The case study is a Brazilian retailer company with hundreds of stores spread throughout the country providing customers with credit cards. The objective of the enterprise is to develop a system that allows to review and modify credit limits for maximize profit in the credit card usage, among other functionalities to be implemented.

The rest of this paper is organized as follows: Sect. 94.2 describes the development of a credit limits method, involving data pre-processing, model construction, and the obtained results. Finally, Sect. 94.3 presents conclusions and suggests future researches.

94.2 Credit Limit Model Development

For the delineation of credit limit revision, the following proposed process with four stages is described as follows: (1) Data Pre-processing; (2) Construction of a Profit Prediction Model; (3) Evaluation of the Model; and (4) Determining of Credit Limit.

In the Data Pre-processing stage, demographic, behavioral, and financial information of the enterprise's customers was used. It was determined that the population involved was related to a product of the company, in this case, a specific credit card type. A sample data set containing 4051 customers were selected, of which 3420 were considered as non-defaulting and 631 defaulting customers.

The objective in the Construction of a Profit Prediction Model stage is to use a credit granting model with a predictive response variable that provides a continuous measure (monetary). This measure is positive if there is profit, and negative if there is loss. It is intended to adequately measure customers with expected profit greater than zero. In this approach, we used Linear Regression, in which one wishes to estimate the profit (or loss) of the proponent on credit in function of the independent variables available.

© Springer International Publishing AG, part of Springer Nature 2018
S. Latifi (ed.), *Information Technology – New Generations*, Advances in Intelligent Systems and Computing 738,
https://doi.org/10.1007/978-3-319-77028-4_94

The approach adopted in this investigation consists in the attribution of financial limit for credit by means of the *Estimated Profit* (*EP*), provided by the regressive model. Initially, it is defined as the population identified in terms of obtained profit, which represents the enterprise's profit obtained with customers identified as non-defaulting (with positive profit) and as defaulting (with negative profit). This population will be used for validation of the proposed regressive model.

The way to define the limit of each customer consists of two steps: the first step is to resize the regression model's response variable *EP* to its corresponding revenue value, by means of Eq. (94.1), equivalent to the value that the customer must acquire in purchases (invoices) in the shopping and/or services, so that the profit forecast is observed.

The *EP* equation has the following format:

$$EP = \alpha * R \qquad (94.1)$$

where:

EP correspond to *Estimated Profit*; *R* represent the enterprise's financial revenue (purchases that the customer must make); and α is the enterprise's profit margin.

In the second step, a limit value is defined for each range of sales and this value is classified in the equivalent class, with standardized values for the credit limit. In this way, negative predicted profit values resulting from the model are automatically classified in the group of defaulting customer and rejected. Only customers classified as non-defaulting, with a positive profit expected value, will have some credit limit assigned.

In the next two stages, the assignment of the limit by means of the expected profit consists of resizing the response variable from the regressive model to its corresponding sales value. The sales value with each customer is obtained by dividing the expected profit by the profit margin, which in this case is estimated by the company in to be 30%. The values obtained represent, in monetary value, how much the customer must acquire in products in order to obtain the expected profit through the estimated profit margin and, therefore, correspond to the limit recommended to the customer.

Table 94.1 shows the average and total limit granted by the enterprise and the new limits suggested by the investigation in each predicted profit range. The results show that the average limits granted by the enterprise in the initial ranges (up to 2000.00) have a high variation in relation to the limits of expected profit, which reveals a misalignment of these limits. Table 94.2 presents the new suggested limits, which are already adequate.

Table 94.1 Current and suggested credit limits

Expected profit		Assigned limit		
Interval	#	Average	Total	Profit
6000	2	4400	8800	0
5500	2	3725	7450	0
5000	2	4000	8000	6133.762
4500	3	2633.333	7900	19,100.51
4000	11	2981.818	32,800	16,655.17
3500	16	2793.75	44,700	44,084.77
3000	27	2042.593	55,150	48,099.9
2500	70	2384.286	166,900	86,927.43
2000	147	1921.088	282,400	241,116
1500	351	1760.826	618,050	328,047.8
1000	776	1702.126	1,320,850	544,403.6
500	1175	1530.936	1,798,850	136,905.5
0	835	1411.317	1,178,450	−33,516
Sum	3417	2560.544	5,530,300	1,437,958

Expected profit		Suggested limit		
Interval	#	Average	Total	Profit
6000	2	6072.095	12,144.19	0
5500	2	5703.806	11,407.61	104.9272
5000	2	5113.188	10,226.38	5825.106
4500	3	4708.95	14,126.85	35,626.53
4000	11	4257.413	46,831.55	5092.989
3500	16	3755.681	60,090.9	49,500.36
3000	27	3290.149	88,834.01	59,772.77
2500	70	2697.06	188,794.2	130,514.2
2000	147	2223.822	326,901.8	407,791.3
1500	351	1700.759	596,966.3	533,210.9
1000	776	1215.907	943,544	799,501.8
500	1175	749.9544	881,196.5	136,112.5
0	835	302.1145	252,265.6	−39,604.3
Sum	3417	3214.684	3,433,330	2,123,449

Table 94.2 New suggested credit limits

	New limit	Sum
6072.095	6075	6125.199
5703.806	5710	11,817.43
5113.188	5115	10,758.43
4708.95	4710	14,687.67
4257.413	4260	22,197.53
3755.681	3755	56,627
3290.149	3290	76,936.72
2697.06	2700	135,121
2223.822	2225	240,553.3
1700.759	1700	596,966.3
1215.907	1215	789,726.6
749.9544	750	976,965.8
302.1145	305	75,250.47

94.3   Conclusion

The credit limit assignments using quantitative methods has been a problem addressed by several investigations in the specialized literature. In this investigation, a heuristic approach was used to determine appropriate credit limits for the customers in the Brazilian retail company. The Linear Regression classifier was used and the results showed that the new suggested limits provide better profit performance for the company.

One area for further work is to use different classifiers and analyze the profit performance. Other area is getting more behavioral/finance attributes.

Acknowledgements The authors wish to thank the Brazilian Aeronautics Institute of Technology (ITA) Software Engineering Research Group (GPES) members for their assistance and advice. In addition, we would like to thank ITA and 2RPNet company for providing the research infrastructure and data needed by this work.

References

1. Y.M. Dirickx, L. Wakeman, An extension of the Bierman-Hausman model for credit granting. Manag. Sci. **22**(11), 1229–1237 (1976)
2. M.C. So, L.C. Thomas, H.-V. Seow, C. Mues, Using a transactor/revolver scorecard to make credit and pricing decisions. Decis. Support Syst. **59**, 143–151 (2013)
3. M.M. Skok, M.P. Bach, J. Zoroja, Credit card spending limit and personal finance: system dynamics approach. Croat. Oper. Res. Rev. **5**(1), 35–47 (2014)
4. J.K. Budd, P.G. Taylor, *Calculating Optimal Limits for Transacting Credit Card Customers* (2015). Papers. arXiv.org. https://EconPapers.repec.org/RePEc:arx:papers:1506.05376
5. U. Paul, A. Biswas, Consumer credit limit assignment using Bayesian decision theory and Fuzzy Logic – a practical approach. J. Manag. **4**(2), 11–18 (2017)
6. Z. Herga, J. Rupnik, P. Skraba, B. Fortuna, Modeling probability of default and credit limits, in *Conference on Data Mining and Data Warehouses*, ed. by K.D.D. Slovenian (2016)
7. L.P.R. Selau, Modelagem para concessão de crédito a pessoas físicas em empresas comerciais: da decisão binária para a decisão monetária. Tese de Doutorado. Escola de Administração. Universidade Federal do Rio Grande do Sul. Porto Alegre. Rio Grande do Sul (2012)
8. A.B. Costa, *Modelo de previsão de risco de crédito com atribuição do limite através do lucro previsto*. Trabalho de conclusão de graduação. Departamento de Estatística, Instituto de Matemática, Universidade Federal do Rio Grande do Sul – UFRGS (2015)

Application of an Effective Methodology for Analysis of Fragility and Its Components in the Elderly

J. L. C. Mello, D. M. T. Souza, C. M. Tamaki, V. A. C. Galhardo, D. F. Veiga, and A. C. B. Ramos

Abstract

Fragility is a syndrome characterized by reduced physical and cognitive reserves making the elderly more vulnerable to adverse events, hospitalizations, falls, loss of independence, and death. Inertia sensors have been applied to quantify motion assessment in Timed Up and Go (TUG) test, accelerometers are used during balance assessment, and algorithms differentiate fragile, pre-fragile, and robust elderly people.

Objective: Developing a multifunctional sensor to evaluate fragility, based on marker phenotype and deficit accumulation index.

Methods: Primary, exploratory, interventional, analytical, and transversal study with a technological approach. The study will be developed, in partnership with researchers from the Federal University of Itajubá-MG using high-tech, multifunctional, and cost-effective sensor equipment in combination with a 3-axis gyroscope, a 3-axis accelerometer, electromyography and frequency meter, analysis of movement quality, energy expenditure, gait velocity, change in balance, heart rate variability during movement, and quality of quadriceps muscle contraction.

The data will be analyzed by software developed after the prototyping of the equipment. The fragility analysis procedure will not cause any damage or impairment to the health of the elderly participants, since the items used during the procedure will be the sensor, the measurement of the instruments, the Barthel Index, the Mental State Examination, and the Self-rated fragility assessment.

The validation of the sensor will not cause damage or impairment to the health of the participants.

Locations: Samuel Libânio Clinical Hospital, in the clinics of Health Clinic, Dementia, and Assistance Nucleus Nursing Education, and in the Basic Health Units of the municipality of Pouso Alegre-MG.

Casuistry: Convenience sample.

Eligibility criteria: 300 elderly people, 60 years of age or older, both sexes, signing the Free and Informed Consent Form (TCLE), and approval by the Research Ethics Committee of University of Vale do Sapucaí (UNIVÁS).

Criteria for non-inclusion: Elderly people with immobility or severe cognitive impairment that impedes understanding of the orientation towards the TUG.

Exclusion criteria: The waiving of continuing the study after the signing of the TCLE.

Keywords

Healthcare information technology · Frail elderly · Medical device · Wearable · Accelerometry

95.1 Introduction

Fragility is a syndrome characterized by reduced physical and cognitive reserves and makes the elderly more vulnerable to adverse events, such as hospitalizations, falls, loss of independence, and death [1, 2].

Although there is no consensus in the literature on the criteria for identifying fragility, the model created by Fried et al., is among the most widely used today. For the author, the presence of three or more criteria classifies the elderly as fragile and the presence of one or two classifies them as pre-fragile, understood here as those that present a high risk to develop the fragility syndrome [3].

J. L. C. Mello · D. M. T. Souza (✉) · V. A. C. Galhardo · D. F. Veiga
University of Vale do Sapucaí, Pouso Alegre, Brazil
e-mail: dibasouz@uai.com.br

C. M. Tamaki (✉) · A. C. B. Ramos (✉)
Federal University of Itajubá, Itajubá, Brazil
e-mail: minoru@unifei.edu.br; ramos@unifei.edu.br

© Springer International Publishing AG, part of Springer Nature 2018
S. Latifi (ed.), *Information Technology – New Generations*, Advances in Intelligent Systems and Computing 738,
https://doi.org/10.1007/978-3-319-77028-4_95

The criteria established by Fried (2001) are:

1. Unintentional weight loss of 4.5 kg or 5% of body weight in the last year.
2. Self-rated fatigue, assessed through questions and the depression scale of the Center for Epidemiological Studies.
3. Reduction of palmar grip strength, measured by manual dynamometer, in the dominant upper limb.
4. Reduced level of physical activity measured by the weekly energy expenditure in kcal and decrease in walking speed.

The Fried (2001) model is based on sarcopenia and immunological and neuroendocrine changes and focuses on the physical dimension of fragility.

Good correlation between the Fried's fragility score and gait speed was evidenced, which makes this functional test adequate to monitor and assist in the diagnosis of fragility syndrome in the elderly [2].

The prompt and accurate identification of a person's state of fragility may allow effective multifactorial interventions that have been shown to improve health outcomes [4].

The TUG test [5, 6] is a standard evaluation of mobility since the time to do it has been a strong predictor of fragility [7] and is commonly used to assess the risk of falls in the elderly [8].

Recent research has investigated the use of inertial sensors to quantify motion assessment in the TUG test and the use of accelerometers during assessment of balance in tasks to examine the utility of derived parameters using an algorithm to discriminate between fragile, non-fragile, and robust. In addition, the accelerometer is a low cost instrument and the test is not restricted to the laboratory environment [8]; "The accelerometry patterns are used to identify normal and pathological gait, with acceleration peaks"; is considered a method of kinematic analysis of human movement [9].

A study published in 2014 investigated the use of inertial sensors in the automatic and quantitative assessment of the fragility state suggested that a protocol using the TUG and said devices can be a fast and effective means for the automatic and non-specialized evaluation of fragility [8].

At present, advances in sensor technology have provided a new method for measuring physical function [10–12] and physical activity in populations. These devices have the benefits of objectivity, portability, and low cost [11], thus making them useful for assessing fragility at home and in the community [13].

95.2 Objective

To develop a multifunctional sensor to evaluate the fragility, based on phenotypic marker and deficit accumulation index, and to validate the use of this sensor in the elderly population to identify it fragile, non-fragile and robust.

95.3 Methodology

95.3.1 Kind of Study

It is a primary, exploratory, interventional, analytical and transversal study with a technological approach.

95.3.2 Casuistry

The sample will be for convenience. Older people aged 60 or older from the community, living in the municipality of Pouso Alegre-MG, those assisted in the outpatient clinics of Clinical Medicine, Dementia, Nursing Assistance and Teaching Nucleus (NAEENF), Basic Health Units (UBS) and Long-term Institutions for elderly within a period of six months, that meet the eligibility criteria.

95.3.2.1 Eligibility Criteria
1. Participants will be patients from the community and attended at HCSL outpatient clinics. The age of the participants will be 60 years and older, both sexes, agreed to participate in the study, and have signed the Free and Informed Consent Form (TCLE).
2. An average of 300 participants.
3. The study is approved by the Research Ethics Committee of UNIVÁS.

95.3.2.2 Criteria for Non-Inclusion
People who have any of the following:

1. Immobility syndrome.
2. Severe cognitive impairment that impedes understanding of the orientation towards the TUG.

95.3.3 Exclusion Criteria

Refusal to continue the study after signing the TCLE.

95.3.4 Development of Multifunctional Analysis Sensor

The Nucleus of Technological Innovation (NIT) of UNIVÁS has as some of its main purposes:

1. To create, manage, and ensure the maintenance of the policy to encourage technological innovation.
2. To enable strategies and actions related to intellectual property rights in both the internal and external environment of the University.

A cost-effective, high-tech, multifunctional, sensor type device was created, in partnership with the Federal University of Itajubá-UNIFEI, can be used in conjunction with a 3-axis gyroscope, a 3-axis accelerometer, electromyography, thermo sensor and frequency meter, analysis of the quality of movement, energy expenditure, gait speed, change in balance, heart rate variability during movement, and quality of quadriceps muscle contraction (Fig. 95.1). The data will be analyzed by specific software which is to be developed after the creation of the equipment prototype.

Accelerometers are sophisticated electronic devices that measure the acceleration produced by body movement [14]. Acceleration is defined as the change in velocity over time, being directly proportional to the external force network involved.

Basically, accelerometers use one or multiple motion sensors to detect accelerations in different body segments [15]. The sensor used by many instruments consists of a piezoelectric element and a seismic mass inside a case. The triaxial accelerometers, in turn, are able to measure the acceleration in each of the three orthogonal planes, providing information for each plane separately as well as in a combined way from all planes [16].

Figure 95.1 show the circuit diagram of the multifunctional analysis sensor that is composed of:

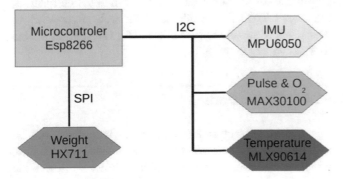

Fig. 95.1 Diagram of the electronic circuit

1. An ESP8266, a firmware and open source development kit that assists in the development of equipment that requires Wi-Fi communication and a micro-controller.
2. An MPU6050 sensor, the IMU Inertial Measurement Unit, features a 3-axis accelerometer and a 3-axis gyroscope that can measure movement.
3. An MAX30100 is an integrated pulse oximetry and heart rate monitor sensor solution for measuring pulse and O_2. It combines two LEDs, an optimized optical photodetector, and low-noise analog signal processing to detect pulse oximetry and heart rate signals;
4. An MLX90614 is an infrared sensor capable of measuring the temperature from $-70\,^{\circ}$ C to $382.2\,^{\circ}$ C, with resolution of 17 bits, i.e., it is able to measure the temperature variation without coming into contact with the object with a resolution of $0.0034\,^{\circ}$ C;
5. An HX711, a 24-bit converter and amplifier module, used to amplify the signal of devices as load cells, making the interconnection between these cells and the micro-controller.
6. The I2C communication protocol, a protocol used between devices that "talk" I2C (Inter-Integrated Circuit). So far we have seen some communication protocols that Arduino supports, such as SPI, One-Wire, and even the serial interface is a well-defined communication protocol.
7. The SPI (Serial Peripheral Interface), a synchronous serial communication interface specification used for serial data communication performed with peripheral devices for quick real time communication.

95.3.4.1 Timed Up and Go (TUG) Test

The TUG test's objective is to evaluate mobility and functional balance. The test quantifies in seconds the functional mobility by analyzing the time that the individual performs the task of getting up from a chair (support of approximately 46 cm in height and arms of 65 cm in height), walking 3 m, turning around, returning to the chair, and sitting again [5, 6].

In the TUG, the initial position of the elderly person is sitting in the chair with the back resting on the chair. The timing is measured after the starting and ending only when the elderly person has returned to the initial position, sitting with his back on the seat.

Bischoff et al. [17] consider that performing the test within 10 s as the time considered normal for healthy, independent adults with no risk of falls; values between 11 and 20 s is expected for the elderly with deficiency or fragility, partial independence, and with low risk of falls; over 20 s implies the test subject has a significant deficit of physical mobility and risk of falls. The same authors determine a performance of up to 12 s as the normal time for the test for community-dwelling elders [17].

The test participants in this study will be divided into three groups, according to the TUG score

1. Up to 10 s
2. Between 11 and 20 s
3. Over 20 s.

95.3.5 Ethical Considerations

The study was approved by the Research Ethics Committee of UNIVÁS (MG), protocol 2.016.179.

As the test is the application of questionnaires and the multi-functional sensor, there are no risks to the physical or psychological integrity of the subjects involved, as no invasive procedures will be performed or that explicitly expose the participants. Thus, there is minimal research risk, which can occur due to constraint arising from some question or sensor placement, which occurs during the test. Whenever the evaluator feels uncomfortable, for whatever reason, he may interrupt the interview at any time he deems appropriate.

95.3.6 Location of the Study

The study will be carried out at the Samuel Libânio Clinic Hospital (HCSL); at the clinics of Health Clinic, Dementia and Nursing Education and Assistance Center (NAEENF); in the city's Basic Health Units; and through calls on weekends for the "Fragility Day", to be held at the Fátima Campus of the UNIVÁS, where several professionals will be involved with evaluation of the elderly, coordinator of the project, graduate student and undergraduate students of the health area.

95.3.7 Instruments

Demographic questionnaire, the Barthel Index [18], the Mental State Examination [19], and the Self-rated fragility assessment [20].

95.3.8 Data Collection Procedures

95.3.8.1 Casuistry Selection
Once the terms of TCLE are signed by the patient and/or responsible party, the instruments will be applied according to protocol to be established after the prototype of the sensor is completed. The application of the instruments will be carried out by the researcher in conjunction with other health professionals and undergraduate students of the health area of UNIVAS.

95.3.8.2 Evaluation of the Elderly with the Application of the Instruments
To fulfill the purposes of the research, the following procedures will be performed:

1. Signing the TCLE by the patient or caregiver.
2. Application of the sociodemographic questionnaire to all test subjects able to communicate verbal or written, as well as their caregivers or legal guardians.
3. Application of the "self-rated assessment of fragility in the elderly", to be answered by the test subjects and possibly confirmed by the responsible caregivers.
4. Application of the MMSE: the test subjects will be classified as having/not having cognitive deficit. For purposes of classification, the cuts of 18 points for illiterates and those with only low schooling and 26 points for eight years or more of schooling will be used.
5. Application of the Barthel Index, for evaluation of mobility and personal care. The elderly will be classified into dependents, partially dependent or independent, according to the score obtained.
6. The calf circumference will be obtained in the sitting or standing positions, with the feet resting on a flat surface, to ensure that the weight is evenly distributed between both sides [21].
7. The parameters of gait velocity, energy expenditure, balance change, heart rate variability, and quality of quadriceps muscle contraction will be obtained by means of a multifunctional sensor coupled to the digital femoral quadriceps, with the patient in motion, running the Timed up and Go (TUG) test in a hallway extensive enough to conduct the measurement. The test subjects will be instructed to walk as fast as possible without running.

In order to avoid the effects of acceleration and deceleration, one meter will be added before and after the three meters of the test.

All test subjects will perform the test three times, being considered for recording the attempt with less time spent for the course. The use of walking sticks, walkers, crutches or even handrail support will be allowed for test subjects unable to walk without them [5, 6].

95.4   Conclusions

The present project is feasible, since the elderly will be recruited from the community at different levels of attention, provided they do not have immobility. Since the test is the application of questionnaires and a multi-functional sensor, there are no risks to the physical or psychological integrity of the subjects involved, as no invasive procedures will be performed or that explicitly expose the participants. Thus, the minimum research risk is considered, which can occur due to constraint arising from some question or sensor placement. However, whenever the evaluator feels uncomfortable, for whatever reason, he may interrupt the interview at any time he deems appropriate.

The results of the study have been analyzed through the use of descriptive and inferential statistics (hypothesis tests). Frequency tables and measures such as mean, median, standard deviation, minimum value and maximum value will be used. The choice of non-parametric or parametric tests will occur according to the type of study variables. The level of significance used as acceptance or rejection criterion in the statistical tests will be 5% ($p < 0.05$). The analysis will be performed in the SPSS program, version 18.0.

References

1. R.C. McDermid, H.T. Stelfox, S.M. Bagshaw, Frailty in the critically ill: a novel concept. Crit. Care **15**, 301 (2011)
2. Y. Schoon, K. Bongers, J. Van Kempen, R. Melis, R.M. Olde, Gait speed as a test for monitoring frailty in community-dwelling older people has the highest diagnostic value compared to step length and chair rise time. Eur. J. Phys. Rehabil. Med. **50**(6), 693–701 (2014)
3. L.P. Fried et al., Frailty in older adults: evidence for a phenotype. J. Gerontol. A Biol. Sci. Med. Sci. **56**(3), 146–156 (2001)
4. M.E. Tinneti et al., A multifactorial intervention to reduce the risk of falling among elderly people living in the community. N. Engl. J. Med. **331**(13), 821–827 (1994)
5. S. Mathias, U.S.L. Nayak, B. Isaacs, Balance in elderly patients: the get up and go test. Arch. Phys. Med. Rehabil. **67**, 387–389 (1986)
6. D. Podsiadlo, S. Richardson, The timed "Up & Go": a test of basic functional mobility for frail elderly pearsons. J. Am. Geriatr. Soc. **39**(2), 142–148 (1991)
7. G.M. Savva, O.A. Donoghue, F. Horgan, C. O'Regan, H. Cronin, R.A. Kenny, Using timed up-and-go to identify frail members of the older population. J. Gerontol. A Biol. Sci. Med. Sci. **68**, 441–446 (2013)
8. B.R. Greene, E.P. Dohener, A. O'Halloran, R.A. Kenny, Frailty status can be accurately assessed using inertial sensors and the TUG test. Age Ageing **43**, 406–411 (2014)
9. D.L.B. Muniz; M.C. De Andrade. *Biomechanical Analysis of the Phases of the March by Accelerometers* (2011)
10. K. Aminian, B. Najafi, C. Bula, P.F. Leyvraz, P. Robert, Spatio-temporal parameters of gait measured by an ambulatory system using miniature gyroscopes. J. Biomech. **35**, 689–699 (2002)
11. B. Najafi, T. Khan, J. Wrobel, Laboratory in a box: wearable sensors and its advantages for gait analysis. Conf. Proc. IEEE Eng. Med. Biol. Soc. **2011**, 6507–6510 (2011)
12. B. Najafi, D. Horn, S. Marclay, R.T. Crews, S. Wu, J.S. Wrobel, Assessing postural control and postural postural control strategy in diabetes patients using innovative and wearabletechnology. J. Diabetes Sci. Technol. **4**, 780–791 (2010)
13. M. Schwenk et al., Wearable sensor-based in-home assessment of gait, balance, and physical activity for discrimination of frailty status: baseline results of the Arizona frailty cohort study. Gerontology **61**, 258–267 (2015)
14. E. Innes, L. Straker, Validity of work-related assessments. Work **13**(2), 125–152 (1999)
15. K.Y. Chen, D.R. Basset Jr., The technology of accelerometry-based activity monitors: current and future. Med. Sci. Sports Exerc. **37**(Suppl 11), S490–S500 (2005)
16. J. Vanhelst, L. Beghin, D. Truck, F. Gotrtrand, New validated thresholds for various intensities of physical activity in adolescents using the Actigraph accelerometer. Int. J. Rehabil. Res. **34**(2), 175–177 (2011)
17. H.A. Bischoff et al., Identifying a cut-off point for normal mobility: A comparison of the timed 'up and go' test in community-dwelling and institutionalised elderly women. Age Ageing **32**(3), 315–320 (2003)
18. F.I. Mahoney, D. Barthel, Functional evaluation: the Barthel index. Md. State Med. J. **14**, 56–61 (1965)
19. M.F. Folstein, S.E. Folstein, P.R. McHugh, Mini-Mental State. J. Psychiatr. Res. **12**, 189–198 (1985)
20. D.P. Nunes, Y.A.O. Duarte, J.L.F. Santos, M.L. Lebrão, Screening for frailty in older adults using a self-reported instrument. Rev. Saúde Pública **49**, 2 (2015)
21. J.L. Fleg et al., Accelerated longitudinal decline of aerobic capacity in healthy older adults. Circulation **112**(5), 674–682 (2005)

A Classifier Evaluation for Payments' Default Predictions in a Brazilian Retail Company

Strauss Carvalho Cunha, Emanuel Mineda Carneiro, Lineu Fernando Stege Mialaret, Luiz Alberto Vieira Dias, and Adilson Marques da Cunha

Abstract

This article presents an investigation about the performance of classification algorithms used for predicting payments' default. Classifiers used for modelling the data set include: Logistic Regression; Naive-Bayes; Decision Trees; Support Vector Machine; k-Nearest Neighbors; Random Forests; and Artificial Neural Networks. These classifiers were applied to both balanced and original data using the Weka data mining tool. Results from experiments revealed that Logistics Regression and Naive Bayes classifiers had the best performance for the chosen data set.

Keywords

Data mining · Classifier algorithms · Area under curve · Logistic regression

96.1 Introduction

In recent years, there have been increases in credit granting by financial institutions and retail companies. This phenomenon is caused by favorable factors like better market conditions, greater consumption inherent to the growth of economies and increases in population incomes [1].

S. C. Cunha
Brazilian Federal Service of Data Processing - SERPRO, RJ, Brazil
e-mail: strauss.carvalho@serpro.gov.br

E. M. Carneiro · L. A. V. Dias · A. M. da Cunha
Computer Science Department, Brazilian Aeronautics Institute of Technology - ITA, Sao Jose dos Campos, SP, Brazil
e-mail: mineda@ita.br; vdias@ita.br; cunha@ita.br

L. F. S. Mialaret (⊠)
Federal Institute of Education, Science and Technology of Sao Paulo - IFSP, Jacarei, SP, Brazil
e-mail: lmialaret@ifsp.edu.br

Regarding predictions of defaulting payments, the use of classification methods have been necessary and mandatory, implemented by the so-called credit scoring systems [2]. Classification methods have been widely implemented, by using algorithms, statistical techniques, and Machine Learning (ML), among other emerging areas of Artificial Intelligence (AI) [3].

In this research, the case study is a Brazilian retailer company with hundreds of stores spread throughout the country providing customers with credit cards. Companies aim to develop systems that allows to identify credit defaulting customers, among other needed functionalities. Computer systems must make use of data mining algorithms for classifying credit card defaulting customers.

The main goal of this paper is to assess classification algorithms for credit analysis in a Brazilian retail company. It is organized as follows: Sect. 96.2 deals with several classification algorithms; Sect. 96.3 describes the data mining experimentation algorithms; and finally, Sect. 96.4 presents some conclusions, recommendations and suggestions for future work.

96.2 Classification Algorithms

Choosing the most suitable classifier for defaulting customers is based on financial data and considered an important decision. Performance's comparison among several classifiers is one way to take this decision.

Louzada et al. [4] and Aniceto [5] have identified in their surveys the following most used classifiers: (1) Artificial Neural Networks (ANN); (2) Support Vector Machine (SVM); (3) Linear Regression; (4) Decision Trees (DT); (5) Fuzzy Logic; (6) Genetic Algorithms (GA); (7) Discriminant Analysis; (8) Bayesian Networks (Naive-Bayes—NB); and (9) Ensemble Methods. Others authors have identified a series of other classifiers used in the credit scoring: (1) Expert Systems; (2) k-Nearest Neighbors (KNN); (3) Clustering; (4)

© Springer International Publishing AG, part of Springer Nature 2018
S. Latifi (ed.), *Information Technology – New Generations*, Advances in Intelligent Systems and Computing 738,
https://doi.org/10.1007/978-3-319-77028-4_96

Case-Based Reasoning; (5) Random Forests (RF); among other types of different classifiers that have been investigated and used in the credit scoring applications [6–10]. In this research, the choice of classifiers was based on their popularity for credit scoring.

96.3 Classification Algorithms Experimentation

For this investigation, a sample of the data set was used, duly validated by the company. The initial sample of the data set used had 6158 records, of which 4461 records were related to the non-defaulting customers and 1696 records were related to the defaulting customers containing eight attributes, including the attribute of the target class.

A series of experiments were carried out, to verify which classifiers best fit the context of granting credit. For experiments, the Weka Experiment Environment was selected from the Weka tool, allowing to perform comparisons between classifiers, duly evaluated by statistical testing.

In this assessment, six sample of data sets were used with the following characteristics:

1. Sample A1, without applying the gain ratio metric, by using the natural imbalance;
2. Sample A2, without applying the gain ratio metric, by using oversampling (the SMOTE technique);
3. Sample A3, without applying the gain ratio metric, by using undersampling;
4. Sample A4, with the application of the gain ratio metric, by selecting the most significant attributes (above the 0.01 threshold);
5. Sample A5, with the application of the gain ratio metric, by using oversampling (the SMOTE technique); and
6. Sample A6, with application of the metric gain ratio, by using undersampling.

In order to evaluate the data sets described above, the following seven classifiers were used: (1) LR; (2) N; (3) DT, also named Algorithm J48 in Weka; (4) SVM; (5) kNN, also named IBK algorithm in Weka; (6) RF; and (7) ANN. Table 96.1 shows assessment results.

The LR classifier was selected as the base classifier for selection because it is traditionally used in credit granting scenarios [11]. For the sample A1, which did not use any attribute selection metrics and was imbalanced, the LR classifier obtained the best performance with the AUC-ROC = 0.89. For the A2 sample, which was available without using any attribute selection technique, but was balanced using the SMOTE technique, the best performing classifier was the RF classifier with the AUC-ROC = 0.91. For the sample A3,

Table 96.1 Classifier evaluation results using AUC-ROC metric

Sample	AUC-ROC values for classifiers						
	LR	NB	DT	SVM	kNN	RF	ANN
A1	0.89	0.89	0.85	0.76	0.85	0.87	0.87
A2	0.9	0.90	0.89	0.82	0.9	0.91	0.9
A3	0.89	0.89	0.87	0.78	0.88	0.88	0.88
A4	0.89	0.89	0.85	0.76	0.88	0.88	0.88
A5	0.89	0.89	0.88	0.78	0.89	0.89	0.89
A6	0.89	0.89	0.87	0.78	0.88	0.88	0.88

where no variable selection metric was applied and it was balanced using the undersampling technique, the classifier that presented the best result was again the LR classifier, along with the NB classifier, with a value of the AUC-ROC = 0.89.

In samples A4, A5, and A6, the gain ratio metric for attribute selection was applied, with attributes discarded with a value lower than 0.01. In the case of the imbalanced A4 sample, the LR classifier, together with the NB classifier, with a value of the AUC-ROC = 0.89, presented the best result in terms of classification. For the A5 sample, which was balanced using the SMOTE technique, the best classifier was also the LR classifier, along with the NB, kNN, and RF classifiers, with a value of the AUC-ROC = 0.89. Finally, for the A6 sample, balanced with the undersampling technique, the best result was the LR classifier, along with the NB classifier, presenting the AUC-ROC = 0.89.

It can be observed that some classifiers obtain an improvement of performance when applying attribute's selection techniques and imbalance's reduction. One example is the kNN classifier, which improves its performance by up to 6%. In other cases, such as the LR classifier, there is no significant improvement in performance, which confirms the resilience of this algorithm to data imbalance [9].

96.4 Conclusion

The main goal of this investigation was to assess classification algorithms for credit analysis in a Brazilian retail company. The following classifiers were used for modelling the data set including: Logistic Regression (LR); Naive-Bayes (NB); Decision Trees (DT); Support Vector Machine (SVM); k-Nearest Neighbors (k-NN); Random Forests (RF); and Artificial Neural Networks (ANN).

Experiments have shown that Logistic Regression (LR) and Naive-Bayes (NB) classifiers have performed better in comparison with other classifiers for a specific data set. It was also possible to verify that class imbalance and attribute selection have affected classification performance for certain classifiers.

As future work, one interesting issue would be to assess the classifiers using others attribute selection metrics. Other line of future research would be the evaluation of classifier algorithms with others performance measures.

Acknowledgements The authors would like to thank: (1) the Brazilian Aeronautics Institute of Technology (ITA); (2) the Casimiro Montenegro Filho Foundation (FCMF); the Software Engineering Research Group (GPES) members; and the 2RP Net Enterprise for their infrastructure, data set, assistance, advice, and financial support for this work.

References

1. V. García, A.I. Marqués, J.S. Sánchez, An insight into the experimental design for credit risk and corporate bankruptcy prediction systems. J. Intell. Inf. Syst. **44**(1), 159–189 (2015)
2. J. Abellán, J.G. Castellano, A comparative study on base classifiers in ensemble methods for credit scoring. Expert. Syst. Appl. **73**, 1–10 (2017)
3. K. Kennedy, Credit scoring using machine learning, Doctoral thesis, Dublin Institute of Technology, 2013
4. F. Louzada, A. Ara, G. Fernandes, Classification methods applied to credit scoring: a systematic review and overall comparison. Surv. Oper. Res. Manag. Sci. **21**(2), 117–134 (2016)
5. M.C. Aniceto, Estudo comparativo entre técnicas de aprendizado de máquina para estimação de risco de crédito, Dissertação (Mestrado em Administração), Universidade de Brasília, Brasília, Brazil, 2016
6. A. Hooman, G. Marthandan, W.F.W. Yusoff, M. Omid, S. Karamizadeh, Statistical and data mining methods in credit scoring. J. Dev. Areas **50**(5), 371–381 (2016)
7. A. Riasi, D. Wang. Comparing the performance of different data mining techniques in evaluating loan applications. Int. Bus. Res. **9**(7), 164–187 (2016).
8. S. Lessmann, B. Baesens, H.-V. Seow, L.C. Thomas, Benchmarking state-of-the-art classification algorithms for credit scoring: an update of research. Eur. J. Oper. Res. **247**(1), 124–136 (2015)
9. I. Brown, C. Mues, An experimental comparison of classification algorithms for imbalanced credit scoring data sets. Expert. Syst. Appl. **39**, 3446–3453 (2012)
10. W. Lin, Y. Hu, C. Tsai, Machine learning in financial crisis prediction: a survey. IEEE Trans. Syst. Man Cybern. C Appl. Rev. **42**(4), 421–436 (2012)
11. H.A. Abdou, J. Pointon, Credit scoring, statistical techniques and evaluation criteria: a review of the literature. Intell. Syst. Accounts Finance Manag. **18**, 59–88 (2011)

Confidentiality, Integrity and Availability in Electronic Health Records: An Integrative Review

97

Mojgan Azadi, Hossein Zare, and Mohammad Jalal Zare

Abstract

Clinical health informatics is a new innovation in healthcare systems to transform paper-based systems to electronic systems. Health information is enhancing care coordination, quality and efficiency, but there are concerns related to protecting security and confidentiality of data. The main aspect of using a different electronic package in hospitals depends on important factors such as confidentiality, integrity and availability of health data.

This paper is an integrative review of the evidence to compare the Confidentiality, Integrity and Availability (CIA) model in different Electronic Health Records [1] and identify the contributing factors in selecting different vendors in hospitals. The Johns Hopkins Nursing Evidence-Based Practice model was used to appraise the quality of studies related to health informatics. Forty-five titles were reviewed and, after reviewing 27 abstracts and contents, seven papers were included in this study. According to the reviewed evidence, a health information framework includes "Confidentiality, Integrity and Availability Triad, MEDITECH, Cerner and EPIC were the most popular hospital software packages because of being user-friendly, accessibility, lower cost and high security.

Keywords

Confidentiality · Integrity and availability · Electronic health records · Integrative review

97.1 Introduction

Transition from paper-based medical records to electronic were initiated over the past few years after hospitals found out about the risk of penalties for not improving their care coordination. The Centers for Medicare and Medicate Services (CMS) mandate that healthcare leaders engage in change strategies for EHRs, which increases the cost and improves patient safety.

Electronic Health Records [1] develop the quality of patient care by increasing the integrity and availability of information for providers; however, the security of health records is still one of the main concerns in healthcare systems.

The US Health Insurance Portability and Accountability Act (HIPAA) privacy rule mandates that users and providers protect patients' information. EHRs contain sensitive patient data along with their identifiers such as diagnosis, past medical history [2].

Healthcare providers must support confidentiality rules while generating multiuser access to EHRs across different settings. There are many vendors to provide EHRs to clinics and hospitals, but according to KLAS in 2014, only three vendors grew this market in clinical health informatics field: Cerner, Epic and MEDITECH [3].

The main characteristics of their suggested information system include Confidentiality, Integrity and Availability [4].

This paper explores some aspects of EHRs based on the evidence and present an integrative review of the advantages of using different electronic records in hospitals.

M. Azadi (✉)
Clinical Informatics, The Johns Hopkins University School of Nursing, Baltimore, MD, USA
e-mail: mazadi2@jhmi.edu

H. Zare
University of Maryland University College, Upper Marlboro, MD, USA

Department of Health Policy and Management, The Johns Hopkins Center for Disparities Solution, Johns Hopkins Bloomberg School of Public Health, Baltimore, MD, USA

M. J. Zare
Department of Computer Science and Engineering, Azad University, Yazd, Iran

© Springer International Publishing AG, part of Springer Nature 2018
S. Latifi (ed.), *Information Technology – New Generations*, Advances in Intelligent Systems and Computing 738,
https://doi.org/10.1007/978-3-319-77028-4_97

97.2 Methodology

A comprehensive search of five major databases was conducted: Scopus, PubMed, CINAHL, Cochrane Library, and Embase. Based on the nature of EHRs, no time frame was entered as an exclusion criterion. The goal was to develop a search strategy and capture a broad match of articles.

Initially, 64 articles were found. After reviewing titles, abstracts, and contents (Fig. 97.1), seven studies met the inclusion criteria and were reviewed in their entirely.

The main approach to appraising the strength and quality of the articles' synthesizing and translating evidence into practice was the "Johns Hopkins Nursing Evidence-Based Practice Evidence Rating Scales." [5] The initial search article types included comparative studies, meta-analyses, research support, observational studies, reviews, and systemic reviews of CIA in EHRs. The majority of retrieved articles were classified in level three and four with good quality.

The inclusion criteria for reviewing studies was defined as [3] English language or at least available in an English version of the article, and [5] related to Electronic Health Records.

97.3 Findings

97.3.1 Situational Analysis

About 99% of U.S. hospitals use EHRs and it is really improving compared to 31% in 2003 [1]. Using paper-based health records has declined to 1% percent but, according to the American Society of Health-System Pharmacists (ASHP), some departments in hospitals continue to expand their paperless improvements. Since health records present variable aspects of human needs, there are some challenges to maintaining this system [1]. Computerized prescriber-order-entry [1], using barcode scanners for administrating medications, rapid access to radiology pictures, electrocardiogram (EKG), and fetal heart rate monitoring are part of EHRs, in which some still use paper-based reports.

According to "2017 best in KLAS: software & services" report, Epic was awarded in 2017 for the best physician practice vendor and earned the top ranking for the seventh consecutive year [6].

97.3.2 Electronic Health Records: Effective Progress

Transition of paper-based health records to electronic health records improves the quality of healthcare and accessibility [2, 4, 7–13]. The majority of articles showed the positive consequences of implementing EHRs in patients' outcomes. A clinical study compared the average of lab errors after using interfaced HER and it showed that it decreased from 2.24 to 0.16 per 1000 specimens (p < 0.001) [14].

Based on the reviewed studies, the ultimate clinical outcomes of using EHRs includes improving the patient outcomes, decrease in medical errors, and less mismanagement of patients. It also helps healthcare providers retrieve patient information in a convenient, timely manner. The EHRs provides a cost-effective method for enhancing patient safety [14].

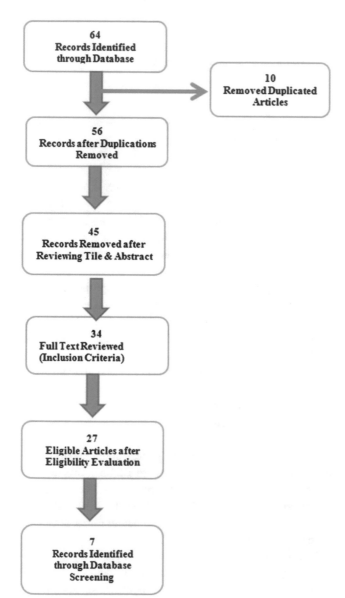

Fig. 97.1 PRIMS flow chart for screening of searched studies

97.3.3 Confidentiality

The main and important rule of EHRs vendors is protecting patient information. Security is the main key in both Epic and Cerner software. The primary purpose of changing paper-based records to electronic records is to support confidentiality with protected accessibility [15]. Patient information cannot be released to others without the patient's permission and it is a priority for every clinician to preserve confidentiality and recognize the authorized persons in the patient plan of care.

97.3.4 Integrity

The ultimate approach in EHRs is to extend the integration between different hospitals across the country, but there are some deficiencies in having unity to use the software. More than 65% of hospitals use computerized prescriber-order-entry [1] instead of hand-written medication orders.

Healthcare providers are willing to focus on integrating EHRs in healthcare system. Both Epic and Cerner have the capabilities to connect different databases and facilitate networking (Fig. 97.2).

97.3.5 Availability

Health information must be available for different clinicians simultaneously. Both Epic and Cerner allow providers to review the information and record their interventions [15]. The information can be stored in EHRs in many different forms: lab reports, radiology pictures, identification data or video files, etc. Thus Epic and Cerner are designed in a way to organize and stratify all this information. Finding the files is not difficult in both Epic and Cerner. It seems both of these software programs need complementary software to store continuous fetal monitoring and the strips of patients who are on cardiac monitoring.

97.3.6 Patient Safety

One of the important goals of implementing EHRs is providing effective patient care and supporting patient safety. Barcode-assisted medication administration systems is one of important feature of using EPIC, CERNER and MEDITEC.

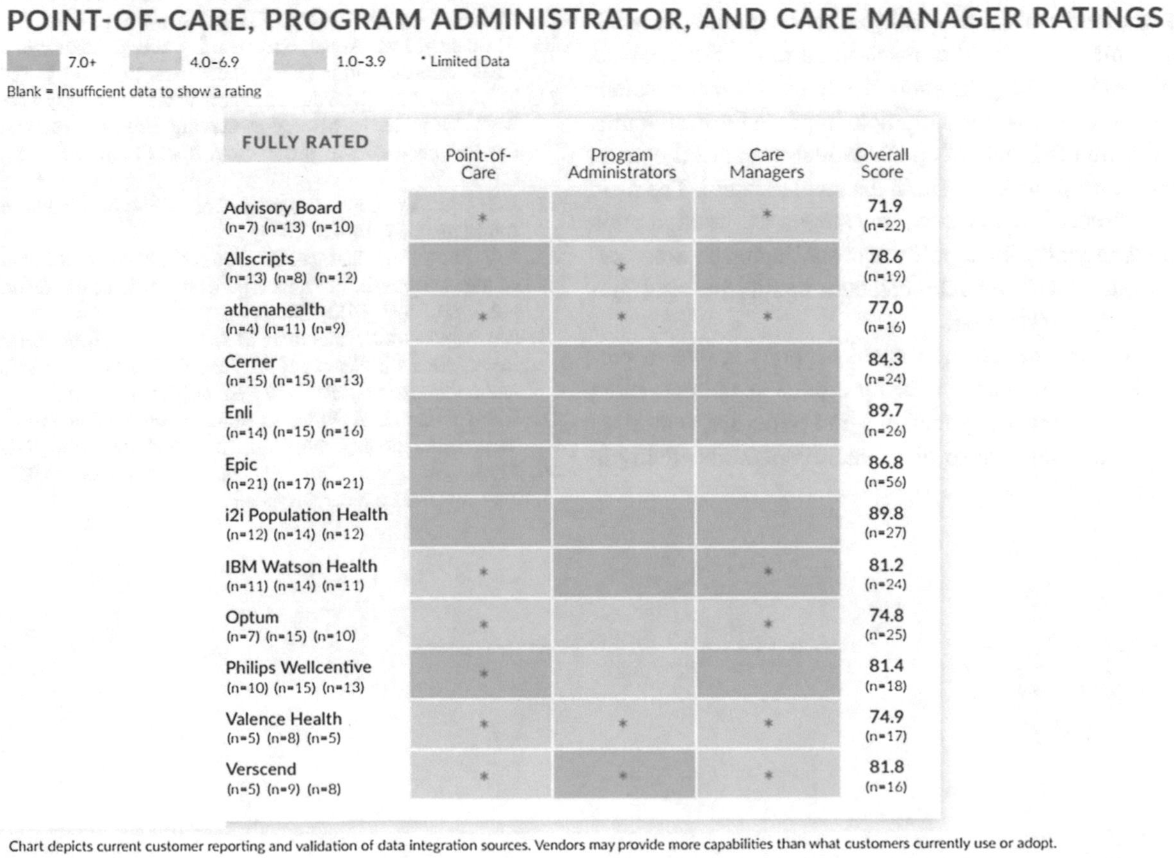

POINT-OF-CARE, PROGRAM ADMINISTRATOR, AND CARE MANAGER RATINGS

Legend: 7.0+ | 4.0-6.9 | 1.0-3.9 | * Limited Data
Blank = Insufficient data to show a rating

FULLY RATED	Point-of-Care	Program Administrators	Care Managers	Overall Score
Advisory Board (n=7) (n=13) (n=10)	*		*	71.9 (n=22)
Allscripts (n=13) (n=8) (n=12)		*		78.6 (n=19)
athenahealth (n=4) (n=11) (n=9)	*	*	*	77.0 (n=16)
Cerner (n=15) (n=15) (n=13)				84.3 (n=24)
Enli (n=14) (n=15) (n=16)				89.7 (n=26)
Epic (n=21) (n=17) (n=21)				86.8 (n=56)
i2i Population Health (n=12) (n=14) (n=12)				89.8 (n=27)
IBM Watson Health (n=11) (n=14) (n=11)	*		*	81.2 (n=24)
Optum (n=7) (n=15) (n=10)	*		*	74.8 (n=25)
Philips Wellcentive (n=10) (n=15) (n=13)	*			81.4 (n=18)
Valence Health (n=5) (n=8) (n=5)	*	*	*	74.9 (n=17)
Verscend (n=5) (n=9) (n=8)	*	*	*	81.8 (n=16)

Chart depicts current customer reporting and validation of data integration sources. Vendors may provide more capabilities than what customers currently use or adopt.

Fig. 97.2 Care manager, program administrators, and clinicians ranking reportSource: [16]

97.3.7 Clinical Intervention

Providers must record all their interventions in EHRs. The left side bar of both software programs help clinicians quickly find their intended tab. In addition to writing orders or progress notes, there are other features such as medication administration, access to previous records and sending patients' prescriptions to the requested pharmacy.

97.3.8 Future Expectation

The most imperative concern to implement EHRs is maintaining privacy of individuals' information in healthcare system [7]. Several security strategies and techniques are recognized that are identified as administrative, physical and technical safeguards [7].

A systematic review study addressed the importance of organizational strategies to protect health information [12].

97.4 Conclusion

The integration between EHRs and outcome improvement was reviewed. The evidence on the EHRs implementation shows improvement in the quality of services and accessibility, but some details need to be clarified more. For instance, unity in implementing the same EHRs in different hospitals or different aspects of networking to improve the availability.

Confidentiality, integrity and availability are the main framework for protecting health data and services. The main security threats include lack of safeguards, configuration weakness, organizational policy and staffing error. Some evidence suggested to use daily database monitoring strategies for protecting information.

Since healthcare staffing plays a significant role in protecting EHRs, it will beneficial for clinicians to know more about the different safety methods and periodical education to enhance the importance of maintaining confidentiality in healthcare systems.

References

1. Survey: Nearly all U.S. Hospitals Use EHRs, CPOE Systems (2017). https://www.healthcare-informatics.com/news-item/ehr/survey-nearly-all-us-hospitals-use-ehrs-cpoe-systems
2. H. Lee, S. Kim, J.W. Kim, Y.D. Chung, Utility-preserving anonymization for health data publishing. BMC Med. Inform. Decis. Mak. **17**, 104 (2017)
3. A. Jammu, H. Singh, Improved AES for data security in E-health. Int. J. Adv. Res. Comput. Sci. **8**, 2016–2020 (2017)
4. T.E. Wesołowski, P. Porwik, R. Doroz, Electronic health record security based on ensemble classification of keystroke dynamics. Appl. Artif. Intell. **30**, 521–540 (2016)
5. Johns Hopkins Nursing Evidence-Based Practice. Appendix C: Evidence Level and Quality Guide (2017). http://www.hopkinsmedicine.org/evidence-based-practice/_docs/appendix_c_evidence_level_quality_guide.pdf. Accessed 08 March 2017
6. KLAS. Bi. Overalll Best in KLAS Awards (2017). http://eds.a.ebscohost.com/ehost/pdfviewer/pdfviewer?vid=1&sid=c2c03d3d-3ec8-4387-9880-b2126c067e4b%40sessionmgr4008
7. C.S. Kruse, B. Smith, H. Vanderlinden, A. Nealand, Security techniques for the electronic health records. J. Med. Syst. **41**, 127 (2017)
8. R. Kullar, D.A. Goff, L.T. Schulz, B.C. Fox, W.E. Rose, The "epic" challenge of optimizing antimicrobial stewardship: the role of electronic medical records and technology. Clin. Infect. Dis. **57**, 1005–1013 (2013)
9. M. Meingast, T. Roosta, S. Sastry, Security and privacy issues with health care information technology, in *Engineering in Medicine and Biology Society, 2006 EMBS'06 28th Annual International Conference of the IEEE* (IEEE, 2006), pp. 5453–8
10. A. Shenoy, J.M. Appel, Safeguarding confidentiality in electronic health records. Camb. Q. Healthc. Ethics **26**, 337–341 (2017)
11. M.R. Tabassum, M.V.K. Burugari, WMSD: towards a new framework approach to privacy-preserving designed for approach in medical patient data. Int. J. Adv. Res. Comput. Sci. **8**, 265–268 (2017)
12. K.T. Win, A review of security of electronic health records. Health Inf. Manag. **34**, 13–18 (2005)
13. L. Zhou, V. Varadharajan, K. Gopinath, A secure role-based cloud storage system for encrypted patient-centric health records. Comput. J. **59**, 1593–1611 (2016)
14. S.R. Lipsitz, A.B. Landman, M.J. Tanasijevic, S.E. Melanson, *The Benefits and Challenges of an Interfaced Electronic Health Record and Laboratory Information System* (2017)
15. L.B. Harman, C.A. Flite, K. Bond, Electronic health records: privacy, confidentiality, and security. Virtual Mentor **14**, 712 (2012)
16. *Cerner vs Epic: Battle of the EHR Titans* (2017). https://blog.capterra.com/cerner-vs-epic/

Operating System Security Management and Ease of Implementation (Passwords, Firewalls and Antivirus)

Hossein Zare, Peter Olsen, Mohammad Jalal Zare, and Mojgan Azadi

Abstract

Recent widely-known hacking exploits have increased the focus on computer and network security. System users need systems to provide confidentiality, integrity, availability and authenticity for their data. Access control, firewalls, and antivirus software are three ways to provide system security. They address different aspects of computer security with complementary advantages and disadvantages.

Keywords

RABC · MD4 · Antivirus · Cyber-attack · Packet-filters

98.1 Introduction

Vulnerability defines a weakness in a computer system that allows an attacker to take advantage of the system. Once he has that advantage he can do such things obtain confidential information, breach the integrity of stored information, and more. He may be able to seize control of the computer or network, subverting it to do even more malicious activities.

Weaknesses in information security are a growing concern around the world, especially for the United States. Many factors contribute to this concern, but poor and inefficient security program management is the major challenge.

Daily changes in hacking techniques force organizations, companies, and individuals to implement more secure operating systems and procedural safeguards. Sometimes these measures combines to yield greater security, other times they yield a pastiche of ill-matched techniques that add little to, and may even decrease, security.

A computer *operating system* (OS) is defined as the software to operate and communicate between computer hardware and software, computer's memory, and processes. Basic functions of OS include but are not limited to device configuration, memory management, file management, interface management, and other utility functions (such as searching files, installing and uninstalling software, problem diagnosis, disk defragmentation, file back up and (not least of all) computer security).

Confidentiality, integrity, and availability. Confidentiality, integrity, and availability (CIA) are three main components of security and are basic requirements for all operating systems [1]. ***Confidentiality*** means the privacy of sensitive data and information—the restriction of reading access only to authorized users. An OS is required to prevent unauthorized access. This protection extends not only sensitive information but also modification of programs that can access this data [2]. ***Integrity*** means consistency and accuracy of data. In a computer security context, integrity is maintained by limiting the ability to make changes (usually write access) only to authorized users. ***Availability*** means that data can be accessed when needed, not only in the main center but also remote locations [2].

H. Zare (✉)
University of Maryland University College, Upper Marlboro, MD, USA

Department of Health Policy and Management, The Johns Hopkins Center for Disparities Solution, The Johns Hopkins Bloomberg School of Public Health, Baltimore, MD, USA
e-mail: Hossein.zare@Faculty.UMUC.edu

P. Olsen
Department of Computer Science and Electrical Engineering, University of Maryland Baltimore County, Catonsville, Baltimore, MD, USA
e-mail: MDolsen@sigmaxi.net

M. J. Zare
Department of Computer Science and Engineering, Azad University, Yazd, Iran

M. Azadi
University of Maryland University College, Upper Marlboro, MD, USA

The Johns Hopkins University, Baltimore, MD, USA

© Springer International Publishing AG, part of Springer Nature 2018
S. Latifi (ed.), *Information Technology – New Generations*, Advances in Intelligent Systems and Computing 738,
https://doi.org/10.1007/978-3-319-77028-4_98

98.1.1 Access Control, Firewalls, and Antivirus Software

This paper describes some of the advantages and disadvantages of three tools used to ensure the confidence, integrity, and availability of information stored on computer systems.

In next section, we review and rank limited access control, firewalls and anti-virus software (AV). We will discuss the ease of implementation and management, level of protection provided, and risk-assessment analysis for each measure.

98.2 Access Control

98.2.1 Access Control Systems (ACSs)

ACSs define the rules that authorize or restrict user access to secured network resources [3].

An ACS defines "who can do what to whom". Access control systems depend on the computer system's ability to *authenticate* each—to ensure that each agent is actually the agent it purports to be. (We use the word "agent" to mean both users and processes). Security experts define some indicators for good access control policy, including but not limited to [4]:

- *Clear understanding of organizational roles*
- *Clear understanding of information systems' architecture and*
- *Ability to anticipate future needs.*

There are three well-known access controls—Role based Access Control (RBAC), Discretionary Access Control (DAC) and Mandatory Access Control (MAC).

98.2.2 Role-Based Access Control

In the Role-Based Access Control (RBAC) model, roles (such as user, owner, or curator) are defined by administrators. RBAC directly works with roles such as these by defining what each roll is allowed to do [1].

98.2.3 Discretionary Access Control

Discretionary access control is defined "as a means of restricting access to objects based on the identity of subjects and/or groups to which they belong. The controls are discretionary in the sense that a subject with a certain access permission is capable of passing that permission (perhaps indirectly) on to any other subject (unless restrained by mandatory access control)" [5]. DAC allows authorized users to change their access control attributes. In this model, end-users or creators of data objects, may define who can have access to the data [3]. DAC is based on an identity management system. Depending on the complexity level of identity-check, these systems are categorized as "simple centralized mode," "meta directions," "virtual direction," "single-sign-on" and "federated identity management" [3].

98.2.4 Mandatory Access Control (MAC)

Mandatory Access Control "refers to a type of access control by which the operating system constrains the ability of a subject or initiator to access or generally perform some sort of operation on an object or target" [6]. MAC is one of the main access control models. This model is "*a militant [strict] style of applying permission.*" [7]

These system, often have a hierarchy of access levels, for example confidential, secret, and top-secret, with access to each level controlled by an *operating system* (OS) implementing a *security policy* (the collection of rules and type of access defining the policy).

98.2.4.1 MAC Systems Divide Users and Data into Classes

Each person in a class has the permission to access data in the corresponding class in which "subject: user" and "object: data/resource are specifically allowed. Classes may overlap, form a hierarchy, or be completely disjoint [3].

Classes can be based on both the classification and type of material. For example, confidential material might be divided into two types of objects: "operations" and "intelligence." People with access to one type might not have access to the other, even if both are authorized to access "confidential material. In this model the combination of classifications and types form a *lattice*.

98.3 Authentication by ID/Password Combinations

Advantages: User IDs and passwords have been recognized as basic minimum requirements for access control because they are inexpensive, easy-to-use, and well-accepted.

Disadvantage: ID/password systems also have some significant disadvantages

- Passwords chosen by users are often common or easy to guess (e.g. wife's name and birthdate.) In 2016 the most popular password was "123,456" with "Password" close behind [8].
- Passwords generated by the system are often difficult to remember.

- Difficult or complex passwords are often written down, sometimes in obvious places (e.g. under a desk pad).
- Often passwords can be obtained by "shoulder surfing" or social engineering.
- Once a miscreant obtains a password he has the same access as the password's owner.

These weakness makes passwords the "weakest link" in cyber-attacks [9].

98.3.1 Type of Algorithm and Size of Password

In most modern systems passwords are stored as hashes of what the user enters. When a user enters a password, its hash is compared to the stored password hash. I Good hash functions prevent passwords being "reverse engineered" even if a miscreant gains access to the system's password files.

Both DES and MD4 are used as the basis for hash functions. MD4 is significantly stronger than DES [10]. However, with rainbow tables and computing power tools (i.e., clouds) passwords could be discovered even with an MD4 hash. Implementation of longer and stronger password—combinations of uppercase, lowercase, numbers, and symbols—could defend a password from rainbow table attacks [11].

Implementing access control through IDs and passwords is easy, but maintaining security of a system requires "continuous updates," "adequate password policy," "minimum age awareness," and "using complicated passwords with combination of small, capital words, character, number and long-enough" [12] Table 98.1.

One problem is that it's difficult to create sufficiently complex passwords that are memorable enough so that users don't write them down. For access control a network admin-istrator must have a clear understanding of "organizational roles," "information systems' architecture," and "ability to anticipate future needs" [4].

98.4 Firewalls

Firewalls are another part of a computer security system designed to prevent unauthorized access [13]. Firewalls can be implemented in software, in hardware, or both. Hardware firewalls have the advantage of prohibiting any access to the machines they protect. Software firewalls are generally cheaper and easier to maintain and install, but they must allow incoming connections to the system on which they run. Security can be increased by cascading firewalls, for example a software firewall behind a hardware one.

All messages entering or leaving the protected network pass through the firewall, which uses specified security criteria to decide to block or pass messages [14] Firewalls provide excellent security if they selected and implemented properly.

There are different types of firewalls and here we will review the most commonly used and describe advantages and disadvantages of both.

98.4.1 Packet Filters

Packet filters are among the most popular basic firewalls. These filters check every packet against a set of access control rules and passes or filters packets to their destinations, using the following conditions:

- Source and destination IP addresses
- Source and destination ports.
- Traffic direction either inbound or outbound.
- Type of protocol
- Packet contents

Advantages. Packet-filtering is simple to set up and provides reasonable security protection. Compared to other firewalls, packet-filtering has the least impact on the bandwidth of the filter."

Packet filters are usually transparent to authorized users. They need know nothing of the packet filter's operation. When set up appropriately packet filters work properly with minimum interference [15].

Disadvantages. Most packet filters are simple. They can detect only attacks in single packets, and then only attacks that have been seen before. Most cannot detect multi-packet attacks.

Another disadvantage is reduction in system functionality. Filters configured to prevent a specific attack may also

Table 98.1 Comparing advantages and disadvantages of passwords as a security measure

Measure	Advantage	Disadvantage
Passwords	• Less expensive for basic passwords. • Easy-to-use. • Well-accepted authentication system. • No need for extra hardware to protect a device. • No need to install additional hardware. • Easy to update by user choice.	• Suffers from being the weakest link and sensitive to guessing and dictionary attack [9]. • Required "*minimum password age*" [12]. • Simple passwords are easy to hack • Depends on the OS' sensitive to different types of attack such as *brute-force* [1], rainbow table for Windows and Linux systems [3]. • Easy to recover by insider threat.

prevent legitimate access to ports and protocols. Packet-filtering firewalls can be "deficient in logging capabilities" and can lack "remote administration facilities." [16]

Most packet filters use regular expressions to define which packets will be accepted and which will be rejected. In some cases, attackers can design packets that will cause the filter's regular expression matching algorithm to cycle infinitely, effectively blocking access to the protected system.

Finally, attackers can take advantage of a system by using the vulnerability in a packet's state; for example, sending acknowledge (ACK) instead of synchronizing (SYN) [17].

98.4.2 Application-Gateway Firewalls

Application-gateway firewalls use different approaches to provide security. Application-gateway firewalls admit only packets for a specific application. This is a type of proxy connection. The most well-known proxy services provide e-mail connections for email and file transfer protocol (FTP). These firewalls use specific sets of rules for each allowed application. Other data (such as IP addresses or ports) also may be used for accepting or rejecting a connection.

There are well-known advantages of these types of firewalls, including but not limited to:

- Properly configured firewalls can make attacks very difficult.
- These firewalls hide a host's information from outsider hackers or users.
- Some of these firewalls benefit from strong authentication methods (e.g., "hand-held" authentication devices) that strongly improve the security of networks.

However, there are some limitations for these firewalls, for instance:

- Application firewalls must know the identity of the computers they serve.
- Application-specific firewalls must know the operation of the applications they protect—"every application needs its own custom proxy" [15].
- Because applications gateways need detailed knowledge of the application they can be difficult to configure and maintain.
- Application filters are expensive, both to install and maintain.
- Not all applications have gateways.

98.4.3 Circuit-Gateways Firewalls

Circuit-gateways firewalls are designed to reduce the limitations of application-gateway firewalls. These use virtual circuits to create an "end-to-end connection between clients and destination application" [15]. This approach uses multiple clients and multiple connections by implementing SOCKS (a tool with a set of client libraries for proxy interface with clients). Circuit-gateway firewalls are more transparent than applicant-gateways connections. In spite of these advantages, there are some disadvantage for these types of firewalls, such as:

- Clients must be aware of the proxy mechanism.
- Application firewalls may admit any connection to a particular application.
- SOCKS has several limitations Most SOCKS are "deficient in their ability to log events" and they are unable to support "access authentication methods and an interface to authentication services" that are used for providing this service [15].

Considering all of the advantages and disadvantages of the three main types of firewalls, most firewalls on the market are hybrid firewalls. These combine two or more approaches such as combining packet-filtering with application gateways.

Using virtual private networks incorporates end-to-end encryption technology into the networks. Even if hackers could pass the firewalls, they must crack the encryption key to gain access (Table 98.2).

98.4.4 Creating Demilitarized Zones (DMZs)

In addition to using firewalls to protect the network, companies can set up multiple DMZs in the environment. A DMZ is another defense-in-depth strategy to separate functionalities and control access privilege, for example:

- DNS-DMZ (Domain Naming Service's DMZ) to direct production traffic to the backup and production sites [3];
- Email-DMZ, to protect system from phishing attacks;
- Web Server DMZ to direct external communications.

Organizations can also use DMZ to FTP DMZ, authentication DMZ, wireless DMZ, DB DMZ, and Security DMZ to protect the data from unsecure transmission outside of the network [18].

Table 98.2 Comparing advantages and disadvantages of firewalls as a security measure

Measure	Advantage	Disadvantage
Firewall	**Packet-filtering** • Simple to set-up. • Little negative impact on the "throughput rate gateway." • Works properly with minimum interference.	**Packet-filtering** • Simplicity. • Uses specific port for connection; increased rate of using other parallel port. • Reduces system performance because of restricted functionality. • Switching acknowledge (ACK) and synchronize (SYN) for cracking system.
	Applicant-gateway • Uses strong authentication technology and provides secure environment. • Hides host's information from outsiders.	**Applicant-gateway** • Expensive. • Needs broad knowledge of network to set up. • Awareness of client and modifying proxy is essential to make a connection. • Limited to specific proxies. • Not easy to "initially configure and update correctly."
	Circuit-gateways • Provide faster connection with higher transparency in comparison with applicant-gateway.	**Circuit-gateways** • Expensive. • Uses generic-access mechanism with lower level of security. • Unable to support "access authentication methods and an interface to authentication services." • "Deficient in their ability to log events."

98.5 Antivirus

The third easily implemented protective measure is antivirus software (AV). "Antivirus is based on signatures in files" [3]. An antivirus scanner can be installed on a server or desktop. Server-based AV cannot scan for malware on local devices such as USB drives, CD, DVDs, and external hard drives. Experts suggest installing AV on both servers and desktops for better results. Most organizations use server-based antivirus and set the program to erase all infected files to protect the system from viruses released by mistake [19]. Using desktop-based antivirus requires users to keep the antivirus updated.

Experts break down antivirus into two main categories; real-time protection and boot-time scanning. Real-time AV software is always active and checks files in real time and suspends or blocks malicious software and infected files. The boot-time scanning checks the system when an operating system becomes active [20].

Organizations must have clear policies for antivirus programs, including but not limited to:

• All machines (desktops and laptops) must run the most updated antivirus.
• All removable media such as external hard disks, floppy disks, CDs, etc., must be scanned before use.
• All encrypted materials need to be decrypted and checked for viruses. Similarly, compressed material must be decompressed.
• All e-mail gateways must have AV installed by a network administrator and suspicious e-mails need to be deleted or quarantined.
• And finally, antivirus is most effective when used with supplemental protection tools such as firewalls, an intrusion prevention system (IPS), an intrusion detection system (IDS), and other network monitoring programs.

Mamaghani (2002) recommends four main criteria for a good antivirus (e.g.,

• installation,
• operation,
• administration,
• notification, and content filtering) [21].

System-wide is much easier to install and maintain than firewalls. Users with basic knowledge of a computer are able to install and maintain on their own computers.

In spite of those advantages, there are some disadvantages and limitations with AV, for example:

• AV systems have a wide range of costs. Some AV packages are expensive to install and maintain while others are free. But "free" systems may have substantial costs if they must be configured and maintained by in-house IT staff.
• Some AV software can reduce computer speed substantially.
• A new study shows that "malware bypassed up-to-date anti-virus software 55% of the time" [22]. Similar to packet-filtering firewalls, pattern matching AV systems can't detect new attacks until they have been recognized and their identifying patterns published.
• "Security countermeasures e.g. antivirus or network IDSs can hardly detect process-related threats as they lack process Semantics" [22] (Table 98.3).

Table 98.3 Comparing advantages and disadvantages of antivirus as a security measure

Measure	Advantage	Disadvantage
Anti-virus	• Easy to install. • Keeps network information and data secure. • With BYOD, antivirus helps employees to keep their own devices. • Useful for signature-based attack.	• Keeping AV software updated needs time and money. • Uses RAM and reduces CPU speed. • AV are behind new technologies. • Not able to detect process-related threats.

98.6 Operating Systems Protection Measurements Implementation

Each of the described protection measures has its own degree of reliability, validity, and effectiveness.

Network administrators benefit from ease of implementation and analysis to make decisions and prioritize each measure. The previous sections discussed each measure in detail. This section highlights the most important indicators for ranking access control list, password, firewall, and antivirus from the viewpoint of ease of implementation.

This section considers two main indicators; cost/benefit and simplicity of implementation.

The easiest tool with reasonable benefits is access control. It is easy to install and to configure in accordance with organization policy. Passwords are easy to use and to update. Successful access control systems require strong passwords, either by imposing rules for password selection or by automatically generating strong passwords. The "cost and effort required to implement a password policy is negligible" [23]. Users understand the process easily, making this a cost-effective tool. Passwords can be complemented with personal authentication devices to yield very strong access control.

AV is the second easiest implement measure on our list. This software can be installed on servers, laptops, and desktops and can cover all users in an organization. AV can be easy to update and often can be updated automatically. Several swell-known AV are inexpensive or free of charge. Disadvantages include the cost of installing and configuring the software and keeping it up-to-date.

The most difficult of the three measures is a firewall. These tools are available in two classes: software and hardware. This paper discusses three well-known types of firewalls. The packet-filtering firewall is the basic level and provides reasonable security, but only for attacks that have been seen before and can be recognized from a single packet. Firewalls require significant resources to install and maintain. (See Fig. 98.1).

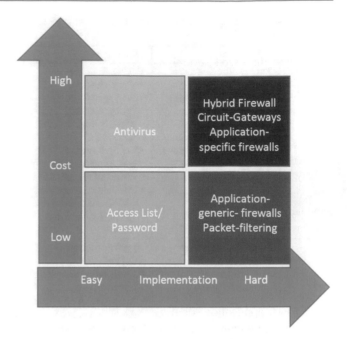

Fig. 98.1 Ease of implementation for three selected measures

98.6.1 Ranking, Discussion and Security Management Issues

The deployment and configuration of operating systems require "accurate information" about devices on the network and "service" they are running [24]. Using these categories places firewalls at the highest rank. Firewalls—particularly software firewalls—can be configured to limit access of both insiders and outsiders. If any connection does not meet required security, it is automatically blocked by the firewall. Considering the risk-model analysis not only are there high-identified risks but also there are high-value assets to be protected by firewalls.

After firewalls, system administrators should require use of advanced antivirus software protection to eliminate malicious software from insiders or outsiders that could pass through the firewall applications. This ensures the network administrator that users are not able to add malicious software to a network whether wanted or unwanted.

The last ranked system is password protection. After setting up the firewall and installing antivirus, the system administrator should require users to have a few authentications measures such as user names and passwords. Additionally, depending on employee level or security level, data access levels could be defined using a role-based access control system. Additional security can be had by complementing password us with secondary security measures such as physical identification (e.g. iris scanners) or user-carried devices, such as one-time passwords. These may be pre-assigned or generated with a special device.

98.7   Summary

This paper discussed several risk-reduction tools such as passwords, antivirus, and firewalls to protect operating systems. Strong passwords can protect the "confidentiality" and "integrity" of valuable files and critical systems, particularly if they are supplemented by secondary security measures such as one-time authentication.

Strong antivirus software should be considered "at the core of a good security program" [23]. Most AV software is signature-based and must be kept updated, otherwise it cannot perform its role effectively. AV can protect "integrity" and "availability" of files and systems. While AV software can be inexpensive and easy to maintain, poorly designed or very strict AV can substantially degrade system performance.

Firewalls are often the best security tool, but they can be both complex and expensive. Firewalls can combine filtering by IP, port, application, or packet. and can enhance both "confidentiality" and "integrity" of the system. By keeping unauthorized users completely out of the system, firewalls can help protect "availability" of data as well [23].

98.8   Conclusion

The increasing number of cyber-attacks world-wide are forcing organizations to worry about confidentiality, integrity, and the availability of networks and data. They use a combination of tools and advanced technologies to keep their systems secure. Three of these well-known security measures are access control/password, AV, and firewall applications. These are the main parts of every security system. In addition, companies benefit from other security tools including a back-up policy, encryption technologies to encrypt important data, and vulnerability scanning to maintain the security of operating systems. The results of this study show that for having the highest security, individuals and organizations are required to use a combination of security tools in addition to updating network administration policies.

References

1. M. Goodrich, R. Tamassia, *Introduction to Computer Security* (Addison-Wesley Publishing Company, Boston, 2010)
2. E. McCallister, T. Grance, K.A. Scarfone, *Guide to Protecting the Confidentiality of Personally Identifiable Information (PII)* (Special Publication (NIST SP)-800-122, Gaithersburg, 2010)
3. J.R. Vacca, *Computer and Information Security Handbook* (Newnes, Oxford, 2012)
4. P.W. Singer, A. Friedman, *Cybersecurity: What Everyone Needs to Know* (Oxford University Press, Oxford, 2014)
5. N. Li, Discretionary access control, in *Encyclopedia of Cryptography and Security*, (Springer, Boston, 2011), pp. 353–356
6. R. Ramakrishnan, J. Gehrke, *Just the Facts 101 (9c), Facts101 Textbook Key Facts*, Database Management Systems, 3rd edn. (Content Technologies, Inc., California, 2014). 9781467297936
7. C. Susan Hansche, C. John Berti, C. Hare, *Official (ISC) 2 Guide to the CISSP Exam* (CRC Press, Boca Raton, 2003)
8. N. Golgowski, *The Most Common Passwords in 2016 are Truly Terrible* (2017). https://www.huffingtonpost.com/entry/2016-most-common-passwords_us_587f9663e4b0c147f0bc299d. Accessed 1 Jan 2018
9. G. Notoatmodjo, *Exploring the 'Weakest Link': A Study of Personal Password Security* (Citeseer, New York, 2007)
10. A. Joux, Multicollisions in iterated hash functions. Application to cascaded constructions, in *Annual International Cryptology Conference*, (Springer, Berlin, 2004), pp. 306–316
11. S. Marechal, Advances in password cracking. J. Comput. Virol. **4**, 73–81 (2008)
12. K. Scarfone, M. Souppaya, *Guide to Enterprise Password Management (Draft): Recommendations of the National Institute of Standards and Technology* (US Dept of Commerce, Technology Administration, National Institute of Standards and Technology, Gaithersburg, MD, 2009)
13. UMUC, *Enterprise Network Intrusion Prevention Systems, CSEC 630 Module 1*, Document posted in University of Maryland University College Prevention and Protection Strategies in Cybersecurity-CSE630 Online Classroom (2016). https://leoprdws.umuc.edu/CSEC630/1306/csec630_01/assets/csec630_01.pdf
14. J. Valacich, C. Schneider, *Information Systems Today: Managing in the Digital World with MyITLab*. Policy Statement (2014)
15. E.E. Schultz, *Types of Firewalls. Previous Screen* (2014). http://www.ittoday.info/AIMS/DSM/83-10-41.pdf. Accessed 2 Jun 2016
16. E.E. Schultz, *83-10-41 Types of Firewalls* (2014). http://www.ittodayinfo/AIMS/DSM/83-10-41.pdf. https://pdfssemanticscholarorg/94f3/b35cc7a47241d8e7677478e01e6c9029fa7dpdf. Accessed 4 Jan 2018
17. J. Brendel, *World-Wide-Web Server that Finds Optimal Path by Sending Multiple syn+ ack Packets to a Single Client*. Google Patents, 2003
18. D. Kuipers , M. Fabro, *Control Systems Cyber Security: Defense in Depth Strategies* (Idaho National Laboratory (INL), 2006). https://pdfs.semanticscholar.org/8876/4aa74474ed67f327c30517f6c91b284d0eac.pdf. Accessed 21 Oct 2017
19. C. Cobb , A. Myers, Antivirus technology. *Computer Security Handbook*, 6th Edn. (2009), pp. 41.1–41.14
20. R.J. Anderson, *Security Engineering: A Guide to Building Dependable Distributed Systems* (John Wiley & Sons, Hoboken, 2010)
21. F. Mamaghani, Evaluation and selection of an antivirus and content filtering software. Inform. Manag. Comput. Secur. **10**, 28–32 (2002)
22. D. Hadziosmanovic, D. Bolzoni, P.H. Hartel, *MEDUSA: Mining Events to Detect Undesirable uSer Actions in SCADA. RAID* (Springer, Berlin, 2010), pp. 500–501
23. L.A. Kadel, *Designing and Implementing as Effective Information Security Program: Protecting the Data the Data Assets of Individual, Small and Large Business* (SANS Institute Reading Room, 2004). https://www.sans.org/reading-room/whitepapers/hsoffice/designing-implementing-effective-information-security-program-protecting-data-assets-of-1398. Accessed 27 Jul 2016
24. Y. Xu , M. Bailey , E. Vander Weele , F. Jahanian, CANVuS: context-aware network vulnerability scanning. *International Workshop on Recent Advances in Intrusion Detection* (Springer, 2010). pp. 138-57

Seilkhan Boranbayev, Assulan Nurkas, Yersultan Tulebayev, and Baktygeldi Tashtai

Abstract

The paper is dedicated to building big data processing methods and image classification using machine learning algorithms. Machine learning methods and their application to computer vision tasks, in particular to image classification, are investigated. Supervised learning applied to image classification is considered. Computational experiments and comparative analysis of various machine learning methods applied to image classification problem are carried out.

Keywords

Model · Method · Modeling · Data · Processing · Classification · Learning · Image

99.1 Introduction

Nowadays with the intensive development of digital technologies, large volumes of unstructured data are being produced. For example, about 70 million photos are uploaded to Instagram daily [1]. 500 million tweets per day, and about 200 billion per year appear in Twitter [2]. 300 h of video are uploaded to Youtube each single minute, and more than one billion users watch millions of hours of video per day [3]. More than 3.5 billion search queries per day and 1.2 trillion queries per year are carried out by Google [4]. Until recently this data was just collected. With the advent of big data analysis technologies a move towards using that data for predictive analytics and pattern detection is

S. Boranbayev (✉) · A. Nurkas · Y. Tulebayev · B. Tashtai
Department of Information Systems, L.N. Gumilyov Eurasian National University, Astana, Kazakhstan
e-mail: sboranba@yandex.kz

happening. Machine learning is the foundation of intelligent data analysis.

99.2 Solution of Image Classification Problem

In the work image classification problem was solved using several methods. Comparative analysis of various classification methods follows below. MNIST [5] data set was used. MNIST contains 60,000 examples for training and 10,000 examples for testing. Images are hand written 20×20 pixel digits that are centered in a square of size 28×28. The digits were written by about 250 people. Digits for training and testing were written by different people. Digit classification task for this data set is a multi-class classification as correct identification of digit from 10 possible categories is needed (0, 1, ..., 9). For MNIST image classification the following models were used: k-NN, linear, neural network, and convolution neural network. To evaluate classification quality, we use accuracy, i.e. number of correctly classified examples from all test examples. Accuracy values range from 0 to 1, where 1 is 100% accurate. k-NN showed accuracy of 0.9681 with hyper parameter values of k = 3, and L2 norm. For each value of $k \in \{1, 3, 5, 7, 10\}$ the accuracy was calculated on validation set. Training set size was 50,000, validation set size 10,000, and test set size 10,000. Test time on average was about 579 s. k-NN shows high accuracy, but requires a lot of time for testing and cannot compare images semantically. The program is written in Python using sklearn library. The results of the experiment are comparable with results shown in [5]. Linear classifier is used as a threshold in many problems. Mini-batch gradient (MGD) descent is used as an optimization algorithm. To verify stability of results experiments are conducted 1000 times (epochs). Python and Theano library that allows computations on graphical video card were used for programming. The best result if 0.92 for batch size of 1000 and $\alpha = 1$ for both GPU and CPU, while the worst result if 0.8517 for batch size of

5000 and $\alpha = 0.001$. Training and testing time on GPU is 10 s, and 21 s for CPU for the best result, and 53 s for GPU and 102 s for CPU for the worst result. Even though the number of parameters is small ($W = 28 * 28 * 10$, $b = 10 \rightarrow 7850$ parameters), difference in time for various settings is considerable. Average training time for all values of α on GPU constituted 22.4 s, and on CPU 36.85 s.

99.3 Discussion

In this work multi-class image classification and computational experiment results are presented. The results are displayed in Table 99.1. Logistic regression is the simplest to implement model. This model along with SGD is the fastest, however, its results is the worst, more than 7% error rate. Multilayer perceptron uses back propagation algorithm and shows good results. Deep convolutional network is the best performer. It is believed that convolutional networks are very well suited for image classification. It is worth to note that image classification is very resource intensive task. Table 99.2 shows results of classification on GPU. Time required to train and test a model has reduced substantially.

Table 99.1 MNIST digit classification results on CPU

Model	Error %	Time
Logistic regression	7.489583	14 s
Logistic regression	7.562500	23.7 s
Multilayer perceptron	1.650000	1328 min
Deep convolutional network	0.94	1146.32 min
Stacked de-noising auto-encoders	1.35	5503.84 min

Table 99.2 MNIST digit classification results on GPU

Model	Error %	Time
Logistic regression	7.5	9.2 s
Logistic regression	7.552083	16 s
Multilayer perceptron	1.65	94.95 min
Deep convolutional network	0.94	27.71 min
Stacked de-noising auto-encoders	1.37	504.64 min

GPU utilization percentage on average was 97%. The most considerable time reduction was with convolutional neural network run on GPU. This is also due to cudnn library from NVidia that is optimized for convolutional operations.

99.4 Conclusion

This work is devoted to the application of machine learning with the supervised learning applied to the task of image classification. Learning process comprises choice of classifier function from a large set of functions. Comparative analysis of various machine learning methods for image classification was conducted. Image classification is a fundamental computer vision problem, and its successful solution makes possible new applications such as visual search systems, video classification, augmented reality systems, and other applications [6, 7]. Also, image classification simulates research in other directions such as multi-modal learning when image classification results are used to automatically describe image using natural language. Experimental results obtained in the work are in correspondence with results obtained by other authors.

References

1. Press page. Instagram. https://instagram.com/press/
2. About Twitter Inc. https://about.twitter.com/company
3. Statistics - Youtube. https://www.youtube.com/yt/press/statistics.html
4. Google Search Statistics - Internet Live Stats. http://www.internetlivestats.com/
5. Y. LeCun , C. Cortes, *The MNIST Database of Handwritten Digits*, (1998). http://yann.lecun.com/exdb/mnist
6. S. Boranbayev, S. Altayev, A. Boranbayev, *Applying the method of diverse redundancy in cloud based systems for increasing reliability. Proceedings of the 12th International Conference on Information Technology: New Generations (ITNG 2015)*, (Las Vegas, Nevada, USA, 2015). pp. 796–799
7. S. Boranbayev, A. Boranbayev, S. Altayev, A. Nurbekov, Mathematical model for optimal designing of reliable information systems. *Proceedings of the 2014 IEEE 8th International Conference on Application of Information and Communication Technologies-AICT2014*, (Astana, Kazakhstan, 2014). pp. 123–127

Software Architecture for In-House Development of a Student Web Portal for Higher Education Institution in Kazakhstan

100

Askar Boranbayev, Ruslan Baidyussenov, and Mikhail Mazhitov

Abstract

The students' portal is a student management information system developed in-house for higher education institution in Kazakhstan. It represents a major part among university information systems. This paper reviews the common features of the general portal structure. The architecture of the new students' portal framework is presented (Boranbayev, Nonlinear Anal. 71:1633–1637, 2009). It consists of a web application developed for the university, dedicated for students and staff members of the department of Student Affairs. It was developed in the last 6 years with such technologies like IBM WebSphere, Java EJB, JavaScript, HTML, and Oracle Database. The university's system designers and application development team constantly work on enhancing and improving it. The software architecture of the developed portal is shared among various web applications at the university (Boranbayev and Boranbayev, Development and optimization of information systems for health insurance billing. *Seventh International Conference on Information Technology: New Generations (ITNG 2010)*, Las Vegas, Nevada, USA, 2010, pp. 1282–1284). This architecture and experience may be used by various development teams developing local applications for universities, either in-house or with the help of suppliers and vendors.

In addition, the paper discusses how the students' portal components were developed. The research contributes towards the higher education field worldwide by providing a solution that could be followed for building university portals with various components.

A. Boranbayev (✉)
Department of Computer Science, Nazarbayev University, Astana, Kazakhstan
e-mail: aboranbayev@nu.edu.kz

R. Baidyussenov (✉) · M. Mazhitov (✉)
Nazarbayev Univesity Library and IT Services, Nazarbayev University, Astana, Kazakhstan
e-mail: rbaidyussenov@nu.edu.kz; mmazhitov@nu.edu.kz

Keywords

Software framework · Web application · Portals · Computer architecture · Information system · Software development

100.1 Introduction

The "Student Portal" was built to create a single information space for university students [1, 2]. The Department of Student Affairs and the Student community of the University are the key stakeholders of the system.

The student portal implements the following functions: creation/publication of news; creating/confirming the publication of events; creation/confirmation of clubs; recording in clubs; search and display of the student in the phone book; an entry to a psychologist; record on psychological trainings; online payment for services; application for room reservation.

100.2 Description and Technologies Used

The student portal consists of an information part and interactive services. The information part is a multi-level set of web pages designed to store and display content. Interactive services—a set of modules and databases, designed to implement the functionality for the needs of the student community. The student portal is integrated with other information systems of the University. It was developed on the IBM WebSphere Portal platform, interactive services are developed in the Java programming language. The system is built using the Java technology stack, EJB3.0, JPA, Javascript, HTML, Oracle Database 11 g. The technical characteristics of the hardware platform are presented in Table 100.1.

Operating systems—on the servers of the Student Portal, "Red Hat Enterprise Linux Server release 6.5 (Santiago)" is used. Web server—the Student Portal server uses a load balancer. As the portal is active, it distributes the load to three web application servers (nodes). On the nodes are installed WebSphere portal 7. Caching—to cache data received from the database and LDAP uses the service Dynamic cache service.

Database—the system uses Oracle Database 11 g. The main components of development of the applied software application are:

JQuery—library for creating interfaces.
ExtJS 4—library for creating interfaces.
EJB 3.0—the framework for building the business logic of an application.
JPA—the Java EE API specification, provides the ability to store Java objects in a convenient way in a database.
Oracle 11 g—data storage and management.

The entry point is a proxy http/https web server. It is responsible for handling requests, transferring static content, and load balancing between nodes. The system uses three separate Oracle, DB2, and LDAP servers. The Oracle database contains a database of installed applications. On the DB2 server, there is a database responsible for the health of the portal. On the LDAP server is a database with data about the users of the university.

The student portal provides communication with the following systems:

1. Identity Management System in the part of authorization and obtaining personal information of the student [3].
2. Billing subsystem in terms of obtaining information on names, codes of paid services, the cost of these services and the transfer of information about paid services.
3. Registrar's office in obtaining information about students (data on the student, a sign of social vulnerability, the form of training, the transfer of information on booking rooms).
4. Subsystem for accounting services in terms of obtaining data for invoicing in the personal account on the Student Portal.
5. HMS (Housing management system) in terms of obtaining information about residence in the dormitory.

Design, implementation and enhancement of an online student portal is an ongoing process. It has become vital for the Department of Student Affairs, Students and the IT department to team up and make use of the system.

The overall IT Ecosystem at our University encompasses both commercial and in-house built systems. The decision rationale that we use for choosing between our commercial, or custom, solutions has largely been driven by two underlying factors—the commercial vendor technology support landscape existing in Kazakhstan as well as the overall University budgeting process. As a result, we have invested significant time, effort and resources towards the development of custom, in-house software solutions to meet many of the operational needs of the University's core administrative functions including admissions, resource management and student services [4]. By designing these systems from the ground up, we have been able to tailor system functionality to specific university's business process requirements and have been able to seamlessly integrate these separate systems with each other to create very effective end-user experiences [5]. These custom solutions have been able to provide most of the core functionality required by our university in our early existence while also proving to be easily supportable and extensible.

References

1. A.S. Boranbayev, Defining methodologies for developing J2EE web-based information systems. Nonlinear Anal. **71**(12), 1633–1637 (2009)
2. A.S. Boranbayev, S.N. Boranbayev, Development and optimization of information systems for health insurance billing. *Seventh International Conference on Information Technology: New Generations (ITNG 2010)*, (Las Vegas, Nevada, USA, 2010). pp. 1282–1284
3. A. Boranbayev, M. Mazhitov, Z. Kakhanov, Implementation of security systems for prevention of loss of information at organizations of higher education. *Proceedings of the 12th International Conference on Information Technology: New Generations (ITNG 2015)*, (Las Vegas, Nevada, USA, 2015). pp. 802–804
4. I. Keynan, Knowledge as responsibility: Universities and society. J. High. Educ. Outreach. Engagem. **18**(2), 179–2014 (2014)
5. A. Boranbayev, S. Boranbayev, S. Altayev, A. Nurbekov, Mathematical model for optimal designing of reliable information systems. *Proceedings of the 2014 IEEE 8th International Conference on Application of Information and Communication Technologies-AICT2014*, (Astana, Kazakhstan, 2014). pp. 123–127

Alexander Hansen and Mark C. Lewis

Abstract

In the interest of minimizing bandwidth usage, a modified Huffman code structure is proposed, with an accompanying algorithm, to achieve excellent lossless compression ratios while maintaining a quick compression and decompression process. This is important as the usage of internet bandwidth increases greatly with each passing year, and other existing compression models are either too slow, or not efficient enough. We then implement this data structure and algorithm using English text compression as the data and discuss its application to other data types. We conclude that if this algorithm were to be adopted by browsers and web servers, bandwidth usage could be reduced significantly, resulting in cut costs and a faster internet.

Keywords

Compression · Bandwidth · Internet · Lossless · Space optimization

101.1 Introduction

In 2016, over 96,000 petabytes of data were transferred across networks in the world [1]. This is up from 72,000 petabytes in 2015, and 12 petabytes in 1998. Shaving off just a kilobyte or even a few bytes off of every server response could have a significant impact on total bandwidth when requests are being processed en masse. We propose a quick, lossless compression algorithm that could work on multiple data types and minimize bandwidth usage.

A. Hansen (✉) · M. C. Lewis
Trinity University, San Antonio, TX, USA
e-mail: ahansen2@trinity.edu

As memory and data storage device prices decrease every year, it is becoming less and less important to be efficient in space complexity. We seek to take advantage of this modern trend by increasing the space complexity of the standard Huffman code in exchange for a smaller compressed file size. The majority of all traffic on the internet is either text, image, audio, or video and these can all be tokenized and used in Huffman encoding schemes. Because of this, our proposed Huffman-based encoding could work with any of these data types. Some extremely useful examples of text-based contexts are Javascript, HTML, and CSS. This solution could deliver compressed web languages very quickly and efficiently, with extremely quick decompression.

101.2 Proposed Solution

101.2.1 Modified Huffman Code

From a high level perspective, the modified version of the Huffman code we present has two major changes. The addition of a variable data context, and the offloading of the Huffman code itself into the implementation specification, so the file does not have to store the code. The addition of a data context has been discussed before, but it has not been as large or offloaded in such a manner as ours is [2]. We also introduce a concept of a compression benefit. That is, the benefit of compressing something big is more than compressing something small.

The prototypical Huffman code encrypts English and uses letters as tokens. The code itself will never be larger than the amount of unique letters in the document. As the size of the code itself is not important in our system, we want to choose a less granular symbol than letters. Sticking with English text, we could choose a word or small phrase. With these less granular symbols, in our case words, we can then construct a much larger tree based on the text. This tree should not be based on one individual file, rather, a corpus based on some subset of the English language as a whole. These subsets should be similar in genre, providing a more accurate tree. As an example, if one were to construct a Huffman code from all papers submitted to a computer science journal and then use that code to compress the next submitted paper, it would probably do a decent job. If that code was then used to compress all tweets made in the past hour, it would not. This context of academic papers is then stored in the compression/decompression program and used to compress similar files in the future.

There is also the consideration of benefits. If the word "a" happens frequently, it will end up towards the top of the Huffman code and be compressed down to a very small size. However, if we compress the word "the" down to that same size, even if "the" is less frequent, we could end up with a smaller file. The benefit of compressing "the" is higher. We calculate the benefit of a symbol as the frequency which it occurs times the size of that symbol. We then use these benefit values instead of the normal frequency value used by a standard Huffman code.

Decoding a file compressed in this manner is very quick [3]. We also considered using different branching factors to minimize the depth of the tree, but this turned out to have no real impact on size.

101.2.2 Implementation Specifications

An encoded file consists of the context identifier, the compressed data, and then any words that were not found in the context at the end, uncompressed. This is necessary because, as the contexts are not generated based on the input file itself, it is possible for an input file to have symbols in it that are not in the context. There will be a node in the Huffman code that is in the least likely position, a very far leaf, that will be a placeholder. The uncontained words are then stored in their original form at the end of the file, in respective to the placeholders. A malicious file could circumvent all available contexts and contain a lot of words that no context contained and cause a file expand instead of compressing. This would be extremely unlikely and easily preventable.

The compression and decompression program would be a Huffman code traverser with all of the contexts loaded into it.

101.2.3 Advantages and Disadvantages

The solution to the problem of bandwidth optimization is the primary advantage. This algorithm can cut down on file sizes in transmission by immense amounts. This algorithm also can be implemented easily, without much more difficulty than a normal Huffman code. This is important, as

Table 101.1 Compression results in various contexts

Wikipedia	Itself	Similar data
With benefits	80.0	63.3
Without benefits	79.4	60.0

Table 101.2 Compression results in various contexts

Social media	Itself	Similar data
With benefits	78.2	79.3
Without benefits	72.3	70.0

Table 101.3 Compression results in various contexts

News article	Itself	Similar data
With benefits	83.9	62.1
Without benefits	81.2	60.1

the adoption of this algorithm would require browsers to implement decoders and servers to implement encoders. It is also adaptable to many formats and can provide many contexts, allowing for the context to fit the input data very well.

The size of the program that compresses and decompresses could get large as it must hold all contexts, but this is not a large concern as the implementer could mitigate this with other forms of compression or only hold the necessary contexts. Corner cases do exist that could cause bad compression rates, but are unlikely.

101.2.4 Results

We did implement this program and achieve good compression results (Tables 101.1, 101.2 and 101.3).

In all examples, the compression ratios are better when the benefits of compressing a symbol are calculated. We can postulate the reasons for these numbers based on the inherent properties of the text, perhaps their likelihood to use the same word more often, or longer words, as well.

101.3 Conclusion

We hope to promote the adoption of this technique by implementing a more fully featured program, with the previously mentioned optimizations for selecting the proper context, handling frequent short phrases as one token, and providing resources such as browser plugins to begin using it. We also hope to implement tokenizers for other forms of audio such as video, audio, and images, so that it can be compressed as well.

References

1. Cisco Systems. *Visual Networking Index*. Available at: https://www.cisco.com/c/en/us/solutions/service-provider/visual-networking-index-vni/index.html, Accessed 10 Mar 2018
2. M.J. Weinberger, G. Seroussi, G. Sapiro, LOCO-I: a low complexity, context-based, loss-less image compression algorithm, in *Proceedings Data Compression Conference, 1996*, pp. 140–149 (1996). https://doi.org/10.1109/DCC.1996.488319
3. C. Hong-Chung, W. Yue-Li, L. Yu-Feng, Memory-efficient and fast Huffman decoding algorithm. Inf. Process. Lett. **69**(3), 119–122 (1999). ISSN: 0020–0190. https://doi.org/10.1016/S0020-0190(99)00002-2. http://www.sciencedirect.com/science/article/pii/S0020019099000022

Erratum to: Information Technology – New Generations

Shahram Latifi

Erratum to:
S. Latifi (ed.), *Information Technology – New Generations*,
Advances in Intelligent Systems and Computing 738,
https://doi.org/10.1007/978-3-319-77028-4

This book was inadvertently published without updating the following corrections:

Chapter 30:

The following Author's name was missing, this has been added now

"Leandro Guarino de Vasconcelos"

Chapter 77:

There was a mistake in the author affiliation in Chapter 77. The affiliation should read as below:

Vanel Lazcano
Núcleo de Matemáticas, Física y Estadística, Facultad de Ciencias, Universidad Mayor, Chile

Chapter 85:

The contributing Authors' names were wrongly presented as "Abd Rahman Al Asmar" and "Abd Al Rahem Jarrah". The correct names should read as below:

"Abdel Rahman Alasmar"
"Abdulraheem Aljarrah"

The updated online version of these chapters can be found under
https://doi.org/10.1007/978-3-319-77028-4_30
https://doi.org/10.1007/978-3-319-77028-4_77
https://doi.org/10.1007/978-3-319-77028-4_85
https://doi.org/10.1007/978-3-319-77028-4

Author Index

© Springer International Publishing AG, part of Springer Nature 2018
S. Latifi (ed.), *Information Technology – New Generations*, Advances in Intelligent Systems and Computing 738,
https://doi.org/10.1007/978-3-319-77028-4

Subject Index

© Springer International Publishing AG, part of Springer Nature 2018
S. Latifi (ed.), *Information Technology – New Generations*, Advances in Intelligent Systems and Computing 738,
https://doi.org/10.1007/978-3-319-77028-4